# VIOLENCE
## IN AMERICA

*An Encyclopedia*

# Editorial Board

# VIOLENCE
## IN AMERICA
### *An Encyclopedia*

RONALD GOTTESMAN
*Editor in Chief*

RICHARD MAXWELL BROWN
*Consulting Editor*

**VOLUME 3**

## Charles Scribner's Sons

An Imprint of The Gale Group
New York

Charles Scribner's Sons
An Imprint of The Gale Group
1633 Broadway
New York, New York 10019

1  3  5  7  9  11  13  15  17  19    20  18  16  14  12  10  8  6  4  2

PRINTED IN THE UNITED STATES OF AMERICA

Library of Congress Cataloging-in-Publication Data

Violence in America : an encyclopedia / Ronald Gottesman, editor ; Richard Maxwell
Brown, Consulting editor . . . [et al.].
    p.  cm.
    Includes bibliographical references and index.
    ISBN 0-684-80487-5 (set : alk. paper)—ISBN 0-684-80488-3 (vol. I : alk. paper)
      1. Violence—United States—Encyclopedias. 2. Violent crimes—United
States—Encyclopedias. 3. Violence in popular culture—United States—Encyclopedias.
I. Gottesman, Ronald.

HN90.V5 V5474   1999
303.6'0973'03—dc21                                                       99-052027


ISBN 0-684-80489-1 (vol. 2)     ISBN 0-684-80490-5 (vol. 3)

The paper used in this publication meets the requirements of ANSI/NISO Z39.48-1992
(Permanence of Paper).

# R

## RACE AND ETHNICITY

Are some racial and ethnic groups more violent than others? To the extent that ethnic and racial differences in rates of involvement in lethal and nonlethal criminal violence are shown to exist, how can they be explained? Criminologists and other social scientists have long wondered if rates of involvement in criminal and other social behaviors differ across racial and ethnic lines; during the 1980s and 1990s, certain societal trends sparked renewed scholarly and public interest in these queries in the United States and many other industrialized nations.

One such societal trend is increasing global migration, which has produced greater ethnic and racial heterogeneity, especially in the most industrialized countries. Since the 1970s Western Europe, once consisting of nations that were racially and culturally homogeneous, has imported laborers from many developing nations. Growing immigration has prompted acts of intolerance among some sectors of the European public, including scrutiny of the criminal behavior of immigrant groups. In the United States, a historically diverse nation, the concern for racial and ethnic disparity in violence is longstanding, but the renewal of interest may be linked to an upswing during the 1980s in rates of homicide, mostly among young, urban minorities, and the extensive media coverage it received.

Despite the intensified effort by scholars to answer the questions posed at the outset, it remains true that objective, scientifically sound analyses aimed at providing such answers face significant obstacles. Foremost among these is the legacy of ethnocentrism and racism that has shaped the way Americans think about ethnic and racial differences in the United States and other Western societies. Often, American beliefs about the relationship among race, ethnicity, and violence or other social behaviors derive much more from this ingrained way of thinking than from the "facts." In addition, once the "facts" are known, these earlier beliefs about race and ethnicity often influence the way in which they are "interpreted," and hence the conclusions drawn from them.

### Outsiders Versus Insiders

Many of the forces that have shaped the American views of the importance of group differences predate U.S. history—and some are perhaps as old as humankind. Human history and development have been marked by periods of both isolation from and intense contact among various groups. One of the abiding legacies of the ages-old interaction and conflict among groups is the belief that members of one's own social group have virtues not possessed by outsiders. One's own group of origin is typically seen as less violent, aggressive, or criminal, and more peace-loving and law-abiding than members of other groups. These ethnocentric beliefs have shaped intergroup relations across lines of what we now think of as race, ethnicity, religion, nationality, and social class for many millennia throughout most of the world.

Despite widespread use of the terms "race" and "ethnicity" to describe groupings of humankind, such usage remains both controversial and scientifically problematic. The idea that humans can be grouped into biologically distinct racial groups has been described as a dangerous myth, and racial distinctions are said to be based less on science than on intergroup politics. Similarly, the notion that humans can be grouped together into culturally homogeneous "ethnic" groups has been disputed by many observers who note the impermanence and arbitrariness of many ethnic categorizations.

Global developments of relatively more recent vintage have shaped contemporary attitudes toward group differences and violence. Among these are the massive population movements of the last millennium, many of which are associated with the "biological expansion" of Europe. One result of this premodern global population shift was the proliferation of more fully developed and articulated beliefs about race, ethnicity, "otherness," and violence. These beliefs became an integral part of larger ethnocentric and racist ideologies of the eighteenth and nineteenth centuries, which also posited notions of inherent group differences in levels of intelligence, sexual morality, industriousness, civilization, culture, economic development, physical attractiveness, temperament, and so on. These ideologies also introduced into public and scholarly discourse throughout the world explicit notions of racial and ethnic superiority and inferiority based on presumed group differences (see Benedict 1940; Montagu 1942).

Historically, however, the question of ethnic and racial differences in violence and aggression has posed something of a dilemma for many proponents of racist ideologies. Whether differences in rates of violence or aggression are seen as evidence of racial or ethnic superiority or as a marker of inferiority depends largely on the social and political contexts in which such acts take place. Depending on the circumstances, greater levels of violence or aggressiveness can be viewed as either a social or personal benefit or as evidence of pathology and disrepute.

For example, race and racial differences in aggressiveness have often served as pretexts for war, the ultimate institution of human violence. Military opponents have often been—and are to this day—depicted as racial or ethnic "outsiders." They are also inevitably described as inherently violent and aggressive. In a given instance of warfare, the violence used by one's own group is seen as a justifiable response to the threat posed by an exceptionally violent and racially or ethnically distinct "other." Official U.S. governmental and media responses to the military hostilities between the United States and Iraq in the 1990s and the Iraqi government's labeling of the U.S. and its allies suggest that racial and ethnic imagery is still a powerful propaganda tool.

Over the last five centuries, long-term militaristic endeavors that were integral to a given nation's imperial, colonial, or expansionist aims were similarly justified on race-based grounds. In colonial settings native populations were frequently described by their colonial masters as not only culturally and socially inferior but also savage and excessively violent. This labeling was especially ironic when struggles involved firearms against spears or other less lethal weapons. Nonetheless, colonial military victories that resulted from the greater levels of violence their weapons afforded and the successful territorial expansion that followed were said to be evidence of divine intervention, "manifest destiny," or proof of the innate superiority of the white race or the specific nationality of the colonizing force. Among Europeans of the sixteenth through nineteenth centuries, it is generally the case that nationalistic violence, colonialism, and war were seen as evidence of ethnic, national, or racial superiority as compared to the conquered groups.

Contemporary social-scientific analyses of violence, race, and ethnicity tend almost exclusively to focus on acts of criminal violence. Yet the historical perspective outlined here highlights the role that race and ethnicity play in other forms of violence in U.S. society—much of it, as criminologists of the 1980s and 1990s were quick to note, perpetrated by males of European ancestry. This violence takes the form of organized warfare, other forms of state-sponsored aggression, and hate crimes committed against racial or ethnic minorities; broadening the definition of violence, one could also include such abuses as harm to the environment and industrial and corporate negligence resulting in deaths or injuries among workers and the public.

## From War to Interpersonal Violence

For the most part, Americans and Western Europeans at the turn of the twenty-first century are not significantly threatened militarily or economically by "outsiders"; concerns about race, ethnicity, and violence now tend to center on internal affairs that are thought to threaten public safety. In both the United States and other nations of the West, the debate over the relationship between race and violence centers on the extent to which racial and ethnic disparity exists for acts of interpersonal violence (homicide, assault, robbery, rape, and so on) committed by citizens during times of peace. In the United States, though events at the end of the twentieth century demonstrated the persistence of organized racial conflict, public attention focused on the race-crime nexus.

This shift in the focus of concern, however, may be largely superficial. The nations in which public discourse about race and crime is most prominent are either agents or products of the colonial expansion of the last several hundred years. Thus, views of racial and ethnic differences may simply shift from an emphasis on the "outsiders" beyond national boundaries to the "strangers" and "aliens" within. Analysts of U.S. race relations have long noted the insider-outsider mentality that has characterized interactions among diverse groupings of European Americans, and between European Americans and those of African, Asian, Native American, or Hispanic origins. This mentality has also affected views of ethnic and racial disparity in crime and violence. Just as crime among the foreign-born was used by policy makers at the turn of the twentieth century to incite fear and mistrust of southern and eastern European immigrants to the United States, Willie Horton–like depictions of crime and criminality serve to maintain the outsider status and exaggerate the threat to society posed by African Americans.

Increasingly, researchers in Western European nations have begun to grapple with the question of racial and ethnic disparity in crime and violence as larger numbers of immigrants of color enter these societies from former colonies. This trend stands in contrast to earlier eras when European criminologists spoke largely of the "dangerous classes" of criminals in terms of socioeconomic disadvantage or as biological misfits without specific regard for their ethnic or racial identity. On the other hand, from the latter decades of the nineteenth century into the first decades of the twentieth, European criminologists were explicit in their beliefs regarding the extent and causes of racial and ethnic differences in crime and violence.

## An Emerging Consensus

Although there is still considerable and fully warranted debate over what is meant by "race"

and "ethnicity" and their importance for the study and explanation of social behavior, many social scientists, especially those in the United States, have presented substantial evidence of racial and ethnic disparity in rates of homicide and other forms of criminal violence. In comparison to European Americans, African Americans, Latinos, and Native Americans show higher rates of both violent offending and victimization. On the other hand, Asian Americans have lower rates of violent offending and victimization than do Americans of European ancestry. For example, national data for 1985 showed homicide arrest rates of 28.5 per 100,000 for African Americans, 15.1 for Hispanics, 7.7 for Native Americans, 4.1 for whites, and 3.6 for Asians and Pacific Islanders. Given these findings, it is no surprise that considerable and heated debate centers on the true extent and causes of ethnic and racial disparity and what can be done to minimize it.

It is worth noting that there is also debate surrounding the extent to which racial discrimination in the administration of justice or faulty measures of violent conduct contribute to observed levels of racial disparity in the committing of crimes. Many researchers have noted the extent to which official counts for such offenses as rape and assault can be affected by nonreporting or underreporting by victims and by changes in police surveillance and record-keeping.

Despite these concerns, during the 1980s and 1990s a consensus emerged among social scientists (Tonry 1995, for example) that differences in actual behavior account for most of the racial disparity seen in arrests in the United States for violent criminal offenses. W. E. B. Du Bois in 1899 and Thorsten Sellin in 1928 reached a similar conclusion regarding the question of whether black Americans were more likely than whites to engage in criminal behavior. Whatever the array of social forces that account for these differences, some racial and ethnic groups have much higher rates of violence than others. In some instances the disparity is quite large. Tonry (1997) concludes that differences in behavior rather than bias in the administration of justice appear to account for the racial and ethnic disparities in imprisonment seen among immigrants in several Western nations.

The accuracy of measures of violent behavior may depend on what type of violence is at issue. Because homicides are more accurately counted and are subject to less discretion in law enforcement than are nonlethal violent offenses, researchers are much more certain of the existence of racial disparity for lethal offending and victimization. Significant racial disparities are more evident for nonlethal offenses committed by adults than by children and adolescents. Some self-report studies have shown little if any difference in rates of violence for young persons of different races.

### The Search for Explanations

The observation that certain groups of racial minorities in the United States, and also in other Western nations, have higher rates of officially reported criminal violence than others raises numerous questions, and certainly more than can be addressed here. Identifying the sources for these differences between groups is a much more complicated task than is commonly assumed by both informed and less informed social commentators and researchers. Interpersonal violence, to a much greater extent than other forms of crime, is largely intraracial. The costs of chronically high rates of violence within a given ethnic or racial group are borne disproportionately by members of that group. Further, in the U.S. and most other industrialized societies, intraracial violence results in significantly greater loss of life than incidents of interracial aggression. Such realities fly in the face of insider versus outsider ideologies that continue to dominate public discourse about race, ethnicity, and violence. To disentangle the various strands of explanations for the connection between race and violence, one must keep in mind two observations that have been borne out by the research into this contentious issue.

*Rates of involvement of various racial and ethnic groups in criminal violence, and hence the level of racial and ethnic disparities, tend to vary from one era to another and across diverse sociocultural contexts.* Let us recall that biological and genetic arguments have been used to explain not only differences in criminal and violent behavior between Europeans and others, but also differences within Europe and among populations of European ancestry elsewhere in the world (Bonger 1943). Yet changes over time in rates of both lethal and nonlethal violence and ethnic disparities among Europeans would appear to argue for the explanatory importance of the role played by shifts in the economy or by universal changes in social values rather than abrupt changes in a nation's gene pool. The major changes in rates of violence in Europe and the European diaspora over the last one and a half

centuries (Gurr 1977) are not consistent with the nineteenth-century American stereotypes that pitted the savage violence of the Irish against the civilized restraint of the English. Indeed, rates of violent crime found in London during the 1830s likely may have exceeded those of turn-of-the-century Londoners. In the United States, both Asian Americans and many groups of ethnic white Americans had much higher rates of criminal violence during the last decades of the nineteenth century than in the last decades of the twentieth. Many of these same groups show higher rates of violence today than do their counterparts living in Asia or Europe. Persons of African ancestry living in the Americas during the 1940s and 1950s had much higher rates of homicide than persons living in West Africa. African Americans living in different parts of the United States also vary in their rates of involvement in homicide and other violence.

*Both during the past and today, high rates of involvement in criminal violence and significant ethnic and racial disparities are associated with economic, political, and social inequality.* Those minority groups with high crime and imprisonment rates are also those that are socially and economically disadvantaged. Although of course not all poor and disadvantaged persons commit crimes or acts of violence, much evidence suggests a causal link between disadvantage and criminal violence (both the violent offender and the victim). The consensus among criminologists is that lack of access to economic and social resources is a prime factor in the tendency to commit violent crime. For instance, in his introduction to cross-national comparison of crime rates, Tonry (1997) reported that those ethnic and racial minorities who had the highest levels of criminal involvement in each nation also had the lowest levels of economic well-being. Numerous studies have also shown that the drop in rates of serious violence among Americans of Irish, Italian, and Eastern European descent during the last century can be attributed to their gradual entry into the economic and social mainstream. On the other hand, both remnants of the tradition of slavery and continuing racial discrimination have posed major impediments to the full social and economic integration of African Americans. Many researchers have concluded that this lack of integration accounts for the persistence of high rates of interpersonal violence among them.

The likely link between economic and social disadvantage and high rates of violent offending and victimization also highlights another dimension of the nexus among race, ethnicity, and violence that has not yet been examined in this discussion. In almost all societies racial and ethnic minorities are also frequent targets of collective violence or themselves resort to acts of collective violence to seek to redress perceived wrongs. In the United States the legacy of intergroup relations has included riots against and by Irish Americans during the middle of the nineteenth century and against and by Latinos and African Americans during many decades of the twentieth century. In addition, more than three thousand—and perhaps as many as six thousand—African Americans have been lynched since 1890. Hate-crime incidents directed against African Americans, Jews, and Asian Americans during the late 1990s are part of a continuing legacy of racial and ethnic oppression and inequality in the United States.

Much research remains to be done to identify which factors contribute to racial and ethnic differences in criminal violence. Social scientists must seek to explain why some ethnic and racial groups who are similar in many respects (e.g., minority status, history of oppression, relative economic disadvantage) do not have similar rates of criminal violence. Other dimensions of the social experiences of these groups—their cultural heritage, presumed racial traits, and the social contexts in which they are found to operate—must be explored. Simplistic and superficial notions about group differences and their relationship to various forms of violence and aggression must be refined and deepened before solutions to the problem of race and violence can be found.

*BIBLIOGRAPHY*

Benedict, Ruth. *Race: Science and Politics.* New York: Modern Age Books, 1940.

Bohannan, Paul. *African Homicide and Suicide.* New York: Atheneum, 1967.

Bonger, Willem A. *Race and Crime.* New York: Columbia University Press, 1943.

Brearley, Horace C. *Homicide in the United States.* Chapel Hill: University of North Carolina Press, 1932.

Crosby, Alfred W. *Ecological Imperialism: The Biological Expansion of Europe, 900–1900.* New York: Cambridge University Press, 1986.

Du Bois, W. E. B. *The Philadelphia Negro: A Social Study.* New York: Benjamin Blom, 1899.

Fingerhut, Lois A., and Joel C. Kleinman. "International and Interstate Comparisons of Homicide Among Young Males." *Journal of the American Medical Association* 263, no. 24 (June 1990).

Gurr, Ted Robert. "Contemporary Crime in Historical Perspective: A Comparative Study of London, Stockholm, and Sydney." *Annals of the Academy of Political and Social Science* 434 (November 1977).

Harries, Keith D. *Serious Violence: Patterns of Homicide and Assault in America.* Springfield, Ill.: C. C. Thomas, 1990.

Hawkins, Darnell F. "Crime and Ethnicity." In *The Socio-Economics of Crime and Justice,* edited by Brian Forst. Armonk, N.Y.: M. E. Sharpe, 1993.

———. "The Nations Within: Race, Class, Region, and American Lethal Violence." *University of Colorado Law Review* 69 (fall 1998).

———. "What Can We Learn from Data Disaggregation: The Case of Homicide and African Americans." In *Homicide: A Sourcebook of Social Research,* edited by M. D. Smith and M. A. Zahn. Thousand Oaks, Calif.: Sage, 1999.

———, ed. *Ethnicity, Race, and Crime: Perspectives Across Time and Place.* Albany: State University of New York Press, 1995.

Herrnstein, Richard J., and Charles Murray. *The Bell Curve: Intelligence and Class Structure in American Life.* New York: Free Press, 1994.

Hindelang, Michael J. "Race and Involvement in Common Law Personal Crimes." *American Sociological Review* 43 (1978).

Lane, Roger. *Roots of Violence in Black Philadelphia, 1860–1900.* Cambridge, Mass.: Harvard University Press, 1986.

———. *Violent Death in the City.* Cambridge, Mass.: Harvard University Press, 1979.

Loeber, Rolf, and David P. Farrington, eds. *Serious and Violent Juvenile Offenders: Risk Factors and Successful Interventions.* Thousand Oaks, Calif.: Sage, 1998.

Mann, Coramae Richey, and Marjorie S. Zatz. *Images of Color, Images of Crime.* Los Angeles, Calif.: Roxbury, 1998.

Marshall, Ineke Haen, ed. *Minorities, Migrants and Crime: Diversity and Similarity Across Europe and the United States.* Thousand Oaks, Calif.: Sage, 1997.

McCord, Joan, ed. *Violence and Childhood in the Inner City.* New York: Cambridge University Press, 1997.

Montagu, Ashley. *Man's Most Dangerous Myth: The Fallacy of Race.* Originally published 1942. Walnut Creek, Calif.: Altamira, 1997.

Parrillo, Vincent N. *Strangers to These Shores: Race and Ethnic Relations in the United States.* 6th ed. Boston: Allyn and Bacon, 1999.

Reiman, Jeffrey H. *The Rich Get Richer and the Poor Get Prison: Ideology, Class, and Criminal Justice.* 5th ed. Boston: Allyn and Bacon, 1997.

Rushton, J. Philippe. *Race, Evolution, and Behavior: A Life-History Perspective.* New Brunswick, N.J.: Transaction, 1995.

Sellin, Thorsten. "The Negro Criminal: A Statistical Note." *Annals of the American Academy of Political and Social Science* 140 (1928).

Takaki, Ronald. *A Different Mirror: A History of Multicultural America.* Boston: Little, Brown, 1993.

Tonry, Michael, ed. *Crime and Justice: A Review of Research.* Vol. 21, *Ethnicity, Crime, and Immigration: Comparative and Cross-National Perspectives.* Chicago: University of Chicago Press, 1997.

———. *Malign Neglect: Race, Crime, and Punishment in America.* New York: Oxford University Press, 1995.

Tonry, Michael, and Mark H. Moore, eds. *Crime and Justice: A Review of Research.* Vol. 24, *Youth Violence.* Chicago: University of Chicago Press, 1998.

Walker, Samuel, Cassia Spohn, and Miriam DeLone. *The Color of Justice: Race, Ethnicity, and Crime in America.* Belmont, Calif.: Wadsworth, 1995.

Wilson, James Q., and Richard J. Herrnstein. *Crime and Human Nature.* New York: Simon and Schuster, 1985.

DARNELL F. HAWKINS

*See also* **African Americans; American Indians; Asians; Extremism; Hate Crime; Ku Klux Klan; Lynching; Poverty; Riots; Simpson, O. J., Murder Trials; Slavery; Structural Violence; Urban Violence;** *and individual ethnic groups.*

# RADIO

*The entry is divided into two subjects:* **Military and Police Uses** *and* **Popular.**

## MILITARY AND POLICE USES

### Military Radios

In the beginning of the twentieth century, the U.S. military recognized radio's potential with respect to violence management, which necessarily involves a complex system of command and control of large numbers of troops across long distances. Accordingly, the first U.S. military-run radio station broadcast a message in 1903. It was not, however, until United States participation in World War I that the military had its first large-scale opportunity to use "wireless" under combat conditions; during the Second Battle of the Marne, a U.S. brigade headquarters broadcast an appeal for assistance while under fire. When U.S. units in the newly formed Tank Corps went into action in 1918, one tank in each company was equipped as the "radio tank" to communicate with tank brigade headquarters. Despite these seemingly robust beginnings, the success of tactical radios during World War I was limited.

Radio technology at the time was still in its infancy. Radios were exceedingly oversized by modern standards. Their range was limited, and power sources were either inadequate or unregulated. Additionally, the instruments themselves were delicate. The pressure created by exploding artillery shells or the loss of the extensive antenna systems that early radios required limited their effective use. Most combat units during World War I relied on three alternative communication tech-

**World War I Radio Alternatives**

In July 1917 the United States Army Signal Corps initiated a pigeon service in anticipation of troop deployment on the western front. Trained carrier pigeons had been used in warfare for some time. The French had even maintained a limited airmail service into and out of Paris while it was besieged by the Prussians in 1870. (Balloons carried Parisian pigeons and mail out; pigeons returning to their roosts carried messages into Paris.) In the assault formations of World War I, if the attack succeeded in reaching the enemy's lines, messages might be sent back by live pigeons carried by the officers for this purpose. Officers commanding tanks had to physically dismount to talk to each other if they wanted to communicate. Communications with the rear, relying upon pigeons, left much to be desired. Pigeons were unreliable and messages did not always make it back. Nevertheless, in its 1920 budget the Signal Corps spent $33,057 on pigeons and only $50,367 on radios.

niques—wire, human runners, and pigeons—depending on the situation.

Changes made in the postwar period were inevitable, given the new technology's demonstrated limitations in combat. Immediately following World War I, the findings of the American Expeditionary Forces Superior Board with regard to the Signal Corps, the branch of the army responsible for military communications, were clear and succinct. Incorporated into the National Defense Act of 1920, they resulted in substantial changes within the army. Based on the premise that the infantry was the center of the army, the act codified two changes that directly resulted in the inhibition of technological innovations and development in the field of communications. The act removed the authorization for trained signalmen to be assigned to front line infantry units and disbanded the Tank Corps, thereby placing tanks under the control of the infantry. Although these changes appeared unrelated at the time, their combined effect had a significant impact over the next two decades. The effect of the changes was reinforced by the incorporation of the theoretical underpinnings of the National Defense Act of 1920 within the army's capstone doctrine, Field Service Regulation 1923.

These changes occurred despite the fact that by 1920, many of the technical problems that had plagued radio during its wartime service had been worked out.

Immediately following the war, radios designed and ordered during the conflict began reaching the field army. These models, while still a long way from the technical proficiency and reliability of today's radios, were technologically far superior to the wartime sets on which the American Expeditionary Forces Superior Board had based its recommendations. As a result of the effectiveness of the new radios, the War Department issued General Order No. 29, dated 18 May 1920, which declared: "Infantry troops will install, maintain and operate all lines of information within the infantry brigade." With one sweep of the pen, the infantry-dominated War Department removed much of the active-duty strength and justification for the Signal Corps, and handed the corps' traditional duties to the infantry.

Problems developed almost immediately when the specially and uniformly trained signalmen were replaced by locally trained infantrymen. Most of the trouble stemmed from the fact that as late as 1920 there were very few radios actually in the infantry brigades. Radios were included in the planned tables of organization and equipment, documents that outlined what equipment and personnel each type of military unit was authorized to have, but had yet to be completely fielded to the active-duty infantry regiments. The army was still moving cautiously in its utilization of this new weapon of war.

There were no radios at platoon, company, or battalion levels and only a few sets at the regimental and brigade level when the National Defense Act of 1920 went into effect. By 1922 new radios were in operation at the battalion level, and technical, as opposed to human or pigeon, means of communication existed all the way down to the platoon level. Still, radios were not used extensively, and their use was not consistently anticipated in the military doctrine being written at the time.

The newly developed and issued radio sets of 1922 were the SCR-77s. Two factors conspired against the successful use of this radio and later models during interwar training. The first was the attitude of the users. A few officers, perhaps braver than they were prudent, published articles in *Infantry Journal* openly stating that their infantry brethren did not recognize the importance of com-

munications and radio maintenance. As early as 1922 the chief of infantry himself identified the problem of infantry unpreparedness with respect to communications equipment:

> A recent inspection of Infantry organizations developed the fact that the personnel of communications platoons, in most cases, have not been trained individually or collectively to a degree of proficiency which would ensure the maximum results from the equipment furnished, and guarantee the proper installation, maintenance and operation of the communications system under field conditions.
>
> *Infantry Journal* 21, no. 5 (1922), p. 563

The situation would only get worse.

In addition to the technical problems that arose from inadequate training of infantrymen, there was also a cultural disdain for radio use in military operations. This disdain stemmed from the fact that the effort required to achieve solid radio communications was perceived to outweigh radio's discernible benefits.

A 1927 article demonstrates this attitude well, while highlighting the decline of the communications elements of the infantry. The author was an observer during the summer maneuvers of the Second Division.

> Radio within the infantry brigade was, as usual, of no value. Its equipment is delicate, and a disproportionate time is required for its personnel to attain proficiency. Then the necessity for coding and decoding all messages renders the radio unfit for practical use because there is always a faster and better means of communications at hand. At present the radio is no better than a very expensive toy. The Infantry and Signal Schools should continue to experiment with it because, very possibly, some years from now, it may have lost its present vital defects. Meantime the troops should not have the burden of its care, and the personnel required for its service should be available for other duty.
>
> *Infantry Journal* 31, no. 3 (1927), p. 537

Thus the army, in a stunning display of shortsightedness, neglected the development of ground-based radios. It would pay a price for this neglect in the coming war. In World War II, radios were essential for the command and control of widely dispersed and quickly moving forces. Although the U.S. army did use FM (frequency modulation) radios to great effect in World War II, it did not pursue radio technology far enough to enable tank radios, which for technical reasons had to use FM, to communicate with infantry radios, which used a mixture of AM (amplitude modulation) and FM and operated at a different part of the radio spectrum. In the words of the architect of the German blitzkrieg, General Heinz Guderian, who had served in a series of positions during World War I, all of them within the German Signals Corps, "Radios with tanks made blitzkrieg possible."

Even as the army suffered through a generation of technical difficulties and problems with respect to radio, radio usage in the civilian market expanded. One obvious application of the technology was to police functions.

### Police Radios and Their Impact on the Military

The first radio used in a police function was an AM radio purchased by the Detroit Police Department at the direction of its commissioner W. P. Rutledge in 1925. Although initially hampered in much the same way as the military by radio's limitations, police benefited—to a greater extent than the army—from the techniques and technologies developed for military use.

Initially the Detroit police radio experiment was slow to get off the ground. It was not until 1928 that the department could boast of a truly useful one-way radio setup that effectively replaced the previous system of scheduled patrols and telephone call boxes. Criminals, who had until then been able to time their activities around known police schedules, were outflanked by the new technology. Based on the eventual success of the Detroit system, several other cities also installed one-way radios.

By 1933 advances in radio transmitters permitted the installation of two-way radios in patrol cars. The first police department thus equipped was that of the city of Bayonne, New Jersey. Despite these advances, and the smaller and smaller sizes of radio receivers and transmitters, police radios still suffered many of the technical limitations that confronted the military. These limitations mainly related to problems of shielding the radios from stray electromagnetic interference (interpreted as static) and the use of amplitude modulation. It was not until the development of frequency modulation by Edwin H. Armstrong, and the subsequent sale of FM-based police radios to the Connecticut state police by the Link Radio Company in 1939 that radios truly came into their own with reliable two-way and mobile communications. It was these very same radios that were later demonstrated to the newly formed Armored

Force of the U.S. Army in 1941. Recognizing the obvious utility of radios that could both send and receive voice messages on the move, the army immediately copied the design for combat use, thus avoiding the heavy costs of design and development normally associated with new technology. Such mobile radios could also convey instructions such as target information to artillery on the battlefield, making it unnecessary for artillery to have their targets in sight in order to fire upon them. The correct angle and charge needed for the shells to reach their targets could be calculated from the front lines and transmitted over the airwaves to artillery positioned more safely farther back. FM radios then became the basis for an entire generation of U.S. Army tactical radios, and by extension affected the army's success at the tactical level during World War II.

*BIBLIOGRAPHY*

Aitken, G. J. *The Continuous Wave: Technology and American Radio, 1900–1932.* Princeton, N.J.: Princeton University Press, 1985.

Almstead, Francis E., Kirke E. Davis, and George K. Stone. *Radio: Fundamental Principles and Practices.* New York: McGraw-Hill, 1944.

Ballard, William C. *Elements of Radio Telephony.* New York: McGraw-Hill, 1922.

Gillie, Mildred. *Forging the Thunderbolt: A History of the Development of Armor.* Harrisburg, Pa.: Military Service, 1947.

Kuhn, Thomas. *The Structure of Scientific Revolutions.* Chicago: University of Chicago Press, 1962.

Schulz, E. H., and L. T. Anderson. *Experiments in Electronics and Communications Engineering.* New York: Harper Brothers, 1943.

ROBERT L. BATEMAN III

*See also* **Journalism; Military Culture; Police.**

## POPULAR

In radio's short history, the medium has featured a wide range of violent fiction and nonfiction programming. Current programming strategies that focus on music, talk, and news minimize but do not eliminate the possibilities for violent programming. In the 1980s and 1990s, moral outrage over violent programming content was for the most part concentrated in the mediums of film and television, but this was not always the case. During radio's heyday as a dramatic medium in the 1930s and 1940s, representations of violence on its airwaves served as a source of continual controversy. Both the programming forms and the attacks on them established patterns that parallel late-twentieth-century concerns over televised depictions of violence.

Violent content is one of the areas that demonstrates conflict over moral standards of a public medium. The historian George Lipsitz has argued that mass cultural texts are not merely a "sideshow" to history but can constitute the "main event." He suggests, "For some populations at some times, commercial culture is history, a repository of collective memory that places immediate experience in the context of change over time. For historians, mass-communication texts provide indispensable information, serving as historical evidence even when the texts display no overt consciousness of their own historicity" (1988, p. 148). Any discussion of radio violence must consider not only the form and content of the medium's representations of violence but also the relationship of these textual forms, in a historical sense, to the larger culture from which they emanate.

## History of Violent Content

Fictional violence on radio has been largely confined to serial thriller-dramas. Encompassing detective shows, children's programs, and science fiction, this wide variety of programming includes some of the best-remembered shows from radio's golden age. *The Shadow* (1930–1954), *Inner-Sanctum* (1941–1952), *Gangbusters* (1935–1957), and *Dragnet* (1949–1956) are some of the best-known serial dramas. Some popular children's shows were *The Lone Ranger* (1933–1955), *Dick Tracy* (1935–1948), and *Buck Rodgers* (1932–1947). Science fiction programming included *The Whistler* (1942–1955), *Suspense* (1942–1962), and *Lights Out* (1934–1947). The common element in these shows was their violent content. Some may have applied a moralizing message, while others used violence gratuitously, but in every case the writers and producers of these shows were attempting to use violence to increase their audiences.

*Serial Dramas.* Radio dramas in the thriller, detective, and science fiction genres especially exploited the popular appeal of violence to attract audiences. These types of serial dramas did not require name talent or guest stars and could therefore be produced very inexpensively, maximizing profits. In the 1930s a variety or comedy show budget may have been $40,000 a week, whereas a detective show could be produced for $6,000 a week. Many of these programs were virtually in-distinguishable as a result, and producers regularly pushed the boundaries of acceptable taste to shock their audiences. While Hollywood production codes during the 1930s and 1940s forbade the visual depiction of acts of violence, radio did not have to follow the same types of restrictions because as an aural medium it was able to represent violent acts without explicitly showing them. An example of radio depicting subjects that film could not address is the inaugural episode of *Lights Out*, entitled "Buried Alive." This episode, written by Arch Oboler and broadcast 10 June 1936, told the story of a paralyzed girl who was buried alive. The show caused such uproar that NBC received over 50,000 letters in protest. The show's ability to disturb its listeners is related to its use of sound effects.

The way in which *Lights Out* uses descriptive techniques to evoke violence demonstrates the singularity of an aural medium like radio. Unlike film, a medium that must continually strive for state-of-the-art visual effects to create convincing fantasies, radio is not limited in what it describes. Context provides the subtle cues that allow listeners to understand radio's aural referents. Listeners are willing to suspend disbelief and accept what characters and narrators tell them they see. Radio producers and sound-effects engineers can use special effects that offer enough evidence for listeners to accept what they hear. For example, chopping a melon could be used to imitate the sound of a head being sliced open, just as frying bacon could convince listeners that they had just heard a body being electrocuted.

*War of the Worlds.* The most famous example of radio's ability to deceive its listeners is Orson Welles's *War of the Worlds*. Broadcast on CBS, this episode of *The Mercury Theater on the Air* was an interpretation of H. G. Wells's book but diverged greatly from the original. Written by Howard Koch and broadcast on 30 October 1938, this episode featured musical interludes interrupted by "live" reports of an alien invasion. Compressing time and space, in just one-half hour Welles and his staff described the arrival of the aliens, faked interviews with scientists and government officials who discussed the situation, and even broadcast the destruction of the eastern half of the United States, terrifying millions of people. Welles could never have convincingly created invading aliens in *War of the Worlds* if he had been obliged to show them. Yet listeners accepted the "reporter's" description

9

of the attacking spacecraft and mobilizing army troops. Moreover, once these things were suggested, people could interpret events in a way that resolved their conflict about whether to believe the radio or tale or not and helped them reconcile whatever incongruity they experienced between what they saw around them and what the radio said was happening around them. While the extent of the panic is still unclear, the *New York Times* reported traffic jams and communications disruptions created by people fleeing their homes and seeking advice on how to protect themselves. The *Boston Globe* and the *Providence Journal* both received reports by eyewitnesses who claimed to have seen the firestorms created by alien attacks. The extent of the hoax can be attributed to radio's descriptive power. Likewise, *War of the Worlds* demonstrated how people listening to radio make inferences from existing knowledge and place that knowledge into the context of a radio program. Many studies of the panic following *War of the Worlds* cite the show's proximity to the Munich crisis as one reason that people were willing to believe that the earth was being attacked. In September 1938, German chancellor Adolf Hitler and British prime minister Neville Chamberlain debated the fate of Czechoslovakia in Munich. During this eighteen-day period the radio networks broadcast up-to-the-minute reports on the situation from their overseas correspondents. Because people had become accustomed to hearing real news reports on world crises from the radio, perhaps they were more willing to accept Welles's fictional ones.

*Struggles over Programming.* Critics of violent programming during the 1930s, 1940s, and 1950s constantly expressed concern about the potential effects of fictional representations of violence. They were unsure whether listeners, especially children, were able to distinguish reality from fantasy. Studies of listening habits found that thriller-dramas were children's favorites. In Azriel Louis Eisenberg's study *Children and Radio Programs* (1936), most children reported thinking about the events of the programs they heard, and a significant percentage stated that radio affected their behavior. Law-enforcement agencies argued that crime programs like *Dragnet* inspired criminal activities. These agencies joined parental groups by calling for boycotts and urging networks to remove violent shows from the air.

Broadcasters responded with programming codes in an effort to avoid legislative regulation.

Unlike other media, radio stations ostensibly had to reciprocate for their use of the public airwaves by providing public service through their programming, making them more vulnerable to lobbying efforts. In 1939 the National Association of Broadcasters amended its code of ethics to include guidelines stating that "programs should reflect respect for parents, adult authority, law and order, clean living, high morals, fair play, and honorable behavior. Such programs must not contain sequences involving horror or torture or use of the supernatural or superstitious or any other material which might reasonably be regarded as likely to overstimulate the child listener, or be prejudicial to sound character development" (quoted in Boemer 1989, p. 8). While these codes may have had some effect, networks continued to program thriller-dramas extensively. Indeed, competition from television during the late 1940s and early 1950s meant that many radio producers were given free reign over content in order to attract listeners. Ray Bradbury and Rod Serling were among the many science fiction writers who began successful careers in radio during this period.

## News and Talk Programming

Unlike most other media that offered fictional representations of violence, radio was at the same time embraced for its ability to quickly transmit news and information. From the early 1920s on, radio served as an important source of news programming. Radio was faster than newspapers, offering immediate coverage of events. In August 1939, *Fortune* reported that 25 percent of Americans relied on radio as their primary source of news. More important, people felt that radio provided more accurate coverage than newspapers, with 40 percent claiming they would believe the radio even if it conflicted with the reports of other media. As with its fictional programming, radio news had unique powers of description. Arguably, radio was the first medium to bring war into people's living rooms. Edward R. Murrow's reports from London have frequently been cited as a factor in swaying public opinion in favor of U.S. entry into World War II. Murrow's homey references and precise, understated descriptions brought the horror of war home to America and provided a model for reporting wars. Decades later, Murrow's influence was still reflected in the delivery of popular radio hosts of the 1990s—for instance in the immediately recognizable solemnity of National Public Radio's Karl Castle and the clipped Italian accent of Sylvia Paggioli.

Although most of radio's current programming is musically based, talk radio emerged in the late 1970s and early 1980s, revitalizing radio's use of sound description. The historian Susan Douglas argues that talk radio is distinct from musical format precisely because it returns to the image-making possibilities of pure sound sets. However, rather than describing events, this genre focuses on conversation. While the range of topics discussed is unlimited, talk radio in the form that gained wide popularity in the 1980s and 1990s focuses on political topics. Radio's smaller scale, relative anonymity, and direct contact with the public allows for the expression of a wider range of political opinion than that typically heard on television news. Many hosts such as Rush Limbaugh and Howard Stern promote controversy to improve their ratings. Much like writers of radio drama in the 1930s and 1940s, these media personalities use graphic descriptions of studio high jinks, voice characterizations, and sound effects to increase their appeal. Likewise, audiences respond to their brand of crude humor and shocking behavior. Their continued popularity suggests that radio retains its powerful appeal as a descriptive medium.

*BIBLIOGRAPHY*

Boemer, Marilyn Lawrence. *The Children's Hour: Radio Programs for Children, 1929–1956.* Metuchen, N.J.: Scarecrow, 1989

Douglas, Susan. *Listening In: Radio and the American Imagination, from Amos 'n' Andy and William R. Murrow to Wolfman Jack and Howard Stern.* New York: Times Books, 1999.

Dunning, John. *On the Air: The Encyclopedia of Old-Time Radio.* New York: Oxford University Press, 1998.

Eisenberg, Azriel Louis. *Children and Radio Programs: A Study of More Than Three Thousand Children in the New York Metropolitan Area.* New York: Columbia University Press, 1936.

Lipsitz, George. "This Ain't No Sideshow: Historians and Media Studies." *Critical Issues in Mass Communications* 5, no. 7 (1988).

MacDonald, F. Fred. *Don't Touch That Dial: Radio Programming in American Life, 1920–1960.* Chicago: Nelson-Hall, 1979.

Nachman, Gerald. *Raised on Radio.* New York: Pantheon, 1998.

Sterling, Christopher, and John Kitross. *Stay Tuned: A Concise History of American Broadcasting.* Belmont, Calif.: Wadsworth, 1978.

ALEXANDER RUSSO

*See also* **Journalism; Music.**

# RAPE

*This entry is divided into two subtopics: **Biosocial Aspects and Incidence** and **Legal and Historical Aspects.***

## BIOSOCIAL ASPECTS

A biosocial theory of rape developed in the late 1980s and early 1990s incorporates evidence from the evolutionary, neurohormonal, and psychological sciences. Its basic premise is that rape is motivated by two evolved drives: the sex drive and the drive to possess and control. All sexually producing organisms possess an unlearned sex drive, although the manner in which it is expressed is mostly learned. The claim of a sexual motivation for rape rests on many facts, the most compelling being (1) most rapists use force only after other tactics have failed, and (2) forced copulation exists in many other animal species. The first fact makes it difficult to claim that the vast majority of rapes are "nonsexual"; the second makes it difficult to claim that human rape is motivated by hatred of women, that it occurs because males and females are socialized differently, or that it is a political act designed to protect male privilege.

Animals also possess a strong drive to possess and control, which is especially strong where sex partners are concerned. Among humans there is substantial evidence that men and women are very possessive of one another. Male jealousy and sexual proprietariness are responsible for most of the spousal and lover homicides around the world. Although the desire to possess and control largely motivates individuals to acquire exclusive access to specific sex partners, under certain conditions this desire can be diffused to include an interest in other sex partners, and may even manifest itself in rape.

Taking into account the logic of natural and sexual selection, as well as the fact that males commit the vast majority of sexual crimes, are the biggest consumers of pornography, constitute nearly all the customers of male and female prostitutes, masturbate more frequently, and are more interested in casual sex, biosocial theory concludes that the male sex drive is stronger than that of the female. The strength of the sex drive is largely determined by neurohormonal events that occur in utero that move the male brain away from its inherent female form. These events are accomplished by androgen hormones, which males secrete more copiously than females. This defeminization—or masculinization—organizes the brain to produce postpubertal hormones in response to environmental cues in sex-typical ways.

Greater male exposure to fetal androgens also results in lessened sensitivity to threats of pain, punishment, and guilt for having harmed someone, which frequently leads males who received excess amounts of androgens to discount the consequences of their behavior for themselves and for their victims. There are differences within, as well as between, the sexes in the strength of the sex drive and in sensitivity to environmental cues. According to the biosocial theory, individuals with the strongest sex drives are usually also the ones most insensitive to cues of suffering by others. These are the individuals who are most likely to rape.

Rape, of course, is not simply a matter of certain types of brain chemistry. Although the motivation for rape is unlearned, the behavior surrounding it is learned. The learning principle stressed by biosocial theory is operant conditioning rather than the attitudinal or imitative learning emphasized by some feminist theorists. A basic tenet of operant psychology is that behavior tends to be repeated when it is reinforced. If a male's "pushy" (not necessarily physically forceful) tactics even occasionally gain him some sexual access, his pushy behavior is reinforced. If he discovers that each time he escalates his pushiness he succeeds in gaining greater sexual access, his behavior is gradually shaped in ways that could lead to rape. Because insensitive males with the strongest sex drive are the most likely to use pushy tactics, these are the males who will learn rape behavior most readily. Unlike other theories of rape, the biosocial theory predicts that a small percentage of females may also learn to employ coercive or deceptive tactics to obtain copulations, and that a fraction of this percentage may actually use forceful tactics (against males or females).

The most effective form of treatment for rapists may be therapeutic castration. A review of the literature involving more than two thousand European sex-offending castrates followed for up to twenty years found recidivism rates ranging from zero to 7.4 percent. Rapists in the United States have rates of known recidivism as high as 50 percent, whether treated psychosocially or not (Walsh 1997).

Chemical castration using anti-androgen drugs such as medroxyprogesterone (Depo-Provera) or cyproterone acetate (Andocur) is an alternative to surgical castration. Offenders with excessive sex drives are good targets for this kind of therapeutic intervention. Depo-Provera reduces libido by drastically reducing testicular production of testosterone, although the adrenals continue to secrete small amounts. Andocur is considered a more effective drug than Depo-Provera because it prevents testosterone from all sources from binding to nerve cell receptors. It is also probably more effective than surgical castration, as removal of the testes does not eliminate adrenal testosterone. Anti-androgens have been called "limbic-hypothalamic tranquilizers" because they "allow the offender to concentrate on his psychosocial problems without the distracting fantasies and urges accompanying androgen-driven limbic-hypothalamic activity." These drugs reduce the level of activating testosterone or prevent its utilization, either of which diminishes responsiveness to sexual arousal and lessens violent tendencies. With limbic-hypothalamic activity dampened, offenders can concentrate on dealing with any psychosocial issues with their counselors.

Chemical castration does not completely eliminate the sex drive. Males on an anti-androgen regimen can become aroused by a partner's patient stimulation, but excessive and compulsive desires are greatly reduced, which is the sought-after result. Unlike surgical castration, chemical castration is reversible when treatment is discontinued.

To summarize the biosocial perspective, the likelihood that an individual will commit rape depends on (1) strength of the sex drive coupled with the desire to possess and control, (2) insensitivity to possible punitive consequences for oneself and to the suffering of others, and (3) a person's history of reinforcement for "pushy" behavior. The first two factors can be called a neurohormonal disposition to sexually assault, and the third factor the mechanism by which the disposition is realized. That the evidence suggests castration is the most effective treatment for rapists is consistent with the view that rape is at least partly sexually motivated.

Rapists come from all classes and ethnic groups. However, large-scale studies of convicted stranger (non-date) rapists have found that these men were what evolutionary psychologists term "competitively disadvantaged males." Competitively disadvantaged males are males who are less likely than average males to attract and hold desirable mates and may thus be more likely to pursue mating opportunities in forceful and illegal ways. Taking an average of a number of studies, it was found that 75 percent of these rapists were under age thirty, 80 percent were either unemployed or employed in lower-blue-collar occupations, and only 20 percent had a high school education or better. Most (about 80 percent) of the convicted rapists also had previous criminal convictions, including about one-third who had convictions for violent crimes. One study comparing non-date rape with date rape found that non-date rapists tend to be significantly younger, of lower class, alcoholics or drug users, more likely to cause harm to the victim, and more likely to have a serious criminal record than rapists who know their victims.

One feminist theory of rape, asserting that rape is a violent, political act that has little or nothing to do with sex, has dominated the social science literature since the 1970s. This view met strong opposition from clinicians and biologically oriented researchers, who claimed that it prevented them from exploring the phenomenon scientifically. Some feminist theorists have withdrawn their insistence that rape has nothing to do with sex as evidence to the contrary has become more compelling.

*BIBLIOGRAPHY*

Ellis, Lee. "Neo-Darwinian Theories of Violent Criminality and Antisocial Behavior: Photographic Evidence from Nonhuman Animals." *Aggression and Violent Behavior* 3 (1998).

———. "A Synthesized (Biosocial) Theory of Rape." *Journal of Consulting and Clinical Psychology* 59 (1991).

Marsh, R., and Anthony Walsh. "Physiological and Psychosocial Assessment and Treatment of Sex Offenders: A Comprehensive Victim-Oriented Program." *Journal of Offender Rehabilitation* 22 (1995).

Palmer, Craig. "Twelve Reasons Why Rape Is Not Sexually Motivated: A Skeptical Examination." In *Taking Sides: Clashing Views on Controversial Issues in Human Sexuality*, edited by R. Francoeur. Guilford, Conn.: Dushkin, 1994.

Walsh, Anthony. *Correctional Assessment, Casework and Counseling*. 2d ed. Lanham, Md.: American Correctional Association, 1997.

ANTHONY WALSH

*See also* **Campus; Endocrinology: Testosterone; Feminism; Legal Definitions of Crimes; Sex Offenders; Sexual Harassment; Women.**

## INCIDENCE AND LEGAL AND HISTORICAL ASPECTS

Prior to the 1980s, the stereotypical rapist was portrayed as a male stranger lurking in the dark waiting to fulfill his sexual needs by preying on a young female victim. Contrary to this characterization, contemporary research has consistently revealed that women are more likely to be raped by people they know (e.g., friends and acquaintances) and sometimes love (e.g., spouses) compared to strangers (Bachman and Saltzman 1995; Koss 1992). In addition, most experts now emphasize that rape is usually a crime of violence, not passion. It is important to be aware of the full range of behaviors that constitute rape according to most criminal codes. A good illustration is the definition of a sexual act that is provided in the sexual assault statute in U.S. federal code (18 U.S.C. § 2245):

*A)* contact between the penis and the vulva or the penis and anus, and for purposes of this subparagraph contact involving the penis occurs upon penetration, however slight; *B)* contact between the mouth and the penis, the mouth and the vulva, or the mouth and the anus; or *C)* the penetration, however slight, of the anal or genital opening of another by a hand or finger or by any object, with an intent to abuse, humiliate, harass, degrade, or arouse or gratify the sexual desire of any person.

### Incidence of Rape

Since the 1970s, researchers and policy makers alike realized that there were more incidents of rape occurring than were being reported to police. As interviewing all individuals about their past victimization experiences is obviously not feasible, researchers rely on the random sample survey. This method is used to estimate the incidence of many types of violent and other phenomena, including rates of rape and sexual assault victimization, within a given population. A sample of the population that is selected randomly from among all eligible respondents will produce estimates of a given phenomenon that are accurate within a measurable range.

As of the late 1990s, the only nationally representative surveys that had attempted to measure the incidence rates of rape were the National Crime Victimization Survey (NCVS), conducted by the U.S. Census Bureau for the U.S. Bureau of Justice Statistics, and the National Women's Study, a survey of adult women supported by the National Institute on Drug Abuse and conducted by Dean Kilpatrick and colleagues at the Medical University of South Carolina. The process of random selection in such studies helps to ensure that those who respond are statistically representative of everyone in the population and that the results can be generalized to the population at large.

However, like the measurement of other violence, estimating the incidence of rape and sexual assault remains fraught with problems. Many methodological factors influence who will be counted as a rape victim in victimization surveys. These factors include variations in the definition of rape used, the type of screening questions used, and the use of the word *rape* versus behavioral descriptions.

The research definition of rape is in a practical sense rendered by and dependent on the questions used by surveys to uncover incidents of rape. For example, regarding "incidents involving forced or unwanted sexual acts," the NCVS asks respondents, "Have you been forced or coerced to engage in unwanted sexual activity by (*a*) someone you didn't know before, (*b*) a casual acquaintance, or (*c*) someone you know well?" If a respondent answers "yes," the interviewer completes an incident report. At this time, the interviewer is instructed to clarify exactly what type of sexual activity occurred by asking the respondent, "Do you mean forced or coerced sexual intercourse?" Again, if the answer is affirmative, the incident is coded as a rape. To avoid confusion about the meaning of "sexual intercourse," interviewers are provided with an explicit definition of rape adopted by the NCVS. This definition can be used for reference or can be read to respondents at any time during the interview: "Rape is forced sexual intercourse and includes both psychological coercion as well as physical force. Forced sexual intercourse means vaginal, anal, or oral penetration by the offender(s). This category also includes incidents where the penetration is from a foreign object such as a bottle."

Both males and females can be classified as rape victims according to this methodology. However, average annual rates of victimization indicate that women (4.6 per 1,000) are significantly more likely to be victimized than men (0.5 per 1,000; Bachman and Saltzman). This estimate indicates that more than five hundred thousand rapes and sexual assaults are committed against women annually. Who are the offenders? An analysis of lone-offender rape and sexual assault victimizations of women identified by the NCVS in 1992 and 1993 revealed that only 18 percent of all victimizations were perpetrated by strangers; 26 percent of all rapes and sexual assaults were committed by intimate partners, 3 percent by other family members and relatives, and 53 percent by friends and other acquaintances (Bachman and Saltzman).

The sexual assault screening questions used by the National Women's Study were much more specific than those in the NCVS. The questions were prefaced by this introduction:

Another type of stressful event that many women have experienced is unwanted sexual advances. Women do not always report such experiences to the police or discuss them with family or friends. The person making the advances isn't always a stranger, but can be a friend, boyfriend, or even a family member. Such experiences can occur anytime in a woman's life—even as a child. Regardless of how long ago it happened or who made the advances . . .

(1) Has a man or boy ever made you have sex by *using force* or threatening to harm you or someone close to you? Just so there is no mistake, by sex we mean putting a penis in your vagina.
(2) Has anyone ever made you have oral sex by force or threat of harm? Just so there is no mistake, by oral sex we mean that a man or boy put his penis in your mouth or someone penetrated your vagina or anus with their mouth or tongue?
(3) Has anyone ever made you have anal sex by force or threat of harm?
(4) Has anyone ever put fingers or objects in your vagina or anus against your will by using force or threats?

It should not be surprising that multiple, behaviorally specific questions such as these were associated with greater disclosure by survey respondents as compared to the NCVS. The estimated rate of rape per 1,000 women from this survey was 7.1. This translates into an estimated 683,000 female victims of rape annually. Although this number is larger than the estimate produced by the NCVS data, when the composition of these rapes was examined by victim-offender relationship, patterns similar to the NCVS results emerged. Results from the National Women's Study indicate that 41 percent of the rape victimizations were perpetrated by husbands or boyfriends, 10 percent by other relatives, 25 percent by friends and other acquaintances, and 24 percent by strangers. Thus, according to both national data sources, fewer than one in four rapes against women in the United States are perpetrated by strangers.

### The Adjudication of Rape: Rape Reform Legislation

"Rape is an accusation easy to be made, hard to be proved, and hard to be defended by the party accused though ever so innocent." This statement by Sir Matthew Hale, lord chief justice of the

King's Bench, is perhaps the most illuminating characterization of laws regarding rape in the formative stages of the U.S. criminal justice system. This concern with protecting defendants from false accusations of rape went beyond the "innocent until proven guilty" standard and informed laws governing the adjudication of rape cases. Historically, both cultural conceptions of rape and early rape laws placed serious impediments in the way of adjudicating the crime.

Until the mid-1970s many state rape statutes required that the victim promptly report her victimization to police, that the victimization be corroborated by other witnesses, and that the victim demonstrate that she physically resisted her attacker; judges could provide cautionary instructions to the jury about the difficulty of determining the truth of a victim's testimony. Prior to reforms, most state statutes also narrowly defined rape as sexual intercourse with a woman not one's wife, by force or against her will.

Beginning in the 1970s, however, efforts by various organizations, including feminist groups and victim's rights groups, led to a growing awareness that the offense of rape had a unique status in the criminal justice system and that extant rape laws in the United States were antiquated. This awareness was the impetus for the rape reform movement. The goals of the rape reform movement were ideological and symbolic as well as instrumental. Ideologically, the focus was to change societal notions about rape and rape victims. These notions included (1) the belief that rape was not a serious and violent offense; (2) the belief that acquaintance rapes or rapes perpetrated by intimates were less serious than and different from "real rapes"—those that fit the stereotypical image of a stranger jumping out from a place of hiding and raping a physically resisting woman; and (3) the various "rape myths," which suggested, among other things, that rape victims were somehow partially to blame for their own victimization. Rape reform was intended by many of its proponents to educate the public about the seriousness of all forms of sexual assault, to reduce the stigma experienced by victims of rape, and to neutralize rape-myth stereotypes.

The more pragmatic goals of reform concerned the fact that, as a result of extant rape statutes, many victims were reluctant to report the offense; thus, too frequently rape offenders were not arrested for their crime. Proponents of reform also believed that many offenders arrested for rape were convicted of a less serious offense or not convicted at all because often it was the victim, rather than the offender, who was put on trial. For example, the victim's own sexual history could be cited to call into question her lack of consent. Many offenders who were convicted of rape or sexual assault did not receive prison sentences because the victim knew the offender. Thus, in addition to changing the public's conceptualization of the crime of rape and the victims of sexual assault, rape law reformers also intended to modify existing criminal justice practices.

Although differing in emphasis, these symbolic and instrumental effects of rape law reform were intended to be complementary. Changes in public conceptions about what rape "really is" and whom rape "really victimizes" were expected to lead to more reports of rape to the police. Simultaneously, jurors were expected to become more sensitive to the stigmatization of rape victims. Rape reports, arrests, convictions, and rates of imprisonment, especially for nonstereotypical date and acquaintance rapes, were all expected to increase.

By the early 1990s most states had passed some form of rape reform legislation. The nature of rape law reforms has varied across state jurisdictions both in comprehensiveness and in specific detail, but Julie Horney and Cassia Spohn have identified four common reform themes: (1) replacing the single crime code of rape with a series of offenses graded by seriousness with commensurate penalties, usually gender- and relationship-neutral; (2) changing consent standards by modifying or eliminating requirements that victims resist their attackers; (3) eliminating corroboration requirements; (4) enacting rape shield laws that place restrictions on the introduction of evidence concerning the victim's prior sexual conduct.

The overall purpose of rape law reforms was to increase the probability that the criminal justice system would treat cases of rape, and rape victims, in the same way as it treats other crimes and their victims. Have reforms been successful? The data is equivocal. In Michigan, for example, where the first and most comprehensive reforms were implemented in the late 1970s and early 1980s, the number of arrests and conviction rates for rape increased, but the number of rapes reported to the police by victims did not significantly change. Incarceration rates at the national level appeared to rise after reforms were instituted, but a nationwide study found no increases in either reporting of rape cases or in arrest and conviction probabilities for rape during the early 1980s. However, data from the 1980s specific to California, New York, and Pennsylvania revealed an increase in both conviction and incarceration rates of rape relative to other violent crimes such as robbery. Moreover, data from the 1990s also suggest that, unlike the 1970s, when victims were more likely to report rapes perpetrated by strangers to the police, rape victims in the 1990s were no longer significantly more likely to report rapes perpetrated by strangers than those by nonstrangers. Nevertheless, less than one-quarter of rape victimizations from this sample of rape cases from the National Crime Victimization Survey were reported to police, regardless of the victim-offender relationship.

There are still significant barriers that discourage individuals from reporting their victimization to police, including the lack of confidentiality provided to rape victims who do report. For example, a survey from the early 1990s suggested that women would be less inhibited to report a sexual assault if they could be assured that their names would not appear in the newspaper and that their anonymity would be protected (Kilpatrick et al. 1992). An obvious policy implication to eradicate this barrier would be legal statutes that guarantee rape victims the right of confidentiality by prohibiting the news media from disclosing their names and addresses. However, because the U.S. Constitution guarantees defendants the right to a public trial and the right to face their accusers, this goal may never be realized, and it is unlikely that the media would take it upon themselves to provide such anonymity without being compelled to do so. A more likely avenue of change may lie in continued educational efforts to increase societal awareness about rape and to eradicate the rape myths that persist in society.

Although attitudes about rape and rape victimization may have become more enlightened since the advent of rape law reform, these attitudes still do not exactly reflect the changes in the criminal justice system. Educational efforts should continue to be directed at aligning societal ideas about rape with existing legal statutes that treat rape like other forms of violent crime. As a result, the stigma historically attached to being a rape victim may further abate, and public attitudes concerning rape might one day catch up to legal norms.

BIBLIOGRAPHY

Bachman, Ronet. "The Factors Related to Rape Reporting Behavior and Arrest: New Evidence from the National Crime Victimization Survey." *Criminal Justice and Behavior* 25, no. 1 (March 1998): 8–29.

Bachman, Ronet, and Linda E. Saltzman. *Violence Against Women: A National Crime Victimization Survey Report.* NCJ-145325. Washington, D.C.: Bureau of Justice Statistics, U.S. Department of Justice, 1995.

Berger, Ronald J., W. Lawrence Neuman, and Patricia Searles. "The Social and Political Context of Rape Law Reform: An Aggregate Analysis." *Social Science Quarterly* 72 (June 1991): 221–238.

Field, Herbert S., and Leigh B. Bienen. *Jurors and Rape: A Study of Psychology and Law.* Lexington, Mass.: Lexington Books, 1980.

Galvin, Jim. "Rape: A Decade of Reform." *Crime and Delinquency* 31 (April 1985): 163–168.

Horney, Julie, and Cassia Spohn. "Rape Law Reform and Instrumental Change in Six Urban Jurisdictions." *Law and Society Review* 25, no. 1 (1991): 117–153.

Kilpatrick, Dean G., C. N. Edmunds, and A. K. Seymour. *Rape in America: A Report to the Nation.* Arlington, Va.: National Victim Center, 1992.

Koss, Mary P. "The Underdetection of Rape: Methodological Choice Influence Incidence Estimates." *Journal of Social Issues* 48 (spring 1992): 61–75.

Largen, M. A. "Rape Law Reform: An Analysis." In *Rape and Sexual Assault.* Vol. 2, edited by Ann Wolbert Burgess. New York: Garland, 1988.

Soshnick, Andrew Z. "The Rape Shield Paradox: Complainant Protection Amidst Oscillating Trends of State Judicial Interpretation." *Journal of Criminal Law and Criminology* 78 (fall 1987): 644–698.

RONET BACHMAN
DIANNE CYR CARMODY

*See also* **Campus; Crime, Legal Definitions of; Prison Violence; Sex Offenders; Sexual Harassment; Women.**

# RAY, JAMES EARL
## (1928–1998)

In the early evening of 4 April 1968, in Memphis, Tennessee, James Earl Ray took aim down the barrel of a 30.06 rifle and fired the bullet that ended the life of Martin Luther King, Jr. The sorrow and anger among blacks, and so many Americans generally, that followed the revered civil rights leader's death are difficult to exaggerate.

King's assassin was born on 10 March 1928 in Alton, Illinois. The first of nine children, James Earl Ray spent his youth living through difficult times on rundown farms near the Illinois-Missouri border. Poverty took a heavy toll. With the exception of one sister, the Ray family members ended up in mental hospitals, early graves, or prisons. James quit school in the eighth grade, when his parents separated; he moved in with a grandmother and eventually got a job at a tannery. In 1946 he joined the army and served in Germany. His military service was the last legitimate occupation he had.

A life of crime followed. His criminal record reveals a history of bungled and ludicrously inept robberies and burglaries, involving little money. From 1949 until his escape from the Missouri State Penitentiary in 1967, Ray spent almost all of his time in local jails and state prisons.

After the 1967 escape, Ray teamed up with his two brothers, Jerry and John, in various illicit schemes to break into the "big time." A bank robbery in Illinois was followed by brief stays in Canada and Mexico, where Ray hoped to capitalize on the burgeoning illicit markets in marijuana and pornography. In November 1967 Ray left Mexico and moved to Los Angeles, where, with no visible means of income, he rented an apartment, enrolled in a bartending school, had plastic surgery on his nose, took dancing lessons, and found a lady friend. In December of that year, Ray learned of a contract on King's life from one of his brothers (it is not clear which one) in St. Louis.

Later that month James traveled from Los Angeles to New Orleans, where he met his brother Jerry. A few days later Ray returned to Los Angeles, where he remained until 17 March, intermittently speaking with his brothers by phone. On that date he headed again to New Orleans, arriving on 20 March. From that time until the assassination, Ray stalked King's movements through Georgia, Alabama, and Tennessee. On 29 March he and Jerry drove to a hardware store in Birmingham, Alabama, where the murder weapon he used six days later was purchased.

After shooting King, Ray made the same sort of foolish mistake that characterized his prior criminal career. Fleeing the crime scene, Ray panicked when he saw a police car and discarded the murder weapon with his fingerprints on it in a doorway where investigators found it. After what was the most intensive manhunt in the history of the Federal Bureau of Investigation, Ray was arrested at Heathrow Airport in London on 8 June 1968 as he was about to board a flight to Brussels. To avoid a trial and the possibility of a death sentence, Ray entered a guilty plea in exchange for a ninety-nine-year prison sentence. Within days of the sentencing, however, he denied his guilt and continued to insist until his death that he had been framed. Whether framed or not, there is convincing evidence to support Ray's claim that others were involved.

**An FBI poster of James Earl Ray.** CORBIS/BETTMANN

The conspiracy to assassinate Martin Luther King, Jr., can be traced back to a wealthy St. Louis patent attorney, a white supremacist with close connections to industrial organizations in the South. John Sutherland was also a major contributor to the 1968 presidential campaign of Georgia governor George Wallace, a segregationist. Sometime early in 1967 Sutherland approached John Kauffmann, a prominent figure in organized crime in St. Louis, with the contract and asked him to find a hit man. Ray's brothers probably learned of the fifty-thousand-dollar contract at the Grapevine Tavern in St. Louis. The Grapevine, owned by Ray's sister Carol, was a well-known underworld hangout where Ray's brothers Jerry and John tended bar.

Although evidence pointing to the conspiracy is compelling, the case against James Earl Ray as the person who fired the weapon also remains overwhelming: he had been stalking King; he had purchased the murder weapon; he had rented a room adjacent to the bathroom from which the fatal shot was fired; witnesses saw a person matching Ray's description fleeing the scene; and Ray's fingerprints were the only ones found on the murder weapon. In the 1990s subsequent ballistics tests, conducted at the insistence of Ray's attorney, failed to support the claim that the rifle Ray left at the scene was not the murder weapon.

The intense and thorough FBI investigation that led to Ray's arrest, however, ended at that on 8 June 1968. The bureau failed to pursue a well-defined trail of evidence that led from the murder scene in Memphis to the meetings in New Orleans, to conversations in the Grapevine Tavern in St. Louis and, earlier, in the Sutherland mansion in the suburbs, and, ultimately, to a curious record of long-distance telephone calls between the mansion and Nashville. Although there is no evidence to indicate that the FBI was in any way involved in King's assassination, some doubts persist as to whether its director, J. Edgar Hoover, suspected who else was involved but chose not to investigate. Hoover's hostility toward King and the Civil Rights movement throughout that period are a matter of public record.

James Earl Ray died on 23 April 1998 of liver disease at a prison medical facility in Nashville, Tennessee.

*BIBLIOGRAPHY*

Clarke, James W. *American Assassins: The Darker Side of Politics.* Princeton, N.J.: Princeton University Press, 1990.
————. *On Being Mad or Merely Angry: John W. Hinckley, Jr., and Other Dangerous People.* Princeton, N.J.: Princeton University Press, 1990.
Pepper, William F. *Orders to Kill: The Truth Behind the Murder of Martin Luther King.* New York: Carroll and Graf, 1995.
Posner, Gerald. *Killing the Dream: James Earl Ray and the Assassination of Martin Luther King, Jr.* New York: Random House, 1998.

JAMES W. CLARKE

*See also* **Assassinations; King, Martin Luther, Jr.**

# RECIDIVISM OF VIOLENT OFFENDERS

*Following the **Overview**, there is a subentry on **Genetic Factors**.*

## OVERVIEW

Recidivism, in a criminal justice context, is the "reversion of an individual to criminal behavior after he or she has been convicted of a prior offense, sentenced, and (presumably) corrected." Recidivism rates are the primary outcome used to evaluate most rehabilitation or treatment programs in correctional settings. Offending is usually measured as contact with the criminal justice system, either through arrest, conviction, or incarceration. Since much of the study on recidivism involves the incarcerated offender, it is useful to gain a sense of the prevalence among the current incarcerated population in the United States of individuals with multiple offenses.

According to a 1991 survey on inmates in state correctional facilities conducted by the Bureau of Justice Statistics (BJS), a full 61 percent of all inmates had been incarcerated for a previous offense, and 81 percent of all inmates had been convicted in the past. Somewhat surprisingly, only 73 percent of those incarcerated for violent crimes had been convicted in the past. This would appear to indicate either that violent first-time offenders were more likely to be incarcerated than other first-time offenders or that violent offenders were less likely to be chronic criminal offenders.

Another way to measure recidivism among the prison population is to follow a cohort of released offenders from the time of their release over a number of years. This approach provides an indication of not only the proportion of those who reoffend but also the speed with which individuals return to crime. The BJS conducted the only study of this type done at the national level, examining a population of 108,589 offenders in eleven states in 1983. As expected, 67.1 percent of these individuals had been incarcerated at least once before the current incarceration. Within three years of their release from prison in 1983, 62.5 percent of these prisoners had been rearrested, 46.8 percent of them had been reconvicted, and 41.4 percent had been reincarcerated. The pattern of rearrest was not evenly distributed over the three-year follow-up period. Instead, nearly 40 percent of those who would ultimately be rearrested were rearrested in the first six months after release, and 63 percent of the offenders were rearrested within one year of release. After the first year, the risk of recidivism for those yet to be rearrested substantially declines. Only 13 percent of those who were rearrested after three years were actually rearrested in the third year after release. Among individuals incarcerated for a violent offense, only 59.6 percent had been rearrested after three years, compared with 68.1 percent for property offenders. This result appears to suggest that violent offenders are somewhat less chronic than property offenders. The BJS study helped to identify the length of the follow-up needed to accurately measure recidivism. In 1984 Michael Maltz had observed that the standard follow-up for recidivism studies was one year. Although the BJS study does show that the majority of recidivists were arrested during the first year of release, fully 37.5 percent of all people who will be rearrested by the end of the third year will be arrested after the first year. Since the 1989 publication of the BJS report, three years of follow-up has emerged as a minimum standard, although some researchers choose to follow their subjects for longer than three years. This study also served to solidify the use of rearrest (rather than reconviction or reincarceration) as the appropriate standard of offending, since it appears to capture the most number of offenses. At the same time, it is important to remember that individuals can offend without being arrested. As a result, the proportion of people with an arrest can be seen as a lower bound on the proportion of people who recidivate.

Besides the methodological debates about how to measure recidivism, there has been considerable interest in determining what kinds of treatment programs might reduce recidivism among the correctional population. In 1974 *Public Interest* published a controversial report by R. Martinson that concluded that no program had been demonstrated to reduce recidivism. Reviews in the 1990s were more hopeful, although it was clear that the stability in offending behavior suggested by the BJS numbers is hard to change with rehabilitation programs. According to Doris MacKenzie's 1997 review of evaluations of correctional programs, a moderate decrease in recidivism in some populations can be achieved through rehabilitation programs that are structured and focused. Such programs also use multiple treatment components; concentrate on developing specific social, educational, and vocational skills; and use cognitive behavioral methods with reinforcements for clearly identified overt behaviors. One example of a particularly effective treatment program is therapeutic community treatment, based in prisons, of drug-involved offenders.

Another area of interest among researchers is whether individual characteristics that might predict recidivism can be identified. A 1998 meta-analysis of recidivism, by James Bonta, Moira Law, and Karl Hanson, showed that prior criminal history is consistently the best predictor of recidivism, followed by age, race, and sex. Family background, histories of drug abuse, clinical assessments, and evaluations of current life situations are sometimes significant predictors but tend to be modest when compared with basic demographics and prior criminal history. Taken as a group, these "risk factors" might have a substantial ability to predict recidivism; but in general the use of combined-risk scales is not well-developed.

The predictors of violent and nonviolent recidivism are fairly similar. A definitive review of the predictors of violence conducted in 1994 for the National Academy of Sciences Panel on Violence agrees, concluding that past violence is among the best predictors of future violence. One interesting implication of this finding is that it is difficult to predict violence among those yet to have been arrested. But since most violent acts are not recorded in official records, we may never be able to develop predictions that do not suffer from a high number of false negatives.

*BIBLIOGRAPHY*

Beck, Allen, and Bernard Shipley. *Recidivism of Prisoners Released in 1983: Bureau of Justice Statistics Special Report.* NCJ-116261. Washington, D.C.: U.S. Department of Justice, 1989.

Beck, Allen, et al. *Survey of State Prison Inmates, 1991.* NCJ-136949. Washington, D.C.: Bureau of Justice Statistics, U.S. Department of Justice, 1993.

Bonta, James, Moira Law, and Karl Hanson. "The Prediction of Criminal and Violent Recidivism Among Mentally Disordered Offenders: A Meta-Analysis." *Psychological Bulletin* 123, no. 2 (1998).

Chaiken, Jan, Marcia Chaiken, and William Rhodes. "Predicting Violent Behavior and Classifying Violent Offenders." In *Understanding and Preventing Violence*, vol. 4, *Consequences and Control*, edited by Albert Reiss, Jr., and Jeffrey Roth. Washington, D.C.: National Academy Press, 1994.

Hanson, Karl, and Monique Bussiere. "Predicting Relapse: A Meta-Analysis of Sexual Offender Recidivism Studies." *Journal of Consulting and Clinical Psychology* 66, no. 2 (1998).

MacKenzie, Doris. "Criminal Justice and Crime Prevention." In *Preventing Crime: What Works, What Doesn't, What's Promising*, edited by Lawrence Sherman. NCJ-165366. Washington, D.C.: U.S. Department of Justice, 1997.

Maltz, Michael. *Recidivism*. New York: Academic Press, 1984.

Martinson, R. "What Works? Questions and Answers About Prison Reform." *Public Interest* 10 (1974): 22–54.

SHAWN BUSHWAY

*See also* **Crime and Punishment in American History; Rehabilitation of Violent Offenders.**

## GENETIC FACTORS

An examination of the empirical evidence for recidivistic, or repeated, violent offending raises two major questions. First, does specialization in crime exist? Second, is repeated violent offending an inherited trait?

### Offense Specialization

Specialization refers to the tendency of an individual to commit certain types of criminal offenses. For example, an executive who frequently embezzles funds from his company may be thought to specialize in white-collar crime. The notion of offense specialization has received much attention in the criminology literature, and the conclusions have varied considerably. Marvin Wolfgang and colleagues (1972) studied a Philadelphia birth cohort and concluded that juvenile delinquents do not specialize. They defined specialization as the tendency to commit two contiguous offenses of the same type, but this definition may present too narrow a parameter with which to test the existence of specialization. G. J. Phillpotts and L. B. Lancucki (1979) expanded this parameter by defining specialization as a higher percentage of single-type offending than would be expected to occur by chance alone. Based on this definition, they found that specialization in fact does exist.

Criminal offenses are thought to fall typically under one of two types: property crimes and violent offenses. With these categories in mind, Sarnoff A. Mednick and E. Kandel (1988) suggested another definition: "Specialization has been observed if an individual who commits a violent offense is more likely to commit a subsequent violent offense than an individual who commits a property offense." This definition is supported by the psychiatric literature on violence that concludes that the best predictor of future violent behavior is a history of past violence.

Operating under this definition, Patricia Brennan, Mednick, and Richard John (1989) set out to determine if specialization existed in a birth cohort of 31,436 men born in Copenhagen, Denmark, from 1 January 1944 to 31 December 1947. Two methods of analysis were utilized to test for the existence of specialization. One method compared first-time violent offenders and nonviolent offenders for their likelihood of later violent offending. The second method examined percentages of violent offending to those expected by chance processes alone, an approach utilized by Phillpotts and Lancucki.

Descriptive analysis revealed that of the 28,879 men still alive and living in Denmark when they reached twenty-seven years of age, 10,918 (37.8 percent) had committed at least one criminal offense, 721 (2.5 percent) had been convicted of at least one violent offense, and 173 (0.6 percent) had been convicted of two or more violent offenses. The 173 repeat violent offenders, although small in number, were responsible for 43.4 percent of the

violent offenses of the birth cohort. These individuals may represent violent specialists.

By comparing individuals with an initial violent offense to individuals with an initial property offense, computations were made of the proportions of each of these groups who committed at least one future violent offense. Controlling for the number of future offenses and number of prior offenses, findings showed a first-time violent offender was almost two times more likely to become a future violent offender than the first-time property offender. This relationship held for both juvenile and adult offenders, which is suggestive of evidence for criminal specialization in both juvenile and adults.

The second method of analysis followed the Bernoulli process, in which the expected level of violent offending was calculated and then compared with the actual percentage of zero-, one-, two-, and three-time violent offenders at each level of recidivism (from one to ten arrests). The data indicated that the observed percentages of two- and three-time violent offenders were significantly higher than expected.

These findings strongly suggest that specialization in recidivistic violent offending is an actual phenomenon. These repeat violent offenders may possess certain traits that predispose them toward serious acts of aggression. Genetic factors may be one potential contributor to the emergence of violent behavior.

## Genetic Factors in Recidivistic Violent Offending

There are three epidemiological methods of studying the transmission of human characteristics: family, twin, and adoption studies. Family studies have consistently shown that the best predictor of criminality of a son is the father's criminality. The methodological approach is an inappropriate method to test genetic versus environmental contributions, because the sons are typically reared by their criminal father. Other research designs, such as twin and adoption studies, may provide a more suitable method for testing the genetic transmission of violent behavior.

The rationale behind twin studies is to assess the role of genetics in the twins who are genetically identical with twins who are not (fraternal twins). For dichotomous variables, such as criminal–not criminal, a concordance rate is calculated separately for the identical and fraternal twins. For example, an 85 percent concordance rate for the identical twins suggests that if one of the identical twins is criminal, then the chance of the identical co-twin being criminal is 85 percent. At least eight twins studies were carried out between 1929 and 1962, reporting considerable variations in the pair-wise concordance rates (among identical twins from 100 percent to 0 percent, and in the fraternal twins from 8 percent to 0 percent).

Several methodological flaws in those twin studies made it difficult to draw conclusions regarding genetic liability to criminal behavior. These flaws included varying definitions of concordance (ranging from mild offenses to long-term incarceration) and use of biased samples. Karl O. Christiansen (1977) sought to address these concerns in his study. Using a sample of 3,586 twin pairs in Denmark, Christiansen found 35 percent concordance for identical twins and 13 percent concordance for fraternal twins. The number of violent offenders were too few to conduct a meaningful analysis.

The twin study design may not be the most appropriate tool for studying genetic factors, however, because twins may share both genes and a common rearing environment. Studies comparing concordance rates in identical twins reared apart and identical twins reared together avoid this problem, but it is difficult to obtain such subjects. Adoption studies may provide an even more compelling test of genetic influence in criminal heritability, because the studies are designed to eliminate most environmental effects.

Several adoption studies have suggested that adopted-away offspring are at greater risk of becoming criminal if their biological parents are criminal than if the biological parents are not. The premise behind the adoption design is that the adoptive parents contribute environmental influences and the biological parents contribute genes.

Sarnoff Mednick, William Gabrielli, and Barry Hutchings examined the criminal records of 14,427 adoptees born in Denmark between 1944 and 1947, along with the records of both sets of biological and adoptive parents. Mednick and colleagues found that adoptees had an elevated risk of court convictions if their biological parents (rather than their adoptive parents) had one or more court convictions. As the number of biological parental convictions increased, the rate of adoptees with criminal convictions also increased. These findings are in agreement with findings from adoption studies carried out in Iowa by Remi Cadoret (1978) and Raymond Crowe (1975). In examining the specialization of offenders, it was also found that a rela-

tionship existed among the male adoptees between criminal convictions in the biological parents and property offending but not for violent offending. This finding proved puzzling, and Mednick and colleagues turned to the existing literature for clues.

Leonard Heston (1966) reported that having a schizophrenic biological parent significantly increased the risk of criminal and violent behavior in the offspring. With the Heston study in mind, Terrie E. Moffitt (1984) found that among the Danish adoptees, violent behavior in the offspring was attributed to the combined effect of violent offending and mental illness in the biological parents. In fact, if the biological father has committed a crime and the biological mother is a substance abuser or has personality disorder, the probability of violent offending is increased threefold in the son. A genetic effect for violence, however, is just one of several plausible explanations. This relationship may also be influenced, in part, by other postconception factors, such as prenatal or perinatal disturbances.

## Conclusions

The findings from the Danish samples may be generalized to other countries as well, including the United States. Findings from the adoption project in Denmark, for example, have been replicated in independent samples of Iowan adoptees. What is less straightforward are the origins of violent offending. A clear genetic relationship has been observed in the case of property offending, but not violent offending. Violent offending among a sample of 6,700 Danish males has been associated with the combined effect of psychiatric hospitalization and criminal behavior in the biological parents. But an examination of a wide spectrum of factors that may influence this finding is needed. For example, an antisocial mother who knows that she will be giving up her child for adoption may be less inclined to take care of her developing fetus. A possible interpretation is that poor nutrition, substance abuse, and other harmful behaviors may negatively affect the developing fetus and predispose the child to late recidivistic violent offending.

*BIBLIOGRAPHY*

Brennan, Patricia, Sarnoff Mednick, and Richard John. "Specialization in Violence: Evidence of a Criminal Subgroup." *Criminology* 27 (1989): 437–453.

Cadoret, Remi J. "Psychopathology in Adopted Away Offspring of Biological Parents with Antisocial Behavior." *Archives of General Psychiatry* 35 (1978).

Christiansen, Karl O. "A Preliminary Study of Criminality Among Twins." In *Biosocial Bases of Criminal Behavior,* edited by Sarnoff A. Mednick and Karl O. Christiansen. New York: Gardener, 1977.

Crowe, Raymond R. "An Adoption Study of Antisocial Behavior." *Archives of General Psychiatry* 3 (1975).

Dalgaard, O. S., and E. Kringlen. "A Norwegian Twin Study of Criminality." *British Journal of Criminology* 16 (1978): 213–232.

Guttridge, P., et al. "Criminal Violence in a Birth Cohort." In *Prospective Studies of Crime and Delinquency,* edited by Katherine T. Van Dusen and Sarnoff A. Mednick. Boston: Kluwer-Nijhoff, 1983.

Heston, Leonard. "Psychiatric Disorders in Foster-Home Reared Children of Schizophrenics." *British Journal of Psychiatry* 112 (1966).

Mednick, Sarnoff A., William F. Gabrielli, and Barry Hutchings. "Genetic Influences in Criminal Convictions: Evidence from an Adoption Cohort." *Science* 224 (1984).

Mednick, Sarnoff A., and Elizabeth Kandel. "Genetic and Perinatal Factors in Crime." In *Biological Contributions to Crime Causation,* edited by Terrie E. Moffitt and Sarnoff A. Mednick. NATO Advanced Study Institutes Series. Boston: M. Nijhoff, 1988.

Mednick, Sarnoff A., Terrie E. Moffitt, and Susan A. Stack, eds. *The Causes of Crime: New Biological Approaches.* New York: Cambridge University Press, 1987.

Moffitt, Terrie E. "Genetic Influences of Parental Psychiatric Illness on Violent and Recidivistic Criminal Behavior." Ph.D. diss., University of Southern California, 1984.

Phillpotts, G. J., and L. B. Lancucki. *Previous Convictions, Sentence, Reconviction.* London: Her Majesty's Stationery Office, 1979.

Rosenhoff, A. J., L. M. Handy, and F. A. Rosenhoff. "Criminality and Delinquency in Twins." *Journal of Criminal Law and Criminology* 24 (1934).

Wolfgang, Marvin, Robert M. Figlio, and Thorsten Sellin, eds. *Delinquency in a Birth Cohort.* Chicago: University of Chicago Press, 1972.

JASMINE A. TEHRANI
SARNOFF A. MEDNICK

*See also* **Genetics.**

# RECONSTRUCTION

Reconstruction, conventionally defined as the period between 1865 and 1877, was an era dominated by questions of reconstructing the American Union and defining the status of the freed slaves. A central irony of the American Civil War is that most of the violence during the postwar period was committed by the losers against the winners. The treatment of the defeated Confederates by the federal government was remarkably mild. Confederate individuals and groups, however, assaulted, shot, and hanged former slaves, white Unionists, and Republicans of both races; these acts were often committed in the name of white supremacy, labor control, and political hegemony. During an era of abnormal and revolutionary politics, violence influenced and sometimes decisively affected election results. Observers of this behavior might well have wondered if the Civil War was really over.

During the summer and fall of 1865, newspapers reported a "crime wave" sweeping through the former Confederate states, but there is no statistical evidence against which to assess these claims. Many former soldiers were still armed with weapons. In Tennessee, both Union and Confederate veterans engaged in acts of reprisal against each other. Southern Unionists complained of threats and assaults, and reports of southern "outrages" soon became grist for political debate. For former Confederates, the frustrations of defeat, economic dislocation, and social upheaval formed the backdrop for the violence of the early Reconstruction period.

## Treatment of Freed People

Much of the violence was specifically racial in character, and African Americans were the principal victims. Reports of intimidation, whippings, and shootings poured into the offices of the Freedmen's Bureau, which was established in 1865 and continued until 1869 and was the first federal social service agency. In many cases whites insisted that freed people follow the same rules of racial etiquette that they had observed as slaves, and when they refused, bitter and often violent confrontations ensued. Whites complained of freed people being "insolent" or "saucy." If a black man did not remove his hat in the presence of a white person or if he said "good morning" to his former owner before being spoken to, he risked being whipped. There were also cases of castration and other forms of mutilation of blacks. Although examples of retaliation by African Americans for such treatment were rare, rumors of black insurrections circulated long after the war and especially during election campaigns. The determination of many white southerners to maintain control of African Americans in the absence of slavery was unmistakable. State legislatures, in 1865–1866, enacted the infamous Black Codes, which established a few basic civil rights for blacks but also severely circumscribed various economic and social government responsibilities toward freedmen and freedwomen. Former slaveholders tried to coerce former slaves into signing restrictive labor contracts that reduced the freed slaves to a condition of quasi-peonage. Thus violence often stemmed from attempts by whites to preserve their supremacy in an era of emancipation and growing black freedom. There was especially strong resentment against black political activity—from voting to officeholding—that began after the passage of the Reconstruction Acts in 1867.

The violence of the early Reconstruction period appeared sporadic and unpredictable. The causes of such violence were rooted not only in the economic and social context of the postwar South but also in local conditions and individual psychology. Yet even this supposedly random violence had political overtones, and by 1866 the larger racial disturbances already began taking on an increasingly partisan cast.

In Memphis, Tennessee, the presence of African American soldiers and impoverished freed people who had recently moved from the surrounding countryside created considerable racial tensions in a river city that had serious crime problems. For three days, from 30 April to 2 May 1866, white policemen and firemen—many of them Irish—assaulted any black people they could find. The murders, rapes, looting, and arson committed by police and private citizens in many ways anticipated the patterns of twentieth-century race riots, but also struck many northerners as fresh evidence of southern rebelliousness and of the failure of President Andrew Johnson's lenient Reconstruction policies.

Three months later, on 30 July, an equally bloody riot in New Orleans illustrated the increasingly political nature of postwar violence. An attempt to reconvene the Louisiana constitutional convention that had last met in 1864 and whose purpose had been to enfranchise blacks and disfranchise Confederates led to police assaults on the delegates and their black supporters. Republicans blamed President Johnson for implicitly encouraging the rioters and not sending federal troops in time to prevent bloodshed. The New Orleans riot was more politically charged than previous violent episodes. Moreover, it symbolized southern resistance to Reconstruction. It also helped unify the Republican Party for the 1866 congressional elections and led Congress to pass the Reconstruction Acts, which placed the former Confederate states under temporary military control and gave black men the right to vote.

White conservatives bitterly attacked this legislation as an illegal usurpation of power designed to foist radical governments on the South and bring on "Negro rule." Some newspaper editors offered analogies to the French Revolution and warned that an oppressed people would strike back against the supposed tyranny of governments dominated by carpetbaggers (northerners who came to the South to engage in Republican politics), scalawags (southern whites who became Republicans), and former slaves.

**A group of men subdue black citizens of Memphis, Tennessee, with gunfire on 2 May 1866.** CORBIS

## Politics and Reconstruction

Although various strategies were adopted to undermine the federal government's program of Reconstruction, such as appealing for black votes and boycotting politics altogether, violence soon became an important political tool. The primary goal of white conservatives was to intimidate newly enfranchised blacks and to frighten white "traitors" in order to reduce the Republican vote. Much of this early terror campaign involved the activities of the recently organized Ku Klux Klan. Founded in Tennessee in the winter of 1865–1866, the Klan soon extended over much of the South, although the loosely organized local dens never coalesced into a well-coordinated body. In Tennessee and Arkansas, the Klan clashed with Republican-controlled state militias. A group similar to the Ku Klux Klan, the Knights of the White Camellia, emerged in Louisiana and was also among the most violent white supremacist organizations of the time.

During the 1868 presidential election campaign, several southern Republicans, including members of the recently convened constitutional conventions, were assassinated. Groups of armed men intimidated potential Republican voters and murdered several party leaders. The violence was particularly intense in Georgia, where mobs spread terror across the state and deterred or forcibly prevented many Republican voters from casting ballots. In Louisiana, night riding ("visiting" Republicans at night for purposes of intimidation) and several bloody clashes in New Orleans had a similar effect. Yet because Congress could throw out electoral votes from states where violence occurred, the political terrorism was unlikely to secure a Democratic victory in a presidential election.

At the state and local level, however, the violence could be chillingly effective—especially when white conservatives continued to deny the legitimacy of state governments that were created under the Reconstruction Acts. The myth of Negro rule became a convenient pretext for counterrevolution. As both Republicans and Democrats moved to the political center in 1869 and 1870, the bloodshed abated for a time. Yet the acceptance of the results of the war, including the postwar constitutional amendments by the Democrats—the so-called new departure—marked at best only a grudging acceptance of Reconstruction by southern Democrats, and the Klan remained active in several states. Despite claims to the contrary, a sig-

nificant number of southern whites from all classes participated in, or at least supported, Klan activity.

The Klan used several means of intimidation. Between 1868 and 1871 local Republican officials were murdered, whipped, or driven from their homes. Black workers who gave their employers trouble or became economically successful often received a visit from night riders. Churches and schools were burned, and ministers and teachers were terrorized. Although many of these acts were never reported, conservative newspaper editors routinely blamed the victims or claimed that "radical incendiaries" from the Union League (a group that organized to register black voters and helped build a southern Republican Party) were inciting African Americans to rise up and slaughter their white neighbors. In areas where blacks did fight back, there were bloody reprisals.

Despite its disorganized and diverse character, the Klan sustained two overriding goals: the overthrow of Republican state governments and the restoration of white supremacy in labor and social relations in the South. The Klan became in essence the military arm of the Democratic Party, and many important Democrats became involved in the organization. Yet the Klan seldom ventured into black-belt areas that were Republican Party strongholds, and even though raids and night riding often reduced the Republican vote, the Klan was not primarily responsible for returning any state to Democratic control.

The violence exacerbated racial divisions in state Republican organizations and also tended to divide the carpetbaggers and scalawags. (Carpetbaggers tended to favor more vigorous efforts by state governments to suppress the violence, but scalawags were reluctant to call out the state—often largely black—militia for fear of inciting a race war.) Republican governors approached this political terrorism in a remarkably timid and cautious way; most refused to call out the militia or take any strong action to suppress the violence. When the state governments failed to protect their citizens, beleaguered Republicans appealed for federal assistance. In 1870 and 1871 Congress adopted three Enforcement Acts that allowed federal district attorneys and military commanders to move against the Klan and to destroy it. Yet the use of these measures to uphold the Fourteenth and Fifteenth Amendments and to protect voters from political terrorism proved remarkably short-lived. Respectable citizens often provided bail for arrested Klansmen and seldom condemned their bloody deeds.

The safety of southern Republicans still depended to an alarming degree on the exercise of federal authority (because the state government proved ineffective in suppressing violence and in preventing the intimidation of voters), but state and local court decisions weakened the Enforcement Acts. Both Congress and President Ulysses S. Grant had grown weary of the perennial question of Reconstruction and increasingly reluctant to intervene in southern affairs despite the successful suppression of the Ku Klux Klan, including the jailing of Klansmen in 1871 and 1872 in South Carolina. In 1874, as Alabama Democrats swept back into power in a campaign based on white solidarity and the selective use of intimidation against Republicans, Washington did nothing. The lesson here was obvious and not lost on conservatives in areas still under Republican control: the federal government would no longer intervene to keep state governments in power or to protect voters from intimidation.

This "white line" strategy soon spread to states where the Republican Party remained strong. Racial appeals and opposition to high taxes steadily eroded white support for the Republicans, but the party's base among African Americans remained solid. In states where African Americans made up nearly half or more of the registered voters, conservatives resorted to fraud and intimidation. The disputed election of 1872 in Louisiana politics was a case in point. With rival governors, legislatures, and even local officials, anarchy reigned for several years. On Easter Sunday 1873 armed whites entered the town of Colfax and killed scores of black Republicans (perhaps one hundred or more) holed up in the courthouse. In the spring of 1874, the newly organized White League began a total assault on Republican power in the state. Armed men forced Republican state officials to resign and generally terrorized the rural areas. In August 1874 six Republican officeholders in Red River Parish were murdered. In September an armed mob took over New Orleans. Even though federal troops belatedly restored the Republican governor William Pit Kellogg to power, the party's hold on the state government remained tenuous. Unlike the violence of the Klan era, the political terrorism here was both overt and better organized.

The "white line" policy in neighboring Mississippi was even more effective. Democratic victories in the 1874 congressional elections encouraged

conservatives to strike at the very base of Republican political power in the state. Attempting to remove an African American sheriff in Vicksburg, armed whites intimidated scores of blacks who had rallied to the sheriff's defense. During the 1875 state election campaign, Democrats were determined to prevent blacks from voting. Mobs attacked Republican meetings and killed several local party leaders. Governor Adelbert Ames vainly begged for federal assistance but refused to call out the militia for fear of inciting a race war. In Mississippi, and other southern states, the white liners succeeded in suppressing the Republican vote—dramatically in some counties—while also greatly increasing Democratic turnout.

By 1876 one conclusion was clear: political terrorism would secure Democratic victories and the federal government was unlikely to intervene. A clash between black militia and armed whites in the village of Hamburg, South Carolina, resulted in the deaths of one white Republican and as many as seven African Americans and set the tone for that state's election campaign. This time, however, the violence was not entirely one-sided. In the low country, black Republicans disrupted Democratic meetings and abused black Democrats, though these outbreaks paled in comparison with the disorder sparked by conservative Red Shirts (armed Democrats bent on intimidating Republican voters). In Aiken and Edgefield Counties armed bands killed as many as one hundred blacks. By early 1877 the period of Republican Reconstruction in South Carolina as well as in Louisiana and Florida came to an end. In returning Democrats to power and preserving white supremacy, violence had played a large and occasionally decisive role. As a New Orleans newspaper editor put it, "Take away from the Democrat his shotgun, and he becomes as weak as Samson with his head shaved." Although historians have often explained the failure of Reconstruction in terms of northern indecisiveness, factionalism, and racism, southern resistance—often accompanied by considerable bloodshed—helped bring an end to this brief experiment in biracial democracy. Former Confederates won during these "battles" of the Reconstruction period what they had failed to secure on the battlefields of the Civil War.

*BIBLIOGRAPHY*

Foner, Eric. *Reconstruction: America's Unfinished Revolution, 1863–1877.* New York: Harper and Row, 1988.

Perman, Michael. "Counter Reconstruction: The Role of Violence in Southern Redemption." In *The Facts of Reconstruction: Essays in Honor of John Hope Franklin*, edited by Eric Anderson and Alfred A. Moss. Baton Rouge: Louisiana State University Press, 1991.

Rable, George C. *But There Was No Peace: The Role of Violence in the Politics of Reconstruction*. Athens: University of Georgia Press, 1984.

Trelease, Allen W. *White Terror: The Ku Klux Klan Conspiracy and Southern Reconstruction*. New York: Harper and Row, 1971.

GEORGE C. RABLE

*See also* **Civil War; Ku Klux Klan; Lynching; South.**

# RED SCARE

Twentieth-century U.S. history saw two major episodes of repression and violence against communists and leftist radicals. Following World War I and beginning in the summer of 1919, federal, state, and local governments targeted a wide range of radical activists and employed a significant level of violence in order to prevent what officials saw as the threat of a Soviet-style revolution in the United States. Almost two decades later, in the late 1940s and early 1950s, the federal government took the lead in repressing the Communist Party USA and rooting out communists (or communist sympathizers) from government agencies, trade unions, the entertainment industry, and some professions, with the aim of strengthening the United States' position in the Cold War with the Soviet Union. The Red Scare of the 1950s, commonly identified with the aggressive tactics and media celebrity of Wisconsin senator Joseph McCarthy, was characterized more by economic repression and jail terms than by physical violence.

**The First Red Scare**

The first Red Scare—the more violent of the two—began in the summer of 1919 and continued through the fall of 1920. The scare was sparked by several events: the successful 1917 Bolshevik Revolution in Russia and subsequent revolutions in central Europe; post–World War I labor unrest at home, including a general strike in Seattle in February 1919; a police strike in Boston and bitter strikes in the American steel and coal industries; and the discovery of a massive mail-bomb plot against three dozen federal judges, senators, and leading businessmen. Federal authorities, led by Attorney General A. Mitchell Palmer and his newly hired assistant, J. Edgar Hoover, drawing on wartime legislation that repressed criticism of U.S. military policy, arrested radical activists and deported several hundred foreign-born anarchists, socialists, and communists in the summer of 1919. Palmer gained national notoriety in January 1920 when he led nationwide raids on Industrial Workers of the World (IWW) halls, Communist and Communist-Labor Party headquarters, and offices of other organizations sympathetic to Soviet Russia. Palmer's raids resulted in thousands of arrests, but his popularity ebbed rather quickly. Palmer's unsuccessful presidential ambitions, liberal and conservative criticism of his methods as unconstitutional, and the machinations of his opponents within the Woodrow Wilson administration all combined to limit his ability to continue his campaign against radicals. In the fall of 1920, when a bomb explosion on Wall Street killed twenty-nine people, no new roundup of radicals occurred, and the Red Scare of 1919–1920 was over.

The bulk of violence during the first Red Scare occurred at the ground level, during strikes, parades, and holidays. Local and state governments, particularly in the West, outlawed radical organizations and utilized or inspired vigilante groups, often composed of veterans' organizations such as the American Legion, to attack striking workers, radical activists, and dissenting organizations' headquarters and meeting halls. Historians agree that the most infamous example of Red Scare mob violence took place in 1919 in Centralia, Washington, in a confrontation between IWW members (Wobblies) and local conservative vigilantes. During a parade marking World War I's Armistice Day, 11 November 1919, American Legionnaires attacked an IWW meeting hall along the parade route. Wobbly activists responded with gunfire, killing four legionnaires. Vigilantes retaliated that evening by lynching a Wobbly activist, Wesley Everest (himself a World War I veteran), and rounding up and terrorizing as many local Wobblies as possible. After a lengthy and irregular trial, a jury convicted seven Wobblies of second-degree murder, and they received stiff prison sentences. Vigilante violence, in conjunction with the Palmer raids, decimated the IWW, forced communist groups underground, and fatally wounded the legal activities of socialist parties.

**The Second Red Scare**

The second Red Scare occurred within a different historical context and exhibited a smaller degree of violence. Although anticommunism in the United States of the 1940s had its roots in the antiradicalism of previous decades, Cold War tensions and partisan politics enlarged the role of the federal government and minimized violence at the local level. Some historians locate the origins of the second Red Scare in the anticommunism of liberals in the late 1940s, noting that in 1947 President Harry Truman, a liberal Democrat, ordered background checks of, and loyalty oaths from, federal employees in order to expel communists from federal government agencies. Americans were shocked in 1949 when the Soviet Union acquired the nuclear bomb and communist rebels captured mainland China. After Alger Hiss, a New Deal–era State Department official, was put on trial for allegedly supplying the Soviet Union with secret information and was later convicted of perjury, the Republicans' anticommunism came into play. They seized upon the charge that Democrats had been "soft on communism" and that domestic radicals, safely ensconced in federal agencies, labor unions, and schools, were working toward Soviet domination of the world. McCarthy was the most skilled practitioner of this Republican counteroffensive against the New Deal, but he was joined by newspaper chains and conservative religious and veterans' organizations.

One of the few violent expressions of American angst over domestic communism and Cold War competition was the Peekskill riot. Paul Robeson, a popular African American actor and singer who was also a civil rights activist and communist, was scheduled in late August 1949 to perform an outdoor concert in New York's Westchester County near the town of Peekskill. Local newspapers and veterans' organizations denounced Robeson's pro-Soviet politics. These expressions of anticommunism fused with local residents' economic resentment of New York City residents to produce a mob of local young men who assaulted concertgoers arriving from the city at the Peekskill train station, forcing the concert to be canceled. Following a rescheduled concert on 4 September, under the cover of darkness, a mob attacked the departing crowd, seriously injuring 150 concertgoers. New York State government officials blamed communist activists for causing the riot. The Peekskill riot was not typical of the era's anticommunism, as it was the federal government, via the House Committee on Un-American Activities, and not local vigilantes, that dominated the campaign to repress dissent against the Cold War.

*BIBLIOGRAPHY*

Duberman, Martin Bauml. *Paul Robeson: A Biography.* New York: Knopf, 1989.

Heale, M. J. *American Anticommunism: Combating the Enemy Within, 1830–1970.* Baltimore: Johns Hopkins University Press, 1990.

McClelland, John M., Jr. *Wobbly War: The Centralia Story.* Tacoma: Washington State Historical Society, 1987.

Murray, Robert K. *Red Scare: A Study of National Hysteria, 1919–1920.* Minneapolis: University of Minnesota Press, 1955. New York: McGraw Hill, 1964.

MICHAEL JONATHAN PEBWORTH

*See also* **Anarchism; Cold War; Foreign Intervention, Fear of; Industrial Workers of the World; McCarthy, Joseph R.**

# REHABILITATION OF VIOLENT OFFENDERS

Rehabilitation, sometimes referred to as *rehab,* of violent offenders (those who commit crimes against persons rather than property) is defined as the programs and treatment approaches geared toward facilitating prosocial and constructive behavioral changes of offenders. Since the 1950s and 1960s, correctional rehabilitation and correctional drug-treatment methods have grown to include a wide variety of programs: psychological and risk assessments; diagnostic assessment and classification into prison programs; substance-abuse counseling; therapeutic communities and medication management; individual behavioral therapy, group counseling, and confrontive group therapy; academic, vocational, and social education; vocational evaluation, training, and placement; family counseling; anger-control programs; work-release programs, study-release programs, and aftercare programs; pretrial intervention; private correctional facilities with an array of treatment programs; specialized treatment programs for mentally ill and violent sex offenders; and diversion programs, which provide a structured, community-based alternative to incarceration for first-time offenders.

## Historical Background

The debate on the pros and cons of punishment versus rehabilitation has gone on for more than a century in the United States. The idea of rehabilitation of violent offenders did not exist in America during the seventeenth and eighteenth centuries, when corporal punishment, public flogging, the branding of convicted felons, and solitary confinement in dungeonlike jails was pervasive. The first attempt at rehabilitation was the introduction of reading instruction in Bible classes at the Elmira Reformatory in upstate New York. When Elmira opened in 1876, individual counseling and vocational training were also provided. Instructors from nearby Wells College also taught the illiterate and semiliterate youthful inmates to read and write. It was not until the post-Depression 1930s and postwar 1940s and 1950s, however, that state and federal prison officials began to develop comprehensive prisoner-education programs and counseling programs. Rehabilitation became synonymous with individual treatment, classification of inmates into personality typologies based on the result of psychological inventories, academic education, and vocational training for offenders.

In the early 1960s the community-based corrections movement emerged. The movement was given a major funding boost with the establishment in 1965 of President Lyndon B. Johnson's Commission on Law Enforcement and the Administration of Justice, particularly the commission's Task Force Report on Corrections. Alternatives to incarceration expanded across the United States, and an increasing number of convicted offenders, including violent offenders, were sentenced to such community alternatives as probation rather than incarceration and work-release programs and residences for inmates prior to release in community-based facilities. Early in the 1960s the federal Bureau of Prisons opened a number of prerelease guidance centers in major cities. These centers housed inmates for a thirty-to-ninety-day reintegration period in preparation for parole. In addition, state prisons developed social education and social skills programs, minimum-security work-release centers, study-release programs, and intensive probation-supervision programs. During the late 1960s the Maryland State Division of Corrections opened its first community correctional center across the street from the Maryland Penitentiary. The most trustworthy prisoners, about 90 percent of whom were murderers who had served long sentences, were transferred into this facility in an effort to ease their return to the community upon release. The primary goal of reintegrating an offender back into society was to bridge the gap between an artificial institutional environment and the community into which an offender was being returned.

By the late 1970s, however, prison rehabilitation programs were being eliminated in many state prisons because of a rising crime rate and a view among politicians that prisoners had been treated too leniently. In addition, the sociologist Robert Martinson and his colleagues Douglas S. Lipton and J. Wilks provided the research rationale to curtail large-scale prison rehabilitation programs. They conducted an analysis of 231 treatment studies (from 1945 to 1967) to determine whether rehabilitation had been successful. Their findings in 1975 indicated that the rehabilitation programs they studied had not reduced the recidivism rate appreciably and that rehabilitation was not working. The desire of state governments to cut spending, combined with the Martinson report, resulted in the slashing of prison rehabilitation budgets. Martinson corrected his pessimistic view of rehabilitation in 1979, when he recognized that treatment programs that focus on learning and cognitive approaches were successful in reducing recidivism and programs that focus on the medical or emotional-disturbance models were not. The rehabilitation cutbacks were already in full swing by that time, however, and Martinson's revised view was ignored by legislators and correctional administrators. In 1982 the criminologists Francis T. Cullen and Karen E. Gilbert documented the perspective that U.S. citizens, legislators, and correctional officials acted too hastily in labeling all prisoner-rehabilitation programs failures. They pointed out that the rehabilitative ideal—humane treatment and recreational therapy, rather than isolation and chain gangs—had led to the improved treatment of prisoners, including better sanitation and food, access to radios and televisions, more freedom of movement, and less rigid disciplinary codes.

By the mid-1980s the conservative administration of President Ronald Reagan was wielding a heavy influence on corrections, and most offender-rehabilitation programs were disbanded. By the early 1990s record numbers of offenders were in state and federal prisons throughout the United States. In 1994 Samuel Walker documented the disastrous effects of the U.S. "war on crime" and the fact that because jail and prison populations had tripled by 1990, many correctional officials were forced to release prisoners early in order to make room for new inmates.

### Treatment Effectiveness of Rehabilitation

Several researchers have conducted meta-analyses that demonstrate some rehabilitation programs are successful with certain types of offenders in particular settings and with particular types of staff. The main finding is that under certain conditions, some rehabilitation programs help reduce the recidivism rate of violent offenders.

D. H. Antonowicz and Robert R. Ross (1994) examined forty-four experimental or quasi-experimental treatment studies published between 1970 and 1991 and found that twenty studies had demonstrated the effectiveness of rehabilitation programs. Several key characteristics were associated with program effectiveness in reducing recidivism: utilization of a sound conceptual model based on a cognitive-behavioral model of treatment; utilization of more than one component in the treatment approach; modification of the offender's antisocial behavior; reduction of the reliance on relationships with lawbreaking peers, facilitation of self-control, and promotion of connections with anticriminal role models; enhancement of social learning or behavioral techniques such as role playing, role rehearsal, and cognitive restructuring; and provision of training for offenders in how to be empathetic and socially appropriate. The meta-analysis of Antonowicz and Ross also determined that when comparing violent and nonviolent offenders no statistical differences were found with regard to studies that varied the setting and the intensity of services provided. Furthermore, the researchers found no empirical support for the view that only motivated offenders who volunteer for rehabilitation programs (as distinguished from those who are mandated into treatment) are successful in having a reduced recidivism rate.

In their 1991 meta-analysis of forty-two studies of juvenile offender treatment, Albert R. Roberts and Michael J. Camasso determined the effect of ten different treatment modalities. They concluded that the two most effective types of programs in reducing recidivism for juveniles were family counseling programs and structured wilderness programs that include physically challenging outdoor activities. These findings are equally applicable to violent and nonviolent juvenile offenders. The key finding from the meta-analysis of more than four hundred studies of juvenile offenders conducted by Mark Lipsey (1992) is that recidivism was lowered 20 to 40 percent by means of skill-oriented, behavioral, and multimodal treatments.

Paul Gendreau and Robert R. Ross (1984) found that the following intervention techniques resulted in a significant decrease in recidivism: contingency contracting (a form of behavior modification), family therapy, training in vocational and social skills, behavioral counseling, cognitive therapy, and knowledge of problem-solving skills.

### Drug-Treatment Rehabilitation Programs

Several studies of substance-abusing offenders have indicated that diversion by the courts to substance-abuse treatment and therapeutic communities is effective in reducing recidivism and is a major cost-saving effort as compared to incarceration. Most of the drug-treatment studies with of-fenders have concluded that prison-based as well as community-based therapeutic programs have had a significant impact on reducing recidivism after release from a facility. A three-year follow-up study by Douglas S. Lipton in 1994 of cocaine- and heroin-using offenders reported a 25 percent decrease in recidivism through the Stay'n Out Program in New York City and the Cornerstone Program in Oregon. The New York program serves violent male and female drug abusers while in prison. When the offenders complete the program in prison, they are transferred to Serendipity House, a halfway house in Brooklyn. The optimal length for the Stay'n Out drug-treatment program is nine to twelve months. In sharp contrast, a group of offenders who received no treatment or traditional counseling for a comparable length of time had a recidivism rate of more than 50 percent.

Treatment Alternative Programs (TAP), a model program for substance-abusing offenders in Wisconsin, is based on the Treatment Alternatives to Street Crime program. TAP utilizes case management and group therapy to break the offender's habitual cycle of drugs and crime. The offender's compliance with his or her individual program is monitored in terms of specific improvements related to staying off drugs (including mandatory urinalysis), employment, and social functioning. This model emphasizes strong coordination between the criminal justice system and the treatment staff. Individuals who completed the program were found to be significantly more likely to avoid further arrest and conviction than those who did not. The reconviction rates ranged from 39 percent to 44 percent for those who successfully completed the program, compared to a 65 percent to 79 percent reconviction rate for those who dropped out.

Although studies have found that prison-based rehabilitation programs for drug users are effective in reducing criminal behavior after release, a 1999 study by the federal Bureau of Justice Statistics reported a sharp decrease in the number of treatment programs in state and federal prisons. The Justice Department study reported a strong relationship between criminal acts and drug use, citing drug use by 73 percent of offenders in federal prisons and 83 percent of offenders in state prisons.

### Conclusion

For decades, legislators had adhered to an incremental form of policy development and new legislation concerning rehabilitation of violent offenders. By the end of the 1990s criminologists agreed that the most promising forms of correctional rehabilitation include intermediate sanctions such as restitution to victims, intensive supervision probation, and electronic monitoring and home confinement; a restorative justice model such as victim-offender mediation; and specific treatment for targeted offender groups, such as drug addicts, sex offenders, and violent juvenile offenders.

*BIBLIOGRAPHY*

Antonowicz, D. H., and Robert R. Ross. "Essential Components of Successful Rehabilitation Programs for Offenders." *International Journal of Offender Therapy and Comparative Criminology* 38, no. 2 (1994): 97–103.

Cullen, Francis T., and Karen E. Gilbert. *Reaffirming Rehabilitation*. Cincinnati: Anderson, 1982.

Gendreau, Paul, and Robert R. Ross. "Correctional Treatment: Some Recommendations for Successful Intervention." *Juvenile and Family Court Journal* 34, no. 4 (1984): 31–40.

Harland, Alan T. *Choosing Correctional Options That Work*. Thousand Oaks, Calif.: Sage, 1996.

Lipsey, Mark. "Juvenile Delinquency Treatment: A Meta Analytic Inquiry into the Variability of Effects." In *Meta-analysis for Explanation: A Casebook*, edited by Thomas D. Cook et al. New York: Russell Sage Foundation, 1992.

Lipton, Douglas S. "The Correctional Opportunity: Pathways to Drug Treatment for Offenders." *Journal of Drug Issues* 24, no. 2 (1994): 331–348.

Lipton, Douglas S., R. Martinson, and J. Wilks. *The Effectiveness of Correctional Treatment: A Survey of Treatment Evaluation Studies*. New York: Praeger, 1975.

Martinson, R. "New Findings, New Views: A Note of Caution Regarding Sentencing Reform." *Hofstra Law Review* 7 (1979): 243–258.

———. "What Works? Questions and Answers About Prison Reform." *Public Interest* (spring 1974): 22–54.

Roberts, Albert R., and Michael J. Camasso. "The Effect of Juvenile Offender Treatment Programs on Recidivism: A Meta-Analysis of Forty-six Studies." *Notre Dame Journal of Law, Ethics, and Public Policy* 5, no. 2 (1991): 421–441.

Walker, Samuel. *Sense and Nonsense About Crime and Drugs*, 3d ed. Belmont, Calif.: Wadsworth, 1994.

ALBERT R. ROBERTS
BEVERLY J. ROBERTS

*See also* **Crime and Punishment in American History; Prisons; Recidivism of Violent Offenders.**

# RELIGION

Given the colonial history of the United States, it would be a fair statement to say that religious violence has been a feature of the American project from its late-fifteenth-century inception. A more balanced reading of history, however, would suggest that religiously inspired violence has been more the exception than the rule in the United States—a state of affairs for which the wisdom of the framers of the American Constitution is in good measure responsible. The First Amendment's establishment clause ("Congress shall make no law respecting an establishment of religion, or prohibiting the free exercise thereof") reflected the founders' determination to avoid the bloody wars of religion that had ravaged Europe. Yet religious violence has taken place in the United States, and these outbreaks may be classified according to distinct patterns. Therefore, this entry will consider what may be deemed (1) expansionist violence, (2) millenarian violence, (3) antinomian violence, (4) violence attendant on questions of sexuality and moral crusades, and (5) vigilante violence.

At the same time it is important to stress the fact that U.S. history provides far more examples of religion as a force for reconciliation than as a cause for violence. One need only reflect on the roles of churchmen and women in the abolitionist movement, in antiwar campaigns throughout the twentieth century, and in efforts to promote social justice and peace in a variety of contexts to reach this conclusion. Thus, in considering incidents of religious violence in the United States, the reader should remain aware of their relative rarity.

## Expansionist Violence

Expansionist violence is a form of religious violence that results from the contact of two civilizations and that often stems from the resistance of indigenous populations to religious conversion. Thus, it might fairly be argued that religious violence came to American shores in the vanguard of European settlement, in that Christianization was a stated objective during the colonization of the New World. This was particularly true in the Spanish territories, where conversion and conquest were deemed two sides of the same coin and where the king of Spain acted under an extraordinary papal grant of authority.

Significantly, however, the first unambiguous act of religious violence to take place in America reflected Old World religious and dynastic controversies rather than intolerance toward Native American religious beliefs. This early clash occurred in 1565, the year in which Spain established the first permanent Catholic mission in North America at St. Augustine, Florida. In that year Spanish forces slaughtered approximately nine hundred Huguenots (French Protestants) who had recently settled in the New World. Here, the European wars of religion, which pitted Catholic against Protestant and which were further complicated by competing dynastic claims, were simply transplanted to the New World. However, as neither side thought of itself as in any sense "American," this event cannot be said to be a precursor of religious violence in America.

From the colonial era through the various Indian wars, religiously sanctioned violence against Native Americans was all too frequent. A distinction must be made, however, between religiously sanctioned violence and religiously motivated violence. In general, religious authorities tended to sanction, often after the fact, violence directed at Native American groups attendant to the "civilizing project" in North America.

Similarly, religious terminology was often used in colonial descriptions of the large-scale killing of settlers by Indians, as occurred for example at Jamestown in 1622 and again in 1644. Yet American history records numerous cases of missionaries and Christian leaders whose denunciations of the treatment of Native Americans continued to resonate powerfully into the twenty-first century. Examples abound: the antislavery campaign of Antonio Montesinos (d. 1530?); the learned writings of Roger Williams (1603?–1683); the passionate sermons of Jonathan Edwards (1703–1758), who spent his most productive years at a mission church; and the remarkable career of John Eliot (1604–1690), who began his career as a missionary only to find that he rather preferred the company of Indians to Europeans.

## Millenarian Violence

Millenarian violence is predicated on the assumption of imminent apocalypse. Millenarian hopes have, from the earliest days of colonization, been attached to the New World. America was perceived by many Puritan colonists to be, in the words of the first governor of the Massachusetts Bay colony, John Winthrop (1588–1649), God's "city on the hill," established for the express purpose of being raised up as the New Jerusalem of the Last Days.

Given the fact of such powerful millenarian currents, it is remarkable that most millennial excitements that have arisen in the United States have been untainted by violence. Rather, the pattern of the nineteenth-century Millerites has been the norm. William Miller (1782–1849), on the basis of his reading of the Bible, prophesied in 1835 that the Second Coming of Christ would occur in March 1843. The Millerite movement soon gained thousands of adherents, who as the great day approached sold their belongings and withdrew from society to await the Great Event. Disappointed, the movement leaders proposed alternative dates; but when the last of these, 22 October 1844, passed without event, the movement peacefully disbanded, only to be gathered together again under the charismatic leadership of Ellen White as the Seventh-Day Adventists, which took organizational form in 1860.

Although peaceful withdrawal from society is more the norm in U.S. religious history, there have been instances of violence or potential violence arising from millennial excitements. These conflicts typically have come in two forms: confrontations with state authority and self-destructive or suicidal violence. Examples of antistate millennial violence (or potentially violent situations) are the Ghost Dance phenomenon among Native Americans in the nineteenth century and the pro-life rescue movement and the Christian Identity movement of the late twentieth century.

**A Native American Ghost Dance.** CORBIS/BETTMANN

31

*Ghost Dance.* The Ghost Dance phenomenon may be classified as a nativist reaction to the imminent destruction of the Native American's traditional way of life. This phenomenon follows a pattern of despairing violence that was seen throughout the colonial world in the nineteenth century. From the Sudan to southern Africa, and from New Zealand to the Americas, this pattern tended to vary remarkably little: the impact of the colonial power reached a point at which the political culture of the colonized people was destroyed and, in the face of aggressive missionizing activity, the religious culture nearly so.

When events reached this stage, and one and all could sense that the passing of an ancient way of life was at hand, a prophet would arise who was fired by a vision that expressed an amalgam of traditional beliefs and Christian apocalypticism. This native prophet would then preach his message of redemption to his people, many of whom would rally to his cause. On occasion the message would be quite violent. More often it would be a redemptive message in which the world would be rectified by supernatural intervention, without the need for the faithful themselves to take up arms. In either case the colonial power invariably interpreted the prophet and his movement as threatening and reacted violently to suppress the movement. Such was the case with the Ghost Dance, which appeared in two distinct waves. The first wave, in 1870, ran its course peacefully, but the second, in 1890, ended in the tragedy of the Wounded Knee massacre. The religious structures of the two waves, however, were identical. In 1870 a Paiute prophet in Nevada named Wodziwob (d. 1872) had an apocalyptic vision of the destruction of the Earth followed by a general resurrection of the dead, the regeneration of game animals, and a reconstituted traditional life cycle for his people. The Christian influences of this vision are as clear to present-day readers as they were to the Native American audience for whom the millennial dream of Wodziwob was intended. To bring about this felicitous denouement, however, the people were urged to renew their age-old traditions by performing dances—dancing being a form of spiritual practice analogous to prayer. The Ghost Dance quickly spread throughout the western United States, with a number of tribes taking part. This first phase of the Ghost Dance phenomenon ran its course and ended without bloodshed.

In 1890 Wovoka (d. 1932), another Paiute prophet, had a vision similar to that of Wodziwob.

In the intervening two decades, however, the situation of the Native American had become more precarious, and Wovoka's vision was consequently darker than that of his predecessor. According to some sources, the Lakota Sioux, who were at the heart of the 1890 events, were faced with the virtual extinction of the buffalo herd, disastrous crop failures on reservation land (which was ill-equipped for agriculture in the first place), epidemic diseases, and the threat of deportation to even less habitable lands. Thus, to the vision of resurrection and the restoration of the world to its pristine condition was added the Lakotas' promised destruction of the white race.

The 1890 phase of the Ghost Dance arose in Nebraska and spread throughout the Midwest, with an epicenter in the Dakotas. This time, however, the U.S. Indian Agency and the military reacted. Through a catastrophic series of misunderstandings and gross miscalculations on both sides, violent clashes flared between the U.S. military, determined to end the Ghost Dance, and Lakotas, equally determined to seize what they viewed as their last, best chance for cultural survival. From the Lakota side, the flavor of this vision may be heard in the words of Short Bull, a medicine man from the Rosebud reservation. James Mooney investigated the Ghost Dance movement for the Bureau of American Ethnology and his 1896 account records Short Bull's promise to his people:

> We must continue this dance. If the soldiers surround you four deep, three of you, on whom I have put holy shirts, will sing a song, which I have taught you, around them, when some of them will drop dead. Then the rest will start to run, but their horses will sink into the earth. The riders will jump from their horses, but they will sink into the earth also. Then you can do as you desire with them. Now, you must know this, that all the soldiers and that race will be dead.
> From Mooney, *The Ghost-Dance Religion and the Sioux Outbreak of 1890*, 1973, pp. 788–789, quoted in Pesantubbee

This promise, and others like it from Short Bull and the Minniconju medicine man Kicking Bear, which assured their people that the wearing of ghost shirts would render them immune to bullets, all played their part in the tragedy that followed. But in the end it was the overreaction of the government and the brutality of soldiers—whose claim to have engaged only armed Indians was belied by the murder of twenty-six children under the age of thirteen and the killing of women and children over a two-mile pursuit—that caused the tragedy at the Rosebud Sioux reservation at Wounded Knee in December 1890, bringing the Ghost Dance to a violent end.

*Christian Millennialism.* Violence emanating from or directed toward Christian millennial movements tends to take on a different dynamic. Millenarians' view of time tends to be distinctly different from that of the dominant culture. Time in this conception is seen as coming to a violent denouement, with a future terrestrial paradise promised to the faithful if they can but persevere in the present time of testing—hence the suicidal audacity of a tiny handful of believers challenging the overwhelming power of the state. Moreover, that edenic paradise—"a new heaven and a new earth" (Rev. 21:1)—will often be posited to resemble the "golden age" that the faithful believe was lost through human sinfulness or because of the malignant conspiracy of a satanic "other" (e.g., the Jews, the Illuminati, the forces of anti-Christ). In this sense the imagined past and longed-for future blend into a single stream of time, with the present a fulcrum at which past and future converge.

Of greatest importance in the millenarian conception is the role of text, most often the Bible, which is seen as the inerrant key to interpreting world events in light of the end-times scenario. The preferred mode of millennialist groups is one of withdrawal, to the greatest possible extent, from the culture they see as beyond redemption and awaiting the chastisement of an angry God; when they are stirred from that mode, it is invariably because the "signs of the times" are such that action is imperative. Two contemporary belief systems from which violence has emerged, the Christian Identity community and the pro-life rescue movement, well illustrate different facets of this form of millenarian violence.

Christian Identity evolved from nineteenth-century British-Israelism, an eccentric form of biblical interpretation that posited the British people as the descendants of the biblical Israelites. Transplanted to the United States, British-Israelism combined with anti-Semitic currents drawn from the nineteenth-century Russian forgery called *The Protocols of the Elders of Zion,* which portrayed the Jews as seeking world domination. In the 1920s Henry Ford circulated the same ideas in the context of the "International Jew" series in his company newspaper, the *Dearborn Independent.* By the 1940s this historical aggregation of virulently anti-Semitic and racist doctrines had coalesced as the Christian Identity movement.

Identity's most distinctive theological motif is the "two seeds doctrine," which posits the Jewish people as the demonic offspring of the biblical Eve and the serpent in the Garden of Eden (Gen. 3:1–4). The nonwhite races in this interpretation of the Book of Genesis are seen as the "beasts of the field" (Gen. 2:19–20), over whom Adam as the first white man was given dominion (Gen. 1:28–30). Identity Christians see the Book of Revelation's dread Tribulation period as imminent; but these believers have no hope of supernatural rescue via the rapture (the rising into the air of the faithful to await the culmination of the Apocalypse at the side of Jesus) as described in the New Testament (1 Thess. 4:17). Thus, the Identity community has a predilection for stockpiling arms and supplies in rural redoubts as they await the end. And from this biblical worldview issues the discourse of the "Zionist Occupation Government," which holds that the Jews have succeeded in establishing control not only over the U.S. government but over the world system itself (Rev. 2:9, Rev. 3:9, John 8:44).

Despite the often violent rhetoric emanating from Christian Identity quarters, the movement has rarely initiated violence. This may be attributed to the faithful's awareness of their own tiny numbers (between ten and fifty thousand worldwide) and to disagreements over the interpretation of world events within the apocalyptic scenario of the Bible. Yet throughout the 1980s there were confrontations between state authorities and Identity communities at several isolated compounds, most notably that of the Covenant, the Sword and the Arm of the Lord in rural Arkansas in 1985. All of these confrontations were resolved with the peaceful surrender of the besieged Identity believers.

A handful of individuals, however, did attempt to take action against the state or against those (such as Jews) whom they identified with the state. The most important of these were the Brüder Schweigen (the Silent Brotherhood, more popularly known as the Order), a revolutionary group centered in the Northwest, which was composed of a mix of Identity Christians and neopagan Odinists under the charismatic leadership of Robert Matthews. In the mid-1980s the Order undertook a brief course of revolutionary violence, which included at least two murders, the robbery of several armored cars, counterfeiting, and sundry crimes and misdemeanors. The group was smashed and

Matthews killed in a shoot-out with federal agents on 8 December 1984.

*Pro-Life Rescue Movement.* The pro-life rescue movement, composed of those who oppose abortion and who practice "interposition" (in rescue parlance "those who interpose their bodies between the killer and his victim"—that is, the abortionist and the unborn child), emerged slowly from the religious opposition to the 1973 *Roe v. Wade* Supreme Court decision legalizing abortion. The first halting attempts at interposition, primarily in the form of minor vandalism, were undertaken in the early 1980s by individuals such as Joan Andrews. The punishments meted out to Andrews and others for these early forays were sufficiently draconian to inspire her and others to attempt to do more serious damage, on the (correct) assumption that the sentences would be no worse for the greater level of destruction.

The example of these early, largely Catholic rescuers was taken to heart, and in 1986–1987 Operation Rescue was formed under the leadership of Randall Terry. Operation Rescue marked both the emergence of a large, organized rescue movement and the shift from a primarily Roman Catholic to a primarily evangelical and fundamentalist Protestant constituency. Operation Rescue's tactical approach involved large-scale demonstrations aimed at shutting down abortion clinics in selected cities for limited periods of time. Thus, in such cities as Buffalo, Fargo, Los Angeles, and Pittsburgh, and culminating in Atlanta during the 1988 Democratic National Convention, Operation Rescue mobilized rescuers throughout the United States. Operation Rescue, however, consciously modeled its actions on the nonviolent civil disobedience of the 1960s-era Civil Rights movement and insisted that anyone seeking to take part in its actions sign a pledge to eschew violence in any form.

The experience of the Atlanta jails split the movement, and after 1988 new rescue groups appeared, some of whom were less committed to nonviolence than Operation Rescue. The Lambs of Christ, for example, a primarily Catholic rescue group, is led by a priest named Norman Weslin, who, like his second-in-command Ron Maxson, has a military background. The Lambs added an element of increased militancy to the rescue movement. The Milwaukee-based Missionaries to the Pre-Born, led by two former Operation Rescue stalwarts, Joseph Foreman and Matt Trewella, added direct confrontations with abortionists, destruction of property, and a form of spiritual warfare they called imprecatory prayer (i.e., calling upon God, through the use of certain Old Tes-

Randall Terry, director of the antiabortion group Operation Rescue, leads hundreds of protesters in prayer at a training session at St. Jude Catholic Church in Atlanta, Georgia, 3 October 1988. CORBIS/BETTMANN

tament psalms, either to show the abortionist the error of his ways or to strike him dead).

Meanwhile, in the mid-1980s and early 1990s, individuals such as John Brockhoeft, Marjorie Reed, Michael Bray, and Shelly Shannon began to take more extreme action by firebombing clinics. They were scrupulous in their determination that the destruction of buildings would be accomplished with absolutely no loss of life. Moreover, all of them explained their actions by reference to biblical text and their passionate belief that abortion was symptomatic of the fact that these were indeed the Last Days and that God's judgment on a fallen nation was nigh. But when Michael Griffin, a peripheral figure in the tightly knit rescue community, shot and killed Dr. David Gunn in Pensacola, Florida, in 1993, the final barrier to lethal violence was broken. In short order, Shannon attempted to kill Dr. George Tiller in Milwaukee and Paul Hill shot and killed another Pensacola doctor, John Britton, and his volunteer bodyguard. In 1998 Dr. Bernard Slepian was shot and killed at his Amherst, New York, home by an unknown sniper.

The core group of rescuers who opted for force—Shannon, Brockhoeft, Bray, Reed, and a few others around the country—created an organizational symbol in the early 1990s called the Army of God (AOG). The AOG produced a manual that contained the experiences of the group as they tried to learn from scratch the methods of domestic terrorism. The AOG manual offered both the optimum recipes for bombs and fervent expressions of religious faith. At the end of the twentieth century, explicit endorsements of the use of force were ubiquitous in the writings and journals of the pro-force wing of the rescue movement (for instance, in *Prayer + Action News* and *Life Advocate*) and on the Internet through a site called the *Nuremberg Files*, which offers both an apocalyptic analysis of American society and the names, addresses, and whereabouts of abortion providers throughout the nation.

## Antinomian Violence

Antinomianism literally means the unbinding of the restraints of the Mosaic Law (i.e., the Ten Commandments). This is most often accomplished by replacing these traditional precepts with a "new revelation." As the source of this new revelation, antinomian leaders often exercise virtually unchecked power over the lives of the faithful. Their specific promise is typically of an ultimate utopia in this or, more often, a better world. The group

thus sees its reward as otherworldly—a place of perfection and happiness far from this world of sorrows. Violence involving antinomian groups may be directed at targets such as symbols of state power or at individuals deemed hostile to the group. However, in late-twentieth-century U.S. history, this violence has more commonly been turned inward. The continuum of violence in this respect ranges from attacks on apostates or dissenters to the phenomenon of mass suicide.

*Jonestown.* The 1978 mass suicide and murder of members of the People's Temple in Guyana was the first such event, and it remains paradigmatic. The People's Temple was led by Jim Jones, a charismatic minister from Indiana who, with his message of racial inclusiveness mixed with extravagant faked healing services, soon wore out his welcome in that conservative region; in 1965 Jones moved the congregation to Ukiah, California. (Always a prophet of apocalypse, Jones chose Ukiah on the basis of a magazine article claiming it to be one of the safest locations in the world in the event of nuclear war.)

In California, Jones veered from his conservative Christian background. He adopted socialist politics while his personal behavior became increasingly antinomian, including beatings and the sexual abuse of his followers. Apprised of a magazine exposé that was about to be published, Jones relocated to Guyana in 1977.

When the U.S. congressman Leo J. Ryan from San Francisco and a contingent of network newsmen arrived in Guyana to visit the People's Temple compound, known as Jonestown, they found a deeply paranoid and drug-addled leader and an explosively unstable mix of followers. Although the events that followed remain in some dispute, the basic outline is this: when Ryan tried to leave with several defectors in tow, he was shot and killed, along with three reporters and one of the defectors. What followed at Jonestown was recorded on audiotape, as Jones urged and cajoled his followers to drink a poisonous mixture of drugs and Kool-Aid in a ritual called a "white night," which the group had rehearsed for years. Jones's explicit final promise was of a paradise "on the other side" in which the group could live together in eternal peace and happiness. Many drank, a few fled, others were shot by teams of guards. In the end, 913 bodies were recovered in Jonestown. In the months that followed, further bloodletting occurred with the murder or suicide of People's Temple members who had not been present at Jonestown, as well as of several prominent defectors.

*Heaven's Gate and Waco, Texas.* The 1997 suicides of the Heaven's Gate flying-saucer cult and the fiery deaths of a group known as the Branch Davidians at Waco, Texas, in 1993 each have pronounced elements of antinomian violence. In the Heaven's Gate case, a millenarian prophet hoped to find a utopian existence beyond the confines of this world. Waco, on the other hand, is unique in that it is a case of an antinomian group that neither threatened others nor had any apparent intention to commit suicide so as to take up a better life together in another existence. Rather, in a grotesque circus of errors and miscalculations, the group's refusal to surrender to federal authorities triggered a violent assault that resulted in the Branch Davidians' deaths.

The significance of the apocalypse at Waco continues to be felt in the United States. In the immediate aftermath of the raid, according to a CNN/Gallup poll, 93 percent of Americans placed blame for the deaths of the Davidians on their leader, David Koresh. But a number of oppositional religious groups drew a different conclusion: they saw the siege as confirmation that the United States government had determined to destroy all forms of dissent, regardless of the cost. Some reacted by inviting scholars and journalists to study their beliefs and lifestyles to show they were not "like Koresh." Others, including Christian Identity groups, armed themselves and prepared for the worst. On 19 April 1995 Timothy McVeigh, who later cited his outrage over Waco, detonated a car bomb at the Oklahoma City Federal Center, killing 168 people in the largest single incident of domestic terrorism in U.S. history.

## The Violence of Moral Crusades

Accusations of sexual misdeeds—in particular, of homosexuality, orgiastic revels, incest, and pedophilia—have always been part and parcel of religious polemic. The early Christians, for example, faced just such accusations, and the medieval Church employed virtually identical charges against heretical sects. Nor have these charges lost their power to mobilize public outrage against minority religions. Anti-Catholic agitation in the 1920s was fed by the publication of the salacious propaganda text *The Awful Disclosures of Maria Monk.* Revelations during the Waco siege of David

Koresh's sexual practices powerfully affected public opinion as to his group's validity.

In the nineteenth century the Mormon practice of polygamy aroused an unprecedented wave of persecution, beginning with scattered cases of vigilantism and culminating in an armed confrontation between the state and believers. Thus the so-called Mormon Wars serve as a prime example of violence resulting from questions of morality.

Almost from the beginning, when the Mormon prophet Joseph Smith (1805–1844) dictated to a small group of witnesses the divine revelation that would become the Book of Mormon in 1827, the Mormons have had external teachings that were disseminated to the public via their missionary outreach and a core of esoteric teachings held only for trusted believers. Polygamy, or the taking of "spiritual wives," was the most incendiary of these internal doctrines, and reports of these teachings—often wildly exaggerated—were from the early days of the community revealed by Mormon dissidents and apostates. It was the local indignation over these reports in the middle years of the nineteenth century that had much to do with the forced exodus of the Mormon faithful from upstate New York ever westward, with important stops in Missouri and Illinois on their way to their ultimate sanctuary in Utah.

The key events of the Mormon Wars—actually a series of vigilante skirmishes and confrontations with state and federal authorities that arguably began in 1838, with Joseph Smith's promise to strike back at the tormentors of his community, and culminated in 1857—were the murder of Joseph Smith near Nauvoo, Illinois, in 1844 and the aftermath of the Mountain Meadows Massacre in Utah in 1857.

Nauvoo, Illinois, was seen by the Mormon faithful as a self-governing refuge, immune to the kind of persecution that had harried them from Ohio and then Missouri (1833–1839). In 1840 the Illinois legislature gave the town a charter that allowed the Mormons under Joseph Smith and John Cook Bennett to produce its own courts and legally to raise a militia in times of crisis. The crisis was not long in coming, as the Mormon community immediately found itself embroiled in conflicts with local residents and the citizens of surrounding townships. At issue were a number of legal and political disputes, but reports of Mormon polygamy provided the rallying cry. Following an intense series of legal skirmishes between the Nauvoo court and those of its neighbors (including the arrest of Joseph Smith and his brother, Hyrum, which was countermanded by a writ from the Nauvoo court), in 1844 Smith made a fatal miscalculation by ordering the destruction of a critical local newspaper, the *Nauvoo Expositor,* and later jailing its editor. The state responded by sending in the Carthage Greys, the local militia, to which Smith responded by raising the Nauvoo Legion. Full-scale hostilities were in the end averted, but the Smith brothers and several others were jailed in nearby Carthage. On 27 June 1844 a mob of local citizens and off-duty Carthage militia members broke into the jail and lynched the prisoners.

What followed these events was a year of low-intensity violence between the Mormons and their neighbors; the violence escalated to house burnings and shootings before the Mormons, under the leadership of Brigham Young, began the trek west in February 1846. By May, sixteen thousand Mormons had departed, leaving only a few thousand Mormon residents of Nauvoo. Then, on 12 September 1846, a "posse" of some six hundred anti-Mormons descended on Nauvoo, and after a battle lasting only an hour, forced the town to surrender, ending the Mormon experiment in Illinois.

The Mormon community regrouped in Utah in 1850, but they had hardly left the polygamy controversy behind. The issue came to a head in 1852, when Brigham Young for the first time publicly proclaimed Joseph Smith's doctrine of polygamy, known to Mormons as the Order of Jacob. The federal government at first reacted mildly, by rejecting repeated applications for Utah statehood. In 1857 President James Buchanan deposed Young as the governor of the Utah territory and replaced him with a non-Mormon. A bloody confrontation followed, culminating in September of that year in the massacre of a group of settlers headed toward California by a Mormon force under the leadership of John Doyle Lee and a band of Paiute Indians. Of the 137 settlers, only the youngest children survived what came to be known as the Mountain Meadows Massacre.

The federal reaction was not long in coming, and in the face of federal troops, overt Mormon control of the Utah territory was ended. The U.S. Supreme Court officially decided against polygamy in 1879, and a series of congressional actions in 1882 and 1884 strengthened the decree. In response, a new revelation in 1890 by Mormon president Wilford Woodruff ended the practice of polygamy by mainstream Mormons. Utah became a state in 1896.

### Vigilante Violence

By far the most common, but at the same time the most amorphous, form of religious violence in the United States is vigilante violence. Vigilante violence has been a common feature of the American scene from its inception; indeed, hate crimes continue sporadically to this day. In this form of violence, an individual, a small group, or a quasi legal organization such as the Ku Klux Klan takes it upon itself to act against minority religious communities.

**The Mountain Meadows Massacre of Mormon settlers in 1857.** CORBIS/BETTMANN

The incidents themselves are legion, but until the late 1980s virtually no effort was made to separate instances of religiously motivated violence from other forms of crime (such as assault, arson, threats, and so forth). Indeed, so prevalent has this form of communal conflict been throughout U.S. history that it would not be an exaggeration to state that many religious communities have been touched by it at one time or another.

Communalist groups have at times experienced vigilante violence, motivated as much by economic fears, social resentments, and suspicions of sexual improprieties as by differences in religious dogma. The Hutterites, Amish, and Mormons come immediately to mind in this context. Religious violence may result as well from social or political competition; for example, eighteenth- and nineteenth-century anti-Catholic sentiment in the western states was primarily a symptom of the territorial competition between Spanish- and English-speaking populations. An even more virulent form of anti-Catholicism appeared in the 1920s as a nativist reaction to the influx of Catholic immigrants from Ireland, Poland, and Germany. At the vanguard of this agitation was the Ku Klux Klan, an organization that had been officially disbanded in 1871 only to rise again in 1915, becoming a political power in the northern states.

In those same years—and for the same reasons—a wave of anti-Semitic sentiment swept the nation in reaction to Jewish immigration from Russia and Eastern Europe. This wave was facilitated by the "Americanization" of *The Protocols of the Elders of Zion* in Henry Ford's company newspaper. This series of articles was later collected in a four-volume work that remains available today under the title *The International Jew.* Although Jews in the United States were never subjected to violence approaching the extremities of that in Europe, beatings, arsons, and threats were not uncommon, and incidents of violent prejudice continue to occur.

Although the problem of religious violence in the United States should not be minimized, it must be reiterated that, throughout the nation's history, religion has always been more a constructive than a destructive force. Religious efforts at conciliation, and religious organizations formed around goals of peace and justice, are more central than ever in the American body politic, while religious calls for violence and intolerance have been banished to the fringes of American society. It may thus be the case that, in these years of increasing global integration, religious violence will come to be seen merely as a dark remnant of the American past.

*BIBLIOGRAPHY*

Adas, Michael. *Prophets of Rebellion: Millenarian Protest Movements Against the European Colonial Order.* Chapel Hill: University of North Carolina Press, 1979.

Ahlstrom, Sydney E. *A Religious History of the American People.* New Haven, Conn.: Yale University Press, 1972.

Anonymous. *The Awful Disclosures of Maria Monk.* London: Canova, 1969.

Barkun, Michael. *Religion and the Racist Right.* Chapel Hill: University of North Carolina Press, 1994.

Bellah, Robert N., and Frederick E. Greenspahn, eds. *Uncivil Religion: Interreligious Hostility in America.* New York: Crossroad, 1987.

Billington, James H. *Fire in the Minds of Men: Origins of the Revolutionary Faith.* New York: Basic, 1980.

Bromley, David G., and Anson D. Shupe, Jr. *The New Vigilantes.* Beverly Hills, Calif.: Sage, 1980.

Coates, James. *Armed and Dangerous: The Rise of the Survivalist Right.* New York: Hill and Wang, 1987.

Cohn, Norman. *Pursuit of the Millennium: Revolutionary Millenarians and Mystical Anarchists of the Middle Ages.* New York: Oxford University Press, 1957.

Dinnerstein, Leonard. *Antisemitism in America.* New York: Oxford University Press, 1994.

Dolan, Jay P. *The American Catholic Experience.* New York: Image, 1985.

Flynn Kevin, and Gary Gerhardt. *The Silent Brotherhood.* New York: Signet, 1990.

Gill, Sam. *Native American Religious Action: A Performance Approach to Religion.* Columbia: University of South Carolina Press, 1987.

Girard, René. *Violence and the Sacred.* Baltimore: Johns Hopkins University Press, 1979.

Kaplan, Jeffrey. *Radical Religion in America.* Syracuse, N.Y.: Syracuse University Press, 1997.

Marty, Martin E. *The Irony of It All, 1893–1919.* Chicago: University of Chicago Press, 1986.

———. *The Noise and the Conflict, 1919–1941.* Chicago: University of Chicago Press, 1991.

———. *Under God Indivisible, 1941–1960.* Chicago: University of Chicago Press, 1996.

Mather, George A., and Larry A. Nichols. *Dictionary of Cults, Sects, Religions, and the Occult.* Grand Rapids, Mich.: Zondervan, 1993.

Melton, J. Gordon. *Encyclopedia of American Religion.* 2d ed. Detroit: Gale, 1987.

Pesantubbee, Michelene E. "From Vision to Violence: The Wounded Knee Massacre." In *Millennialism, Persecution, and Violence,* edited by Catherine Wessinger. Syracuse, N.Y.: Syracuse University Press. In press.

Pitzer, Donald E., ed. *America's Communal Utopias.* Chapel Hill: University of North Carolina Press, 1997.

Sims, Patsy. *The Klan.* New York: Stein and Day, 1978.

Smith, Jonathan Z. *Imagining Religion.* Chicago: University of Chicago, 1982.

St. Clair, Michael J. *Millenarian Movements in Historical Context.* New York: Garland, 1992.

Tabor, James D., and Eugene V. Gallagher. *Why Waco? Cults and the Battle for Religious Freedom in America.* Berkeley: University of California Press, 1995.

Walls, Roy, ed. *Millenarianism and Charisma.* Belfast, U.K.: Queens University, 1982.

Wilson, Bryan R. *Magic and the Millennium.* New York: Harper and Row, 1973.

JEFFREY KAPLAN

*See also* **Abortion; American Indians; Catholics; Cults; Extremism; Heaven's Gate; Jehovah's Witnesses; Jews; Jonestown; Mormons; Nonviolence; Vigilantism; Waco.**

# REMINGTON, ELIPHALET
## (1793–1861)

Son of a frontier housewife and a man skilled in carpentry and blacksmithing, Eliphalet Remington II would become widely known as a manufacturer of firearms. Called "Lite" by those closest to him, Eliphalet was born on 28 October 1793 in Suffield, Connecticut. In 1800 his family moved from New England to upstate New York, settling near Crane's Corners, a dozen miles from Utica. There, in 1816, working at his father's forge, Eliphalet turned from farm implement repair to gun making, fashioning a flintlock rifle that evoked much admiration. Local gunsmiths, marksmen, and hunters began to ask him to make barrels and rifles for them, and soon the Remington family was decidedly active in the gun business. By 1828 the Remingtons were making plans to move a few miles and enlarge operations by building a factory at a site (now the city of Ilion) beside the Erie Canal. Before this move was accomplished, the elder Remington died, and Eliphalet thus assumed full control of a rapidly growing business.

Much greater growth occurred in 1845, when Remington purchased the machinery and carbine contracts of the N. P. Ames Company in Springfield, Massachusetts, and in 1847, when he introduced the popular Remington pistol. By the late 1840s Remington's three sons—Philo, Samuel, and Eliphalet III—had become involved in the business, and in 1856 the three young men and their father established the firm of E. Remington and Sons, which became renowned for guns of uncompromising quality. When the Civil War began in 1861, the Remingtons received huge government orders for revolvers and Springfield-type rifles. (Springfield-type rifles refers to rifles similar to those manufactured by the government arsenal in Springfield, Massachusetts.) Such orders created great demands and pressures that quickly undermined the father's health. Eliphalet Remington died in Ilion on 12 August 1861, leaving his life's work in the hands of his sons.

Even while Eliphalet Remington was alive, his company tried to diversify and manufacture something in addition to firearms. In 1856, for example, the firm branched out into agricultural implements—Sayre cultivators, mechanical mowers, rolling rakes—as well as security devices, such as locks, safes, and vault doors for banks. After Eliphalet died, the company periodically developed and marketed such products as sewing machines, typewriters, cash registers, and bicycles. The Remington typewriter was hailed by the likes of Mark Twain and was one of the mechanical marvels to be found at the Centennial Exhibition (1876) in Philadelphia. Nevertheless, since the early nineteenth century the Remington name has most often been associated with firearms. According to Alden Hatch, Eliphalet's 1816 rifle was the first of ten million guns bearing the name of Remington. Many of these guns were used for hunting or sport or "civilizing a continent," but the majority of them ended up in wars. The Remington Company supplied the U.S. Army with Jenks carbines in the Mexican War and sold breech-loading rifles to the French in the Franco-Prussian War. It supplied a large share of the small arms used by the Union army in the Civil War and by the U.S. government in World Wars I and II.

*BIBLIOGRAPHY*

Hatch, Alden. *Remington Arms in American History.* New York: Rinehart, 1956.

DONALD D. KUMMINGS

*See also* **Colt, Samuel; Deringer, Henry, Jr.; Gatling, Richard Jordan; Weapons.**

# REPRESENTATION OF VIOLENCE

*Representation* is a remarkably capacious concept, embracing the entire range of art, literature, and media; the realm of symbolic, signifying, and communicative behavior; and the sphere of legal and political theory, specifically in notions of representative government. It has been a key concept in aesthetics since Aristotle, linked with notions of imitation or mimesis, and it is fundamental to all conceptions of signs and semiosis, the very activity of making one thing "stand for" or "act for" another thing.

Representation may be thought of, then, as roughly commensurate with the entire range of cultural activity insofar as it is constituted by symbolic practices. Raymond Williams's distinction between culture and society is helpful here. If society consists in the network of "face to face" relations among a group of people, culture is the whole body of mediating signs, symbols, images, practices, institutions, narratives, habits, and customs—in short, representations—that make it possible for a society to exist.

Representation has had a very mixed reception in contemporary discussions of culture and politics, however. Representational practices are inexorably linked with power, ideology, and domination: "They cannot represent themselves; they must be represented," is Karl Marx's epitaph for the powerless in *The Eighteenth Brumaire of Louis Bonaparte* (1898). So insidious and pervasive is the power of representation that it has sometimes played the role of a political enemy to be overcome. A great deal of polemical energy in contemporary theory has been expended in "getting beyond" representation. Old-fashioned notions of mimesis, along with "copy" or "correspondence" theories of truth, mechanical notions of empowerment, and representational (mirror) models of knowledge have been treated as pariahs to be expelled by contemporary philosophy and aesthetics. Although the concept of representation applies equally well to literature and verbal media more generally, there is a powerful tendency to "specularize" the concept and to think of representation primarily as a matter of vision and mimesis, spectacle and similitude. Paradigmatic examples of representation—pictures, images, and visual media generally—are routinely characterized as contemporary "idols" that must be smashed by clearheaded iconoclastic critique or ironically celebrated as a kind of frenzy of images.

Representation should probably be treated as a highly problematic but unavoidable concept in the analysis of culture and society. We gain little by "getting beyond" representation to the sign, to language, to materialism, or to authentic, essential identities. If representation has become the scapegoat figure in much contemporary cultural theory, this makes it all the more interesting and central for reflections on violence.

### Cause, Cure, or Both?

Discussions of violence and its representation tend themselves to be filled with the most violent contradictions and paradoxes. Representations of violence in the media are widely supposed to be important causes of violence. Much of the discussion around representations of violence is oriented toward censorship, containment, immunization against, or outright banning and destruction of certain kinds of images. Representation is thought of as itself a form of violence, traumatizing, numbing, imprinting, and even transforming the spectator through mimesis. The viewer subjected to the violence of the image becomes a kind of image, a passive automaton, imitating the hypnotizing spectacle. Contemporary analyses of pornography (as in the work of Catharine MacKinnon and Andrea Dworkin) and hate speech (as in the work of Judith Butler) have a tendency to literalize the equation of violence and representation, so that words and images in themselves are seen as inflicting actual bodily or mental trauma, or as directly inciting or causing violent behavior in those who wield violent representations as weapons.

And yet at the same time, representation is commonly understood to be significantly distinct from violence: an alternative or substitute, a mere simulacrum of violence, a pretended or merely apparent violence, a rehearsed or ritually repeated and remembered violence, a cathartic nonviolent release for violent impulses. Representation itself is often thought of as inherently nonviolent: the most sadistic horror film does not literally inflict any visible, physical wounds on the spectator. The blood is just as illusory (and perhaps of the same order of reality) as stage ketchup. For every account of "words that wound" and images that violate the sensibilities of their beholders or models, there is the proverbial reminder that sticks and stones may break your bones, but words will never harm you.

Representation is thus itself represented as both the cause and the cure of violence. Even more emphatically, some theorists claim that representation simply is an instrument of violence, like an offensive weapon that transmits and translates physical acts and behavior and thereby traumatizes both its immediate recipients and the wider circle of those in turn affected by them. At the same time, representation is that which wards off violence, the shield that defends us from the violence of representation. Censorship, too, may be viewed as a shielding act of representation, a re-presenting of some prior representation as that which will not be countenanced or tolerated.

This encyclopedia of violence is itself a representation whose explicit aim is to describe, categorize, and survey the entire field of violence in a single nation, and thus (the hope is) to control, ameliorate, and perhaps pacify the tendencies toward violence in the culture and society of the United States. There is no guarantee, however, that a book like this will not become a best-seller among violent individuals who will savor the wide range of examples and the intricate analyses of their favorite subject. Like the 1986 Meese Commission Report on Pornography in the United States, sponsored by the attorney general's office under President Ronald Reagan, the representation aimed at containment of the "bad object" may wind up letting the cat out of the bag.

It is important to note, finally, that even before violence is represented in words or images, in arts or media of any kind, it is already, in its "raw" natural state, already saturated with representational issues. Animals, especially primates, often produce displays of mock violence, threatening postures, gestures, and sounds, as a substitute for the real thing. Violence is never just a pure activity separated from mimesis or semiosis, devoid of meaning, purpose, motivation, or significance. There is, as the psychiatrist James Gilligan observes, "a symbolic language of . . . violent acts" even in (or especially in) apparently "senseless" acts of violence. Even when violence is unmotivated and arbitrary, it mimics the fundamental character of the linguistic sign in the moment of its institution. We routinely characterize violence as a way of communicating or performing or expressing a message. The United States, for instance, declared that it would "send a message" to the Iraqi president Saddam Hussein with bombs and missiles. The violence of child abuse is often rationalized by parents as a way of "teaching a lesson" to their children. From the bully on the playground to the aggressor on the geopolitical stage, the agent of violence typically portrays himself as engaging in symbolic or mimetic acts calculated to impress, intimidate, and communicate with his enemies.

When the aggressor is not staging himself as a forceful communicator, he may portray himself as being engaged in self-expression of a deep nature or in making idealistic statements about fundamental moral principles. Indeed, that is why acts of violence are often rationalized as acts of pacification: World War I was "the war to end all wars," and the bland paradox of the U.S. military in Vietnam was that "we had to destroy the village in order to save it." The official aim of violence in Vietnam was never simply destruction but persuasion, "winning the hearts and minds" of the Vietnamese people. The argument of force and the force of argument, the twin weapons of words and deeds, have been the principal instruments of war since Thucydides. The end of violence is always peace and tranquillity; the aim of conflict, struggle, and aggression is always the subduing of the antagonist and the elimination of his will or ability to fight. It was not by accident that the six-gun on the American frontier was called the peacemaker, and that this central instrument of violence had (and has) a symbolic, even mythic importance in American culture.

## Political Representation

There is no possibility, then, of producing a critique of violence, a historical, political, philosophical understanding of its causes and consequences, without engaging the problem of representation. Violence and representation as concepts do not merely exist in some kind of adventitious relation, as if we could understand one without recourse to the other or reduce their relation to sound-bites about the tendency of media representations to cause violence. Representation and violence are engaged with one another from the ground up: violence is a form of representation and vice versa. Representation is also a key player in the legal and political portrayal of violence as legitimate or illegitimate, just or unjust, and in the creation of a governmental system capable of sustaining these portrayals. The central insight of Hobbes's political theory is grounded in the dialectic of violence and representation. The state of nature is, for Hobbes, a state of pure violence, a war of all against all, "nasty, brutish, and short." This violent world is antithetical to political forms of representation: it lies outside oaths, covenants, contracts, laws, and sovereign representatives such as assemblies or monarchs. Representation, as we see in Hobbes's *Leviathan*, is the key activity in the transformation of this state of nature into a commonwealth with a civil society:

> Nature (the art whereby God hath made and governes the World) is by the *Art* of man, as in many other

things, so in this also imitated, that it can make an Artificial Animal ... that great Leviathan called a Common-wealth, or State.

Imitation and artifice create a collective representation, an "Artificiall Man" whose "soul" is the "soveraignty" that "personates" the collective and whose will is embodied in the person of the sovereign, the "representative" of the totality. But this act of representation, far from spelling an end to violence, is actually its concentration in the hands of a central authority. As the figure of the Leviathan itself suggests, the commonwealth or collective body and the sovereign representative that is its soul is a monstrous artificial being characterized by overwhelming power, a monopoly on the means of violence, and a control over the legitimation of those means. Whether or not they agree with the details of Hobbes's political philosophy, all modern states, the United States included, are predicated on some narrative of this sort, in which the (natural) right of individuals to exert violence in their own interests is renounced and divested, transferred to some representative authority—the military or the police—that then has the power to make war and keep the civil peace with the appropriate instruments of (legitimate) violence. (The "right to bear arms" in the U.S. Constitution is a conspicuous deviation from the sovereign representative's monopoly on violence and a symptom of a fundamental contradiction in U.S. culture: the continuing belief, manifested everywhere in popular media and everyday life, that every U.S. citizen reserves the right to the private control of instruments of deadly force.) Despite the "right to bear arms" and the renunciation of private, individual acts of violence, the delegation of violence to representatives of the social whole is such a self-evident fact of life that we rarely reflect on the extent to which it, and all social orders, are grounded in processes of representation—the representative who "acts for" the society, the legal representation of acts as legal or illegal. The discrimination between legitimate and illegitimate violence is conducted by means of representations (prohibitions and injunctions, laws and contracts, oaths and vows); the exertion of legitimate violence is restricted to those who act as representatives of the community.

## Agent, Instrument, Patient

Violence, like representation, is always a three-way affair, involving an agent, an instrument, and a patient (or victim), just as communication of symbolic meaning or value goes from a sender through a medium to a receiver. Something is transmitted in violence from one person to another, just as something is transmitted in every communicative act. That is why violence is often characterized as communication (sending a message) or in economic terms (the exchange of blows or "an eye for an eye"). Sometimes the victim position is the addressee of the representation (the audience listening to an offensive statement or the viewer of a horrific spectacle); sometimes the victim is the "model" represented (most notably in caricatures that disfigure or mutilate what they represent). Clearly it is possible to be doubly wounded by representation, to be violated as the (disfigured) model and as the (offended) beholder.

The representational model of violence also helps us see how it is that representation generally plays the role of instrument in an action. The author and political scientist Hannah Arendt argues that "violence is by nature instrumental; like all means, it always stands in need of guidance and justification through the end it pursues." Representation is also a means: as mediator or medium it serves as a prosthesis for the audience, a veil or screen for a symbolic appearance—a narrative, spectacle, or event. But representation (words and images) cannot be confined so easily to the instrumental position in the agent-instrument-patient structure of action. The representation is often regarded as itself an agent, as when the media or some specific image or text is blamed for authorizing and initiating violence. It is only a small step from representation-as-agent to representation-as-patient, or victim, most notably in cases where an image is subjected to defacement, destruction, or desecration. Hanging in effigy, vandalism, and the disfiguring of public monuments are obvious examples of the image as victim. The ongoing effort to pass a constitutional amendment protecting the American flag from burning or desecration testifies to the extent to which this symbol has become a kind of living icon in U.S. culture, capable of playing the victim's role in political rituals. Since every interesting account of representation as communication is interactive and dialectical, involving two-way or multiple-routed transactions and "feedback loops" among agents, it is not surprising that violence turns out to be a phenomenon that moves in cycles, with rehearsals, repetitions, and escalations, or that it is often represented as a kind of contagion or virulent plague in which mimesis is the vehicle of transmission. Copycat murders, in which one violent act (especially one widely represented in news media) seems to generate a host of imitators, are a common feature of American life. The right to bear arms and the right to free speech and a free press are thus deeply implicated with one another in American culture. The gun and the camera participate in analogous rituals of "shooting" that are not confined to the obvious linkages of war and visual technologies. Contemporary "rapid-cam" journalism is rapidly becoming indistinguishable from entertainment in its lurid representations of violence. The entire apparatus of the mass media seems ineluctably drawn to scenes of disaster and violence, as if expressing a collective form of morbid fascination with words and images linked to horror or scandal.

## The Media

At times, the media themselves seem to become agents of violence, in overaggressive violations of privacy (as with Princess Diana) or in the providing of a stage to exhibitionistic aggressors (as with the Unabomber). The death of Princess Diana in August 1997 might seem to be a British example; but the event occurred in Paris and was instantaneously reported worldwide by the American-owned CNN television network, which continued coverage of the event and its aftermath seemingly without end. It hardly seems an exaggeration to say that Princess Diana was "killed by photography," so long as we understand that statement as shorthand for a complex feedback loop of mediation and representation. That is, Princess Diana first had to be created by the media as an attractive object, a star image whose privacy was worth violating; the craving for that violation had to be expressed by a mass market for the consumption of her image; and a whole industry (tabloid journals with their image providers, the paparazzi) had to be willing to obtain and circulate her image.

The location of agency and responsibility in this whole cycle of representation is extraordinarily slippery. Although it was popular to blame the paparazzi for the death of Princess Diana, the pursuing photographers were probably just doing their jobs in a fairly routine way. The high-speed pursuit of celebrities is a well-established part of the game. Insofar as the paparazzi were mere instruments of the tabloid publishers, and insofar as the tabloids merely cater to mass taste—the taste of the same masses who cried their eyes out in a weeklong escalation of spectacular mediatized grief, the location of guilt and agency becomes problematic. The paparazzi are merely the eyes of the masses; they are prosthetic extensions of a collective desire to see, to consume images of star personalities.

Nevertheless, the point of linking the logic of violence and representation is not to produce an evasion of agency or responsibility. Rather, the value of making such a linkage is that it helps

**The mangled car of Princess Diana after the fatal crash in Paris, August 1997.** Gamma/Liaison Agency

avoid an all-too-familiar strategy in critiques of violence, which starts with the assumption that violence is evil, to be stamped out or contained, and that representation is merely one means to this end. If representation encourages violence, it is to be destroyed; if it has the effect of pacification, it is to be encouraged. Far from leading to a critique of violence (or of representation), this procedure already knows its outcome from the beginning and substitutes any possibility of actual analysis of violence with a sentimental assurance that it is against it.

### Ends and Means

Walter Benjamin's "Critique of Violence" (written in 1920) comes at this intuition from the side of political theory and the question of "ends and means." Benjamin demolishes the common assumption that the critique of violence can be carried forward as "the question whether violence, in a given case, is a means to a just or an unjust end." The critique (and justification) of violence by an appeal to the realm of ends is all too obvious and tempting. If violence is exerted on behalf of a good end, it is good; if exerted on behalf of a bad end, it is bad. "Violence," as Benjamin notes, becomes "a product of nature, as it were a raw material," in itself ethically and politically neutral. This line of thinking, associated with natural law in legal philosophy, leads immediately away from any possible critique of violence itself into questions about the good life or the good state. Once those questions are answered, any violence (notoriously, the 1793–1794 Reign of Terror during the French Revolution) may be justified as long as its linkage to the good end may be made plausible.

Benjamin also considers the alternative of "positive law, which sees violence as a product of history," and which rejects the critique of "just ends" for that of "legal means." This approach has at least the virtue of being historical and of leading to an examination of the socially constructed character of legitimate and illegitimate violence. It leads, in other words, toward the question of how violence is imbricated with legal and political representation. The limitation of the positive law tradition in Benjamin's view is that it cannot reflect on its own relation to the sphere of justice (the realm of ends and natural law), nor can it transcend its limitations to assess the value of legal or legitimated forms of violence. Writing his "Critique of Violence" in the wake of World War I and the Russian Revolution, Benjamin saw the need for an immanent critique of violence, one that would not defer examination of violence itself in favor of debates about justice (the way things ought to be) or legality (the way things are and have been). His was a critique of violence that wanted to keep open the possibility of a "divine violence" (the bloodless revolution or general strike or the nonviolent overturning of a regime). The closest thing in U.S. political culture is probably the Jeffersonian legacy of continuing revolution with its corollaries, the need for a weak central government, local autonomy, and the right to bear arms.

Benjamin's emphasis was on violence and representative institutions (police and the military) and transgressive representatives such as the romantic figure of the "great criminal" who "arouses . . . the sympathy of the public against the law." American culture provides many examples of such figures from Billy the Kid to Bonnie and Clyde. It is clear, however, that representational institutions (media, the arts, ritual, performance, and mimicry in everyday life) provide the aesthetic and semiotic ligatures that shape popular ideas about the nature of representative institutions and consequently determine how the violence that emanates from these institutions is enacted. War and crime, the military and the police, are not merely sociopolitical institutions, but cultural ones as well. Mafia thugs learn how to walk and talk by watching "mob" films like *Scarface* (1932), *The Godfather* (1972), and *Goodfellas* (1990). Ronald Reagan was evidently convinced (despite all facts to the contrary) that he had "seen action" in World War II very much like the action he could have seen in the movies. (See Michael Paul Rogin's 1987 study, *Ronald Reagan, the Movie*.) Mortally wounded soldiers in Vietnam would sometimes ask medics for a last cigarette, even when they had never smoked before in their lives, as a way of reenacting standard scenes from war movies.

### What We Talk About When We Talk About Violence

What conclusions can we draw from this survey of the relations between violence and representation? First, it should be clear that the critique of violence within a representational model is not very fully developed. Despite the hosts of experts on violence and media, public health, youth, ethnic minorities, criminal subcultures, and gender (especially male perpetrators and female victims), there is a conspicuous lack of interdisciplinary theoretical reflection across the numerous domains

A scene from *The Godfather* (1972). Corbis/Bettmann

of violence and representation. Legitimate or sanctioned forms of violence (military and police power) tend to be bracketed off as external to the problem, which is focused on crime, terrorism, and civil disorder as the privileged, even exclusive terrain of violence. Systemic forms of violence (poverty and racial or sexual discrimination) are rendered invisible by forms of representation that rationalize them as natural and portray their victims as inherently, genetically violent. When the subject of representation enters a conversation about violence, the discussion tends to be limited to cries of alarm over some movie or television show, followed by calls for censorship of violent media spectacles as "entertainment." (Scenes of violence on the news, by contrast, are rarely seen as issues for concern.)

Second, it seems clear that in U.S. culture the official attitude toward representation and violence is primarily instrumental and pragmatic. The refrain "Guns don't kill. People do" is oft-heard from the National Rifle Association; given the uncanny parallels between debates over the control of guns and the control of images, one almost anticipates that a slogan along the lines of "Images don't kill. People do" might someday be taken up by the American Civil Liberties Union. Opponents of gun control often argue that guns prevent as

much violent crime as they cause, and defenders of free speech argue that the cure for hateful, violent speech is more speech (here understood as encompassing both words and images, the whole field of representation). The similarity of these arguments is all the more interesting given their typical location in diametrically opposed political positions. Instead of assuming that words and guns are straightforwardly distinguishable as figurative and literal weapons that wound the spirit and the body respectively, we need to explore the extent to which the roles are reversed, with guns playing the role of cultural symbols (of manhood, autonomy, and independence) while symbols (that is, words and images) serve as weapons that exert a real, not imaginary, violence.

Third, we need a critique of representation and violence that attempts a more capacious understanding of the twin role of representation as both cause and cure, weapon of and shield against violence. Particularly relevant here would be the small body of theoretical literature that goes against the grain of pragmatic, problem-solving approaches to violence and explores the questions of social function, individual pleasure, and historical repetition involved in representations of violence. René Girard's *Violence and the Sacred* (1977) provides one crucial opening in its argument that violence is endemic to the human condition and that it can never be eliminated, only contained by representations and ritual reenactments involving surrogate victims. If representation itself sometimes seems to play the role of scapegoat in discussions of media violence, Girard may help us to understand how such discussions are themselves rituals of substitution. Leo Bersani and Ulysse Dutoit's *The Forms of Violence* (1985) calls into question the common appeal to "narrative justification" for violent scenes. Drawing on the example of the highly formalized, abstracted patterns of violence in the much-reviled Assyrian palace reliefs of the ninth to seventh century B.C., Bersani and Dutoit argue for a mobilized, de-centered, and playful form of sadomasochistic pleasure that refuses the fascination, fixation, and narrative legitimation so typical of violent stories. The distinction to which they appeal might be exemplified by the difference between Rambo and Jackie Chan films—that is, between self-righteous narratives of vengeance and the self-reflexive play of virtuosic mayhem.

Also worth mentioning in this context are the new attempts to analyze what might be called "cultures of violence," social orders in which violence has become not an anomaly or problem but a way of life that seems to perpetuate itself indefinitely. Notable work has been done in Colombia (where a discipline known as "violentology" has sprung up), in the former Yugoslavia, and in Northern Ireland, where Allan Feldman's *Formations of Violence* (1991) offers a striking new model of anthropological fieldwork and theoretical reflection on ritualized cycles of religious and political violence.

## The Metaphor of Public Health

One compelling attempt to understand the entire phenomenon of individual and social violence, James Gilligan's *Violence: Our Deadly Epidemic and Its Causes* (1996), comes from the field of psychiatry and criminology. Gilligan regards violence as a consequence of shame and humiliation. Rejecting sociobiological accounts of violence as genetic, racial, or gender determined, Gilligan argues that violence is a product of systemic inequality, degradation, and despair. He applies a "public health" model to the problem of violence, treating it quite literally as an epidemic in which the pathogens are not microorganisms but emotions.

One can argue that Gilligan's theory needs to be supplemented by a fuller recognition of exactly what the vehicle of contagion is in the epidemic of violence. The "germ" model does not, in fact, perfectly apply; rather, it works best as a bold analogy, a metaphor, a way of picturing violence. The medium in which the plague of violence is literally spread is neither germs nor emotions, but the process of representation itself. Gilligan says as much when he notes that "there is a symbolic language of . . . violent acts" that one has to decipher "like a cryptologist"; when he portrays legal punishment as a "mirror of crime" that enacts a ritual exchange of "an eye for an eye"; and, indeed, in the very phenomenon of shame itself.

Shame is the loss of control over one's self-presentation, an exposure to hostile, degrading forms of representation. That is why "losing face" is such a powerful incitement to violence, and why violence so often seems disproportionate or irrational, an extreme response to a trivial provocation—a "mere" word or gesture or symbolic act. Violence becomes intelligible (and therefore treatable) only within a framework that recognizes the extent to which it is a mimetic and symbolic process. We need to explore the implications of the commonplace observation that the contemporary epidemic of violence is accompanied by (perhaps sustained by) an epidemic of images, what Fredric Jameson has called the "mediatization" of everyday life. The culture in which the germs of violence flourish is constructed by practices of representation. Since the elimination of mimetic and symbolic behavior is out of the question, the only way left to imagine a "cure" for violence is through what Nelson Goodman (1968) might call the "routes" of representation, its pathways of mediation, reference, repetition, and substitution. If violence and images are "pathogens" in mutually reinforcing epidemics, the traditional cures are either homeopathic or allopathic medicines, that is, medicines either similar to the disease (thus stimulating the immune system) or antithetical to it (antigens, antibiotics, anaesthetics). A promising area of investigation would then be the realm of what we might call "metapictures" of violence, representations of representation of violence.

## Metapictures

The ironic or reflexive doubling of representation in films such as Oliver Stone's *Natural Born Killers* (1994), which continually crosses the boundary between real and mediatized violence, actual and fantastic scenes of destruction, offers a place in which critical reflection on this issue may be carried on. Nothing guarantees, of course, that irony or self-reference will serve as anything more than an alibi for the same old spectacles of mayhem. *Natural Born Killers* may simply be providing a set of role models for self-destructive copycat couples who find serial killing a basis for good sex. It is a film about immunization and resistance: if a spectator can withstand the sensory assault of this picture, its relentless effort to render "senseless" violence as a hyper-mediated spectacle, then one's immune system is clearly in working order.

Wim Wenders's 1997 film *The End of Violence* takes the "antigen" route. It is an attempt to reference runaway police violence without imitating or displaying it directly, foregrounding the apparatus of representation itself. Based on the premise of instantaneous video surveillance of the entire city of Los Angeles with high-powered remote-control rifles carrying out equally instantaneous executions of lawbreakers as they are caught in the act, *The End of Violence* is itself almost completely devoid of violent spectacle (the image repertoire is one of glowing television monitors, and remote-control video cameras sweeping over panoramas of Los Angeles at night). It is as if Wenders set himself the task of critical reflection without representation, perhaps the most utopian goal imaginable in a culture that thrives on violent spectacle.

The concept of the metapicture, what Foucault called a "representation of representation," might help us then consolidate and particularize the fragmented array of critiques of representation and violence, especially those that rely on received notions of media or culture as the key agent or instrument in cycles of violence. We need to keep in mind that there is no such thing as "the media," in any homogeneous or monolithic sense. Media are complex social institutions with ongoing histories and internal cultures; they cannot be defined simply in terms of their sensory address (visual or auditory), their mode of representation (image or text), or their putative audience (mass versus elite). All media are mixed media, and the challenge is to describe and analyze specific mixtures with maximum precision. "The" media that made possible the Monica Lewinsky sex scandal that threatened the presidency of Bill Clinton in 1998, for instance, included wiretapping, photojournalism, network news, the Internet, talk radio, digital imaging and virtual reality technologies, daily newspapers, weekly news magazines, supermarket tabloids, spin doctors, media experts, lawyers, the presidency (in which the nation "personates" itself in the physical body of the sovereign representa-

tive), and that curious legal representative known as a "special prosecutor."

Metapictures make visible the "nesting" of different media inside one another, the way, for instance, that one medium (the law, government) overlaps with others (photography, television, cinema) or the way that technical advances in media (computers, biogenetic engineering) make previous technologies appear obsolete and introduce the possibility of new events into the world.

The film *Wag the Dog* (1997), which appeared contemporaneously with the Lewinsky scandal, is a metapicture, a filmic representation of the various modes of representation that might be mobilized to contain a runaway media scandal. *Wag the Dog* adds Hollywood and its special-effects arsenal to the media mixture, and suggests that the most efficacious form of representation for containing a high-level political sex scandal is (unsurprisingly) a war. The image of the president molesting a "Fire Fly girl" during a moment of privacy in the Oval Office can only be checkmated by something as extreme as vivid images of terrorism and mass destruction. If sex sells, violence sells even better (which may explain why the film industry has more success in censoring sex than violence). The president's body is as much an image and a medium of representation as the "media" that make his body into a spectacle.

Metapictures of this sort may also help us understand that peculiar phenomenon of representation that Jean Baudrillard (1995) has called "the precession of simulacra," in which media images seem to precede the events they represent. *Wag the Dog* seemed uncannily to describe the renewal of the Persian Gulf War at the height of the Monica Lewinsky scandal—before renewed bombing in the Middle East in fact began. Baudrillard argues provocatively that "the Gulf War did not take place," that it was a simulated "event" staged for the audience of globalized media. More accurate would be to say that there is no event without representation; the Gulf War *did* happen—as representation from beginning to end.

To bowdlerize Karl Marx and Nathaniel Hawthorne: every historical event happens at least twice, and every tale is "twice-told" at a minimum. The metapicture makes this doubleness of representation visible, open to description and analysis. Putting representation on the table for inspection might perhaps also help us to comprehend and to break the cycles of violence in which representation plays a crucial role, as putative agent, runaway instrumentality, and surrogate victim.

*BIBLIOGRAPHY*

Arendt, Hannah. *On Violence.* New York: Harcourt, Brace, 1969.

Armstrong, Nancy, and Leonard Tennenhouse. *The Violence of Representation: Literature and the History of Violence.* New York: Routledge, 1989.

Barker, Francis. *The Culture of Violence: Tragedy and History.* Chicago: University of Chicago Press, 1993.

Baudrillard, Jean. *The Gulf War Did Not Take Place.* Translated from the French by Paul Patton. Bloomington: Indiana University Press, 1995.

Benjamin, Walter. "Critique of Violence." In his *Reflections: Essays, Aphorisms, Autobiographical Writings.* New York: Harcourt, 1978.

Bersani, Leo, and Ulysse Dutoit. *The Forms of Violence.* New York: Schocken, 1985.

Bryson, Norman. "The Essential Copy." In his *Vision and Painting: The Logic in the Gaze.* New Haven, Conn.: Yale University Press, 1983.

Butler, Judith. *Excitable Speech: A Politics of the Performative.* New York, Routledge, 1997.

Caillois, Roger. *The Mask of Medusa,* translated by George Ordish. New York: C. N. Potter, 1964.

Derrida, Jacques. *Given Time.* Chicago: University of Chicago Press, 1992.

Feldman, Allen. *Formations of Violence: The Narrative of the Body and Political Terror in Northern Ireland, 1991.* Chicago: University of Chicago Press, 1991.

Gilligan, James. *Violence: Our Deadly Epidemic and Its Causes.* New York: Putnam, 1996.

Girard, René. *Violence and the Sacred.* Baltimore: Johns Hopkins University Press, 1977.

Goodman, Nelson. *Languages of Art: An Approach to a Theory of Symbols.* Indianapolis, Ind.: Bobbs-Merrill, 1968.

Jameson, Fredric. *Postmodernism.* Durham, N.C.: Duke University Press, 1991.

Jay, Martin. *Downcast Eyes: The Denigration of Vision in Twentieth-Century French Thought.* Berkeley: University of California Press, 1993.

Lacan, Jacques. *Four Fundamental Concepts of Psychoanalysis.* New York: Norton, 1977.

Mitchell, W. J. T. "Metapictures," "The Violence of Public Art: *Do the Right Thing,*" and "Representation and Responsibility." In his *Picture Theory: Essays on Verbal and Visual Representation.* Chicago: University of Chicago Press, 1994.

Pitkin, Hannah. *Representation.* New York: Atherton, 1969.

Rorty, Richard. *Philosophy and the Mirror of Nature.* Princeton, N.J.: Princeton University Press, 1979.

Said, Edward W. *Orientalism.* New York: Pantheon, 1978.

Shapiro, Michael J. *The Politics of Representation: Writing Practices in Biography, Photography, and Policy Analysis.* Madison: University of Wisconsin Press, 1988.

Stewart, Susan. "The Marquis de Meese." *Critical Inquiry* 15, no. 1 (1998).

Virilio, Paul. *War and Cinema: The Logistics of Perception.* New York: Verso, 1989.

Wilden, Anthony. *System and Structure: Essays in Communication and Exchange.* London: Travistock, 1972.

Williams, Raymond. *Keywords: A Vocabulary of Culture and Society.* New York: Oxford University Press, 1976.

W. J. T. MITCHELL

*See also* **Dance; Film; Fine Arts; Language and Verbal Violence; Painting; Popular Culture; Sculpture; Serial Killers, Representations of; Shame; Television; Theater.**

**REVOLUTIONARY WAR.** *See* American Revolution.

# RIGHT TO BEAR ARMS

The Second Amendment to the U.S. Constitution provides: "A well regulated Militia, being necessary to the security of a free State, the right of the people to keep and bear Arms, shall not be infringed." This part of the Bill of Rights was originally intended to reduce violence in society by enabling the people to protect themselves from foreign invasion, domestic tyranny, and private crime. At the close of the twentieth century, great controversy existed over this right.

## The American Revolution

The Glorious Revolution of 1689 ended the unlimited power of the monarchy in England and resulted in the adoption of the Declaration of Rights, which decried the disarming of the Protestant majority and guaranteed the right to petition and the right of Protestants to "have arms for their defense." William Blackstone wrote in his *Commentaries on the Laws of England* (1765–1769) that this declaration protected all English citizens in "the right of having and using arms for self-preservation and defense."

In 1768, as British soldiers sailed to occupy Boston, the American colonists feared that they would be disarmed and that leading patriots would be taken to England to stand trial. Arming themselves, they insisted on their rights as English subjects. The Boston Massacre and other continuing conflicts boiled over by 1774, when King George III banned the importation of arms into the American colonies and British soldiers began to execute searches and seizures of firearms in Boston. The

The statue of a minuteman stands at the end of the Old North Bridge in Concord, Massachusetts, the site of "the shot heard around the world" at the first battle of the American Revolution. CORBIS/LEE SNIDER

colonists seized arms and gunpowder from royal armories, and the conflict escalated.

The British march into the countryside to seize the colonists' arms resulted in the "shot heard round the world" at Lexington and Concord on 19 April 1775. In occupied Boston, General Thomas Gage decreed that all citizens must entrust their firearms temporarily to their selectmen and that anyone would be allowed to leave Boston after complying. The 2,500 firearms turned in were confiscated by British troops. Gage then refused to allow anyone free passage from Boston. This perfidy was cited on 6 July 1775 by the Continental Congress in its Declaration of Causes of Taking Up Arms.

During the American Revolution about half of the states adopted bills of rights. Pennsylvania and Vermont declared that "the people have a right to

bear arms for the defense of themselves and the state." North Carolina declared that "the people have a right to bear arms, for the defense of the state," while the Massachusetts guarantee provided that "the people have a right to keep and bear arms for the common defense." The Continental army, state militias, and guerrillas played varying roles in the road to independence.

**Adopting the Bill of Rights**

When the Constitution was proposed in 1787 without a bill of rights, the federalists argued that such a bill was unnecessary, since Congress had no power to control rights such as freedom of the press and the right to bear arms. In *The Federalist Papers* (1787–1788), number twenty-nine, Alexander Hamilton wrote that a standing army could never rule "while there is a large body of citizens, little if at all inferior to them in discipline and the use of arms, who stand ready to defend their rights and those of their fellow citizens."

In *The Federalist*, number forty-six, James Madison alluded to "the advantage of being armed, which the Americans possess over the people of almost every other nation," adding that, "notwithstanding the military establishments in the several kingdoms of Europe, which are carried as far as the public resources will bear, the governments are afraid to trust the people with arms." If the people were armed, "the throne of every tyranny in Europe would be speedily overturned in spite of the legions which surround it."

Noah Webster, the influential federalist and lexicographer, in *An Examination into the Leading Principles of the Federal Constitution* (1787), wrote: "Before a standing army can rule, the people must be disarmed; as they are in almost every kingdom in Europe. The supreme power in America cannot enforce unjust laws by the sword; because the whole body of the people are armed."

Similarly, Tench Coxe, another prominent federalist, explained in the *Pennsylvania Gazette* on 20 February 1788 that the militia was the people at large and that "Congress have no power to disarm the militia. Their swords, and every other terrible implement of the soldier, are *the birth-right of an American*."

Insisting on a bill of rights, the antifederalist Richard Henry Lee wrote in *Additional Letters from the Federal Farmer* (1788) that "to preserve liberty, it is essential that the whole body of the people always possess arms, and be taught alike, especially when young, how to use them."

A great compromise was reached in which the Constitution would be ratified and a bill of rights would be taken up by the first Congress. True to this bargain, in 1789 James Madison rose in the House of Representatives and proposed what became the Bill of Rights. Days later, on 18 June 1789, in an article in the *Federal Gazette* approved by Madison, Tench Coxe wrote of the Second Amendment: "As civil rulers, not having their duty to the people duly before them, may attempt to tyrannize, and as the military forces which must be occasionally raised to defend our country, might pervert their power to the injury of their fellow citizens, the people are confirmed . . . in their right to keep and bear their private arms." The Bill of Rights, containing the first ten amendments, was ratified in 1791.

St. George Tucker, the first major commentator on the Bill of Rights, explained the Second Amendment in his edition of *Blackstone's Commentaries* (1803) as follows: "The right of self-defense is the first law of nature. . . . Wherever . . . the right of the people to keep and bear arms is, under any color or pretext whatsoever, prohibited, liberty, if not already annihilated, is on the brink of destruction."

## Freedmen and Reconstruction

The right to bear arms generated little controversy in antebellum America. The federal and state militia laws required every citizen to keep a musket or pistol. The only restriction applicable to citizens was the antebellum prohibitions in the southern states against carrying concealed weapons, in order to enforce the code of honor for dueling.

Abolitionists argued that slavery was unconstitutional because the Constitution, including the Second Amendment, protected "the people." Yet the slave codes prohibited firearm possession by blacks and deprived them of other basic rights. In *Dred Scott v. Sandford* (1857), the Supreme Court held that African Americans were not citizens, for if they were, they would have the rights to "full liberty of speech" and "to keep and carry arms wherever they went."

After the Civil War the southern states reenacted slave-code bans on blacks exercising basic rights, including firearm ownership. State militias enforced the law by conducting searches and seizures of the homes of freedmen. Congress responded by passing the Freedmen's Bureau Act of 1866, which protected the rights to "personal liberty, personal security, and [estate], including the constitutional right to bear arms."

The same Congress proposed what became the Fourteenth Amendment to the Constitution, which prohibits states from abridging "the privileges or immunities of citizens" and from depriving "any person of life, liberty, or property, without due process of law." Senator Jacob Howard, introducing the amendment on 23 May 1866, explained that its purpose was to protect "personal rights" such as "the right to keep and bear arms."

At the end of the Reconstruction, the Supreme Court ruled in *United States v. Cruikshank* (1876) that the rights of the people to assemble and to bear arms for a lawful purpose were not "granted" by the Constitution because these rights existed long before its adoption. While these rights were protected from infringement by the federal government, they were not protected against private violation except under state law. Thus, the federal government could not prosecute whites who had disarmed and then murdered blacks.

A decade later, in *Presser v. Illinois* (1886), the Supreme Court held that a state law that required citizens to obtain a license from the governor in order to have an armed march in a city did not violate the rights to assemble and to bear arms. Critics charged that the state law was passed to restrict membership in the National Guard to "trusted" citizens who would repress the labor movement and to criminalize workers marching with unloaded rifles to protest police violence.

## From Prohibition to World War II

No federal law restricting firearm ownership existed until the National Firearms Act of 1934. This law was spawned by Prohibition, which created organized crime and Depression-era gangsterism. As proposed, the bill would have virtually banned pistols and revolvers, but a compromise with the National Rifle Association restricted the act to a ban on machine guns and short-barreled shotguns and rifles.

In *United States v. Miller* (1939), the Supreme Court avoided determining whether restricting the short-barreled shotgun was consistent with the Second Amendment. The district court had declared the restriction contrary to the Second Amendment, but the Supreme Court remanded the case for fact-finding because there was no evidence in the trial court that "this weapon is any part of the ordinary military equipment or that its use could contribute to the common defense." The

## Jack Miller

Born in 1897, the defendant in *United States v. Miller* (1939) was charged with transporting a short-barreled shotgun from Oklahoma to Arkansas. Jack Miller had been the getaway car driver for a gang that robbed banks in Arkansas, and he later turned state's evidence against some associates. After the district court in the Western District of Arkansas dismissed the weapon-transporting charges against him, Miller went into hiding.

Miller's attorney did not have the funds to file a brief or to argue in the Supreme Court, so the Court heard arguments only from the U.S. government. In the meantime, Miller's former associates broke out of jail and apparently caught up with him. Six weeks before the 1939 Supreme Court ruling, which would have reinstated his indictment, Miller's body was found on a creek bank, with two shots in the chest.

Supreme Court did not suggest that the possessor of such a firearm must be a member of the militia; it asked only whether the arm could have militia use.

In 1941, just before the Japanese attack on Pearl Harbor, Congress authorized President Franklin D. Roosevelt to requisition private property with military uses. However, in reaction to Hitler's repression and disarming of political opponents, Jews, and the people of occupied countries, the Property Requisition Act of 1941 guaranteed against the requisition or registration "of any firearms possessed by any individual for his personal protection or sport" and against any action "to impair or infringe in any manner the right of any individual to keep and bear arms."

During World War II, with the National Guard shipped overseas, the reserve militia was called out by the states for civil defense. Able-bodied males, using their own sporting firearms, organized under state sanction to guard and defend against sabotage, subversion, and fifth-column activity.

### Whither the Right to Keep and Bear Arms?

Few restrictions on firearm transactions existed until civil unrest and the assassinations of John

Kennedy and Martin Luther King, Jr., led to the enactment of the Gun Control Act (GCA) of 1968. In addition to creating new categories of "victimless crimes" (such as the transfer of a firearm to a person in another state), this law prohibited possession of firearms by felons and by those in other narrow categories. To uphold the GCA, the argument blossomed that the Second Amendment only protected the collective state "right" to have a militia, not individual rights.

By the 1980s, gun collectors and the National Rifle Association charged that the GCA was being enforced against law-abiding citizens instead of criminals. Congress enacted the Firearms Owners' Protection Act of 1986, a reform designed to protect "the rights of citizens to keep and bear arms under the second amendment."

By the late twentieth century, the Supreme Court had yet to decide a major case on the Second Amendment. In a 1990 case, the Supreme Court stated that "the people" as used in the First, Second, and Fourth Amendments "refers to a class of persons who are part of a national community."

The former chief justice Warren E. Burger wrote in *Parade* magazine in 1990 that the view that the Second Amendment guarantees individual rights is a "fraud." On the other hand, in *A Matter of Interpretation* (1997), Justice Antonin Scalia wrote that the Second Amendment protects "the individual's right to bear arms for self-defense." In *Sheriff Jay Printz v. United States* (1997) the Supreme Court declared part of the Brady Handgun Act of 1993 in violation of the Tenth Amendment powers reserved for the states. In his concurring opinion, Justice Clarence Thomas challenged the Supreme Court to decide whether the nineteenth-century justice Joseph Story was correct when he wrote that the right to bear arms is "the palladium of the liberties of a republic."

It is worth remembering that in ancient Greece Aristotle advocated a polity of armed citizens, while Plato maintained that the ideal state restricted arms possession. This issue will continue to be debated as long as humans are organized into political societies.

*BIBLIOGRAPHY*

Cottrol, Robert, ed. *Gun Control and the Constitution.* New York: Garland, 1994.

Halbrook, Stephen P. *Freedman, the Fourteenth Amendment, and the Right to Bear Arms, 1866–1876.* Westport, Conn.: Praeger, 1998.

———. *A Right to Bear Arms: State and Federal Bills of Rights and Constitutional Guarantees.* Westport, Conn.: Greenwood Press, 1989.

———. *That Every Man Be Armed: The Evolution of a Constitutional Right.* Albuquerque: University of New Mexico Press, 1984. Reprinted in 1994 by Independent Institute, Oakland, Calif.

Malcolm, Joyce L. *To Keep and Bear Arms: The Origins of an Anglo-American Right.* Cambridge, Mass.: Harvard University Press, 1994.

Reynolds, Glenn H., and Don B. Kates. "The Second Amendment and States' Rights." *William and Mary Law Review* 36 (August 1995): 1737.

U.S. Congress. Senate. Committee on the Judiciary. Subcommittee on the Constitution. *The Right to Keep and Bear Arms.* 97th Cong., 2d sess., 1982.

STEPHEN P. HALBROOK

*See also* **Civil Liberties; Gun Control; Gun Violence: Culture; Militarism; Militias, Authorized; National Rifle Association; Weapons: Handguns.**

# RIOTS

Riots as a form of social violence are both fascinating and a source of fear. The total number of deaths from all of America's riots is modest compared with mortality from vehicular accidents, yet the impact of riots on U.S. culture and attitudes about violence and human rights has been immeasurably more important. It is possible to suggest, but not to demonstrate, that riots have facilitated positive social change that might otherwise not have occurred. The significance of rioting—whether as a form of violence or as a catalyst for social change—is suggested in the extent of academic, scientific, and governmental research that has been done on riots and riot-related behavior and events, and even in the way riots appear as a theme in fiction, ranging from Edward Bellamy's now quaintly antiquated *The Duke of Stockbridge: A Romance of Shays' Rebellion* (1879) to Ralph Ellison's *Invisible Man* (1952). What might seem a disproportionate interest in riots can probably best be explained by the fact that automobile deaths happen to other individuals, and riots, even riots in faraway places without major casualties, dramatically raise questions about the very viability of a society.

## What Is a Riot?

The *Oxford English Dictionary* defines *riot* as "a violent disturbance of the peace by an assembly or body of persons; an outbreak of active lawlessness or disorder among the populace." T. A. Critchley quotes an 1884 definition of unlawful assembly as a meeting "of great numbers of people with such circumstances of terror as cannot but endanger the public peace . . . as where great numbers complaining of a common grievance meet together, armed in a warlike manner." Actual violence was not necessary to make an assembly unlawful; the threat was enough. Paul Gilje (1996) combines legal and customary definitions and comes up with a working definition: "a riot is any group of twelve or more people attempting to assert their will immediately through the use of force outside the natural bounds of law."

---

### Individual and Collective Action

Every conceivable variety of human action could presumably occur in the course of rioting. Some are more likely than others, however, and some are primarily things individuals do, while others are collective.

Consider asking someone who had been in a riot, whether as victim, rioter, or control agent, "What did you *do?*" Some of the acts in the following list make more sense as answers (activities that would surprise an interlocutor are in italics): *administer,* assault, blame, boo, burn, chant, *clean, compose, cook,* cooperate, coordinate, destroy, *dine,* escape, *exercise,* exhort, explain, gather or assemble, *jog,* judge, listen, loot, march, *meditate,* mill around, monitor, plan, protect, report, *sail, sculpt, sew,* share or exchange rumors, *sleep, study,* sympathize, teach (for example, how to minimize the effects of tear gas), watch, *work.* Individuals assemble, listen, monitor, watch. Collectivities chant, march, and cooperate to raise barricades.

Clark McPhail has pointed out that individual and collective behaviors alternate in the temporary gatherings constituted by riot participants. Authority, control, technology, and beliefs concerning what constitutes permissible behavior all constrain the range of behaviors that are likely to occur in such gatherings. On the other hand, the occurrence of individual and collective behaviors outside the range of the expected or traditionally acceptable is likely to have long-range effects in transforming society, perhaps toward more openness, perhaps toward greater repression.

---

Legal definitions of riots are not very helpful. They often encompass events that most people would not regard as riots and do not provide useful ways of distinguishing riots from other varieties of collective violence (physical assault and assault on property). Statutory- and common-law definitions usually include some minimum number of participants, as few as three and seldom more than twelve. Few people would consider a dozen or so drunken college students noisily trying to find their way home, urinating on bushes, and knocking over trash cans a riot, but under some definitions such activity would constitute a riot. Riots are generally limited to public places; most legal definitions include intent to commit illegal acts and the occurrence of illegal behavior. Most legal treatments also mention disruptiveness, tumultuousness, and so on—behaviors that are clearly not limited to riots and are no easier to define than riots themselves. Many violent events have elements of riot-like behavior, but most strikes, protests, and demonstrations are not riots, although they may become riotous.

Are pogroms riots? What about postvictory slaughters in conquered cities or on the battlefield or large-scale killing of indigenous populations by colonizing peoples? What about violence by criminal gangs? More broadly, what distinguishes riots from social movements, insurrections, rebellions, protests, and demonstrations? The criterial considerations for calling an event a riot are clearly not those that define the term *riot* legally. It is not numbers, though some consideration of scope must be involved. It is not a temporal dimension, since riots often occur in series. If it is the occurrence of violence, it must be acknowledged that protestors and demonstrators who have no intention to commit violence sometimes are drawn into riotous behavior. It can be argued that riots become revolutionary incidents when participants have as their goal not redress or remedy but overthrow and replacement of government authority. I have no space to address these questions; readers should keep them in mind.

## Types of Riots

While changing population characteristics, urban geographies, technologies, and ideologies have influenced the occurrence, nature, and outcomes of riots, almost every type of contemporary riot in the United States has identifiable precursors in earlier times and different locales. Indeed, much of the rioting in late-colonial America before the

Revolutionary War was so similar to that in late-seventeenth- and eighteenth-century France and Britain that it is likely it was modeled on the European phenomena. Riots in the late twentieth century manifested many of the same patterns of those two hundred years earlier.

*Riots Based on Issues and Interests.* These disturbances are primarily of two types: class riots, which often occur over access to economic resources, and antigovernment riots, primarily over issues of political power. Economic riots, which arise from issues having to do with people's livelihoods, can become very violent. Some of the most bitter rioting in the years before and after the American Revolution was over control of land: homesteaders challenged rights granted by one or another of the colonies; tenants and sometimes squatters challenged the often tremendous land grants given by royal or other charter and claimed rights to the land by virtue of occupancy, uncompensated labor equity, or the absentee status of putative owners. Such assaults on the class structure worried even those members of urban elites involved in challenging crown policies on matters related to commerce; land usurpers seemed to generate the same fear among the upper classes as anarchists and communists did in later periods.

Commodity riots in England and France, particularly the bread riots of the eighteenth century, were accompanied by more violence than commodity-related riots in the United States; at the end of the twentieth century riots occurred over such items as hard-to-find toys and tickets for popular events. Much more consistently and sometimes lethally violent have been riots during strikes over fundamental issues of workers' rights to employment and fair wages and employers' rights to control the workplace. In 1877 rioting was so endemic that many worried about class war and revolution; government troops, state militias, state and local police, and company police and Pinkertons, or private security guards, intervened on the side of capitalist owners, wounding and killing (sometimes peaceful) strikers and their families and destroying their homes and property. Bitter strikes continued through the end of the twentieth century, but they were seldom accompanied by riots and large-scale violence. (Violent confrontations did occur over newspaper-delivery rights and seizure of property by miners in the last quarter of the twentieth century.)

In the three decades preceding the Civil War, antiabolitionist riots in the American South and antislavery riots in support of fugitive slaves in the North ran into the hundreds. David Grimsted (1998) claims that hundreds were killed in this violence: for the most part abolitionists were victims of mobs in the South and mob participants were victims of authorities in the North. The draft riots in New York City and other urban centers during the Civil War resulted from combined working-class outrage over the inequity of richer men being able to purchase draft substitutes, fear of competition from former slaves, prejudice against blacks, and general disaffection over conditions of life. Pitched battles were fought, sometimes with firearms as well as clubs and rocks. Neighborhoods were torched and government buildings assaulted, while scores of people were killed and hundreds injured.

Antigovernment riots were commonplace in the late-colonial years and in the initial decades after independence; they were less frequent and received less media coverage in the late twentieth century. Pre–Revolutionary War urban centers saw riots against ordinances for animal control, over the raising and tearing down of liberty poles (an activity that began around 1765 and continued until the beginning of the war), and over the Stamp Act (1765–1766). Houses were pulled down, personal property and trade items were burned or destroyed (Boston had more than one tea party, and the event was emulated elsewhere), customs agents and other officials and "collaborators" were harassed, occasionally beaten, tarred and feathered, and ridden out of town on rails—but seldom killed. Independence did not bring an end to antigovernment rioting, some of which, like the Shays's Rebellion and the Whiskey Rebellion in the late eighteenth century, approached rural insurrections and were accompanied by occasional fatalities and considerable destruction of property. Similar damage and mayhem occurred in riots during the Civil War and Reconstruction. In the latter part of the nineteenth century there was widespread violence and occasional rioting over *where* government (specifically, county seats) was to be located, and election riots continued well into the twentieth century.

Two of the largest race riots in the twentieth century, those in Chicago (1919) and Detroit (1943), began in disputes over access to recreational facilities. In the decade following World War II, rioting often accompanied efforts at desegregating public (but previously "white only") swimming pools and similar community resources. A few years later large-scale protests and occasional rioting accompanied the desegregation of schools and the busing of children to schools away from their neighborhoods, particularly in the North—and in venues as widely scattered as Boston, Louisville, and Pontiac (Michigan). Disputes over busing continued in the late twentieth century.

The most spectacular antigovernment rioting in the latter part of the twentieth century arose as a reaction to U.S. participation in the war in Vietnam. While there were protests and demonstrations across the country in urban areas and on college and university campuses, for many people the most memorable antiwar event was the collage of demonstrations, guerrilla theater, police baiting (and responsive police violence and hippie bashing), bombastic political rhetoric from left and right, journalistic hyperbole, and public near-hysteria associated with the Democratic National Convention in Chicago in the summer of 1968. When, in May 1970, National Guardsmen killed demonstrators at Kent State University in Ohio and at Jackson State College in Mississippi, demonstrations, which often turned into rioting, became endemic on campuses. After these events and in the following years, protests and demonstrations against nuclear installations (for example, Seabrook in 1970) and in support of other environmental causes, and the sometimes obstreperous behavior that accompanied them, resulted in hundreds of arrests and occasional scuffling, but they never approached the anti–Vietnam War disturbances in scale or in media visibility.

Other issues that have exercised Americans to the point of rioting have been disputes over the relative merits of stage actors (twenty-two people reportedly died in New York's so-called Astor Place rioting in 1849) and sports teams. Many people also have been killed in prison riots.

*Riots Based on Social Categorical Membership.* While religious violence was not uncommon in England, the much greater diversity of religions as well as the diversity of races and nationalities in the United States have led to widespread prejudice and social violence in which individuals participate because of their membership in these socially identifiable groups or categories. While such prejudice is frequently associated with economic competition, it would be difficult to demonstrate that fear of economic competition is at the root of prejudice against homosexuals or variously disadvantaged populations.

**National Guard field training in Washington, D.C., 1968.** LIBRARY OF CONGRESS

Whatever its roots, social rioting has accounted for many of the casualties and much of the property damage resulting from rioting in the United States. It began when early settlers exploited and killed their Native American neighbors. It continued with the initial appearance of substantial numbers of "different" populations from Europe in eastern cities, particularly the wave of Irish immigrants at the end of the first half of the nineteenth century. The Know-Nothing movement, which was motivated in part by hostility to the perceived political influence of recent immigrants and Roman Catholics, generated attacks on Irish and Roman Catholic institutions, including pitched battles employing cannon as well as small arms and arson. In the 1830s and 1840s Mormons were hounded, from New York to Ohio to Missouri (where the governor of the state ordered them expelled or exterminated) to Illinois and then farther west, by assault (including murder), arson, and large-scale attacks by mobs of local citizens (and even state militia in Missouri) until they finally found sanctuary in Utah. Later in the century, when Chinese laborers were brought into the country to build railroads, they in turn became the focus of violence, culminating in anti-Chinese rioting by hoodlums in San Francisco in 1877. During World War II American servicemen in Los Angeles were responsible for attacking Hispanic citizens in what became known as the Zoot-Suit Riot.

Racial violence, specifically that involving blacks and whites, has arguably been the social categorical violence that has been most pervasive over time and the most costly in terms of casualties and personal and societal assets. (It is probable that more Native Americans died from widespread settler and military violence than members of other groups, but the exact magnitude of this violence is undocumented.) From the first institution of slavery in colonial America in 1619, there were assaults based on race and on white fears of slave uprisings. The disruption of traditional patterns of race relations that accompanied the Civil War and emancipation of the slaves resulted in major confrontations such as the New York draft riots and Reconstruction violence in New Orleans (1866). Reconstruction also saw the beginning of lynchings of blacks, which sometimes developed into general assaults on black communities. In the period around World War I a new pattern emerged in which urban areas became centers of mutual assault sometimes approaching warfare. These riots, in which members of both races died, can be attributed to blacks' refusal to accept a status of permanent subordination. (Indeed, the *New York Times* opined of the 1919 riot in Washington, D.C., that it never would have occurred had "negroes" kept their place.) While casualties never reached the hundreds initially reported after rioting in East St. Louis (1917), many *were* killed in rioting during the period, and there was substantial property damage. Prejudice and deep-seated hostility were manifest in acts of brutality by law-enforcement agencies as well as by small groups of both races.

A 1943 riot in Detroit, Michigan, was the last large-scale instance of the "mutual assault" type of violence in which interracial pursuit and attack—as opposed to the violence taking place largely within population concentrations—were widespread. After a number of minor and generally nonlethal riots over desegregation of housing, schools, and recreational facilities (primarily swimming pools) following World War II, there was a brief hiatus in which violence subsided. Violence—generally one-way violence, initiated by white civilians, white law-enforcement personnel, or both—flourished again during the civil

rights struggles of the 1960s; indeed, blacks and their white supporters learned how to respond nonviolently to verbal and physical assault. It is ironic that the assassination in 1968 of Martin Luther King, Jr., a proponent of nonviolence, was followed by a wave of inner-city rioting across the United States.

In the middle of the same decade there emerged a new model for large-scale urban racial violence, so-called ghetto rioting or uprisings. In these riots, usually precipitated by allegations of discriminatory treatment of blacks (in the prototype of such riots, that of Harlem in 1935, it was rumored that a black child had been killed by whites in an altercation over alleged shoplifting), assault by blacks on white (or Asian) property in the form of looting or arson occurs, but most, though not all, of the casualties are blacks shot, or occasionally beaten, by white police or National Guardsmen. Figures published in the final report of the Eisenhower Commission state that between June 1963 and May 1968, 200,000 people in 237 cities participated in riots that resulted in 190 deaths and 50,000 arrests. Among the principal disturbances in the 1960s were riots, sometimes recurrent, in Detroit, Los Angeles, and Newark (New Jersey); smaller or less intense events occurred across the country. Many hours of television coverage of this rioting were broadcast, and there may have been contagion effects. While there was at least as much media coverage of the so-called Rodney King riots in Los Angeles in 1992 (in which more than fifty people were killed), the "copycat" violence was relatively limited.

Other examples of rioting caused by conflict directed against social categories include assaults on antiwar dissidents, which occurred during every major U.S. war except World War II (when there was some assault on individual pacifists and Japanese but no rioting); loyalists during the American Revolution, copperheads (northerners who sympathized with the South) and pacifists during the Civil War, pacifists and members of the Nonpartisan League during World War I, and anti–Vietnam War protestors and hippies have all come under assault. In 1969, patrons at the Stonewall Inn, a gay bar in New York City, resisted a police raid; the melee spilled into the streets and grew into neighborhood rioting in protest of police harassment of homosexuals. Interservice and interunit rioting of military personnel and disputes between members of the military and civilians were almost common in places where there were large

**Illinois National Guardsmen try to disperse a large crowd consisting mostly of teenagers in Cicero on 12 July 1951 after someone tossed a flare atop a building in which an African American family has rented an apartment.** LIBRARY OF CONGRESS

concentrations of military personnel waiting to enter combat in World War II and occurred again in later U.S. military involvements. This sort of rioting seldom results in fatalities or substantial property damage.

*Riots of Opportunity.* Riots of opportunity occur when the risk of apprehension and punishment for illegal activities, such as looting or vandalism, is sharply reduced. Examples are the 1919 police strike in Boston and the 1977 blackout in New York City. The Boston riots brought thousands into the streets and ended only after the National Guard had been called in and nine rioters had been shot and killed. In New York the police had been ordered to avoid confrontation during the blackout; looting and relatively minor property damage occurred, but there were few and only minor casualties. There are probably opportunists in all major riots.

*Expressive Riots and Emergent Riots from Exuberance.* Although some expressive riots turn ugly, they are more generally characterized by the party

atmosphere putatively describing the 1977 blackout riot in New York. In 1766, in what may have been the first college food fight, students at Harvard College riotously protested rancid butter and college rules. In the years since, students have been involved in a variety of riotous disturbances. The second half of the twentieth century witnessed the phenomenon of spring-break rioting, panty raids (in which male students raid women's residences in defiance of authority to obtain panties or other intimate apparel as trophies), end-of-term disturbances, riots associated with both victory and defeat in traditional athletic rivalries, and town-gown rioting.

Rioting has also accompanied professional athletic competition in the United States, sometimes with considerable violence and destruction but not with the fatalities that have occurred in conjunction with soccer (known as "football" outside the United States) in other parts of the world. Alcohol is often a major ingredient in such riots. Other types of riots of exuberance include concert and other entertainment riots (for example, the melee

57

at the end of Woodstock '99), outbursts at Mardi Gras and other carnivals, and brawls aboard excursion steamers. These types of riots have sometimes been associated with relatively more vandalism and other property damage and personal injuries than the kinds of riots mentioned earlier, such as spring-break riots and panty raids. Fatalities have been rare in riots of exuberance and usually accidental when they do occur.

### Some Patterns in U.S. Riots

While riots vary substantially over time and space in terms of focus, intensity, and the long- and short-term change they effect, it is nonetheless possible to discern some consistencies in patterns of onset, development, behavior, and participation—characteristics that are often interrelated.

*Ecological, Technological, and Demographic Features.* A major factor influencing a number of riot characteristics is community size. One reason that earlier riots tended to have more heterogeneous participation was because people of different sorts lived much closer together than is the case in the late twentieth century. If a venue of potential rioting is within walking distance, people are more inclined to participate, but if participation requires driving or using public transport, people may be concerned about becoming targets. Indeed, in many riots public-transportation transfer points have become centers both for gathering potential mob members and for isolating members of target groups. At the same time, modern transport facilitates rapid movement of police and the military. Natural barriers (rivers with widely separated bridges, for example) can stem the spread of violence. On the other hand, telephones facilitate both communication of rumor and planning.

In addition to absolute size and distribution of populations, two other important demographic factors are absolute and proportionate size of minority populations and patterns of concentration. Quantitative studies have found that there are thresholds of proportionate size of particular populations below which certain sorts of riots are not likely to occur (so-called ghetto riots, for example) and that high-density concentrations of populations, such as urban housing, campuses, and venues for spectator crowds, serve as breeding grounds for temporary gatherings.

*Temporal Patterns.* Historically, riots have been concentrated in periods when patterns of intergroup accommodation are under maximum stress. This is perhaps most obvious in the case of commodity riots, which occur when production and distribution structures have broken down, and in riots before a revolution, when the very legitimacy of a government is questioned. But riots associated with strikes have occurred when the economy is depressed and employers are trying to reduce labor costs—with the exception of postwar periods of prosperity, when demands deferred by no-strike agreements are let loose. While there was antiblack rioting as early as the eighteenth century and while lynching took the lives of thousands of blacks during Reconstruction and into the twentieth century, the two major periods of widespread and large-scale race riots in the United States occurred when there were major assaults on the accommodative structure of black subordination (blacks were subordinate, while whites had always been superordinate): first, at the time of World War I as blacks moved into northern cities and challenged white monopolies of employment and housing; second, in the 1960s, when aspirations encouraged by the Civil Rights movement and the rhetoric of equality came up against the realities of massive unemployment and continuing discrimination, including violent acts of repression in response to demonstrations.

Riots in different social arenas differ in degrees of spontaneity but share common constraints on occurrence. Labor disturbances, which are most often tied to management decisions, and antigovernment disorder, which most often occurs in reaction to regulations and laws, often require periods of assembly, milling and discussion, exhortation, and planning before there is action. Campus eruptions and race riots, in contrast, usually occur in situations where large numbers of people are already gathered and are precipitated by some highly visible event (for example, a National Collegiate Athletic Association basketball championship or police harassment). This variable spontaneity interacts with mundane circumstances like the weather (and thus, also, time of year) and the day of the week. There have been many more riots, of all sorts, on evenings and weekends in July and August than on weekday mornings in December and January (see, for example, Spike Lee's 1989 film, *Do the Right Thing*). Statistics on the temporal distribution of riots are influenced both by contagion effects (imitation) and by heightened journalistic attention. Assaults are more likely during daylight hours, especially when people are going to work. Looting most often occurs at night.

While it has been claimed that riots unfold in stages, there is so much variability in individual cases and across social arenas that it would be difficult to specify a pattern. Gathering or assembling will precede listening, which in turn will precede actions of various sorts. There may be multiple gatherings and dispersals over the course of a major riot, milling and rumor exchange may occur among spectators watching attacks on buildings or on individual victims, or riots in the making may be suddenly terminated. In fact, riots end very differently, sometimes because of the appearance of overwhelming force (state police, National Guardsmen, and paratroopers have all played this role), sometimes because of exhaustion (or boredom) although some rioters go home for lunch or to nap, or sometimes because it starts to rain (just as rioters are loath to walk very far to riot, they are loath to participate when wet or cold). On the other hand, riots may be invigorated by real or imagined control-agency excesses (police beatings, shooting of bystanders), the appearance of unanticipated allies (roaming mobs in widely dispersed rioting), the excitement of watching buildings burn (perhaps to the chant "Burn baby, burn!"), or improvement in the weather.

*Patterns in Participation.* A great deal has been written about participants in riots, often by people who feel threatened by what they perceive as attacks on established and normative order. Such commentators often refer to riffraff, criminal elements, offenders, or atomistic individuals temporarily out of control. Commentators in sympathy with rioters are more likely to characterize them as heroes and heroines of the people (or race or movement) and to conceive of control agents as cossacks or murderers. In actuality, rioters in the late twentieth century, like those of past centuries, are ordinarily rational actors with short- or long-term goals (or both) who monitor their environments in deciding how best to achieve those goals. Participants are neither alone nor anonymous; most people at temporary gatherings, including gatherings that turn into riots, are there with friends, acquaintances, or family members and are likely to act in concert with them. The extent to which rioters (as opposed to victims or control agents) are homogeneous or heterogeneous depends on such factors as the ecological variables mentioned earlier and the presence or absence of participant pools (as in the cases of prisons, college campuses, or neighborhoods, as contrasted with faraway groups watching rioting on television or hearing about it on the radio), as well as considerations of ideology and the presence or absence of agencies of control. (When control agents are present, particularly in force and with visible weapons, they have the effect of dampening adult participation.) In some instances participation can be, for all intents and purposes, coerced ("You are either for us or against us"). Motivation for participation may be sympathetic, opportunistic, recreational, or, for those following a riot in the media, vicarious.

The period of involvement in a riot may be of varying duration: (1) short, because one's presence is accidental or because of injury, fear (of physical harm or of being recognized, for example), or horror and revulsion about what is transpiring; (2) as long as is convenient (for example, until public transportation comes, some immediate event is over, or crowds move on); (3) until exhaustion sets in or it is time to keep an appointment; (4) episodic; (5) for a day or a night; or (6) until the event ends. Some participants may try to keep a dying disturbance going. It may be that time of involvement is related to the nature of one's participation—as a spectator, for example, versus as a verbal supporter egging others on.

Some participants have characteristics that set them off from others. Leaders (particularly those who operate behind the scenes) have sometimes come from more elite sectors of society than rank-and-file rioters. Leaders also emerge from those gathered. Such emergent leaders often have no previous experience as leaders and may become leaders as a result of happenstance. Indeed, leadership may be transitory, as when, as excitement (or hostility) grows, leaders cautioning moderation are overthrown by individuals with more extreme agendas.

Social-control agencies, including city, county, and state police, state militia, the National Guard, the federal military, company police, and private security agencies, have played different roles as national attitudes have changed. While subordinated groups continue to complain about brutality (including unwarranted shooting) by some members of control agencies, control agencies in the late twentieth century were both more neutral and more restrained than those involved in nineteenth-century disturbances. Studies of the socioeconomic characteristics of those rioters detained, arrested, indicted, and convicted indicate that they are not very different from other people present at a riot. Fleetness of foot, the density and nature of illegal behaviors at the time of possible apprehension, physical appearance (including fitting stereotypes), and being known to authorities influence the likelihood of being stopped and arrested.

The comparative information on women in earlier riots, even if in England and France, provides a context for comments on participation by women in the late twentieth century. In those early riots women usually were major participants and were frequently arrested. Although women were less likely to be arrested in the 1990s, in general, the treatment of women was based on where and what they were doing. A woman looter carrying bags of groceries or other subsistence items, for example, was not placed in the same category as a woman wielding a weapon or looting a jewelry store.

Participants in and observers of riots have often assigned various villains' roles to people from outside the community in which the disturbances take place. During the course of strikes moving toward violence, for example, labor often blamed scabs and toughs for heightening tensions while management might blame Wobblies, communists, or more vaguely, "outside agitators." Police and politicians responsible for maintaining public order have frequently blamed outsiders for breakdowns in that order; in the course of the anti–Vietnam War disturbances at the time of the 1968 Democratic Party convention, the claim that all protestors were outsiders who had "invaded" Chicago was widely broadcast and a later court trial attempted to prove that the rioting had resulted from a conspiracy of outsiders.

Helping-agency personnel, elected officials, firemen, and members of attacking groups have all worked to rescue individuals and groups under attack. Blacks have hidden whites, neighbors have hidden ethnics of opposing groups, and strikers have helped their supervisors. Neighbors' attacking and informing on one another have not been typical of U.S. rioting. But succor has costs; firemen have been shot at and protecting neighbors beaten. Members of the media have also been accorded highly variable treatment.

*Casualties.* Riot fatalities in the United States have never come close to the estimated five thousand plus killed in India's Great Calcutta Killing during violence at the time of independence and partition in 1947 (five thousand were killed in the city of Calcutta alone, and possibly as many as a million were killed in India and Pakistan combined) or to late-twentieth-century genocidal killing in a variety of world locations. Indeed, while initial newspaper estimates of deaths in some U.S. riots ran into the hundreds and in the case of the New York draft riots to more than one thousand, postriot records generally show fewer than fifty deaths. The 120 dead listed in the record for the draft riots is probably the highest confirmed figure. (By contrast, ten hostages and thirty-two inmates were killed in New York's 1971 Attica Prison uprising.)

With some exceptions, the bulk of those killed in race riots have been blacks, and the deaths most often have been recorded as "justifiable police homicide" (that is, they have been killed allegedly in the course of looting or other criminal behavior) or a similar category. In labor violence, strikers make up the bulk of fatalities—again killed largely by public or private police or occasionally by troops (mainly U.S. Army troops in the nineteenth century and the National Guard in the twentieth). Killings by civilians have been largely of isolated individuals caught on the turf of another group. Most people killed and injured are male adolescents and young adults, although women have occasionally been killed and some old people get caught up in riotous behavior. Patterns of injury are similar; reports are probably distorted because the injured may avoid hospitals if afraid of arrest.

While several thousand people have probably been killed in U.S. riots since before the Revolutionary War, and while injuries have probably run to the tens or even hundreds of thousands, casualties have been less injurious to American society than the damage done to intergroup attitudes and relations. In the United States, as elsewhere, there have been many riots, protests, demonstrations, and other collective actions in which no one was injured for every riot in which people were seriously hurt or killed. When people have been killed, it is usually by police and other agents of social control. Finally, the total number of fatalities from riots and other social violence has generally been dwarfed by that of casualties from participation in international wars or, as noted earlier, other forms of internal violence.

*Property Damage and Looting.* In pre–Revolutionary War disorders, rioters broke windows and threw filth. They sometimes razed houses or emptied them of contents, which they then burned in the street. Sometimes houses or whole neighborhoods were burned. Arson became more frequent and more costly with larger urban concentrations and continued wood construction. Attacks on corporate and government property sometimes involved the use of explosives. Generally, looting has been an accompaniment of rioting. Occasionally, rioters have intentionally or inadvertently destroyed their own property.

There are few good data on property loss (insurance records are underutilized). It is probably safe to say that property damage has run into many billions of dollars. Pictures of some cities after rioting are evocative of post–World War II photographs of bombed-out cities.

*Aftermath.* Nonrioting members of groups involved in riots have often approved of the rioting even when they have, themselves, suffered from it. Some sympathy has come from members of superordinate groups and there have sometimes been moves in the direction of amelioration. There have also been moves in the direction of firmer suppression. There are often deeply entrenched hostilities that remain long after violence has ended.

**Causes of Riots**

Explanations abound to account for the occurrence of civil violence, particularly during periods when it is a visible and painful part of public life. While common threads can be found, popular explanations, behavioral-science perspectives, and postriot commissions often offer quite different conclusions and recommendations for solutions. This brief treatment will focus on popular explanations. Donald Black, Lewis A. Coser, Ted Gurr, Morris Janowitz, George Rude, Georg Simmel, Neil J. Smelser, Seymour Spilerman, and Charles, Louise, and Richard Tilly are excellent beginnings for exploration of scholarly interpretations.

*Popular Explanations.* Popular explanations come from ordinary individuals; formal organizations (for example, activist organizations across the political spectrum and professional organizations); emergent spokespersons or experts who have opinions, share them freely, and come to be asked as a phenomenon continues; representatives of affected corporations, governments, or populations; and the print and electronic media. As riots continue, popular explanations increasingly incorporate elements of behavioral-science theories and the conclusions of postriot commissions.

Folk explanations may be favorable and sympathetic to rioters, opposed to disorder, or neutral. Perspectives ordinarily reflect location in the social structure, but there are cross-class and cross-race sympathies. Scholarly views have crept into popular currency. The downtrodden and exploited often find Marxist interpretations persuasive; elites are more attracted by psychological interpretations that focus on group contagion or the negative characterization of "demented" rioters. Some interpretations are consistent with commission reports and reflect the realities of worlds in which rioters live. In his 1968 novel *The Algiers Motel Incident,* John Hersey wrote, "There are four main causes of racial violence: unequal justice, unequal employment opportunities, unequal housing, unequal education." Riot commissions agree, as do black people. Other interpretations reflect personal fears or ideologies, or are simply arbitrary. Many white people, including some law-enforcement personnel, would maintain that riots result from conspiracies (including communist plots), criminal elements, activities of individuals with special agendas or axes to grind, fear of crime, summer heat, overreaction by socially disvalued categories or classes of people to imagined slights, and so on. Whites have also invoked "insults against the white race" as an explanation for riots targeting blacks.

*Behavioral-Science Perspectives.* There are two major behavioral-science perspectives on rioting: those that focus on the individual, which are associated primarily with psychology and related disciplines and generally look for explanations in the characteristics and past experiences of violent individuals; and those that theorize about groups and the social structure. Two excellent volumes, *The Myth of the Madding Crowd* by Clark McPhail and *Theories of Civil Violence* by James Rule, contain comprehensive discussions that together cover numerous theoretical perspectives.

*Riot Commissions and Other Investigative Bodies.* In the pre–Revolutionary War period informers, spies, military authorities, local officials, and loyalists reported to both crown and colonial authorities about increasingly frequent assaults on the public order in the American colonies. Both disorder and its reporting continued after independence. From about the mid-nineteenth century onward, official reports on class and race rioting in the United States became more or less routinized. In the second half of the twentieth century the same was true of student disturbances. At the national level there have been presidential, Senate, House, departmental, bureau (including the Federal Bureau of Investigation), agency, and military

61

commissions, boards, and reviews. State governors and legislatures have ordered inquiries, often involving departments of corrections, state police, militia and national guard, and various social agencies. On the municipal level mayors, city managers, and city councils have made similar requests of police, hospitals, and miscellaneous agencies, including housing and public-transport agencies. Autonomous organizations, such as the National Association for the Advancement of Colored People, the Urban League, the American Bar Association, employers' organizations, and unions, have mounted investigations, as have an equivalently wide range of ad hoc citizens' groups of neighbors, merchants, physicians, educators, and so on. The judiciary has been involved in studies of the justice system. These bodies, which sit from periods of weeks to periods of years and which receive funding that ranges from none at all to millions of dollars, are all charged with finding causal explanations, solutions, and, particularly, ways of restoring and maintaining civil order.

The interpretations and recommendations of these reports reflect (1) the political climate when investigating bodies are appointed; (2) the composition of the commissions (or other investigative bodies) and their staff; (3) the support, both moral and financial, provided; (4) the time allowed for the body to investigate and write its report; (5) whether or not there were open hearings, particularly hearings in which public participation was invited; and (6) what sort of dissemination of the findings was projected. All four members of the Governor's Committee to Investigate the Riot Occurring in Detroit on 21 June 1943 were heads of law-enforcement agencies at various levels. Their final report concluded that those agencies had generally behaved well and that the riots were caused by riffraff and criminals. Investigating bodies with a more balanced composition tend to be more evenhanded in their assessments of responsibility and to look for root causes. Nonetheless, they also are likely to make recommendations facilitating prompter and stronger controls. Similar differences in causal assessments appear in the reports of congressional committees investigating cases of major labor violence at the end of the nineteenth century and the beginning of the twentieth, as well as those of student disorders during the years of Vietnam protest. The 1970 Scranton Report on campus unrest, for example, was considered too liberal and was disowned by the administration of Richard M. Nixon, which had appointed the committee that wrote it.

While there are continuities in the contexts and causes of all of the major kinds of rioting in the United States, greater changes have occurred in the nature of class and labor struggle than in that of racial violence. In 1741 workers were tried in New York City for a "conspiracy to raise wages"; at the time of the 1892 Homestead strike in Pennsylvania some investigators still argued that secret organizations, by which they meant unions, constrained the freedom of individuals to work. Combinations—that is, alliances formed with the intention of achieving social, political, or economic ends—and clubs were for a long time illegal. While some late-twentieth-century owners bitterly fought over the right to control what goes on in the workplace, few publicly argued that individuals have no right to unionize. In the second decade of the twentieth century a minority position on the cause of widespread labor violence in Colorado listed four sources of industrial unrest: unequal distribution of wealth and income; unemployment and denial of the opportunity to earn a living; denial of justice; and denial of the right and opportunity to form effective organizations. The report concluded that the killing had been "directly and proximately" caused by refusal of the operator (the Rockefeller Foundation in the instance under investigation) to meet with representatives of the workers. This same commentator proposed, among other recommendations, the abolition of private ownership of public utilities, women's suffrage, a six-day workweek, and an eight-hour day. The parallels to Hersey's four main causes of racial violence are obvious.

Tens of thousands of pages have been published about causes and cures for riots. There have been basically two varieties of recommendations for riot prevention, having to do either with justice for categories or classes of citizens victimized by prejudice and discrimination or with increasing strength for social-control agencies and improved technologies for control. Observations regarding the riots during the Vietnam War that resources expended in the war could have been directed to reducing inequities in U.S. society never made their way into commission reports, nor was ending the war recommended as a solution to inner-city rioting. Recommendations on strengthening social control have much more frequently been implemented. With reference to more fundamental changes in society, Kenneth Clark's oft-quoted observation in testimony given before the 1968 National Advisory Commission on Civil Disorders (and cited in the report summary) is apt:

> I read that report . . . of the 1919 riot in Chicago, and it is as if I were reading the report of the investigating committee on the Harlem riot of '35, the report of the investigating committee on the Harlem riot of '43, the report of the McCone Commission on the Watts riot. I must again in candor say to you members of this Commission—it is a kind of Alice in Wonderland—with the same moving picture re-shown over and over again, the same analysis, the same recommendations, and the same inaction.

Some observers have even suggested that by appearing to take action investigations deflect pressures for actual change.

There are four major themes in causal analyses of riots in the United States. Claims are made that riots are caused by prejudice; a combination of prejudice, discrimination, and injustice; weakness of social-control agencies, sometimes coupled with contentions of failures of will on the part of authorities; and conspiracies, foreign or domestic, and assaults on U.S. values. A claim is also occasionally forwarded that certain rioting, such as some of that protesting slavery or involvement in war, results from U.S. values and ideals of justice.

*Comparative Issues.* The United States has been a lawless and violent nation. However, the same could be said for many other places in the world. In cases such as the Great Calcutta Killing and in communal violence in Ceylon or Rwanda and Burundi at the end of the twentieth century, it is difficult to determine where race or ethnic rioting ends and genocide begins. The numbers of communal riots in India during the British period and at its end ran into the thousands. But commodity riots with no obvious overtones of communalism were endemic from the times of early empires at least until modern transportation facilitated movement of foodstuffs. Even then, as we have seen above, government pricing policies contributed to rioting over food into the eighteenth century in western Europe and in North America. Overall it may be safe to say that rioting involving race, ethnicity, and religion has produced more casualties than other varieties. The total number of riots is impossible to estimate; because of the populations involved, it is probably safe to say that there have been fewer student riots than class riots over the years. Political riots have been more bitter, but perhaps no more frequent, in authoritarian states in

the making than in democracies. It is impossible to know for sure.

## Morality and Inevitability

Caution is needed in extrapolating from one variety of rioting in the United States to another or across historical periods. One thing is sure: some social change in past times has come about following social disorder. Given the organization of state authority in the modern world, it may well be that the attainment of justice *requires* social disruption, sometimes including rioting. Readers should keep these conundrums in mind in thinking about the inevitability and morality of riots.

*BIBLIOGRAPHY*

Black, Donald. *The Social Structure of Right and Wrong.* New York: Academic, 1989.

Chicago Commission on Race Relations. *The Negro in Chicago.* Chicago: University of Chicago Press, 1922.

Coser, Lewis A. *The Functions of Social Conflict.* Glencoe, Ill.: Free Press, 1956.

Countryman, Edward. *A People in Revolution: The American Revolution and Political Society in New York, 1760–1790.* Baltimore, Md.: Johns Hopkins University Press, 1981.

Critchley, T. A. *The Conquest of Violence.* New York: Schocken, 1970.

Gilje, Paul A. *Rioting in America.* Bloomington: Indiana University Press, 1996.

———. *The Road to Mobocracy: Popular Disorder in New York City, 1763–1834.* Chapel Hill: University of North Carolina Press, 1987.

Governor's Commission on the Los Angeles Riots. *Violence in the City—an End or a Beginning? A Report by the Governor's Commission on the Los Angeles Riots.* Los Angeles: State of California, 1965. Also known as the McCone Commission Report.

Grimshaw, Allen D. "National Commission on the Causes and Prevention of Violence: Reports." *American Sociological Review* 36, no. 4 (1971): 716–724.

———, ed. *Racial Violence in the United States.* Chicago: Aldine, 1969.

Grimsted, David. *American Mobbing, 1828–1861: Toward Civil War.* New York: Oxford University Press, 1998.

Gurr, Ted. *Why Men Rebel.* Princeton, N.J.: Princeton University Press, 1970.

Heineman, Kenneth J. *Campus Wars: The Peace Movement at American State Universities in the Vietnam Era.* New York: New York University Press, 1993.

Janowitz, Morris. *Social Control of Escalated Riots.* Chicago: University of Chicago Press, 1968.

Lipsky, Michael, and David J. Olson. *Commission Politics: The Processing of Racial Crisis in America.* New Brunswick, N.J.: Transaction, 1977.

McPhail, Clark. *The Myth of the Madding Crowd.* New York: Aldine de Gruyter, 1991.

Platt, Anthony M., ed. *The Politics of Riot Commissions, 1917–1970: A Collection of Official Reports and Critical Essays.* New York: Collier, 1971.

Rude, George. *The Crowd in History: A Study of Popular Disturbances in France and England, 1730–1848.* New York: Wiley, 1964.

Rule, James B. *Theories of Civil Violence.* Berkeley: University of California Press, 1988.

Rushton, Herbert I., William E. Dowling, Oscar Olander, and John H. Witherspoon. *Committee to Investigate the Riot Occurring in Detroit, June 21, 1943: Factual Report.* Detroit, Mich.: mimeograph form, n.d.

Schellenberg, James A. *Conflict Between Communities: American County Seat Wars.* New York: Paragon, 1987.

Simmel, Georg. "Conflict." In *Conflict and the Web of Group Affiliation,* edited and translated by Kurt Wolff. 1908. New York: Free Press, 1955. Pages 11–123.

Smelser, Neil J. *Theory of Collective Behavior.* New York: Free Press, 1963.

Spilerman, Seymour. "The Causes of Racial Disturbances: A Comparison of Alternative Explanations." *American Sociological Review* 35 (1970): 627–649.

Tilly, Charles. *The Contentious French: Four Centuries of Popular Struggle.* Cambridge, Mass.: Harvard University Press, 1986.

———. "Invisible Elbow." *Sociological Forum* 11, no. 4 (1996): 589–601.

Tilly, Charles, Louise Tilly, and Richard Tilly. *The Rebellious Century, 1830–1930.* Cambridge, Mass.: Harvard University Press, 1975.

U.S. Commissioner of Labor. *Third Annual Report, 1887.* Washington, D.C.: Government Printing Office, 1888.

U.S. House of Representatives. *Employment of Pinkerton Detectives.* 52d Cong., 2d sess., 1893. H. Rept. 2447.

U.S. Senate. *The Colorado Coal Miners' Strike: Report of the Commission on Industrial Relations.* 64th Cong., 1st sess., 1916. S. Doc. 415.

Yellen, Samuel. *American Labor Struggles.* New York: S. A. Russell, 1936.

Young, Alfred F., ed., *The American Revolution: Explorations in the History of American Radicalism.* De Kalb: Northern Illinois University Press, 1976.

Thanks for various sorts of collegial assistance are due to Donald Black, John Bohstedt, Paul Gilje, Polly Grimshaw, George Juergens, Clark McPhail, Karl Schuessler, and particularly Art Stinchombe and are gratefully given.

ALLEN D. GRIMSHAW

*See also* **Agrarian Violence; Civil Disorder; Draft Riots; Frontier; Haymarket Square Riot; Los Angeles Riots of 1992; Prisons: Riots; Slave Rebellions; South; Watts Riot; Zoot-Suit Riot;** *and individual city articles.*

# ROAD RAGE

Road rage is a popular psychological term, used to designate the most extreme states of mind and behavior in aggressive driving incidents. Distinctions between road rage and the "aggressive driving" targeted by legislation in the late 1990s are unclear and may not be useful. Both include acts such as yelling at other drivers, making obscene gestures, blocking vehicles, flashing high beams, and tailgating. While some motorists are thought to be more prone to road rage than others, psychologists and policy makers view even the most extreme behaviors as exacerbated expressions of the routine antagonisms of driving, especially in high-density traffic areas.

Journalists, watchdog groups, and traffic-safety officials use sensational road rage incidents to signal the absolute loss of emotional control that distinguishes such behavior from more modest expressions of driving-related stress and anger. In these highly publicized cases, cars have been rammed or run off the road, and motorists have been shot, stabbed, beaten, and run over for trivial infractions of driving etiquette. In one paradigmatic incident on 20 February 1994, Donald Graham, a fifty-four-year-old bookkeeper and church deacon, pulled off the interstate highway in Massachusetts and murdered forty-two-year-old Michael Blodgett with a crossbow in a traffic dispute.

### History

Intersections between automobiles, highways, and violence are nothing new. Violent contests on American open roads and urban traffic jams have long been imagined as epicenters of strife. Psychological studies about aggressive driving began to appear in the late 1960s, and articles lamenting the loss of driving civility and car wars have appeared sporadically since the late 1970s. Films such as *Duel* (1971), *Death Race 2000* (1975), *Road Warrior* (1982), and *Crash* (1996, based on J. G. Ballard's 1973 novel) have in different ways evoked psychological and fantasy elements of car-related violence. Representations of vehicular mayhem in newspapers and movies have informed popular perceptions of social breakdown on the road at least since the 1970s.

Despite a history of associations between cars and violence, maniacal drivers first loomed as a national epidemic in the late 1980s and early 1990s. A rash of California freeway shootings in 1987 introduced the threat of random violence to commuting. As these incidents spread to other cities, they became associated with other urban, car-related fears of the late 1980s and early 1990s surrounding phenomena such as carjackings and drive-by shootings.

Following this wave of freeway violence in the United States, Great Britain saw a series of violent traffic incidents during the mid-1990s, and journalists and traffic-safety officials lamented the arrival of a violent "American phenomenon" to British expressways. The term *road rage* became a popular sensationalist shorthand for these episodes of vehicular aggression. The British press, early studies by the British Automobile Association, and government traffic safety programs all made use of road rage as an organizing concept to describe the loss of civility and self-control while driving. In responses to British traffic safety campaigns and a rash of U.S. incidents during 1996, journalists, watchdog groups, and law enforcement officials became increasingly concerned with road rage and aggressive driving.

The Automobile Association of America (AAA) and the U.S. Department of Transportation (DOT) commissioned studies, the House of Representatives convened a 1997 hearing, Road Rage: Causes and Dangers of Aggressive Driving, and several anti–road rage groups were formed. The AAA found that aggressive-driving incidents had increased by 51 percent between 1990 and 1996 and that nearly 90 percent of all motorists surveyed had experienced an aggressive-driving incident during 1996. In a report given before Congress, the DOT estimated that one-third of all traffic accidents and two-thirds of all traffic fatalities between 1990 and 1997 had resulted from aggressive driving. Public awareness led to law enforcement crackdowns on aggressive driving through driver education, the use of red-light cameras and photo radar, and an increased police presence in high-density traffic areas. Programs such as the Smooth Operation and Road Sharks efforts in the Washington, D.C., area combined waves of increased enforcement of traffic laws with education and information gathering. In conjunction with such programs, law officers encouraged private citizens with cellular phones to report aggressive drivers. Meanwhile, private groups developed Web sites to post license plate numbers and names of aggressive drivers, proposing to link such posts to the insurance premiums of offending drivers.

**Explanations and Remedies**

In seeking to explain road rage, policy makers have cited traffic congestion and decaying highway infrastructure. According to the DOT, the number of miles of road increased by 1 percent between 1987 and 1996, while the number of vehicle miles driven increased by 35 percent. Increases in both population and in the numbers of vehicles on the road intensified congestion in urban areas. Downsizing and the growing necessity of commuting between multiple part-time jobs made additional losses of time through traffic delays seem more catastrophic. In the 1990s a shift of law enforcement resources away from traffic control to violent crimes may also have made it possible for these frustrations to find expressions in violence.

Psychological approaches to road rage recognize material causes of traffic congestion but emphasize the reactions of drivers to this given set of conditions. By imagining their cars to be extensions of themselves, motorists can perceive infractions of driving etiquette as aggressive acts by other drivers. In contrast, the anonymity of the other drivers makes their own infractions seem comparatively insignificant. These conflicting perceptions facilitate the escalating violence that characterizes road rage incidents. In the 1990s, the military chic of sport utility vehicles enhances driver illusions of vehicular invulnerability and, simultaneously, makes traffic collisions far more deadly for drivers of smaller vehicles.

Perceptions of other people's actions as threatening and one's own actions as accidental inform the moral outrage that legitimates aggressive actions on the road. Outrage crystallizes around the clichéd pet peeves of motorists: slow drivers clogging the fast lanes, punitive tailgating, passing on highway shoulders, talking on cell phones while driving, and reckless speeding. Such vocabularies of moral outrage justify urges to teach other drivers violent lessons in highway etiquette. Accordingly, therapeutic approaches to road rage emphasize "cooling off" periods and regarding oneself as an imperfect driver in order to forgive the driving faults of others.

**Conclusion**

While traffic accidents are far more likely than sensational road rage incidents, the latter phenomenon elicits fascination and fear out of measure with its actual likelihood. Other types of rage were sensationalized in the 1990s. Road, sky, mall, and phone rage are all quasi-syndromes of uncontrollable frustration that cast fears of random violence over everyday experiences and that figured prominently in a 1990s culture of urban and suburban fear.

BIBLIOGRAPHY

AAA Foundation for Highway Safety. *Aggressive Driving: Three Studies*. Washington, D.C.: AAA Foundation for Highway Safety, 1997.

Davis, Mike. *Beyond Blade Runner: Urban Control, the Ecology of Fear*. Westfield, N.J.: Open Magazine Pamphlet Series, 1992.

Davis, Patricia, and Leef Smith. "A Crisis That May Not Exist Is All the Rage." *Washington Post*, 29 November 1998.

Kermode, Mark, and Julian Petley. "Road Rage." *Sight and Sound* 7, no. 6 (June 1997).

Massumi, Brian, ed. *The Politics of Everyday Fear*. Minneapolis: University of Minnesota Press, 1993.

U.S. Congress. House. Committee on Transportation and Infrastructure. *Road Rage: Causes and Dangers of Aggressive Driving*. Washington, D.C.: U.S. Government Printing Office, 1997.

BILL DOTSON

*See also* **Aggression; Carjacking; Drive-by Shooting.**

# ROBBERY

The Federal Bureau of Investigation defines robbery as "the use or threat of force to deprive another person of their property." This formal definition includes several important subcategories: robberies with and without injuries, and attempted and completed acts of robbery. Robberies are also distinguished by target, such as persons or commercial establishments.

In its most common form, robbery occurs on a street between strangers. The robber is typically armed with a gun and gets a relatively small amount of money. (The average robbery nets just under $1,000.) The key ingredient is the creation of fear by the robber. Robbery is the quintessential street crime, and one of the chief insecurities of most citizens is worry over armed predators lurking on street corners. The common perception of robbery is that of a bank robbery. However, the 8,046 bank robberies reported by the FBI in 1996 make up just over 1 percent of all robberies known to the police that year. Robberies range from minor "snatch-and-grab" incidents to home invasions with armed intruders holding family members hostage.

It is important to put U.S. rates of robbery in an international context. For the years 1988–1991 the U.S. rate was lower than Poland's but between 100 and 130 percent of the robbery rates of Italy, Australia, Czechoslovakia, Canada, and England. The gradual convergence of European and U.S. and Canadian robbery rates suggests that forces similar to those that created the high U.S. rates are pushing robbery rates elsewhere as well.

## Statistical Profile

The 1996 National Crime Victimization Survey estimated that 1,134,000 robberies occurred in the United States, a rate of 5.4 per thousand households. Two-thirds of robbery attempts were completed, and 29 percent resulted in injuries to the victim. Many fewer robberies—537,050 (or 202 per 100,000 residents)—were actually reported to the police that year. And only a small fraction of the robberies reported to the police resulted in an arrest: 156,270 (or 29 percent of all robberies known to the police). Arrests for those over eighteen years of age comprised approximately three-quarters of all robbery arrests for 1996, and 90 percent of all arrests for robbery were of male suspects. Robbery is the most racially disproportionate of all serious crimes; involvement in robbery by black Americans far outstrips their representation in the population both as offenders and victims. The 1996 arrest data show that blacks represented 58 percent of all persons arrested for robbery, despite comprising just 12.6 percent of the total population.

In 1994 there were 46,028 felony convictions in state courts for robbery, 5.3 percent of all state felony convictions. In federal court 48,069 robbery convictions were obtained. This offense constituted 4.2 percent of all state and federal felony convictions. Most often, those convicted were male, black, and in their twenties. And those convicted of robbery in state courts were most likely to have entered a guilty plea. Indeed, 85 percent of all robbery convictions in state courts were obtained by this means. The sentences for robbery reflect the seriousness of the offense. Only murder and manslaughter resulted in a higher percentage of prison sentences than robbery. While slightly less than half of all felony convictions resulted in a prison term, 77 percent of those for robbery did. And robbery results in longer prison terms than lesser crimes: the average maximum length of sentence received by robbers in state courts was 116 months (just under ten years), ranking third behind murder and rape.

The numbers for offenders closely resemble those for convicts: they are overwhelmingly male, single, most often black, in their twenties or late teens, and the products of low-income households. Rates of robbery are considerably higher in urban than in suburban or rural areas. In injuries resulting from robberies, African Americans are even more heavily represented, both as offenders and victims.

The 1996 surveys reveal many distinctive aspects of robbery. Some 78 percent of robberies involve victims and offenders who are strangers, a higher proportion than for any other serious crime. Following murder and nonnegligent homicide, robbery has the second highest proportion of offenses committed with a weapon. It is also the violent crime second most likely to be committed alone (56 percent of robberies are one-person jobs) and on the street (44.4 percent in the street, 11 percent in a residence). Drugs or alcohol also figure prominently in robbery: 53 percent of incarcerated robbers reported that they acted under the influence of drugs or alcohol, a figure roughly equal to that for serious assault and the highest for any crime category except drug offenses.

## Changing Definitions

The legal definition of robbery has evolved over time. Robbery could not exist until the concept of private property came about, and this emerged in feudal times in England, when the serfs were freed from the land. Robbery in the modern sense thus emerged in feudal England as roving bands of robbers, later to be known as bandits, terrorized people in transit from one village to another. Historically robbery has often represented a rebellion against traditional order, particularly in peasant societies. Those who robbed the ruling class were often viewed as heroes within their own social order. The process of "social differentiation," or the creation of social classes, is a necessary precursor to such a development. Robbers have been identified as "highwaymen" in some literature, as they preyed on individuals who traveled from town to town, typically by carriage. The processes of urbanization and modernization that accompanied the eighteenth-century Industrial Revolution lay at the foundation of the social changes that produced such robberies.

## Patterns of Robbery

Several significant patterns have emerged from the study of robberies. One concerns robbery mur-der, which constitutes 10 to 20 percent of all murders. This crime is typically the result of a robbery gone awry. Convenience-store robberies are also an important subcategory of robbery. While such offenses are a relatively small fraction of all robberies—approximately 4 percent took place at commercial establishments in 1995—they represent a serious public threat. Research suggests that these offenses take place when a single clerk is present, when cash is available, and at times when surveillance of the convenience store is likely to be low.

A number of studies have addressed robbery from the perspective of the robber, employing interviews with active or imprisoned robbers. This research highlights three significant steps in the robbery process: being motivated to commit a robbery, selecting the target, and committing the offense. Robbers appear to be motivated by a variety of short-term concerns, chiefly the desire to obtain gratification through drugs or alcohol, but also the desire to maintain an image for friends and neighbors. Keeping up images is an important part of the street-life culture in which many robbers are immersed. Target selection is usually based on ease of execution and potential gain. We have already noted that most robberies net under a thousand dollars, and street robberies usually yield far less than that. The short-term need for gratification that motivates most street robberies means that robbers generally do not wait for lucrative targets; rather they are satisfied with getting what they can from the first sufficiently vulnerable and defenseless target. The final step, committing the offense, is the most straightforward. Robbers attempt to take their victims by surprise, overpower them with force or the threat of force, take their cash, and exit quickly. The actual completion of a street robbery can take less than a minute.

*BIBLIOGRAPHY*

Conklin, John. *Robbery*. Philadelphia: Lippincott, 1972.
Cook, Phil. "Robbery Violence." *Journal of Criminology and Criminal Justice* 78, no. 2 (1987): 357–376.
———. "The Technology of Personal Violence." In *Crime and Justice*, edited by M. Tonry. Chicago: University of Chicago Press, 1992.
Einstadter, Walter. "The Social Organization of Robbery." *Social Problems* 17 (1969): 64–83.
Hobsbawm, Eric. *Bandits*. New York: Delacorte, 1969.
Lejune, Robert. "The Management of a Mugging." *Urban Life* 6 (1977): 123–148.
Luckenbill, David. "Generating Compliance: The Case of Robbery." *Urban Life* 10 (1981): 25–46.

Maguire, Kathleen, and Ann L. Pastore, eds. *Sourcebook of Criminal Justice Statistics, 1996.* Washington, D.C.: U.S. Department of Justice, Bureau of Justice Statistics. U.S. Government Printing Office, 1997.

Miller, Jody. "Up It Up: Gender and the Accomplishment of Street Robbery." *Criminology* 36 (1998): 37–66.

Wright, Richard T., and Scott H. Decker. *Armed Robbers in Action: Streetlife.* Boston: Northeastern University Press, 1996.

Zimring, Franklin E., and Gordon Hawkins. *Crime Is Not the Problem: Lethal Violence in America.* New York: Oxford University Press, 1997.

SCOTT H. DECKER

*See also* **Crime, Legal Definitions of.**

# RUBY, JACK
## (1911–1967)

On 24 November 1963, as presidential assassin Lee Harvey Oswald was being moved from downtown Dallas, Texas, local businessman Jack Ruby slipped into the crowded jail's garage and shot the cuffed prisoner on live television. The murder manifested all the contradictions bound up in national grief. Equal parts retribution and denial, Ruby's action sought to erase with swift vengeance the shock of President John F. Kennedy's assassination only two days earlier. This was Jack Ruby in a nutshell: thoughtlessly violent, full of misguided good intentions.

A one-man caricature of American extremes, Ruby had a hair-trigger temper coupled with an urge to defend, an attention-seeking egotism expressed in extravagant generosity, and an almost puritanical sense of decorum defended by a street-tough code of honor. Born Jacob Rubenstein on 25 March 1911 in a poor Jewish neighborhood in Chicago, the fifth of Joseph Rubenstein and Fanny Rokowsky's eight children quickly learned to throw the first punch. His father drank heavily and beat his mother; the family moved frequently, from ghetto to ghetto. By the time he was ten, Jacob's parents had separated, but Fanny's emotional problems made this less an escape than a minor alteration of circumstances (she was later institutionalized). The children spent a brief period in foster homes. Jacob was constantly in trouble for truancy and gang-related fighting, quickly earning (or assuming, in boasts) a reputation as the toughest kid around; his nickname was "Sparky" as a result of his intense temper. But Jacob's delinquency, explained in an early psychological profile

**Jack Ruby, in 1965.** CORBIS/BETTMANN-UPI

that found him extremely aggressive, egocentric, and obsessive, was also defined against a strong sense of communal identity. Jacob was his sisters' protector and fought at the drop of a hat against any perceived bigotry.

Jacob left school after the eighth grade but avoided real trouble, skirting the fringes of legitimate business. He failed for years to find a long-term job or residence. Jacob later served an honorable stint in the army during World War II, despite constant hustles and a brutal beating he administered to an anti-Semitic soldier. In 1947, following his brothers, Jacob legally changed his name to Ruby to avoid anti-Semitism in his business ventures; he also moved to Dallas to help his sister Eva manage her nightclub. Until 1963, Jack Ruby ran clubs; only his last venture, a three-runway strip joint called the Carousel, achieved modest success.

His life was a persistent string of slightly shady, generally ineffectual business deals, outbursts of extreme but short-lived violence, and a constant striving for class. But Ruby was also known for moments of eccentric compassion. Reading of local disasters, he would hurry to the scene to donate food or money. Employees could always hit him up for loans; he gave shelter to assorted drifters and unfortunate friends. Despite this generosity, Ruby had no close relationships and only limited connections with his sister and two brothers.

These contradictions set the stage for Ruby's action: an impulsive rage; his worries about the widowed Jackie and little Caroline and John, Jr.; and shame for his adopted Dallas, a code of community that Oswald, the outsider, had violated. However, Ruby failed to accomplish any of his possible goals, self-aggrandizing or self-sacrificing, by killing the assassin. Questions and concerns about the death of Kennedy still circulate, some think as a result of Oswald's untimely death. Worse, approval for Ruby shifted to distrust and loathing; the "hero" himself became indelibly associated with the death of the president and the assassin. Ruby spent his last three years in prison awaiting appeals to his 1964 conviction and suffering from a worsening paranoia, expressed in worries about anti-Semitic conspiracies behind the Kennedy assassination. He died of cancer in 1967.

*BIBLIOGRAPHY*

Posner, Gerald. *Case Closed: Lee Harvey Oswald and the Assassination of JFK.* New York: Random House, 1993.

*Report of the Warren Commission on the Assassination of President Kennedy.* With additional material prepared by the *New York Times.* New York: McGraw-Hill, 1964.

Wills, Garry, and Ovid Demaris. *Jack Ruby.* New York: New American Library, 1968. Reprint, New York: Da Capo, 1994.

MIKE REYNOLDS

*See also* **Assassinations; Kennedy, John F.; Oswald, Lee Harvey.**

# RUBY RIDGE

The 1992 confrontation between federal agents and the Randy Weaver family at Ruby Ridge, Idaho, has become one of the most widely debated and bitterly contested examples of the abuse of federal power. Often overlooked in this controversy is the fact that the conflict at Ruby Ridge was the result of an ongoing federal crusade against the radical right in the American Northwest—a campaign that began in the early 1980s, when the Federal Bureau of Investigation set its sights on a runaway neo-Nazi terrorist cell (from the remote mountains of eastern Washington) known as the Order. Led by thirty-one-year-old Robert Mathews, the Order was responsible for a string of assassinations, bombings, and bank robberies. Following an intensive manhunt, federal agents killed Mathews during a December 1984 standoff on Whidbey Island, Washington, and then won a massive sixty-seven-part indictment against twenty-nine individuals who had helped Mathews carry out a conspiracy of terror. The investigation revealed that the conspiracy originated at the Aryan Nations compound near Coeur d'Alene, Idaho, and brought Randy Weaver to the attention of the Bureau of Alcohol, Tobacco, and Firearms (ATF).

**Preceding Events**

The initial engagement with Weaver was a gun deal. In October 1989 Weaver sold two shotguns, both with sawed-off barrels—about five inches shorter than the law allows—to Kenneth Fadeley, a gun dealer and a paid informant of the ATF, who had encouraged the indigent Weaver to manufacture and sell the guns. On 12 June 1990 two ATF agents approached Weaver in Naples, Idaho, saying they had evidence of illegal gun dealings and that they had presented the case to the U.S. attorney. The agents indicated that there was a good chance Weaver would be indicted on federal firearms violations and lose his property. They offered to have the charges dropped if Weaver would provide the agents with information about the gun-running activities of two of his friends, Aryan Nations members John Trochmann and Chuck Howarth. Weaver refused.

In January 1991 Weaver was arrested on the gun charges by two ATF agents near Naples, and then released on a bond. Several days later an event occurred that transformed this $300 gun deal into what federal authorities saw as a neo-Nazi conspiracy to incite revolution. The U.S. attorney's office received an envelope addressed to the "Servant of the Queen of Babylon." Inside was a handwritten letter reading, in part, that "we will not bow to your evil commandments." This was followed by two quotes—one from the biblical Book of Jeremiah and one from the writings of Robert Mathews. The letter, signed "Mrs. Vicki

Weaver," was accompanied by the signatures of Randy Weaver and the three Weaver children.

On 20 February a failure-to-appear warrant went out for Randy Weaver. The case was assigned to the U.S. marshals, one of whom wrote of Weaver's potential to be "another Bob Mathews and his homestead another Whidbey Island stand-off."

After his failure-to-appear warrant was issued, Randy Weaver retreated to his isolated cabin atop Ruby Ridge and did not leave for the next eighteen months. During this time, consumed with fear over Randy's impending arrest and the possibility of losing their home, the Weaver family became more militant than ever. Randy and his thirteen-year-old son, Sammy, shaved their heads. The entire Weaver family—Randy, Vicki (now pregnant again), fifteen-year-old Sara, Sammy, ten-year-old Rachel, and a young houseguest named Kevin Harris—constantly armed themselves with guns.

**The Confrontation**

At about 4:00 A.M. on Friday, 21 August 1992, a team of six marshals, split into two groups and armed with military-style machine guns, began a preliminary inspection of the woods around the Weavers' cabin. Their objective was not to arrest Weaver at this time but to search for places to hide snipers for implementation of that ultimate goal. Upon completing their assignment at 10:45 A.M., one of the marshals threw rocks at the cabin to see how much noise was required to agitate the Weavers' dogs. A few minutes later, Randy Weaver, Kevin Harris, and Sammy Weaver came out of the cabin and began following the dogs. Three marshals began running through the woods.

At this point, Marshal Larry Cooper stopped and told the others that he did not want to "run down the trail and get shot in the back." He urged them to take up ambush positions and wait. Moments later, they were confronted by a big dog, baying wildly. An agent took aim and killed the dog with one shot. Then they heard the angry voice of Sammy Weaver, who opened fire with his rifle. Randy Weaver shouted to the boys from the ridgetop, telling them to go home, and fired four shots into the air. Sammy turned and started running up the hill. Agent Cooper fired, killing Sammy. Marshal William Degan saw a man dressed in black running through the woods with a rifle. After pulling his badge and identifying himself, Degan fired at Kevin Harris. Harris returned fire, killing Degan.

The Marshals Service immediately issued a report saying that officer Degan had been "ambushed" in a firefight begun by the Weavers from the back of a pickup truck. The report said that the Weavers were "of the Aryan Nations kind," that they were heavily armed, zealous, extremely dangerous, and that they had vowed they would never be taken alive. The report concluded that Randy Weaver was a "crazy skinhead" in charge of a "crazy skinhead family."

On 22 August, the day after the shooting of Marshal Degan, the associate director of the U.S. Marshals Service, Duke Smith, and the leader of the FBI Hostage Rescue Team, Richard Rogers, arrived at Ruby Ridge and took charge. Under standard policy, FBI agents are allowed to shoot at suspects only if another's life is in danger. That is, there must be some provocation on the part of a suspect, and verbal warning must be given, before agents can engage with firearms. However, because of the momentous nature of the crisis, Smith and Rogers—with the knowledge and consent of FBI assistant director Larry Potts—agreed to a new shoot-on-sight rule of engagement.

Shortly after 5:30 P.M. on Saturday, 22 August, twelve camouflaged FBI snipers and advisers moved into position around the cabin. One sniper, Lon Horiuchi, took a position two hundred yards away from the front door of the cabin. Just before 6:00 P.M., Harris along with Randy and Sara Weaver emerged from the cabin. As Randy Weaver reached for the door latch of the birthing shed, Horiuchi fired a bullet into the soft part of his underarm. The three raced back to the cabin door, where Vicki was standing with her baby in her arms and a pistol strapped to her hip. Another FBI sniper's shot went through Kevin Harris's left arm and into his body, penetrating his lung. Horiuchi's second bullet hit Vicki in the head, killing her instantly. The siege ended when Weaver was persuaded to leave the cabin by James "Bo" Gritz, a well-known figure in the American radical-right movement.

**The Legacy of Ruby Ridge**

The aftershocks of Ruby Ridge began immediately, and in many ways continued to reverberate through U.S. law and society. The state of siege continued for eleven more days. Protesters gathered at the Ruby Creek bridge. Weaver's neighbors were joined by more than a hundred bikers, woodsmen, constitutionalists, Christian patriots, Vietnam veterans, and neo-Nazis from the Aryan

## Getting Back at Government: Events of the 1990s

All terrorism begins with a grievance, and Ruby Ridge provided an unparalleled grievance to the far right. In direct response to the Ruby Ridge tragedy, John Trochmann organized the Militia of Montana, the first citizen militia group in the United States, and other militias sprang up across the nation. Following the FBI attack on the Branch Davidians at Waco, Texas, on 19 April 1993, Trochmann began disseminating information on bomb-making and calls for revenge with "great coldbloodedness."

Meanwhile, out on the southwestern gun-show circuit, an alienated Gulf War veteran named Timothy McVeigh was distributing fliers with the name and private address of Lon Horiuchi. Less than a month after the bombing of the Oklahoma City Federal Building on 19 April 1995, McVeigh declared to members of his defense team that he took "responsibility for the bombing," adding that he had been motivated by his anger over the events at Waco and Ruby Ridge.

flawed" law enforcement operations and an interpretation of the rules of engagement that permitted a violation of FBI policy and the Constitution. The U.S. attorney general determined that the threat posed by Randy Weaver was exaggerated and that the FBI's response was clearly an overreaction. Twelve FBI employees were disciplined for their conduct related to the incident at Ruby Ridge. Subsequently, Freeh "ended forever" the use of the rules of engagement by the FBI and replaced them with a revised deadly-force policy that permits the use of lethal force only in the face of imminent death or injury to an officer or another person.

*BIBLIOGRAPHY*

Bovard, James. "Ruby Ridge: The Justice Report." *Wall Street Journal*, 30 June 1995.

Hamm, Mark S. *Apocalypse in Oklahoma: Waco and Ruby Ridge Revenged.* Boston: Northeastern University Press, 1997.

Spence, Gerry. *From Freedom to Slavery: The Rebirth of Tyranny in America.* New York: St. Martin's Griffin, 1996.

Walter, Jess. *Every Knee Shall Bow: The Truth and Tragedy of Ruby Ridge and the Randy Weaver Family.* New York: Regan, 1995.

MARK S. HAMM

*See also* **Bureau of Alcohol, Tobacco, and Firearms; Extremism; Government Violence Against Citizens; Militias, Unauthorized; Oklahoma City Bombing; Waco.**

Nations. Clearly, Vicki and Sam Weaver had taken their places alongside Robert Mathews as martyrs of the radical right. Clearly, too, the distinguishable features of the American right were becoming blurred. Not only did this solidarity fit the radical sensibilities of such groups as the skinheads, but in time it would allow antigovernment sentiment to become nationalized, thus gaining a larger and more moderate constituency.

Randy Weaver and Kevin Harris were acquitted of murder charges related to the death of U.S. Marshal William Degan. Weaver was convicted on two counts of failing to appear in court on the weapons charges, for which he served a sixteen-month sentence. On his release, Weaver filed a $170 million lawsuit against the federal government for the wrongful deaths of Vicki and Sammy Weaver. A settlement was reached awarding $1 million to each of Weaver's three daughters. Weaver himself received a $100,000 settlement.

During the October 1995 Congressional hearings on Ruby Ridge, the FBI director, Louis J. Freeh, admitted to "serious deficiencies in the FBI's performance during the crisis." Among the deficiencies noted by Freeh were a series of "terribly

# RURAL VIOLENCE

There is a stereotype of rural America as peaceful and crime-free, in contrast to life in the city. In early America, rural areas were comparatively dangerous and lawless places, made even less safe by the practice of banishing troublesome people from the cities to the countryside, people who then might prey on innocent travelers. The image of rural areas as safe and peaceful appears true when one consults police records and statistics, but the picture is more complex when other types of data are considered. Unfortunately, most studies of violence have focused on urban violence, either ignoring rural areas or failing to differentiate between the two. Consequently, our understanding of rural violence is less complete than our understanding of urban violence, and many dimensions of rural violence remain unexamined.

Although the term *rural* is in itself difficult to define, defining *violence* is also an important task that will shape the conclusions we draw. For example, when lethal violence is broadly defined to include homicide, suicide, highway automobile accidents, and deaths from drowning, falling, and fires, the rate of lethal violence among young white males in the most dangerous rural counties in the West is higher than that among young black males in the six most dangerous inner cities.

Rural areas can be dangerous places, but when accidents and death caused by nature are excluded and one examines criminal acts of violence, a very different picture emerges. Criminal violence takes many forms and can be measured in a variety of ways. Among the most easily accessible and most frequently cited data are official police records. Each year the Uniform Crime Reports assembles data from police departments throughout the country, although urban departments are more likely to report data than are rural departments. In 1996, 97 percent of urban departments reported data while 87 percent of rural departments did. Data are reported for a variety of crimes, but the greatest detail is presented for the so-called index offenses—the eight most serious crimes that occur with enough frequency to allow for meaningful year-to-year comparisons. Among these eight index offenses are four crimes of violence—murder, rape, robbery, and aggravated assault. For each of these offense categories, the largest cities report substantially higher rates than do rural areas. In 1997, for example, the rate of murder was four times higher in urban areas, the rate of rape was twice as high, the robbery rate was twenty-six times higher, and the rate of aggravated assault was four times higher. Overall, the rate of violent index offenses reported by police was five times higher in urban areas than in rural areas. The late twentieth century witnessed declines in homicides in the largest cities, but homicides in rural areas have maintained relatively low rates with little fluctuation. Thus, whatever convergence is occurring between rural and urban homicide rates is primarily the result of declines in urban rates. In the case of homicide, comparisons between rural and urban areas are further complicated because the response time of emergency vehicles is often longer in rural areas. When emergency vehicles do respond, the hospital may be farther away, which also increases the likelihood of an assault case becoming a homicide. In other words, differences in

the availability of emergency medical care may exaggerate rural homicide levels.

Differences in the rates of violent index offenses in rural and urban areas are consistent with popular stereotypes, but there are factors concerning these differences that challenge simplistic explanations of violence. First, violence is lower in rural areas, despite the fact that guns are more readily available in rural areas and that a much higher percentage of rural citizens are familiar and comfortable with their use. Homicides, robberies, rapes, and aggravated assaults are less likely to be committed with a gun in rural areas than in the largest cities. Second, while drug use is linked with violence in the public's mind, drug use is about as frequent in rural areas. Violence, however, including drug-related violence, is less frequent. Third, while the public often makes a connection between crime and persistent poverty, some of the poorest areas of America are rural areas. Despite generations of poverty, compared with large cities, crime remains low in these areas. While the direct impact of poverty on crime continues to be debated among scholars, there is no doubt that rural poverty means a small tax base. These circumstances, in turn, mean fewer resources for rural police and prosecutors, including less manpower, less equipment, fewer resources for investigation, and less money for in-service training of officers.

Another source of information about rural violence is the National Crime Victimization Survey. Analysis of these data show that city residents are more frequently the victims of violent crime than are residents of suburban and rural areas. While these data reveal a modest convergence of rural and urban rates of violent victimization between 1981 and 1996, patterns of violence in urban, suburban, and rural areas are quite similar. When violence drops in cities, it generally drops in suburban and rural areas as well. This suggests that although rural violence is persistently less frequent than urban violence, both areas are influenced by some set of larger forces in American society.

While police reports and general victimization data suggest rural violence is less frequent than urban violence, some forms of violence are of particular concern in rural communities. These types of violence include spousal abuse, child abuse, and domestic terrorism.

### Spousal Abuse

In contrast to police reports of index offenses, surveys of domestic violence have generally reported only small differences between rural and urban areas in the percentage of households reporting spousal abuse, a finding duplicated in a 1992 reanalysis of National Crime Victimization Survey data. These data may be a problematic source because many of those people interviewed answer questions while another member of the family is in the room. This situation is likely to suppress reports of intimate abuse.

Ethnographic or field studies are not equipped to tell us about the relative number of spousal abuse cases in rural areas, but they can describe the nature of the problem. Perhaps the most thorough of these ethnographies is Neil Websdale's (1998) work in rural Kentucky. He found that abuse was facilitated by physical isolation, a tendency toward patriarchy, and isolation from potentially supportive institutions, including child care, health care, and other social services. The distances involved in traveling to these institutions and the lack of public transportation complicate providing counseling or other services that might help these battered women.

**Child Abuse**

Domestic-violence surveys also suggest that the size of a community has only a small effect on the rate of child abuse in that community. Surveys conducted in the mid-1970s found child-abuse rates were highest in urban areas, next highest in suburban areas, and lowest in rural areas. Surveys conducted in the mid-1980s and later, again by community size, found no significant differences in self-reported child abuse.

The problem of identifying lethal child abuse may be complicated by the scarce resources and close social networks in which such investigations take place. There is evidence that a child's death is less often investigated with an autopsy in rural areas than in cities. This difference may partly be explained by the fact that urban areas are more likely to have medical examiners or forensic pathologists—trained medical professionals who exclusively focus on crime and who can conduct their own autopsies. In contrast, rural areas more often rely on coroners who are usually elected and for whom no medical training is required. In many rural areas coroners are part-time officials who are most often funeral directors but could just as easily be farmers or shopkeepers. Within the close social confines of a rural community, and given that the funeral director's business depends on good relationships with members of the community, a fam-

ily's objections to an autopsy on their child may often be respected. In jurisdictions covered by coroners with no experience in forensic pathology, conducting an autopsy may require sending the body to a medical examiner in another jurisdiction and paying a high price for the service. This can place a substantial hardship on a financially strapped rural county, since not all states will cover these costs for the county. These conditions effectively discourage autopsies in cases where there is nothing immediately suspicious about a child's death. These circumstances, in turn, can lead to an underestimation of the number of children killed.

**Domestic Terrorism**

Rural America has a long history of mistrusting centralized government and of using violence against the government. Thomas Jefferson was said to believe that, to keep democracy alive, a violent revolution would be necessary about every twenty years. When Timothy McVeigh was arrested on a traffic violation, which eventually led to his being charged and convicted for the 1995 bombing of the Alfred P. Murrah Federal Building in Oklahoma City, he was said to be wearing a T-shirt printed with words adapted from a Thomas Jefferson quote: "The tree of liberty shall be fertilized by the blood of tyrants and patriots."

Antigovernment sentiments in the western states have led to threats against federal forest and wildlife officials, and antitax groups have sometimes been linked to violence. While the number of people who would directly engage in antigovernment violence is quite small, what is of concern is the extent to which these individuals are viewed by rural citizens with a sympathetic eye. On 5 April 1985 a highway patrolman in Missouri was shot and killed by an antigovernment extremist in his rural jurisdiction. The trooper had lived in the area for many years, as had the trooper who was his backup. In an interview with the backup officer years later, he reported that the most discouraging outcome of the incident was the unwillingness of members of the trooper's own church to condemn the shooting. These were people he considered personal friends.

Researchers have only begun to appreciate the importance of the rural context for understanding these specific forms of violence. Several factors may help explain what attracts extremists to rural areas. First, the physically remote settings typical of many rural areas are logical places to avoid routine contact with the government and to escape dependence on the larger society that depends on the government to maintain highways, water supplies, and other necessities of urban life. Second, many extremists are connected with ultraconservative religious groups, such as the Christian Identity movement, and rural areas have traditionally been more tolerant of conservative religious movements. Finally, many of these conservative groups harbor strong racist sentiments. Compared with cities, rural areas are racially homogeneous, and therefore, racists can live in rural areas without having to interact directly with the groups they cannot tolerate. In the rural areas of industrial states such as Michigan, Illinois, and New York, for example, more than 97 percent of the population is white.

## Understanding Rural Violence

Scholars have only begun to examine the patterns of violence in rural America and have yet to focus on understanding those patterns, with one important exception. Richard Nisbett and Dov Cohen (1996) have attempted to explain both general differences in urban and rural violence and large variations in violence within rural areas. These authors have suggested that high homicide rates in the South reflect a "culture of honor," in which responding violently to threats that challenge one's honor is considered more acceptable than it is in the North. Nisbett and Cohen argue that higher rates of violence in the South are almost entirely explained by the substantially higher number of white males in rural areas and that studies must simultaneously consider race, gender, and community size to understand cultural variations in American violence. The authors argue that southerners do not approve of violence in general, but they are more likely to endorse violence in cases involving an affront to one's home, family, or person. Using multiple research methods, they systematically examine the relatively higher levels of violence in the South and parts of the West. They also argue that regional differences are most substantial in rural areas, while urban areas show much less regional and subcultural variation. Carefully ruling out such factors as gun ownership and a history of oppression through slavery, Nisbett and Cohen suggest that the culture of honor is a product of the type of agricultural activity practiced by the forefathers of current residents. Groups with ancestors who herded animals and lived a relatively nomadic lifestyle were much more violent than those with ancestors who cultivated and tended crops. Nisbett and Cohen and others make a powerful case for incorporating community size and regional history, as well as race and gender, in subsequent analyses of violence in America.

## Conclusion

Rural violence is a seriously understudied phenomenon. Understanding rural and urban variations in violence, as well as differences within rural areas, can improve our understanding of violence in general. Violence in the form of traditional street crime appears to be less frequent in rural areas than in cities. In contrast, family violence appears to be as frequent in rural areas as in cities, but resources for police, support for victims, and social services may be less readily available in rural areas. Antigovernment sentiments have a long history in rural America and seem to be an integral part of rural culture. Although these sentiments do not usually lead to violent actions, the potential for such actions is high, particularly in the rural West. Finally, research that links violence to rural culture provides an interesting starting point for examining more closely the factors that shape rural violence.

*BIBLIOGRAPHY*

Dyer, Joel. *Harvest of Rage: Why Oklahoma City Is Only the Beginning.* Boulder, Colo.: Westview, 1997.

Fischer, David H. *Albion's Seed: Four British Folkways in America.* New York: Oxford University Press, 1989.

Greenberg, Michael R., George W. Carey, and Frank J. Popper. "Violent Death, Violent States, and American Youth." *The Public Interest* 87 (1987).

Nisbett, Richard E., and Dov Cohen. *Culture of Honor: The Psychology of Violence in the South.* Boulder, Colo.: Westview, 1996.

Stock, Catherine McNicol. *Rural Radicals: Righteous Rage in the American Grain.* Ithaca, N.Y.: Cornell University Press, 1996.

Unnithan, Prabha. "The Processing of Homicide Cases with Child Victims: Systemic and Situational Contingencies." *Journal of Criminal Justice* 22 (1994).

Websdale, Neil. *Rural Woman Battering and the Justice System: An Ethnography.* Thousand Oaks, Calif.: Sage, 1998.

Weisheit, Ralph A., David N. Falcone, and L. Edward Wells. *Crime and Policing in Rural and Small-Town America.* 2d ed. Prospect Heights, Ill.: Waveland, 1999.

RALPH A. WEISHEIT

*See also* **Agrarian Violence; Child Abuse; Geography of Violence; National Crime Victimization Survey; South; Spousal and Partner Abuse; Suburban Violence; Terrorism; Uniform Crime Reports; Urban Violence; West.**

# S

## SACCO-VANZETTI CASE

The legacy of Nicola Sacco and Bartolomeo Vanzetti has continued to be felt in the realms of law, literature, history, and politics. These two Italian immigrants, dedicated anarchists, were tried, convicted, and executed for the murder of two men during a holdup and robbery at a shoe factory in South Braintree, Massachusetts, on 15 April 1920. From their conviction in 1921 to their execution on 23 August 1927, their fate provoked intense questioning of American justice, the capitalist system, and governmental ethics.

Authorities believed the South Braintree payroll holdup a repeat of an earlier attempted holdup in Bridgewater, Massachusetts. Five men, supposedly Italians, were responsible for these crimes. (Vanzetti was also charged, convicted, and sentenced as one of the perpetrators of the Bridgewater crime.) On the night of 5 May 1920, Sacco and Vanzetti and two other anarchists, Mike (Mario) Buda and Riccardo Orciani, met at a garage in Bridgewater to pick up Buda's car, which the police suspected had been used in the robberies. Sacco and Vanzetti left town on the trolley and were arrested on it by police. They were not told the charges against them until four months later when they were arraigned by the grand jury.

Buda disappeared; because the police could not find any witnesses to swear that anyone of Buda's description had been at either holdup, they did not attempt to trace him. Orciani had an alibi on 15 April. Instead of searching for the culprits, police concentrated solely on gathering circumstantial evidence to convict the two Italian anarchists who happened to be picking up a car that in any event turned out not to be connected to the holdups.

### Background

To understand the complexity of Sacco and Vanzetti's situation, one must recall the events of 1918 and 1919, when the U.S. government censored publications containing "subversive" materials and systematically targeted immigrants and their organizations who opposed U.S. involvement in World War I, the capitalist system, and its politics. Hundreds of people were deported. It is also essential to keep in mind the war against labor organizations then being waged by corporate America. Citing foreign anarchist extremists, Congress enacted restrictive immigration laws that substantially reduced immigration by southern and eastern Europeans.

In 1919 a series of mail bombs addressed to prominent businessmen and government officials were intercepted. On 2 June, bombs exploded in eight cities, including a bomb that damaged the home of Attorney General A. Mitchell Palmer. Copies of an anarchist pamphlet, *Plain Words,* were found near these explosions. Two Italian immigrant printers in New York, Andrea Salsedo and Roberto Elia, both anarchists, were arrested by the Justice Department after the typeface from *Plain Words* was discovered in their workplace. Salsedo either was pushed or jumped from the building in which he was detained; fearing further reprisals, Vanzetti and other anarchists decided to hide incriminating printed materials.

### Reactions to the Trial

The radical community of anarchists and syndicalists rallied to the aid of Sacco and Vanzetti. They established a Defense League and hired a prominent labor lawyer, Fred Moore, to defend the men. When a guilty verdict was delivered on 11 September 1920, violence and mass protests followed. While doubt regarding the conclusiveness of the evidence against him remains, many scholars believe that on 16 September 1920, Mario Buda set off a bomb on the corner of Wall and Broad Streets in New York City, killing thirty people and injuring more than two hundred. In October 1921, a bomb exploded at the American embassy in Paris, and another was intercepted at the U.S. consulate in Lisbon. Similar violent responses occurred when the court rejected appeals of the verdict in 1927.

The defense plea for a new trial was based on the concept of consciousness of guilt (the prosecution used against them the manner in which the accused acted and spoke at the time of their arrest); the highlighting of the accused's political beliefs during in-court examinations and cross-examinations; and

charges of Judge Webster Thayer's overt bias during the trial and subsequent appeals. Eminent scholars, including Harvard Law School professors Felix Frankfurter (writing in 1927) and Edmund M. Morgan (writing in 1948), echoed these concerns.

In its review, the State Supreme Court could rule only on the legal procedures of the case, not the content or the verdict. In November 1927, the Massachusetts Judicial Council recommended changes in the review procedures in provisions in capital cases. However, not until 1939 was the statute amended to require that in reviewing capital cases the Supreme Court consider both the law and the evidence.

### Legacy of the Case

In the rhetoric of those convinced of their innocence, Sacco and Vanzetti became symbols of the failure of the U.S. justice system and the evils of capitalism. Some groups, like the Communist Party, used the case as a soapbox to condemn the system. The writer Katherine Anne Porter recalled how a party member, reacting to her hopes that Sacco and Vanzetti would be saved from execution, remarked, "Saved, who wants them saved? What earthly good would they do us alive?" Novels by John Dos Passos and Upton Sinclair under-

**Bartolomeo Vanzetti (middle) and Nicola Sacco (right), in 1923.** CORBIS/BETTMANN

scored the anarchist as idealist. The artist Ben Shahn painted a series of pictures depicting Judge Thayer and other Massachusetts officials as cruel, stony, puritanical avengers. These themes reflected the disenchantment of intellectuals with U.S. justice. Sacco and Vanzetti's own words, later printed in *Letters of Sacco-Vanzetti* (1928), helped to perpetuate the image of martyrs who died defending their beliefs in social justice and commitment to the working class.

Debates over legal and evidential aspects of the case continued, as revisionists examined trial transcripts and interviewed the principal participants. Ballistic tests performed in the 1960s and 1980s seemed to establish that Sacco's gun fired the bullet that killed the guard in the robbery, leading some to question the innocence of the two men, particularly Sacco. In addition, remarks attributed to supporters, such as Carlo Tresca, who years later stated that Sacco was guilty, seemed to represent "inside" information.

Historians of the anarchist movement have questioned the aptness of the term "philosophical anarchists" as applied to Sacco and Vanzetti by their supporters. Paul Avrich, in his definitive 1991 study, documented their commitment to the principles of Luigi Galleani, who advocated violent overthrow of the system. Vanzetti's and Sacco's statements from prison encouraged their followers to avenge their names, and acts of violence continued. On 15 August 1927 an explosion demolished the home of Lewis McHardy, a juror in the Sacco-Vanzetti trial. Judge Thayer's home was bombed in September 1932.

Others continued to insist on the men's innocence, saying that two men unfamiliar with criminal tactics could not have planned this robbery—and that in any case bombing, not robbery, was the hallmark of anarchists—and questioning the prosecution witnesses and the withholding of information on evidence and on witnesses by the prosecution.

Katherine Anne Porter in 1977 summed up the Sacco-Vanzetti legacy:

> I cannot even now decide by my own evidence whether or not they were guilty of the crime for which they were put to death. . . . We do know now, all of us, that the most appalling cruelties are committed by apparently virtuous governments in expectation of a great good to come, never learning that the evil done now is the sure destroyer of the expected good. Yet, no matter what, it was a terrible miscarriage of justice; it was a most reprehensible abuse of legal power, in

their attempt to prove that the law is something to be inflicted—not enforced—and that it is above the judgment of the people. (p. 57)

In 1977, Governor Michael Dukakis of Massachusetts ordered a review of the Sacco-Vanzetti matter. In his report, legal counsel Daniel Taylor maintained that a pardon would give the impression that the men were guilty of the crime. Instead, Taylor recommended that the governor issue a proclamation admitting the unfairness of the trial, citing factors such as the prevailing prejudicial atmosphere against foreigners and radicals, the questionable conduct of many officials involved with the trial, and the limited scope of appellate review. The proclamation declared 23 August 1977 Nicola Sacco and Bartolomeo Vanzetti Memorial Day and declared "that any stigma and disgrace be forever removed from [their] names, from the names of their families and descendants, and so, from the name of the Commonwealth of Massachusetts."

The public demonstrations provoked by what was seen as Sacco and Vanzetti's victimization by the system echoed decades later in protests against authority and public policy during the Vietnam War; the violent and terroristic acts of the 1920s were recalled when terrorist attacks and bombings occurred in the United States in the 1980s and 1990s. Perhaps the greatest legacy of the Sacco-Vanzetti case concerns state-authorized violence: the methods used to bring criminals and terrorists to justice and efforts to ensure fair trials continue to place the political and judicial system in a delicate balancing act, attempting to protect the rights of the accused while also ensuring the public right to safety.

*BIBLIOGRAPHY*

Avrich, Paul. *Sacco and Vanzetti: The Anarchist Background.* Princeton, N.J.: Princeton University Press, 1991.

Ehrmann, Herbert B. *The Case That Will Not Die: Commonwealth vs. Sacco and Vanzetti.* Boston: Little, Brown, 1969.

Frankfurter, Felix. *The Case of Sacco and Vanzetti: A Critical Analysis for Lawyers and Laymen.* Boston: Little, Brown, 1927.

Joughin, G. Louis, and Edmund M. Morgan. *The Legacy of Sacco and Vanzetti.* New York: Harcourt, Brace, 1948.

Pernicone, Nunzio. "Carlo Tresca and the Sacco-Vanzetti Case." *Journal of American History* 66, no. 3 (December 1979).

Porter, Katherine Anne. *The Never-Ending Wrong.* Boston: Little, Brown, 1977.

Russell, Francis. *Sacco and Vanzetti: The Case Resolved.* New York: Harper and Row, 1986.

*Sacco-Vanzetti: Developments and Reconsiderations—1979.* Boston: Trustees of the Public Library of the City of Boston, 1982.

Taylor, Daniel. *Report to the Governor in the Matter of Sacco and Vanzetti.* Boston: Office of the Governor's Legal Counsel, 1977.

VINCENZA SCARPACI

*See also* **Anarchism; Immigration; Italian Americans; Wall Street, Bombing of.**

## SADISM AND MASOCHISM

The term *sadism* was first used in France in the mid-nineteenth century to denote sexual pleasure derived from the infliction of cruelty and pain on others. The term comes from the name of the Marquis de Sade (1740–1814), whose notoriety is based on his lifestyle and his writings, *The 120 Days of Sodom* (1785) and *Justine* (1791) among others. The term *masochism* was first used in 1886 by the Viennese pathologist Richard von Krafft-Ebing (1840–1902) to describe sexual pleasure derived from subjecting oneself to cruelty and pain. Krafft-Ebing coined the term from the name of the writer Leopold Sacher-Masoch (1835–1900), whose best-known novel, *Venus in Furs*, describes this behavior. The novel tells the story of a male masochist, Severin, who lives out his fantasies before finally being cured by a sadistic mistress. Acts of sadism and masochism later came to be associated with each other and eventually were referred to as sadomasochism. In present-day usage *sadomasochism* is a consensual sexual arrangement in which scenes of violence, domination and subordination, humiliation, and bondage—sometimes to the point of self-mutilation—are enacted according to an implicitly or explicitly scripted agreement. Because of the consensual and scripted nature of sadomasochism, with its elements of role-play and shared fantasy, it is essential to distinguish it from sexual violence. Yet the boundary between consensual and nonconsenual sexual violence may become blurred.

### Historical Background

If sadomasochistic sexuality is taken to include religious rituals that eroticize pain or power and powerlessness, such as flagellation, self-mutilation, and various other practices in which bodily pleasure and pain are confounded, sadomasochism is probably as old as human society. Often-cited ex-amples of this kind of practice include initiation rituals, Roman deity rites, and medieval flagellation. But in the sense defined here, there is little evidence of the practice of sexual sadomasochism prior to the sixteenth century. The first systematic attempt to define sadism and masochism as clinical pathologies was made by Krafft-Ebing in 1886. He shared the common view that male sexuality was naturally aggressive and female sexuality was naturally passive. Consequently, he concluded that sadism was normal behavior in the male and pathological in the female, while masochism was normal behavior in the female and pathological in the male. The psychoanalyst Sigmund Freud drew on these ideas, but writing in 1924, he made three important interventions. He saw masochistic sexuality as a performance; his theories departed from the common idea that sadism and masochism are complementary opposites; and he sought to explain how individuals need to deal with self-inflicted suffering in the process of socialization. William Stekel (1925) appears to have been the first to speak consistently and purposefully of sadomasochism. The current understanding of sadomasochism owes much to developments after Stekel. Among these are the idea of masochism as a socially conditioned performance put forth by Theodor Reik in 1940; the study of social mechanisms of control and how they affect sexuality by Karen Horney in 1947; the abandoning of biological theories of female masochism as propagated by Helen Deutsch in 1925 and Marie Deutsch in 1935; and Wilhelm Reich's 1933 concept of masochism as a defense maneuver.

Since the 1950s empirical studies have provided information on the frequency and nature of sadomasochistic practices in American society. Alfred Kinsey in his famous 1953 work on sexual behavior asserted that humans have a biological propensity to violent sexual play, and he extended the definition of sadomasochism to include acts of physical aggression and violence of the kind found in the sexual behavior of mammals, singling out biting as the most common example. Kinsey observed that attitudes toward sexual sadomasochism were tied to social class; he found sadomasochism more frequently practiced in those sectors of American society with better incomes and education. The percentage of people involved in this behavior, however, remained low according to Kinsey: 4 percent of the women in his sample masturbated with sadomasochistic fantasies; 3 percent of the women and 10 percent of the men were definitely or frequently aroused by sadomasochistic stories. In the *Janus Report* (1993) there is a significant increase: 14 percent of the men and 11 percent of the women sampled reported having engaged in sadomasochistic sex, while it was estimated that between 8 and 10 percent of American homes have sadomasochistic equipment, such as masks, whips, and ropes.

## In the Culture

By the mid-1980s sadomasochism had become visible in society in mainstream magazines like *Penthouse* and *Vogue;* in the music videos of such pop megastars as Madonna and Duran Duran; in the fashion world with the photography of Helmut Newton and the fashion shows of Gianni Versace; and in advertising. In 1994 *New York* magazine claimed that sadomasochism was the sexual mode of the 1990s. Lynn Chancer (1992) suggests that this trend reflects a general feeling of individual powerlessness in private life and interpersonal relationships in American society; sadomasochism may thus offer a way to seize or negotiate power. According to Chancer the individual may feel he or she exercises little control over his or her own life and environment; public images of harmonious and happy family life thus often contrast with private realities of hidden violence. Barbara Ehrenreich (1986) suggests that the rise in sadomasochism is related to a general tendency to treat sex as a marketable commodity.

In the United States, gay, lesbian, and heterosexual practitioners of sadomasochism have all developed their own symbolism, myths, and codes. Common to many of the sadomasochistic subcultures is a display of leather, chains, piercings, and iconography from historical stereotypes of violence, such as Nazi insignia.

One of the best known and most sophisticated sadomasochistic novels is *Story of O* (1954) by Pauline Réage (the nom de plume of Anne Delos). It tells the story of a young Parisian woman who lives out her masochistic desire to be a slave lover. This brings her into a community of libertines whose sadistic urges are a source of satisfaction and sexual pleasure for O. The submission and humiliation she experiences seem well suited to her sexual taste, and at the end of the story, she has completely abandoned her own willpower, to the point of wishing her own death. The controversial scenes of sexual violence as well as the portrayal of women in this novel led to conflicting interpretations. For many years the novel's graphic descriptions of sexual violence—particularly the violence against women—caused it to be sharply criticized, even banned. It has also been described as a parable of how individuals place themselves under the power of others in order to achieve protection and recognition. A work of literary merit, *Story of O* demonstrates some of the problems that sadomasochism raises in modern society.

Sadomasochistic themes run through a good deal of late-twentieth-century American literature, as for example in works by Kathy Acker (*Kathy Goes to Haiti*, 1993) and Thomas Pynchon (*Gravity's Rainbow*, 1973). The same is true of films such as David Lynch's *Blue Velvet* (1986) and *Wild at Heart* (1990), Adrian Lyne's *9½ Weeks* (1986), and Paul Verhoeven's *Basic Instinct* (1992). Sadomasochistic imagery also appears in television advertising. The Internet—particularly conducive to role-play and anonymity—has proved to be a popular medium for communicating sadomasochistic fantasies; it is also a high-risk venue for initiating meetings where these fantasies can be played out.

## Legal Issues

The legal implications of sadomasochistic sexuality are complex, centering on the issue of consent and extending to issues of legal ethics and of normative sexuality. In the 1970s certain relaxations were instituted in legislation affecting consensual exercise of "perverse" activities. One attempt to treat sadomasochistic relations adequately has been to regard injuries ensuing from sadomasochistic relations in the same light as sports injuries, that is to say, the injury itself may not have been anticipated—perhaps not even desired—but the injured person had voluntarily and knowingly entered a situation where injuries of a particular kind were not only possible but likely. Nevertheless, the question of violence remains a real problem: the protection that criminal law affords individuals from acts of violence must be balanced with the fundamental human right of individuals to exercise their own discretion in the conduct of their private lives.

## Feminist Issues

The need to accord individuals certain freedoms in the realm of sexuality while at the same time protecting human rights became a serious issue for feminist views of sadomasochism in the 1980s, when a heated debate erupted concerning the feminist interpretation of masochism among women, and the ethical acceptability of sado-masochism. On the one hand sadomasochism was seen as a legitimate expression of female sexuality, while others argued that it simply reinforced the conditions that lead to violence against women in American society. In this connection some feminists and reformist psychiatrists claimed that sadist and masochist sexuality simply perpetuated the way violence is exercised in society at large; to deal with such behaviors without examining the underlying social causes of violence against women would potentially disadvantage women or infringe on personal rights in the choice of sexual practice.

The feminist controversy over masochism and self-defeating behavior had important repercussions for the psychiatric profession. The American Psychiatric Association instituted a series of reforms of the concept of masochism in its *Diagnostic and Statistical Manual of Mental Disorders* (DSM). These were prompted by the observation that the definition of masochism in the 1980 and 1987 editions of the DSM could be used by the judiciary as well as in medicine and insurance claims to condone violence against women. The critique of the older definitions rested on the recognition that sadomasochism and violence against women are two distinct things. The diagnostic category of sexual masochism in the 1994 version of DSM remains problematic, since it relies on an easy distinction between real and simulated violence, something that most theories of sadomasochism regard as difficult to uphold.

Although it has become increasingly more visible, sadomasochistic sexuality is still highly controversial. In a 1993 U.S. survey, 60 percent of men and 67 percent of women still regarded it as "kinky" sex, while only 2 percent of men and 1 percent of women regarded it as "very normal." If sadomasochism is to provide those who engage in it with the thrill they require, this aura of the forbidden needs to be maintained.

BIBLIOGRAPHY

Bonaparte, Marie. "Passivity, Masochism, and Femininity." *International Journal of Psycho-Analysis* 16 (1935).
Caplan, Paula J. *The Myth of Women's Masochism.* New York: Dutton, 1985.
Chancer, Lynn S. *Sadomasochism in Everyday Life: The Dynamics of Power and Powerlessness.* New Brunswick, N.J.: Rutgers University Press, 1992.
Deutsch, Helene. *Psychoanalysis of the Sexual Functions of Women.* 1925. Reprint, London: Karnac, 1991.
Ehrenreich, Barbara, Elizabeth Hess, and Gloria Jacobs. *Remaking Love: The Feminization of Sex.* New York: Anchor, 1986.
Ellis, Havelock. *Studies in the Psychology of Sex.* Vol. 3, *Analysis of the Sexual Impulse; Love and Pain; The Sexual Impulse in Women.* 1903. Reprint, Philadelphia: F. A. Davis, 1913.
Freud, Sigmund. "The Economic Problem of Masochism." In *Standard Edition of the Complete Works of Sigmund Freud,* vol. 19, edited by James Strachey. London: Hogarth, 1924.
———. *Three Essays on the Theory of Sexuality.* In *Standard Edition of the Complete Works of Sigmund Freud,* vol. 7, edited by James Strachey. London: Hogarth, 1905.
Gebhard, Paul H. "Fetishism and Sadomasochism." In *Dynamics of Deviant Sexuality,* vol. 15, edited by Jules H. Masserman. New York: Grune and Stratton, 1969.
Horney, Karen. *New Ways in Psychoanalysis.* London: Kegan Paul, Trench, Trubner, 1947.
Janus, Samuel L., and Cynthia L. Janus. *The Janus Report on Sexual Behavior.* New York: Wiley, 1993.
Kinsey, Alfred C., et. al. *Sexual Behavior in the Human Female.* Philadelphia and London: W. B. Saunders, 1953.
Krafft-Ebing, Richard von. *Psychopathia Sexualis: A Medico-Forensic Study.* 1890. Reprint, New York: Pioneer, 1944.
Leigh, L. H. "Sado-Masochism, Consent, and the Reform of the Criminal Law." *Modern Law Review* 39 (1976).
Linden, Robin Ruth, et al., eds. *Against Sadomasochism: A Radical Feminist Analysis.* East Palo Alto, Calif.: Frog in the Well, 1982.
McArdle, David. "A Few Hard Cases? Sport, Sadomasochism, and Public Policy in the English Courts." *Canadian Journal of Law and Society* 10 (1995).
Noyes, John K. *The Mastery of Submission: Inventions of Masochism.* Ithaca, N.Y.: Cornell University Press, 1997.
Reich, Wilhelm. *Character Analysis.* 1933. Reprint, New York: Farrar, Straus, 1949.
Reik, Theodor. *Masochism in Modern Man.* 1940. Reprint, New York: Farrar, Straus, 1949.
Stekel, Wilhelm. *Sadism and Masochism.* 1925. Reprint, New York: Liveright, 1929.

JOHN K. NOYES

*See also* **Fashion; Mutilation of the Body; Self-Destructiveness.**

## ST. LOUIS

Violence in St. Louis reflects the city's position as a Midwestern transportation and industrial center. Its transformation from frontier town to modern metropolis, its historically diverse population, and the shifts in its economy over time have all provided contexts for several periods of intense racial and ethnic tension.

Early generalizations about violence in St. Louis were made when political control shifted from France to the United States following the Louisiana

Purchase in 1803. Many inhabitants argued that the Americanization of the city led to an increase in acts of random physical violence. Longtime city residents of French and Creole descent, and some American observers, noted that the new American traders and riverboat workers were hard-drinking, quick-tempered, and well-armed men whose fondness for gambling often led to brawls and shootouts. Conflict between factions of the city's elite over land claims and political power was another source of violence in St. Louis in the early nineteenth century. Grudge matches between prominent attorneys, land speculators, newspaper editors, and aspiring politicians often led to physical attacks and duels. The newspaper editor Thomas Hart Benton, later Missouri's most famous senator and proponent of westward expansion, twice dueled with rival Charles Lucas in 1817 on "Bloody Island," a Mississippi River islet that was the site of dozens of elite duels in the 1810s and 1820s.

Crime, crowd violence, and vigilante activity also contributed to St. Louis's reputation as a violent frontier town, although these patterns of urban violence were similar to those of other growing American cities. Economic booms and busts in the 1810s and 1820s created affluence and poverty, and hence crime, well before the city had constructed municipal services such as police and fire protection. Eastern newspapers warned travelers that the citizens of St. Louis were heavily armed and that stabbings in the street were common. In the late 1810s the Regulators, an armed vigilante group organized to combat the circulation of counterfeit paper money, rounded up city residents they deemed guilty of a wide range of crimes and punished them with whippings. In addition, in the 1830s and 1840s public drunkenness and civil disorder were not uncommon, as evidenced by the frequent brawls between volunteer fire-fighting companies and the mob that chased the abolitionist Elijah P. Lovejoy out of town in 1836.

Nativism, race, and ethnicity shaped the patterns of violence in St. Louis in the mid-nineteenth century. The city attracted national attention in 1836 when a mob lynched Francis McIntosh, a free, mixed-race riverboat worker who had killed one white deputy sheriff and wounded another. The mob forcibly removed McIntosh from jail and burned him alive. Abolitionist newspapers decried the racist attack, but a grand jury failed to issue indictments in the case. The Know-Nothing Party,

**National Guardsmen escort a man to safety during a St. Louis race riot, June 1917.**
Corbis/Bettmann

81

a short-lived but influential national nativist political movement, was popular with native-born white St. Louisans. By 1860 over half of the city was foreign born, and Irish and German Catholics were the largest immigrant groups. These populations clashed with white nativist mobs several times in the early 1850s, especially during elections. In 1852 nativists charged Germans with stuffing ballot boxes, which led to rock throwing and an exchange of gunfire between the two sides. A three-day anti-Irish rampage during the 1854 election, the worst riot in St. Louis prior to the Civil War, caused ten deaths. During the Civil War, despite the carnage and brutality throughout Missouri and the threats of pro-Confederate conspiracies, St. Louis remained relatively free of war-related violence.

St. Louis's transformation from a riverport and agricultural processing center to a major railroad and industrial hub gave rise to violence associated with class conflict. A nationwide railway strike in 1877 sparked a peaceful citywide general strike. Thousands of railway, riverfront, and manufacturing and service workers marched through the city demanding wage increases and political reforms, effectively taking control of the city. The press denounced the strikers, but the mayor and police refrained from using force. Within a few days, the strike's leadership wavered and the strikers' momentum started to fade. The police and a militia drawn from the city's upper class arrested several participants but did not successfully prosecute them. Despite the strikers' threats to seize the federal arsenal, and the possession of an artillery battery by the citizen militia, the 1877 strike did not result in violence. In contrast, a transit workers strike in 1900 produced violent clashes, including exchanges of gunfire between strikers and out-of-town replacement workers. Three people died when a posse called in by a federal judge and composed of upper-class residents battled with strikers. Liberal elites helped mediate a tenuous resolution that ended the violence, but many union members remained dissatisfied.

In the twentieth century, race continued to be the major factor shaping violence in the St. Louis metropolitan area. Beginning after the failure of Reconstruction in the South and continuing until World War I, African Americans from the rural South migrated to St. Louis, where they occupied the lowest rungs of the expanding industrial labor force. White St. Louis residents enforced racial segregation in housing, education, and many public accommodations. One of the worst race riots in American history took place across the Mississippi River in East Saint Louis, Illinois, in 1917. Striking whites attacked black replacement workers, leading to a wider antiblack melee that claimed the lives of approximately thirty-nine blacks and nine whites. During the struggles of the Civil Rights era, the city's predominantly white police department was seen as a cause of violence against blacks. In the summer of 1965 six African Americans were shot in the back by St. Louis police. Throughout the 1970s the decline of good-paying blue-collar manufacturing jobs devastated working-class African American neighborhoods. Several St. Louis public housing projects, such as the Pruitt-Igoe project, the product of graft by crooked politicians and shoddy construction by predominantly white unions, became violent, crime-ridden traps that illustrated the outcomes of class- and race-based discrimination.

*BIBLIOGRAPHY*

Lipsitz, George. *The Sidewalks of St. Louis: Places, People, and Politics in an American City.* Columbia: University of Missouri Press, 1991.

Primm, James Neal. *Lion of the Valley: St. Louis, Missouri.* Boulder, Colo.: Pruett, 1981.

Troen, Selwyn K., and Glen E. Holt, eds. *St. Louis.* New York: New Viewpoints, 1977.

Van Ravenswaay, Charles. *Saint Louis: An Informal History of the City and Its People, 1764–1865.* St. Louis: Missouri Historical Society, 1991.

MICHAEL JONATHAN PEBWORTH

*See also* **Nativism; Urban Violence.**

# ST. VALENTINE'S DAY MASSACRE

The St. Valentine's Day Massacre of 14 February 1929 was the climax of a decade of violence among gangs battling for control of Chicago's organized-crime revenues. When Prohibition, implemented in 1920, created an unprecedented market for illegal liquor, it also tempted countless criminal entrepreneurs to form bootlegging operations. In the first few years of the decade there was wide-open competition, but a handful of gangs—generally ones that had additional illegal income from gambling, racketeering, prostitution, or political corruption—soon came to dominate bootlegging by frightening off, cooperating with, or killing their competitors. By 1924 the two dominant cartels in Chicago were a South Side group headed by Johnny Torrio and Al Capone and a North Side group that included Dion O'Bannion, Earl "Hymie" Weiss, and George "Bugs" Moran. By 1929 a succession of murders and attempted murders left Capone and Moran the recognized leaders of the two gangs.

The massacre took place when four men disguised as policemen entered a Moran Gang facility at the S.M.C. Cartage Company, ordered the assembled gangsters to line up against a wall, and sprayed their surprised and defenseless victims with tommy guns. Six Moran associates died: Pete and Frank Gusenberg, Adam Heyer, James Clark, John May, and Albert Weinshank; a seventh victim, Reinhardt Schwimmer, had no apparent connection to the gang other than that he enjoyed their company. Frank Gusenberg lived long enough to be interviewed by police, but, in a caricature of the gangland code that kept gangsters from talking to

**Victims of the St. Valentine's Day Massacre, 14 February 1929.** CORBIS/BETTMANN

the authorities, he refused to furnish any information about the gunmen.

The murders remain officially unsolved, but generations have speculated about the killers' identities. Moran's widely quoted observation, "Only Capone's gang kills like that!"—which he might not actually have uttered—pointed to his rival as the obvious suspect, but Capone had an ironclad alibi: in Miami at the time, he had spent the morning talking with Dade County solicitor Robert Taylor. Suspicion also fell on "Machine Gun" Jack McGurn, a Capone lieutenant reputed to be his most effective killer. McGurn, however, produced a girlfriend, Louise Rolfe—his "blonde alibi"—who claimed to have been with him at the time of the murders. McGurn himself was later murdered on the eve of Valentine's Day in 1936, his killers leaving a valentine on his corpse in reference to his purported involvement in the massacre. Others immediately or eventually suspected of planning or taking part in the crime included several reputed Capone gunmen, various St. Louis gangsters, and members of Detroit's Purple Gang. One Chicago Prohibition officer said that Chicago police might have been behind the massacre; Alabama senator J. Thomas Heflin even suggested that the Italian Fascist premier Benito Mussolini might have ordered it.

The massacre has fascinated historians, fiction writers, and filmmakers almost from the moment it took place. With photographs of the murder scene widely available and the massacre reimagined in films such as *Scarface* (1931), *Some Like It Hot* (1959), *Al Capone* (1959), *The Scarface Mob* (1959), *The Saint Valentine's Day Massacre* (1967), and *The Untouchables* (1987), it has remained in the public consciousness. Although it was only one episode in a long campaign of violence, it has come to symbolize 1920s Chicago-gangster rule in general and the career of Al Capone in particular.

*BIBLIOGRAPHY*

Bergreen, Laurence. *Capone: The Man and the Era.* New York: Simon and Schuster, 1994.
Kobler, John. *Capone: The Life and World of Al Capone.* New York: Putnam, 1971.
Schoenberg, Robert J. *Mr. Capone: The Real—and Complete—Story of Al Capone.* New York: Morrow, 1992.

JOE KRAUS

*See also* **Capone, Al; Chicago; Moran, George "Bugs"; Organized Crime; Prohibition and Temperance.**

## SALEM WITCH TRIALS

"Thou shalt not suffer a witch to live" (Exodus 22:18). Seventeenth-century New England Puritans lived by this biblical injunction. Convinced that witches were real and threatening, they sought to rid their community of such evil influences. The Salem, Massachusetts, witchcraft episode began in the winter months of 1692, when several young girls accused three women of be-

---

### From the Confession of Abigail Hobbs, 19 April 1692

Are you not bid to hurt folks?

Yes.

Who are you bid to hurt?

Mercy Lewes and Ann Putman.

What did you do to them when you hurt them?

I pinch't them.

How did you pinch them, do you goe in your own person to them?

No.

Doth the Devil go for you?

Yes.

And what doth he take, your spirit with him?

No. I am as well as at other times: but the Devil has my consent, and goes and hurts them.

Who hurt your mother last Lord's day, was it not you?

No.

Who was it?

I heard her say it was Goody Wilds at Topsfield.

Have you been in company with Goody Wilds at any time?

No, I never saw her.

Well, who are your companions?

Why I have seen Sarah Good once.

How many did you see?

I saw but two.

Did you know Sarah Good was a witch, when you saw her?

Yes.

How did you know it?

The Devil told me.

*Source: The Salem Witchcraft Papers: Verbatim Transcripts of the Legal Documents of the Salem Witchcraft Outbreak of 1692, p. 407.*

---

witching them, and ended the following year. In that interval 156 people were accused of witchcraft, fourteen women and five men were hanged, and one man was pressed to death. The agonies allegedly endured by the victims of the "witches" and reproduced in court were deemed effective evidence against the accused, and confessions by the "witches" were seen as justifying the entire proceedings.

Witchcraft accusations appeared periodically in New England earlier in the seventeenth century, but the number of charges and the severity of official reaction in Salem distinguished this episode from previous cases. The relentless pursuit of witches, endorsed and encouraged by the magistrates, was guided by intense Puritan religious beliefs concerning sin, damnation, and the devil's perceived presence in their world. According to the Puritan worldview, a witch has signed a pact with the devil, thereby enlisting in his army against the godly and aiding in his effort to recruit others for his service. Witches gave Satan permission to take their shape, and then, using the bodies of the witches, Satan tortured others, anxious to dominate first bodies and then souls. Violence characterized witchcraft accusations as well as punishments. The language of the indictments brought against the accused at Salem illustrates the extent of the agonies supposedly inflicted by Satan; its nearly formulaic repetition attests to the ubiquitous belief in Satan's physical powers. The indictments stated that the victims were "Tortured Afflicted Consumed pined Wasted and Tormented." At the trials one woman testified that the devil "did tortor me most cruelly . . . and allmost ready to pull all my bones out of joynt." The Salem court records indicate that 78 percent of the accused witches were women; women and men encountered the devil differently. Women uniformly described physical torture at the hands of Satan or a specter, the shape of one of his witches. One woman swore that the apparition of an accused woman "hurt me and tortord me most dreadfully by pinching and choaking of me and twesting of my nick several times" in order to persuade her to sign a covenant with Satan and to renounce God. Men were rarely victims of the devil's direct physical assault. Generally men's descriptions of their encounters with accused witches centered on bizarre acts of maleficence or on harm to their wives and children, rather than on the physical harm allegedly caused by the witch's shape. When men were victims of physical violence at the hands of

**Hysteria marked the Salem witch trials of 1692 and 1693.** LIBRARY OF CONGRESS

the accused, the scenes were far less dramatic; on the rare occasions when male victims complained of severe physical abuse, it was usually at the hands of another man. Apparently, even with the aid of the devil, women were not physically capable of doing great harm to the bodies of men. Puritans believed that Satan designed his attacks to fit his prey, and so they expected that women and men would experience Satan's tortures differently.

Approximately fifty people confessed to charges of witchcraft in Salem. Scholars have long wondered what motivated these admissions. Why would (mostly) women confess to signing the devil's pact in blood, riding on poles through the air to witches' meetings, and giving their souls to the devil in exchange for his services? Certainly one explanation is that, in Salem, confessors' lives were spared. The magistrates hardly intended to trade witches' confessions for reprieves, but they kept confessors imprisoned in the hope that they might reveal the names of others involved in the devil's wicked plan. It is likely that by the time this pattern was noticed some fraudulent confessions had been tendered to avoid hangings.

Some have speculated that the accused were tortured until they told the magistrates what they wanted to hear: that witches had indeed invaded their godly community, and thus, by implication, the court's relentless witch-hunting was justified. Yet evidence of violent torture is scant. Court records indicated that two brothers, Richard and An-

drew Carrier, confessed after they had been tortured. Shortly after being "Carried out to another Cambbre and there feet & hands bound," Richard Carrier told the court everything he knew—or everything he thought the court wanted to hear—in order to avoid more pain. One woman, Sarah Churchill, admitted that her confession was motivated by fear. She had been threatened and told "thay would put her in to the dongin." Churchill did not mention physical torture, but like many others seemed resigned to confession because persistent denials simply were not believed.

Most people in Salem, women as well as men, imagined that women like Churchill were more likely than men to succumb to the devil. So conditioned, women sometimes confessed without the aid of torture. Honestly searching their souls for evidence that they had signed the devil's pact, Puritan women may have confused ordinary sin with the extraordinary offense of witchcraft, which implicitly bonded one to the devil. Amid the extreme stress of the trials, women's sense of their own mundane complicity with Satan convinced some that they were indeed witches and deserving of their fates.

Surely Salem has become an icon in American culture. Even to this day we want to see people publicly admit wrongdoing, whether imagined or real, and get on with their redemption. Perhaps this is one of the legacies of the Puritan witch-hunts: we need confessions to corroborate our own understanding of right and wrong. The term "witch-hunt," applied to contemporary social problems such as the false accusation of child abuse or to political persecutions like McCarthyism, is used to invoke memories of a grim past, a time when concocted accusations were rife and innocent lives were rashly extinguished. Obviously, the trials have had a much broader effect than their actual scope and duration might lead us to expect.

*BIBLIOGRAPHY*

Boyer, Paul, and Stephen Nissenbaum. *Salem Possessed: The Social Origins of Witchcraft.* Cambridge, Mass.: Harvard University Press, 1974.

Boyer, Paul, and Stephen Nissenbaum, eds. *The Salem Witchcraft Papers: Verbatim Transcripts of the Legal Documents of the Salem Witchcraft Outbreak of 1692.* 3 vols. New York: DaCapo, 1977.

Reis, Elizabeth. *Damned Women: Sinners and Witches in Puritan New England.* Ithaca, N.Y.: Cornell University Press, 1997.

Rosenthal, Bernard. *Salem Story: Reading the Witch Trials of 1692.* Cambridge, U.K.: Cambridge University Press, 1993.

ELIZABETH REIS

*See also* **Cults; Religion; Witchcraft.**

# SAND CREEK MASSACRE

On 29 November 1864 Colorado volunteers attacked the village of the Cheyenne chief Black Kettle and killed between 150 and 200 men, women, and children. Initially heralded as a major victory, the Sand Creek attack soon became the subject of a military investigation and two congressional hearings. In time, the Sand Creek Massacre became both a symbol of the failure of American Indian policy to the nation at large and an emblem of frontier justice to westerners.

The Sand Creek affair had its origin in the Indian War of 1864, which erupted on the central plains that spring, due more to misunderstanding, distrust, and lack of communication between whites and Indians than to any overt cause. It proved to be a costly conflict that for a time interrupted commerce and spread panic. In Colorado the war became an issue in a bitter political battle over statehood. John Evans, Colorado's governor and superintendent of Indian Affairs, and John Milton Chivington, commander of the Military District of Colorado, were ambitious players in the statehood movement. Faced with anti-Indian panic in Colorado and growing disapproval (both of Chivington at Department of Kansas headquarters and of Evans' handling of Indian policy in Washington), both men advocated a punitive Indian policy.

Evans gained permission to raise a regiment of one-hundred-day volunteers. But before the troops could be organized for action, the Cheyenne and Arapaho made a peace overture at Fort Lyon, in southeastern Colorado. The fort commander escorted the chiefs to Denver for a conference with the governor, and Evans reluctantly told the chiefs that they would be safe if they brought their people into Fort Lyon. They did so, but a new commander told them to move to Sand Creek, where they could wait until further instructions were received from department headquarters.

Evans left for Washington, D.C., and Chivington, faced with the imminent end of the one hundred days of service required of the Third Colorado Volunteers, decided to act. He assembled his forces at Bijou Basin and marched down the Arkansas River to Fort Lyon. When he announced his intention to attack the Sand Creek camp, officers of the First Colorado Cavalry protested vehemently, but the following evening, reinforced by the Lyon Battalion, Chivington and his forces rode and marched all night, arriving at the Indian camp at dawn.

The fight that followed could scarcely be called a military action. Units of the First Cavalry did operate as military units, but the "Thirdsters" quickly degenerated from soldiers into a body of individual vigilantes bent on killing Indians. Many Cheyennes and Arapahoes escaped, but when the day's fight was over nearly two-thirds of the dead were women and children. Many of the soldiers mutilated bodies while they collected "souvenirs" such as clothing accoutrements, scalps, and body parts, including the genitals of men and women. Only the company of the First Cavalry, commanded by Captain Silas Soule, refused to participate in the action.

The Chivington affair was not the only massacre of Indians by whites, but it did have far-reaching effects. Instead of ending Indian troubles on the plains, it set off a winter war and virtually closed the Overland Trail. It attracted attention in the midst of the Civil War, when thousands were dying every day. It stimulated a review of American Indian policy and provided a symbol of military brutality for reformers in the years that followed. Although the Sand Creek massacre showed that volunteers who held frontier prejudices were more likely to massacre Indians than were regular troops who did not share the settlers' attitudes, it was used by reformers as a rallying point against the military establishment, and it was viewed by frontier newspaper editors as a model that should be followed in all campaigns against Native Americans. The Sand Creek tragedy remains the subject of bitter controversy among historians and a politically charged topic in Colorado and among American Indian activists.

*BIBLIOGRAPHY*

Hoig, Stan. *The Sand Creek Massacre.* Norman: University of Oklahoma Press, 1961.

Svaldi, David. *Sand Creek and the Rhetoric of Extermination: A Case Study in Indian-White Relations.* Lanham, Md.: University Press of America, 1989.

GARY L. ROBERTS

*See also* **American Indians; Mass Murder: Collective Murder.**

# SAN DIEGO

### Frontier Town

Although typically thought of as a peaceable city, San Diego has known spates of violence that reflect broader themes about violence in the American experience. Before the city came into being, mission and other Indians attacked a Spanish mission in 1775. During the nineteenth century, San Diego was a frontier town on the edge of settlement. Its population grew from a few hundred at the American takeover in 1846 to about sixteen thousand by 1900 (with a temporary 1880s boom, fed by the arrival of the Santa Fe Railroad and by land speculation, when the town exploded to over forty thousand residents). During that era of westward expansion, rife with intense racism, San Diego and environs experienced what might be called "frontier" violence, much of it directed against Native Americans, who were frequent victims of beatings, shootings, hangings, and rapes. The perpetrators justified their actions by alleging Indian drunkenness, theft (usually of cattle or horses), Indian murder of whites, conflict over scarce resources, or fears of Indian uprisings. Few whites were brought to justice for their actions, although Indians were convicted for killing whites.

The overall level of disorder and violence of this frontier settlement was so severe that the historian Pliny Castanien, writing about the San Diego police department, titled a chapter on the pre-1880 period "Early Lawmen Lose Control." In San Diego between 1850 and 1900, that violence included,

in addition to the attacks on Indians, 220 documented homicides; burglary and theft; personal assaults; and considerable street fighting, often accompanied by gunfire.

The frontier violence intensified during the boom of the 1880s. The 13 March 1888 *San Diego Union* complained that the town "contains too many of that class of individuals who have 'no visible means of support,' and from whose ranks are recruited the assassins, footpads, burglars and criminals that now infest the city." So prevalent were gangs and juvenile delinquency that some parts of town were unsafe after dark; robbers struck laborers returning home and even train passengers. Fights between sailors and constables were common, with the police often posing as big a danger as the hoodlums. Only the decline of the frontier and the maturing of the town dissipated the rowdyism of boomtown San Diego.

As white-dominated frontier violence declined in the last decades of the nineteenth century, it began to be superseded by another kind, the chief targets of which were Indian, Mexican, black, and Chinese residents. In the 1880s the rate of murder victimization was 18.96 per 100,000 for the Anglo population, 140 for the Mexican, 45.10 for Indians, 38.85 for African Americans, and 30.34 for Chinese, and that disparity between white and nonwhite victim rates endured for the following half century. These figures overwhelmingly reflected killing within each ethnic group and were probably byproducts of the frustration from social displacement, ghettoization, poverty, and the concentration of most crime (such as gambling, prostitution, and liquor smuggling) in minority-dominated neighborhoods. Such statistics suggest that San Diego's mistreatment of its minorities contributed to some of the town's violence.

### The Industrial Workers of the World

The only episode of San Diegan violence that garnered national headlines grew out of the efforts by the Industrial Workers of the World (IWW), or the Wobblies, to unionize some local workers in 1912. By this time San Diego had become a conservative, prosperous, middle-class, predominantly white community of about fifty thousand residents, most of whom regarded the IWW as a radical, violent, subversive threat to capitalism and public order. The corner of Fifth and E streets, traditionally a forum for public debate, was flooded with IWW speakers advocating their cause and denigrating the established order. In 1912 the alarmed city council prohibited all public speaking in a six-block area around the intersection, precipitating a nationwide drive to support free speech in San Diego. Soon the city was aswarm with some five thousand outside activists, against whom the local police and vigilantes massed a counterforce in defense of the status quo. There followed a series of demonstrations that resulted in arrests, police brutality, vigilante abuses, incarceration, deportation of IWW sympathizers, and eventually the death of one IWW supporter in an altercation with policemen. The repressive measures quelled the radical movement and by mid-1912 the disorders had tapered off. But San Diego was left with a national reputation for police brutality, vigilantism, and archconservatism.

### Calm in the Storm

Despite San Diego's spasms of violence, the city has been equally notable for its avoidance of bloodshed at times when it might have seemed most likely. In the 1870s and the 1890s, for example, when whites violently attacked Chinese communities throughout the West, there were no such episodes in San Diego. During Prohibition, when, as Castanien put it, alcohol "poured into the city by land and sea" and "made bootlegging big business," there was no notable increase in violence. When World War II led to a doubling of San Diego's population and unprecedented crowding, the police force was able to contain crime and prevent the racial violence that afflicted other towns swollen by wartime activities.

### Violence after World War II

Major violence did not resurface in San Diego until it grew into a major urban community after World War II. According to the 1990 U.S. Census, San Diego had a population of 1,110,549, making it the sixth largest city in the nation. That postwar growth encompassed a nonwhite component whose burgeoning presence fostered a new generation of racial and ethnic tensions, some of them associated with "urban guerrilla" violence arising from drug trafficking and a proliferation of illegal firearms (thirteen of the fourteen police officers killed in the line of duty between 1970 and 1991 died of gunshot wounds). Especially after 1970, there were increases in violence related to narcotics, gang activity, and prostitution. This strain of contemporary urban violence is more anonymous, typically involving impersonal crime, such as a rash of thirteen drive-by shootings that occurred within six days in 1988.

While some forms of violence became prevalent after World War II, some forms of violence that erupted in other cities did not occur in San Diego. For instance, in the 1960s and 1970s, when many American cities exploded with racial violence, San Diego remained relatively calm, with limited damage and few deaths or injuries. Likewise, despite plenty of military targets, the city avoided significant violence during the years of militant protests against the Vietnam War.

Thus, although San Diego's history has not been characterized by a high degree of violence, that which occurred helped to define the city at the various stages of its development.

*BIBLIOGRAPHY*

Castanien, Pliny. *To Protect and Serve: A History of the San Diego Police Department and Its Chiefs*. San Diego, Calif.: San Diego Historical Society, 1993.

Lewis, Michael Andrew. "Ethnic and Racial Violence in San gDiego, 1880–1920." Master's thesis, San Diego State University, 1991.

Shanks, Rosalie. "The I.W.W. Free Speech Movement, San Diego, 1912." *Journal of San Diego History* 19 (winter 1973).

RAYMOND G. STARR

*See also* **Industrial Workers of the World; Urban Violence.**

## SAN FRANCISCO

The worst violence in the early history of San Francisco took place during the gold-rush era, when the city fell under the control of two extralegal committees of vigilance in 1851 and 1856. The committees hanged eight men and deported several dozen others. A reputation for rough-and-ready unconventionality and its role as a world-famous port with a wide-open market for drugs, alcohol, and sexual adventure ensured that the city would continue to attract large numbers of young single males. This demographic group, which exhibits higher than usual rates of risk taking, including criminal behavior, dominated the population during the gold-rush period and continued to assert itself in the public life of San Francisco.

The participation of adventurous young men was a distinguishing feature in the more notable episodes of violence in the city. Even when they did not initiate the violence, their presence in large numbers—for instance, during the notorious late-nineteenth-century Tong wars between rival groups in Chinatown—contributed to both the substance and the style of violent activities.

From the gold-rush era to the early twentieth century, many young Roman Catholic Irishmen sought out opportunities in San Francisco and made it a major center of Irish Roman Catholic life in the United States. They developed a street culture that highly valued public displays of white working-class empowerment and demanded respect for white wage earners, whether skilled or unskilled. This culture contributed to the violence that accompanied the Workingmen's Party of California's mass protest demonstrations during the summer of 1877. The party leader Denis Kearney's intemperate speeches against the Central Pacific Railroad and its Chinese workers set in motion attempts to burn down Chinatown and destroy the railroad's waterfront terminal. The rioters failed to achieve their objectives, but their work rejuvenated the vigilante spirit, and a law-and-order committee worked with the city police force to restore calm to the streets of San Francisco.

From the 1850s to the mid–twentieth century, the city played host to many sailors and workers in port-related occupations. Many of these men were sojourners rather than permanent residents, and many brought political and sexual radicalism to San Francisco. The result was a culture of adventure and thrill seeking that made the city's South of the Slot, Barbary Coast, and, much later, Castro districts famous (or infamous) throughout the world.

So many anarchist, socialist, and communist political radicals and sexual radicals lived in San Francisco during the twentieth century that their proportion of the city population was substantially higher than in most U.S. cities and in the nation. This demographic reality fostered a cultural division in San Francisco life. On one side lived the settled, married, family-oriented, property-owning, and religious people. On the other side stood the unmarried, transient adventure seekers, many of whom flaunted their sexual and political radicalism and, if and when they settled permanently in the city, typically expected to reshape it to their tastes and preferences.

### Violence in the Twentieth Century

During the twentieth century this social and cultural division shaped the character of noteworthy incidents of collective social violence. In 1901 violent altercations involving city police, company guards, strikers, and strikebreakers marked the nearly four months of conflict between the new and aggressive antiunion Employers' Association and unions of machinists, waiters, cooks, butchers, and teamsters. Most of the violence occurred between young men on or near the waterfront during conflicts between strikebreakers and unionists after employers locked out union teamsters and Mayor James D. Phelan allowed private police to guard wagons driven by the strikebreakers. The Employers' Association suffered defeat, but two strikers and two strikebreakers died, and hundreds were injured.

Six years later, in May and June 1907, as the city struggled to rebuild after the disastrous earthquake and fire of April 1906, an even more violent labor conflict occurred. When members of the streetcar operators union struck the United Railroads, management brought more than a thousand young men to the city to replace them. The strikebreakers received an enthusiastic welcome from city residents who criticized the striking unionists for interfering with the city's efforts to recover from the 1906 disaster. A boycott against the United Railroads fizzled, and unionists and their sympathizers reacted forcibly against the strikebreakers. The ensuing violence left thirty-one dead, including twenty-five passengers, and over eleven hundred injured, of whom some nine hundred were passengers. The strike destroyed the streetcar union, and the city was more bitterly divided for and against labor unions than in the past.

Nine years later a bomb explosion killed ten and wounded forty people during the Preparedness Day Parade on Saturday, 22 July 1916. The parade called on residents to support Britain and its allies in World War I, which the United States would enter nine months later. A vigilante-inspired law-and-order committee, headed by the conservative Roman Catholic president of the chamber of commerce, worked with the district attorney to secure a speedy trial and conviction. The two men convicted, thirty-four-year-old Thomas J. Mooney and twenty-two-year-old Warren K. Billings, newcomers to the city who were activists in anarchist and socialist circles, eventually received pardons but not until decades after the testimony that placed them at the scene was proved perjured. The identity of the person who left the bomb at the foot of Market Street was never discovered. The best hypothesis is that the suitcase containing the bomb was abandoned there by a German agent who was blocked by the parade crowds from reaching his original target: a munitions ship destined for the British side docked on the Embarcadero a few blocks away.

The San Francisco waterfront exploded with violence again in the summer of 1934 during an eighty-two-day West Coast maritime strike. Seven men died during the strike, including one sailor who was stabbed to death by a strikebreaker in Hong Kong. In San Francisco three died on 5 July, which became known as Bloody Thursday, when six thousand strikers and supporters protested the police-enforced opening of the port by employers. One man died when a salesman demonstrating a new weapon shot him in the head with a tear-gas canister. Two others died of gunshot wounds in what the city coroner declared "justifiable homicide by an unknown officer in lawful performance of his duty in suppressing a riot." The city's hospitals treated hundreds of strikers, strikebreakers, and bystanders for injuries and wounds, and thousands experienced tear-gas-related symptoms. The violence of Bloody Thursday caused Governor Frank Merriam to send fifteen hundred National Guard troops to the city; on 30 July the leaders of the Sailors Union authorized their members to return to work, which they did on 31 July, thereby ending the strike.

During the 1960s and 1970s racial tensions and sexual politics sparked violence in San Francisco. In 1966 African American demonstrators in the Hunters Point district took to the streets for three days, protesting the 27 September 1966 fatal shooting by a police officer of a car thief during a chase in that black neighborhood. The press characterized the demonstrations as a riot, but no fatalities occurred, and the city escaped the deadly consequences of similar events in Los Angeles, Detroit, Newark, and hundreds of other communities during this period.

In the 1970s violence associated with racial tensions did occur during a 179-day reign of terror by four African American men influenced by Black Muslim teachings and motivated by hatred of white people. They assaulted twenty-one white men and women and three white children in late 1973 and early 1974. Fourteen died, seven were wounded, and the three children escaped unharmed. The Zebra killings, the name derived from the police radio channel used in the case, ended with the arrest and conviction of the four men after a 376-day trial, the longest criminal trial in California history.

The Zebra killings may be considered the city's worst series of murders, but the worst murderous violence in a single incident took place on 1 July 1993 at a law firm at 101 California Street. Gian Luigi Ferri, dressed in a business suit and armed

**Aftermath of San Francisco firebombing and police response, September 1966.** CORBIS/
BETTMANN

with three semiautomatic weapons, murdered eight people, wounded six others, and then killed himself, all in a fifteen-minute period. Ferri apparently harbored a grudge against the law firm due to losses in a real-estate transaction in which the firm played a part. The 101 California Street slayings stemmed from the deranged mind of an aggrieved individual. Similar deadly attacks with high fatalities, due to the use of semiautomatic weapons, plagued other U.S. communities in the 1990s.

Tensions related to sexual politics sparked the city's most serious riotous violence of the late twentieth century: the White Night Riot of Monday, 22 May 1979. The event followed the voluntary manslaughter verdict in the trial of a former city supervisor, Dan White. White, a conservative Irish Roman Catholic and a former firefighter and police officer, smoldered with resentment against perceived slights by the city's first openly gay supervisor, Harvey Milk, and Mayor George Moscone. On 27 November 1978 White smuggled his police revolver into city hall by climbing through a basement window. He then shot and killed Milk and Moscone. Demonstrators were outraged that the court failed to deliver a verdict of first-degree murder, and they marched in the thousands from the Castro district to city hall. They smashed the glass in the massive doors of the Beaux Arts building, torched eleven police cars, and attacked police officers. A genuine battle between police and demonstrators then ensued both in the streets around city hall and in the Castro Street area uptown, where police smashed up gay bars and attacked customers. No one died, but some 120 people, both police officers and protesters, were injured.

It would be absurd to claim that young men, leftist political radicals, advocates of alternative sexual orientations, Irish Roman Catholics, sailors, and dockworkers as individuals had an innate propensity to cause or provoke violence in San Francisco. However, it would not be an exaggeration to conclude that the presence of high proportions of residents in each of those demographic categories has contributed to a distinctive history of violence in the city.

BIBLIOGRAPHY

Fracchia, Charles A. *Fire and Gold: The San Francisco Story.* 2d ed. Encinitas, Calif.: Heritage Media Corporation, 1996.

Frost, Richard H. *The Mooney Case.* Stanford, Calif.: Stanford University Press, 1968.

Howard, Clark. *Zebra: The True Account of the 179 Days of Terror in San Francisco.* New York: Richard Marek, 1979.

Issel, William, and Robert W. Cherny. *San Francisco, 1865–1932: Politics, Power, and Urban Development.* Berkeley: University of California Press, 1986.

Selvin, David. *A Terrible Anger: The 1934 Waterfront and General Strikes in San Francisco.* Detroit: Wayne State University Press, 1996.

Weiss, Mike. *Double Play: The San Francisco City Hall Killings.* Reading, Mass.: Addison-Wesley, 1984.

WILLIAM ISSEL

*See also* **Chinese Americans; Gay Bashing; Irish Americans; Urban Violence.**

# SATANISM, MODERN

The era of modern American Satanism (as distinguished from nineteenth-century British forms of Satanism) began on Walpurgisnacht, 30 April 1966, by proclamation of Anton Szandor LaVey, who on that night officially founded the Church of Satan. (In folklore, Walpurgisnacht is the night when witches fly to Sabbats.) The year 1966 thus became the year 1 of the Satanic Era. Since that night, the Satanic subculture has grown remarkably, developing a number of branches representing many shades of belief. Two areas of Satanism have particular implications for the study of violence: the Satanic "churches" and youth Satanism.

LaVey's Church of Satan, composed of equal parts of Nietzsche, Epicurus, Jung, Aliester Crowley, and P. T. Barnum, arrived at the perfect moment in history. The mid-1960s in the United States was a fertile period of social and religious experimentation, and LaVey's vision of Satan as an archetype representing man's immemorial quest for freedom and guilt-free gratification perfectly suited the temper of the times.

LaVey operated with a shrewd media savvy. He created a demonic persona, shaved his head, grew a goatee, instituted services in his San Francisco church that prominently featured a nude woman serving as an altar, became a Hollywood consultant (notably on *Rosemary's Baby*), and had a brief romance with the actress Jayne Mansfield, which may or may not have ended with a death curse before her tragic death. By the time of his own death in October 1997, Anton LaVey and the Church of Satan could rightly claim to have fathered the modern satanic subculture.

It was not long before the Church of Satan would split into hostile factions. Its most important offshoot was the Temple of Set, founded in

1975 by Michael Aquino, a military intelligence officer who had been one of LaVey's most intimate associates. Aquino, along with a dissident group that followed him out of the Church of Satan, found LaVey's vision of Satan as a mere psychological construct unacceptable; they wished to develop the magical side of Satanism to a greater extent than LaVey was willing to countenance. Set was an ancient Egyptian deity from which, the Temple of Set claimed, the biblical Satan was derived. Other less successful rivals included the Werewolf Order, a group centered in Europe that was led by Nikolas Schreck and LaVey's daughter, Zeena. None of these rivals has had the impact of the Church of Satan.

No Satanic church has been implicated in acts of violence (although the Werewolf Order has on occasion appeared to advocate violence). However, the words of Anton LaVey and the cumulative message of *The Satanic Bible* and other Church of Satan literature "to do as thou wilt," when combined with the powerful strain of social Darwinism implying that the "superior man" has the right to gratify his whims at the expense of the weak, has an undeniable appeal to a population of adolescents—especially adolescent males—in search of a meaningful identity. It is from this population that most acts of violence that may be linked to Satanism have come.

To be sure, very few self-styled youth Satanists have been involved in violence. Most content themselves with a copy of *The Satanic Bible* or a collection of compact discs from bands associated with the Satanic subculture. For these young people, it is enough to dream of power, of revenge on those who have slighted them, and most of all, of sexual gratification. Much the same can be said of the European youth Satanism scene, where black clothing and sallow complexions have become a uniform for alienated young people. A few, however, have gone considerably farther.

Three points should be noted as a preface to a discussion of Satanist violence. First, there is no body of statistics upon which to base a reliable estimate of the level of violence associated with youth Satanism. Moreover, police reports often confuse youth Satanism with such manifestations of youth culture activity as the gothic scene or role-playing games. Second, studies of youth Satanists indicate that most began their involvement either with material from the Satanic churches, which they soon found too tame, or through involvement

with the black or death metal music scene. Third, thanks to the transnational appeal of popular music and the ubiquity of the Internet, the youth Satanism subculture today knows no borders. For this reason, the violence of youth Satanists in Scandinavia has had a considerable impact on American youth.

The violence that does emerge from the youth Satanist subculture tends to take stereotypical forms. By far the most common is violence against property. Graffiti with satanic symbols such as "666," pentagrams, and the like have been used to deface gravestones, churches, and public buildings. These may be accompanied by animal bones or signs of a "ritual" having taken place.

The apex of violence to property involves the burning of churches. The American South in the late 1990s saw an epidemic of church burnings, but few of these cases were traced to youth Satanists. In Norway, however, Varg Vikernes, of the one-man black metal band Burzum, was responsible for burning Fantoft church near Bergen in 1992. Forty-five to sixty arsons or attempted arsons followed in Norway, with a number of copycat instances in Sweden and Germany.

More serious is the sacrifice or mutilation of animals. Evidence of animal sacrifice is often confused with the practice of Santeria or Candomblé, two African-based religions in which animal sacrifice plays a central role. Rituals involving the killing or maiming of animals in the youth Satanist subculture, by contrast, tend to be relatively opportunistic, demonstrating little advance planning and leaving clear signs that the intent was to torture rather than simply dispatch the sacrificial animal.

Serious violence against persons is quite rare in the youth Satanist subculture, but a number of high-profile cases have emerged. Here it is important to differentiate between two forms: self-inflicted violence and violence against others. Since the 1980s the media have carried a number of reports of suicides by young people influenced by heavy metal music with Satanic themes. Drugs are invariably a part of the mix, and several of these cases have ended in civil litigation. In the 1990s the parents of a boy who killed himself after listening to one of Judas Priest's records filed an unsuccessful civil suit against the group.

The most serious instances of youth Satanist violence are not so easily dismissed. On both sides of the Atlantic, charges of rape made by women who changed their minds about participating in youth Satanists' self-styled black masses have been substantiated. More serious still are cases of murder attributed to youth Satanists. Excluding from the discussion self-described Satanist serial killers like Richard Ramirez, the Night Stalker, who were adults when committing their crimes, youth Satanist killings tend to fall into two general scenarios: (1) opportunistic killings by Satanists of presumed enemies, defectors, or simply innocent bystanders, and (2) killings performed in a ritual context. The former are by far the most common.

The paradigmatic case of a youth Satanist killing is the 1985 case of Sean Sellers, on death row in Oklahoma for the murder of a convenience store clerk in the course of a robbery. Sellers subsequently became a born-again Christian and attributed his crime to Satanism. A number of similar cases could be adduced. In 1994 in Eugene, Oregon, Michael Hayward, Joel Brock, Jason Brumwell, and Daniel Paul Rabago also robbed and murdered a convenience store clerk. In 1984 Ricky Casso in Northport, New York, killed a classmate for allegedly refusing to declare allegiance to Satan. Varg Vikernes in Norway murdered another Satanist in 1993, allegedly in a personal and business dispute, and several killings of homosexuals have been attributed to the black metal subculture in Norway and Sweden. Running the gamut of youth Satanist crime was a group of teenage Satanists calling themselves the Lords of Chaos in Fort Myers, Florida, who imitated the Norwegian black metal subculture by burning a church before graduating to murder and an attempted robbery that was planned to finance the murder of black visitors to Disney World. They were convicted in 1997.

In all of these cases Satanism was a factor in the killings; but this factor was invariably less important than other motives. The Fort Myers case and the killings of homosexuals in Scandinavia represented the first public manifestation of a convergence of youth Satanism and racist politics that is a feature of a small segment of the Satanic subculture.

Murder in a ritual context is extremely rare. Only one underground Satanist organization, the British-based Order of the Nine Angles, condones human sacrifice, although there is no evidence that the leaders of the group, Anton Long and Christos Beest, have themselves committed murder. Moreover, Ken Lanning, an FBI agent who authored a report on the charges of Satanic killings, discounts such activities because of the lack of forensic confirmation. Despite widespread popular fears of Satanic cults practicing human sacrifice, there is no reliable evidence of the practice. It is noted here in recognition of the fact that in the idiosyncratic world of youth Satanism, it is possible that one or more such cases may have occurred in the past or may occur in the future.

*BIBLIOGRAPHY*

Aquino, Michael A. *The Church of Satan*. 3d ed. San Francisco: Michael A. Aquino, 1993.
Hicks, Robert D. *In Pursuit of Satan*. Buffalo, N.Y.: Prometheus, 1991.
LaVey, Anton Szandor. *The Satanic Bible*. New York: Avon, 1969.
Moynihan, Michael, and Didrik Søderlind. *Lords of Chaos*. Venice, Calif.: Feral House, 1998.
Richardson, James T., et al. *The Satanism Scare*. New York: De Gruyter, 1991.

JEFFREY KAPLAN

*See also* **Child Abuse: Ritual; Cults; Religion; Witchcraft.**

# SATURDAY NIGHT SPECIALS

The concept "Saturday night special" (SNS) is denounced by the gun lobby, antigun advocates, and neutral experts alike as undefinable, inaccurate, and even racist. The term derives from "niggertown Saturday Night." The phrase evokes the era when police and public officials generally gave little protection to ghetto areas and paid scant attention to violence therein. Such violence had always peaked on Saturday nights and in homes and bars where liquor was freely imbibed. A typical and traditional expression of official indifference to shootings and killings was "Oh well, that's just niggertown Saturday night," the implicit message being that those people's lives are not worth anything (notwithstanding the fact that the very same kind of activity went on in poor white areas). In 1996 Franklin Zimring, a leading academic gun-control advocate, avowed: "I have been studying 'Saturday Night Specials' for twenty-five years and have yet to find one. There is no content to the term other than a gun that poor people with dark skins can use to shoot each other. . . . There is no principled way to define or ban 'Saturday Night Specials.' " Nevertheless, attempts to ban them have been frequent in U.S. history.

Banning certain handguns using the excuse that they are SNSs would be unnecessary if inexpensive handguns really were, as some claim, dangerous to their users, because personal-injury lawsuits would drive manufacturers out of business. But relative to the number of SNSs in the United States, their makers are sued less often than makers of expensive firearms. As a former director of the federal Bureau of Alcohol, Tobacco, and Firearms testified to Congress in 1971, "In all my experience, I do not recall a single complaint of a handgun user being injured from a faulty weapon. The gun almost always performs in the manner for which it is made."

Perverse though it may seem, society would actually benefit if the so-called SNS brands were especially attractive to criminals. As the authors of a National Institute of Justice prison survey wrote, "If someone intends to open fire on the authors of this study, our *strong* preference is that they open fire with a handgun, and the junkier the handgun, the better. The possibility that even a fraction of the predators who now walk the streets armed with handguns would, in the face of a handgun ban, prowl with sawed-off shotguns instead causes one to tremble." But whether criminological studies define SNSs as inexpensive handguns, low-caliber handguns, or short-barreled handguns, they find that SNSs are used less than the proportion they make up of the total handgun stock. The National Institute of Justice survey found that gun criminals strongly prefer large-caliber guns for their high resale and "intimidation" value.

Banning SNSs nevertheless remains popular with both the public and legislators. It offers an intermediate position between banning no firearms and banning all. Racial issues may also be involved. The original SNS laws appeared in the South after the Civil War, as part of a group of laws that one state supreme court candidly said "were never intended to be applied to the white population" (*Watson v. State* 4 So. 2d 700, 703—exonerating a white defendant). They banned all but military-model handguns, which freedmen could not afford but whites could (Confederate veterans already had them). A southern senator who introduced a similar law in Congress in 1924 openly avowed its racial purpose, as did a University of Virginia *Law Review* article urging disarmament of "the Son of Ham." By 1968 such sentiments were no longer politically acceptable, but the journalist and gun-control advocate Robert Sherrill saw them as the real reason that Congress forbade importation of inexpensive handguns in 1968.

*BIBLIOGRAPHY*

Brill, Steven. *Firearms Abuse: A Research and Policy Report.* Washington, D.C.: Police Foundation, 1970.

Cottrol, Robert J., and Raymond T. Diamond. " 'Never Intended to Be Applied to the White Population': Firearms Regulation and Racial Disparity, the Redeemed South's Legacy to a National Jurisprudence?" *Chicago Kent Law Review* 70, no. 3 (1995): 1307–1335.

Kates, Don B. "Toward a History of Handgun Prohibition in the United States." In *Restricting Handguns*, edited by Don B. Kates. Croton-on Hudson, N.Y.: North River Press, 1979.

Kessler, Raymond. "Gun Control and Political Power." *Law and Policy Quarterly* 4, no. 3 (July 1983): 381.

Kleck, Gary. "Evidence That 'Saturday Night Specials' Not Very Important for Crime." *Sociology and Social Research* 70, no. 4 (July 1986): 303.

———. *Targeting Guns: Firearms and Their Control.* New York: de Gruyter, 1997.

Kopel, David B. *The Samurai, the Mountie, and the Cowboy: Should America Adopt the Gun Control of Other Democracies?* Buffalo, N.Y.: Prometheus, 1992. Pp. 332–340.

Sherrill, Robert. *The Saturday Night Special and Other Guns with Which Americans Won the West, Protected Bootleg Franchises, Slew Wildlife, Robbed Countless Banks, Shot Husbands Purposely and by Mistake—Together with the Debate over Continuing Same.* New York: Penguin, 1975.

DON B. KATES

*See also* **Gun Control; Weapons: Handguns.**

# SCALPING

The use of enemies' body parts, especially their heads, as trophies is a widespread custom of warfare—for example, American soldiers took enemy ears during the Vietnam War. However, the taking of the skin and hair of an enemy's scalp as a trophy was one of many customs the Euro-American invaders and settlers of North America adopted from the Indians. Thus the English, French, and Dutch in colonial times offered bounties to European settlers and Indians for the scalps of Indians and Europeans. Guns and metal knives introduced by Europeans facilitated the taking of scalps. Warfare between Indian tribes and between Indians and Euro-Americans resulted in the spread of the custom of scalping beyond the areas of eastern North America (where the custom dated back to pre-Columbian times) to the Indians of the Plains and the West, where it continued among

Timucua Indians shown mutilating enemy corpses and preparing scalps by smoking. Engraving by Théodore de Bry (1591), based on the 1564 reports of Jacques Le Moyne de Morgues in Florida. SMITHSONIAN INSTITUTION. PHOTO NO. 57555

both sides in inter-Indian and U.S.-Indian warfare until about 1900.

In the 1960s and 1970s it was sometimes said that the Indians did not scalp until Europeans introduced the custom, but there is excellent evidence that the custom was common among eastern Indians when Europeans first arrived. Early written and pictorial sources show that scalping was well integrated in Indian custom and ritual. Some Indian skulls of proven pre-European dates show cut marks consistent with scalping, especially where the cuts had partially healed (there is also historical evidence that victims sometimes survived after being scalped—for example, an 1805–1806 doctor's description of how to treat such survivors). European languages had no words for the process or its results until the meaning of the English word *scalp* was modified and incorporated into French, Dutch, and German. The terminology in several Indian languages of the eastern United States is ancient, sometimes containing unanalyzable terms and never showing European influence (as would be expected if the practice had been recently borrowed from Europeans).

When Europeans arrived, scalping was especially important among southeastern tribes, among which the taking of scalp trophies gave men warrior status and placated the spirits of their own dead tribesmen. Among northeastern tribes scalps were often taken, but war captives were more highly valued. On the Plains, all tribes took scalps. There, the taking of a scalp was one of a series of war honors, but it was not as highly valued as more risky feats, such as touching a live enemy. Scalping occurred among southwestern Indians but was considered spiritually dangerous. In the East and on the Plains either the whole scalp was removed, sometimes including the ears, or else a circle a few inches in diameter was removed from the top of the head. Men of many Plains tribes cut their hair short except for a long scalp lock left as a challenge to the enemy. After removal the scalp was usually stretched on a small hoop and often painted red and then carried on a pole in a victory dance. Plains tribes often used scalps for decoration on clothing, weapons, and horse gear.

BIBLIOGRAPHY

Axtell, James, and William C. Sturtevant. "The Unkindest Cut, or Who Invented Scalping?" *William and Mary Quarterly*, 3d series, 37, no. 3 (1980): 451–471.

Friederici, Georg. *Skalpieren und ähnliche Kriegsgebräuche in Amerika*. Braunschweig, Germany: Friedrich Vieweg und Sohn (1906).

Owsley, Douglas W., and Hugh E. Berryman. "Ethnographic and Archaeological Evidence of Scalping in the Southeastern United States."*Tennessee Archaeologist* 31, no. 1 (1975): 41–58.

Robertson, James. "Remarks on the Management of the Scalped Head."*Philadelphia Medical and Physical Journal* 2, no. 2 (1805–1806): 27–30.

WILLIAM C. STURTEVANT

*See also* **American Indians.**


# SCAPEGOAT

The earliest known appearance of the term *scapegoat* is in Leviticus, chapter 16, where the Hebrew word 'azazel describes one of the rites for the Day of Atonement. The sins and transgressions of the Israelite people are transferred onto the scapegoat, which is then released into the wilderness: "and Aaron shall lay both his hands on the head of the live goat, confess over it all of the iniquities of the children of Israel, and all their transgressions, concerning all their sins, putting them on the head of the goat, and shall send it away into the wilderness by the hand of a suitable man" (Leviticus 16:21). Anthropologists have found similar scapegoating rituals in most human societies; James Frazer devotes several chapters to traditions of scapegoating in *The Golden Bough* (1890).

In the twentieth century René Girard developed a compelling theory of the scapegoat. In his seminal *Violence and the Sacred* (1972), Girard examines the foundational role that violence plays in human society. At the outset he makes two crucial claims about the nature of violence: (1) violent impulses are more difficult to subdue than to arouse, and (2) when the object that initially provoked the violent impulses is out of reach, "violence seeks and always finds a surrogate victim." For Girard, all violence can ultimately be understood through the model of sacrificial violence. In *Violence and the Sacred* and his other works of the 1970s and 1980s, such as *Things Hidden Since the Foundation of the World* (1978), *The Scapegoat* (1982), and *Job, the Victim of His People* (1985), Girard traces representations of the surrogate victim throughout Western and non-Western history and finds that the essential story of the scapegoat remains the same. A society finds itself faced with a "sacrificial crisis" that threatens to bring about a collapse of the social order. The community reacts to this violent threat by thrusting total blame upon an individual or a small group that must then be sacrificed. The scapegoat, charged with crimes that "attack the very foundation of cultural order," is condemned as "extremely harmful to the whole of society." The overblown severity of these accusations serves to bridge "the gap between the insignificance of the individual and the enormity of the social body" (*The Scapegoat*, p. 15). The scapegoats must be community members, but decidedly marginal ones; often they are drawn from the ranks of the physically and mentally ill or ethnic and religious minorities: "If the gap between the victim and the community is allowed to grow too wide . . . the victim will no longer be capable of attracting the violent impulses to itself; the sacrifice will cease to serve as a 'good conductor.' . . . On the other hand, if there is *too much* continuity the violence will overflow its channels." (*Violence and the Sacred*, p. 39; emphasis in original). The scapegoat must be enough of an insider to be convincingly blamed for the internal problems of the community, yet enough of an outsider to be easily singled out as a target of violence. By concentrating all violent impulses onto a single target, scapegoating provides a surrogate victim for all members of the community. This process makes possible the reestablishment of harmony and social order, often resulting in the scapegoat's transformation into a hero after death. For Girard, all violence is scapegoating, and scapegoating is a recurring and fundamental feature of human society and, therefore, human history; indeed, this "generative violence constitutes at least the indirect origin of all those things that men hold most dear and that they strive most ardently to preserve . . . in short, of all those cultural forms that give man his unique humanity" (*Violence and the Sacred*, p. 93).

BIBLIOGRAPHY

Frazer, James George. *The Golden Bough*. London: Macmillan, 1890.

Girard, René. *The Scapegoat*. 1982. Translated by Yvonne Freccero. Baltimore: Johns Hopkins University Press, 1986.

———. *Violence and the Sacred*. 1972. Translated by Patrick Gregory. Baltimore: Johns Hopkins University Press, 1977.

TODD HERZOG

*See also* **Theories of Violence: Religion.**

# SCARBOROUGH, GEORGE ADOLPHUS
## (1859–1900)

George Adolphus Scarborough, western frontier peace officer and gunfighter, was tried for murder three times. Although at each affray he wore a badge, sufficient controversy surrounded the cases to warrant indictment and trial. Born in Natchitoches Parish, Louisiana, on 2 October 1859, he witnessed at the age of thirteen one of the most violent episodes of the turbulent Reconstruction period: his family was involved in the 1873 Colfax Riot, a bloody Louisiana racial battle in which several whites and scores of blacks were killed. Following the riot, the Scarboroughs moved to McLennan County, Texas, where young George began work as a cowboy.

In a marriage ceremony conducted by his father, a southern Baptist minister, he married Mary Frances McMahan on 30 August 1877. Seven children were born of this union. In 1883 Scarborough took his family to Anson, Jones County, Texas, and began his career in law enforcement as the town constable and deputy sheriff. In November 1884 he was elected to the first of two terms as Jones County sheriff. On 15 October 1887 A. J. Williams, a notorious desperado and frequent guest in the Jones County calaboose, walked into a Haskell, Texas, saloon where Scarborough, according to a contemporary account, "was facing a mirror with his back to the door when he saw Williams come in. Williams drawed [sic] his gun. But George whirled and drew his gun and killed him." Scarborough was indicted for murder and stood trial in Haskell in March 1888. The jury deliberated less than five minutes before bringing in a verdict of not guilty.

Failing in his bid for reelection in 1888, Scarborough worked as a stock detective, patrolling the ranges in search of stick rustlers and overseeing roundups in the interest of large cattlemen, until 1893 when he was appointed deputy U.S. marshal in El Paso, Texas. On 29 June 1895 he enticed the fugitive cattle rustler Martin Mroz across the Rio Grande bridge from his Juarez, Mexico, hideout. When Mroz resisted arrest on the El Paso side, Scarborough and fellow officers Jeff Milton and Frank McMahan shot him dead. The three lawmen were tried for murder and cleared.

While making an arrest on 9 March 1896, Scarborough was shot in the face. The gunshot wound was bloody and painful but not critical, and he made his arrest. On 5 April 1896 Scarborough shot and killed the gunman John Selman, who a few months before had assassinated John Wesley Hardin, the most deadly Texas gunfighter of them all. Tried for murder a third time, Scarborough was again acquitted.

In 1897 Scarborough moved to Deming, New Mexico, where he took employment as stock detective and held commissions as deputy sheriff, deputy U.S. marshal, and state ranger. In 1898 he wounded and captured notorious outlaw Bronco Bill Walters. In an April 1900 gun battle with an outlaw gang in the mountains near San Simon, Arizona, he was shot in the leg. After a cold and lonely night alone, he was taken to Deming, where his gangrenous leg was amputated, but he died on the operating table on 5 April 1900. George Scarborough typifies the dedicated professional frontier lawman to a far greater degree than the Earps, Hickoks, and Mastersons of song and legend.

**George Adolphus Scarborough in 1870.** Western History Collections, University of Oklahoma Library

*BIBLIOGRAPHY*

DeArment, Robert K. *George Scarborough: The Life and Death of a Lawman on the Closing Frontier.* Norman: University of Oklahoma Press, 1992.

Haley, J. Evetts. *Jeff Milton: A Good Man with a Gun.* Norman: University of Oklahoma Press, 1948.

Scarborough, Jewel Davis. *Southern Kith and Kin: A Record of My Children's Ancestors.* Vol. 3. Abilene, Texas: Abilene Printing Co., 1957.

ROBERT K. DEARMENT

*See also* **Gunfighters and Outlaws, Western.**


**SCARFACE.** *See* Capone, Al.


# SCHOOLS

*Following the* **Overview** *are two subentries:* **Antiviolence Curricula** *and* **Integration.**

## OVERVIEW

Violence and aggression in U.S. schools—in contrast to the more generic topic of youth violence—was not the focus of extensive scholarly research until the late twentieth century. Of the 260 titles listed in the Library of Congress catalog under the rubric "school violence" in 1999, twenty-two books were published in the 1970s, fifty-nine in the 1980s, and one hundred seventy-nine in the 1990s. The evolution of the subjects covered during this time span is indicative of the escalating severity of the problem. Prior to the late 1960s, authors wrote about school disturbances, disruptive behavior, vandalism, classroom discipline, unruly conduct, and other disorders. Since then, writers have felt compelled to deal with topics like "dangerous schools," "guns in schools," "school crime," "trauma response," "designing safe schools," as well as rape, murder, and hostage-taking. Prior generations of researchers presupposed that schools were normally safe; in the 1990s, they began with the assumption that violence is a taken-for-granted entity with which schools must learn to cope.

Prior to the 1990s, the general public rarely discussed school-related violence. Traditionally, infractions of school discipline were mostly associated with immature behavior patterns rather than with seriously aggressive acts. Both academicians and the public at large commonly assumed that crime in schools was largely limited to the inner cities. Criminal incidents in suburban or rural public schools were usually dismissed as pathological aberrations by disturbed individuals, and U.S. schools generally maintained their image as safe sanctuaries. Even in urban areas, school violence was considered to be a deviation from the norm, although the use of firearms by school-age youths was much greater among those who live in the inner city. And it has become a reality that school-age youth in any U.S. community can obtain firearms fairly simply if they wish to.

Starting in late 1997, a series of appalling incidents in state after state shattered these innocent assessments. Following each incident, Americans saw tragic television images of weeping children and parents outside rural schools in which students or teachers had been killed or grievously wounded by students who had opened fire at them with a shocking array of rifles, handguns, and automatic weapons. Within a span of eight months names like Pearl (Mississippi), Paducah (Kentucky), Jonesboro (Arkansas), and Springfield (Oregon)—to mention only the sites where multiple gunshot murders by students took place—became household names throughout the country. Even placid school districts that had hitherto considered themselves havens from urban violence began developing safety plans and taking other precautions.

Then shortly before 11:25 A.M. on 20 April 1999, two students—Eric Harris, age eighteen, and Dylan Klebold, age seventeen—dressed in black trench coats, stormed into the highly regarded Columbine High School in the very desirable middle-class suburb of Littleton, Colorado. Armed with a TEC DC9 semiautomatic pistol, two sawed-off shotguns, a 9-millimeter semiautomatic rifle, and over thirty pipe bombs, grenades, and other explosives, they proceeded to carry out a meticulous plan apparently intended to destroy the entire school and as many of its two thousand occupants as possible. As the nation—and a good part of the world—watched the live television images in horror, and as terrified students hiding inside the building desperately called for help on cellular phones, the two killers continued to discharge round after round of rapid-fire ammunition into the bodies of their teachers and fellow students, from whom they had long felt alienated. Several reports later said that the pair laughed as they roamed about the school, threatening and terrorizing their victims before shooting them. Although

**Surrounded by the news media, students from Columbine High School in Colorado console each other after the April 1999 shootings.** MONICA ALMEIDA/ NYT PICTURES

the rampage was over in less than forty-five minutes, the rescue operation was hindered by the utter confusion the siege had produced. Police were unable to rescue a teacher who lay dying on the library floor, and it was not until 3:30 P.M. that SWAT teams recovered all of the bodies. It was only at 4:30 P.M. that they declared the school "safe." In all, thirteen people were murdered (twelve students and one teacher), twenty-three were wounded, and the two youthful gunmen had killed themselves.

It was the worst school shooting in U.S. history. Commentators and analysts could not find the language to describe what had happened. Without hyperbole, it could be said that two very disturbed

boys had waged total warfare on their school and community. The unthinkable had happened but had not yet become thinkable, as the nation reacted with utter disbelief. Other nations asked how it was possible that the most powerful country on earth was unable to control its own schools. Embarrassed Americans had no coherent answers. Suddenly all of the dominant discourses about U.S. education and pedagogical practice had lost their authority. This single event at Littleton would alter more than just U.S. perceptions about the nature of school violence; it would call into question the innocence of schooling in the United States, and, indeed, the nature of U.S. culture. A whole new epistemic framework was required to rethink the school-violence epidemic, as parents, teachers, and students everywhere suddenly felt vulnerable.

Not everyone is comfortable with the analysis that the "total culture" needs to be "fixed," although most serious students of school violence do agree that no single cause can explain these phenomena. Despite the various destructive elements in U.S. society, many respected scholars are skeptical about engaging in sweeping explanations about an American "culture of violence" to account for these tragic shootings. They prefer to look at more limited ways in which U.S. society can anticipate and prevent these harmful incidents. But many respected criminologists view these events as essentially unpredictable and doubt if very much can be done to prevent repetitions.

Thus, behind all the glib analyses of the talk shows, the topic of school violence reveals two opposing worldviews at work: one wherein the culture is basically sound (and therefore is only in need of limited repairs), and another that claims that the culture exhibits violence as the norm rather than the exception (and therefore is in need of complete transformation). Those who hold the latter weltanschauung—that Americans' phantasmagoria of a stable, peaceful society is a mere cover-up for a permanent underlying savagery— would accuse the former group of singling out one cause (e.g., guns or media violence) and neglecting all the rest. But talk about fixing the "total culture" can also be merely a way of diverting attention from a particularly sensitive topic. Gun advocates, for example, are fond of making statements like "school violence is a much more complex problem than guns," as a way of shifting attention from the fact that the firearms-related homicide rate for children less than fifteen years of age in the United States is nearly sixteen times higher than that of the other twenty-five leading industrialized countries of the world combined.

The list of potential items that have been identified as "causes" of school violence has become almost unsurveyable: too little emphasis on spiritual and moral values in the home; too much violence in movies, television, and entertainment; too little moral instruction in schools; too few school counselors; too few after-school programs; the growing ubiquity of and easy access to all types of guns in U.S. homes; the use of drugs (both legal and illegal); too little teaching of tolerance; too little training of school staff to recognize the warning signs of seriously disturbed youth; lack of metal detectors, closed-circuit televisions and other technological aids; unmanageable class and school sizes; lack of sufficient parental involvement in children's lives; lack of a comprehensive school-safety plan; too few security guards or school police; lack of a clear school discipline code and the willingness to enforce it; unsupervised access to video games and the Internet; lack of laws holding parents accountable for children's actions; a generalized U.S. "permissiveness" in the home, at school, and in the judicial system; refusal to take adolescents' destructive threats seriously; lack of teacher access to students' prior criminal records; poorly conceptualized school-safety programs.

But to accept the multifaceted nature of school violence does not mean that one must accept all causes as equally contributory. In Europe, for example—where it is difficult for youth to get access to firearms—one finds many of the same alleged cultural deficiencies as in the United States (such as permissiveness, decline of traditional religious values, and rising youth violence) but not the massive school killings. It is true that sixteen small children and one teacher were killed and twelve other children were wounded when a gunman with two semiautomatic pistols entered a school gymnasium in Dunblane, Scotland, in 1996. But the British government responded quickly and firmly with a total ban on the possession of handguns, and as of late 1999 there had been no further incidents. And when gun proponents attempt to shift the primary blame for school violence onto the entertainment industry, they find it impossible to explain away the case of Japan, which does not have massive school shootings or easy access to guns, despite the fact that Japanese children are bombarded with violent video games and cartoons.

Most people outside the gun lobby, then, believe that the primary cause of massive school-related murders is the ubiquity of guns in U.S. society. They see the biggest question as whether the nation has the will to give human life a higher priority than the recreational pleasures of powerful interest groups. For them, the chief lesson of Littleton is clear: banning firearms (and not just handguns) completely—or at the very least regulating them rigorously—should be the highest priority for public officials concerned for the future of U.S. education.

But the question remains why these school massacres occurred in the late 1990s even though firearms have been accessible in the United States for many years. The simplest answer would seem to lie in the fact that it is only since the 1990s that the rapid-fire automatic weapons, designed solely for killing a large number of people quickly, have proliferated. One indication of the growing "normalization" of violence in U.S. society was that single-death school murders often did not even make the front page of newspapers in the late 1990s. Such considerations illustrate the need to define exactly what is meant by the term *school violence.*

### Defining Terms

This article deals exclusively with the topic of school violence in elementary, junior high, and high school. Topics related to violence at the college or university level (such as date rape, campus security, fraternity crime, and so on) are covered in the article on "Campus Violence."

How does U.S. law define school violence, as opposed to mere immature adolescent behavior? In 1999 the Supreme Court, in holding that schools may be held liable for a student's persistent sexual harassment (certainly one form of school violence), drew a clear line between immature or inappropriate adolescent deportment and behavior "that is so severe, pervasive, and objectively offensive, and that so undermines and detracts from the victims' educational experience, that the victim-students are effectively denied equal access to an institution's resources and opportunities" (*Davis v. Monroe County Board of Education*). Always sensitive to the limited power of the federal government to intervene in the area of education, the Court nonetheless held that the maintenance of discipline in schools requires not only that students be restrained from assaulting one another, abusing drugs and alcohol, and committing other crimes, but also that they conform themselves to the standards of conduct prescribed by school authorities.

The national problem had already become so pervasive by 1994 that Congress, finding that "approximately 3,000,000 thefts and violent crimes occur in or near our Nation's schools every year," deemed it necessary to enact the Safe and Drug-Free Schools and Communities Act, designed in support of the National Education Goals, which stated that "by the year 2000, every school in the United States will be free of drugs, violence, and the unauthorized presence of firearms and alcohol and will offer a disciplined environment conducive to learning." That same year Congress also enacted the federal Gun-Free Schools Act, requiring that schools receiving federal funds expel for a minimum of one year any student who brings a firearm to school. Earlier generations took it for granted that U.S. schools would be "gun-free"; now the country operates from the opposite assumption: that schools are potentially violent settings. The Safe and Drug-Free Schools Program, whose annual appropriation has grown to over $500 million, is the federal government's primary vehicle for reducing school violence. Like the presence of the metal detector at the individual school level, its very existence as a routine component of the federal bureaucracy signals the broad extent of the normalization of violence in U.S. schools.

The official legal definitions become translated, at the local level, into extremely detailed codes of conduct drawn up by various school districts in order to ensure a safe and secure school environment. In 1997 the New York City Board of Education, for example, developed an itemized discipline code listing thirty-seven different possible infractions, ranging from making excessive noise and cutting class to inflicting serious injury, intimidation, extortion, rape, arson, causing a riot, selling drugs, and possessing and using a firearm. Possible penalties have a range of eight levels of severity, from mere reprimands to suspension and expulsion.

Because definitions of violence vary from society to society and even within societies, defining violence raises a host of questions. The literature in many Western European countries, as well as in Australia and New Zealand, long identified school violence almost exclusively with "bullying" and was silent on serious issues such as weapon-carrying, an item of frequent mention in the United States. Just as fighting domestic violence and sexual harassment required consciousness-raising movements, so, too, did bullying. Beginning in the 1970s, Professor Dan Olweus of the University of Bergen began a national campaign to eliminate bullying in Norway. His groundbreaking research and activism were followed by parallel studies in Britain, the United States, Canada, the Netherlands, Italy, Spain, Japan, and Australia. Bullying at school, instead of being accepted as natural, came to be redefined as "repeated oppression, psychological or physical, of a less powerful person by a more powerful person." At the same time, a whole range of behaviors—aggressive play-fighting, disparaging remarks, yelling and pushing in school corridors—that had been condoned as part of adolescence began to be understood as reiterations of media violence and as actions potentially leading to violence (Rigby 1996, p. 15). Student fistfighting is usually considered the most widely accepted form of school violence. Verbal violence, threats, and harassment are, however, potent forms of aggression that are often excused in the permissive atmosphere of many U.S. schools as "freedom of speech."

Another reason school violence is so difficult to define is that those teachers and students who are forced through economic or geographic circumstances to live under the constant menace of violence also have to engage in psychological denial or even outright acceptance of a culture of violence. If a girl has to ride to school on a deserted and dangerous subway train, for example, carrying a switchblade may begin to make sense to her. Thus the "culture of violence" begins to become normalized. Inner-city and, increasingly, even suburban students develop ideologies, understandings, and definitions surrounding violence that differ radically from those of the professional world of academia and middle-class America. At the same time, students often express the wish that adults would enforce school regulations and supervise disruptive students more closely. In the wake of several of the school massacres, school officials were severely criticized for their laxity in allowing one student clique (e.g., the athletes or the outcasts) to taunt another group or for failing to challenge student misbehavior generally. U.S. students are not always tolerant of teachers' fearfulness and permissiveness and register disappointment when teachers neglect their "in loco parentis" role.

Studies have shown that more than half the children in violence-prone neighborhoods suffer from post-traumatic stress disorder. But even if they do not develop the full-blown symptoms of post-traumatic stress disorder, youth who grow up in housing projects in which they hear gunshots sounding in the middle of the night may have experienced traumatic stressors that cause them to appraise ordinary school disciplinary procedures (e.g., the presence of security guards) as extremely threatening and react accordingly. Conversely, students habituated to living in such circumstances may perceive school metal detectors, violence-saturated videotapes and movies, or even tumultuous gang activity as part of everyday life.

U.S. teachers are therefore faced with an unprecedented challenge. They must learn to recognize that different children may have been exposed to severe stressors and abusive experiences in early childhood, and that they may react to these in different ways. They must also be aware that their students come from a wide variety of cultural and social backgrounds, some of which may condone behaviors (e.g., direct sexual advances) that the fast-changing, dominant U.S. culture is beginning to condemn and prosecute. It is also important to recognize that teachers or administrators desperately trying to cope with chaotic student behavior in many larger, overcrowded schools often employ a tough street style themselves, as a mechanism for control, and thereby become complicit in expanding the culture of violence.

**Causes of School Violence**

How can the etiology of this disease of school violence in the United States be interpreted? What are the explanations for the underlying causes of both the long-standing violence in inner-city schools and the more recent massacres in Littleton and other suburban or rural areas? Many scholars have questioned why violence should be defined —as the medical model would have it—as resulting from the individual child (or the child's family) rather than from the structure of the school (or society at large). Some conservative commentators place the responsibility for school violence on the student and the predispositions that she or he brings into the school from family, neighborhood, or peer group. Other conservatives place blame directly on weak leadership of the principal—or on the entire public education system itself.

A more radical pedagogy interprets violence— usually termed *symbolic violence* or *structural violence*—as fundamental to the very practices of schools or to the structures of industrial society as a whole, traceable ultimately to capitalism or to the whole enterprise of modernity. This view of violence, in which the institution of the school cov-

ertly constructs an unjust, undemocratic, and ultimately violent society, is most often contrasted with the narrower and more literal sense of physical violence as a direct act of aggression likely to cause the death or injury of another.

The pivotal debate surrounding the roots of school violence is between the "social reproductionists," who see public school not as a route to upward mobility but as a violent means by which a dominant society contains the lower classes, and other theorists, who are more inclined to see the causality as located within the individual student. The latter group bifurcates into two wings: the conservative, which calls for more stringent school and classroom discipline and for severe punishment of student perpetrators of school crime, and the more liberal, which would like to see more careful diagnosis and treatment of student pathologies. Reproductionists argue that concentrating on individual pathologies distracts from reforming the oppressive social conditions under which these young "perpetrators" of school violence must live. In the late 1990s there was a good deal of political support for a severe policy (known as "zero-tolerance") for school violence; this tough-sounding approach tended to obscure other important causes that require investigation. Deep-rooted social maladies such as child abuse, family emotional distress, unemployment, homelessness, and inadequate nutrition need to be recognized as preconditions for aggressive and belligerent behavior. The irresponsible proliferation of guns and the incessant glamorization of violence in television, movies, gangster-rap music, video games, and the Internet all need to be taken into account.

Many mainstream educational theorists and school reformers are unwilling to recognize the role the school itself plays; they tend to view violence, harassment, and aggression as foreign elements imported into the secure domain of the school from the surrounding community. Even after Littleton this viewpoint considers violence as something that happens to children on the way to and from school. The possible violence of the school itself is not addressed.

The narrowness of this view tends to shift blame away from the educational and political establishment and permits the dominant ideologies latent in U.S. culture to escape scrutiny. Human rights and gay right advocates as well as feminists have long criticized schools as primary sites for constructing and reproducing sexual, ethnic, and gender stereotypes. Often one school clique, with the tacit approval of authorities, will taunt another with homophobic or racial slurs that are frequently the trigger for explosively violent acts. Also, although not so frequently commented on, class prejudices operate inside schools as they do throughout U.S. society. Stratifications observable in the country as a whole are reproduced within the school culture in the form of expensive clothes, exotic vacations, automobiles, and other commodities.

One common denominator of all the 1990s school killings was the fact that after the event, surviving classmates indicated that they had some foreknowledge of the incident. But the adults in the school appear to have been totally in the dark concerning the tensions, frustrations, and animosities among the youth. Cliques have been part of the American high school social scene for many years. What appears to be new is the lack of ability or even the desire on the part of principals and teachers to engage the youth culture in order to influence its sometimes negative, destructive, and self-destructive aspects. Youths need the close involvement of mature adults to help them think through the consequences of their projected actions. In some of the schools, the principal and teachers appear to have had no interest in interacting with the adolescents on an emotional level or in learning what was transpiring in students' fantasy lives—until it was too late.

**Statistical Data**

School violence is grossly underreported. Often principals are accused of covering up serious incidents for the sake of appearances or simply to spare teachers the extra work of reporting and following up. Therefore, some cities have taken the reporting responsibility away from the principal and vested it in the school's chief security officer, who reports to a central bureau. When a school attains a reputation for violence, more than just the principal's reputation is at stake. Adolescents tend to identify with their schools, and thus the reputation of the school can greatly affect how the students feel about themselves. In the very large urban schools with student populations of three to five thousand, there may be five or six very serious incidents in a single day, only one of which gets reported. A teacher in one part of such a school may not be aware of the turmoil that is taking place elsewhere in the building.

If the vast majority of incidents are kept secret at the school level, clearly they will not be reported even in the local newspapers, let alone on large-scale national questionnaires. Reporting problems abound for other reasons as well. If a member of the school basketball team is killed on a subway on the way home from a game, should the crime be reported as a school-related crime? What if the basketball coach neglected to accompany the team back home from the game? (This hypothetical case is very similar to one that took place in New York City.) Statistical data collection strips such incidents of the "thick description" that ethnographic research would provide. In examining the data provided through large-scale national surveys, it is important to keep in mind that each of these incidents is ripped out of the existential context necessary for meaningful interpretation.

Until the succession of multiple school murders during the 1997–1998 academic year, there was no single source of information about crime and violence in schools. Neither the National Center for Educational Statistics nor the Bureau of Justice Statistics collected comprehensive data. When this gap became apparent, President Bill Clinton brought together the Departments of Justice and Education and mandated a single, annual document on the topic of school violence; as a result, the *Indicators of School Crime and Safety* report was produced (Kaufman 1998). But detailed data on the single most serious item—school-associated violent death—is still not collected on a national basis. To access the most accurate information on that topic, one must consult the National School Safety Center's *School Associated Violent Deaths (SAVD)* report, which, although not a scientific study, is the most comprehensive accumulation of information taken from newspaper accounts around the country.

From the *SAVD* report we learn that in the seven academic years from 1992–1993 to 1998–1999 there were a total of 251 school-associated violent deaths, of which the overwhelming majority were deaths by firearms (195). Every year, over 35 violent deaths occur on the grounds of U.S. schools or at school-related functions. Of the 195 firearms deaths on school-related property (grounds, buses, official events), 122 were student killings (of which 7 were accidental firearms deaths), 28 student suicides, 22 teacher (or staff) homicides, and 23 homicides of persons not related to the school. In all there were 166 students killed (including 44 killed by means other than guns), or an average of more than 23 students killed each academic year (National School Safety Center 1999).

Notable School Killings of the 1990s

| Date | Place | Dead/ Wounded | Weapons | Description of Incident |
|---|---|---|---|---|
| 2 Feb. 1996 | Frontier Junior High School Moses Lake, Wash. | 3/1 | • High-powered rifle | The alleged perpetrator, who had been teased by other students for being a "nerd," was quoted as saying that it would be "cool" to go on a killing spree like characters in the movie *Natural Born Killers*. He shot and killed two fellow students and a teacher. |
| 19 Feb. 1997 | Bethel Regional High School Bethel, Alaska | 2/2 | • 12-gauge shotgun | A student shot and killed a fellow student, who was reported to have called him names, as well as the high school principal. |
| 1 Oct. 1997 | Pearl High School Pearl, Miss. | 2/7 | • Rifle • Kitchen knife | After stabbing his mother to death, the gunman went on a shooting spree at school, killing or wounding nine students, including a girl he had dated. Five other students, who belonged to what authorities called a "cult-like group," were charged with conspiracy and accessory to murder. |
| 1 Dec. 1997 | Heath High School West Paducah, Ky. | 3/5 | • .22-caliber handgun | A student opened fire on a daily prayer meeting held before school. At his trial, he pleaded guilty but claimed mental illness; when asked why he had committed the crimes he said he did not know. |

*(continued)*

In a more detailed study of this same database for a two-year period, between 1992 and 1994, 105 school-associated violent deaths were identified. Secondary-school students, racial and ethnic minorities, and students in urban school districts had higher levels of risk. Homicide was the predominant cause of death, and firearms were responsible for a majority (77 percent) of the deaths. Both victims and offenders tended to be male (Kachur et al. 1996).

The multiple murders of the late 1990s all demonstrate the availability of devastating firepower. The youth in the Springfield, Oregon, shooting possessed a .22-caliber semiautomatic rifle; a .22-caliber handgun; a 9-millimeter Glock handgun; and a .32-caliber handgun. But the bare statistics obscure the full horror of the incidents: in the same Springfield murders the youth also killed his parents and injured twenty-two others at school, nine critically. Time and again, it is only by happenstance that a full-blown disaster is averted. A security guard discovers a loaded Uzi submachine gun in a schoolbag in the nick of time. A student shoots into a crowded corridor and misses his intended targets. A list of gun near-disasters would be far longer than the list of real ones.

Violent deaths at schools tend to overshadow the large number of nonfatal student-victimization incidents. According to the *Indicators* study, in 1996 students aged twelve through eighteen were vic-

Notable School Killings of the 1990s (continued)

| Date | Place | Dead/ Wounded | Weapons | Description of Incident |
|---|---|---|---|---|
| 24 Apr. 1998 | Westside Middle School Jonesboro, Ark. | 4/11 | • Handguns and rifles, including a high-powered 30.06 hunting rifle | Armed with weapons stolen from one boy's father and grandfather and from a neighbor's garage, the boys pulled the school fire alarm and then hid in the woods, opening fire on the students who exited the building. Motive unknown. |
| 21 May 1998 | Thurston High School Springfield, Oreg. | 2/22 | • .22-caliber semiautomatic rifle<br>• .22-caliber handgun<br>• 9-millimeter Glock semiautomatic handgun<br>• .32-caliber handgun | The day after being expelled for bringing a stolen .32-caliber gun to school, a young student killed his parents at home and then opened fire in the school cafeteria. A police videotape shows him being asked why he began firing and responding, "I had no other choice." |
| 20 Apr. 1999 | Columbine High School Littleton, Colo. | 15/23, including two suicides | • TEC DC9 modified semiautomatic pistol<br>• Sawed-off double-barrel shotgun<br>• Sawed-off pump-action shotgun<br>• 9-millimeter semiautomatic rifle<br>• More than 30 homemade explosives (pipe bomb, hand grenades, and a propane gas tank with explosives attached) | Two members of a group calling themselves the "Trenchcoat Mafia" went on a bloody rampage as students and teachers hid within the school or risked their lives to escape. After creating the worst school massacre in American history, Dylan Klebold and Eric Harris killed themselves, leaving behind homemade bombs set to explode later. |

SOURCE: *School Associated Violent Deaths: In-House Report of the National School Safety Center* (1999).

tims of about 255,000 incidents of serious, though nonfatal crimes at school, including rape, sexual assault, robbery, and aggravated assault. In 1996–1997, 10 percent of all the public schools in the country reported at least one of these same serious offenses to the police. Over the five-year period 1992–1996, teachers were victims of 1.58 million nonfatal crimes, including 962,000 thefts and 619,000 violent crimes. Each year teachers are victims of 123,800 violent crimes (rape, sexual assault, robbery, aggravated and simple assault). Between 1989 and 1995 an increasing percentage of students (from 6 percent of all students to 9 percent) felt unsafe while they were at school or while they were going to and from school. In that same period

the percentage of students who reported that street gangs were present at their schools increased. In 1989, 15 percent of students reported gangs being present in their schools. By 1995 this percentage had risen to 28 percent.

Preliminary findings from the "National Longitudinal Study on Adolescent Health," one of the most comprehensive and rigorous quantitative studies performed on this topic, describe relationships among the student, family, school, and several preventable health outcomes, including suicide, violence, substance use, and sexual behaviors (Resnick et al. 1997). The study surveyed more than ninety thousand U.S. adolescents in schools throughout the country during the 1994–1995 school year using state-of-the-art measurements and methods. The data provide solid evidence for ways that families and schools can be protective in the lives of teenagers. The authors found that adolescents who are well-connected to schools (for example, those who take part in extracurricular activities) were consistently found to engage in less risky activities than those less well-connected to schools. The presence of connected, caring parents was associated with lower levels of interpersonal violence. Easy access to firearms in the homes of school-age youth was associated with increased risk for both suicide and violence.

Although most junior and senior high school students in the "National Longitudinal Study" reported never having been victims of violent behavior at school, 24.1 percent indicated that they had been victims. Additionally, 12.4 percent of students indicated that they had carried a weapon during the previous thirty days. (Several other surveys estimate much higher percentages.) Connection to school was associated with lower levels of violence. "Among both younger and older adolescents, involvement in violence was associated with having been a victim or a witness to violence, frequency of carrying a weapon, involvement in deviant or antisocial behaviors, and involvement with marijuana or other drugs. Interpersonal violence was associated with a lower grade-point average and higher perceived risk of untimely death"(Resnick et al. 1997).

Many large-scale statistical studies ask participants whether they have had direct personal experience of threats of actual harm. As a result, they have a built-in tendency to portray both teachers and students as passive victims of school violence rather than as active perpetrators. These analyses are sometime enlarged to ask whether participants have witnessed crime or bullying in schools. Such studies do not yield new insights into the nature of the problem, nor do they contribute much to a national conversation on ways to combat violence. Nevertheless, the massive amount of accumulated statistical data can jar us into realizing that the proportions of the problem have become shocking. About one public school teacher in four rates physical conflicts among students as a serious school problem. Since 1970 the American public, when asked which are the most serious problems facing public schools, has consistently ranked "lack of discipline" and "use of drugs" along with fighting, violence, and gangs at the top of the list.

In one survey, released in 1996, 26 percent of American high school students reported that physical fights in school were a very serious problem for them. Only half of American students reported that they "felt very safe" at school. In another survey of teachers' perceptions about school conditions, over 44 percent of public school teachers throughout the country complained that the level of student misbehavior interfered with their teaching, while only half that number of private school teachers had similar complaints. Among public high school students, 24.5 percent reported that fights often occur between different ethnic or racial groups within the school, whereas only 8.3 percent of Catholic school students and 3 percent of other private school students made similar statements.

The data also seem to indicate that misbehavior toward teachers is on the rise. In the academic year 1993–1994, 18.5 percent of public school teachers said that "student disrespect for teachers" was a serious school problem, up from 13 percent in 1990–1991. The most commonly perceived problems were pushing, shoving, grabbing, or slapping (28 percent); verbal insults (26 percent); and stealing (18 percent). Teachers perceived that 3 percent of students carried weapons to school, most commonly knives and handguns. Violence was perceived as more likely to occur at the secondary level and in urban schools. The majority of teachers (77 percent) reported feeling very safe at school; however, 11 percent had been the victim of a violent act. In New York City, the largest school system in the United States, 3,984 teachers were the victims of crime in the 1994–1995 school year, according to the teachers' union; incidents ranged from criminal mischief to sex offenses and assault. Despite sign-in procedures at many schools, suspended students or other intruders can easily manage to get into school buildings and roam the corridors at will.

Such bland statistics that identify "types of incidents," often for law-enforcement data-collection purposes, purport to present just the objective facts. In doing so, however, they lump the more serious with the less serious and, in divesting the violent episode of its social context, cripple attempts at interpretation. In the process, a U.S. "culture of violence" becomes further normalized.

Consider some of the extreme cases faced by American schools in the late twentieth century. On 17 January 1989, a man killed five children and wounded twenty-nine others and one teacher at an elementary school in Stockton, California. In less than two minutes, he fired 106 rounds from a semi-automatic AK-47 assault rifle. In West Paducah, Kentucky, on 1 December 1997, a fourteen-year-old walked into his high school with an armful of stolen weapons—a semiautomatic pistol, two rifles, two handguns, and spare ammunition clips—and opened fire into a prayer circle, killing three girls and wounding five other classmates. In the aftermath, the press attention focused on such items as the forgiving spirit of the town or whether the boy had been an atheist; the fact that the boy was able to break into a neighbor's garage and find a small arsenal to loot was deemed to be so normal that it received very little media attention. A few weeks earlier, in Pearl, Mississippi, a sixteen-year-old boy stabbed his mother to death with a butcher's knife before driving to school, where he shot his former girlfriend and another girl dead and wounded seven other students. The main focus of the investigations was on the other students who might have been conspiring with the accused, on evidence of a secret society and satanic worship. The town was silent on the issue of easy access to guns. These incidents happened in small towns in middle America, far from the urban areas typically associated with school violence.

In a 1993 national survey of junior high and high school students, 59 percent reported that they could get a gun if they needed one; two out of three of these students said they could get a gun within twenty-four hours. Illegal guns can be readily purchased within most neighborhoods, even in close proximity to schools. Nearly 20 percent of all students in grades nine to twelve reported that they had carried a weapon at least once during the thirty days preceding the survey. Knives or razors (55 percent) were carried significantly more often than clubs (24 percent) or firearms (20 percent). In another survey, 4.4 percent of high school students reported that they had missed at least one day of school during the prior thirty days because they felt unsafe at or en route to school. The main reason given by adolescents for obtaining or carrying guns is self-protection. From 1989 to 1998 homicide rates among school-age children increased dramatically, and suicide rates among adolescents more than tripled since the early 1950s —in both cases the increases correlate with firearms availability.

Some national surveys seem intent on reassuring the American people that their schools are still essentially safe by emphasizing the fact that "the large majority of teachers and students feel safe and have not been personally involved in a violent incident." Others focus on the fact that there is far more crime outside the schools than inside. These positive studies do little to comfort American parents, who feel that school violence has become an overwhelming problem, far more serious than ever before in U.S. history and far more deadly than in any other nation in the world.

**Violence Prevention**

There are some causes of school violence over which the schools have little or no direct control (the expanding gun market, the production of media violence, drugs in the community). Other problems can be reasonably managed within the schoolhouse. Educators need to know which factors they can reasonably control.

School security and safety experts have been more active than ever in helping schools to perform security needs assessments, develop and implement practical school security policies and strategies, train school staff in security and threat procedures, formulate crisis guidelines, promulgate safety tips for reducing risks to teachers and other staff, explore ways to collaborate with the community, learn how to deal with the media in the event of a crisis, and, in general, manage a full-blown security program. When extreme violence (for example, murder or assault) occurs within a U.S. school, the response of many school districts is often technological and security-based. Metal detectors are introduced along with X-ray machines, closed-circuit television, and other devices used for detecting weapons and keeping out intruders. Large squads of school-safety officers are brought into the schools with their own administration, training, and police-based practices. Their presence has drastically changed the pedagogical landscape of the public school, especially in the inner cities, where employment as a security guard has become a promising position for many young adults. In both urban and suburban areas, police have also been introduced into the schools to maintain order. Some U.S. school districts have their own police forces with authority to carry weapons.

The school security industry is lobbying for higher working standards for the "school safety officers," including better pay, more training, supervision by security professionals (rather than by the principal), crisis-preparedness plans, sign-in and visitor policies, the installation of card access

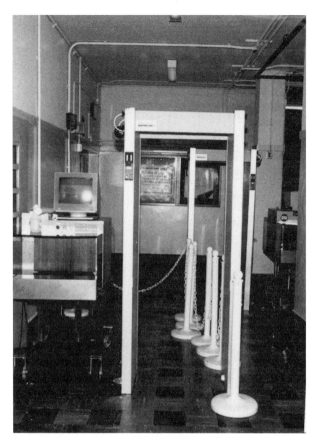

Metal detector at school entrance. From John Devine, *Maximum Security: The Culture of Violence in Inner-City Schools.* © 1996 UNIVERSITY OF CHICAGO PRESS

machines, and independent maintenance of security statistics. Although the stated motivation for inaugurating metal detectors and professional security systems is the concern for the safety of the school population, the main forces propelling these extraordinary increases in techno-security are economic, legal, and political: the threat of lawsuits and of large financial liability settlements is very real.

The enormous financial expenditure on technology and extra security guards has done little to solve the many problems associated with school violence. On the contrary, there is much evidence to suggest that the metal detectors and other security hardware have exacerbated them and contributed to a mentality of despair. The technology present in school lobbies has become an immutable part of the educational scene and sends the double message: "we will keep the school safe" and "we expect violence."

As if to counterbalance this "police state" mentality, many schools have simultaneously initiated conflict-resolution or peer-mediation programs as well as curricula dealing with human rights and peace studies. There was an enormous increase in the number of such programs during the 1990s. As federal funding became available for such projects, many local community-based agencies developed their own unique approaches to "conflict resolution." Despite the popularity of the programs, the claims of effectiveness by advocates are largely untested. Still, there seems to be some evidence that with proper training in conflict resolution, students do resolve their disputes through discussion and negotiation, and discipline problems and suspensions tend to decrease. Such programs appear to make students' attitudes toward conflict more positive, and their self-esteem tends to increase.

Since the late 1980s school violence has also been conceptualized as a serious public health problem. Using the model of the antitobacco campaign, this approach emphasizes primary preventive care and takes steps to educate the community and the school about the behavioral or environmental risk factors associated with school violence. Public-health advocates also underscore the importance of identifying the aggressive child as early as possible in order to provide appropriate intervention and treatment.

Many psychiatrists and child-health leaders see a common theme in all of the school shootings in recent years: the schools' inability to recognize psychological illnesses in children. Schools sometimes make the children's problems worse by not being sensitive enough to those with mental disorders. Critics of this approach argue that some of the recent school killers were, in fact, under the care of psychiatrists who utilized prescription drugs, and that there has been little public debate about the potential risks of youth taking these medications or about withdrawal symptoms.

The federal government put its imprimatur on this psychological approach when, in response to the killings of 1997–1998, it published a guide to violence prevention. The guide lists some of the early warning signs: social withdrawal; excessive feelings of isolation and being alone; excessive feelings of rejection; being a victim of violence; feelings of being picked on and persecuted; low school interest and poor academic performance; expressions of violence in writings and drawings; uncontrolled anger; patterns of impulsive and chronic hitting, intimidating, and bullying behavior; history of discipline problems; past history of violent and aggressive behavior; intolerance for differences and prejudicial attitudes; drug and alcohol abuse; affiliation with gangs; inappropriate access to, possession, and use of firearms; and serious threats of violence. But the guide is also careful to warn that these "signs" should not be used as a rationale for excluding, isolating, or punishing a child or for labeling or stereotyping children. The warning signs should be understood within a developmental context with the recognition that violence-prone children typically exhibit multiple warning signs.

The country employs a wide spectrum of technological and psychological strategies to combat school violence. Some schools attempt to bring together local social, health, drug-prevention, and victim-service agencies to combat and alter abusive behaviors. Some states create detailed incident-reporting systems for school districts. In other places zero-tolerance policies are enacted. School buildings are redesigned. In the New York City Board of Education, special schools, labeled euphemistically "Second Opportunity Schools," are being created for the most violent offenders who have been expelled from other schools.

**Strategies for Change**

In the wake of the Littleton nightmare, political leaders asked every institution in U.S. society to examine itself and consider how it might be contributing to the problem of school violence. But critics of this plan pointed out that it is naive to think that Hollywood will magnanimously forgo the profitable production of movie violence, or that the gun industry will unilaterally regulate itself. To confront media horror and the virtual universality of guns throughout America, many believe that the government will have to place reasonable restrictions on film and video-game violence and reasonable eligibility requirements and restrictions on firearms.

Meanwhile, the legal profession has intruded inside the schoolhouse. The reaction of parents to serious student-on-student sexual harassment and to the mass murders has introduced lawyers and the courts—even the Supreme Court—into daily decision-making processes that were formerly the exclusive province of educators. In the late 1990s, some prominent public figures were using these incidents to further the cause of vouchers, home schooling, or the abandonment of the public school system altogether. Conservatives have tried to capture the moral high ground by insisting on a

return to traditional pre–Progressive Era values, while liberals have remained focused on curricular debates and cognitive issues. Mainstream educational reformers who became visible in the early 1980s have largely ignored the full dimensions of the school violence problem, choosing to label much of the chaotic behavior mere adolescent feistiness. Universities and their schools of education have largely ignored the issue of violence and instead promoted schools with "success stories."

Moreover, the educational community—at both the level of theory and of everyday praxis—has not begun to reflect on the meaning and consequences of the intrusion of a uniformed paramilitary entity (the security apparatus) into the schools. Independent school security units are entities with their own ideologies, political bases, organizations, procedures, languages, rules, equipment, resources, and lines of authority, most of them more closely related to the juvenile justice system than to traditional pedagogy. One question to consider is how this police presence in schools has altered the role of the teacher.

The school of thought known as "critical pedagogy" interprets student violence as "resistance" to the oppressive hegemony of the state as mediated through the educational system. Prolonged ethnographic fieldwork in schools suggests the contrary, that students are looking for more structure and discipline and finding neither. Both students who are recent immigrants and overseas visitors to American schools are often appalled at what appears to be the lack of any code of school behavior. When parents or teachers stop getting closely involved with adolescents and cease setting the limits that youth expect, societal controls begin to break down. William Damon has called this a "culture of indulgence" involving misguided child-rearing practices that shield children at home and at school from hard work, firm rules, and consistent disciplinary practices.

There are, however, few voices calling for a national conversation to discuss how the United States can begin to extricate itself from this culture of violence that tends to dominate all aspects of school life. School systems are desperately seeking answers for schools that have spun out of control, but neither theoreticians nor politicians seem willing to question some of their most basic and cherished assumptions on the topic, such as those pertaining to the inevitability of firearms and reliance on technology.

Alternatively, peer-mediation programs are touted as effective ways of teaching students of all ages how to mediate conflicts among peers. Some high governmental officials, perhaps looking for a quick fix, have proclaimed such programs successful and declared that if only students can learn how to talk through their disputes, "they won't have to resort to fists and guns." One assumption underlying such views, however, is that students themselves must be responsible for eliminating violent confrontations in schools, meaning that educators can retreat from discipline to concentrate on academics.

Schools' earlier "in loco parentis" role depended on the principal and teachers taking a sense of ownership of a school and accepting responsibility for making it safe. Teachers' unions and many intellectuals rejected this concept and redefined the teachers' function as purely instructional. By default, all responsibility came to fall on the guards, and the dispute-resolution burden has been consigned to the students. Persuaded by unions, graduate schools of education, and even local education boards that their jobs should be aimed exclusively at academic achievement, many teachers have renounced the task of supervising adolescents in cafeterias, washrooms, and schoolyards.

When teachers deliberately turn a blind eye to students' misbehavior in and around the school, and as educators continue to delegate the crucial work of supervision to the professional security personnel, unanticipated changes take place throughout the structure of the school. If the regular patrols of the guards of the corridors do nothing to enhance a real sense of security, a sense of fear pervades the hallways and stairwells. The students, sensing that no legitimate authority is in control of the public space, realize that they have no one to rely on for safety but themselves and perhaps their friends. They report that they have to "be their own backup" and can depend on no one but their "homeboys" (Devine 1996, p. 146). The result is that they feel the need to act tough and engage in ganglike behavior, including sexually aggressive behavior, even when they are not members of a gang. It is at this point that they begin considering bringing weapons to school for self-protection. Thus the educational system itself becomes complicit in constructing aggressive student attitudes.

At the same time, students—especially immigrant students—complain that teachers are reluc-

tant to challenge even the most flagrant misbehaviors inside and outside the classroom. Ethnographic research has demonstrated that students expect schools to be structured environments, and that they quickly sense it when teachers appear afraid to correct rude and inappropriate behavior. In a curious way, the extreme positions of both the reproductionists and the conservatives (described above under "Causes") become validated; the "hegemonic" system creates the very agency it fears the most and purports to desire to eliminate: the violent student.

In school situations where legitimate authority has absented itself and students are left to fend for themselves for safety, adolescent boys and girls are denied any legitimate rites of passage such as preliterate societies enjoyed; instead they are abandoned to the aggression inherent in a masculinized Western culture stripped of all responsible adult supervision. In short, violence may not be merely a problem extrinsic to the school and imported into it, rather, the school may be a site in which violent, macho masculinities are produced and reproduced.

What can schools do to bring about fundamental change? Many educators feel that reducing school size may be the best means under their control for reducing school violence. In smaller schools, where it is easier for teachers and students to develop strong, meaningful relationships, students feel less alienated and anonymous. Several larger U.S. school districts are allowing schools to restructure themselves into smaller entities as part of their school-improvement plans. Statistically, smaller learning milieus offer many advantages: fewer dropouts, improved attendance, and greater student identification with the school. Moreover, students, teachers, and parents all report feeling a greater sense of security in the smaller settings. With fewer students, teachers are able to give more individualized and personalized instruction and are able to enforce school regulations in a more consistent and fairer way. The Small Schools Coalition, a Chicago-based advocacy group, estimates that the preferable school size is no more than 350 students in elementary schools and 500 in high schools. With an inclusive admissions policy and sufficient autonomy, schools of this size can foster environments in which parents, teachers, and students get to know one another well. Teachers not only design the instructional component; they also work collaboratively to manage the school. In these smaller contexts, teachers begin to reassert their "in loco parentis" role. Several types of smaller schools have been devised, and some have formed partnerships with businesses, foundations, and universities.

Small schools are no panacea, but in smaller settings adults have more opportunity and motivation to become closely connected to the students and the day-to-day issues and problems they face; the adult community also has a reasonable opportunity to formulate an acceptable code of behavior and to enlist the entire teaching staff to enforce it consistently. In such a setting, every teacher has the opportunity to know every student in the school by name. It is this combination of structure and empathy that creates the relaxed atmosphere in which behavioral standards can be made clear, a school community can be constructed, and no one feels excluded. Then it is possible for youth to experience a sense of incorporation into the school as a community whose members—youth and adult—respect each other.

*BIBLIOGRAPHY*

Board of Education of the City of New York. "Citywide Standards of Conduct and Uniform Disciplinary Measures." Resolution adopted by the Board of Education of New York City on 21 May 1986; amended 22 May 1991, 23 June 1993, 7 June 1995, and 19 March 1997.

Centers for Disease Control and Prevention. "Youth Risk Behavior Surveillance—United States, 1997." *Morbidity and Mortality Weekly Report* 47, no. 5503: 001 (14 August 1998).

Connell, R. W. *Masculinities.* Berkeley: University of California Press, 1995.

Damon, William. *Greater Expectations: Overcoming the Culture of Indulgence in America's Homes and Schools.* New York: Free Press, 1995.

Devine, John. *Maximum Security: The Culture of Violence in Inner-City Schools.* Chicago: University of Chicago Press, 1996.

Farrington, David P. "Understanding and Preventing Bullying." In *Crime and Justice.* Vol. 17, edited by Michael H. Tonry and Norval Morris. Chicago: University of Chicago Press, 1993.

Friedman, Matthew J. *Neurobiological and Clinical Consequences of Stress: From Normal Adaptation to Post-Traumatic Stress Disorder.* Philadelphia: Lippincott-Raven, 1995.

Giroux, Henry A. *Schooling and the Struggle for Public Life: Critical Pedagogy in the Modern Age.* Minneapolis: University of Minnesota Press, 1988.

Hamburg, Margaret A. "Violence Is a Public Health Concern." In *Violence in American Schools: A New Perspective,* edited by Delbert S. Elliott, Beatrix A. Hamburg, and Kirk R. Williams. Cambridge: Cambridge University Press, 1998.

Hylton, J. Barry, and Kenneth S. Trump. "Hard Lessons in School Security." *Security Management* (December 1997).

Johnson, David W., and Roger T. Johnson. "Conflict Resolution and Peer Mediation Programs in Elementary and Secondary Schools: A Review of the Research." *Review of Educational Research* 66, no. 4 (1996).

Kachur, S. Patrick, et al. "School-Associated Violent Deaths in the United States, 1992 to 1994." *Journal of the American Medical Association* 275, no. 22 (12 June 1996).

Kann, L., et al. "Youth Risk Behavior Surveillance—United States, 1993." *Morbidity and Mortality Weekly Report* 44, no. SS-1 (24 March 1995).

Kaufman, P., et al. *Indicators of School Crime and Safety, 1998.* Washington, D.C.: U.S. Departments of Education and Justice, 1998.

Klonsky, Michael. *Small Schools: The Numbers Tell a Story.* Chicago: Small Schools Workshop, 1995 (privately distributed).

Koplewicz, Harold S. *It's Nobody's Fault: New Hope and Help for Difficult Children and Their Parents.* New York: Times Books, 1996.

LH Research, Inc. *A Survey of Experiences, Perceptions, and Apprehensions About Guns Among Young People in America.* Cambridge, Mass.: Report to the Harvard School of Public Health Under a Grant from the Joyce Foundation, 1993.

Mercy, James A., and Mark Rosenberg. "Preventing Firearm Violence in and Around Schools." In *Violence in America's Schools: A New Perspective,* edited by Delbert S. Elliott, Beatrix A. Hamburg, and Kirk R. Williams. Cambridge: Cambridge University Press, 1998.

Metropolitan Life/Louis Harris Associates, Inc. "Part I: Students Voice Their Opinions on Violence, Social Tensions, and Equality Among Teens." In *The Metropolitan Life Survey of the American Teacher.* New York: Metropolitan Life Insurance Company, 1996.

Nadel, Helen, et al. "The Cycle of Violence and Victimization: A Study of the School-Based Intervention of a Multidisciplinary Youth Violence-Prevention Program." *American Journal of Preventive Medicine* 12, no. 5 (1996).

National Association for Mediation in Education. *Conflict Resolution: Solving Conflicts Without Violence.* Amherst, Mass.: National Association for Mediation in Education, 1994.

National School Safety Center. *School Associated Violent Deaths. In-House Report.* Westlake, Calif.: NSSC, 1999.

Nolin, Mary, and Elizabeth Davies. "Student Victimization at School." In *National Household Education Survey.* NCES 95–204. Washington, D.C.: U.S. Department of Education, National Center for Education Statistics, 1993.

Olweus, Dan. *Bullying at School: What We Know and What We Can Do.* Oxford, U.K.: Blackwell, 1993.

Price, James H., and Sherry A. Everett. "Teachers' Perceptions of Violence in the Public Schools: The MetLife Survey." *American Journal of Public Health* 21, no. 3 (1997).

Prothrow-Stith, Deborah. *Deadly Consequences.* New York: HarperCollins, 1991.

Resnick, Michael D., et al. "Protecting Adolescents from Harm: Findings from the National Longitudinal Study on Adolescent Health." *Journal of the American Medical Association* 278, no. 23 (10 September 1997).

Rigby, Ken. *Bullying in Schools: And What to Do About It.* Melbourne: Australian Council for Educational Research, 1996.

Trump, Kenneth S. *Practical School Security: Basic Guidelines for Safe and Secure Schools.* Thousand Oaks, Calif.: Corwin, 1997.

U.S. Department of Education. "Early Warning, Timely Response: A Guide for Safe Schools." Washington, D.C.: Office of Special Education and Rehabilitative Services, 1998.

————. "National Educational Longitudinal Study of 1988: Base Year and First and Second Followup Survey, 'Eighth, Tenth, and Twelfth Graders Attitudes About School Climate.' " Washington, D.C.: National Center for Educational Statistics, 1989.

————. "Schools and Staffing Survey, 1993–94: Teachers' Perceptions About Teaching and School Conditions." *Digest of Educational Statistics.* NCES 98-015. Washington, D.C.: National Center for Educational Statistics, 1997.

Webster, D. W., P. S. Gainer, and H. R. Champion. "Weapon Carrying Among Inner-City Junior High School Students: Defensive Behavior Versus Aggressive Delinquency." *American Journal of Public Health* 83, no. 11 (November 1993).

JOHN DEVINE

*See also* **Campus Violence; Children; Corporal Punishment; Mass Murder; Teenagers.**

## ANTIVIOLENCE CURRICULA

In the late twentieth century, the United States focused on the problem of violence in schools by providing school antiviolence curricula. Perhaps this was because research showed that the people most likely to be violent were teenagers. Or perhaps it was because of national media attention to shootings in schools around the country in the 1990s. While it is impossible to say whether particular instances of violence—especially those by troubled youth with access to guns—could ever have been prevented, research began to show that certain types of prevention activities could reduce aggression and violence in youth. As a result of these findings and in response to the increased public attention to this problem, in the late 1990s there was a virtual explosion in the number of school-based curricula designed to reduce violence. Some of these curricula were designed to prevent certain types of violence—hate crimes, dating violence, gun violence, media-influenced violence—but the vast majority of these curricula were designed to prevent interpersonal violence in general.

A 1998 guide to violence-prevention curricula written and published by Drug Strategies identifies a total of eighty-four school prevention curricula targeting violence, and this was not an exhaustive list. It was an astonishing number, especially given that the field of violence prevention was very young. Indeed, the earliest violence-prevention programs only began appearing in the late 1980s, and most curricula available to schools appeared on the scene in the mid-1990s and later.

As a point of comparison, drug-abuse prevention programs existed in the late 1970s, yet a 1996 Drug Strategies guide to drug-abuse prevention identified only forty-seven programs available to schools. On the surface this would appear an anomaly: Why would violence prevention—a newer field than drug abuse prevention—have almost twice as many programs? The answer, according to experts, was that the programs that did not work had probably not been weeded out. While drug-abuse prevention curricula were subjected to rigorous evaluation studies in the 1980s and 1990s, in the late 1990s very few curricula in the field of violence prevention had been evaluated, and little was known about what would work. Out of the eighty-four curricula identified, only six had been evaluated using pretest- and post-test control group designs, with outcome measures of aggressive behavior. None of these had followed students beyond the initial post-test.

Most curricula available to schools in the late 1990s used a broad definition of violence that included fighting, intimidation, and bullying, as well as other acts of aggression; the curricula helped students learn how to resolve conflicts peacefully. A limited number of programs focused on more specific issues relating to violence, including hate crimes and dating violence. While serious acts of violence (homicide, rape) were relatively rare in schools, aggression and intimidation were usually all too familiar. Curricula that addressed these everyday problems, or promoted peace, were therefore welcome and immediately relevant to teachers and students.

While effective curricula were not identified in completed evaluation studies, it was possible, based on studies of the causes of violence as well as studies of other types of prevention programs (e.g., delinquency prevention, drug-abuse prevention), to develop a list of the likely ingredients of effective violence-prevention curricula. Critical elements of promising programs include:

1. The content of the most promising prevention curricula would be organized into two major areas: normative education and life-skills

training (described below). While programs often focused only on normative education or life-skills training, experts believed that the best programs would come to combine these two approaches.

Normative education (including school climate programs) is designed to promote a positive, peaceful norm and to correct misperceptions that students often have about violence. Violent norms are pervasive in the media and in our culture. Attitudes such as "only wimps walk away from a fight" or "fighting is cool" abound. Students often overestimate the number of peers who carry weapons. During adolescence, when being accepted by a peer group becomes so important, such misperceptions can have profound and dangerous implications for a student's own behavior. School administrators also send powerful messages about whether aggression and bullying will be tolerated. Suggesting to students that they need to handle bullies on their own and stand up for themselves actually may make the problem worse. Teachers and administrators have to be involved in eliminating violence. Good normative programs help schools communicate a strong message that violence will not be tolerated by adults and that the consequences for violations of school rules concerning violence will be swift and sure.

The second promising content area is life-skills training. Life-skills training teaches young people how to make decisions, solve problems, cope with stress and anxiety, set goals for the future, communicate effectively, get along with others, be assertive, and resist negative social influences. A number of prevention studies have demonstrated that life-skills training approaches enhance personal and social competence as well as reduce a variety of problem or risk behaviors, including smoking, drinking, other drug use, delinquency, and premature sexual behavior. Certain life skills—anger management, empathy training, and social problem solving—are especially important to violence prevention. Skills for resisting media and interpersonal influences to fight or be violent also are important, as are general communication and social skills.

2. Life skills and positive norms need to be developed and reinforced in various settings. Within the school, well-designed curricula provide ways of infusing materials across different subject areas, as well as in different settings (e.g., playground, cafeteria). Ideally there should be complementary programs for families, as well as communities, so that new norms and skills are reinforced outside school. Media campaigns can also help to generalize and institutionalize prevention strategies.

3. Prevention programs should begin early in the primary grades and be reinforced across grade levels. Research has not determined the minimal number of sessions needed to reduce aggression or violence. Because life-skills approaches are effective at reducing risk for a variety of problem behaviors, including drug use and premature sexual behavior, one way of providing a sufficient dosage and adequate follow-up is to develop an integrated strategy that addresses multiple problem behaviors within the context of a single program. Life-skills development and behavioral change can take multiple sessions; an integrated approach helps minimize the number of sessions required for addressing different problem behaviors by providing some skills training each year in school and by building on and reinforcing skills developed in previous years.

4. Material must be relevant, culturally sensitive, and developmentally appropriate to the students who use it. Prevention programs are more likely to be accepted and to be effective if they address important developmental issues of their audience and if they are sensitive to cultural issues and norms. For example, programs that recognize the importance of peers and teach skills for resisting negative peer influence while at the same time maintaining friendships are more likely to be effective than prevention programs that suggest that young people should "just say no."

5. Personal and social skills are most effectively taught using modeling and coaching; in addition, students need opportunities to practice new skills. Interactive techniques that use discussion, cooperative learning, behavioral rehearsal, and role play have greater impact on behavior. Peer mediation is an element of some violence-prevention programs; this involves providing peer leaders with the interactive skills needed to mediate student conflicts. Training peers in this way may also help to develop and reinforce positive norms.

113

6. For prevention strategies to have impact, they must be implemented effectively. Teachers need to understand what the critical elements are and how to develop them using interactive techniques. Educator training that includes modeling and on-site coaching helps teachers to master the program and impart violence-prevention skills to students.

A handful of methodologically rigorous evaluation studies of violence-prevention programs were under way in the late 1990s. Several of these were funded by the Centers for Disease Control and Prevention. None had been completed by the turn of the century, though preliminary findings from several of them suggested that certain strategies may reduce aggressive behavior in students. On the basis of these preliminary studies, it seemed reasonable to expect that violence-prevention curricula would be an effective component of our national violence-prevention strategy. However, experts expected that it would probably be early in the twenty-first century before studies would identify programs that work or begin to answer a number of important questions about the various skills areas that need to be covered or the minimum number of sessions.

Meanwhile, there were a few efforts designed to assist schools in choosing promising programs. For example, *Blueprints for Violence Prevention* (1997) identifies exemplary prevention programs shown in rigorous research studies to reduce risk behaviors associated with violence. Although the research did not directly address violence prevention, several programs identified in *Blueprints for Violence Prevention* contain the elements experts believed would come to be important in practice. *Safe Schools/Safe Students: A Guide to Violence Prevention Strategies* (1998) reviews eighty-four nationally available violence-prevention curricula and assesses how completely each addresses the key elements of violence prevention. Both works have provided schools with information for making more informed decisions as they developed violence-prevention strategies.

*BIBLIOGRAPHY*

Drug Strategies. *Making the Grade: A Guide to School-Based Drug Abuse Prevention Curricula.* Washington, D.C.: Drug Strategies, 1996.

———. *Safe Schools/Safe Students: A Guide to School-Based Violence Prevention Curricula, Policies, and Environmental Changes.* Washington, D.C.: Drug Strategies, 1998.

Dusenbury, Linda, et al. "Nine Critical Elements of Promising Violence Prevention Programs." *Journal of School Health* 67, no. 10 (December 1997): 409–414.

Elliott, Delbert S., and Sharon W. Mihalic. *Blueprints for Violence Prevention and Reduction: The Identification and Documentation of Successful Programs.* Boulder, Colo.: Center for the Study and Prevention of Violence, 1997.

Gottfredson, D. "School-Based Crime Prevention." In *Preventing Crime: What Works, What Doesn't, What's Promising: A Report to the United States Congress,* edited by Lawrence W. Sherman et al. Washington, D.C.: U.S. Department of Justice, National Institute of Justice, 1997.

LINDA DUSENBURY
ROGER WEISSBERG

*See also* **Prevention; Schools; Teenagers.**

### INTEGRATION

In 1954, in *Brown v. Board of Education of Topeka*, the U.S. Supreme Court reversed the Court's 1896 *Plessy v. Ferguson* decision, effectively ending federal tolerance of racial segregation. In *Plessy v. Ferguson* the Court had ruled that "separate but equal" accommodations for black travelers on railroad cars did not violate the Fourteenth Amendment's guarantee of equal protection. That decision was used to justify the racial segregation of all public facilities, including schools. Moreover, most school districts, ignoring *Plessy's* "equal" requirement, tended to neglect African American schools. When the Court issued its 1954 decision, strong local opposition (what came to be known in the South as "massive resistance") resulted in long delays in school desegregation and bitter conflicts often marked by violence. In 1956, for example, more than a hundred southern members of Congress signed a "manifesto" denouncing the *Brown* decision and urged their constituents to defy it.

In 1957 an angry white mob in Little Rock, Arkansas, tried to prevent the implementation of a federal court decision ordering the desegregation of Central High School. Governor Orville Faubus refused to prevent this obstruction. In response, President Dwight D. Eisenhower was forced to federalize the National Guard and send troops to the school. In May 1962, in Birmingham, Alabama, civil rights leader Martin Luther King, Jr., organized a series of demonstrations, whose participants included numerous African American schoolchildren, to protest the continued segregation of the city's public facilities, including its schools. Birmingham's police commissioner, Eugene "Bull" Connor, personally supervised a brutal effort to break up the peaceful marches, arrest-

**Paratroopers from the 101st Airborne Division protect students entering Central High School in Little Rock, Arkansas, 26 September 1957.** CORBIS/BETTMANN

ing hundreds of demonstrators and using attack dogs, tear gas, electric cattle prods, and fire hoses —at times even against the schoolchildren—as much of the nation watched the events unfold on television.

Two months later Alabama governor George Wallace, who had won election in 1962 by promising staunch resistance to integration, pledged to stand in the doorway of a building at the University of Alabama to prevent the court-ordered enrollment of several African American students. Only after the arrival of federal marshals and a visit from Attorney General Robert Kennedy did Wallace give way. In October 1962, after a federal court ordered the University of Mississippi to enroll James Meredith, an African American, Governor Ross Barnett refused to enforce the order. When angry whites in Oxford, Mississippi, began rioting to protest the court's decree, President John F. Kennedy sent federal troops to the city to restore order and protect Meredith's right to attend the university.

The historic decision in the *Brown* case had specifically stated that only de jure segregation was illegal. Consequently, the North—where the practice of de facto segregation was widespread—was spared federal attempts at school integration until

the 1970s. In 1971 the Department of Health, Education, and Welfare began collecting figures on school desegregation; research revealed that, primarily due to white migration to the suburbs, many northern cities no longer had white majorities. In twelve major northern cities there were approximately 380,000 African American students, all in African American schools. The numbers showed that in that year segregation in the North was in fact more widespread than in the South. By the end of 1971 federal judges in the North had begun to issue orders forcing northern public schools to integrate. The principal means used to integrate northern schools was the controversial practice of busing African American students to white schools and white students to African American schools. The struggle between those who opposed busing, both white and black, and those who supported the practice developed into a protracted conflict lasting until the latter part of the 1970s. Whites mounted massive opposition to busing, staging angry protests that sometimes turned into violent confrontations with police. In the 1970s violence between black and white students was not uncommon, as many schools in the North became the battlegrounds on which the nation's struggle over school integration was fought.

Although antibusing movements formed in virtually all of the northern cities in which the federal government had implemented busing, the city of Boston's experience with the practice was the most highly publicized. Boston, in fact, came to symbolize the painful and violent conflicts over the issue in the North. A 1974 decision by a federal judge to integrate several of the city's schools was met with widespread opposition from white parents, who greeted the African Americans bused to their children's schools with racist chants and the throwing of rocks and bottles, a scene that was repeated in Boston over the next several years. Moreover, violence between black and white students in the neighborhoods of South Boston and Charlestown led to police presence on school grounds during much of the controversy. In 1976 a young African American man, Theodore Landsmark, was attacked by a group of white students leaving a city council meeting. The man's nose was broken, and he was beaten with a flagpole. Fourteen days later, a white auto mechanic, Richard Poleet, was dragged from his car in the African American neighborhood of Roxbury by a gang of twenty-five African Americans and beaten. The man, who spent two years in a coma, eventually died.

The integration of the nation's schools remained an open-ended issue. In a few areas desegregation attained widespread public support and became an accepted part of daily life. In Boston, once the hotbed of resistance, biracial committees such as the Boston Home and School Association were formed in the 1970s by parents and community leaders to help ease the transition to integrated schools, foster interracial cooperation, and ease racial tensions among students and parents. Interracial committees were also formed in cities such as Detroit, Chicago, and Philadelphia. Educational programs designed to ease racial tensions and encourage diversity in schools, paid for with federal, state, and local funds, became commonplace in the 1980s and 1990s. But in some areas, intense, unyielding resistance continued, notably in the form of resegregation. Supreme Court decisions in the late twentieth century—such as *Riddick v. School Board of Norfolk, Virginia* (1986); *Board of Education of Oklahoma City v. Dowell* (1991); *Freeman v. Pitts* (1992); and *Missouri v. Jenkins* (1995), among others—made it easier for school districts under desegregation court orders to resegregate their schools. De facto resegregation may also have been caused by the effects of white enrollment loss due to, for example, white flight. School districts that

## Desegregating School Spending

Jonathan Kozol's 1991 book, *Savage Inequalities: Children in America's Schools,* revealed that most efforts to desegregate our nation's public schools have been dismal failures. According to Kozol, who spent two years investigating the public schools in thirty urban and suburban American communities, his most startling discoveries were the degree to which racial segregation was evident in most of the places he visited—especially outside the South—and the enormous discrepancies in equipment, curriculum, and staff between schools in poor neighborhoods and schools in wealthy ones. In most of the urban schools that Kozol observed, 95 to 99 percent of the students were nonwhite, textbooks were scarce, chemistry labs, if they existed at all, lacked basic supplies such as beakers and Bunsen burners, and playgrounds had no equipment. Suburban schools, on the other hand, were remarkably better equipped. New Trier High School outside of Chicago, for example, offers students seven gyms, an Olympic-size swimming pool, and a television studio and has one faculty adviser for every twenty-four students.

Kozol concludes that because of the widespread disparities in expenditures between poor schools and wealthy ones, efforts to redress the inequities and bring urban schools up to suburban standards must equalize school spending rather than alter the organizational structure of public schools.

dismantled their court-ordered school desegregation plans included Denver, Colorado; Cleveland, Ohio; and Oklahoma City, Oklahoma.

A haunting reminder of desegregation's troubled history is the fact that Linda Brown, the girl for whom the *Brown* case was named, as a parent alleged that her children's constitutional rights were violated by a state's failure to fully desegregate its public schools.

*BIBLIOGRAPHY*

Formisano, Ronald P. *Boston Against Busing: Race, Class, and Ethnicity in the 1960s and 1970s.* Chapel Hill: University of North Carolina Press, 1991.

Huckaby, Elizabeth. *Crisis at Central High.* Baton Rouge: Louisiana State University, 1980.

Kozol, Jonathan. *Savage Inequalities: Children in America's Schools.* New York: Crown, 1991.

Lukas, J. Anthony. *Common Ground: A Turbulent Decade in the Lives of Three American Families.* New York: Knopf, 1985.

Metcalf, George R. *From Little Rock to Boston: The History of School Desegregation.* Westport, Conn.: Greenwood, 1983.

Orfield, Gary. *Dismantling Desegregation: The Quiet Retreat of Brown v. Board of Education.* New York: New Press, 1996.

NANCY A. BANKS

*See also* **African Americans; Race and Ethnicity.**

# SCHULTZ, "DUTCH" (ARTHUR FLEGENHEIMER)

## (1902–1935)

A one-time petty thief—his specialty was stealing packages from delivery wagons—Dutch Schultz, born Arthur Flegenheimer, took advantage of Prohibition to become one of New York City's leading beer barons and racketeers. Although he wielded considerable power within the underworld, Schultz did not look the part of a spectacular criminal. Clad in baggy trousers and ill-fitting jackets, he seemed to be a "perfect example of the unsuccessful man" (as the crime reporter Meyer Berger described him in the *New York Times*). Only suckers, Schultz liked to say, spent money on expensive silk shirts.

Born on 6 August 1902 in the Bronx, New York, to hardworking Jewish parents, Schultz got only as far as the sixth grade before leaving school. He went on to hold a succession of odd jobs, from roofer's apprentice to office boy, before landing in jail in 1917 for burglary. Upon his release, he returned to his old neighborhood, where, when not hauling trunks for a local mover, he spent much of his time frequenting poolrooms in the company of the so-called Bergen Avenue gang, a crowd of hoodlums believed to have given Flegenheimer his sobriquet. "He wasn't Dutch. His father and mother were German Jews. But the name sounded tough," wrote Berger, explaining that "Dutch Schultz" had been the title of a "rough-and-tumble fighter famous in the Bronx back in the days of the old Frog Hollow gang."

In 1928 Schultz became a partner in a Bronx speakeasy; within three years, he owned seventeen garages and beer drops, one of which featured a "disappearing elevator." Attracting the attention of the city's midtown moguls, he was soon taken under their wing and, in due course, prospered

"Dutch" Schultz at New York Federal Court, 1935.
CORBIS/BETTMANN

mightily. With his growing—and tax-free—profits, Schultz then moved in on the Harlem numbers or policy racket, completely taking it over and streamlining the enterprise. He also seized control of several unions that serviced the food and restaurant industry, among them the local of the Delicatessen, Counterman, and Cafeteria Workers. At the time the authorities confessed to being puzzled by Schultz's rapid ascent. He had far less animal courage than those who drove his trucks or did his bidding, the police conceded. Instead, as Berger wrote in the *New York Times*, they attributed his success "partly [to] accident and partly [to] his native business sense. He did have a gift for organization."

The Dutchman's career, however, was short-lived. Indicted in the early 1930s for income tax evasion, Schultz went into hiding. Eventually he surfaced to face trial two times: the first trial ended in April 1935 in a mistrial; the second ended in an acquittal in July 1935. The racketeer was preparing his triumphal return and the resumption of his criminal career when, in October 1935, he was mortally wounded in Newark, New Jersey, at the Palace Chop House, a restaurant he often used to conduct business and hold conferences; Schultz died the next day. Fearful that Schultz might become too much of a liability, New York's reigning gangsters, including Louis Lepke and "Lucky" Luciano, had ordered his execution. As the police searched the premises looking for clues, they came across a piece of adding machine tape. It showed a tally of $827,253.

Schultz's death made front-page news, giving rise to animated public discussions about the strange ways of the underworld. According to the *New York Times*, Schultz, who was thirty-three at the time of his demise, "fulfills the tradition that a gangster chieftain never dies of old age. They seldom ever reach even middle age." More to the point, Shultz's death, a watershed in American criminal history, pointed to one of the most salient characteristics of the modern underworld: its ability to mix business with violence.

*BIBLIOGRAPHY*

Berger, Meyer. "Schultz Reigned on Discreet Lines," *New York Times*, 2 October 1935.

Fried, Albert. *The Rise and Fall of the Jewish Gangster in America*. New York: Columbia University Press, 1993.

Sann, Paul. *Kill the Dutchman*. New Rochelle, New York: Arlington, 1971.

JENNA WEISSMAN JOSELIT

*See also* **Lepke, Louis; Luciano, "Lucky"; Organized Crime.**

## SCOTTSBORO CASE

What became known to history as the Scottsboro case began on 25 March 1931, when nine black teenagers—Olen Montgomery, Clarence Norris, Haywood Patterson, Ozie Powell, Willie Roberson, Charlie Weems, Eugene Williams, Andy Wright, and Roy Wright—were accused of raping two white women—Ruby Bates and Victoria Price—on a freight train traveling through northern Alabama. Twelve days after their arrest, the defendants were put on trial in Scottsboro, Alabama,

and in four days four juries found eight of them guilty and sentenced them to death.

The Communist Party U.S.A., whose southern field organizers were on the scene, called the trials "legal lynchings" and announced its intention to fight in the courts and in the streets to free the "Scottsboro Boys." The party organized meetings, marches, and a massive letter-writing campaign; it fended off a challenge from the National Association for the Advancement of Colored People for control of the defense; and then it appealed the convictions. The Alabama Supreme Court upheld the convictions, but in *Powell v. Alabama* (1932) the U.S. Supreme Court ordered new trials on the grounds that the defendants had been denied counsel in violation of the rights guaranteed by the equal protection clause of the Fourteenth Amendment.

In Decatur, Alabama, in April 1933, Haywood Patterson was tried for a second time, before Judge James Horton. The Communist Party hired Samuel Leibowitz, a brilliant New York criminal lawyer, to represent Patterson. Victoria Price stuck to her story, but Ruby Bates testified for the defense, insisting that she and Price had made up the story of the rape and that none of the defendants had even touched them. Nonetheless, the jury found Patterson guilty and sentenced him to death. Liberals and radicals decried Alabama bigotry, while countless southerners protested northern, Jewish, and communist interference in Alabama's affairs.

In June 1933 Judge Horton granted the defense's motion for a new trial. The verdict, Horton argued, clearly contradicted the evidence. Alabama officials forced Horton to recuse himself, and in late 1933 Judge William Callahan, who was openly hostile to the defense, presided over Patterson's third trial and Clarence Norris's second trial. Both were quickly convicted and sentenced to death. The defense appealed, and in *Norris v. Alabama* (1935), the Supreme Court reversed Norris's second conviction (and, in effect, Patterson's third) on the grounds that the grand jurors who indicted Norris and trial jurors who convicted him had been drawn from jury rolls that excluded black men.

In July 1937, after four more trials, Alabama dropped charges against four of the defendants. Between 1943 and 1951, Alabama paroled four more. In 1948, Haywood Patterson staged a daring escape from Kilby Prison and fled north to Detroit. Not until 1976, when Alabama granted Clarence Norris a full and unconditional pardon, did the

Scottsboro defendants Eugene Williams, Olen Montgomery, and Andy Wright at Birmingham Jail, 1931. HULTON GETTY/LIAISON AGENCY

state finally acknowledge that he and his fellow defendants had been falsely accused and wrongly convicted.

The Scottsboro case brought the horrors of Jim Crow justice to the attention of people all over the world, and it encouraged many white Americans to join black Americans in their long struggle for freedom and equality.

BIBLIOGRAPHY

Carter, Dan T. *Scottsboro: A Tragedy of the American South.* Baton Rouge: Louisiana State University Press, 1969.
Goodman, James. *Stories of Scottsboro.* New York: Pantheon, 1994.

JAMES GOODMAN

*See also* **African Americans.**

# SCULPTURE

Violence does not immediately leap to mind as a prevalent theme in American sculpture but, upon reflection, reveals itself as a consistent undercurrent. During the nineteenth century, violence was frequently alluded to and occasionally depicted.

Sculpted objects themselves took on an increasingly violent tone in the twentieth century, at times even posing a physical threat to the spectator. While the materials used to create sculpture have always affected the ways violence could be portrayed or embodied, the ever-increasing diversity of media has continued to unleash new creative possibilities.

The early years of American nationhood corresponded with Neoclassicism, a movement of subdued emotions. Violence could be rendered, but only with great restraint. Johann Winckelmann, the great German neoclassical theorist, particularly admired *Laocoön* (c. 150 B.C.) because the writhing agony of the figures being attacked by serpents is relatively controlled, both physically and emotionally. Well into the second half of the nineteenth century, American sculptors valued the study and emulation of antique sculpture and frequently trained in Italy. The emphasis on the use of marble also influenced the subjects chosen, as the weight of the material lent itself to tempered poses and gestures resistant to breakage.

American sculptors of the late eighteenth and early nineteenth centuries worked mostly in wood and were often viewed as craftsmen rather than fine artists. William Rush tried to bridge the gap

**The Laocoön Group (first century** B.C.**), a major influence on early American sculptors.** Corbis/Araldo de Luca

between art and craft by carving ambitious wooden works that he then painted white to resemble marble. His *Allegory of the Schuylkill River in Its Improved State* (1825), which is made of painted Spanish cedar, is based on classical allegorical figures. The sculpture depicts a reclining, bearded man whose wrists are manacled. He represents the Schuylkill being controlled by locks and dams, an instance of human engineering winning a battle in the war to harness the powers of nature.

Two decades later, in *The Greek Slave* (1843), Hiram Powers also used chains as a symbol of control. This image of a Greek maiden held in bondage by the Turks downplays the violence of captivity and concentrates instead on the beauty of an ideal female nude. Powers produced this work (based on antique prototypes, including the *Medici Venus*, created in the first century B.C.) while living in Florence, a city that attracted foreign sculptors because of the availability of fine marble and accomplished stone carvers. The nudity provoked an outcry when the work was first shown in Victorian America. But the sculpture ultimately became one of the most celebrated works of its age because the woman was interpreted as being figuratively clothed by her Christian faith and virtue.

As the century progressed, American sculptors frequently chose to study in France rather than Italy. Howard Roberts attended the Pennsylvania Academy of the Fine Arts before voyaging to Paris, where he learned the vigorous naturalism and technical virtuosity that became the hallmarks of his style. *Hypatia* (1873–1877), his earliest life-size marble sculpture, was inspired by an 1853 novel set in fifth-century Alexandria. Roberts chose to depict Hypatia (a Neoplatonic philosopher who upheld the ancient pagan beliefs of the Roman Empire) at the moment when, driven into the church, she turns to face the monks who are about to kill her. The sculptor has included an intricately carved crucifix, censer, and candlestick as a means of locating the scene. The sculpture anticipates the violence that awaits Hypatia but also evokes her proud defiance: her pose can read at once as a defensive recoil or a cobralike coil. The independent Hypatia was just one of many threatening heroines sculpted at this time, a trend that Joy S. Kasson has attributed to contemporary anxiety over changing gender roles.

Americans were also influenced by Antoine-Louis Barye, France's famed *animalier*, who pioneered a revival of sculpture in bronze, a medium that offered sculptors the freedom to create complicated and dynamic compositions. William Rimmer's *Fighting Lions* (1870–1871) bears a strong resemblance to *Lion Crushing a Serpent* (1832) by Barye. In Rimmer's sculpture two lions are violently locked together, their bodies forming a single unified mass. Rimmer, moreover, imbued these beasts with an anthropomorphic quality.

While Rimmer made his animals resemble people, John J. Boyle evoked the bestiality of certain humans. In his *Stone Age in America* (1887), a Native American woman holds a small child in her left arm and a stone ax in her right hand while a slightly older child kneels by her side and grasps her right leg. The presence of a dead bear cub by her left foot attests to an act of violence, and the woman's firm grasp on her weapon suggests that she is fully prepared to attack the unseen adult bear, presumably poised to retaliate for the death of the cub. This seemingly noble action has been actually interpreted as a denigration of Native Americans, implying a dependence on force rather than intellect for survival. The theme of *Stone Age,*

*The Greek Slave,* **marble by Hiram Powers, 1846.**
CORBIS/THE CORCORAN GALLERY OF ART

as well as the juxtaposition of human and bear, may have been inspired by the work of Emmanuel Fremiet, a French sculptor whose *Bear-Cub Thief* (1885) depicts the battle between a mother bear and the prehistoric man who has just strangled her cub.

Paul Wayland Bartlett was also influenced by Fremiet, with whom he studied, as well as by Auguste Rodin, for whom he served as an assistant. In *The Indian Ghost Dancer* (1888–1889), Bartlett depicts a Native American as a savage. The dancer, worked into a frenzied trance, seems neither fully rational nor completely human. As Thomas P. Somma has explained, the sculpture drew on contemporary racist beliefs and ideas about degeneracy in order to convey the idea of Native Americans as inherently "other."

Kirk Savage has noted that African Americans, who were also categorized as "other," were seldom portrayed in the nineteenth century because of what contemporaries regarded as their physical and physiognomic deviations from Western ideals of perfection and beauty. When they were depicted in sculpture, even in monuments to emancipation such as Thomas Ball's *Freedmen's Memorial to Abraham Lincoln* (1876), blacks were often shown in a subjugated position while the focus was placed on the controlling power of white men. In the 1930s, sculpture finally began to address the aftermath of slavery and the violent effects of racism more directly. Seymour Lipton's *Lynched* (1933) and Isamu Noguchi's *Lynched Figure* (1934) dramatically underscore the violence inflicted on blacks during the Depression. Both works highlight the rope used to hang the figure and the distortion of the body resulting from violent death.

At the turn of the century sculptors offered vicarious physicality and violence to an increasingly sedentary middle-class public. Frederic Remington's *The Broncho Buster* (1895) depicts a cowboy breaking a wild horse. This intricately detailed and extremely popular bronze tabletop statuette drew on myths about the American West and reworked the age-old theme of man against nature, symbolized here by the untamed steed. Meanwhile, Mahonri Young's *Right to the Jaw* (1926–1927) and *The Knockdown* (1927) glorified the sport of boxing. While Young was compared with the painter George Bellows, his works did not emphasize the brutishness of the sport as seen in such Bellows paintings as *Stag at Sharkey's* (1909). By focusing on the physiques of the athletes more than the violence of their sport, Young recognized that boxing was beginning to stress style and finesse more than sheer barbaric power.

The brutality of warfare, on the other hand, was addressed more directly in twentieth-century monuments than ever before. While Daniel Chester French's *Minute Man* (1873–1875) and Augustus Saint-Gaudens's *Robert Gould Shaw Memorial* (1884–1897) had honored armed Revolutionary War and Civil War fighters, respectively, these men were not shown in combat. Karl Illava's *The 107th Infantry Memorial* (1927), however, depicts doughboys charging into battle during World War I and includes wounded and dying soldiers in poses patterned after traditional pietà scenes. By drawing on religious imagery alluding to the life of Christ, the sculpture portrays death in battle as a noble and patriotic self-sacrifice.

The twentieth century also brought more personal reactions to war and, in at least one instance, the subversion of a codified commemorative form. David Smith used the traditional lost-wax process to produce his fifteen *Medals for Dishonor* (1937–1940), medallions that bespeak the horrors of war rather than its glories. In this series Smith uses surreal imagery to condemn ruthless practices specified in his titles: for example, *Bombing Civilian Populations* (1939) and *Sinking Hospital and Civilian Refugee Ships* (1939).

Sculpture in the twentieth century also began to implicate the viewer in new and often menacing ways. In *Gift* (1921), Man Ray turned a mundane object into a threatening one. Influenced by Marcel Duchamp's "assisted readymades," in which everyday objects were combined in unconventional ways, Ray attached a row of tacks to a flatiron, creating an object that looks more like a weapon than a work of art. *Gift* was a precursor of violent surrealist objects portraying violence, such as Alberto Giacometti's *Disagreeable Object* (1931). The work also foreshadowed Walter De Maria's *Beds of Spikes* (1968–1969), in which the artist attached varying numbers of obelisk-shaped spikes to five sheets of stainless steel. When exhibited, these works were considered so potentially harmful that visitors had to sign a legal release form in order to enter the gallery.

The violence of sculpture by De Maria and other minimalists has been recognized by Anna C. Chave, who has commented on the ominous qualities of many of their works. Richard Serra's *Delineator* (1974–1976) juxtaposes two steel plates. As the viewer walks on the plate placed on the floor, he or she cannot help but hope that the plate hanging from the ceiling is firmly attached. The all-too-real physical menace of such works was brought home in 1988, when a sixteen-ton sculpture by

**Maya Ying Lin's Vietnam Veterans Memorial Wall, Washington, D.C.** CORBIS/JAMES P. BLAIR

Serra fell while being installed and severely injured two workers. In addition, the use of industrial materials by Serra and others, who often ordered their works from factories rather than personally fabricating them, was seen as an attack on the very concept of art.

*Given: 1. The Waterfall, 2. The Illuminating Gas* (1946–1966), created by Duchamp, a French artist who emigrated to the United States, involves the viewer by turning him or her into a voyeur. The viewer approaches an old wooden door and peers through two holes situated at approximately eye level. Beyond one sees a lifelike sculpture of a naked woman lying on her back in a bed of twigs. Her legs are open, revealing a smooth, unnaturally split pubis. This mixed-media assemblage brings to mind a crime scene where a rape or murder has taken place and leaves the viewer feeling disconcerted and uncomfortable.

Maya Lin's *Vietnam Veterans Memorial* (1980–1982) involves visitors in a different way. The human sacrifice of the Vietnam War is poignantly conveyed in the chronological listing of the 57,939 names of those Americans who died or were reported missing in action. The fact that visitors can see themselves reflected in the two black granite walls encourages them to remember the violent loss of life that is part of every armed combat and to take responsibility for avoiding similar conflicts in the future.

The history of sculpture in the United States has often been seen as an evolution from figuration to abstraction, from the use of traditional media to unconventional materials. In terms of violence, American sculpture has, over time, gravitated from the direct and indirect representation of violence to works that seem to embody it, challenging and even threatening the viewer's mind, spirit, and body. In and through sculpture, humans enact violence on nature, other humans, and ideas about art, thus causing viewers to question the role of violence in American society.

*BIBLIOGRAPHY*

Chave, Anna C. "Minimalism and the Rhetoric of Power." *Arts Magazine* 64, no. 5 (1990).

Fort, Ilene Susan. *The Figure in American Sculpture: A Question of Modernity.* Los Angeles: Los Angeles County Museum of Art in association with University of Washington Press, 1995.

Kasson, Joy S. *Marble Queens and Captives: Women in Nineteenth-Century American Sculpture.* New Haven, Conn.: Yale University Press, 1990.

Reynolds, Donald Martin. *Masters of American Sculpture: The Figurative Tradition from the American Renaissance to the Millennium.* New York: Abbeville Press, 1993.

Savage, Kirk. *Standing Soldiers, Kneeling Slaves: Race, War, and Monument in Nineteenth-Century America.* Princeton, N.J.: Princeton University Press, 1997.

Somma, Thomas P. "The Myth of Bohemia and the Savage Other: Paul Wayland Bartlett's *Bear Tamer* and *Indian Ghost Dancer.*" *American Art* 6, no. 3 (1992).

MARIA P. GINDHART

*See also* **Fine Arts; Painting.**

# SEATTLE

Despite its reputation in the late twentieth century as one of the nicest places in America to live, Seattle has experienced dramatic outbreaks of violence that reflect the unique character of the city. From the late nineteenth century until World War II, Seattle's position as a rapidly industrializing city in a region marked by a boom-and-bust economy created the context for crowd violence against racial minorities and political radicals. Since the 1960s, group violence shaped by politics and race has persisted, but violence has also become more diffused and atomized.

The most notorious example of mob violence in late-nineteenth-century Seattle was the expulsion of the city's immigrant Chinese population. Seattle's economic growth attracted diverse peoples. Many of Seattle's working class believed that Chinese laborers, who often worked at pay scales below those of whites, were an economic threat to white working people. Throughout 1885 Daniel Cronin, a California-based organizer associated with the Knights of Labor, the nation's largest union in the 1880s, encouraged anti-Chinese sentiment in Seattle's working-class neighborhoods. Cronin helped organize a grassroots movement that demanded the expulsion of all Chinese laborers. Seattle's commercial and political elite perceived anti-Chinese mob action as part of an attempt to foment anarchy and class war. They deputized themselves and formed a Home Guard that opposed the immediate expulsion but agreed in principle to Chinese removal. A meeting on 5 November 1885 between the leaders of the anti-Chinese group, Seattle's mayor, and several Chinese representatives resulted in the voluntary departure of 200 Chinese, leaving some 350 in the city.

Ironically, Seattle's period of anti-Chinese agitation gave rise to violence between competing white factions and relatively little between whites and Chinese. Within a few months of the deal brokered in the fall, working-class residents acted on their belief that the agreement had failed to remove enough of the city's Chinese laborers. On the morning of 7 February 1886 a mob rounded up the city's entire Chinese community and escorted it to the Ocean Dock at Seattle's waterfront, planning to send the group to San Francisco. After locking the Chinese in a warehouse, the anti-Chinese mob took up a collection in order to purchase steamer tickets for the captives; this delay gave the city elite time to call together the Home Guard. When the Home Guard attempted to march those Chinese who had not boarded the steamer back to their homes in the Chinese district, the two white groups exchanged gunfire, wounding four and killing one. The Home Guard, in concert with the territorial militia and aided by the imposition of martial law, helped to dismantle Seattle's organized anti-Chinese movement, but by late February 1886 virtually the entire Chinese population had left Seattle of their own volition.

Crowd and group violence continued to leave a mark on Seattle in the early twentieth century, although it often took place within a political, rather than racial or ethnic, context. One example of antiradical political violence occurred in the summer of 1913 during the city's annual potlatch. On 17 July several sailors who had heckled Annie Miller, a local pacifist and speaker, were chased out of downtown Seattle by a crowd of onlookers. Colonel Alden J. Blethen, the staunch antiradical publisher of the *Seattle Times*, published a fallacious account of the Miller fracas that accused members of the radical union the Industrial Workers of the World (IWW, or "Wobblies") of murdering one of the sailors. The following day, 18 July, a mob of military personnel and festival participants numbering several thousand destroyed an IWW hall, a radical newsstand, and several offices of socialist organizations. Most scholars agree with the historian Murray Morgan's assertion that apart from one broken Wobbly nose, IWW and socialist activists escaped physical harm.

Although Seattle-based radicals experienced violence in other parts of Washington State, antiradical crowd violence in the city ebbed in the 1920s. During the fall of 1916 Seattle Wobblies vigorously supported and intervened in a vicious timber industry strike in the nearby community of Everett. In October over two hundred local vigilantes—the majority of them businessmen—met forty-one Wobblies arriving by boat from Seattle and viciously beat them. On 5 November 1916 an armed group of Wobblies from Seattle attempting to dock at Everett exchanged gunfire with waiting vigilantes, resulting in twelve deaths. Given the association between antiradicalism and violence, it is somewhat surprising that Seattle's most infamous radical event, the general strike of 1919, was not marked by bloodshed. Despite the press and business community's claims that Bolshevik agents were attempting to produce anarchy, the five-day walkout by sixty thousand Seattle workers was peaceful.

Violence in Seattle following World War II mirrored national patterns. Like the rest of the nation, Seattle witnessed violence associated with the Civil Rights, Black Power, and antiwar movements. In the summer of 1968 conflict between the Seattle police and the African American community, including the Seattle Black Panther Party, resulted in the Central Area riots. Snipers shot at police officers and civilians, but no deaths resulted. In October of that year, one Panther threatened several police officers, and another Panther activist was killed during his arrest. In January 1969 an unknown assailant gunned down Edwin Pratt, a leader of Seattle's Urban League and an outspoken civil rights activist.

Violence associated with campus radicalism also impacted Seattle. In February 1970 student radicals who were aligned with the Seattle Liberation Front sparked a riot at the federal courthouse in downtown Seattle. Several leftist activists were charged with planting bombs on the University of Washington campus in the spring of 1970, although some claim that undercover Seattle police agents planted the devices in order to frame the radicals.

Outside of political or racial contexts, Seattle has also experienced pathological, individual violence. In the mid-1970s serial killer Theodore "Ted" Bundy murdered nine women in the Pacific Northwest, including three women from Seattle. As the city shifts into the service economy of the information age, its patterns of violence may change.

*BIBLIOGRAPHY*

Berner, Richard C. *Seattle in the Twentieth Century.* Volume 1, *1900–1920.* Seattle: Charles Press, 1991.

Crowley, Walt. *Rites of Passage: A Memoir of the Sixties in Seattle.* Seattle: University of Washington Press, 1995.

Michaud, Stephen G., and Hugh Aynesworth. *The Only Living Witness.* [A profile of Ted Bundy.] New York: Simon and Schuster, 1983.

Morgan, Murray. *Skid Road: An Informal Portrait of Seattle.* Rev. ed. New York: Viking, 1960.

Sale, Roger. *Seattle, Past to Present.* Seattle: University of Washington Press, 1976.

Taylor, Quintard. *The Forging of a Black Community: A History of Seattle's Central District, 1870–1970.* Seattle: University of Washington Press, 1994.

MICHAEL JONATHAN PEBWORTH

*See also* **Chinese Americans; Urban Violence; Wobblies (Industrial Workers of the World).**

# SECOND AMENDMENT. *See* Right to Bear Arms.

# SELF-DEFENSE AND SECURITY

Biblical texts have variously urged "an eye for eye, a tooth for a tooth" and "turn the other cheek." The law regarding self-defense and the history of the concept of self-defense vacillate between, reflect, and are informed by these conflicting principles without ever completely embodying either. Self-defense is neither vengeance nor pacifism; it is an amalgamation of conflicting rationales and contradictory principles and is a product of a melting pot of historical and societal influences.

There is widespread agreement that self-defense is a fundamental, inalienable, moral, and legal right. Self-defense is recognized in all fifty states and nearly all jurisdictions worldwide. Indeed, it is difficult to imagine a legal system, political authority, or moral paradigm barring the right of self-defense to a person facing a murderous assault. The English philosopher Thomas Hobbes's rationale for the defense of duress provides a cogent explanation for the illogic of denying legitimate claims of self-defense:

> If a man by the terrour of present death, be compelled to doe a fact against the Law, he is totally Excused; because no Law can oblige a man to abandon his own preservation. And supposing such a Law were obligatory; yet a man would reason thus, *If I doe it not, I die presently; if I doe it, I die afterwards; therefore by doing it, there is time of life gained.* (*Leviathan* 1651, chapter 27)

In other words, where a man is facing a Hobson's choice of certain present death at the hands of a villainous assailant or possible subsequent death from the state's executioner, it would be futile to criminalize self-defense because of the will to live that is inculcated in human nature. Though perhaps self-evident, and a necessary adjunct to such other self-evident truths as the right to life and liberty extolled in the Declaration of Independence, the right to self-defense is curiously not a constitutional right.

Despite the fact that self-defense was recognized as far back as Roman law and is nearly universally accepted in modern times, there is substantial disagreement among scholars and variance among jurisdictions as to the necessary (that is, indispensable or required) conditions for self-defense. However, the following jointly sufficient (adequate) conditions for a successful claim of self-defense are uncontroversial: (1) a blameworthy or non-innocent (2) initial aggressor (3) wrongfully, and without provocation, attacks (4) an innocent victim (5) who uses minimally necessary (6) proportional (7) nonlethal force (8) which force does not include either an illegal weapon or the illegal use of a legal weapon (9) against the aggressor's present or imminent attack (10) from which there is no retreat (11) with the intention, purpose, or motive of defending himself or herself (12) and which does not endanger any innocent bystanders. Not a single one of these collectively sufficient elements is a necessary condition in all formulations of self-defense. Even if all of these conditions are satisfied, there is some disagreement as to whether self-defense is right, proper, and good or merely permissible, tolerable, and not wrongful.

The debate over which conditions are necessary arises from the delicate balancing of the aggressor's and the defender's interests. The disagreement is testament to the quandary self-defense represents to those who hold onto the belief in the sanctity of life and the suppression of violence: the goal is to craft a formulation of self-defense that maximally protects the autonomy of innocent victims while not authorizing such excessive violence as to turn the aggressor into another victim. This delicate balance has been shaped by history and buffeted by the changing tides of racial, gender-based, cultural, and societal attitudes toward violence and crime.

## History

The origin of self-defense in Anglo America is believed to stem from the cross-fertilization by the Normans, subsequent to their conquest of England in 1066, of the Anglo-Saxon conception of the sanctity of life with more nuanced European ideas.

Previously, any killing was culpable regardless of the circumstances or whether it was by accident or without malice. Once the accused was found liable, regardless of blameworthiness, the remedy was either monetary compensation to, or personal vengeance wrought by, the victim's family. Over time, the personal-injury nature of a homicide became a public crime against the king, a breach of the king's peace. Private vengeance and reparations gave way to public punishment and forfeiture of the accused's land and possessions to the crown.

Gradually, English jurists began to wrestle with the issue of the relevance of the circumstances of a killing. The promulgation of the Statute of Gloucester in 1278 allowed defendants who killed by accident or in self-defense to apply to the king for a pardon. By the beginning of the fourteenth century, justifiable homicide preserving the king's peace—the execution of a felon sentenced to death or one resisting capture—was distinguished from excusable homicide or *se defendendo* (in self-defense). In 1532 the Parliament of Henry VIII enacted a statute that eliminated the forfeiture of property as a form of punishment. In 1769 William Blackstone, the great English legal scholar, explained that justifiable homicide could only be killings required by law that promoted the social good. Personal killings, for example, in self-defense, could qualify only as excusable homicide because they could not be absolutely free from guilt. Interestingly, the killing of a murderer in defense of another person was therefore justifiable, but the killing of the same murderer in self-defense was tainted with some guilt. In excusable homicide, the accused had to retreat to the "wall" before killing (except if he was in his home), but in justifiable homicide, the accused need not retreat and could even pursue the felon.

Blackstone's interpretation was imported into the New World and became quite influential; indeed, it was often the only source of law. As the frontier expanded westward, however, sentiment grew that retreat before using force in the face of a wrongful assault was cowardly and unmanly, and gradually the retreat requirement dissolved in western areas. (Cynthia Gillespie, an advocate for battered women, contends that this male perspective infuses modern self-defense law to the detriment of women.) Even in the late twentieth century, while eastern states generally retained some form of retreat requirement, most western states did not. Gradually, self-defense became justified,

even though it did not further the public good in Blackstone's sense.

The criminal-law scholar George Fletcher has termed Blackstone's view the social theory of self-defense in which the rights of the victim are tempered by acknowledging the rights and humanity of the aggressor; self-defense is only legitimate when it promotes social welfare. In contrast, the individualist theory of self-defense posits that the right to resist aggression and violations of one's autonomy is absolute and little concern need be given to the aggressor's interests. The individualist theory finds its champions in the philosophers John Locke and Immanuel Kant. Locke claimed that yielding to aggression would enslave the victim; Kant argued that an unfettered right to self-defense was the cornerstone of a legitimate legal system. Fletcher notes that the social theory's heyday was in the 1950s and 1960s and that the individualist theory was ascendant at the end of the twentieth century.

## Modern Law

As to which of the jointly sufficient conditions for self-defense listed above are necessary varies among different legal theories and formulations. For example, the leading formulation of self-defense in the United States is contained in the Model Penal Code (MPC), which has influenced the criminal codes of more than thirty-five states. Section 3.041 of the MPC is, in part, as follows:

> The use of force upon or toward another person is justifiable when the actor believes that such force is immediately necessary for the purpose of protecting himself against the use of unlawful force by such other person on the present occasion.

The MPC's definition of self-defense departs from the jointly sufficient conditions listed above in a number of ways. First, a blameworthy aggressor is not required. Self-defense may be used against an assailant who is not responsible because of youth, insanity, or duress, among other things. Second, neither a wrongful attack nor an actual attack is required. If the defender reasonably but mistakenly believes that he or she is being attacked, defensive force may be justified. Third, the aggressor's attack need not be present or imminent. The MPC broadens the time frame under which self-defense may be used to when defensive force is "immediately necessary" even if the aggressor's attack is not imminent.

Section 3.04 (2)(b) also departs from the list of sufficient conditions by not requiring retreat and allowing lethal force. A defender need not retreat before using nonlethal force. Lethal force may only be used against lethal force or to protect against serious bodily injury, kidnapping, or rape. But deadly force generally may not be used when the defender can retreat with complete safety, except when he or she is at home or in a place of business.

**Deterrence of Violence**

Does the right to self-defense deter violence? Or does the use of self-defense, which is a form of violence, increase the amount of violence? These questions parallel the issue of gun control. Some criminologists cite the correlation between high levels of gun ownership and criminal violence in the United States (which has some of the highest rates of both among western industrialized nations) to assert a cause-and-effect relationship. Others argue that criminals will always obtain guns and that putting more guns in the hands of law-abiding citizens will decrease violence and crime through the ability of these citizens to protect themselves and prevent crime. Florida, the nation's leading state in licensing the carrying of concealed handguns to citizens with no felony convictions, enacted a statute licensing concealed weapons in 1987. In that year Florida's homicide rate was 11.4 per 100,000 people; in 1993 the rate had declined to 8.9 homicides per 100,000 (the national homicide rate over the same period increased from 8.3 to 9.5 per 100,000).

The legal scholar Garrett Epps maintains that a substantial restriction in the right of self-defense would deter violence. Echoing Blackstone, Epps asserts that most claims of self-defense involve culpable conduct. The distinction between a wrongful aggressor and a rightful defender is often illusory.

Women threatened with rape or spousal abuse face an especially difficult choice as to whether or not the use of self-defense will deter or prevent the attacks. Statistics show that women who resist with self-defense are less likely to be victimized. However, those who use defensive force are more likely to sustain serious injuries. Fifty-eight percent of those women who resist rape will be injured compared with 46 percent among those who do not resist. In these contexts, self-defense may be both an effective deterrent and a dangerous inducement to serious harm.

In two unique arenas where violence is endemic, the use of self-defense is viewed as pro-

moting further violence. Prisons typically bar fighting and can punish infractions with increased sentences. In two separate cases, a prisoner who was punished for fighting claimed self-defense, which the prison authority acknowledged. Federal appellate courts upheld the prison's right to deter violence by barring all fighting—including self-defense, which had never been held to be a constitutional right—and the prisoner's claim of a constitutional right to self-defense was denied. In sports, the other arena, steps also have been taken to deter violence. For example, the National Hockey League, in an effort to deter fighting during games, penalizes equally the initial aggressor and the victim of the assault who acts in self-defense.

*Bernhard H. Goetz.* In an incident harking back to the 1974 film *Death Wish* (in which Charles Bronson's character, after his wife is murdered and his daughter raped, rides the New York City subway enticing criminals to prey upon him so that he might kill them), Bernhard Goetz in 1984 shot and wounded four black youths who asked him, in an arguably menacing fashion, for five dollars on a New York City subway. Public support for Goetz's action was overwhelming in New York City, even among blacks, and a nationwide poll revealed that 78 percent of U.S. citizens would have acted the same way Goetz did. Clearly, many people, including the jury that acquitted him of attempted murder and found him guilty only of illegal gun possession, cared little that Goetz's shooting may not have satisfied many of the necessary conditions of self-defense in New York State: using the minimally necessary force, using proportional force, perceiving an imminent threat, and failing to retreat, among others.

Though there were anecdotal reports that subway crime immediately after the shooting decreased, crime rates were soon back to their previous levels. Speculation that the anointing of Goetz as a folk hero, "the subway vigilante," would ignite copycat "crimes of self-defense" proved false. A seeming anomaly in the Goetz jury findings, also reflected in opinion polls, demonstrates the ambivalence and conflict in self-defense as a form of security. Though initially puzzled by why "you can't have it, but you can use it," the jury found legal Goetz's use but not his possession of a handgun. Opinion polls also reveal this sentiment: U.S. citizens want an expansive right to self-defense but at the same time oppose the easy access to handguns that might facilitate self-defense as an effective deterrent to violent crime.

*Weapons.* In addition to handguns and community crime-prevention organizations (which in the late twentieth century criminologists placed in the vanguard of crime prevention), U.S. citizens have sought other means to protect themselves from violent crime. To defend both lives and property, home owners sometimes install spring guns or trap guns, mechanical devices set up to go off automatically when an intruder enters. Though effective in their capacity to kill or injure seriously, their use is problematic in that they can also harm those lawfully or innocently entering a building. Although their use is legal under some circumstances, the installer of such a device is placed in legal jeopardy: if the intrusion is such that were the home owner present he or she would not have been justified in inflicting the same harm personally, then he or she is liable.

Other weapons that have been held illegal, at least under some circumstances, include switchblades; stun, shock, or laser guns; box cutters or utility knives used by minors in New York City; and realistic-looking toy guns in Los Angeles. Among the most popular weapons marketed to women for self-defense are personal chemical weapons, including tear-gas aerosols, tear-gas pens, pepper sprays, and mace. Some of these devices contain an ultraviolet dye, which, when staining the clothes or body of the assailant, will aid police apprehension. Though some form of these chemical weapons is legal in the majority of states, they are subject to even greater regulation than firearms for a variety of political, historical, and constitutional reasons. As chemical weapons are of more recent origin than firearms, arguably the Second Amendment may protect the right to possess a firearm but not a chemical weapon. To the extent that any group has lobbied for the legality of the use of personal chemical weapons, no group as of the late twentieth century has been as influential as the National Rifle Association has been with handguns. Among the states still prohibiting their use in the late twentieth century were New York, Kansas, Virginia, Massachusetts, and Wisconsin.

To avoid the dangers and potential legal liability associated with using handguns and other weapons, an increasing number of people have turned to the "weaponry" of their bodies, that is, the martial arts. However, the use of martial arts is not altogether free of criminal responsibility. Justifiable self-defense requires proportional, and the minimally necessary amount of, force. A martial arts expert faced with an assault from an unskilled assailant might be tempted to use excessive, and thus unjustified, force in self-defense.

Does self-defense deter violence, or does it beget more violence? The question is as old as the hills and reflects the tension between the competing views of the Old and New Testaments. Each generation must devise its own answer and find the appropriate balance in forging its rules of self-defense.

*BIBLIOGRAPHY*

American Law Institute. *Model Penal Code and Commentaries: Official Draft and Revised Comments.* Philadelphia: The American Law Institute, 1985.

Brown, Richard Maxwell. *No Duty to Retreat: Violence and Values in American History and Society.* New York: Oxford University Press, 1991.

Dressler, Joshua. *Understanding Criminal Law.* 2d ed. New York: Matthew Bender/Irwin, 1995.

Epps, Garrett. "Any Which Way but Loose: Interpretive Strategies and Attitudes Toward Violence in the Evolution of the Anglo-American 'Retreat Rule.'" *Law and Contemporary Problems* 55 (winter 1992).

Fletcher, George P. *A Crime of Self-Defense: Bernhard Goetz and the Law on Trial.* New York: Free Press, 1988.

Gillespie, Cynthia K. *Justifiable Homicide: Battered Women, Self-Defense, and the Law.* Columbus: Ohio State University Press, 1989.

Jacobs, James B. "The Regulation of Personal Chemical Weapons: Some Anomalies in American Weapons Law." *University of Dayton Law Review* 15 (1989).

Meyerhofer, William. "Statutory Restrictions on Weapons Possession: Must the Right to Self-Defense Fall Victim?" *Annual Survey of American Law* (1996).

RUSSELL L. CHRISTOPHER

*See also* **Goetz, Bernhard H.; Martial Arts; No Duty to Retreat; Weapons; Women.**

# SELF-DESTRUCTIVENESS

The majority of behaviors classified as self-destructive, self-injurious, and self-mutilative, such as anorexia and bulimia, tobacco dependence, chronic alcoholism, tattooing, and body cutting and piercing, are often not perceived as life threatening by those who engage in them, in part because these behaviors frequently begin in adolescence or young adulthood, when individuals often feel invincible, immortal, healthy, and resilient.

People who display such behavior often claim that it is "within my control," that "I can give it up whenever I want," or that "it is just a passing phase in my life." The slippery slope from experimentation to chemical dependence can be gradual, as with alcohol, or swift, as with tobacco, cocaine, or heroin.

These behaviors are willful or deliberate. A major issue in the study of self-destructive behaviors relates to defining and measuring intent or motivation for the behavior, especially in individuals under the influence of alcohol or other drugs that can alter mood, reasoning, orientation, reality testing, and coordination. Intent is also difficult to assess when individuals are unable to organize and communicate their desires and wishes in a clear, logical, and goal-directed manner, as is the case with people suffering from a major depressive disorder, personality disorder, or psychosis. Such distortions of logic and reality testing are associated with anorexia nervosa, psychotic depression, and borderline personality disorder.

Part of the difficulty in clinically assessing, understanding, and treating self-destructive behaviors relates to establishing objective and clinically applicable criteria and reliably labeling these behaviors as self-directed and self-destructive. Not everyone who engages in these behaviors considers them self-destructive. For example, people who cut, scratch, and burn their bodies often say such behavior relieves tension and is even therapeutic in that it lessens internal psychological pain and allows them to gain control and mastery over their bodies and immediate environments. Those who engage in suicidal acts, such as overdoses or wrist cutting, might say that these actions are reactive (to punish others), attention getting, or cries for help. Such individuals, although acknowledging the potential for self-destruction, do not label these behaviors as such because they are not perceived as life threatening. The intent is not to destroy oneself but to draw attention to oneself—a self in psychological pain due to the frustrations of not having one's psychological needs met.

From a public health perspective, these behaviors are self-destructive because they are associated with an increased morbidity and mortality. In addition, these behaviors affect the quality of life within a family unit or community. Their associated economic costs can be enormous, as measured by such indexes as years of potential life lost, absenteeism from work, decreased productivity, in-

creased utilization of health-care services and resources, and increased injury potential on the job.

Patrick O'Carroll et al. (1996) have attempted to develop a nomenclature for commonly used and often confused terminology, such as *suicide attempt* and *self-destructive behaviors*, that can be applied and attached to behaviors commonly seen in clinical settings. The difficulty has been in reliably classifying a range of behaviors for which the health consequences—in both the short and the long term—are potentially negative. Suicide attempts and other self-destructive behaviors can result in disability, dysfunction, pain, and suffering that are not planned or predicted. From an epidemiological as well as a clinical perspective, there is a great need to develop a nomenclature as a first step toward a classification scheme for all self-destructive behaviors.

In the 1990s there was an explosion of research exploring the biological foundations for violence and other forms of self-destructive behavior. Moving beyond the contributory roles of childhood trauma, post-traumatic stress responses, and unresolved psychological conflicts to the development and expression of violent behaviors, these studies have identified abnormalities in biological functioning that are quantifiable and reproducible in animal models, such as abnormalities in the endocrine system, structural lesions in the brain, and changes in central nervous system amine metabolism (particularly neurotransmitters, such as serotonin). Additional research has established genetic predispositions for some of these behaviors. For example, impulsivity, aggressiveness, and mood disorders tend to be genetically transmitted in families.

Some have understood self-destructiveness as violence turned inward. Just as outwardly directed violence occurs for multiple reasons, self-destructive behaviors are multidetermined and multifactorial.

*BIBLIOGRAPHY*

Mann, John J. "The Neurobiology of Suicide." *Nature Medicine* 4 (1998): 25–30.

Mann, John J., et al. "Neurobiological Insights into the Pathogens of Self-Mutilation and Suicidal Behavior." In *Suicide: Biopsychosocial Approaches*, edited by Alexander J. Botsis, Constantin R. Soldatos, and Costas N. Stefanis. Amsterdam: Elsevier, 1997.

O'Carroll, Patrick W., Alan L. Berman, Ronald W. Maris, Eve K. Moscicki, Bryan L. Tanney, and Morton M. Silverman. "Beyond the Tower of Babel: A Nomenclature for Suicidology." *Suicide and Life-Threatening Behavior* 26, no. 3 (1996): 237–252.

Stoff, D. M., and John J. Mann, eds. "The Neurobiology of Suicide: From the Bench to the Clinic." *Annals of the New York Academy of Sciences* 836 (1997).

MORTON M. SILVERMAN

*See also* **Alcohol and Alcoholism; Anorexia and Bulimia; Assisted Suicide; Drugs: Drugs and Violence; Mutilation of the Body; Sadism and Masochism; Suicide.**

# SENTENCING

Sentencing is the imposition of a criminal sanction or punishment on an individual who has been found guilty of a crime. Judges typically hand down sentences, but in some instances, as in the case of capital punishment, it is the jury that does so. The sentencing of an offender is a key step in the criminal justice process. The type of punishment has an impact not only on the future of the individual but on that of society. It may determine whether the individual offends again or lives crime free.

## History

Sentences have not always involved imprisonment. Often, the body of the offender bore the punishment. For example, in ancient Athens a sentenced offender could be stoned to death, thrown from a cliff, bound to a stake and left to a slow death, or shunned. This last form of punishment forbade any communication with the offender, effectively banishing that person from the community. Sentences in Babylon were much less complicated: the typical criminal sanction was to force the offender into slavery. Often individuals were subject to branding and flogging.

In ancient Rome, a criminal could be sentenced to death only if caught in the act. Otherwise, most convicted offenders were fined or given another form of economic sanction. Fines were also used in the early Middle Ages. To maintain public order, a manslayer was required to pay a *wergild*, or "man-price." There were fines for disturbing the peace and fines paid as compensation to the victims or their family. The goal was to preserve public order by preventing blood feuds between warring parties.

European expansion increased toward the end of the seventeenth century, and in England criminals were often sentenced to work in the colonies. Torture and execution, the preferred methods of dealing with offenders, were limited in favor of forced exile. The free labor source afforded by this punishment enabled ship captains to man their vessels with galley slaves and offered plentiful labor for the colonies. The new policy encouraged widespread deportation, often for offenses as simple as vagrancy.

With the increasing use of machinery and the rising population, the call for convict labor declined in the new American nation. At the same time, the separation between the wealthy and poor in England grew sharper; living conditions worsened for the poor, and crime increased, as did the call for harsher punishments. Hanging sentences became common, and toward the end of the eighteenth century in England more than 350 types of crime involved a sentence of death. As the death penalty flourished, there arose a countervailing movement to humanize the process of criminal punishment. Cesare Beccaria's *Dei delitti e delle pene* (On crime and punishment, 1764) and the influence of the Pennsylvania Quakers are two of the best-known factors in this movement. Legal philosophers in this period felt that the interests of the state and society could be better served by housing offenders in reformatories or penitentiaries. In the United States, imprisonment has remained the primary method of punishment since the development of the first jail in the Virginia colonies in the late eighteenth century and the birth of the prison system in Pennsylvania.

## Sentencing Goals

When an offender is placed behind bars, fined, or subjected to an alternative form of punishment, the sentence is meant to fulfill certain goals, either singly or in combination. The six traditional goals of criminal punishment are specific deterrence, general deterrence, retribution, restitution, rehabilitation, and incapacitation.

*Deterrence,* which aims to discourage the offender from committing further crimes, can be viewed from a specific or general perspective. Specific deterrence relies on the effect the punishment will have on the criminal: if the punishment outweighs the criminal gain, there is less likelihood of repetition. For example, an individual who receives a simple warning for drunk driving is more likely to repeat the offense than one who is forced to spend the night in jail. General deterrence is much broader in scope and aims to influence societal attitudes toward the commission of crime. By using the offender as an example, general deterrence affects the future behavior of those who have not yet been arrested.

*Retribution*, based on the notion of just deserts, involves the use of punishment to restore equity to society. Since the offender is thought to have benefited from crime, punishment must erase that advantage. For example, an individual may profit by stealing money from his place of business, but that benefit is counteracted by the period of incarceration.

*Restitution* seeks mainly financial redress. Offenders are often required to pay the victim for tangible losses. For example, vandals are assessed for the cost of damage or clean-up or both. In cases involving drug trafficking, where there is no identifiable victim, offenders are often required to perform community service to reimburse the state for the cost of the criminal proceedings.

*Rehabilitation* involves the notion that society has failed the offender, who is thus likely to commit more crimes if put back into the same environment. Rehabilitation may take place behind bars or under community supervision. The offender is usually put through a series of programs designed to restore confidence, personal responsibility, and compliance with social norms.

*Incapacitation* is enforced when judges feel that a convicted offender poses a significant risk to society. Confinement to a correctional facility affords offenders little or no opportunity to commit new crimes. They are thus penalized not only for the crimes they have committed but also for those they might commit if free. Although it is difficult to predict future behavior, frequent offenders are often targeted for long sentences on the assumption that the more an individual has offended, the more likely he or she is to offend again in the future. This practice is known as selective incapacitation.

### Sentencing Systems

When sentencing an offender, judges rely on a sentencing strategy or combination of strategies. An *indeterminate* sentence involves the imposition of a sanction that could, in its literal form, involve a term of one day to life behind bars. Often judicial personnel are guided by state legislation that sets the maximum or minimum sentencing boundaries for a given offense. As there is no set time for release, the offender may earn parole before the sentence is completed by demonstrating good be-

havior or other signs of rehabilitation. Though popular, the indeterminate sentencing model came under fire in the late 1990s for its inequities. A defendant tried before a "tough" judge may spend more time behind bars than a similar defendant tried by a judge who favors alternative sentencing. Also, the use of indeterminate sentences has contributed to the public impression that offenders get off too easily. A sentence of five to ten years may find the inmate being released after only a few months once credits for time served and good behavior are taken into account.

The use of *mandatory* sentences, also known as mandatory minimums, increased in the 1990s. Mandatory sentencing allows for little judicial discretion; rather, the length of the sentence is usually predetermined by the state legislature, based on the severity of the crime. The turn to this type of sentencing has been inspired primarily by increasing crime rates, especially for violent crime, and by the public's belief that the criminal justice system is little more than a revolving door. Mandatory sentences are not without their critics. Charges of racism were voiced in the mid-1990s when an examination of drug sentences revealed that possession of powdered cocaine carried a lighter sentence than possession of the equivalent amount of crack cocaine, which is essentially the same drug. Those who defended the difference in sentencing did so on the basis of crack's social impact, arguing that, as much more violent crime is associated with crack, a harsher penalty is warranted. However, the majority of people arrested and prosecuted for crack cocaine, which is much cheaper than other forms, are inner-city minorities. Critics have called the sentencing discrepancy patently racist, as it effectively punishes minorities more harshly because they could not afford powdered cocaine. The Supreme Court, however, has declined to endorse that argument.

Another criticism of mandatory sentences is that they do not guarantee the offender will serve the prescribed time. *Plea bargaining* is the process by which a defendant cooperates with the prosecution for a reduction in the charge. Such bargains sometimes lead to dismissal of charges. A high-ranking member of a drug ring who offers information on others in the organization may spend less time in prison than a low-level courier, who might receive ten to twenty-five years simply for possessing a certain amount of drugs.

Mandatory sentences, though originally designed to deter the violent crime associated with the drug culture, have mainly affected the low-level drug dealer. To deal more effectively with the violent repeat offender, a newer sentencing strategy was developed. The policy known as "three strikes," developed first in California after the 1993 abduction and murder of Polly Klass by a career criminal who had been in and out of jail for most of his life, requires a harsher sentence for a second violent offense and life without parole for a third. Though the policy was designed to remove the violent offender from society, it has often caught the petty criminal in its wake, potentially meting out life sentences to repeat shoplifters. Additionally, the three-strikes policy is expensive to implement fully. A RAND Corporation study found that in California the costs would run between $4.5 billion and $6.5 billion every year.

In response to the large number of minor drug offenders moving through the justice system, some jurisdictions have advocated the use of *split sentences*. These sentences usually entail a period of incarceration followed by probation. Although minor offenders do not spend a great deal of time in jail, they know that further offenses will result in longer periods of incarceration.

## Alternatives to Prison

The use of incarceration as the primary form of punishment in the United States has created an ever-increasing financial burden for many states. A rising prison population has prompted calls for alternative forms of punishment, the most prevalent of which—applying to just over three million people at the turn of the century—is probation. Offenders sentenced to probation do not serve any time in prison but are subject to a number of conditions set forth by the court. Usually the conditions involve finding employment, abstaining from the use of drugs and alcohol, and reporting regularly to a probation officer. Failure to comply with any of the conditions of the sentence would, in theory, result in incarceration.

From the mid-1980s there has been increasing public skepticism about probation and rehabilitation as press reports feature more and more parolees violating some condition of the probation contract. Public support for probation has thus eroded, and many have called for its abolition.

Along with probation have come a number of *intermediate* sentences. These sanctions fall somewhere between incarceration and probation. Included in this category are intensive supervision probation (ISP), boot camps, and electronic moni-

toring. Aside from boot camps, all these programs have the offender living in the community.

*Intensive supervision probation* is probably the most widely used of these sanctions. As the name implies, ISP is highly restrictive program. Offenders are subject to multiple weekly meetings with probation officers, unscheduled drug tests, and strict curfews.

*Electronic monitoring* is not really a punishment in itself but is used in conjunction with other programs. As a condition of their probation contract, offenders sentenced to house arrest or ISP wear a bracelet that allows a probation officer to track their movement simply by telephoning the house; electronic signals from the bracelet confirm that the offender is home.

*Boot camp*, also known as shock incarceration, is used primarily for young first-time offenders. In a military-style setting, offenders are roused early in the morning, then marched to a silent breakfast. Their day consists of drills and six to eight hours of manual labor. Evening includes more drills and exercise followed by five or six hours of educational or treatment programs before lights-out. The offender's stay in boot camp is usually 90 to 180 days. Upon successful completion, offenders are typically moved into some type of community supervision. "Failures" are often moved into the general prison population.

Indeterminate sentencing has gained popularity. As prison populations continue to rise, it seems clear that modifications must be made to our current method of sentencing. Options such as intensive probation, day reporting centers, electronic monitoring, and diversion are not without their problems, but they seem a necessary step as we approach the reality of housing nearly two million of our citizens behind bars.

*BIBLIOGRAPHY*

Anderson, David C. *Sensible Justice: Alternatives to Prison.* New York: New Press, 1998.

Byrne, James M., et al., eds. *Smart Sentencing: The Emergence of Intermediate Sanctions.* Newbury Park, Calif.: Sage, 1992.

Donziger, Steven R., ed. *The Real War on Crime: The Report of the National Criminal Justice Commission.* New York: Harper Perennial, 1996.

Maguire, Kathleen, and Ann L. Pastore, eds. *Sourcebook of Criminal Justice Statistics, 1996.* U.S. Department of Justice, Bureau of Justice Statistics. Washington, D.C.: U.S. Government Printing Office, 1997.

Morris, Norval, and David J. Rothman, eds. *The Oxford History of the Prison: The Practice of Punishment in Western Society.* New York: Oxford University Press, 1995.

Newman, Graeme. *The Punishment Response.* New York: Harrow and Heston, 1985.

Reid, Sue T. *Criminal Justice.* 4th ed. Madison, Wisc.: Brown and Benchmark, 1996.

Senna, Joseph J., and Larry J. Siegel. *Introduction to Criminal Justice.* Minneapolis: West, 1996.

LARRY SIEGEL
ERIK DIETZ

*See also* **Capital Punishment; Criminal Justice System; Prisons and Prisoners.**

# SERIAL KILLERS

The term *serial killer* was coined in the early 1970s by a special agent of the Federal Bureau of Investigation, Robert K. Ressler, one of the pioneering members of the FBI's Behavioral Science Unit. The phenomenon itself, however, is undoubtedly as old as human history—and possibly even older. Research into primate behavior clearly indicates that random "stranger murder," sadistic cruelty, cannibalism, vampirism, and other atrocities associated with serial killing are a standard feature of chimpanzee behavior—a finding that suggests that a bent for savagery is part of our prehuman heritage (Wrangham and Peterson 1996).

## In European History and Legend

Sadistic sex-killers appear in the annals of crime from ancient times onward. Historical surveys of the subject, like Robert E. L. Masters and Eduard Lea's *Sex Crimes in History,* generally commence with the outrages of Caligula, Justinian, and other Roman monsters. During the Middle Ages and the Renaissance, this tradition of aristocratic depravity was perpetuated by the likes of Erzsebet Báthory—the infamous Transylvanian countess whose beauty regimen required a daily bath in the blood of a freshly slaughtered virgin—and Gilles de Rais, who, following a heroic career as Joan of Arc's comrade-in-arms, returned to his ancestral castle in Brittany where, during a nine-year reign of terror, he freely indulged his tastes for child-murder, torture, and necrophiliac sex.

Whereas the atrocities of these highborn psychopaths were extensively (if not always reliably) documented, there are few extant records of sex-killers among the peasantry, though their existence can be readily inferred from a study of folklore and legend. The collections of Jacob and Wilhelm Grimm are full of cautionary tales about unwary girls who fall prey to homicidal maniacs. (In "The Robber Bridegroom," for example, the heroine sneaks into her betrothed's hideaway, where she watches in horror as he and his crew of robbers bring home another young woman and—after plying her with wine—kill her, butcher the body, and preserve the dismembered pieces for future consumption.) Certain scholars have also theorized that European werewolf legends are rooted in the atrocities of real-life monsters like Peter Stubbe (d. 1573) and Gilles Garnier (d. 1589), two extraordinarily vicious killers with a shared taste for mutilation-murder and cannibalism. The sensational crimes recounted in the popular genre of "murder ballads" also make it clear that the phenomenon we now call serial killing existed in premodern times.

The prototype of the modern serial murderer was "Jack the Ripper," the anonymous sex-slayer whose butchery of five London streetwalkers in the fall of 1888 sent shock waves throughout England and indeed much of the world. In Victorian times the press relied on terms like "human monster," "murder-demon," and "blood-fiend" to describe the Ripper. In Germany such killers became known as *Lustmörderen* (lust-murderers), and their deeply aberrant psychology was documented for the first time in Richard von Krafft-Ebing's pioneering study of sexual deviation, *Psychopathia Sexualis* (1886). The Weimar era produced several notorious examples of such psychopaths, including Peter Kürten, the "Monster of Düsseldorf"—whose year-long reign of terror (part of a forty-year career of violence and blood lust) inspired Fritz Lang's classic crime movie, *M*—and Fritz Haarmann, the "Vampire of Hanover," who confessed to the slaughter of nearly fifty adolescent boys, whose bodies he butchered and peddled as black-market beef.

## In U.S. History

Though lust-murderers have probably always existed in the United States, there are no documented examples prior to the late nineteenth century, when the country was riveted by stories of the Boston "boy-fiend," Jesse Pomeroy, a juvenile sadist who tortured a string of young children and was convicted of the savage murder of a ten-year-old girl and a four-year-old boy. (Pomeroy's death sentence in 1875 was commuted to life in prison, and he spent the next forty-one years in solitary confinement—the longest such term in U.S. penal history.) An even more sensational case was that of Herman Mudgett, alias Dr. H. H. Holmes, the

133

Gilded Age "multi-murderer" whose three-story "Horror Castle" in suburban Chicago became the site of countless atrocities. (In his best-selling novel *The Alienist* [1994], Caleb Carr skillfully captures the public hysteria generated by the Holmes case.)

That nineteenth-century Americans were familiar with the kind of criminals we now call serial killers is confirmed in Herman Melville's tale of a shipboard killing, *Billy Budd*. Contemplating the nature of John Claggart, the malevolent master-at-arms, Melville writes:

> Though the man's even temper and discreet bearing would seem to intimate a mind peculiarly subject to the law of reason, not the less in heart he would seem to riot in complete exemption from that law, having apparently little to do with reason further than to employ it as an ambidexter implement for effecting the irrational. That is to say: Toward the accomplishment of an aim which in wantonness of atrocity would seem to partake of the insane, he will direct a cool judgment sagacious and sound. These men are madmen, and of the most dangerous sort, for their lunacy is not continuous, but occasional, evoked by some special object. (Phoenix edition, p. 76)

As Melville clearly understood, creatures like Claggart are not, by and large, psychotically deranged (that is, subject to visual and aural hallucinations). Rather, they are *psychopaths*—cunning, often highly intelligent, individuals possessed of monstrously sadistic appetites and absolutely devoid of conscience or remorse. The coolly deliberate way in which they plan and execute their crimes—as well as the utter banality of their lives when they are not in the grip of their hideous passions—makes them exceptionally hard to detect. (It also makes it nearly impossible—when they are finally caught and tried—to persuade a jury that they are legally insane.)

The history of serial murder in twentieth-century America begins in 1918, with the still-unsolved case of the "Axe-Man of New Orleans," a homicidal night prowler who terrorized the city for two-and-half years. The Axe-Man murdered seven people and savagely wounded another eight, breaking into their homes at night and attacking them in bed.

The Roaring Twenties produced a notable pair of American sociopaths. During an eighteen-month spree that began in February 1926, a nomadic sex-killer named Earle Leonard Nelson (whose build and features earned him the nickname the "Gorilla Murderer") roamed from coast to coast, strangling nearly two dozen boarding-house landladies and violating them by using their corpses for sex. His contemporary, Carl Panzram—arguably the most incorrigible criminal in U.S. history—proudly confessed to twenty-one murders, countless felonies, and more than one thousand acts of sodomy. Panzram's lifelong defiance of authority has made him something of a folk hero to certain self-styled rebels, who particularly prize the written remarks he once addressed to a pious representative of the Society for the Abolishment of Capital Punishment: "I have no desire whatever to reform myself. My only desire is to reform people who try to reform me, and I believe the only way to reform people is to kill 'em. My motto is: 'Rob 'em all, rape 'em all, and kill 'em all.'"

One of the most terrifying of all twentieth-century serial killers, in the United States or elsewhere, was Albert Fish, a sexagenarian with the demeanor of a kindly grandfather and the sexual proclivities of the Marquis de Sade. In 1928 Fish abducted a twelve-year-old girl, strangled her, butchered her body, and—after smuggling some of her flesh back to his Manhattan boardinghouse—cooked it into a cannibal stew. It took the New York City homicide detectives six years to capture Fish, whose 1935 trial was a nationwide sensation. Another notorious Depression-era serial killer was the so-called Mad Butcher of Kingsbury Run, who preyed on homeless men in Cleveland and, in spite of the efforts of Eliot Ness (of *The Untouchables* fame, at that time Cleveland's director of public safety), was never identified or apprehended.

Among the most infamous American serial killers of the 1940s and 1950s were Jake Bird, a homicidal burglar who confessed to a dozen ax murders; William Heirens, famous for his desperate, lipstick-scrawled plea, "For heaven's sake catch me before I kill more. I cannot control myself"; and Harvey Murray Glatman, who photographed his bound, terrorized victims before raping and murdering them. The Eisenhower era also produced perhaps the most bizarre and culturally influential psychokiller of modern times: Ed Gein, the mild-mannered midwestern necrophile whose ghoulish crimes, uncovered in 1957, not only held the country in thrall but also inspired arguably the three most terrifying films of the postwar era—*Psycho* (1960), *The Texas Chainsaw Massacre* (1974), and *The Silence of the Lambs* (1991).

Although in the social revolution of the 1960s sexual liberation was seen by countercultural idealists as purely redemptive, the erotic energies

A police officer searches the Plainfield, Wisconsin, home of Ed Gein in November 1957. Human remains are found. CORBIS/BETTMANN

thus unleashed possessed a dark and destructive aspect that may have manifested itself in a surge of sensational lust killings. Among other atrocities, the 1960s witnessed the murderer Albert DeSalvo, known as the Boston Strangler; the still-unidentified San Francisco killer known as Zodiac, and, most notoriously, Charles Manson and his blood-crazed acolytes.

By the early 1970s there was a growing sense among criminologists that the problem had reached crisis proportions. In response, the FBI established its Behavorial Science Unit to study the newly named phenomenon of serial murder. This was the decade of some of the most infamous psychopaths in American history: Ted Bundy, John Wayne Gacy, David "Son of Sam" Berkowitz, Kenneth Bianchi and Angelo Buono (the "Hillside Stranglers"), and Henry Lee Lucas.

Since then, the ranks of Ripper-style sex-killers in the United States have grown so large that their opportunistic crimes (often committed against defenseless victims like crack-addicted prostitutes) stir up little more than local interest. Still, a number of the most sensational cases have garnered nationwide attention: the forty or more savage murders committed by the elusive "Green River

Killer" in the Seattle-Tacoma area in the mid-1980s; the killing spree by Richard Ramirez, the "Night Stalker," in Los Angeles during the spring and summer of 1985; and the atrocities of Joel Rifkin, who slaughtered a string of prostitutes in the Long Island home he shared with his adoptive parents. In July 1991 the discovery of Jeffrey Dahmer's collection of human remains made him into an overnight sensation. The case was front-page news throughout the country, *People* magazine ran the serial killer's picture on its cover, publishers scrambled to print lurid "instant books," and morbid jokes about "Jeff the Chef" abounded.

### Understanding the Pathology

In July 1997 the country was riveted by the bloody rampage of Andrew Cunanan, whose victims included the celebrated fashion designer Gianni Versace. Whether Cunanan could actually be categorized as a serial killer, however, was a matter of debate among specialists. Certain experts argued that he did indeed fit the profile, basing their opinion on a quantitative definition of the term—that is, three or more killings of unrelated victims with a distinct hiatus (or "cooling-off period") separating each homicide. This definition, however, ignores the all-important issue of motivation. According to most criminologists, true serial murder is always a crime of extreme sexual pathology—essentially nothing more or less than a new name for old-fashioned *Lustmörd*. Indeed, in the typical pattern of serial murder, after a period of increasingly intense fantasizing the perpetrator is driven to stalk and snare a victim. He achieves his gratification (generally to the point of orgasm) by degrading, torturing, and finally murdering the victim. The so-called cooling-off period corresponds to the satiated lull that follows sexual release. Having subsided for a while (days, weeks, months, or even years), his blood-lust begins to build again, at which point the pattern is repeated. Since serial killers derive active sexual pleasure from their atrocities, they generally make every attempt to remain at large for as long as possible.

The profound sexual psychopathology of the serial killer is what distinguishes him from the mass murderer—the human time bomb who erupts in a sudden burst of apocalyptic violence, slaughtering a whole group of people all at once in a single confined area—as well as from the so-called spree killer, who is essentially a mass murderer on the move (this is the category into which Cunanan falls). This sexual psychopathology also helps explain the fact that serial murder appears to be an exclusively male crime. Although there have been many prolific female killers throughout history—"black widows" who dispatch a succession of husbands, homicidal nurses who poison dozens of patients, lethal nannies who dispose of entire families, and so on—few if any women have engaged in the kind of sadistic, serial lust-murder perpetrated by the likes of Ted Bundy. With its quality of extreme, penetrative, phallic aggression, such behavior is essentially a perversion of the male erotic impulse. As the cultural critic Camille Paglia puts it in her controversial *Sexual Personae*, "there is no female Jack the Ripper" (p. 247).

What is the etiology of serial murder? Every decade seems to bring a different theory, from Cesare Lombroso's highly influential (if thoroughly eccentric) notion of "criminal man" to the once-popular (though now totally discredited) belief that violent male murderers possess an extra Y chromosome. Some criminologists have put the blame on childhood head injuries, others on overexposure to ultraviolent entertainment. Ultimately, the only possible answer may be the one offered in *Billy Budd*, where Melville—citing the Epistle to the Thessalonians—defines Claggart's evil as a "mystery of iniquity."

One factor does seem to be, if not a sufficient cause, certainly a necessary condition: virtually every serial killer on record has been subjected to forms of childhood abuse (emotional, physical, sexual) so extreme that they verge on torture. Indeed, in certain cases—like that of Henry Lee Lucas, whose prostitute mother enjoyed dressing him as a girl and forcing him to watch her have sex with her customers—the question is not how a person could grow up to be a sexual psychopath but rather how such a person could not. Because of their horrific upbringings, future serial killers almost always display symptoms of severe emotional disturbance from a very early age, most prominently juvenile sadism (generally directed against small animals), youthful pyromania, and bed-wetting that persists into adolescence.

Social conditions in the United States are arguably conducive to this form of criminal behavior. The breakdown of the traditional nuclear family often contributes to emotional instability that in turn can promote violent psychopathology. The often-noted mobility of American life may make it easier for nomadic killers like Ted Bundy or Henry Lee Lucas to commit their atrocities on the run. And the isolation and anonymity that have become features of modern society may enable killers like Jeffrey Dahmer and John Wayne Gacy to conduct their at-home atrocities for years without attracting the notice of their neighbors.

Though the late-twentieth-century craze for fiction and films about psychopathic sex-killers—a phenomenon sometimes referred to as "serial chic"—has been widely deplored as a symptom of the country's moral decay, it is important to keep in mind that literature dealing with sensational real-life crime has been popular since at least the 1600s, when John Reynolds's *God's Revenge Against Murder and Adultery* was an English best-seller. During the eighteenth century the British public devoured the lurid true-crime accounts in the *Newgate Calendar*, while the *Illustrated Police News*—a sensational Victorian tabloid that makes modern-day counterparts seem like models of journalistic restraint—was the most popular periodical of its day. By the mid-nineteenth century sensational accounts of murder and mayhem were appearing in the pages of the penny press.

Clearly, ordinary, law-abiding men and women have always required a vicarious way of venting their most lawless impulses. (As Freud, citing

Plato, writes in *The Interpretation of Dreams*, "the virtuous man is content to dream what the wicked man really *does*.") Indeed, it might be argued that, if anything, we have become far more refined in our tastes, since we no longer insist on viewing actual gore and violence (in the form, say, of gladiatorial combat and gruesome public executions) but are willing to settle for the graphic simulations provided by cinematic special effects.

For similar psychological reasons—that is, as a way of managing primal fears and taboo fantasies—people from a very early age tend to be fascinated by monsters. Of course, it is also true that the specific type of monster that haunts a given era reflects not only the primitive, perennial desires of the id but the particular anxieties of the moment. Thus, the classic American horror films of the 1930s and 1940s, with their dark European settings—*Dracula, The Wolf Man, Frankenstein*—seemed to embody a mounting dread about the menace arising overseas. The scary science fiction movies of the 1950s—*Invasion of the Body Snatchers, Them!, The Thing from Another World*—were the nightmarish product of extreme Cold War anxieties. Similarly, the societal appetite for portrayals of the serial killer suggests that he incarnates the deepest and most pervasive dreads of a particular cultural moment—fears about random violence, social disintegration, and sexual danger. And, in a culture increasingly obsessed with staying young at any cost, the serial killer may represent the inevitability of extinction. In effect, novels and movies like *The Silence of the Lambs* function as our modern-day version of the medieval *danse macabre*, reminding us that—even with "abs of steel"—our bodies remain appallingly vulnerable to the ravages of death.

BIBLIOGRAPHY

Freud, Sigmund. *The Interpretation of Dreams.* Translated by James Strachey. New York: Avon, 1965.

Krafft-Ebing, Richard von. *Psychopathia Sexualis.* Translated by Franklin S. Klaf. New York: Stein and Day, 1965.

Masters, Robert E. L., and Eduard Lea. *Sex Crimes in History: Evolving Concepts of Sadism, Lust-Murder, and Necrophilia from Ancient to Modern Times.* New York: Matrix House, 1966.

Newton, Michael. *Hunting Humans: An Encyclopedia of Modern Serial Killers.* Port Townsend, Wash.: Loompanics Unlimited, 1990.

Paglia, Camille. *Sexual Personae: Art and Decadence from Nefertiti to Emily Dickinson.* New York: Vintage, 1991.

Schechter, Harold, and David Everitt. *The A–Z Encyclopedia of Serial Killers.* New York: Simon and Schuster, 1996.

Wrangham, Richard, and Dale Peterson. *Demonic Males: Apes and the Origins of Human Violence.* Boston: Houghton Mifflin, 1996.

HAROLD SCHECHTER

*See also* **Berkowitz, David "Son of Sam"; Bundy, Ted; Cunanan, Andrew; Dahmer, Jeffrey; DeSalvo, Albert; Lucas, Henry Lee; Manson, Charles; Mass Murders: Individual Perpetrators; Panzram, Carl; Zodiac Killer.**

# SERIAL KILLERS, REPRESENTATIONS OF

Crime and violence are conventionally treated by mass media as aberrations that speak a deep truth, in a diagnostic way, about various social ills (from economic inequality to parental permissiveness). Thus it may be odd but is perhaps not surprising that film and television tend to represent the perpetrators of violence as having a particular form of insight—a unique and privileged relation to knowledge that allows criminals as characters to serve as the agents for delivering an indictment on society. For example, a staple in many crime genres is the apprehended criminal's speech implying that some particular social origin is culpable for his crime; the same effect can be achieved visually through the mise-en-scène, which may reveal the criminal's milieu as a burned-out housing project or a family of rich, indifferent parents.

One type of criminal in particular was accorded special diagnostic powers in media representations of the late twentieth century: the serial killer. The paradigmatic instance of this character trope was Hannibal Lecter, the notorious and brilliant psychiatrist and serial killer of Thomas Harris's *Red Dragon* (1981) and the 1991 film version, *The Silence of the Lambs.* Lecter's insight and diagnostic expertise are so acute he can infer the psychological formation of a young Federal Bureau of Investigation trainee by the style of her handbag, his predictive powers so invincible that he can turn his captors into his victims at will. This was a character who seemed so inevitable, so somehow perfect, that the cannibal-psychopath immediately entered the popular social lexicon as a new form of cultural hero.

## The Knowledge of Violence, the Violence of Knowledge

It is not insignificant that Hannibal Lecter was a psychiatrist, because it is the psychoanalytic

## Class Consciousness

One of the most prevalent tendencies in the study of popular culture is to assume that the lower down the cultural ladder one descends, the more literally the cultural product under discussion should be taken. "Higher" forms of culture—great literature, opera, serious theater—are known to be awash in symbolism, metaphor, or themes that lurk beneath the surface and can be made the subject of intense critical discussions or interpretation. "Lower" forms of culture (cartoons, pornography, and "exploitation films") are assumed to wear their meanings on the surface, to be straightforwardly literal and thus not particularly worthy of analysis, other than for their putative social effects.

Research that purports to study the effects on viewers of mass-media entertainment compounds this assumption by studying only lower cultural forms: researchers do not hook subjects up to galvanic skin monitors to test their responses to violent scenes in Kurosawa films or Shakespearean drama. Is there some degree of class prejudice implicit in the presumption that only violent low culture causes effects, that the art-house crowd is somehow less susceptible to violent suggestion than the audience for *Texas Chain Saw Massacre?*

category of transference that is foregrounded in popular representations of serial criminals and enacted in the relationship between the psychopathic criminal and the cop. *Transference* describes a situation—typically a psychotherapeutic situation—in which ideas and wishes are transferred by one person to another, often fantasies of knowledge and omniscience. What kind of knowledge could serial killers possess? As with the analyst, it is the fantasy of knowledge from which no one can escape.

For instance, in *Serial Killer* (1995)—the title tells us that this movie intends to be paradigmatic of its genre—a brilliant and culturally refined serial killer has trapped the female "profiler," a cop specializing in serial-killer psychology, in her apartment, and proceeds to torment her with his knowledge of her conflicted inner life. "Very good work, Agent Younger," Morrano tells her. "You got so close so quickly. But did you crawl far enough inside my head to anticipate that I'd come looking for *you*?" When he quotes Shakespeare to her, she

recognizes the quote. "You have a love of the poets," he says admiringly. "Did you put a face on the devil when you were in religion class? Like mine? I think the little Catholic girl likes to play in the repulsive mind of killers. Too bad we'll never find out."

We next encounter Agent Younger two years after this traumatic encounter, in a scene that opens tight on her crucifix necklace, while she explains to her former boyfriend that she is unable to restart a relationship with him. "Morrano said some things that night that I never told you about. He implied that I was good at my job because something in me was attracted to what he is, that I enjoyed exploring the dark side, playing with the devil. . . . I think maybe he was right. . . . I quit us because I was afraid of facing what was inside me." The story and the mise-en-scène itself (the shot of the crucifix) work to confirm the serial killer's diagnosis. It is Morrano who has the goods on her, knows more about her than she knows about herself. And when Morrano comes after her once more, he insists, "You know we were destined for this moment, Selby. Any two people who understand each other the way we do belong together. . . . You *are* like me, everyone is in some way. Why don't you come to me, Selby, why don't you give in to that part of you inside that frightens and fascinates you so much?"

Granted, *Serial Killer* is a poorly made, straight-to-video exploitation film. It has none of the cachet of *Silence of the Lambs*, the work of a "serious" director and featuring an Oscar-winning performance. But scenes like these from *Serial Killer* are repeated, with strikingly little variation, in numerous films and television cop shows. The question of where the violence is—in here or out there?—seems to plague media cops confronted with violent serial crimes.

In the film *Manhunter* (1986), which features Hannibal Lecter in a story line that precedes *Silence of the Lambs*, another profiler tells of his encounter with an earlier incarnation of Lecter to his young son, and explains why it caused him to have a mental breakdown:

I tried to build feelings in my imagination like the killer had so that I would know why he did what he did, because that would help me find him. When I was sitting in Lecter's office, I looked up and I saw a book on his shelf. It had pictures of war wounds in it and I knew it was him. I went down the hall to a pay phone to call the police, and that's when he attacked me. . . . But after my body got okay I still had his thoughts going around in my head.

The son then asks, "And the way he thought felt that bad?" to which the father replies, "Kevin, they're the ugliest thoughts in the world."

In *Tightrope* (1984), Clint Eastwood is a New Orleans cop who indulges his penchant for rough sex until the women he has sex with start getting killed, one by one, in scenarios that use elements of his own sexual encounters with them—strangled while bound with handcuffs. Tracking down the killer is a journey through his own sexuality, which the killer seems to know far better than the cop himself does. "He [the killer] said you were just like him," a female prostitute tells the cop, handing him a whip. In another encounter in a gay bar, a male prostitute tells him: "He said this was your first time. He bought me for you. You don't want it?" Cop: "No." Prostitute: "He said you did, you just don't know it yet." Cop: "Well he's wrong." Prostitute: "How do you know if you haven't tried it?" Cop: "Maybe I have."

In an interrogation scene from the television cop show *NYPD Blue* (1993–), Detective Sipowitz, one of the series regulars, beats a suspected serial rapist-killer into a confession, only to have the man turn on him and scream: "Burn your sick mind for giving people beatings! *I* couldn't help myself, but *your* sick mind doesn't have to. You do it because you *want* to. I raped that girl from a monstrous force, I'm a monstrous force. You *want* to, but I'm a helpless force!" "Yeah," acknowledges Sipowitz, "I *want* to!" In the following scene, he breaks down before his fellow cops gathered in the locker room, expressing anguish at his skill at extracting confessions with beatings. Betraying a self-loathing not so unlike the serial killer's, he confirms the killer's accusation and knowledge of his not-so-hidden sadism: "One good slap to the back of his head is how he knew that both of us were sick," he explodes at himself in the mirror, scrubbing his hands compulsively in the sink.

Detached from their narrative contexts these examples may seem slightly overwrought, but the convention of cop-criminal identification is hardly a media invention. The criminological field of profiling is quite real, and, at least as represented by the former FBI agent John Douglas in his 1995 best-seller *Mindhunter*, the operations of the FBI's behavioral sciences unit, like the film and television examples, produce scenes of psychological strain and self-torment brought on by living so close to the criminal psyche. Indeed, the nonfiction *Mindhunter* is remarkably close to the fictional *Manhunter*: *Mindhunter* also opens with an account of a massive physical and mental breakdown, while the rest of the book goes on to recount the emotional difficulty of the work that brought Douglas to that crisis, that is, the strain of getting "inside" all those serial killers' minds.

### Getting Inside the Killer's Mind

Why is it "inside" the killer's mind that we want to be? The convention of cop-criminal identification is relatively new. In the 1968 film *No Way To Treat a Lady*, an early example of the serial-killer theme, the subject is approached with irony and distance rather than intensity and psychical sharing. That the cop has an annoying mother, and the killer kills middle-aged women because of his own mother problem, suggests a not-so-subtle prefeminist joke along the lines of "Who *wouldn't* want to

---

### Shifting Identifications

Do viewers simply and immediately identify with the perpetrators of violence? Or (as psychoanalytic theory would complicate the question) do viewers vacillate in their identifications—between figures embodying power and figures embodying powerlessness, between victimizer and victim—because these oppositions represent competing and ambivalent aspects of each of our psyches? The universal experience of childhood ensures that all of us have experienced the trauma of powerlessness as an intrinsic aspect of our formation as selves; these are precisely the memories prone to a high degree of distortion and fascination when we view violence on television and in film.

Media representations complicate the terrain of identification further by their use of a range of point-of-view devices that work to shape viewer identifications: at various moments, through the use of particular camera angles for instance, a male viewer may be put into the position of a female rape victim, or a female viewer into the position of a male psychopath, or any number of other possibilities. The range of visual and narrative "positions" offered by most films can unsettle any easy certainty about what the film's particular "message" about violence is.

kill his mother?" In this film the cop, not the killer, is firmly in the position of knowledge: he is the one who diagnoses the criminal rather than the other way around. The killer has no particular knowledge to impart other than a certain way with wigs and accents. The detective does not have to delve into his own heart of darkness to apprehend him.

The question "Who would I have to be to commit this crime?" dates back to the invention of the detective genre. The fascination with the adjacency of the criminal and the normal mind gives crime genres their edge and, at times, their moral ambiguity. Crime genres also routinely dwell on the fine line between state-sanctioned violence and criminal violence, through hinge figures like Clint Eastwood's Dirty Harry or others from the endless rogues' gallery of violent and corrupt policemen. The tormented-cop figure plagued by alcoholism, self-loathing, and bad marriages is a staple of h the genre. The more the detective and the serial killer "share" certain things—tastes, affinities, predilections—the closer the two figures come to trading places.

Still, why is the serial criminal granted the privilege of saying the "truth"—and what exactly is that truth? Often it seems to be a way of indicating that cops have legal methods of venting the same impulses that drive the criminal, or further, that being a cop is a way of fulfilling a similarly compulsive need to *play a role* in violent scenes. The cop can be simultaneously virtuous and violent, while maintaining an institutional position that allows for conferring that predilection for violence onto someone else. The violence isn't *here*, it's over there. However, typically this analysis is advanced by rapists or killers—somewhat degraded sources of knowledge. This allows for two competing impulses on the part of the audience: "This is true; this can't be true," or the classic rhetorical structure of disavowal.

"Freud suggests that psychoanalysis, if it lives on, will live on not as the straightforward life of a known and understood theory, but as the endless survival of what has not yet been understood" (Caruth 1996, p. 72). Popular culture, obsessed with violence as something very much "not yet understood," is an example of this Freudian migration. By putting viewers in imaginary proximity to those who act out violent scenarios, pop culture raises a range of questions that more traditional schools of jurisprudence, morality, and criminology do not address.

BIBLIOGRAPHY

Caruth, Cathy. *Unclaimed Experience: Trauma, Narrative, and History*. Baltimore: Johns Hopkins University Press, 1996.

Clover, Carol. *Men, Women, and Chain Saws: Gender in the Modern Horror Film*. Princeton, N.J.: Princeton University Press, 1992.

Douglas, John (with Mark Olshaker). *Mindhunter: Inside the FBI's Elite Serial Crime Unit*. New York: Scribner, 1995.

Freud, Sigmund. "A Child Is Being Beaten: A Contribution to the Origin of Sexual Perversions." In *Sexuality and the Psychology of Love*. New York: Macmillan, 1963.

Kipnis, Laura. *Bound and Gagged: Pornography and the Politics of Fantasy in America*. New York: Grove, 1996.

Seltzer, Mark. *Serial Killers: Death and Life in America's Wound Culture*. New York: Routledge, 1998.

LAURA KIPNIS

*See also* **Literature: Fiction; Representation of Violence; Television: Violent Genres.**

# SEX DIFFERENCES

Throughout history and across cultures, men have collectively and individually been more violent than women; this article will examine the difference in the extent to which men and women intentionally harm others physically. This is not to say that women are never violent, or that they do not express hostility in other ways; but they are far less likely to injure physically or kill others. A range of theories has attempted to explain this sex difference, variously emphasizing cultural, biological, and environmental factors.

### Origins of Male Violence

Evolutionary psychology, and the related field of evolutionary biology, posits that young males are naturally the most violence-prone members of any society: the violence stems directly or indirectly from reproductive competition for access to desirable mates and for the status and resources that enable a man to attract and keep a mate.

This argument is derived from Darwin's principle of sexual selection. As set out by Robert Trivers, the principle states that because females will invest more time, resources, and energy in the care of progeny, they are choosy about with whom they mate; they will have more to lose by a choice resulting in poor genes or poor protection for their offspring. Thus, they control reproductive access by the other sex. Males, who will invest less in the future progeny, are in the position of competing with other members of their sex for the attentions of and access to females, which for them constitutes a scarce resource.

Modern sexual selection theory predicts that under certain circumstances male competition will be particularly risky and dangerous—for example, when a disadvantageous sex ratio limits access to females and makes it difficult for males to achieve the status or resources necessary for reproduction.

Evolutionary psychology also addresses the inherent biological imbalance that males can never be certain of paternity, whereas females are always certain of maternity; as a result males, human and animal, frequently show mate-guarding behavior, which can be violent. Men's sexual jealousy and possessiveness are likewise potent motives for violence toward women partners. In humans, many arguments between mates that lead to violence concern perceived neglect of responsibilities or lack of commitment to the relationship.

Most of the variation in homicide rates in different nations arises from different rates of same-sex killings; these killings account for most homicides in the United States and other countries with high homicide rates. But a greater consistency is seen across nations in the numbers of women killed by their male partners. Evolutionary theories, along with cultural and environmental influences, can be used to explain why this is so.

### Gender-Related Patterns of Violence

A body of quantifiable evidence enables a comparison of the sexes in terms of violence. Homicide statistics are perhaps the most useful crime figures, as there is a clear criterion for the degree of force involved. Less solidly reliable are self-reports of all acts of physical aggression; these may be subject to reporting biases but can be informative as to the occurrence of more common types of behavior.

Violence between people of the same sex is different from that between the sexes in terms of where it occurs, to whom it occurs, and the motives behind it. The two forms of violence are thus best considered separately.

*Same-Sex Violence.* Most same-sex violence is violence between men, tending to occur outside the home between strangers or those not well known to one another. In twelve sets of same-sex homicide figures from North America, male cases ranged from 93.3 to 100 percent of the total (Daly and Wilson 1988). Analysis of twenty studies,

involving 13,680 same-sex homicides, in which killings by family members were excluded—thus removing cases of women killing dependent children—showed that 97.2 percent were male (Daly and Wilson 1990).

This pattern is consistent across nations, despite great differences in the absolute rates of same-sex homicides. For example, the same-sex homicide rates for Chicago from 1965 to 1981 are about thirty times higher than those for England and Wales from 1977 to 1986, yet the percentage of male same-sex homicides is similar.

Male-male homicides are concentrated during young adulthood—beginning shortly after puberty, with a peak during the twenties, and declining from the late thirties onward. Again, this occurs irrespective of the absolute rate of same-sex homicide in a given society (see figure 1).

Statistics for nonlethal violent crimes are typically expressed in terms of the sex of the person arrested or convicted of an assault, without an indication of the sex of the victim. They show the characteristic pattern of age and sex differences reported for same-sex homicides (see figure 2). Self-report measures of physical aggression also seldom specify the sex of the person against whom the aggressive act is made. One exception was a study of a sample of U.S. students: 81 percent of those who said they had fought someone of their own sex during the previous three years were male (Gergen 1990). Such studies typically involve young subjects; there is no research on how individuals' tendency to commit nonlethal physical aggression changes over time.

A range of causal influences can together account for young male violence. A large proportion of homicides result from exchanges about something that seems trivial in retrospect, such as an insult or an argument between neighbors over parking or noise. Sensitivity about reputation or honor, characteristic of many masculine subcultures, looms large in the background of such cases. A concern about honor is generally found among men from cultures that originated in herding economies without an effective rule of law. For example, many areas in the South and West have been populated by groups who have come from herding economies overseas, such as Ireland. Valuable livestock could be and often were stolen, and no centralized or governmental institutions existed to prevent such theft. This necessitated the "every man's his own sheriff" situation, vestiges of which still exist.

FIGURE 1. Graph of Homicides According to Age and Sex for Two Areas Whose Absolute Rates Differ Greatly

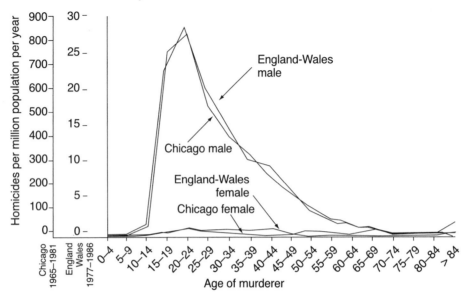

SOURCE: Cronin, Helena, *The Ant and the Peacock* (New York: Cambridge University Press, 1991), based on Daly and Wilson (1990).

In the United States a culture of honor has been identified among southern white males and is associated with other American male subcultures from the frontier cowboy to the present-day inner-city gang. Mining and frontier towns in the latter half of the nineteenth century had high homicide rates in part because much of their population consisted of males who lacked the restraining influences of family obligations and religion. The propensity toward violence in these concentrated male groups was exacerbated by sensitivity about reputation, the disinhibiting influence of alcohol, and the habit of carrying guns. David Courtwright alleges a continuity between these young men and those living in armed and undisciplined groups in the inner cities of the late twentieth century. There is the same sensitivity to honor, lack of family ties, associations with like-minded males, lack of religion, possession of weapons, and tendency to drink. Added to these is the impact of the drug trade. These cultural variables all operate primarily within young male subcultures. Statistically they will both increase the absolute rates of violence and exaggerate the sex difference.

*Violence Between Men and Women.* Among adults, most opposite-sex violence occurs between men and women who are sexual partners. Interpretation of the statistics related to violence between the sexes is a contentious topic. Researchers

from a feminist perspective (e.g., Walker 1989) emphasize that men are the usual perpetrators and women the victims. Their evidence is typically derived from victims' reports, crime statistics, or interviews with men referred by the court to treatment programs. Researchers from a family-interaction perspective (e.g., Stets and Straus 1990), who examine family dynamics and responses to interpersonal conflicts, emphasize the mutuality of physical aggression between partners. Their evidence is typically derived from samples from national populations of married and cohabiting couples or from studies of dating couples (e.g., Morse 1995).

The different conclusions are a result of different statistical approaches and different samples. Feminist research tends to focus on victimization—for example, the injuries sustained—whereas family interaction research typically examines all acts of physical aggression regardless of context or consequences. Studies involving both measures show that as many women as men report having engaged in some form of physical aggression against their partners, ranging from slapping to using a weapon, yet more women are injured. Among samples selected for their likelihood of high levels of marital violence or conflict, whatever analytical approach is taken, a much higher frequency of male than female violence is reported. This is in

FIGURE 2. Graph of Arrest Rates for Assault According to Age and Sex for the United States, 1989

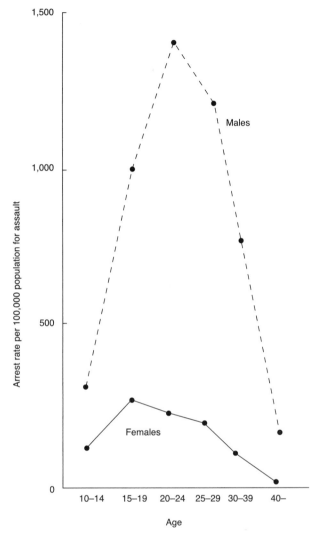

SOURCE: Campbell, Anne, "A Few Good Men," in *Ethology and Sociobiology* 16, no. 2 (1995).

portion of these cases of violence against men probably results from self-defensive actions taken by their female spouses in response to violence from the male. More recent figures (for 1976–1985) show a lower, but still substantial, proportion of male victims—30 percent (Gondolf and Shestakov 1997). Spousal violence in the United States, then, is less of an overwhelmingly male phenomenon than is same-sex violence. This generalization cannot be applied to other nations: Among other English-speaking and European nations such as Canada, England, Wales, Scotland, Denmark, and Australia, 79 percent of 2,913 spousal homicides were committed by men (Wilson and Daly 1992); figures for Russia from 1991 show 86 percent of spousal homicides committed by men (Gondolf and Shestakov 1997). Scant evidence for nonlethal violence is available for countries other than the United States.

*BIBLIOGRAPHY*

Campbell, Anne. "A Few Good Men: Evolutionary Psychology and Female Adolescent Aggression." *Ethology and Sociobiology* 16, no. 2 (1995).

Courtwright, David T. *Violent Land: Single Men and Social Disorder from the Frontier to the Inner City.* Cambridge, Mass.: Harvard University Press, 1996.

Cronin, Helena. *The Ant and the Peacock.* New York: Cambridge University Press, 1991.

Daly, Martin, and Margo Wilson. *Homicide.* New York: Aldine de Gruyter, 1988.

———. "Killing the Competition: Female/Female and Male/Male Homicide." *Human Nature* 1, no. 1 (1990).

Gergen, Mary. "Beyond the Evil Empire: Horseplay and Aggression." *Aggressive Behavior* 16, no. 6 (1990).

Gondolf, Edward W., and Dmitri Shestakov. "Spousal Homicide in Russia Versus the United States: Preliminary Findings and Implications." *Journal of Family Violence* 12, no. 1 (1997).

Leyton, Elliott. *Men of Blood.* London: Constable, 1995.

Morse, Barbara J. "Beyond the Conflict Tactics Scale: Assessing Gender Differences in Partner Violence." *Violence and Victims* 10, no. 4 (1995): 251–272.

Nisbett, Richard E., and Dov Cohen. *Culture of Honor: The Psychology of Violence in the South.* Boulder, Colo.: Westview, 1996.

Stets, Jan E., and Murray A. Straus. "Gender Differences in Reporting Marital Violence and Its Medical and Psychological Consequences." In *Physical Violence in American Families: Risk Factors and Adaptations to Violence in 8,145 Families,* edited by Murray A. Straus and Richard J. Gelles. New Brunswick, N.J.: Transaction, 1990.

Trivers, Robert L. "Parental Investment and Sexual Selection." In *Sexual Selection and the Descent of Man,* edited by Bernard B. Campbell. Chicago: Aldine, 1972.

contrast to findings from community-based samples not selected for problems with marital violence, suggesting that concentrating on selected samples has led to a neglect of the extent of women's physical aggression. In fact, an analysis of seventeen published studies providing the numbers of men and women injured by their spouses shows that 65 percent of those injured were women, leaving a substantial minority of male victims.

Homicides resulting from marital violence in the United States also show a large proportion of male victims—44 percent, according to figures for 1948–1989 (Wilson and Daly 1992). A large pro-

Walker, Lenore E. A. "Psychology and Violence Against Women." *American Psychologist* 44, no. 4 (1989): 659–702.

Wilson, Margo, and Martin Daly. "Who Kills Whom in Spouse Killings? On the Exceptional Sex Ratio of Spousal Homicides in the United States." *Criminology* 30, no. 2 (1992).

JOHN ARCHER

*See also* **Developmental Factors; Endocrinology; Gender; Masculinity; Sex Offenders; Sociobiology; Women.**

# SEX OFFENDERS

A *sex offender* is an individual who has been convicted of violently victimizing another person by means of sexual assault, including child molestation, incest, or rape. In the late twentieth century, *sex crimes* were generally understood to indicate these types of violent sexual offenses, which were an increasing source of public fear in the United States.

In a broader view, the understanding of *sex crimes* sometimes includes all sexual acts (including acts of consensual sex, or "victimless" crimes) that are proscribed by law. These include prostitution and sodomy, as well as some instances of statutory rape (that is, sexual intercourse with a person who is below the statutory age of consent).

Of course sexual deviance, in the sense of sexual behavior contrary to a culture's prevailing public norm, has always existed and persistently been criminalized. Bestiality and sodomy are attested (and condemned) in the biblical books of Genesis and Leviticus. But just as cultures change, so do the norms of what is tolerated as acceptable and what is ostracized or criminalized as an "offense." This pattern of conflicted change has prevailed in American history. "Buggery" and sodomy were capital offenses in all of the New England colonies, although homosexual persons were generally treated leniently. Illegitimacy was a major public concern in the nineteenth and twentieth centuries.

At the dawn of the twenty-first century, homoerotic and premarital sexuality have attained widespread social tolerance, although many restrictive laws have been retained or enacted. Inevitably, however, a number of deviant behaviors continue to challenge society's shifting norms. One index of those norms is the ever controversial *Diagnostic and Statistical Manual of Mental Disorders*, published by the American Psychiatric Association since 1952. The legal-political sphere is naturally even more prone to conflict and change than the psychiatric community. Among the behaviors most frequently subject to both sanction and criminalization are exhibitionism, voyeurism, bestiality, sadomasochism, and pedophilia.

## Characteristics of Sex Offenses and Offenders

Data provided by the U.S. Department of Justice (available on the Internet at the Bureau of Justice Statistics home page) provides the following profiles of sex offenses and offenders:

- The victims of sex offenders are most often teenagers and children.
- Rape and sexual assault offenders serving time in state prisons reported that two-thirds of their victims were younger than eighteen. Among the sex offenders whose victims were seventeen or younger, nearly six in ten (58 percent) said their victims were twelve or younger.
- In 90 percent of the rapes of children less than twelve years old, the child knew the offender.
- Among sexual assault victims eighteen to twenty-nine years old, two-thirds had a prior relationship with the rapist.
- Several sources point to a sex offender who is older than other violent offenders, generally in his early thirties, and more likely to be white than other violent offenders.
- On a given day there are approximately 234,000 sex offenders under the care, custody, or control of corrections agencies; nearly 60 percent of these offenders are under conditional supervision in the community. The median age of the victims of imprisoned sexual assaulters is less than thirteen years, and the median age of rape victims is about twenty-two years.
- An estimated 24 percent of those serving time for rape and 19 percent of those serving time for sexual assault had been on probation or parole at the time of the offense for which they were in state prison.

## Legal and Legislative Trends

Protecting society from the predations of violent sexual offenders while at the same time protecting the constitutional rights of those offenders, regardless of the repugnance with which society views their crimes, poses one of the most difficult dilemmas faced by the criminal justice system.

*Megan's Law.* The legal and legislative journey toward today's sexual predator and registration and notification laws began in 1990, when public concern was aroused with the abduction of eleven-year-old Jacob Wetterling in Minnesota. Congress enacted the 1994 "Jacob Wetterling Act," which mandated that each state register its released sex offenders.

In July 1994 the nation was shocked again by the abduction, molestation, and strangulation of a seven-year-old New Jersey girl, Megan Kanka, by her neighbor, a twice-convicted child sex offender. Following Megan's death, New Jersey legislators concluded that registration of sex offenders was not arming the public with enough information to protect children. Hence, legislation was enacted not only to register sex offenders but also to notify those community members (by distributing flyers, alerting local organizations, and conducting door-to-door campaigns) who were most likely to come into contact with such offenders. Then, the omnibus federal Violent Crime Control and Law Enforcement Act of 1994—known as the Crime Bill, at 42 U.S.C. 140719 (d)—mandated that each state establish a system for registering released sex offenders but allowed states to devise their own systems for notification. Under the law, all such offenders are required to notify state law-enforcement agencies of their whereabouts for ten years after their release from prison, and states are required to notify appropriate agencies of an offender's release.

In 1996 the Crime Bill provision regarding sex-offender registration was amended under the title "Megan's Law" (H.R. 2137) to give states broad discretion over disclosing the names of registered sex offenders (allowing disclosure "for any purpose permitted under the laws of the state") and to furthermore require that states notify community members who are most likely to come into contact with such offenders. Thus the federal Crime Bill provided the foundation on which Megan's Law rests.

Megan's Law, however, does not require public notification of all sex offenders. The law assigns each offender to one of three tiers depending on the expected risk of recidivism. The first tier, classified as low risk, results in annual registration, and only law-enforcement agencies can access the sex offender's file. The second, or moderate risk, tier, allows for limited notification to specified entities. Last is the high-risk tier, which predicts that the offender will recidivate. Sex offenders classified in this tier must constantly reregister, and vulnerable populations (e.g., preschools, small communities, churches, and even the public at large) will be notified. Many people praise the theory underlying Megan's Law; indeed, her father stated that Megan would be alive today had he known of the offender's record and forbidden her to cross the street.

However, many legal observers vehemently reject the Megan's Law on grounds of double jeopardy (saying the law affords additional punishment for past crimes), violation of the right to privacy (citing the public notification provision), and the equal protection clause (asserting that the law unfairly singles out child sex offenders). They feel Megan's Law is vulnerable on these grounds and is unconstitutional, and therefore void, if placed under judicial scrutiny. In fact, a federal judge in New Jersey challenged a portion of the law in February 1995, approving the requirement that sex offenders register with police but finding that community notification was unconstitutional.

On a broader scale, although Megan's Laws are in place in all fifty states and have provided communities with offender information, their fate in other federal courts—where challenges to state notification laws have found success—remains to be seen. In several such challenges, sex offenders subjected to these notification requirements have been granted injunctions against state and local agencies attempting to report moderate- and high-risk offenders to the communities. This trend of judicial interdiction against the law-enforcement agencies' notification of sex offenders to the community shows the federal courts' apparent disdain for this potential constitutional infringement on sex offenders' rights. In addition, others wonder whether this law truly prevents sex offenders from committing their crimes or simply gives parents a false sense of security. Clearly a debate continues over such so-called "scarlet letter" databases and over whether the provisions of Megan's Law represent the best means for controlling sex offenders.

*Sexual Predator Laws.* In June 1997, the United States Supreme Court upheld (in *State v. Hendricks*) a Kansas statute establishing civil commitment procedures for sexually violent predators who had completed their prison sentences. The ruling meant that such offenders with a "mental abnormality" and who pose a danger to the community may be confined even if they are not found to have a "mental illness." The defendant, five-time convicted child molester Leroy Hendricks, had stated that his death was the only way to guarantee that he would not molest again. The Kansas decision spurred other states to enact similar legislation. This decision also offered the Supreme Court's first implicit approval of Megan's Laws, which are based on the same legal foundation.

*Chemical Castration.* On 1 January 1997, California became the first state in the nation to enact a chemical-castration law for child molesters. The law requires that persons convicted for a second molestation offense against a child under age thirteen receive weekly injections of Depo-Provera, a drug which lowers testosterone levels and thereby reduces sex drive in men. Proponents of the law say it is the only way to stop criminals known for being repeat offenders. Opponents claim such a law violates the offender's right to privacy, undermines the constitutional guarantee of equal protection, and represents cruel and unusual punishment. While other states have considered enacting such laws, there appears to be a wait-and-see attitude until the legal issues are resolved in the federal courts.

**Effectiveness of Treatment Models**

The successful treatment of sex offenders would have the general goals of preventing recidivism (or at least delaying the onset of a future offense) and reducing the numbers of persons who are victimized. It would also be helpful to be able to measure such indicators as denial or minimization, the frequency of intensity of sexually abusive or violent fantasies, and the degree of social intimacy. Only in the early 1970s did researchers begin to attempt such behavioral programs.

No effective treatment program for sex offenders has yet been developed. Several issues confound outcome research on treatment for sex offenders, including lack of adequate databases (due to low reporting rates by victims and low arrest and conviction rates for offenders), lack of a uniform definition of recidivism, lack of adequate selection criteria for placing subjects into treatment versus placing them in a control group, and lack of a useful measure of treatment protocol (including skills training, stress management, and techniques to target denial, inappropriate attitudes, deviant sexual preferences, victim impact and empathy, social skills, anger control, relationship issues, life skill, and so on). Given these problems, it is not surprising that few researchers choose to devote their careers to determining "what works" with sex-offender treatment models.

Furthermore, methodological problems exacerbate the difficulties in determining which treatment model(s) will work. For example, scientific method requires two groups in order to study whether treatment is effective—one group of sex offenders that receives treatment and a control group receiving no treatment. However, many states require that incarcerated sex offenders participate in a treatment program if they are to be paroled. Also, treatment-outcome studies have been conducted within a single setting; they should be conducted across several sites to enhance generalizability of findings. Other procedural concerns have been noted—for example, some programs have returned treated offenders to their ward, where they live in the company of many untreated offenders, often for many years, before being released without any transitional process or follow-up attention. While there are some successes with sex-offender treatment, generally speaking there is no evidence that treatments developed in the face of these kinds of methodological and procedural issues will effectively reduce sex-offense recidivism.

Some sex offenders do respond to treatment, however; indeed, one program for child molesters that was deemed "disappointing" in outcomes still achieved the goals of treatment with half of its subjects. Several other reports evaluating the efficacy of sex-offender programs agree that sex offenders who have engaged in specialized treatment reoffend at lower rates than do offenders who have not participated in treatment (Maletzky 1991; Marques et al. 1993; Marshall et al. 1991; Pithers and Cumming 1991). However, at present researchers cannot identify who will respond effectively.

Clearly the problem of sex offenses has long-term antecedents, with no short-term solutions yet on the horizon.

*BIBLIOGRAPHY*

American Psychiatric Association. *Diagnostic and Statistical Manual of Mental Disorders.* 4th ed. Washington, D.C.: American Psychiatric Association, 1994.

Cox, Douglas J. "Incidence and Nature of Male Genital Exposure Behavior as Reported by College Women." *Journal of Sex Research* 24 (1988).

Feldman, D. L. "Scarlet Letter Laws of the 1990s: A Response to Critics." 60 *Alabama Law Review* 1081 (1997).

Furby, Lita, Mark R. Weinrott, and Lyn Blackshaw. "Sex Offenders Recidivism: A Review." *Psychological Bulletin* 105 (1989).

Kabat, A. R. "Scarlet Letter Sex Offender Databases and Community Notification: Sacrificing Personal Privacy for a Symbol's Sake." *American Criminal Law Review* 35 (1989): 333.

Karpman, Benjamin. *The Sexual Offender and His Offenses: Etiology, Pathology, Psychodynamics, and Treatment.* New York: Julian Press, 1954.

Maletzky, Barry M. *Treating the Sexual Offender.* Newbury Park, Calif.: Sage, 1991.

Marques, J. K., D. M. Day, C. Nelson, and M. A. West. "Findings and Recommendations from California's Experimental Treatment Program." In *Sexual Aggression: Issues in Etiology, Assessment, and Treatment,* edited by Gordon C. Nagayama Hall et al. Washington, D.C.: Taylor and Francis, 1993.

Marshall, William L., Audrey Eccles, and Howard E. Barbaree. "Treatment of Exhibitionists: A Focus on Sexual Deviance Versus Cognitive and Relationship Features." *Behavioural Research and Therapy* 29, no. 2 (1991).

Marshall, William L., and W. D. Pithers. "A Reconsideration of Treatment Outcomes with Sex Offenders." *Criminal Justice and Behavior* 21 (March 1994).

Morneau, Robert H., and Robert R. Rockwell. *Sex, Motivation, and the Criminal Offender.* Springfield, Ill.: Charles C. Thomas, 1980.

Oaks, R. F. "'Things Fearful to Name': Sodomy and Buggery in Seventeenth-Century New England." *Journal of Social History* 12 (winter 1978).

Pithers, W. D., and G. F. Cumming. "Can Relapses Be Prevented? Initial Outcome Data from the Vermont Treatment Program for Sexual Aggressors." In *Relapse Prevention with Sex Offenders,* edited by D. Richard Laws. New York: Guilford, 1989.

Smith, S., and C. Braun. "Necrophilia and Lust Murder: Report of a Rare Occurrence." *Bulletin of the American Academy of Psychiatry and the Law* 6, no. 3 (1978).

West, Donald J. *Sexual Crimes and Confrontations: A Study of Victims and Offenders.* Brookfield, Vt.: Gower, 1987.

KENNETH J. PEAK
JASON W. PEAK

*See also* **Child Abuse: Sexual; Incest; Pornography; Rape.**

# SEXUAL HARASSMENT

Although inappropriate sexual behavior in the workplace has been a part of the American landscape for many years, it was not until the 1970s that such behavior was defined in a legal context as *sexual harassment.* Throughout the 1970s and 1980s sexual harassment was acknowledged by both employers and employees, but it was not taken very seriously. However, in 1991 the issue of sexual harassment exploded into the American consciousness. The American public was bombarded with news coverage focusing on sexual harassment during the Senate hearings of Clarence Thomas, who was ultimately confirmed as a justice of the United States Supreme Court. Anita Hill, then a law professor at the University of Oklahoma, testified that Thomas had sexually harassed her on numerous occasions in the early 1980s while she was under his supervision at the Civil Rights Division of the Department of Education and the U.S. Equal Employment Opportunity Commission (EEOC).

At about the same time, charges of sexual harassment and abuse were emanating from the ranks of the military. In September 1991 the Tailhook Association, an organization of American military pilots, held a convention in Las Vegas. During the convention, women were subjected to sexually and physically assaultive behavior by a group of drunken servicemen. Women who entered a particular hallway were forced to walk a "gauntlet" while being grabbed, pushed, and fondled. Although the military had "zero tolerance" policies on sexual harassment, this behavior had occurred at previous conventions without repercussions. The scandal following the Tailhook convention exposed all branches of the military to extensive criticism.

Although the charges of sexual harassment did not prevent the confirmation of Thomas, and it took years before the Tailhook scandal was resolved, the publicity surrounding these events created a new atmosphere in which women who came forward with complaints about harassment were taken seriously. In spite of the awareness generated by these events, however, confusion and ambiguity continued to surround the question of what constitutes sexual harassment.

**Defining Sexual Harassment**

Sexual harassment is a civil offense covered under federal legislation and state statute. Although the behavior that constitutes sexual harassment may be a criminal offense under state penal code, traditional criminal statutes have been unsatisfactory in providing recourse to sexual harassment victims. The level of behavior in sexual harassment cases often does not fit the definition of sexual assault. Furthermore, relying on criminal statutes to prosecute an offender for a criminal offense leaves

## Paula Jones v. Bill Clinton

In May 1994 Paula Jones filed a sexual harassment lawsuit against President Bill Clinton, alleging that while he was governor of Arkansas and she was a low-level state clerk, he deprived her of her civil rights by sexually harassing her. Jones claimed that on 8 May 1991 Clinton summoned her to his Little Rock hotel room, dropped his pants, and propositioned her. In 1998 an Arkansas federal judge, Susan Webber Wright, dismissed the lawsuit, stating that Jones failed to prove quid quo pro harassment, that a hostile work environment ensued from his conduct. Wright ruled that, even if Clinton did make a crude and offensive proposition, it did not constitute sexual assault; there was no proof that Jones was emotionally afflicted or punished in the workplace for refusing his offer. Specifically, the judge found that Jones never filed a grievance about the behavior, never sought counseling or missed a day of work. There was no proof that Clinton ever sought retribution against her. In addition, a single hotel-room proposition—that was brief in duration, did not involve coercion or threats of reprisal, and was abandoned as soon as Jones indicated it was not welcome—was not severe enough to constitute a hostile workplace.

unresolved the issues of protecting the victim's employment and providing damages to the victim.

The Civil Rights Act of 1964 prohibits discrimination in employment on the basis of race, color, sex, religion, and national origin. Although sexual harassment is not specifically mentioned in this legislation, the Supreme Court has found that under the act, sexual harassment constitutes sex discrimination. Early efforts to file sexual harassment suits under Title VII of the Civil Rights Act proved to be unsuccessful; however in 1976, discrimination based on sex was found for the first time when an employee was fired after she refused to have sex with her supervisor.

Sexual harassment is also prohibited by Title IX of the 1972 Education Acts Amendment. Title IX prohibits sexual discrimination in universities and other schools receiving federal funds. This legislation is important because it allows students, who are not covered under Title VII, to seek recourse for sexual harassment. An example of where a

claim under Title IX would exist is when a professor demands sex from a student in exchange for a better grade.

The Civil Rights Act of 1964 also created the EEOC, which issued a series of guidelines on sexual harassment in 1980. Two basic categories of sexual harassment were defined, quid pro quo and hostile work environment. Quid pro quo involves a direct exchange of sexual favors for a job-related benefit, while a hostile working environment can exist even without the loss of a tangible job benefit. The EEOC guidelines on sexual harassment are as follows:

> Harassment on the basis of sex is a violation of the law. Unwelcome sexual advances, requests for sexual favors and other verbal or physical conduct of a sexual nature constitute sexual harassment when: (1) submission to such conduct is made either explicitly or implicitly a term or condition of employment, (2) submission to or rejection of such conduct by an individual is used as the basis for employment decisions affecting such individual, or (3) such conduct has the purpose or effect of unreasonably interfering with an individual's work performance or creating an intimidating, hostile or offensive work environment.

In 1984 the EEOC guidelines were expanded to include educational institutions.

The U.S. Supreme Court has addressed the issue of sexual harassment in several major cases. In 1986 the Court ruled in *Meritor Savings Bank v. Vinson* that sexual harassment on the job is illegal sex discrimination even if the victim suffers no economic loss. In a 1993 case, *Harris v. Forklift Systems, Inc.*, the Supreme Court ruled that a hostile work environment can exist absent psychological harm, if the work environment can be reasonably perceived as abusive or an interference with a person's work. In 1998 the Supreme Court ruled that Title VII of the Civil Rights Act of 1964 applies to same-sex harassment. The Court stated in *Oncale v. Sundowner Offshore Services* that nothing in the law prohibits a claim of discrimination simply because the victim and offender are both men or both women. In *Burlington Industries Inc. v. Ellerth*, decided the same year, the Court found that an employee who refuses the unwelcome and threatening sexual advances of a supervisor yet suffers no adverse, tangible job consequences may recover against an employer without showing the employer is negligent or otherwise at fault for the supervisor's actions.

Victims of sexual harassment are entitled to sue and recover from harassers and employers for

## Same-Sex Harassment

*Oncale v. Sundowner Offshore Services* (1998) involved a man employed on an offshore oil rig who was subjected to sexual humiliation, assault, and threats of rape by his boss and coworkers, all of them men. The victim, Joseph Oncale, claimed the men grabbed him in the company shower, forced a bar of soap between his buttocks, and threatened to rape him. The victim complained to the company, but it did nothing; he then quit his job. In its ruling, the Supreme Court said that nothing in the law prohibits a claim of sexual harassment on the grounds that the victim and offender are the same sex. The Court wrote that "common sense" should prevail in all harassment cases and that courts should not mistake ordinary socializing, such as male-on-male horseplay, for sexual harassment. Title VII of the Civil Rights Act of 1964 forbids only that behavior so objectively offensive as to alter the conditions of employment.

compensatory and punitive damages that may result from emotional pain and suffering, illness, medical costs, and loss of employment. The 1991 Civil Rights Act limits the amount of damages based on the size of the employer: damages range from $50,000 for employers with less than one hundred employees to $300,000 for employers with more than five hundred employees.

In cases involving the uniformed military personnel, Title VII is not the appropriate remedy. Although employees of the Department of Defense are federal workers and under the purview of Title VII, uniformed personnel are beyond the scope of the statute, absent congressional inclusion. This rule is based on the premise that disruption to the unique military mission would result if service members were allowed to sue for actions involving military duties. As a result of public pressure, the Department of Defense began to implement sexual harassment policies in the early 1980s. All branches of the military have adopted guidelines based on the EEOC regulations and civilian employment definitions.

Although the courts have defined sexual harassment, employees and employers alike continue to express confusion about the type of behavior that actually constitutes sexual harassment

under the law. Susan Webb defines sexual harassment as deliberate, perhaps repeated, sexual or sex- or gender-based behavior that is not welcome, not asked for, and not returned. This definition encompasses a continuum of behavior ranging from joking and innuendo to fondling, assault, and rape, and includes verbal, nonverbal, and physical behavior. Generally speaking, the responsibility for determining whether behavior is sexually harassing falls on the receiver of the behavior, in that if the behavior is unwelcome to the receiver, then it is harassment. However, as Webb points out, the more severe the behavior, the less responsibility falls on the receiver to define the situation. In other words, the more severe the behavior (attempted rape, for instance), the more responsibility falls on the offender to know that the behavior in question is offensive.

In 1995 Michele Paludi and Richard Barickman categorized sexual harassment according to five levels of seriousness. Here, sexual harassment is viewed as a continuum of behavior with mildly offensive behavior at one extreme and severe behavior at the other. Gender harassment consists of generalized sexist remarks or insulting and degrading comments. Seductive behavior is defined as unwanted and offensive sexual advances. Sexual bribery is the solicitation of sexual activity by threat of punishment, while sexual coercion is coercion by threat of punishment. The most serious behavior is termed sexual imposition, which includes sexual assault and rape.

### Prevalence of Sexual Harassment

Sexual harassment occurs in workplaces across the United States. Although there are few national random samples, the existing data suggest that sexual harassment occurs with unsettling frequency. Surveys of college undergraduate and graduate students, business employees, and military service members indicate that women and men have been subjected to sexually harassing behavior. In several studies conducted in academic environments, students reported that they had skipped classes, dropped classes, and even changed academic majors to avoid sexual harassment by professors. Students have also reported harassment by their peers.

In a major survey conducted in 1980 by the National Merit Systems Protection Board in which over twenty-three thousand workers were surveyed, 42 percent of women reported that they had experienced sexual harassment. In 1988 this organization performed a follow-up study of thirteen thousand workers and found similar results.

Studies have also been conducted in the military. In a 1980 study conducted of enlisted women in the navy, 90 percent said that they had been verbally harassed and 61 percent indicated that they had been physically harassed. Results of a survey conducted of fifteen thousand enlisted air force personnel found that 27 percent of the women and 7 percent of the men had been harassed within the prior four-week period. A nationwide survey of thirty-five thousand service members conducted by the Department of Defense in 1988–1989 indicated that 64 percent of the females and 17 percent of the males had experienced some form of harassment at least once in the previous year (Chema 1993).

Moreover, sexual harassment claims filed with the EEOC more than doubled in the two-year period following the Thomas confirmation hearings, from thirty-three hundred in 1991 to seventy-three hundred in 1993. The EEOC statistics for 1995 show that the number of claims doubled again to more than fifteen thousand. The majority of complaints involved hostile work environments. The army has also received an increase in sexual harassment complaints. As of January 1997, almost seven thousand complaints had been filed, one thousand of which were referred for investigation. Researchers continue to speculate that many cases of sexual harassment go unreported; therefore relying on formal complaints may underestimate the prevalence of sexual harassment.

### Sexual Harassers

Research studies indicate that the majority of harassers are men, although little is known about men who harass women. Available data come from victim self-reports and indicate that men who harass are likely to be married, older than their victims, and the same race as their victims (Pryor 1987). Harassers also have a reputation for sexually exploitative behavior. Coworkers are more likely than supervisors to harass women; however, harassment from supervisors tends to be more severe. Coworkers are also more likely to engage in persistent offensive behavior.

### Impact of Harassment

For many years the behaviors now known as sexual harassment were viewed as innocuous, on the order of bantering between men and women. This view has changed, with researchers now recognizing sexual harassment as part of the larger context of violence against women. Although sexual harassment does not usually reach the level of physical violence, its impact on victims can be severe in terms of emotional and psychic damage. Studies that have been conducted on the impact of harassment show that employees have quit their jobs, have been transferred or reassigned, or have been fired because they failed to comply with the harasser's demands. Other consequences include deterioration of relationships at work, lowered job satisfaction and motivation, and lack of access to information at work, all of which can affect job performance. Victims have also reported emotional and physical consequences associated with being harassed, including depression, anxiety, irritability, loss of self-esteem, and in severe cases, posttraumatic stress disorder.

The impact of harassment upon organizations is less clear. Financially, organizations stand to lose money from lack of worker productivity, absenteeism, and high job turnover. Additionally, victims of harassment can cost companies thousands of dollars in medical expenses. The most obvious loss is if a company has to pay damages due to a successful sexual harassment claim.

### Conclusion

The issue of sexual harassment has revolutionized the workplace. Confusion about what constitutes harassment continues to cause strain between men and women and employers and employees. Cases continue to be filed, prompting ongoing debate. Whatever court decisions and new legislation are to come, ambivalence about sexual behavior in the workplace is likely to remain.

*BIBLIOGRAPHY*

Chema, Richard L. "Arresting Tailhook: The Prosecution of Sexual Harassment in the Military." *Military Law Review* 140, no. 1 (1993): 1, 18.

Cleveland, Jeanette N., and Melinda E. Kerst. "Sexual Harassment and Perceptions of Power: An Underarticulated Relationship." *Journal of Vocational Behavior* 42 (1993): 49–67.

Greenwald, Juliana. "Army Defends Record on Harassment." *Congressional Quarterly Weekly Report* 55, no. 6 (February 1997): 376.

Gutek, Barbara, and Mary P. Koss. "Changed Women and Organizations: Consequences of and Coping with Sexual Harassment." *Journal of Vocational Behavior* 42 (1993): 28–48.

Paludi, Michele A., and Richard Barickman. "Sexual Harassment Definitions Apply to Academia." In *What Is*

*Sexual Harassment?* edited by Karin Swisher. San Diego: Greenhaven, 1995.

Pryor, John. "Sexual Proclivities in Men." *Sex Roles* 17, no. 5/6 (1987): 269–289.

Siegel, Deborah L. "Legal Definitions of Sexual Harassment Must Be Broad." In *What Is Sexual Harassment?* edited by Karin Swisher. San Diego: Greenhaven, 1995.

Webb, Susan. "Sexual Harassment Should Be Defined Broadly." In *What Is Sexual Harassment?* edited by Karin Swisher. San Diego: Greenhaven, 1995.

KAREN A. CASEY

*See also* **Corporations; Rape; Sex Differences; Women; Workplace.**

# SHAME

The connection between shame and violence is not immediately apparent. Most of us when embarrassed turn away quietly from whoever has exposed what we had wanted to keep secret and hope we might fall into the safe obscurity of a hole so no one can see our discomfort. It is true that one who has been treated violently by another or made to feel helpless in the face of overwhelming power of any sort may feel shame. Yet there is a far more important logic, through which shame itself comes to be a trigger for violent action; Donald L. Nathanson (1992) has estimated that more than 90 percent of the arguments or fights we see in our shared world have been set in motion as a response to shame.

For each of the basic clusters of emotions named by Nathanson, there seems to be a range of expression we understand intuitively as normal and a level of reaction most people would consider pathological. The shame family of emotions, as noted by Leon Wurmser (1987), includes embarrassment, shame, mortification, humiliation, and the experience of being put down or treated with contempt. In banter two people conversing may characterize each other with labels that are embarrassing but within socially accepted limits; when those limits are exceeded, the labels are redefined as insulting. The Chinese proverb "He who lands the first blow was the first to run out of arguments" suggests that both the type and intensity of our reaction to shame are highly variable. Despite the ubiquity of this most social of emotions, shame has come under intense investigation only in the last quarter of the twentieth century.

Like all emotions, what we call shame is a matter of both biology and biography. Even infants several weeks old, far too young to know that they have been "embarrassed," will drop their eyes, turn away from whatever had been occupying their attention only a moment before, show the peculiar lack of muscular tone in the neck and upper back associated with the slump of shame, blush, and for a moment become unable to pay attention to anything. This is a genetically programmed, evolved response to a stimulus that interferes with attention to an already interesting or enjoyable stimulus; the physiology of shame is a highly amplified version of that interference. Yet from the moment we are born, we start learning to handle our emotions. How we are raised in a family, a neighborhood, and an era determine to a large extent how we will react emotionally to any stimulus.

## The Compass of Shame

Although the physiology of shame has evolved to make us pay attention to whatever has interfered with the previously pleasant stimulus, quite often we ignore this built-in warning system. When thus ignored, this physiological reaction points to an array of possible responses known as the compass of shame (see figure 1). At each point of this compass is stored a library of behavior and attitudes through which we have learned to deal with any conceivable moment of shame. The *withdrawal* pole contains a storehouse of information about all those times we have obeyed the physiological shame mechanism without thinking about its cause, and turned away from a pleasant experience that had suddenly become conflicted. It is our personal history of situations in which this

FIGURE 1. **The Compass of Shame**

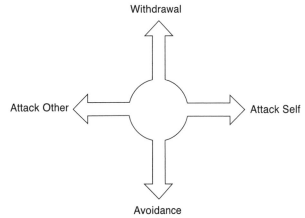

SOURCE: Nathanson 1992.

151

SHAYS'S REBELLION

physiological mechanism had been so triggered as to bring to mind the sense of exposure and personal defect or deficiency that we so often associate with the moment of shame.

At the *attack self* pole lie the ways in which we can become subservient to others so as to reduce or prevent whatever danger might be associated with the sense of isolation that might be felt if we were to withdraw in shame. Here lies behavior over a range from simple, reasonable, and harmless deference toward a more powerful other to masochistic submission to a truly dangerous other; at either end of this spectrum we are spared from abandonment and isolation. The *avoidance* pole contains all the ways we disavow the bad feeling and try to make it go away without dealing with its message. This approach is linked to narcissism, which also entails reluctance to deal with certain information about ourselves. Alcohol, amphetamines, cocaine, and heroin are just a few of the chemicals that can assist avoidance, whereas bragging, macho behavior, and the search for excitement and danger may be understood as ways we distract both ourselves and the others before whom our defects or deficiencies have been exposed.

For those moments when there seems to be no way to limit the pain brought by shame or to bring on countervailing pride, we can mobilize actions from the *attack other* library of scripts. An individual may try to put down, humiliate, injure, or abuse another, or otherwise reduce another's self-esteem to feel bigger and better than that person (if only for a moment). Whereas the actions, drugs, and psychological devices mobilized at the *avoidance* pole of the compass predispose us to violence by reducing the degree to which any of us may be held in check by shame expressed as reticence, it is only the responses associated with the *attack other* pole that transform shame into violent action. Although emotion is a combination of ancient physiological mechanisms and our personal history of the scenes in which each of these mechanisms may have been triggered, violence is always learned behavior.

**The Public World of Shame**

Public and private behavior prompted by the shame responses delineated here have varied greatly over the course of history. In medieval times bumping into someone unintentionally in the town square might set off a fight to the death. From the early days of the Renaissance until the beginning of the modern era, standards of public decency provided behavioral controls that limited such expressions of anger and violence. These constraints eroded significantly during the last half of the twentieth century, as the social control of behavior met with increasing public disfavor and the drug culture grew explosively. Both of these trends intensified a shift from the *withdrawal* and *attack self* modes of response to shame toward the *avoidance* and *attack other* poles of the compass. Although violent action may of course be carefully planned and as dispassionate as shooting in a target range, most of the spontaneous anger and explosive violence seen in public life may be understood as a response to shame.

Nathanson (1995) has found that programs that educate adults about the connection between shame and violence have proved useful in promoting effective communities. Formal education of grade-school children about the nature of emotion and the compass of shame has begun to offer a long-term solution to a problem long buried beneath strident attention to the more easily visible problems of drug use. Education must also address the often ignored and legally excused ways in which movies and television teach children, if only by example, to respond to increasingly trivial instances of shame with studied violence as if it were a normative response to insult.

*BIBLIOGRAPHY*

Nathanson, Donald L. "Crime and Nourishment: When the Tried and True Becomes the Tired and False." *Bulletin of the Tomkins Institute* 2 (summer 1995).
———. *Shame and Pride: Affect, Sex, and the Birth of the Self.* New York: Norton, 1992.
Tomkins, Silvan S. *Affect Imagery Consciousness.* Vol. 2, *The Negative Affects.* New York: Guilford, 1963.
———. "Shame." In *The Many Faces of Shame*, edited by Donald L. Nathanson. New York: Guilford, 1987.
Wurmser, Leon. "Shame: The Veiled Companion to Narcissism." In *The Many Faces of Shame*, edited by Donald L. Nathanson. New York: Guilford, 1987.

DONALD L. NATHANSON

*See also* **Emotion; Poverty; Psychological Violence.**

**SHAYS'S REBELLION.** *See* Agrarian Violence; Civil Disorder; Depressions, Economic.

**SHORT, ELIZABETH.** *See* Black Dahlia.

152

# SIBLING ABUSE

Sibling abuse, though the most prevalent form of family violence in the United States, for the most part has been overlooked and ignored or simply accepted. Sibling violence is so commonplace that very few people consider it abuse. Parents may see sibling violence as inevitable because of its existence throughout history. Sibling violence exceeds the level of violence that parents use on children or that spouses use on each other. Murray Straus estimated more than thirty-six million attacks in 1980 would have been considered assaults had they not occurred between siblings: research in a single year showed 5.8 million siblings beaten up; 14.5 million hit with an object; 15.2 million kicked, bitten, or punched; close to 300,000 threatened with a gun or a knife; and more than 100,000 attacked with a gun or a knife.

One sibling may be more likely to abuse another if parents are absent or unavailable, if parents practice authoritarian punishment, and if parents abuse drugs or alcohol or have marital dysfunctions. Violence in the family—spousal abuse, child abuse, elder abuse, and incest—also influences how siblings treat each other. Sibling abuse manifests itself in physical, emotional, and sexual behavior. Physical abuse includes hitting, choking, biting, slapping, holding down, striking with objects, throwing objects, destroying personal property (usually favorite toys and other objects), and maltreating pets. Emotional abuse includes name-calling, cursing, blaming, demeaning references and insults (humiliation), threats, isolation, and controlling conversations and gestures. Sexual abuse includes fondling, manipulated sexual stimulation (usually by an older sibling), coerced masturbation, forced oral sex, and intercourse.

Victims of sibling abuse suffer from low self-esteem, greater levels of depression and anxiety, guilt, distrust of authority figures, difficulties with intimacy, isolation, self-destructiveness and self-hating, and other problems. Society pays consequences as well. According to a report issued at the 1984 national conference of the American Association for Marriage and Family Therapy, 90 percent of all criminals in the United States report having been physically abused as children. Suzanne K. Steinmetz's study of thirty-three adolescents who had committed murder found that the adolescents shared a similar childhood background of relentless brutality (by inference this would include sibling abuse), personal experience

## Jacob and Esau

The story of Cain killing his brother Abel is most often cited in reference to sibling abuse. However, the story of the biblical twins Jacob and Esau (Genesis 25:19–33:20) is more pertinent to such abuse and its systemic dysfunction. Rebekah, who favored her younger son Jacob over Esau, instigated Jacob in a plot to steal Esau's birthright and blessing. When their father, Isaac, learned of the deception, he did nothing to establish integrity and fairness. Estranged from his father, abandoned by his mother, and deceived and humiliated by Jacob, Esau suffered his entire life. The story illustrates the key concepts of sibling abuse, parental influence, and passive acceptance.

with violent death, and extremely unfavorable home conditions.

Violence is a learned pattern of behavior that has its roots in early childhood experiences. It is a result of intergenerational transmission of repetitive, habitualized abuse. When violent behavior is the everyday experience of growing up, it likely will become the modus operandi of later adult relationships. According to the Georgia Council on Child Abuse, children who were abused by their parents are six times more likely to abuse their own children. An older brother who physically abuses his sister is likely to do the same to his future wife. Until the incidence of sibling abuse becomes more accurately reported and documented, other forms of family violence will continue to receive the focus of attention. Prevention and treatment programs for victims of sibling abuse await society's awakening to the detrimental effects of sibling abuse on individuals and society.

*BIBLIOGRAPHY*

Gelles, Richard J., and Claire Pedrick Cornell. *Intimate Violence in Families.* Beverly Hills, Calif.: Sage, 1985.
Gelles, Richard J., and Murray A. Straus. *Intimate Violence.* New York: Simon and Schuster, 1988.
Steinmetz, Suzanne K. *Family Violence: Past, Present, Future.* Newark: University of Delaware Press, 1988.

JERRY L. BRINEGAR

*See also* **Birth Order and Birth Spacing; Child Abuse; Domestic Violence; Incest.**

## SIEGEL, BENJAMIN "BUGSY"
### (1906–1947)

Benjamin "Bugsy" Siegel personified the under-world's post–World War II transformation from a society of hot-tempered, ill-mannered hoodlums into smooth-talking exemplars of "gangster capitalism." A poorly educated punk from Manhattan's Lower East Side, Siegel fashioned himself into a "Hollywood gentleman" who counted movie producers, film stars, and even a countess among his friends. Nattily attired and socially adroit, with an easy, affable manner, he was said to have "handled a big cigar as nimbly" as any mogul. Born in 1906 in Brooklyn, New York, to poor Jewish parents, Siegel drifted into a life of petty crime while still a youngster. With his childhood chum Meyer Lansky, he spent much of his adolescence robbing pushcarts and rolling drunks and dice. It was also during this period in his life that the hot-headed Siegel acquired the nickname "Bugsy," a sobriquet that he hated. Because of his volatile temper, the young hoodlum was thought

**Benjamin 'Bugsy' Siegel.** LIBRARY OF CONGRESS

to be "crazy as a bedbug," and in short order, he became known as "Bugsy." Prohibition unleashed the duo's talents. Using their fists and wits, the Bugs and Meyer Gang, as they were known at the time, protected rival bootleggers from one another. They became "specialists in the dangerous occupation of transporting booze."

Shortly after the repeal of Prohibition in 1933, Siegel left for the West Coast. Some say he acted on his own, others that he departed on instructions from Lansky, who was eager to expand his empire. Whatever his motivation, the New York gangster took to Tinseltown, making it his own. Eschewing violence in favor of more gentlemanly forms of persuasion, Siegel seized control of the wire services, or what the *New York Times* euphemistically called the "racing information business." An extremely lucrative enterprise, Siegel's company, the Trans-American, was believed to have generated as much as $25,000 a month in revenue. Siegel also invested heavily in the track and other gaming establishments, including a string of tumbledown casinos in what was then the sleepy desert town of Las Vegas.

In 1946, with a keen eye toward the future, Siegel and his underworld associates built the Flamingo, a fabulous resort and casino, for the then-staggering price of more than $6 million. With its plush carpets, deluxe accommodations, and acres of slot machines, the Flamingo heralded Las Vegas's metamorphosis into America's gambling mecca.

A few months after the Flamingo's gala opening, Siegel's life and career came to a brutal end. In June 1947 he was shot to death in the Beverly Hills mansion of his girlfriend and confidante, Virginia Hill, with a fusillade of bullets. Speculation ran riot about the identity of his killer, prompting *Time* magazine to write that "readers could take their pick of a dozen theories." Today, most historians believe that Siegel was killed by his underworld associates, investors in the Flamingo, for exceeding his authority and cheating them of their money. Siegel's untimely demise—he was only forty-one at the time—also generated a great deal of discussion about his true identity. He lived the life of a gentleman, reported *Life* magazine, but he met the bloody end of a "public enemy."

Eventually, Bugsy Siegel receded into the "romantic mists of early Las Vegas" history. All that remained of the Hollywood legend was an illuminated memorial, a "chaste ziggurat" that towered over his beloved Flamingo.

*BIBLIOGRAPHY*

"End of a Gangster." *Life,* 7 July 1947.

Fried, Albert. *The Rise and Fall of the Jewish Gangster in America.* New York: Columbia University Press, 1993.

"The 'Inside' on Bugsy." *Time,* 7 July 1947.

Liebling, A. J. "Our Far-Flung Correspondents: Out Among the Gangsters." *New Yorker,* 27 March 1954.

JENNA WEISSMAN JOSELIT

*See also* **Gambling; Lansky, Meyer; Las Vegas; Murder, Inc.; Organized Crime.**

# SIMPSON, O. J., MURDER TRIALS

During the early morning hours of 13 June 1994, two slashed and mangled bodies—a white woman and white man—were discovered lying in pools of their own blood outside a condominium on Bundy Drive in one of Los Angeles's most fashionable neighborhoods. The woman had suffered seven stab wounds to the neck and scalp in what police described as a "rage killing." Her neck had been lacerated so deeply that her head was nearly severed from the rest of her body. The male victim had suffered dozens of stab wounds to the neck, chest, abdomen, thighs, scalp, face, and hands.

Shortly after the gruesome discovery, news quickly spread around the nation about the murders of Nicole Brown Simpson and Ronald Goldman, and about evidence pointing toward the guilt of the black football legend Orenthal James (O. J.) Simpson, Nicole Brown Simpson's ex-husband. Unnamed sources informed the news media that Los Angeles Police Department (LAPD) detectives had found blood matching Simpson's outside his ex-wife's Bundy Drive condominium and at his nearby Rockingham Avenue estate. Also, a bloody glove reportedly discovered behind Simpson's house was said to match one found at the Bundy Drive crime scene. But Simpson's attorneys steadfastly proclaimed the Hall-of-Famer's innocence.

On 17 June an LAPD commander made an announcement to the media: the prime suspect had failed to turn himself in to police as promised. Hours later Simpson was spotted south of Los Angeles, on Interstate 5, in the backseat of a Ford Bronco with his friend A. C. Cowlings at the wheel. Ninety-five million viewers across the nation—one of the largest television audiences in U.S. history—watched helicopter video images of Simpson and Cowlings slowly leading a growing contingent of law enforcement vehicles back up the interstate. In Los Angeles spectators lined the freeway, hoping to get a glimpse of Simpson's vehicle. Many cheered on the fugitive. When the caravan finally made its way to Simpson's home, the celebrity suspect was swiftly arrested. Simpson plead "100 percent not guilty" in Los Angeles Superior Court a month later (22 July 1994) and became the most famous murder defendant in U.S. history. Denied bail, Simpson was confined for the duration of the trial to Los Angeles County Jail.

**Motorists observing O. J. Simpson and his white Ford Bronco followed by police, 17 June 1994.** GAMMA

155

### The Criminal Trial

Opening arguments in *People of the State of California v. Orenthal James Simpson* began in Los Angeles Superior Court on 24 January 1995. Prosecutors mounted a long, tedious case in which they called fifty-eight witnesses in their attempts to prove that O. J. Simpson had murdered Nicole Brown Simpson and Ronald Goldman. The jury consisted of nine blacks, two whites, and one Latino. Christopher Darden, a black man who critics charged was added to the prosecution team primarily to appeal to the predominantly black jury, began the case against Simpson in an unconventional manner. Rather than begin with evidence tying Simpson directly to the murders and crime scenes, prosecutors decided to open with a focus on Simpson's motive. Accordingly, Darden characterized Simpson as an enraged, obsessed wife batterer who committed the final act of control by murdering his ex-wife and her male friend. Darden pointed out, for example, that Nicole Brown Simpson had left behind a diary describing her ex-husband's abuse, as well as a safety deposit box containing photos of her bruised face and apology letters from Simpson. To this motive, the lead prosecutor, Marcia Clark, added what she described as a "mountain" of circumstantial blood and fiber evidence linking Simpson to the Bundy Drive murder scene and linking the victims to his Ford Bronco and Rockingham Avenue estate. When police first interrogated Simpson, for example, investigators noticed an oozing cut on the middle finger of his left hand. The location of this cut seemed to correspond to the location of blood drops at the Bundy Drive crime scene. That is, the drops appeared to the left of bloody, size-twelve footprints from rare Bruno Magli shoes—Simpson's size. Although prosecutors were unable to prove that Simpson ever owned such shoes, DNA from one of the blood drops could have been produced only by about one in 170 million persons, and Simpson's blood matched it. Clark also introduced other evidence suggesting that a trail of Simpson's and the victims' blood led from the Bundy Drive crime scene to Simpson's Ford Bronco, up his Rockingham Avenue driveway, through his foyer, and into his master bedroom.

In contrast, Simpson's defense team called fifty-three witnesses in an attempt to show that a "rush to judgment" and willful misconduct by LAPD detectives worked to incriminate an innocent Simpson. The media dubbed this group of eleven attorneys and numerous investigators Simpson's Dream Team because of the participation of high-profile attorneys and legal scholars such as Johnnie Cochran, F. Lee Bailey, Robert Shapiro, Alan M. Dershowitz, and Gerald Uelman. Led by Cochran, a prominent black attorney based in Los Angeles, the team mounted a three-pronged attack. First, it argued that Simpson had no motive to kill his ex-wife and that the prosecution's depictions of Simpson's obsession with his ex-wife were false. Second, the team argued that LAPD evidence collection practices in the case could not be trusted and that all the astronomical DNA statistics the prosecutors embraced were thus invalid. Finally, the attorneys reasoned that the detective Mark Fuhrman—the white officer credited with discovering key evidence in the case (e.g., the bloody glove)—harbored a racial hatred toward blacks that prompted him to plant evidence against Simpson. During a controversial cross-examination by the defense attorney F. Lee Bailey that took place toward the beginning of the trial, Fuhrman denied that he had referred to African Americans in the past ten years as "niggers." But audiotapes surfaced late in the trial on which the detective could clearly be heard using the racial epithet dozens of times. To avoid perjury prosecution, Fuhrman pleaded his Fifth Amendment right against self-incrimination to all the questions the defense attorney Gerald Uelman posed, including, "Detective Fuhrman, did you plant or manufacture any evidence in this case?" The discrediting of Fuhrman formed the cornerstone of the defense's so-called conspiracy theory. During his closing arguments to the jury, Cochran compared Fuhrman's alleged actions and his audiotaped statements to those of Adolf Hitler. When Cochran told the primarily black jury that it could take a stand against racism in the LAPD by acquitting Simpson, outraged critics immediately accused him of soliciting jury nullification (that is, ignoring the evidence and subverting the law in the name of a political cause).

The trial judge, Lance A. Ito, permitted the trial to be televised live to the world via a courtroom camera operated by the cable television network Court TV. Some 1,159 journalists from the United States and more than a dozen foreign nations covered daily developments in the trial using a makeshift production facility outside the courthouse dubbed Camp O. J. One major development that received recurring media attention was a series of opinion polls suggesting the existence of a "racial divide" in opinion about Simpson's innocence or guilt. Dozens of national and regional opinion polls taken in the months following the murders and throughout the trial found that most white Americans believed in the prosecution's case against Simpson, while their black counterparts were more sympathetic to his defense. This latter group was influenced by concerns about possible racial inequities in the criminal justice system— for example, the statistic that black males faced a 28 percent chance of entering state or federal prison in their lifetimes, compared with only a 4.4 percent chance for white males. Throughout the trial, media pundits, scholars, and the public debated what this schism might mean for the future of U.S. race relations.

Women activists cited the murder of Simpson's ex-wife as a tragic example of what can happen when society allows domestic violence to escalate unchecked. They noted, for example, that nearly one-third of all women homicide victims in the United States are killed by a husband or boyfriend. As a result of their campaign, calls to domestic-violence shelters across the nation increased, the U.S. Congress held a series of hearings on domestic violence, and many judges across the country handed down unusually tough sentences in domestic-violence cases.

Other activists saw the unfolding case as an example of how wealth can buy justice. Three months into the trial an editorial in *Newsweek* made the point: "If Simpson walks, as most lawyers think he will, what will have decided the outcome is not that O. J. is black, but that he is rich." Even before the verdicts some activists called for the institution of professional juries, nonunanimous verdicts, and disclosure of compensations for expert witnesses—all changes designed to facilitate criminal convictions.

On 3 October 1995, nearly sixteen months after the murders, Los Angeles and much of the nation came to a halt as the verdicts in the criminal trial were about to be read. Deliberating for less than four hours, the jury found Simpson not guilty of murdering his ex-wife and her male friend. As television news media canvassed for public reaction to the verdicts, the racial divide was again highlighted. Several local and national news media juxtaposed images of elated black trial observers with those of somber whites. Blacks generally embraced the verdicts as a sign that the criminal justice system may have finally worked as it should for a black defendant: for them, the prose-

cution had not proven Simpson's guilt beyond a reasonable doubt and the system had justly acquitted him. Whites, however, were in general convinced that the prosecution had amassed a "mountain of evidence" that proved Simpson's guilt beyond almost any doubt: for them, the verdicts were a miscarriage of justice facilitated by the defense's cynical playing of the "race card" before a predominantly black jury.

**The Civil Trial**

On 4 February 1997—in what continued to be a racially charged atmosphere—the nation again awaited the readings of verdicts in an O. J. Simpson case. This time, however, the legal venue was a civil court and the verdicts would determine Simpson's liability for the deaths of Nicole Brown Simpson and Ronald Goldman. The burden of proof ("the preponderance of the evidence") was significantly lower in this trial than in the criminal trial ("beyond a reasonable doubt") that preceded it. And in the civil trial Simpson could be compelled to testify. The public, however, would have to rely solely on news media accounts of Simpson's testimony and other evidence because the trial judge, Hiroshi Fujisaki, had banned all cameras and audio recorders from his courtroom to avoid the media circus that he believed plagued the criminal trial.

This new trial differed from the earlier trial in another important respect: whereas the criminal trial had been held in a downtown Los Angeles courthouse serviced by a largely minority jury pool, the civil trial was held in a Santa Monica courthouse and featured a jury pool dominated by whites. Indeed, a predominantly white jury would listen to streamlined prosecution and defense cases (e.g., the judge forbade the lead defense attorney, Robert C. Baker, from exploring many of the conspiracy theories defense attorneys successfully argued in the criminal case). Photos of Simpson apparently wearing the Bruno Magli shoes and Simpson's own performance on the witness stand (e.g., in the face of seemingly incontrovertible evidence, he denied that he and his ex-wife had a troubled relationship or that he had ever hit her) were identified by some observers as decisive in the trial. Just weeks after an Orange County judge had granted Simpson custody of his two young children, the civil trial jury agreed with prosecutors that he had probably murdered the children's mother and awarded the victims' families $8.5 million plus $25 million in punitive damages.

In the aftermath of this latest verdict, the racial divide in perceptions of the case remained. Domestic-violence and victim's rights activists continued to travel the talk-show circuit, a forum that the Simpson case dominated for over two years. And despite a conviction rate well above 90 percent in all criminal cases in Los Angeles, activists continued to lobby for changes to the criminal justice system that would facilitate the conviction of "obviously guilty" defendants like Simpson.

O. J. Simpson was eventually forced to vacate his Rockingham Avenue estate after he fell behind in mortgage payments, thanks to an estimated $6 million in legal expenses for the criminal trial alone. To the delight of his ex-wife's sister, Denise Brown, and many who were convinced of his guilt, the estate he had called home for two decades would eventually be demolished by its new owner. But Simpson continued to maintain his innocence. He filed an appeal to the civil verdicts in July 1998. Later that year the decision granting Simpson custody of his two young children was overturned, paving the way for a fourth trial in the case.

*BIBLIOGRAPHY*

Abramson, Jeffrey, ed. *Postmortem, The O. J. Simpson Case: Justice Confronts Race, Domestic Violence, Lawyers, Money, and the Media*. New York: Basic, 1996.

Dershowitz, Alan M. *Reasonable Doubts: The O. J. Simpson Case and the Criminal Justice System.* New York: Simon and Schuster, 1996.

Elias, Tom, and Dennis Schatzman. *The Simpson Trial in Black and White*. Los Angeles: General Publishing, 1996.

Hunt, Darnell M. *O. J. Simpson Facts and Fictions: News Rituals in the Construction of Reality*. Cambridge, U.K.: Cambridge University Press, 1999.

Morrison, Toni, and Claudia Brodsky Lacour, eds. *Birth of a Nation'hood: Gaze, Script, and Spectacle in the O. J. Simpson Case*. New York: Pantheon, 1997.

Petrocelli, Daniel, and Peter Knobler. *Triumph of Justice: The Final Judgment on the Simpson Saga*. New York: Crown, 1998.

Schiller, Lawrence, and James Willwerth. *American Tragedy: The Uncensored Story of the Simpson Defense*. New York: Random House, 1996.

Schmalleger, Frank. *Trial of the Century: People of the State of California v. Orenthal James Simpson*. Upper Saddle River, N.J.: Prentice Hall, 1996.

Spence, Gerry. *O. J.: The Last Word*. New York: St. Martin's, 1997.

DARNELL M. HUNT

*See also* **Los Angeles; Spousal and Partner Abuse.**

# SIRHAN SIRHAN
## (1944– )

Shortly after midnight on 5 June 1968, the evening of the California Democratic presidential primary election, Sirhan Sirhan stepped from behind a tray rack in the pantry of the Ambassador Hotel in Los Angeles and into the path of Senator Robert F. Kennedy. Snarling, "Kennedy, you son of a bitch," he raised a .22-caliber pistol to within an inch of the senator's head and fired a fatal bullet into his brain. Five other persons were wounded before Sirhan was subdued. As he was being driven to police headquarters, he was asked why he had murdered Kennedy. Sirhan's reply, "I did it for my country," was the same comment he had made at the scene of the crime. Sirhan was tried and convicted of first-degree murder and sentenced to die in the California gas chamber. His sentence was reduced to life imprisonment in 1972 when the U.S. Supreme Court declared the death penalty unconstitutional.

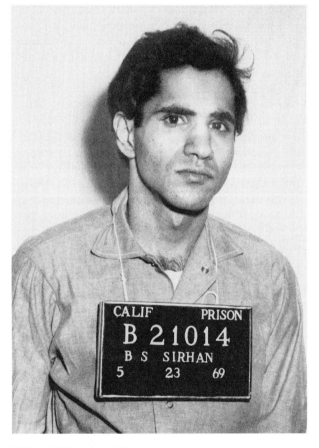

**Sirhan Sirhan in 1969.** CORBIS/BETTMANN

Sirhan Sirhan, a Palestinian Arab, was born on 19 March 1944 in Jerusalem. As a child he witnessed the brutal, often bloody struggle between Arabs, Jews, and the British forces that foreshadowed the establishment of the new State of Israel. The deafening explosions and chaos of war, the mutilated bodies of Arab neighbors, and the sight of a brother being crushed under the wheels of a truck driven by a Zionist, left wounds that would never heal. Shortly after Israeli independence was declared on 14 May 1948 Sirhan's family—his parents and four brothers and a sister—were forced to abandon their home as Jews took over that section of the city. For the next nine years they survived as poverty-stricken refugees, living on the fringes of a hostile Israeli society, on land that was no longer theirs. In 1956, when Sirhan was twelve years old, the family immigrated to the United States, but the terror, trauma, and anger caused by those experiences remained. Sirhan hated Jews and Israel.

With the aid of relief agencies, the Sirhan family settled in Pasadena, California, where he completed his elementary and secondary education in the city's public schools. Classmates, teachers, and neighbors recalled him as cooperative, courteous, and enthusiastic. Later, his enrollment at Pasadena City College proved less successful. A series of marginal jobs followed, including a stint caring for horses at the Santa Anita racetrack, where his desire to become a jockey was never realized. Throughout this period, however, he lived with the hope of someday returning to his homeland.

The chances of doing that seemed even more remote after the devastating Arab defeat by Israeli forces in the Six-Day War of 1967. Later, Sirhan was appalled and enraged when he learned that a man he had admired, Senator Robert F. Kennedy, supported the sale of jet fighter bombers to Israel to replace planes it had lost in that war. Evidence reveals that on 31 January 1968 he decided the senator should be assassinated. When Kennedy, some six weeks later, announced plans to seek the Democratic presidential nomination, Sirhan vowed to himself to take matters into his own hands. Convinced that Kennedy would succeed if he was not stopped, Sirhan acquired the murder weapon and began preparing himself for the event. Mind-control exercises and long practice sessions at a local firing range followed. Sirhan began stalking Kennedy during the final two weeks of the California primary campaign, following the senator from one engagement to another and waiting for an opportunity to strike. It came on 5 June 1968, the first anniversary of the Six-Day War.

*BIBLIOGRAPHY*

Clarke, James W. *American Assassins: The Darker Side of Politics.* Princeton, N.J.: Princeton University Press, 1982. Reprint, 1990.
———. *On Being Mad or Merely Angry: John W. Hinckley, Jr., and Other Dangerous People.* Princeton, N.J.: Princeton University Press, 1990.
Klaber, William, and Philip H. Melanson. *Shadow Play: The Murder of Robert F. Kennedy, the Trial of Sirhan Sirhan, and the Failure of American Justice.* New York: St. Martin's, 1997.

JAMES W. CLARKE

*See also* **Assassinations; Kennedy, Robert F.; Politics: Political Campaigns.**

# SITTING BULL
## (c. 1831–1890)

Sitting Bull (Tatanka Iyotake) was a preeminent leader of the Lakotas (one of seven divisions of the Sioux). He is best known today as an uncompromising advocate of militant resistance to U.S. expansion into Lakota territory. Sitting Bull was also a religious and political leader who further advanced his people's interests through war with other tribes to obtain horses and control of buffalo ranges. Through his many roles, he exemplified Lakota virtues of bravery and generosity.

Born sometime between 1831 and 1834 in what is now South Dakota, Sitting Bull quickly attained prominence among the Hunkpapas (a subdivision of the Lakotas) as a fearless fighter in warfare with other Indian tribes, especially Assiniboines and Crows. While in his twenties, Sitting Bull also became a *wicasa wakan* (holy man). Living in the northern regions of Lakota territory, Sitting Bull was removed from the conflict between the Lakotas and the United States along the Oregon Trail in the 1850s. In the early 1860s, however, gold miners began to travel through Hunkpapa hunting grounds on their way to the Rocky Mountains. At the same time, U.S. troops invaded northern Lakota territory in pursuit of Santee Sioux fleeing reprisals in the aftermath of the 1862 Minnesota Uprising. Although some Lakota leaders signed the Treaty of 1868 and began to live near government

**Sitting Bull. Photo © 1884 by Palmquist and Jurgens.**

agencies where they received food and clothing, Sitting Bull favored armed struggle.

Following the discovery of gold in the Black Hills in 1874, a new wave of miners moved into Lakota territory in violation of the 1868 treaty. Instead of stopping this illegal incursion, the government demanded that Lakotas abandon unceded hunting grounds in present-day Wyoming and Montana. When they refused to do so, government officials authorized a military expedition to subjugate the militants. It was in this context that George Armstrong Custer attacked a large encampment of Lakotas, Cheyennes, and Arapahoes on 25 June 1876. Although Sitting Bull did not play a crucial military role in the defeat of Custer's Seventh Cavalry at the Battle of Little Bighorn, days earlier he had given his people courage through foretelling their victory.

As the army continued to harass the militants, Sitting Bull took refuge in Canada in 1877. Four years later he surrendered and settled on the Standing Rock reservation (in South Dakota), where he became a steadfast opponent of U.S. policies to force his people to assimilate to American cultural norms and cede additional lands. In 1889–1890, many Lakotas began to participate in the Ghost Dance, an anticolonial religious movement that promised the return of the buffalo and dead ancestors as well as the removal of whites through supernatural means. In November 1890 U.S. troops tried to suppress the Ghost Dance on western Sioux reservations; officials ordered Sitting Bull's arrest. On 15 December, when Standing Rock Indian police tried to carry out these orders, one of Sitting Bull's supporters opened fire. Two policemen fired at Sitting Bull, killing him instantly. Sitting Bull's death set off a chain of events that culminated in the Wounded Knee massacre on 29 December 1890.

*BIBLIOGRAPHY*

Anderson, Gary Clayton. *Sitting Bull and the Paradox of Lakota Nationhood.* New York: HarperCollins, 1996.
Utley, Robert M. *The Lance and the Shield: The Life and Times of Sitting Bull.* New York: Henry Holt, 1993.
Vestal, Stanley. *Sitting Bull, Champion of the Sioux: A Biography.* Boston: Houghton Mifflin, 1932.

JEFFREY OSTLER

*See also* **American Indian Wars; Wounded Knee, 1890.**

# SKINHEADS

### English Origins

Skinheads as a group phenomenon with a sense of internal cohesion and a particular style of appearance and mode of behavior were one of a number of youth subcultures evolving from the early 1950s in an economically troubled England attempting to rebuild from its devastation in World War II. These subcultures, which included Teddy Boys, Mods, Rockers, and Greasers, tended to view their native land, with varying degrees of distaste and hostility, as a weakened authority with little vitality or hope to offer them. In his analysis *Folk Devils and Moral Panics: The Creation of the Mods and Rockers* (1980), Stanley Cohen cites the repugnance with which institutional England (including politicians, clergy, and the press) observed the emergence of these groups as a classic example of "moral panic." Opposition between community forces and these youth groups occasionally produced violent clashes, and countercultural gangs sometimes battled each other for primacy on the increasingly autonomous youth scene.

Early on, the youth groups adopted characteristic modes of preferred dress and musical styles as signs of their distinct identity and their rebellion. The Teddy Boys of the early 1950s—the most visible of whom were young working-class males, although young women and men higher up the socio-educational ladder were included—affected gaudy, Edwardian fashions and listened mainly to loud (and sometimes ersatz) early American rock and roll. By the early 1960s in England, Teddy Boys had given way to Mods (mainly young working-class males with short, clean hair who, according to Dick Hebdige, "affected dandyism" and at first wore conservative, "fastidiously neat and tidy clothing, perhaps to parody their elders") and Rockers (who wore motorcycle regalia like Marlon Brando's in *The Wild One* [1954]). Their participation in street fights in London and various seaside resort towns in the early 1960s and in the infamous rioting in Clacton on Easter Sunday 1964, though perhaps sensationalized to exploit public fears, affirmed the youth groups' willingness to participate in a culture of violence.

Skinheads emerged from a branch of Mods, called "hard Mods," who affected heavy boots, jeans with suspenders, and short hair, and they were generally poorer, angrier, and edgier than "smooth Mods." By the mid-1960s the skinhead style had rigidified to consist of closely shaved heads, Ben Sherman shirts, and Dr. Martens boots (with inserted steel toe tips, used for kicking, that police could not legally claim were concealed weapons). By 1968, according to a report noted by the ex-skinhead and writer Nick Knight, as many as four thousand skinheads were observed behaving violently as a group after a London soccer match.

Some evidence indicates that during a very early period when the skinheads were developing as a recognizable, belligerent group of mainly young, white, working-class English males, they sometimes shared subcultural space with or even occasionally included ethnic minority youth. More often, however, from their inception they seem to have been willing or even eager to engage in violent acts against minorities, as well as local authorities and those they considered social deviants. One of the first English skinhead gangs, described in Susie Daniel and Pete McGuire's *The Paint House*

(London, Penguin, 1972), for example, listed young blacks, Pakistanis, and hippies as people who oppressed them. In time, gays would be added. On 25 May 1970 several hundred Pakistanis marched to Prime Minister Harold Wilson's house to protest skinhead Paki bashing, and in the summer of 1972 skinheads joined with other militant whites in a series of attacks against young blacks in the Toxteth area of Liverpool.

The mid-1970s saw a waning of the subcultural attraction of skinheads, who at this time were not apparent on the American scene, an unusual phenomenon since the relationship between youth subcultures in the United States and the United Kingdom was usually symbiotic. The situation changed late in the decade with the advent of the punk rock scene, which was amorphous but very open to extreme, anti-authoritarian, and often violent behavior. As the tide of the punk scene flowed between the United States and the United Kingdom, skinheads were re-emerging in England with a more focused political agenda. Bands such as Brutal Attack, Skullhead, Prime Suspects (English), Brutal Combat (French), Bohse Onkelz (Evil Uncles, German), banged messages of hate into the ears of (often drunk) skinheads thrash-dancing in the "pit," bashing into each other or anyone who got into their way. They would find American counterparts in the 1980s skinhead bands White Pride, Final Solution, Tulsa Boot Boys, and Hammer Head.

By the late 1970s and early 1980s, the violence of skinhead groups in England was being given emotional support and ideological direction by right-wing organizations such as the fascist National Front. Skrewdriver's lead performer, Ian Stuart, for what he said was "the survival of our

**Skinhead or neo-Nazi graffiti.** COURTESY OF JEFF FERRELL

161

[white] race," backed up his hate charges against Jews and blacks both in his songs and in his actions—the street fighting for which he was jailed together with fellow skinheads.

## American Developments

Young Americans embracing skinhead styles were observable on the punk scene in the late 1970s and early 1980s—for example, in Penelope Spheeris's documentary about punk Los Angeles, *The Decline of Western Civilization*. The number of American skinheads, however, never exceeded four thousand, far fewer than that of their English counterparts, and American skinhead gangs generally were smaller and their constituencies more middle-class. With the exception of gangs of nonracist skinheads (a variety in many ways separate and often antagonistic to racist skinheads, though sometimes violent themselves), American skinheads would seek out and commit violence against members of so-called mud races—blacks, Jews, and nonwhite minorities—in addition to indigents, liberals, and homosexuals. One of the earliest skinhead gangs of any size in America named itself Romantic Violence. Centered in Chicago, the group sold tapes of Skrewdriver and other skinhead bands and marched along with the American Nazi Party in protest of a 1985 Gay and Lesbian Pride Day rally. Skinhead Clark Martell declared that Romantic Violence stood "for war," and in 1986 at a training camp for right-wing extremist groups, he announced that he himself was "a violent person" who "love[d] the white race, and if you love something, you're the most vicious person on earth."

By the end of the 1980s and throughout the 1990s, national organizations such as the Anti-Defamation League and the Southern Poverty Law Center issued statistics chronicling the violent activities of skinheads and skinhead gangs. Their offenses ranged from defacing property (such as splattering swastikas on synagogue walls) and making threats to carrying out assaults (including the incident on the nationally broadcast Geraldo Rivera television show on 3 November 1988, when a skinhead broke host Rivera's nose) to committing murder. One of their victims was an Ethiopian immigrant, Mulegeta Seraw; he was killed 13 November 1988 in Portland, Oregon, by Ken Mieske and two other skinheads who helped bash Seraw's skull open with a baseball bat. While their deadly acts often spring spontaneously from their hatreds and a willingness or desire to commit violence,

evidence suggests that (as in the murder of Seraw, the murder of antiracist skinheads near Las Vegas in 1998, and the unsuccessful plot to blow up the Southern Poverty Law Center headquarters in Montgomery, Alabama, in the same year) skinhead violence often entails conscious and purposeful planning. Communication between skinhead groups is common and has been greatly facilitated by the advent of the Internet, although the majority of skinheads are not strongly organized beyond local levels. Their near worldwide presence, however, has been dramatized in a number of films, including *Skinheads, Scourge of the Nation* (United States, 1989), *Romper Stomper* (Australia, 1992), *La haine* (Hate; France, 1995), and *American History X* (United States, 1998).

Duplicating the skinhead experience in England and many European countries, American racist skinheads became increasingly politicized as they evolved. In the late 1980s and 1990s, they were courted by and drawn into alliances with right-wing extremists and hate organizations such as the Ku Klux Klan, Aryan Nations, White Aryan Resistance, Aryan Brotherhood, and National Alliance. The names of these groups change, but their activities remain violent and hostile to a just, tolerant, peaceful, multicultural, multiethnic democracy.

*BIBLIOGRAPHY*

The Anti-Defamation League and the Southern Poverty Law Center periodically issue publications on skinhead activities. In addition see the following:

Anti-Defamation League. *The Skinhead International: A Worldwide Survey of Neo-Nazi Skinheads*. New York: Anti-Defamation League, 1995.

Hebdige, Dick. *Subculture: The Meaning of Style*. London: Methuen, 1979.

Moore, Jack B. *Skinheads Shaved for Battle*. Bowling Green, Ohio: Bowling Green State University Popular Press, 1993.

JACK B. MOORE

See also **Extremism; Hate Crimes; Ku Klux Klan; Nativism; Neo-Nazis; Race and Ethnicity.**

# SLAVE REBELLIONS

The development of slavery as a coercive system naturally led to attempts by those enslaved to break the chains of their oppressors. Since antiquity, slaves have expressed their dissatisfaction with being held against their will by revolting against their oppressors. Rebellions were a constant threat in all slave societies and were never far from the minds of the masters, who were aware that violent societies bred violence. Indeed, even the rumor or hint of revolt often led masters to take dramatic measures against their slaves. Slaves were usually disorganized, isolated, and unarmed; their attempts to escape enslavement were desperate acts that usually ended in tragedy.

## Conditions for Success

Some slave rebellions did meet with success. The most important factors in large-scale slave insurrections were the ratio of slaves to their masters, the topography of the area, and the origin of the slaves themselves. For example, slave rebellions were quite common on islands such as Jamaica, where the black population was much larger than the white population, and where the rebel slaves could escape to the mountains. Also, most West Indian slaves had experienced freedom in Africa before being seized and forced to suffer the horrors of the Middle Passage in the holds of slave ships; therefore, it was both natural and possible for them to run away and unite in isolated communities, from whence they conducted raids against their former masters. The tradition of black militancy began in these outlaw societies of runaway slaves, or *maroons*.

Unquestionably the most successful slave insurrection in all of history was the Haitian Revolution of 1791–1804, where former slaves such as Toussaint Louverture and black leaders such as Jean Jacques Dessalines eliminated slavery from the island. The Haitian Revolution left an indelible impression of fear in the minds of whites in all the other slave societies in the Caribbean and in the Americas. The slave colonies of Spain, Portugal, the Netherlands, and Great Britain, including the former American colonies, did everything in their power to keep the race war that broke out in Haiti from spilling over into their colonies.

## Rebellion in North America

The West Indian tradition of slave insurrection and violence against the oppressor only infrequently translated into the same behavior in the southern United States. By the beginning of the nineteenth century, most slaves in the United States were born into slavery and had not experienced freedom in their ancestral homeland. The only life they knew was that into which they were born. In addition, slaves in the United States rarely

outnumbered the white population, with South Carolina being the most notable exception. Even in the more populated slave states, such as Virginia, and later Mississippi, slavery never took on the West Indian pattern of a small minority of whites attempting to control a significantly larger majority of slaves. Furthermore, slaves who revolted in the United States had few accessible mountainous or isolated areas to flee to, particularly with Amerindians bordering most settlements.

In spite of these conditions, however, slave revolts, or rumors of them, did occur often enough to keep whites edgy. Many plots were discovered and suppressed before they had a chance to be carried out. Although individual acts of defiance such as sabotage, malingering, or running away were everyday occurrences in the southern slave system, any time that slave conspirators attempted to expand their number of plotters they ran the risk of being discovered or betrayed. It was often the case that loyal or greedy slaves would divulge a plot, and the authorities would quickly move in to eliminate the threat of insurrection. Far more slaves were charged, and often executed, as rebels than actually carried out their plots. Another factor that militated against the use of violence to overthrow the slave system was the extent to which Christianity was assimilated into African American culture, particularly in the American South. The church taught slaves to "turn the other cheek" and that the "meek shall inherit the earth," hardly doctrines that would encourage violence, even for a just cause. Ironically, it was also a religious impulse that caused white Americans in the eighteenth century to begin questioning the morality of slavery.

While there were literally hundreds of minor slave revolts in American history, rarely were they significant beyond the expression of slaves' discontent with their oppression. Several do stand out as capturing the imagination of the American public. One of the first in the North American colonies took place in New York as early as 1712, when Africans recently arrived led a short-lived revolt one April night that ended in eight white deaths, scores wounded, and twenty-five slaves either killed or executed as a result of the violent outbreak. The Stono revolt in South Carolina in 1739 resulted in the deaths of twenty-five whites and scores of slaves. Another scare swept through New York City in 1741, resulting in the execution of over thirty slaves—nearly one in five of the city's eleven thousand residents were slaves—and several white conspirators. In Virginia in 1800, a shrewd, religiously devout slave named Gabriel Prosser, as depicted in Arna Bontemps's novel, *Black Thunder,* planned to organize hundreds of his brethren to kill their masters, beginning on a plantation near Richmond. As often happened, several slaves betrayed the plot to the authorities, who arrested the plotters before they could act. Over thirty alleged conspirators were tried and executed, including "General" Prosser, who was apprehended trying to escape. Finally, the largest slave insurrection in the United States, in terms of number of slaves involved (estimates range from 150 to 500), occurred in two isolated parishes of Louisiana in early 1811. Federal troops were employed to put down this insurrection before it spread throughout the territory.

One of the most famous near-conspiracies that took place in the slaveholding South was the Denmark Vesey plot in Charleston, South Carolina, in May 1822. Vesey, a free black (who had traveled to Haiti as a seaman), was accused of planning an elaborate plot to overthrow the harsh slave system in that state with its black majority. Over one hundred slaves were arrested, and Vesey and over thirty of his coconspirators were executed. Thereafter, South Carolina and other states passed harsh laws prohibiting contact between slaves and freed blacks as a way to reduce the likelihood of rebellion. To whites, Vesey represented the dangers of a free black population in an urban area, where supervision was more lax. It was soon after the Vesey plot that the mysterious David Walker, a free black of Boston, wrote his militant *Appeal* (1829), the first written plea for blacks to throw off their chains violently.

In southeastern Virginia in August 1831, a revolt led by Nat Turner involved well over a hundred slaves and resulted in the deaths of sixty whites. Turner was a slave preacher who inspired his companions with his vision of freedom. His band wreaked havoc by killing all the whites that they met as they moved toward the Dismal Swamp in southeastern Virginia. Uncharacteristically, it took six weeks for the slaveholding authorities to capture the rebels.

This revolt marked a turning point in the history of slavery in the South: Virginia and the rest of the South became more aggressive in their defense of slavery and in their control of slaves. As

*The Discovery of Nat Turner.* **Woodcut from** *Popular History of the United States,* **by William Cullen Bryant and Sidney Howard Gay (1876–1880).**
LIBRARY OF CONGRESS

**Contemporary woodcut of Nat Turner rebellion of 1831.** LIBRARY OF
CONGRESS

if to legitimize southern fears, free northern blacks joined John Brown in his raid on Harpers Ferry in Virginia in 1859, hoping to initiate a slave revolt in the South by providing the slaves with arms. Instead the raid helped initiate a civil war.

Successful or not, rebellions in the slave states were a constant reminder to most Americans of the denial of freedom that slavery represented in the South. To abolitionists hostile to "the peculiar institution," slave revolts were a warning of what might happen to those who would not repent their slaveholding sins. The violent attempts to escape or overthrow slavery also negated the proslavery contention that blacks were docile, content, and well-cared for in the slave system. To free blacks of the north, these rebellions were a reminder of

the need to continue the fight against the slave system.

Though rarely successful, slave rebellions indicated the lengths to which ill-prepared slaves were willing to go to obtain their freedom, and they served as a constant reminder that a society willing to ignore the brutality of slavery did so at its peril.

BIBLIOGRAPHY

Carroll, Joseph. *Slave Insurrections in the United States, 1800–1865*. 1938. Reprint, New York: Negro University Press, 1968.

Egerton, Douglas R. *Gabriel's Rebellion: The Virginia Slave Conspiracies of 1800 and 1802*. Chapel Hill: University of North Carolina Press, 1993.

Frey, Sylvia. *Water from the Rock: Black Resistance in a Revolutionary Age*. Princeton, N.J.: Princeton University Press, 1991.

Genovese, Eugene. *From Rebellion to Revolution: Afro-American Slave Revolts in the Making of the Modern World*. Baton Rouge: Louisiana State University Press, 1979.

Jones, Howard. *Mutiny on the* Amistad. New York: Oxford University Press, 1997

Lofton, John. *Insurrection in South Carolina: The Turbulent World of Denmark Vesey*. Yellow Springs, Ohio: Antioch, 1964.

Mullin, Gerald. *Flight and Rebellion: Slave Resistance in Eighteenth-Century Virginia*. New York: Oxford University Press, 1974.

Oates, Stephen B. *The Fires of Jubilee: Nat Turner's Fierce Rebellion*. New York: Harper and Row, 1975.

Pearson, Edward, ed. *Designs Against Charleston: The Trial Record of the Denmark Slave Conspiracy of 1822*. Chapel Hill: University of North Carolina Press, 1999.

ALFRED HUNT

---

## Nat Turner

Nat Turner dictated his confession before his execution in November 1831. William Styron's novel *The Confessions of Nat Turner* (1967) renewed interest in one of the most visible slave rebellions in U.S. history. Like Arna Bontemps's *Black Thunder* (1935), the novel suggests that fiction may be as legitimate as "nonfiction" in dealing with the subject and getting to the essence of the problem. Styron's book, however, elicited strong criticism from the black intellectual community during the turbulent 1960s because it stressed Turner's motivations as perhaps more spiritual than political.

See also **Abolition; Amistad Case; Harpers Ferry, Raid on; Slavery.**

## SLAVERY

Slavery—involuntary servitude—means hard, perpetual, unpaid labor for someone else's benefit; without coercion, no one would be a slave. Over the millennia slavery has required the use or threat of force, although an ever changing cast of peoples has been enslaved. In the period of New World slavery, the enslaved have been of Native American, African, or mixed ancestry, but one identity stuck. Reflecting the demographics of 1865, when slavery finally became unlawful in the United States, African Americans have been most closely linked to the concept of enslavement. In American intellectual and social history, slavery implicates race, and the race in question is Negro.

During the era of slavery and after emancipation, African Americans were subject to a great deal of personal violence in the form of whipping, lynching, rape, riot, assault, homicide, occupational injury, family violence, police brutality, and hate crimes. As the poorest people in the United States over the course of four centuries, blacks have fallen easy prey to communicable diseases and the ailments of poverty: parasites, venereal diseases, diabetes, respiratory ailments, infant and maternal mortality, and malnutrition. Nonblacks who experience violence on the scale endemic to the lives of black Americans—soldiers in combat, rape victims, abused women, or abused children—may be diagnosed with post-traumatic stress disorder (PTSD). Yet despite psychologists' correlation of trauma with powerlessness in the face of overwhelming force, neither the term *trauma* nor the symptoms associated with PTSD have been associated with African Americans as a consequence of their enslavement.

Nineteenth-century abolitionists, such as Frederick Douglass, Angelina Grimké, and Theodore Weld, dwelled on the violence of slavery: the whippings, rapes, and shacklings. The twentieth-century historiography of African slavery in the New World, however, has averted its gaze from this river of blood and gore. During the early twentieth century, professional historians concentrated largely on the sectional politics and economics of southern slavery; slaves as people did not interest most nonblack scholars. After the Civil

Rights movement of the 1950s and 1960s, when the connection was made between mid-nineteenth- and mid-twentieth-century events, historians began to focus on slave culture, family life, and resistance to oppression. But these efforts to see slaves as more than mere victims strengthened rather than weakened our unwillingness to confront the violence to which they were routinely subjected.

Up to the late twentieth century, a student of American slavery was more likely to learn about slaves transcending violence rather than about the devastating physical and psychological assaults against which they struggled. Americans now have the resources to discover what enslaved people were able to make of themselves, given their dismal situation. This became all the more true after the controversy stirred by Stanley Elkins's *Slavery: A Problem in American Institutional and Intellectual Life* (1959), still the major psychological study of American slaves, which characterized enslaved people as childlike "sambos" dependent on their masters and severed from their own kin. Despite Elkins and beyond the healthy reorientation of historical inquiry away from victimization, American historians must, nonetheless, grapple with the pervasiveness of violence in slave society and with its sequelae in American society.

### Slave Trade

The violence began with the capture of Africans for the Atlantic slave trade through war or kidnapping. Villages were burned and villagers taken prisoner, and individuals were abducted as they went about their daily work. In the fifteenth century Portuguese traders went ashore to capture people, but once the trade was established, Europeans were able to leave the work of abduction to other Africans and merely trade goods or money for people.

As the volume of the slave trade increased in the sixteenth and seventeenth centuries, African coastal peoples, such as the Fanti of what is now Ghana, reoriented their economies around the exigencies of the Atlantic slave trade with Europeans. In time, the violence endemic to the slave trade devastated these coastal peoples, and stronger kingdoms more distant from the coast, like the Ashanti, delivered captives by the hundreds in exchange for European cloth, metals, alcohol, and firearms. In what are now Senegal, Gambia, Ghana, Benin, Nigeria, the Congos, and Angola, inland kingdoms rose and flourished because of the Atlantic slave trade. By the late seventeenth century and through the mid-nineteenth century, African traders and empires such as the Lunda of northeast Angola used guns and staged raids to capture people for the overseas trade. The captives who were the raw material of this trade would be subject to inhuman treatment for the rest of their lives.

In the coastal barracoons and slave "castles" (warehouses for captives awaiting shipment to the Americas), such as Cape Coast castle in Ghana, European and mixed-race Afro-European and Afro-Brazilian merchants stockpiled captives until a full shipload could be collected. During the wait captive Africans were marked indelibly by branding or other obvious scarification (cut ears, for example) and chained in dark, damp, overcrowded pits. The arrival of tall sailing ships, which by the eighteenth and nineteenth centuries were usually English or French, signaled the beginning of the "triangular trade" between Europe, Africa, and America. The second leg was the infamous Middle Passage. Herded into slave ships, captives were packed as densely as possible in holds divided into decks as low as eighteen inches, but normally four to five feet high. Captives were chained together so they might sit but not stand, unable to get out of their own or others' vomit, excrement, and menstrual blood. The English abolitionist Thomas Clarkson's 1808 sardine-can depiction of slave ships made the abominable conditions of transatlantic slavers infamous.

A voyage from Africa to the New World normally took four to twelve weeks. In the Middle Passage, crew and cargo equally fell casualty to conditions of filth, crowding, and shortages of food and water. While in transit, about thirteen percent of the captives and crew would die of dysentery, malnutrition, communicable diseases, and personal violence. Historians estimate that of the more than twelve million Africans who embarked on the coasts of Africa, roughly ten million arrived in the New World alive. High rates of mortality serve as one index to the bodily ravages of the Middle Passage.

Casualty rates fail to capture fully the psychological toll of capture, incarceration, branding, exile, sale, and seasoning. Because importation alone did not transform Africans into slaves, what was called *seasoning* in the New World meant teaching an immigrant the language of the land and accustoming him or her to unremitting labor, insufficient food, and inadequate clothing and housing.

Normally this process included enough whipping and shackling to convince the new arrival that she or he was no longer autonomous. Not surprisingly, many new immigrants attempted to escape, but they were usually unsuccessful because of their unfamiliarity with their strange new surroundings.

## Violence Suffered by the Enslaved

In the Caribbean sugar islands, overwork and skewed sex ratios impeded the formation of families by slaves. As slaves usually were worked to death within seven to ten years, the workforce could be maintained only by continual importation of new slaves. North American demographics were different: African Americans began reproducing their numbers in the mid-seventeenth century at the same rate as their nonblack immigrant neighbors. By the early nineteenth century, the majority of those enslaved in America were native born, and the dislocations of capture and the Middle Passage receded into memory. But the violence did not end.

American slaves, especially in the southern states, were subject to a variety of injuries, tortures, and punishments. Their owners branded them as they would cattle—to indicate ownership and to restrain or punish. Runaway-slave advertisements describing fugitives as branded, scarred, burned, broken, and whipped reveal such practices to have been commonplace. Runaway slaves often had torn or missing ears, eyes, front teeth, finger joints, and toes. Advertisements enumerated wounds of all sorts, from lost hands, dented foreheads, cuts, sores, limps, and ruptures to the marks of having been shot or whipped.

Slaves were whipped for many kinds of infractions, real or imagined, but two were particularly common: insufficient work and running away. The usual punishment for failing to complete one's tasks was flogging, which could be inflicted with any of several kinds of whips. Most vicious were rawhide whips, three feet long, tapered to a flexible point, and known for cutting into the skin, even to the point of pulling out strips of mangled flesh. A leather strap eighteen-by-two-and-one-half inches or a three-foot-long braided whip attached to a wooden handle would not break the skin so badly. If a long, narrow piece of soft, dry buckskin was attached to the end of a whip, it would make a snapping sound as it burned the skin but not bite deeply into the flesh. Some masters used paddles with holes cut in them that sucked up and broke the skin and pulverized the flesh.

Before being flogged, victims were chained to whipping posts or strung up to a limb or beam, wrists tied together, feet barely touching the ground. Sometimes they were stretched out flat on the ground, face down, arms and legs outstretched and tethered. Habitually whipping meant fifteen to twenty strokes on a bare back, regardless of the sex or age of the victim, but severe punishment could exceed one hundred blows. Afterward turpentine, salt, or hot brine would be poured over the wounds to increase the pain and counter sepsis. Whipping was the most common form of punishment, but slaves were also punched; slapped; beaten with cudgels, tree limbs, and farm tools; and burned with hot irons—in sum, assaulted with whatever instruments of torture lay at hand. Slaves did not always know the motive for beatings, but they knew that running away merited some of the worst penalties.

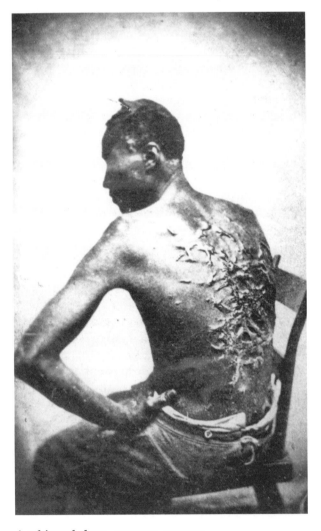

**A whipped slave.** NATIONAL ARCHIVES

Recaptured runaways were whipped repeatedly, sometimes by professional whippers, and locked in stocks or imprisoned, not only for attempting to escape but also to serve as a lesson to other slaves. Runaways might also be branded, shackled, and maimed to impede future flight. Iron collars with or without long, sharp prongs, rings, clogs, bars, and gags lacerated the skin and interfered with sleep. But while they encumbered movement, irons sometimes failed to constrain. A survey of southern newspapers in the mid-1830s turned up numerous descriptions of fugitives with "marks of lashing" and shackled with such instruments as "a large lock chain," an iron band around a left leg, a "large neck iron with a huge pair of horns and a large bar or band of iron on his left leg," "handcuffs," "a pair of handcuffs and a pair of drawing chains," and so on.

In *Stolen Childhood* (1995) the historian Wilma King likens slave societies to war zones, where slave children learned hypervigilance and dissimulation as toddlers and where masters beat grownups to make them hard workers and beat children to make them into good slaves. In this world of violence, slave parents beat children to make obedience second nature and render them first and always submissive. Parents and owners taught slave children to quash their anger at being mistreated, for anger was a forbidden emotion for slaves to display before owners. It is now understood that suppression of this kind of anger gives rise to fairly predictable effects in its victims, like feelings of degradation and humiliation, impaired identity formation, suppression of vitality and creativity, deadening of any feeling of self, anger, hatred, self-hatred, and outbreaks of violence. Escaped slaves recognized these weaknesses in other slaves they knew.

Runaway-slave advertisements also bear witness to the psychological trauma of enslavement. Slaves are described as having a "gloomy down look," a "downcast look," and a variety of "surly" expressions. Scores of runaways, all "country born" (that is, native born), were described as either having a stutter or speaking with various impediments. Twentieth-century oral histories, collected by Fisk University students, Works Progress Administration interviewers, and historians, bear witness to the legacy of violence and anger in the families of former slaves, in which wives and children bore the brunt of violent abuse. Psychologists note that victims of violence and trauma do not necessarily turn into batterers, but they are at great risk of doing so.

*Flogging the Negro,* **nineteenth-century woodcut from** *The Suppressed Book About Slavery!* **(1864).** LIBRARY OF CONGRESS

## Violence Suffered by the Enslavers

Tyrannical authority abounded in slave societies between white masters and black slaves, between white husbands and white wives, between white men, and between black parents and black children. The violence that owners inflicted on their slaves also damaged their own families and, ultimately, their whole society, because owners as well as owned families paid a high psychological and physical cost for the child abuse and the sexual abuse concomitant with slavery. Despite the assumptions of both black and white scholars about the rigidity of the color bar, witnesses testify to its porousness. Personal feeling, positive and negative, often transcended barriers of race and class and flowed in both directions. Attacks on slaves hurt nonslaves as well as slaves, especially children, by forcing witnesses to identify with either the victim or the perpetrator.

As slave-owning children grew into adults, their identification with victims or victimizers often accorded to their gender. While mistresses could torment their slaves cruelly, in comparison with masters white women were also more likely to side with the slaves, in words and occasionally in actions. When daughters of masters recognized the humanity of slaves, they were learning from their mothers. Fathers ordinarily did the work of inculcating manhood by snuffing out white children's identification with injured slaves. White

boys learned to identify with being the aggressor, for to be masculine and to own slaves required the ability to "inflict stripes," that is, to whip one's workers without pity.

Thomas Jefferson, in *Notes on the State of Virginia,* questioned whether slavery contributed to Virginians' overall welfare, though his reservations pertained to owners, not to slaves, whom he considered stupid and ugly. When Jefferson stated his objections to involuntary servitude, he was recognizing the perniciousness of one person's unlimited power over another. By inculcating habits of tyranny—what Jefferson called "odious peculiarities"—in the masters, slavery corrupted their morals and manners.

Two "odious peculiarities" were adultery and family violence. Church records and petitions for divorce in the South show that wife beating commonly motivated attempts to dissolve marriages or to expel people from church. Slaveholding regions held no monopoly on fornication and family violence, but the laws and mores of slave societies supported the absolute power of the master, as slave owner and as patriarch. In the slave South, legislators and church leaders routinely urged wives to remain in abusive unions and bear the abuse in a spirit of submission—not the same submission exacted from slaves, but submission nonetheless. In the hard-drinking antebellum South, white women had little recourse when their husbands beat them, for these states long withheld

169

women's legal rights to divorce or to custody of their children in cases of separation.

In incest cases, as in wife beating, southern judges preferred to investigate the shortcomings of the female petitioner; even extremely young girls were construed as consenting accomplices. The slave-owning class that blamed incest on privileged young white girls also portrayed enslaved women as temptresses; Mary Chesnut, the Civil War diarist from South Carolina, for instance, saw women like herself as victims of their husbands' adultery with slaves. Reversing the actual balance of power, slave owners like Chesnut transformed enslaved black victims of their masters' sexual predation into the instigators of trespass.

The inability of white mistresses like Mary Chesnut to acknowledge the primacy of violence in relationships between masters and slaves foreshadows and encapsulates the pervasive but half-hidden role of violence in American society. Slavery made violence an everyday matter, even while training Americans to avert their gaze.

*BIBLIOGRAPHY*

Douglass, Frederick. *Narrative of the Life of Frederick Douglass: An American Slave.* Boston: American Antislavery Society, 1845.

Kolchin, Peter. *American Slavery, 1619–1877.* New York: Hill and Wang, 1993.

Painter, Nell Irvin, ed. *Narrative of Sojourner Truth.* New York: Penguin, 1998.

Stampp, Kenneth M. *The Peculiar Institution.* New York: Knopf, 1956.

Thomas, Hugh. *The Slave Trade: The Story of the Atlantic Slave Trade, 1440–1870.* New York: Simon and Schuster, 1997.

NELL IRVIN PAINTER

*See also* **African Americans; Amistad Case; Civil War; Race and Ethnicity; Slave Rebellions; South.**

# SMITH, SUSAN
## (1971– )

At the age of twenty-three, Susan Smith came to national attention shortly after she reported her children missing from Union, South Carolina, on 25 October 1994. She appeared on national news shows pleading for the safe return of her sons, three-year-old Michael Daniel and fourteen-month-old Alexander Tyler, who she claimed had been kidnapped by a black carjacker. Nine days later, Smith confessed to drowning her boys; she had rolled her car into John D. Long Lake with the children strapped into their car seats.

Smith was born in Union in 1971 to Harry and Linda Vaughn. Her parents divorced, and her father shot himself shortly thereafter, when Susan was six years old. When she was fifteen, she accused her stepfather, Beverly Russell, of molesting her; at her trial for the murder of her sons, he admitted to this abuse. As a teenager, Susan attempted to take her life at least twice, at thirteen and again at eighteen.

When Susan became pregnant at nineteen, she and David Smith decided to marry. Throughout their on-again-off-again relationship, Susan frequently moved back in with her mother, and both Susan and David pursued extramarital relationships. They separated formally in 1994 and divorced on 25 May 1995. Susan supported her two young sons on the roughly $17,000 per year she made as an office worker at a local mill, plus $115 per week child support that David contributed from his salary as an assistant manager of a supermarket. Shortly before her children's deaths, Smith's boyfriend, Tom Findlay, broke up with her, saying he was not interested in pursuing a long-term relationship, citing differences in their backgrounds and her children as principal reasons.

After confessing to the murder of her sons, Smith underwent a psychiatric evaluation and was found capable of standing trial. Although the defense stipulated that Smith had killed her children by drowning, to avoid the death penalty they attempted to show that she had dependent personality disorder in addition to a history of mistreatment by men, both of which made her suicidal. She was found guilty of murder and was sentenced to life imprisonment. She is serving her sentence at the Women's Correctional Institution in Columbia, South Carolina, and will not be eligible for parole until 24 November 2024.

The general acceptance of Smith's claim in the days before her confession illustrates the public's impression that child abduction is most often committed by strangers. In fact, according to a Department of Justice study of crimes such as murder, rape, negligent manslaughter, and sexual assault that involve minors as victims, about a third of child victimizers were the parents or stepparents of the victim. More than 40 percent of those offenders whose victims were under the age of eighteen were related to their victims.

BIBLIOGRAPHY

Burritt, Chris. "Focus on Union, S.C." *Atlanta Journal and Constitution*, 10 July 1996.

Greenfeld, Lawrence A. "Child Victimizers: Violent Offenders and the Victims." United States Department of Justice report. NCJ-153258. Washington, D.C.: Bureau of Justice Statistics; jointly published with the Office of Juvenile Justice and Delinquency Prevention, March 1996.

Rekers, George. *Susan Smith: Victim or Murderer?* Lakewood, Colo.: Glenbridge, 1996.

NIKKI SENECAL

*See also* **Child Abuse; Infanticide and Neonaticide.**

# SMOKING

In addition to its known detrimental effects on physical health, cigarette smoke may also be connected to increased aggression. Research in this area, though limited, has exhibited this link; however, the causal direction remains unclear: Does smoking cause aggression, or do inherently aggressive individuals choose to smoke?

Several studies have shown increased antisocial behavior in offspring whose mothers smoked during pregnancy. Studies have shown that a mother's smoking during pregnancy significantly increases the likelihood of psychiatric symptoms, such as conduct disorder, in male children (Wakschlag et al. 1997; Fergusson et al. 1998). Mothers who smoked more than ten cigarettes daily were more than four times as likely to have a child that fit the criteria for conduct disorder defined in the third edition of the American Psychiatric Association's *Diagnostic and Statistical Manual of Mental Disorders*. This increased risk was found even when controlling for socioeconomic status, demographic factors, parental psychopathology, pregnancy complications, and other parenting variables. Prenatal exposure to smoking was also associated with attention problems and motor hyperactivity (including attention deficit hyperactivity disorder, ADHD) and impulsivity. Brennan and colleagues (1999) found similar effects in the adult offspring of mothers who smoked during pregnancy. Maternal smoking significantly predicted violent and nonviolent arrests and life-course persistent offending for males who were measured at thirty-four years of age. All of these studies evidenced a dose-response relationship in which increased maternal smoking resulted in higher rates of symptoms. These findings are consistent with similar studies on animals, which have also suggested a connection between cigarette smoke and increased motor activity along with decreased learning efficiency.

There is also evidence of a causal effect of smoke on human aggression. Nonsmokers exposed to secondhand smoke were reliably more aggressive in a laboratory situation than nonsmokers exposed to clean air (Jones and Bogat 1978). This study strongly suggests causal effects of cigarette smoking on observed aggression. However, it does not rule out the possibility that prior aggressive tendencies may exist in individuals who smoke.

One possible mediator between smoking and aggression is monoamine oxidase (MAO), an enzyme involved in the metabolism of neurotransmitters important to impulsivity, arousal, and aggression. There are two MAO subtypes, MAO-A and MAO-B, which are different in structure, function, and localization in the brain. MAO-A acts primarily on norepinephrine and serotonin, while MAO-B is more important to dopamine breakdown. There is significant evidence that smoking decreases the activity of MAO-A in the brain. Heavy smokers have decreases in peripheral tissue as well (Shih et al. 1999). Studies of animals, as well as of humans in utero, have also provided evidence that cigarette smoke decreases MAO-A and MAO-B activity. With the exception of platelet MAO, which remains constant in former smokers (Ward et al. 1987), MAO activity levels increase in former smokers after quitting, and overall levels become comparable with those in nonsmokers (Sher et al. 1994). Thus, the decrease in MAO may be caused by smoking itself, rather than the propensity to smoke being solely a function of decreased MAO.

There is also evidence that MAO influences aggression. Researchers have observed that animals with decreased MAO activity are unequivocally more aggressive than those with normal activity levels. MAO-A knockout mice (i.e., mice bred to have a specific lack of the normal MAO-A knockout allele) show enhanced offensive aggression and elevated levels of brain serotonin (Shih et al. 1999). These researchers postulate that increased aggression is due to changes in the serotonin receptors, including a decrease in number, which results in an increase of serotonin remaining in the synapses, leading to elevated levels in the somatosensory system. The aggressive behavior of these mice is consistent with the highly aggressive behavior of eight Dutch males with a point deletion (i.e., omission of a single DNA base-pair) in the gene responsible for encoding MAO-A, thus rendering them completely MAO-A deficient (Brunner et al. 1993).

While MAO is clearly related to both aggression and smoking, the causal nature of this relationship is not completely understood. Although one possibility is that smoking reduces MAO activity, which in turn increases aggressive behavior (as supported by animal research), other possibilities exist. For example, individuals with naturally low MAO levels may have characteristics that lead them to smoke in the first place. In fact, individuals with decreased MAO activity score higher on sensation-seeking scales (Sher et al. 1994; Ward et al. 1987), suggesting that smoking may be part of their sensation-seeking behavior. It is also possible that sensation seekers would tend to smoke, hence decreasing MAO activity. Also, if the relationship between MAO and smoking was completely mediated by sensation-seeking tendencies, then the relationship between sensation-seeking scores and smoking would be stronger than that between MAO activity and smoking. In actuality, however, the relationship between MAO activity and smoking is stronger (Sher et al. 1994). This was found even after controlling for personality traits and examining the joint influence of MAO and sensation seeking on smoking. Thus, there is likely some direct relationship between MAO and smoking, independent of sensation seeking.

Studies examining smokers' personality characteristics also suggest the possibility of a reverse causal relationship—aggressive tendencies may cause certain individuals to smoke. There is evidence that children diagnosed with ADHD or conduct problems are at increased risk to start smoking early (Milberger et al. 1997; Breslau 1995). Researchers have also suggested that smokers, or at least a large subgroup of them, are different from nonsmokers in that they are extroverted and impulsive and have antisocial tendencies (Patton et al. 1997; Lipkus et al. 1994). Similarly, Zaimov and colleagues (1994) studied motivation to smoke and found that older men reported a tendency to smoke to stimulate aggression. These studies, coupled with those on sensation seeking, suggest that the differences observed between smokers and nonsmokers are caused not entirely by smoking but by personality traits that lead individuals to become smokers.

The mechanisms underlying the relationship between smoking and aggression are not entirely clear. In terms of increased aggression, nicotine does not appear the culprit, since it reduces aggression. Studies have demonstrated that nicotine exposure decreased aggression in squirrel monkeys, rats, and ants (Schechter and Rand 1974). The researchers who conducted these studies also found that acute deprivation of smoke in habitual smokers caused significant increases in aggression. Ague (1973) found similar results with smokers using a mood-adjective checklist. The smokers reported decreases in aggression after smoking cigarettes with the highest content of nicotine. However, these changes in aggression observed in human subjects may not be a function of nicotine, since studies on smokers may be confounded by the symptoms of withdrawal. It is possible that other components of cigarette smoke (e.g., cyanide and formaldehyde) are responsible for increased aggression while nicotine actually causes it to subside. This would be consistent with the finding by Shih and colleagues (1999) that though smoking was linked to decreased MAO activity, nicotine was not responsible for the change, and with the study by Sher and colleagues (1994) that failed to decrease MAO levels in vitro by administering nicotine. If it is true that some components of cigarettes increase aggression while nicotine decreases it, then the two directions of causality could exist simultaneously. An inherently aggressive individual may choose to smoke for the calming effect of the nicotine but subsequently become more aggressive due to the decrease in MAO activity. This could lead the person to need to smoke more to quell this increased aggression. A cycle would then evolve, possibly functioning as one pathway to addiction.

## BIBLIOGRAPHY

Ague, C. "Nicotine and Smoking: Effects upon Subjective Changes in Mood." *Psychopharmacologia* 30, no. 4 (1973): 323–328.

Brennan, Patricia A., Emily R. Grekin, and Sarnoff A. Mednick. "Maternal Smoking During Pregnancy and Adult Male Criminal Outcomes." *Archives of General Psychiatry* 56, no. 3 (1999): 215–219.

Breslau, Naomi. "Psychiatric Comorbidity of Smoking and Nicotine Dependence." *Behavior Genetics* 25, no. 2 (1995): 95–101.

Brunner, Hans G., et al. "Abnormal Behavior Associated with a Point Mutation in the Structural Gene for Monoamine Oxidase A." *Science* 262, no. 5133 (1993): 578–580.

Fergusson, David M., Lianne J. Woodward, and L. John Horwood. "Maternal Smoking During Pregnancy and Psychiatric Adjustment in Late Adolescence." *Archives of General Psychiatry* 55, no. 8 (1998): 721–727.

Jones, John W., and G. Anne Bogat. "Air Pollution and Human Aggression." *Psychological Reports* 43 (December 1978): 721–722.

Lipkus, Isaac M., et al. "A Short MMPI Scale to Identify People Likely to Begin Smoking." *Journal of Personality Assessment* 62, no. 2 (1994): 213–222.

Milberger, Sharon, et al. "Further Evidence of an Association Between Attention-Deficit/Hyperactivity Disorder and Cigarette Smoking: Findings from a High-Risk Sample of Siblings." *American Journal on Addictions* 6, no. 3 (1997): 205–217.

Patton, David, Gordon E. Barnes, and Robert P. Murray. "A Personality Typology of Smokers." *Addictive Behaviors* 22, no. 2 (1997): 269–273.

Schechter, Martin D., and Michael J. Rand. "Effect of Acute Deprivation of Smoking on Aggression and Hostility." *Psychopharmacologia* 35, no. 1 (1974): 19–28.

Sher, Kenneth J., et al. "Platelet Monoamine Oxidase (MAO) Activity: Personality, Substance Use, and the Stress-Response-Dampening Effect of Alcohol." *Experimental and Clinical Psychopharmacology* 2, no. 1 (1994): 53–81.

Shih, Jean C., Kevin Chen, and Michael Ridd. "Monoamine Oxidase: From Genes to Behavior." *Annual Review of Neuroscience* 22 (1999): 197–217.

Wakschlag, Lauren S., et al. "Maternal Smoking During Pregnancy and the Risk of Conduct Disorder in Boys." *Archives of General Psychiatry* 54, no. 7 (1997): 670–676.

Ward, Philip B., et al. "Low Platelet Monoamine Oxidase and Sensation Seeking in Males: An Established Relationship?" *Acta Psychiatrica Scandinavica* 75, no. 1 (1987): 86–90.

Zaimov, Kosta Alexandrov, Fertcheva Anita, and Vanev Plamen Ivanov. "Motives of Smoking and Inborn Behavioral Preprogram of the Personality." *International Journal of the Addictions* 29, no. 7 (1994): 957–970.

MICHELLE WARD
LAURA A. BAKER

*See also* **Health and Medical Factors: Diet and Nutrition; Neurotransmitters; Tobacco Industry.**

## SNAKE HANDLERS

A variant within the holiness-pentecostal movement, snake handlers (also known as serpent handlers) derive their biblical warrant from a literal interpretation of Mark 16:18, in the King James Version of the Bible: "They shall take up serpents; and if they drink any deadly thing, it shall not hurt them; they shall lay hands on the sick, and they shall recover!" The earliest recorded incident of snake handling in a religious context took place in 1910, when George W. Hensley picked up a serpent during a revival near Cleveland, Tennessee. The practice spread to eastern Kentucky and, even-tually, throughout Appalachia, especially among those of Scots-Irish descent. Because of the radical independence of these groups—they have no denominational affiliation—it is difficult to judge their numbers, but it was estimated that there were approximately two thousand snake handlers in Appalachia in the late 1990s.

In the course of the snake handlers' religious gatherings, as the service reaches a climax amid the sounds of tambourines, guitars, clapping, and ecstatic dancing, snake handlers, also known as Holy Ghost people, take poisonous snakes—usually copperheads and rattlesnakes—out of boxes and pass them among members of the congregation. Some place the serpents on their heads or inside their shirts or toss them back and forth to other members of the congregation. The vipers are in no way bound or anesthetized. When someone is bitten, the congregation seeks to "pray them through," and survival is seen as a confirmation of the presence of the Holy Spirit. Variations of snake handling include the drinking of strychnine and the use of fire, sometimes with blowtorches—the purpose once again being to demonstrate the faith and the righteousness of the believer.

In common with others in the holiness movement, most snake-handling congregations also believe in divine healing; they anoint the afflicted with oil and pray for healing. They emphasize biblical literalism and spiritual simplicity. Women, for example, are not allowed to cut their hair because, according to 1 Corinthians 11:15, it is given to them as a "covering." Similarly, women wear no cosmetics or jewelry, with the occasional exception of wristwatches.

Snake-handling congregations, primarily descendants of English and Scots-Irish pioneers, typically meet in small buildings or in members' homes and tend to be poorly educated. Many snake handlers are, or were, coal miners; one of the rites of initiation for a new miner is for fellow miners to throw poisonous snakes at him.

The association of violence with snake handling derives from the implicitly violent nature of the act and the fact that some snake handlers have died from bites sustained in the course of snake-handling services. Sixty-three deaths of this nature were confirmed as of 1996. A court case in the early 1990s, albeit aberrant, made the connection between serpent handling and violence more explicit. In the fall of 1991 Glenn Summerford, pastor of a snake-handling congregation near Scottsboro, Alabama, called the Church of Jesus with Signs

Following, was arrested for trying to murder his wife with snakes. According to court testimony, Summerford, who frequently handled snakes, drank strychnine, and poked his fingers into live electrical sockets to demonstrate his faith to the congregation, had fallen into a drunken, jealous rage and, at gunpoint, forced his wife to write a suicide note and then to plunge her hand into one of the cages where he kept the rattlesnakes he used in church services. Summerford was convicted of attempted murder and sentenced to ninety-nine years in prison.

*BIBLIOGRAPHY*

Covington, Dennis. *Salvation on Sand Mountain: Snake Handling and Redemption in Southern Appalachia.* New York: Addison-Wesley, 1995.

Kane, Steven M. "The Holy Ghost People: The Snake-Handlers of Southern Appalachia." *Appalachian Journal* 1 (spring 1974).

McCauley, Deborah Vansau. *Appalachian Mountain Religion: A History.* Urbana: University of Illinois Press, 1995.

RANDALL BALMER

*See also* **Religion.**

# SOCIAL CONTROL

*Social control* refers to an array of activities, from secular and religious education, to socialization in the home, to gossip, to mass media messages, to engineered physical environments such as walls and alarms, to formal agencies such as police, courts, and prisons, intended to encourage conformity to rules.

## Agents of Social Control as Unintentional Contributors to Violence

Contrary to the conventional view in which the role of the police—as agents of social control in a democratic society—is to prevent or limit violence, under some conditions police may cause or contribute to unnecessary violence. In some cases, this violence is associated with clear violations of ethical and legal standards, as with the extremes of police brutality, torture, vigilante groups, death squads, or corrupt police using violence in pursuit of their ends. Another, broader, argument suggests that social controllers as agents of economic and political elites may contribute to violence on a vast scale, both directly and indirectly, by perpetuating social orders perceived to be unjust based on class,

racial, ethnic, and religious grounds. Yet another perspective addresses the "labeling argument," in which social control agents are seen to contribute to rule infractions by defining some of a wide range of behavior as illegal or violent, using their discretion about which laws will be most actively enforced, and singling out some of those who violate these laws for processing by the criminal justice system.

The argument developed here, however, will be restricted to the concept of unintended consequences, in which the end result (violence) is not one that is publicly sought or justified by the agency or agent. (Whether the end result may sometimes be consistent with private goals is a different question.) This argument is an element of a broader, counterintuitive view of the working of social institutions in which outcomes may be very different from intentions. For example, in medicine there is the phenomenon of iatrogenesis, in which medical interventions create or worsen illnesses. Under some conditions, schools may impede learning and mental hospitals may contribute to mental illness. So too may the criminal justice system contribute to crime.

The perspective on social control presented in this article stresses understanding the interaction of the involved parties. Violent outcomes are not necessarily predetermined. They reflect social conditions and exchanges among those involved. Those who are a part of a violent setting can be seen to form a system with varying degrees of reciprocal influence. For instance, one could look at crime or violence from a victim-precipitated view, in which the actions of the victim contribute to the crime (for example, by provoking an aggressor). This article offers an equivalent social control–precipitated view of violence. The argument here is but one strand of an approach that considers the possible criminogenic consequences of social control actions, most of which do not result in violence. Social control efforts may unintentionally contribute to violence in at least three broad ways, involving (1) covert facilitation, (2) escalation, and (3) nonenforcement.

## Covert Facilitation

Covert facilitation involves hidden or deceptive action on the part of law enforcement. Ironically, as with undercover actions, authorities may become involved in rule breaking in order ostensibly to better control it. Yet these covert actions may have unexpected results.

1. *Covert facilitation may result in violence or the threat of it as a result of generating a market for stolen goods.* For example, a ruse in which undercover agents in Idaho claimed to be Mafia members interested in purchasing guns apparently generated a wave of gun store burglaries.

2. *Covert facilitation may result in the generation of collateral offenses carried out in pursuit of the undercover operation's goal.* For example, police may pretend to be fences purchasing stolen items. In a 1980 Lakewood, Colorado, case, two young men learned that a local fence—in reality a police sting—was buying stolen cars. They stole several cars and sold them to the sting. The undercover officers initially took no action, even after seeing a .45-caliber automatic taken in a burglary. The young men stole another car after killing its owner with the same gun. They sold this car to the fence. They did this again and were finally arrested.

3. *Covert facilitation may generate violence (or resistance leading to violence) on the part of persons unaware of an undercover operation or police presence.* For example, in Los Angeles a narcotics agent was shot while trying to purchase drugs in the early 1980s. His assailants were members of a neighborhood group trying to rid their community of drugs. A New Jersey schoolteacher was shot in the head as he tried to escape from the shabbily dressed drug enforcement agents in unmarked cars who pulled him over. He did not believe they were agents. When more than one police agency is involved, or police do not know that an undercover operation is present, authorities may unknowingly use violence against each other. For example, during a Houston drug arrest in the early 1980s, an undercover policewoman with her gun drawn was shot to death by a uniformed officer who did not realize who she was. Minority police officers in undercover roles have been disproportionately injured and killed in such incidents.

4. *Covert facilitation may result in the provision of a scarce skill or resource contributing to violence.* In the 1960s there were cases of agent provocateurs, knowledgeable about the use of explosives, who offered encouragement, training, and supplies to impressionable young activists. One well known case involved "Tommy the Traveler," an agent working for a sheriff in upstate New York, who persuaded students to destroy a Reserve Officers' Training Corps (ROTC) building.

5. *Covert facilitation may generate a motive for a crime.* Authorities may falsely spread the word that an individual is an informant, leading to retalia- tory violence. Authorities (with infiltrators on both sides) may encourage infighting among members of radical social movements, as was the case with some civil rights groups such as the Black Panthers. Police may seek to increase conflict among rival criminal groups in the hope that they will attack each other.

**Escalation**

Escalation occurs when a conflict deepens as a result of inappropriate control actions. In the language of cybernetics this involves a "deviation amplifying feedback," or put more simply, snowballing or mushrooming. Escalation may stem from initial or postapprehension enforcement efforts. Police involvement in family conflict, crowd, and automobile chase situations can contribute to violations when none were imminent, or increase their seriousness. Dirty Harry's (Clint Eastwood) famous line in the 1983 film *Sudden Impact*—"Go ahead. Make my day"—asks the criminal to act in such a way that the police officer is justified in taking aggressive action. But beyond the high-minded waiting of Eastwood, such action can also be provoked by the officer. In response to challenges or to interpersonal conflict situations, preemptive police actions (sometimes euphemistically, or sardonically, called "constructive coercion" or "preventive violence") may lead to further violence.

Police responses to protest and celebratory crowds offer many examples of escalation. Provocative overreaction—"oiling the fire"—can turn a peaceful crowd into a disorderly one. For example, in New Haven, Connecticut, during a 1967 civil rights protest, a small group of angry, but as yet law-abiding citizens marched in the street and were met by police tear gas; this overreaction provoked a riot. In Detroit, riotous behavior occurred during a 1968 protest against poverty after police inside a meeting hall tried to push people outside at the same time that mounted police outside were trying to push people back inside. Such police reactions and subsequent crowd violence may occur in the most benign of circumstances, such as at sporting events or concerts.

In some cases, the police solution to crowd violence has been to withdraw law enforcement, or to lower the level of police involvement. In communicating indifference, the failure to stop violence may contribute to it, by sending a signal that it is acceptable. This was often the case with nineteenth-century mob violence directed against

African Americans. When lynchings occurred, police generally were absent (or sometimes "police" were present only as active participants in the mob). Police strikes can have the same effect, as in 1919 Boston, when several days of looting and rioting took place during a police work stoppage. More recently, the 1992 Rodney King riots in Los Angeles, which followed a not-guilty verdict for several of King's attackers, were attributed partly to a lack of police preparation and the absence of an initial forceful police presence, despite expectations that street violence might follow acquittals in the case.

High-speed chases offer other tragic examples. They sometimes result in injuries or deaths or long prison sentences for persons who, in the absence of the chase, might have faced minimal or no charges. For example, in a Boston suburb in 1975, a car being chased by two police cruisers at speeds up to ninety-five miles per hour killed a footpatrolman. The same day, a jailed fifteen-year-old hung himself in a nearby town. He had been arrested the week before, following a high-speed chase in which his car killed two people. In some of such chases (particularly when the initial offense is minor and police know who the offender is or have a license plate number), police could have served a summons or made an arrest at a later time, thus avoiding the escalation.

### Nonenforcement

In the case of nonenforcement, the contribution of authorities to rule breaking is more indirect than with escalation or covert facilitation. Those involved in nonenforcement relationships with police may break rules partly because they believe they will not be punished. In an exchange relationship, offenders perform services for police and in return police may look the other way with respect to some violations. This is often the case with informants, particularly when they face arrest or after they have been arrested. Sentencing may be deferred for a period of time while the informant "works off" the charges. In some cities this is referred to as "flipping" or "turning" a person.

Nonenforcement is difficult to document. As a social control strategy, it may be realistic and effective. A justification of the lesser of two evils often accompanies the practice. But it also can be illegal, and it is not something one finds spelled out in detail in official policy. Police, after all, are sworn to uphold the law; not to do so may involve them in malfeasance, aiding and abetting a felon,

compounding a felony, perjury, and other violations. Some anticorruption policies are in reality anti-nonenforcement policies. Those violating the law will often claim that they are working for police and hence entitled to break the law. This may be a correct assumption or a misperception (when the violator wrongly assumes privileged status). Or it may simply be an excuse.

Police nonenforcement may take the form of failure to take enforcement action, offering information (including tips on planned raids), using procedures that will result in a case being rejected by the court, giving ineffective testimony, dismissing charges or helping a person obtain leniency by encouraging lower charges, or taking enforcement action against a criminal's competitors. Such actions receive some encouragement from the legitimate discretion in the police role and relatively high standards of proof and rules of evidence required for conviction in the United States.

A policy of nonenforcement is seen most often with respect to (1) informants offering information on the law breaking of others, or offering to help in facilitating the controlled commission of a crime, or both; (2) vice entrepreneurs agreeing to keep their own illegal behavior within agreed-upon bounds; and (3) individuals who either directly or indirectly control others by using resources or means police do not have, or who take actions desired by authorities but considered too politically risky for the authorities themselves to undertake. The literature on prisons gives many examples that fit the third category, describing the way selected prisoners often play a significant role in the running of a prison. Concessions may be given to key prisoners in return for their regulation of the behavior of others. An elaborate system of informal social control is present. Authorities need this cooperation and are willing to pay a price for it.

Pressure on police to solve crimes may lead them to delegate information and other techniques that they would not directly use themselves. For example, in 1963 police allowed an active burglar to kidnap a key figure in the plot to assassinate the civil rights leader Medgar Evers. The kidnapped suspect was told that he would be killed unless he provided information for police about the plan, which he did. The kidnapper had been promised leniency for his crime.

Another example of nonenforcement takes the form of police toleration of vigilante-type groups. In some urban areas police apparently tolerate violence among criminal gangs, perhaps because the gangs do more harm to each other than police ever could, or because police want to see one gang become dominant. In the same vein, police sometimes seem less than aggressive in pursuing the murderers of drug dealers thought to be vigilantes seeking to rid their communities of drug dealing.

The fact that criminals may possess unique skills and access or share enemies with the government can also be a factor in nonenforcement. For example, in Italy during World War II some mafiosi were active in the underground and provided the Allies with intelligence. Antifascist Mafia were appointed to important positions in many towns and villages. Alliances between the Central Intelligence Agency (CIA) and anticommunists in Asia or Latin America, some of whom were engaged in drug dealing and other illicit activities, are another example. This was the case with the unsuccessful CIA-organized plot to kill Fidel Castro.

### Conclusion

Social control responses are just one part of the interactive and systemic aspects of some types of violence. Interdependence often exists between social control agents, victims, and aggressors (categories that sometimes shift and overlap) in the precipitation of violence. While the examples in this article illustrate how social control efforts can lead to violence, this is certainly not to suggest that if social control were absent, violence would disappear, nor that on balance the violence-facilitative consequences of social control outweigh the violence-inhibiting consequences. But it does call attention to social control as a factor that can be crucial in creating or escalating social violence and one that is usually unseen in the face of good intentions and official rhetoric.

*BIBLIOGRAPHY*

Becker, Howard. *Outsiders: Studies in the Sociology of Deviance.* Glencoe, Ill.: Free Press, 1985.

Chevigny, Paul. *Edge of the Knife: Police Violence in the Americas.* New York: New Press, 1995.

Higgins, Martha K. *Political Policing: The United States and Latin America.* Durham, N.C.: Duke University Press, 1998.

Marx, Gary T. "Ironies of Social Control: Authorities as Contributors to Deviance Through Escalation, Nonenforcement, and Covert Facilitation." *Social Problems* 28, no. 3 (1981).

———. *Undercover: Police Surveillance in America.* Berkeley: University of California Press, 1988.

Merton, Robert K. *Social Theory and Social Structure.* Glencoe, Ill.: Free Press, 1968.

GARY T. MARX

*See also* **Civil Disobedience; Civil Disorder; Police; Riots.**

## SOCIOBIOLOGY

Sociobiology is a theory of human social behavior based on neo-Darwinian (gene-based) evolutionary principles; it is closely aligned with other neo-Darwinian perspectives such as evolutionary psychology and Darwinian anthropology.

The mechanisms of evolution can be summarized as follows: (1) Populations of organisms contain variations in gene-based morphological and behavioral traits and characteristics. (2) Some variations provide individual organisms with advantages over the rest of the population that improve their chances of surviving and reproducing. (3) Because populations tend to produce more offspring than the environment can support, the proportion of favorable variants surviving and reproducing will be larger than the proportion of unfavorable variants. (4) Eventually, the genes for the advantageous trait will become relatively fixed (invariant) in the population. Such advantageous traits are called adaptations, although as environments change, some formerly adaptive (fitness-enhancing) traits may become maladaptive (fitness-reducing).

Because it rests on the firm foundation of the theory of evolution by natural selection and sexual selection, sociobiology can claim to be the only scientific explanation for basic behavioral design. The basic premise of sociobiology is that behavior, like morphology, reveals the adaptive history of the species. That is, behaviors favored by natural selection, such as altruism, cooperation, nurturance, as well as deceit, aggression, and violence, are those that led to reproductive success (fitness) in environments of evolutionary adaptation (EEA). EEA refers to the roughly 2.5-million-year Pleistocene epoch, during which the most relevant hominid features, such as rapidly expanding brain size and bipedalism, were evolving. This essay is limited to summarizing the evolutionary basis for violence, the adaptive significance of the use of violence, and differences between the sexes in the propensity to commit violence.

Sociobiology differs from other biological approaches to behavior, such as behavioral genetics, in that it seeks to explain commonalities within species rather than differences. It also differs from other biological approaches in that it focuses on *ultimate* causes of behavior (its adaptive history) rather than its *proximate* causes (variables that arise out of the situation of the organism or the organism itself). These two foci are complementary, not antagonistic. Sociobiologists posit that behaviors (or, more correctly, the physiological mechanisms that support them) most relevant to reproductive success should have minimal heritable variation (that is, minimal variance in the quantitative properties of human traits) because natural selection moves organisms toward genetic fixity for such mechanisms. That is, because certain traits and behaviors have such important reproductive consequences, genes conducive to them are uniform in the population. The alternative view is that the approximately two thousand generations that have lived during our approximately fifty-thousand-year history as *Homo sapiens sapiens* are very few relative to other species, and thus there may be a lot less genetic fixity than is often supposed. The fact of so few generations leaves room for oscillation of gene frequencies. Indeed, behavioral genetic studies of aggression, a necessary if not sufficient cause of violence, put the heritability coefficient for aggression at around 0.50, although this varies depending on how aggression is measured.

The sociobiological view does not deny individual differences in thresholds (which may be heritable) for the emergence of fitness-relevant behavior; it simply denies that these differences are adaptations per se. Sociobiologists tend to see a normal distribution of individual thresholds (e.g., differences in impulsiveness, aggression, capacity for empathy, and so on) for engaging in fitness-relevant acts dispersed around an adaptive mean. (A species will vary in its traits, but the mean, or average, of these traits will, by definition, be the threshold for most organisms in the species.) Whether or not the species-typical behavior emerges depends on evolutionarily relevant environmental triggers interacting with (a) individual differences in traits that facilitate that behavior and (b) cultural practices, such as moral injunctions and legal and other penalties, that constrain it. Sociobiology is thus far from being, as some critics maintain, the theory of "genetic determinism." Sociobiologists fully agree that genes produce proteins—hormones, enzymes, and neurotransmitters—not behaviors or emotions. Nor do these gene products produce behaviors or emotions, but they do produce tendencies to respond to environmental cues in ways favored over alternatives.

Violent behavior (behavior designed to inflict injury on another) is an extreme form of aggression. The ubiquity of violence across cultures, historical periods, and species strongly implies that such behaviors have served important evolutionary purposes: that is, they have been adaptive. Widespread acts of violence across a wide range of animal species include infanticide, cannibalism, siblicide, lethal and injurious male fights, rape of females and other forms of courtship violence between males and females (such as spousal abuse and emotional violence), xenophobia, "primitive warfare" among chimpanzees, and "war" and "slavery" among the eusocial insects (insects, such as ants and bees, that will sacrifice their lives for the colony). However, when food, territory, and mates are plentiful and readily available, violence is an unnecessary waste of energy that is to be avoided because it involves the risk of serious injury or death. Gratuitous violence was as maladaptive in EEA as it is today, which is why we see relatively little of it in typical environments. When resources become scarce, violent competition to acquire them may become necessary. The human brain evolved in the context of overwhelming concerns for resource and mate acquisition. Males who were triumphant in these sometimes violent competitions gained rank and status, and thereby access to a disproportionate number of females. Because rank and status brought more copulation opportunities, genes inclining males to violence enjoyed greater representation in subsequent generations. According to the sociobiologist, human males (as well as males in numerous other species) are thus designed by nature to be violent under certain circumstances.

### Homicide and Assault

Although killing rival suitors and rival claimants to resources and territory doubtless conferred a reproductive advantage on the killers, sociobiologists do not view homicide per se as adaptive. (An adaptation is an evolved mechanism derived to solve a specific adaptive problem; homicide is far too rare to be considered an adaptation.) However, behaviors that were adaptive in EEA, such as male sexual propriety, jealousy, aggressive resource acquisition, and status-striving, occasionally manifest themselves in homicide. Intrasexual competition for access to reproductive opportunities leads to violence only in certain environments and under certain circumstances. Thus, although there are genes governing psychophysiological processes that facilitate violence, their expression is contingent on environmental circumstances. Most competition between males is for power, wealth, and status, the acquisition of which draws females to males who are successful and obviates any necessity for these males actually to fight other males for access. Within human and nonhuman primate groups with established dominance hierarchies, social rules restrain the emergence of widespread violent conflict.

Sociobiologists predict that violent confrontations over issues ultimately related to reproductive success usually will be observed in the most disadvantaged environments—those that are lacking in firmly established dominance hierarchies and in which social restraints have dissolved. Annual Federal Bureau of Investigation crime statistics consistently show that crimes of assault and homicide are highly concentrated among the uneducated, unmarried, unpropertied, and unemployed young males in our society who have little to lose, and often much to gain, by acting violently. Serious assaults and homicides among this group are generally the result of seemingly trivial altercations over matters of honor, respect, and reputation in the context of a culture where the violent defense of such intangibles is a major route to status—it lets others know that "you can't push *me* around!" Status, however it is defined in a given culture, has positive fitness consequences and will be sought after in culturally prescribed ways. When viewed in the light of evolutionary theory, the cost/benefit ratio of violent behavior engaged in by culturally disadvantaged males for some of the most trivial reasons, and which seems to defy assumptions of rational choice, becomes quite understandable. Experiments with a variety of nonhuman primates have shown that efficiency of serotonergic mechanisms (brain mechanisms having to do with the neurotransmitter/modulator serotonin) underlies dominance hierarchies, with the highest-ranking males having the highest levels of serotonin (which, among other things, promotes confidence and self-esteem), and the lowest-ranking having the lowest levels. In established dominance hierarchies, low-ranking members typically defer without much fuss to higher-ranking members over access to females and other resources. However, when the hierarchy is disrupted, lower-level members tend to become the most impulsively vi-

olent in the competition for status. Those rising to positions of status in the new dominance hierarchy tend to be the most aggressive, and their serotonin rises to levels commensurate with their new status. The same kinds of relationships between serotonin levels and self-esteem, status, impulsivity, and violence are consistently found among human males. This is not to say that rising in a new hierarchy is simply a matter of individual combativeness. Ambitious individuals form alliances, coalitions, and "gangs," just as aspiring human leaders do, to help them achieve their aim. Serotonergic mechanisms may have been naturally selected to equip us for the social status we find ourselves having attained within well-ordered groups and also to equip those who have little to lose with the necessary mechanisms to attempt to elevate their status when social restraints are weak by taking violent risks.

### Spousal or Lover Assault

Spousal or lover assault also has evolutionary underpinnings, with male sexual propriety, jealousy, and suspicion of infidelity probably being the fitness-promoting mechanisms driving it. Males in several nonhuman animal species have been observed attacking females who show interest in other males. Human males in EEA who did not react emotionally when their mates showed interest in other males and who did not seek to control their mates' sexual behavior risked being cuckolded (unwittingly raising a child carrying another male's genes). Females are always certain of their maternity; males can only infer their paternity. To the extent that males invested resources in females and their offspring, assaultive tendencies aimed at maintaining a mate's fidelity will have been favored by natural selection. Males who were nonchalant about the sexual behavior of mates in whom they invested resources probably had their genes culled from the gene pool long ago.

Consistent with evolutionary principles, evidence from many cultures around the world indicates that the single most important cause of spousal or lover assault and homicide is male jealousy and suspicion of infidelity. Also consistent with evolutionary principles are laboratory findings indicating that males in bonded relationships, when told to imagine their mates engaging in sexual intercourse with another male, are more jealous (as measured by readings of brain waves and self-reports) than females told to imagine their mates engaging in sexual intercourse with another female. Females in bonded relationships were more jealous when imagining their mates falling in love with another female. Although both sexes became jealous when imagining both scenarios, it is interesting to note that males were more emotionally upset by actions carrying the threat of cuckoldry and females by actions that threatened the loss of paternal investment.

If spousal or lover assault is ultimately a male tactic to prevent real or imagined infidelity, sociobiological theory would predict that it would be most common in environments where the threat of cuckoldry is most real: that is, environments in which marriages are precarious, where moral restrictions on pre- and extramarital sexual relationships are weakest, and where out-of-wedlock birth rates are highest. These are precisely the same deprived environments in which intrasex assault and homicide (often directly or indirectly over women) are most common. Spousal or lover assaults are not only more frequent in such environments, they also tend to be more serious. Strictly environmental theories would also predict that most incidents of spousal or lover assault would occur in the most deprived environment, but such explanations would invoke discrimination, status-frustration, and the notion of a "subculture of violence." Sociobiologists would not necessarily dismiss these factors as proximate facilitators (that is, the event or events that most immediately precede the event in question in a manner likely to make it possible), but they would point out that such explanations fail to account for the cross-cultural and non-human animal data pertinent to this issue.

## Rape

The behavior of all animals is ultimately about reproductive success, and forced copulation is the act of violence that can have the most direct reproductive consequences. Sociobiology posits that all males possess a genetically invariant predisposition toward sexual aggression, although they may argue about whether the disposition is an adaptation per se or a side effect of other adaptations that may promote sexual assault. Neither viewpoint avers that every man is equally likely to rape, even under the same environmental conditions, but both contend that all men share the propensity because they all share the same evolutionary history. Rape, a high-risk behavior, is most likely to occur among low-status young males living in environments with high rates of other forms of violence.

The key to understanding rape behavior and the different reproductive strategies of human males and females is to recognize the tremendous disparity in parental investment between men and women. The only necessary male investment in reproducing his genes is the time spent copulating. The optimal strategy for maximizing male reproductive success is therefore to seek copulations with multiple partners, and throughout human evolution males have had a propensity to do so. Female parental investment is enormous, and they cannot increase their fitness by copulating with multiple partners. The female's best fitness strategy is to secure male parental investment in exchange for exclusive sexual access. Female promiscuity would reduce fitness because few males would invest resources in offspring that in all likelihood are not theirs. Because females in EEA faced this problem, women in the modern epoch evolved with a tendency to resist casual copulation, or at least to be much more circumspect about it than males. Thus, two different and often conflicting reproductive strategies have evolved: the careful and discriminating female strategy and the reckless and indiscriminate male strategy. Rape was and is sometimes the result of this disparity. Males in EEA who were most inclined to pursue multiple copulation opportunities with multiple partners, forcefully or otherwise, enjoyed greater fitness than those who did not, thus passing on these inclinations to their offspring.

Although forced copulation is found among nonhuman mammals, especially among some primates, and few would argue that the strategy does not result in increased fitness among them, there is much resistance to applying similar reasoning to humans. Critics claim that to assert that rape (or any other violent behavior) is a natural phenomenon (i.e., a product of natural selection) is to dignify and justify it, or even to imply that it is morally acceptable. Philosophers of science call this confusion of *is* with *ought* the naturalistic fallacy. Nature simply is; what ought to be is a moral judgment. To say that forced copulation is natural mammalian behavior no more constitutes moral approval than to claim that we approve of disease and death because we call them normal and natural. Rape is a maladaptive consequence of a mating strategy that was probably adaptive in EEA; it is a morally reprehensible crime that requires strong preventative legal sanctions. Calling something natural does not place it beyond the power of society to modify.

Just as the naturalistic fallacy is a misunderstanding of evolutionary logic, so is the assertion that because the putative motive for rape is reproductive success, the theory cannot explain the rape of men, children, and postmenopausal women, or sexual attacks not including vaginal intercourse. This point overlooks the fact that organisms are not adapted by natural selection to directly seek ultimate goals (fitness); they are adapted to directly seek proximate goals (in this case, sexual pleasure) that themselves blindly serve ultimate goals. Evolution is a mindless algorithmic process operating without any sort of conscious input from those on whom it operates. Indeed, we often, through the use of contraceptives, consciously attempt to thwart maximizing our fitness even as our Pleistocene-evolved brains continue to seek and enjoy the mechanism that promotes it.

### Child Abuse and Neglect

Child abuse and neglect (including infanticide) appears to be thoroughly inconsistent with evolutionary logic. Selection for abuse and neglect of one's own genetic offspring is almost a contradiction in terms. However, in EEA there are environmental conditions under which such behavior may have enhanced *inclusive fitness* (personal fitness plus the fitness of close genetic relatives). Studies have found that the probability of abuse, neglect, and infanticide among nonhuman animals increases when the food supply is low, when the litter size is large, when an infant has low reproductive viability, and, in biparental species, when the female lacks the assistance of a mate. These are precisely the conditions under which we find most human incidences of abuse and neglect—that is, under conditions of poverty, within large families, in single-parent families, in families with children born out of wedlock, and in families with physically or mentally handicapped children.

Stepparenting is a very strong additional risk factor in human abuse and neglect. In many animal species, a new male claiming a female commences to kill any offspring sired by the female's previous mate. This prompts the female's return to estrus and an opportunity for the new male to produce his own offspring. In some preliterate cultures, human males acquiring wives may also kill any dependent children from a previous relationship, thereby increasing the fitness of the killer at the expense of the fitness of the father of the victims. Although human males tend to be the only males who routinely invest resources in genetically

unrelated children, the abuse, neglect, and murder of stepchildren is as much as one hundred times more likely than the abuse, neglect, and murder of biological children in every country where it has been studied.

Abuse, neglect, and killing of offspring may increase inclusive fitness in several ways. When a mother in EEA had too many mouths to feed, lacked a mate, or had children who were unlikely to be able to contribute, a triage strategy may have been the best one available in terms of maximizing the probability of the survival of her genetic material. Such a strategy increases the probability of the survival of the most reproductively viable of her offspring, while a strategy of trying to nurture each offspring equally may have resulted in the survival of none.

### Differences Between the Sexes

Across time and national boundaries, males are consistently found to be more violent than females by a very large margin. Theories stressing differential gender socialization as an explanation for difference in propensity to commit violence by men and women imply that there could be cultures, past or present, in which women are equally as violent as men. No such culture has been found. Socialization theories also ignore the fact that males in almost all animal species are more violent than females, and in many cases the difference between the sexes is greater than it is among humans. We cannot, of course, invoke differential gender socialization to explain this pattern among nonhuman animals.

The sociobiological explanation for the sex difference in violent behavior is the asymmetry in fitness variation between the sexes. Male fitness is limited by access to fertile females; female fitness is limited by access to resources. A female could copulate with a different partner every night without increasing her fitness, whereas a male doing the same would increase his fitness tremendously. This is why males throughout most of the animal kingdom seek copulations with multiple partners despite the risk of injury and death from competitors and why they have evolved the mechanisms (most specifically, testosterone-driven size, strength, and aggression) to pursue that strategy. This is also why female animals have evolved tendencies to choose the males most likely to provide them with the best genes and the ability to provide parental investment—an evaluation indexed by the male's status in the group, which may have been achieved through violent means. Given our evolutionary history of much greater parental investment by females compared with males and our sexually dimorphic reproductive strategies, it is almost impossible to imagine human males and females *not* evolving widely different propensities to engage in violence.

Buttressing the parental investment thesis is evidence from species (mostly bird and insect species) in which males make greater parental investment than do females. In these species it is females who show evidence of greater fitness variance than males and who have been selected to seek multiple partners, to fight other females over access to males, and to be larger and more aggressive than the male of the species. Thus, the different nature of parental investment between the sexes, not sex per se, appears to be the ultimate cause of differences in the propensity to commit violence.

## Conclusion

It is important to emphasize again that none of the behaviors described as either adaptive or as side effects of other adaptations are *directly* motivated by concerns of reproductive success. Humans are adapted to seek the immediate means of achieving specific goals, not ultimate ends. Evolution is a process that inevitably perpetuates any trait, characteristic, or behavior that resulted in its possessors' leaving more offspring than those not possessing such traits, or those who expressed the same ones less forcefully. Males who were unwilling to withdraw when threatened by rivals; males who sought copulation with multiple partners using whatever strategies at their command; males who became jealous and reacted if their mates flirted; males who took strong actions to avoid cuckoldry; males who favored their own offspring at the expense of the offspring of others; and males who sought status by acting fearlessly and building coalitions were males who enhanced their genes' representation in future generations.

Sociobiology is not about how violence is "in the genes" and therefore inevitable. It simply points to the adaptive significance of violence in environments of evolutionary adaptation; such a task is not incompatible with pointing out the adaptive significance of cooperation, nurturance, and altruism, human characteristics that also have strong genetic underpinnings. Sociobiology is not an "imperial" discipline seeking to swallow the social sciences; rather, it fully recognizes the remoteness of its motivational claims and the

need to complement them with more proximate explanations from both the biological and social-behavioral sciences. Sociobiologists know that substances associated with violence, such as testosterone (high) and serotonin (low), fluctuate as much in accordance with environmental variation as (and perhaps more than) they do with genetic variation. Sociobiology enables us to predict the kinds of unstable environments in which violence will be relatively common and nurturance and altruism uncommon. For these as well as other reasons, sociobiology has even been called an "environmental discipline."

*BIBLIOGRAPHY*

Buss, David, et al. "Sex Differences in Jealousy: Evolution, Physiology, and Psychology." *Psychological Science* 3 (1992).

Crawford, Charles, and Judith Anderson. "Sociobiology: An Environmental Discipline?" *American Psychologist* 44 (1989).

Daley, Martin, and Margo Wilson. *Homicide: Psychological Aspects.* New York: de Gruyter, 1988.

Ellis, Lee. "Neo-Darwinian Theories of Violent Criminality and Antisocial Behavior: Photographic Evidence from Nonhuman Animals and a Review of the Literature." *Aggression and Violent Behavior* 3 (1998).

Ellis, Lee, and Anthony Walsh. "Gene-Based Evolutionary Theories in Criminology." *Criminology* 35 (1997).

Lepowsky, Maria. "Women, Men, and Aggression in Egalitarian Societies." *Sex Roles* 30 (1994).

Pater, Polemoss. "The Study of Conflict." In *Sociobiology and Conflict: Evolutionary Perspectives on Competition, Cooperation, Violence and Warfare,* edited by J. Van der Dennen and V. Falger. London: Chapman and Hall, 1990.

Raleigh, Michael, et al. "Serotonergic Mechanisms Promote Dominance Acquisition in Adult Vervet Monkeys." *Brain Research* 559 (1991).

Rasche, Christine. "Minority Women and Domestic Violence: The Unique Dilemmas of Battered Women of Color." In *The Criminal Justice System and Women: Offenders, Victims, and Workers,* edited by B. Price and N. Sokoloff. New York: McGraw-Hill, 1995.

Rushton, J. Philippe, et al. "Altruism and Aggression: The Heritability of Individual Differences." *Journal of Personality and Social Psychology* 50 (1986).

Thornhill, Randy, and Nancy Thornhill. "The Evolutionary Psychology of Men's Coercive Sexuality." *Behavioral and Brain Sciences* 15 (1992).

Tooby, John, and Leda Cosmides. "On the Universality of Human Nature and the Uniqueness of the Individual: The Role of Genetics and Adaptation." *Journal of Personality* 58 (1990).

Virkkunen, Matti, and Markku Linnoila. "Serotonin in Early Onset, Male Alcoholics with Violent Behaviour." *Annals of Medicine* 22 (1990).

ANTHONY WALSH

*See also* **Child Abuse; Developmental Factors; Nature vs. Nurture; Neurotransmitters: Serotonin; Rape; Sex Differences; Spousal and Partner Abuse; Theories of Violence.**

**SON OF SAM.** *See* Berkowitz, David "Son of Sam."

# SOUTH

Violence and the American South have always shared a special relationship. Throughout history, southerners considered violence part of the natural order and not an aberration. The Virginian Thomas Jefferson recognized its presence in the personality of the white southerner. As he wrote in 1785, "The manner of training children at the South accounts for that pugilistic spirit and uncontrollable temper . . . [that] we all know is a characteristic of the Southerner." More than one hundred and fifty years later, the journalist Wilbur J. Cash—the self-proclaimed voice of the South—reaffirmed the centrality of violence to the region's character. In *The Mind of the South* (1941), he wrote that a southerner was "full of the chip-on shoulder swagger and bray of a boy—one, in brief, of which the essence was the boast, voiced or not, on the part of every southerner, that he would knock the hell out of whoever dared to cross him." The social scientists Richard E. Nisbett and Dov Cohen (1996) confirmed these observations. Southerners in the 1990s commit more violent crimes, fight more barroom brawls, and organize more of their leisure activities around blood sports than other Americans. They also authorize the use of corporal punishment for criminals more than other Americans, and they are more likely to consider violence as an acceptable form of self-defense. Nisbett and Cohen even discovered that "southerners showed psychological preparedness for dominant and aggressive behaviors, as indicated by their rise in testosterone levels" in response to verbal insults. Something in the southern character continues to perpetuate a predisposition for violence.

Scholars disagree over the sources of the southern affinity for violence, but they emphasize the region's relative poverty, rural character, warm climate, heightened sense of individualism, scattered population, system of honor, means of physically disciplining children, lack of education, peculiar history of immigration, economic structure, and prolonged frontier character. None of these factors can be understood apart from the South's explosive racial history, in regard to both Native Americans and African Americans. Despite heated debates over its origins, the idea of a violent south is accepted by sociologists, historians, journalists, and other observers. The region's image remains one of slave beatings, duels, rough-and-tumble fights, race riots, feuds, frontier wars, lynchings, shotgun weddings, cockfighting, church burnings, and capital punishment. H. C. Brearley's assertion about the South in *Homicide in the United States* (1932), that it is "that part of the United States lying below the Smith and Wesson line," accurately describes the region's past and present.

## Colonial Times to the Civil War

Southern violence began early in colonial Virginia. The peaceful relations initiated by the 1614 marriage of the Indian princess Pocahontas to the English colonist John Rolfe did not last long. In 1622 a series of bloody Anglo-Powhatan wars erupted. The Carolinas and Georgia went through similar experiences with the Cherokees, Chickasaws, and Creeks. Although colonial governments often initiated campaigns against neighboring Native Americans, the violence sometimes stemmed from local populations. Bacon's Rebellion (1676–1677), for example, erupted when Virginian colonists disagreed with the colony's official Anglo-Indian policy. A trade dispute between a planter and local Indians led to the murder of the planter's servant. When demands for vengeance were unmet by the colonial government, followers of Nathaniel Bacon retaliated against neighboring Indians of all nationalities. The bloody disagreement over Indian affairs became an internal civil war between Baconians and Governor William Berkeley. The rebels burned Jamestown, made hostages of the wives of Berkeley supporters, and threatened the lives of all who opposed them. The prevalence of guns within Virginia society made the uprising especially dangerous. William Blathwayt wrote in 1691 that "there is no Custom more generally to be observed among the Young Virginians than that they all Learn to keep and use a gun with a Marvelous dexterity as soon as ever they have strength enough to lift it to their heads." The colonial tendency to resort to violence was not particular to Virginians, or even to southerners. North Carolinians erupted in Culpepper's Rebellion (1677–1678), and northern colonists also experienced extralegal disturbances. During England's Glorious Revolution, most of

**Rebels led by Nathaniel Bacon set fire to Jamestown, 1676.** HULTON GETTY/LIAISON AGENCY

the colonies, both northern and southern, erupted in political violence.

Underneath this similarity of colonial violence in the North and the South were the roots of a distinctively southern attitude toward violence. Whereas physical violence was one of the grounds for divorce in seventeenth- and eighteenth-century Massachusetts, settlers in the southern backcountry condoned physical violence between spouses if the wife did not fulfill her marital duties, disgraced her family, or disobeyed her husband. Such a trend continued into the late twentieth century. In Texas until the 1970s it remained "justifiable homicide" for a husband to kill his wife and her lover if they were found in "a compromising position." Also, whereas northern colonists usually invoked the law for protection, southerners increasingly turned to individual acts of vengeance. Nearly all aspects of southern life centered upon violence, and southerners even organized much of their leisure time around violence. Horse racing, cockfighting, gambling, and drinking all promoted frequent fights by spectators and participants. The system of indentured servitude also relied on violence for masters to maintain their authority. Much like the African slaves who replaced them, indentured servants lived in a precarious position; they were property whose misdeeds encouraged a range of corporal punishments.

During the American Revolution, the South experienced what might be called an "uncivil war." The backcountry, where the vigilante Regulator movement had recently flourished, erupted into chaos. Revolutionaries aggressively forced Tories from their midst, confiscating their land, issuing physical threats, and pursuing legal retribution. Britain's invasion of the South and its occupation of Charles Town, South Carolina, in 1780 further heightened the internal dissent. In the Carolina and Georgia countrysides, where the war was fiercely contested, private bands of bandits confused matters through acts of personal vengeance and widespread looting. To avoid these extralegal and legal acts of war, many loyalists fled to Florida, Canada, the West Indies, and local Indian nations.

After the Revolution, the southerner's peculiar relationship with violence became even more pronounced. While northern colonists slowly abolished slavery, pushed the frontier further west, and abandoned dueling, white southerners continued to exalt the virtues of masculinity, honor, and violence. African slavery ensured that violence would remain a part of the southern fabric. Masters used the whip and the branding iron or the threat of them to maintain control over their slaves. Bondspeople lived in fear of punishment and violent intrusion into their family lives. On a daily basis slave women faced the terrifying threat of rape, and most slaves feared that they would be separated from their children, parents, and spouses. Violence was also endemic to black southerners. Its use by slaves served a logical response to their condition. The abolitionist David Walker, born in North Carolina the son of a slave father, appealed to southern blacks to resist with a violent rebellion: "They want us for their slaves, and think nothing of murdering us in order to subject us to that wretched condition—therefore, if there is an *attempt* by us, kill or be killed. Now, I ask you had you not rather be killed than to be a slave to a tyrant, who takes the life of your mother, wife, and dear little children?" (*Walker's Appeal*, 1829). Although protest in the slave quarters often occurred passively, violent resistance by African American slaves also surfaced. Large-scale rebellions or plots in Richmond (led by Gabriel Prosser in 1800), Charleston (led by Denmark Vesey in 1822), and Southampton County, Virginia (Nat Turner's rebellion in 1831), all contributed to heightened racial tensions in the South. In each case the consequences of rebellion were chilling. At least twenty conspirators were executed for their roles in the Prosser conspiracy, thirty-five after the Vesey conspiracy, and another twenty after Turner's revolt. Southerners turned to the local militias and slave patrols to tighten their control over the African American population. The regularity of the patrols, the martial training of their members, and the authority to suppress unruly slaves increased after the rebellions. For example, after Virginians suppressed Turner's revolt, they brought more than one hundred suspected slave instigators to the gallows in the name of "justice." Many more faced personal acts of vengeance administered behind the walls of the planter's house. Out of necessity, violence underpinned the institution of slavery.

The scope of antebellum southern violence extended beyond the issues of slavery. Diplomatic concerns, including the constant threat of Indian and European invasions, also ensured a militant flavor in the South. During the early part of the nineteenth century, bloody and relentless Indian campaigns with Cherokees, Creeks, and Seminoles made mutual atrocities the norm. In between the wars, Indian attacks and the desire to dispossess Indian lands heightened the perceived need of southerners for frontier defenses. Potential warfare with European rivals also promoted the need for a strong local militia in the South. Until France ceded Louisiana to Great Britain in 1763, the

French threatened the southern borderlands. The Spanish occupation of Florida also posed a constant threat until Florida's purchase by the United States in 1819. During the War of 1812 all of these concerns converged as southeastern Indians, escaped slaves, and British soldiers united against the citizens of South Carolina and Georgia.

White southerners also directed their violence at other white southerners. In 1804, after the duel between Alexander Hamilton and Aaron Burr, after which Hamilton died, northerners outlawed dueling, but honorable southern gentlemen continued to use the ritual to defend their good names and reputations. Movements against dueling existed in the South, but duels with pistols, rifles, and swords remained the antebellum southern way. Many challenges were never fought and few duels ended in death. However, a man's willingness to throw down the gauntlet or accept the challenge showed his unflinching courage in the face of violence—a sure indication of his masculinity. For politicians such a trait endeared him to his contemporaries. Admired men such as Andrew Jackson, Thomas Hart Benton, William Crawford, Louis T. Wigfall, Judah Benjamin, John Randolph, Albert Sidney Johnston, and William Yancey all fought duels before entering the public sphere.

Affairs of honor were not confined to the political class or to the elite. For poor southern whites a different type of ritualized fighting served as a means of proving and defending one's masculinity. During the antebellum era, rough-and-tumbles settled disputes in the southern backcountry. Eye-gouging, hair-pulling, and nose-biting were so common in these encounters that one eighteenth-century French observer commented that the backcountry was inhabited by "Anglo-Americans of a peculiar sort, called Crackers or Gougers who are nearly all one-eyed." The scars from these battles, whether missing eyes, torn ears, or lost teeth, served as badges of honor for the community to respect. The violent rough-and-tumbles, like duels, was part of the southern social fabric, not an aberration.

The difference between the southern and northern means of settling disputes in the antebellum era became clear in the 1856 caning of the Massachusetts senator William Sumner by the South Carolina congressman Preston Brooks. Two days after abolitionist Sumner issued his fiery "Crime Against Kansas" speech, Brooks assaulted him with his own cane until Sumner fell bloodied on the Senate floor. Brooks justified his actions by citing his outrage at Sumner's disrespect for the South. More important, Brooks also felt obliged to avenge the dishonor done to his cousin, South Carolina senator Andrew Butler. For Brooks and his fellow southerners, Sumner's reference to the "thugs" from South Carolina and "the harlot, Slavery" demanded a violent answer. Although Sumner and other northerners saw the caning as nothing less than a sign of southern barbarity, Brooks answered Sumner's oratory in the language of the South—personal violence.

The Civil War also illuminated the southern penchant for violence. Southern attitudes toward violence influenced military strategy and allowed for a well-armed, if not well-disciplined, military. General Robert E. Lee exemplified the southern attitude toward war. He dismissed any notion of waiting for the fight to come to him. Instead, he was known for "never defending when he could attack." The Confederate army's aggressive tendency led the historian Grady McWhiney to characterize it as an "attack and die" strategy. During the Civil War, white southerners benefited from their long martial traditions. The temperament of the South led to many bloody victories and prolonged even lost battles. Union soldiers heard the South's violent spirit in the rebel yell, which they thought a perfect complement to the southern soldier. A northern veteran recalled that "there is nothing like it on this side of the infernal region. The peculiar corkscrew sensation that it sends down your backbone under these circumstances can never be told. You have to feel it." Some two hundred and fifty thousand Confederates died during the war, nearly one in three soldiers, and one in two survivors returned home with serious injuries. Few families were spared. The Civil War certainly brought the consequences of violence to every home in the South, but the realities of war did not lessen the region's martial ardor.

Violence was also used to control dissent within the Confederacy. In many regions of the South the war created legendary fights within families and between brothers. Both Unionists and slaves faced pressures to support the Confederate cause. Whites who refused to support the South faced violent threats, angry mobs, and often exile. One Confederate voiced the desire of many southerners that any "darned Old Union son of a bitch . . . ought to be hung." Southerners would not tolerate dissent. For slaves, too, the war was dangerous. The violence associated with slavery continued throughout the war, and often increased as masters

felt the cornerstone of the Confederacy crumble beneath them. Southern white women worked to prolong the fight. Many urged deserters back into the Confederate army, often publicly shaming those who did not fulfill their masculine duty.

**After the Civil War**

During Reconstruction, white southerners resisted changes to the antebellum racial order through both legal and extralegal violence. The Ku Klux Klan, formed in 1866 in Tennessee, and other paramilitary groups defiantly fought to keep "Black Republicans" and carpetbaggers out of power. In many ways they served the same function as the informal antebellum slave patrols. These white supremacists sought to control what the law could not or would not. The Klan, along with "home guards, " helped impeach the North Carolina governor William W. Holden, prevented thousands of African Americans from asserting their Thirteenth, Fourteenth, and Fifteenth Amendment rights, and tried to enforce the tenets of white supremacy. Many white southerners threatened political candidates, often literally killing their opposition, and intimidated voters. Nevertheless, the white supremacists did not end Reconstruction; they did, however, ensure its violent nature. Not all Reconstruction violence occurred outside of the law. For example, on 30 July 1866 a police-supported white mob killed thirty-seven blacks who had met for a suffrage convention in New Orleans. Over the next ten years, more than seventy similar riots occurred throughout the South. In all of these instances, the local police force actively assisted the white mob.

After Reconstruction, violence continued to ensure the solidity of the racial order and the complete disfranchisement of African Americans. Although poll taxes, fraud, literacy tests, and understanding clauses (laws passed throughout the South that required voters to prove that they "understood" American law and what they were voting for) prevented black participation and representation, violence and intimidation by whites also backed the "new" order. The Jim Crow laws that created segregation in the South also relied on extralegal and legal violence for their enforcement. Local southern governments found a partner in the rebirth of the Ku Klux Klan of the 1920s. Together they solidified their vision of racial order through a system of lynchings, chain gangs, convict leasing, debt peonage, and vagrancy laws. In each case the state instituted systems characterized by vigilante justice, racial oppression, constant whippings, and violence. When southern politicians wavered on issues of segregation, white supremacy, and civil rights, the Klan and individual white southerners responded promptly and violently. (Extreme political partisanship was behind the assassination of Governor William Goebel of Kentucky in 1900, while personal and political factors motivated the assassin of Senator Huey P. Long of Louisiana in 1935.)

Postbellum lynchings, used to maintain the racial order, epitomized the use of violence in the New South. Eighty-two percent of the nation's lynchings in the 1880s and 95 percent in the 1920s occurred in southern states. Victims in Texas alone outnumbered those in the entire "wild West." Usually lynchings occurred under the guise of protecting the purity of white womanhood and avenging a rape. In reality, whites tended to target blacks whom they perceived as "dangerous" to the southern order. One southerner wrote a Louisiana newspaper to claim that stopping lynchings and interracial violence was easy. "If the black man will stay where he belongs, act like a Negro should act, work like a Negro should work, talk like a Negro should talk . . . there will be very few riots, fights or clashes." Blacks who refused to stay in their "place" became targets of white aggression.

In 1954, when *Brown v. Board of Education of Topeka, Kansas* rattled the underpinnings of southern society by overturning the basis for segregation, the white South again resorted to violence. Black leaders throughout the South received death threats for their "insolence," and several threats were quickly fulfilled. In 1955 Elmer Kimball killed an African American, Clinton Melton, and, despite testimony by eyewitnesses, Kimball was acquitted. One local white man understood what the next few years would look like. "There's open season on the Negroes now. They've got no protection, and any peckerwood who wants can go out and shoot himself one, and we'll free him." This statement proved prophetic. The 1955 murders of the Reverend George Lee and Emmett Till and the 1956 murder of Lamar Smith all demonstrated that white murderers of blacks would be protected by the southern white community.

In the 1960s white policemen, who were ordered to "serve and protect," used violence to prevent the Jim Crow order from tumbling. During the spring of 1963 the police commissioner Eugene "Bull" Connor turned firehoses on black demonstrators in Birmingham. Although his actions out-

raged many white northerners and some white southerners, others felt that the threat of integration justified such actions. Soon after this, Governor George Wallace threatened to personally block the court-ordered integration of the University of Alabama. Only a greater threat of force, that of the federal marshals, forced him to back down. That very night, shortly after midnight on 12 June, Medgar Evers, a National Association for the Advancement of Colored People official and civil rights activist, was gunned down outside his Mississippi home. Although the white assassin bragged about his escapade, he was not convicted by two all-white juries. During the Freedom Summer of 1964, three civil rights workers—whites Andrew Goodman and Michael Schwerner and black James Chaney—disappeared during an investigation of a church burning and were later found dead. While Martin Luther King, Jr., preached passive resistance, white opponents to civil rights followed the paths of violence and militancy that characterized their region's past. King's assault on the southern order was radical in more than its racial objectives.

Southerners did not direct all of their violence toward blacks. Throughout the twentieth century, southern states had higher homicide rates, larger gun-owning populations, and greater military participation than the other states of the nation. During the 1920s the homicide rate in the South was two and a half times that of the rest of the nation. In 1968, 52 percent of white southern families and 34 percent of black southern families owned firearms. In contrast, 27 percent of northern white families and 15 percent of northern black families owned guns. This coincided with higher homicide rates. In 1969 Alabama, South Carolina, Georgia, Florida, Texas, and North Carolina had the six highest murder rates in the nation. Regional trends continued over the next decades. In 1997, seven of the states with the ten highest murder rates were in the South, and only three southern states (Kentucky, Texas, and West Virginia) did not have murder rates higher than the national average. The military tradition in the South also continued into the twentieth century. In 1910, 93 percent of army generals had a southern heritage, and during World War II southern enlistment in both the army and navy far exceeded the national average. At the end of the twentieth century, West Point, the Reserve Officers' Training Corps, and private military academies continued to attract a disproportionate number of southerners.

Firefighters break up an African American demonstration in Birmingham, Alabama, **1963.** CORBIS/BETTMANN

## Conclusion

Scholars continue to ask what constitutes the South and whether it will survive into the twenty-first century. Not surprisingly, southern violence continues to be used as proof of the region's vibrancy. The South still supports a disproportionate number of military academies, including the Virginia Military Institute and the Citadel. Secondary-school students also evidence the southern predisposition for violence. As most of the nation tries to get guns out of the schoolyard, some southern school districts mandate gun-safety classes for all of their male students.

Although in 1999 thirty-eight of the fifty states had the death penalty, the South employed it more frequently than ever, executing more criminals than the rest of the states combined. When the U.S. Supreme Court called for a temporary moratorium on capital punishment in 1972, it cited Georgia for using "cruel and unusual punishment," and southern states participated in the first five Supreme Court challenges to this ruling. Between 1976 and 1998 Texas executed more than one hundred convicted criminals. In 1992 two southern gubernatorial races focused on the ability to implement capital punishment, and each candidate sought to

convince the public that he or she would execute criminals as quickly as possible. These contests occurred in Texas, which uses the death penalty more than any other state, and in Florida, where the state's electric chair is colorfully known as "Old Sparky."

Violence in the South has undergone many changes over the past few centuries. The gaps between southern homicide rates and those of the rest of the country have lessened. White-on-white and black-on-black violence have replaced interracial violence as the central characterization of southern violence. Even so, southerners today commit more violent crime than the people in the rest of the nation, and these acts have a regional flavor. Homicides in the South are usually personal, involving friends, families, and neighbors. Southerners continue to believe more than others that violence is an acceptable form of behavior. A National Opinion Research Council poll in the 1990s revealed that two-thirds of white southern men owned guns as compared to less than half of northern white men. Similarly, gun control laws in the South remain much weaker than the national norm. If violence indicates the region's vibrancy, then the South is alive and well. H. C. Brearley's belief in 1932 that in due time "the resort to violence will no longer be a distinguishing feature of the southern scene" apparently jumped the gun.

BIBLIOGRAPHY

Ayers, Edward. *Vengeance and Justice: Crime and Punishment in the Nineteenth-Century American South.* New York: Oxford University Press, 1984.

Bruce, Dickson D., Jr. *Violence and Culture in the Antebellum South.* Austin: University of Texas Press, 1979.

Brundage, W. Fitzhugh. *Lynching in the New South: Georgia and Virginia, 1880–1930.* Urbana: University of Illinois Press, 1993.

Franklin, John Hope. *The Militant South, 1800–1861.* Cambridge, Mass.: Harvard University Press, 1970.

Greenberg, Kenneth. *Honor and Slavery: Lies, Duels, Noses, Masks, Dressing as a Woman, Gifts, Strangers, Humanitarianism, Death, Slave Rebellions, the Proslavery Argument, Baseball, Hunting, and Gambling in the Old South.* Princeton, N.J.: Princeton University Press, 1996.

Lundsgaarde, Henry P. *Murder in Space City: A Cultural Analysis of Houston Homicide Patterns.* New York: Oxford University Press, 1977.

Nisbett, Richard E., and Dov Cohen. *Culture of Honor: The Psychology of Violence in the South.* Boulder, Colo.: Westview, 1996.

Reed, John Shelton. *One South: An Ethnic Approach to Regional Culture.* Baton Rouge: Louisiana State University Press, 1982.

Wyatt-Brown, Bertram. *Southern Honor: Ethics and Behavior in the Old South.* New York: Oxford University Press, 1982.

ANDREW KEVIN FRANK

*See also* **Church Bombings; Civil War; Dueling; Feuds; Honor; Ku Klux Klan; Lynching; Reconstruction; Slave Rebellions; Slavery.**

# SOUTHERN CHRISTIAN LEADERSHIP CONFERENCE

After the conclusion of the Montgomery, Alabama, bus boycott in late 1956, a coalition of southern black leaders met in Atlanta on 10–11 January 1957 to form an organizational arm of the Civil Rights movement. Martin Luther King, Jr., who had been slated to preside over the conference, left on its eve to survey the destruction caused by opponents of bus desegregation. King called the bombing of Montgomery's black homes and churches a reign of terror. The Atlanta coalition, originally called the Southern Leadership Conference on Transportation and Nonviolent Integration, quickly made nonviolent direct action its principal objective and named King its president.

Recognizing the broad base of support from black church leaders, King renamed the organization the Southern Christian Leadership Conference (SCLC) in August 1957. Its association with Christian churches distinguished SCLC from other civil rights organizations and highlighted its philosophy of nonviolent direct action based on the teachings of Jesus Christ and Mohandas Gandhi. Nonviolence involved organizing large groups of people into campaigns of direct-action protest, thereby creating social disruption and public recognition of oppressive conditions. King and SCLC cofounders desired an inclusive organization responsive to the struggles of blacks in the South. Social Gospel conceptions of "beloved community," which King found so attractive as the basis for social and political reforms, would underscore SCLC philosophy.

Montgomery's bus boycott, which had resulted in the Supreme Court ordering an end to bus segregation in Montgomery in November 1956, had convinced SCLC members that a mass protest movement could desegregate the South. By 1958 SCLC was promoting a Crusade for Citizenship while encouraging the federal government to take oversight responsibility for civil rights. SCLC's twofold goal became enlarging the black electorate in the South and increasing political support for civil rights. Violence dogged SCLC's crusade in 1958 when the Reverend Ralph Abernathy, a prominent member of the organization, was beaten in his office; King was arrested for loitering in the Montgomery courthouse as he sought legal help for Abernathy.

In 1960 SCLC helped underwrite a student grassroots movement for sit-in demonstrations and supported creation of the Student Nonviolent Coordinating Committee (SNCC). In turn, SNCC helped turn SCLC's focus from boycott action to voter registration campaigns. In late 1961 SCLC began desegregation campaigns in Albany, Georgia, where violence erupted in August 1962 when Ku Klux Klan members burned Albany's black churches. SCLC undertook citywide campaigns in Birmingham, St. Augustine, and Selma during 1963 and 1965, calling for desegregation of lunch counters and public facilities, fair hiring practices, and the formation of biracial committees to further desegregation. After his 1963 arrest in Birmingham, King wrote "Letter from a Birmingham Jail," underscoring that injustice anywhere threatened communities everywhere.

SCLC helped promote the 1963 civil rights march on Washington, D.C., where King delivered his "I Have a Dream" speech, an elaboration of his Birmingham letter in broader economic and social terms. With the passage of the Civil Rights Act of 1964 and the 1965 Voting Rights Act, SCLC extended its citizenship education and voter registration programs. Although maintaining its philosophy of nonviolent social change after King's assassination in April 1968, SCLC no longer initiated national mass actions. After King was assassinated, Ralph Abernathy became head of the SCLC and directed SCLC's efforts toward the Poor People's Campaign. This project focused national attention upon the needs of poor people in America, especially food aid and low-income housing. At the SCLC's twenty-fifth anniversary in 1982, its members expressed continued commitment to economic and political justice as well as peace. King had steered this course for SCLC when he championed a poor people's campaign before his death. The SCLC continues to focus on problems within the black community, including crime and drug abuse. Although most SCLC affiliates are church and civil rights groups, membership in the SCLC remains open to all.

*BIBLIOGRAPHY*

Garrow, David J. *Bearing the Cross: Martin Luther King, Jr., and the Southern Christian Leadership Conference.* New York: William Morrow, 1986.

Peake, Thomas R. *Keeping the Dream Alive: A History of the Southern Christian Leadership Conference from King to the 1980s.* New York: Peter Lang, 1987.

*Records of the Southern Christian Leadership Conference, 1954–1970.* Bethesda, Md.: University Publications of America, 1995. Microfilm.

DELORES NASON MCBROOME

*See also* **Civil Rights Movements; King, Martin Luther, Jr.**

# SPANISH-AMERICAN WAR

The Spanish-American War, or the War with Spain, was a four-month war in 1898 between the United States and Spain that took place in the Spanish possessions of Cuba, Puerto Rico, and the Philippines. It resulted in the U.S. acquisition of an overseas empire, at a cost of $250 million and more than three thousand American lives. The immediate cause of the war was the sinking of the U.S. battleship *Maine* in Havana harbor on 15 February 1898, but the primary causes were U.S. economic interests in Cuba, which were threatened by the

**U.S. soldiers near Manila, 1898.** HULTON GETTY/LIAISON AGENCY

**Theodore Roosevelt and his Rough Riders atop San Juan Hill, July 1898.** THE GRANGER COLLECTION, NEW YORK

Cubans' rebellion that had erupted in 1895 against Spanish misrule, and the brutal treatment of Cubans.

### Cuba and Puerto Rico Campaigns

On 25 January 1898, the *Maine* was sent to Havana officially as an "act of friendly courtesy" but actually to protect U.S. citizens and property in Cuba. At 9:40 P.M. on 15 February, an external explosion caused by a Spanish mine below the ship's ammunition magazine destroyed the *Maine*, killing 266 sailors and marines. American public opinion erupted into demands for Spanish expulsion from Cuba and was fueled by yellow journalism in the American press. Spain agreed to arbitrate the matter but would not promise Cuban independence, which led to President William McKinley's request on 11 April for armed intervention in Cuba. On 19 April, Congress passed a joint resolution that declared Cuba independent, demanded Spanish withdrawal, and approved the request for armed intervention. On 24 April, Spain declared war on the United States, and the following day

Congress declared that a state of war had existed since 21 April.

Meanwhile, the U.S. North Atlantic Squadron, under the command of Rear Admiral William T. Sampson, was ordered to blockade Cuba and did so on 22 April, while Cuban insurgents (about 50,000) would continue to fight against 150,000 Spanish troops. As a Spanish fleet of seven vessels approached the eastern coast of the United States, a call went out for 125,000 American volunteers. The Spanish fleet eluded the American blockade and sailed into Santiago de Cuba on 20 May. Sampson's ships and those of Commodore Winfield Scott Schley's flying squadron bottled up the Spanish ships in Santiago harbor on 28 May. There were five Spanish artillery batteries in the city of Santiago on the heights overlooking the harbor.

During the blockade U.S. forces took Guantánamo Bay (11–14 June) and the Cuzco Hills (14 June), despite stubborn Spanish resistance. From 22 June to 26 June, seventeen thousand troops of the Fifth Army Corps under Major General William R. Shafter landed in Cuba. They were eventually joined by five thousand Cuban revolutionaries. Two of the major battles in Cuba took place on 1 July. Brigadier General Henry W. Lawton attacked El Caney, a Spanish garrison with 520 defenders. Later in the day, an assault was made on two hills of the San Juan Heights: San Juan Hill and Kettle Hill. A Gatling gun detachment fired on the summit; and as U.S. troops—including the First U.S. Volunteer Cavalry (the Rough Riders)—advanced up Kettle Hill, they were fired on by Spanish snipers, who also shot wounded men on litters and their stewards. But the Spanish were outnumbered at El Caney twelve to one and at the San Juan Heights by sixteen to one. The Spanish lost more than one-third of their 1,700 defenders, whereas U.S. losses were 205 dead and 1,180 wounded. The American troops then began their overland march to Santiago.

On 3 July, the Spanish ships tried to escape Santiago de Cuba harbor one by one through a narrow channel to the open sea. Within two hours, only two Spanish ships remained afloat after the U.S. fleet's seventy-six big guns finished firing. Only one U.S. sailor was killed, but nearly 500 Spanish were dead and 1,720 were taken prisoner and detained in the United States. After repeated refusals by the Spanish garrison commander to surrender Santiago, there was a naval bombardment on 10–11 July, followed by a formal capitulation of the garrison on 17 July.

Major General Nelson A. Miles then began an expedition to Puerto Rico. He landed near Ponce on 25 July, taking this largest of Puerto Rico's cities, and began to march to the capital, San Juan, virtually unopposed. There were only six minor engagements, resulting in 41 U.S. casualties.

### Philippines Campaign

In the Pacific, Commodore George Dewey arrived with his Asiatic Squadron on 30 April 1898 at Subic Bay in the Philippines. He moved south to Manila Bay, where the next day his heavier and better-armed ships easily destroyed the Spanish squadron anchored there. Dewey lacked the troops to move against the twenty-six thousand Spanish soldiers and fourteen thousand Filipino militia in Manila. While Dewey waited for reinforcements, the Filipino insurgent leader, Emilio Aguinaldo y Famy, organized his rebels; and on 12 June, he declared the independence of the Philippines and established a military dictatorship.

By the end of July, twenty thousand men under Major General Wesley Merritt had reached the is-

### The Philippine War

During treaty negotiations to formally end the Spanish-American War, relations between U.S. troops occupying the Philippines and the Filipino insurgents worsened. While Emilio Aguinaldo and his men were forced to remain outside Manila, he strengthened his armed forces to more than twenty thousand. The Philippine War opened on 4 February 1899, when a rebel patrol approached the American line and a U.S. guard killed one man. Thus began three years of war in which 4,224 Americans died and 2,818 were wounded. The insurgents' losses were 16,000 killed and wounded, and perhaps 100,000 civilians died from starvation and war-related calamities. During 1901 and 1902, U.S. troops, angered by Filipino terrorist tactics—which included hacking men to death, burying prisoners alive, mutilating corpses, and creating trailway pits filled with sharpened stakes—also resorted to torture. One of the American interrogation techniques was the "water cure," in which water was forced down the throat or nose of the prisoner. Resistance declined after Aguinaldo was captured on 23 March 1901, but mop-up operations and atrocities continued. Brigadier General Jacob ("Hell-Roaring Jake") Smith used ruthless measures at the Battle of Samar on 28 September, ordering his troops to kill all males aged ten and older: "I want you to burn and kill. The more you burn and kill, the better it will please me." After the war ended in July 1902, a U.S. commission found fifty-seven verifiable atrocities by U.S. troops, although the number may have been much higher. Smith was court-martialed and forced to retire.

lands. Meanwhile, a small contingent of American troops sailing for Manila Bay had stopped at Guam, another Spanish possession, and took its poorly manned garrison without resistance.

Although firefights broke out near Manila on 31 July, secret negotiations for surrender were going on between Dewey and the Philippine governor-general Dom Fermín Jaudenes y Alvarez, who suggested that if a mock battle were staged to preserve the garrison's honor and if Aguinaldo's troops, which had surrounded the city, were not permitted inside the city, he would capitulate. A sham battle, with some naval artillery fire occurring away from the city, took place on 13 August; and the city surrendered. Because of a cut cable line, Dewey and Merritt were unaware that the war was over, a peace protocol having been signed the day before by President McKinley and the Spanish ambassador.

The formal Treaty of Paris was signed on 10 December. It established the independence of Cuba, ceded Puerto Rico and Guam to the United States, and required that $20 million be paid to Spain for the annexation of the Philippines.

*BIBLIOGRAPHY*

Allen, Thomas B. "Remember the Maine?" *National Geographic* (February 1998).

Cosmas, Graham A. *An Army for Empire: The U.S. Army in the Spanish-American War.* Columbia: University of Missouri Press, 1971.

Dyal, Donald H., Brian B. Carpenter, and Mark Thomas, eds. *Historical Dictionary of the Spanish-American War.* Westport, Conn.: Greenwood, 1996.

Linn, Brian M. *The U.S. Army and Counterinsurgency in the Philippine War, 1899–1902.* Chapel Hill: University of North Carolina Press, 1989.

Miller, Stuart Creighton. *"Benevolent Assimilation": The American Conquest of the Philippines, 1899–1903.* New Haven, Conn.: Yale University Press, 1982.

Musicant, Ivan. *Empire by Default: The Spanish-American War and the Dawn of the American Century.* New York: Holt, 1998.

O'Toole, G. J. A. *The Spanish War: An American Epic, 1898.* New York: Norton, 1984.

Trask, David F. *The War with Spain in 1898.* New York: Macmillan, 1981.

LOUISE B. KETZ

*See also* **Hearst, William Randolph; Puerto Ricans; War.**

# SPECK, RICHARD
## (1941–1991)

Richard Speck, the mass murderer who killed eight Chicago nurses, was born in December 1941 in Kirkwood, Illinois. One of seven children, he was raised with an adoptive stepfather after the death of his father when he was six years old. In 1961 he married a fifteen-year-old girl and fathered a daughter. His marriage soon failed, and Speck, an alcoholic and drug addict, went through several jobs in the Great Lakes area.

On the night of 13 July 1966, high on an unknown substance and reeking of alcohol, he ar-

rived at the door of a South Chicago Community Hospital residence for young female student nurses. Three young women opened the door to Speck, and Speck, knife and gun in hand, forced his way into their home. Upstairs, he found three more residents. Assuring the young women that he would not harm them and that he only intended to rob them, he tied their hands and feet with strips torn from a bedsheet. Within the next hour three more women arrived at the house and were tied up and deposited with the others.

Speck became increasingly nervous and agitated. He untied Pamela Wilkening and led her from the room. Speck then stabbed Wilkening and strangled her to death. Next he led Mary Ann Jordan and Suzanne Farris to another room. He stabbed Jordan three times and then stabbed and strangled the resisting Farris. Nina Schmale, the next to be led from the room, was also stabbed and strangled. Speck then found the five remaining women attempting to hide themselves anywhere possible. Valentina Passion and Merlita Gargullo, two Philippine women who had just arrived in the

**Richard Speck.** CORBIS/BETTMANN

United States for the first time the previous month, were the next to be murdered. He then returned for Patricia Matusek and later Gloria Davy. Corazon Amurao, the lone survivor, had hidden beneath the bed. From her hiding place Amurao witnessed Speck rape Gloria Davy before he led her, naked, downstairs to be anally assaulted and strangled to death.

Speck had arrived at the house at 11 P.M., and after killing the eight women, he probably left in the early hours of the following morning. Amurao, terrified to leave her hiding place, climbed out on a window ledge around 5 P.M., screaming for help.

Through the use of a police sketch, officials were able to discover the name of the murderer, and Speck made his capture easier after a suicide attempt landed him in an emergency room. He was recognized by the "Born to Raise Hell" tattoo on his arm, and the police quickly had him in custody. It is possible, although never proven, that Speck was also responsible for four similar murders that had taken place around the same time. Speck was noted to have been unintelligent and to have had little insight into the reasons for his crimes. He never showed any remorse for his actions. Speck was sentenced to death by electrocution; however, this was commuted to life imprisonment after the U.S. Supreme Court ruled the death penalty unconstitutional in 1972. He remained in the Joliet, Illinois, prison until he died of a heart attack the day before his fiftieth birthday.

*BIBLIOGRAPHY*

Altman, Jack, and Marvin Ziporyn. *Born to Raise Hell: The Untold Story of Richard Speck*. New York: Grove, 1967.

Breo, Dennis L., and William J. Martin. *The Crime of the Century: Richard Speck and the Murder of Eight Student Nurses*. New York: Bantam, 1993.

Kelleher, Michael D. *Flash Point: The American Mass Murderer*. Westport, Conn.: Praeger, 1997.

Ressler, Robert K., and Tom Shachtman. *Whoever Fights Monsters*. New York: St. Martin's, 1992.

TRACY W. PETERS

*See also* **Mass Murder: Individual Perpetrators.**

# SPECTACLE, VIOLENCE AS

According to an oft-quoted statistic, by the age of fourteen the average American child will have witnessed approximately eleven thousand murders and countless other less lethal acts of violence. Few of these violent acts will have been "real"; rather, they will appear in the form of entertainment on television, in films, at sporting events, and in video games. But widespread fascination with violence as spectacle, as entertainment, is not a new phenomenon. Today it is television and video games that are the chief arenas for vicarious belligerence. In the 1950s it was comic books, before World War II it was films, and before that it was the gothic novel. Popular culture seems always to have been awash in violent representations. Saint Augustine relates the story of a young man who, after being taken against his will to a Roman gladiator fight, finds himself returning repeatedly to the arena to slake his growing thirst for violent spectacle. This process of taking pleasure in violent spectacles and being driven to continually repeat the experience remains remarkably constant across times, spaces, and genres.

"Every people," according to a Balinese proverb, "loves its own form of violence." In Clifford Geertz's estimation, what the Balinese love about their favored display of violence, the cockfight, is that it manages to separate itself from the everyday in order to focus assorted experiences and say something not so much about how men actually are as about how they imaginatively are. If, as Norbert Elias has argued, a general "civilizing process" has gradually strengthened social prohibitions against violence, then violent spectacles have become socially sanctioned spheres in which spectators can "let off steam" and express violent emotions that are otherwise prohibited. Violent spectacles thus serve to enact a sort of "catharsis," by which the violent urges rooted deep in the human—or at least male—psyche are safely discharged. However, the catharsis theory fails to account for the overwhelming evidence pointing to a clear correlation between witnessing and committing violent acts.

## Sports

Sporting events are a fertile ground for examining the catharsis theory. Violence has always been a central aspect of both sporting events and sports spectatorship. Elias and others have argued that in societies that have become increasingly intolerant of violent behavior, sports play a crucial role in providing an outlet for "pleasurable excitement." Through fervent identification with a team or athlete, the sports spectator becomes intimately involved with the actions taking place on the field, in the ring, or on the court. Immersed in the uninhibited mass of the sports arena, the sports spectator is able to indulge in aggressive behavior—such as excessive drinking, caterwauling, and braying crude insults at opposing teams or athletes—that is not tolerated in other spheres of life. Opponents of this catharsis theory argue that the roiling partisan passions fomented by sporting events stoke rather than exhaust violent impulses. They point to the growing tendency for the sublimated violence of the athletic arena to provoke the real thing outside the arena. Athletes convicted of criminal activities, for example, often commit crimes not directly related to sports, and fans will often attack athletes, officials, or other fans and sometimes riot following important victories, thus expressing their "pleasurable excitement" at winning by embarking on a destructive rampage. It has become commonplace to see American fans burn and blow up buildings and cars following a baseball, basketball, football, or hockey title. This phenomenon of hooliganism, which was once associated solely with behavior following European soccer matches, has received considerable attention in the 1990s. Several theories have been advanced to explain this form of "extracurricular" violence that occurs around sporting events, ranging from blaming the violence on existing animosity between members of different classes to the old standby, the madness of crowds, which holds that a mass gathering takes on an irrational, libidinal, and often destructive energy of its own. Here, as with other spectacles of violence, a clear causal relationship is elusive. Some have argued that the legitimized violence of the sporting event leads to a general loosening of internal restraints on violent acts. But the fact that the most violent sports—boxing, for example—do not seem to prompt the greatest violence in fans would seem to speak against this. Soccer hooliganism is especially notable for its elaborate rituals, complete with well-defined roles (chant leader, novice, clown, and so on) and hierarchies (based upon aggressive masculinity). This ritualization of violence among the hooligans—which, through media reports, has itself become something of a spectacle—echoes the ritualized, sublimated violence of the athletic competition itself.

**Video Games**

The vicarious violence of the spectacle is even more pronounced in video games than in sporting events. A review of eighteen popular video games in the December 1982 issue of *TV Guide* determined fourteen of the games to be violent, two

nonviolent, and two "mixed" (the goal was to *avoid* being a victim of violence). Though gaming technology has evolved significantly over the past two decades, the centrality of violent actions—generally, defending oneself against attackers through the use of various types of weapons—remains a constant feature. Technological developments have enabled depictions of violence to become increasingly realistic, to the point where games that were considered scandalous in the 1980s, such as *Death Race* (the object of which was to hit and kill pedestrians), now seem positively tame in comparison with more recent games such as *Mortal Kombat* or *Doom.* An especially interesting facet of video games is that the distinction between spectator of and participant in violence is dissolved. One does not simply observe violence, as on television; nor does one merely support an aggressor, as at a sporting event. Here, one *is* the aggressor. Video gaming promotes an essentially paranoid worldview that not only permits violent behavior toward perceived threats (be they asteroids, aliens, monsters, or humans) but demands and rewards it (nonviolence is never a winning option). If there is a sphere that lends support to the "role-modeling" theory of violence—that is, the notion that violent behavior is learned by observation and imitation—then surely it is the sphere of violent video games, for in that universe everyone is a potential threat, and the player hones his skills at committing violent acts by compulsively repeating traumatic life-and-death sequences.

In a 1994 statement before a House subcommittee examining video-game violence, the American Medical Association (AMA) warned that "like violence depicted elsewhere in the media, video game violence has a horrifying potential to coarsen society, promote acts of violence against real victims, and desensitize children to the real thing"; the report recommended preventive measures, such as the introduction of a rating system and the inclusion of statements warning of the "real-life" effects of killing people (U.S. House Committee on Energy and Commerce, p. 24). The AMA, however, went beyond such traditional measures, advocating that "scenes should be incorporated into games in which the consequences of violent acts are depicted . . . such as an ambulance rushing the character to a hospital or cemetery, and other characters representing the family and friends of the injured or killed character crying and grieving" (p. 25). That such scenes would be unthinkable in the world of video games, as well as in other violent spectacles, is worth pondering. For spectacles of violence, whether in fictional films, reality-television programs, sporting events, or video games, rarely focus on the sufferings of the victims, their families, and friends. Perhaps this traumatic fear of being the victim of violence is precisely what spectacles of violence, in their ritualized replaying of violent scenarios, are intended to accomplish: to protect against the trauma by playing it out.

*BIBLIOGRAPHY*

Elias, Norbert, and Eric Dunning. *Quest for Excitement: Sport and Leisure in the Civilizing Process.* London: Blackwell, 1986.

Geertz, Clifford. "Deep Play: Notes on the Balinese Cockfight." In his *The Interpretation of Cultures.* New York: Basic, 1973.

Twitchell, James B. *Preposterous Violence: Fables of Aggression in Modern Culture.* New York: Oxford University Press, 1989.

U.S. House of Representatives. Committee on Energy and Commerce. *Violence in Video Games: Hearing Before the Subcommittee on Telecommunications and Finance.* Washington, D.C.: Government Printing Office, 1994.

TODD HERZOG

*See also* **Boxing; Copycat Violence; Film: Violent Genres; Representation of Violence; Sports; Television: Violent Genres; Theater; Ultimate Fighting; Video Games; Wrestling, Professional.**

# SPILLANE, MICKEY
## (1918– )

Mickey Spillane is one of the most commercially successful authors in U.S. history, having sold more than 150 million books. Born in Brooklyn in 1918, Spillane began writing for pulp magazines and comic books soon after high school. But it was after World War II, in which he served as a fighter pilot instructor, that he published the books that made him famous, beginning with *I, the Jury* (1947) and continuing in rapid succession with *My Gun Is Quick* (1950), *Vengeance Is Mine!* (1950), *One Lonely Night* (1951), *The Big Kill* (1951), *The Long Wait* (1951), and *Kiss Me, Deadly* (1952). All but one of these novels were narrated by the private detective Mike Hammer, an ex-cop and World War II veteran in passionate pursuit of truth and justice. Unlike earlier detectives of hard-boiled fiction, who often solved crimes through logic and allowed the law to punish wrongdoers, Hammer

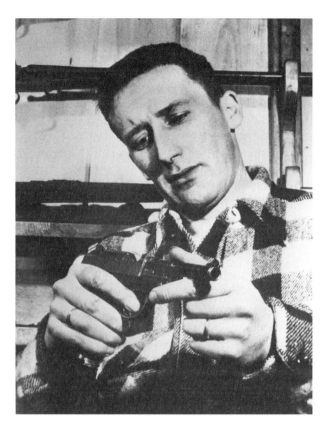

**Mickey Spillane, in 1953.** CORBIS/BETTMANN

tracked down criminals by following his unerring instincts, then exacted retribution himself. These books offered readers sensational action, raw emotion, and dramatic surprise endings (because, as Spillane explained, people read mysteries "to get to the end. . . . The first page sells that book. The last page sells your next book.")

*I, the Jury* was based on a comic-book project, and some readers see the influence of the comics in the exaggerated violence, simple characters, and black-and-white morality of the Hammer novels. Also indebted to the pulps and hard-boiled detective fiction of the 1920s and 1930s, the Hammer novels were central to the paperback boom of the postwar decade, inspiring many imitators and much commentary. Spillane's writing has been denounced as a pernicious influence on both fiction and behavior but also praised as a harmless outlet for male aggression. Mike Hammer has been analyzed as, among other things, the embodiment of the male reader's resistance to changing gender roles as well as of his disillusionment with the legal system and his longing for vigilante justice.

Whatever their significance, both Spillane and Hammer have been an enduring presence. Although Spillane did not publish another novel for nine years after the appearance of *Kiss Me, Deadly*, he wrote short fiction throughout the 1950s, along with stories for a comic strip, "From the Files of Mike Hammer," which appeared in 1953 and 1954. Hammer also had incarnations in a radio series and in film versions of three of the novels.

Spillane returned to novel writing in 1961, with *The Deep*, and to Mike Hammer a year later with *The Girl Hunters*. His output since then has been eclectic, including detective, spy, and Mafia thrillers as well as children's books. Periodically, he has written installments in the life of Mike Hammer, including *Black Alley* (1997).

Despite a life that has included diverse writings, three marriages, four children, and a 1951 conversion to the Jehovah's Witnesses, Spillane remains strongly linked in the American imagination with the persona of his fictional detective, that violent, independent man of action. Spillane has often encouraged this identification: he posed as Hammer for several book jackets and starred in the 1963 film of *The Girl Hunters*. These associations were revived in the 1980s, when Spillane promoted a remake of *I, the Jury*, and a television series and several television movies introduced Hammer and Spillane to a new generation.

*BIBLIOGRAPHY*

Collins, Max Allan, and James L. Traylor. *One Lonely Knight: Mickey Spillane's Mike Hammer.* Bowling Green, Ohio: Bowling Green State University Popular Press, 1984.

Van Dover, J. Kenneth. *Murder in the Millions: Erle Stanley Gardner, Mickey Spillane, Ian Fleming.* New York: Frederick Ungar, 1984.

KIMBERLY R. GLADMAN

*See also* **Comics; Literature: Pulp Fiction.**

# SPORTS

Sports have been closely linked to violence throughout history. From the Roman circus and arena to the English foxhunt, sporting culture has prized physical prowess, aggressiveness, competitiveness, thirst for victory, and often brutality. Some have argued that sport is a microcosm of society, that it mirrors social patterns of violence and interpersonal aggression. In America this connection is evident in traditional and new sports, including extreme sports and, especially, ultimate fighting. Sport in America has been shaped by a wide array of issues, including religious ideals, class status, republican ideology, race relations, gender theories, mass culture, and modern media spectacle. These concerns have redefined the meanings and roles of sport throughout America's history and reshaped the connections between sports and violence.

## Defining Sport Violence

Sport violence is an elusive concept. Can violent acts on the playing field or in any sport setting be construed as violence? Robert C. Yeager notes in *Seasons of Shame* (1979) the difficulties of distinguishing between "unacceptable viciousness and a game's rough-and-tumble." He explains that this debate is often used as an attempt to defend the violence of sport. Toby Miller (1997) argues that certain sports, by their very nature (e.g., boxing, hunting, shooting, car racing, and football) are "intrinsically dedicated to violence." Peter C. Terry and John J. Jackson (1985), by contrast, define sports violence as behavior that transgresses the rules of sport and is unrelated to the objectives of sports.

Michael D. Smith (1983) has developed a "typology of sport violence" based on a scale that ranges from "relatively legitimate violence" to "relatively illegitimate violence." Despite such efforts to define what constitutes legitimate or illegitimate sport violence, these concepts remain difficult to operationalize because they change as the rules change. For example, in football, spearing (tackling or blocking with the head as initial point of contact) was legal until 1976, when the rule changed after research revealed a correlation with spinal injury.

## Theoretical Explanations of Violence in Sport

Scholars have advanced various biological, psychological, and social-learning theories as explanations of violence in sport. The biological view is often referred to as an instinctive or "drive discharge" view, where aggression is an innate rather than learned quality. Most support for this view is based on the research of the Austrian ethologist Konrad Lorenz (1966), who concluded that violence is not learned because it is evident in animals raised in isolation. Supporters of this view believe that participation in sports (both active and vicarious) can act as a catharsis, venting pent-up aggressions through relatively harmless competitions. However, the catharsis principle has not been strongly supported by research. For example,

Leonard Berkowitz (1964) found that allowing children who became angry to "let off steam" through harmless aggressive acts promotes aggressive behavior rather than dissipating it. Ruth E. Tandy and Joyce Laflin (1973) also dispute the catharsis theory, arguing that the tension from the game is unconsciously absorbed by spectators and might result in displaced aggression, which may lead to postgame rioting or other antisocial behavior.

On the other hand, Bob Andelman (1993), using a nonprobability sampling technique (wherein data are collected on a few members of the population in a nonrandom way and then those individuals are asked to suggest other subjects), conducted interviews in the twenty-eight cities with National Football League franchises and found that violence was the reason many fans love football, and "for most men, a cathartic release occurs when watching a defensive back as he snares a wide receiver in mid-air and slams him back down to earth." Andelman's respondents felt that this "attachment to vicarious violence" is healthy, allowing them to release pent-up energy without hurting themselves. Even though the catharsis principle has not been substantiated by empirical research, there still remains the belief that watching the aggressive behavior of contact sports has therapeutic value.

The psychological view of violent behavior, often referred to as the "frustration-aggression hypothesis," originated in the early research of John Dollard and his colleagues (1939) and assumes that frustration always leads to some form of aggression. More recent social psychological research, however, has "discovered that frustration is neither a necessary nor sufficient condition for aggression to occur." Researchers do contend, however, that this frustration theory is an attractive means for rationalizing sports violence, but many theorists accept the frustration-aggression hypothesis insofar as it suggests that in contact sports the level of aggression is higher, therefore the risk of violence is greater.

Albert Bandura's (1963) social-learning theory states that socialization is based on reinforcement and modeling. In this respect, violence and aggression, like other forms of conforming behavior, are learned. Reinforcement can emerge from a variety of sources, such as coaches, teammates, family, the sport structure, and fans. The modeling perspective, often called the "cultural pattern model," implies that social learning of violent or aggressive behavior can occur by simply observing another's behavior, especially if that behavior is rewarded. Wilbert M. Leonard II (1988) refers to the modeling of the aggressive playing style of professional athletes by youth in organized team sport as "vicarious reinforcement."

Of the three theories, the social-learning theory has enjoyed the most extensive empirical validation. The anthropologist Richard G. Sipes (1973) found that the cultural pattern model worked best in explaining warlike societies with a preponderance of violent sports and more pacific societies with a predilection for nonviolent sports. Such cases seemingly undermine the drive-discharge model, according to which warlike societies, having spent their aggressive energies in actual combat, would be less inclined toward aggressive activity in their sports. In addition, research has shown that imitative behavior does include the simulation of violence. Michael D. Smith reported that junior hockey players claimed they learned and incorporated illegal aggressive techniques from watching professional hockey.

### Sport and Violence in the Ancient World

The links between sport and violence extend back to the ancient world. While Greek sport most often is associated with the agility, grace, and athleticism of track and field events celebrated in the Olympic Games, it also incorporated combat sports, including wrestling, boxing, and pancratium (techniques in unarmed fighting, including pressure locks, kicking, strangling, and punching). Combat sports illustrated the athlete's mastery of the martial virtues of courage, cunning, and endurance. While wrestling called for skill and craft, boxing emphasized power and strength, and pancratium highlighted ferocity, all of these sports reflected and shaped skills and attitudes conducive to the creation of a warrior elite. While all classes participated in sporting activity, the nobility dominated; through their exhibition of athletic prowess, especially in combat sports, they reinforced their social status and honor.

Roman sport illustrates the importance of spectacle and the role of spectators in the sporting experience. The two most popular Roman sports, gladiator contests and chariot races, thrived on stirring the emotions of the crowd. The first gladiatorial combats, believed to have taken place in 246 B.C., were funeral games in which the dead were honored with additional deaths in the form of gladiator duels. Chariot races left more room for spectator violence, because spectators were divided over which team they supported. The size of the events also fueled mass frenzy. The Circus Maximus, for example, reportedly held over a quarter of a million spectators. According to the sport scholar Allen Guttmann, these spectacles represented divided loyalties that were in part social, economic, and political in origin. The race results, then, had the potential to expose deeper fissures in Roman society and explode into violence. The worst riot took place in Constantinople in 532 A.D., when close to thirty thousand died as a result of mob violence.

### Festive Culture and Sport in Britain

This legacy of violence in sport, and its connections to economic and political status, has also been evident in British sports. Sport became an integral element of what the historian Richard Holt has called "festive culture" in Britain. Seventeenth- and eighteenth-century villagers created a culture of holidays and celebrations around the harvest, the church calendar, and parish feasts that incorporated food, drink, and folk games. Blood sports such as cockfights and bullbaiting dominated village celebration and brought spectators together in a common ritual of wagering. Another rural tradition that promoted shared village customs was the early game of football, today called soccer. Scholars trace British football to medieval Europe. Players kicked an inflated cow bladder, often from one village boundary line to the boundary of another village, ostensibly with the purpose of advancing the ball between predetermined goals and scoring points. In many villages the game had few if any rules and often became little more than a ritualized brawl, with players kicking, scratching, and even maiming opponents.

While football emerged primarily as a rural sport, modern pugilism has its roots in the British city. According to the historian Elliott Gorn, boxing drew its strength from the tradition of blood sport and violent competition in the villages, but it evolved as an urban phenomenon. The emergence of commercialized leisure in urban centers helped make boxing the national sport of England. Like the combat sports in Greece and Rome, boxing in England represented the display of the martial values of courage, physical prowess, and valor, embodied in champions like "Gentleman" John Jackson at the end of the eighteenth century.

The fights also reasserted class privilege at a time when it was declining. Unlike hunting, which was a sporting privilege reserved exclusively for nobles and gentry, prizefighting brought all classes together. According to Gorn, "Prize fights and other popular recreations momentarily reestablished elite authority among the masses. They allowed gentlemen at once to mingle with the multitude, cementing the loyalty of their inferiors, but simultaneously to distance themselves through displays of wealth and largess." In prizefights violent display helped to shape a hierarchical male sporting culture.

### Blood Sports, "Lawful Sports," and Gambling in Colonial America

The class dimensions of sport, along with the ritualization of masculine values, were equally evident in sporting culture in colonial America. In the southern colonies in particular, settlers sought to emulate the values and pageantry of the British gentry. For the southern gentry, grandiose displays of leisure activity and recreational brutality further cemented the racial and economic divides in the South. Southern planters reveled in many of the same blood sports as the British did, including cockfights and gander pulling, and often did so in the company of poor white farmers.

Fox chases and hunting, however, were the exclusive privilege of the gentry in the South, just as they were in England. In addition, gambling was reserved for men of property. One of the most popular wagering sports in the South was quarter-horse racing. Gambling on public spectacles like horse racing also exemplified the gentry values of independence, materialism, and intense competition, along with the element of chance that governed life in the South. Indeed, this intense desire to win at any cost often led southern gentlemen to break their own rules of fair play; jostling, whipping, and kneeing opponents were not unheard of. Southern planters thus recognized violence as a part of the world they created and ritualized this violence and competition in their culture of gambling.

Sport played a much different role in the New England colonies. The Puritan settlers who established these colonies challenged what they perceived as the frivolity, ostentation, and brutality of the British sporting tradition. Both in England and the American colonies, Puritans enforced strict codes of Sabbatarianism that reviled idleness and recreation. New Englanders censured games associated with animal baiting, gambling, and drinking but approved of and even promoted what they called "lawful sport and recreation." The historian Benjamin Rader explains that Puritans encouraged participation in sports that glorified or honored God and that promoted one's sense of spiritual calling. Fishing and hunting were permitted, for example, as long as these activities were carried out for the purpose of obtaining food, refreshing the mind and body, or ridding the colony of vermin. New England bore a greater resemblance to Greek sporting tradition (at least the noncombatant side of it), with its emphasis on athleticism as a symbol of godly pursuits, while the South's gambling and blood sports were much closer to Roman sporting culture.

## Male Subcultures and Elite and Working-Class Leisure

Changes in the structure of the American economy in the middle of the nineteenth century spurred a renewed interest in assertions of manliness through sport. A few wealthy Americans began to acquire the resources to establish large-scale manufacturing enterprises. This new gentry in American cities displayed its new wealth, much as the southern planters had during the colonial period, through involvement in male sporting traditions. They joined athletic clubs like the New York Athletic Club, founded in 1866 by three upper-class merchants to arrange various competitions, especially in track and field, among men of similar backgrounds. Soon membership in these clubs was less about skill and athletic prowess and more about social prestige.

Working-class groups organized their own athletic clubs, which came to play a central role in community life. Urban working-class male subcultures were centered on saloons, which provided spaces for men to gather outside of the purview of their bosses, wives, or reformers. Drinking, gambling, and blood sports helped solidify the connections among urban male workers into a community that challenged the industrial values of regimentation, discipline, and sobriety. Athletic clubs, which often helped to strengthen ethnic cohesion, grew out of this saloon culture.

Athletic competitions sponsored by the clubs ranged from boxing matches to track and field competitions to the blood sport of "ratting" (a terrier was placed in a ring with rats and wagers were made on how many rats the dog could kill in a given amount of time). Clubs were backed by prominent local politicians, who would sponsor fighters from their ethnic groups, especially the Irish, in exchange for their muscle on election day. Indeed, many fighters soon capitalized on their ring reputations by entering local politics. Because nineteenth-century prizefighting had few rules

(bare-knuckle fighters often boxed to the death), the violence in the ring often spilled out into the streets. One observer described bare-knuckle fights as bouts in which biting, eye gouging, groin kicking, and hair pulling were the norm.

## Middle-Class Reform

By the end of the nineteenth century, middle-class reformers, appalled by the gruesomeness of much of fraternal male culture, pressed for sporting reform. Their efforts included temperance campaigns and attempts to outlaw blood sports and prizefighting. Unable to ban prizefighting, they pushed for the introduction of the Marquis of Queensberry Rules. These rules, published in England in 1867 and first used in a tournament in 1872, mandated the use of gloves, three-minute rounds, and the ten-second rule for a knockout. The first championship fight in America to use these rules was in 1892, between the famed boxing champion John L. Sullivan and the challenger, James J. Corbett. Despite Corbett's defeat of Sullivan and the growing acceptance of boxing in all social circles, most scholars argue that boxing never overcame the stigma of its association with the often violent and vice-ridden world of working-class and ethnic urban subcultures.

## Gender, Athleticism, and Women's Bodies

While reformers tried to curb sport violence, they recognized the importance of athleticism for the health of both the men and women of the nation. Many physicians, however, argued that competitive athletics were potentially harmful to women. In fact, according to Dudley Allen Sargent, writing in 1912, competitive sports could undermine women's femininity and thereby pose a threat to the human race. By engaging in competition, women might take on masculine characteristics, including aggression, violence, and a drive to win at all costs. Sargent argued that while swimming, tossing a ball, or even bicycling might be beneficial for women, competitive sports might cause too great a drain on women's limited energy. Women also could be injured in competitive games like baseball if they fell to the ground. While some women's colleges were sponsoring baseball and basketball teams by 1900, most schools confined their athletic programs for women to noncompetitive exercise. By the 1920s, however, team competition was pervasive in women's athletics.

Since the 1980s there has been an increase in the number of women entering the traditionally non-female sports of "combat/body contact events which involve combinations of power, strength, aggressiveness, and speed" (Dunning and Maguire 1996). This phenomenon can be attributed to Title IX legislation, which ensured legal protection against discrimination on the basis of gender as it applies to, among other things, admission and recruitment of scholarship athletes, and thus led to an increase in female participation in sports. Owing to the passage of this legislation in 1972, women's participation in intercollegiate sports increased fourfold. However, the experiences of women appear to be very different from those of men in similar sports. In a qualitative examination of female athletes involved in either rugby, rock-climbing, wrestling, ice hockey, or martial arts, Kevin Young noted, "some of the women clearly articulated a desire to distinguish strategy from force and violence. . . . They reported enjoying the physical and aggressive aspects of competition" and yet still affirmed a dislike of dominant "unethical" models of sport.

## Intercollegiate Football and Violence on the Gridiron

Early college football games exhibited few of the patriotic and moralistic values that its promoters emphasized. Football promoters, including college presidents like William Rainey Harper at the University of Chicago and coaches like the legendary Walter Camp at Yale, argued that the skills learned in football would prove valuable in off-the-field endeavors. But early college football games bore little resemblance to this world of duty, sacrifice, and moralism. With few rules, the games often ended in melees between the teams, with broken bones, black eyes, and bloody noses the result of the contest and drinking parties the reward. Walter Camp played a leading role in transforming football from this early game of male roughhousing and revelry into a more disciplined, if only marginally less violent, game of rules. Camp's rules included the introduction of the line of scrimmage, which separated the offensive and defensive teams (1880); the down-yardage system (1883), which gave the offensive team three tries to get five yards (later changed to ten yards) before it had to give the ball to the other team; and low tackling (1888), which created a mass-momentum style of play and was largely responsible for the game's continued brutality. As Michael Oriard explains, Camp not only was responsible for most of the rule changes that shaped modern football but also

played a key role in structuring the narrative of nationalism that placed football firmly at the center of American ideals. According to Oriard, "Camp's own narrative of football's development had a central plot: the rationalization and tactical development of the game's action, driven by the object of winning, developed in young men the character and experiences essential for success in America."

The importance of winning, however, undermined the value of the game for many observers because excessive competitiveness fueled numerous rules violations. Critics also charged that the central place of football within universities, coupled with the desire to win at all costs, fostered brutality. In 1905 and 1906 muckraking journalists in popular magazines like *McClure's* exposed the underside of collegiate football. The articles charged football teams with extreme roughness and foul play and explained that teams often tried to knock out opposing players in efforts to achieve victory. The *Chicago Tribune* reported that eighteen students lost their lives and that 159 were injured in the 1905 season. This evidence of brutality led to even more rule changes but failed to assuage the sentiments of many Americans who believed that the game of football itself was fraught with violence.

## Baseball, Professionalism, and National Identity

Many advocates of athletics and organized play were appalled by the brutality associated with football and turned to baseball and its rules promoting discipline, order, and self-sacrifice as a means of inculcating nationalism and loyalty. Reformers, however, worried that the values of cooperation and discipline would be corrupted when athletes played for money. Owners of professional baseball clubs, especially Albert G. Spalding of the Chicago White Stockings (later Cubs), attempted to overcome these objections and concerns by linking commerce with professionalism and baseball with decorum. They used the language of expertise that dominated the worlds of the university and the corporation to illustrate the role of professional sports in the modern marketplace. Club owners established codified rules and regulations, statistical measures of talent, and strict prescriptions for training. At the same time, however, they were unable to remove the elements of aggressiveness that were associated with male sporting culture. As a result, bench-clearing fights between players, taunting of players by fans, and frequent disregard for the authority of umpires remained central elements of professional baseball.

### Race, Prizefighting, and Social Upheaval

Much like baseball, boxing has served as a means of social mobility for many poor and working-class Americans. And its emphasis on sheer physicality, strength, and power has made it the quintessential manly sport. Yet Americans could imbue boxing with a variety of meanings and its heroes with seemingly contradictory characteristics, depending on the social climate of the nation. African American champions, in particular, have been held up to intense scrutiny. The violence of the ring could easily spill over into the streets, especially when motivated by racial conflict. Such was the case when the African American fighter Jack Johnson defeated Jim Jeffries, a white man, in 1910. The press played up the bout as a contest for racial supremacy. At a time when lynchings of black men averaged sixty per year and the eugenics movement had gained a foothold over national racial discourse, the Johnson-Jeffries match represented the desire among many whites to demonstrate their superiority. After Johnson defeated Jeffries, riots raged in at least a dozen cities.

### Media, Spectatorship, and Sports Violence

In the mid-nineteenth century, the rise of mass-circulation sporting magazines like William T. Porter's *Spirit of the Times* helped link fans across the nation in a shared culture of sport. In the twentieth century, with the successive rise of the newsreel, radio, and television, a media-spawned culture of celebrity made sports figures into cultural heroes and superstars. And sporting spectacles, especially violent ones, made headlines and sold papers.

New media also created new styles of play. First radio, and then television, altered the ways Americans experienced sports. Roone Arledge of ABC television became the leading figure in transforming sport in the 1960s and 1970s into mass entertainment through innovative approaches to televised coverage. His *Wide World of Sports* series included coverage of both popular and obscure sports. New sports emerged explicitly for their entertainment value, including professional wrestling and roller derby, both of which centered on

**Wrestling match between Jack Dempsey and Bull Montana, 1925.** HULTON GETTY/LIAISON AGENCY

**Jim Jeffries before his 1910 world heavyweight title fight against Jack Johnson in Reno, Nevada.** HULTON GETTY/LIAISON AGENCY

gratuitous violence as the basis of the game. Spectacle made the best television, and television executives and advertisers wanted the highest market share. As a result, some critics charged, the broadcasting of sporting events highlighted power over strategy, sensationalism over humbleness, and violence over controlled play.

The televising of professional ice hockey has encouraged greater violence in that sport. Numerous studies have measured the degree of air time given to rough play over normal play. These studies suggest that violence in hockey not only gets more coverage but is also glorified by announcers. Sports announcers analyze the qualities of a body check and raise their voices in excitement as more players become involved in the resulting melee. Numerous camera angles show close-up shots of the violence, and replays allow viewers to watch the incident over and over again. Television thrives on the promotion of drama and excitement, which are often fueled by aggressiveness, violence, and brutality. In the era of modern mass media, then, violence in sport serves the function of entertainment and in doing so helps elevate the cultural and economic power of the athletes who provide the most excitement.

**New Wave of Violent Sports: Extreme Sports and Ultimate Fighting**

The growth and popularity of so-called extreme sports worldwide, especially during the 1980s and 1990s, was said to represent an "athletic revolution" that values the "wagering of life and limb." Included among the sports considered as "extreme" are hang gliding, in-line skating, mountain biking, mountain climbing, sky surfing, skydiving, snowboarding (which was included in the 1998 Winter Olympics), skateboarding, bungee jumping, street or road luge (referred to as a "skateboard on steroids"), and eco-challenge (a seven-to-ten-day race of teams on mountain bikes, white-water rafts, kayaks, horses, and so on, televised by the Discovery Channel). Some of these sports have reached a level of popularity that has brought them close to the mainstream of American sporting culture.

Carolyn Flemming (1998) explains that extreme sports are not only redefining the way sports are played but are also aggravating the problem of sports injuries, a prominent part of the extreme sports subculture, which features entire Web sites, some accompanied by hard-rock music, devoted to demonstrating injuries. A four-part video series by

**The Red Devils skydivers, about 1990.** CORBIS/CHRIS
SIMPSON; CORDAIY PHOTO LIBRARY

elbowing, butting, slamming, and choking were permissible. Inevitably, the Ultimate Fighting Alliance was formed, complete with its own rules and regulations and commissioner. The new rules included three separate weight classes and mandatory use of martial-arts gloves. Now, in addition to the original rules, kicking a downed opponent, striking pressure points, yanking fingers and toes, pulling hair, and hitting in the groin are prohibited.

Ultimate fighting has become extremely popular in the United States, with over two hundred thousand people paying $20 or more to watch the sport on pay-per-view cable television. It is profitable both for the promoters and the fighters, who can make from $50,000 to $150,000 for winning tournaments. Many athletes turn to ultimate fighting after their competitive careers are over.

Although promoters contend that ultimate fighting is no more dangerous than boxing, others claim that ultimate fighters can suffer more brain damage than other athletes because of repeated blows to the head. They can suffer "other serious injuries because of the array of tactics they can use, including kicking and choking." Because of the high likelihood of broken bones, brain damage, and spinal-cord injury, the American Medical Association has called for a national ban on ultimate fighting. In 1996 Lonnie R. Bristow, president of the American Medical Association, declared that the AMA "actively supports efforts to ban these brutal and repugnant contests as posing an imminent danger to the health and lives of the participants."

### Rationalizing Violence in Professional Sports

Since the early 1970s there have been many examples of sport violence reported in the media that reveal the magnitude and severity of the problem. For example, in a 1978 preseason game that had no bearing on the team's record or subsequent entry into the playoffs, the Oakland Raiders defensive back Jack Tatum viciously (although legally) hit New England Patriots receiver Darryl Stingley, leaving him a quadriplegic; afterward, Tatum was quoted as saying, "I like to believe that my best hits border on felonious assault." Football player Alex Karras stated that he had a "license to kill for sixty minutes a week," and the boxer Ron Lyle claimed that "America was not built on going to church. It was built on violence. I express America in the ring." These views of violence in the 1980s

T-Bone Productions entitled "Black and White and Red All Over" was originally advertised on the Internet as "all fun and games until someone gets hurt . . . then it's hysterical."

Ultimate fighting is the name for the newest trend in brutal contests that mix boxing, martial arts, and street brawling techniques. A fixture in Brazil, Thailand, and Japan for decades, ultimate fighting was introduced in the United States only in 1993. The barbarity of this "sport," once dubbed "human cockfighting," prompted the governor of New York to call for a statewide ban, and ultimate fighting is now banned in other states as well.

The original U.S. rules of ultimate fighting were simple: two men battle in a thirty-two-foot, caged octagonal ring until one of them submits or a referee determines a fighter is unable to defend himself; not permitted were biting and gouging the eyes, but kicking, punching, chopping, squeezing,

were relatively common among athletes participating in contact sports.

In 1975 the president of the National Hockey League, Clarence Campbell, justified fighting as "a well-established ingredient for the economic well-being of the game ... if violence ceases to exist, it will not be the same game." The demand for violence in hockey has been supported by research conducted by K. G. Stewart and his colleagues (1992), who found that violence in hockey games could be explained economically. They contend that there is an economic need for violence as it is a factor when explaining game attendance, where the "blood lust of fans" is related to sport attendance.

James Bryant (1980) refers to this phenomenon as an "economic violence hype." This "hype" begins with the media reports of violent acts that occur in various athletic events, which leads to additional fans attending future games. Bryant argues that one of the worst of these hypes is the instant replay of violent acts on television, followed by the showing of highlight clips without interpreting the events so graphically displayed. Bryant refers to this as "glamorizations of bad blood," which he claims "encourage violence through emulation of role models by youth, by encouraging fans to seek situations that are violent prone, and by constantly exposing viewers and readers with violent acts that eventually seem to be commonplace."

## Spectator Violence

There are numerous examples of incidents of violent crowd behavior that predominate in sport. Such spectator violence reflects the fans' perception that the opposing team is the enemy. Wilbert M. Leonard II (1988) explains that this tendency might be the result of the trend of "superfans," who want to be both participant and spectator. This type of behavior has also been referred to as "hooliganism," where spectators physically challenge opposing players and officials.

Hooliganism has often been attributed to British soccer spectators, who have been guilty of throwing beer cans at the opposing team's goalie when their team falls behind or running out onto the field when it becomes apparent that their team will lose. In some cases hooliganism has turned into excessive violence; fans have "carried their rowdiness into the streets and tossed a wide variety of artillery—beer cans, bottles, and bricks—through windows." Death has even been a result. In Cairo,

Egypt, forty-nine people were killed and forty-seven injured when the stadium for a soccer game where one hundred thousand tickets were sold was switched at the last minute for a stadium that was not large enough to accommodate all the ticket holders.

Some have argued that there is a distinction between the types of spectator violence. Allen Guttmann (1983) argues for a distinction between sports violence and sports-related spectator violence. He questions, in fact, whether or not sports-related spectator violence has much to do with the actual sporting event. He argues that "knifing fans of rival teams and throwing beer cans at the umpire are not examples of sports violence" but are characteristic of the spectators themselves. Guttman explains that when examining spectator violence, emphasis must be placed on society's disorganization, rather than on the sport itself. He argues that the resolution and elimination of the problem of spectator violence would be best attained by addressing the issues of unemployment and racial discrimination in society, rather than by changing sports. Melvin Mark and his colleagues (1983) have noted how spectator violence has also been attributed to the reaction of the fans to a perceived injustice, such as when fans feel that an official decision has been unfair. They claim that reducing the amount of perceived injustice "should result in a concomitant reduction in sports violence."

## Domestic Abuse and Sexual Assault

Sport has also been associated with such antisocial behavior as domestic abuse and sexual assault. Accounts of violence by male athletes against women have been portrayed extensively throughout the media. The *Harvard Law Review* even published a report on professional sports leagues and domestic violence, and they list various accounts of such violence. The review quotes Penn State football coach Joe Paterno speaking at a press conference following a loss: "I'm going home ... and beat up my wife." Such statements, whether truthful or not, are not uncommon in the sports world. In the late twentieth century accounts of domestic abuse and sexual assault against women made big news stories when they involved such sports celebrities as Mike Tyson, O. J. Simpson, and José Canseco. The former football player O. J. Simpson had been charged several times with spousal abuse and battering before he was indicted in 1994 for the murder of his ex-wife.

Research, however, has not substantiated that the proportion of male athletes who abuse their wives or other women is higher than that of males in the general public. New research is needed to differentiate between types of domestic violence (i.e., rape, sexual abuse, stalking, and battering) and to discern whether certain situations make it more likely for an athlete to be involved in domestic abuse. Some research has shown that men in sex-segregated groups such as sport teams, fraternities, and the military are more likely to commit acts of group sexual assault. There is, however, little research on athletes' individual acts of sexual assault. In their analyses of official reports on college campuses, Todd W. Crosset and his colleagues (1995) found a higher percentage of sexual assault committed by male student athletes than the rest of the male student population.

It has also been argued that prosecutors are increasingly inclined to dismiss or water down sexual assault charges against professional and college athletes. In their research on arrest and conviction rates of athletes accused of sexual assault, Jeffrey Benedict and Alan Klein (1997) found that college and professional athletes charged with sexual assault are more likely to be charged and arrested but less likely to be prosecuted. They attribute this discrepancy to the many legal advantages that attend the status of "celebrity athlete."

*BIBLIOGRAPHY*

Adelman, Melvin L. *A Sporting Time: New York City and the Rise of Modern Athletics, 1820–1870.* Urbana: University of Illinois Press, 1990.

Andelman, Bob. *Why Men Watch Football.* Lafayette, Louisiana: Acadian, 1993.

Bandura, Albert, and Richard H. Walters. *Social Learning and Personality Development.* New York: Holt, Reinhart, and Winston, 1963.

Benedict, Jeffrey. *Athletes and Acquaintance Rape.* Newbury Park, Calif.: Sage, 1998.

Benedict, Jeffrey, and Alan Klein. "Arrest and Conviction Rates for Athletes Accused of Sexual Assault." *Sociology of Sport Journal* 14 (1997): 86–94.

Berkowitz, Leonard. "Aggressive Cues in Aggressive Behavior and Hostility Catharsis." *Psychological Review* 71 (1964): 104–122.

Brackenridge, Celia. "He Owned Me Basically . . . Women's Experience of Sexual Abuse in Sport." *International Review for the Sociology of Sport* 32 (1997): 15–130.

Bredemeier, Brenda Jo. "Athletic Aggression: A Moral Concern." In *Sports Violence*, edited by Jeffrey H. Goldstein. New York: Springer-Verlag, 1983.

Breen, Timothy H. "Horses and Gentlemen: The Cultural Significance of Gambling Among the Gentry of Virginia." In *Sport in America: New Historical Perspectives,* edited by Donald Spivey. Westport, Conn.: Greenwood, 1985.

Bryant, James. "The Business World and Sport Violence." *Physical Educator* 37 (1980): 44–146.

Cahn, Susan. *Coming on Strong: Gender and Sexuality in Twentieth-Century Sport.* New York: Free Press, 1994.

Crosset, Todd W., Jeffrey R. Benedict, and Mark A. McDonald. "Male Student-Athletes Reported for Sexual Assault: A Survey of Campus Police Departments and Judicial Affairs Offices." *Journal of Sport and Social Issues* 19 (1995): 126–140.

Davies, Richard O. *America's Obsession: Sports and Society Since 1945.* Fort Worth, Tex.: Harcourt Brace, 1994.

Dollard, John L., et al. *Frustration and Aggression.* New Haven, Conn.: Yale University Press, 1939.

Dunning, Eric, and Joseph Maguire. "Process-Sociological Notes on Sport, Gender Relations, and Violence Control." *International Review for the Sociology of Sport* 31 (1996): 295–321.

Ehrhart, Julie K., and Bernice R. Sandler. *Campus Gang Rape: Party Games?* Washington, D.C.: Center for Women Policy Studies, 1992.

Flemming, Carolyn. "The Most Dangerous Games." *Chatelaine* 71, no. 8 (1998): 22.

Goldstein, Warren. *Playing for Keeps: A History of Early Baseball.* Ithaca, N.Y.: Cornell University Press, 1989.

Gorn, Elliott J. *The Manly Art: Bare-Knuckle Prize Fighting in America.* Ithaca, N.Y.: Cornell University Press, 1986.

Gorn, Elliott, and Warren Goldstein. *A Brief History of American Sports.* New York: Hill and Wang, 1993.

Guttmann, Allen. *From Ritual to Record: The Nature of Modern Sports.* New York: Columbia University Press, 1978.

———. "Roman Sports Violence." In *Sports Violence*, edited by Jeffrey H. Goldstein. New York: Springer-Verlag, 1983.

———. "Sports Spectators from Antiquity to the Renaissance." *Journal of Sport History* 8 (summer 1981): 5–27.

———. *A Whole New Ball Game: An Interpretation of American Sports.* Chapel Hill: University of North Carolina Press, 1988.

Harvard Law Review. "Out of Bounds: Professional Sports Leagues and Domestic Violence." *Harvard Law Review* 109 (1996): 1048–1065.

Holt, Richard. *Sport and the British: A Modern History.* New York: Oxford University Press, 1989.

Karp, David, et al. "Sports and Urban Life." In *Being Urban: A Sociology of City Life.* New York: Praeger, 1991.

Koerner, Brendan I. "Extreeeme." *U.S. News and World Report,* 30 June 1997.

Kupelian, Vartan. "Sprewell Incident Latest in Disturbing Trend," *Detroit News,* 3 December 1997.

Leonard, Wilbert M., II. *A Sociological Perspective of Sport.* New York: Macmillan, 1988.

Lester, Robin. *Stagg's University: The Rise, Decline, and Fall of Big-Time Football at Chicago.* Urbana: University of Illinois Press, 1995.

Lorenz, Konrad. *On Aggression.* New York: Harcourt, Brace, and World, 1966.

Mark, Melvin M., Fred B. Bryant, and Darrin R. Lehman. "Perceived Injustice and Sports Violence." In *Sports Vi-*

olence, edited by Jeffrey H. Goldstein. New York: Springer-Verlag, 1983.

Miller, Toby. "Sport and Violence: Glue, Seed, State, or Psyche?" *Journal of Sport and Social Issues* 21 (1997): 235–238.

Oriard, Michael. "In the Beginning Was the Rule." In *The New American Sport History: Recent Approaches and Perspectives*, edited by S. W. Pope. Urbana: University of Illinois Press, 1997.

———. *Reading Football: How the Popular Press Created an American Spectacle*. Chapel Hill: University of North Carolina Press, 1993.

Pfeiffer, Ronald P., and Brent C. Mangus. *Concepts of Athletic Training*, 2d edition. Sudbury, Mass.: Jones and Bartlett, 1998.

Poliakoff, Michael B. *Combat Sports in the Ancient World: Competition, Violence, and Culture*. New Haven, Conn.: Yale University Press, 1987.

Pope, S. W., ed. *The New American Sport History: Recent Approaches and Perspectives*. Urbana: University of Illinois Press, 1997.

Rader, Benjamin G. *American Sports: From the Age of Folk Games to the Age of Television*, 3d ed. Upper Saddle River, N.J.: Prentice Hall, 1996.

Riess, Steven A. *City Games: The Evolution of American Urban Society and the Rise of Sports*. Urbana: University of Illinois Press, 1989.

———. *Sport in Industrial America, 1850–1920*. Wheeling, Ill.: Harlan Davidson, 1995.

———. *Touching Base: Professional Baseball and American Culture in the Progressive Era*. Westport, Conn.: Greenwood, 1980.

Roberts, Randy, and James Olsen. *Winning Is the Only Thing: Sports in America Since 1945*. Baltimore: Johns Hopkins University Press, 1989.

Rosenzweig, Roy. *Eight Hours for What We Will: Workers and Leisure in an Industrial City, 1870–1920*. Cambridge, U.K.: Cambridge University Press, 1983.

Sipes, Richard G. "War, Sports, and Aggression: An Empirical Test of Two Rival Theories." *American Anthropologist* 75 (1973): 64–80.

Smith, Michael D. *Violence and Sport*. Toronto, Canada: Butterworths, 1983.

Smith, Ronald A. *Sports and Freedom: The Rise of Big Time College Athletics*. New York: Oxford University Press, 1988.

Spivey, Donald, ed. *Sport in America: New Historical Perspectives*. Westport, Conn.: Greenwood, 1985.

"Sports: Ultimate Fighting Adding Restrictions for Safety." *Atlanta Journal/Atlanta Constitution*, 20 June 1997.

Stewart, K. G., Donald G. Ferguson, and J. C. H. Jones. "On Violence in Professional Team Sport as the Endogenous Result of Profit Maximization." *Atlantic Economic Journal* 20 (1992): 55–64.

Tandy, Ruth E., and Joyce Laflin. "Aggression and Sport: Two Theories." *Journal of Health, Physical Education, and Recreation* (June 1973): 19–20.

Terry, Peter C., and John J. Jackson. "The Determinants and Control of Violence in Sport." *Quest* 37, no. 1 (1985): 27–37.

Twin, Stephanie. "Women and Sport." In *Out of the Bleachers: Writings on Women and Sport*, edited by Stephanie Twin. Old Westbury, N.Y.: Feminist Press, 1979.

Yeager, Robert C. *Seasons of Shame: The New Violence in Sports*. New York: McGraw-Hill, 1979.

Young, Kevin. "Women, Sport, and Physicality: Preliminary Findings from a Canadian Study." *International Review for the Sociology of Sport* 32 (1997): 297–305.

ROBIN F. BACHIN
JAN SOKOL-KATZ
JOMILLS HENRY BRADDOCK

*See also* **Boxing; Hunting; Martial Arts; Simpson, O. J., Murder Trials; Spectacle, Violence as; Ultimate Fighting; Wrestling, Professional.**

## SPOUSAL AND PARTNER ABUSE

Violence in intimate relationships, often referred to as either domestic violence or spousal and partner abuse, has always existed. Historically, a wife was often viewed as her husband's property. Marital partners, cohabitants, and dating partners have been abused and battered in almost every society in the world. Following English as well as European law, in 1824 Mississippi made wife beating legal. Several other states followed, with court cases reaffirming the right of a husband to chastise and beat his wife in keeping with the tradition established in English common law.

The term *spousal and partner abuse* refers to intentional abuse by adult men or women of their intimate partners by methods that cause bruises, scratches, cuts, bleeding, injuries, pain, or suffering. The most frequent types of physical battering are slapping, grabbing, pushing, shoving, hair pulling, kicking, choking, biting, head banging, and striking with a bat. Studies in the 1990s indicate that 80 to 90 percent of the victims of domestic violence are women.

The turning point in modern American society's response to the abuse of women occurred in 1885, when the Chicago Protective Agency for Women was established to provide legal assistance for rape victims, and to advocate for and shelter women who were victims of physical abuse at the hands of their husbands. Between 1915 and 1920, twenty-five cities followed Chicago's pioneering lead in developing agencies for the protection of abused women. However, after World War II most of these protective agencies disappeared owing to the war effort and changes in funding priorities.

It was not until the 1970s, as a result of the women's movement, pioneering books on battered women by Del Martin and Maria Roy, and increased media attention, that services for battered women and rape victims were initiated; these services included innovative crisis-intervention programs for rape victims, reforms in courtroom procedures and sexual assault laws, and the emergence of federally funded shelters for battered women and their children. The first twenty-four-hour crisis intervention hotline for rape victims was established in Berkeley, California, in 1972. Chiswick Women's Aid, the first modern shelter for abused women, was opened in London by Erin Pizzey in 1971. One of the first consciousness-raising groups for battered women in the United States, Women's Advocates of St. Paul, Minnesota, started a telephone hotline and housed battered women in group members' homes starting in 1974. Also in 1974 Marjory D. Fields, a former legal-aid attorney at the Brooklyn Legal Services Corporation, learned that, though many of her clients had called the police after being beaten by a husband or ex-husband, the police refused to respond to these emergency calls, viewing each situation as a private family matter rather than an illegal act. Judge Fields was so outraged by the lack of action from police officers that she alerted a *New York Times* reporter. The 1974 article was syndicated in newspapers across the United States. Following this media attention, the New York City Police Department created special teams that included women officers and social workers to handle domestic-violence complaints.

Although police departments were starting to respond to family violence complaints, for the most part their response was limited to helping the battered woman get emergency medical attention, informing her of safe housing at the new local shelters, and sometimes warning or counseling the abusive husband. But batterers were almost never arrested. At the same time, in Oakland, California, feminist attorneys sued the police department on behalf of a group of battered women. In New York City the court's decision in the *Bruno v. Codd* case in 1978 resulted in more police responsiveness to battered women's requests for police assistance and protection. It also clearly demonstrated that victims of family violence "could not be denied their rights as crime victims." Between 1975 and 1981, forty-four states enacted legislation in support of the legal rights of battered women. State-wide domestic-violence coalitions advocated and lobbied their representatives until legislation was passed to make it easier for battered women to receive temporary and permanent restraining orders as well as to increase funding for emergency shelters.

Two significant events led to widespread social and legal reforms in the area of spousal abuse. The first, the 1984 Minneapolis Police Experimental Study, indicated that arresting batterers deters further family violence. The police in two precincts randomly assigned abusive partners to one of the three experimental conditions: arrest, separation, or advice and mediation. The follow-up data demonstrated that the arrested abusers had the lowest recidivism rate of the three groups. The National Institute of Justice widely disseminated the preliminary results of this study, including numerous press releases and articles in the *New York Times*. During the next six years (1984–1990) there was a dramatic increase in mandatory and presumptive arrests of batterers.

The second influential event was the landmark Supreme Court decision in *Thurman v. City of Torrington* (1984), which held the police liable for their negligence in failing to protect a woman from severe and repeated injuries from her husband. In 1983 Tracy Thurman had regularly called the police in Torrington, Connecticut, to protect her from the severe beatings she suffered at the hands of her estranged husband. The police failed to respond to her call in a timely manner and initially failed to restrain her husband from kicking, stomping, and knifing Thurman's face, neck, and chest, resulting in permanent injuries. Tracy Thurman was awarded $1.9 million in damages from the city of Torrington. Other lawsuits were filed in the mid-1980s against city and town police departments for failing to protect battered women victims.

As a result of media attention to both the Minneapolis police experiment and the 1984 U.S. Attorney's Report on Family Violence, as well as increased state and federal funding for police training on domestic violence, by 1992 forty-seven states and the District of Columbia had passed statutes authorizing arrest in cases of misdemeanor simple assault and battery domestic violence; in fourteen of these states arrest was mandatory when the police officer made a determination that domestic-violence crime had occurred. In addition, statutes in all fifty states provide for protective orders or temporary restraining orders in domestic-violence cases. Many of these state statutes expressly allow police enforcement of a restraining order by warrantless arrest.

Before discussing the problems associated with spousal abuse, it may be helpful to define a set of several terms commonly used by professionals:

1. *Marital rape* and *partner rape* refer to forced sexual intercourse or sexual intercourse obtained by intimidation or threat of force. In addition, in chronic battering relationships, the abusive partner intermittently or on a regular basis controls the type and frequency of sexual activity. Chronically and severely battered women have reported being frequently forced into degrading and sadistic sexual acts or having had objects forced into their vaginas.

2. *Emotional abuse* and *mental abuse* describe a pattern of intense insults, degrading statements, harangues, threats of repeat abuse, and aversive and intimidating demands upon one's intimate partner. The intensity and repetition are key elements.

3. *Lesbian* and *gay abuse/battering* applies to a pattern of coercive, physically abusive, and violent acts perpetrated by same-sex adult partners who attempt to control, humiliate, physically punish, sexually assault, or psychologically abuse their partners.

4. *Date abuse* describes unwanted physical abuse or a pattern of emotional abuse in dating relationships. Abusive acts include pushing, shoving, slapping, throwing objects, punching, hair pulling, kicking, biting, scratching, choking, head banging, stabbing, and hitting with a heavy object.

5. A *restraining order* or *order of protection* is a court order signed by a judge that usually forbids the alleged batterer from making contact with the victim; in some cases the court order specifies the distance that the abuser must maintain from the victim who requested the order. Depending on the state law, the restraining order may mandate that the abusive spouse or partner immediately vacate the residence, refrain from threats of abuse or further abusive acts, pay support for the victim and minor children, or be court-mandated to participate in group counseling or in a chemical-dependency treatment program.

## Scope of the Problem

Spousal and partner abuse constitute a pervasive and severe social problem in U.S. society, estimated to occur in some 25–30 percent of couples. Estimates of sexual assault by intimate partners

vary widely, clustering around 15–20 percent of adult women in the general population and approximately 50 percent of physically battered women. The scope of the problem is illustrated by national estimates indicating that "8.7 million women are victimized by partner abuse in their homes each year." Paula Nurius and her colleagues found that domestic violence causes injuries to more women victims than accidents, muggings, and cancer deaths combined. According to a 1993 Commonwealth Fund report, in the United States a woman is physically abused by her husband every nine seconds. Pregnancy is a risk factor for battering; the Council on Scientific Affairs of the American Medical Association reported in 1992 that as many as 37 percent of obstetrics patients are physically abused during pregnancy. A majority of female homicides are related to domestic violence.

Medical costs for battered women and children were $1,633 per person, or an annual total of $857.3 million (Valentine, Roberts, and Burgess 1998). The human costs of spousal and partner abuse are impossible to quantify. The costs to society of woman battering include medical bills and lost wages due to absenteeism and disabilities. But the long-term health and mental-health costs to the children who witness marital violence are almost impossible to measure.

## Shelters

Since the first emergency shelters for battered women opened their doors in the mid-1970s, increased awareness of the chronic and severe nature of battering relationships has led to an increasing number of short-term shelters. In 1975 there were only a half dozen shelters for battered women; by January 1998 there were more than fifteen hundred such shelters throughout the United States. The scope of services provided has also enlarged. In the late 1970s the most frequent type of services available in shelters were the twenty-four-hour crisis hotlines and emergency housing. Upon leaving the shelter, a woman was usually referred to welfare or legal agencies, but the service stopped there. Shelters now offer support groups and legal advocacy for women, and education, crisis counseling, and trauma treatment for children. In addition, family-crisis programs and shelters employ clinical social workers and licensed mental health counselors. Outreach has been expanded to include specialized training of police officers and efforts at prevention of date abuse and acquaintance rape at secondary schools and colleges. Shelters once drew on the original grassroots movement of paraprofessionals and former battered women; staffing is now more commonly by trained clinicians and managers. By 1998 many comprehensive family crisis programs had secured funding for transitional second-stage communal housing, usually lasting from six months to one year, and vocational training and job-placement services.

The zealous and committed advocacy and lobbying efforts of statewide victims' rights and domestic-violence coalitions has led to significant legislative reform and federal funding of domestic violence and sexual assault treatment programs. The federal 1984 Victims of Crime Act (VOCA) gave priority block-grant funding to states that were responsive to both domestic-violence and sexual-assault victims. As of November 1995 payments to the Federal Crime Victims Fund by criminal offenders had exceeded $1 billion, with more than half of these funds allocated through block grants to the states for rape-crisis programs, battered women's shelters, and child-abuse treatment programs.

Among significant developments in the 1990s, the U.S. Congress passed the Violence Against Women Act in 1994, allocating $1.3 billion for statewide and local domestic-violence and rape-crisis programs between 1995 and 1999. In addition, in 1995 President Bill Clinton helped establish a federal office on violence against women in the U.S. Department of Justice. In 1996 Ann W. Burgess, chairwoman of the National Research Council's Panel on Research on Violence Against Women, recommended a research agenda and priorities for preventing domestic violence and sexual assault in the twenty-first century.

Emergency shelters for battered women and their children can provide a promising exit point from a battering relationship as well as a new beginning for abused women who are determined to break the cycle of violence and change their lives. Battered women who are successful in ending the abusive relationship usually gain the necessary strength and self-confidence from domestic-violence advocates and clinicians, or in support groups with other women who have had similar experiences. Unfortunately, state legislatures have either totally ignored this problem or moved very slowly in drafting legislation to meet the service and counseling needs of abusers. As of 1999 there were approximately two hundred counseling programs for batterers, usually located in highly pop-

ulated cities throughout the United States. By 1995 all fifty states were providing substantial funding for family-crisis programs and shelters for battered women. Although important progress has been made, much remains to be done to help groups of battered women who are still underserved: these include children and adolescents, victims living in rural areas, and those who are poor, elderly, lesbian, African American, Asian, Latino, and Orthodox Jewish.

## Programs and Services for Children

According to P. Lehmann and B. E. Carlson (1998), two-thirds of the shelters for battered women in the United States have children's programs, while only 31 percent of the 433 shelters in Canada have children's programs. Programs for children range from short-term child care to comprehensive trauma assessment and group therapy for children who have witnessed violence against their mothers. Effective treatment programs for children of violent families include group therapy aimed at crisis intervention in order to relieve feelings of isolation, alienation, and trauma among the children; parenting education to strengthen the relationship between mother and child; and psychoeducational groups, art therapy, and play therapy focused on crisis management and fostering attitudinal changes and adaptive coping. Domestic violence is frequently chronic in nature, and can lead to serious injuries to mother or child. Battering witnesses often experience hypervigilance and startle reactions, sleep disturbances and nightmares, cognitive confusion and revenge fantasies, panic attacks, intense fear, agitation, and regression. Therefore, it is critical that community family-crisis programs develop model trauma-assessment and crisis-intervention programs for the ten million children estimated each year to witness domestic violence between their parents.

## Police Involvement

Most police calls for domestic violence come from women who have been abused by their partners several times before. In most cases, several months or years pass, with the women suffering in silence. In the beginning, with the first or second incident, the majority of battered women believe the batterers' apologies and false promises and remain dependent by staying in the relationship, particularly when they have children. Many of these women live in a state varying from complete denial to constant fear and terror, which may result

**A deputy sheriff responds to a domestic-violence call in Polk County, Florida.** CORBIS/NUBAR ALEXANIAN

in depression, anxiety, or somatic complaints. The abusive relationship can be endured for a few months or many years. Then, as a result of a sudden crisis, they seek help from relatives, neighbors, or friends. Some are helped and leave the batterer permanently. It is such an acute crisis event that usually results in the police being called.

Throughout the United States there has been a major change in police attitudes and responses to domestic-violence calls. The batterer is usually arrested when the battered woman shows visible signs of injury, when the officer or neighbors of the victim overhear threats, or when there is probable cause to believe a crime has been committed. Several research studies have indicated that arrest and prosecution alone are not effective in reducing battering. Mandatory arrest seems to reduce future battering by minor offenders, but it has the opposite effect on more serious offenders, whose violence escalates, particularly when the couple are unmarried and unemployed. A Milwaukee police experimental study of twelve hundred domestic-violence cases indicated that, "among individuals with a high stake in conformity (married and employed), arrest reduces the annual rate of subsequent violence by 25.2 percent. Among those with a low stake in conformity (unmarried and unemployed), arrest is associated with a 53.5 percent increase in the annual rate of subsequent violence."

Cities and towns with high employment rates may offer greater stakes in conformity. The threat of arrest does not deter domestic violence in the long term; rather, it must be part of a comprehensive approach to lessening and eventually eliminating domestic violence. Such an approach must incorporate crisis intervention, cognitive-behavioral therapy, restraining orders, court-mandated batterers' counseling, victim assistance and concrete services, prosecution, and group counseling. All new programs should have mandated program evaluations and outcome studies required by their funding sources. With further research and evaluation studies, we will be in a much better position to predict which types of comprehensive programs are likely to lessen and prevent domestic violence.

*BIBLIOGRAPHY*

Carlson, B. E., and L. A. McNutt. "Intimate Partner Violence: Intervention in Primary Health Care Settings." In *Battered Women and Their Families: Intervention Strategies and Treatment Programs*, edited by Albert R. Roberts. 2d ed. New York: Springer, 1998.

Eisenberg, S., and P. Micklow. "The Assaulted Wife: Catch 22 Revisited." *Women's Rights Law Reporter* 3, nos. 3–4 (1977).

Koss, M. P., and C. Oros. "The Sexual Experiences Survey: A Research Instrument Investigating Sexual Aggression and Victimization." *Journal of Consulting and Clinical Psychology* 50 (1982).

Lehman, P., and B. E. Carlson. "Crisis Intervention with Traumatized Child Witnesses in Shelters for Battered Women." In *Battered Women and Their Families: Intervention Strategies and Treatment Programs*, edited by Albert R. Roberts. 2d ed. New York: Springer, 1998.

Nurius, Paula, et al. "The Single Greatest Health Threat to Women: Their Partners." In *Future Issues in Social Work Practice,* edited by Paul Raffoul and C. Aaron McNeece. Boston: Allyn and Bacon, 1996.

Pirro, J. F. "Domestic Violence: The Criminal Court Response." *New York State Bar Journal* 54 (October 1982).

Pleck, Elizabeth. *Domestic Tyranny: The Making of Social Policy Against Family Violence from Colonial Times to the Present.* New York: Oxford University Press, 1987.

Roberts, Albert R. *Helping Battered Women: New Perspectives and Remedies.* New York: Oxford University Press, 1996.

———. *Sheltering Battered Women: A National Study and Service Guide.* New York: Springer, 1981.

Roberts, Albert R., ed. *Battered Women and Their Families: Intervention Strategies and Treatment Programs.* 2d ed. New York: Springer, 1998.

———. *Crisis Intervention and Time-Limited Cognitive Treatment.* Thousand Oaks, Calif.: Sage, 1995.

Roberts, Albert R., and Sandra Burman. "Crisis Intervention and Cognitive Problem Solving Therapy with Battered Women: A National Survey and Practice Model." In *Battered Women and Their Families: Intervention Strategies and Treatment Programs,* edited by Albert R. Roberts. 2d ed. New York: Springer, 1998.

Roberts, Albert R., and B. S. Roberts. "A Comprehensive Model for Crisis Intervention with Battered Women and Their Children." In *Crisis Intervention Handbook: Assessment, Treatment, and Research,* edited by Albert R. Roberts. Belmont, Calif.: Wadsworth, 1990.

Russell, Diana E. H. *Rape in Marriage.* Bloomington: Indiana University Press, 1990.

Sherman, L. W. *Policing Domestic Violence.* New York: Free Press, 1992.

Valentine, Pamela V., Albert R. Roberts, and A. W. Burgess. "The Stress Crisis Continuum: Its Application to Domestic Violence." In *Battered Women and Their Families: Intervention Strategies and Treatment Programs,* edited by Albert R. Roberts. 2d ed. New York: Springer, 1998.

Wallace, H. *Family Violence: Legal, Medical, and Social Perspectives.* Needham Heights, Mass.: Allyn and Bacon, 1996.

ALBERT R. ROBERTS

*See also* **Domestic Violence; Rape; Women.**

# STALKING

Termed *psychological rape* in the 1980s, *stalking* has no single legal definition. It is generally understood to refer to a course of conduct directed at a specific person that would cause a reasonable person to fear bodily injury. One example of such behavior is the willful, malicious, and repeated following and harassing of another person. Increasingly, states are including surveillance, lying in wait, vandalism, and nonconsensual communication, such as telephone harassment, as stalking. Of-

ten the legal emphasis is placed on the victim's experiencing a high level of fear of bodily harm rather than on the stalker's making a credible threat of violence. In the late 1990s stalking was recognized as a worldwide problem; most of the research on it was being done in the United States.

## History of Antistalking Laws

In 1990 California became the first state to pass antistalking laws, following the sensational media coverage of the 1989 murder by an obsessed male fan of Rebecca Schaeffer, the star of the sitcom *My Sister Sam.* By 1993 all states and the District of Columbia had antistalking laws. In 1994, largely as a response to lobbying from women's groups, Congress passed the landmark Violence Against Women Act (VAWA). Designed to eradicate violence against women, this federal statute was also intended to enhance the safety of victims and to hold perpetrators of domestic violence, stalking, and sexual assault accountable for their actions. By the mid-1990s some of the original state antistalking laws were being strengthened because they had been found ineffective. In 1996 a federal law banning interstate stalking strengthened the VAWA.

The legal status of stalking is well established, but laws against it are continually challenged, usually for vagueness and constitutional violations. In April 1998 the U.S. Supreme Court denied without comment the free-speech appeals of two men—one from Virginia, the other from the District of Columbia—convicted of threatening women by phone and letters while the two were in prison. Presumably someday the justices will review a challenge to an antistalking law, in order to set forth a decision that stands as a national precedent. At that time the U.S. Supreme Court may recognize the research that has reported links between stalking and domestic violence.

## Demographics of Stalking

While stalking is theoretically gender-free, overwhelmingly women are the victims and men are the stalkers. The National Violence Against Women Survey, based on interviews with a cross section of eight thousand adult females and eight thousand adult males conducted between November 1995 and May 1996, estimated that 1,000,976 women and 370,992 men had been stalked. The NVAW survey indicated that one out of every twelve women and one out of every forty-five men in the United States have been stalked sometime in their lives (Violence Against Women Grants Office 1997). These figures imply that approximately 8 percent of adult women in the United States were stalked sometime in their lives and that, overall, women are nearly four times more likely than men to be stalked. A 1998 survey based on interviews with sixteen thousand men and women, sponsored by the federal Centers for Disease Control and Prevention and the Department of Justice, found similar results.

Survey data indicate that women and men are stalked by different types of persons. Women are more likely than men to be stalked by an intimate, including a spouse or former spouse (38 percent), a current or former cohabiting partner (10 percent), or a current or former date or boyfriend (14 percent). Perhaps not surprisingly, domestic assault is closely linked to stalking: 80 percent of women who said they had been stalked also reported that they had been assaulted by intimates or former intimates.

Most stalkers are men; 94 percent of the stalkers identified by female victims and 60 percent of the stalkers identified by male victims were male. The motivations for men stalking intimates have not been explicitly addressed by researchers, but it appears that stalking by an intimate involves issues of control. Domestic violence is most often about control, power, and domination; women who leave their abusers are often stalked in an effort by abusers to regain control.

Research has also identified links between stalking and age and between stalking and race or ethnicity. According to the NVAW survey, only 12 percent of the women who had been stalked were eighteen years of age or younger when first stalked. The largest portion of women (54 percent) reported being first stalked when they were between eighteen and twenty-nine years of age; 47 percent of the men in the survey who reported being stalked were also in this age-group. In the age categories of thirty to thirty-nine and forty and older, more men than women reported being stalked for the first time. The explanation for this difference is open to debate. It may be that males in these age categories are stalked because of domestic conflicts that have involved emotional, physical, and fiscal abandonment of female intimates and dependents. On average, female victims were twenty-eight years old and males thirty years old when they were first stalked.

Caution is in order when evaluating the accuracy of survey research and official statistics on stalking. Unlike many crimes that consist of discrete acts such as stranger-on-stranger murders, stalking by intimates or strangers consists of a series of acts that taken separately may not be illegal. Moreover, the individual acts may not appear threatening until they are linked together. Offenders charged separately with harassment, trespassing, criminal mischief, terrorism, or violation of protective orders may go undetected as stalkers. Furthermore, stalking by intimates is often part of domestic violence, which itself is underreported. Thus survey results may give only some indication of the demographics of stalking.

The links between stalking victimization and race and ethnicity are more complex. White women report a higher percentage (8.1 percent) of victimization by stalkers than do African American women (6.5 percent). However, Native American and Alaskan women report a significantly higher rate of stalker victimization at 17 percent. Mixed-race women also report a higher rate of victimization (10.6 percent) than white or African American women. Unfortunately, the women reporting double-digit percentages of stalking are from socioeconomic and cultural groups that have been relatively neglected by the research. We have little data to help explain why their rates are so much higher. The socioeconomic and cultural factors behind these high rates need further study. For example, are mixed-race women in domestic relations more likely to be both disadvantaged economically and low in prestige and thus viewed as more socially marginal and without power and worth, relatively speaking, than white or African American women? There is virtually no data on violence against mixed-race men or women. It is a neglected area of research.

**Celebrity Stalking**

In the past celebrities were rarely threatened either by fans or by the press. More recently, however, in the late twentieth century, celebrities were so routinely subjected to various forms of threats and invasions, including stalking, that an office of the Federal Bureau of Investigation was set up in Los Angeles to specialize in celebrity stalking. Some observers attribute this development to the real—and imagined—accessibility of celebrities that is enhanced by seeing them in our living rooms. Television programs such as *Life Styles of the Rich and Famous* and *Entertainment Tonight* have allowed celebrities to become our "friends" and "neighbors".

Psychiatric diagnoses of fans who have approached and threatened celebrities indicate that in many cases, perhaps as many as 95 percent, the subject is mentally ill. One study concluded that people who are obsessed with celebrities are ultimately more likely to kill themselves, a family member, or a friend than a celebrity.

For photojournalists, celebrities are commodities whose public and private lives can make good copy and profits. In 1999, for example, a bare-breasted photo of the fiancée of Britain's Prince Edward was sold to a tabloid for a reported $4 million. Paparazzi photography has always been big business in world-class cities. Some of their aggressive tactics were referred to as stalking in 1997, when Britain's Princess Diana died in a Paris car crash while she was being pursued by paparazzi.

**Electronic Stalking**

A relatively new form of stalking developed as telecommunications technology made new types of harassment possible. Electronic stalking first came to national attention in 1994, when a thirty-two-year-old male, Andy Archambeau, was charged with a misdemeanor for stalking a female schoolteacher after they met through a chat room on the Internet. Following their electronic introduction, they met in person, and five days later the teacher found she had no interest in continuing the relationship. She attempted to terminate it, but the man continued sending her electronic messages and leaving messages on her answering machine. In one message he told her that he had been watching her leave work. At this point she filed a police report, and he was ordered to have no more communication with her. He failed to comply with the order and sent her about twenty more computer messages, one of which reportedly contained the sentence: "I've been trying to court you, not stalk you." He also threatened to e-mail their story to all her friends on America Online, her family, and her old boyfriend. It was also reported that he wrote that his e-mail messages were the least of things he could do to annoy her. Two years later Archambeau pled "no contest" to stalking in a case referred to as a "crime of the nineties." He was sentenced to a year's probation and ordered to undergo a psychiatric evaluation and to abstain from directly or indirectly contacting the teacher.

During the final hearing the teacher said the case had shattered her personally and professionally and that she had been afraid for her life. She also stated that she resented the media circus Archambeau had "stirred up" and "took great pleasure in." Before he was ordered to stop talking about the case, Archambeau had become a media darling by telling his tale of "love gone wrong" to the *National Enquirer,* national radio, the *New York Times,* and *Time* magazine.

Another landmark electronic-stalking case involved Abraham Jacob Alkhabaz, a University of Michigan student who in 1995 posted a short fictional story of sexual violence on the Internet using the real name of a female classmate. While Alkhabaz did not contact the woman personally or through the Internet, he was charged with electronic stalking because his story included graphic language about rape with a hot curling iron. The federal government charged him with threatening to injure, an abuse of his First Amendment privileges, which constitutes a felony and carries a five-year sentence.

One of the unique features of this case is that the felony was not generated by the posted story per se. The charges resulted from a subsequent search of his electronic mailbox, which disclosed a chilling correspondence between Alkhabaz and a man in Ontario, Canada. The mailbox contained the men's plans, which involved abduction, bondage, torture, humiliation, rape, sodomy, murder, and necrophilia.

In early 1997, after what appeared to be clear violation of the federal law's three-pronged test to convict Alkhabaz for threatening injury, the U.S. Court of Appeals, Sixth Circuit, with a split vote dismissed the indictment. The court concluded that the electronic mail messages between Alkhabaz and another, expressing sexual interest in violence against women, did not constitute "communications containing a threat." In a vigorous dissent, Judge Robert Krupansky included examples of the sadistic short stories that Alkhabaz transmitted to Canada.

One of the most sensational stalking cases involved a man suspected of being a computer stalker who not only used his skills anonymously to terrorize women in several states but also created scores of false credit-card numbers to open Internet accounts for on-line services. He was never arrested for electronic stalking because in 1995, when he was charged with 112 federal felony counts of fraud, there were few if any laws that addressed stalking using a computer for fraud in cyberspace.

Various issues involved in prosecuting electronic stalking were still under debate in 1999. One of these had to do with whether laws regulating the use of the U.S. Postal Service for sexually explicit materials, including child pornography, should hold for electronic mail. Some advocates of strict enforcement of antidecency laws saw no difference between stalking in person, using regular mail, and using e-mail. Another issue had to do with identifying stalkers, because Internet chat rooms allow users to remain anonymous. Law-enforcement officials also faced the problem of prosecuting offenders across multiple jurisdictions. As the telecommunications industries develop new technologies and markets, they simultaneously provide more and more opportunities for a wide variety of electronic harassment.

**Technology for Prevention**

Early intervention is one of the most effective ways to control stalking. Toward this end, various devices have been developed to aid potential victims: cellular phones that are preprogrammed to call only 911 emergency numbers; video cameras; phone systems equipped to trace calls automatically; and small personal-alarm transmitters that can be worn around the neck and activated to alert a security firm, which in turn notifies the police. But according to *Domestic Violence and Stalking: The Second Annual Report to Congress Under the Violence Against Women Act*, intervening in stalking cases is perhaps the "most difficult and dangerous aspect of addressing this crime." The crucial issue is how to provide a balance between the objectives of preventing the stalking from escalating and protecting the victim from injury or death. Some forms of intervention may actually result in alerting stalkers that they are losing more and more control over their victims and thus may increase the aggressive behavior of the stalkers.

*BIBLIOGRAPHY*

Cone, Tracie. "Snap Judgments: Miami Beach Is Heating Up as a Celebrity-Stalking Ground for Paparazzi." *Chicago Tribune*, 5 May 1993.

Ginsburg, Marsha. "Tougher Law Takes New Aim at Stalkers." *San Francisco Examiner*, 2 January 1994.

Kessler, Ronald. *The FBI: Inside the World's Most Powerful Law Enforcement Agency.* New York: Pocket Books, 1993.

Kuntz, Tom. "Sugar and Spite and a Legal Mess Not Nice." *New York Times*, 7 December 1997.

Lilly, J. Robert. "Selling Justice: Electronic Monitoring and the Security Industry." *Justice Quarterly* 9, no. 3 (1992): 493–503.

Lilly, J. Robert, and Richard A. Ball. "The Development of Home Confinement and Electronic Monitoring in the United States." In *Community Corrections: A Community Field Approach*, edited by David E. Duffee and Edmund F. McGarrell. Cincinnati, Ohio: Anderson, 1990.

Lowney, Kathleen S., and Joel Best. "Stalking Strangers and Lovers." In *Images of Issues: Typifying Contemporary Social Problems*. New York: Aldine de Gruyter, 1995.

Masley, Ed. "Death Becomes Them: Horror Fans Find Gore and More at Zombie Jamboree '93." *Pittsburgh Post-Gazette*, 30 August 1993.

Piccoli, Sean. "Celebrating Italian Heritage." *Washington Times*, 31 October 1994.

Rosenlind, Stevan. "Fraud Charges May Tie Computer Stalker to Fresnan." *Fresno Bee*, 25 July 1995.

U.S. Department of Justice. *Project to Develop a Model Anti-Stalking Code for States*. Washington, D.C.: National Institute of Justice, 1993.

Violence Against Women Grants Office. *Domestic Violence and Stalking: The Second Annual Report to Congress Under the Violence Against Women Act*. Washington, D.C.: U.S. Department of Justice, 1997.

Wolff, Isabel. "Stalked by a Terrible Obsession." *Observer*, 27 November 1994.

J. ROBERT LILLY

*See also* **Domestic Violence; Internet; Private Security: Private Police.**

# STARKWEATHER, CHARLES, AND CARIL ANN FUGATE
## Starkweather (1938–1959); Fugate (1943– )

Born in 1938 to a poor family in Lincoln, Nebraska, Charles Raymond Starkweather was a small child who was taunted by his classmates from an early age. Bowlegged and standing only five feet two inches tall at age seventeen, Starkweather dropped out of school and worked as a garbage collector. He had an angry disposition and his behavior was volatile; he displayed antisocial tendencies in public, sometimes shouting obscenities at passersby. The only person to whom he displayed any affection was his girlfriend, Caril Ann Fugate, whom he began dating when she was thirteen. Problems in that relationship stemming from Starkweather's rage were compounded by the Fugate family's disapproval of his extreme mood swings and the fact that he carried a rifle.

On 1 December 1957 Starkweather held up a gas station in Lincoln, abducting the attendant and then killing him with a close-range shotgun blast. Starkweather was not named a suspect in the crime, and a few weeks later, on 21 January 1958, he and Fugate set out on a murderous rampage across the Plains states. The killing spree lasted

**Charles Starkweather (age nineteen) and Caril Ann Fugate (age fifteen) in a photograph used in a 1958 wanted flyer.** CORBIS/BETTMANN

eight days and claimed the lives of ten people. Three of the victims were Fugate's parents and baby sister.

Although the nation was shocked by the murders, Charlie Starkweather and Caril Fugate quickly became macabre characters of twentieth-century American folklore. People were fascinated with the seemingly matter-of-fact way in which the killing had been done. After shooting and stabbing three members of Fugate's family, for example, the teenage couple reportedly ate sandwiches and watched television only a few yards from where their victims' bodies lay hidden.

The nineteen-year-old Starkweather was a projection of the then-popular James Dean image. Af-

ter his death in an automobile crash in 1955 at age twenty-four, Dean became a symbol of the young outsider too uncompromising to survive in a conformist adult society. Similarly, for the rebellious youth of the 1950s for whom individuality and status were to be gained through confrontation by brute force, Charles Raymond Starkweather was a hero. Like Robin Hood, Jesse James, and Billy the Kid, he had defied the established order, and done so in a most visible and savage way. And like Dean, he became a martyr. When Starkweather was executed in the Nebraska State Penitentiary electric chair on 25 June 1959, his death was mourned by those who identified with him across the country.

Caril Ann Fugate was sentenced to life imprisonment for her role in the murder spree and was ultimately paroled in 1976. In later years Starkweather and Fugate were the subjects of the title song of Bruce Springsteen's 1982 album, *Nebraska,* and Terrence Malick's 1973 film, *Badlands;* Oliver Stone's 1994 film, *Natural Born Killers,* controversial for its violent content, was also based on the Starkweather-Fugate killing spree.

*BIBLIOGRAPHY*

Allen, William. *Starkweather: The Story of a Mass Murderer.* Boston: Houghton Mifflin, 1976.
Reinhardt, James M. *The Murderous Trail of Charles Starkweather.* Springfield, Ill.: Charles C. Thomas, 1960.

JAMES A. INCIARDI

*See also* **Mass Murder: Individual Perpetrators.**

# STATISTICS AND EPIDEMIOLOGY

Statistics on crime and violence are used by a wide range of people for a variety of purposes. Humans' understanding of the world, including its violence and crime, is shaped by a number of sources, among them personal experiences, friends, acquaintances, family members, and the mass media. In fact, for most people the mass media constitute the primary source of information on violence and criminality. Violent crime is a favorite topic of the news media, and journalists frequently use various statistics on crime rates and trends to contextualize stories within a larger societal framework, both to inform and, often, to sensationalize. Policy makers and politicians also reference statistics on violence to make a point, get elected, or garner support for certain pieces of legislation. Law-enforcement agencies cite statistics on decreasing crime rates to showcase their own effectiveness, or point to increased rates of crime to highlight a need for more resources and personnel. The public, in turn, often relies on these statistics when voting or lobbying for various types of social or legal change, while criminologists and other social scientists rely on statistics to conduct research and answer important questions about the causes and consequences of violence in American society. Medical and health-care professionals have also begun using statistics on violence to develop strategies aimed at reducing violence.

In the 1990s violence has been defined and managed not only as a criminal justice problem but as a public-health issue as well. This epidemiological approach (that is, originating from a medical health care perspective) to violent crime has been spurred on by the recognition that violence in the United States has a tremendous impact on the country's medical-care systems. Epidemiological studies of violence are much more proactive and preventive in orientation than conventional criminal justice approaches. In the same way that smoking, alcohol, and drug abuse are public-health issues and are attacked through education and intervention strategies, so too is violence increasingly perceived and treated in much the same way. This approach, however, is contingent upon specific and detailed knowledge about the trends, patterns, and characteristics of violent crime within specific targeted populations. Racial and ethnic groups often differ in the particular correlates and patterns of violent crime and public health, meaning that epidemiological approaches must, therefore, generate group-specific data so that social policy can be implemented to target the specific causes of violence for different populations.

Since statistics constitute such an important source of information on violent crime, as well as the foundation for effective intervention strategies, several important questions need to be asked. First, where do the statistics come from? In other words, who gathers these numbers? Second, how are they collected? What are the methods utilized to piece together these data? Third, how accurate are sources of violent-crime statistics? These critical questions address the reliability and validity of the information collected. The answers to these questions determine whether the numbers gathered and statistics generated truly illustrate the nature and frequency of violent crimes in this

country. Social-policy initiatives and violence-prevention strategies derived from faulty data have little hope of successfully ameliorating violent-crime rates. Such policies also waste money and divert attention.

An examination of data-collection methods and sources of statistics reveals that statistics on violence and crime suffer from various shortcomings that seriously affect the quality of the knowledge gathered. The purpose of this entry is to examine the ways in which information on violence is gathered and to discuss some of the strengths and weaknesses of these sources of data.

## Measuring Crime and Violence

One issue in the statistical study of violence concerns the nature of scientific analysis and its ability to measure reality. Statistics on violent crime tell us the frequency of violent acts, trends over time, and patterns of perpetration. Yet how well do these numbers capture the reality and totality of the experience of violence? Each act of violence is a complex phenomenon that is situated in a particular spatial and historical context, and each act involves its own unique microdynamics and meanings. Violence is a process, not just an event. It involves various actors for whom the violence may mean many different things. Murderers, for example, may see themselves as acting in self-defense, while rapists may believe that their victims solicited and encouraged their advances. Similarly, parents who use violence against children may not see their actions as violent or criminal; instead, they may define their actions as a form of physical discipline necessary to maintaining moral order. The interactions that lead up to violent behavior are guided and shaped by individual circumstances, beliefs, and the setting within which the violent interaction is played out. In short, violence is comprised of intricate patterns of thought and behavior. Thus, the numbers that are used to ostensibly represent these acts are not always the best tools to help us understand the full reality of violence. Statistics on violence can be perceived as a form of "abstracted empiricism" in which the data generated fall far short of measuring the full experience and meaning of violent crimes. These numbers, then, may offer only limited insight into violent behavior.

Additionally, numbers can be manipulated and distorted to support misleading or false conclusions. In one case, the National Rifle Association, trying to show a need for more prisons, wanted to establish a link between rates of imprisonment and violent offending by showing that during the 1980s, when the rate of imprisonment increased dramatically, there had been a corresponding decrease in violent crimes. Accordingly, burglary was included in a measure of violent crime that also included murder, rape, robbery, and assault. Even though burglary is a nonviolent offense, it was incorporated into the measure of violent crime because burglary rates experienced a significant reduction during the decade, while the rates of truly violent offenses decreased only by very small amounts. The organization then put forth the argument that the massive increase in the prison population had resulted in significant decreases in the number of violent crimes being perpetrated. Even though this conclusion was patently false, at first glance it seemed to be supported by the statistics that had been generated.

All attempts to measure violent crime also suffer from various methodological problems that affect the caliber of the information gathered. In fact, one could argue that no statistics on violence can ever be perfect for the simple reason that it is impossible to measure every act of violence committed. All types of violent crime suffer from different degrees of underreporting. Estimates from various Bureau of Justice Statistics studies suggest that police statistics, for example, measure approximately one-third of all burglaries and about half of all robberies, aggravated assaults, and rapes. If our understanding of these crimes is shaped by statistics based on underreporting, it is clear that our knowledge is far from complete. As might be expected, the more serious the violence, the more likely it is to be reported. The presence of a weapon and injuries requiring medical attention, for example, increase the likelihood of acts of violence being reported. On the other hand, if the violent crime is not completed or if the victim feels that nothing can be done by authorities in response to a report, the chances of reporting are lowered.

Another factor associated with the decision to report violence concerns the relationship between the actors involved in the violent interplay. Many instances of violence occur between family members or acquaintances, and these acts of violence often go unrecorded because they occur in the privacy of a home, out of sight of a public audience. The individuals involved, both victims and perpetrators, may well define the violence as personal and not want or seek outside intervention. Spousal violence, for example, was historically perceived as a private matter between a husband and wife and of no concern to the community or law-enforcement agencies.

Another reason for nonreporting of violence may be that witnesses simply do not want to get involved. A famous example of this happened in 1964 in Queens, New York, when Kitty Genovese was stalked and repeatedly attacked by a knife-wielding assailant for over thirty minutes. Even though she screamed and called for help, not one of the thirty-eight witnesses who saw or heard the assault helped her or even called the police until it was far too late to save Genovese. When later questioned, many of these individuals asserted either that they defined what they witnessed as a domestic quarrel and therefore none of their business or that they simply did not want to get involved. For these reasons, most data sets on violence record only a fraction of all of the acts perpetrated, resulting in incomplete and potentially biased understandings.

Most crime statistics can be broken down into two major categories: official statistics and surveys. *Official statistics* refer to data gathered by various official criminal justice agencies and include the records collected in prisons, courts, and police departments. Police records are by far the most commonly used type of official statistics. Of these, the Uniform Crime Reports are the preeminent source of information on crime and violence. *Surveys,* because they bypass the filtering of the criminal justice system and go directly to those individuals involved in the crime, are generally more complete than statistics derived from various criminal justice agencies. Surveys may be conducted by official agencies but are as likely to be administered by researchers and private organizations. Generally speaking, there are two primary kinds of surveys: victimization and self-report. Victimization surveys ask a sample of respondents if they have been the victims of various types of violence, while self-report surveys question whether respondents have ever perpetrated the kinds of violence and criminality being studied. The most comprehensive example of the former type is the National Crime Victimization Survey. A discussion of these sources provides a good overview of the strengths and problems associated with the major sources of statistics on violent crime.

*Uniform Crime Reports.* The Federal Bureau of Investigation's Uniform Crime Reporting (UCR) program is one of the best known and most widely used sources of information on crime and violence. Begun in 1927 when the International Association of Chiefs of Police formed a committee to create a nationwide system for collecting police records of crime, it is also the oldest national-level source of statistics on crime and violence. Since each state defines crime somewhat differently, the committee's mandate was to find a method to compile consistent crime statistics. After evaluating the record-keeping practices in place at the time, the committee in 1929 developed a plan based on what became known as the seven index offenses. Because of their seriousness, their frequency of perpetration, as well as their likelihood of being reported, the following seven crimes were chosen to provide an indication or index of the amount of crime in the United States: murder and nonnegligent manslaughter, forcible rape, robbery, aggravated assault, larceny-theft, burglary, and motor-vehicle theft. In 1978, arson was added as the eighth index offense.

Participating police agencies are required to produce monthly and annual reports recording details of crimes that are reported to them. In these reports, police must use a generic definition of the crime provided by the FBI. The UCR program is also designed to gather information on property stolen and recovered; on the age, sex, race, and ethnic background of persons arrested; on all police employees; and on homicides. Each year this material is collated, analyzed, and published by the FBI in the book *Crime in the United States*, which is made available to libraries, agencies, scholars, and citizens alike across the country. Even though the Uniform Crime Reports are among the most used sources for information on violence in the United States, they have various limitations in addition to the problems of underreporting.

One significant issue concerns the fact that police departments sometimes fail to substantiate a crime. In other words, even though a crime is reported to them, the police do not record it as such. This may occur because an officer may misjudge a case and incorrectly decide that it is not a crime. Research has found that up to half of crimes judged unfounded by the police should have been recorded as crimes. The reasons why police do not acknowledge crimes range from a belief that the crime is too trivial or that prosecution is too unlikely to a perception that the crime is too difficult to investigate. This "unfounding" of crimes results in less than complete and accurate statistics, and

has significant consequences for our understanding of violence in U.S. society.

Similarly, changes in reporting practices can also affect the information recorded. When New York City changed its reporting procedures in 1950, for example, various crimes showed dramatic increases in the reports. A similar procedural change in Chicago in 1959 also resulted in sudden escalations in specific crimes. While these upswings reflected only a change in official reporting practices, an unaware consumer of this data may well assume that they reflected a dramatic change in the frequency of the affected crimes. With official statistics it can be easy to confuse a reporting wave with a true crime wave.

Reported trends may not match the reality of changes in perpetration for other reasons as well. A good example of this involves the crime of rape. Since the 1960s the rape rate, as reported by official statistics, has increased over 400 percent. It is problematic, however, to decipher whether this reflects a massive increase in perpetration, or whether it reflects other, more methodological changes. The evidence suggests that much of the increase may in fact be more a reflection of changing definitions and reporting than of any real escalation in perpetration. Since the 1960s the legal and social definitions of rape have expanded to include date or acquaintance rape. Whereas "real" rape was once believed to be solely perpetrated by strangers, increasingly U.S. society recognizes that women are often raped by men they know and whom they may even be dating or otherwise involved with. Similarly, it is now also accepted that husbands can rape their wives. This type of rape gained national attention in 1978 when Greta Rideout accused her husband of marital rape. Even though her husband, John, was acquitted, the case provided a powerful impetus for elimination of the marital-exemption rule, to the extent that today virtually all jurisdictions recognize marital rape as a crime. As rape is defined more broadly and includes more behaviors, official statistics on this form of violence increase.

Similarly, when examining the tremendous increase in official rape rates, it must be pointed out that many late-twentieth-century changes in U.S. society made it more likely that a rape would be reported. Much of the social stigma that automatically blamed rape victims for their victimization was eliminated or reduced, for example. Attitudes that suggested women provoked their victimization because of clothing or demeanor became less prevalent or overt than they were in the past. Many states passed shield laws that protect rape victims from being victimized in court through questioning about their past sexual behavior. Counselors and victims-advocates who advise and assist rape victims are now also often provided. These changes resulted in rape victims being more likely to report the crime. The reported numbers on rape in the Uniform Crime Reports, therefore, reflect an increase in the reporting of rape more than an escalating pattern of perpetration.

For all of these reasons, the Uniform Crime Reports are a significantly flawed source of information on crime and violence. This does not mean, however, that they have no value. Judicious use of this source of crime statistics has helped increase the state of knowledge about crime and violence. However, those who rely on the Uniform Crime Reports must recognize the limitations of the data and accept that results may be questionable or that they do not allow for broad and conclusive generalizations.

*National Crime Victimization Survey.* For those seeking national-level information on violent crime, there exists another important source of knowledge: the National Crime Victimization Survey (NCVS). In 1965 the President's Commission on Law Enforcement and the Administration of Justice sponsored several surveys of crime victims to determine the extent of the shortcomings of official statistics. They found that police statistics dramatically underenumerated various crimes. In response to these findings, the Department of Justice established the NCVS.

Begun in 1972, the NCVS was intended as a more accurate alternative to the UCR program. Officially, its objectives are to ascertain the amount of underreporting suffered by the Uniform Crime Reports, establish the accuracy of the Uniform Crime Reports in reporting trends and patterns of offending, discover the significant factors involved in decisions not to report crimes to the police, and profile the demographic characteristics of offenders and victims.

Conducted by the U.S. Bureau of Census on behalf of the Bureau of Justice Statistics, the survey in 1999 was composed of approximately 56,000 households. This translates to roughly 120,000 individuals over twelve years of age living within those households who are interviewed about their experiences with personal and household robberies, burglary, motor-vehicle theft, assaults, and

various other violent victimizations. Those respondents who have been victimized are asked for specific information on where the victimization occurred, the time of day, how many perpetrators were involved, and whether weapons were present. The NCVS gathers very detailed information on the specifics of victimization as well as demographic information on the victims of crime. Not only can victimizations be described and understood better because of this data, but the information can be used to predict who is most at risk for being the victim of various crimes as well as the situations, locations, and times that are the most hazardous. This is especially important for those utilizing an epidemiological approach to violence in order to implement effective reduction strategies. Being able to pinpoint locations and situations conducive to violence is the first step in designing productive preventative approaches.

In conducting the survey, trained interviewers personally visit or sometimes telephone selected households. Approximately ten thousand households are replaced in every six-month period, which means that each household is included in the sample for approximately three years. (The sampling procedure selects housing units through a multistage clustering design that makes use of the detailed information the Bureau of the Census has for all households in the United States.) The sample is surveyed twice a year to determine victimizations in the past six-month period; given the sophisticated sampling techniques employed as well as a 90 percent response rate, it is generally considered to present a fairly realistic portrayal of crime and violence in the United States.

This project is also important because it elicits information on whether the victimization was reported to the police and what factors were involved in making that decision. In this way, the NCVS provides a reference point for the Uniform Crime Reports to help determine the levels of underreporting for different offenses. For all of its strengths, however, the NCVS still has significant weaknesses that affect the quality of the data collected.

Some of the drawbacks of the NCVS are ones common to all survey research. The wording of questions, for example, can dramatically affect the responses received. Vague, misleading, judgmental, or complexly worded questions can confuse or inhibit the respondents. In 1992, the NCVS was redesigned to more directly ask about rape and sexual assault precisely for these reasons. Whereas in the past the survey only indirectly alluded to rape and sexual assault by questioning whether "anything else" had happened to the respondent, the present form directly asks whether the respondent has been sexually assaulted or raped. Survey research with adolescents, or individuals for whom English is not their first language, can also pose problems, since these participants may have difficulty in understanding and interpreting specific terms and questions.

Similarly, the demeanor of the interviewer can influence the responses that people give. The expressions and reactions of interviewers can encourage or discourage open and honest responses to the survey questions in ways that are sometimes difficult to predict and control. If a respondent feels that the person asking the questions may judge him or her for answering affirmatively, for example, that respondent may not want to risk the negative reaction of the interviewer and instead may deny being victimized.

Another potential problem with the NCVS concerns the issue of truthfulness. Some participants may feel that their victimization is embarrassing and that it reflects poorly on them and therefore do not report it. This is especially true for some types of victimization, such as rape, an incredibly intimate violation. Historically, the burden of rape victimhood has been compounded by the reaction of family, friends, and the larger community; rape victims have been subject to a great deal of social stigma placing much of the blame on them. Assertions that a woman must have provoked the rape or that she must not have resisted enough have been very common. Consequently, rape victims may not want to admit to having been raped because of derogatory assumptions and consequences. This is especially true if the attacker is a friend or acquaintance of the victim. Similarly, evidence exists that other forms of assault perpetrated by family, friends, and acquaintances are also often not reported because of a fear of reprisal or not wanting a loved one to get into trouble. Although surveys may not suffer from underreporting as dramatically as official statistics, it nonetheless remains a problem.

The issue of truthfulness may also work the opposite way. Some respondents may actually inflate their victimization experiences for various reasons. This is more of a problem with self-report surveys in which respondents are asked about their experiences perpetrating various offenses, rather than with victimization surveys. Young males may ex-

aggerate their activities to appear tougher, more dangerous, or simply to pull a fast one on officials. Overreporting may also occur, not because of the lack of truthfulness, but because the respondents incorrectly report as crimes events that were simply accidents. For example, a person who lost a wallet, camera, or some other valuable may believe it to have been stolen. On the other hand, stolen items may sometimes be falsely believed to have been lost or misplaced. In either case, the quality of the information gathered is somewhat compromised.

The problem of recall is also important. Because of simple memory lapses, various respondents may not report victimizations, even violent ones, because they do not remember them. Even though NCVS respondents need only remember victimizations that occurred within the last six months, it is not unusual for people to forget some events, especially the most minor forms of theft. Additionally, it is also quite possible that many victims of such violent crimes as rape seek to protect themselves psychologically by actively suppressing the criminal event. In short, surveys are dependent upon the vagaries of human memory, which are clearly fallible.

## Conclusion

The NCVS and the UCR are not the only sources of statistics on crime and violence. They are, however, two of the more comprehensive sources of information and are among the most widely utilized collections of data. The strengths and weaknesses they suffer from are also to some extent representative of the strengths and weaknesses common to all data sets on violence and crime. There are no sources of perfect information on these issues. Criminologists and epidemiologists continue to rely on imperfect instruments and measures because the alternative is to forego research on these issues entirely and give up on implementing programs and strategies intended to reduce the problem of violence. Knowledge about crime and violence in the United States increases slowly and incrementally, constrained as it is by the nature of the data-gathering enterprise. Consumers of crime statistics, be they scholars, healthcare professionals, or private citizens, must always take the information presented with a grain of salt and recognize that, because of the flawed sources of data, the conclusions and implications are often somewhat tentative and subject to revision as methods of gathering and compiling statistics on violent crime continue to change and evolve.

BIBLIOGRAPHY

Barlow, Hugh. *Introduction to Criminology.* 5th ed. Mill Valley, Calif.: Scott, Foresman, 1990.

Biderman, Albert D., and James P. Lynch. *Understanding Crime Incidence Statistics: Why the UCR Diverges from the NCVS.* New York: Springer Verlag, 1991.

Blumstein, Alfred, et al. "Trend and Deviation in Crime Rates: A Comparison of UCR and NCS Data for Burglary and Robbery." *Criminology* 29 (May 1991).

Bureau of Justice Statistics. *New Directions for the National Crime Survey.* Washington, D.C.: U.S. Department of Justice, 1989.

Koss, Mary P. "The Measurement of Rape Victimization in Crime Surveys." *Criminal Justice and Behavior* 23 (March 1996).

McDowall, David, and Colin Loftin. "Comparing the UCR and NCVS over Time." *Criminology* 30 (February 1992).

MacKenzie, Doris Layton, Phyllis Jo Baunach, and Roy R. Roberg, eds. *Measuring Crime: Large-Scale, Long-Range Efforts.* Albany: State University of New York Press, 1990.

National Criminal Justice Commission. *The Real War on Crime: The Report on the National Criminal Justice Commission.* Edited by Steven R. Donziger. New York: HarperPerennial, 1996.

Orcutt, James D., and Rebecca Faison. "Sex-Role Attitude Change and Reporting of Rape Victimization, 1973–1985." *Sociological Quarterly* 29, no. 4 (1988).

ALEXANDER ALVAREZ

*See also* **Incidence of Violence; Methodologies of Violence Research; National Crime Victimization Survey; Rape; Uniform Crime Reports.**

# STERILIZATION, INVOLUNTARY

Involuntary sterilization is the use of surgical or other means to destroy reproductive potential in persons considered unfit to bear children. In the United States, laws authorizing the compulsory sterilization of criminals, the mentally compromised, and the mentally ill led to the coerced sterilization of more than sixty thousand American men, women, and children in the years between 1907 and 1970.

Restricting the reproductive ability of the "socially inadequate" represented one feature of the American eugenics movement, the effort in the late nineteenth and early twentieth century to curtail the threat of growing numbers of "degenerate" persons predisposed by biology to lives of crime, poverty, disease, and dependency. Introduced in 1897, vasectomy, a surgical technique that rendered men incapable of fathering children, offered eugenic reformers an attractive solution. Unlike tubal ligation in women, which entailed greater risk of infection to the patient, expense, and surgical skill, vasectomy could be performed in a doctor's office or prison infirmary. Before the Great Depression, the majority of persons sterilized in the United States were male; the harsh economic conditions of the 1930s, in addition to medical advances in infection management, encouraged physicians to sterilize women in greater numbers.

In 1907 Indiana became the first state to implement coercive sterilization of "confirmed criminals, idiots, imbeciles, and rapists." By 1932, thirty-two American states had laws requiring the sterilization of the "unfit." The number of sterilizations performed by American surgeons escalated after 1927, when the U.S. Supreme Court, in *Buck v. Bell,* upheld the constitutionality of the Virginia involuntary-sterilization statute. German racial hygienists admired American leadership in the field of coercive sterilization; the American eugenicist Harry Laughlin boasted that his "model" sterilization law inspired the German sterilization program implemented in 1933 when Adolf Hitler came to power.

In the United States involuntary sterilization declined during World War II and in the postwar decades, although the laws remained in force. In 1961 the American Bar Foundation reported that involuntary sterilization for eugenic purposes remained lawful in twenty-six states. In the 1970s fears that sterilization was being selectively performed on poor women without their knowledge and consent prompted an overhaul of federal regulations. Inspired by reports that an Alabama physician had sterilized black teenage girls without their consent at government-sponsored health clinics, the U.S. Department of Health, Education, and Welfare issued regulations that prohibited using federal funds to sterilize persons who were under the age of twenty-one, mentally incompetent, or institutionalized. In the 1980s, parents and guardians of the mentally retarded have advocated sterilization as a right, as a form of social and physical protection for these vulnerable individuals.

The principle that sustains compulsory vaccination, wrote Justice Oliver Wendell Holmes in the *Buck v. Bell* decision, is broad enough to cover cutting the fallopian tubes (female sterilization). Coercive sterilization continues to be seen as an avenue for promoting social welfare; in the 1990s sterilization as a condition for parole was proposed for prison inmates in Colorado. In South Dakota, Medicaid (state medical assistance) covered insertion—but not removal—of the contraceptive Norplant for women receiving welfare payments.

*BIBLIOGRAPHY*

Lombardo, Paul A. "Medicine, Eugenics, and the Supreme Court: From Coercive Sterilization to Reproductive Freedom." *Journal of Contemporary Health Law and Policy* 13, no. 1 (fall 1996).

Reilly, Philip R. *The Surgical Solution: A History of Involuntary Sterilization in the United States.* Baltimore: Johns Hopkins University Press, 1991.

SUSAN E. LEDERER

*See also* **Eugenics; Medicine and Violence: Medical Experimentation on the Mentally Ill; Tuskegee Syphilis Study.**

# STRATEGIC DEFENSE INITIATIVE

In a 23 March 1983 televised address, President Ronald Reagan proposed to develop a ballistic missile defense system that would render nuclear weapons "impotent and obsolete." The Strategic Defense Initiative (SDI) research program, promoted more aggressively during Reagan's second term (1985–1989), promised a technological solution to Cold War fears of global destruction through a massive exchange of nuclear missiles between the United States and the Soviet Union. Through SDI, the Reagan administration sought to shift the arms race toward defensive technologies while promoting offensive programs such as the MX missile. Despite Reagan's vision of SDI as a shield impervious to nuclear attacks, its goals remained vague and SDI was often described as simply a strategy to defend U.S. missile silo sites.

Supporters saw defensive "star wars" technologies (X-ray lasers, "smart" projectiles, and particle-beam weapons) as humane successors to a Cold War logic of mutually assured destruction (MAD). They also claimed that increased Soviet intercontinental ballistic missile (ICBM) forces opened a "window of vulnerability," in which a massive first strike could prevent the United States from retaliating with sufficient numbers of its own nuclear warheads. SDI would maintain nuclear deterrence, ensure against accidental launches, and eventually trump the arms race altogether. Despite the dependence of SDI upon offensive nuclear weapons in the short term, Reagan referred to the film *Star Wars* (1977) explicitly, evoking the futuristic cleanliness of SDI technology and its potency against a Soviet "evil empire."

Critics saw SDI as a dangerous, costly, and technologically unworkable fantasy that underplayed the horrors of nuclear war. Critics saw SDI not as an escape from MAD but as an extension of strategic plans for limited nuclear exchanges in which the United States could prevail with "acceptable" civilian and military casualties. MAD kept nuclear war strategically unthinkable while SDI seemed like an effort to acquire a first-strike capability. SDI required vast defensive commitments to an array of satellites and orbiting battle stations that would have made conflicts more likely. Additionally, countermeasures (decoys, chaff, and more missiles) were far cheaper than unproven star wars technologies.

By 1987 annual funding had reached $6 billion, and the Defense Department estimated that this figure would reach $12.5 billion by 1990. The disintegration of the Soviet Union led President George Bush to greatly reduce funding in 1991, and President Bill Clinton officially ended SDI in 1993. But SDI never entirely disappeared. Research continues under the Ballistic Missile Defense Program and the total spent on star wars and its "sequel" programs reached $50 billion in 1998. Its legacy could be seen in the depictions of "smart" weapons destroying military hardware and not people in the 1991 Gulf War and in the air strikes against Serbs in 1999.

Under congressional pressure, Clinton was committed to develop and deploy a limited national defense system by the year 2003. Using missiles to intercept and destroy nuclear or biological warheads, the system would guard against ballistic missile threats that some analysts thought would come from Iraq or North Korea during the next decades. Test results have been mixed. Both the army and navy are developing theater-wide defense systems against medium-range missiles, and the air force plans to mount missile-burning lasers on 747 aircraft. The programs are more limited but their multibillion-dollar combined annual budget approaches that of the more ambitious predecessor of the Reagan administration.

*BIBLIOGRAPHY*

Boffey, Philip M., et al. *Claiming the Heavens.* New York: Times Books, 1988.

Chalfont, Alun. *Star Wars: Suicide or Survival.* Boston: Little, Brown, 1985.

Graham, Bradley. "A Bumpy Path for Missile Defenses." *Washington Post*, 27 April 1998.

Jessup, John E., and Louise B. Ketz, eds. *The Encyclopedia of the American Military.* New York: Scribners, 1994.

Reagan, Ronald. "Peace and National Security." 23 March 1983. Televised address.

Reiss, Edward. *The Strategic Defense Initiative.* New York: Cambridge University Press, 1992.

Rogers, Paul. "The Myth of the Clean War." In *Incorporations: Zone 6*, edited by Jonathan Crary and Sanford Kwinter. New York: Urzone, 1992.

Rogin, Michael. *Ronald Reagan, the Movie, and Other Episodes in Political Demonology.* Berkeley: University of California Press, 1987.

BILL DOTSON

*See also* **Cold War; Literature: Nuclear War Fiction; Weapons: Nuclear.**

# STRIKES

Two powerful myths have shaped our images of the American past. One suggests that the United States has been among the most violent of societies in the developed world. The second depicts U.S. labor history as having been punctuated by a greater number of violent and destructive strikes than has any other developed industrial society. The second myth deserves closer scrutiny.

Between the 1870s and the 1930s the United States experienced a history of especially violent strikes. In nearly every decade one or more strikes resulted in the loss of lives, shattered bodies, uprooted families, and the destruction of property. Evidence suggests that strikes in the United States were in the main more violent than comparable events in Canada, Great Britain, and the latter's Australasian dominions. For other comparable industrial nations, however, the data is less clear and subject to dispute. And even in the United States the vast majority of industrial disputes passed uneventfully.

The violence associated with labor conflicts in the United States can be demarcated into two distinct eras and two forms of mayhem. In the years before the Civil War, when the nation remained overwhelmingly agrarian and only a minority of wageworkers toiled in factories, industrial disputes rarely erupted into violence. Most violence occurred on neighborhood streets or in public spaces separate from places of work and flowed from community notions about customary rights.

Similar eruptions of crowd violence plagued Europe simultaneously. A second type of antebellum labor violence had an ethnic or racial edge. Irish immigrant workers employed in the construction of canals often rioted in response to mistreatment by the contractors who hired and exploited them. Such riots, moreover, often pitted immigrant Catholics against American-born Protestant bosses and local residents. And sometimes the Irish immigrant workers competed for jobs with enslaved and free African Americans, a competition that could degenerate into violence, as demonstrated most notably by the New York City draft riot of 1863.

## The Transition to Modern Forms of Labor Violence

After the Civil War labor violence changed in form and character. As the nation industrialized and urbanized, industrial conflict came to be associated with trade unions and collective action directed at places of work. The Molly Maguires, who appeared in the coalfields of northeastern Pennsylvania in the 1870s, served as a transitional element in the shift from older forms of collective action to more modern styles of labor violence. Composed largely of immigrant Irish Catholic workers who felt exploited by their Protestant and Welsh-origin bosses and neighbors, the Mollies, unable to sustain union organizations broken by recalcitrant employers in the "long strike of 1875," resorted to customary forms of rural Irish collective action to accomplish their goals. Their economic and social grievances led the Mollies to use guns and dynamite. A response to the policies of obdurate antiunion employers, the Molly Maguire incidents retained the character of ethnically based, communal crowd actions.

The first major strike of the modern era, the railroad labor conflict of 1877, also shared traits characteristic of earlier forms of crowd action. Largely a response by aggrieved railroad workers to a series of wage cuts, combined with intensification in the pace of work instituted by employers in reaction to the depression of 1873–1877, the strike rapidly spun out of control, moving away from the rail lines and directly onto the streets of large and small cities. Rather than bargain with their employees or rescind wage cuts, the railroads tried to keep operating with the assistance of military power. Wherever governors dispatched state militia, violence followed, spreading from the Baltimore and Ohio Railroad in West Virginia, where the conflict originated, to the streets of Baltimore, Pittsburgh, and St. Louis. In Pittsburgh mobs torched the properties of the Pennsylvania Railroad, turning the skies over the city into a haze of smoke. In Baltimore mobs of unemployed and transient workers waged street warfare with state militia. And in St. Louis crowds of local citizens besieged the city hall, demanding bread and jobs. Only the dispatch by President Rutherford B. Hayes of more disciplined regular federal troops quelled the rioting, ensured that railroad traffic moved unimpeded, and ended the strike.

The pattern of violence that manifested itself during the railroad strikes of 1877 recurred repeatedly during the long era of industrial conflict that followed. Strikes ebbed and flowed in a cyclical rhythm, intensifying when labor markets were tight and unemployment low, and abating as unemployment rose. The years 1885–1886, 1898–1904, 1910–1913, 1916–1922, 1934, 1937, 1940–1941, and 1945–1946 saw strikes surge in number, from 1,572 strikes in 1885–1886 to as many as 4,985 in 1945–1946. Yet the vast majority of strikes passed without incident. Whenever employers recognized unions, bargained with their representatives, and shut down during disputes, conflict rarely caused violence. But when management refused to recognize or bargain with unions and insisted on using strikebreakers (replacement workers) to maintain operations during a strike, violence often erupted. And when employers used police or troops to protect strikebreakers, the level of violence intensified.

The Haymarket riot in Chicago in 1886, although itself not a strike or industrial conflict, resulted from two disputes in which employers tried to maintain production by using strikebreakers protected by city police. A group of anarchists called a mass meeting at Haymarket Square to protest brutality by Chicago police sent to protect strikebreakers during disputes at the McCormick Harvester works and other sites. As the peaceful mass meeting ended, an unknown individual threw a bomb into the crowd, which injured police as well as bystanders. The police responded by shooting and clubbing the fleeing crowd members, causing even more injuries and deaths. In the aftermath of the bombing, city authorities conducted a dragnet for suspects in which they rounded up hundreds of anarchists and radicals, choosing eight anarchists for arraignment, indictment, and trial. The trial, conducted during the nation's first large-scale Red Scare, brought the quick conviction of all eight defendants, four of whom were hanged.

More typical of the pattern of violent strikes in the late nineteenth century, however, were the Homestead steel strike of 1892 in Homestead, Pennsylvania, and the Pullman boycott and strike of 1894. In the former, Andrew Carnegie and his right-hand man Henry Clay Frick concluded that the union representing the skilled workers at Homestead diminished company profits, and they decided to eliminate it. Frick devised a strategy in which he fortified the plant, recruited strikebreakers to keep it operating, and hired armed Pinkerton agents to protect the replacement workers. When the Homestead strikers learned that Frick intended to replace them with outsiders and to use armed guards, they armed themselves and awaited the arrival of the strikebreakers and Pinkertons. When the barge carrying the Pinkertons neared the bank of the Monongahela River, the Homestead workers opened fire. In the ensuing battle, the Pinkertons paid a heavy price in casualties before surrendering to the strikers who, together with their local

Pinkerton men surrendering to workers during the Homestead strike. Engraving by W. P. Snyder after a photograph by Dabbs. From *Harper's Weekly* (16 July 1892). Library of Congress

sympathizers, ruled Homestead. The governor of Pennsylvania responded to Frick and Carnegie's pleas for assistance, dispatching state militia to Homestead, where they instituted martial law and took control of the community away from local officials and strikers. From then until 1937 effective unions remained absent from the steel industry. Whenever workers resisted their employers or walked out, steelmasters replaced them with strikebreakers and used private police or military force to break strikes.

The Pullman strike and boycott of 1894 resembled the Homestead strike. Once again a recalcitrant employer, in this case George Pullman, refused to bargain with his workers at the Pullman Palace Car Company or to negotiate with the union that represented them, the American Railway Union (ARU). Unable to bring Pullman to the bargaining table through conventional tactics, ARU president Eugene V. Debs asked all union members employed on the railroads to refuse to handle Pullman sleeping cars.

The boycott of Pullman cars brought the railroads and the federal government into the dispute between Pullman and his employees. As the boycott of railroad traffic spread from Chicago west and south, tying the nation's railroads into knots, the railroad managers appealed to President Grover Cleveland for assistance. The president responded to their appeal. Cleveland's attorney general obtained a judicial injunction interdicting all forms of union and strike activity, and the president dispatched federal marshals and troops to enforce the injunction. The presence of troops caused rioting, property damage, and the loss of lives. Federal power, however, broke the strike-boycott, and a federal judge sentenced its leader, Debs, to prison for violating the injunction.

## Age of Industrial Violence

Haymarket, Homestead, and Pullman were only the most egregious of a wave of violent labor conflicts that scarred industrial relations in the United States. Nearly all of the most violent conflicts resulted from the practices of employers who refused to recognize the right of workers to unionize, or sought to eliminate unions already established in the workplace, or replaced strikers and

**Pennsylvania State Police disperse striking Pittsburgh steelworkers, September 1919.**
UPI/CORBIS/BETTMANN

continued to operate the enterprise. Workers who were denied a voice at work or saw their jobs and livelihoods imperiled often resorted to violence to redress their grievances and uphold their rights as free and equal citizens.

Between 1892 and 1905 such a history plagued the hard-rock mining regions of the Mountain West. Beginning in the Coeur d'Alenes mining district of northern Idaho in 1892, spreading to Cripple Creek, Colorado, in 1894, moving back to the Coeur d'Alenes in 1899, and encompassing nearly all the hard-rock mining regions of Colorado between 1903 and 1905, miners and their employers fought a decade-long, no-holds-barred industrial war. Familiar with dynamite and accustomed to guns, miners battled recalcitrant antiunion employers by destroying company property and intimidating strikebreakers. Mine operators, in turn, hired armed guards and sought state militia and ultimately federal troops. They broke the 1892 strike in the Coeur d'Alenes by using state troops to arrest and incarcerate hundreds of strikers and union sympathizers; in the more tumultuous and violent strike of 1899, mine operators used federal troops to accomplish the same end. In the Colorado labor war of 1903–1905, the mine owners, the governor, and the commander of the National Guard united to defeat the strikers. The governor declared martial law in the mining districts, dispatched troops to administer military justice, and allowed the mine owners to pay the cost. The military suspended due process, arrested hundreds of union members, evicted and expelled hundreds more across state lines, and offered summary military justice to union leaders. Over the ensuing two decades, the antiunion intransigence of western mine and mill operators caused their workers in Montana, Utah, Arizona, and New Mexico, as well as Idaho and Colorado, to use violence to claim their human rights as workers and citizens.

The bituminous and anthracite coal industries repeated the hard-rock mining story. Coal miners, like metal miners, were experienced in using explosives. And in the isolated, rural regions where most coal in the United States was mined, residents were accustomed to a culture of guns and hunting. Hence, when mine operators refused to recognize their workers' right to unionize and miners demanded the right to act collectively, dynamitings and shootings punctuated relations between employers and employees. Between 1894 and 1919, as mine owners in Pennsylvania's an-

## Age of Industrial Violence

In the years from the turn of the century through the end of World War I, industrial violence scarred every region of the nation and affected every sort of worker. Clashes between employers and workers precipitated violence—from the streets of New York City's garment industry (1910–1913), to woolen mills in Lawrence, Massachusetts (1912), and silk mills in Paterson, New Jersey (1913), to the piney woods of Louisiana (1912–1913), to the coal country around Ludlow, Colorado (1914), to the iron mines of the Mesabi Range in Minnesota (1916), to the copper mines of Montana, Arizona, and Utah (1914–1919), to the wheat fields of the high plains (1917–1918), to the Douglas fir forests of the Pacific Northwest (1916–1918), to the telephone exchanges of San Francisco (1917). Everywhere the story was the same: the harder employers resisted the efforts by their workers to unionize, the more likely that violence ensued. In the parlance of labor economists, enterprises obtained precisely the sort of unions and industrial relations that they deserved.

thracite district and in the northern bituminous region recognized and bargained with the United Mine Workers of America, both the incidence of strikes and the violence associated with them diminished. But in southern Appalachia, where mine operators resisted unionism, labor violence remained common, culminating in a West Virginia labor civil war (1921–1922) that featured an army of union sympathizers, equally numerous and well-armed company forces, and the intervention of the U.S. Army Air Force. Even in the heavily unionized Illinois coalfields, the actions of an aggressive antiunion mine owner could precipitate outbursts of raw violence, as happened in "bloody Williamson County" in 1922. And as the United Mine Workers lost contracts between 1922 and 1930 in the northern fields, striking miners resorted to violence and also became its victims.

The primary case in which violence marred industrial relations in a sector of the economy where unions had a strong presence affected the construction trades. Many building and construction trades workers had sufficient power to compel smaller

**Ohio National Guardsmen protect entering workers during a strike at the Univis Lens Company of Dayton, Ohio, August 1948.** LIBRARY OF CONGRESS

local construction companies to recognize and bargain with them. However, larger nationwide construction companies linked to powerful antiunion firms in the steel industry sought to dilute the power of building trades workers, especially the International Association of Bridge, Structural, and Ornamental Iron Workers. In response, union leaders organized a coordinated plan of violence against antiunion employers that culminated in the dynamiting of the *Los Angeles Times* building in 1910. That bloody event produced two significant results. First, it led to the trial of two officers of the Iron Workers' union who confessed their guilt, and to subsequent trials and guilty verdicts for other union officials for their part in similar episodes of violence. Second, and perhaps more important, it resulted in the appointment of a federal commission to investigate industrial relations in the United States; in 1915 the commission produced an eleven-volume final report, its findings prompting one historian to aptly characterize the years 1910–1915 as "an age of industrial violence."

The last great wave of strike violence occurred during the labor upheaval associated with the Great Depression and New Deal of the 1930s. Once

again, when employers resisted their workers' demand to unionize, violence followed. In Minneapolis–St. Paul, the waterfront of San Francisco, and southern textile mills in 1934; in Flint, Michigan; Chicago; and several smaller steel towns in 1937; and everywhere in the South throughout the decade, employers' efforts to beat back unionism precipitated violence. As world war approached, however, strike violence began to diminish, and during the war relations between unions and corporations grew more routinized.

### Industrial Conflict as Ritual

For a quarter of a century after World War II, strikes remained at peak levels, yet violence proved the exception. Employers accepted unionism and collective bargaining, did not hire strikebreakers, and declined to continue operating. Indeed, whenever employers honored the principles of unionism and collective bargaining, strikes served more as a ritual in which workers affirmed their brotherhood (and sisterhood) and solidarity and less as a form of class war in which the means justified the ends.

Nevertheless, some employers continued to resist unionism, and in those cases, especially when workers evinced a strong desire to organize, violence ensued. Such was the case in Kohler, Wisconsin, where the Kohler Company during the 1950s and 1960s waged war against a local of the United Automobile Workers, and the adversaries both resorted to violence. And such was often the case everywhere in the South where employers, backed by the state, firmly resisted unionism. But for the most part, between 1945 and 1973 large well-organized unions managed to live peacefully with employers, even when the former saw no alternative to strikes as a weapon in collective bargaining.

Beginning in the 1970s, however, unions began to lose members. As union power diminished, employers operated during strikes with replacement workers. But even frustrated and defeated strikers now rarely turned to violence. Why is not entirely clear. Perhaps police (private as well as public) and military forces had grown more efficient and effective in regulating violence during industrial disputes. Whatever the reason, not only did strike violence abate, but by the 1990s the number of strikes, especially large ones, fell to levels not seen since the late 1920s or prior to the industrial era.

*BIBLIOGRAPHY*

Avrich, Paul. *The Haymarket Tragedy.* Princeton, N.J.: Princeton University Press, 1984.

Brecher, Jeremy. *Strike!* Boston: South End, 1997.

Bruce, Robert V. *1877: Year of Violence.* Chicago: Ivan R. Dee, 1989.

Dubofsky, Melvyn. *Industrialism and the American Worker, 1865–1920.* Arlington Heights, Ill.: Harlan Davidson, 1996.

Edwards, P. K. *Strikes in the United States, 1881–1974.* New York: St. Martin's, 1981.

Fine, Sidney. *"Without Blare of Trumpets": Walter Drew, the National Erectors' Association, and the Open Shop Movement, 1903–57.* Ann Arbor: University of Michigan Press, 1995.

Krause, Paul. *The Battle for Homestead, 1880–1892: Politics, Culture, and Steel.* Pittsburgh: University of Pittsburgh Press, 1992.

Lukas, J. Anthony. *Big Trouble: A Murder in a Small Western Town Sets Off a Struggle for the Soul of America.* New York: Simon and Schuster, 1997.

Taft, Philip, and Philip Ross. "American Labor Violence: Its Causes, Character, and Outcome." In *Violence in America: Historical and Comparative Perspectives,* edited by Hugh Davis Graham and Ted Robert Gurr. New York: New American Library, 1969.

MELVYN DUBOFSKY

*See also* **Anarchism; Bombings and Bomb Scares; Civil Disorder; Depressions, Economic; Haymarket Square Riot; Haywood, William; Labor and Unions; Los Angeles Times Building, Bombing of; Molly Maguires; Pullman Strike.**

## STRUCTURAL VIOLENCE

Throughout history and around the world, in every society in which wealth and income have been unequally distributed, the poor have suffered deaths and disabilities at higher rates than the wealthy. These excess rates of mortality and morbidity have been called *structural violence* by Johan Galtung and others: structural because they are caused by the social and economic structure of society (its division into rich and poor), and violence because they are injuries to people that are caused by acts of man, not acts of God. Deaths and illnesses from natural causes are not considered to be "violent" if they are not caused and could not be prevented by people's behavior. Violent deaths and injuries, by contrast, can be defined as those that are inflicted on people by people. By that definition, the increased rates of death and disability that are suffered by the poor as a result of the social and economic structure of society are a form of violence, because the division of any given society into rich and poor is caused not by God or nature but by the collective decisions made by people concerning how to share, or not share, their collective wealth and income.

Structural violence can be contrasted with behavioral violence—that is, violent behavior, such as homicide, suicide, capital punishment, and warfare—from which it differs in at least three major respects. First, its lethal effects operate continuously rather than discontinuously or sporadically (one at a time), as the various forms of behavioral violence do. Second, structural violence can occur more or less independently of any intention or wish to kill anyone. It can be an inadvertent by-product of the pursuit of other goals, such as maximizing one's own wealth and power. Third, structural violence is normally invisible, as compared with behavioral violence, in the sense that the deaths caused by structural violence (which include both natural and violent deaths) may appear to have had other (natural or violent) causes. Neither the existence nor the scope and extent of structural violence may be discerned, or even be discernible, until there is a shift from a perspective in which the focus is on the highly visible deaths that occur one individual or war at a time to the epidemiological perspective of public health and preventive medicine. That approach, rather than examining just the individual violent event or case history, also compares the vital statistics of different groups—noticing, for example, the extreme differentials among demographic groups, such as social classes and castes, in their life expectancies and death rates.

All the wars, murders, suicides, and genocides throughout history have not even begun to kill as many people as have been killed by the economic deprivations to which the poor are subjected. Gandhi was correct, then, when he observed that the deadliest form of violence is poverty. Thus structural violence is the most destructive form of violence, for it kills far more people than behavioral violence. However, all forms of violence, like all human behaviors, both healthy and pathological, are multidetermined; they have biological, psychological, and social causes. Structural violence is the main social cause of behavioral violence. As Plato put it, poverty is the mother of crime (although that relationship is complicated by the mediation of an intervening psychological cause—the feeling of shame, humiliation, and inferiority—which is itself stimulated by being in a humble and inferior social and economic class or caste).

Most behavioral violence is committed by those who are the victims of structural violence—that is, the poor and disadvantaged. Most of the victims of behavioral violence are also poor. From that perspective, behavioral violence itself is simply a subset of the various forms of structural violence. In other words, structural violence does not kill people only by subjecting them to the lethal effects of malnutrition, ignorance, polluted water, toxic chemicals, poor medical care, hazardous working conditions, rat bites, substandard housing, homelessness, and the psychophysiological effects of the stresses associated with poverty—all of which have been shown to increase death rates among the lower classes and castes—but also by increasing the likelihood that they will be subjected to the various forms of behavioral violence—murder, rape, assault, capital punishment, child abuse, police brutality, lynching, war, and so on.

### The Deadliest Form of Violence

In the United States the poverty rate among blacks is three times as high as it is among whites,

and the unemployment rate is twice as high, decade after decade. These facts are directly related to the fact that black babies die at two to three times the rate of white babies, and black mothers die at three to five times the rate of white mothers—year after year. The age-adjusted death rates for blacks as a whole have exceeded those for whites by about 300 per 100,000 population per year ever since those comparisons started being made in 1960. In 1993, for example, the age-adjusted death rate for whites was 490, but for blacks it was 790. From the 1960s to the 1990s the U.S. national murder rate, which never rose above 10 or 11 per 100,000, was considered virtually a national emergency and a major factor in presidential elections, and yet the death rate from structural violence among blacks was around 300 per 100,000. Such comparisons make it clear how distorted a picture is painted of the true nature, location, and dimensions of violence in the United States when attention is paid only to the type that is defined by the legal system as criminal.

But what reason do we have for assuming that relative poverty causes death? Could it be that the excess deaths among blacks are caused by their own behavior patterns (as if those were independent of social and economic circumstances, which we know they are not) or by hereditary biological differences between blacks and whites? Several lines of evidence suggest that both of those hypotheses are not the explanation and that both absolute and relative poverty can have lethal consequences independent of the behavior or heredity of the victims. For example, a nationwide study conducted by the U.S. Public Health Service from 1971 to 1984 found that only about one-third of the "excess mortality" suffered by blacks aged thirty-five to fifty-four was associated with the six known major health risks: smoking, obesity, alcohol consumption, hypertension, diabetes, and elevated cholesterol levels. The remaining two-thirds could be accounted for only by the direct and indirect effects of low socioeconomic status itself, that is, the relative deprivation or poverty that blacks suffer from at vastly higher rates than whites: such factors as low family income, unequal access to health care, and the pathogenic (indeed, lethal) psychophysiological stresses caused by lower class and caste status.

Colin McCord and Harold P. Freeman, in a study published in 1990, found that death rates between the ages of five and sixty-five were higher in Harlem, New York, than in Bangladesh. The lethal effects of being a black in Harlem were especially strong for men, who were substantially less likely to reach the age of sixty-five (in fact, less likely to live beyond the age of forty) than were men in Bangladesh. Comparing the death rate in Harlem's almost entirely black population with that of the white population of the United States, they found that only 45 percent of the excess deaths in Harlem could be attributed to behavioral, nonnatural causes (homicides, accidents, and substance abuse); the remaining 55 percent were attributed to natural causes such as heart disease and cancer but occurred at rates two to three times higher than in the white population in this country. McCord and Freeman pointed out that the number of excess deaths in Harlem and the poorest areas of other cities was considerably larger than the number of deaths in places the U.S. government had designated as natural-disaster areas, so why was this devastation not treated with the same degree of urgency?

Both of the studies of excess black death rates found that the most important natural cause of death in this group was cardiovascular disease, especially hypertension. Hussein A. Bulhan has reviewed several studies showing that while high blood pressure is common among American, West Indian, and urbanized African blacks, it is infrequent among rural Africans—that is, those least exposed to the social and economic structure and traditions of colonialism, slavery, inferior class and caste status, and white domination. That suggests that the excess deaths caused by hypertension among blacks in our society are at least in part a psychophysiological response to a lifetime of being treated as inferior and subjected to the systematic rejections, humiliations, and insults of racial discrimination and lower class and caste status rather than heredity. There are also other causes of the excess death rate in the black community. Bulhan, for example, has summarized studies from industrial and military medicine showing that blacks are disproportionately assigned to more hazardous industrial jobs, giving them the highest exposure to carcinogenic smoke and fumes, and to higher-risk military assignments.

### An International Perspective

The finding that structural violence is far deadlier than behavioral violence is not limited to the United States. Gernot Kohler and Norman Alcock (1976) devised two ways to measure the number of excess deaths caused by socioeconomic inequities on a worldwide basis. The first measure used Sweden as the nation that had come closest to eliminating structural violence, because Sweden had the least inequity in living standards and the lowest discrepancies in the various indices of morbidity and mortality between people at the extreme ends of the socioeconomic spectrum; it also had the highest overall life expectancy for a country as a whole. When Kohler and Alcock compared life expectancies everywhere else in the world with that of Sweden, they found that 18 million deaths a year could be attributed to the "structural violence" to which the citizens of all the other nations of the world were being subjected by the socioeconomic systems in which they were living.

The second measure, the "egalitarian" model, began with the empirical finding that life expectancy throughout the world is, on average, a function of relative social position; that is, the higher one's relative socioeconomic status, the longer one can expect to live. They then asked what would happen if there were a complete and equal redistribution of currently available global resources; that is, if the gross world product were equitably distributed so that every country had the same gross national product (GNP) per capita and every individual in the world had the same income. By plotting life expectancy against GNP per capita for each nation on earth, they were able to show that the life expectancy for nations with a GNP per capita that corresponded to the world average was 68.3 years. Comparing that with the actual life expectancies of the different nations on earth, they were able to calculate a worldwide total of 14 million deaths a year due to structural violence as of 1965. As they put it, "Wealth cannot only buy a higher standard of living, it also buys life itself."

The 14 million to 18 million deaths a year estimated to be caused by structural violence were about two orders of magnitude (that is, a hundred times) greater than the death toll from behavioral violence (including war and murder) in that same year. In fact, when Kohler and Alcock compared the frequency of deaths from structural violence to the frequency of those caused by World War II (an estimated 49 million military and civilian deaths, or about 8 million per year from 1939 to 1945) or even by a hypothetical nuclear exchange between the United States and the former Soviet Union (232 million), it was clear that very few actual or hypothetical forms of even the most deadly military violence could begin to compare with structural violence—especially since the latter continues year after year, during times of peace as well as of war.

In other words, every fifteen years, on average, as many people die because of relative poverty as would be killed in a nuclear war that caused 232 million deaths, and every single year at least two to three times as many people die from poverty throughout the world as were killed by the Nazi genocide of the Jews. This is, in effect, the equivalent of an ongoing, unending, in fact accelerating thermonuclear war, or genocide, perpetrated on the weak and poor every year of every decade throughout the world. But perhaps the most astonishing result of Kohler and Alcock's research was that while the 68.3 years of life that could be expected if the world's wealth were equitably distributed was about forty years higher than the lowest recorded national average, it was only six years less than the highest life expectancy (74.7 years, in Sweden). In other words, under conditions of complete global equality, the rich countries would lose only minor amounts of life expectancy, whereas the poor would gain tremendously.

More recent figures bear out that conclusion even more startlingly. The United Nations Human Development Report for 1998 points out that it would only cost about $40 billion a year beyond what is already being spent to provide universal access to basic education and health care and adequate food, safe water, and sanitation for everyone in the world and reproductive health care for all women. This is less than 4 percent of the combined wealth of the 225 richest individuals in the world, whose total net worth is more than $1 trillion. And at a more mundane level, Europeans spend $50 billion a year on cigarettes and $11 billion on ice cream; the United States and Europe together spend $20 billion on perfumes and cosmetics and $17 billion on pet foods. Whatever may be the reason for failing to prevent much of the structural violence in the world, expense is not one of them.

**The Main Cause of Behavioral Violence**

The rates of murder and other violent crimes are far higher among the lower classes and castes than they are among the rich and powerful. In the United States, for example, blacks commit murder and other violent crimes six to fourteen times as frequently as whites (almost always against other blacks, which leads to the tragic irony that the main victims of structural violence are also the main victims of behavioral violence). As the political scientist Hannah Arendt put it, violence is inversely proportional to power. Those who have power do not need to engage in violent behavior themselves in order to get what they want; it flows to them automatically through the normal operations of the socioeconomic system, and when it does not, or when violence is needed in order to enforce that system, they can always pay other people, such as police, prisons, and armies, to commit it for them.

Throughout the world and throughout the United States, the most powerful predictor of the individual homicide rate is the size of the gap in income and wealth between the rich and the poor—the higher the gap, the higher the murder rate—whether one is comparing the different nations of the world or the different states, counties, or cities of the United States. And the most powerful predictor of the frequency and severity of collective violence (war, civil war, insurrection) is the size of the gap in income and wealth between the rich and poor nations. In other words, the greater the degree of structural violence, the greater the degree of behavioral violence.

Since the end of World War II, when every developed nation except the United States adopted a system of social democracy (or a "welfare state," as it is sometimes called), their murder rates have remained on average only about one-tenth as high as that of the United States. This is not surprising, given that Americans have the highest poverty rate, and the largest gap between the rich and the poor, of all those countries, and the United States is the only one not to have provided universal health insurance and other methods of preventing structural violence. Or consider an even more extreme example. The Hutterites, an Anabaptist sect that practices "primitive Christian communism" (the communal sharing of wealth) so that its practitioners are as classless as any society in history, have experienced no murders, rapes, robberies, or even serious assaults during the century since they emigrated to North America from Europe in 1874.

All of those facts can be understood when one considers the individual psychology of violence and how it is related to the social phenomena of class and caste. The most powerful psychological cause of violent behavior is the feeling of being shamed, humiliated, insulted, slighted, disrespected, rejected, and treated as if one were inferior and a failure. The most powerful social cause of those feelings is the experience of belonging to a lower, or inferior, social class or caste. That is why structural violence (relative poverty, lower class or caste status) is the most powerful social cause of behavioral violence. Structural violence does not cause behavioral violence directly; the causal mechanism operates indirectly, via an intervening psychological variable, the feeling of shame.

The concept of structural violence not only explains the social cause of behavioral violence (and therefore its social epidemiology, or distribution among different social groups) but also shows how both forms of violence can be prevented—namely, by distributing income and wealth more equitably. In the nineteenth century we discovered that cleaning up the water supply was more effective in preventing contagious disease than all the doctors, hospitals, and medicines in the world. Now we can see that cleaning up our social and economic system by sharing our collective income and wealth equitably will do far more to prevent violence than all the police, prisons, and punishments—and all the armies, armaments, and artillery—in the world. In fact, it is precisely those methods of attempting to prevent violence through more violence that have been the main causes of violence, because the violence of the state and the legal system is precisely what maintains the structural violence that causes the behavioral violence that the state and its violence are ostensibly needed to combat.

*BIBLIOGRAPHY*

Arendt, Hannah. *On Violence.* New York: Vintage, 1969.

Bulhan, Hussein A. "Structural Violence and Premature Death." In *Frantz Fanon and the Psychology of Oppression.* New York: Plenum, 1985.

Galtung, Johan. "A Structural Theory of Aggression" and "Feudal Systems, Structural Violence, and the Structural Theory of Revolution." In *Essays in Peace Research.* Vol. 3, *Peace and Social Structure.* PRIO Monographs from the International Peace Research Institute, Oslo. Copenhagen: Christian Ejlers, 1975.

———. "Violence, Peace and Peace Research" and "Structural and Direct Violence: A Note on Operationalization." In *Essays in Peace Research.* Vol. 1, *Peace: Research, Education, Action.* PRIO Monographs from the International Peace Research Institute, Oslo. Copenhagen: Christian Ejlers, 1975.

Gilligan, James. *Violence: Our Deadly Epidemic and Its Causes.* New York: Putnam, 1996. Also published in paperback as *Violence: Reflections on a National Epidemic.* New York: Vintage, 1997. See esp. chap. 8, "The Deadliest Form of Violence Is Poverty."

Graubard, Stephen R., ed. "Health and Wealth." *Proceedings of the American Academy of Arts and Sciences* 123, no. 4 (1994).

James, Oliver. *Juvenile Violence in a Winner-Loser Culture: Socio-Economic and Familial Origins of the Rise of Violence Against the Person.* London and New York: Free Association Books, 1995.

Kaplan, G. A., et al. "Income Inequality and Mortality in the United States." *British Medical Journal* 312 (1996).

Kohler, Gernot, and Norman Alcock. "An Empirical Table of Structural Violence." *Journal of Peace Research* 13 (1976). Reprinted in *Peace and Violence: Quantitative Studies in International and Civil Conflict,* edited by Anita Kemp. New Haven, Conn.: Human Relations Area Files, 1980.

McCord, Colin, and Harold P. Freeman. "Excess Mortality in Harlem." *New England Journal of Medicine* 322, no. 3 (1990).

Margalit, Avishai. *The Decent Society.* Cambridge, Mass.: Harvard University Press, 1996.

Otten, Mac W., Jr., et al. "The Effect of Known Risk Factors on the Excess Mortality of Black Adults in the United States." *Journal of the American Medical Association* 263, no. 6 (1990).

Reiman, Jeffrey. *The Rich Get Richer and the Poor Get Prison: Ideology, Crime, and Criminal Justice.* 4th ed. Boston: Allyn and Bacon, 1995.

Sennett, Richard, and Jonathan Cobb. *The Hidden Injuries of Class.* New York: Vintage, 1973.

Smith, M. Dwayne, and Margaret A. Zahn, eds. *Homicide: A Sourcebook of Social Research.* Thousand Oaks, Calif.: Sage, 1999.

———. *Studying and Preventing Homicide: Issues and Challenges.* Thousand Oaks, Calif.: Sage, 1999.

Townsend, Peter, Nick Davidson, and Margaret Whitehead, eds. *Inequalities in Health: "The Black Report" and "The Health Divide."* London: Penguin, 1992.

Wilkinson, Richard G. *Unhealthy Societies: The Afflictions of Inequality.* London and New York: Routledge, 1996.

JAMES GILLIGAN

*See also* **Capitalism; Class; Developmental Factors; Drugs: Drugs and Violence; Health and Medical Factors; Homelessness; Nature vs. Nurture; Poverty; Shame; Theories of Violence: Behavioral Sciences.**

# SUBURBAN VIOLENCE

The widely held belief that suburbs are safer—especially as regards violent crime—than urban areas is borne out by statistics. But the issue of suburban violence is more complex than any set of numbers can convey.

## Early American Suburbs

The term *suburban* is ambiguous at best. Most urban historians look to the mid-nineteenth century for the first trends in American suburbanization. At that time, although most Americans still lived in rural areas, cities were growing rapidly. Before the cultural development of the suburban ideal, the division of city and countryside was stark. The rich were nestled in the city center, and outlying urban areas had a reputation for unsavory characters—wage earners, immigrants, and other undesirables. Nineteenth-century suburban areas—labeled "suburban slums" by the urban historian Kenneth Jackson—were regarded by city dwellers as danger zones.

In the mid-nineteenth century technological advances in transportation combined with reform movements that romanticized nature to foster a suburban ideal that added the convenience and culture of the city to the comfort and cleanliness of rural living. For those who could afford it, this "suburban ideal" was found in planned, private, racially homogenous communities of single-family, detached dwellings on the urban fringe. Free from the perceived problems and violence of urban life—both crimes and accidents—yet retaining proximity to the city with rail transit, suburban life became fashionable among wealthy exiles from the city center.

## The Postwar Suburban Ideal

The initial suburban impetus was a trickle compared to the widespread suburbanization of the twentieth century, especially after World War II, when urban racial tensions increased and the federal government began to subsidize suburbanization with federal highways and guaranteed home loans. The postwar era marked what some historians called the "urban crisis" in America, when cities—especially inner-city areas—suffered abandonment, rising unemployment, and segregation as wealthy residents and corporations left for the suburbs. Essentially, the suburbanization movement was a self-fulfilling prophecy of doom for the major cities and their disadvantaged minorities. The urban exodus, fleeing the central cities' growing unemployment, racial conflict, and violent crime, aggravated all of these problems by draining wealth and a tax base from areas most in need of them.

A key motivation in postwar suburbanization, as it was in the nineteenth century, was quest for greater safety. In large part, suburbs were and are safer; violent crimes are usually lower in suburban areas. For example, in 1993 personal victimization rates for crimes of violence—defined as rape, robbery, and assault—for American cities was 73.4 victimizations per thousand people; for suburban areas the rate was 47.5 victimizations per thousand (U.S. Department of Justice 1996, p. 54). Other studies corroborate this urban-suburban disparity. In all of these studies suburban areas are defined as areas outside central cities.

## Complicating the Safe Suburb

A few violent crimes are higher in suburban areas, though. For example, in 1992 children in suburban areas were more likely to be sexually abused. However, in urban areas, the percentage of children kidnapped or assaulted was higher. The overall percentage of children victimized in city areas was 59.6 percent, compared with 53.6 percent in suburban areas—a marginal difference (Dobrin 1996, p. 144). In addition, in 1993 females were more likely to be victims of verbal threats of assault in suburban areas, although almost all other kinds of female victimization were significantly higher in urban areas (p. 157).

The statistical safety of suburbs is offset by a few other factors. For example, suburbanites usually drive more often and longer distances than urban dwellers (some of whom do not drive at all), thus increasing their chances of dying violently in an auto accident, particularly drunk-driving accidents.

Moreover, the clear dichotomy between suburban and urban areas has blurred in recent years as certain suburban settlements have developed urbanlike crime rates and cities with suburbanlike densities have developed urban crime rates. In the case of Camden, New Jersey (an eastern suburb of Philadelphia), and Inglewood, California, violent crime rates have risen to levels more typical of urban "problem" areas. Los Angeles and other southwestern cities, meanwhile, with their suburban densities, remain plagued by urbanlike levels of violence.

Other suburban areas were witnessing increases in violent crime in the 1990s. A 1997 article in New Jersey's *Newark Star-Ledger* stated that in that state, overall suburban crime was decreasing while suburban violent crime was increasing, making violent crime a greater proportion of crime in these areas. If the suburbs are safer than cities, then certainly some suburbs are safer than others. Coupled with decreasing crime rates found in many cities, the rise in some suburban crime rates has corroded the suburban mantle of serenity and security. In addition many urban planners have questioned the isolated lifestyle fostered by suburban living, especially in relation to adolescents. School shootings—like the 1999 mass murder in the suburban community of Littleton, Colorado, by two students—have confirmed the worst fears of many, placing suburban violence on the national agenda. It is doubtful, however, that this or other incidents confirm any inherent murderous tendency in suburban youth.

### Conclusion

Statistical evidence supports the statement that suburbs are safer than urban areas. According to Department of Justice statistics, from 1973 to 1990 the rate of urban and suburban violent crimes for the country as a whole has decreased almost uniformly. Some violent crimes are more likely in the suburbs, however, and some suburban areas are equaling urban areas in violent crime rates.

*BIBLIOGRAPHY*

Dobrin, Adam, et al. *Statistical Handbook on Violence in America.* Phoenix, Ariz.: Oryx, 1996.

Jackson, Kenneth T. *Crabgrass Frontier: The Suburbanization of the United States.* New York: Oxford University Press, 1985.

Sherman, Ted. "New Jersey Crime Down—Except for Violent Crime in Suburbs." *Newark (N.J.) Star-Ledger,* 18 May 1998.

U.S. Department of Justice. *Criminal Victimization in the United States: 1973–1992 Trends.* Washington, D.C.: U.S. Department of Justice, 1994.

U.S. Department of Justice. *Criminal Victimization in the United States, 1993.* Washington, D.C.: U.S. Department of Justice, 1996.

GREGORY L. PARKER

*See also* **Geography of Violence; Rural Violence; Urban Violence.**

# SUFFRAGE

Americans, it has been said, have historical amnesia about violence. This is especially true when one considers the violence associated with the suffrage movements of women and of African Americans. The frequently forgotten battles over suf-

frage, both in law and in practice, were hard fought, dangerous, and often bloody.

### Women's Suffrage

The history of the women's suffrage movement begins at the 1848 Seneca Falls Convention in New York State, among whose goals were full voting rights. Women suffragists expected to attain their goal with the passage of the Fifteenth Amendment (1870) to the U.S. Constitution but were bitterly disappointed when the amendment only gave African American men the franchise. Suffrage activists had already formed the radical National Women's Suffrage Association and the more conservative American Woman Suffrage Association in 1869, and in 1888 the two associations merged to become the National American Woman Suffrage Association (NAWSA), which continued to lobby Congress peacefully to take up the cause of women's suffrage. Although a women's suffrage amendment was introduced in Congress every year from 1879 to 1919, senators and representatives rarely debated the issue and voted on the issue only once; the amendment failed to pass in 1914.

By the turn of the twentieth century, a new generation of women reformers was ready to add its voice to the chorus calling for another voting amendment to the Constitution. These younger activists such as Harriot Stanton Blatch and Alice Paul were veterans of the British suffrage movement. They had been arrested with their English counterparts, jailed, and force-fed while on hunger strikes. Both brought that intense commitment to suffrage to the United States.

Initially, these suffragettes were a part of NAWSA. During President Woodrow Wilson's first inauguration in Washington, D.C., in 1913, they led a parade down Pennsylvania Avenue. The march drew the ire of male onlookers who attacked the women while police watched idly. Such hostile activities eventually sparked a division between NAWSA's radicals and conservatives. By 1916 Paul and her followers had left the association and formed the National Woman's Party (NWP), which continued to demand publicly for the right of women to vote. Their chosen method of protest was picketing in front of the White House. Frequently, men seeing the demonstrations would attack the suffragists. Rather than apprehend their male assailants, the police arrested the women on trumped-up charges. The NWP sentinels, as they were called, were convicted and sent to Virginia's

Occoquan Workhouse, where many were beaten and mistreated. When Paul was finally arrested in 1917 and detained at Occoquan, she began a hunger strike. After moving her to the psychiatric ward, prison officials subjected her to force-feedings, a violent and painful procedure. Despite the torture and terror, which included the destruction of NWP headquarters, radical suffragists continued to pressure President Wilson and Congress to act on their demand. At first, Wilson maintained the police repression. Over the three years that the NWP staged pickets, more than 500 women were arrested and 168 were jailed. The brutality caused congressmen and eventually Wilson to reconsider their positions on suffrage, which then paved the way for the passage of the Nineteenth Amendment (1920). After the women gained the franchise, the fears of antisuffrage men who thought that women voting would disrupt American politics were never realized, and the violence subsided.

**African American Suffrage**

In some ways, the African American suffrage movement had the opposite problem of the women's movement. The passage of the Fifteenth Amendment was a relatively peaceful act. During the century that followed, however, exercising the vote was a dangerous and at times deadly enterprise for blacks. Until the 1820s free blacks had voted frequently in several northern and southern states, but by 1830 most state legislatures had made suffrage a white privilege. The Reconstruction amendments to the Constitution (the Thirteenth, Fourteenth, and Fifteenth Amendments, passed in 1865, 1868, and 1870, respectively) allowed for a return of African American political participation. But exercising one's rights came at a cost. By extralegal means southern whites, organized in groups such as the Ku Klux Klan, opposed black suffrage. For instance, in 1870 and 1874, whites rioted in Alabama to terrorize Republicans, to disenfranchise blacks, and to give electoral victory to the Democrats. On both occasions the violence produced the intended results. The federal government did little to stop the terrorism. By the end of the nineteenth century, black voting was infrequent and only took place where the number of blacks was sparse.

The nature of black suffrage shifted shortly after 1914. The manpower demands of World War I drew approximately half a million blacks from the South to northern and western cities, where they voted more freely. By the late 1940s African Amer-

icans were a political force not only in cities such as Chicago, New York, and Los Angeles but also in many states, including Georgia and North Carolina as federal judges began to enforce voting rights laws. The rise in black voting coincided with an increase in white violence. Undaunted, a voting rights movement emerged as part of the postwar Civil Rights movement. The Voter Education Project (VEP), coordinated by the Southern Christian Leadership Conference, the Student Nonviolent Coordinating Committee, and the Congress of Racial Equality, attempted to register voters in the Deep South. Activists such as Bob Moses led marches and instructional seminars to foster black voter participation. In an attempt to maintain black disenfranchisement, whites established new vigilante groups such as citizen's councils and resuscitated the Klan. Violence was also perpetrated by southern police who commonly arrested, jailed, and beat civil rights workers. By the early 1960s whites were also resorting to murder. One of the most gruesome incidents occurred during the 1964 Freedom Summer, when white and black civil rights workers from around the country, many of them college students, tried to register black voters. In Mississippi a group of whites abducted, tortured, and shot Andrew Goodman, Michael Schwerner, and James Chaney. Again, violence against those pushing for suffrage prompted federal action. By 1965, when Congress passed the Voting Rights Act, which put the Justice Department squarely behind those seeking to exercise the franchise, there had been in the South more than a thousand arrests, eighty beatings, thirty-five shootings, and thirty bombings related to the VEP.

By the 1990s, as the federal government had strongly enforced voting rights, violence relating to suffrage dissipated for both African Americans and women as well.

*BIBLIOGRAPHY*

Branch, Taylor. *Parting the Waters: America in the King Years, 1954–1963.* New York: Simon and Schuster, 1989.
Shapiro, Herbert. *White Violence and Black Response: From Reconstruction to Montgomery.* Amherst: University of Massachusetts Press, 1988.
Stevens, Doris. *Jailed for Freedom: American Women Win the Vote.* Edited by Carol O'Hare. Troutdale, Oreg.: New Sage, 1995.

ANDREW E. KERSTEN

*See also* **African Americans; Civil Disobedience; Civil Rights Movements; Women.**

# SUICIDE

*Suicide* (from the Latin *sui,* "of oneself," and *caedere,* "to kill") can be defined briefly as the act of intentionally ending one's own life. Accounts of men and women taking their own lives appear throughout recorded history, going back to Greco-Roman literature and the Old and New Testaments.

From earliest accounts it seems that suicide, although prohibited for criminals and slaves (for whom it was seen as an attempt to escape punishment or duty), was at times viewed as the honorable or noble solution to a problem or set of circumstances. The fact that neither the Old Testament nor the New Testament specifically prohibits suicide may reflect its relative infrequency in biblical times. Concern about suicide emerged later, when Christian theologians feared it might be encouraged by the promise of blissful immortality. This led to a strong condemnation of the practice by church leaders in the fourth century, most vigorously expressed by Saint Augustine. Suicide was seen as precluding the possibility of expiation, violating the Sixth Commandment—Thou shalt not kill—and usurping God's power to control man's life, death, and resurrection.

As recently as 1823 in England, suicide was punishable by refusal of proper burial, by forfeiture of one's property to the crown, and sometimes by punitive mutilation of the corpse. An exception was made in cases of insanity, and throughout the 1800s mental health professionals played an increasing role in the treatment of suicidal individuals. Nevertheless, suicide was considered a felony and attempted suicide a misdemeanor in English common law until 1961, when laws criminalizing both were abolished. In the United States most states had laws treating suicidal behavior as a crime, but these were seldom enforced and almost all had been repealed by 1960.

## Durkheim and Freud

Contemporary investigation of suicidal behavior could be said to have begun with the French sociologist Émile Durkheim, whose book on the subject, *Le suicide* (1897), addressed suicide as associated with a person's relationship to society. Durkheim formulated three main categories of suicide: *egoistic,* resulting from an individual's lack of integration into society (living alone, being unemployed); *altruistic,* following upon oversubmission to social norms (suicide for the "good" of one's society, such as hara-kiri and suttee); and *anomic,* stemming from the disruption of a person's social norms (divorce, financial reversal).

The first major contribution to understanding the psychological dimension of suicide was made by Sigmund Freud. In *Mourning and Melancholia* (1916), Freud stated that the self-hatred observed in depression originated in anger toward a love object that the individual turned back on himself. Freud postulated that suicide, the extreme outcome of such a process, reflected the repressed desire to kill someone else.

Although Durkheim's and Freud's contributions are still relevant, today we understand suicidal behavior as emerging from the complex interaction of epidemiological, psychiatric, biologic, genetic, personality, and social factors.

## Epidemiology

Suicide is the ninth leading cause of death in the United States. It is the third leading cause of death among young people ages fifteen to twenty-four, and the fourth leading cause of death among young adults ages twenty-five to thirty-four. There are over thirty-one thousand deaths by suicide in the United States each year, representing about 1.4 percent of all deaths in the country. The U.S. suicide rate of over eleven suicides per one hundred thousand deaths is in the middle range of industrialized countries, whose rates vary from less than three in one hundred thousand in Greece to over forty-five per hundred thousand in Lithuania.

*Age.* In general, the overall suicide rate in the United States increases with age. This is due largely to the high suicide rate of older white males. White men over fifty, comprising 10 percent of the population, are responsible for a third of all suicides. Women are responsible for fewer than 20 percent of all suicides. The female rate also rises with age, but only until ages forty to fifty-five; it then gradually declines.

*Attempted Suicide.* It is estimated that there are ten attempted suicides for every one completion. This ratio decreases with age from approximately 50:1 in adolescents to 2:1 in the elderly. While males complete suicide more than four times as often as females, females attempt suicide twice as often as males. A previous attempt greatly increases the likelihood of eventual suicide; about 10 percent of people who make a suicide attempt go on to kill themselves later in life.

## Youth Suicide

Although the overall U.S. suicide rate remained remarkably constant in the second half of the twentieth century, the suicide rate for males ages fifteen to twenty-four more than tripled, from 6.4 per 100,000 in 1957 to 22.6 in 1995. During this period, the suicide rate for this group became higher than the rate for the country as a whole (see figure 1). The rate for young females of the same age doubled during this period, from 1.8 per 100,000 in 1950 to 3.7 in 1995. Although white males were responsible for most of this long-term increase, the most dramatic increases in the late twentieth century were among young black males ages fifteen to nineteen, whose rate more than doubled between 1980 and 1995, from 5.6 per 100,000 to 13.8.

In the late twentieth century, suicide began to be seen at younger ages. The suicide rate of children ages ten to fourteen doubled in fifteen years from .8 per 100,000 in 1980 to 1.7 in 1995.

*Methods.* More than 60 percent of all people who kill themselves in the United States use a gun to do so. In fact, each year in the United States guns are used in more suicides than homicides. Hanging, gas, and sleeping pills are the other most commonly used suicide methods.

### Etiology

*Violence and Suicide.* Freud's theory seemed to link murder and suicide, but psychological thought on the subject over the next fifty years became dominated by the notion that the murderer expressed what the suicide repressed. Suicide and homicide were said to reflect opposite types of adjustment. Behavioral and social scientists posited an inverse relationship between suicide and violence. Social groups were presumed to deal with certain high levels of frustration or aggression by either suicide (committed by those at the upper end of the socioeconomic scale) or homicide (committed by those at the lower end). The high homicide rates and low suicide rates of American blacks were used as evidence in support of this view, as were the low homicide and high suicide rates in countries such as Sweden and Denmark.

Experience has invalidated such claims. Although homicide appears primarily in groups in the lower end of the socioeconomic scale, suicide is high in this group as well. Young urban blacks have high suicide and homicide rates. Among other cultures, there are those like Finland that have ranked high in both suicide and homicide, and others like Norway that rank low in both. Finally, taken as a group, individuals who kill themselves have committed homicide at a much higher rate than the population as a whole, and individuals who kill others have a suicide rate several hundred times greater than that of the overall population.

*Mental Illness.* Studies of adolescents and adults reveal that 90 to 95 percent of those who commit suicide have some diagnosable psychiatric illness. This illness is most often a depressive disorder (a factor in over 60 percent of all suicides), or a drug or alcohol substance-abuse disorder (a factor in 25–30 percent of adult and 50–70 percent of adolescent suicides). Other disorders often associated with suicide are schizophrenia and organic brain disorders in adults and conduct disorders and borderline personality disorder in adolescents.

Yet most people who are depressed, alcoholic, or schizophrenic do not die from suicide. Research has thus begun to focus on the risk factors within a diagnosis that distinguish those who are suicidal from those who are not. Feelings of hopelessness and aggressive and impulsive behavior are such factors that are often present in suicidal individuals.

*Biological Factors.* Neurobiologists have come to view suicide as a separate syndrome whose features can occur in a variety of diagnoses. Evidence for this conclusion has come from several sources: despite new effective treatments for specific psychiatric disorders, there has not been a reduction in the suicide rate; suicide occurs across a wide variety of psychiatric diagnoses; and biochemical findings suggest that there are abnormalities specific to suicidal behavior found regardless of the particular psychiatric diagnosis.

The most dramatic such finding came in the mid-1970s when Marie Åsberg and her colleagues at the Karolinska Institute in Sweden discovered that suicidal patients had low cerebrospinal fluid levels of 5-hydroxyindoleacetic acid (5-HIAA), a metabolite of the neurotransmitter serotonin that transmits nerve impulses across synapses. Al-

FIGURE 1. U.S. Suicide Rates for Total Population and for Males Ages 15–24

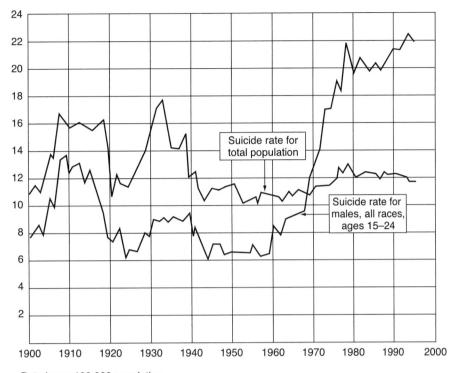

Rate is per 100,000 population.

SOURCE: U.S. Bureau of Vital Statistics.

though originally studied in depressed patients, low levels of 5-HIAA were observed in suicidal patients who were not clinically depressed but had a variety of disorders ranging from borderline and antisocial personality disorders to schizophrenia. Among patients who attempt suicide, those with low cerebrospinal fluid levels of 5-HIAA, regardless of diagnosis, have more than a 20 percent chance of killing themselves within a year. This risk factor is one of the strongest predictors of mortality in all of medicine.

Low levels of 5-HIAA were also found in arsonists, violent criminals, and murderers who committed their crimes in an impulsive manner. This finding has led researchers to consider poor impulse control and inability to regulate aggression as risk factors in suicidal behavior. It also seems to account for the overlap between those who are violent toward others as well as themselves.

The correlation between low levels of 5-HIAA and suicide does not, however, necessarily indicate a causal relationship. Both may result from a common, as yet unrecognized, cause. Nevertheless, the predictive capacity of low 5-HIAA levels in suicidal patients permits us to identify and con-

centrate treatment on those most at risk. Such advances give hope that our ability to pharmacologically influence serotonin levels may yet prove therapeutic in preventing suicide.

*Genetic Factors.* A family history of suicide is associated with an increased risk for attempted and completed suicide at all stages of the life cycle. Exactly what is being transmitted in these families has been open to question. Psychological factors, genes for depressive disorders, and genes for certain personality traits have all been implicated.

Studies of identical twins reveal that when one commits suicide, in more than 10 percent of cases the other twin commits suicide as well. With fraternal twins such concordance is rare, ranging in different studies from 0 to 2 percent.

Adoption studies, in which genetically related individuals have been separated soon after birth, show that there is significantly more suicide among the biological relatives of adoptees who commit suicide than in the families who adopt them. The fact that the suicides occur independent of the presence of psychiatric disorders in the biological families suggests that there may be a

239

genetic predisposition for suicide independent of, or in addition to, the psychiatric disorders associated with suicide.

Another study looked at suicide and affective disorder over a one-hundred-year period in the Amish population. The vast majority of the suicides were diagnosed as having a major affective disorder and the suicides occurred in multigenerational families with a high frequency of affective disorders. The clustering of the suicides, however, in only four of the affective disorder family trees suggested that there might be genetic factors for suicide apart from those for affective disorders.

Further evidence is provided by molecular genetic studies. Molecular variation in the gene on chromosome 11 responsible for serotonin synthesis has been shown to be strongly correlated with suicidal and other impulsive behavior. Impulsivity may be the inherited factor that makes some individuals particularly vulnerable to suicide, with a psychiatric disorder or environmental stress serving as a trigger mechanism. This would be consistent with the finding of low concentrations of serotonin in both suicidal patients and individuals with impulsive disorders.

*Psychodynamic Factors.*  Although suicide is often described imprecisely as an escape from life, it is the possibility of escaping from an intolerable affective state that usually leads patients to commit or contemplate suicide. Among depressed patients, for example, the seriousness of suicidal intent has been shown to be related more to one specific aspect of depression—hopelessness about the future—than to the severity of the depression.

In addition to hopelessness, desperation, rage, and guilt predominate in suicidal patients. The nature and intensity of these emotions help us to distinguish further patients who are suicidal from those who are not.

Some patients who feel hopeless about the future are resigned to the situation. Desperation implies not only hopelessness about change but also a feeling that life is impossible without such change. Anxiety and urgency are an integral part of this desperation. The importance of these clinical affective elements is confirmed by research that demonstrated that among patients with a major depressive disorder, anxiety is a stronger predictor of short-term risk for suicide than is hopelessness.

Rage that threatens to overwhelm the individual is often a precipitant of suicide. Such individuals often alternate between a lifeless depression and outbursts of rage. Some are terrified at their inability to control their rage and see death as the only solution.

Guilt as a trigger for suicide is seen in depressed patients and has been perhaps best described in Vietnam combat veterans. Guilt over actions in combat, usually the killing of civilians—and most often when the soldier was feeling out of control—is the most consistent explanation for these veterans' suicidal behavior.

The cognitive component of the meaning of suicide helps clarify the affective aspects of the suicidal act. For example, the guilt of Vietnam veterans over their combat actions complements their widely shared view of suicide as a deserved punishment. "Cognition" generally refers to conscious ideation, whereas "meaning" includes both conscious and unconscious affects and perceptions. The meanings of suicide can be usefully organized around the conscious and unconscious meanings given to death by the suicidal patient.

We have learned that suicidal patients give a special meaning to death, using it to help adapt to life. They use, or fantasize using, their own death to control others or to maintain an illusory control over their own lives. Many see death as an act of reunion, rebirth, retaliatory abandonment, revenge, and self-punishment or atonement.

Although psychiatrists continue to see a wider range of psychodynamics producing suicide, Freud's seminal insight into the relationship of abandonment, loss, and suicide has stood the test of time. All of these meanings ascribed to death by suicidal patients can be conceptualized as responses to loss, separation, or abandonment.

- Rebirth and reunion fantasies undo or deny such a loss.
- Becoming the one who leaves avoids the feeling of having been left.
- Feelings of rage that are repressed, suppressed, or expressed may derive from the experience of loss.
- Self-punishment may express both guilt at provoking a loss and the fantasy of rapprochement through atonement.
- Numbness or deadness and the insistence that one is already psychologically dead may reflect determination not to live without the lost object.
- For most suicidal patients a rejection of life usually includes a rejection of the parents from whom it originated (whether or not

they are alive). Persons so doing are likely to feel in a deep way that they themselves were abandoned first.

### New Social Factors

*Firearms.* Gun accessibility makes it possible for impulsive persons to act on suicidal impulses. Higher suicide rates in some states correlate with higher rates of gun ownership in those states—especially handguns. The states with more restrictive gun laws have lower rates of firearm suicides, and, although they have higher rates of suicide committed by other means, their suicide rate is lower overall. Studies have also found that suicide rates, particularly among the young, fall in the years following the enactment of laws restricting handgun ownership. The presence of a gun in the home and a previous suicide attempt have been shown to be the two strongest predictors of adolescent suicide.

A high percentage of those who survive suicide attempts with guns indicate that their attempts were impulsive, and many occurred under the influence of alcohol. A strong association has been demonstrated between firearm suicide and intoxication at the time of death.

The importance of guns in youth suicide is not surprising, since impulsive suicide attempts are common among the young and the availability of a gun makes it more likely that such an attempt will be fatal. It is a mistake to attribute the increase in youth suicide in this country entirely to the increased availability of firearms, since the greater availability of firearms is largely a U.S. phenomenon, and youth suicide worldwide is on the rise. More significant is the increased incidence since the 1960s in substance abuse both in the United States and globally.

*Suicide Pacts.* Although suicide appears to be a very personal, isolated act, it sometimes claims pairs of victims and, even less frequently, large groups. Most who die in suicide pacts are not impulsive young lovers but codependent couples over the age of fifty. Suicide committed by couples is usually planned, and is often motivated by such factors as isolation or fear of separation owing to serious physical or mental illness; fantasies of reunion after death are common. Most often the man initiates the pact and the woman is coerced into joining as proof of her devotion.

Suicide pacts involving large groups of people —"mass suicides"—are rare. The 960 Jews who committed suicide at Masada in A.D. 73 to elude torture and enslavement by the Romans are a historic example. In modern times, however, such occurrences have been somewhat more frequent, and have included the 913 followers of the People's Temple in Jonestown, Guyana, in 1978, and the 39 members of the organization Heaven's Gate, who committed suicide in southern California in March 1997. The two latter mass suicides involved the political and psychological control and manipulation of alienated and vulnerable people and are often referred to as cult suicides. The extent of the manipulation and coercion used by often delusional group leaders is elucidated by the fact that although most of the group members agreed to commit suicide, some resisted. Half of those who died at Jonestown were murdered by other group members.

*Media Coverage of Suicide and Contagion.* Prominent news coverage of suicides has been found to increase suicidal behavior, particularly among young people, within the area of the coverage through an effect referred to as contagion. The size of the increase has been related to the celebrity of the suicide victim and the amount of publicity given to the story. Shortly after the suicide of Marilyn Monroe and the murder of John Lennon, a number of people expressed, in their suicide notes, a desire to link their death to that of the celebrity. A sense of sharing the tragic death or suicide of someone famous, or of identifying suicide with a cause, may enable vulnerable persons to feel that their deaths—and lives—have a larger significance. Further confirmation of media influence on suicide has come from research showing a decrease in suicide in cities where extended newspaper blackouts owing to a strike diminished coverage of the dramatic deaths of famous people.

Sensational and dramatic reporting of suicides was evidently responsible for a substantial increase in suicides, committed by young people in Vienna, from 1984 to 1987, by throwing themselves in front of subway trains. At that time the Austrian Association for Suicide Prevention created reporting guidelines for the press to follow when covering a suicide. The guidelines delineated the features that are likely to encourage imitative suicide: detailed depictions of methods employed; minimization or lack of presentation of the physical consequences of an attempt; lack of coverage of the victim's mental health problems; romantic or simplistic rationales for suicide, such as reunion with a deceased loved one or distress over low marks in school or "pressure"; emphasis on the victim's engaging qualities; mention of the "rewards" associated with the suicide (getting even, gaining attention). The guidelines also requested that the reporters mention possible alternatives to the suicide as well as strategies for prevention. More immediate, the newspapers stopped covering the subway suicides. Within six months of implementation of the guidelines, the number of subway suicides decreased by 75 percent and remained at this level when subway suicide rates were examined five years later.

## Suicide Prevention

The first step in suicide prevention is identifying individuals at risk. Indicators range from symptoms of depression to drug or alcohol abuse (see sidebar).

The treatment of suicidal individuals has concentrated on treating their underlying mental disorders, most often depression. While antidepressant medications are effective in treating depression, there is not yet convincing evidence of their ability to reduce the incidence of suicide. Researchers are now focusing on combining antidepressant medications with other treatments that are specific for suicidal behavior. The one medication shown consistently to prevent suicide is lithium, which is used in treating bipolar (manic-depressive) disorder. In the 1990s the antipsychotic medication clozapine had been shown to reduce suicidal behavior in schizophrenic patients.

---

**Indicators for Suicide Risk**

- symptoms of depression—depressed mood; changes in eating or sleeping habits; lack of concentration, interest, or energy; feelings of worthlessness, self-reproach, or guilt
- talk of suicide or preoccupation with death in general
- feelings of hopelessness or desperation
- feelings of anxiety and agitation
- history of aggressive or impulsive behavior
- past suicide attempt
- having a detailed plan for suicide
- firearm present in home
- current alcohol or drug abuse

Source: American Foundation for Suicide Prevention

---

Preventing suicide also entails trying to influence the social factors that contribute to it, such as unrestricted firearm access and reckless or irresponsible media coverage of suicides. Providing adequate care for seriously ill patients is another such preventive measure, since without it suicide often seems like a patient's only option.

## Survivors of Suicide

For the more than thirty thousand people who commit suicide each year, there are millions more who have lost someone due to suicide and who bear the social stigma long associated with the act. Those left behind by the suicide often feel obliged to suffer alone with their grief, anger, and guilt.

Suicide survivors have become increasingly less isolated in American society. The growing awareness that suicide is the outgrowth of an illness, combined with the alarming increase in the rate of youth suicide, has transformed public perception of suicide from a matter of private shame to a subject for public discussion. In the late twentieth century, dealing with the issue of suicide—particularly youth suicide—began to be seen as a moral imperative in the United States. Survivors of suicide began to form support groups to cope with their loss. Many became involved in the effort to fund research, education, and treatment programs to help others avoid such tragedy. Efforts at suicide prevention now extend well beyond the mental health community. It can be expected that wider public engagement with the circumstances, and predictors of suicide will benefit survivors of the act while also contributing to the goal of suicide prevention.

*BIBLIOGRAPHY*

Åsberg, Marie, L. Traskman, and P. Thoren. "5-HIAA in the Cerebrospinal Fluid: A Biochemical Suicide Predictor?" *Archives of General Psychiatry* 33, no. 10 (1976): 1193–1197.

Beck, Aaron T., et al. "Hopelessness and Eventual Suicide: A Ten-Year Prospective Study of Patients Hospitalized with Suicidal Ideation." *American Journal of Psychiatry* 142 (1985): 559–563.

Brent, David, et al. "The Presence and Accessibility of Firearms in the Homes of Adolescent Suicides: A Case-Control Study." *Journal of the American Medical Association* 266, no. 21 (1991): 2989–2995.

Durkheim, Émile. *Suicide.* New York: Free Press, 1951.

Egeland, J. A., and J. N. Sussex. "Suicide and Family Loading for Affective Disorders." *Journal of the American Medical Association* 254, no. 7 (1985): 915–918.

Fawcett, Jan, et al. "Time-Related Predictors of Suicide in Major Affective Disorder." *American Journal of Psychiatry* 147, no. 9 (1990): 1189–1194.

Freud, Sigmund. "Mourning and Melancholia." In *The Standard Edition of the Complete Psychological Works*, edited and translated by J. Strachey. Vol. 14. London: Hogarth, 1957; New York: Norton, 1976.

Hendin, Herbert. "Psychodynamics of Suicide, with Particular Reference to the Young." *American Journal of Psychiatry* 148, no. 9 (1991): 1150–1158.

———. *Suicide in America.* New York: Norton, 1995.

National Center for Health Statistics. *Monthly Vital Statistics Report,* 12 June 1997, p. 45.

Robins, Eli. *The Final Months: A Study of the Lives of 134 Persons Who Committed Suicide.* New York: Oxford University Press, 1981.

Sonneck, G., E. Etzersdorfer, and S. Nagel-Kuess. "Imitative Suicide on the Viennese Subway." *Social Science and Medicine.* 38, no. 3 (1994): 453–457.

World Health Organization Statistical Data Base. www.who.dk

HERBERT HENDIN
MATTHEW K. NOCK

*See also* **Anorexia and Bulimia; Assisted Suicide and Euthanasia; Euthanasia; Heaven's Gate; Jonestown; Self-Destructiveness.**

# SWEATSHOPS

A sweatshop is a workplace where unskilled and unorganized workers toil long hours for low pay in unhealthy and unsafe working conditions. In the United States, sweatshops have been a metaphor for exploitation in the needle trades, manufacturing, and food industries. The term *unskilled* is an unfair characterization of harsh, demanding jobs that require dexterity and mastery of special skills to be productive. However, by labeling sweatshop jobs "unskilled," some employers justify the low wages and bad working conditions prevalent in sweatshop production. When these conditions cause death and disease, workers are victims of economic exploitation and direct physical assault on their lives. Clearly, these are forms of violence. Sweatshop violence has two aspects: chronic violence, characterized by long-term fatiguing of workers by overwork, malnutrition, and disease; and acute violence, manifested as tragic incidents where inhumane conditions have caused a number of deaths in a working population.

## Historical Perspective

*The Seamstress, 1820–1880.* Seamstresses were pieceworkers in the garment industry who stitched precut fabric into clothing while working at home. As opposed to dressmakers who produced a complete garment and earned a better wage, seamstresses were paid poorly and worked as many as sixteen hours a day. Economic hardships of these workers (almost exclusively women) were legendary in the garment industry. Seamstresses were not organized into unions and were almost completely isolated. Working conditions for the seamstresses were harsh. The women first had to carry home the heavy bundles of garments. The work was performed mostly at night after domestic chores were finished. Fifty- to sixty-hour workweeks, sewing in cramped, dark, and unventilated places, were not uncommon, as this volume of piecework was necessary to earn enough to survive. The harsh working conditions to which seamstresses were subjected are an example of underground chronic violence inflicted by employers.

*The Tenement Sweatshop, 1880–1940.* The collectivization of the garment industry took place in many U.S. cities in this period. Newly arrived immigrants—Jews from Germany, Poland, and Russia and Catholics from Italy and Ireland—provided cheap and plentiful labor. Immigrants typically converted small apartments into contract shops that doubled as living quarters. Competition and need for employment kept wages down and hours of work up. Although a small number of immigrant workers became wealthy, the great majority suffered disease, malnutrition, and exhaustion. Intensive efforts to organize these workers into unions faced strong opposition from the garment industry. Accounts of indiscriminate violence against garment workers (and their families) during strikes for recognition or to obtain decent working conditions are fully documented. This violence was perpetrated by garment companies often in collusion with state and local authorities.

One of the most tragic events of this period was the notorious fire at the Triangle Shirtwaist Company of New York, where 146 young immigrant women died on 25 March 1911. It was a clear case of criminal negligence by a typical garment company employing an immigrant labor force. Triangle was known for its harsh working conditions and antiunion stance. When the fire started, the workers could not escape because the company had locked the doors to the stairs. The company had kept their workers in a virtual prison, purportedly to prevent theft and absenteeism. There was no equipment in the building with which to extinguish the fire and

**A New York "sweater's factory." Reproduced from** *Frank Leslie's Illus-trated Newspaper* **(3 November 1888).** LIBRARY OF CONGRESS

only one fire escape. Most of the women jumped seven floors to their deaths or were burned beyond recognition.

*The Resurgent Sweatshop, 1940–1990s.* In the 1940s the number of sweatshops in the United States dwindled, but it increased again in the 1960s with an upsurge in immigration from Asia (China and the Philippines) and Latin America (Mexico and South America). Again, a large pool of immigrants arrived in the United States and new sweatshops appeared in the garment industry. The food industry also produced their products (especially meat and chicken) under sweatshop conditions.

On 3 September 1991 a fire at Imperial Food Products, Inc., a chicken-processing factory in Hamlet, North Carolina, resulted in twenty-five deaths and fifty-six injuries. After the fact, the federal Occupational Safety and Health Administration (OSHA) proposed $808,000 in fines and the plant manager was indicted on twenty-five counts of involuntary manslaughter. Imperial was a nonunionized company of two hundred workers earning a maximum wage of $5.50 an hour. The company did not have a fire-sprinkler system, emergency lighting, or an emergency evacuation plan. Of the nine exit doors, seven were bolted from the outside, again purportedly to prevent theft. On the day of the fire, a natural gas line near a deep-fat fryer leaked and ignited. The fire fed on the grease accumulated on factory surfaces. All

lights went out and workers died trying to escape through the bolted doors.

It is ironic that after eighty years of industrial achievements in the United States, the same violent conditions that claimed the lives of 146 women in a New York sweatshop in 1911 were repeated in a modern sweatshop in North Carolina in 1991.

**Violence Prevention**

What forces in the United States and abroad promote sweatshops? Greed and opportunism have contributed to this type of production in the United States since the nineteenth century, but the forces of competition in the global economy also drive sweatshops abroad under the control of U.S. corporations.

The U.S. General Accounting Office (GAO) and the U.S. Department of Labor identified numerous sweatshops in the 1990s where employers did not comply with federal laws. GAO defines sweatshops as "businesses that regularly violate both safety and health laws (OSHA) and wages (minimum wage, overtime) and child labor regulations (U.S. Department of Labor)." Table 1 summarizes labor law violations in 1994 and 1996 in garment factories inspected in southern California. A 1995 federal raid in an El Monte, California, garment shop documented graphically how immigrants from Thailand were held in virtual slavery in an apartment complex under armed guards. The raid

TABLE 1. Percentage of Violations of Federal Labor Law in Southern California Garment Industry, on Inspections Conducted 1994–1996

| Violation Category | 1994 Percentage in Violation | 1996 Percentage in Violation |
|---|---|---|
| Less Than Minimum Wage | 61 | 43 |
| Failure to Pay Overtime | 78 | 55 |
| OSHA Violations | 98 | 96 |
| Serious OSHA Violations | 35 | 72 |

SOURCE: The National Museum of American History's exhibition *Between a Rock and a Hard Place: A History of American Sweatshops, 1820–Present*, April–October 1998.

freed the workers and led to guilty pleas from the operators to charges of conspiracy and compelling involuntary servitude.

Unsafe working conditions are a form of chronic violence, often as terrifying as fires that can kill dozens of workers in a single incident. Prevention of both chronic violence and acute violence may be accomplished by three strategies: unionization of sweatshop operations; awareness campaigns to inform the public that the violence perpetrated on workers in sweatshop industries in the United States and abroad is an inherent part of cheap labor; and strict enforcement of U.S. regulations at home and international regulations abroad by the International Labor Organization.

*BIBLIOGRAPHY*

Baxandall, Rosalyn, and Linda Gordon, eds. *America's Working Women: A Documentary History, 1600 to Present.* 2d ed. New York: Norton, 1995.

Boris, Eileen, and Cynthia R. Daniels, eds. *Homework: Historical and Contemporary Perspectives on Paid Labor at Home.* Urbana: University of Illinois Press, 1989.

Boyer, Richard O., and Herbert M. Morais. *Labor's Untold Story.* 3d ed. New York: United Electrical, Radio, and Machine Workers of America, 1970.

LaBar, Gregg. "Hamlet, N.C.: Home to a National Tragedy." *Occupational Hazards* 54 (September 1992).

National Museum of American History. *Between a Rock and a Hard Place: A History of American Sweatshops, 1820 to Present.* Washington, D.C.: Smithsonian Institution, April–October 1998.

Ross, Andrew. *No Sweat.* New York: Verso-Norton, 1997.

RAFAEL MOURE-ERASO

*See also* **Child Labor; Labor and Unions; Strikes; Workplace.**

# SYMBIONESE LIBERATION ARMY

The Symbionese Liberation Army (SLA), one of the most notorious American terrorist organizations of the twentieth century, emerged out of the swirl of revolutionary politics in the northern California of the 1960s. In early 1973 Donald DeFreeze, an escapee from Soledad Prison, formed the SLA with his lover, Patricia "Mizmoon" Soltysizk, fusing his connections from the Black Cultural Association, a prisoners' rights organization at Vacaville Prison, with friends in a Maoist group called Venceremos.

The SLA's platform called for the violent destruction of capitalism and the division of the United States into racially distinct states. At first, DeFreeze, who renamed himself Field Marshall Cinque Mtume, attempted to create a "war council" of leftist groups in the San Francisco Bay area. Other leaders balked, seeing DeFreeze as unstable and lacking revolutionary credentials. Isolated, the SLA sought to recruit new members alone. Among the new recruits was Joseph Remiro, a Vietnam veteran, who led the group's military training.

The group captured headlines with the 6 November 1973 assassination of the Oakland School superintendent Marcus Foster. SLA members Remiro, Russell Little, and Nancy Ling Perry ambushed Foster and his deputy, Robert Blackburn, as they exited a meeting. The trio fired a hail of cyanide-filled bullets, killing Foster and wounding Blackburn, who escaped. Four days later the SLA took responsibility in a letter identifying Foster as "guilty of supporting and taking part in crimes against the children and the life of the people" for his support of a system of school student ID cards. The letter warned that a "shoot on sight" order remained in effect for other officials.

Though Foster's assassination brought the SLA to the public's attention, its next action brought it worldwide notoriety. On 4 February 1974 the group kidnapped the mathematician Peter Benenson as he walked to his car. After blindfolding and beating Benenson, his captors threw him in the back of his 1963 Chevrolet convertible. The group then sped to its prime target, the home of Patricia Hearst, daughter of the publisher of the *San Francisco Examiner* and granddaughter of legendary media mogul William Randolph Hearst.

Hearst's boyfriend, Stephen Weed, opened the door to a woman asking to use the phone to report an accident, only to be thrown to the ground as SLA soldiers swept in. Weed was beaten and bound as Hearst was dragged screaming from the

**Patty Hearst caught on surveillance camera during a bank robbery in San Francisco, 1974.** HULTON GETTY/ LIAISON AGENCY

apartment. During the confusion Benenson escaped, but Hearst was sped to an SLA safe house. In letters to the media, the SLA demanded the Hearst family distribute $70 million worth of food to California's poor to stave off their daughter's execution.

For Hearst the captivity was a brutal two months. She was kept bound and blindfolded in a closet, tortured physically, sexually, and mentally. Taking the name Tania, Hearst went from captive to revolutionary, participating in SLA communiqués and actions. During a dramatic robbery of the Hibernia Bank in San Francisco, security cameras recorded the "new" Patricia Hearst armed with an assault rifle.

The SLA managed to evade authorities until 17 May 1974, when the Los Angeles Police Department closed in on the group's hideout in Compton, California. The police unleashed over 3,700 rounds into the house, killing all six members inside and setting the house ablaze. Only Hearst, along with Bill and Emily Harris, who had been out running errands, escaped the massacre. The three remained on the run for more than a year, until they were finally captured on 18 September 1975 in San Francisco, ending the SLA's reign of terror.

Hearst's trial became one of the great media events of the century. Debates raged about whether she was a victim or, as the prosecutor argued, a revolutionary. The famed defense lawyer F. Lee Bailey tried unsuccessfully to claim that Patty had been brainwashed and was therefore not responsible for her criminal actions; she received a sentence of thirty-five years, which was reduced almost immediately to seven. Hearst served a prison term until President Jimmy Carter commuted her sentence in 1979.

*BIBLIOGRAPHY*

Baker, Marylin. *Exclusive! The Inside Story of Patricia Hearst and the SLA.* New York: Macmillan, 1982.
Boulton, David. *The Making of Tania.* London: New English Library, 1975.
Bryan, John. *This Soldier Still at War.* New York: Harcourt Brace Jovanovich, 1975.
Hearst, Patricia. *Every Secret Thing.* Garden City, N.Y.: Doubleday, 1982.
McClellan, Vin. *The Voices of Guns.* New York: Putnam, 1976.
McGuire, John. *Patty Hearst: From Heiress to Revolutionary.* North Miami Beach, Fla.: Success, 1975.

MATTHEW TAYLOR RAFFETY

*See also* **Extremism; Kidnapping; Terrorism.**

# SYMBOLIC VIOLENCE

The study of violence has traditionally focused on variables that are statistically related to offenders' biological, psychological, or social backgrounds. For example, homicide rates are often "explained" in terms of neighborhood levels of poverty or social disorganization. In the hopes of illuminating aspects of violence that traditional explanations have ignored, scholars have turned to the subjective meanings participants give to violent events. James Gilligan (1997) notes that violence is often a tragic, self-destructive, and seemingly irrational act, but from the perpetrator's point of view "all violence is an attempt to achieve justice." Several prominent strains of this research address symbolic violence: this work is grounded in the theoretical writings of the *Verstehen* tradition of Max Weber, the symbolic interactionist perspective associated with George Herbert Mead and Herbert Blumer, Harold Garfinkel's ethnomethodology, and work by postmodernists such as Pierre Bourdieu. For these writers, all forms of social action (including violence) must be explained according to the meanings and understandings that are experientially constructed by actual participants. Theories of violence based on statistical studies of background factors, these writers would argue, strip violence from its symbolic context and can therefore provide only partial explanations at best.

Although the study of symbolic violence has generated important insights, it has not produced a unified body of work but rather multiple distinct subfields. Imposing order on a diverse, even chaotic body of work is necessary to delineate the two dominant strands of research on symbolic violence. Thus, the first subject addressed here is the symbolic meanings participants assign to specific violent acts; this topic is epitomized by the work of the sociologist Jack Katz. The second subject addressed is the writings that have grown out of the postmodernist conception, such as the work of Pierre Bourdieu and Loic J. D. Wacquant (1992), of symbolic violence, holding that the control of discourse marginalizes some viewpoints and facilitates certain categories of violence.

### Symbolic Meanings of Violence

Theories of violence often assume that offenders are motivated by the rational pursuit of material gain (e.g., the purpose of robbery is to acquire money) or are merely responding to unfortunate "background" conditions (e.g., violence relieves the frustration of those living in poverty). Yet when one examines what violence means to the offender, such assumptions often appear unwarranted. How can we explain the consistent finding that women are equally as likely as—if not more likely than—men to experience background conditions such as poverty or poor educational training yet are much less likely to be involved in most types of interpersonal violence, as both victims and offenders? One attempt is to study symbolic meanings and the subjective interpretations of participants in violent events. A development largely of the 1980s and 1990s, this kind of violence research has already greatly increased our understanding of central issues in the study of violence, such as the striking gender differences in involvement. The contributions of this kind of work can be illustrated by the following four examples.

*The Emotional and Symbolic Attractions of Robbery.* The clearest example of research on the symbolic meanings of violence can be found in Jack Katz's

---

### The Organizational Context of Symbolic Violence

The dominance of organizations in modern society has had a significant impact on the nature of symbolic violence. Generic features of organizations—the centralization of authority, hierarchical chains of command, reward structures, and so forth—have increased both the speed and scope of violence against worldviews and identities. One example of symbolic violence within an organization occurred when the identities of museum workers were altered by changes in the nature of their work. Curators of museums who once saw their role as preserving artifacts to increase society's base of knowledge about the past were forced to contend with the profit-oriented worldview of new managers. Changes in the operation of museums were justified by managers in terms of market pressures and the need to make museums more economically competitive with other forms of entertainment, such as sporting events. This is an act of symbolic violence in the sense that over time it reorganized the identities and worldviews of museum workers against their will and in ways that shifted their professional identities and led them to accept less control over their work. The fact that authority was centralized and museum workers were made subordinate to managers increased the efficiency and reach of this violence so that identities were altered in less than three years.

---

1988 study of the "seductions of crime." This perspective directs attention to the offender's subjective interpretation of the criminal act rather than the offender's background characteristics. Katz argues that offenders engage in crime, particularly violent crime, primarily for emotional and symbolic reasons: for excitement, to restore honor, to transcend one's place in society, to feel morally superior to one's victim, and so on. The materialistic emphasis of most theories of violence seems to miss the most fundamental meanings of violence. The purpose of robbery, for example, goes beyond the acquisition of money (most robbers could get more of it by working at one of the plentiful entry-level jobs in the fast-food business, albeit the payoff is not as quick). The principal rewards of robbery are emotional (e.g., there is a thrill in dominating the victim) and symbolic (e.g., the robber constructs an identity as a "hardman"). According to Katz, by attempting to dominate victims and embracing the chaos inherent in robberies, the hardman "discovers, fantasizes, or manufactures *an angle of moral superiority* over the intended victim." The hardman (most robbers are men) cultivates an image of ferocity and control that symbolizes a victory over society, whereas submitting to the demands of a conventional job would represent a failure. Because many of these offenders have been brutalized, violence of this kind follows an identifiable logic: it is revenge on an unfair world for a thousand (perceived) past injustices, a means of overcoming feelings of inadequacy, or a desperate attempt to overcome chronic feelings of shame.

*Masculinities and Domestic Violence.* The idea of constructing "masculinities" refers to the process by which men use power to create a public image that differs from that of women and the attributes women are thought to possess (passivity, emotionality, and so forth). According to this perspective, masculinities can be constructed in a number of ways—through dominance in the workplace, or for those whose position in the occupational structure precludes this, through involvement in violent crime. Because domestic violence, like most forms of violence, has been an almost exclusively male activity, it is one practice men can use to construct a masculine identity. Thus, for men who work in low-status, demeaning jobs, domestic violence can become a way to demonstrate "maleness." This is not to suggest that low-status jobs necessarily "cause" violent crime. But when men fail to demonstrate masculinity by securing an adequate, stable income for their family, in accordance with the traditional male role as family provider, domestic violence becomes one option for symbolically restoring their maleness. Obviously, this is not the only explanation for domestic violence, but it illuminates at least part of the male motivation to act violently against women.

*Homicide and Honor Contests.* The majority of homicide victims and offenders are male, and a large proportion of homicides are in fact the result of what Kenneth Polk calls "honor contests" among males. These contests begin with some provocation, such as an insult or a disrespectful look, which the target of this instigation takes as a challenge to his sense of honor. Whereas the insult

may appear trivial to outsiders, research has shown that for many young, working- or lower-class males it takes on a grave symbolic meaning involving the obligatory maintenance of the participants' manhood and reputation in the community. Honor contests often occur in leisure settings such as bars or parties because such settings contain an essential ingredient: an audience of young, male peers who recognize the symbolic importance of male honor. This audience often facilitates a violent resolution of the contest by antagonizing the participants. In a classic study of homicide, Henry Lundsgaarde (1977) found that participants in the legal system also understood the symbolic importance of honor and frequently legitimated the practice of using lethal violence in the defense of honor. Prosecutors often refused to charge offenders with murder, while juries routinely acquitted. Despite the importance of honor contests to participants, most studies of homicide continue to ignore the prominent causal role of symbolic meanings.

*The Meaning of the 1992 Los Angeles Race Riot.* The acquittal in April 1992 of four white Los Angeles police officers tried for the beating of African American motorist Rodney King touched off a massive race riot in and around South Central Los Angeles, resulting in more than fifty deaths, thousands of injuries and arrests, and hundreds of millions of dollars in property damage. Although the verdict sparked the riot, the violence had symbolic significance beyond simple outrage. The racial composition of the neighborhoods where the most serious damage and loss of life occurred, and the types of businesses targeted by rioters, suggest that the riot represented "backlash violence" against the perceived economic successes of Latino and Asian immigrants in African American neighborhoods. The L.A. riot is better understood as a defensive response by members of African American neighborhoods to the in-migration of Latinos and Asians rather than as a primarily political protest against the verdict in the King case or, more generally, against police brutality and economic injustice as in the Civil Rights–era riots of the 1960s. There is a historical precedent for this kind of "communal riot"; for example, Irish immigrants were the targets of riot violence in the 1840s, and African Americans were subjected to reactionary violence when they moved into predominantly white neighborhoods in the 1900–1920 period. Ex-

Volunteers "Rebuild Los Angeles" following the Rodney King riots of 1992. CORBIS/JOSEPH SOHM

ploring the symbolic—especially racial—meanings of riot violence is critical to understanding why it occurs.

## The Postmodern Conception of Symbolic Violence

In postmodernist writings *symbolic violence* has a meaning very different from that suggested by the foregoing discussion. In contrast to scholars who emphasize scientific rationality and positivist representations of objective facts, postmodernist scholars generally favor research narratives based on subjective meanings and a plurality of viewpoints. However, it should be noted that a precise definition of *postmodernism* remains elusive (the term originated in France and has been variously adapted by academics in other countries). Thus, whereas sociologists tend to dominate research into the symbolic meanings of violence as discussed in the previous section, studies informed by the postmodern conception of symbolic violence are of a more interdisciplinary nature. Fields as diverse as psychology, political science, literary criticism, sociology, business management, and cultural studies have contributed to the postmodern debates.

Postmodernist scholars disagree as to the appropriate meaning of *symbolic violence*, partly be-

cause of different national academic traditions and translation difficulties. For our purposes, symbolic violence is the suppression of certain conceptions of reality (or worldviews) that compete with the dominant worldviews. Symbolic violence has the effect of marginalizing certain social identities, forms of expression, and ideological perspectives. This process of marginalizing or suppressing can do symbolic damage to a person's entire outlook on existence. Sander L. Gilman (1986) shows, for example, how thousands of years of writing by non-Jews (often hostile Christians) have done symbolic violence to Jewish self-identities. In these writings Jews were depicted as scheming liars and inferior to other groups of people; over time this damaged the worldview of Jews and fostered an intense self-hatred among them that can be clearly identified in the works of Jewish writers. Postmodernists see this damage as a form of violence, much as physical or emotional violence harms victims' bodies or emotional well-being.

Some writers have attempted to trace the ways in which symbolic forms of violence facilitate physical violence against oppressed groups or generate self-destructive behaviors among members of these groups. For example, it has been argued that the judicial system uses symbolic violence to marginalize or silence the political viewpoints of subjugated groups. By "destroying" alternative interpretations of the world, the judiciary reproduces patterns of domination, and this, in turn, facilitates legal violence and repression. A review of four applications of the postmodernist concept of symbolic violence can further an understanding of violence in general.

*Symbolic Violence and Gang Rape.* One of the defining characteristics of the postmodern conception of symbolic violence is that it is "exercised upon a social agent with his or her complicity." A notable case involved the community response to a Portuguese woman who was raped by six men in Massachusetts in 1983. In the aftermath of the rape, Portuguese women marched in defense of the rapists—an indication of the effects of symbolic violence on the worldviews of women within the male-dominated community. One woman remarked, "They did nothing to her. Her rights are to be at home with her two kids and to be a good mother. A Portuguese woman should be with her kids and that's it." Thus, the rape victim was subjected to the physical and psychological violence of the rapists, and also to the symbolic violence of the larger community, which had denied her the validity that the rape was wrong. The victims of symbolic violence often come to believe that their outlook is inferior and ultimately accept the dominant perspective as the legitimate one. At that point they will actively suppress alternative values or beliefs, as shown by the way the Portuguese women acted contrary to their self-interests and justified the use of physical violence by men against a woman.

*Symbolic Violence and Health Care.* The field of health care has been the setting for several prominent studies of symbolic violence. Arthur Kleinman (1988) describes the way social reality is organized by the health care establishment's "radically materialist pursuit of the biological mechanisms of disease." This orientation does symbolic violence to patients' values and beliefs because it marginalizes worldviews that stress the interconnectedness of mind, body, and soul in determining the trajectory of an illness. Patients often attach physiological, psychological, and social meanings to the illness experience that are ignored by doctors, who, as a function of their training, "interrogate" patients simply to identify a specific biological disease. This symbolic violence is even more pronounced when American doctors treat patients from different cultural backgrounds. Doc-

tors trained according to the Western rational medical model tend to reject medical outlooks that stress the spiritual causes of illness. In one example, instead of working with shamans when treating Hmong patients—the Hmong are originally from Southeast Asia and South China— Western doctors "did everything they could to discomfit them and undermine their authority." Since the doctors had the power to define the nature of the illness and set the course of treatment, the doctors' deeds and words represented violence against Hmong worldviews, caused patients and their families psychological stress, and interfered with the effectiveness of medical treatments.

Inquiries into the nature of community mental-health centers have also focused attention on symbolic violence. In these settings, diagnostic schemes are commonly used to enforce the mental-health professional's worldview at the expense of the patient's. The practices of professionals may exclude the patient's input, and the patient may eventually withdraw from meaningful dialogue. Invasive methods of control are then justified in terms of a treatment plan that patients have not helped develop, even though patient involvement is one of the key assumptions of the community mental-health movement. In time, patients learn to suppress clinically inappropriate thoughts, values, or behaviors, thereby participating in the regime of social control that seeks to suppress them.

An ever-present danger is that this symbolic violence can be used to achieve the goals of custodial care (e.g., care of docile patients), in the absence of treatment intended to benefit the patient. In this way, symbolic violence provides the social-control functions once secured by lobotomies or "chemical straitjackets." Such violence can lead to self-destructive behavior on the part of patients, yet this institutionally produced harm is often not recognized as "real" violence. Moreover, as noted by John Murphy and his colleagues (1994), "the self may be systematically dismantled and reconstructed according to a clinical ideal"; this process represents violence directed at a person's identity.

*Symbolic Violence in Television Advertising.* When television advertising practices seek to control viewers through the manipulation of symbolic phenomena, they too can be viewed as symbolic violence. One example can be found in a case study of television advertising aimed at women that was produced by the Jenny Craig Weight Loss Center. According to Kathleen M. Torrens (1998), the center's advertisements represented an attempt to achieve social control of female bodies through the "promulgation of idealized images" that have become taken for granted as the norm. Presenting a single conception of how women should look promotes the objectification of women and thus can be understood as symbolic violence. Such uniform imagery suggests that weight loss and physical beauty are the solutions to all women's problems; alternative female worldviews, by implication, are inferior. The drive to imitate the beauty ideals projected in the ads can lead to a woman's destructive concern with her weight or body shape and result in depression, eating disorders, and other problems. Thus, violence at the symbolic level can then manifest at the physical and emotional levels.

*Symbolic Violence and Race Relations.* Symbolic violence has played a central role in perpetuating systems of racial domination and inequality in the United States. In a white-dominated society the viewpoints, forms of expression, and social identities of racial minorities are regularly suppressed or silenced. This kind of coercive and exclusionary control is the hallmark of symbolic violence. Minorities are violated by the portrayal of their cultural practices and identities as inferior, while the violent history of racism (including the issues of slavery, segregation, and the staggering differences in living conditions between whites and certain minorities) is denied or minimized. This symbolic violence provides the ideological underpinnings for overt acts of aggression. As Ward Churchill reported (1993), the U.S. government's Indian Health Service was forced to admit in 1975 that it had been conducting a program of involuntary sterilization that might have affected an estimated 40 percent of the population of American Indian women.

Symbolic violence exists in the apolitical language and use of the passive voice in many writings on race and race relations. For example, a number of undergraduate texts, such as Martin N. Marger's *Race and Ethnic Relations: American and Global Perspectives* (1991), use the passive voice to describe the experiences of African American slaves. Likewise, a 1994 article in the *New Republic*, "Race, Genes, and I.Q.: An Apologia," neutralizes the brutality of the slave system by referring to slaves as "involuntary immigrants." This writing style allows the perpetrators of violence to remain hidden and unacknowledged, so that "racism, past

and present, can be referred to without implicating or alluding to those who are responsible."

By controlling discourse in this manner, writers mask the political nature of past actions, overwhelm competing versions of events through their sheer number, and confer a neutral status on current patterns of inequality and discrimination. Thus, writers may cast certain actions or policies (e.g., welfare reform) that result in physical and emotional harm to members of minority groups in terms of abstract forces rather than as the political acts of identifiable groups. The symbolic violence accomplished by such writers prevents minorities from challenging this dominant conception of anonymous action and represents an important barrier to effective social change.

## Conclusion

The study of the symbolic meanings of violence and the postmodern conception of symbolic violence remain controversial but fruitful areas of academic investigation. Creative and innovative approaches to the study of violence have emerged out of the apparent disunity of viewpoints, and scholars have generated important insights that other approaches might not have produced. We now understand a great deal more about the emotional inducements and subjective underpinnings of violence on the one hand, and the complex relationship between symbolic, physical, and emotional violence on the other. A better integration of these newer subjective projects with the voluminous research being collected by more traditional, "objective" methods would further that understanding.

*BIBLIOGRAPHY*

Anderson, Elijah. *Streetwise: Race, Class, and Change in an Urban Community.* Chicago: University of Chicago Press, 1990.

Bergesen, Albert, and Max Herman. "Immigration, Race, and Riot: The 1992 Los Angeles Uprising." *American Sociological Review* 63, no. 1 (1998).

Bourdieu, Pierre, and Loic J. D. Wacquant. *An Invitation to Reflexive Sociology.* Chicago: University of Chicago Press, 1992.

Brisbin, Richard A. "Antonin Scalia, William Brennan, and the Politics of Expression: A Study of Legal Violence and Repression." *American Political Science Review* 87, no. 4 (1993).

Callaghan, Karen A. "Symbolic Violence and Race." In *Postmodernism and Race,* edited by Eric Mark Kramer. Westport, Conn.: Praeger, 1997.

Chancer, Lynn S. "New Bedford, Massachusetts, March 6, 1983–March 22, 1984: The 'Before' and 'After' of a Group Rape." *Gender and Society* 1, no. 3 (1987).

Churchill, Ward. "Crimes Against Humanity." *Z Magazine* (March 1993).

Fadiman, Ann. *The Spirit Catches You and You Fall Down: A Hmong Child, Her American Doctors, and the Collision of Two Cultures*. New York: Farrar, Straus and Giroux, 1997.

Gilligan, James. *Violence: Reflections on a National Epidemic*. New York: Vintage, 1997.

Gilman, Sander L. *Jewish Self-Hatred: Anti-Semitism and the Hidden Language of the Jews*. Baltimore: Johns Hopkins University Press, 1986.

Janowitz, Morris. "Patterns of Collective Racial Violence." In *Violence in America*, edited by H. D. Graham and Ted Robert Gurr. New York: New American Library, 1969.

Katz, Jack. *Seductions of Crime: Moral and Sensual Attractions in Doing Evil*. New York: Basic, 1988.

Kleinman, Arthur. *The Illness Narratives: Suffering, Healing, and the Human Condition*. New York: Basic, 1988.

Lundsgaarde, Henry P. *Murder in Space City*. New York: Oxford University Press, 1977.

Marger, Martin N. *Race and Ethnic Relations: American and Global Perspectives*. Belmont, Calif.: Wadsworth, 1991.

Messerschmidt, James W. *Crime as Structured Action: Gender, Race, Class, and Crime in the Making*. Thousand Oaks, Calif.: Sage, 1997.

Murphy, John W., et al. "Symbolic Violence and Social Control in the Total Institution." *Journal of Sociology and Social Welfare* 21, no. 4 (1994).

Murray, Charles, and Richard J. Herrnstein. "Race, Genes and I.Q. — An Apologia." *New Republic* (October 1994).

Oaks, Leslie B., Barbara Townley, and David J. Cooper. "Business Planning as Pedagogy: Language and Control in a Changing Institutional Field." *Administrative Science Quarterly* 43, no. 2 (1998).

Polk, Kenneth. "Males and Honor Contest Violence." *Homicides Studies* 3, no. 1 (1999).

Torrens, Kathleen M. "I Can Get Any Job and Feel Like a Butterfly! Symbolic Violence in the TV Advertising of Jenny Craig." *Journal of Communication Inquiry* 22, no. 1 (1998).

Matthew T. Lee
Ramiro Martinez, Jr.

*See also* **Graffiti; Language and Verbal Violence; Representation of Violence.**

# T

## TAMPERING, PRODUCT

Product tampering became a national issue in 1982 when cyanide-laced Tylenol capsules caused seven deaths in the Chicago area. These deaths were the first confirmed homicides resulting from drug tampering. Later that year, an unrelated incident of tampering, with strychnine-laced Tylenol, resulted in the death of a California man. The near public hysteria that followed forced Johnson and Johnson, the maker of Tylenol, to pull the product from the nation's shelves. The Tylenol incidents led to a proliferation of copycat attempts, an increase in reported tampering incidents, a concern over food-product tampering, and action by the Food and Drug Administration (FDA). In 1983 the Federal Anti-Tampering Act made it a federal crime to tamper or threaten to tamper with a consumer product, supplanting many existing state laws.

In the 1980s and 1990s, four more drug tampering incidents resulted in deaths, all caused by cyanide poisoning. Contaminated Tylenol (in Westchester County, New York) and Excedrin capsules (in the Seattle area) killed one and two respectively in 1986; in 1991 and 1992 cyanide-tainted Sudafed and Goody's Headache Powder resulted in more deaths. Other acts of tampering were either discovered before the products were consumed or resulted in illness short of death.

In addition to the 1983 act, the FDA requires drug companies to adopt tamper-proof or tamper-resistant packaging to thwart contamination. But individual companies cannot be held solely responsible for prevention of tampering, because no package can be designed to be fully tamper-proof.

Motives of extortion, terrorism, and murder fuel tamperers. One man, James Lewis, was jailed for attempted extortion following the 1982 Chicago Tylenol scare. In 1986 in Washington State, Stella Nickell was convicted for the murder of her husband and a stranger, both of whom took Excedrin capsules she had laced with cyanide.

Most of the negative effects from drug tampering are the result of public hysteria rather than actual casualties. In his analysis of FDA statistics and drug-tampering incidents and trends, Park Dietz points out that reported tampering incidents increased markedly immediately after national scares occurred. In some cases, faked, copycat tamperings have been attributed to those seeking to injure drug companies or simply to gain personal attention. Even faked tamperings may compel a company to pull its inventory, often at extreme cost. At least one suicide was designed to look like a drug-tampering death. The food industry has also been affected by tampering; aside from repeated incidents over several decades of tamperings with Halloween candy, in 1986 a death from cyanide in Lipton Cup-A-Soup marked the first of a series of food-related tampering incidents.

Dietz's report indicates that the FDA receives around ten tampering complaints every week; as of 1988, all forty-five drug companies in the Fortune 500 had experienced tampering threats or incidents. Major drug companies have developed task forces to manage potential tampering crises, especially in terms of media relations, which is crucial in shaping public reactions to tampering scares. Some companies have purchased insurance policies against tampering, because even threats of the action can have dire financial consequences.

*BIBLIOGRAPHY*

Dietz, Park. "The Proliferation of Product Tampering." FACSNET, *www.facsnet.org*, 12 May 1999.
Greenberg, Eric. "The Legal Framework of Product Tampering." FACSNET, *www.facsnet.org*, 12 May 1999.
Lance, David. "Product Tampering." *FBI Law Enforcement Bulletin* (April 1988): 20–23.
Mitroff, Ian I., and Kilmann, Ralph H. *Corporate Tragedies— Product Tampering and Other Catastrophies.* New York: Praeger, 1984.

GREGORY L. PARKER

*See also* **Crime, Legal Definitions of.**

# TARRING AND FEATHERING

The first historical reference to tarring and feathering was made in 1189, when King Richard I of England declared on his way to fight in the Crusades that "thieves were to have their heads shaved, to have boiling Pitch dropped upon their Crowns; and after having Cushion Feathers stuck upon the Pitch, they were to be set on shore, in that figure, at the first place they came to" (Mackenzie 1930). Although a legal form of punishment in Europe, tarring and feathering was rarely employed there. In contrast, this punishment was never legal in the United States but was commonly used in the eighteenth and nineteenth centuries as a form of mob justice toward those who violated the norms of the ascendant or majority group.

Based on the evidence of historical accounts, tarring and feathering was most often administered during the Revolutionary War, when it was deployed by mobs of angry American patriots to punish informants, customs officials, and British tax collectors. Tarring and feathering, because of the social stigma it carried, proved a most effective deterrent, which many argue helped bring about the repeal of most of the British taxation laws. However, by the end of the war and even into the twentieth century, tarring and feathering came to be associated with more violent and ritualized forms of communal justice in the United States.

American patriots tar and feather the excise-man in protest against new taxes. Lithograph by D. C. Johnston. Boston, 1774. CORBIS

In the South tarring and feathering played an integral role in purification ceremonies known as charivari, or shivaree. In fact, lynching and charivari were the preferred methods of cleansing the wicked in the South between 1800 and 1860. Both were forms of social control carried out not by the law but by the people—usually in the form of a mob. The unfortunate victims included those whose actions threatened basic community norms regarding family, honor, and hierarchy. Race played a crucial role, as southern whites—fearing the general economic and social advances of blacks—invoked the purification ceremonies as a way of asserting white supremacy. Tarring and feathering was utilized for "lesser offenses" (or those committed by whites), while lynching was favored for "serious offenses" (or those committed by blacks).

Thus tarring and feathering evolved into a ritualized, symbolic activity to alleviate general social tensions and increase group solidarity. In the 1830s a member of an antislavery organization was kidnapped, tarred and feathered, and returned in a state of near delirium. Similarly, Mormons attempting to spread their gospel to southerners often suffered this fate. In short, anyone perceived as hostile or threatening to the established way of life was subjected to this ritualized punishment. Even as late as the 1920s, tarring and feathering, as well as whipping and branding, was a form of punishment used by the Ku Klux Klan.

*BIBLIOGRAPHY*

Mackenzie, Frederick. *Diary of Frederick Mackenzie.* Cambridge, Mass.: Harvard University Press, 1930.
Wyatt-Brown, Bertram. *Southern Honor: Ethics and Behavior in the Old South.* New York: Oxford University Press, 1982.

JARRETT PASCHEL

*See also* **American Revolution: Overview; Crime and Punishment in American History; Cruel and Unusual Punishment.**

# TEENAGERS

In the early to mid-1990s, the United States witnessed an epidemic of violence among young people. While the incidence of juvenile violence actually dropped slightly in both 1995 and 1996, this decrease was widely regarded as a temporary phenomenon since it occurred at a time when the teenage population (thirteen- to nineteen-year-olds) was declining. If demographic projections made in the late 1990s prove accurate, the population of American teenagers will increase 15 percent from 1999 to 2005. The number of violent crimes committed by juveniles, therefore, will likely increase.

In any event, there can be little question that juvenile violence in the United States reached pandemic proportions in the 1990s. The rate of violent crime committed by juveniles quadrupled over the last quarter of the twentieth century. Moreover, according to Federal Bureau of Investigation data, the juvenile arrest rate for violent crime exceeded the adult rate by nearly one-third. In 1996 teenagers made up over 38 percent of those arrested for murder and nonnegligent manslaughter; approximately 45 percent of those arrested for robbery; and more than 20 percent of those arrested for forcible rape, assault, and aggravated assault.

Unfortunately, there is little reason to believe that violence ends with the teenage years. For example, among those arrested for the most serious crimes in 1996, 31 percent were under eighteen

years old, 45 percent under twenty-one, and 56 percent under twenty-five.

## Roots of the Problem

Juvenile violence in America appears to be rooted in the confluence of a number of factors, including increases in child abuse and neglect, juvenile poverty, juvenile substance abuse, access to firearms by young people, and the exposure of youths to violence.

*Child Abuse and Neglect.* It seems no coincidence that in the past twenty-five years, while the annual rate of juvenile violence has quadrupled, according to the U.S. Department of Health and Human Services, reports of child abuse and neglect have risen from six hundred thousand annually to over three million each year, a 500 percent increase.

Numerous studies and case reports state that many seriously violent juvenile offenders have been the victims of child abuse, often at early ages. Most have also been seriously neglected by their parents.

The link between child maltreatment and juvenile violence, though not well-researched, seems intuitive. Some children learn to become violent from their abusive parents, who serve as role models. Other abused children suffer psychological or physical trauma, or both, which leads to impaired functioning of the sort that has been empirically linked to juvenile violence—for example, brain damage, neurological dysfunction, psychiatric illness, and learning disabilities. Children also commit acts of violence in direct response to the abuse they suffer. For example, each year between four and five hundred juvenile Americans kill their parents, and it has been estimated that in 90 percent of these cases the killer had been previously abused by the adult victim.

*Juvenile Poverty.* In 1980, prior to the tremendous increase in juvenile violence in America, an estimated 18 percent of the children in the United States lived in poverty. By the mid-1990s, in the midst of one of the greatest periods of economic prosperity ever experienced in the United States, as many as one out of every four American children was being raised in poverty. Moreover, in many large urban areas, where rates of juvenile violence were the highest in the nation, the percentage of children living in poverty was said to be 40 percent or higher. Indeed, in some major cities the majority of children were being raised in economically impoverished homes.

The link between poverty and crime, including violent crime, is universally recognized. It is a link undoubtedly mediated by a host of factors related to poverty—for example, an increased likelihood of child abuse and neglect; greater exposure to crime, including violent crime, both in the home and in the community; and a higher incidence of substance abuse. While not all violent juveniles have been raised in poverty, many have. Poverty does not directly cause juvenile violence, but it often sows the seeds for such behavior by limiting the legitimate opportunities of many youngsters, thus making them more vulnerable to the kinds of social and economic pressures that lead to criminal, sometimes violently criminal, conduct.

*Substance Abuse.* Surveys conducted in the late 1990s repeatedly found that drug abuse in the United States was declining, except among one segment of the population: children and adolescents. According to the National Institute on Drug Abuse, drug abuse (including alcohol abuse) among high school students reached its low point in 1992 at 21.7 percent. Thereafter in the 1990s, the incidence of high school drug and alcohol abuse rose steadily to more than 40 percent nationally.

It is not known how many juveniles commit crimes of violence while under the influence of drugs, but the percentage is likely quite high. For example, informed estimates indicate that between 25 and 50 percent of all juvenile murderers are under the influence of alcohol or other substances at the time they kill.

The link between substance abuse and violence among teenagers is not only well recognized but also readily explained. Developmentally, teenagers have limited impulse control. Many drugs, including alcohol, have a disinhibiting effect on the central nervous system that reduces what little self-control many young people already have, thereby significantly increasing the likelihood of violent acting-out.

*Access to Firearms.* The vast majority of juvenile homicides are committed with firearms, as are a large proportion of other juvenile crimes of violence. Thus, it comes as no surprise that at the same time the United States began to experience this ep-

**Teenage gang members charged with the fatal stabbing of a New York City rival, 1957.**
CORBIS/BETTMANN

idemic of juvenile violence, juvenile access to guns grew to unprecedented levels. In the late 1990s, it was estimated that there were nearly as many guns as people in the United States. And more than ever before, these guns had fallen into the hands of teenagers, many of whom used them to commit violent crimes.

In one study of public and private elementary, middle, and high school students (grades six through twelve) conducted by the Harvard University School of Public Health, 59 percent of the teenage respondents said they had access to a handgun. In other recent studies conducted or funded by the federal government, results also indicated the ease with which juveniles could obtain guns. In a survey conducted by the Centers for Disease Control and Prevention, almost 14 percent of male high school students polled said they had carried a gun to school during the preceding thirty days. According to data released by the U.S. Education Department in May 1998, 6,093 students, including some 500 elementary students, were expelled for bringing a gun to school during the 1996–1997 year.

*Exposure to Violence.* Violent behavior, like most behavior, is learned, and juvenile violence is no exception. Many children undoubtedly learn to be violent by observing or being directly victimized by violence in their homes; abusive parents provide powerfully negative role models. American children and adolescents, however, are also exposed to violence in entertainment media, including television, movies, video games, comic books, and lyrics of popular music.

In some instances exposure to media violence has led directly to juvenile violence, as in cases of so-called copycat crimes committed by teenagers. However, media violence also seems to have a more insidious and widespread influence as the frequency of exposure to violence creates the illusion (and gives children the message) that violence is a commonplace and a normal, if not acceptable, part of life.

## Social and Legal Response

Although teenage violence achieved national attention in the United States only toward the end of the twentieth century, it is a phenomenon older than the country itself. Young people committed violent crimes in colonial America as early as the 1600s. Initially these juvenile offenders were treated as adults and subjected to the same pen-

alties as their adult counterparts: prison and execution. Indeed, the first legally sanctioned execution of a child that was recorded in the United States occurred in 1644. Thomas Grainger, a sixteen-year-old boy, was put to death after confessing to sexual conduct with a sheep.

Over the next two hundred years, as the American system of justice evolved, the treatment of violent youths became more standardized and in many ways more humane. In the early nineteenth century, many states developed special institutions to deal with criminal and so-called incorrigible juveniles. Known as houses of refuge, houses of reformation, or more commonly, reform schools, these early juvenile facilities received abused, neglected, abandoned, and criminal youths. Still, in most jurisdictions, serious juvenile offenders were subject to the same criminal proceedings as adults and could, in the discretion of the courts, be sent to jails, penitentiaries, and reformatories.

The "refuge" movement, in various incarnations, dominated the social and legal response to violent youths until nearly the end of the 1800s. In 1899 the first juvenile court in the United States was established in Chicago. The Juvenile Court of Cook County was granted jurisdiction over all juveniles, whether neglected, abandoned, abused, or delinquent. Thereafter, every other state created similar juvenile courts, children's courts, or (most recently) family courts. These institutions usually have exclusive jurisdiction over cases involving juveniles, including those who have committed violent crimes. The juvenile court movement also led virtually all states to develop separate, special institutions for juvenile offenders aimed at rehabilitating rather than punishing or merely warehousing the guilty.

This "rehabilitative model" for dealing with juvenile offenders, including violent youths, dominated the legal landscape throughout the first half of the twentieth century. Even the most violent juvenile offenders were generally tried only in juvenile court and, if found delinquent, subjected at most to confinement in secure facilities until they reached the age of majority. Upon reaching that age (usually eighteen or twenty-one), these youths were released outright.

During the 1960s and 1970s, however, in response to a perceived increase in juvenile violence, virtually every state amended its laws as part of what has been called the move to "recriminalize" serious delinquency among young people. The new laws provided that children and young teenagers, previously immune from criminal prosecution, could, in some cases, be prosecuted in adult criminal court and, if convicted, be subjected to adult criminal sanctions. These laws, variously termed waiver, transfer, or certification statutes, allow prosecutors and courts to consider factors such as the nature of the crime, the youth's background, and the likelihood of rehabilitation in deciding whether to try a juvenile as an adult.

Although these relatively harsh laws had been on the books since the 1970s, the epidemic of juvenile violence in the last decade of the twentieth century brought about a renewed call for even greater criminalization of violent juvenile offenses. Some states responded by further lowering the age at which violent juveniles could be tried as adults or by expanding the number of violent crimes for which juveniles could be criminally punished. As a result, more teenagers than ever before are being tried in adult criminal courts, sentenced to lengthy prison terms, and in some cases, sentenced to death. Many commentators argued seriously for dismantling the juvenile justice system altogether and treating all young criminals as adults. Others, however, urged legislators, courts, and policy makers to temper these criminalization efforts with an eye toward preventing juvenile violence. Those urging a more preventive approach noted that more punitive legal responses to violent juveniles are quite unlikely to decrease the overall incidence of juvenile violence. These commentators noted that juvenile offenders, especially those who commit violent crimes, do not seem to be deterred in any large measure by the threat of criminal punishment.

While the trend at the end of the twentieth century was toward increased criminalization of juvenile violence, many schools, agencies, and institutions began to make efforts to prevent or at least control this epidemic by other means.

Many government agencies attempted to prevent juvenile violence by making serious attempts to decrease the incidence of child abuse. In many jurisdictions, parents at risk began to be identified before or shortly after the births of their children; they were provided with in-house nursing and educational services aimed at improving their parenting. Schools implemented parenting courses; educational and family planning efforts led to a decrease in the number of children born to teenage mothers.

Efforts at welfare reform, including job training and increased availability of child care, began to break the cycle of poverty that had for so long trapped generation after generation of American children, thereby placing them at grave risk of delinquent behavior, including violent crime.

Educational efforts at reducing juvenile substance abuse also led to positive results. Legislators at both the state and national levels gave serious thought to effective gun control measures that would at least keep the most dangerous firearms out of the hands of children and teenagers. Goaded by the threat of legislation, the entertainment industry finally gave serious consideration to reducing the violent content in television programming, movies, and other media.

During the 1990s, however, most of these preventive efforts were in their infancy, their viability often depending on the changing state of politics and the economy.

*BIBLIOGRAPHY*

Bok, Sissela. *Mayhem: Violence as Public Entertainment.* Reading, Mass.: Addison-Wesley, 1998.
Ewing, Charles Patrick. *Kids Who Kill.* New York: Avon Books, 1995.
———. *When Children Kill: The Dynamics of Juvenile Homicide.* Lexington, Mass.: Lexington Books, 1990.
Federal Bureau of Investigation. *Crime in the United States: Uniform Crime Reports, 1996.* Washington, D.C.: U.S. Government Printing Office, 1997.
Kaar-Morse, Robin, and Meredith S. Wiley. *Ghosts from the Nursery: Tracing the Roots of Violence.* Boston: Atlantic Monthly, 1998.
Singer, Simon I. *Recriminalizing Delinquency: Violent Juvenile Crimes and Juvenile Justice Reform.* New York: Cambridge University Press, 1996.
Wodarski, John S., and Lois Ann Wodarski. *Preventing Teenage Violence.* New York: Springer, 1998.

CHARLES PATRICK EWING

*See also* **Age and the Life Cycle; Children; Developmental Factors: Puberty and Adolescence; Domestic Violence; Schools; Thrill Crime.**

# TELEVISION

*Following the **Historical Overview** are three subentries: Censorship, Children's Television, and Violent Genres.*

## HISTORICAL OVERVIEW

The debate over television violence is a long and storied one. Media violence—whether in comic books, movies, or radio—as a contributor to social problems has been studied since the 1920s; for as long as television has been used as a mass medium, it too has been the subject of concerns about its effects. Parents worry that children who watch television are exposed to undesirable messages regarding sex and violence. Social scientists, law enforcement agents, and physicians have joined the ranks of those concerned that television reinforces antisocial behaviors by teaching youths that violence is an acceptable way to deal with conflict. Others counter these concerns with the argument that television is merely an entertainment medium—not a teacher—and that the responsibility to teach right and wrong falls to parents, not to television networks and program producers.

Television, like radio, is a point-to-multipoint medium; multiple viewers receive the same message. What attention they pay to the message, and how they process it, may vary a great deal, but at a base level, the message (or content) is the same for all who choose to tune their televisions to a particular channel at a specific time. This technical aspect of television makes it a particularly powerful medium. And the element of visual images is the source of television's great appeal to children.

At its advent, television, with its singular message to the masses (or at least those who had access to a television), had a unifying effect on disparate elements of society. Viewers of different races, classes, and geographic locations were informed about important news events and entertained by comedy and drama shows; all were receiving a common message, something that rarely happened with the print media. Sometimes referred to as the "watercooler effect," television provided employees from all walks of life with a shared experience that they could then talk about, often while taking a break around the watercooler or, in more contemporary times, the coffee machine. Managers and subordinates alike could share a laugh over last night's favorite sitcom or variety show.

As television, with its powerful combination of audio and visual images, had the great potential to bring people together with a single message, the content of that message soon became the object of concern. For if television's positive messages had the power to unite and inform people, it was likely that negative messages and portrayals could have an equally strong impact. The most common concern over television violence has been its potential effects on young people, who are generally believed to be more impressionable and less able to

distinguish between such abstract concepts as good and evil, reality and fantasy, and right and wrong behavior. Specific concerns related to children include the following:

1. Children may not be able to tell the difference between real violence and fictional violence such as that portrayed in cartoons. When a cartoon character shakes off the effects of falling off a cliff or having a boulder land on its head, children may not understand that the real life consequences of such events are a great deal more serious. This may be even more confusing when cartoon characters have a human form, further blurring the distinction between real and make-believe characters.

2. Television often portrays unrealistic consequences of violence, so that children may not understand the true potential of violent acts. Characters often do not exhibit true harm when injured or assaulted. Whereas the cowboy who is shot may be back in the saddle after the commercial break, real gunshot victims rarely make such a rapid recovery. Children may also become confused about the realistic and long-lasting effects of physical violence when they see an actor who was killed on one show appear on a new one. The finality of death may be diminished.

3. Television, some believe, encourages "copycat violence"—some children mimic behaviors seen on their favorite programs. This is potentially dangerous if they also have a diminished understanding of the real effects of violent behavior. Shortly after the debut of the popular program *Power Rangers*, many parents and teachers observed an alarming increase in martial-arts-style aggression toward other children. The program was subsequently banned in many day-care centers and schools and by government officials in several countries.

4. Television relies heavily on violence as a plot device because it is a quick and easy way to resolve conflict and to establish power. Consequently, heavy television viewers are saturated with gratuitous violence and may lack knowledge of prosocial methods of conflict resolution. A child may glean that it is much easier to shoot, and possibly even kill, the bad guy than to

pursue other, more time-consuming ways to apprehend him.

As broadcasting is a unique medium with special qualities, it also has its own legal restrictions and protections. The airwaves used to transmit broadcast signals are essentially owned by the citizens, much as public parks are the property of the people; frequency space is merely loaned to broadcasters through the licensing process. Broadcasters theoretically are held to a strict standard of public service, more so than the print media and cable television networks that are privately owned and distributed. But broadcasting, like other media, is also a form of speech that is fully protected from government censorship by the First Amendment of the U.S. Constitution. And therein lies the great obstacle to any easy solution to the potential effects of such a ubiquitous and pervasive medium. At the heart of the issue is the conflict between, on the one hand, the well-intentioned desire to protect children from potentially harmful images, and, on the other, First Amendment protections of free speech and Section 326 of the Communications Act, which prohibits government censorship of television programming.

**Historical Context**

Concerns over television violence, voiced ever since the medium's beginnings in the 1950s, resurface virtually every time a particular act or series of violent acts captures the nation's attention, ironically often through the national news media. Such violent events or trends often renew the public debate; they have sometimes instigated government interest and even congressional hearings. For example, the first congressional inquiry into television violence followed a 1954 Justice Department study that reported an increase in juvenile delinquency in the United States. Although television was a relatively new medium, crime and horror shows were popular with children, leading many senators to make the "logical" connection between it and the increase in youth violence.

Following years of political and social unrest during the Civil Rights movement, and the assassinations of John F. Kennedy and Martin Luther King, Jr., the United States was searching for answers to the causes of violent behavior. An extensive investigation of television violence came after the assassination of Robert Kennedy in 1968. Immediately following the assassination, President Lyndon Johnson announced the formation of the National Commission on the Causes and Preven-

tion of Violence, and suggested that television might be a good place to start the investigation. In countless Capitol Hill speeches, television violence, including that which was shown during newscasts, was blamed for desensitizing Americans to violence; polls indicated that many Americans believed that television was too violent and did indeed contribute to societal aggression by normalizing a climate of violence. Although a number of congressional bills aimed at curbing television violence failed to pass, the sentiment remained that something had to be done to reduce the amount of violence in television programming.

One of the most famous, if not embarrassing, efforts to discover the true effects of television violence came with the Surgeon General's Scientific Advisory Committee on Television Behavior. In 1972, after nearly three years of study, the committee released a 279-page report titled "Television and Growing Up: The Impact of Televised Violence," comprising inconsistent findings and weakly recommended actions. Many considered the investigative effort a failure, but it did serve to highlight the real difficulties in media-effects research and the need for continued, long-term studies.

The concern over television continued into the 1970s, but there was also a move away from indicting television as the singular cause of societal violence. In the closely watched 1977 trial of Ronnie Zamora, accused of the brutal murder of an elderly Florida woman, the broadcast industry found itself on trial as Zamora pleaded insanity due to "subliminal television intoxication." Zamora's attorney said that his client, an avid viewer of television crime shows, had seen so many crimes without realistic consequences that he did not understand the true impact of his actions. The jury quickly rejected Zamora's defense, and observers suggested that personal, social, and economic issues affect behavior far more than does television viewing.

As with the Zamora jury, the courts have been reluctant to place the blame on television for violent behavior. In two separate cases ultimately decided in 1981 and 1982, the NBC network came under scrutiny for an assault and a suicide that had been blamed on their programming. In the first case the mother of a nine-year-old girl assaulted by fellow students claimed the young boys reenacted a rape scene from the 1974 NBC movie *Born Innocent*, which aired on the network the evening before the attack. The network was accused of negligence and reckless conduct for broadcasting

Dallas, 22 November 1963. The traumatic assassinations of the 1960s led to several investigations of television violence. CORBIS

the film in the early evening, when it was likely that children would be among the viewing audience. A few years later NBC was again accused of negligence by the parents of Nicky DeFilippo, a teenager who hanged himself after viewing the *Tonight Show*. The 23 May 1979 episode featured a segment in which the host, Johnny Carson, was "hanged" by a guest professional stuntman, who even warned viewers not to reenact the stunt. In both cases, the court ruled that in the absence of incitement to violence (action), a television show and network cannot be liable for the actions of its viewers.

Still, many were unwilling to let television off the hook altogether. The 1989 Central Park jogger incident, in which a New York City woman was brutally gang-raped, was cited by congressional members as the very type of societal violence caused by the continual exposure to violent television programming. A death caused by a child allegedly emulating an episode of MTV's *Beavis and Butt-Head* became the target of Attorney General Janet Reno in 1993. Although the after-school program was on a cable—not a broadcast—network, the incident prompted intense scrutiny; in response, MTV moved the show to an evening hour when children were not likely to be watching it unsupervised.

A series of school shootings in the late 1990s again led to fingerpointing at television. Although

the need to find a cause for senseless acts of violence, especially tragedies involving children, is understandable, the general consensus has moved away from an indictment of a particular television show or network toward concerns over long-term exposure to television violence in combination with a number of other social conditions, including familial, socioeconomic, and cultural status. By the end of the twentieth century, fully two generations of children had grown up on television, and not all of them exhibited violent behaviors. Identifying those who are likely and those who are unlikely to mimic television violence appears to be key to gauging media effects.

The "TV made me do it" defense did not hold much credibility in the case of Ronnie Zamora; nor is there credibility in making television the scapegoat for societal violence. The violent acts cited do not necessarily imply a direct cause-and-effect relationship between societal violence and television violence. A more realistic approach is to examine the slow, almost insidious effect that develops over long periods of exposure to television violence.

### Studies of Television's Effects

Virtually all mass media have been blamed for having a negative social effect at one time or another; but none has been scrutinized as much and by such a wide variety of sources as has television. Although it is difficult to give an exact number, one

President Bill Clinton speaking about youth violence in May 1999 (after the Littleton shootings). He announced that half of the televisions sold in the United States that year would contain the v-chip. CORBIS/AFP

government source in the 1980s estimated that 3,500 studies had investigated the social and behavioral effects of television violence. In addition to the government-commissioned studies by the Surgeon General, the Centers for Disease Control and Prevention, and the National Institutes of Mental Health, private agencies studying television violence include the American Medical Association, American Psychological Association, Parent-Teacher Association, National Council on Churches of Christ, National Coalition for Television (NCTV), and the National Citizen's Committee on Broadcasting. Most of these studies were conducted under the supervision of research teams or agencies. Others were less scientifically directed, such as the study directed by NCTV's executive director, the Reverend David Wildmon. Assembling a national team of four thousand coders (viewers who recorded the context and content of shows), the study registered the names of companies that advertised during programs that NCTV had labeled as violent. These companies were then targeted by Wildmon's organization for a one-year consumer boycott.

Despite the plethora of studies, few absolutes can be said of the effects of television violence on the viewing public. For every study that has claimed proof that television has a significant effect on aggressive behavior, another study counters that it is impossible to establish a direct cause-and-effect correlation between the two. Comparisons have also been difficult because of varying operational definitions of violence. Should violence be defined

as physical abuse, or verbal or mental abuse as well? Only actual, or also threatened, assault? Involving only humans, or animals also, or even acts of God? The use of different methodological approaches (quantitative, qualitative, and experimental) have also posed problems. When University of Washington researcher Brandon Centerwall reported that homicides doubled in South Africa after television was introduced, critics of the study dismissed the methodological approach and suggested that a host of issues could have attributed to the increased violence.

The truth of television's impact on viewers probably lies somewhere between the two extremes of no effect and an absolute effect. Although it is hard to prove that television violence has a direct effect on behavior, it certainly cannot be dismissed as one among a host of societal issues that have led to a violent culture. For example, law enforcement agencies have long voiced their concern over the environment of "happy violence" that is fostered by American television, movies, and video games—that is, violence depicted with no apparent serious or real consequence. They argue that young people inured to such presentations do not fully consider the repercussions of their own violent actions. Beginning in the 1970s, a group of researchers headed by University of Pennsylvania professor George Gerbner compiled a yearly index that tracked both the amount and the context of violent acts in television programs. They also conducted surveys of television viewers' attitudes. Gerbner concluded that the way heavy users of television saw the world (their level of social reality) was largely shaped by the world as portrayed on television. If, as Gerbner later contended, the world as portrayed on television was both inaccurate and disproportionately violent, it could lead to a false notion of the world as an ultraviolent and dangerous place.

It should be noted that, like most studies, Gerbner's had its critics. Still, the concept that television's effect was not immediate but rather developed over continued and intense exposure won favor among many social scientists. Ellen Wartella, dean of the College of Communication at the University of Texas at Austin and coprincipal investigator on the National Television Violence Study, summarized three major findings in television effects research:

1. The learning effect—viewers learn the aggressive attitudes and behaviors depicted in the programs they see.
2. The desensitization effect—prolonged viewing of media violence can lead to emotional desensitization toward real violence and real victims, which may result in callous attitudes and a decreased likelihood that desensitized individuals will take action to help victims when real violence occurs.
3. The fear effect—viewing violence may increase the fear of being victimized, leading toward self-protective behavior and an increased mistrust of others.

**Legislative Efforts**

After years of debate in Congress over legislative remedies for violence on television, the first concrete step was taken in 1990 with the passage of the Television Improvement Act. This measure released the television networks from antitrust constraints, thereby enabling them to explore collectively voluntary measures to reduce the amount and the nature of violence in television programming. Although Congress was promoting industry self-regulation, it was implied that if the networks did not take steps to reduce television violence, government would step in and introduce formal regulatory measures to force such a reduction.

By 1993 it was clear that the networks had few intentions of instituting any programming changes, and it was widely reported that no formal meetings had ever taken place. Acting on its earlier threats to enact regulation, Congress revisited the issue of television violence in a series of hearings led by Senator Paul Simon of Illinois. Faced once again with criticism by politicians and the viewing public, the broadcast and cable industries agreed to provide a yearly report on violence, facilitated through two independent monitoring groups.

Although the monitoring reports were informative, the industry took little action to further reduce its violent programming. The issue continued to be an important, if not clear-cut, political issue. While those decrying violence on television had to skirt the issue of censorship, even the most impassioned First Amendment supporters felt justified in taking broadcasters to task for failing to

The *Jerry Springer Show* was awarded a TV-MA rating for televising sex, strippers, fighting, and general adult content. CORBIS/MITCH GERBER

program in the public's best interest. The bipartisan criticism came to the forefront during the campaign preceding the 1996 presidential election, as both incumbent president Bill Clinton and Republican nominee Bob Dole called on broadcasters to do something or risk government intervention.

The opportunity for government intervention, or at least "voluntary" self-regulation, came shortly after Clinton was elected to a second term. Approaching a new era in communications with the convergence of digital technologies, Congress seized the opportunity to enter a pact with the television industry. In exchange for industry deregulation and relaxed government oversight, Congress expected programmers to clean up their violence- and sex-laden programming.

### The V-Chip

The voluntary self-regulation agreement became law on 8 February 1996, when President Clinton signed the Telecommunications Act of 1996, a sweeping reform of the communications industry. Among the host of regulatory initiatives was Section 551, which required the television industry to establish guidelines and procedures for rating its programs, and then encode that ratings information in the vertical blanking device of newly manufactured television sets. The transmitted ratings systems would be used in conjunction with the "v-chip," an electronic blocking device that would enable parents to block programming they believed harmful to their children. Although these initiatives were labeled as voluntary, the legislation required the Federal Communications Commission to review and approve the ratings system and design its own if not satisfied with the television industry's efforts.

Not wanting to bite the government hand that had just handed it a lucrative deregulatory package, the broadcast and cable television industries quickly assembled a panel of executives to establish the required ratings system. The appointment of Jack Valenti, president of the Motion Picture Association of America, as head of the panel drew criticism from politicians and children's advocates who feared the adoption of an age-based ratings system similar to the one used for movies. These critics favored a system that also included information about the content of programming (such a system had been tested for nearly a year in Canada) and thus would be more useful to parents wishing to screen out specific elements such as sex, violence, and offensive or adult language.

When the age-based ratings system was unveiled as expected, its critics mounted a lengthy and vocal campaign in favor of content-based ratings. Many detractors complained about the voluntary nature of the ratings system and feared inconsistencies, or downright lack of compliance, among cable and broadcast networks. Soap operas, talk shows, and adult dramas, programs with similar themes and content, were often found to receive different ratings, often depending on which network aired them. It was also widely believed that networks and program producers would use the ratings system as an open door to more violent and vulgar television. If the audience was given fair warning, why not push the envelope of sex and violence? Indeed, after the *Jerry Springer Show* was awarded a TV-MA (Mature Audiences) rating, it promptly began a daily dose of sex, strippers, adult language, and fights among the show's guests.

**Jimmy Smits in the realistic police drama** *NYPD Blue*, **1997.** CORBIS/MITCHELL GERBER

## TV Parental Guidelines

TV-Y (All Children)—This program is designed to be appropriate for all children. Whether animated or live-action, the themes and elements in this program are specifically designed for a very young audience, including children from the ages of 2–6. This program is not expected to frighten younger children.

TV-Y7 (Directed to Older Children)—This program is designed for children age seven and above. It may be appropriate for children who have acquired the developmental skills needed to distinguish between make-believe and reality. Themes and elements in this program may include mild fantasy and comedic violence, or may frighten children under the age of seven. Therefore, parents may wish to consider the suitability of this program for their very young children. Note: For those programs where fantasy violence may be more intense or more combative than other programs in this category, such programs will be designated TV-Y7-FV.

TV-G (General Audience)—Most parents would find this program suitable for all ages. Although this rating does not signify a program designed specifically for children, most parents may let younger children watch this program unattended. It contains little or no violence, no strong language, and little to no sexual dialogue or situations.

TV-PG (Parental Guidance Suggested)—This program contains material that parents may find unsuitable for younger children. Many parents may want to watch it with their younger children. The theme itself may call for parental guidance, or the program may contain one or more of the following: moderate violence (V), some sexual situations (S), infrequent coarse language (L), or some suggestive dialogue (D).

TV-14 (Parents Strongly Cautioned)—This program contains some material that many parents would find unsuitable for children under fourteen years of age. Parents are strongly urged to exercise greater care in monitoring this program and are cautioned against letting children under the age of fourteen watch unattended. This program contains one or more of the following: intense violence (V), intense sexual situations (S), strong coarse language (L), or intensely suggestive dialogue (D).

TV-MA (Mature Audiences Only)—This program is specifically designed to be viewed by adults and therefore may be unsuitable for children under seventeen. This program contains one or more of the following: graphic violence (V), explicit sexual activity (S), or crude language (L).

Source: "Commission Finds Industry Video Programming Rating System Acceptable; Adopts Technical Requirements to Enable Blocking of Video Programming (the 'V-Chip')." CS Docket No. 97-55, CS Docket 97-321, ET Docket 97-206. Federal Communications Commission, 12 March 1998.

Still other critics believed the system would be applied unfairly against shows with minority characters and unconventional plotlines. Gay and lesbian organizations complained when the ABC network gave *Ellen*, a sitcom with a lead lesbian character, mildly suggestive dialogue, and virtually no violence, the same TV-14 rating given the adult police drama *NYPD Blue*. And as was true with other labeled media, including movies and music compact discs, researchers found that children were actually attracted to programs with the most restrictive ratings. In an apparent manifestation of the forbidden-fruit syndrome, youths felt more grown-up watching programs that were labeled as restricted to "mature audiences."

Many broadcasters doubted that most parents would pay much attention to the ratings, let alone learn how to program the v-chip to block objectionable shows. Indeed, an Annenberg Public Policy Center poll found that six months after the ratings system's debut fully two-thirds of parents were not using it; another six months later that number had decreased, although 51 percent of parents polled by the Associated Press reported that they paid little to no attention to the television ratings.

The public's lukewarm response to the ratings system, coupled with continued public and political protests, eventually resulted in a revised system known as the TV Parental Guidelines, formally approved by the FCC in March 1998. The new system combines six descriptive labels to indicate appropriateness based on age and maturity (TV-Y, TV-Y7, TV-G, TV-PG, TV-14, TV-MA) and content indicators concerning fantasy violence (FV), violence (V), sexual situation (S), strong language (L), and suggestive dialogue (D). An on-screen ratings icon is broadcast for fifteen seconds at the beginning of every program, and the rating is encoded at intervals throughout the program so that a show can be blocked even after it has begun.

Compliance by individual broadcast and cable networks remains voluntary, but once a network or show commits to labeling its programming it must continue to do so. Sports and news programs are exempt, even though many believe these are among the most violent genres on television. It was successfully argued that the realistic portrayal of violence is essential to truthful and accurate news reporting, just as it is also a realistic element of professional sports.

The ultimate test of the ratings system will come once the v-chips are in widespread use. Without a way to electronically block objectionable programming, parents have only half a system. It is likely that parents who acquire the v-chip will begin to pay more attention to the ratings and to block programs based on them. Yet pre-v-chip televisions will remain in people's homes for a while. Thus, the public's verdict on the ratings system and the v-chip will not be known for quite some time.

*BIBLIOGRAPHY*

Clark, C. "TV Violence: Will Hollywood Tone It Down—or Face Regulation?" *Congressional Quarterly Researcher* 3, no. 12 (26 March 1993).

Cooper, Cynthia A. *Violence on Television: Congressional Inquiry, Public Criticism, and Industry Response: A Policy Analysis.* Lanham, Md.: University Press of America, 1996.

Dyk, Timothy, and R. Goldberg. "The First Amendment and Congressional Investigations of Broadcast Programming." *Journal of Law and Politics* 3, no. 4 (1987).

Federal Communications Commission. "Commission Finds Industry Video Programming Rating System Acceptable; Adopts Technical Requirements to Enable Blocking of Video Programming (The 'V-Chip')." CS Docket No. 97–55, CS Docket 97–321, ET Docket 97–206, 12 March 1998.

———. "Joint Reply Comments in the Matter of Joint Voluntary Proposal for Video Programming Rating System of National Association of Broadcasters, National Cable Television Association and Motion Picture Association of America." CS Docket No. 97–55, 8 May 1997.

Gerbner, George, and L. Gross. "Living with Television: The Violence Profile." *Journal of Communication* 26, no. 2 (1976).

Levin, Gary. "Even with V-Chip Ahead, System Earns Few Fans." *USA Today*, 13 January 1998.

National Institutes of Mental Health. "Television and Behavior: Ten Years of Scientific Progress Implications for the Eighties." Vols. 1 and 2. Washington, D.C.: U.S. Government Printing Office, 1982.

Pecora, Norma O. *The Business of Children's Television.* New York: Guilford, 1998.

Postman, Neil. *Amusing Ourselves to Death: Public Discourse in the Age of Show Business.* New York: Viking, 1986.

"Ratings Have 'Forbidden Fruit' Effect—Study." *Reuters News Service*, 26 March 1997.

Wartella, Ellen A. "The Context of Television Violence. The Carroll C. Arnold Distinguished Lecture." Speech Communication Association Annual Convention, San Diego, Calif., 23 November 1996.

CYNTHIA A. COOPER

*See also* **Advertising; Journalism; Language and Verbal Violence; Photography; Popular Culture; Sports.**

## CENSORSHIP

From the time of the acceptance of television as the dominant form of American entertainment, in the early 1950s, questions have been raised about the medium's content, especially its portrayal of violence. Serious investigations into the causal link between television violence and real-life aggression have been mounted in each succeeding decade. Television's representation of minorities and its openness to controversial ideas have also been disputed throughout the years. All segments of American society have gotten involved in these discussions—government officials, network executives, Hollywood producers, advertisers, scientists, advocacy groups, and concerned citizens. Changes in technology and distribution have only intensified the debate about how well television reflects the real world. Campaigns have been waged for some type of censorship of the airwaves, calls that critics say go against the right of free expression guaranteed by the First Amendment.

From the beginning, radio and television have been treated differently from other means of communication, for several reasons. First, since there is a limit to the frequency spectrum, broadcasters must apply to the Federal Communications Commission (FCC) to use the public airwaves. Second, since both media are transmitted directly into the home, provisions must be made to safeguard children from objectionable programs. The FCC was created in 1934 as an independent government agency to regulate broadcasting and determine whether a licensed station is serving the "public interest, convenience, and necessity." The commission is prohibited from interfering with the right of free speech but has the responsibility to determine if a licensee is serving the interests of its community.

The FCC has been prominent in determining what constitutes public morality and especially in safeguarding against "obscene, indecent, or profane language." A landmark case begun in the early 1970s prohibited broadcasters from airing sexual or excretory epithets, which the comedian George Carlin called "the seven dirty words," when children would be in the audience. The Supreme Court upheld the ruling, for the reason that radio and television are "uniquely pervasive in the lives of all Americans." Visual images have been more difficult to regulate, and what constitutes indecent television programming has been debated in every branch of government.

The House Committee on Interstate and Foreign Commerce conducted the first examination of television content in 1952. Its hearings addressed the gratuitous violence in such live adult series as *Man Against Crime* and in such filmed children's shows as *Hopalong Cassidy*. The investigation prompted the television industry to adopt a censorship code modeled after the Hollywood Production Code. *TV Guide* remained unconvinced of the effect of violence on children and declared in its first editorial on the subject that "physical action, excitement, and adventure are part of every child."

During the 1950s sponsors controlled the production of most evening programs. They vigorously combed all scripts, searching for ways in which their products were cast in a bad light. The most notorious interference occurred during *Playhouse 90*'s live production of *Judgement at Nuremberg,* when the American Gas Company blipped out "gas chamber" from this play about Nazi atrocities because the term reflected poorly on the sponsor. Sponsors were susceptible to special-interest groups and participated freely in the blacklist, which banned performers whose political opinions or associations were deemed controversial. Much television censorship during the 1950s occurred behind the scenes, with the unpublicized excising of troublesome content and talent from productions.

Disturbed by the rising rate of teenage crime, the Democratic senator Estes Kefauver of Tennes-

see convened a public hearing in 1954 to determine the causes of juvenile delinquency. The Senate subcommittee listened to the findings of psychiatrists and police officers to probe the detrimental effect that popular culture, including comic books, movies, and television, had on the behavior of adolescents. Kefauver's report, released in 1955, warned that television was potentially the most harmful of all media. The networks expressed their concern and promised remedies, but television was undergoing a major structural transformation that would have the effect of increasing violent content in television programming.

During the mid-1950s the production axis of television shifted from New York City to Hollywood, California, resulting in a switch from live anthology dramas to filmed episodic series. Instead of producing character studies based on a theatrical tradition, the West Coast studios, in consultation with the networks, relied on familiar generic formulas, notably Westerns and detective stories, and utilized action to resolve dramatic conflict. Newton Minow, appointed chairman of the FCC by President John F. Kennedy, described the genre of the telefilm (a motion picture produced to be broadcast on television), which at the time was dominating the airwaves, as "a vast wasteland," an endless procession of "blood and thunder, mayhem, violence, sadism, murder, western badmen, western good men, private eyes, gangsters, more violence, and cartoons." Each new Hollywood series upped the action quota of the last, until the watershed mayhem of *The Untouchables,* which focused on the murderous exploits of 1930s gangsters in Prohibition Chicago. Dr. Fredric Wertham, a psychiatric consultant to the Kefauver subcommittee, warned that Americans had been conditioned to enjoy merciless violence, to the imperilment of democracy.

With *The Untouchables* as his chief target, Democratic senator Thomas Dodd of Connecticut conducted a series of hearings on television violence during the early 1960s. His committee produced thousands of pages of testimony and even subpoenaed secret documents from network producers. Quinn Martin, the producer of *The Untouchables*, was quoted as saying "I like the idea of sadism." The heads of the three networks—CBS, ABC, and NBC—were castigated for injecting sex and violence into popular programs. Although Dodd did not recommend specific legislation, his probe led indirectly to a shift from action-adventure programs to lighter situation comedies.

The television business had never been so scrutinized, and executives took voluntary action to clean up the airwaves, keeping the government at bay.

After years of little success, advocacy groups began to influence television programming in the 1960s. The National Association for the Advancement of Colored People had been protesting the television adaptation of *Amos 'n' Andy* since its 1951 debut. The series was withdrawn from syndication in 1966, when its derogatory stereotypes of blacks from the minstrel era helped to flame urban unrest. A group of Italian American associations objected to the negative ethnic stereotyping of *The Untouchables*. After boycotting a sponsor of the series, Liggett and Myers Tobacco Company, the group met with producers, who agreed to eliminate from the program "fictional characters as hoodlums with Italian names." Over the years many television executives have welcomed advocacy groups such as the National Gay and Lesbian Task Force and the National Organization for Women into the creative process, discussing story lines and characters with their former adversaries.

The unremitting turbulence of the late 1960s, marked by the assassinations of Martin Luther King, Jr., and Robert Kennedy, prompted a national attempt to get to the roots of what seemed like an era of violence. For many critics, television was a prime culprit. Between 1968 and 1972 three federal task forces were commissioned to study the amount and effects of media violence. The National Commission on Causes and Prevention of Violence, headed by Milton Eisenhower (the brother of former President Dwight Eisenhower and retired president of the Johns Hopkins University), discovered that eight out of every ten programs on television contained violent content, and that episodes of violence occurred at the rate of seven times an hour. The study, organized by George Gerbner, a professor and dean of the Annenberg School of Communications at the University of Pennsylvania, defined violence as "the overt expression of force intended to hurt or kill" and quantified for the first time acts of violence on network dramatic shows. Television executives did not release research this time but promised greater self-regulation.

While academics were preparing more thorough analyses of broadcast violence, network television went through a period of turmoil over political censorship. Tom and Dick Smothers, hosts of their own series *The Smothers Brothers Comedy*

*Hour,* clashed repeatedly with the management of CBS over segments of their variety show that overtly criticized the Vietnam War, most notably in their comments on the folksinger Pete Seeger's return to television after having been blacklisted in the early 1950s. Although the ratings were high, the show was abruptly canceled in 1969, and questions about freedom of speech were raised. At the same time, the major network stations and public television received a barrage of criticism from the Nixon administration over unfair news coverage. Vice President Spiro Agnew attacked the concentration of network power and threatened to revoke licenses if liberal journalistic policies did not change. Although the networks were reluctant to explore political controversies in entertainment, they continued to produce hard-hitting documentaries, most notably *The Selling of the Pentagon,* broadcast by CBS on 23 February 1971, which prompted a House committee investigation into liberties taken in the editing of interviews.

During the 1970s the surgeon general's Inquiry on Violence and congressional hearings overseen by Senator John Pastore of Rhode Island established that television violence had an adverse effect on certain members of the population, especially juveniles. For the first time the results were verified scientifically. Family groups, notably the coast-to-coast Parent Teacher Association, declared war on television sex and crime, threatening boycotts of advertised products on action series. The FCC and the Senate pressured networks to make substantive changes, leading to the removal of violent cartoons from Saturday-morning programming and the creation of "family hour." The National Association of Broadcasters (NAB) and the networks agreed that the first hour of evening programming (8:00 P.M.–9:00 P.M.) would be reserved for shows suitable for the entire family. Hollywood writers and producers, who found that networks were also censoring serious themes, challenged the family-viewing concept. In 1976 the federal judge Warren J. Ferguson of the District Court for Southern California declared that the adoption of the family viewing hour "constituted a violation of the First Amendment."

Transformations in the industry during the 1980s quieted governmental demand for network restraint. Cable television, which was increasingly prevalent and unregulated by any public interest, brought into the home violent theatrical movies with stronger language and more graphic images than those that any commercial network had ever delivered. The deregulation fervor generated by the election of President Ronald Reagan took hold of the FCC, which allowed media mergers and almost any transgression in taste. Cold War rhetoric and violent action reentered the television picture with the success of *The A-Team* (1983–1987), *He-Man and the Masters of the Universe* (1983), and later the *Mighty Morphin Power Rangers* (1993–present), whose action-toy spin-offs were heavily merchandised to children. As laissez-faire assumptions dominated the television marketplace, research into media violence became more exacting. George Gerbner developed an "enculturation" thesis, positing that frequent viewing of television crime made people excessively fearful of violence in their own world.

In the 1980s conservative religious groups began to campaign vigorously against any sexual innuendo and profanity on commercial and public television. In previous decades the National Legion of Decency, which became the National Catholic Office for Motion Pictures in 1965, reviewed and rated movies and television programs, assigning an *MO* for morally offensive material. Donald Wildmon, a United Methodist minister, took a more activist approach when he created the Coalition for Better Television in 1981 with funding from the Reverend Jerry Falwell's Moral Majority. From his base in Tupelo, Mississippi, he waged mail-in campaigns and boycotts against the advertisers of offending shows. Outraged by PBS's 1990s fictional series on gay lifestyles, *Tales of the City*, he petitioned state legislatures not to fund public television because PBS "promotes the homosexual agenda" and "mocks traditional Judeo-Christian values." Capitulations to Wildmon's pressure by such companies as Procter and Gamble and Bristol-Myers inspired individuals to take up the cause. A Michigan housewife, Terry Rakolta, organized a boycott against the sponsors of the Fox network's *Married . . . With Children* in 1989 when she was outraged by the show's raunchy humor. The series was moved to a later time slot and attracted more viewers and more potential sponsors.

As in decades past, the next crusade against television violence began with the outrage of a single senator, Democrat Paul Simon of Illinois. Shocked by an outrageous murder scene, Simon was determined to put media brutality back on the national agenda. In 1993 he brought together the broadcast and cable industries to discuss the issue with congressional representatives and media activists. Reports on this new television environ-

ment, which sustained hundreds of channels, followed quickly. The National Television Violence Study conducted by Mediascope, a national nonprofit public policy organization founded in 1992 to promote constructive depictions of health and social issues in the media, found that 57 percent of programs aired in 1994 featured some sort of violence, with perpetrators going unpunished in 73 percent of all violent scenes. President Bill Clinton joined the fray and urged his Hollywood supporters to begin "deglamorizing mindless sex and violence."

During this round of congressional negotiations, technology offered a solution. A small computer transistor, called the v-chip (the *v* stands for *violence*), was developed to screen out programs that were coded as harmful to children. With President Clinton's support, Representative Edward Markey of Massachusetts pushed for legislation in the House making v-chips mandatory in all new television sets. Steven Bochco, a writer-producer representing the creative community, led a fight against this microchip, stating that such a requirement would ultimately result in bland programs. On the other side, more than forty organizations

---

## The National Association of Broadcasters

The National Association of Broadcasters is one of the most active media lobbies in the United States, representing the commercial networks and more than nine hundred local television stations. Concerned about the legal and social problems that affect the industry, the board has written standards for its members so that broadcasters can maintain the trust and confidence of the general public. The following are program principles relating to the depiction of violence:

Violence, physical or psychological, should only be portrayed in a responsible manner and should not be used exploitatively. Where consistent with the creative intent, programs involving violence should present the consequences of violence to its victims and perpetrators.
Presentation of the details of violence should avoid the excessive, the gratuitous, and the instructional.
The use of violence for its own sake and the detailed dwelling upon brutality or physical agony, by sight or sound, should be avoided.
Particular care should be exercised where children are involved in the depiction of violent behavior.

concerned about the impact of television and the computer on children's lives demanded a major change.

Seeking a comprehensive vision for future technologies, Congress updated the responsibilities of the FCC with the passage of the Telecommunications Act of 1996. The bill revised existing policies to regulate the burgeoning information industries, including the Internet and telephone services. Television executives were given new ownership freedoms in exchange for creating standards to control indecency. Section 351 of the act mandated the installation of the v-chip in every television receiver having a diagonal screen size greater than thirteen inches. The television industry was required to devise voluntarily a rating system to identify violent, sexual, and objectionable material. The bill, encompassing broadcasting, cable, and on-line services, also created criminal penalties for anyone who knowingly transmitted "any comment, request, suggestion, image, or other communications, which is obscene, lewd, lascivious, filthy, or indecent."

Jack Valenti, the president of the Motion Picture Association of America and the architect of the film industry's voluntary movie ratings, headed a fifteen-member board to devise the television rating system. Unlike the movie system, which rates several hundred films a year, the television system would need to cover more than two thousand hours of programming a day. In March 1998 the FCC accepted the proposals of Valenti's group, which featured six levels of parental indicators for all broadcast and cable programming except news and sports. The guidelines ranged from TV-Y (programs for all children, including those between two and six years old) to TV-MA (programs designed for mature audiences only that contain one or more of the following: graphic violence, explicit sexual activity, or crude language). These parental guidelines would appear for fifteen seconds at the beginning of all rated programs and would work with v-chip technology so that parents could block programs with a certain rating. Many remained unconvinced of the legality and efficacy of the v-chip, especially the American Civil Liberties Union, which held that the depiction of violence in books and films is protected from government restriction by the First Amendment.

Television is America's most pervasive and powerful mass medium of information and entertainment. Part of its heritage has been a debate and struggle over how accurately it represents the values and ideals of all Americans. The industry and government have always relied on voluntary reform to correct programming problems, a self-regulation that sometimes results from exhaustive investigations and public outcry. In its vital position in contemporary society, American television has always relied on a complex negotiation among networks, the creative community, big business, government, and the public. Whenever television oversteps boundaries of taste in the sensitive arenas of sex and violence, there will be calls for some type of restraint by one or more of its many different audiences, and always the possibility of governmental intrusion.

*BIBLIOGRAPHY*

Barnouw, Erik. *Tube of Plenty: The Evolution of American Television.* 2d rev. ed. New York: Oxford University Press, 1990.

Cole, Barry, and Mal Oettinger. *Reluctant Regulators: The FCC and the Broadcast Audience.* Reading, Mass.: Addison-Wesley, 1978.

Comstock, George, and Eli Rubinstein. *Television and Social Behavior.* 5 vols. Washington, D.C.: National Institute of Mental Health, 1972.

Cowan, Geoffrey. *See No Evil: The Backstage Battle over Sex and Violence on Television.* New York: Simon and Schuster, 1979.

Gerbner, George, et al. *Television's Mean World: Violence Profile No. 14–15.* Philadelphia: University of Pennsylvania Annenberg School of Communications, 1986.

Gunter, Barrie. *Dimensions of Television Violence.* Aldershot, U.K.: Gower, 1985.

Montgomery, Kathryn C. *Target: Prime Time Advocacy Groups and the Struggle over Entertainment Television.* New York: Oxford University Press, 1989.

Rowland, Willard D. *The Politics of TV Violence: Policy Uses of Communication Research.* Beverly Hills, Calif.: Sage, 1983.

Watson, Mary Ann. *Defining Visions: Television and the American Experience Since 1945.* Fort Worth, Tex.: Harcourt Brace, 1998.

Wober, J. Mallory, and Barrie Gunter. *Television and Social Control.* Aldershot, U.K.: Avebury, 1988.

RON SIMON

*See also* **Film: Censorship.**

## CHILDREN'S TELEVISION

The effect of television violence on children has been a subject of debate in the United States almost from the time of television's introduction to the consumer market in the late 1940s, in part because the new medium's early success depended on the child viewer. Needing to sell television sets if their business was to survive, the broadcast networks marketed television as a family-friendly product, including in their schedules many exemplary children's programs. As television penetration increased, however, those programs were dropped in favor of more profitable ones, with more mature subject matter, aimed at the larger adult audience. Criticism soon followed.

In 1954 Senator Estes Kefauver, chairman of the Senate Subcommittee on Juvenile Delinquency, held the first congressional hearings to examine television's portrayal of crime and sexuality and its influence on children. Network executives testified that little research was available on the subject and promised to look into the matter. They did not, and in 1961 they were again called to testify before the subcommittee and its new chairman Thomas Dodd, who chastised the industry for its failure to honor its research promises. Dodd held another round of hearings in 1964 and issued a report stating that there was a relationship between the viewing of crime and violence on television and antisocial behavior.

Beginning in 1970, the federal government began to fund its own research on television violence. That year, the National Commission on the Causes and Prevention of Violence asked a number of social scientists to review existing research on tele-

vision's effects on viewers; the commission issued a statement that suggested the "constant portrayal of violence" (NCCPV 1970, p. 160) had an adverse effect on all viewers, but especially on children. With respect to children, the commission urged eliminating violence from cartoons and decreasing the programming hours given to detective shows, Westerns, and other adventure programs.

About the time that the commission issued its report, another national examination on television violence was begun by the U.S. surgeon general Jesse Steinfeld at the urging of Senator John Pastore, chairman of the Senate Subcommittee on Communications. Congress allocated $1 million to conduct research on the issue and recruited a committee of twelve distinguished social scientists, five of them with direct ties to the television industry. The panel's research consisted of twenty-three studies using several different methodologies. The surgeon general's 1972 report *Television and Growing Up: The Impact of Televised Violence* stated unequivocally that there was a causal relationship between aggressive behavior and watching violence on television.

News coverage of the report suggested a different conclusion. The *New York Times* received a leaked copy of the final report and erroneously

**Senate subcommittee hearing on juvenile delinquency led by Senator Estes Kefauver, 1956.** CORBIS/BETTMANN-UPI

## Violence Concerns in Early Children's Television

The television programs that have been most sharply criticized for their violent content have never been children's programs, but adult programs that children also watch.

In 1961 the first comprehensive study of children and television found that viewers under eighteen made up 21 to 40 percent of the audiences for many dramas made for adults—among them *Cheyenne, Maverick, 77 Sunset Strip,* and *Peter Gunn.* In one city, the researchers found, first-graders devoted 40 percent of their viewing time to adult programs; sixth-graders, 79 percent. Other dramas with violent content, such as *Roy Rogers, The Lone Ranger,* and *Sky King,* had audiences that consisted primarily of children.

Although the researchers reserved judgment on their findings, that same year the Federal Communications Commission chairman, Newton Minow, won public acclaim when he charged that "blood and thunder, western bad men, private eyes, gangsters and cartoons" had turned television into a "vast wasteland."

Children's cartoons, until recently the anchor of Saturday morning television, have come in for criticism since at least 1956, when researchers claimed that *Woody Woodpecker* contributed to aggression in children. In the mid-1960s famed CBS programmer Fred Silverman drew criticism when he invented the hard-action superhero cartoon series, a genre that was both violent and geared to selling toys and other merchandise.

reported in a front-page story that the "Surgeon General has found that violence in television programming does not have an adverse effect on the majority of the nation's youth," an error compounded by the *Times* headline, "TV Violence Held Unharmful to Youth." The *Times* report caused a furor in Washington and in the research community, leading Senator Pastore to convene hearings to publicly review the report's findings.

In the end, perhaps, the most important contribution of the surgeon general's report was that it greatly increased what was known about television and children; the ensuing controversy fueled more research. By 1975 some one thousand studies

had been done in the field; by 1980, about three thousand. In 1976 the American Medical Association issued a statement saying that television violence was a risk factor threatening the health and welfare of American children and urging boycotts of companies that sponsored violent programs. The American Psychological Association (APA) and the National Parent-Teacher Association called for similar boycotts.

In the 1970s and early 1980s federal regulators also weighed the issue, with a net effect that, from the standpoint of many critics of the broadcast industry, was probably negative. In 1975, prodded by the then Federal Communications Commission chairman Richard Wiley, the three major television networks (ABC, CBS, and NBC) announced a "family viewing" policy in which the early hours of prime time would be devoted to programs suitable for all family members, and especially young viewers. Claiming the policy violated the First Amendment, the Writers Guild sued the FCC in federal district court and won, forcing the networks to drop the policy in 1976. In 1982, as the result of a separate action brought by the U.S. Justice Department, the National Association of Broadcasters (NAB) disbanded its long-standing code of ethics and good practice when the code's commercial-time restrictions were found to violate the Sherman Anti-Trust Act. In so doing, the NAB also abandoned the code's recommendations concerning broadcasters' responsibilities to families and especially to young viewers.

The same year, the National Institute of Mental Health (NIMH) published a comprehensive review of the research in the field and concluded that "in magnitude, television violence is as strongly correlated with aggressive behavior as any other behavioral variable that has been measured" (quoted in Federman 1996, p. 5). Among its findings, the NIMH found it particularly significant that 80 percent of programs made specifically for children, such as cartoons, included some sort of violent act. Subsequent studies have noted that cartoons depicting violence, while not the bloodiest or most realistic programs, are nonetheless detrimental for children under the age of seven, an age when children have difficulty distinguishing between reality and fantasy. A 1997 study by a team of researchers at the University of California at Santa Barbara found that the average American preschooler who watches mostly cartoons sees about ten thousand violent incidents each year. Of those incidents, five hundred are considered to be "high-risk portrayals" that teach aggressive attitudes and behaviors (NTVS 1998, p. 34).

Since the NIMH report, other major reports on television violence and children have been done by the Centers for Disease Control (1991), the APA (1992), and the National Academy of Science (1992). One researcher, Edward Donnerstein, testifying on the APA's findings before Congress in 1993, reported that "by the time a child leaves elementary school they would have seen 8,000 murders and more than 100,000 acts of violence. As they near the end of their teenage years they have been witness to over 200,000 violent acts within the media," among them eighteen thousand homicides (Donnerstein 1993, p. 3). The authors of the APA report published their findings in *Big World, Small Screen,* in which they described a consensus among medical, public health, and scientific researchers as to the effects of violence in entertainment media on children and adolescents. The findings can be summarized as follows:

> *Viewing violence on television influences aggressive attitudes and behaviors, both subsequent to viewing and over the long term.* Television and film violence affects young children of all ages, at all socioeconomic levels, and at all levels of intelligence. The effect is not limited to children who are predisposed to aggressive behavior, though among those children the effects can be most pronounced.
>
> *Prolonged viewing of media violence can lead to emotional desensitization toward real-world violence and its victims.* As viewers become accustomed to violent content in entertainment media, their appetite for violence increases. So, too, does the likelihood that they will become involved with or expose themselves to real violence.
>
> *Viewing violence increases one's fear of becoming a victim of violence, with a resultant increase in self-protective behaviors and increased mistrust of others.* The leading researcher in this area, George Gerbner, describes this finding as the "mean world syndrome," in which viewers' own perceptions of reality and of their risks match what is presented on television.

In 1993, following the APA report, Senator Paul Simon and Representative Edward Markey again opened congressional hearings on the subject of television violence and its effects on children. This time the impetus for the hearings was the major broadcast networks' failure to take advantage of a 1990 antitrust exemption Senator Simon had persuaded Congress to give the industry specifically so it could address the issue of violent programming. In December 1992 the Network Television Association had issued a statement in which it listed ten Standards for Depiction of Violence in Television Programs. In June 1993, threatened with several congressional bills on television violence and sensing public frustration, ABC, CBS, and NBC announced that they would take the additional step of labeling programs for their violent content. Two months later Senator Simon convened a nationally televised "summit meeting" in Hollywood to discuss the issue, at which time the Fox Television Network, the Turner Broadcasting System, and several independent broadcasters announced that they, too, would begin labeling violent programs. The summit meeting, though little remembered, marked the first time the broadcast television industry acknowledged that its programming might in fact be causally connected to behavior.

**The Multichannel Video Environment**

In its 1992 report the APA noted its expectation that children would soon be exposed to greater amounts of even more graphic violence through exposure to cable television and to R-rated films through home VCR use. According to the cable-industry-sponsored National Television Violence Study (1994–1997), the greatest number of violent programs are found on premium cable channels, followed by independent broadcasters, basic cable, and the broadcast networks. More important, the NTVS found that over the three years in which the study was done overall levels of violence on television increased; according to the researchers' final report (1998), 60 percent of all television programs contained violence. Most of that violence, the report said, was "glamorized, sanitized, and trivialized" (p. 29). Less than 5 percent of violent programs, the study said, contained any corresponding antiviolence theme.

Of particular concern in the new video environment, researchers agree, is explicit sexual violence against women, including images of rape, torture, murder, and mutilation. Cable channels that are popular with children, such as MTV, have been criticized by researchers both for their sexual content and for their portrayal of women, often shown in some coercive or otherwise violent context.

**The MTV cartoon *Beavis and Butthead* has been criticized by parents as a bad influence on children.** GAMMA/LIAISON AGENCY

Specific programs, such as MTV's *Beavis and Butthead*, have been criticized not only for their vulgarity but also for their depictions of dangerous and easily imitated behavior. Though sexual violence is still most common and most graphic in rental videos, pay-per-view movies, and premium cable offerings, it is no longer taboo, or uncommon, on broadcast television. The reason for the change is competition: broadcasters have responded to cable and video competition in part with programs mimicking some of the adult themes and storytelling techniques used in those media.

Other important new media for children are video games for use on television sets and personal computers. Since 1992 VCR and video-game use have together resulted in a significant overall decrease in children's television viewing and in the late 1990s represented the primary source of video entertainment for children ages two to eleven. In response to congressional pressure, in 1994 two major classification systems were introduced for interactive electronic entertainment.

Television ratings were written into federal law in the 1996 Telecommunications Act, which instructed broadcasters to develop a ratings system to inform parents about programs containing "sexual, violent, or other indecent material." The ratings are to be used in conjunction with discretion technology (known as the v-chip) in television sets, and though the industry has condemned the rat-

ings requirement as unconstitutional, it has not yet challenged it in court. In July 1997 the industry unveiled an age-based ratings system, rather than a content-based one, resulting in harsh criticism from children's advocacy groups and several members of Congress. The industry responded by agreeing to add some content information to its ratings, and Congress postponed further consideration of the issue until the discretion technology becomes widely available and parents have had an opportunity to use it.

At the close of the twentieth century, the debate over television violence and its effects was international. Television was a global business, and the United States was the world's largest exporter of video programming. Many nations found programming in the United States, and particularly its children's fare, objectionable for its violence and chose to regulate it through a variety of mechanisms: outright bans; mandatory ratings and scheduling restrictions; and subsidies for domestically produced, high-quality children's programming.

BIBLIOGRAPHY

Centerwall, Brandon. "Television and Violence: The Scale of the Problem and Where to Go from Here." *Journal of the American Medical Association* 267, no. 22 (10 June 1992).

Donnerstein, Edward. Testimony on behalf of the American Psychological Association before the Committee on

Commerce, Science, and Transportation on Media Violence. United States Senate, 20 October 1993.

Federman, Joel. *Media Ratings: Design, Use, and Consequences.* Studio City, Calif.: Mediascope, 1996.

Gerbner, George, and L. Gross. "The Violent Face of Television and Its Lessons." In *Children and the Faces of Television—Teaching, Violence, Selling,* edited by E.L. Palmer and A. Dorrs. New York: Academic Press, 1980.

Huston, Aletha, et al. *Big World, Small Screen: The Role of Television in American Society.* Lincoln: University of Nebraska Press, 1992.

Minow, N., and C. LaMay, *Abandoned in the Wasteland: Children, Television and the First Amendment.* New York: Hill and Wang, 1995.

National Commission on the Causes and Prevention of Violence. *To Establish Justice, to Insure Domestic Tranquillity: Final Report of the National Commission on the Causes and Prevention of Violence.* Washington, D.C.: U.S. Government Printing Office, 1970.

*National Television Violence Study,* Vol. 3. Santa Barbara, Calif.: Center for Communication and Social Policy, University of California, 1998.

Surgeon General's Scientific Advisory Committee on Television and Social Behavior. *Television and Growing Up: The Impact of Televised Violence.* Report to the Surgeon General. United States Public Health Service. Washington, D.C.: U.S. Government Printing Office, 1972.

*Television and Behavior: Ten Years of Scientific Progress and Implications for the Eighties.* Vol. 1, *Summary Report.* Rockville, Md.: National Institute of Mental Health, 1982.

Zillman, Dolf, et al. *Media, Children, and the Family.* Hillsdale, N.J.: Lawrence Erlbaum, 1994.

CRAIG L. LaMAY

*See also* **Film: Animation; Literature: Children's and Young Adult Literature.**

## VIOLENT GENRES

Television genres are both an industrial practice and an object of critical activity. When a network needs new programming for an upcoming season, it expects that independent production companies will create new programs according to a commonly accepted set of elements and structures—that is, they will fulfill the expectations of a given genre. Critics group programs in a given genre so as to understand their development, significance, and appeal. For example, a historian can construct the development of the situation comedy from *I Love Lucy* to *Roseanne* in order to understand evolution of gender identity in American culture. Violent television genres are groups of programs that are produced to contain violent content or are understood by critics and viewers to contain violent content.

Violence of many kinds and degrees has been a consistent programming feature throughout the history of American television; nonetheless, the violence depicted on broadcast television is of a lower level of intensity and explicitness than theatrical film violence. Where feature films depict injury to the body through special effects such as squibbling (using explosives to simulate the impact of weapons), network television has largely avoided depicting wounds or blood. Television violence is typically represented by fistfights, gunshots viewed from a distance, or explosives; these representations lack the graphic detail of film violence. Like the American film industry, which from 1934 until 1966 used the Production Code to regulate film content, the television industry adopted a code in the early 1950s in response to congressional investigations into violent television content. Although the 1952 Code of Censorship remained in place only until 1976, network standards and practices departments continue to oversee television content to this day, reviewing all non-news broadcasts for compliance with legal, factual, and community standards. Further congressional hearings were held from 1961 to 1964, in which Senator Thomas J. Dodd condemned the depiction of violence in television programs such as the ABC series *The Untouchables* but did not address film violence. Television was understood by government and the industry itself to require greater oversight because of its direct entry into the home.

Television's ascendance as the dominant audio-visual mass medium of the latter half of the twentieth century contributed to film's reconceptualization of its audience, which in turn led to changes in film's depiction of violence. With the adoption of a ratings system in 1968, the film industry embraced audience differentiation, opening up possibilities for more explicit depiction of violence in categories of film restricted to adults. Television, by contrast, was until the 1980s dominated by three networks that conceived of their audiences as an undifferentiated mass; thus, from the 1950s through the 1980s—when the rise of cable television and the small-screen presentation of uncut theatrical films changed the television landscape—control over the depiction of violence was greater in television than in film.

It is important to distinguish between television genres that sometimes feature violence and violent television genres—that is, between incidental and constitutive violence. Though situation comedies, comedy-variety shows, dramas, soap operas, news programs, sports, commercials, music videos, and animation may feature some violent content some of the time, the violent content is usually subordinate to other, more defining content, whether devised to provoke laughter, tears, or the impulse to buy something. For example, in a 1953 episode of CBS's top-rated sitcom *I Love Lucy* (1951–1957), Lucy (Lucille Ball) attempts to get Ricky's (Desi Arnaz) attention by claiming that a man has tried to break into their apartment. After determining that Lucy has "cried wolf," Ricky ignores her cries when she is actually being assaulted and dragged into the basement of their building. Through Ball's physical exaggeration of a struggle, the abduction is played for laughs, and its disturbing implications are defused. By contrast, violent television genres feature violence as a constitutive element. The most prominent violent television genres are actually subgenres of the larger mode of action, which includes police-detective-crime shows, Westerns, and programs based on science fiction–fantasy.

### Westerns and Science Fiction–Fantasy Genres

Adapted from radio serials, the police-detective-crime genre was among television's earliest programming forms and has been consistently popular throughout the history of American television production. In contrast, the Western enjoyed a limited period of intense popularity, the late 1950s and early 1960s. During the 1958–1959 season, eight of the top-ten-rated shows were Westerns, led by *Gunsmoke* (CBS, 1955–1975). *Gunsmoke*'s opening sequence typified the Western's violence: a main-street shoot-out between Marshall Dillon (James Arness) and an unnamed opponent, who was killed every time. Though *Gunsmoke* remained popular until the 1970s, production of television Westerns largely ceased in the mid-1960s. The Western survives in hybrid combination with the detective genre in programs such as *Walker, Texas Ranger* (CBS, premiered in 1996).

Early examples of the science fiction–fantasy genre include *The Twilight Zone* (CBS, 1959–1965), *The Outer Limits* (ABC, 1963–1965), and *Alfred Hitchcock Presents* (CBS, 1955–1960, 1962–1964; NBC, 1960–1962, 1964–1965), which also contain elements of the horror and crime genres. These programs regularly featured murder and other violent acts, often in order to produce fantastic effects and ironic reversals. In an episode of *The Twilight Zone* entitled "Escape Clause," a man makes a pact with the devil, exchanging his soul for physical immortality. This man then commits

murder simply because, even if caught, he could not be put to death; instead, he is sentenced to life in prison.

In the 1970s science fiction and fantasy programs featured superheroes who operated as specially enhanced detectives. *The Six Million Dollar Man* (ABC, 1974–1978), *The Bionic Woman* (ABC, 1976–1977; NBC, 1977–1978), *Wonder Woman* (ABC, 1976–1977; CBS, 1977–1979), and *The Incredible Hulk* (CBS, 1978–1982) each featured main characters with superhuman strength who used their powers to violently subdue variously evil antagonists. In the 1990s syndicated programs such as *The Adventures of Hercules* and *Xena: Warrior Princess* renewed the theme of hyperbolic physical violence. Also in the 1990s science fiction–fantasy programs such as *Twin Peaks* (ABC, 1990–1991) and *The X-Files* (Fox, premiered in 1993) reemphasized the genre's early interest in the mysterious, weird, and occult. Incorporating elements of the detective-police-crime genre as well as the melodramatic serial, both shows featured special government agents attempting to understand and explain graphic violence committed by spirits, ghouls, and aliens.

### Cops and Private Eyes

Police, detective, and crime programs have dominated the representation of violence on television, influencing other genres that have incorporated their generic elements. As noted, detective serials were adapted from radio to provide programming during the first years of post–World War II broadcasting. In 1949 CBS debuted *Man Against Crime* (1949–1956), a hard-boiled detective series starring Ralph Bellamy. Bellamy used violence as often as logic to solve crimes, and the live broadcasts always included a gunshot or a punch. As television historian Erik Barnouw has noted, the production constraints of live television prevented the depiction of more extensive violence: "physical struggle was hardly feasible amid flimsy sets" (1990, p. 132). As telefilms began to replace live broadcasts in the early 1950s, the genre's focus shifted from private detectives to police detectives; the use of film created new possibilities for television violence, including expanding beyond the limits of a set. NBC's *Dragnet* (1952–1959) was shot in Los Angeles, often featuring location filming. Though a police procedural, a subgenre that focuses on the routines of police work, *Dragnet* occasionally allowed Jack Webb, as Sergeant Joe Friday, to see violent action.

By the end of the 1950s, ABC was using telefilmed Westerns and detective-crime shows to garner ratings and approach parity with its more established competitors, NBC and CBS. ABC returned the genre's focus to the private eye in top-rated shows such as *77 Sunset Strip* (1958–1964) and *Hawaiian Eye* (1959–1963), which combined violence with sex and exotic locations. ABC's most controversial show of the early 1960s was *The Untouchables* (1959–1963), which featured Eliot Ness (Robert Stack) and his band of Treasury agents engaging in perpetual gun battles with various mob figures. Tim Brooks and Earle Marsh quote an early 1960s *TV Guide* description of the show's violent formula: "'In practically every episode a gang leader winds up stitched to a brick wall and full of bullets, or face down in the parking lot (and full of bullets), or face up in the gutter (and still full of bullets), or hung up in an ice box, or run down in the street . . .'" (1992, p. 938). Indeed, in the pilot for the series, broadcast in 1959 as an installment of *The Westinghouse Desilu Playhouse* (CBS, 1958–1960), the climactic scene depicted a shoot-out in a brewery, resulting in a dozen corpses lying among the spilled suds. *The Untouchables* represented the extreme of television violence during the 1960s. Yet it is worth noting that, compared with the film *Bonnie and Clyde,* which came out in 1967 and broke new ground in depictions of violence in feature film, the violence in *The Untouchables* was far less detailed and explicit, with none of the wound-simulating special effects of the film.

In the 1970s *Mannix* (CBS, 1967–1975) continued the tradition of the violent private eye begun by *Man Against Crime* and the syndicated *Mickey Spillane's Mike Hammer* (1957–1959). A Los Angeles detective, Mannix (Mike Connors) was quick to employ his fists when questioning failed. Some programs of this era focused on individual cops, for example *Kojak* (CBS 1973–1978), while others focused on the crime-fighting unit. ABC's *S.W.A.T* (1975–1976) featured an elite Los Angeles Police Department unit of Vietnam veterans who employed special weapons and tactics to violently subdue threats too difficult for the force's regular Joe Fridays. As David Marc has observed, *S.W.A.T* expanded the type of violence depicted on television by targeting crimes of terrorism and civil disobedience rather than homicide or robbery: "the viewer is more likely to run into the PLO [Palestine Liberation Organization] than a pickpocket" (1984, p. 88). By the end of 1970s, Aaron Spelling's *Starsky and Hutch* (ABC, 1975–1979) and *Charlie's Angels* (ABC, 1976–1981) merged charisma and violence, the popularity of the shows resting as much on sex appeal as on action.

**Realism and Fantasy**

In the 1980s *Hill Street Blues* (NBC, 1981–1987) reworked *Dragnet*'s focus on the everyday business of police work into serial form, with a large ensemble cast and multiple subplots stretching across episodes. One of the decade's most critically acclaimed shows, *Hill Street Blues* used violence to advance plot and develop character. For example, in the first episode of the show, Officers Hill (Michael Warren) and Renko (Charles Haid) are shot while investigating a crime. Unlike most violent television genre programming, *Hill Street Blues* engaged the consequences of violence. Hill and Renko had difficulty readjusting to police work after recovering from their wounds.

If *Hill Street Blues'* realism, its drama leavened with comedy, added dimension to television's depiction of violence, *The A-Team* (NBC, 1983–1987) emphasized fantasy and disconnection. Like *S.W.A.T.*, *The A-Team* featured a group of Vietnam veterans utilizing special weaponry, only in this case not as police but as soldiers of fortune. Where *Hill Street Blues'* violence was personal and meaningful, *The A-Team*'s violence was spectacular and superficial. A typical episode would feature B. A. (Mr. T) building a rocket launcher from junkyard parts in order to blow up an enemy's stronghold. Typical of cartoonish violence, *The A-Team* elided the consequences of violence, as buildings exploded and cars crashed without injury to anyone.

Combining elements of both realism and fantasy, *Miami Vice* (NBC, 1984–1989) brought a new audiovisual style to television violence during the 1980s. Building on Brian DePalma and Oliver Stone's *Scarface* (1983), *Miami Vice* reconceptualized the city of Miami: no longer seen as a retirement community, Miami was depicted as the glamorous center of an economy based on drug dealing. Vice detectives Sonny (Don Johnson) and Rico (Philip Michael Thomas) worked undercover as drug dealers, enabling them to spend much of their time in Miami's most fashionable clubs and bistros. When violence erupted between the police and drug dealers, it was accompanied by a rock-music soundtrack. Drawing on video aesthetics popularized by MTV (the cable channel that debuted in 1981, featuring twenty-four hours of promotional music videos), *Miami Vice* occasionally eschewed narrative for beautiful and horrible images and sounds: violent death was synchronized to hit music. This stylization allowed for some of the most explicit violence depicted in the police-detective-crime genre.

In the 1990s *NYPD Blue* (ABC, premiered in 1994), created by Stephen Bochco (one of the creators of *Hill Street Blues*) and David Milch, combined *Hill Street Blues'* focus on the everyday lives of police officers with stylized visuals and sounds. In its presentation of the psychological and physical costs of violence, *NYPD Blue* emphasizes not only action but also its consequences. Though shots are fired and blows exchanged, the show makes a point of lingering on the casualties of violence. Nearly every episode begins with the investigation of a crime scene, including an inspection of the victim's dead body.

The use of multiple elements and conventions in a single program is typical of television generally, and of violent television genres in particular. Exemplifying this hybrid, *NYPD Blue* regularly features comedy in addition to conflict, and while each episode begins with the discovery of a dead body, it often ends with a seduction featuring partial nudity. Undeniably, violence has been one of the central appeals of American television since its origins. In 1949 Camel brand cigarettes, the sponsor of *Man Against Crime*, encouraged the show's writers to include generous portions of violence: "It has been found that we retain audience best when our story is concerned with murder. Therefore, although other crimes may be introduced, somebody must be murdered, preferably early, with the threat of more violence to come" (quoted in Barnouw 1990, p. 132). Images and sounds of conflict—ranging from the fistfight to machine-gun battles—continue to be effective at retaining the American audience.

BIBLIOGRAPHY

Barnouw, Erik. *Tube of Plenty: The Evolution of American Television.* New York: Oxford University Press, 1990.
Boddy, William. "Senator Dodd Goes to Hollywood: Investigating Video Violence." In *The Revolution Wasn't Televised: Sixties Television and Social Conflict,* edited by Lynn Spigel and Michael Curtin. New York: Routledge, 1997.
Brooks, Tim, and Earle Marsh. *The Complete Directory to Prime Time Network TV Shows, 1946–Present.* New York: Ballantine, 1992.
Feuer, Jane. "Genre Study and Television." In *Channels of Discourse, Reassembled,* edited by Robert Allen. Chapel Hill: University of North Carolina Press, 1992.
Marc, David. *Demographic Vistas: Television in American Culture.* Philadelphia: University of Pennsylvania Press, 1984.

BERNIE COOK

*See also* **Film: Violent Genres; Serial Killers, Representations of.**

# TEMPERAMENT

Why did I abandon my own weapons, violent savagery, anger, and threats, and make humble prayers, quite unsuited to my character? Violence is natural to me!

Tereus in Ovid's *Metamorphoses*

While most people agree that aggressive behavior arises more "naturally" for some individuals than for others, philosophers, scientists, and laypeople have long debated the relative importance of biology versus experience in explaining an individual's propensity for violence. Scientific thinking now acknowledges the combined effect of biology and experience on the emergence of aggression. Although the methods available to test such an inquiry directly are relatively new (e.g., brain imaging, blood assays), the philosophical principle has been brought to bear on the topic for almost two thousand years. The ancient Greek physician Galen of Pergamon first introduced the notion that distinct personality types, such as the sanguine and melancholic personalities, result from innate, biological dispositions that the environment shapes. Twentieth-century research indicates that the propensity for violence may similarly find its roots in early childhood temperament.

## The Concept of Temperament

Temperament refers to the bias in an individual toward a moderately stable display of emotional and behavioral reactions as a result of inherited physiological and psychological processes. The labeling of specific temperament types varies across researchers but generally reflects the affective behavior (e.g., easy versus difficult; positive versus negative emotionality; inhibited versus uninhibited; overcontrolled versus undercontrolled) that a child readily exhibits, particularly with regard to novel or discrepant stimuli. Those who have difficult or negative temperaments are more likely to display anger, irritability, and anxiety than are those with easy or positive temperaments. Those with uninhibited or undercontrolled temperaments generally approach unfamiliar situations with readiness and ease, whereas those with inhibited or overcontrolled temperaments generally approach unfamiliar situations with caution or distress. In addition, inhibited and uninhibited temperaments are moderately stable between infancy and middle childhood.

Differences in psychophysiological response to stimuli, which have a genetic basis, have also been identified between inhibited and uninhibited children. Uninhibited children tend to show less physiological response (i.e., less heart-rate acceleration or increase in diastolic blood pressure, less muscle tension, lower levels of salivary cortisol or urinary norephinephrine) than do inhibited children during various psychological challenges. Autonomic underarousal, which is found in 35 percent to 40 percent of uninhibited children, is commonly interpreted as a biological correlate of fearlessness (Kagan 1994).

The potential heritability of fearlessness and fearfulness in humans is supported by animal research. Scientists have repeatedly demonstrated that birds and rats can be bred to be fearless (or fearful). Reliable temperamental differences regarding fearlessness, fearfulness, and aggression have also been observed in different breeds or strains of animals (i.e., dogs, primates). These behavioral differences have been linked, in turn, to the amygdala, which plays a critical role in fear and sympathetic nervous system activity. Thus, for both humans and animals, the inherited excitability of the limbic system, particularly the amygdala, may mediate the genetic predisposition toward, and expression of, fearless or fearful behavior. In addition, it should be noted that animal research has also demonstrated that environmental factors can influence the development of the limbic system. In short, the overall findings seem to indicate that biology and environmental factors have an interactive effect on the expression of fearlessness or fearfulness.

## Temperament and Aggression

Research has demonstrated that certain temperaments carry an increased probability that an individual will become aggressive. Individuals described as having uninhibited, negatively emotional, or undercontrolled temperaments in childhood appear to be more aggressive later in life than those described as having other types of temperaments. Furthermore, studies have suggested that difficult temperament is more strongly linked to aggression that is life-course persistent than to ag-

gression that discontinues over time or that occurs only during certain developmental stages or milestones (Rutter, Giller, and Hagell 1998). Individuals who commit violent offenses in late adolescence or early adulthood are also more likely to have been classified as undercontrolled children; temperament does not appear to correlate with nonviolent offending.

In addition, both cross-sectional and longitudinal studies have found that those who engage in violent offending show less autonomic-nervous-system activity than do other individuals (Kagan 1994). Antisocial adolescents who are later convicted for violent crimes have lower heart rates than do adolescents convicted for nonviolent crimes and adolescents who have never been convicted. In addition, delinquent boys who engage in frequent fighting have lower resting heart rates than do nonaggressive delinquents sampled from the same urban neighborhood. This autonomic underarousal is similar to the psychophysiological functioning of a subset of uninhibited children.

## Understanding the Temperament-Aggression Link

Although research has identified a link between an uninhibited or negatively emotional temperament and later aggressive behavior, the link is nevertheless a modest one. Clearly, not all children with an uninhibited temperament grow up to become violent, and it is estimated that only one-third of unusually aggressive older children grow up to become antisocial adults (Kagan 1994). Because temperament emerges as a consequence of continuing growth in early childhood, particular experiences that shape both physical and psychological development may be necessary before an uninhibited temperament results in stable aggression. In particular, being raised in a family or community that does not punish, and perhaps even models, aggressive behavior may place an uninhibited child at greater risk for engaging in later violent behavior.

Although this hypothesis suggests that punishment for inappropriate behavior may deter the uninhibited child from aggression, uninhibited children actually appear to be less responsive to admonishment than do inhibited children. Twenty-one-month-old uninhibited children are less likely to exhibit apprehension after receiving adult disapproval than are inhibited children. In fact, some uninhibited children even vocalize in protest or smile at the disapproving adult. In addition, undercontrolled children who are aggressive later in life are more prone to danger seeking, impulsivity, and interpersonal alienation than are other children. Taken together, these findings suggest that uninhibited children possess an exaggerated sense of fearlessness that leads to difficulties with respect to their socialization. Thus, the link between an uninhibited childhood temperament and later violence appears to be mediated, in part, through poor socialization and exposure to aggression. Furthermore, poor socialization may result from the biological correlates of fearlessness that are observed in a subset of uninhibited children. Future research that focuses on particular neurophysiological functions and environmental conditions may demonstrate greater specificity in the temperament-aggression link.

*BIBLIOGRAPHY*

Caspi, Avshalom, and Phil A. Silva. "Temperamental Qualities at Age Three Predict Personality Traits in Young Adulthood: Longitudinal Evidence from a Birth Cohort." *Child Development* 66, no. 2 (1995).

Henri, Bill, et al. "Temperamental and Familial Predictors of Violent and Non-Violent Criminal Convictions: Age Three to Age Eighteen." *Developmental Psychology* 32, no. 4 (1996).

Kagan, Jerome. *Galen's Prophecy.* New York: Basic, 1994.

Rutter, Michael, Henri Giller, and Ann Hagell. *Antisocial Behavior by Young People.* New York: Cambridge University Press, 1998.

SHARON S. ISHIKAWA
ADRIAN RAINE

*See also* **Aggression; Developmental Factors; Emotion; Psychological Violence; Psychophysiology.**

# TERRORISM

Although the word dates from the French Revolution, terrorism was a conspicuous phenomenon of the twentieth century and likely to persist beyond it. Certainly terrorism was not unknown in previous centuries, but rarely with the destructive power, the ability to transcend national boundaries, and the appeal to the media it displayed during the twentieth century.

Actual terrorist incidents in the United States have been relatively uncommon since the mid-1980s, but when dramatic and devastating ones occur, as with the bombing of the World Trade Center in New York City in 1993 and the bombing of the Alfred P. Murrah Federal Building in Oklahoma City in 1995, they can be traumatic, shattering Americans' sense of invulnerability and security. Overseas, U.S. citizens and properties are among the leading targets of terrorism, most notably with the 1998 blowing up of the embassies in Kenya and Tanzania.

Scholarly efforts to address the issue of terrorism are bedeviled by the question of how to define the term. There seem to be as many definitions of *terrorism* as there are terrorist groups. From the commonalities of these definitions one can define *terrorism* as the use of violence, or threats of violence, for coercion. At its severest, terrorism is a kind of sporadic waging of war.

Beneath this broad definition, terrorism and its perpetrators differ significantly in terms of types of organization, rationales for their behavior, goals, targets, and tactics. The following discussion of these elements rests on the assumption that although most acts of terrorism are executed by one or a few terrorists, these individuals commonly belong to, plan, and carry out their activities as part of a terrorist organization. Moreover, although they differ in resources, numbers, and even dedication, such organizations conventionally have leaders, some degree of hierarchy, division of labor, and allocation of operations, as well as sources of financing and ways of acquiring their weapons of destruction. Terrorist organizations are not necessarily monolithic: some members are liable to disagree on issues such as tactics and goals or to leave the group altogether.

## Types and Rationales

There are essentially two types of terrorist organizations: domestic (homegrown) and international. The former, for example the animal rights activists in the United States, are organized and operate within a particular country. Sometimes domestic terrorists extend their activities outside their country's borders; for example, the Irish Republican Army (IRA) functions within Northern Ireland but, aiming to put pressure on the British government, which controls the province, has extended its bombing campaign to England. International terrorist organizations attack their enemy anywhere and everywhere it may be vulnerable. In the 1990s those targeting the United States struck the World Trade Center in New York City, U.S. troops bases in Lebanon and Saudi Arabia, and U.S. embassies in Kenya and Tanzania. (For a history of international terrorist attacks on Americans both at home and abroad from the 1950s through the 1990s, see Tucker 1997.)

Terrorist groups can be categorized more specifically according to their essential organizational purpose. It is possible to type them as predominantly social-revolutionary, nationalist, separatist (including those militias in the United States committed to violence), ideological, political, single issue (the Ku Klux Klan's avowed purpose was to protect white womanhood), and idiosyncratic (such as the Symbionese Liberation Army). These types are not necessarily mutually exclusive: a group can be simultaneously separatist, nationalist, and ideological.

Terrorists invoke various rationales for their actions. These usually stem from their purposes and include ideology, nationalism, political or religious beliefs, and reactions against real or imagined oppression. These rationales can also apply to lone terrorists unconnected with any organization; such individuals, though, are commonly diagnosed as suffering from severe mental illness (for example, Lynette "Squeaky" Fromme and John Hinckley, Jr., who attempted to assassinate Presidents Gerald Ford and Ronald Reagan, respectively, in 1975 and 1981).

### Goals and Targets

Terrorists' goals include trying to gain an independent state or more limited freedom from a government whose control they reject; undermining and demoralizing a regime or some other enemy; creating chaos and generating general fear among the public; gaining sympathy by raising public awareness of the group and its grievances; demonstrating the movement's strength and building momentum; and vengeance. Many of these goals, such as demonstrating the organization's strength and wreaking vengeance, overlap. But others can be contradictory: killing people and blowing up buildings frighten the public but are unlikely to gain the terrorists much public sympathy. Sometimes terrorists' goals are based on unrealistic assumptions. Thus, in the 1970s the IRA in Great Britain and the Baader-Meinhof gang in Germany behaved on the assumption that their violence would force the rulers of Britain and Germany, respectively, to reveal their states' true fascist natures. But neither state displayed fascist tendencies, and no significant repression took place.

Terrorism necessarily has victims. Common terrorist tactics include hostage taking and hijacking, bomb threats and bombings at public places or against particular individuals or locations, and assassinations or random killings. The choice of targets has one or more of three communicative functions—attention getting, symbolic, or instrumental—and usually depends on the terrorists' goals and to whom they want to send a message. Government leaders, often directly or symbolically responsible for the policies that terrorists are fighting against, are common targets. Eliminating one or more of them may mean the end of a disputed policy when someone else takes over. Arguably, the assassination of Abraham Lincoln in 1865 falls into this category. An assassination attempt, whether successful or unsuccessful, can undermine or demoralize the leader's regime or coerce a change in policy. Sometimes an attack on a leader may simply be an act of vengeance. Terrorists might target a person for intimidation or coercion so that he or his colleagues will not perform a particular action or engage in a profession; judges are sometimes targeted for this reason.

Sometimes, to generate widespread fear and chaos, terrorists target ordinary citizens selected at random. The public may then pressure its leaders to end the violence. At times well-known individuals such as U.S. presidents are chosen to garner the most attention. Destructively violent acts committed in prominent locations that serve as powerful symbols are sure to gain worldwide publicity and notoriety. The federal office building in Oklahoma City bombed in 1995 represented the national government, whom the terrorists viewed as the enemy. The bombing at Centennial Olympic Park in Atlanta during the 1996 Olympic Games has been interpreted as an attack on internationalism and multinationalism. For the Islamist terrorists who bombed the World Trade Center in New York City in 1993 in reaction to American policies in the Middle East and elsewhere, the landmark served as a symbol of U.S. business might.

### The Media

"Because [terrorism] is political, it is theoretically and practically rhetorical" (Leeman 1991, p. 13)—hence, in addition to acts of violence, many terrorists seek media attention as a means of achieving their goals. Terrorists garner publicity from the news media in various ways: by devising actions specifically for their newsworthiness, choosing symbolically charged targets and prominent times and places for their actions, and releasing statements or giving interviews directly to the press claiming responsibility for terrorist acts such

**U.S. embassy in Beirut, Lebanon, after the 18 April 1983 bomb attack.** CORBIS/BETTMANN

as plane hijackings. Of those who claim that media coverage significantly affects terrorism, most view the problem as one of exacerbation; some take a harsher view, blaming the media's presence at and reporting of terrorist incidents for damaging effects—prolonging incidents, hindering police operations, providing terrorists with tactical and strategic information, placing the lives of hostages and police in jeopardy, and putting inappropriate pressure on authorities to resolve incidents, that is, to settle with terrorists or meet their demands. In these ways, the media can become participants in rather than simply chroniclers of the events.

Some observers go even further, viewing the media as vital to terrorism's survival and the accomplishment of terrorists' goals; curtail media coverage, and terrorists' efficacy is diminished. As Margaret Thatcher insisted when she was Britain's prime minister, it is necessary to "find ways to starve the terrorist and the hijacker of the oxygen of publicity on which they depend" (R. W. Apple, Jr., "Thatcher Urges the Press to Help 'Starve' Terrorists," *New York Times*, 16 July 1985, p. 3). Others have argued that squelching media coverage, instead of discouraging acts of terrorism, would increase the incentive for violence.

That terrorists often attempt to use the media to achieve their goals and that journalists often give terrorist actions extensive news coverage does not necessarily mean that the media are conduits for

terrorism. An analysis of surveys sent to broadcasters around the world found several common themes in media attitudes toward terrorism. Although the journalists surveyed believed that terrorism was a newsworthy event, they also strove to be prudent in their coverage. They voiced a need to maintain their credibility as journalists and avoid legitimating terrorists. One of the most established attitudes was caution so as not to endanger hostages.

It has been argued at the other end of the spectrum that the media hinder the aims of terrorists. By focusing on terrorists' acts of violence and their effects on individuals without adequately explaining the terrorists' grievances, objectives, and causes, the media lead the public to concentrate on the violence alone (Paletz, Fozzard, and Ayanian 1982). In this view, it is not the terrorists who use the media to promote their propaganda but the government or those whom the terrorists oppose who use the media to disseminate antiterrorist messages. Witness the negative way terrorists are usually depicted in Hollywood feature films. And when terrorists are brought to trial, the media serve as a conduit for the government to discredit those being charged.

### "Faceless" Terrorism

The conventional wisdom that terrorists always desire publicity and therefore seek credit for attacks has not gone unchallenged. Some have detected a movement since the 1980s toward "faceless" terrorism, in which no one claims responsibility for major acts of terrorist violence; this is thought to have come about because fewer states are likely to provide safe havens for terrorists (Hoffman 1997). Others have argued that unclaimed attacks are not new developments and that terrorists have never universally claimed credit for their actions (Pluchinsky 1997 and Rapoport 1997).

An organization associated with terrorist acts may seek publicity at certain junctures and avoid it at others. The timing often depends on the organization's stage of development, for terrorist groups are dynamic organizations whose tactics change over time. In the early stages of development publicity is usually essential, but in later stages one sector of a group may become institutionalized and recognized as legitimate and so want to separate itself from the violent acts of the terrorist wing. This legitimate sector could be harmed by the negative publicity that results from association with terrorist acts. So its leaders, for example, Yasir Arafat, while acknowledging the reasons for the violence, deny knowledge of, express regret for, and even disavow, the violence itself. Another situation in which the perpetrator of a terrorist act may not want publicity is an attack that claims unintended victims. The adverse publicity associated with the accidental casualties may cause a backlash among potential sympathizers who share the terrorists' grievances.

## Combating Terrorism

The United States has taken many measures over the years to combat terrorism and terrorists: international legal conventions, defensive actions, addressing the causes of terrorism, adopting a public policy of no concessions to terrorists' demands, applying economic sanctions to countries allegedly involved in terrorist activity or harboring terrorists, attempting to disrupt terrorist movements, and military retaliation. The U.S. government, through the Federal Bureau of Investigation and the Central Intelligence Agency, is particularly dedicated to capturing those suspected of engaging in terrorist activities against it no matter how long it takes. The government frequently offers rewards for aid in apprehending suspects; captured suspects are then extradited to the United States for trial.

Some of the most obvious attempts to prevent terrorism can be seen in Washington, D.C. Physical changes, such as closing part of Pennsylvania Avenue, where the White House and other government buildings are located, to traffic, were made in the 1990s to make attacks more difficult. But most attempts to thwart terrorists take place out of public view. Whenever a suspected terrorist attack occurs in the United States, the FBI is brought in to investigate. Certain laws give government agencies special powers to gather information on suspected and potential terrorists; thus the FBI will infiltrate and monitor domestic organizations viewed as possible threats and make use of paid informants, as it did with the Ku Klux Klan.

Acts of terrorism suspected of being generated in or by foreign countries prompt special responses by the U.S. government, which will pressure countries suspected of harboring or supporting terrorists or engaging in terrorism against the United States. This pressure includes quiet diplomacy, public protest, and claims for compensation. Some countries are placed under an economic embargo, while others, such as Libya, are the subject of military retaliation as punishment.

Fearing and anticipating terrorists' ability to disrupt civilian and military computer networks (thereby shutting down telephone networks and transportation systems, for example), unleash chemical and biological agents, and attack with nuclear weapons, the U.S. government has also significantly increased federal spending to equip military, intelligence, criminal justice, and public health agencies to combat such "unconventional" threats from terrorist organizations.

## Limiting Liberties?

Governments can react to the threat of terrorism or actual terrorist actions by diminishing or even suspending civil liberties—thereby reducing the freedom of their own citizens. In an attempt to curtail terrorists' ability to recruit members and publicize their causes, a government might preempt rights such as freedom of association and freedom of the press. In Britain, for example, in response to terrorist acts in the 1980s, the government passed a law that forbade the broadcast of live interviews with members of the IRA or its political wing, Sinn Fein.

No such laws exist in the United States, where the government relies on the media voluntarily to cooperate in the fight against terrorists. However, the United States did respond to the spate of terrorist incidents in 1995 and 1996 (the bombing of the federal building in Oklahoma City and the Centennial Olympic Park pipe bombing in Atlanta) with new antiterrorism laws. These include stopping suspected terrorist groups from raising money in the United States, granting new authority to the Immigration and Naturalization Service to turn people away at the border, and authorizing $1 billion over four years to help the FBI and other agencies fight terrorism. More significant expansions of federal law-enforcement powers, including authority for federal agents to conduct multipoint wiretaps, were requested by President Bill Clinton but not passed by Congress, in part because they were seen as unnecessary and undesirable infringements on civil liberties.

It is not unknown for politicians, particularly presidents, to trade on terrorism by exaggerating its threat, creating or magnifying the image of a dangerous enemy against whom they are fighting. They thereby seek to increase their public support and facilitate the achievement of their domestic- and foreign-policy goals, whether or not directed at terrorism.

### State Terrorism

Terrorism is not limited to insurgents fighting the government or some other group but is also engaged in by countries; this type of terrorism is known as state terrorism. State terrorism may be aimed at intimidating certain residents of the country or preventing them from undertaking (usually, but not invariably) violent activities. Governments have been known to authorize massacres of their own people as an object lesson to discourage rebellion or deter dissent.

More often, state-sponsored terrorism is directed externally at aiding those involved in violent acts against people in other countries. The least incendiary type of aid that countries give to international terrorists is tacit and rhetorical support and the use of diplomatic assets. More vigorous support includes financing, transportation, and allowing the use of territory. Direct involvement includes intelligence support, training (both specialized terrorist and basic military training), provision of high technology, and supplying weapons and explosives (Murphy 1989).

The U.S. government has been accused of involvement in terrorist activities against foreign leaders, such as assassination attempts against Fidel Castro of Cuba. During the 1980s the Reagan administration supported groups like the contras,

the revolutionary band of guerrillas whose aim was to overthrow the Sandinista government in Nicaragua.

In contrast to insurgent terrorist groups, governments often eschew publicity for their terrorist activities. When a government wants to eliminate or intimidate individuals or groups but does not want widespread public knowledge of its actions, it will carefully avoid the media. The CIA has been involved in such activities over the years, reportedly including attempted assassinations of leaders and the fomenting of insurrections in foreign countries. Because of possible backlash in public opinion at home and the angry reaction of other nations, these tactics are used covertly.

### Freedom Fighters

A group or an individual called "terrorist" by some may be called "freedom fighter" by others, thus avoiding the former term's negative connotations. The Nicaraguan contras were a case in point. Though some claimed that they were committing acts of terrorism, the Reagan administration and many of its supporters labeled the group freedom fighters.

Another prominent twentieth-century revolutionary group that was the subject of much controversy was the African National Congress (ANC). Some labeled the ANC terrorists, but this group gained worldwide support for its struggle to end the rule of apartheid, the policy of segregation and political and economic discrimination against non-European groups in the Republic of South Africa. After the South African government finally succumbed to pressure and ended the policy, Nelson Mandela, the leader of the ANC who had spent twenty-seven years in prison for his role in the organization, was elected to lead the government. Mandela, considered by some the leader of a "terrorist" organization, was ultimately recognized and lauded as a statesman.

### Terrorism's Effectiveness

Many terrorist groups are crushed, buried in the rubble of history. A few achieve legitimacy and widespread support and, as with the ANC, ultimately take over the government through a democratic election. Clearly, it helps if the terrorists are waging a war of national liberation against an oppressive minority or a foreign power. Legitimacy is most likely to be achieved when the group's objectives (freedom, democracy) are valued by others; the regime being fought stands for an unpopular policy (such as apartheid) or engages in oppressive domination over a group (for example, Serbian actions in Kosovo in the late 1990s); and violence appears to be the only way to achieve change. Conversely, if the terrorist group is seeking to establish autocratic rule and is fighting against a democratically elected government that respects dissent, it is less likely to succeed.

Between these two extremes of total success and abject failure, there are a host of possibilities. Terrorists are in some instances so determined, so persistent in their violence, and so skillful at demonstrating their movement's strength that the government they oppose ultimately becomes more flexible, responding with a willingness to listen to and even enter into negotiations with them. One could argue that this has happened with the British government and the IRA and with the Spanish government and the Basque freedom movement, ETA.

Terrorists do sometimes achieve limited goals, but the success is often temporary. They may cause minor disruptions in international and multinational business. They may generate fear among the public, threatening its sense of security, although they rarely create long-lasting chaos. They may demoralize or compel harsh reactions from a government but not topple it.

Vengeance is perhaps the easiest goal for terrorists to achieve. People are hard to protect all the time, symbolic buildings are plentiful and cannot all be guarded, and developed countries that rely on the latest technologies can be disrupted. But vengeance rarely leads to the achievement of larger goals. Indeed, it often provokes retaliation —witness the 1998 U.S. bombing of targets in Afghanistan and the Sudan in response to attacks on U.S. embassies in Kenya and Tanzania.

Nonetheless, terrorist actions can reinforce the commitment of the organization's members, confirming their purpose and potency. Failures can be an incentive to try again; success can produce a contagion effect, inspiring similar actions by other terrorists.

## Research

The study of terrorism has long been the preserve of antiterrorism experts, who are often associated with putatively nonpartisan research institutions and write from a governmental perspective. Much of this work is propagandistic, replete with tendentious examples and unexamined assumptions.

The journals *Terrorism and Political Violence* and, on occasion, *Studies in Conflict and Terrorism* present more dispassionate research into terrorists' origins, philosophy, organizations, strategies, and tactics. Empirical work in this area is increasing. Terrorists' perspectives, however, remain largely unrepresented except in their memoirs.

Another category of research concerns terrorism and the media. Commonly condemning the media as proterrorist, such indictments are rarely based on systematic research. Recommendations for better coverage of terrorism usually mean coverage that is more critical of terrorists and less willing to present their (mis)deeds. Further research could "specify and test for possible media influences . . . by examining source reliance, verbal and visual content, program formats, fiction versus nonfiction programming, audience exposure patterns and reactions, terrorist goals and strategies, and state interests and responses" (Paletz and Boiney 1992, p. 24).

That terrorism is inherently politicized and, like most forms of violence, highly contentious should not mean that fulminations against it are the only proper response; it is to be hoped that the controversies around the subject will lead to further serious inquiry and research.

*BIBLIOGRAPHY*

Crelinsten, Ronald D. "Victims' Perspectives." In *Terrorism and the Media*, edited by David L. Paletz and Alex P. Schmid. Newbury Park, Calif.: Sage, 1992.

Gerrits, Robin P. J. M. "Terrorists' Perspectives: Memoirs." In *Terrorism and the Media*, edited by David L. Paletz and Alex P. Schmid. Newbury Park, Calif.: Sage, 1992.

Guelke, Adrian. *The Age of Terrorism and the International Political System*. London: Tauris Academic Studies, 1995.

Heymann, Philip B. *Terrorism and America*. Cambridge, Mass.: MIT Press, 1998.

Hoffman, Bruce. "Why Terrorists Don't Claim Credit." *Terrorism and Political Violence* 9, no. 1 (spring 1997).

Leeman, Richard W. *The Rhetoric of Terrorism and Counterterrorism*. New York: Greenwood, 1991.

Livingston, Steven. *The Terrorism Spectacle*. Boulder, Colo.: Westview, 1994.

Murphy, John Francis. *State Support of International Terrorism: Legal, Political, and Economic Dimensions*. Boulder, Colo.: Westview, 1989.

Paletz, David L., and John Boiney. "Researchers' Perspectives." In *Terrorism and the Media*, edited by David L. Paletz and Alex P. Schmid. Newbury Park, Calif.: Sage, 1992.

Paletz, David L., and Laura L. Tawney. "Broadcasting Organizations' Perspectives." In *Political Terrorism: A Research Guide to Concepts, Theories, Data Bases, and*

*Literature*, edited by Alex P. Schmid. Amsterdam, Netherlands: North-Holland, 1983.

Paletz, David L., Peter A. Fozzard, and John Z. Ayanian. "The I.R.A., the Red Brigades, and the F.A.L.N. in the *New York Times*." *Journal of Communication* 32, no. 2 (spring 1982).

Pluchinsky, Dennis A. "The Terrorism Puzzle." *Terrorism and Political Violence* 9, no. 1 (spring 1997).

Rapoport, David C. "To Claim or Not to Claim: That Is the Question—Always!" *Terrorism and Political Violence* 9, no. 1 (spring 1997).

Smith, Brent L. *Terrorism in America: Pipe Bombs and Pipe Dreams*. Albany: State University of New York Press, 1994.

Tucker, David. *Skirmishes at the Edge of the Empire*. Westport, Conn.: Praeger, 1997.

DANIEL LIPINSKI
DAVID L. PALETZ

*See also* **Atlanta Centennial Olympic Park, Bombing of; Bombing and Bomb Scares; Crime, Legal Definitions of; Extremism; Hijacking; Oklahoma City Bombing; Symbionese Liberation Army; Unabomber; World Trade Center Bombing.**

# TET OFFENSIVE

On the night of 30 January 1968, South Vietnamese insurgents (dubbed "Vietcong" by the U.S. military) invaded America—at least that symbolic extension of American territory represented by the U.S. embassy in Saigon. It was a minuscule incident in a night full of battles. "A piddling platoon action," one officer called it; nineteen Vietcong guerrillas from the National Liberation Front (NLF) against five U.S. marine guards. The attackers seized the grounds but did not break into the Chancery building. At dawn on 31 January U.S. troops counterattacked, and all the guerrillas were killed. Perhaps the incident's symbolic importance outweighed its real importance. The real violence, marked by dead U.S. soldiers, symbolically encapsulated the challenge to U.S. power coming from a small nation halfway around the world.

## Background

Once U.S. troops took a direct combat role in March 1965, a certain grim normalcy settled over the war in Vietnam. The South Vietnamese insurgents, operating with the aid of the North Vietnamese Army (PAVN), held effective control of much of rural South Vietnam and engaged in continual, low-intensity conflict with U.S. forces and the Army of the Republic of South Vietnam (ARVN). There was guerrilla war in the country-side, occasionally punctuated by large-scale battles; in the cities there were acts of terrorism and political assassination.

In the United States support for the administration's conduct of the war was fading. In the fall of 1967, at President Lyndon Johnson's request, General William Westmoreland (commander of U.S. forces in South Vietnam) went on a public-relations tour of the United States, announcing, "We have reached an important point where the end begins to come into view" (Oberdorfer 1971, p. 105).

## Tet 1968

Tet, the lunar New Year celebration, is Vietnam's most important holiday, and in its honor a cease-fire had been agreed to by both sides. On the night of 30 January to the early morning of 31 January, the cease-fire was broken by 80,000 NLF and PAVN soldiers attacking more than a hundred cities and towns throughout the Republic of South Vietnam. The ensuing nationwide chaos was displayed to Americans on their television sets each night. After the public had been fed so much official optimism, this crisis seemed to demonstrate the bankruptcy of government claims to be "pacifying" Vietnam. Within a month Walter Cronkite, America's most prominent newscaster, who had been loyally supporting the war effort, declared that the war was "mired in stalemate."

While there was a new skepticism about official claims of victory, it perhaps was misplaced in this instance. The superior firepower and numerical advantage of U.S. and South Vietnamese forces led to an overwhelming tactical victory. Most of the attacks were repulsed in a few days. The chief exception was the major city of Hue, which was held by North Vietnamese forces for a month; they were driven out only after intense bombing and house-to-house warfare. PAVN and NLF forces carried out one of the worst atrocities of the war during the occupation, killing approximately three thousand noncombatants.

The insurgent strategy, called "General Offensive–General Uprising," was to inspire a popular revolt on the part of the citizens of South Vietnam that would overthrow their government and force the departure of U.S. troops. This plan failed, however; the people of South Vietnam remained passive, and ARVN troops remained loyal to the government. It took years for the NLF to recover from its losses, and one consequence of this decimation of the southern resistance was the domination of the eventually unified Vietnam by northerners.

## Khe Sanh

The first phase of the Tet Offensive actually began in late 1967, when North Vietnamese Army (PAVN) troops began to concentrate around the small, remote marine base at Khe Sanh, located in the northwest corner of South Vietnam. The U.S. command thought that that the enemy was preparing a major battle to seize the base. Military leaders thought that this concentration of PAVN forces would finally lead to a pitched battle, in which U.S. forces would have the advantage. The siege of the base riveted the attention of the world for weeks in early 1968, and U.S. television carried regular reports on the marines living "in the V-ring"—at the center of a marksman's target.

Khe Sanh took on an importance that transcended any realistic appraisal of its strategic value. It echoed a critical battle that took place in 1954, when Vietnamese nationalist forces won a decisive victory over the French colonial army by capturing their base at Dien Bien Phu. This victory led directly to the collapse of French control in Indochina and creation of the two independent Vietnamese states. The parallel between the two embattled outposts became an obsession for some journalists, soldiers, and politicians, particularly President Lyndon Johnson. In an unprecedented move, Johnson required the Joint Chiefs of Staff to sign a pledge that the base at Khe Sanh could be successfully defended.

As it turned out, the threat to Khe Sanh appears to have been a feint designed to draw U.S. troops to the periphery of the country, leaving urban areas vulnerable to attacks by the National Liberation Front and the PAVN during the Tet Offensive. Even after the outbreak of the Tet Offensive, the United States was reluctant to divert troops to urban areas because the Tet attacks were believed to be only a diversion leading up to a decisive battle in the highlands.

The Tet Offensive had a high cost. General William Westmoreland's optimism about U.S. supremacy in a stationary battle was justified. In Operation Niagara, B-52 bombers dropped almost sixty thousand tons of bombs around the base at Khe Sanh. Approximately ten thousand PAVN soldiers were killed, while only about five hundred U.S. marines were lost.

In July 1968 the base at Khe Sanh was quietly abandoned. The focus of international attention for weeks during the winter because of its vital strategic significance, every structure was plowed under by bulldozers; all that was left were the craters.

The offensive drove a wedge between South Vietnam and the United States. Many in the United States blamed the South Vietnamese for passively observing the communist infiltration and military buildup beforehand. Tet 1968 also produced one of the most famous images of the war: the still photograph and film footage of General Nguyen Ngoc Loan, chief of police for South Vietnam, shooting a captured Vietcong guerrilla in the head at point-blank range. This scene fostered doubt about the virtues of the ally that Americans were sacrificing themselves to protect.

On the other side of this alliance, many South Vietnamese felt less confidence in their government, which had failed to maintain safety in the cities, and they became disillusioned with the United States. In driving communist forces out of some urban areas, U.S. troops wreaked terrible devastation, leading to one of the most infamous remarks of the war, an American officer's description of the battle to retake the town of Ben Tre: "We had to destroy the village in order to save it."

Studies of poll data indicate no uniform response among Americans to the Tet Offensive. The immediate reaction was a boost in support for the war effort, as people rallied to the cause of beleaguered U.S. soldiers. Approval of the war did decline after Tet, but this decline was only a

**A Vietnamese man surveys the wreckage of his home and shop after the battle for Hue, 1968.** HULTON GETTY/ LIAISON AGENCY

*BIBLIOGRAPHY*

Gilbert, Marc Jason, and William Head, eds. *The Tet Offensive.* Westport, Conn.: Praeger, 1996.

Karnow, Stanley. *Vietnam: A History.* New York: Penguin, 1984.

Oberdorfer, Don. *Tet.* New York: Doubleday, 1971.

*Reporting Vietnam, Part One: American Journalism 1959–1969.* New York: Library of America, 1998.

Wyatt, Clarence R. *Paper Soldiers: The American Press and the Vietnam War.* Chicago: University of Chicago Press, 1995.

BRIAN ZIMMERMAN

*See also* **Vietnam War.**

# TEXAS RANGERS

In the Lone Star State, a land "below the Smith and Wesson line" (Brearley 1970, p. 678), violence arose out of a heritage that was both southern and western. In the nineteenth and twentieth centuries Anglo Texas underwent vast changes: from settlement by pioneers from the Old South to development as a cattle kingdom to industrialization and the growth of urban centers. This cultural mix produced Texans who were not only southern in their beliefs about honor and vengeance but western in their ability to strap on six-shooters and stand their ground and fight. A Texas male who refused to take up arms and defend family members and fellow citizens "ain't no man" (Brearley 1970, p. 687).

The Texas Rangers modified their operations through state law to fit the changing times. Their history can be divided into three distinct yet interrelated periods. From 1823 to 1874 Rangers were citizen-soldiers who acted as scouts, spies, and fighting columns in sporadic warfare with Native Americans and Mexican nationals. In this era Rangers gained national prominence for their exploits both on and off the battlefields during the Mexican War. In 1874 legislation was passed vesting the Rangers with authority as a protective force. First the Frontier Battalion and then the Ranger Force used their statewide authority as peace officers to investigate crimes, arrest felons, and testify in courts. At this time, the Rangers found themselves in gun battles in the towns and countryside and along the Mexican border. The third period began in 1935, when the Rangers merged with the highway patrol and other agencies to form the Department of Public Safety (DPS). Since that time, the Rangers have modernized their operations as a police detective force through the use of crime labs

continuation of a trend that had started long before. Its effect on President Johnson's popularity, however, was dramatic. Even supporters lost faith in Johnson's ability to conduct the war.

While there has been a long controversy over the American media's depiction of the Tet Offensive as a catastrophe, given the military victory that ensued, the attack demonstrated that claims that the U.S. strategy was working were greatly inflated. A month after the offensive, U.S. military leaders requested 206,000 more troops in addition to the half million already in Vietnam. President Johnson denied the request and shortly afterward announced he would not seek reelection. Within two years the United States began to withdraw combat forces from Vietnam. The result of the Tet Offensive was a strategic victory for the North Vietnamese, although not the one they had planned. The Tet Offensive demonstrated that despite its overwhelming military power, the United States was not always powerful enough to subdue third-world nations resistant to its will.

and high-tech weaponry. Violence remains a part of the everyday life of Rangers, as seen, for example, in their participation in the 1997 shoot-out near Fort Davis, in which one member of the Republic of Texas separatist group was killed.

In any age, the work of police involves life-threatening encounters with violent criminals. Social and economic conditions in the United States after the Civil War and during the Great Depression were especially conducive to the rise of bandit gangs. Here Texas Rangers gained fame and notoriety in numerous clashes with badmen. Some of the celebrated cases are as follows: Ranger John Armstrong joined other law officers in capturing the outlaw John Wesley Hardin in Florida in 1877, and Armstrong knocked Hardin unconscious with his revolver; Rangers and local officers shot and killed Sam Bass and several companions as they attempted to rob a bank in Round Rock in 1878; in a running gun battle, on horse and on foot, Rangers killed one desperado and captured three others, including Jesse Evans of Lincoln County War fame, in the mountainous region of West Texas in

1880; and former Ranger Frank Hamer took part in the barrage of gunfire that ended the crime spree of Clyde Barrow and Bonnie Parker in 1934, bringing to a close the old-time Texas outlaw tradition. The most devastating loss for the Rangers occurred in 1887, when Captain William Scott and five of his men were ambushed by the Connor gang in East Texas, resulting in one Ranger dead and three wounded; one bandit was also killed. In such violent clashes the Rangers proved to be unexceptional gunfighters. Captain John Hughes ranked among the best of the Old West gunmen, as he and his Ranger company gunned down white outlaws and a number of Hispanics involved in criminal acts. The reputations of other Rangers as gunfighters rested not only on their publicized encounters with armed desperadoes but also upon their easily demonstrated marksmanship, their flair for using their weapons to intimidate opponents, and their ability to inspire romantic tales that captured the public's imagination.

Controversy has surrounded the Rangers' involvement with minority groups. Captain William

Texas Rangers in El Paso, 1896. The front row shows Adjutant General William Mabry with the "Four Great Captains" of the Frontier Battalion: John Hughes, John Brooks, Bill McDonald, and John Rogers. TEXAS STATE LIBRARY AND ARCHIVES COMMISSION

J. McDonald at the turn of the twentieth century, for example, disliked lawbreakers of all creeds and colors and took a paternalistic view of black Texans. McDonald took a strong stand against third-degree methods and white lynch mobs and investigated some criminal cases involving blacks with an open mind, some with a closed mind. The Ranger captain was unable to analyze evidence in crimes involving black and white suspects—the Brownsville raid of 1906, for example—with the same soundness of judgment that he could apply to cases involving only African American suspects, such as the Conditt murder case of 1905.

In the nineteenth century a special law-and-order problem arose in southern Texas, where territorial ambitions, the drive for economic and political power, and the hostility between Tejanos (Hispanic inhabitants of Texas) and Anglos created a violent environment. Three periods stand out: (1) the decade of the 1870s, when Captain L. H. McNelly, with his view of the border as a war zone, executed Tejano prisoners and carried out a bloody invasion of Mexico in 1875 in his drive against cattle rustlers; (2) the years 1910 to 1920, when Mexican revolutionaries and raiders crossed the Rio Grande to seek support (arms and men) and plunder and the Rangers kept the Hispanic populace in line through intimidation, pistol whippings, and cold-blooded killings (as revealed in the Canales hearings of 1919, an investigation by the Texas legislature into alleged abuses of the Rangers); and (3) the era of the 1960s, when militant Mexican American agricultural workers in the Rio Grande Valley charged that the Rangers under Captain Alfred Y. Allee violated their civil rights through the use of strong-arm tactics. Over the years some participants in border clashes, such as Juan "Cheno" Cortina and Gregorio Cortez, have been viewed by Anglos as brigands and by Texas Mexicans as social bandits trying to preserve a way of life.

Throughout American history lawmen have come to blows with other lawmen. This happened in Texas and the West when base personality traits surfaced; when drinking, gambling, and fighting over women in saloons took place; and when social issues polarized throughts and actions. The Ranger-versus-Ranger equation was not unknown in Texas, as evidenced by several violent events, all of which were alcohol related: Buck Guyse's shoot-out with fellow Rangers in 1881; Bass Outlaw's shooting of another Ranger and subsequent death at the hands of a constable in 1894; and Captain K. F. Cunningham's gunfight with another

Ranger in 1919. Rangers were also known to fight with local and national police officers. Perhaps the most dramatic gun battle between Old West lawmen took place in Quanah in 1893. For personal and professional reasons, Ranger Captain Bill McDonald met Sheriff John Matthews of Childress County in a classic street gunfight that left McDonald badly wounded and Matthews dead.

Since their inception the Texas Rangers have been shaped by the times in which they lived. In frontier Texas they were schooled by Jack Hays in irregular warfare against the Comanches. Under the leadership of John Jones, commandant of the Frontier Battalion, they gained a reputation as intrepid—and brutal—law enforcement officers. And in contemporary Texas, as amply demonstrated in the career of M. T. "Lone Wolf" Gonzaullas, who chased killers, tamed oil-boom towns, and became a specialist in forensic science, they have earned a reputation as shrewd detectives.

*BIBLIOGRAPHY*

Brearley, H. C. "The Pattern of Violence." In *Culture in the South,* edited by W. T. Couch. Reprint Westport, Conn.: Greenwood, 1970.

Cox, Mike. *Stand-off in Texas: "Just Call Me a Spokesman for the DPS."* Austin, Tex.: Eakin, 1998.

Procter, Ben. *Just One Riot: Episodes of Texas Rangers in the Twentieth Century.* Austin, Tex.: Eakin, 1991.

Webb, Walter Prescott. *The Texas Rangers: A Century of Frontier Defense.* Boston: Houghton Mifflin, 1935.

Weiss, Harold J., Jr. "The Texas Rangers Revisited: Old Themes and New Viewpoints." *Southwestern Historical Quarterly* 97 (April 1994).

HAROLD J. WEISS, JR.

*See also* **Frontier; Mexican War; Police: Overview.**

# THANATOLOGY

"I think it extremely probable that the scientific study of old age and of death, two branches of science that may be called *gerontology* and *thanatology,* will bring about great modifications in the course of the last period of life." With these words in 1903, Elie Metchnikoff, Louis Pasteur's protégé and successor, called for the establishment of two new fields of systematic scientific inquiry and provided the terms by which they would become known. Fellow scientists, with a few exceptions, were slow to follow Metchnikoff's lead. Gerontology did not become a thriving field of research until the end of World War II and even then did not immediately attract much attention to death-related issues. More firmly established disciplines such as medicine and psychology continued their neglect of the meaning of death in human life.

The opportunity for thanatological inquiry and innovation arose in the 1960s as part of a larger shift in attitudes and values. The Vietnam War renewed public awareness of death and grief while also contributing to distrust of authority in general. Bureaucratic control of dying and death was challenged by the converging power of civil rights, consumerism, and back-to-nature movements. Some families and care providers decided that the act of giving birth should occur in a more natural and family-oriented setting. The same view would soon be applied to dying and death.

The death awareness movement in the United States was sparked by Jessica Mitford's critique *The American Way of Death* (1963) and Evelyn Waugh's *The Loved One* (1948), a parody of the funeral industry. The social and emotional isolation of terminally ill people then came into focus in Elisabeth Kubler-Ross's *On Death and Dying* (1969), while Ernest Becker called attention to the consequences of society's systematic avoidance of confrontation with mortality in *The Denial of Death* (1973).

Pioneering studies soon provided compelling evidence that dying people were often abandoned to suffer pain and despair alone, while professional health service providers and the general culture remained locked in a rigid denial of death. The psychologist Herman Feifel (1959) characterized death as a taboo topic in the United States and spearheaded a movement toward open communication and dialogue. The first death education courses appeared in the 1960s and *Omega*, a scientific journal focusing on dying, death, and grief, was established in 1970. At the same time two new developments occurred, one raising anxiety and the other hope. The prospect of being maintained in a vegetative state on life support devices aroused concerns that continue to resonate in the realm of suicide and physician-assisted death. On the positive side, the hospice model of palliative care demonstrated that pain and suffering can be alleviated and that the terminally ill can continue to live fulfilling lives.

Thanatology today draws upon the work of anthropologists, bioscientists, communication scientists, historians, nurses, physicians, psychologists, and sociologists. The most systematically researched topics are anxiety and other attitudes toward dying and death, coping with dying and grief, funeral customs, and the child's understanding of death. Attention has also been given to preparing health care providers and counselors for working with dying, grieving, and suicidal people. The concept of a death instinct, central both to Metchnikoff and Sigmund Freud, has not attracted much interest in recent years. Salient controversies have centered on the validity of the stage theory approach to dying (not well supported by the evidence); the near-death experience (evidence or counterevidence for the soul's survival after death); and death anxiety (existential fear, learned response, or adaptive function). There is a developing consensus that thanatology is most useful when it does not focus on death as an isolated topic but rather as a condition of individual life and a test of sociocultural resiliency.

*BIBLIOGRAPHY*

Feifel, Herman, ed. *The Meaning of Death.* New York: McGraw-Hill, 1959.

Kastenbaum, Robert. *Death, Society, and Human Experience.* 6th ed. Boston: Allyn and Bacon, 1998.

Metchnikoff, Elie. *The Nature of Man.* New York: G. P. Putnam, 1903.

ROBERT KASTENBAUM

*See also* **Forensic Psychiatry; Suicide; Theories of Violence.**

# THEATER

The centrality of violence in dramas from cultures around the world and across centuries is nearly universal. Conflict lies at the very heart of most dramatic narrative, a situation that has aroused impassioned critiques of theater. The earliest Western playwrights (525–406 B.C.E.), Greek tragedians such as Aeschylus, Sophocles, and Euripides, built their dramas around the agon, a debate or contest that leads inexorably to a scene of physical or psychological suffering. The extreme violence enjoyed by the successive Roman culture (including actual maiming and death before an audience) led the Christian polemicist Tertullian (c. 200 C.E.) to implore Christians in the second century to eschew the violence of the spectacles and to find these pleasures instead in the Bible and Christian liturgy. ("Would you have blood? You have Christ's.") In the modern era, feminist critics such as Lynda Hart and practitioners such as Megan Terry have objected to the constant struggle that animates traditional theater as a reflection of patriarchy and have proposed in its stead a theater built upon celebration or consensus, a drama in which no one loses and a comedy devoid of humiliation and triumphalism.

## Native American Performance

As with most other cultures of the world, violence was central in many of the theatrical rituals or dance-dramas that were being performed by Native Americans at the time of European exploration and conquest of the North American continent. Ancient dramas such as the midsummer Sun Dance of the Sioux, a highly theatrical rite that survived into the twentieth century, involved extreme feats of painful endurance, with some dancers volunteering to have bits of flesh cut from their bodies and other male dancers hanging suspended from a sacred tree trunk by tethers laced through the flesh of their pectoral muscles.

Other cultures developed more purely theatrical forms that required no physical harm, such as the cosmic battles enacted among dancers wearing enormous, hinged beak masks in the Pacific Northwest. In ceremonies of the Kwakiutl society, dancers representing various animal spirits pretend to take bites from spectators and to suck out brains through the long, clacking beaks of their brightly painted masks. The Northwest traditions, along with various dance dramas of the Hopi and Zuni people of the Southwest, are among the relative few to survive the European conquest. With the virtual extermination by Europeans of more easterly Native American cultures in the eighteenth and nineteenth centuries, and with the confinement of surviving peoples into reservations, hundreds, possibly thousands, of ancient dance dramas were lost along with their cultural contexts.

## European Dramas

The earliest theater performed in the North American colonies by Europeans followed the patterns of European tradition and experienced no discernible influence from Native American arts. As England established dominance in the eastern part of North America, the plays performed by pioneering acting companies were representative of the literary traditions of that nation. English Renaissance playwrights such as Thomas Kyd, Christopher Marlowe, and William Shakespeare had ignored the advice of classic authorities such as

Aristotle, who in his *Poetics* (c. 335 B.C.E.) argued that acts of violence and death should be kept offstage. Aristotle offered this advice not out of squeamishness—in fact, he felt that violent outcomes were essential in tragedy for the successful purgation of the audience's pent-up emotions—but because he believed it impossible to stage violent acts in a believable way.

The English playwrights preferred the model of Roman dramatists such as Seneca, who did not bother with maneuvering characters offstage before having them carve out their eyes or cut the throats of political or romantic rivals. Kyd, Marlowe, and Shakespeare pioneered a modern tragedy in which such acts were performed on stage, with plays such as Shakespeare's *Hamlet* featuring multiple stabbings and a poisoning. Shakespeare's tragedies were the cornerstone of the repertory of the first professional companies to perform in the colonies—one headed by Walter Murray and Thomas Kean, whose theatrical company emerged in 1749, and another headed by Mr. and Mrs. Lewis Hallam, who arrived from London in 1752. Both companies favored such plays as Shakespeare's *Richard III*, with its climactic battle scene and death of the eponymous character; the Hallams, whose company persisted into the nineteenth century, performed a repertoire featuring that play as well as Shakespeare's *Othello, Hamlet,* and *Romeo and Juliet.*

## Melodrama and Spectacular Violence

Though Shakespeare continued as the most performed dramatist in the United States in the nineteenth century, a new form was imported from Europe and soon swept the nation. Melodrama emphasizes the conflict between clearly defined representatives of good and evil and exploits the scenic possibilities of violent stage spectacle. Physical violence is more typically threatened than carried out, but the means of threat are far more dramatic than the stabbings, poisonings, garrotings, and smotherings of Shakespeare's theater.

The new playwrights and their producers competed in inventing monstrous means of human destruction: demonic villains were ingenious in the novel methods they devised for the destruction of sympathetic characters who stood in the way of their evil plans. Heroes and heroines and occasionally more minor innocent characters were tied up in mills set to explode, strapped to logs and sent on conveyors toward gigantic buzz saws, trapped below erupting volcanoes, and—in one noteworthy work—tied to the back of a crazed steed sent racing toward a precipice. This last spectacle, *Mazeppa,* was a mainstay at the Bowery Theater in New York City in the 1830s, where a program of spectacular melodramas proved a sensational success. Spectacular violence was seen by elite observers as a threat to the very existence of more literary theater: one St. Louis critic decried the degradation of theaters to "show shops" that produced nothing but "pasteboard pageantry, conflagrations, bombardments, springing of mines, blowing up of castles and such like accumulations of awful nursery horrors" (Grimstead 1968, p. 79).

Despite its high level of scenic violence, melodrama was, in many ways, a gentler drama than was Renaissance tragedy. Characters were rarely tortured or killed in nineteenth-century melodrama. The stage versions of Harriet Beecher Stowe's novel *Uncle Tom's Cabin* (1852) were unusual in their depictions of torture and murder. These "Tom plays," which became the most performed stage pieces in the nineteenth century, featured the savage beating of the elderly slave Uncle Tom by the satanic plantation owner, Simon Legree. After Tom was beaten to death, Legree himself was shot dead in a highly coincidental and fateful encounter. The stage versions, of which George Aiken's was most durable, made a strong statement in favor of the necessity of violence in a moral cause: Phineas, recently converted to Quaker pacifism through his love for a Quaker woman, assists fleeing slaves in a moment of crisis. Exclaiming, "Friend thee is not wanted here!," he throws a bounty hunter over the edge of a cliff. The record-breaking popularity of the "Tom plays" contributed to a climate of confrontation that would foster the outbreak of the Civil War. President Abraham Lincoln was said to have remarked, upon meeting Mrs. Stowe, "So, you are the little lady who made this big war!"

More typical than violent death in American melodrama were last-second rescues of the innocent through their own ingenuity or through the efforts of another sympathetic character. Augustin Daly's *Under the Gaslight* (1867) was an enormously successful melodrama of the post–Civil War period, and its stage imagery offers insight into the subtle means that mimetic violence provides for working through cultural anxieties such as sudden poverty, homelessness, loss of power, social inequality, and the threat to labor posed by technology. The play turns upon the expulsion of the heroine (Laura) from respectable society based on evidence offered by a powerful villain, Byke, who claims to have sold the infant Laura to her now dead parent. One of the few remaining loyal to Laura is Snorkey, a homeless Union veteran of the Civil War who suffered the loss of one arm in that conflict. In one of the most famous scenes of nineteenth-century theater, Laura rescues Snorkey from bloody bifurcation, freeing him from the tracks to which he has been tied by Byke just before a steam engine, perfect image of the machine age, rushes across the stage. Beaming with gratitude toward his rescuer, Snorkey ends the act with the exclamation, "And these are the women who ain't to have a vote!"

## Opera

Melodrama's domination of the popular American stage continued into the twentieth century, until much of its popular appeal was drained away by the widespread introduction of motion pictures. But melodrama's pattern of menace and retribution was extended on the operatic stage in the late nineteenth and early twentieth centuries. Though they aspired to tragic proportions, European works such as Giuseppe Verdi's *La Traviata* (1853) and *Otello* (1887) were essentially melodramatic, with their simplified plots of love, honor, revenge, and violent conclusions. Such works were played to the economic and cultural elite in New York and a handful of other major cities soon after their European premieres. The close relations between American popular melodrama and Italian opera became obvious when Giacomo Puccini created two highly successful operas—*Madame Butterfly* (1904) and *The Girl of the Golden West* (1910)—that were based on plays by the American playwright-producer David Belasco. *Madame Butterfly* followed the more "tragic" path, building as it does through a thin plot toward the suffering heroine's suicide. *The Girl of the Golden West* follows the gentler melodramatic path, the hero being wounded in a gunfight but surviving to marry the heroine and ride together with her into the sunset.

## Musical Theater

As cinema lured away audiences in the second decade of the twentieth century, theater was forced into a more specialized position in American culture, a trend that intensified after the introduction of national television programming in the 1940s. Plays and musicals gradually increased in sophistication as playgoers came to expect in live theater qualities that were not available in the cheaper and more conveniently available electronic entertainments.

One measure of this change toward a more elitist American theater was the transformation of the musical play in the 1940s. What had been a determinedly light entertainment form characterized by sprightly songs, sketchy and often arbitrary plots, and the display of women's legs was transformed in the 1940s into a more serious art form. Broadway insiders predicted failure for a musical based on Lynn Riggs's cowboy melodrama *Green Grow the Lilacs*, the crisis of which is the murder of the villain in a knife fight. When the show opened in 1943 as *Oklahoma!*, produced by the high-toned Theatre Guild, critics and audiences were ecstatic, recognizing a new standard in musical narrative. Violent dance was a major innovation of *Oklahoma!*, the story's climax foreshadowed in a haunting "dream ballet" choreographed by Agnes de Mille. Though murder did not become a commonplace plot solution in musical theater, it arose regularly as the form evolved, with shows such as Leonard Bernstein and Stephen Sondheim's *West Side Story* (1957) reaching for tragic proportions with the death of the Romeo-like hero in a gang war.

Sondheim became virtually synonymous with serious and violent musical theater. His *Sweeney Todd* (1979) musicalizes the story of a mass murderer whose accomplice serves up human meat pies to a hungry public; *Into the Woods* (1987) emphasizes nightmarish violence in its use of Grimms' fairy tales: toes are cut off, eyes are plucked out, a sympathetic character is murdered by a blow to the head, and a rampaging giant kills the story's narrator; *Assassins* (1991) is a study of president-killers.

## Modern Drama

As theater became a more complex, intellectual, and elite art form in the twentieth century, violence took on an artistic air in spoken drama. Whereas violence was used by playwrights of previous centuries to "purge" the audience of its deep-seated aggressions, violence now lost a redeeming narrative purpose and served instead to show the meaninglessness of existence. Desires for revenge are no longer clear, nor is justice neatly restored with an eleven-o'clock stabbing.

The play of philosophical despair and violence was developed during the 1930s by the Broadway dramatist Robert E. Sherwood, whose world-weary central characters sought out violence as a means for something decisive to happen to them. In *The Petrified Forest* (1935), a spiritually exhausted poet begs a fugitive gunman to kill him. The gangster obliges. In *Idiot's Delight* (1936), a young couple, cynical about the future of humankind, remain in the path of an air attack, singing "Onward Christian Soldiers" as the bombs fall around them.

A related phenomenon of the Depression era was the proliferation of comic violence in Broadway entertainments. Plays such as the gruesome and laughable *Tobacco Road* (Erskine Caldwell and Jack Kirkland, 1933) and the manic "scream-lined revue" known as *Hellzapoppin'* (Ole Olsen and Chic Johnson, 1938) were examples of what the critic Eric Bentley calls "hostility enjoying itself." Such violently funny, grotesque spectacles seemed to capture the nation's fears of poverty and a new war and to expel those anxieties through laughter.

In the 1970s David Rabe emerged as the outstanding representative of a violent, angst-ridden style of playwriting in his trilogy about America's encounter with Vietnam. *The Basic Training of Pavlo Hummel* (1971) concerns a violence-loving soldier who is himself brutally killed in a Saigon whorehouse. *Sticks and Bones* (1971) satirizes an absurd American family who have no understanding of a son's experiences in the war and who eventually assist him in slashing his wrists. *Streamers* (1976) examines the relation between masculinity, war, and violence. That play's depiction of a homosexual rape and multiple bloody murders in a U.S. barracks so shocked New Haven audiences in its premiere at Connecticut's Long Wharf Theatre that large numbers of audience members walked out of the performances, some shouting protests at the events taking place on stage.

Other notable examples of the violent play of spiritual despair are Edward Albee's *The Zoo Story* (1958), about a young man's gambit to trick an older man into stabbing him; Amiri Baraka's *Dutchman* (1964), which suggests the secret rage of both black and white Americans and culminates in a sudden act of violence in a subway car; Marsha Norman's *'night Mother* (1983), in which a daughter informs her mother that she will kill herself later in the evening and then does so; and Wallace Shawn's *Aunt Dan and Lemon* (1985), a disturbing parable linking Nazi atrocities, America's actions in Vietnam, and the onstage strangulation of an arms dealer during sex.

## Violence in Theaters

Riots, murders, and other violent acts have occurred during or surrounding theatrical performances. Theater is a symbolic art, not only in the sense of symbols on stage, but in the social meaning that people attach to attendance at certain performances at certain times. John Wilkes Booth, an actor by profession and possessed of a romantic if morbid sense of symbolism, was quite deliberate in choosing a theater performance as the site for his assassination of Abraham Lincoln on 14 April 1865. Frequently the symbolic meaning of who attends a theater (and where and when) is of greater historical significance than the comparatively trivial matter of the narrative content of the play that was staged. In May 1766 a mob attacked theatergoers leaving a performance, ransacked the building, destroyed it, and then burned the remains in a nearby common. Attendance at a theater was seen as a statement of Tory sympathies and the destruction of the building itself an act of revolutionary zeal. Class feeling was evidenced by the crowd's physical attack on theater patrons, during which the patrons' wigs and fancy clothes were torn off—actions similar to those carried out by mobs who had attacked the elite attending Harvard commencements in the 1750s.

Riots were fairly common in the late eighteenth and early nineteenth centuries, when theater became an acceptable site for verbal and even physical confrontation between Republican and Federalist, elite and populist. Political motives combined with race hatred in interventions against performances of the African Company in 1821–1823. This company of free blacks were harassed in their performances by white theatergoers who seem to have been organized by a coalition of Tammany Hall politicians and white theater managers who saw the company as both a political and economic threat. After New York's sheriff ordered police to quell a series of "riots" at the company's performances, police arrested the actors rather than the harassers. Authorities eventually closed down the African Company's operations, calling the theater a threat to public safety.

Most famous and deadly among theater riots in American history were events that took place at New York City's Astor Place Opera House in 1849. On 10 May of that year, a long-simmering feud between English actor William Charles Macready and American star Edwin Forrest reached a peak. Forrest, whose gruff and muscular performances had made him a star at the working-class Bowery Theater, had accused Macready of turning audiences against him during his tour of Britain in 1845. When Macready attempted to perform the role of Macbeth at Astor Place on 7 May 1849, forces had been marshaled against him. Class feeling and anti-English sentiment motivated crowds of working-class Irish to buy up large numbers of seats, from which they heckled Macready and prevented the play from going on. Macready's upper-class sponsors persuaded him to attempt another performance on 10 May, filling the theater with sympathetic audience members and so preventing havoc inside the theater. The tactic only increased social tension and a crowd of between ten and fifteen thousand gathered outside. Local authorities called in the militia to control the mob and, in response to stone-throwing from the crowd, ordered the militia to fire into the crowd. As a result of gunfire and the violence of the ensuing panic, between twenty-two and thirty persons were killed and countless others injured.

## Public Violence as Theater

Cultural historians have begun to consider acts of public violence, in particular those with a strong element of self-conscious performance and display, as theatrical events. This interdisciplinary approach to performance brings the study of theater into contact with the fields of anthropology, philosophy, and religious studies over issues of scapegoating, community "cleansing," and ritual sacrifice.

Grisly events such as the public burnings and hangings of Africans convicted in a mass hysteria that seized the white population of the New York colony in 1741 reveal an underpinning of ritual and performance. Victims were paraded through the streets on their way to the fire or the gallows. The execution itself was carried out before a mass audience, and some of the resulting corpses were displayed for weeks or months, hanging in gibbets. Analysis of the social meaning of spectacles has also been applied to such events as the destruction of buildings by patriot mob action in the 1760s, public tarring and featherings, and the abuse and burning of effigies during political demonstrations.

Regardless of the rubric of "theater"—which can be applied by observers removed by time, space, or culture from the events—the participants in these events are unaware of any aspect of "acting" or fictive circumstances. The performance demands unquestioned belief in the reality of the victim's guilt. "We have only legitimate enmities," writes the philosopher René Girard, "and yet the universe swarms with scapegoats."

*BIBLIOGRAPHY*

Butsch, Richard. "American Theatre Riots and Class Relations, 1754–1849." *Theatre Annual* 48 (1995).

Fearnow, Mark. "American Colonial Disturbances as Political Theatre." *Theatre Survey* 33, no. 1 (1992).

———. *The American Stage and the Great Depression: A Cultural History of the Grotesque.* New York: Cambridge University Press, 1997.

———. "Theatre for an Angry God: Public Burnings and Hangings in Colonial New York, 1741." *Drama Review* 40, no. 2 (1996).

Gilje, Paul. *The Road to Mobocracy: Popular Disorder in New York City, 1763–1834.* Chapel Hill: University of North Carolina Press, 1987.

Grimsted, David. *Melodrama Unveiled: American Theater and Culture, 1800–1850.* Chicago: University of Chicago Press, 1968.

Hay, Samuel A. *African American Theatre: A Historical and Critical Analysis.* Cambridge: Cambridge University Press, 1994.

Hoerder, Dirk. *Crowd Action in Revolutionary Massachusetts, 1765–1780.* New York: Academic Press, 1977.

McConachie, Bruce. *Melodramatic Formations: American Theatre and Society, 1820–1870.* Iowa City: University of Iowa Press, 1992.

MARK FEARNOW

*See also* **Music: Musicals; Performance Art; Representation of Violence; Spectacle, Violence as.**

# THEORIES OF VIOLENCE

*The entry begins with a two-part* Overview *and then discusses theories in these areas of study:* **Anthropology, Behavioral Sciences, Biology, Feminism, History, Philosophy, Political and Social Sciences, Psychology,** *and* **Religion**

## OVERVIEW I

Existing theories of violence, the psychologist W. S. Davidson II has observed, are "laden with interpersonal and political as well as scientific overtones." In proposing their hypotheses, social, behavioral, and natural scientists have disagreed significantly concerning the origins, nature, legitimacy, and consequences of violence, as well as about strategies for its prevention.

The Harvard physiologist Walter B. Cannon persuasively demonstrated (with experiments in the early 1940s) that any organism perceiving itself threatened will respond in one of three ways: "fight," "flight," or "delayed response." In all three cases, the organism reacts with a rush of adrenaline, a rise in blood pressure, and an increase in heartbeat rate, resulting in a sudden and powerful burst of energy that permits performance at a supernormal level. Which of these three courses an individual chooses at any given time, however, depends upon a complex dynamic of genetic and environmental elements, whose relative strength varies significantly over time and in differing situations. "When individuals feel that they are backed to the wall and there is no escape, they become violent," the sociologist Stuart Palmer has concluded. "Depending upon environmental conditions and their perception of these conditions, individuals aggress against others, against the social system, or against themselves" (1972, p. 13). This perception of having no alternative to the "fight" response is highly subjective, residing almost entirely in personal perceptions rather than in objective reality. Consequently, the imposition of social restraints often produces an overwhelming sense of frustration or impotence, exacerbating the very behavior that they were designed to prevent.

While the bulk of research and public concern has focused on theories about individual criminal acts, violence, per se, is a considerably more complex phenomenon. The psychologist Rollo May (1998) has identified at least five varieties of violence:

1. *Simple*—immediate response to feelings of frustration or impotence;
2. *Calculated*—another name for Cannon's "delayed response";
3. *Fomented*—mass outbreaks incited by demagogues;
4. *Absentee* or *Instrumental*—actions committed by the minions of authority at the behest of their superiors;
5. *Repressive*—that unleashed against the lower social orders in maintenance of the status quo.

As these last three categories suggest, violence is frequently collective, as exemplified by race riots, lynch mobs, wars, or armed rebellions. Collective violence, in turn, can be repressive, such as using the police or the army to keep down strikers or demonstrators, or radical, as in the case of "revolutions from below," in which the populace overthrows a leader. While violence is almost always destructive, it can also be psychologically constructive when engaged in by people suffering from deep-seated neuroses or psychoses, or chafing under brutal political or social repression. In such cases, violence can be "life-giving," says May, a "uniting of the self in action." Although violence is usually associated with criminality and antisocial behavior, much of it is legally, morally, or culturally sanctioned as the only feasible means to a higher good, as the only language understood by adversaries, or as the court of last resort. Mass or mob violence results when people are caught up in a fantasy-like experience induced by high emotional excitement, intense propaganda that "dehumanizes" potential victims, and excessive stress, fear, or fatigue.

Theories of violence generally fall into three broad categories: neurobiological, psychological, and sociological. Although there is no single marker predisposing people toward violence, certain genetic combinations or processes may account for some individual or familial deviations from normal social patterns. Genetically based electrical and chemical dysfunctions within specific regions of the brain, hormonal imbalances, or low overall intelligence are likely causative conditions. These malfunctions may be generated or worsened by severe head injuries, exposure to lead, or fetal damage owing to alcohol, drugs, or tobacco. Children who are hyperactive, impulsive, restless, demanding of immediate gratification, lacking in empathy, enamored of unreasonable risk taking, or suffering from attention deficit disorder are more prone to become violent. So are those whose psychological development has been arrested by denial of parental love and nurturing or by persistent physical or emotional abuse. Individuals manifesting low self-esteem, feelings of inadequacy, or frequent bouts of depression frequently seize upon violent outbursts as their only means of asserting a sense of identity. People severely damaged by any combination of genetic or environmental factors often "split off" those parts of themselves perceived as negative, "project" them onto other individuals or groups, and then "dehumanize" and brutalize those others in a ritual of expiation.

Without denying the importance of neurobiological or psychological factors, sociologists, anthropologists, and historians emphasize the importance of the macro level of social and cultural influences on individuals and groups. Many have attributed violent criminal behavior primarily to the existence of a "subculture of violence," characterized by dense concentrations of socioeconomically disadvantaged persons with few legitimate avenues of social mobility, lucrative illegal markets for forbidden goods and services, a value system that rewards only survival and material success, and private enforcement of the informal rules of the game. The sociologist Robert K. Merton has attributed most urban, lower-class violence to a pervasive ambience of anomie—a sense of alienation and purposelessness induced by the huge disparity between the professed ideals of equal rights and opportunities and the harsh realities imposed by institutional barriers, especially against racial and ethnic minorities. According to the 1993 Panel on the Understanding and Control of Violent Behavior of the National Academy of Sciences, violence constitutes a "learned response to frustration" engendered by the imposition of one-sided, top-down restraints on the lower social orders, who lash out against their inability to engage in reciprocal social rituals with mainstream society. Although physical isolation and such palliative expressions as "bread and circuses" and "opiates of the masses" serve to keep some groups marginalized and maintain the social status quo, when these seem insufficient, the dominant factions of society readily resort to repressive violence to preserve supremacy.

Whatever their differences in interpretation, social scientists generally agree that the United States has been among the most violent societies in recent world history, that violence permeated the course of American development, and that it has been a major ingredient in shaping the character of American life. This nation's persisting frontier experience; its revolutionary national birth; its celebration of individualism, competition, social and spatial mobility, and material success; its moral ambivalence toward crime and criminals; its easy sanctioning of the use of force in furtherance of a "higher good" (whether conservative or radical); its consistently low position on international indices of social well-being; and its unqualified commitment to economic growth and modernization are among the major ingredients cited by those scholars seeking to formulate a comprehensive theory of American violence.

BIBLIOGRAPHY

Brown, Richard Maxwell. *Strain of Violence: Historical Studies of American Violence and Vigilantism.* New York: Oxford University Press, 1975.
May, Rollo. *Power and Innocence: A Search for the Sources of Violence.* New York: Norton, 1998.
Palmer, Stuart. *The Violent Society.* New Haven, Conn.: Yale University Press, 1972.
Reiss, Albert J., Jr., and Jeffrey A. Roth, eds. *Understanding and Preventing Violence.* Washington, D.C.: National Academy Press, 1993.

JOHN D. BUENKER

*See also* **Fight-or-Flight Syndrome; Genetics; Nature vs. Nurture; Psychological Violence; Shame; Sociobiology.**

## OVERVIEW II

What are the causes of violence? What motivates a person to resort to violence? Can institutions and even nations be violent? Does violence usually take the form of random acts committed by predatory individuals, or is most violence organized violence? Social scientists and philosophers involved in the study of violent behavior have been haunted by these questions, and their answers have taken different forms. Naturalistic explanations have been based on religious and medical views, while social-constructionist approaches have focused on violence as created by social arrangements and structured hierarchies, arrangements that often favor those who have the power to define what behaviors and what actors are to be considered violent.

### Historical Interpretations of Crime and Violence

Early American philosophical explanations of violent behavior were heavily influenced by religious or theological views. Criminals, especially violent criminals, were seen as possessed by demonic forces out of their control. In the United States, the witch trials in Salem, Massachusetts, during the late 1600s were based on the premise that crime was the work of evil spirits that possessed a person's soul. Although discredited today, the demonic view of violent crime still persists in popular culture and among conservative groups and was exemplified in the use of everyday expressions such as "the serial killer Jeffrey Dahmer is a demon."

Social scientists such as Kai Erikson have argued that demonic views emerge in a society during periods of rapid social change in which social boundaries have been challenged. For example, at the time of the Salem, Massachusetts, witch trials of 1692, women were trying to gain access to rights such as the economic right to land ownership. The fact that a majority of those accused of witchcraft at Salem were women suggests that one of the concerns confronted by the Puritans was the definition of gender roles. Hanging witches was a way to keep women under control in a society that was facing radical social and political changes.

During the eighteenth century in Europe, the philosophy of the Enlightenment, with its emphasis on finding explanations for physical as well as social phenomena through means of logic and reasoning, strongly influenced Western views on crime and punishment. Naturalistic philosophical explanations about laws that governed the cosmos—for instance, as reflected in the writings of Rousseau, Montesquieu, and Voltaire—replaced demonic views of violence and crime. Viewed from within this framework, crime and violence in society not only could be understood but could also be eradicated by using reasoning and logic.

One of the founders of the field of criminology, Cesare Beccaria (1738–1794), applied the political philosophy of the Enlightenment to the subject of criminal justice in his native Italy, in a classic treatise titled *On Crime and Punishment* (1764). Beccaria characterized the eighteenth-century Italian system of punishment not only as ineffective and corrupt, but as criminogenic, or crime producing. Justice that was violent and barbaric, argued Beccaria, will lead to a population that is violent and barbaric. In particular, he opposed the death penalty, arguing that the punishment should *fit* the crime, not duplicate it. Demonstrating the public's abhorrence of homicide by punishing murderers with state-sponsored homicide struck Beccaria as not only cruel and barbaric but absurd. Certainty of punishment was more important than severity of punishment, he insisted. The idea that people will embrace violence and crime if they are not deterred by the certainty of punishment remained the primary model for dealing with crime and punishment over the next two and a half centuries.

Enlightenment philosophy laid the groundwork for the introduction in Europe and in the

United States of exhaustive penal reforms. However, as major social transformations began to occur as a result of industrialization, urbanization, and population growth, urban violence in the United States increased as well. The legalism of the classical school, with its ideal that individuals are free to choose their behavior and its emphasis on law and punishment as a way to control crime, was inadequate as a theory for explaining the increase in crime rates.

## Pathological Explanations of Violence

During the mid-nineteenth century, a new philosophical paradigm known as positivism took preeminence in the study of social problems. Positivism focused on using empirical science—observation, measurement, and analysis—to determine what about the world could be "positively" known, as opposed to surmising natural laws by means of theology or metaphysics. The scientific method through observation and analysis was the best tool with which to study crime and violence.

*Biological Theories.* The work of biological positivists such as Cesare Lombroso in Italy and the Harvard anthropologist Ernest Hooton in the United States attempted to explain violence as the work of individuals with biological characteristics that made them prone to crime. An entire generation of Americans grew up with popular images transmitted through the media of violent individuals as mental deviants or biological misfits.

Many have also criticized biological theories for linking racial characteristics associated with people of color to violence and crime. However, these theories still enjoy preeminence among criminologists and policy makers. Some insist in locating the causes of violence in the brain, the nervous system, the extra Y chromosome, the hormonal system, or the genetic makeup of an individual. More recently, biochemical factors—such as chemical and mineral deficiencies, allergies, hypoglycemia, and even dangerous amounts of copper, lead, or mercury in the body—have been explored as possible explanations of violence. One of the most controversial and widely read books exploring crime and violence from the perspective of biological positivism is James Q. Wilson and Richard J. Hernstein's *Crime and Human Nature* (1985). Wilson, a political scientist, and Hernstein, a psychologist, argue that constitutional factors can be associated with criminal behavior. They maintain that criminals may be born with physiological characteristics such as low intelligence, mesomorphic body type, and aggressive personality that predispose them to criminal behavior. Wilson and Hernstein conclude that a combination of social circumstances and biological factors cause crime and violence.

*Psychological Theories.* Biological theories focus on deviance as being an individual trait, literally located in the body of a person. But the pathological model also encompasses individual psychology, in which the abnormality that causes deviance is located in the mind. Psychologists also have jumped onto the bandwagon of individualistic explanations of crime and violence, looking back into the lives of violent criminals for causes such as childhood trauma, maternal deprivation, abnormal personality development, psychosis and neurosis, or even penis envy in the case of female offenders. Rather than focusing on biological factors, these theories emphasize the relationship between mental and subconscious processes and violence. Violent criminals are seen as deranged individuals who commit their violent crimes because of mental problems, even mental illnesses.

Sociopsychological theories also place importance on the way individuals learn violence from others through a process of imitation. The cycle-of-violence approach offers evidence that those who live in violent homes have a much higher chance of becoming violent themselves. However, not only can violence be learned from witnessing significant others committing violent acts, but also from movies, television, and other media influences. Freudian explanations dealing with repression, inferiority complex, and latent delinquency have also found a place on the long list of psychosocial dynamics associated with violence.

## Sociological Theories of Violence

Until the late nineteenth century, the major approaches to the study of crime and violence focused on individual factors, in which the units of analysis were certain categories of persons, small groups, and even families. These micro explanations focused on face-to-face interactions, individual behavior, and small-group dynamics. During the late nineteenth century, however, the first macro theories emerged, with their emphasis on political and social organizations, institutions, and structures. While micro theories focus on why certain individuals engage in violent behavior, macro theories try to explain why violence occurs in a certain society.

Not surprisingly, the development of macro theories of violence took place during and after the Industrial Revolution, especially following the observation that rates of violence are higher in metropolitan than in rural areas. In other words, demographic changes led the way to the development of different crime patterns. Beginning with Émile Durkheim's pioneering work, *The Division of Labor in Society* (1893), late-nineteenth-century criminologists and scholars preoccupied with the study of violent behaviors looked at factors such as population density and the greater need for occupational specialization as factors leading to crime and violence. Living anonymously in large cities was linked to a decrease in social solidarity and an increase in anomie, or normlessness, a situation that provides fertile ground for crime and violence to flourish.

Durkheim's work paved the way for the emergence of a set of ideas that came to be known as disorganization theory, based on the observation that social problems are caused by social change, which creates social disorganization. Foremost among early-twentieth-century thinkers examining crime and violence through the lens of this kind of ecological theory—which focused on what made violent places rather than on what made violent people—were Clifford R. Shaw and Henry D. McKay, working at the University of Chicago in the early 1920s. Shaw and McKay called attention to the existence of urban zones with higher rates of juvenile delinquency and crime and noted that violence and crime tend to be higher as one moves toward the business center of the city. Their studies were carried out in U.S. cities including Philadelphia, Boston, Cincinnati, Cleveland, Richmond, and Chicago. In Chicago, their research received government funds and was developed into a massive project of crime-prevention programs; the Chicago project led to major policy changes in the state of Illinois and was imitated in other cities nationwide. Durkheim's concept of social solidarity was the foundation of the Chicago project, which tried to prevent crime and violence by finding ways to build a sense of community in inner-city neighborhoods—most visibly, through the creation of community centers.

During the 1960s other scholars attempted to explain the higher rates of violence among young lower-class African Americans. Marvin E. Wolfgang and Franco Ferracuti's *The Subculture of Violence*, which first appeared in Italian in 1966, combined several theoretical approaches to conclude that young lower-class African Americans possess a value system that deviates from that of the larger society, mainly in the way that violence has become an acceptable part of everyday life in the black ghettos of the United States. Some of these young people view carrying weapons as a reasonable form of protection and survival. In Wolfgang and Ferracuti's view, this subculture breeds higher rates of violent behavior by accepting violence as "normal." At the same time, this subculture of violence is self-reinforcing, because it rejects outside influence and is suspicious of outsiders and of the criminal justice agencies.

Criticisms of the work of Wolfgang and Ferracuti abound. Some have questioned the assumption that there is something inherently violent in African American youth subcultures. Others have seen their work as stereotyping young African American males and ignoring that violence among young white males can be perceived and treated differently by the agencies of criminal justice and by the mass media.

Some authors, such as Marvin Dawkins, have focused on the relationship between violence and abuse of drugs and alcohol, suggesting the existence of a pharmacological relation. However, Paul Goldstein, in his study of homicides in New York City, found that as many as 84 percent of these incidents were motivated by drug trafficking and by interpersonal conflict linked to drug abuse. He maintains that drug users trying to obtain money for drugs account for a very small proportion of homicides.

Firearms availability has also been included as a major cause of violence. The Federal Bureau of Investigation's annual Uniform Crime Reports indicate that about half of the murders and one third of the robberies in the United States every year involve the use of firearms. Moreover, the presence of firearms at home significantly increases the risk of suicide among adolescents as well as the chances of being killed by a family member or other intimate. A logical conclusion is that gun control would result in a reduction in the rate of violence.

## Structural Theories of Conflict and Power

The explanations for violence offered by the pathological and sociological models do not take into account human choice and the sociohistorical and political context in which such choice takes place. Violent behavior and its complexity in these models are reduced to biological and psychologi-

## A Recipe for a Violent Society

In a 1996 essay "Confronting Crime: New Directions," the criminologist Elliot Currie sketches the imaginary blueprint of a violent society: It should encourage a distribution of wealth that increasingly separates the rich from the poor. It should deny meaningful and fulfilling employment to large portions of its population, particularly to its youth. It should consider its human resources "replaceable," by shifting work to those areas in which labor is cheaper, with total disregard for the consequences of these relocations on communities or on people's lives. It should promote competition rather than cooperation among its members, and it should deny basic benefits to those who are unable to work or to those who have problems finding fulfilling jobs, either because of discrimination or because they lack skills.

To Currie's list it is important to add: It should promote racist and sexist attitudes and it should scapegoat certain persons, such as immigrants and people of color, blaming them for the maladies existing in that society.

cal processes or to specific external factors, and the political dimension embedded in the definition of violence is completely ignored. For example, these models do not address the way violence by the state is often seen as legitimate—or not viewed as violence at all—since the state has a monopoly on defining violence. Meanwhile, violence committed by dissident groups as a form of political protest is usually defined as illegitimate violence. (In some countries, political dissidents have been defined as mentally ill and treated as such.)

A humanistic theory of violence shifts the focus of inquiry from individual factors to structural determinants of violence. Violence and control are treated as political definitions because they are based on power. Among the most important approaches within this humanistic tradition is the conflict view of crime, which maintains that crime and violence are the result of unequal power relations. Influenced by Marxist analysis, the conflict view explains how violent acts committed by dominant groups in society, such as nuclear testing, police brutality, corporate crime, and unsafe working conditions, are not defined as violence in a culture

in which such definitions are controlled by the powerful. The definition of what is violent and what is not is aimed at controlling those with no power, who are often presented as "dangerous." Therefore, individual acts of violence committed by poor people, such as mugging, are portrayed as more harmful and detrimental to society than collective acts of violence, such as environmental pollution, which are usually committed by those holding political and economic power. However, such acts of collective violence cause more harm and have more detrimental consequences on the larger society than do individual crimes.

Moreover, powerful institutions and governments resort to violence as way of keeping intact social hierarchies which favor the status quo. In *Criminology as Peacemaking* (1991), Harold E. Pepinski and Richard Quinney outline the way in which the U.S criminal justice system is founded on violence. Violence not only underlies the justice institutions in the United States but also guides political and economic international policies. Individual and structural violence, international conflicts in the form of war and warfare, and crimes committed by the U.S. Central Intelligence Agency all share a common denominator—the need to keep intact the overlapping structures of power.

For instance, the U.S. government used violence, defended as foreign policy, to suppress movements for social justice in Central America because powerful economic groups in the United States benefit from the current hierarchical structures existing in that part of Latin America. (The United Fruit Company, to name an example, has benefited economically from the cheap labor of Central Americans and from the appropriation of lands that belonged to indigenous peoples of the area.)

Internally, the U.S. government has regularly suppressed and repressed movements for social equality and social justice. Leaders of the Civil Rights movement, for example, were consistently harassed, imprisoned, even killed. During the 1970s, in universities across the country progressive professors and students were singled out for surveillance and control. Moreover, students at Kent State University in Ohio and Jackson State College in Mississippi were gunned down during political protests. This governmental violence, however, was presented to the public as justified on the grounds that students were disruptive or that they were engaged in activities defined as "criminal" by those in power.

The humanistic perspective has been influenced by feminism, which has called attention to acts of criminality and violence committed against women that serve to preserve the patriarchal structure of society—in which men essentially hold the monopoly on violence. In this light, acts of resistance committed by women against their aggressors are seen as crime; for instance, acts of self-defense committed by women who kill their abusive partners are treated as murders. Feminist theory has helped explain acts of violence against women—such as rape, torture, sexual slavery, prostitution, stalking, and sexual harassment at work and in the streets—as means of coercing the marginalization and powerlessness of women.

The activism of gay men, lesbians, and bisexuals has also been a factor in the development of critical thought. On 27 June 1969, riots broke out in the Greenwich Village neighborhood of New York City following a police raid on a gay bar called the Stonewall Inn. The Stonewall riots marked the beginning of a visible movement for gay and lesbian rights. Nonetheless, three decades later, nearly twenty U.S. states still had sodomy laws that could be used to convict homosexuals of consensual sexual activities. Moreover, hate crimes and murders committed against homosexuals, such as the killing of Matthew Shepard in Wyoming in 1998, are still prevalent on the streets of this country.

One of the major shortcomings of early humanistic theories of violence was an overemphasis on the role of sociostructural arrangements on individual actions. Human life is not entirely determined by impersonal hierarchies of power. Free will and human agency play a substantial role in individual actions. A useful theory of violence cannot neglect the role of reflexive human agency or treat free will as being completely subsumed by larger political and economic historical forces. Critical and feminist scholarship has, in fact, evolved toward views that are less rigidly deterministic, recognizing individuals as both creative and created agents of their own destinies.

*BIBLIOGRAPHY*

Bureau of Justice Statistics. *Changes in Criminal Victimization, 1994–1995: National Crime Victimization Survey.* Washington, D.C.: U.S. Department of Justice, 1997.

———. *Violence Between Intimates.* Washington, D.C.: U.S. Department of Justice, 1994.

Currie, Elliot. "Confronting Crime: New Directions." In *Crime and Society.* Vol. 1, edited by Robert Crutchfield, George S. Brides, and Joseph G. Weis. Thousand Oaks, Calif.: Pine Forge, 1996.

Dawkins, Marvin. "Drug Use and Violent Behavior Among Adolescents." *Adolescence* 32 (1997): 395–406.

Erikson, Kai T. *Wayward Puritans: A Study in the Sociology of Deviance.* New York: Wiley, 1996.

Hooten, Ernst. *The American Criminal.* Cambridge, Mass.: Harvard University Press, 1939–.

Lombroso, Cesare. *Criminal Man.* 1863

Madriz, Esther. *Nothing Bad Happens to Good Girls: Fear of Crime in Women's Lives.* Berkeley: University of California Press, 1997.

Pepinski, Harold E., and Richard Quinney. *Criminology as Peacemaking.* Bloomington: Indiana University Press, 1991.

Reiss, Albert J., Jr., and Jeffrey A. Roth, eds. *Understanding and Preventing Violence.* Washington, D.C.: National Academy Press, 1993.

Shaw, Clifford R., and Henry D. McKay. *Juvenile Delinquency and Urban Areas.* Rev. ed. Chicago: University of Chicago Press, 1972.

Wilson, James Q., and Richard J. Hernstein. *Crime and Human Nature.* New York: Simon and Schuster, 1985.

Wolfgang, Marvin E., and Franco Ferracuti. *The Subculture of Violence: Towards an Integrated Theory in Criminology.* London: Tavistock, 1967.

ESTHER MADRIZ

*See also* **Crime and Punishment in American History; Prevention: Violent-Crime Prevention.**

## ANTHROPOLOGY

Anthropologists view topics from a cross-cultural or worldwide perspective; they seek generalizations that pertain to all cultures. Violence is a universal feature of human life; of the many types of violence, anthropologists are particularly interested in the causes and manifestations of child abuse, spouse beating, rape, assault, homicide, suicide, and capital punishment, as well as feuding and warfare. Each topic has its own literature and an accompanying set of theories within the field. This article will selectively review some anthropological perspectives relevant to three particular forms of violence in the United States: homicide, wife beating, and capital punishment.

### Theories of Homicide

*Cultural.* An anthropologist typically proceeds by describing a culture (i.e., the way of life of a particular group of people), showing how the parts of that culture fit together, tracing its origins (historical and environmental factors that led to its rise), and showing the impact of the culture on its own members as well as on other cultures. From an anthropological perspective, culture is seen as causing a particular effect—for instance, violence.

An approach known as the culture of violence, with origins in the field of sociology, has been used to understand homicide, for instance, as it is manifested in the American South. Societies with cultures of violence have social orders in which violence is a way of life that seems to perpetuate itself indefinitely. Such societies often have fraternal interest groups (see below). High rates of homicide in southern states are attributed to a propensity among southern males to use violence to settle disputes; violence is seen as a means to preserve honor in what has been called a "culture of honor" (Nisbett and Cohen 1996). William Montell (1986), in a field study of homicides in an area on the border between Kentucky and Tennessee, refers to retaliatory killings as a folk system of justice. Houston's high homicide rate is attributed by Henry Lundsgaarde (1977) to the southern cultural emphasis on honor and justice and to the practice of gun carrying; indeed, the spread of violence through migration from the South to other regions has been treated as a causal factor both in high nineteenth-century homicide rates in the West and in high twentieth-century urban homicide rates (Butterfield 1995).

The roots of southern violence are traced to the Scotch-Irish, more appropriately referred to as *borderers*, bearers of a distinct culture that developed in the borderland counties of England, Scotland, and Ireland that touched on the Irish Sea, who immigrated from this region to the American colonies in a wave lasting from about 1717 to about 1775. To their new home in the upland eastern region of North America they brought a culture developed over many centuries—a culture molded by hundreds of years of fighting by rival monarchs over the border between northern England and southern Scotland, numerous battles between warlords, and incessant livestock raiding by predatory clans (technically, in anthropological jargon, ambilineages).

Under these conditions, survival for a man and his family meant the ability and willingness to use weapons. Once settled in the Appalachian mountains extending from what was to become southwestern Pennsylvania to Tennessee and Georgia, they continued to live as they had in the borderlands (Fischer 1989). This cultural pattern of self-reliance, based on violent retaliation, raiding of livestock, and feuding between clans, persisted into the twentieth century, probably because environmental conditions were similar: isolated mountain settlements and livestock herds, attacks by Native Americans, and paucity of governmental control.

Historians who study the feuds in the Appalachian highlands, which ended in the 1890s with the dismemberment of the clans (due to the onset of state militias, industrialization, out-migration, and, later, the World War I draft), point out that the descendants of the warring clans are law-abiding citizens; on the other hand, those who study contemporary crime note the speed with which confrontations between the descendants of borderers, who often carry guns, turn violent (Nisbett and Cohen 1996). Fox Butterfield (1995) has argued that because borderers were sometimes owners and often overseers of slaves, the pattern of homicidal retaliation was adopted by southern African Americans and transported to northern cities.

One can accept the formulation that homicide patterns in the American South have their roots in the violent culture of the borderers of the Irish Sea, who transported this culture to the New World, where it persisted in the Appalachian highlands until the end of the nineteenth century. But the notion that present-day urban crime can also be traced to these roots is more difficult to accept. Three factors seem much more likely to be causative in the case of black urban violence: First, the brutalization of African Americans, both during and after slavery, led to dehumanization. Segregation and continuing discrimination have compounded the problems afflicting portions of the African American community (Rosenfeld 1971). Those who have been dehumanized have little regard for their own lives or for those of others. Second, the ready availability of firearms and the incessant demonstrations of their use in movies and television have not only made it easy to obtain the means of killing but have provided models for violent-prone individuals. Gang killings to control drug traffic occur with great frequency, a person under the influence of drugs may kill, and felony murder may be committed to obtain money for drugs.

*Social.* Societies with fraternal interest groups, power groups of related males, have been found in numerous case studies and cross-cultural studies to be characterized by violence of several kinds within the local community: rape, feuding, and warfare between culturally similar, independent political units (Otterbein 1994). Members of such groups defend each other's interests; they may also, as a group, perpetrate violent acts against members of other groups, including women. The borderers of the Appalachian highlands formed clans or ambilineages, which are fraternal interest groups. The fraternal-interest-group theory can be expanded to include nonkinship groups, such as criminal gangs and police forces. A classic anthropological study of feuding criminal gangs in Chicago is *The Vice Lords* (Keiser 1969). Two categories of societies can be delineated and contrasted: those with fraternal interest groups, which demonstrate much conflict and feuding and little or no law, and those without fraternal interest groups, which show little conflict, no feuding, and the flourishing and enforcing of law (Otterbein 1994). Within the United States such peaceable enclaves as the Amish and the Hutterites are examples of the latter category (Dentan 1994). Thus, social as well as cultural theories can be used, in part, to explain the patterns of southern feuding: the clans or ambilineages are fraternal interest groups.

*Psychological.* The frustrations of everyday life create an aggressiveness that can erupt into violence. Frustration-aggression theory posits that *"aggression is always a consequence of frustration. . . .* [T]he occurrence of aggressive behavior always presupposes the existence of frustration and . . . the existence of frustration always leads to some form of aggression"* (Dollard et al. 1939, p. 1; emphasis in original). The poverty of African Americans and other minority groups who live in inner cities and the concomitant frustrations they endure are viewed by some anthropologists as a root cause of homicide and other forms of violence (Sharff 1998). The battering of women by their male partners is frequently attributed to the frustrations that men often suffer in the workplace. In particular military socialization in the United States (the boot camp experience) engenders violence against women.

## Theories of Wife Beating

When certain factors are present in a society, wife beating becomes a likely occurrence in the households of that society, as it is in the United States, where 2.1 million to 8 million women are abused by their partners each year (McBride 1995, p. 12). An inequality-conflict model, which predicts wife beating, is derived by David Levinson from a cross-cultural study of ninety societies in a worldwide sample. The model combines four sets of factors that are the strongest predictors of frequent wife beating: economic inequality between the sexes, violent conflict resolution, male domestic authority, and divorce restrictions for women. Each of these factors alone is correlated with wife beating, but the combined effect is even stronger. Levinson does not apply his model to the present-day United States. If one did, the model would suggest that wife beating should be on the decline, since gender-based economic inequality is decreasing, violent conflict resolution is more and more disapproved of, male domestic authority has eroded, and divorce restrictions for women are nearly gone. Given the imprecision of data on the frequency of spouse abuse, it is impossible to determine, at the present, if wife beating is on the decline.

Culture of violence theory would predict that for groups in the United States like the borderers, wife beating would be a less likely form of violence. In such groups where there are high levels of male aggression, that aggression is more often aimed at targets outside the family. Furthermore, if one applied Levinson's cross-cultural study and looked for economic inequality between men and women as a predictor of wife beating, that form of violence again seems unlikely in a self-reliant culture such as that of the Scotch-Irish in Appalachia—where gender-based economic inequality was rarely an issue since women were major subsistence producers.

## Theories of Capital Punishment

The death penalty in the United States is used for the most heinous crimes, usually murder. A cross-cultural study of sixty societies in a worldwide sample found that societies with decentralized political systems were most likely to execute recidivist criminals. It also revealed a distinction between what may be called *early states* and *mature states* as defined by their use of capital punishment. *Early states*—that is, societies that have recently developed into states—were likely to be despotic, using execution for many offenses and using torture as part of executions. After two centuries as a state, torture was no longer used; these *mature states* retained capital punishment, but for far fewer crimes (Otterbein 1986). Conceivably, the term *mature state* should be reserved for only those polities that do not practice capital punishment.

Most anthropologists do not see capital punishment as a general deterrent to homicide, and thus they do not believe that it is a solution to the high homicide rate in the United States. An anthropological view of violence would posit that reducing poverty and discrimination, and the dehumanization that accompanies these conditions, would be foremost as a potential solution to the homicide problem.

*BIBLIOGRAPHY*

Butterfield, Fox. *All God's Children: The Bosket Family and the American Tradition of Violence.* New York: Knopf, 1995.

Dentan, Robert Knox. "Surrendered Men: Peaceable Enclaves in the Post-Enlightenment West." In *The Anthropology of Peace and Nonviolence,* edited by Leslie E. Sponsel and Thomas Gregor. Boulder, Colo.: Lynne Reinner, 1994.

Dollard, John, et al. *Frustration and Aggression.* New Haven, Conn.: Yale University Press, 1939.

Fischer, David Hackett. "Borderlands to the Backcountry: The Flight from North Britain, 1717–1775." In *Albion's Seed: Four British Folkways in America,* edited by David H. Fischer. New York: Oxford University Press, 1989.

Keiser, R. Lincoln. *The Vice Lords: Warriors of the Streets.* New York: Holt, Rinehart and Winston, 1969.

Levinson, David. *Family Violence in Cross-Cultural Perspective.* Newbury Park, Calif.: Sage, 1989.

Lundsgaarde, Henry P. *Murder in Space City.* New York: Oxford University Press, 1977.

McBride, James. *War, Battering, and Other Sports: The Gulf Between American Men and Women.* Atlantic Highlands, N.J.: Humanities Press International, 1995.

Montell, William Lynwood. *Killings: Folk Justice in the Upper South.* Lexington: University Press of Kentucky, 1986.

Nisbett, Richard E., and Dov Cohen. *Culture of Honor: The Psychology of Violence in the South.* Boulder, Colo.: Westview, 1996.

Otterbein, Keith F. "Crime." In *The Encyclopedia of Cultural Anthropology,* edited by David Levinson and Melvin Ember. New York: Holt, 1996.

———. *Feuding and Warfare: Selected Works of Keith F. Otterbein.* Langhorne, Penn.: Gordon and Breach, 1994.

———. *The Ultimate Coercive Sanction: A Cross-Cultural Study of Capital Punishment.* New Haven, Conn.: Human Relations Area Files, 1986.

Rosenfeld, Gerry. *"Shut Those Thick Lips!": A Study of Slum School Failure.* New York: Holt, Rinehart, and Winston, 1971.

Sharff, Jagna Wojcicka. *King Kong on Fourth Street: Families and the Violence of Poverty on the Lower East Side.* Boulder, Colo.: Westview, 1998.

KEITH F. OTTERBEIN

*See also* **Capital Punishment; Homicide; Spousal and Partner Abuse.**

## BEHAVIORAL SCIENCES

An adequate explanation of violence first requires a definition of the act, process, or condition to be explained. Consider the following definition of violence the National Academy of Sciences' Panel on the Understanding and Control of Violent Behavior offers: "behaviors by individuals that intentionally threaten, attempt, or inflict physical harm on others" (Reiss and Roth 1993, p. 2). It is important to note what this widely adopted definition of violent behavior includes and what it leaves out. It includes such acts of conventional criminal violence as homicide, rape, assault, and robbery (theft accompanied by force or the threat of force). Other examples of violence that also fit the panel's definition are war, torture, capital punishment, and boxing. A heterogeneous range of behaviors falls within the panel's definition, and it is unlikely that a single theory would be capable of explaining all of them. Most analysts and policy makers insist, for example, that different theories are required to explain murder and lethal injection, even though both involve intentional physical harm. At the same time, the panel's definition omits behaviors that reasonably might be considered "violent," for example, extreme psychological abuse or certain kinds of malicious property crime, such as destruction of religious property or crossburning. One influential definition of violence encompasses any activities that inflict "damage on persons or property" (Blumenthal et al. 1972, p. 71 n.).

An important facet of a theory of violence, then, is the definition of violence that it presupposes. The same definition may underlie different theories, and the same theory may be applied to different definitions. This discussion will adopt the panel's definition, but please bear in mind that plausible alternatives could have been selected and that the choice of a definition necessarily directs attention toward some theoretical perspectives and away from others.

A second important dimension of any theory concerns its scope conditions, that is, the conditions under which the theory's propositions are presumed to apply. A key scope condition of theories in the behavioral and social sciences is the level of analysis at which they are formulated. Some theories are restricted to the microlevel of analysis, meaning that they are intended to explain the characteristics of individuals and perhaps those of the immediate social setting. Other theories are more macrolevel in their focus on the properties of groups, communities, and societies. Very few behavioral or social theories encompass both levels of analysis, although some perspectives are highly consistent with what may be viewed as companion perspectives at a different level of analysis. This is the case with the major behavioral theories of violence.

The major theories of violence at the macrolevel of analysis are the cultural, disorganization, and anomie perspectives. Their microlevel companions are social learning theory, control theory, and strain theory. Pairing the theories across levels of analysis yields three multilevel perspectives: cultural-learning, disorganization-control, and anomie-strain theory. Cultural-learning theory posits that, like other behaviors, violent behavior is learned, or scripted, under specific cultural conditions. We should expect to observe from this perspective high levels of violent behavior in situations, groups, or communities where such behavior is widely regarded as appropriate or even mandatory under certain circumstances. By contrast, disorganization-control theory proposes that, like other deviant or criminal behavior, violence results from the absence or breakdown of social control or self-control. Violence does not have to be culturally motivated; it merely has to be released, and it emerges when the regulatory capacity of community institutions (families, schools, neighborhoods) or the internal controls of individuals are weakened.

Finally, in Robert K. Merton's classic anomie-strain perspective (1968), crime and violence result from the strain associated with blocked access to the legitimate means for attaining social success, or from an excessive emphasis on the success goals relative to the culturally approved means for achieving them. In a later microlevel formulation, strain is associated not only with the failure to achieve highly valued goals but with the presence of negative stimuli and the absence of positive stimuli (Agnew 1992). Unlike cultural-learning theory, anomie-strain theory does not explain violent behavior in terms of the prevalence or strength of violence-promoting values. Rather, violence emerges from the adoption of conventional values when access to the legitimate means (education, employment, income) is restricted. Unlike disorganization-control theory, the anomie-strain perspective does not envision persons as "freed" to behave violently when controls are diminished, but as motivated to do so by a disjuncture between goals and means or by stressors of various kinds.

A lively debate existed in the late 1980s and the 1990s over the desirability of integrating different theories of violence and crime into a single framework. Wherever one might come down in the debate, however, it is important to recognize that the three violence perspectives described here share a fundamental orientation: they all direct attention to the causes and distribution of violence across individuals or populations. Like most such etiological theories, these three perspectives take the meaning of violence for granted and assume that a behavior is violent if it meets a specified definition of violence, such as the panel's definition. Yet the meaning of violent behavior does not reside in the behavior itself. The definition of a behavior as violent and the theoretical explanation of behavior so defined are part of a social process consisting of sometimes conflicting values, interests, and appraisals. It is unlikely that the same theory would be used to explain the crime of murder and the lawful act of lethal injection; indeed, some readers will question the designation of lethal injection as an act of violence.

We tend to reserve the term *violence* for socially condemned behaviors that harm others, and theories of violence are nearly always, implicitly or explicitly, limited to deviant or antisocial behavior. This limitation does not invalidate the theories. Rather, as with other scope conditions, it specifies the boundaries within which they are appropriately applied, in this case the boundary between normative and deviant violence. One of the most valuable contributions of the behavioral and social sciences to the study of violence is to remind us that such socially constructed distinctions are always subject to change.

*BIBLIOGRAPHY*

Agnew, Robert. "Foundation for a General Strain Theory of Crime and Delinquency." *Criminology* 30, no. 1 (1992).

Akers, Ronald L. *Deviant Behavior: A Social Learning Approach.* Belmont, Calif.: Wadsworth, 1985.

Blumenthal, Monica D., et al. *Justifying Violence: Attitudes of American Men.* Ann Arbor, Mich.: Institute for Social Research, 1972.

Braithwaite, John. *Crime, Shame, and Reintegration.* Cambridge, U.K.: Cambridge University Press, 1989.

Gottfredson, Michael R., and Travis Hirschi. *A General Theory of Crime.* Stanford, Calif.: Stanford University Press, 1990.

Kornhauser, Ruth. *The Social Sources of Delinquency: An Appraisal of Analytic Models.* Chicago: University of Chicago Press, 1978.

Merton, Robert K. *Social Theory and Social Structure.* New York: Free Press, 1968.

Messner, Steven F., and Richard Rosenfeld. *Crime and the American Dream*. 2d ed. Belmont, Calif.: Wadsworth, 1997.

Miethe, Terance D., and Robert F. Meier. *Crime and Its Social Context: Toward an Integrated Theory of Offenders, Victims, and Situations*. Albany: State University of New York Press, 1994.

Reiss, Albert J., Jr., and Jeffrey A. Roth, eds. *Understanding and Preventing Violence*. Washington, D.C.: National Academy Press, 1993.

Wolfgang, Marvin E., and Franco Ferracuti. *The Subculture of Violence: Towards an Integrated Theory in Criminology*. New York: Tavistock, 1967.

RICHARD ROSENFELD

*See also* **Nature vs. Nurture; Sociobiology.**

## BIOLOGY

Biological influences in aggression and violence have been clearly established in studies of humans and other animals. These factors have been extensively reviewed elsewhere (e.g., Raine 1993, 1995; Miczek et al. 1994; Niehoff 1999) and are summarized in detail throughout this encyclopedia. Key biological variables include genetic predispositions, hormones, physiological underarousal (autonomic-nervous-system functioning), brain function (and dysfunction), and neurotransmitters. These biological variables are not independent from one another and are highly interrelated, often in complex ways. Moreover, the interaction between social and biological factors appears to be of critical importance in understanding human violence.

Some of the earliest scientific attempts to link violence to physical characteristics were made at the beginning of the nineteenth century. In what eventually became known as phrenology, a Viennese physician, Franz Joseph Gall, proposed links between behaviors and mental characteristics (including "destructiveness") with the size and shape of bumps in the skull overlying certain functional regions. Although seemingly farfetched compared to more complex biological theories nearly two centuries later, Gall's work inspired other research into brain function and violence, including that of an American physician John Bell (see Finger 1994). Charles Darwin (1859; 1871) also considered aggression and violence in his theory of evolution and natural selection, which became the basis for popular evolutionary and genetic explanations of violence in the 1990s. Konrad Lorenz and E. O. Wilson brought an ethological perspective to human aggression and violence by emphasizing the position of humans in the larger animal hierarchy.

By the end of the twentieth century, there were several theories or explanatory models attempting to integrate the findings from research into biological bases of aggression and violence. Human violence itself, however, is a heterogeneous phenomenon, and there is no single theory that can explain all forms of violence in all individuals. Most researchers of the biological underpinnings of violence consider that there may be different etiologies, or causes, for varying forms of violent behavior. In fact, there is support from animal studies for distinct biological pathways underlying violence in predatory attack and in defensive behaviors (Niehoff 1999). Several major theories or explanatory models encompassing the biological bases of human violence are reviewed in this article: (1) sociobiology, (2) brain function and dysfunction, (3) neurochemical models, (4) autonomic underarousal, (5) endocrinological (hormone) models, (6) genetic predispositions, and (7) biosocial interaction models.

### Sociobiology

Sociobiology is a comprehensive biological explanation of human violence based on Darwin's theory of evolution. This explanation focuses on the profound implications of people's desire to maximize their individual reproductive status through gains or protection of resources and access to mates. That is, humans have evolved with mechanisms for ensuring that their genes are passed on to subsequent generations through reproduction. Two important consequences of sexual reproduction, in which differential investment in offspring occurs between sexes, are (1) competition between males for ultimate access to desirable females, and (2) female choice for desirable males. In their book *Homicide* (1988), Martin Daly and Margo Wilson provide an excellent account of the profound implications of these consequences for many important issues in human violence, including infanticide; intermale conflict; and greater violence, aggression, and sexual jealousy in men than in women.

One limitation of the Darwinian explanation of violence is that it focuses on ultimate (evolutionary) rather than proximate (immediate) causes. Although a great deal of explanatory power is derived from evolutionary approaches to understanding human behavior, including violence, there is little to say about the specific biological mechanisms that account for individual behavior in specific instances. Evolutionary causes explain *why* humans may behave violently, but proximate causes are needed to understand *how* individual behaviors occur. Thus, other biological theories are needed to provide greater details regarding proximal mechanisms, which may ultimately have an evolutionary basis.

### Brain Function and Dysfunction

Two major areas of the brain have received a great deal of attention in violence research. First, the limbic system (including amygdala and hypothalamus) appears to be essential in violent behaviors, both in humans and animals. Both the amygdala and hypothalamus have been implicated in predatory and defense attack behaviors, although different regions and pathways appear important to each type of aggressive behavior. Second, the more recently evolved neocortex has shown important relationships to human violence. Of particular interest are the frontal and temporal areas of the cerebral cortex, which have been identified with emotional responding and executive functioning, including impulse control. Violent behavior has been linked to abnormalities in these areas using electroencephalographic (EEG) studies (see the entry "Psychophysiology: EEG"), brain injuries (see "Neuropsychology: Head Injury"), and brain imaging (see "Neuropsychology: Brain Imaging"). An excellent account of the neurological pathways involved in violent behavior may be found in Debra Niehoff's *The Biology of Violence* (1999). These brain abnormalities in violent offenders may indicate a disruption in neural development during gestation, pregnancy and delivery complications, or other traumas. It is especially difficult to establish cause-effect relationships in head injuries.

Brain mechanisms may be involved in perceptions of threat and subsequent responses. There may also be indirect effects of brain dysfunction on aggressive and violent behavior, via cognitive deficits. Propensities toward violence may be the direct result of neurological damage or may be indirectly influenced—that is, mediated through other factors. For example, cognitive deficits resulting from dysfunction in these areas may lead to school failure, dropouts, or alcohol and drug use, which may in turn increase propensities toward antisocial behavior, including violence.

### Neurochemical Models

Several neurotransmitters (chemical messengers that facilitate communication between nerve cells), as well as their related enzymes and byproducts after breakdown, have demonstrated importance in human violence. In particular, violent behavior has been associated with high levels of dopamine (which is involved in reward pathways in the brain), low levels of serotonin (which is important to impulse control), low levels of monoamine oxidase (MAO, an important enzyme in the breakdown of serotonin), or high levels of norepinephrine (which excites the central and peripheral nervous systems during high arousal states, and initiates the fight-or-flight response). There have also been studies of gamma-aminobutyric acid (GABA, an inhibitory amino acid transmitter), which has been shown to play an important role in alcohol metabolism, and thus perhaps indirectly in alcohol-related violence (see "Neurotransmitters: GABA").

Some neurochemical factors, such as elevated norepinephrine, may be involved in defensive responses, while others, for example, MAO deficiency, may be more important in proactive forms of aggression and violence. Thus, neurotransmitters and their metabolic pathways themselves may explain different forms of violence in different individuals in different situations.

The causal nature of these relationships is not always apparent, however. For example, neurotransmitter levels may increase as a result of violent behavior, or violent behavior itself may be the result of neurotransmitter increases. Some genetic defects in loci involved in various aspects of neurotransmitter systems (including MAO, dopamine, and serotonin) have also been reported in several studies (see the entries "Genetics: Molecular—Human" and "Neurotransmitters: Dopamine, Norepinephrine, and Their Metabolic Enzyme, Monoamine Oxidase"), suggesting at least some causal effect of neurotransmitter systems on violence.

Genetic defects in dopamine metabolism have been found in excessive and compulsive behaviors of many forms that often coincide with violence, including drug abuse, conduct disorder, Tourette's syndrome, obsessive-compulsive disorder, and post-traumatic stress disorder. A group of investigators has suggested a "reward deficiency" model in which an inherited imbalance in the dopaminergic system alters the intercellular signaling in the brain's reward process. The dopamine deficiency leads to replacement of an individual's feeling of well-being with anxiety, anger, or a craving for a substance that can alleviate the negative emotions. A possible genetic aberration involves a variant form of the gene for the dopamine D2 receptor, called the A1 allele, which has been found to be associated with alcoholism and, to a lesser extent, with a spectrum of impulsive, compulsive, and addictive behaviors (Blum et al. 1996).

## Autonomic Underarousal

One well-replicated finding is that of autonomic underarousal (i.e., reduced activity or emotional responding of the autonomic nervous system) in antisocial (including violent) individuals. This result has been found for both heart rate (see "Psychophysiology: Heart Rate") and skin conductance (see "Psychophysiology: Autonomic Activity"), in both institutionalized and noninstitutionalized samples. Violent individuals tend to show lower resting heart rates, lower electrodermal responding (i.e., skin conductance), and smaller changes in these factors in response to novel stimuli (e.g., auditory presentation of tones). These findings have been interpreted in a number of ways. First, low heart rates may reflect "fearlessness" or reduced anxiety, lack of socialization (i.e., poor conditioning due to cognitive deficits or emotional withdrawal), or reduced brain functioning in areas involved in mediating psychophysiological responding. Another explanation is that low arousal may lead to stimulation-seeking behaviors, including violence, in an attempt to raise autonomic levels to optimal levels.

## Endocrinological Models

"Raging hormones" have been a popular explanation for human violence. In fact, the endocrine (hormone) system has been shown to play an important role in human aggression. However, these effects are not simple, as endocrine glands and resulting hormones interact with one another as well as with other systems, including the central nervous system and the sensory systems.

In hormone-behavior research, a distinction is made between organizational influences (i.e., structural changes), which may occur especially, but not exclusively, during prenatal and perinatal development, and later activational influences, which occur in response to circulating hormones. In the entry "Endocrinology: Overview," the various ways in which hormones may exert their influences on aggressive behavior are discussed.

Testosterone and another androgens have been of particular interest in research on violence, due to their relatively high levels in males, who display greater violence and aggression than females in most species. There are clear organizational effects of prenatal exposure to testosterone on physical structures (including the brain) as well as on some aspects of behavior. However, organizational effects on aggressive outcomes are not particularly strong, and may be limited to particular subcategories of aggressive behavior (e.g., athletic and other competitive situations). Moreover, although some associations between circulating levels of testosterone and aggression (i.e., activational influences) have been found in adolescent and adult males, these effects have not been consistently replicated across studies.

The role of estrogen, particularly in female violence, has also been considered, although in a much more limited way than testosterone. Higher estrogen levels have been associated with hostile outbursts in adolescent females, but not in adolescent males (Inoff-Germain et al. 1988). However, a greater proportion of crimes by women are committed just before or after the beginning of their monthly menstruation, a time when estrogen levels are *lower* compared to other portions of the cycle (see "Endrocrinology: PMS and Female Violence"). As in the case of testosterone, then, the effects of estrogen on human aggression and violence are not simple causal ones.

One theory is that hormones play a role in victims' ability to cope with stress, including threats of violence. Testosterone in males and estrogen in females have been noted to fluctuate in response to stress and competition (Niehoff 1999). Also, the ability to regulate physiological responses to stress (including the stress hormone cortisol) appear to be diminished in sexually and physically abused children (see the entries "Child Abuse: Physical"; "Child Abuse: Sexual"; and "Endocrinology: Hormones in Child Abuse").

## Genetic Predispositions

Genetic predispositions to aggression are clearly evident in both animal and human studies (see the entries "Genetics: Twins, Families, and Adoptions" and "Animal Studies of Aggression and Violence"), although genetic effects vary somewhat across definitions and measures of aggression. Evidence for a genetic basis for human aggression comes primarily from twin, family, and adoption studies. However, research on specific pathways from individual genes to aggressive behavior is still in its infancy. Although some genetic markers for aggression (and possibly violence) have been recently suggested (see the entry

"Genetics: Molecular—Humans"), most of these studies have not focused on aggression or violence per se but on disorders for which aggression may play some role (e.g., Tourette's syndrome, substance abuse, and conduct disorder). One noteworthy exception is the Dutch study (Brunner et al. 1993) in which an omission of a single chemical base-pair in the MAO-A structural gene was associated with a variety of antisocial behaviors, including violence. This result, however, has yet to be replicated in other samples. Thus, there is no clearly established gene (or set of genes) for human aggression or violence.

How might genetic and environmental factors mediate the relationships between violence and its biological risk factors? While many of the biological risk factors important to human violence, as described in detail throughout this encyclopedia, may be functions of genetic predispositions, they are almost certainly not entirely genetically based. In particular, environmental factors that cannot be transmitted (e.g., brain trauma and other experiences) may be of considerable influence in the biological risk factors for violence.

In the same vein, it should be noted that social risk factors (such as lack of parental supervision and involvement or delinquent peer group associations) may not exclusively represent environmental influences. For example, individuals genetically predisposed toward antisocial behavior may selectively affiliate with delinquent peers, and may elicit negative behaviors from their parents (O'Connor et al. 1998). These possibilities call into question the traditional assumptions about the nature of peer and parental effects on youth violence—that is, they may not represent pure environmental effects but may reflect a complex interplay between genes and environment. Much research is still needed to understand how genes and environment may underlie the relationships between biological and social variables and their relationships to human violence.

Most important, the interactions among biological (including genetic) and social (environmental) factors appear to be of critical importance in understanding human violence. Genetic factors, in particular, appear to exert their greatest influence in the presence of adverse environmental conditions. It is noteworthy that antisocial behavior is the one behavioral domain in which gene X environment interactions have been consistently replicated in many samples, including the United States. That is, the effects of genetic predispositions for antisocial behavior appear to be amplified un-

der adverse environmental conditions. Moreover, negative environmental factors often appear *not* to be particularly influential, except in the presence of individual genetic predispositions toward antisociality.

## Biosocial Interaction Models

The importance of biological factors in general (not just genetic factors) may depend very much on environmental or social conditions. In fact, there is considerable evidence that many biological effects described above and throughout this encyclopedia may be small or nonexistent under certain environmental conditions. For example, Adrian Raine has found that birth complications (which are considered to be primarily environmental factors), in combination with maternal rejection, are most important to violent outcomes (Raine et al. 1997). Even adult neurotransmitter levels may be altered by early rearing experiences, as discussed by Marcus J. P. Kruesi (Kruesi and Jacobson 1997; also "Neurotransmitters: Overview"). Moreover, the single domain in behavioral genetics in which gene-environment interactions have been found repeatedly is the study of antisocial behavior, including violence. In both Scandinavian and U.S. samples, genetic predispositions for criminal behavior appear to be of greatest importance when adverse environmental factors are present.

An excellent overview of biosocial models may be found in *Biosocial Bases of Violence* (1997), edited by Adrian Raine et al. The book summarizes four specific theories that have been articulated on biosocial interactions. Three of the theories (Eysenck 1964, Mednick 1977, and Buikhuisen 1988) propose enhanced conditioning and learning of prosocial behavior as a function of biological characteristics, particularly those related to the functioning of the autonomic nervous system. The fourth biosocial theory, by Terrie Moffitt (1993), proposes that neuropsychological problems (manifested as cognitive deficits, difficult temperament, and motor difficulties) combine with adverse social conditions to produce the greatest risk for criminal outcomes in what she terms "life-course persistent offenders." Further elaboration on biosocial models, including Moffitt's developmentally based theory, may be found in the entry "Age and the Life Cycle."

## Summary

The causes of human violence must certainly include biological factors at some level. There is a wide range of influences with well-established associations to violence, including brain dysfunction, hormones, and neurotransmitters. These factors, however, are likely to differ across both individuals and situations. Although genetic factors have been clearly demonstrated to play a role in some forms of violence, much is still to be learned about exactly how genes and environment may mediate the relationships between violence and many of the biological factors. Biosocial models of violence, which consider the complex interplay of both inherited conditions and life experiences, are likely to become of greatest importance in explaining human violence.

*BIBLIOGRAPHY*

Blum, Kenneth, et al. "Reward Deficiency Syndrome." *American Scientist* 84 (March–April 1996): 132–145.

Brunner, Hans G., et al. "Abnormal Behavior Associated with a Point Mutation in the Structural Gene for Monoamine Oxidase A." *Science* 262 (22 October 1993): 578–580.

Buikhuisen, Wouter. "Chronic Juvenile Delinquency: A Theory." In *Explaining Criminal Behavior: Interdisciplinary Approaches,* edited by Wouter Buikhuisen and Sarnoff A. Mednick. Leiden, the Netherlands: E. J. Brill, 1988. Pp. 27–50.

Daly, Martin, and Margo Wilson. *Homicide.* Hawthorne, N.Y.: Aldine de Gruyter, 1988.

Darwin, Charles. *On the Origin of Species.* London: Murray, 1859.

———. *The Descent of Man and Selection in Relation to Sex.* London: Murray, 1871.

Eysenck, Hans Jurgen. *Crime and Personality.* London: Methuen, 1964; 3d ed., St. Albans, U.K.: Paladin, 1977.

Finger, Stanley. *Origins of Neuroscience: A History of Explorations into Brain Function.* New York: Oxford University Press, 1994.

Inoff-Germain, Gale, et al. "Relations Between Hormone Levels and Observational Measures of Aggressive Behavior of Young Adolescents in Family Interactions." *Developmental Psychology,* 24, no. 1 (1988): 129–139.

Kruesi, Marcus J. P., and Teresa Jacobson. "Serotonin and Human Violence: Do Enviromental Mediators Exist? In *Biosocial Bases of Violence,* edited by Adrian Raine, Patricia A. Brennan, and Sarnoff A. Mednick. New York: Plenum Press, 1997. Pp. 189–205.

Lorenz, Konrad. *On Aggression.* New York: Harcourt, Brace and World, 1966.

Mednick, Sarnoff A. "A Biosocial Theory of the Learning of Law-Abiding Behavior. In *Biosocial Bases of Criminal Behavior,* edited by Sarnoff A. Mednick and Karl O. Christiansen. New York: Gardner, 1977. Pp. 1–8.

Miczek, Klaus, et al. "An Overview of Biological Influences on Violent Behavior." In *Understanding and Preventing Violence.* Vol. 2, *Biobehavioral Influences,* edited by Albert J. Reiss, Jr., Klaus Miczek, and Jeffrey A. Roth. Washington, D.C.: National Academy Press, 1994.

Moffitt, Terrie E. "Life-Course Persistent and 'Adolescence-Limited' Antisocial Behavior: A Developmental Taxonomy." *Psychological Review* 100 (1993): 674–701.

Niehoff, Debra. *The Biology of Violence.* New York: Free Press, 1999.

O'Connor, Thomas G., et al. "Genotype-Environment Correlations in Late Childhood and Early Adolescence: Antisocial Behavioral Problems and Coercive Parenting." *Developmental Psychology* 34 (summer 1998): 970–981.

Raine, Adrian. *The Psychopathology of Crime: Criminal Behavior as a Clinical Disorder.* San Diego, Calif.: Academic Press, 1993.

Raine, Adrian, Patricia A. Brennan, and David P. Farrington. "Biosocial Bases of Violence." In *Biosocial Bases of Violence,* edited by Adrian Raine, Patricia A. Brennan, and David P. Farrington. New York: Plenum, 1997.

Wilson, Edward O. *Sociobiology: The New Synthesis.* Cambridge, Mass.: Belknap Press, 1975.

LAURA A. BAKER

*See also* **Animal Studies of Aggression and Violence; Child Abuse: Physical; Developmental Factors: Perinatal** *and* **Prenatal; Endocrinology; Fight-or-Flight Syndrome; Genetics: Chromosomal Abnormalities** *and* **Molecular—Human; Health and Medical Factors; Nature vs. Nurture; Post-Traumatic Stress Disorder; Psychopathy, Biology of; Psychophysiology; Sociobiology.**

## FEMINISM

Although the suffrage movement, or "first wave" of American feminism, did encounter and attempt to address certain types of violence, it was not until the mid-1960s that feminists extensively theorized about and created new policy to deal with men's violence against women. The analysis of violence played an important part in the development of various branches of "second wave" feminism. Late-twentieth-century feminists focused on demonstrating that violence against women was pervasive and proving that it was a product of culture—especially patriarchy.

Different feminist analyses of the causes of violence suggest widely different ways of eradicating violence: If violence is an extreme form of power relations, violence could be abolished by eliminating authority and hierarchy. If violence is learned culturally, culture must be changed (for example, men could learn to be more like women). If violence is biological, men should be eradicated. Nonetheless, although second-wave feminists divided into several theoretical groups (radical, liberal, socialist, Marxist), feminist analyses of issues related to violence—including rape, pornography, and battery—overlapped between and among groups, perhaps as often as they conflicted.

### Sexual Violence Against Women

The anti-rape movement worked to change beliefs about the causes of sexual violence against women, beginning by demonstrating that rape did not result from out-of-control male sexuality or behaviors by the victim. Feminists such as Susan Brownmiller and groups such as the New York Radical Feminists in the early 1970s asserted that rape was political rather than sexual, an act of violence committed against women because they were women, rather than a crime against (male) property. They argued that rape, and especially the threat of rape, was a systematic form of oppression that affected women's daily lives.

Rape crisis centers begun by feminists in the early 1970s demanded legal and institutional reforms (changing courtroom procedures, police attitudes, and hospital practices, for example). While liberal feminists worked toward changing laws against sexual assault, radical feminists felt that modifying the system was less important than attacking the root causes of sexism and violence in society. Early feminist martial-arts and self-defense groups felt that violence against women would not end until it was dangerous to attack women. Although some believed this meant imitating men's violence, others felt that feminist violence was justifiable, but only when it was used as a way to end violence.

Black feminists have critiqued ideas about rape that construct black men as rapists and invalidate black women as victims of rape, also pointing a finger at white feminists who can maintain a form of privileged innocence. For example, the distinguished African American intellectual Bell Hooks was among those who criticized Susan Brownmiller's work *Against Our Will: Men, Women, and Rape* (1975) because of its white, middle-class bias. Hooks points out the way Brownmiller's text, considered a feminist classic, acknowledges the rape of black women by white men but focuses on the experience of black women during slavery, without considering the far-reaching implications these acts had in devaluing black women over the course of nearly two centuries after the end of slavery.

Poststructuralist feminists are interested in the way that discussion of rape inherently portrays women as objects of desire and violence; they view this discourse as a revealing cultural narrative in which women are always already raped or vulnerable to rape. Radical feminists object to poststructuralist focus on discourse, criticizing it as theory that ignores women's actual experience.

The cultural analysis of rape led to a movement shaped around opposition to negative images of women conveyed by the popular culture. Although early radical feminists protested pornography as degrading to women, they also felt that many other media representations such as sexist advertisements were oppressive. They believed that all of these representations contributed to violence against women by helping to create or reinforce antiwoman attitudes in the viewers, and so they attempted to boycott and protest these representations.

More specifically, however, some feminists narrowed their scope to pornography as the primary cause of violence against women. Charging that "pornography is the theory; rape is the practice," they lobbied for legislation that would eliminate pornography by making it illegal. The prominent antipornography activist Catharine MacKinnon claimed that pornography itself is an act of violence against women and that it is therefore not protected by the constitutional guarantee of freedom of speech.

### Battered Women

As late as the 1970s, women who were physically abused at home in the context of a private relationship were generally not recognized as victims of crime. Neither the police nor social-welfare institutions took this violence seriously, and battered women often refused to press charges, due in part to the lack of services available to them. In 1973 a grassroots movement emerged in which feminists (often in partnership with nonfeminist social agencies) began to create shelters for battered women and their children. These shelters provided temporary care but also helped women train for and find work so that they could take control of their lives. At the same time, liberal feminist groups such as the National Organization for Women (NOW) sought to change legal and social mechanisms for dealing with battery.

Like feminists in the anti-rape movement, radical feminists working with battered women sought to address the politics of the problem at hand and to demonstrate (both to their clients and to social-service providers) that domestic abuse stemmed from a wide acceptance of male violence in society; the problem was social rather than individual. Feminists also began to consider violence committed by women, and some battered women's shelters became aware of the need to make a place for lesbian clients and acknowledge the issue of domestic violence involving lesbian partners. At the same time, addressing the social roots of this newly visible feminist issue, feminists began to extend their political efforts to educating against homophobia and on behalf of lesbian human rights.

Intertwined in the late-twentieth-century feminist debate around violence between women was a polarization of views on lesbian sadomasochism. Some feminists, notably Pat Califia, argued that a relationship between two women is essentially equal and that lesbian sadomasochism represents a choice—thus they saw it as a liberating form of multifaceted feminine desire and sexuality rather than oppression. The opposition argued that to assume that any two women must be equal ignores class, race, and ethnic differences among women; they felt that sadomasochism often disguises battery in lesbian relationships.

## Peace Work and the Myth of Feminist Nonviolence

The battered women's movement of the 1970s was by no means the first instance of women in the United States joining forces and working separately from men to oppose violence. Women have organized alongside the peace movement dating back to at least the mid-1800s, when they were often excluded from peace organizations. These women's peace groups, like the Olive Branch Circles, often lacked a feminist analysis of their work. Many women's abolitionist groups (like the regional Female Anti-Slavery Societies), temperance societies (including the Women's Christian Temperance Union), and women's rights activists (such as Julia Ward Howe and Elizabeth Cady Stanton) had connected women's oppression with the violence of war, but it was not until 1914 and the onset of World War I that the first feminist peace organization formally evolved: the Women's Peace Party of New York. The Women's International League for Peace and Freedom was formed soon after, as women recognized the limited sphere of influence of a local group.

Some radical and ecofeminists of the late twentieth century advocated that women were better suited for peace activism than men, arguing that women's biology gives them a specific connection to all life. Socialist feminists, however, maintain that this essentialist association between women and peace is ahistorical; they point out the ways that women also have been involved with milita-

rism and violence. Most feminists who work for peace recognize that sexism and violence both have roots in patriarchy; therefore, they feel they must work against both.

While most feminist theorizing about violence focuses on women as victims, this should not suggest that no feminists engaged in or advocated violence. In 1971, at a gathering billed as the Violence Meeting, feminists in New York discussed the possibility of government infiltration into the women's liberation movement. They believed that violence would be used against women's groups in order to undermine feminist efforts. Several prominent feminists spoke that evening about the possibility of the feminist use of violence in retaliation or as a forestalling measure. Some felt that violence, because it was an instrument of patriarchy, could not be used by feminists. Others believed that their oppression left them, like other oppressed groups, no choice but to use violence. In the end, there was no infiltration by government agencies, and second-wave feminists did not need to respond to it, violently or otherwise.

Although the Violence Meeting seemingly marked the beginning and the end of feminist arguments advocating violence, the lack of discussion should not allow the impression that the second wave of feminism was entirely antiviolent. For example, the lesbian feminist essayist Robin Morgan once suggested that paramilitary training would best prepare feminists for the coming revolution (she later recanted). At the beginning of the twenty-first century, however, feminists have begun to rethink how the existence of women who commit violence challenges feminist ideas about women. The issue of women's violence is being addressed by feminist sociologists, criminologists, and cultural and literary theorists.

*BIBLIOGRAPHY*

Alonso, Harriet Hyman. *Peace as a Women's Issue: A History of the U.S. Movement for World Peace and Women's Rights.* Syracuse, N.Y.: Syracuse University Press, 1993.

Bart, Pauline B., and Elizabeth Geil Moran, eds. *Violence Against Women: The Bloody Footprints.* Thousand Oaks, Calif.: Sage, 1993.

Brownmiller, Susan. *Against Our Will: Men, Women, and Rape.* New York: Simon and Schuster, 1975.

Castro, Ginette. *American Feminism: A Contemporary History,* translated by Elizabeth Loverde-Bagwell. New York: New York University Press, 1990.

Echols, Alice. *Daring to Be Bad: Radical Feminism in America, 1967–1975.* Minneapolis: University of Minnesota Press, 1989.

Haag, Pamela. " 'Putting Your Body on the Line': The Question of Violence, Victims, and the Legacies of Second-Wave Feminism." *Differences: A Journal of Feminist Cultural Studies* 8, no. 2 (1996).

Hooks, Bell. *Feminist Theory: From Margin to Center.* Boston: South End Press, 1984.

Linden, Robin Ruth, et al., eds. *Against Sadomasochism: A Radical Feminist Analysis.* East Palo Alto, Calif.: Frog in the Well, 1982.

Lobe, Kerry, ed. *Naming the Violence: Speaking Out About Lesbian Battering.* Seattle: Seal Press, 1986.

MacKinnon, Catharine. *Feminism Unmodified: Discourses on Life and Law.* Cambridge, Mass.: Harvard University Press, 1987.

NIKKI SENECAL

*See also* **Rape; Women.**

## HISTORY

Historical studies of violence have generally focused on several interrelated tasks: documenting and categorizing the extent and types of violence over a significant span of time; discerning patterns and processes in incidence and types of violence over time; assessing the historical conditions that have produced violence; situating American violence within a wider, comparative context; and debating whether violence ever "succeeds." Almost universally, historians agree that the United States has always been an extremely violent nation and that violence usually redounds to the ultimate advantage of those who control the levers of power.

### Categorizing Violence

According to Hugh Davis Graham and Ted Robert Gurr (1969), American historians of violence face four powerful obstacles: insufficient and inadequate historical evidence; the lack of reputable, applicable models and theories derived from present-day data; the increasingly narrow specialization of historical studies; and the powerful strain of "optimistic parochialism" that regards violence as an aberration rather than as the product of "the same ostensibly benevolent forces which contributed to our uniqueness." Especially critical of his fellow historians' efforts to "construct highly interpretive syntheses of violence" has been Robert Brent Toplin, who divides the results into the "handkerchief approach" ("long catalogues of atrocities from American history"), the "ideological approach" ("neat, supposedly air-tight explanations that require acceptance of a few fundamental assumptions"), and the various "disciplinary approaches" (in which scholars "tend to explain varied manifestations of violence under the rubric of

their favorite professional subjects"). David T. Courtwright in his 1997 work excoriates fellow historians for their reluctance to consider seriously that violence is, at least to some degree, a vestige of our animal origins that has yet to be eliminated by evolution.

Contending that violence "has accompanied virtually every stage and aspect of our national existence," Richard Maxwell Brown established a typography that subsumes its various manifestations under the categories of positive ("means to ends that have been widely accepted and applauded") and negative ("in no direct way connected with any socially or historically constructive movement"). Under the former rubric, he includes the Revolutionary War and the Civil War, the conquest of Native Americans, vigilantism, agrarian and labor uprisings, and law enforcement. The latter encompasses criminal activity; feuds; lynching; racial, ethnic, and religious strife; urban riots; assassination; and "freelance multiple murder." Graham and Gurr argue that violence can be judged "good, bad, or neutral, depending on who engages in it and against whom." They also distinguish between legal ("determined by formal procedures of community decision making") and legitimate ("if members of a community regard them as desirable or justifiable") acts of violence. Irving J. Sloan (1970) proffers a taxonomy based upon the categories of political, economic, or ethnic, with the caveat that elements of all three are usually present in some combination. The urban historian Charles Tilly contends that group violence has evolved over time from primitive (preindustrial, apolitical "brawls and communal clashes") to reactionary (loosely organized revolts of common people to protect traditional lifeways) to modern (specialized associations with relatively well defined economic and political objectives). Whatever their resultant typology, most historians have concentrated their attention on group or collective, as opposed to individual, patterns of violence.

### Identifying Sources of Violence

By the same token, they have almost universally located the historical sources of American violence in various combinations and permutations of large-scale demographic, ethnocultural, socioeconomic, ideological, and political forces. Much emphasis has been placed upon rapid and massive industrialization and urbanization, which have periodically dislocated and disoriented millions of people, frustrating their efforts to achieve prosperity, security, and social mobility. Equal attention has been paid to our ethnocultural diversity, which has virtually guaranteed the persistent presence of millions of unassimilated people and fueled successive waves of violence and discrimination against and among a wide variety of ethnic groups. The attendant dynamics of chain migration have also produced a country populated consistently with a disproportionate number of young, single males largely unrestrained by socializing influences and institutions. This demographic bulge has always been most pronounced in the two areas that have been the main theaters of violence: the frontier and the inner city. Moreover, the nation's frontier experience has been continuously replicated over a vast expanse of time and space, while the rapidly morphing inner city always serves as the primary habitat and workshop for the unassimilated. Only in the United States, according to Graham and Gurr, has "an interminable stream of relatively propertyless individuals, armed with bourgeois-liberal values and a powerful acquisitive instinct, marched 3,000 miles to the Pacific in an epic migration lasting 2½ centuries" (1969, p. 104). It is more than coincidence that the quintessential heroes of American fiction, usually males, have been the cowboy and the private eye—rootless young men operating in a frontierlike environment who almost always take the law into their own hands and use violent means to achieve laudable goals.

Equally exacerbating has been the country's deliberately weak institutional base—no established church; weak, fragmented government; the absence of an aristocracy with some sense of noblesse oblige; no permanent class of civil servants protecting the commonweal; no authoritative and politically influential intelligentsia—no universal institutions empowered and entrusted to ameliorate conditions and mediate conflict. Completing the picture is a virtually uncontested Lockean-Jeffersonian value system that places individual self-fulfillment above all other obligations, elevates property to a status equal or even superior to life and liberty, celebrates limited government, and defines freedom as the absence of societal and governmental restraints. Liberty and equality have proven to be in frequent conflict, as have life and liberty on the one hand, and property and "the pursuit of happiness" on the other. Perhaps because of its ethnocultural diversity and worship of individualism and competition, the United States

has never ranked fraternity and equality (at least in an economic sense) on par with liberty. Few historians of violence, apparently, would seriously dispute Courtwright's claim that in the United States violence has been the "dark side of its coin of freedom and abundance" or Brown's that it "has been a determinant of both the form and the substance of American life."

*BIBLIOGRAPHY*

Adams, Graham. *Age of Industrial Violence, 1910–1915.* New York: Columbia University Press, 1966.

Bingham, Jonathan B., and Alfred M. Bingham. *Violence and Democracy.* New York: World, 1970.

Brown, Richard Maxwell. *No Duty to Retreat: Violence and Values in American History and Society.* Norman: University of Oklahoma Press, 1994.

———. *Strain of Violence: Historical Studies of American Violence and Vigilantism.* New York: Oxford University Press, 1975.

Courtwright, David T. *Violent Land: Single Men and Social Disorder from the Frontier to the Inner City.* Cambridge, Mass.: Harvard University Press, 1997.

Graham, Hugh Davis, and Ted Robert Gurr, eds. *The History of Violence in America: Historical and Comparative Perspectives.* New York: Praeger, 1969.

Hofstadter, Richard, ed. *American Violence: A Documentary History.* New York: Vintage, 1971.

Jeffreys-Jones, Rhodri. *Violence and Reform in American History.* New York: New Viewpoint, 1978.

Sloan, Irving J. *Our Violent Past: An American Chronicle.* New York: Random House, 1970.

Toplin, Robert Brent. *Unchallenged Violence: An American Ordeal.* Westport, Conn.: Greenwood, 1975.

JOHN D. BUENKER

*See also* **Frontier; Urban Violence.**

## PHILOSOPHY

Violence, as usually defined, involves intentional injury of a serious nature by one entity against another. Beings or forces that do not have intentional states cannot actually inflict violence. Thus, when we speak of a violent storm or an animal turned violent, we are speaking metaphorically. It is also the prevailing view among theorists that violence involves coercion but that not all coercion is violent; similarly, violence involves the infliction of pain, but not every painful act is violent. Thus, coercion and the infliction of pain are neither necessary nor sufficient for the existence of violence.

Denying that intentional injury is a necessary condition for violence greatly increases what can be considered violence. Unintentional bodily movement that results in injury—say, when a car steered by a driver having a seizure strikes a pedestrian—would qualify as violence; so, too, would behaviors by nonhuman animals that result in significant injuries. To those theorists of violence who view intentionality as essential to its definition, widening the definition in this way robs violence of any clear meaning.

## Types of Violence

*Individual and Collective Violence.* Although the adjective *violent* is commonly applied both to individuals—"Dirty Harry is a violent man"—and to groups—"the Ku Klux Klan is a violent organization," theorists of a school called methodological individualism emphasize the distinction between the group and its constituent individuals (Brodbeck 1968), while critics of this school emphasize the nature of the group itself (Held 1972; McGary 1991). Under what conditions is it valid to call a group violent—must each and every member of the group have acted in a violent manner, or only some of them?

A group with a clearly stated commitment to violence, in which all of its members condone violence, can reasonably be described as a violent group: even if some members never commit an act of violence, they are connected to such acts by their solidarity with members of the group who do behave violently. Where a group's commitment to violence is ambiguous, however, a methodological individualist can reasonably argue that we should not apply the term *violent* to the group as a whole, but only to members who have acted violently or condoned the violence.

*Psychological Violence.* Another source of theoretical controversy is the question of whether acts other than physical acts should be described as violent (Barcalow 1994). For instance, we might say that "Sally shook Timothy in a violent way"; we might also say that "John speaks to his wife in a psychologically violent way." Some prominent feminist theorists have pointed to the legal and moral consequences of failing to recognize psychological violence *as* violence (Gillespie 1989). They believe that this failure places women at risk of harm not experienced by men (Bell 1993). African American theorists have made similar arguments about the psychological violence brought on by a prolonged system of racial oppression (McGary 1997).

The critics of the notion of psychological violence recognize that mental distress is a serious matter and that people can intentionally or predictably cause serious harm by inflicting such distress on their victims, but in the legal context they believe that juries are correct when they are reluctant to excuse physical violence committed in response to psychological violence. For example, in murder trials juries have not responded favorably to mentally abused women who have claimed that they acted in self-defense when they killed their abusive husbands. However, these jurors do find that such abuse might justify less drastic measures. But even the more radical ethical and legal theorists who accept that psychological abuse can justify an individual's using physical violence to end that abuse are reluctant to accept this self-defense plea when the abuse is brought on by social institutions and practices. An example of such abuse is a subtle and covert system of racial discrimination such as the Jim Crow system in the American South (Nielsen 1981).

## Morality and Violence

For thousands of years people have debated the nature and cause of violence in human beings (Tiger 1969). Some claim that humans are by nature violent. Others claim that violence is not natural but the result of social conditioning. Yet positing that people are by nature violent does not settle the issue of the relationship between violence and morality.

Pacifists like Mohandas K. Gandhi and Martin Luther King, Jr., claimed that violence is always morally impermissible; this prohibition extends to self-defensive violence. The pacifist position is controversial. Is pacifism justified on consequentialist grounds—that is, is it always true that refraining from violence brings about better consequences than violence? Or is the justification deontological in nature? Deontological moral theories claim that some actions are inherently right or wrong independent of their consequences. But is every violent act inherently wrong? Neither pacifists nor those who challenge pacifist theories have provided totally persuasive arguments for their points of view.

Attempting to explain why violence is sometimes morally permissible, nonpacifists most commonly cite the necessity of self-defense. The argument in support of self-defense asserts that all persons have a fundamental right to protect their lives, bodies, and property from transgressors; to do so, violence can be used when it is the only or most effective means available. However, supporters of this view are quick to stipulate that morally decent people do not prefer violence but consider it a last resort.

Self-defense as a legitimate reason for violence is often relied on not only in disputes involving individuals but also in political contexts. Nation-states sometimes maintain that they are morally justified in using violence against lawbreakers and enemies of the state. Individuals sometimes claim moral legitimacy for their use of violence to end political oppression by the state. It has even been argued that the victims of colonial oppression must act violently toward their oppressors if they are to eliminate the oppressive state of mind that the system imposes upon its victims (Fanon 1963).

Critics of pacifism further claim that the view is self-contradictory: given that people have a right not to be killed or assaulted, if the only way to prevent this from happening is to resort to violence, then violence is permissible in these circumstances (Narveson 1975. In response to this objection, pacifists challenge the claim that violence is necessary to prevent violence. They point to what they see as the false assumption that the language of rights is the only way to understand morality. The supporters of the ethics of care and love maintain that morality often requires self-sacrifice (Wolgast 1987); thus, in their view morality defined strictly in terms of rights fails to appreciate the caring and dependent relationships that exist between human beings. Expressing love toward one's violent enemies has the potential to transform them (King 1986). Such ethicists point to violence within families as a case where developing loving and caring relationships among family members is far more effective than getting them to acknowledge and respect one another's rights.

The history of violence is as old as the history of human affairs. Pacifists have provided thoughtful arguments for the belief that a morally good society is one that strives in principle to eliminate all violent behavior. Nonpacifists counter that to condemn all violence is to render all wars unjust and all cases of self-defense illegitimate. To non-pacifists this view of human events is unacceptable, with no reasonable person capable of condemning all violence on moral grounds.

## BIBLIOGRAPHY

Arendt, Hannah. *On Violence.* New York: Harcourt Brace, 1969.

Barcalow, Emmett. *Moral Philosophy: Theory and Issues.* Belmont, Calif.: Wadsworth, 1994.

Bell, Linda A. *Rethinking Ethics in the Midst of Violence.* Lanham, Md.: Rowman and Littlefield, 1993.

Brodbeck, May. "Methodological Individualisms: Definition and Reduction." In *Readings in the Philosophy of Social Sciences,* edited by May Brodbeck. New York: Macmillan, 1968.

Fanon, Frantz. *The Wretched of the Earth,* translated by C. Farrington. New York: Grove, 1963.

Gandhi, Mohandas K. *Non-Violent Resistance.* New York: Schocken, 1961.

Gillespie, Cynthia K. *Justifiable Homicide: Battered Women, Self-Defense, and the Law.* Columbus: Ohio State University Press, 1989.

Held, Virginia. "Moral Responsibility and Collective Action." In *Individual and Collective Responsibility: The Massacre at My Lai,* edited by Peter A. French. Cambridge, Mass.: Schenkman, 1972.

King, Martin Luther, Jr. *A Testament of Hope: The Essential Writings of Martin Luther King, Jr.,* edited by James M. Washington. New York: Harper and Row, 1986.

McGary, Howard. "Morality and Collective Liability." In *Collective Responsibility: Five Decades of Debate in Theoretical and Applied Ethics,* edited by Larry May and Stacey Hoffman. Lanham, Md.: Rowman and Littlefield, 1991.

———. "Psychological Violence, Physical Violence, and Racial Oppression." In *Existence in Black: An Anthology of Black Existential Philosophy,* edited by Lewis R. Gordon. New York: Routledge, 1997.

Narveson, Jan. "Pacifism: A Philosophical Analysis." In *Moral Problems,* edited by James Rachels. New York: Harper and Row, 1975.

Nielsen, Kai. "Violence and Terrorism: Its Uses and Abuses." In *Values in Conflict,* edited by Burton M. Leiser. New York: Macmillan, 1981.

Tiger, Lionel. *Men in Groups.* New York: Random House, 1969.

Wolgast, Elizabeth H. *The Grammar of Justice.* Ithaca, N.Y.: Cornell University Press, 1987.

HOWARD MCGARY

*See also* **Mass Murder: Collective Murder; Non-violence; Psychological Violence.**

## POLITICAL AND SOCIAL SCIENCES

The Greek philosophers believed that the proper end of politics was the good and happy life of the citizens of the polis. For both Plato and Aristotle, the aim of politics seemed to be the good life for a minority, since freedom, leisure, and property were necessary for the kinds of political and intellectual activity that produce happiness. In this context, violence might be permissible if it benefits the ends of the city-state because some citizens may need to be controlled by those who know the "truth." Ultimately, violence could be cured only by changing human nature by restricting desires through education, selective breeding, and removing from the "philosopher-kings" all manner of temptation. In Platonic terms, the institution of a civic religion would also emphasize communitarian values that would reduce the need for violence.

The rise of Christianity as a distinct institution saw the emergence of two types of duties—spiritual and secular. Civic obedience became a central Christian virtue, but one that was clearly subordinate to obedience to God, especially in the event of a conflict between the two. During the fourth century, the philosophers Saint Ambrose and his student Saint Augustine stressed the autonomy of the church in spiritual matters and the independence of the state in secular affairs. Augustine also elaborated the doctrine of original sin, the view that all human beings are sinful because of Adam's original fall from God's grace. According to this view, our sins, which include violence toward others, deserve eternal punishment in hell and render futile any attempts for happiness in this life. The most we can aspire to is an imperfect peace that brings some order to the chaos and anarchy that results from sin. Rulers may have to use warfare against those threatening disorder or heresy.

While the sixteenth-century Italian philosopher Niccolò Machiavelli might have agreed that violence was innate to human beings, he was politically indifferent to morality and religion except as they affected politics. Living in a time of political and social disorder, Machiavelli was concerned with establishing the principles under which competent political leadership could preserve the security and well-being of the community. The most successful princes, emulating the example of ancient republican Rome, recognized violence as part of political life, accepting it as an integral part of human nature while striving to control it. Machiavelli stressed that princes must not shirk from using violence; indeed, they must become proficient in its use, preparing for war even in times of peace.

Machiavelli's indifference to religion should not obscure the fact that for two centuries after the publication of his book *The Prince* (1513), the Protestant Reformation led to a merger of religious and political concerns. Yet while Martin Luther and John Calvin in the sixteenth century upheld the notion that resistance to rulers is sinful, some Protestants, such as John Knox, were formulating the view that resistance, even violent resistance, could be justified in circumstances where monarchs act contrary to God's will. In Europe, a social and political structure based upon divine right of kings and the power of the church was giving way to the idea that human beings as individuals could be active citizens and not just passive subjects.

## Violence and Political Individualism

In historical terms, this trend toward political individualism was the result of struggles over political authority, peasant revolts, the development of trade and industry, the emergence of the nation-state, and disputes between church and state. Reflecting on the turbulence of seventeenth-century English society, Thomas Hobbes argued that self-interest is the driving force of human nature, a self-interest that produces a war of all against all. Hobbes marks the beginning of liberalism in that the existence of society is explained by reference to free and equal individuals who consent to regulate their attempts to find the best expression for their egotistical natures.

John Locke, also writing in the seventeenth century, argued that there were no obstacles to the potential violence and oppression of an absolute ruler in Hobbes's work and sought to arrange political institutions in such a way that a system of checks and balances would ensure that the self-interest of one group would come up against the self-interest of another. For him the end of politics was to create a legal framework within which free, property-owning individuals could pursue their private ends. If individual rights are consistently undermined, he argued, then people have the right, even the obligation, to resist and form a new government. The French philosopher Jean-Jacques Rousseau, writing in the mid-eighteenth century, believed that "peace" under despotic rule could not be tolerated and that people are justified in using force to restore their liberties. Among classical liberals, Thomas Jefferson is often celebrated as the most ardent supporter of rebellion. He argued that even unjustified rebellion can prevent the lethargy that is the "forerunner of death to the public liberty."

While the right to rebellion might be used to defend bourgeois political rights, it did not imply any right to resist the violence produced by social inequalities that were a feature of the emerging capitalist system of production. The radicalism of Thomas Paine, James Mackintosh, William Godwin, and Mary Wollstonecraft in the late eighteenth century might see lower-class violence as a response to power inequalities in the political structure, but they did not advocate using revolution to abolish the violence in exploitative economic relations.

## Violence and Social Structure

According to Karl Marx and Friedrich Engels, writing in the mid-nineteenth century, political violence is only the instrument and reflection of the violence of the class struggle. Revolutionary violence aimed at the capitalist state is designed to end the violence inherent in the capitalist mode of production. Only the collective ownership of the means of production by the proletariat and the withering away of the state can alleviate this system. In Marxist theory revolution is justified as a response to the violence of private capital accumulation. Although neo-Marxists such as Antonio Gramsci, György Lukács, Theodor Adorno, Max Horkheimer, Herbert Marcuse, Jean-Paul Sartre, Heidi Hartmann, and Juliet Mitchell have given greater prominence to noneconomic components (the state, gender, race, and ideology), most have agreed that the economic issues of capital accumulation and private ownership have priority.

Many have been quick to condemn revolutionary violence, but as Maurice Merleau-Ponty argued: "In advocating nonviolence one reinforces the established violence of a system of production which makes misery and war inevitable." Marx and Engels believed that proletarian violence had the specific purpose of overthrowing the capitalist state and would be superseded by a democratic, nonviolent, cooperative system. Only in the most advanced capitalist countries was there the slim possibility that capitalism could be peacefully transformed. Unfortunately, when presented with political power, Lenin's vanguard party showed little signs of relinquishing its monopoly of violence in favor of democracy, raising the question of whether violence is absolutely necessary to social transformation.

Other macrosociological theories of violence emerged in the context of political, economic, social, and cultural changes that took place in the early twentieth century. In looking at the role of cultural values and religious beliefs in the emergence of Western capitalism, the German sociologist Max Weber stressed the state's control over the means of violence within a given territorial jurisdiction. He viewed control of the means of violence as a key to power that operated independently of social class and that was crucial in shaping the social order. He further argued that the legitimization and organization of violence and coercive authority were also crucial factors in social, political, and economic development. The French sociologist Émile Durkheim also believed that the transition from rural and agricultural to urban and industrial societies had profoundly unsettling effects on people's lives. In *The Division of Labor in Society* (1893), Durkheim argued that industrial society broke down traditional ways of life without providing a clear set of new norms and values. Anomie, or normlessness, was a feature of modernity that left individuals without rules on how to live. Unfortunately, as the bonds of social solidarity declined, people were left only with a competitive individualism and inner loneliness that led to a rise in various social problems such as drug abuse, mental illness, suicide, and violence. Durkheim's later work stressed the importance of culture, stressing the ways in which we are socialized into a group's language, values, beliefs, and symbols. Later social scientists, especially demographers and criminologists, used Durkheim's theories to analyze violent crime's relationship to the conditions of urban life.

More recently, Michael Mann (1988) has examined the concept of "embedded militarism" within modern states, where institutions regard war or the preparation for war as normal and desirable. The American sociologist C. Wright Mills (1958) analyzed the continual preparation for war as a structured feature of U.S. society, and the American economist Seymour Melman has described the United States as a "permanent war economy."

## Violence and Social Psychology

While the social systemic theories examined characteristics of societies that produce violence, psychologists and psychiatrists developed theories of violence that focused on the individual personality and individual behavior. The psychoanalytic perspective of the twentieth-century Austrian psychiatrist Sigmund Freud is based on instincts and drives. Freud thought that humans had an innate aggressive drive residing in the id component of the tripartite personality, mediated by a realistic ego and a moralistic superego. Human aggression could be accounted for by the drive, an insufficiently developed superego, or a weak ego. Most social psychologists, however, agree that Freud's theory relies too heavily on biological factors.

Physical anthropologists such as Konrad Lorenz and Robert Ardrey also developed a variant of the instinct or drive theory, contending that evolution produced humans who were naturally aggressive. But as the Seville Statement on Violence (Adams et al. 1992) indicates, no scientific evidence demonstrates that an aggressive drive exists apart from social conditions, nor is there evidence that aggression must take violent forms. In addition, cultural anthropologists and sociologists have demonstrated that societies vary in their levels of violence, arguing that it is not innate, as the instinctivists contend.

Behaviorists, drawing on John Watson's notion of the newborn child as tabula rasa, reacted against such notions of drives, introspection, and mentalistic concepts. They give an alternative explanation: violence is learned behavior. Albert Bandura's social learning theory (1973) suggested that children learn violent behavior through modeling, or imitation of behavior that is reinforced. The idea that vicarious learning accounts for the process by which humans become violent has widespread appeal and has contributed to debates about television violence and its potential effects on viewers. Exchange theory adds that violence may become a reciprocal process wherein participants become caught up in an action-reaction cycle of violence, and that when distributive justice does not prevail, anger is aroused.

Studies on obedience to authority suggest that persons may be violent in compliance with orders from an authority figure. Stanley Milgram's work (1974) on obedience to authority has been invoked in relation to tragedies such as the Holocaust and Adolf Hitler's command of authority. Research on obedience also has implications for the launching of nuclear weapons, which may include the order to an inferior officer by someone in command. Structural role theory suggests that when individuals play out roles, their behavior is highly determined by social structures. This idea was demonstrated in the study of a mock prison conducted at Stanford University by Craig Haney, Curtis Banks, and Philip Zimbardo (1984). The experiment had to be terminated because their subjects became so absorbed in their roles that mock prison guards acted exceedingly violently, and mock prisoners became fearful and compliant.

Psychologists who have studied problems of genocide and war have done so primarily by addressing the internal psychological mechanisms at work when individuals inflict or suffer from violence. Others, such as Bruce Berkowitz and Robert Jay Lifton (1962), have explored the internal processes leading to aggressive or violent behavior. Irving Janis (1982) has attempted to link psychology and international relations in cases of foreign policy fiascoes that involved violence and warfare. Janis identified small-group processes that undermine efficient decision making and have led to such consequences as the failed Bay of Pigs invasion and the escalation of the war in Vietnam. Janis also noted a tendency for groups to stereotype the enemy as evil or stupid. This process effectively depersonalizes the enemy, possibly facilitating violent acts. Randall Collins (1974) has stated that modern violence is very different from direct violence involving human contact. Thus, the depersonalization of violence may facilitate large-scale violence such as bombings.

From the symbolic interactionist tradition, labeling theory suggests that once a deviant act has been committed, persons may be labeled or defined as deviant. The labeling process serves to maintain the deviant behavior or encourage a "deviant career." From this perspective, persons who commit violent acts may continue to do so in part because of the labeling process.

While these theories provide no definitive answer to the question of violence, they offer some insights into the social context of violence. They have been augmented by theoretical developments that link the study of social systems with social psychology.

## Contemporary Theories: Humanism, Feminism, Postmodernism, and Interdisciplinary Studies

The humanist tradition focuses on structural causes of violence and is particularly influenced by Marxist thought. Humanists tend to emphasize the unequal distribution of power in society as a foundation for violence against subordinate groups.

Feminists add the idea that in patriarchal societies, men commit most of the violence, from the interpersonal to the international level. They view violence as a means of maintaining social control over women, who are situated in positions of lesser social, economic, and political power than men are in society. Feminists have also pointed to the cultural practices and institutions that sustain ideologies of male dominance in contemporary societies, including the family, work, and political and religious institutions.

*Postmodernism* is a very broad term used to describe the new cultural, theoretical, and aesthetic practices that emerged in the 1980s and 1990s. It celebrates the popular and vernacular, fragmentation and difference, and pastiche and ephemerality, particularly in commercial media representations of contemporary life. Movements against domestic violence, violence against animals, and environmental violence have come to the fore.

Some postmodernists believe that the plurality of new social movements may make the formation of alliances among groups difficult, particularly under the impersonal conditions of late capitalism, in which, they contend, it is hard to discern and define who the enemy is. Postmodernist theorists believe that under these conditions the structural causes of violence may become increasingly hidden from popular and academic gaze.

Four interdisciplinary fields have developed that have made important theoretical contributions to our understanding of violence: critical criminology, peace and conflict studies, gender studies, and public health. Each draws on earlier theoretical traditions but analyzes violence in more holistic terms. These fields link micro and macro causes of violence and widen the lens to include interpersonal, collective, and global forms.

Critical criminologists explicitly link macrostructures and culture to violent crime. In their definition crime is broadened to include not only those acts officially outlawed by the state but also officially sanctioned and unpunished acts that are committed by the state and other organs of the power elite. These researchers have thus developed social justice approaches to the study of crime, which link micro and macro issues; they argue that undemocratic and unequal social arrangements, rather than insufficient social control, lead to criminal violence.

Gender studies have also linked micro and macro issues, arguing that patriarchal culture, in which masculine dominates feminine, creates both microlevel violence, committed mostly by men, and macrolevel violence such as war. Gender scholars have explored the gender nature of violence and its relationship to gender socialization and the gender division of resources at all levels of society.

Peace and conflict studies have focused primarily on critiquing approaches to the study of war and developing alternatives to war. Increasingly, the field attends to the problem Johan Galtung (1969) calls "structural violence." Galtung developed the concept to account for violence that occurs when people are harmed because of inequitable social arrangements rather than by overt physical violence.

Physicians and other scholars doing research on public health issues also address problems of violence. In addition to studying problems of interpersonal violence, public health researchers have also examined the consequences of structural violence, such as unequal development, racism, food policy, and health care. Educators concerned with public health believe that humans' capacity to destroy the globe is dramatically increasing, and some argue that preventing that is the greatest contemporary health priority.

## BIBLIOGRAPHY

Adams, David, et al. "The Seville Statement on Violence." *Peace Review* 4, no. 3 (1992): 20–22.

Bandura, Albert. *Aggression: A Social Learning Analysis.* New York: Atheneum, 1973.

Berkowitz, Leonard. *Aggression: A Social Psychological Analysis.* New York: McGraw-Hill, 1962.

Caws, Peter, ed. *The Causes of Quarrel: Essays on Peace, War, and Thomas Hobbes.* Boston: Beacon Press, 1989.

Collins, Randall. "Three Faces of Cruelty: Toward a Comparative Sociology of Violence." *Theory and Society* 1 (1974): 415–440.

Durkheim, Émile. *The Division of Labor in Society.* New York: Free Press, 1984.

———. *The Elementary Forms of the Religious Life.* New York: Free Press, 1965.

Elias, Norbert. *The Civilizing Process: State Formations and Civilization.* Vol. 2. Oxford, U.K.: Basil Blackwell, 1982.

Elias, Robert, and Jennifer Turpin, eds. *Rethinking Peace.* Boulder, Colo.: Lynne Rienner, 1994.

Galtung, Johan. "Violence, Peace, and Peace Research." *Journal of Peace Research* 6, no. 3 (1969): 167–191.

Hall, Stuart, David Held, Don Hubert, and Kenneth Thompson, eds. *Modernity: An Introduction to Modern Societies.* Cambridge, Mass.: Blackwell, 1996.

Haney, Craig, Curtis Banks, and Philip Zimbardo. "A Study of Prisoners and Guards in a Simulated Prison." In *Readings About the Social Animal,* edited by E. Aronson. New York: W. H. Freeman, 1984.

Janis, Irving. *Groupthink: Psychological Studies of Policy Decisions and Fiascoes.* 2d ed. Boston: Houghton Mifflin, 1982.

Kurtz, Lester R., and Jennifer Turpin. "The Social Psychology of Warfare." In *The Nuclear Cage,* edited by Lester R. Kurtz. Englewood Cliffs, N.J.: Prentice-Hall, 1989.

Lifton, Robert Jay. *The Genocidal Mentality: Nazi Holocaust and Nuclear Threat.* New York: Basic, 1990.

Lorenz, Konrad. *On Aggression.* New York: Harcourt, Brace, and World, 1966.

Mann, Michael. *States, War, and Capitalism.* Oxford, U.K.: Basil Blackwell, 1988.

Melman, Seymour. *Profits Without Production.* New York: Knopf, 1983.

Milgram, Stanley. *Obedience to Authority.* New York: Harper and Row, 1974.

Mills, C. Wright. *The Causes of World War Three.* New York: Simon and Schuster, 1958.

Prothrow-Stith, Deborah, with Michaele Weissman. *Deadly Consequences.* New York: HarperCollins, 1991.

Reardon, Betty. *Sexism and the War System.* New York: Teachers College Press, 1991.

Ritzer, George. *Postmodern Social Theory.* New York: McGraw-Hill, 1997.

Sabine, George H. *A History of Political Theory.* 4th ed. Hinsdale, Ill.: Dryden Press, 1973.

Turpin, Jennifer, and Lester R Kurtz. *The Web of Violence: From Interpersonal to Global.* Urbana: University of Illinois Press, 1997.

Watson, John B. *Behaviorism.* 1930. Chicago: University of Chicago Press, 1957.

Weber, Max. *Sociological Writings.* New York: Continuum, 1994.

Weiner, Philip, and John Fisher. *Violence and Aggression in the History of Ideas.* New Brunswick, N.J.: Rutgers University Press, 1974.

MICHAEL J. WEBBER
JENNIFER TURPIN

*See also* **Sociobiology; Structural Violence.**

## PSYCHOLOGY

Psychological theories of aggression and violence are rooted in a long-standing debate about whether humans are innately brutal or benign. Two contrasting views of human nature are found in the classical writings of philosophers and scientific thinkers. On the one hand, Thomas Hobbes argued in *Leviathan* (1651) that humans are naturally brutal and that societal laws and their enforcement are consequently required to curb our natural aggressive instincts. Conversely, Jean-Jacques Rousseau in 1762 conceptualized the noble savage, who is naturally benign, happy, and good. According to Rousseau, the restrictions imposed by society lead to aggression and corrupt behavior.

These opposing viewpoints emerge in psychological theories of human aggression. The pessimistic Hobbesian view of innate aggressive instincts is found in Sigmund Freud's psychoanalytic theory, developed in the 1920s. Rousseau's perspective is more clearly seen in social psychological theories of the 1960s, which emphasize the role of external factors in producing aggressive outcomes. It is noteworthy, however, that most psychological theories of aggression and violence, including those that emphasize situational factors and learning, place some importance on underlying biological processes.

### Instincts and Innate Aggressive Drives

In his psychoanalytic theory Freud (1930) argued that each human is born with equally powerful instincts toward life (Eros) and death (Thanatos). When the death instinct is turned inward, it results in self-punishment (in the extreme, suicide). When directed outward, it results in hostility and anger, leading to destructive behavior and even murder. Freud believed that aggressive energy would build up and produce illness unless released, ideally in acceptable behavior.

The idea of innate, biologically based aggressive instincts dominated psychologists' thinking during the first quarter of the twentieth century. Support for this view was provided by discoveries of brain mechanisms in aggressive behavior (e.g., Cannon 1925), as well as studies demonstrating that animals could be bred for high levels of aggression. In fact, the biological basis for aggression was explored throughout the twentieth century and remained an important and popular perspective in the broader scientific community (including many psychologists).

Konrad Lorenz (1966) and E. O. Wilson (1975) later developed an evolutionary perspective of human aggression, by emphasizing the place of human beings within the animal kingdom and pointing to the apparent universality of aggression among vertebrates. Aggression is considered a valuable instinct necessary for survival, because it enhances the ability to hunt, defend territories, and compete successfully for desirable mates. However, strong inhibitory mechanisms coevolved, enabling humans to suppress aggression when needed.

Although most psychologists accept the role of biological factors in aggression at some level, some have focused on the external factors that elicit such behaviors. The frustration-aggression hypothesis was the first systematic explanation of human aggression as a reaction to environmental factors. This theory was originally formulated, in 1939, by John Dollard et al., who proposed that frustration always leads to aggression and vice versa. Other research demonstrated, however, that frustration does not necessarily lead to aggression and instead may cause depression and lethargy (Seligman 1975). In his revised frustration-aggression hypothesis, Leonard Berkowitz (1980) proposed that frustration leads to anger, which may in turn instigate aggression in the presence of certain external cues.

To social psychologists of the 1990s biological factors provided "background conditions that moderate the effects of aversive stimuli in the individual's immediate situation, particularly those that involve conflict with other people" (Geen 1998). In this regard, aggression is viewed not simply as an innate drive but as a response to external stimuli.

## Situational Factors Important to Aggression

Extensive research in the last half of the twentieth century demonstrated that a variety of social situations may lead to aggression, including frustration. Frustration may indeed increase the chances of aggressive behavior. Frustration may be exacerbated by the proximity of desired goals or objects, the attainment of which has been thwarted: the closer the goal when blocked, the greater the frustration and its aggressive outcome. However, while frustration may not always produce aggression, it may produce anger, annoyance, or readiness to aggression if the situation is conducive (for example, if the victim seems unlikely to reciprocate, due to small size or physical distance). Also, if the frustration is understandable, legitimate, or unintended, there may be less chance of aggression.

Provocation, such as that arising from the need to reciprocate in reaction to another's aggressive behavior, can also produce aggression, but not always. Reciprocation is more likely if the victim perceives the provocation as intentional. Objects of aggression, such as weapons, might also stimulate human aggression. In a classic experiment conducted by Berkowitz and Anthony LePage (1967), college students were more aggressive (delivered more shocks to a victim) when made angry in the presence of a gun than in the presence of a badminton racket. Dane Archer and Rosemary Gartner (1984) have also shown a correlation between handgun availability and homicide rate across countries.

## Psychological Processes Involved in Aggression

Beyond considering the external stimuli that may invoke aggression, several lines of research have explored the psychological processes and underlying mechanisms involved in aggression. The importance of cognitive processes, including perception, memory, and appraisal, in responding aggressively has been emphasized in social cognition. Examples of this focus include Berkowitz's (1989) theory of cognitive neo-associationism, which posits that negative affective states (elicited by aversive conditions) become associated in long-term memory with specific motor tendencies to fight or flight. Individual reactions to aggress or flee depend on genetic predispositions, prior conditioning and learning, and recognition of situational factors that inhibit or promote aggression.

The acquisition and maintenance of aggressive-response tendencies are also emphasized in Albert Bandura's social-learning theory (1963; 1973; 1983), which considers the effects of learning via modeling and imitation. Through observation of role models at home, at school, and through the media, children learn social-conduct rules and a repertoire of social behaviors, including aggression. Rewards and punishments then shape the child's behavior, determining the chances of responding aggressively in future situations. In the presence of suitable incentives the probability of aggressive behavior increases.

## Reducing Aggression

Psychologists have considered various methods for reducing aggressive behavior in both children and adults. Much of this research has focused on the effects of punishment. Mild threats of punishment appear to have a greater effect than severe threats in reducing the attractiveness of aggressive actions (Aronson and Carlsmith 1963). Also, teacher-training programs that emphasize the use of swift and nonsevere punishment have significantly reduced bullying behavior in schoolchildren (Olweus 1991). In adults severe punishment does not seem to deter violent crimes, in part because it is not swift and not certain for most violent acts (for example, countries with the death penalty do not have lower violent-crime rates). An interesting study by the Minneapolis police found that the immediate arrest of domestic abusers dramatically reduced the chances of repeat offense (Sherman and Berk 1984).

Another psychological concept thought to be important in reducing aggression is catharsis. Several theorists, including Freud (1933) and Dollard et al. (1939), have proposed that unreleased aggressive impulses lead to a buildup of pressure. Thus it is necessary to release this pressure, ideally through socially acceptable forms of behavior, to avoid the risk of illness or uncontrollable behavior. This aggressive energy is thought to be released in various ways, including physical activity, such as competitive sport; watching other people engage in aggressive play—in other words, experiencing a vicarious discharge of aggressive energy; and engaging in direct aggression—lashing out, hurting someone, saying something nasty. Research has provided no evidence, however, to support the idea that participation in competitive sports has any effect. For example, football players do not become less hostile over the course of a season or immediately after a game. Moreover, some research suggests an increase of aggression among spectators at sports events (e.g., soccer matches) or immediately following a game (one study reported greater rates of domestic abuse after Super Bowl games). Similarly, the majority of studies on the effects of direct aggression suggest no reduction but sometimes an increase in the tendency toward future aggression (see Geen and Quanty 1977). Thus, catharsis is not a viable mechanism for reducing aggression.

## Summary

Throughout the twentieth century the pendulum swung between nature or nurture as more important in determining human aggression. At the turn of the millennium a more balanced perspective was prevalent, in which both nature and nurture were considered essential in understanding the causes of individual aggressive and violent behavior. While aggression most likely evolved as a strategy in many species, whether or not it is expressed depends on previous social experiences, as well as the specific social context in which the animal finds itself. There are also important individual differences in the propensity for aggression, depending on both genetic and environmental factors, as well as their interaction. Any psychological explanation for aggression and violence must consider the role of both biological and situational factors.

*BIBLIOGRAPHY*

Archer, Dane, and Rosemary Gartner. *Violence and Crime in Cross-National Perspective.* New Haven, Conn.: Yale University Press, 1984.

Aronson, Elliot, and J. Merrill Carlsmith. "Effect of Severity of Threat in the Devaluation of Forbidden Behavior." *Journal of Abnormal and Social Psychology* 66, no. 6 (1963): 584–588.

Bandura, Albert. *Aggression: A Social Learning Analysis.* Englewood Cliffs, N.J.: Prentice-Hall, 1973.

———. "Psychological Mechanisms of Aggression." In *Aggression: Theoretical and Empirical Reviews,* edited by Russell G. Geen and Edward I. Donnerstein. Vol. 1. New York: Academic Press, 1983. Pp. 1–40.

Bandura, Albert, and Richard H. Walters. *Social Learning and Personality Development.* New York: Holt, Rinehart and Winston, 1963.

Berkowitz, Leonard. "Frustration-Aggression Hypothesis: Examination and Reformulation." *Psychological Bulletin* 106, no. 1 (1989): 59–73.

———. *A Survey of Social Psychology.* 2d ed. New York: Holt Rinehart and Winston, 1980.

Berkowitz, Leonard, and Anthony LePage. "Weapons as Aggression-Eliciting Stimuli." *Journal of Personality and Social Psychology* 7, no. 2 (1967): 202–207.

Cannon, Walter B. *Bodily Changes in Pain, Fear, Hunger, and Rage.* New York: D. Appleton, 1925.

Dollard, John, et al. *Frustration and Aggression.* New Haven, Conn.: Yale University Press, 1939.

Freud, Sigmund. *Civilization and Its Discontents,* translated by Joan Riviere. London: Hogarth Press, 1930.

———. *New Introductory Lectures on Psycho-analysis.* New York: Norton, 1933.

Geen, Russell G. "Aggression and Antisocial Behavior." In *The Handbook of Social Psychology,* edited by Daniel T. Gilbert, Susan T. Fiske, and Gardner Lindzey. Oxford, U.K.: Oxford University Press, 1998. Pp. 317–356.

Geen, Russell G., and Michael B. Quanty. "Catharsis of Aggression: An Evaluation of a Hypothesis." In *Advances in Experimental Social Psychology,* edited by Leonard Berkowitz. Vol. 10. New York: Academic Press, 1977. Pp. 1–36.

Hobbes, Thomas. *Leviathan.* 1651. Harmondsworth, U.K.: Penguin, 1986.

Lorenz, Konrad. *On Aggression.* New York: Harcourt, Brace and World, 1966.

Olweus, Dan. "Bully/Victim Problems Among Schoolchildren: Basic Facts and Effects of a School-Based Intervention Program." In *The Development and Treatment of Childhood Aggression,* edited by D. J. Pepler and Kenneth H. Rubin. Hillsdale, N.J.: Erlbaum, 1991. Pp. 4110–4448.

Rousseau, Jean-Jacques. *The Social Contract and Discourses.* 1762. New York: Dutton, 1913.

Seligman, Martin E. P. *Helplessness: On Depression, Development, and Death.* San Francisco: Freeman, 1975.

Sherman, Lawrence W., and Richard A. Berk. "The Specific Deterrent Effects of Arrest for Domestic Assault." *American Sociological Review* 49, no. 2 (1984): 261–272.

Wilson, Edward O. *Sociobiology: The New Synthesis.* Cambridge, Mass.: Belknap Press of Harvard University Press, 1975.

LAURA A. BAKER

*See also* **Aggression; Fight-or-Flight Syndrome; Nature vs. Nurture; Neuropsychology: Brain Function; Psychological Violence; Psychopathy, Biology of; Psychophysiology: Autonomic Activity; Sociobiology.**

## RELIGION

Archaic religion emerged in the midst of violence. By acquiring a monopoly on legitimate violence, archaic religions were able to create and sustain reasonably ordered societies. To understand the rising tide of violence that washed over the world in the twentieth century, therefore, one must begin with a clearer understanding of the enormous anthropological shift that is taking place beneath the surface events of contemporary history. As the work of René Girard has made clear, that understanding rests on the recognition of the role violence has played in generating the kind of social consensus upon which all cultural life depends. The ideas here are based on Girard's work and are meant to call attention to its value for those working to better understand and to address the problem of violence. While most modern religious thinking treats violence simply at the moral level and most secular thinking interprets it politically, economically, sociologically, or psychologically, Girard insists that only a genuinely anthropological perspective can illuminate the issues we face.

Rudimentary forms of human culture emerged when acts of collective violence of the kind we call "scapegoating" generated humanity's first crude forms of intense social unanimity. Only as our ancestors gradually acquired the ability to recollect these acts of violence mythologically, and to reenact them in their rituals of blood sacrifice, were they able to sustain these first episodic forms of social bonding, thus making culture possible. The ritual or quasi ritual by which a society focused all its roiling rancor on one figure and vented this violence on him functioned to unify the society and purge it of its various animosities at the same time. These systems of sacred violence were the ancient world's only tool for preventing the rampages of violence that would have otherwise left the social landscape in ruins and that today are doing just that in many places all over the world.

The challenge, therefore, of freeing humanity's religious structures from their historical complicity with violence and its mystifying power is an exceedingly complex one, a challenge, moreover, from which both religious fundamentalism and irreligious secularism have taken flight. Of all the factors contributing to the waning power of the ancient systems of sacred violence, by far the most historically decisive has been the demythologizing spirit whose moral and religious epicenter is the spectacle of sacred violence—seen from the point of view of its innocent victim—which is at the center of the Christian New Testament. In comparison with archaic myths, the Greek tragedians, and the pre-Socratic philosophers, the Judeo-Christian tradition is unique in two ways. The first is the specificity with which it awakens to the moral problem of the victim *as* victim. The second is that it fosters religious traditions that have the effect of arousing in their host cultures this same moral concern, thus gradually depriving these cultures of the social benefits the scapegoating mechanism provides as long as its practitioners believe the myths that lend it moral and religious legitimacy. Not only is the

exposé of sacred violence in the Christian Gospels anthropologically unique, but the historical effect of this exposé is unique as well, for Christianity's constituent events gradually undermine the myths and rituals of sacred violence in ways that are largely independent of the conscious aim or moral wherewithal of Christian believers.

In awareness of how readily both the defenders and detractors of Christianity might misconstrue these matters, it is important to point out that the role the Gospel is playing in undermining the old sacred system means neither that Christianity is to blame (as Nietzsche insisted) for the crisis of culture we are now facing nor that historical Christians are exempt from the moral reproach against sacred violence that the Gospel has let loose on the world.

In dealing with the problem of violence, therefore, the issue that must be faced is the waning power—for better or worse—of the old sacred systems and the corresponding diminution of our ability to use "holy" violence (or invoke its cultural prestige) to keep "godless" violence in check. As proximity to the Gospel revelation (and the cultures suffused with its moral ethos) continues to undermine the myths of sacred violence, the affected societies, in varying degrees, suffer from an upsurge in the kind of random violence which the old sacred systems existed to preclude. In other words, today's mounting level of "bad" violence is directly related to the waning of the sacred aura that once surrounded officially sanctioned "good" violence and endowed it with the moral and cultural prestige upon which its power to keep or restore order depended.

The fact remains, however, that collective violence is the most ancient and primitive source of camaraderie, the only one on which deeply crisis-ridden societies could rely for restoring unity. Moreover, as a glance at any newspaper will confirm, many of our most powerful social and psychological reflexes predispose us to it. When the officially sanctioned forms of violence are stripped of their justifying myths, the social aggravations they once restrained fester, heightening both the propensity for violence and the predilection to conjure up some new myth or ideology to justify it. One must recognize this resurgence of violence for what it is: an unwitting and desperate attempt to resuscitate the crude and fierce solidarity that raw violence engenders and to fall again under the spell of the justifying myths that endow such violence with moral and religious legitimacy.

Although non-Western cultures have been somewhat insulated from the New Testament's demythologizing and desacralizing effects, the West has largely failed to recognize the source of its own moral intelligence with regard to violence. In failing to recognize the problem at an anthropological level—in conceiving of violence in terms of politics, economics, sociology, and psychology, and in turning to the laudable but morally fickle assertion of individual "rights" as an antidote—the West has left itself vulnerable to the great ideological scourges of the twentieth century, unable to recognize them for what they really were—namely, the irreligious resurgence of sacred violence whose myths were secular and whose appetite for victims was almost insatiable.

Modern rationalism, secularism, and subjectivism, on one hand, and postmodernity's rigidly enforced normlessness, on the other, appear obviously unequal to the historical responsibilities facing humanity at the beginning of the twenty-first century. The work of René Girard suggests that to confront the challenge for which these projects lack the moral and intellectual vigor, we humans must free ourselves and our cultures from the structures of sacred violence upon which we have always depended, and we must do so without precipitating the very social catastrophes that the ancient systems of sacred violence existed to avert. From a Girardian perspective, the best way to begin facing this challenge is to discover or rediscover the deeper anthropological, moral, and religious significance of the New Testament, and to assess its staggering historical ramifications.

*BIBLIOGRAPHY*

Bailie, Gil. *Violence Unveiled: Humanity at the Crossroads.* New York: Crossroad, 1995.
Girard, René. *Things Hidden Since the Foundation of the World.* Stanford, Calif.: Stanford University Press, 1987.
Williams, James G., ed. *The Girard Reader.* New York: Crossroad, 1996.

GIL BAILIE

*See also* **Religion.**

# THRILL CRIME

The term *thrill crime* first came into wide journalistic use following the 1924 murder of a fourteen-year-old schoolboy, Bobby Franks, by his cousins Nathan Leopold and Richard Loeb, then college students. All three were members of wealthy Chicago families and were described in the press as "children of privilege."

Although Leopold and Loeb had prepared a ransom note, kidnapping was readily dismissed as a ruse. After discovery of the victim's body, police investigation uncovered neither robbery, sexual abuse, nor a long-standing grudge (whether between the victim and his killers or their respective families) as a motivation for the killing. Instead, Leopold and Loeb claimed in their confessions that they had committed the murder merely to demonstrate their superiority to ordinary people—not only the victim but also police and prosecutors. The killers fully expected to escape detection, prosecution, and sanction; they had convinced themselves that they had committed "the perfect crime," because the killing would seem to investigators (and the press) to have no discernible motive.

The state of Illinois sought the death penalty. Although the pair entered pleas of guilty, a court proceeding was conducted to determine sentence, during which Leopold and Loeb were represented by the famous attorney Clarence Darrow. Darrow, whose summation included a ringing condemnation of the death penalty, argued that the two had acted in response to an "irresistible impulse" to kill. Although the defendants were spared execution, both the presiding judge and the press were profoundly disturbed that the killers had expressed no remorse—not over the death of their victim or about the impact of their crime on the families (their own and the victim's).

Not all thrill crimes end in homicide; indeed, not all thrill crimes are offenses against persons—the "joy rider" might steal an automobile that he or she later returns to the owner. Social scientists have refined the definition of a thrill crime to include the following key criteria:

1. There must be apparent purposelessness, a lack of any motive discernible to investigators and other observers. Moreover, since an offense that is instrumental to another crime (such as robbery or rape) clearly has a purpose other than the exhilaration of the offender, only acts of *gratuitous aggression* fall within this definition.
2. Absence of remorse is also a distinguishing characteristic.
3. An expectation of impunity is also common. The exhilaration that accompanies the

thrill crime, according to many experts, arises not merely from the criminal act itself but also from the offender's expectation, however delusional, that he or she will escape apprehension and punishment. Indeed, this expectation is itself a source of exhilaration. In extreme cases, the thrill-crime offender (like some serial offenders) will, intentionally or not, engage law enforcement agents in a cat-and-mouse exercise by leaving a trail of "clues" (perhaps false ones) in order to goad or taunt investigators. Such behavior seems calculated to arouse an exciting fear of apprehension that is nevertheless offset by the conviction of invulnerability. That oscillation itself may become a source of exhilaration; as the novelist Aldous Huxley put it, "Fear itself is a hideous kind of fun." To that extent, the motive that indirectly drives the thrill crime may well be self-aggrandizement. Thus, in this view the thrill crime is a declaration of freedom from the conventional mores and moral codes of society, propelled by the self-exalting illusion of soaring beyond any human law.

4. For such reasons, some (but not all) experts hold that another psychological element in the thrill crime is a deeply embedded narcissism.

5. Because sadism is commonly associated with narcissism and because elements of domination, control, torture, or mutilation often attach to thrill crimes, some experts consider sadism as a hallmark of these crimes. In cases of homicide, attempted murder, or assault the victim is often tortured or mutilated. In the most bizarre cases mutilation may follow the actual slaying.

6. Solitary perpetration is another distinguishing mark of the thrill crime. A thrill crime committed by a group might provide excitement for the leader of the pack, but the followers may be acting out of a wish to demonstrate solidarity with the leader and with other members of the group. If so, the Leopold-Loeb murder could be construed as a thrill crime for only one of the perpetrators, with "followership" (or "other-directedness") as the motive ascribed to the other. Under such a formulation, the experience of thrill or exhilaration by the second ("other-directed") offender (if it occurs at all) is quite secondary to the approval he or she seeks from the first actor, sometimes referred to as the "instigator."

Overall, then, *apparent purposelessness* and *lack of remorse* are widely regarded as the hallmarks of a thrill crime. *Narcissism, grandiosity,* and *sadism* (or some combination thereof) are often regarded as the interpersonal traits within the offender that give rise to such apparent purposelessness and lack of remorse. Some experts insist that only crimes committed by a *single offender acting independently* fall within the definition of a thrill crime. These criteria exclude crimes that may provide an incidental sense of exhilaration to the perpetrator but that have clearly discernible purposes, such as greed, or the exhilaration experienced by the 125-pound armed robber before whom the 200-pound shopkeeper cowers. These are often regarded as offenses merely having some features of a thrill crime.

Although the term *thrill crime* has been in popular usage for decades, no reliable data on frequency are available. Classification of an offense as a thrill crime requires knowledge of offender motivation, typically not available until long after a crime has been committed and reported, an arrest made, and formal proceedings (interrogation, arraignment, perhaps even plea bargaining or trial) conducted. Government agencies charged with data keeping on criminal justice are understandably reluctant to retroactively reclassify criminal events months or even years later. Precisely the same cautions and caveats apply in the case of serial offenses of any sort (whether homicides, sexual assaults, or even serial burglaries). As a result, journalistic estimates of frequency of thrill crimes or of serial offenses are devoid of empirical support and often fanciful in the extreme. The plain fact is that trustworthy data on frequency are not available, and any estimate is guesswork.

Nor do psychologists and psychiatrists agree on the personality type or psychopathology of thrill-crime offenders. They do agree that such criminals present "some features" of psychopathy (antisocial personality disorder), in which the principal dynamic is rejection of the customary mores of society, a posture that implies both grandiosity and narcissism. But although it may be the case that all offenders who perpetrate thrill-crimes are psychopathic, it is far from the case that all psychopaths commit thrill crimes—witness the highly sophisticated financiers who construct "junk bond" schemes that defraud hundreds of victims of millions of dollars. Similarly, thrill-crime offenders have "some features" of sadistic personality disorder, a diagnostic category that was, however, eliminated from the official psychiatric nosology with the publication in 1994 of the fourth edition of the American Psychiatric Association's *Diagnostic and Statistical Manual of Mental Disorders*. Because the diagnostic categories in that document (and only those categories) are employed in official and formal mental health record keeping and census taking and because the relevant diagnostic category is no longer available, thrill-crime offenders are as uncountable as thrill crimes.

A comprehensive conceptualization of the antecedents to offending in thrill crime is offered in the book *Tinder-Box Criminal Aggression* by Nathaniel J. Pallone and James J. Hennessy (1996). The "tinderbox" model analyzes biological, psychological, and social antecedents that interact with one another to produce frequent risk-taking behavior in general and antisocial thrill seeking in particular. Whether antisocial, asocial (e.g., rock climbing, bungee jumping), or prosocial (e.g., heroism), thrill-seeking behavior pivots on systematic minimization of costs and risks and magnification of anticipated benefits. Since the mid-1960s, a consensus has developed in the neurosciences that consistently unrealistic assessment of ways of behaving (typically, the magnification of benefits and the minimization of costs and risks associated with a particular piece of behavior) arises from impairments in neurologic or neuropsychologic processes. Major advances in research utilizing advanced brain-imaging technology (e.g., computer-assisted tomography, or the CAT scan) strongly suggest that those impairments arise most frequently from anomalies in the production of the ubiquitous neurohormones monoamine oxidase and serotonin, or in anatomical damage to (or naturally occurring variations in) the structures within the brain where these neurohormones are metabolized. Such anomalies incline the person toward habitual thrill seeking and risk taking. According to the Pallone-Hennessy model, those anomalies produce an inclination that remains dormant until activated by psychological, social, and environmental variables. The model, depicted graphically in figure 1, attributes thrill crime to a complex interplay among the following bio-psychosocial variables:

(*a*) *Neurologic anomaly* affecting realistic assessment of costs, risks, and benefits associated with behavior of various sorts

(*b*) perpetuating as *impulsivity* expressed as persistent underestimation of costs and risks and perhaps supported by a condition of *alexithymia* (or verbal deficit in cognitive functioning that is not in the least synonymous with cognitive or mental deficiency), interacting with

(*c*) a persistent *need for self-aggrandizement* likely born of psychosocial developmental experiences, leading to

(*d*) sensitization to interpersonal environments that provide *role models* for and positively reinforce *antisocial thrill-seeking behavior* (including those provided through the entertainment media, which, through ubiquitous action films, glamorize exhilarating aggressive behavior, even on the part of characters who are presumably prosocial in orientation), yielding to

(*e*) the manipulative creation of an *opportunity to behave* without deterrence in such fashion so as to engender risk or harm to others and exhilaration for the self, whatever the costs to the self (e.g., long prison sentence, even execution) or to others (grievous physical harm, death).

On the basis of substantial evidence from criminological and psychometric studies and what they term "suggestive" evidence from the neurosciences, Pallone and Hennessy assert that thrill-crime offending (indeed, thrill-seeking behavior generally) is essentially a time-limited phenomenon, escalating through adolescence and early adulthood but declining precipitously after the age of thirty.

Although anomaly in neurological functioning affecting the capacity to assess costs, risks, and benefits realistically is integral to their conceptual model, Pallone and Hennessy exclude from thrill crimes those apparently motiveless offenses that occur *solely* as the result of acute organic brain disorder. In offenses in which violent behavior is driven exclusively by severe neuropathology, it is doubtful that the offender is able either to consciously embrace thrill seeking as a goal or to experience thrill or exhilaration. Hence, the mass murderer Charles Whitman—the "Texas Tower sniper" who killed eighteen people and wounded thirty-one others by rifle fire before being slain by police during a ninety-minute shooting spree in 1966—is not considered a thrill-crime offender. Whitman had earlier consulted psychiatrists with complaints of uncontrollable violent impulses end-

FIGURE 1.   **An Interactive Progression from Neurobiology to Thrill Crime**

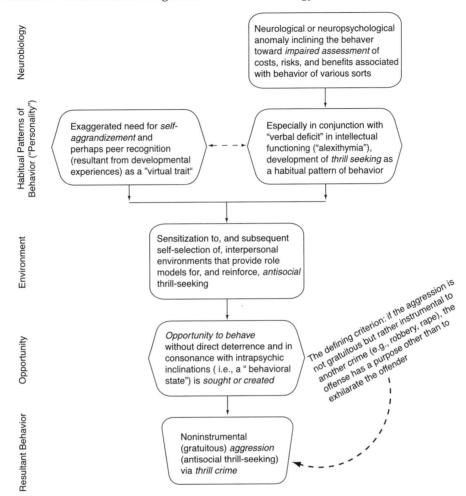

ing in explosive rage, but he received neither an accurate diagnosis nor relief. Before he mounted the clock tower at the University of Texas at Austin, Whitman had written a note specifically asking that after his death (which he fully anticipated at the hands of law officers, quite in contrast to the expectation of impunity associated with thrill crimes) an autopsy be performed to learn "if there's something wrong with my brain." Whitman's autopsy revealed a walnut-sized tumor pressing upon the nucleus of the amygdala, the brain structure principally responsible for the control of aggression.

Some scholars and clinicians regard *wilding* as a subspecies of thrill crime. In wilding, the offense (often a single offense with multiple victims or perhaps a series of offenses) is committed by an ad hoc aggregate (not necessarily a "gang" with relatively stable membership) that has been purpose-

fully formed to pursue criminal ends. The term *wilding* became popular through the 1954 motion picture *The Wild One,* in which a group of motorcyclists (the leader is played by Marlon Brando) terrorizes, or, in the language of the film, "trees," a town in California for several hours, during which citizens are subjected to various indignities, thefts, and minor sexual abuses. Collectively, members of the group are exhilarated by their cowing of the town's citizens, including law enforcement officers, but the sense of membership in a cohesive, purposive group that shapes and binds their behavior is also an important reward. In this case the leader's chief satisfaction is the demonstration of his capacity to command and direct the behavior of members of the group rather than the exhilaration of dominating or mutilating victims. In the 1990s version of wilding, groups of teenagers, often mounted on roller blades, skate in and

329

out of mall stores snatching at goods and at customers, apparently to induce a pervasive sense of fear, vulnerability, and helplessness in customers, staff, and the private security officers who patrol the malls. Greed or theft is evidently not the main motive for such wilders, most of whom come from financially secure homes. Some commentators, however, regard *Kristallnacht* (the night of 9 November 1938, during which members of the Nazi party looted stores owned by Jewish merchants, set fire to synagogues across Germany, and randomly killed ninety-one persons) as an example of wilding. That party members unquestioningly followed their leaders in violating German law is taken as a precursor of the behavioral lockstep that swept up many Germans in the chain of events leading to the Holocaust. Even apart from such retrospective analysis, it seems evident that similar psychosocial dynamics clearly operate within and among paramilitary terrorist organizations in the United States and abroad. Without question, political terrorism achieves its aims precisely because its apparent randomness induces a pervasive sense of fear, vulnerability, and helplessness.

*BIBLIOGRAPHY*

Eysenck, Sybil B. G., and Hans J. Eysenck. "Impulsiveness and Venturesomeness: Their Position in a Dimensional System of Personality Description." *Psychological Reports* 43 (1978): 1247–1255.

Farley, Frank. "The Big T in Personality." *Psychology Today* (May 1986): 44–52.

Levenson, Michael R. "Risk Taking and Personality." *Journal of Personality and Social Psychology* 58 (June 1990): 1073–1080.

Pallone, Nathaniel J., and James J. Hennessy. *Tinder-Box Criminal Aggression: Neuropsychology, Demography, Phenomenology.* New Brunswick, N.J.: Transaction, 1996.

Raine, Adrian, et al. *Biosocial Bases of Violence.* New York: Plenum, 1997.

Schlesinger, Louis B. *Explorations in Criminal Psychopathology.* Springfield, Ill.: Charles C. Thomas, 1996.

NATHANIEL J. PALLONE
JAMES J. HENNESSY

*See also* **Crime, Legal Definitions of; Loeb, Richard, and Nathan Leopold; Serial Killers; Starkweather, Charles, and Caril Ann Fugate; Teenagers; Wilding and Berserking.**

# TOBACCO INDUSTRY

Consumers who purchase cigarettes and other tobacco products often become addicted, and many die of tobacco-related illnesses. Can it be said, then, that the tobacco industry is guilty of violence against the consumer?

The answer to this question depends on which definition of violence is in play. A key legal and social definition is "unwanted physical force or threat of physical force." This definition might expand to include inflicting psychological injury by rendering someone incapable of exerting rational judgment: for example, administering alcohol or drugs to impair a victim's ability to refuse a sexual advance. The word *violence* has also been frequently applied to acts such as driving under the influence of alcohol, which can lead to unintentional but devastating harm. Repeated acts of driving under the influence implies gross disregard for the safety of others.

An assault is an attempt, with unlawful force, to inflict bodily injury upon another, accompanied by the apparent ability to carry out that attempt. As a tort, an assault may be found to have taken place even where no actual intent existed (e.g., a practical joke) if the actor placed the victim in reasonable fear. Negligence, on the other hand, consists of failure to exercise the degree of care that a reasonable person would exercise under the same circumstances. Larry C. White (1991) notes that cigarettes are the only products on the market that are harmful when they are used as intended. They are not harmful because of any error in design but because they are intrinsically harmful to health. Is the tobacco industry, then, guilty of a violent assault on the consumer?

A definitive answer to this question would entail an investigation of the following issues: (1) Is the industry trying to inflict injury on its consumers through repeated acts and with knowledge of consequences of the product, such that the consumer is placed in reasonable fear? (2) Is there evidence of the use of unlawful force, such as an effort to exert will over the consumer or to engage in action that would result in injury to the consumer? This second issue might be settled by evidence of consumer injury or by attempts to prevent injury through consumer or third-party action. The following sections examine each component of this argument.

## History of Tobacco

Is there evidence that the tobacco industry, with full knowledge of the consequences, has engaged in acts that might injure consumers or cause them to be afraid? A brief history of tobacco use may help answer this question. Tobacco smoking in pipes entered Europe through the Spanish explorers of America, who acquired tobacco from Native Americans. As tobacco use became widespread on the European continent in the seventeenth century, it was alternately touted for its medicinal qualities, supposedly for preventing various illnesses and curing cancer (e.g., by Jean Nicot, the French ambassador to Lisbon, in 1556), and decried as a noxious drug that was dangerous to the heart and lungs (e.g., by Dr. William Vaughn in 1617 and by Dr. Tobias Venner of Bathe in 1650).

The modern cigarette industry began in the 1880s with the invention in Virginia of the cigarette-rolling machine, which was capable of mass production of cigarettes. James Duke's American Tobacco Company, which controlled the tobacco business in the United States, was broken up into four competing companies under the Sherman Anti-Trust Act in 1911. In the United States cigarettes were more expensive than in Europe, so their use did not outstrip that of cigars, pipes, and smokeless tobacco until 1921. Cigarettes' convenience made them popular among U.S. soldiers during World War I, and their general use increased steadily until the 1960s.

Despite persistent claims that tobacco might be addictive and harmful, there was little scientific confirmation of such fears until the 1950s, when a tobacco "health scare" led to the popularity of lower-tar brands and filtered cigarettes (which often contained stronger tobacco to counteract the benefit of the filter). Scientific publications began reporting the negative consequences of tobacco use, and tobacco industry spokespersons launched a concerted public relations campaign to discredit such reports as the propaganda of moralists or stock manipulators. On the defensive, the industry also advanced advertising claims of advanced filters and ever-lower levels of tar and nicotine.

The first cigarette-related lung cancer case to be brought to trial by a victim was the 1960 suit of Otto Pritchard against Liggett and Myers (one of the major American tobacco companies), based on a claim that the company had misleadingly advertised its product as safe. The jury ruled that the plaintiff bore responsibility for taking the risk of smoking. In other cases companies claimed that they could not have known the relation of cancer to cigarette smoking at the time of manufacture.

Congress began requiring warnings on cigarette packages in 1965, and increasingly stringent and diverse printed caveats were mandated in 1969 and 1984. But until the 1990s the tobacco industry continued denying addictive or carcinogenic consequences of smoking, even though its own private memos show that the companies were aware of the health risks. The tobacco industry's behavior was deceptive, if not fraudulent.

Documents from the files of the major tobacco companies disclosed in the 1990s show that they conspired for at least forty years to conceal the dangers of smoking, sought to enhance the addictive properties of their products, and purposely targeted youth to build brand loyalty ("Joe Camel" being one of the most successful and notorious campaigns directed at teenagers). Lawsuit and settlements abound; the main active ingredient of tobacco, nicotine, is now generally recognized by scientists, legal authorities, the tobacco industry, and the general public as an addictive drug. The tobacco companies argue that if the government tolerates other forms of addiction (e.g., gambling and alcoholism) and other potentially harmful products (e.g., red meat), then why single out tobacco for restrictive measures?

Although tobacco is clearly addictive and 80 to 90 percent of adult tobacco users want to quit, fearing for their lives, many tobacco users, including children, are aware of long-term consequences of use. Certainly, though, the tobacco industry has been trying to sell an addictive and harmful product while concealing its dangers and even portraying it as glamorous. Many consumers have felt misled by a continual barrage of advertisements shown over the years, as is evidenced by the proliferation of lawsuits against the tobacco industry.

Tobacco use is the world's leading behavioral cause of death. Some 10 to 15 percent of the world's population will die from a tobacco-related illness. Approximately a half million deaths per year are attributed to tobacco-related causes in the United States alone. Smokers are ten times more likely than nonsmokers to die of lung cancer, four times more likely to die from chronic respiratory diseases, and have nearly double the chance of dying from bladder cancer, cancer of the pancreas, and cardiovascular disease. The effects of smoking on respiratory and cardiovascular functions have been observed in adolescents as well as adults. As a result, tobacco-prevention programs have proliferated in schools, clinics, work sites, media, and community organizations throughout the world.

**Tobacco Industry's Influence**

Between 1996 and 1998 the number of individual plaintiffs or class-action suits against the tobacco industry quadrupled. State settlements with the tobacco industry by Minnesota, Mississippi,

Florida, and Texas yielded $35.3 billion. The Multistate Master Settlement Agreement (MSA) package with the tobacco industry provides many protections for the consumer (e.g., raising the price of cigarettes, removal of cartoon and human images from advertisements, removal of vending machines, restriction of mail-order sales, and careful monitoring of ingredients by the Food and Drug Administration) and payments for tobacco-related damages. The MSA would restrict future state claims to criminal ones, for tax liabilities, and to enforce settlement commitments. All of these developments in the 1990s suggest the tobacco industry's acknowledgment, however implicit, of the injury to consumers.

The tobacco industry is powerful. The five largest tobacco companies brought in between $800 million and $55.9 billion dollars in total assets in 1997, a largesse that supports high-powered lobbyists and top-flight legal talent to defend its interests. During the 1980s and 1990s, of the first 174 pieces of legislation developed to restrict the activities of the tobacco industry, only two passed. Maintaining that tobacco is a crop rather than a drug, the federal government until 1998 regulated the industry under the Department of Agriculture rather than the more restrictive Food and Drug Administration. To counter increasing antitobacco pressures on the government, tobacco companies spent some $12 million on lobbying efforts in 1996.

The tobacco industry spends $4 billion on advertising in the United States each year, targeting the young as well as adults by portraying smoking as "cool" while downplaying its addictive and hazardous properties. By the time many young people realize that the tobacco advertisements are "hype," they might already be hooked.

Big Tobacco has flexed its promotional muscle overseas as well. In 1981 Philip Morris, R. J. Reynolds, and Brown and Williamson formed the United States Cigarette Export Association, in part to pressure the U.S. government to force Asian countries to repeal laws restricting the importation of U.S. tobacco products. Accordingly, the United States government threatened trade sanctions against Japan, South Korea, Taiwan, and Thailand unless they opened up their markets to U.S. cigarettes and cigarette advertising; the countries complied.

### Tobacco Industry and Violence

The tobacco industry has a long history of selling a product it knows to be dangerous, using various means of influence—lobbying, advertising, public-relations campaigns—to steer public attitudes and consumer behavior. Even though tobacco remains a legal product, some have argued that the tobacco industry is socially irresponsible, engaging in an immoral business that has seized every legal opening to foist a lethal, addictive product on credulous consumers, avoiding the issuance of any warnings that were not imposed on it by government regulation. This argument suggests that the tobacco industry is a perpetrator of dangerous activity.

One can argue that, by its deceptive practices, the tobacco industry has, metaphorically, committed violence on the health of generations of Americans, but this view requires a loose definition of violence. If the tobacco industry were placing poisons into its products that caused immediate death or injury, an accusation of violence against the tobacco industry would carry more weight; in fact, the industry and its executives would most likely be subject to criminal sanctions. But the fact that tobacco's hazards often take decades to surface cushions the industry from such allegations. Moreover, smoking just one cigarette (or using one dip or smoking one cigar or pipe) is not likely to cause any lasting harm. Even smoking one cigarette per day ("chipping") is most likely harmless, even when done over many years, although only 5 percent of tobacco users are able to smoke at this low rate. It is only smoking several cigarettes per day over many years that triggers tobacco-related diseases. Thus the tobacco industry, however grave its misdeeds, is not guilty of pushing a weapon that will hurt everyone no matter how it is used.

Moreover, advertising seeks to manipulate consumer behavior but is not equivalent to outright coercion. To what extent should tobacco users themselves be held accountable for their habit? Although many consumers acknowledge that tobacco use is dangerous to others, many feel that they are personally invulnerable. Such perceptions, however illusory, further complicate any accusations of blame against the tobacco industry, which can plausibly argue that any violence suffered by such consumers is freely self-inflicted. Other consumers feel that they have the personal right to smoke even if they do injure themselves by doing it. Given more than thirty years of printed warnings on cigarette packages, one could even argue that smokers are exhibiting a form of self-destructive behavior. Certainly the tobacco industry has been grossly negligent, but the purchase of tobacco is a voluntary activity.

The tobacco industry should change in many ways; for example, advertising should be restricted, and the industry should promote low levels of tobacco intake per day. The consumer, the policy maker, and society at large must also evaluate the known consequences of this product.

*BIBLIOGRAPHY*

Advocacy Institute. *Evaluating the Proposed Settlement: A Comparison with the Koop-Kessler Report and with Current Public Policies and Efforts.* Washington, D.C.: Advocacy Institute, 1997.

Brecher, Ruth, et al. *The Consumer Union Report on Smoking and the Public Interest.* Mount Vernon, N.Y.: Consumers Union, 1963.

Kelder, Graham E., and Richard A. Daynard. "The Role of Litigation in the Effective Control of the Sale and Use of Tobacco." *Stanford Law and Policy Review* 8 (1997): 63–98.

Kessler, David A., et al. "Nicotine Addiction: A Pediatric Disease." *New England Journal of Medicine* 335 (1996): 931–937.

Sussman, Steve, et al. *Developing School-Based Tobacco-Use Prevention and Cessation Programs.* Thousand Oaks, Calif.: Sage, 1995.

U.S. Department of Health and Human Services. *Preventing Tobacco Use Among Young People: A Report of the Surgeon General* (Publication no. S/N 017–001–0049100). Washington, D.C.: Public Health Service, 1994.

White, Larry C. *Ethical Considerations of Accepting Financial Support from the Tobacco Industry.* New York: American Council on Science and Health, 1991.

STEVE SUSSMAN

*See also* **Corporations; Drugs: Drugs and Violence; Smoking.**

# TOMBSTONE. *See* O.K. Corral Gunfight.

# TONKIN GULF RESOLUTION. *See* Gulf of Tonkin Resolution.

# TORTURE

Torture, according to the United Nations Declaration Against Torture, involves severe pain or suffering intentionally inflicted by a public official to obtain information or confession, to punish, or to intimidate. Other definitions restrict the term to physical pain, expand it to nonofficial inflictions, require excruciating rather than merely severe pain, or recognize different purposes. Related terms for practices that may or may not amount to torture include: "cruel, inhuman, or degrading treatment" (in international treaties); "cruel and unusual punishment" (in American constitutional law); "coercion" (in American interrogation law); "abuse," "brutality," and "hazing" (in common parlance).

Americans seem generally to regard torture as a medieval, fictional, or foreign practice, assuming "it can't happen here." The rack and wheel is a device consigned to history. The horror genre of novels and films provides imagery of torture that affords a safe thrill of fantasized danger. Media coverage associates political torture with dictatorships, or perhaps with the coercive interrogation of suspected terrorists in democratic states like Northern Ireland and Israel.

**Torture Before the Twentieth Century**

As H. Rap Brown noted, however, violence is as American as apple pie. Even before the War of Independence, the American experience included torture—or at least candidates for that designation, requiring us to decide just what severity and purpose we require to thus label the infliction of pain. Native Americans sometimes scalped or burned alive captive soldiers; various colonial governments likewise offered bounties for Indian scalps, and, in several battles, burned stockades with hundreds of Indian men, women, and children inside. In New England, judicial torture was outlawed in the 1640s, except "in some capital case where [the defendant] is first fully convicted by clear and sufficient evidence to be guilty." One man accused in the Salem witch trials was pressed with heavy stones to force him to agree to stand trial—the ancient British practice of *peine forte et dure.*

In New York City in 1741, at least one group of thirteen slaves was burned at the stake, and throughout the slavery period, masters and public officials punished slaves by whipping them. After Emancipation, African Americans continued to be subject to whipping, tarring and feathering, and other cruelties inflicted by the Ku Klux Klan and by lynch mobs, sometimes with the cooperation of local jailers. According to the conservative estimates of the Tuskegee Institute, 3,426 African Americans were lynched in the United States from 1882 through 1947; in 1892, the peak year of violence, 161 lynchings occurred.

Police interrogation of suspects in the nineteenth and twentieth centuries often used force and threats, popularly called the "third degree." Under President Herbert Hoover, the National Commission on Law Observance and Enforcement (the Wickersham Commission) declared such methods to be widespread in 1931, and in 1936 the U.S. Supreme Court deemed some instances torture.

**Torture in the Modern Era**

In the modern era, several violent or coercive practices might contestably be deemed torture, including certain acts of the military. Colonial burnings have lineal descendants in World War II firebombings and flamethrowers and in Vietnamese War napalm. The U.S. Army School for the Americas taught torture techniques to a number of South American officers. (The official position is that there were few such manuals and that they were repudiated as soon as headquarters knew of them.) To prepare army, navy, and air force personnel to resist torture as war prisoners, the Survival, Evasion, Resistance, and Escape program (SERE) uses techniques that themselves approximate torture, including sleep deprivation, controlled drowning, and sometimes sexual harassment. In 1991 and 1993, some West Pointers and some marine paratroopers engaged in a form of hazing that included pinning decorations into the bare chests of newcomers—ceremonies that were later revealed in a well-publicized videotape.

Central Intelligence Agency involvement in torture is often alleged. Instances of torture of suspected Vietcong were admitted by participants in Operation Phoenix, a Vietnam War intelligence program conducted by the CIA, U.S. Special Forces, and South Vietnamese police. A CIA training document, the *Human Resource Exploitation Training Manual—1983,* was reported to describe torture methods that included stripping suspects naked, keeping them blindfolded, depriving them of food and sleep, and making them stand at attention for long periods. CIA and U.S. State Department personnel cooperated with a secret Honduran military unit in the 1980s, the 316th Battalion, knowing it used such practices on dissidents, but a CIA inspector general report found that notifications by field agents to CIA headquarters, and by it to Congress, were incomplete and inaccurate. The CIA has cashiered roughly one hundred foreign agents, about half in Latin America, acknowledging that their acts of torture and

other crimes outweighed their value as informers. Americans abroad have themselves been subjects of torture—examples include World War II prisoners of war in Japan and Southeast Asia, as well as individual U.S. officials such as CIA station chief William Buckley, who died of torture after being kidnapped by terrorists in Lebanon in 1984, and U.S. Drug Enforcement Agency agents in Mexico tortured by drug dealers or corrupt local police.

State government actions also raise issues of torture. Some regard as equivalent to torture the U.S. use of capital punishment, or prolonged stays of inmates on death row and the use of the gas chamber or electric chair—especially electrocutions requiring repeated applications of electric current. In two horrifying instances in 1990 and 1997, the Florida state electric chair set afire the head of a condemned man. Law enforcement sometimes uses excessive violence—in the field, during interrogation, in jails and in prisons—which can rise to the level of torture. While most complaints against police violence are filed locally, about eight thousand complaints of excessive force reach federal officials annually. The complaints relate disproportionately to police violence against racial minorities and come primarily from California, Louisiana, and Texas, followed by New York, Georgia, Florida, Alabama, and Mississippi. In addition, torture of immigrants by agents of the U.S. Immigration and Naturalization Service occurs along the Mexican border, according to 1992 reports by the American Friends Service Committee and Human Rights Watch.

In the field, police use of force during searches, arrests, traffic stops, or at the end of police pursuits is sometimes labeled "police brutality." In one well-publicized 1997 incident in Humboldt County, California, sheriff's deputies rubbed pepper spray into the eyes of antilogging demonstrators to induce them to submit. The paradigm case is the 1991 police beating of Rodney King, a black resident of Los Angeles, after King had led police on a traffic chase. A witness videotaped the beating, which received media coverage around the world. The four officers charged in the case, all of them white, were ultimately acquitted, setting off race riots in Los Angeles in April 1992. A widespread pattern of excessive force was documented in official reports on the Los Angeles Sheriff's Department (Kolts report, 1992) and Police Department (Christopher Commission report, 1991). Decades before, a class-action lawsuit brought by the Western Center on Law and Poverty in 1968 had alleged police brutality by the Los Angeles Police Department against blacks. Two white Detroit police officers were convicted on murder charges for the fatal beating of a black motorist in 1992. In Miami, police beatings or shootings of black suspects have led to civil unrest four times between 1980 and 1990.

Reports by Amnesty International and Human Rights Watch document the subjection of suspects held in temporary custody in police stations or jails to beatings or other brutalities, including improper use of tasers, stun guns, mace, and pepper spray. Restraints or positions that restrict breathing can be life-threatening; a 1992 San Diego police study found that nationwide during the prior ten-year period, more than ninety suspects died from being hog-tied while in police custody. A New York City police officer was convicted of forcing the handle of a toilet plunger up the rectum of a Haitian immigrant who had been arrested in 1997 during a fight outside a Brooklyn nightclub, bringing rare front-page headlines concerning use of torture by police in American cities.

A police report, juries, and appellate courts have concluded that two Chicago police stations, Areas 2 and 3, systematically tortured suspects, primarily African Americans. There were complaints of brutalities against sixty-five individuals between 1972 and 1991; the brutality included electric shocks, kicking and beating, burning a suspect against a radiator, and placing plastic bags over the heads of suspects. New Orleans police received the most citizen complaints of police brutality according to a 1991 U.S. Justice Department report. According to Human Rights Watch reports, New Orleans police tortured and killed several African Americans in 1980 and one in 1990, in reaction to the killing of white officers; a police officer was sentenced to death for a 1994 contract killing of a person who had complained of brutality.

Prisoners in long-term institutions also have been tortured or beaten by guards and other prisoners, sometimes resulting in death, according to Amnesty International. Rape of male prisoners by other prisoners, without official redress, has been acknowledged by courts to be a serious problem. Georgia Women's Correctional Institution guards were the subject of a lawsuit and U.S. Justice Department investigation in 1992 and 1993 charging rape of female inmates and coercion of them into prostitution. Conditions in new "super-maximum security" prisons, in at least thirty-six states and the federal system, are deemed by Human Rights

Watch excessively brutal: confining inmates to twenty-three hours daily in sealed or windowless cells, without work or training programs, and with severe limitations on human contact. Some thirty prison guards in four Texas prisons were accused in 1994 press reports of systematically mistreating inmates. Some practices sound medieval: according to news reports and photos, some county jail prisoners in Knox County, Tennessee, were left suspended for lengthy periods with their feet barely touching support, shackled in uncomfortable positions, and other inmates were placed in special restraining chairs wearing sealed helmets that were beaten on by guards. According to Physicians for Human Rights, prisoners in Syracuse, New York, were also suspended for lengthy periods, their bodies barely touching support, in addition to being deprived of drink, food, and toilet facilities.

## Legal Status of Torture

Torture, not always specifically named as such, is covered directly or indirectly by various U.S. laws. In constitutional law, the Eighth Amendment of the Bill of Rights prohibits "cruel and unusual punishment," words usually limited to punishment inflicted as part of a judicial sentence. The Supreme Court has ruled that the amendment also applies when prison officials' inaction amounts to unnecessary, wanton infliction of pain, but the clause has not been applied to investigational cruelties involving the police.

Coerced confessions are addressed using other constitutional provisions in many Supreme Court cases dealing with the admissibility of evidence, often using the touchstone of "voluntariness" (the opposite of coercion). The Fifth Amendment recognizes a right against compelled self-incrimination (which does not cover the compulsion of a person to be a witness against others) and has been interpreted as asking whether the suspect chose to speak by a "purely voluntary mental action" rather than out of "hope or fear." The due process of law guaranteed by the Fifth and Fourteenth Amendments is held to prohibit convictions based on coerced confessions, not merely because such confessions are unreliable but also "because the methods used to extract them offend an underlying principle."

The Supreme Court did not overturn state convictions based on coerced confessions until the 1930s. In the 1936 Supreme Court case *Brown v. Mississippi*, African American defendants had been whipped severely and threatened with lynching until they confessed; the Court used the term "torture" and referred to medieval practices, condemning what happened as "revolting to the sense of justice." Some police action is regarded as "inherently coercive," so that "there is no need to weigh or measure its effects on the free will of the individual victim," but in most coerced confession cases, the Court looks to the "totality of the circumstances," including not just the actions of the police but also the defendant's susceptibility.

The United States has ratified some of the international treaties against torture. The International Covenant on Civil and Political Rights, recognizing a right against torture derived from "the inherent dignity of the human person," obligates countries to adopt effectual measures against torture and provide remedies for violations. The UN Convention Against Torture and Other Cruel, Inhuman, or Degrading Treatment or Punishment goes further, requiring nations to ensure that "all acts of torture are offenses under its criminal law." Both treaties declare that no exceptional circumstances whatsoever can derogate from the prohibition of torture. (By contrast, some scholars justify torture if the situation is sufficiently extreme.)

A limited amount of federal law deals with torture. A modern statute criminally prohibits torture by name, but only if it is committed outside the United States. The Torture Victim Protection Act authorizes civil suits against those who commit torture under apparent authority of any foreign nation. Torture is also included within the acts that can amount to the crime of genocide. And U.S. policy ostensibly is to deny foreign aid to governments that engage in torture. The U.S. Justice Department may bring federal criminal civil rights charges against state officials acting "under color of law," but only if specific intent to violate a protected right can be proven. Convictions, and even prosecutions, are rare. A victim of police abuse may also sue civilly for damages.

Surprisingly, it is rare for state codes—the basic laws of the United States—to specifically outlaw torture as an independent crime or directly prohibit torture as a means of interrogation. In California, a 1990 citizen initiative declared torture a crime punishable by life imprisonment; in Connecticut, a statute declares "cruelty to persons," defined so as to include torture, a misdemeanor. Some private violence may on occasion be extreme enough—painful and sometimes fatal—to be deemed torture, including child abuse, spousal abuse, fraternity hazing, and sadomasochistic rituals. Thirteen states prohibit the torture and cruel treatment of children by including such acts in their definition of child abuse. Some, though not all, states explicitly prohibit torture of prisoners by their jailers; a few states outlaw sexual torture or torture of the young, elderly, or helpless.

While torture is rarely criminalized per se, it is covered by general statutes such as assault and battery, and many state laws (and the Federal Sentencing Guidelines) enhance punishment for other crimes when torture is used. In twenty-two states murder laws include fatal torture, either within the definition of first-degree murder or as an aggravating circumstance in sentencing. In a few states, use of torture aggravates the sentence for certain other specified crimes; in a few other states, for any felony. Occasional statutes criminalize ritualized torture, toys that depict torture, or school employment after conviction of torturing a child. Thirty-six states include depictions of sadomasochism in their definitions of criminal obscenity. Thus, to the extent that U.S. law explicitly deals with torture, stories about torture are more widely criminalized than torture itself.

*BIBLIOGRAPHY*

*Human Rights Violations in the United States: A Report on U.S. Compliance with the International Covenant on Civil and Political Rights.* New York: Human Rights Watch and the American Civil Liberties Union, 1993.
*Shielded from Justice: Police Brutality and Accountability in the United States.* New York: Human Rights Watch, 1998.
*United States of America: Human Rights Violations: A Summary of Amnesty International's Concerns.* London: Amnesty International, 1995.

MARTIN LYON LEVINE

*See also* **Confessions, Coerced; Crime and Punishment in American History; Foreign Police, U.S. Training of; Militarism; Police; Prison Violence; Weapons: Stun and Shock Devices.**

# TOYS AND GAMES

Across the United States, the last decades of the twentieth century saw increasing public concern over toys and games of a violent nature. Such toys have a long history in the United States, and concern over their connection to real violence is not entirely new. The debate as to whether such toys lead to aggressive behavior is deadlocked: psychologists and other interested researchers on both sides have provided ample but often inconsistent evidence to support their positions.

Parents of the baby-boom generation, who believe themselves to have been unaffected by watching cartoon violence or playing "cowboys and Indians," tend to believe that the stakes are higher for the next generation—their children—because of the intensification of violent imagery, especially in computer games and toys spawned by television shows. The best research to date, however, has increasingly emphasized the contextual nature of any effects. How violent a toy is seen to be, how closely related to reality, how likely to stimulate violent sorts of play, how likely to exert a damaging influence on attitudes or behavior beyond the realm of play—these are all factors that can easily change from one context to another. A toy Gulf War grenade and a toy *Star Trek* "phaser" belong in very different contexts: whereas the Gulf War was a real event, *Star Trek* is a fictional television and movie series, in which the violence depicted is carefully restrained, infrequently deadly, and filtered through a liberal sensibility. Children have been found capable of quite specific contextual discriminations of this kind. Particular family, peer, and community contexts, with dominant values that color a child's thinking and feelings, alter the meaning a specific toy is capable of generating for that child. A toy gun in a violent urban neighborhood may offer a child the frisson of immediate realism (and the risk of being shot); the same toy in some other community may be wholly an object of make-believe, belonging only in the world of television shows as a prop for stereotypical heroes and villains. As the contextual determinants proliferate, it becomes impossible to legislate for a specific effect that can be attached to any particular toy.

### The Context of Toys

Two major categories of context determine the meanings and, therefore, the effects of toys. Constitutive contexts—particular historical, social, and cultural settings—produce the toys' meanings, which are then subject to regulative contexts—particular communities, families, or peer groups—that interpret, support, modify, challenge, or alter those meanings. Determining the effects of any particular toy—especially one with violent connotations—entails understanding not only its formation as a meaningful object within a particular constitutive context but also how it is

## The Aesthetic of Violence

Violence as the basis for action is a convenient device to keep television narratives going—battle scenes offer the sorts of audiovisual climax, especially in animated series, that transform Saturday morning television viewing into something aesthetically closer to a computer game. There is an emerging stylistic form here based on rapid-cutting, short bursts of action, fragmented plots, and audiovisual elaboration that draws together the music video, the computer game, and children's television into an overlapping aesthetic that children seem to recognize as theirs in some barely conscious sense. Violent plotlines and character interactions may well have emerged as the most obvious narrative justification of this aesthetic, written by adults who do not interpret the style in any other way. As a preferred audiovisual style in the minds of children, it may have more to do with abstract perceptual stimulation and a high-energy, attention-focusing level of cognitive arousal than with the violent narrative content in itself. Nonetheless, the violent content is insistently present and is distilled in many computer games into protracted sequences of violent interaction with only minimally explanatory plot to justify them.

dealt with in any regulative contexts that apply in the specific instance. Thus, the toy guns buried at the Peace Toy Fair (see sidebar "Questioning Violent Toys") will have had their original meanings formed within the particular constitutive context of contemporary American popular culture and new meanings allocated to them by the particular community's regulative context—its dominant values. Most of the research on children and violence from the 1940s to the 1970s, whether concerned with toys or television, completely ignored the issue of contextual location (the actual circumstances of play) and, as a consequence, failed to provide any lasting guidance on the matter. On the other hand, those correlational and laboratory studies fairly convincingly demonstrated that in the confines of the laboratory—that is, in the absence of any regulative context, or real-world situations, to modify the process of how a toy is received—war toys (like violent incidents in television programs) do have the capacity to trigger isolated aggressive actions when a child models his or her behavior on the given stimulus. But children do not live in laboratories, where cause-and-effect chains can be artificially isolated from other influences, and thus the research has not transferred convincingly to the real world.

Some research has been informed by the so-called catharsis hypothesis, which holds that controlled violence in play healthily vents inner pressures. But this perspective has also failed to produce convincing evidence of such an effect and has been undermined by its dependence on a crude Freudian model of relevant "repressions" that has not worn well. A more subtle perspective emerges from a related practice known as sand-play therapy. A therapist offers a young patient an array of toy objects in a sandbox; the child's undirected arrangement of those objects tells a revealing story (for the therapist trained to read it) about that individual's inner life. Especially revealing from sand-play studies is the fact that the exclusion of "violent" objects (for example, a toy soldier) from the available repertoire can severely distort the achievable representations. This is unsurprising in the therapeutic context—how is a young patient to deal with violent memories, feelings, or impulses if the representational means have been censored?—but it should be allowed to tell us something about "normal" play as well. In fact it was the psychologist Erik Erikson who first clearly articulated the idea that play is about symbolically reconciling what are in fact irreconcilable, problematic, stress-inducing aspects of the child's experience. Erikson's description of the symbolically harmonizing achievements of play remains powerfully resistant to any suggestion that play should be sanitized in order to remove potentially harmful cause-and-effect results in a child's behavior. Indeed, if we take Erikson's insight to its logical conclusion, the child who can experience only a sanitized repertoire of playthings will not have access to the symbolic tools needed to come to terms with a highly unsanitized reality and may be, as a result, less behaviorally adjusted to that reality. Sand-play therapy provides an example of a regulative context in which violent representations, when they occur in the sandbox, can be reframed, explored, defused, and made genuinely productive for the child by working through conflicts and unresolved feelings. The public's concern over isolated playthings and potential cause-and-effect relationships between play and behavior misses an important issue: the violent nature of some toys can be reframed in productive ways by means of contextual interventions and reconstructions. Nancy Carlsson-Paige and Diane Levin (1987) have provided parents and teachers with useful practical advice on how to achieve such interventions.

## Historical Contexts

It was in the early years of the nineteenth century, with the development of the modern American observance of Christmas after the German fashion, that toy making—and indeed the word *toy* itself—became firmly established in the United States. By 1838 the Philadelphia Tin Toy Manufactory had inaugurated the new industry—a distinction often more romantically if erroneously attributed to William Tower of Massachusetts, whose charming wooden toys of the 1840s appeal more to today's sense of an appropriate ancestry. But it was the tinplate manufacturers who, by the end of the century, were mass-producing the toy steamboats, locomotives, wagons, and pull-toys that have become so recognizably American, including the famous Ives clockwork and mechanical playthings. The constitutive context for these toys was clearly the dawning of the Machine Age.

The late nineteenth century saw a tension, familiar to modern sensibilities, appear between the mass-produced tinplate toys and an emerging parental interest in "philosophic" toys—playthings with some educative or scientific principle to teach. One of the earliest examples of a violent plaything is a pull-toy of this period (a wheeled mechanical toy with a mechanism worked by the motion) on which two upright metal frogs with articulated legs kick each other incessantly. One can imagine concerned parents of the time trying to interest their children—vainly no doubt—in the alternative pleasures of a kaleidoscope or some other "philosophic" toy. The tinplate steamships of the same period had particular appeal; Mark Twain captures the symbolic power of the originals in his fiction. Erikson uses the example of playing at being a steamboat (a famous scene in *The Adventures of Tom Sawyer*) to suggest how play's symbolic resources seek to capture and control the great forces that children see unleashed in the world around them—in this case the forces of machine-driven progress. Unsurprisingly, then, it was the tinplate steamboats that became gunboats and battleships, such as the Ives "Destroyers" manufactured in 1915, as warfare began to offer powerful imagery to intrigue young imaginations.

With World War I came a new constitutive context and the precursors of the "dimestore soldier"—small lead figures that continued to be popular into the 1920s and 1930s, from companies such as Grey Iron, Ideal, and Soljertoys, culminating in Barclay's mid-1930s line of soldiers that are recognizably modern in weaponry and posture (notably a seated figure with a heavy-duty machine gun). Barclay's main competitor, Manoil, released a catalog of toy soldiers in 1939 that included gas-masked figures redolent of World War I and of further horrors to come.

World War II brought restrictions on the use in toy making of tin, lead, and other "strategic" materials; a few manufacturers, notably Hubley, had managed to produce lines of metal toy guns in 1940 and 1941 before the restrictions tightened, but with the return to manufacturing in wood came the arrival en masse of the toy gun. A wartime magazine advertisement depicted a boy clutching a one-dollar wooden machine gun: "'Take aim . . . FIRE! you'll route out the enemy with this nifty Raid Gun,' says Billy. 'It has a swell repeating action. Makes loud popping noises when you move the pistol grip handle backward and forward.'" Billy looks rather glum below his slogan: "Come on good little sports. Be physically active and you'll keep vitally fit!" The popular Hubley Army .45 pistol in cast iron was almost a replica of the real thing, but it was cruder wooden guns that proliferated during the war, firmly establishing a market for this kind of toy. Hubley returned to making metal toy guns throughout the 1950s, in increasingly well-tooled and realistic models with working triggers and ribbons of tiny explosive "caps" for insertion under the hammer.

It must be kept in mind that the material restrictions of World War II meant shortages of other toys, from bicycles to balloons, and that, given what was happening in the adult world, children unsurprisingly found the toy guns compelling. The climate of the subsequent Cold War no doubt sustained the militaristic imagery of the toy guns, but additional factors were coming into play. One of Hubley's most popular products was the Roy Rogers cap pistol, first made in 1941, along with subsequent cowboy guns of a similar kind. Few men born in the 1950s will forget the metallic, oily feel of these guns, the smell of the caps, or the imagery that came to mind while handling one. Hollywood had come to toytown, and television would follow. Cowboy and military toy guns were soon joined by science fiction variants—the Marx

**Advertisement for a toy coastal defense gun that hurls wooden projectiles, Christmas 1941.** CORBIS/BETTMANN

company, in particular, producing successful lines such as its Flash Gordon pistol—until, by 1959, the toy pages of the Sears Christmas catalog were giving pride of place to spin-off toy figures and other paraphernalia related to popular television science fiction and Western series.

Since the late 1950s this intimate relationship with popular cinema and television has become the single most important factor driving a succession of popular toy lines, especially what would later come to be known as action figures—plastic sets of figures representing characters from popular films and series. A plastic figure of cowboy star Roy Rogers in that 1959 catalog was among the earliest examples; in the same year the Barbie doll made her appearance.

In summarily charting the two-hundred-year history of the toy in the United States, it becomes evident that violence was not a conspicuous theme until the appearance of war toys that reflected global events. Even then, one must be careful not to assume too potent an influence. The Ives clockwork boats—the "Destroyers" from the World War I period—were not a successful line and were sustained more by the firm's patriotism than by children's interest. Over the years, toy construction sets (such as the Erector Set, patented in 1913), automobiles, animals, and girls' dolls have all had an enduring popularity unmatched by any of the war toys until the appearance of the GI Joe doll in 1964. The little toy soldiers, while never quite engaging with the older European tradition of marshaling and parading miniature armies in splendid colors, remained illustrative of contemporary events and, as such, tell us as much about how a society chooses to represent its military realities as about children's interest in warfare.

The historian Stephen E. Ambrose (1976) encapsulates the transformation of the nation's military realities between the 1930s and the 1960s:

> As Franklin Roosevelt began his sixth year as President, the United States had an army of 185,000 officers and men with an annual budget of less than $500 million. America had no military alliances and no American troops were stationed in any foreign country.... One generation later the United States had a standing Army of well over one million men, with an Air Force and a Navy almost as large. The budget of the Department of Defense was almost $80 billion. The United States had military alliances with 48 nations, had 1,517,000 soldiers and sailors stationed in 119 countries, and had an offensive capability sufficient to destroy the world many times over.

Against the background of this rise to militarily sustained globalism on the part of the United States, it is hardly surprising that the same generation saw the arrival of the toy gun and the increasing popularity of the toy soldier, whose numbers increased along with those of his real counterparts. Indeed, what may be surprising is that American society did not see a more explicit militarization of toys in this period. On the other hand, nations devoting vast and increasing resources to their armed forces often tend also to invest symbolically in representations of "home" as an ideological construct to explain what a million soldiers are out there defending. So Marx's toy convertibles, Ertl's farm toys, Keystone's garages, and so on populated a reassuring image of America—of aspiration and mobility on a bedrock of hard work and enduring values. Barbie and GI Joe would emerge as the perfect symbolic couple to traverse that symbolic landscape.

So how violent was GI Joe, the most popular boy's toy for much of the period between his appearance in 1964 and his disappearance by the early 1980s, following a national loss of confidence in military imagery induced by the Vietnam War? Essentially only a doll, eleven inches high, GI Joe's military status was represented by the extensive range of uniforms and weapons available to dress him. He could not be deployed as a violent object per se in play, like a toy gun. Rather he had to be dressed, equipped, and then posed in various imaginary scenarios in order to produce a viable play experience for a child. Those scenarios, cued by the available uniforms, tended to be from the World War II of popular imagination—the version propagated by Hollywood and by comics from DC or Marvel that, in turn, represented in ideologically acceptable ways the transformation of the United States into a global military power. In action, Joe became John Wayne storming the sands of Iwo Jima or DC's Sgt. Rock. As such, he was inextricable from the imagery of popular culture, no more and no less violent than any of these other representations: even as a Green Beret in Vietnam he seemed more in keeping with Wayne's 1968 reimagining of Vietnam (in the film *The Green Berets*)—as just another winnable theater from World War II—than with the television news images beginning to disturb America's conscience. It is difficult to argue that GI Joe carried any inherently violent implications other than those already widely available in American culture, for which he may have become a focal point in the hands of children but for which he can hardly be held accountable. Removing him from the hands of a child would not have removed the child from the culture—the constitutive context—that made GI Joe meaningful and attractive in the first place.

## The Closed Circuit of Media Culture

The replacement of the large GI Joe doll by a range of small, plastic action figures in the early 1980s signaled a new relationship between toys and popular culture. "Total marketing" had arrived, in part as a consequence of new dynamics in consumer culture generally. Now toys, comics, films, and television series increasingly fed off each other to create integrated marketing campaigns, often highly cyclical and aimed at creating temporary fads, in which the toy's only meaningful existence was as a character normally resident in a television series, supported by merchandising lines that could include everything from food cartons to wallpaper. The film *Star Wars* inaugurated this development in 1977, but it has continued unabated through such phenomena in children's popular culture as Thundercats, GI Joe (the new version, based on a team of futuristic warriors), Masters of the Universe, Transformers, Teenage Mutant Ninja Turtles, and Mighty Morphin Power Rangers. All of these, and others like them, have seen television series function as extended advertisements for toy lines and other merchandise, usually peaking for a Christmas buying season to be replaced by a similar multimedia product in the

## Questioning Violent Toys

In 1986 one parents' group organized a Peace Toy Fair in Eugene, Oregon, whose central event was a ceremonial burying of war toys in a "grave" dug at the end of a church parking lot. A spokeswoman for the giant retail chain Toys R Us, when questioned by a reporter about the company's response to the Peace Toy Fair, replied, "There are some psychiatrists who think war toys are positive for children, and that's about it" (Bishoff 1986). Community activism against violent toys is not always untainted by commercial interests—manufacturers of alternative toys for concerned parents sometimes support such events as the Eugene fair. While retailers on both sides benefit, parents are left with the dilemma of whether to err on the side of caution in the absence of absolutely convincing evidence for or against the effects of war toys.

Some models for public reframing of violent toys have emerged. Farideh Kioumehr-Dadsetan, an Iranian immigrant, is an educator and sponsor of a campaign against toy guns. At the center of this campaign in the late 1990s was the theme "Replacing Violence with Art." Kioumehr-Dadsetan and her colleagues, in collaboration with schools, government agencies, parents' groups, and artists, instigated a series of events in which toy weapons were collected and transformed into works of art, such as collages or three-dimensional constructions (for example, on 6 April 1997 at the Los Angeles Children's Museum, in cooperation with the Los Angeles County Health Department). Transforming violent toys is much closer to sand-play's therapeutic reframing than simply burying them.

The work of New York–based artist and photographer David Levinthal, who constructs miniature tableaux with toys and photographs them using a spare, shallow-focus technique, has the potential to awaken the viewer's visual imagination to the subtle but powerful relationships between toy imagery and history. Levinthal has drawn on the imagery of Hollywood Westerns and Nazi Germany to mine the latent power of toys as historical objects embedded in people's individual and collective imaginings. Such public recontextualizations of violent toys can serve to open up the debate about their role in American society.

next marketing cycle. Although there have been many nonviolent examples, notably Disney products but also others such as the environmentally themed *Captain Planet,* violent themes remain central to many of these lines of television-linked toys.

The little articulated action figure, with its fiddly accessories, and the omnipresent video-game control pad both seem to demand not only violent intent but a high degree of physical dexterity from children. Yet a serious issue remains. Both forms of amusement function in densely inhabited contexts where the only referents are the narratives endlessly elaborated through television series, comics, films, and so on. Industrial development once provided the context in relation to which toy machines became meaningful; later, militarily sustained globalism in U.S. foreign policy

provided the constitutive context for war toys. But in the last quarter of the twentieth century, popular culture has become the dominant context for determining the meaning of toys.

Although this trend is traceable back to the 1950s, it is only with the emergence of total marketing that it has become dominant. What this amounts to is a displacement of the potentially regulative contexts, such as home, school, and community, where toy objects have had to find their place in relation to the powerful stories children are offered about themselves and the world they live in. In those regulative contexts, any connotations of violence attached to a particular toy would be open to interpretation and the forming of new associations. Now popular culture has become both a constitutive and a regulative context for

## Movies and Merchandising

Toys are now central to the merchandising blitzes that accompany many popular movies. Since the original *Star Wars* largely began this process in 1977, it is not surprising that *Star Wars Episode 1: The Phantom Menace* took this to unprecedented heights in 1999. While the violence in the Star Wars films is highly stylized, it is nonetheless central to the plots. The overarching theme of galactic warfare gives the spin-off toys their meanings. Most of the toys based on *The Phantom Menace* remain essentially war toys, thinly disguised by their science fiction setting. Militaristic machines and weaponry are especially celebrated as essential to the appeal of the Star Wars movies.

However, toy sales related to *The Phantom Menace* were falling far short of the expected totals by the end of the summer 1999 marketing extravaganza, and other merchandising, such as clothing, was failing to attract consumers at all. *The Phantom Menace* demonstrates that media merchandising is a central context for today's toys and that this is not a simple cause-and-effect process, where a hit movie causes massive merchandising sales. There is growing circumstantial evidence that toys, and probably other spin-off merchandise, have to provide meaningful symbolic resources for children at the particular moment in order to be successful. The director George Lucas evokes the idea of timeless myth to explain *Star Wars*, but it is beginning to look as if the popular is determined by a closer fit between the "myth" and the moment. Toy manufacturers may find that capturing the imaginations of children remains an elusive and unpredictable goal, despite the sophistication of their mass-marketing techniques.

toys—both generating the toys and telling the interpretive stories about them through the dense elaborations of other media forms. Alternative regulative contexts continue to exist but are no longer dominant. Media culture has become a closed circuit.

The culmination of this process has been the computer game, where the toy and the context are no longer separable—the former is reduced to a sprite, a frenetically active little object manipulated by remote control in the sealed world of the media environment. This is a distillation of the contemporary toy world down to its essence. As such it reveals the central process that has, undoubtedly, always been at work in war toys and in other connotations of violence associated with particular toys—the projection of a socially constructed masculinity and a "boy culture" into play. Starkly revealed by the computer game, gender is the regulative context that has finally emerged as central to determining whether violent toys can have negative effects.

### Boys and Girls

Nineteenth-century boy culture, expressed through outdoor peer-group interactions, was romanticized in the figure of Tom Sawyer; whereas girls had little choice but to remain "naturally" and socially confined, boys could explore a liminal zone where they were temporarily free from maternal influence but not yet recruited to adult male activity.

> The boy's world countered with energy, self-assertion, noise, and a frequent resort to violence. The physical explosiveness and the willingness to inflict pain contrasted so sharply with the values of the home that they suggest a dialogue in actions between the values of the two spheres—as if a boy's aggressive impulses, so relentlessly opposed at home, sought extreme forms of release outside it; then, with stricken consciences, the boys came home for further lessons in self-restraint.
>
> (Rotundo 1994, p. 37)

As the streets became less safe venues for a boy culture of pranks and daring, which too readily shaded over into serious crime, for most American boys at the end of the twentieth century, the computer game became an alternative setting for the same interests. In the nineteenth century and for much of the twentieth, boy culture was as much concerned with games as with toys, except where the latter offered appropriate totems of male power, such as the toy machines and guns. Ironically, the gradual domestication of boy culture since the late nineteenth century—notably through suburbanization—has brought playing with such props increasingly under the influence of regulative contexts other than the outdoor peer group. But the computer game has turned this process finally inside out—opening up an electronic adventure space in the child's own bedroom. This cyclical return to the rough values of nineteenth-century boy culture, however, does not mark a return to the peer group as a regulative context for play. This is predominantly a space for solitary play, whether in the home or the games arcade, where things make sense in relation to the regulative context of popular culture—where narratives, themes, characters, and styles migrate around the closed circuit of games, films, television series, and comics. Role-playing games, with their careful scripting of violence in fantasy settings, were a brief interlude of social play for teenagers and young adults but have been largely overtaken by computer game versions.

This leaves violence, which is inescapable in the majority of contemporary computer games, at the center of boy culture. In the late 1990s, women have actively intervened to challenge this situation, through what has come to be known as the girls' games movement in the United States, spearheaded by software companies such as Purple Moon and Girl Games. For the most part, these alternative games are based on social interaction, "lifestyle"-related activities, and storytelling. The girls' games movement has been criticized for its supposed contribution to a ghettoization of boys' and girls' gaming, leaving the violent predispositions of the former unchallenged.

Yet the issue remains not whether violence in computer games, toys, and children's television programs *causes* violent behavior in children, but whether the constitutive contexts for such violence leave room for regulative contexts to counterbalance and redirect any such potential. Where home, school, and community, however troubled in particular instances, nonetheless serve to filter, to reinterpret, the game experience, the content of such material can fulfill its cultural function as the raw material for symbolic resolutions of otherwise unresolvable tensions. Both boys and girls, however, are now caught up in an increasingly closed circuit of media-generated meanings where the dominant regulative context for material in one medium is provided by the interconnected media environment generally—a toy or computer game character is contextualized by television programs, films, and comics. The computer-game company Purple Moon has taken a radical step forward by breaking the media closed circuit and reconnecting the gaming experience with the other regulative contexts. In Purple Moon games the characters interact in representations of the home, school, and community or in imaginary variants of these places that do not refer solely to the closed world of other popular media. Readmitting the regulative contexts that exist outside media culture, these girls' games point to a socially responsible way forward for computer games generally.

A productive cultural response to the dominant boy culture of media-defined toys and games must stem not from a panicky and censorious knee-jerk reaction but from an imaginative reconstruction of the cultural role of toys. Such cultural work is capable of recapturing the equilibrium between the constitutive and the regulative contexts in which toys find their meaning, while allowing representational violence to play its role as a symbolic resource of which a mature democracy need have no fear.

*BIBLIOGRAPHY*

Ambrose, Stephen E. *Rise to Globalism: American Foreign Policy, 1938–1976.* Harmondsworth, U.K.: Penguin, 1976.

Bishoff, Don. "Waging War on War Toys." *Register Guard* (Eugene, Oreg.), 20 November 1986.

Bradway, Katherine, et al. *Sandplay Studies: Origins, Theory and Practice.* Boston: Sigo, 1990.

Carlsson-Paige, Nancy, and Diane Levin. *The War Play Dilemma: Balancing Needs and Values in the Early Childhood Classroom.* New York: Teachers College, 1987.

Cassell, Justine, and Henry Jenkins, eds. *From Barbie to Mortal Kombat: Gender and Computer Games.* Cambridge, Mass.: MIT Press, 1998.

Erikson, Erik. *Childhood and Society.* London: Paladin, 1977.

Fleming, Dan. *Powerplay: Toys as Popular Culture.* New York: Manchester University Press, 1996.

Kinder, Marsha. *Playing with Power in Movies, Television, and Video Games.* Berkeley: University of California Press, 1991.

Kline, Stephen. *Out of the Garden: Toys and Children's Culture in the Age of Television Marketing.* New York: Verso, 1993.

O'Brien, Richard. *The Story of American Toys.* London: New Cavendish, 1990.

Provenzo, Eugene F. *Video Kids: Making Sense of Nintendo.* Cambridge: Harvard University Press, 1991.

Rotundo, E. A. *American Manhood: Transformations in Masculinity from the Revolution to the Modern Era.* New York: Basic, 1994.

Rushkoff, Douglas. *Playing the Future.* New York: HarperCollins, 1996.

Smith, Peter K. "The War Play Debate." In *Toys and Child Development,* edited by Jeffrey H. Goldstein. Cambridge: Cambridge University Press, 1994.

Sutton-Smith, Brian. *Toys as Culture.* New York: Gardner, 1986.

———. "War Toys and Childhood Aggression." *Play and Culture* 1 (1988).

DAN FLEMING

*See also* **Children; Television: Children's Television; Militarism; Popular Culture; Video Games.**

# TRAIL OF TEARS

The term *trail of tears* describes the forced removal of Native Americans from their traditional homelands east of the Mississippi River to newly established "Indian territories" in the West. Removal was advocated as a "humanitarian and civilizing" policy to protect Indian people from westward expansion while opening tribal lands to white settlement. Scholars describe the actual removal, lasting from 1830 to about 1859, as a "genocide-at-law" because one-quarter to one-third of removed Indian populations died from the forced migration.

Although Indian removal was advocated by Thomas Jefferson, the 1828 election of Andrew Jackson to the U.S. presidency provided the impetus. Despite a conciliatory inaugural address, Jackson demanded that Indians remove to the West; in his first annual message he urged a voluntary removal. On 28 May 1830 the Indian Removal Act passed against strong opposition arguing for the sanctity of Indian tribes. It authorized the president to exchange U.S. territory west of the Mississippi for the eastern lands of native peoples. Refusal to emigrate meant the end of federal protection for Indians and transfer of tribes to state jurisdiction.

This conflict climaxed before the U.S. Supreme Court in *Cherokee Nation v. Georgia* (1831) and *Worcester v. Georgia* (1832). Although the ultimate decision supported the Cherokee, Jackson had the troops and thus was able to drive the Cherokee and other native peoples from their homelands.

The story of the Cherokee forced march, which is perhaps the most infamous of removals and which became known as the Trail of Tears, is one of death and dying—for old men, young women, small children, and expectant mothers, all under the bayonets of white troops. The Cherokee were hunted down, herded into stockades, organized in wagon trains, and sent forth under military guard. Their journey stretched over six months, from October 1838 to March 1839, covering more than a thousand miles from Georgia to present-day Oklahoma. The exiles died in the tens and twenties every day. The very old and the very young could not stand the brutal winter, and relentless blizzards and driving snow weakened even the most able-bodied. The story of crossing the frozen Mississippi was etched in the minds of those who suffered the trail. The Cherokee knew the symbolism of crossing a river toward the west, for west in Cherokee mythology is the way of death.

The shadow of the trail forever darkened Indian history. More than half a century after removal, the chronicler James Mooney recorded the events described by Cherokee survivors in *Myths of the Cherokees* (1897–1898):

*The Trail of Tears.* **Oil on canvas by Robert Lindneux.** THE GRANGER COLLECTION, NEW YORK

Families at dinner were startled by the sudden gleam of bayonets in the doorway and rose to be driven with blows and oaths along the many miles of trail that led to the stockade. Men were seized in their fields or going along the road, women were taken from their [spinning] wheels and children from their play. In many cases, on turning for one last look as they crossed the ridge, they saw their homes in flames, fired by the lawless rabble that followed on the heels of the soldiers to loot and pillage. (pp. 124–125)

In this widely repeated description of Indian removal, Mooney reported the human story of the beginning of the "trail of tears." He concluded that the "history of this Cherokee removal of 1838, as gleaned . . . from the lips of actors in the tragedy, may well exceed in grief and pathos any other passage in American history." First-person accounts from non-Indians echoed this sentiment. A Georgian former colonel recalled that he had "seen men shot to pieces and slaughtered by the thousands [in the Civil War], but the Cherokee removal was the cruelest work I ever saw."

Sixteen thousand Cherokee began the trek; twelve thousand finished. Modern demographers believe that in the decade following removal, ten thousand more Cherokee would have been alive were it not for the Trail of Tears. Even for the survivors, removal was devastating. These traditional people were ripped from their homeland, from the sites of their spiritual strength, and from the graves of their ancestors. Furthermore, removal divided the tribe and ignited a bitter internal fratricide that followed the Trail of Tears.

Although it is the Cherokee march that has come to symbolize the brutality of Indian removal, other tribes faced the Trail of Tears (which included several routes), including the other so-called civilized tribes—Creek, Choctaw, Chickasaw, and Seminole. The Delaware, Kickapoo, and Quapaw were also forced to cede their lands in exchange for smaller parcels in the West. In 1832 the Winnebago joined the Sauk and Fox in hostilities against white settlers to protest the sale of their tribal lands during their winter hunting absence. Defeated, the Winnebago were driven from all their lands east of the Mississippi and the Sauk and Fox were forced to cede nearly all of eastern Iowa. In 1837 the Potawatomi were removed from their lands in Indiana, Illinois, and Michigan.

The factual record of removal is unambiguous. Alexis de Tocqueville, a contemporary French observer who witnessed the beginning of the Choctaw removal, observed ironically that "if an Indian nation happens to be so encroached upon as to be unable to subsist upon their territory, [the Americans] kindly take them by the hand and transport them to a grave far from the land of their fathers." For thousands of Indian people, the Trail of Tears was the path to a grave in the West.

*BIBLIOGRAPHY*

Carter, Forrest. *The Education of Little Tree*. Albuquerque: University of New Mexico Press, 1976.

De Rosier, Arthur H., Jr. *The Removal of the Choctaw Indians*. Knoxville: University of Tennessee Press, 1970.

Foreman, Grant. *Indian Removal: The Emigration of the Five Civilized Tribes*. Norman: University of Oklahoma Press, 1932.

Jahoda, Gloria. *The Trail of Tears*. New York: Holt, Rinehart and Winston, 1976.

Mooney, James. *Myths of the Cherokees*. Washington, D.C.: Government Printing Office, 1897–1898.

Satz, Ronald N. *American Indian Policy in the Jacksonian Era*. Lincoln: University of Nebraska Press, 1975.

RENNARD STRICKLAND

*See also* **American Indian Holocaust; American Indians.**

**TRAUMA.** *See* Medicine and Violence: Emergency Medicine; Victims of Violence.

# TUSKEGEE SYPHILIS STUDY

Beginning in 1932, more than four hundred African American men participated, without their knowledge or consent, in a forty-year study of the effects of untreated syphilis. Conducted in Tuskegee, Alabama, by researchers from the U.S. Public Health Service Venereal Disease Division, the study involved both periodic medical examinations and, following the deaths of the men, autopsies or postmortem dissections. When President Bill Clinton apologized in 1997 on behalf of the American people to the participants of the Tuskegee Syphilis Study and their families, he acknowledged how the study and other experiments that exploited African Americans had fostered intense suspicion of the white medical research establishment and its goals. This climate of suspicion created black distrust of such clinical and research activities as AIDS treatment trials and organ transplantation.

When the study began in 1932, many people believed that syphilis, a sexually transmitted disease with potentially devastating complications and few effective therapies, affected blacks and whites differently. By following the progress of untreated disease in the men, researchers sought to demonstrate specific racial differences. In order to ensure cooperation with the study, white researchers deceived their subjects by labeling such diagnostic procedures as lumbar puncture (the insertion of a needle into the spinal column to withdraw fluid for analysis) as "special free treatments." In addition to the deception that the subjects were receiving treatment for their "bad blood," investigators actively prevented the men in the study from receiving penicillin, an antibiotic newly available in the 1940s and dramatically effective against syphilis; government scientists, for example, contacted local draft boards, explaining how the men should be exempted from military duty because of their participation in the study. This exemption ensured that the men would not receive the treatment for syphilis routinely administered to all military personnel. Realizing that cooperation from families was essential to gain permission to perform autopsies, researchers offered surviving family members $50 in burial insurance. This money, rides in a government car, ointments, hot lunches, and in 1958 a certificate from the Public Health Service in recognition of twenty-five years of participation in the study were viewed by researchers as incentives crucial to maintaining the men's participation in the project.

Evidence from the Tuskegee Syphilis Study demonstrated that the death rate of untreated syphilis (or undertreated disease, as some men did gain access outside the study to penicillin and other forms of therapy) in black men aged twenty-five to fifty was 17 percent higher compared with the control group (black men who remained uninfected). More important than this clinical information was the effect of the Tuskegee Syphilis Study on the development of research guidelines in the United States. Amid the public outrage fostered by the public revelation of the study in 1972, several surviving participants in the study testified before the U.S. Senate about their exploitation at the hands of government scientists. Their testimony, together with reports of other abuses of human subjects, sparked the passage of the National Research Act in 1974, the first federal legislation for the protection of human subjects of medical research.

In 1997, speaking on behalf of the survivors assembled to hear the presidential apology, Herman Shaw, a Tuskegee participant, explained, "We were treated unfairly, to some extent like guinea pigs. We were not pigs. We were all hard-working men, not boys, and citizens of the United States."

*BIBLIOGRAPHY*

Jones, James H. *Bad Blood: The Tuskegee Syphilis Experiment.* New York: Free Press, 1993.
Reverby, Susan, ed. *Tuskegee's "Truths": Rethinking the Tuskegee Syphilis Study.* Chapel Hill: University of North Carolina Press, 2000.

Susan E. Lederer

*See also* **Medicine and Violence; Sterilization, Involuntary.**

# U

## ULTIMATE FIGHTING

In the fall of 1993 the Ultimate Fighting Championship (UFC) introduced American audiences to a sport that would soon be labeled no-rules, or ultimate, fighting. Unlike boxing, judo, karate, wrestling, and other sportive martial arts, ultimate fighting had far fewer rules. The format was simple: two fighters were placed in an octagonal ring enclosed by a six-foot-high, chain-link fence. In the beginning, the rules were minimal and included no biting, no eye gouging, no gloves, and no time limits. The contestants could fight standing up or grapple on the ground.

### The Ultimate Fighting Championship

The UFC was the creation of Rorion Gracie, whose family had dominated Brazilian *vale tudo*, or anything-goes, fighting for more than fifty years. In fact, Gracie's father, Helio, and uncle Carlos all but invented the modern sport. The former Japanese jujitsu champion Esai Maeda taught the brothers the then-secret art of jujitsu. The brothers modified the traditional martial art into a practical system of self-defense and opened their first academy in Rio de Janeiro in the 1920s. From that day, the Gracies offered a standing invitation to any fighter who wanted to test his style against what would come to be known as Gracie jujitsu. From 1930 to 1960, the brothers fought numerous challenges in public rings, in their academy, and in the street. Helio Gracie fought and lost a three-hour-and-forty-eight-minute bout against a former student named Valdemar Santana.

Under Rorion Gracie's direction, the UFC was designed to introduce Americans to the Gracie family's martial art. The first UFC tournament, held in Denver, Colorado, on 12 November 1993, brought together twelve fighters of very different styles: a 410-pound sumo wrestler, Teila Tuli; the boxer Art Jimmerson; the shootfighter Ken Shamrock; the Dutch kickboxer Gerard Gordeau; and eight others fought in a single-elimination tournament. At 180 pounds, Rorion Gracie's younger brother Royce was the smallest man in the tournament. The slight Brazilian threw few punches and kicks but easily defeated three much larger opponents by using a very sophisticated series of chokes and arm locks to capture the first UFC title. At the second UFC tournament, held in Denver in March 1994, Royce Gracie's mystique grew as he defeated four more opponents with similar ease. The young Brazilian's seven fights lasted a total of ten minutes, and he earned $110,000. Royce's quick victories over much larger opponents caused a paradigm shift in the world of martial arts. It soon became apparent to all prospective ultimate fighters that to be competitive in the UFC, a participant had to be able to grapple and fight on the ground. Besides Royce, the second generation of Gracie fighters included his brothers Rickson and Royler and his cousins Renzo and Ralph. Ironically, Royce was not the best fighter in the family; that honor was reserved for his older brother Rickson.

## A Predecessor to Ultimate Fighting

One of the first organized mixed-martial-arts competitions in the United States took place at the Salt Lake City Fairgrounds on 2 December 1963. The match came about as the result of a *Rogue* magazine article that charged, "Judo . . . is a complete fraud," and offered $1,000 to any judo player who could defeat a boxer (August 1963). The challenge was accepted by the 1954 and 1955 Amateur Athletic Union judo champion, Gene LeBell. The judoka was pitted against a high-ranking middleweight boxer named Milo Savage. The fight was scheduled for five three-minute rounds. LeBell wore a GI top and was allowed to employ any judo technique; Savage wore boxing trunks and extremely light, speed-bag gloves. The fighters battled inconclusively until the fourth round, when Savage left his neck exposed and LeBell choked him unconscious. Savage was from Salt Lake City, and his hometown fans began to riot. Bottles and chairs were thrown into the ring, and as LeBell made his way to his locker room, someone tried to stab him. It would be more than thirty years before mixed martial arts fighting returned to American shores.

The introduction of ultimate fighting was perfectly timed, because the credibility of professional boxing under Don King's stewardship was dropping to new lows. In addition, by 1994, as a reaction to the seemingly widespread corruption in boxing, fans helped make ultimate fighting a fast-growing sport. The second UFC tournament was broadcast live to more than 120,000 homes across America, and the cable subscription rates for the UFC events quadrupled in the first year. Ironically, it was this popularity that ultimately led to the sport's demise in the United States. In trying to capture an audience from outside the martial arts, promoters began to draw attention to the brutality of the sport. Semaphore Entertainment Group Sports (parent of the UFC) advertised its early tournaments as "the bloodiest, most barbaric show in history," and its anthem became, "There are no rules." The inaccurate hype surrounding the UFC created a great deal of interest in the tournaments.

A split soon began to emerge between Rorion Gracie and his partners over the future direction of the show. After a thirty-minute draw in UFC V, a battered Royce Gracie retired from the organization, and the UFC began to suffer from an identity crisis. Under the direction of businessmen and entertainment executives such as Art Davie, Bob Meyerwitz, and David Isaacs, the UFC began to feature less elite athletes and began to look more like the World Wrestling Federation. The promoters were less interested in drawing world-class competitors and more interested in cultivating personalities. What behemoths like Tank Abbot, Scott Ferrazzo, and Paul Varlens lacked in technique, they more than made up for with raw power. In the absence of a serious venue, rival ultimate-fighting leagues quickly filled the void.

### Extreme Fighting

Extreme fighting was the most serious challenger to the UFC. Under the direction of the former kickboxer John Perretti, extreme fighting treated no-rules fighting as a serious sport. The single-elimination tournament featured three weight divisions. The rules were similar to the original UFC: no rounds, no gloves, no eye gouging, no biting, and no judges. The first extreme-fighting tournament was scheduled for 15 November 1995 at the Brooklyn Armory in New York City. Perretti put together an impressive fight card, which included the Brazilians Mario Sperry, Ralph Gracie, and Carolson Gracie, Jr.; the former Russian judo team captain Igor Zinoviev; the American Greco-Roman wrestling world champion Gary Meyers; and eight others. Even though the New York State Athletic Commission had no jurisdiction over the event, the Republican state senator Roy Goodman called it a "human cockfight" and demanded a total ban on such events in New York State. Goodman described the event as "animalistic and hazardous to the contestants." Owing to the negative publicity, the New York Division of Naval Affairs revoked the lease for the armory, and extreme fighting was instead held in a sound stage in Wilmington, North Carolina. This relocation was a preview of things to come. There were so many objections in the United States that tournaments migrated to Japan, Brazil, and Canada. Again, promoters shared some of the blame, because they went to great lengths to highlight the sport's more brutal side.

### Decline of Ultimate Fighting

By 1995, politicians and pundits found an easy target in ultimate fighting. Not only did all but a handful of states outlaw these events, cable companies such as TCI and Time Warner refused to sell air time. The Republican U.S. senator John McCain (Arizona) sent a letter to the governors of all fifty states, requesting a total ban on "a brutal and repugnant blood sport." In an effort to appease politicians, the UFC abandoned the tournament format, added gloves, judges, rounds, weight limits, and more rules. Ironically, as the UFC teetered on the brink of extinction, the quality of competition improved markedly with the introduction of world-class wrestlers, such as Mark Coleman, and kickboxers, such as Maurice Smith. Still unable to get extensive cable coverage, the UFC limped along, holding events in Puerto Rico, Japan, and Brazil. Although the promoters of ultimate fighting are partly to blame for the sport's demise, the political attacks were inaccurate and opportunistic.

After an American competitor named Douglas Dredge was killed in a dubious, nonsanctioned ultimate-fighting tournament in Russia in 1998, the outcry over perceived violence in ultimate fighting increased once again in the United States. Government leaders, including McCain, led the charge and all but succeeded in driving the Ultimate Fighting Championship out of the United States. There was, however, something hypocritical about the politicians' actions. For example, although his criticisms of no-rules fighting were often inaccurate, Senator McCain actively supported professional boxing on the grounds that "Some people may not like boxing, but at least it is supervised and regulated."

There is a widespread misconception that boxers wear gloves to soften their blows. In fact, taped hands and gloves are worn to protect the fighters' hands. The end result is that boxers often sustain twelve rounds of frequent trauma to the head. Although boxing leads to less soft-tissue damage than does ultimate fighting, many boxers suffer from brain damage and have even died inside the ring in fully sanctioned events. After more than five years and hundreds of bouts, the UFC fighters suffered significantly fewer serious injuries than have boxers or even high school football players —no competitor has been paralyzed or seriously injured, much less had part of his ear bitten off, in any of the American no-rules fighting events.

BIBLIOGRAPHY

Berkow, Ira. "A Fight Better Than a Stick in the Eye." *New York Times*, 14 November 1995.

Douglas, Jeffrey. "Gracie Jiu-Jitsu: Still King of the Mountain." *Black Belt*, July 1994.

Luff, Bob. "Brooklyn Brawl Has Pol Fighting Mad." *Daily News*, 10 November 1995.

PETER MAGUIRE

*See also* **Boxing; Martial Arts; Spectacle, Violence as; Sports.**

# UNABOMBER
## (1942– )

In January 1998 the serial bomber Theodore John Kaczynski, also known as the Unabomber, saved himself from the prospect of execution. In the plea bargain with federal prosecutors, he accepted a sentence of life in prison without the possibility of appeal or release. Denied his late request to defend himself in court, he gave up on a plan to argue that his coast-to-coast killing spree was necessary to save the environment. He entered into his plea in part to protect himself from having his mental health called into question. Kaczynski was given a life sentence and ordered to pay $15,026,000 to his victims.

Kaczynski was born on 22 May 1942 to Theodore Richard Kaczynski and Wanda Theresa Kaczynski (née Dombek) of Evergreen Park, Illinois, a neat, working-class suburb of Chicago. David, the second son, was born in 1950. Kaczynski's father, who committed suicide in 1990 after being diagnosed with cancer, worked in a sausage plant in downtown Chicago and later managed a company called Cushion Park near Cedar Rapids, Iowa.

Little "Teddy John," as his parents called him, breezed through high school and went off to Harvard. By 1962 Kaczynski had finished his undergraduate degree, and at age twenty, he set off for the University of Michigan, where he earned a master's and a doctorate in mathematics. Kaczynski's prizewinning dissertation was on a pure mathematical problem about circles and functions. In 1967 he arrived at the University of California at Berkeley to teach mathematics. He lasted just two years, leaving of his own choice despite efforts by the university—which saw in him a potentially great mathematician—to lure him back. In 1971 he moved to Montana and purchased with his brother 1.4 acres in Florence Gulch, near Lincoln. He built his cabin in 1975.

For almost twenty-five years, Kaczynski lived the life of a hermit in a ten-by-twelve-foot shack with no heat or running water. The cabin was just below the largest stretch of unbroken wilderness in the continental United States. There were no cars, no roads, no buildings other than a shelter or two, and more bears than people. This territory was pristine, just the kind of place Kaczynski wanted America to be.

To his neighbors Kaczynski was known as an intensely private man, polite but aloof. It was hard for them to imagine that this bearded eccentric had a Ph.D. in mathematics and had once taught at a leading university. One neighbor from Lincoln said that Kaczynski was not mechanically inclined. When the Unabomber started his reign of terror, the bomb-squad cops insisted they were looking for a "junkyard bomber" because his inventions were patched together from lamp cords, bits of pipe, recycled screws, and match heads.

Kaczynski's first letter bomb, bearing the name of a professor at Northwestern University's Technological Institute, went off at the university in 1978, injuring a security guard. A year later, a second bomb was left at the institute, injuring a graduate student who had the misfortune to open it. After that, bombs were sent to an airline executive, to a University of Michigan professor, and to the computer science departments at Vanderbilt University and the University of California at Berkeley, among other places; each bomb was more sophisticated than the last. In the 1980s, as it became clear that the attacks were the work of one man—serial bombers are mostly males—a Federal Bureau of Investigation task force was born. Its name was UNABOM, after the nickname Kaczynski was given for his penchant for targeting university and airline personnel.

Every bomb maker, experts say, develops a signature: He may cut and loop wires in a certain way, or set his switches at a certain angle, or, in the Unabomber's case, create his contraptions out of wood and inscribe the letters FC on the metal parts that survive the blast (in a letter to a San Francisco newspaper, Kaczynski had identified himself as a member of a group called the Freedom Club). When he targeted the president of United Airlines in June 1980, it was not lost on students of his obsessions that the man's name was Percy Wood and that the bomb came disguised in a 1979 book called *Ice Brothers* (by Sloan Wilson), published by Arbor House, whose symbol is a leaf. Kaczynski was ob-

sessed with wood; he surrounded himself with it. For his targets, he selected people who had wood associated with their names, addresses, or businesses. His friends near his wood cabin had wood-associated names. The boxes that were part of the bombs he fashioned were made of wood.

In April 1995, the California Forestry Association president Gilbert Murray became Kaczynski's last victim when he was killed while opening a package bomb at the association's headquarters in Sacramento. Investigators suggested that the bomb was calculated to divert attention away from the Oklahoma City bombing five days earlier. Five months later, Kaczynski broke his silence with a windy, taunting letter to the *New York Times* in which he threatened that the terrorist group FC would make more powerful bombs and do more damage unless a lengthy political statement was published in acceptable forums. In exchange for this publication, the Unabomber said he would "permanently desist from terrorist activities" except for "sabotage." In September 1995, the *New York Times* and the *Washington Post* published the Unabomber's 35,000-word manifesto decrying the evils of modern, technological society. "The Industrial Revolution and its consequences have been a disaster for the human race," he wrote. "They have . . . made life unfulfilling, have subjected human beings to indignities, have led to widespread psychological suffering . . . and have inflicted damage on the natural world."

At the family home in Lombard, Illinois, David Kaczynski found letters from his brother replete with Unabomber-like rhetoric and alerted a childhood friend. The friend passed the letters over to experts, who compared them with the turgid manifesto and concurred that the sources probably matched. Soon thereafter, David was persuaded to talk to FBI agents. In April 1996, after a nearly two-month stakeout following almost two decades of avoiding detection, federal agents took Kaczynski into custody. Searches of his Montana cabin turned up a do-it-yourself bomb lab.

Altogether Kaczynski killed three people and wounded twenty-three others. He struck in sixteen different places across the country, from New Haven, Connecticut, to Tiburon, California. Federal agents developed twelve million bytes of information on Kaczynski and spent more than $50 million, as well as one million work hours, trying to catch him. Some FBI agents worked most of their careers chasing him and retired, despairing.

BIBLIOGRAPHY

Graysmith, Robert. *Unabomber: A Desire to Kill*. Washington, D.C.: Regnery, 1997.

Mello, Michael. *The United States of America Versus Theodore John Kaczynski: Ethics, Power, and the Invention of the Unabomber*. New York: Context, 1999.

Waits, Chris, and Dave Shors. *Unabomber: The Secret Life of Ted Kaczynski*. Helena, Montana: American World Geographic Publishing, 1999.

HARVEY W. KUSHNER

*See also* **Bombing and Bomb Scares; Letter Bombs; Terrorism.**

# UNIFORM CRIME REPORTS

The Uniform Crime Reports (UCRs) are the product of a national program of standardized crime-related record keeping that has made a significant contribution to our understanding of crime in the United States. Containing widely publicized criminal statistics based on crimes known to federal, state, and local police and on arrests, the UCRs provide detailed geographic coverage of crime trends and crime rates nationwide. UCR information is used extensively by criminal-justice policy makers, planners and researchers, sociologists and other members of academia, businesses, the media, tourism agencies, and private citizens.

## History and Methodology

The UCRs were not the first attempt at a national system to measure crime. An earlier effort began in the 1850s when the U.S. Census began counting persons living in correctional facilities. This endeavor failed because it was determined that a simple count of prisoners would not produce a methodologically sound crime index (that is, reliable statistics indicating the volume and distribution of crime). Instead, a method of recording crime incidence was needed, and the utilization of standard definitions of crime in the data collection process became a major goal of police and social scientists. In the late 1920s initiatives by the International Association of Chiefs of Police and the Social Science Research Council, as well as public administration and philanthropic organizations, were instrumental in the creation of the first uniform, reliable system for gathering crime statistics. The Uniform Crime Reporting System was officially established in 1930, and the Federal Bureau of Investigation was authorized to serve as the national clearinghouse for UCR data.

Participation in the UCR program is voluntary and continues to increase with technological advances in data management. At its inception in 1930, four hundred cities, with a total population of twenty million people, sent reports to the FBI. By 1983 the FBI received reports from agencies representing 226 million people, or 97 percent of the total U.S. population. UCR statistics in the late 1990s were based on reports by more than sixteen thousand city, county, and state law-enforcement agencies. The UCR presents crime data for the nation as a whole, as well as for regions, states, cities, and college and university campuses.

UCR data are compiled annually and published as *Crime in the United States*. Categories included in *Crime in the United States* are the numbers, rates, and percent changes in crimes over previous years; crime volume; violent-crime index; property-crime index; arrests; crime clearances (a crime is considered cleared when at least one person is arrested, charged with the offense, and turned over to the court for prosecution); and number of law-enforcement employees in the United States. A prominent chart included in each year's UCR is the Crime Clock, which represents the annual ratio of crime to fixed time intervals (for example, in 1996 one violent crime occurred every 19 seconds—see figure 1).

## UCR Index Crimes

The UCR records information on several major index crimes as an indication of changes, geographical differences, and the nature of the total crime picture in the United States. The seven original index crimes, also known as Part I crimes, are murder and nonnegligent manslaughter, rape, robbery, aggravated assault, burglary, larceny-theft, and motor-vehicle theft. Arson was added to the index crimes by congressional mandate in 1979. The UCR also collects information on what are referred to as Part II crimes. The Part II crimes include forgery, fraud, embezzlement, vandalism, weapons violations, sex offenses, drug- and alcohol-abuse violations, gambling, vagrancy, curfew violations, and runaways. Data on the age, sex, race, and ethnic origin of persons arrested are kept for both Part I and Part II offenses, while more detailed data are recorded for Part I offenses, such as type of weapon used, time and place of the offense, and relationship of the person arrested to the

FIGURE 1.   Crime Clock, 1997

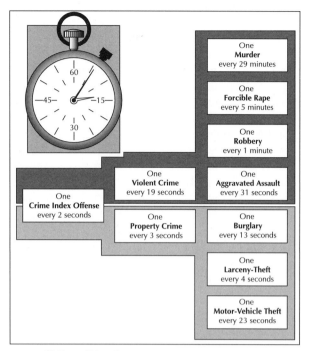

One
**Murder**
every 29 minutes

One
**Forcible Rape**
every 5 minutes

One
**Robbery**
every 1 minute

One
**Violent Crime**
every 19 seconds

One
**Aggravated Assault**
every 31 seconds

One
**Crime Index Offense**
every 2 seconds

One
**Property Crime**
every 3 seconds

One
**Burglary**
every 13 seconds

One
**Larceny-Theft**
every 4 seconds

One
**Motor-Vehicle Theft**
every 23 seconds

SOURCE: Uniform Crime Reports

victim (in murder cases). Most UCR statistics are based on the Part I index crime.

The UCR "hierarchy rule" indicates that only the most serious or highest ranking (in the order listed in the previous paragraph) of the index crimes committed in the same incident is recorded. The following scenario illustrates this rule: During an armed bank robbery the offender strikes a teller with his gun and then runs outside and steals an automobile. Three incidents have occurred: robbery, aggravated assault, and motor-vehicle theft. However, since robbery is ranked the highest, only robbery is recorded and the other two offenses are ignored. Arson is an exception to the hierarchy rule in that all arsons are recorded, even in multiple-offense situations.

### Imperfections of the UCR

The accuracy and utility of the UCR as the primary gauge of the national crime problem has been questioned by criminologists. Much crime information is systematically excluded by the nature of the data-collection approach. Based on the hierarchy rule, homicide, the highest-ranking Part I crime, would not be underreported in the UCR, but robbery would often be neglected. In addition,

not all crimes are reported to, or discovered by, the police. Thus, since the crime of rape is significantly underreported, the UCR rates for this crime are considerably lower than the actual frequency. The reliability and validity of the data reported to the UCR have also been questioned because of differences in recording practices and biases across individual law-enforcement agencies. Other weaknesses of the UCRs are that only limited information is available regarding the characteristics of offenders and that no data are collected on the victims of crime (with the exception of murder victims).

*BIBLIOGRAPHY*

Biderman, Albert D., and James P. Lynch. *Understanding Crime Incidence Statistics: Why the UCR Diverges from the NCS.* New York: Springer-Verlag, 1991.

O'Brien, Robert M. *Crime and Victimization Data.* Beverly Hills: Sage, 1985.

Rosen, Lawrence. "The Creation of the Uniform Crime Report: The Role of Social Science." *Social Science History* 19, no. 2 (1995).

U.S. Department of Justice. Federal Bureau of Investigation. *Crime in the United States: 1997 Uniform Crime Reports.* Washington, D.C., 1998. On the Internet at www.fbi. gov/ucr/ucrquest.htm and www.fbi.gov/ucr/ucreports.htm.

CHRISTINE A. SAUM

*See also* **Incidence of Violence; Methodologies of Violence Research; National Crime Victimization Survey; Statistics and Epidemiology.**

# UNRUH, HOWARD
## (1920– )

The prototype of the modern mass murderer, Howard Unruh detoured from a seemingly quiet existence in 1949 to plunge into a brief, mad episode of violence. At a time when the country was sick of war and eager to embrace a tranquil prosperity, Unruh's crimes proved to be a disquieting reminder of the murderous impulses that may lie just beneath a civilized veneer.

Although killing eventually earned Unruh infamy, it had qualified him for commendation a few years earlier. During World War II he was considered a war hero; he had served as a tank machine gunner and fought bravely and effectively in the rescue of the besieged Americans at the Battle of the Bulge. Nevertheless, his distinguished performance in the field did not translate into popularity with his fellow soldiers. The tall, thin young man was quiet and solitary. Instead of carousing with other men in his unit, he preferred to read the Bible and clean his rifle. He also kept a diary in which he noted every one of the Germans that he killed and their appearance at death.

Unruh's diary-keeping continued when he returned to his hometown of Camden, New Jersey, after the war. He recorded every grievance he held against his neighbors, every perceived slight or insult. Living alone with his mother in a second-floor apartment, he at first applied himself to studying pharmacy at nearby Temple University, but he stuck with it for only three months. Unemployed, he filled his time with churchgoing, Bible study, and target practice in the basement of his building. The notations in his journal began to focus on his next-door neighbor, Maurice Cohen. Following his entries about Cohen and some others, he began to jot down "retal," his abbreviation for "retaliate."

On the night of 5 September 1949, Unruh spent hours in an all-night movie theater watching the same double-bill over and over again. When he returned home at 3:00 A.M., he discovered that the gate to his backyard fence had been stolen. He could not get any sleep that night. At 9:20 on the morning of 6 September, he left his house armed with a 9-mm German Lugerand and strolled down his block and started shooting people.

Among the people Unruh killed was Cohen, his imagined enemy, along with Cohen's wife and mother. Other victims included three children. In all, during his twelve-minute walk he murdered thirteen people. Retreating to his apartment, he held out briefly against the police but then surrendered when overcome with tear gas.

Upon his arrest Unruh seemed chillingly unfazed by the horrific extent of the carnage he had wrought, calmly explaining that his neighbors had been making "derogatory remarks about my character." One thing he was defensive about was his mental state. "I'm no psycho," he was quick to point out. Local authorities took a different view. Judged psychologically unfit to stand trial, Unruh was committed to a maximum-security mental institution. Nearly fifty years later, in 1998, Unruh attempted to persuade a judge that he no longer posed a danger to others and should be transferred to a less stringent facility. The judge ruled that the mental condition of the seventy-seven-year-old

**Howard Unruh.** CORBIS-BETTMANN/UPI

murderer had not improved since 1949 and that he should remain under prisonlike supervision.

Howard Unruh proved to be a precursor of a criminal type that became all too common in postwar America: the human time bomb who explodes in a flash of random slaughter. Charles Whitman followed Unruh's pattern in 1966, when he climbed to the top of a University of Texas watchtower and began firing on people below. Another notorious example was James Oliver Huberty, who opened fire in a crowded McDonald's in San Ysidro, California, in 1984. Typically this crime had been the domain of men in their twenties, thirties, and forties. By the late 1990s, however, the phenomenon took on an even more disturbing dimension. By then the perpetrators were often teenage boys, as seen in the horrific high school killings committed in such otherwise quiet communities as

Jonesboro, Arkansas (in March 1998), and Little-ton, Colorado (in April 1999).

BIBLIOGRAPHY

Everitt, David. *Human Monsters.* Chicago: Contemporary Books, 1993.
Nash, Jay Robert. *World Encyclopedia of Twentieth-Century Murder.* New York: Paragon House, 1992.
"The Quiet One." *Time,* 19 September 1949.

DAVID EVERITT

*See also* **Mass Murder: Individual Perpetrators.**

# URBAN VIOLENCE

A salient characteristic that distinguishes urban violence from other forms or types of violence in the United States is the component of race and ethnicity. One form of violence that has been exclusively associated with cities in the United States—the urban riot—often erupts in a context of antagonistic social class and race relations. Urban violence, contrary to popular perception, is thus not always random but often is patterned by prevailing social conditions, including social inequality compounded by issues of race and ethnicity. At times involving labor strife, depending on the historical period and attendant social circumstances, ethnic or racial identity may be either accentuated or downplayed. For much of U.S. history, save for relatively brief periods during the Civil War and Reconstruction in the nineteenth century and during the post–World War II Civil Rights era in the twentieth century, the employing of particularist strategies—that is, those favoring one's particular group—has seemed especially beneficial to the groups involved.

## Approaches to Urban Violence

Scholars of urban crime and violence have attempted to identify a number of aspects of society that can affect the prevalence and type of violence in urban areas. This research is strongly linked to more general theories on racial and ethnic relations and can be divided into three generations of ideas. The first, formulated at the University of Chicago, was linked to theories of crime and deliquency. These theories elevated the cultural norms of middle-class and upper-class Protestant behavior to universal standards and attributed violence to the degraded state of black and immigrant popu-lations, whether that degradation was said to be due to biological or social causes.

In the middle of the twentieth century, the second generation of theories stressed the economic and cultural assimilation of urban migrant populations as a result of the post–World War II national expansion. In this "melting pot" model, a prosperous America found room for all second- and third-generation urban residents, and ethnic and racial antagonisms correspondingly declined over time. As the children and grandchildren of white ethnic immigrants moved up the socioeconomic ladder, African American migrants from the rural South were simplistically viewed as the "last of the immigrants." Toward the end of the twentieth century, speculation about the impact of renewed immigration and the invention of the term *underclass* to describe poor, inner-city black populations have led to a return in theory and policy to arguments about deep, enduring biological and social differences between the races. This is the third generation of thinking about racial and ethnic relations.

## Historical Patterns

Urban development and urban violence can be divided into four rough historical periods: antebellum (to 1860); the era of first ghetto formation following the Civil War and Reconstruction (about 1880–1930); the era of the Great Depression, the second ghetto formation, and the Civil Rights movement (1930–1968); and the era of new polarization (from the late 1960s on). In each period, a distinctive configuration of politics, economics, and culture combines to produce new group settlement and interaction patterns and a characteristic morphology of violence.

The antebellum decades are among the most violent in American history. In Philadelphia, for example, there were over a dozen violent mass disturbances and riots during the 1830s and 1840s. The formal mechanisms of social control and political processes were severely strained in the few decades before the Civil War. As were other cities of the new republic, Philadelphia was beset by youth gangs, by the influx of Irish and German immigrant workers, and by Protestant-Catholic antagonisms. In a changing economy the replacement of skilled native artisans by unskilled, and often immigrant, factory workers produced a series of strikes in the 1830s and 1840s. The police lacked professionalism, and jurisdictional boundaries hampered their ability to pursue criminals; in fact, the need to create a more effective police force was the main impetus behind the consolidation of the county into an expanded City of Philadelphia in 1854.

In these years an urban strategy of internal community control coupled with a defensive posture vis-à-vis neighboring communities first appeared. Three sociocultural forces fueled the development of this urban organization. First, the long-standing antipathy between Protestants and Catholics in England and Ireland was transplanted to the United States and took root among the native-born as well as among the immigrants. Second, the spectacular growth in the city of a culturally diverse population challenged the previously dominant values. And third, the conflict between artisans and unskilled workers on the one hand, and between workers and employers on the other, meant that the newly forming working classes could take advantage of the weakening systems of social control to build their own autonomous cultures. In this era, religion and ethnicity combined as bases of group identity to form a potent, unstable mix. Race provided a subordinate dividing line; white Catholics and Protestants often united around racial antipathy toward black people, but their own mutual antagonism usually kept them divided over the long run.

Though all forms of violence occurred at high rates in this era, particularly noteworthy were both large and small intergroup confrontations. Gangs of Protestant and Catholic young men regularly clashed in the streets. When these clashes coincided with institutional rivalries, such as those between fire companies or those in the workplace over labor issues, few means were available to prevent them from exploding into full-fledged communal riots. Native Protestant artisans in particular, their livelihood threatened by growing industrialism, rioted against Catholics and blacks by invading the residential areas of both groups, beating pedestrians, breaking into houses, and setting fire to buildings. These are classic communal riots, with direct confrontations between members of conflicting groups.

In the era of the growth of the industrial city (1880–1930), cities assumed the size, shape, and character on which the earliest urban theories were based and which continue to provide much of our urban imagery. The years 1880 to 1920 saw mass immigration to the United States from southern and eastern Europe, with millions of new workers arriving each decade, especially Jews, Italians, and Poles. Social networks linking immigrants who were faced with language barriers combined with employers' swiftly rising demand for large, coordinated workforces to promote group hiring in factories. Though these immigrant "white ethnics" were rarely fully segregated from each other or from native whites, neighborhoods that grew up around the factories did develop distinct ethnic identities. At the same time, longer-established immigrants like the Irish were assimilating the dominant native traditions and cultural patterns, in the process forming a new white racial consciousness and culture. For the most recent immigrants, therefore, a model of how to understand their own identity as whites rather than as Poles or Hungarians or Italians was becoming available.

A great expansion of formal social, economic, and political institutions took place during this period, primarily in the cities. Most dramatically, the new industrial order was irrevocably established, as small workplaces were replaced by giant factories turning out cheap, mass-produced goods. The modern service and retail industries, which are the backbone of white-collar employment, were also established, as was mandatory schooling for most urban children. The fire gangs, which were responsible for so much antebellum violence, were also transformed into the more restrained, if not less corrupt, men's political clubs; these clubs formed the grassroots basis of powerful urban political machines. In fact, it was the strong organization of the ethnic neighborhoods that enabled professional politics to mobilize votes by manipulating patronage.

Blacks, however, as Roger Lane points out, formed a unique subgroup, one that was shunned by both the white elites and the working classes. As a result, they were excluded from both blue-collar and white-collar employment in the new large workplaces as well as from most other institutions. Furthermore, though blacks obtained the vote in many cities, their participation in patronage networks and party reward systems was severly restricted. This economic, political, and social exclusion formed the social-structural basis for rising intragroup violence among African Americans—at the same time as intragroup violence among white ethnic groups, who were finding places in the growing American institutional and industrial order, was declining. Infamous examples of violence related to organized crime, such as the 1929 St. Valentine's Day Massacre in Chicago, were notable in part because they were

355

increasingly exceptional. Intergroup violence was declining as well. The communal riot declined rapidly after the Civil War, except for a spate of race riots from 1917 to 1921 (including Philadelphia in 1918 and Chicago in 1919) and a final occurrence in Detroit during World War II. These twentieth-century riots occurred as the spike in industrial employment induced by the two world wars drew large numbers of southern blacks into northern cities, where they often encountered serious white resistance. The area of black settlement expanded quickly, but the riots, which occurred mainly along the color line, served to cement the boundaries of ghettoes through the 1960s.

The middle decades of the twentieth century, roughly from 1930 to 1970, saw the country's most sustained attempts to institutionalize democracy and equal opportunity for all citizens. The Depression was a nationwide shock that left no group of people untouched. In American cities virtually no new housing was built from 1930 to 1947. World War II brought massive urban industrialization, and the labor demand again brought great numbers of African Americans out of the South and into cities to work in war factories. After the war, southern agricultural industrialization pushed even more blacks off the land; simultaneously, new suburban construction, subsidized by federal mortgage and highway assistance, pulled middle- and working-class whites out of many urban neighborhoods. As the more affluent African Americans took advantage of the resulting hous-

ing vacancies to move out of crowded ghettoes, the frontier of black settlement again began to expand. Threatened whites remaining in these neighborhoods, many of whom could not afford to leave for the suburbs, in turn resorted to vandalism, arson, and direct attacks on blacks in an attempt to keep their blocks all white.

Politically at this time there was a remarkable shift toward a greater role for the federal government, begun by the New Deal and firmed up by World War II. At first, federal urban renewal and housing policies actually contributed to segregation in the North—by redlining black neighborhoods so that they received limited mortgage assistance, by promoting new housing for whites in the suburbs, and by allowing local control of urban renewal funds. The original social purpose of public housing—to alleviate poverty by improving the physical environments of the poor, and later, the black poor—was subverted over time as massive projects in fact concentrated great numbers of black poor people in areas with few resources other than governmental social service agencies. Mayors and other local politicians generally refused to use urban renewal and other public funds to integrate neighborhoods, choosing instead to erect segregated housing projects. Furthermore, in the 1950s these monies were used to destroy tens of thousands of low-income housing units that were never replaced. Welfare rights activists undertook to reverse this process by using the recently expanded and invigorated federal govern-

**White rioters overturn a car owned by an African American in Detroit in 1943.**
CORBIS/BETTMANN

ment as an ally against state and local politicians who used local control over policy to enforce segregation. This strategy had great success in the South, where the movement was able to combine it with an ideology of nonviolence that made southern segregationists look like the aggressors. However, it largely failed in the North, as was demonstrated by the stalemate, rather than victory, that resulted from the campaign by Martin Luther King, Jr., against housing discrimination and segregation in Chicago.

Various forms of violence were sparked by the release of these social forces. There were widespread interracial clashes between small groups of white and black youths along the residential color line and in the few urban high schools that had been integrated. Loosely organized "gangs" of whites and blacks were responsible for some of this violence, though gang violence was overwhelmingly intragroup rather than intergroup. Widespread police brutality was another source of violence. Police abuse on the street or during arrests provoked many of the commodity riots of the 1960s, as black onlookers decided to act on growing feelings of alienation, exclusion, and frustrated mobility. The targets of the commodity riots were precisely those entities that represented the institutions most directly seen as impeding black advancement: law enforcement as the representative of the local government and businesses as the representatives of blocked employment opportunity. In this sense, it is possible to view the riots as the culmination of the Civil Rights movement. The Kerner Commission, appointed by President Lyndon Johnson, concluded in 1968 that white racism was ultimately, if indirectly, responsible for the riots; it was in fact in response to these riots that government at all levels adopted a number of policy changes, including voting rights legislation and affirmative action, to open up the political and occupational system to greater black participation. The entrance of African Americans into highly visible occupational and political positions, like mayoralties, had implications for future acts of violence: the presence of blacks in these leadership positions may have helped to prevent or defuse potentially violent situations in the 1970s and 1980s.

## The New Polarization and the Code of the Street

During Richard Nixon's presidency (1969–1974), it became increasingly clear that the post–World War II arrangements that had been governing and promoting sustained economic growth, rising real wages, and better living conditions for all Americans were becoming less and less effective. America entered a period of profound social and economic restructuring, the most notable aspects of which were the decline of manufacturing jobs, the shift to a service-based economy, the rise of the global economy, and the great expansion of Latino, Asian, and Caribbean immigration.

The dislocations brought on by deindustrialization, specifically layoffs and rising unemployment, were most pronounced in urban communities. Unemployment among African American men has always been higher than that among whites, but since the late 1960s it has rarely, if ever, been less than twice that of whites. The decline in manufacturing jobs that caused the substantial rise in black male unemployment was accompanied by the simultaneous rise of households headed by women and the expansion of the welfare rolls. The 1970s and early 1980s were thus a period not of recession but of depression for many black neighborhoods. The ultimate effects of recession, deindustrialization, and restructuring have been (1) to limit the number of African American males able to take advantage of the opportunities created during the 1960s and participate in individual and intergenerational socioeconomic mobility, (2) to encourage those blacks who became solidly middle class or professional to take good advantage of their economic gains to move out of the inner-city ghetto, and (3) to create competition, polarization, and tension between urban blacks and newly arrived immigrants. Though middle-class African Americans have not necessarily thereby moved into a life of integration—discrimination, police harassment, stereotyping, and white reluctance to mix still abound—the exodus from the community of these blacks has meant that lower-class blacks have become increasingly isolated from the middle classes, black as well as white.

As a result, many inner-city black neighborhoods have suffered from prolonged flight of capital of diverse kinds. Deindustrialization and the suburbanization of employment have meant the flight of investment and corporate capital. The departure of middle-class blacks for black suburbs combined with the reluctance of banks to lend money for mortgages in poor and working-class urban neighborhoods have meant the flight of home-owner capital. The flight of the middle class, black and white, to the suburbs has drained the inner city of substantial amounts of the human capital that is associated with highly educated and well-paid professionals. Declining, underfunded public schools have difficulty providing students with the human and cultural capital necessary for success in the service sectors that are the most swiftly growing sources of jobs, while the underground economy provides an alternative, if risky, source of income. And the increasing socioeconomic differentiation of neighborhoods means that poor people are increasingly spatially separated from the middle-class and professional people who provide a community with social capital—that is, interpersonal networks that can informally link residents to jobs and support social institutions.

The result of all these developments is that a great many inner-city black neighborhoods are experiencing a lost sense of security, as—to a lesser extent—are many working-class and poor white urban neighborhoods. Many people in these neighborhoods are not effectively adjusting to new labor-market requirements provoked by the shift from manufacturing to services. As neighborhood resources decline, as residents become ever poorer, the social breakdown spreads. Competition for available resources increases, and the drug trade becomes more pervasive; some of the most desperate people see few alternatives to engaging in the underground economy. In fact, the introduction of crack cocaine in itself has had an enormous deleterious impact on inner-city neighborhoods. Along with the proliferation of guns, the competition over drug markets and turf has greatly escalated the violence in these and adjoining areas. In addition, the police when summoned may not respond; they even often tolerate obvious drug dealing and disrespect for the law, thus encouraging the cynicism of many black residents toward both the police and the criminal justice system.

Urban politics often become a racial conflict over a shrinking economic pie. Suburbanites are increasingly self-sufficient and reluctant to see any money leave their communities to benefit the cities they purposely left behind. Cuts during the era of the Reagan presidency (1980s) in federal aid to cities have combined with globalization and deindustrialization to make the historic mode of ensuring urban peace—patronage—obsolete. Instead, city mayors scramble to give tax breaks to businesses to locate within the city limits. It is only in the 1990s that immigrant communities have exercised more political pull, but up to that time they lacked the electoral strength to generate greater federal aid.

Spurred on by this persistent high poverty rate, the sociospatial isolation of the inner cities, a rampant drug trade, and lack of faith in the police, the level of violence, particularly among youth, increased in the 1970s and 1980s. Many residents now take personal responsibility for their safety, at times arming themselves, and this reality has given rise to a "code of the streets" that orders social relations in public often through the use of the implied threat of violence. As noted above, part of the increase in violence can be traced to the spread of crack cocaine and of unregulated firearms. But social scientists have also been correct in pointing to the influence of neighborhood conditions on violent conduct and on propensities for violence. Living under conditions of capital flight, unemployment, poverty, and social isolation, residents of "ghetto poverty" neighborhoods come into contact with potential danger on a daily basis, and living by the code is a cultural adaptation to this reality. As a result, public spaces cease to be truly communal areas and become instead hazardous zones shared by people who lack trust in or who even fear one another, forcing them always to watch their backs, judge other's motives from subtle cues, be suspicious of outsiders, and remain guarded about what personal information they reveal to others, lest it be used against them.

But the decline in local public spaces is not just the result of capital flight; it is also intertwined with cultural shifts that can be characterized as a decline of public culture, public engagement, and public ideologies. Civil rights and the movement for integration failed to stop housing segregation or to get better urban public schools for black students. Instead, whites fled mixed neighborhoods and shifted their children to private schools. Interpretations vary: on the one hand, some black nationalists claim that the difficulties in urban black communities are the result of integration policies that fragmented black neighborhoods; on the other hand, white conservatives tend to blame liberalism and the social programs of the 1960s for urban poverty and social problems. The ideals of integration and multiculturalism are further betrayed in mixed-race and gentrified neighborhoods by a public culture of "street etiquette," a veneer of the recognition of public diversity that in reality seeks to preserve social distance and avoid public interaction. So even residentially mixed neighborhoods often lack real integration in terms of social relations. In marginalized areas, public spaces like parks, playgrounds, vacant lots, and street corners are now littered with brown paper bags, empty liquor bottles, crack vials, condoms, and the occasional shell casing—evidence that they have been coopted by people who see them not as belonging to everyone but as areas that can be controlled by those with the greatest clout.

With the influx of immigrants from Latin America, the Caribbean, and South and East Asia, many of whom are highly skilled and educated, the United States is now much more of a multiracial and multiethnic society than it was in the 1960s, and it is possible that the 1990s marked a new phase of the era of ethnic and racial polarization. Yet it is also true that in the 1990s some cities—Boston and New York in particular—witnessed extraordinary declines in violence; and it appears that this decline is related to a decline in intragroup violence stemming from the code of the streets. Some evidence suggests, however, that we may be trading intragroup violence for heightened intergroup tensions. The commodity riot of 1992 in Los Angeles, in the wake of the acquittal of police officers accused of beating motorist Rodney King, may be taken symbolically as evidence that polarization has come full circle and that national diversity is combining with urban economic distress to provoke greater interracial and interethnic antagonisms.

Moreover, many whites, provoked by politicians who fan the flames of racial antipathy in a search for votes, continue to attack with renewed vigor policies and ideas intended to foster equal opportunity. Low-level, small-scale interracial clashes, now sometimes called hate crimes, are on the rise. African Americans have publicly clashed with immigrant Korean store owners in many cities. In the general population, social distance from persons of other races, political rhetoric, and lurid television accounts of crime have increased fear among whites of hostile encounters in public spaces and have made streets and parks seem more dangerous than they really are.

The situation of blacks in poor inner-city neighborhoods seems to be considerably more daunting than that of other groups, past or present. In the early years of the twentieth century, Italian and Irish neighborhoods experienced similar levels of violence, but as these new immigrants settled into jobs and family life, the neighborhoods became more organized and social relations more orderly. A parallel cannot be drawn with the blacks of the 1990s, however, since the system itself has changed. The occupational ladder does not exist for poor blacks as it did for earlier immigrants because jobs now require much higher levels of skills and education, while inner-city schools are failing to provide that education. And those unskilled jobs at the bottom rarely pay an adequate wage. Coupled with racial prejudice that has been more persistent than the ethnic prejudice directed against immigrant groups, this economic predicament leaves the most desperate to gravitate to, if

The aftermath of the Los Angeles riot of 1992. CORBIS/JOSEPH SOHM; CHROMOSOHM INC.

not fully embrace, the receptive underground economy. However, this mode of survival, which is to a large extent organized around the code of the streets and violence, leads ultimately not to socioeconomic incorporation but to ever greater alienation and higher rates of incarceration.

*BIBLIOGRAPHY*

Anderson, Elijah. *Code of the Street: Decency, Violence, and the Moral Life of the Inner City.* New York: Norton, 1999.

———. *A Place on the Corner.* Chicago: University of Chicago Press, 1976.

———. *Streetwise: Race, Class, and Change in an Urban Community.* Chicago: University of Chicago Press, 1990.

Davis, Allen F., and Mark Haller, eds. *The Peoples of Philadelphia.* Philadelphia: Temple University Press, 1973.

Du Bois, W. E. B. *The Philadelphia Negro.* 1899. Reprint, Philadelphia: University of Pennsylvania Press, 1996.

Hirsch, Arnold. *Making the Second Ghetto: Race and Housing in Chicago, 1940–1960.* New York: Cambridge University Press, 1983.

Horowitz, Ruth. *Honor and the American Dream.* New Brunswick: Rutgers University Press, 1983.

Janowitz, Morris. *Political Conflict.* Chicago: Quadrangle, 1970.

Katznelson, Ira. *City Trenches: Urban Politics and the Patterning of Class in the United States.* New York: Pantheon, 1981.

Lane, Roger. *Roots of Violence in Black Philadelphia, 1860–1900.* Cambridge, Mass.: Harvard University Press, 1986.

National Advisory Commission on Civil Disorders (the Kerner Commission). *Report of the National Advisory Commission on Civil Disorders.* New York: Bantam, 1968.

National Research Council. *Understanding and Preventing Violence.* 4 vols. Washington, D.C.: National Academy Press, 1994.

Reiss, Albert J., and Michael Tonry, eds. *Communities and Crime.* Chicago: University of Chicago Press, 1986.

Shaw, Clifford R., and Henry D. McKay. *Juvenile Delinquency and Urban Areas.* 1942. Reprint, Chicago: University of Chicago Press, 1969.

Short, James F., Jr. "Gangs and Adolescent Violence." Center for the Study and Prevention of Violence, paper 4. Boulder, Colo.: Institute for Behavioral Sciences, 1996.

———. *Poverty, Ethnicity, and Violent Crime.* Boulder, Colo.: Westview, 1997.

Wilson, William Julius. *The Truly Disadvantaged: The Inner City, the Underclass and Public Policy.* Chicago: University of Chicago Press, 1987.

———. *When Work Disappears.* New York: Knopf, 1996.

JEROME HODOS
ELIJAH ANDERSON

*See also* **Geography of Violence; Graffiti; Police; Poverty; Riots; Rural Violence;** *and entries on individual cities.*

# V

## VALACHI, JOSEPH
### (1903–1971)

Joseph Valachi became one of the first members of the Mafia to violate *omertà*, the organization's code of silence, when he testified in 1963 before the U.S. Senate Permanent Subcommittee on Investigations about the inner structure of the Mafia and organized crime. Valachi testified not only to his own participation in a number of murders, but also to his position as a "soldier" of the Mafia. Overnight, this relatively insignificant underworld figure became an international celebrity whose testimony was widely accepted as the gospel on organized crime in the United States.

Born in New York City in 1903 to immigrant parents from Naples, Italy, Valachi quit school when he was fifteen and soon turned to a life of crime. By age nineteen he was an accomplished burglar. In the 1920s Valachi joined Salvatore Maranzano's Sicilian Mafia organization; after Maranzano's assassination in 1931, he moved to the Luciano family to serve under Vito Genovese. As a "soldier," or "button man," Valachi worked as a hit man, enforcer, numbers operator, and drug pusher until 1959, when he was sentenced to fifteen to twenty years on drug-trafficking charges.

In the federal penitentiary in Atlanta, Valachi shared a cell with Genovese, who he would later testify had become head of the Luciano crime family's operations after Lucky Luciano's deportation to Italy in 1946. In 1962 Valachi became convinced that Genovese wrongly suspected him of being an informer and had ordered his assassination. Par-

anoid, Valachi mistook a prisoner named Joe Saupp for Joe Beck, the man he believed had been sent by Genovese to kill him, and bludgeoned Saupp to death. Valachi subsequently received a life sentence for the killing. Still fearing for his own life, he decided he would indeed turn informer and thus receive federal protection.

Valachi's appearance before Senator John McClellan's subcommittee made for excellent theater. Guarded by a contingent of some two hundred U.S. marshals, Valachi revealed often chilling details about mob murders, which simultaneously fascinated and horrified the national television audience. Valachi also introduced the American public to the term *Cosa Nostra* (our thing), insisting that *Mafia* was used only by outsiders.

All in all, Valachi identified 317 syndicate members. Many of the incidents and facts that Valachi described were known to police, and a substantial amount of this history had previously appeared in books, magazine articles, and newspapers. Moreover, because he was a low-level member of organized crime, his knowledge of high-level Mafia decisions and operations was limited and its accuracy questionable. Nevertheless, Valachi offered an inside view of the struggle for power within the Mafia and of the double-dealing characteristic of organized crime. He also helped law enforcement officials link previously unconnected events and provided a better understanding of the dimensions of organized crime.

Joseph Valachi died of a heart attack in prison in 1971. Just before his death, a reporter asked him what would have happened if prison authorities

**Joseph Valachi before the Senate Investigating Subcommittee, September 1963.** CORBIS/BETTMANN

had not taken special precautions while he was in custody. "I'd have to kill or be killed," he replied. "If they got me, I wouldn't last five minutes."

BIBLIOGRAPHY

Fox, Stephen P. *Blood and Power: Organized Crime in Twentieth-Century America.* New York: Morrow, 1989.

Humbert, Nelli S. *The Business of Crime: Italians and Syndicate Crime in the United States.* New York: Oxford University Press, 1976.

Maas, Peter. *The Valachi Papers.* New York: Putnam, 1968.

Peterson, Virgil W. *The Mob: 200 Years of Organized Crime in New York.* Ottawa, Ill.: Green Hill, 1983.

NANCY A. BANKS

*See also* **Genovese, Vito; Luciano, "Lucky"; Mafia; Organized Crime.**

# VANDALISM AND VIOLENCE AGAINST PROPERTY

Vandalism has been defined as the "willful destruction of property without the consent of the owner." Damage to property that results in injury or death to individuals is treated more seriously and generally is not considered to be vandalism. Acts of vandalism occur throughout the United States, in rural and urban areas, in public and private spaces. The financial costs are staggering: it costs taxpayers an estimated $8 billion per year to fight graffiti alone, and hundreds of millions more for repairing, replacing, and rebuilding equipment and property, and providing security (equipment and personnel) to prevent vandalism.

Research on vandalism has focused largely on graffiti; considerably less is known about other forms of vandalism. The lack of research in this area has contributed to misguided policies. Controversies persist over the very definition of vandalism: some people believe that certain kinds of graffiti should be viewed as art rather than destruction, creativity rather than criminality. For example, taggers, graffiti artists steeped in hip-hop culture, consider themselves artists and consider their work to be public displays of creativity. Public officials, however, usually view this form of graffiti as vandalism. Consequently, most intervention strategies have focused on the construction of environmental deterrents to graffiti, the implementation of expensive graffiti-removal methods, and penalties for graffiti offenses.

This article (1) describes the targets and patterns of vandals and graffiti writers; (2) reviews possible explanations for their activities; (3) critically examines traditional strategies that communities have developed to address graffiti and other forms of vandalism; and (4) recommends a number of innovative approaches to reducing vandalism and graffiti.

## Targets and Patterns

Just as the motivations for acts of vandalism and graffiti vary widely, so do the choice of targets and associated patterns of behavior. Whereas vandals are likely to target hidden as well as visible spaces, graffiti writers are most attracted to public spaces such as buses, railways and subways, elevators, billboards, highway overhead signs, and public restrooms. The "tagging" form of graffiti that emerged in the 1970s, distinguished by individualistic signatures or "tags" that identify the writer (often with a street name or alias), has been the focus of a number of studies, one of which suggests that tagging developed from hip-hop culture. Tags with greater detail are known as "throw-ups" (messages that use multiple colors or block letters) or as "pieces," (murals or tags containing several words). Taggers often choose prominent public spaces from which the graffiti cannot easily be removed and where the execution of their project entails great risk. Tagging in such locations earns the writer/artist respect and esteem from peers.

In some respects tagging differs from other forms of graffiti. For example, taggers view their work as expressive artistry, whereas gang members use graffiti to mark territory. Also, some taggers prefer to work alone rather than with a tagger crew; by contrast, group involvement and a sense of belonging is important to gang members. Moreover, the violent behavior of some gangs diverges sharply from the nonviolent subculture of the taggers.

Whatever the legitimacy of its aesthetic claims, tagging stands in sharp contrast to forms of vandalism whose sole purpose is destruction. Some such acts occur in sprees. For example, one night of group vandalism can result in intense damage within a limited neighborhood area: windows smashed, a number of cars "keyed" (that is, the fine point of a key is used to scrape the side of a car), or several tires deflated or sliced. In other typical instances, specific properties might be targeted for days, weeks, or months. Tagging, however, usually occurs over long periods, during which writers target several locations; the number of tags in part contributes to the tagger's reputation. In California one tagger wrote his name more than ten thousand times in various places from San Francisco to Orange County over the course of several months.

Vandalism and graffiti can be motivated by politics. After the Pacific Lumber company was permitted to remove dead and dying trees from Headwaters Forest in California, militant environmentalists poured and ignited gasoline in the pool of the company president. "Save Headwaters" was written on his house. Vandalism has also been a common tactic during strikes and other labor disputes. Clinics that offer abortion also have been targeted by vandals. The National Abortion Federation reports that from 1992 to 1994, incidents of chemical vandalism (that is, spraying clinics with butyric acid or purposely exposing a clinic staff to anthrax) resulted in damages worth more than $800,000, a figure that does not include the costs of damage resulting from other forms of vandalism, such as arson.

Hate and bigotry are other common motives for vandalism and graffiti. For several years the Southern Poverty Law Center, in its Klanwatch Intelligence Reports, has documented such acts, which include racist or anti-Semitic graffiti, arson, and other property destruction. Several churches with predominantly African American membership have been vandalized in southern states. In Boligee, Alabama, the destruction of an African American church by arson was a severe emotional blow to the community, where many congregants' families had worshipped in the church for generations. Other churches in the area also were destroyed by suspicious fires. In 1995 two white males admitted using a sledgehammer to smash pews, windows, and equipment in a local church.

Vandals have targeted other groups as well. At Michigan State University a fire of suspicious origin damaged the Jewish student center in 1995. Elsewhere, Jewish gravestones have been overturned and broken and temples targeted by vandals. During the Gulf War, Muslim mosques and businesses were vandalized.

University and college campuses across the United States have experienced considerable property damage from vandalism. Some vandals have no campus affiliation, but there are many instances of students, mostly males, damaging their own living environments. The purposeful destruction of university property is commonly linked to alcohol use among student vandals, although formal studies of this correlation are lacking.

## Explanations

Research into the causes and correlates of vandalism has been limited. A 1979 study by Pamela Richards focused on vandalism among middle-income students in a junior and a senior high

**Hip-hop graffiti mural on a railroad tanker car. Painting on cross-country trains widens the graffiti artist's exposure.** COURTESY OF JEFF FERRELL

school. The results showed that vandalism was more common in the younger group and more common inside the school than outside. More important, the research showed that vandalism was not a byproduct of issues like self-esteem, boredom, and students' "general outlook on life"; it was, rather, bound up with peer-group deviance patterns and perceptions of conflict with adults.

According to Richard Cloward and Lloyd Ohlin, delinquent acts reflect the frustration experienced by youth whose opportunities for material success are blocked by inequities inherent in the social order; the social system thus serves as a target on which to vent their frustration. This theory assumes that lower-income youth are disproportionately involved in delinquency; in fact, studies of both vandalism and graffiti have found that these activities are common among members of all socioeconomic groups. Still, schools are middle-class institutions and often are targeted by vandals and graffiti writers. Research has found that the targets of youth vandals reflect their perceptions about an unfair system. For example, two twelve-year-old students in Connecticut scrawled "Die Joel" on the property of the Lewin G. Joel, Jr., Elementary School, perhaps out of frustration with school authority. In Philadelphia vandals destroyed a school, a library, and the building that housed a local police athletic league—all venues that are part of the authority system with which some youths feel frustrated.

In one study, school tracking (the segregation of students by presumed level of academic ability) was found to be a better predictor of school vandalism than academic achievement, although peer relationships also were a contributing factor. However, the relationship between tracking and vandalism is complex. It is possible, for example, that students engage in acts of vandalism before tracking occurs and that tracking decisions are influenced by students' deviant behavior as well as by their scores on standardized tests. School tracking may be thus one aspect of the educational system that fosters the alienation and frustration involved in vandalism. Jeff Ferrell's extensive fieldwork with taggers confirms the notion of graffiti as a form of resistance. He argues that because public space has become more restricted and authorities have stepped up their attempts to control and govern youth, graffiti can be viewed as a reflection of frustration with the social system. In addition, youth who challenge authority at times gain respect from some of their peers. Graffiti in some

venues is a form of communication for persons who are denied legitimate avenues of expression. For example, at Brown University the names of male sexual attackers were written on the walls and stalls of women's restrooms. Here graffiti served as an alternative method of communication to express the women's frustration with the system's inadequate response to sexual victimization. Similarly, because taggers generally are denied access to art galleries, tagging provides an alternative venue for displaying their work.

Jane Gadsby has noted that graffiti is viewed by some scholars as the collective expression of a particular subculture. As has been noted, tagging, for example, is an outgrowth of the hip-hop culture in some areas. Tagger subcultures have developed their own norms, language, and values. One important subcultural norm is that taggers are expected to develop their own creative style of writing rather than use the work or letter style of another artist. Taggers evaluate one another's work and disdain the drip marks and lack of originality that are typical of inexperienced artists. Tagger mentors assist newcomers in mastering the art.

Of the four principal values that have been identified with the hip-hop graffiti subculture—fame, artistry, power, and rebellion—fame is the most important. One way that fame is achieved by taggers is through the placement of tags in a variety of hard-to-reach locations. The tagger subculture also has its own distinctive argot. For example, to "bite" is to copy the writing style of another. Names or acronyms are used to identify particular tagger crews or the targets they seek.

Although some graffiti writers and vandals work alone, others operate in peer groups. In fact, peer involvement in the activity appears to play an important role in individual acts of vandalism and graffiti. Taggers, for example, are often part of a tagger "crew," an informal organization of writers. Tagging and other forms of graffiti help to promote identity in a peer group that rewards achievements and risks. Self-praise also is an important dimension. In Philadelphia a young adult male and two adolescents videotaped their destruction of property in three sites.

Most research concentrates on vandalism and graffiti work among adolescents or young adults, since these activities typically decline with age. Motives and targets differ across age categories. Anecdotal evidence suggests that vandalism among adults is more likely to reflect political or ideological conflict with the social system. Clearly, more research is needed into adult vandalism.

## Community Responses

Vandalism and graffiti have received considerable public attention, much of it focused on prevention, surveillance, and reducing the costs of repairs. In 1997 widespread concern over the issue was expressed at the National Graffiti Prevention Conference in Phoenix. Consulting firms such as the National Graffiti Information Network have surfaced across the country and provide strategies to reduce and prevent graffiti and other vandalism. Yet to date few empirical studies have investigated the impact of such strategies on reducing and preventing vandalism.

Traditional antidotes to vandalism—e.g., arrest, fines, and other penalties—often fail to address the dynamics of youth culture. Increased surveillance designed to deter or capture graffiti writers at work often fuels the excitement and "rush" of writers. According to one study, traditional educational programs geared toward reducing vandalism were the least effective strategy.

When vandals are apprehended by police, charges can include trespass, criminal mischief, or vandalism. Between 1984 and 1993, the number of vandalism arrests increased by 31 percent among youths and by 27 percent among adults (U.S. Department of Justice 1994). However, the increase may reflect a change in the allocation of police resources rather than a rise in incidents. For example, the increased availability of police surveillance equipment (e.g., infrared cameras) in some areas has made it easier to locate vandals and graffiti writers. Another limitation of arrest data is that acts perceived as vandalism might be attempted burglaries or attempted thefts of motor vehicles. Still, most vandals and graffiti writers are never apprehended, in part because eyewitness or videotaped accounts of the behaviors are lacking. The effectiveness of arrest as a deterrent to vandalism is uncertain. In Devon Brewer's 1992 study, some graffiti artists and writers persisted despite repeated arrests. And the famous (or infamous) "Chaka" was found tagging in the elevator of a Los Angeles court building while on his way to visit his probation officer.

Many communities construct environmental deterrents such as razor wire, foliage, and improved lighting. At one university officials spent $11,000 to construct an observational tower in a parking lot. Complete with one-way windows, the structure was designed to deter car theft and vandalism. Other areas use a neighborhood watch system. Prevention efforts that focus on modifying the physical environment in order to prevent vandalism may produce a displacement effect. For example, inaccessible targets may lead persons to alter their behavior by seeking other targets within or outside the area. However, because crime displacement is not easily measured, studies of it are of limited value.

Elsewhere, communities have employed "rapid cleanup," known among taggers as "buffing." This strategy focuses on the removal of graffiti as quickly as possible. The purpose is twofold. First, quick removal deprives the writers of self-gratification and peer recognition. Second, clean public space allows for residents to feel less anxious and less fearful; more residents use the public space, and, in turn, more people are present to monitor and prevent the actions of others. Most communities, however, lack the resources to remove graffiti quickly. Moreover, the strategy fails to recognize Jeff Ferrell's 1995 findings that tagging followed by increased surveillance was often followed by more tagging. Stated differently, graffiti writing and other forms of vandalism are often provoked, rather than deterred, by increased authority and surveillance. In some areas graffiti telephone hotlines have been established and are well publicized on highways and streets. In Miami local officials have erected signs on public highways that list telephone numbers and ask cell-phone and other callers to report graffiti. In 1996 a sign located on a main thoroughfare was continuously sprayed with graffiti, replaced by officials, and defaced again.

In some areas sales of spray materials or marking pens to minors are monitored or banned. This measure has proved ineffective, because many of the items can be found in households or shoplifted from stores. In other communities parents are held financially responsible for children's acts of vandalism on school property, an approach that has had little impact because of the low rate of arrest for such offenses. Moreover, the strategy is discriminatory in that, similar to other restitution schemes, parents who head lower-income households are less able to pay for damaged property. All such traditional "Band-Aid solutions" fail to address and understand the youth culture that motivates the activities. Traditional strategies might even have unintended consequences. For example, Jeff Ferrell has concluded that tagger crews may be an important alternative to gang involvement; hence, community responses that seek to eliminate tagger crews may actually contribute to gang involvement among former taggers.

Surveillance, reduction, and removal efforts all appear to be increasing. Information is shared through conferences, workshops, and public meetings. Yet vandalism and graffiti continue. Graffiti writers counter such efforts with their own information networks; dozens of graffiti magazines are marketed and sold to domestic and international audiences. Internet sites warn viewers that some magazines may be hoaxes, with subscriptions intended only to identify and police graffiti writers.

**Finding New Solutions**

Although studies of vandalism and graffiti are few, the findings are important and should be considered by policy makers. Youth must be involved in the decision-making process, especially since youthful writers and artists perceive all too clearly the ineffectiveness of traditional strategies. Involving youth in policy formation would serve two purposes. First, policy makers would have the opportunity to develop a better understanding of youth culture. Second, youth involvement in the decision-making process would send a powerful message, one of dialogue rather than control. Devon Brewer interviewed fifteen graffiti writers from four cities and asked them to evaluate a number of approaches for preventing illegal graffiti. The writers indicated that the best strategy involved the providing of legal walls controlled by the artists, establishing areas for graffiti work, supplying materials for writers and artists, and organizing competitions. (The effectiveness of this intervention method has not been examined thoroughly.) Brewer also found that writers' and artists' recommendations for reducing illegal graffiti differed across geographic areas. A similar strategy could be used in schools. Involving youth in the formation of school policy might contribute to self-esteem and identity. It might also curtail resentments engendered by authoritarian postures and regulations.

Vandalism and graffiti motivated by hate and bigotry are the toughest challenge. Some have suggested mandatory school curricula designed to enlighten students about cultural diversity and tolerance. The educational program "Teaching Tolerance," developed by the Southern Poverty Law Center, could serve as a model. Such programs, which seek to address the causes of the social unrest of which graffiti and vandalism are mere symptoms, seem to offer the best hope for a thorough long-term solution.

*BIBLIOGRAPHY*

Brewer, Devon D. "Hip Hop Graffiti Writers' Evaluations of Strategies to Control Illegal Graffiti." *Human Organization* 51, no. 2 (1992).

Brewer, Devon D., and Marc L. Miller. "Bombing and Burning: The Social Organization and Values of Hip Hop Graffiti Writers." *Deviant Behavior* 11, no. 4 (1990).

Castleman, Craig. *Getting Up: Subway Graffiti in New York.* Cambridge, Mass.: MIT Press, 1982.

Chalfont, Henry, and James Prigoff. *Spraycan Art.* New York: Thames and Hudson, 1987.

Cloward, Richard A., and Lloyd E. Ohlin. *Delinquency and Opportunity: A Theory of Delinquent Gangs.* New York: Free Press, 1960.

Ferrell, Jeff. "Urban Graffiti: Crime, Control, and Resistance." *Youth and Society* 27, no. 1 (1995).

Hagan, Frank E. *Introduction to Criminology.* 3d ed. Chicago: Nelson-Hall, 1994.

Nwoye, Onuigbo G. "Social Issues on Walls: Graffiti in University Lavatories." *Discourse and Society* 4, no. 4 (1993).

Richards, Pamela. "Middle-Class Vandalism and Age-Status Conflict." *Social Problems* 26, no. 4 (1979).

Sloan-Howitt, Mary-Alice, and George L. Kelling. "Subway Graffiti in New York City: 'Gettin Up' vs. 'Meanin It and Cleaning It.'" *Security Journal* 1 (1990).

Tygart, Clarence E. "Strain Theory and Public School Vandalism: Academic Tracking, School Social Status, and Students' Academic Achievement." *Youth and Society* 20, no. 1 (1988).

———. "Youth Vandalism: Toward a Collective Behavior Approach to the Study of Delinquency." *International Journal of Group Tensions* 19, no. 2 (1989).

Wooden, Wayne S. *Renegade Kids, Suburban Outlaws.* Belmont, Calif.: Wadsworth, 1995.

KAREN McELRATH

*See also* **Arson and Fire; Environment, Violence Against; Graffiti; Crime, Legal Definitions of.**

**VERBAL VIOLENCE.** *See* Language and Verbal Violence.

# VICTIMS OF VIOLENCE

*Following the* **Overview** *is a subentry,* **Social Suffering.**

## OVERVIEW

**Trends in Victimization**

People of all ages, all races, all socioeconomic classes, and all ethnic groups have a chance of becoming victims of violent crime. However, victimization statistics from the Bureau of Justice Statistics (BJS) at the U.S. Department of Justice reveal that not all groups have an equal likelihood of becoming a crime victim. Young black males (sixteen to twenty-four years of age) living in low-income housing in high-crime urban areas are the Americans most likely to become a victim of a crime, according to 1990s data from the Federal Bureau of Investigation's Uniform Crime Reports and the BJS's National Crime Victimization Survey, while white females (and especially elderly white females) who live in wealthy, low-crime areas are the least likely to become a victim of a violent crime.

*Race.* Income and education, place of residence, age, gender, and race are all to some extent predictors of who is most likely to become a victim of violence, but race is one of the primary predictors. Black murder victimization rates, as well as rates for other violent crimes, including aggravated assault, exceeded those of whites throughout the twentieth century; black murder rates are higher than white murder rates for all age groups. Victimization rates for individuals age twelve and older follow a similar pattern when identifying race and family income as affiliated factors. For example, for all victimizations in 1992, whites experienced a rate of 63.5 (per 1,000) for families with incomes less than $7,500 while the rate for blacks in the same socioeconomic bracket was 70.2 (per 1,000) (Dobrin et al. 1996). However, it is necessary to recognize that while the victimization rate for blacks is significantly higher, blacks only make up 13 percent of the population. Justice Department statistics indicate that rates of victimization steadily decrease both for whites and blacks as annual family income increases to $50,000 or more.

*Age.* As individuals age, the likelihood of their being victimized by crime decreases. Although some three-fourths of all murder victims are age twenty-four or older when killed, teenagers and young adults are more likely than older adults to be murdered. The largest number of victims of aggravated assault consistently falls within the sixteen-to-nineteen-year-old age category. Those children at greatest risk for any violent victimization, according to 1990s statistics from the BJS, are children of families whose household income is less than $20,000, black children, and children in large cities (Dobrin et al. 1996).

Elderly members of society are also a vulnerable victimization subgroup. For individuals over age sixty-five, those at greatest risk of violent victimization in the period 1987–1990 were males, blacks, divorced or separated individuals, and persons residing in the city (Dorkin et al. 1996). In the 1990s the seventy-five-and-older age group was the fastest growing segment of the U.S. population. The rapidly increasing numbers of frail elderly people in U.S. society made it likely that the incidence of elder abuse and neglect will also rapidly increase. The type of abuse inflicted most frequently on elders is neglect, followed by physical abuse.

*Gender.* Women have approximately one-third the risk of men of being murdered, but women are four times as likely as men to be killed by a spouse or intimate partner. The rates of nonfatal violent victimization among women were highest for black women (58.5 per 1,000), for females age twelve to fifteen (102.3 per 1,000), and for divorced or separated women (86.2 per 1,000) (BJS 1997; Rand, Lynch, and Cantor 1997).

Female children are victims of resoundingly higher levels of physical, sexual, and emotional abuse than are male children. The greatest difference exists in the category of sexual abuse. Moreover, in instances where the assault is identified as a "family assault," girls tend to be victims more often than boys. However, among child victims, the incidence for all victimizations, especially nonfamily assault, is higher for boys than for girls (Dobrin et al. 1996).

*Income and Education.* When trends are assessed from the perspective of income, BJS data from the 1990s indicates that the highest violent crime victimization rates generally exist for those earning less than $7,500 annually while those least at risk are members of households with annual income above $25,000. Individuals with no more than an elementary school education consistently experience the highest rates of crime victimization, and persons with a college education, the lowest.

## Changing Views Toward Victims

The injury experienced by victims of personal violence is not limited to the immediate experience of the crime. The crime victims may have been robbed, raped, murdered, assaulted, or had their automobile stolen, but the perpetrator's actions also have a residual effect: the crime usually causes psychological pain and torment, medical injuries, and trauma and intense fear in the victims (or in the victims' survivors) that they will be victims again.

## Three Typical Cases of Crime Victimizations

- Sam, a twenty-one-year-old automobile parts salesman, was robbed at gunpoint upon returning to his apartment in Yonkers, New York. Sam recalls looking down the barrel of a nine-millimeter semiautomatic gun. The criminal took $169 in cash, several credit cards, and Sam's coat, watch, glasses, and shoes. Sam had nightmares several times each week for about four weeks after the crime. He finally went for counseling at the local mental health center. In addition, the victim advocate at the local victim-assistance agency in Westchester County helped Sam complete a victim compensation application so he would be compensated for his monetary and property losses. Victim compensation also eventually reimbursed him for six weeks of mental health counseling.
- Julie, a twenty-eight-year-old advertising executive, was raped at knifepoint when she returned from work to her apartment in Brooklyn, New York. It was midnight, and Julie had worked late. The lock on the front door to her building was broken, and she was concerned, but she went inside, stopping off at the alcove that held the tenants' mailboxes. She unlocked her mailbox, took the mail out, and proceeded to walk toward the steps when someone grabbed her from behind. She later recalled that her rapist put a knife to her throat and told her that if she did not immediately remove her skirt and panties he would cut her clothes off and stab her in the throat. She removed her clothes quickly, and closed her eyes when the rapist penetrated her. She recalled the rapist whispering in her ear that he might be back in a week or two because Julie had a great body just like his sister, with whom he had had a lot of sex before she got married. Julie told the female detective in the sex crimes unit that she was worried that the rapist might have AIDS or another sexually transmitted disease, and she was fearful that he would return.
- Mr. Stevenson owned a liquor store with his brother-in-law. He was robbed on Christmas eve. The criminal had a gun, and Mr. Stevenson was shot to death as he struggled to take the gun away from him. The California State Victim Compensation Board reimbursed Mrs. Stevenson for all funeral expenses. In addition, Mrs. Stevenson got support from other survivors in a support group in Los Angeles.

These three typical cases depict the unpredictable nature of becoming a victim of a violent crime and the psychologically painful and sometimes fatal outcome of being victimized. When violent crime is covered in the media, however, the victims of violence who receive the most attention tend to be those who are least typical. For example, Ronald Goldman and Nicole Brown Simpson were certainly victims of violent crime when they were murdered in 1993, a case that generated the trial of the former football star O. J. Simpson and months of sensational media coverage. But the murders of these two victims were not typical in at least two aspects: the victims were white, and they were residents of California neighborhoods (Beverly Hills and Brentwood) that are among the nation's wealthiest.

A field called victimology began in the 1940s and 1950s with the research of Benjamin Mendelsohn and Hans Von Hentig. Early victimologists, working in a field that was considered a branch of criminology, focused their analysis and writing on typologies of crime victims and the different ways in which the victim contributes, knowingly or unknowingly, to his or her own victimization. Von Hentig identified types of people who seemed to be prone to becoming crime victims. A highly regarded doctoral dissertation by Marvin Wolfgang at the University of Pennsylvania in the 1950s built on Von Hentig's theory of victim-proneness and led to Wolfgang's influential conclusion that the majority of criminal homicides in the city of Philadelphia were victim-precipitated because the vic-

The 1987 trial of Bernhard H. Goetz evoked conflicting viewpoints. See also the entry on Goetz. CORBIS/BETTMANN

tim either provoked the perpetrator or the victim was motivated by an unconscious desire to commit suicide.

The crime victims movement of the 1970s, 1980s, and 1990s gradually led to a discrediting of the idea that victims were somehow responsible for what had happened to them and resulted in increased attention to and positive changes in the social, economic, and political forces that caused harsh and neglectful treatment of crime victims by the criminal justice system. The victims movement led to landmark federal legislation that resulted in major funding initiatives throughout the nation for prosecutor-based victim and witness assistance programs, state crime victim compensation programs, police victim assistance programs, shelters for battered women, restitution programs, and sexual abuse treatment and prevention programs. Most important, the Victims of Crime Act was passed in 1984. This significant federal legislation led to the development and funding of several thousand victim assistance programs nationwide. By 1996 deposits from criminal penalties and fines into the federal Crime Victims Fund reached $525 million, which was made available to state victim compensation programs, federal victim assistance programs, state and local victim and witness assistance programs, technical assistance programs, and the training of victim advocates. During 1997 the fifty states received more than triple the amount of federal crime victim funds than they had received in any previous year.

In the last decades of the twentieth century, the United States saw a rapid expansion of theory, research, and legislation to protect victims' rights and provide services for survivors. Community leaders, legislators, and victims' rights advocates in America successfully lobbied for thousands of laws and state constitutional amendments protecting the rights of crime victims. Community-wide coalitions, elicited governmental hearings, crime-commission reports, conferences, media attention, and the passage of important victim-rights legislation at the state and federal levels.

By the 1990s, the federal government and most states had adopted some sort of victim-rights legislation. Most statutes identified specific rights held by victims and their families, such as:

- To bring the accused to a speedy trial
- To be present at all critical stages of a suspect's trial, including sentencing and appeals hearing
- To be treated with dignity, respect, courtesy, and sensitivity
- To be notified in advance of scheduled or rescheduled court proceedings
- To be given a waiting area separate from the one used by the alleged offender and his or her family during any stage of the investigating process
- To receive information of their rights promptly; just as criminal suspects must be read their rights

- To be informed of monetary assistance and concrete services (e.g., emergency food coupons), crisis counseling, criminal injury compensation, and other services available for crime victims
- To have property promptly returned unless the police have a compelling reason to delay the return
- To receive full restitution from the offender if possible
- To be informed of a defendant's release or escape
- To testify at any parole or probation hearing or plea bargaining process
- To require the offender to undergo a blood test if bodily fluid capable of transmitting the HIV virus may have been transferred during the criminal act (Roberts 1997; Wallace 1998).

### The 1984 Victims of Crime Act

Increased public sensitivity about the trauma and loss experienced by victims of violent crime, a growing fear of crime, and the influence of the women's movement all combined in the early 1980s to elicit a task force from the attorney general's office under President Ronald Reagan to study the needs of victims of crime. The 1982 report of this task force set the stage for passage of the Federal Victim and Witness Protection Act of 1982, and ultimately for the landmark Victims of Crime Act (VOCA), passed by Congress in 1984.

A major component of the VOCA legislation was the creation of a large federal fund within the U.S. Treasury, known as the Crime Victims Fund, that would amass money from federal criminal fines, penalties, and asset forfeitures in order to finance services and assistance for victims of crime. Over the next fifteen years, a total of more than $2 billion from this victims' fund was made available to agencies at the federal, state, and local levels in support of services such as victim compensation programs and victim and witness assistance, domestic violence, and sexual assault prevention programs. By the late 1990s the fund was worth several hundred million dollars a year, and disbursement of money to states was growing almost exponentially, funding thousands upon thousands of victim-advocacy agencies and services nationwide.

*Victim and Witness Assistance Programs.* Victim and witness assistance programs are usually located either within the local county prosecutor's

---

## Putting a Price on Victimization

Is it possible to place a monetary value on losses as a result of victimization? Tangible losses consist of direct expenses from victimization such as the cost of medical and mental health services, the cost of victim assistance and other concrete social services, and losses of the victim's own productivity—for instance in terms of lost wages or salary or lost time from school or work. One estimate calculates that these kinds of tangible economic losses due to victimization from crime in the United States amounts to $105 billion annually; along with intangible psychological costs estimated at $450 billion and tangible criminal justice costs of roughly $70 billion, the cost of U.S. crime in the 1990s could be figured at some $625 billion yearly.

One group of researchers (Miller, Cohen, and Wiersema 1996) measured and quantified the tangible losses from a rape-related death as $1.03 million, while estimating the intangible cost of a human life at $1.91 million. The tangible value of a crime victim's life was measured in terms of the person's occupation and age (e.g., a twenty-five-year-old homicide victim translates into forty years of wages and income lost) and the amount of money spent to reduce the risk of death (e.g., emergency medical care and ambulance), among other variables.

The economic, health, mental health, and criminal justice costs of victimization are astronomical. The billions of dollars lost as a result of violent crime victimization is an important indicator of this major social problem.

---

suite of offices, the county courthouse, or across the street from the court building. These programs are designed to encourage witness cooperation in the filing of criminal charges as well as testifying in court. In general, these programs include a witness-notification and case monitoring system, in which staff keep witnesses advised of indictment, continuances, and postponements; specific trial and hearing dates; negotiated pleas; and trial outcomes. In addition, many of these programs provide secure and comfortable reception rooms for witnesses waiting to testify in court, as well as transportation services and court escort (that is, someone accompanies the witness to court and remains with that individual in order to explain and interpret the court proceedings). These programs also prepare and distribute court-orientation pamphlets about the adjudication process; examples typically include titles such as "Crime Victims' Bill of Rights," "Witness Guidelines for Courtroom Testimony," "What You Should Know About Your Criminal Court and the Court Process," and "Information Guide for Crime Victims" (Roberts 1997).

One element that is often lacking in victim and witness assistance programs is that many do not offer any form of childcare for the children of victims and witnesses while the parents testify in court (Roberts 1990). Providing responsible and structured childcare for a parent while they are testifying in court can provide an important service. Most criminal justice agencies, unlike social work agencies, do not realize that victims and witnesses' children are affected by their parents' emotional reactions, losses, physical injuries, and disruptions due to being a victim of a crime. Victim or witness assistance programs should be concerned with the needs of children not only because many parent witnesses will not be able to testify if they can not find childcare during a traumatizing court ordeal, but because it is the humane thing to do. An added benefit is that some children may have witnessed the crime and noticed additional identifying characteristics of the perpetrator.

The overriding objectives of victim and witness assistance programs are to assist witnesses in overcoming the anxiety and trauma associated with testifying in court, while encouraging witness cooperation in the prosecution of criminal cases. The primary objectives of these programs are:

1. Providing victims and witnesses with the message that their cooperation is essential to crime control efforts and successful criminal prosecution
2. Informing victims and witnesses of their rights to receive dignified and compassionate treatment by criminal justice authorities
3. Providing information to witnesses on the court process, the scheduling of the case, the trial, and the disposition
4. Providing orientation to court and tips on how best to recall accurately the crime scene and testify.

*Victim-Service Programs.* Victim-service or crisis intervention programs for crime victims are not as common as victim and witness assistance programs. This type of program is usually lodged in a police department, sheriff's office, hospital, probation department, or nonprofit social service agency. Typically, these programs attempt to intervene within the first twenty-four hours after the victimization to provide a comprehensive range of essential services for crime victims. Most victim-service programs maintain twenty-four-hour mobile response teams to aid crime victims. They offer crisis intervention at the crime scene, the hospital, or the local battered women's shelter. Other services include help in completing victim compensation applications; emergency financial assistance; transportation (to court, a battered women's shelter, a hosptial, or the victim assistance program office); repairing or replacing broken locks and windows; assistance in replacing lost documents (e.g., birth certificates, marriage licenses, wills); and referrals to community mental health centers and social service agencies for extended counseling and short-term treatment.

Violent crime leaves its victims with psychological consequences that include not only fear and distress but also a tarnished view of the world, distorted by negative cognitions and irrational beliefs. Recovery for the victim of violent crime depends largely on building on inner strengths and developing positive coping skills; it involves a process of "coming to terms with . . . shattered assumptions and reestablishing a conceptual system that will allow victims to once again function effectively" (Janof-Bulman 1992, p. 22). Further research is needed to determine which programs are most effective with which type of crime victims in facilitating recovery, allaying fears of further victimization, and lowering stress and acute crisis reactions. But a major step in this direction came in May 1998, when U.S. Attorney General Janet Reno and the federal Office of Crime Victims released a comprehensive report titled *New Directions from the Field*, which surveyed the government's progress in fulfilling recommendations set forth in the 1982 report from the Reagan task force on victims of crime. The 1998 volume issued more than 250 new recommendations to set the agenda for expanding victim rights, victim advocacy, and victim services for the twenty-first century.

*BIBLIOGRAPHY*

Brownell, Patricia J. "Domestic Violence in the Workplace: An Emergent Issue." *Crisis Intervention and Time-Limited Treatment* 3, no. 2 (1996).

Bureau of Justice Statistics. *Criminal Victimization in the U.S.: 1973–1992 Trends.* Washington, D.C.: U.S. Department of Justice, 1994.

———. *National Crime Victimization Survey: Changes in Criminal Victimization, 1994–1995.* Washington, D.C.: U.S. Department of Justice, 1997.

———. *National Crime Victimization Survey: Criminal Victimization in the U.S., 1990: A National Crime Victimization Report.* Washington, D.C.: U.S. Department of Justice, 1992.

———. *Sourcebook of Criminal Justice Statistics 1992.* Washington, D.C.: U.S. Department of Justice, 1993.

———. *Sourcebook of Criminal Justice Statistics 1996.* Washington, D.C.: U.S. Department of Justice, 1997.

Dobrin, Adam, et al. *Statistical Handbook on Violence in America.* Phoenix, Ariz.: Oryx, 1996.

Janoff-Bulman, Ronnie. *Shattered Assumptions: Towards a New Psychology of Trauma.* New York: Free Press, 1992.

Miller, Ted R., Mark A. Cohen, and Brian Wiersema. *Victim Costs and Consequences: A New Look.* Washington, D.C.: National Institute of Justice, 1996.

Perkins, C., and P. Klaus. "Criminal Victimization 1994." *Bureau of Justice Statistics Bulletin.* Washington, D.C.: U.S. Department of Justice, 1996.

Rand, Michael R., James P. Lynch, and David Cantor. *National Crime Victimization Survey: Criminal Victimization, 1973–1995.* Washington, D.C.: U.S. Department of Justice, Bureau of Justice Statistics, 1997.

Roberts, Albert R. *Battered Women and Their Families: Intervention Strategies and Treatment Programs.* 2d ed. New York: Springer, 1998.

———. *Helping Crime Victims: Research, Policy, and Practice.* Thousand Oaks, Calif.: Sage, 1990.

———. "Myths and Realities Regarding Battered Women." In his *Helping Battered Women: New Perspectives and Remedies.* New York: Oxford University Press, 1996.

———. "The Role of the Social Worker in Victim/Witness Assistance Prorgams." In *Social Work in Juvenile and Criminal Justice Settings,* edited by Albert R. Roberts. Springfield, Ill.: Charles C. Thomas, 1997.

Roberts, Albert R., and Beverly J. Roberts. "A Model for Crisis Intervention with Battered Women and Their Children." In *Crisis Intervention Handbook: Assessment, Treatment, and Research,* 2d ed., edited by Albert R. Roberts. New York: Oxford University Press, 1999.

Roth, Jeffrey. *Firearms and Violence.* Washington, D.C.: U.S. Department of Justice, 1994.

Wallace, Harvey. *Victimology: Legal, Psychological, and Social Perspectives.* Boston: Allyn and Bacon, 1998.

Zawitz, Marianne W., et al. *Highlights from Twenty Years of Surveying Crime Victims: The National Crime Victimization Survey, 1973–1992.* Washington, D.C.: Bureau of Justice Statistics, U.S. Department of Justice, 1993.

ALBERT R. ROBERTS

*See also* **Costs of Violent Crime; Domestic Violence; Folk Narratives: New York City Crime-Victim Stories; Medicine and Violence; National Crime Victimization Survey; Post-Traumatic Stress Disorder; Prevention: Violent-Crime Prevention; Rape; Urban Violence; Women: Overview.**

## SOCIAL SUFFERING

Late-twentieth-century social science straddled two trends in the study of violence. As a new geography of political violence emerged in the world, partly as a result of the rebirth of genocide in parts of Africa and Central Europe, complex issues about aesthetic, moral, and political representation came to the fore. The former Yugoslavian republics of Bosnia-Herzegovina and Croatia, as well as Serbia (and Kosovo), Sri Lanka, Cambodia, and Rwanda loomed large in the popular imagination as places caught within a spiral of violence. Such specters of violence were accompanied by questions about the loss of the "human." There was a tendency to use stereotypes designating "civilized" and "savage" spaces, both in the media and in discussions of international relations.

A counterpoint to this was a focus on violence as embedded in the "normal" social practices of society. Some scholars have suggested that it is the way violence is normalized and naturalized in the minutia of social life that accounts for the fact that individuals do not speak up against the more spectacular violences when these occur. Taken together, these two strands challenge us to conceptualize the continuity between "everyday violence" and more explicit political terror. The concept of social suffering seems particularly apt in bridging this distinction between the two kinds of violence.

*Social suffering* refers to an assemblage of human problems that have their origin and consequence in the devastating injuries that social force can inflict on human experience. While much of the literature on suffering defines it as an *individual* experience, albeit one that is embedded in social life, the concept of social suffering recognizes that suffering is produced and distributed by societal institutions as much as by exigencies of life implicated in the human condition. Violence creates social exclusions, reifies people, and often strips victims of the cultural resources to represent and ameliorate their suffering. To understand the complex interconnections between violence and social suffering, one must first look at the social logic of space. Questions on how representations of violence and suffering circulate among the aesthetic, moral, and political values of a society can then be considered in the light of the global media and the shaping of collective experience through images and text.

## Space, Boundaries, and Everyday Life

Just as the new political geography of the world divides spaces in which violent conflicts and ethnic cleansing have occurred from the more "safe" areas of the world, a language of zoning, seen in such terms as *inner city* in the literature on urban poverty, is pervasive in North America. The processes set in motion after World War II and the massive migration of African Americans into northern and midwestern cities created zones of poverty in which race, urban violence, and crime came to be configured as normal. Ethnographic work in some of these areas suggests that violence in the inner cities is deeply embedded in the processes of illicit activities such as the drug trade. The more dramatic acts of violence in these spaces make it to the headlines of metropolitan newspapers and are widely disseminated by the electronic media. The demographic trends in violent crime in North America show the increase in black intraracial violence. Dramatic events of violence must be understood, however, in relation to what happens routinely, uneventfully, and repeatedly in the everyday life of these places.

From the perspective of the residents in these zones, the conflation of poverty and race overdetermines the character of these spaces. First, the African Americans living in inner cities do not command the material and symbolic capital, such as assets, work experience, and education, or even the correct body language, necessary to move into the formal economy and hence they develop important stakes in the underground economy, especially the illegal drug trade. Second, the marking of these spaces as violent predisposes societal institutions such as the police, the schools, and the courts of law to withdraw except for purposes of "keeping the order." The ecology of fear blights the lives of those who are caught between the everyday violence of the ghetto and the institutional practices of the state. The constant presence of death affects not only the perpetrators and the victims but also those who as witnesses become marked by the social logic of these spaces. Without a sense of the unremitting engagement with violence there—learning how to avoid being recruited in gangs, learning how to avoid the police, learning how not to be in the wrong place at the wrong time—it would be difficult to understand the social suffering produced.

There is an obsession in the Western tradition with the question of the communicability of pain. From the perspective of social suffering, the issue is not whether pain can be represented or not, but rather what kind of genres of representation are available in a society through which suffering can be given recognition or denied such recognition. The development of the global media has made people in American society much more aware of the violent and catastrophic events taking place in other parts of the world. The camera increasingly brings scenes of violence into the homes of the relatively affluent. Images of disaster circulate widely, connecting not only distant spaces but also, through analogy, different kinds of events. Icons of Nazi savagery, which stand for extreme violation and horror, are offered in newspaper accounts along with more recent examples of the savagery of war in Bosnia, Kosovo, or Rwanda. There is, thus, an immediate appeal to the experience of suffering but there is also a demand from the audience for ever more detail to authenticate reality. Yet this sense of authenticity is constantly destroyed by the interspersing of advertisements and editorial comments, which re-create the viewer as a *consumer* of images. This raises important questions about how suffering is authorized in the contemporary world.

## Retrieval of Voice

What is at stake for the survivor of violence, as distinct from the consumer of images of violence created through the media? Studies suggest that experiences of suffering are structured by local narrative styles and are distinctive cultural productions. The choke and sting of experience only becomes real—is only heard—when it is narrativized. Experience moves from inchoate social and psychological processes to definable, even memorable, cultural representations through its evocation or realization in stories. But stories, like other social phenomena, are not simply individual productions. They are shaped by the cultural genres, by the subtle workings of power that authorizes some ways of telling and silences others, and the spaces within which stories may be told or heard. For example, the Truth and Reconciliation Commission in South Africa created a public space in which stories of cruelty and violation against the black population during apartheid could be heard. Such creation of new publics around events of atrocity may enable victims to reclaim their suppressed voices, and sometimes out of such desperate and defeated experiences stories may emerge that call for, and even at times bring about, change that alters utterly the commonplace—at both the level of collective experience and of individual subjectivity.

At its best, the deep call of stories may create spaces for those whose experience of violence was delegitimized by powerful social forces. At its worst, when stories of violence are elicited from victims but then rearranged and appropriated by powerful agencies of the state or by commercial interests, survivors may feel doubly betrayed. This was the situation with the veterans of the Vietnam War during the Agent Orange case; the suffering of those who had gotten ill after exposure to the defoliant was elicited in the course of the trials but then subtly denied. Similar experiences have been recorded in the case of women subjected to violence in the intimacy of domestic space. This shows that not only the infliction of violence but its recognition is part of contested domains—the very mechanisms of amelioration through courts of law or service bureaucracies may contribute to the social suffering of the victims.

While courts of law, public commissions, and the media provide ways of constructing different kinds of publics for the articulation of violence and social suffering, communities blighted by violence often evolve their own local mechanisms of articulation. It is often in the "work" performed away from public eyes —in families, schools, places of worship, neighborhoods—that the stereotypical conventions through which grief is addressed are transcended and recognition given to the pain created through both spectacular acts of violence and the routinization of violence. What one may expect from such everyday acts of engagement with suffering is not some miraculous process of healing but simply the capacity for survivors to engage the future. Indeed, the events of the twentieth century alert us more to the recalcitrance of tragedy than to the diminishment of social suffering.

*BIBLIOGRAPHY*

Bourgois, Phillippe. *In Search of Respect: Selling Crack in El Barrio.* London: Cambridge University Press, 1995.

Das, Veena, Arthur Kleinman, et al. *Violence and Subjectivity.* Berkeley: University of California Press, 1999.

Devine, John. *Maximum Security: The Culture of Violence in Inner City Schools.* Chicago: University of Chicago Press, 1989.

Kleinman, Arthur, Veena Das, and Margaret Lock. *Social Suffering.* Berkeley: University of California Press, 1997.

Kleinman, Arthur, and Joan Kleinman. "The Appeal of Experience; the Dismay of Images: Cultural Appropriations of Suffering in Our Time." *Daedalus* 125, no. 1 (1996).

Minow, Martha. *Between Vengeance and Forgiveness: Facing History After Genocide and Mass Violence.* Boston: Beacon Press, 1998.

Morris, David. "About Suffering: Voice, Genre, and Moral Community." *Daedalus* 125, no. 1 (1996).

Scheper-Hughes, Nancy. "Peace-time Crimes." *Social Identities* 3, no. 3 (1997).

Schuck, Peter. *Agent Orange on Trial: Mass Toxic Disasters in the Court.* Cambridge, Mass.: Harvard University Press, 1987.

VEENA DAS

*See also* **Costs of Violent Crime; Representation of Violence.**

# VIDEO GAMES

Video games are a pervasive phenomenon in contemporary U.S. culture. The game industry made $6.1 billion from software alone in 1998, a 20 percent increase over the year before. There have been concerns raised over levels of violence in video games, especially given the influence that these games may have on children.

The term *video games* includes many different formats and genres: there are coin-operated arcade games, home console units (like Nintendo's Super NES), home computer games, and games played over the Internet. The games' contents vary widely: there are sports games, fighting games, puzzle games, simulations, and so on. Not all video games are violent; the Entertainment Software Rating Board, a trade organization, had given an *E* rating (suitable for all audiences) to 70 percent of the five thousand games it had rated as of 1998. Violence appears in many different forms in the games: there are war games where the player has a general's abstract view of combat, and there are others where from a first-person perspective the player shoots, punches, and chainsaws realistic opponents.

For the most part, the concerns about violence raised by video games are the same as those raised by other forms of popular media, such as television or movies. There is a particular concern about video games, however, because instead of passively observing violence, the player actively takes on the role of a violent agent. Research in this area is inconclusive. Studies have shown that children who play violent video games are more likely to be aggressive than their peers, but causation has not yet been demonstrated. It has also been suggested that playing video games (the proper kinds in the proper amounts) can have beneficial effects such as providing early exposure to computers and enhancing problem-solving skills.

## Video Game History

Violence has been a symbolic part of games since the Persians developed the original war game, chess, thousands of years back. The first game developed for a computer, *Spacewar*, created on a mainframe computer at the Massachusetts Institute of Technology in 1962, was part of a long tradition and the beginning of a new one. Video games became a big business in the 1970s, when Atari's *Pong* became a hit first as a coin-operated arcade game and then as a home console device. During the video game boom of the late 1970s, many games adopted violent themes. Both *Space Invaders* and *Missile Command* are considered classics, and both end every game with the apocalyptic destruction of the planet Earth. In the early 1980s a crisis of overproduction led the video game industry to crash, but in 1986 the Nintendo Entertainment System was introduced in the United States, which began a period of growth for the industry through the 1990s. The Internet has become both a medium and a distribution mechanism for games. Many games, both violent and nonviolent, can be played with or against other people via the Internet. Samples of games (often generous in size) can be downloaded for trial; ID Software's *Doom* was a trendsetter in this marketing strategy in the early 1990s.

In early 1994, after the release of the arcade hit *Mortal Kombat* for home play, growing concerns over game violence led to congressional hearings on developing a rating system for games. (*Mortal Kombat* is famous for its "finishing moves," in which, for instance, a defeated rival has his still-beating heart ripped from his chest and displayed.) These hearings led directly to the development of industry-regulated ratings systems. Some 90 percent of video game purchasers are over eighteen, so parents, informed by ratings, should be able to control the games their children play. While concerns about violence focus on children, little attention is paid to ultraviolent computer games like *Doom* that are often played on business computers, where they presumably would not affect impressionable children and would desensitize only corporate America.

The most pronounced trend in the industry in the 1990s was technological progress, which raised the stakes in relation to violence; new technology permitted greater realism, which meant that the depiction of violence could become more lifelike.

## Video Games and Gender

Women and girls make up a third of game players, but video games have been seen as largely a male pursuit, both in their production and consumption. The violence in the games has roots in traditions of adolescent masculinity in America and has raised two concerns: first, that girls are missing out on the beneficial aspects of video games, such as early exposure to computers, and second, that games offer unhealthy images of women to their players. Studies have shown that many girls are put off by violent games, and the industry has slowly responded by creating games that appeal to girls' interests and styles of play, such as the hit game *Barbie Fashion Designer*. One lesson of the trend toward girls' games was the commercial viability of nonviolent action.

Critics of video games noted that a large proportion of females in games played the role of passive "damsels in distress." This changed strikingly with the advent of violent video game heroines. These video game "babes" are gorgeous women, usually with enormous breasts and tight costumes, who are every bit as dangerous and violent as their male counterparts. These characters, like Lara Croft of *Tomb Raider*, are often popular among both male and female players. Some suggest that these heroines provide assertive role models for girls and raise the consciousness of the adolescent boys who adopt their personae. It is also clear, however, that a disturbing element of violent sexual fantasy is involved.

## Combat Simulations

The early history of video games, like that of the Internet, has links to Department of Defense funding. The military has not only developed its own computer simulations but has also directly adopted commercial entertainment software for training purposes. Many simulations of jet or tank warfare boast of their fidelity to the experience of modern warfare, which itself increasingly takes on the feel of a video game. As J. C. Herz (1997) points out, "In a submarine, all information is mediated by electronics." Dave Grossman (1995) has pointed out that this convergence may be far from benign. It probably does little harm for a commuter to exorcise road rage by indulging the fantasy of driving a tank through the desert. Games like *Lethal Enforcer*, however, have a gun as their controller. The player points and pulls the trigger to kill terrorists and criminals. The character loses a health point when an innocent bystander is killed. The U.S. Army uses similar conditioning under closely controlled conditions to overcome recruits' inhibitions about killing. Most Americans have no access to M-1 tanks or jet fighters, but guns are notoriously common in America, and such games release inhibitions about their use without instilling much in the way of discipline.

*BIBLIOGRAPHY*

Alloway, Nola, and Pam Gilbert. "Video Game Culture: Playing with Masculinity, Violence, and Pleasure." In *Wired-Up: Young People and the Electronic Media,* edited by Sue Howard. London: UCL Press, 1998.

Cassell, Justine, and Henry Jenkins, eds. *From Barbie to Mortal Kombat: Gender and Computer Games.* Cambridge, Mass.: MIT Press, 1998.

Cohen, Scott. *Zap: The Rise and Fall of Atari.* New York: McGraw Hill, 1984.

Grossman, Dave. "B. F. Skinner's Rats and Operant Conditioning at the Video Arcade." In *On Killing: The Psychological Cost of Learning to Kill in War and Society.* New York: Little, Brown, 1995.

Gunter, Barrie. *The Effects of Video Games on Children: The Myth Unmasked.* Sheffield, U.K.: Sheffield Academic Press, 1998.

Herz, J. C. *Joystick Nation: How Videogames Ate Our Quarters, Won Our Hearts, and Rewired Our Minds.* New York: Little, Brown, 1997.

Kinder, Marsha. *Playing with Power in Movies, Television, and Video Games: From Muppet Babies to Teenage Mutant Ninja Turtles.* Berkeley: University of California Press, 1991.

Provenso, Eugene F., Jr. *Video Kids: Making Sense of Nintendo.* Cambridge, Mass.: Harvard University Press, 1991.

Traiman, Steve. "Multimedia Roundup: Software Firms Gear Up for a Smash Follow-up to 'the Biggest Year Ever.' " *Billboard,* 20 February 1999.

U.S. Senate Subcommittee on Juvenile Justice and Subcommittee on Regulation and Government Information. *Rating Video Games: A Parent's Guide to Games.* Washington, D.C.: U.S. Government Printing Office, 1995.

BRIAN ZIMMERMAN

*See also* **Popular Culture; Spectacle, Violence as; Television: Children's Television; Toys and Games.**

# VIETNAMESE AMERICANS

At the time of the collapse of the American-supported Republic of Vietnam in 1975, there were very few Vietnamese in the United States. But with the arrival of nearly 130,000 that year and many more in subsequent years, the Vietnamese rapidly became one of the largest populations of Asian origin in the United States. Most came as formally designated refugees, although many have also arrived as regular immigrants, largely through family-reunification provisions of U.S. immigration law or through the special provisions of the Amerasian Homecoming Act of 1987. By 1999 close to a million people from Vietnam had arrived in the United States. They were initially scattered across the country but soon developed particularly strong representation on the West Coast and in Texas, such East Coast cities as Boston, New York, Philadelphia, and Washington, D.C., and—in an unusual pattern for Asian immigrants—New Orleans.

For the relatively well-educated Vietnamese immigrants, the American promise has been a real one, especially for their children. For others, however—especially those with limited education or those suffering from the trauma of broken family ties—the experience has been more problematic. Amerasian children in particular often face special developmental difficulties, both emotional (e.g., sharp racial discrimination in both Vietnam and the United States) and practical (e.g., lack of schooling in Vietnam and living in single-parent households or foster homes in the United States). Much of the violence that penetrates the lives of Vietnamese in America arises from those disadvantages, from the stresses of adaptation to a new culture, and from the psychological and political scars of decades of war.

## A Trail of Violence from the Vietnam War

Vietnamese refugees lived through a generation of violence in a war that inflicted widespread losses on civilians as well as active combatants. Many of these Vietnamese have been personally brutalized by the war, their lives twisted, families fractured, futures lost; many had already been transplanted within Vietnam only to be later driven to foreign countries of which they have had little experience, faced with monumental tasks: reweaving a coherent identity after years in reeducation camps; returning to normal life after the assaults, rapes, and killings they endured during escape; or re-creating the structure and feeling of traditional extended families when members have died or disappeared.

These refugees must also contend with spasms of war-related violence in America. Political feelings, for example, run very high in the Vietnamese community, and the accusation of leftist leanings can be devastating. The threat is real: offices have been bombed and people occasionally killed because of political conflicts transposed to the United States. Even in 1999, a picture of Ho Chi Minh and a North Vietnamese flag in the window of a Vietnamese video store in Westminster, California, were enough to incite two months of large demonstrations by the Vietnamese community. Although the demonstrations were relatively peaceful, there were physical assaults on the store owner, Truong Van Tran, and numerous arrests for disorderly conduct. This political acrimony is not confined to the Vietnamese. Americans' anger and confusion about the Vietnam War occasionally erupts in violent form: for example, the 1977 kidnapping, interrogation, rape, and murder of Le My Hanh, a young Vietnamese woman, in New York by Louis Kahan, an American veteran who mistook her as one of the "enemy." That the most notorious New York Vietnamese gang took its name —Born to Kill—from the words on the helmets of American soldiers in Vietnam is another sharp reminder of the ties of violence that bind Vietnamese and Americans together.

## Violence and Gangs

One pervasive aspect of violence for Vietnamese in America involves criminal behavior within the ethnic community. Of particular importance are gangs. Vietnamese gangs are typically flexible and mobile, less concerned with turf and the attendant drug selling and more preoccupied with burglary and robbery. In the gangs' familial hierarchy the more established members act as older brothers, and the group as a whole offers practical and emotional support to members. The gangs recruit heavily from those refugees who came to the United States in their teens, lacked family stateside, and faced language barriers in school. According to some analysts, the growth of gangs stems from the Vietnamese ethnic community's emphasis on success, which drives the less successful to drop out of the system. The histories of gang members, however—particularly their lack of direct kin and consequent moves among foster homes in poor neighborhoods—suggest that although the structure of the gangs may be attributable to specifically Vietnamese cultural factors,

recruitment might simply thrive on some youths' insecure living arrangements.

The victims of gangs are usually other Vietnamese. Small, easily identified operations with little formal security, Vietnamese businesses are tempting targets for extortion and robbery. Furthermore, the owners can usually be traced from their businesses to their homes and subjected to the frequent centerpiece of ethnic Vietnamese crime: "home-invasion" robbery, a tactic based on the assumption that here, as in Vietnam, people keep large amounts of cash in their homes. By invading a home and threatening violent assault, the gang seeks to extract the location of that money. Hauls of $10,000 to $20,000 have been reported. Finally, the threat of retribution by a violent gang, mistrust of the police, and difficulties in communicating with authorities often combine to discourage victims from reporting such crimes.

## At Risk in America

Violence can also impinge on Vietnamese from outside their communities. Sometimes that violence has resulted from Vietnamese intrusion into neighborhoods or economic niches occupied by other groups. Vietnamese fishermen on the Pacific and Gulf Coasts, for example, initially faced hostility when their unauthorized nets and extended working hours cut into the livelihood of the existing fishing communities. Those who are in marginal economic circumstances and live in crime-prone neighborhoods might be seen as less likely to resist and report a crime or identify the criminals. Such risks of violence may have a specifically anti-Asian component. Reports by the U.S. Commission on Civil Rights have noted the problems of bigotry and violence faced by Asian Americans, whether because of racial prejudice, misplaced anger over past wars or over current economic competition, or stereotypes about Asians in America. The brutal California killing of a young Vietnamese man in early 1996 was a gruesome example. Thien Minh Ly, a graduate of the University of California at Los Angeles who had recently completed an M.A. at Georgetown University, was rollerblading in his hometown of Tustin, California, when he was attacked by Gunner Lindberg and Dominic Christopher. Lindberg's subsequent letter to a friend noted—in excruciating detail—how he had "killed a jap a while ago." Although some doubted that racism motivated this slaying, others saw an especially brutal instance of anti-Asian prejudice. For Vietnamese, survivors of the violence

377

of war and the escape from it, this new anonymous violence and the violence of gangs within their own community are particularly bleak sides of life in their land of refuge.

BIBLIOGRAPHY

Ahrin, Mishan, and Nick Rothenberg. *Bui Doi: Life Like Dust.* 16 mm, 29 min. San Francisco: Urban Nomad Productions. 1994.

DeVoe, Pamela A. "Crime and Safety Among Vietnamese Business People." In *Beyond Boundaries: Selected Papers on Refugees and Immigrants.* Vol. 5, edited by Diane Baxter and Ruth Krulfeld. Arlington, Va.: American Anthropological Association's Committee on Refugees and Immigrants, 1997.

English, T. J. *Born to Kill: The Rise and Fall of America's Bloodiest Asian Gang.* New York: Avon, 1995.

Hung, Nguyen Manh, and David W. Haines. "Vietnamese." In *Refugees in America in the 1990s: A Reference Handbook,* edited by David W. Haines. Westport, Conn.: Greenwood, 1996.

Long, Patrick Du Phuoc, with Laura Ricard. *The Dream Shattered: Vietnamese Gangs in America.* Boston: Northeastern University Press, 1996.

Smith, Michael Peter, and Bernadette Tarallo. "Who Are the 'Good Guys'? The Social Construction of the Vietnamese 'Other.'" In *The Bubbling Cauldron: Race, Ethnicity, and the Urban Crisis,* edited by Michael P. Smith and Joe R. Feagin. Minneapolis: University of Minnesota Press, 1995.

Vigil, James Diego, and Steve Chong Yun. "Vietnamese Youth Gangs in Southern California." In *Gangs in America,* edited by C. Ronald Huff. Newbury Park, Calif.: Sage, 1990.

DAVID W. HAINES

*See also* **Asians; Gangs; Immigration.**

# VIETNAM WAR

Until the Vietnam era Americans generally took violence in wartime for granted. As U.S. involvement in Vietnam grew, a great national debate arose not only over the wisdom of intervention but also over the nature of the war itself. As scenes of killing and destruction entered American homes nightly via television, the character of violence in warfare came under closer scrutiny than ever before.

Vietnam was a different kind of war. To the Vietnamese people, it was a long-term war for national liberation, full of anguish and sacrifice. Millions had died during the French and Japanese occupations of Vietnam, so by the time the United States took over the war in the early 1960s to prevent a nationalist-communist victory, the Vietnamese were accustomed to suffering on a mass scale. Over the course of the next decade, however, until the 1973 U.S. withdrawal and the 1975 victory of the Vietnamese communists, many millions more would die, and Vietnam and the neighboring countries of Laos and Cambodia would be invaded and bombed at levels unparalleled in the history of modern warfare.

The U.S. military was not well prepared for Vietnam. The enemy—variously called the Viet Minh, Viet Cong (VC), or National Liberation Front (NLF)—consisted of nationalist and communist Vietnamese waging a guerrilla war in the southern half of the country to overthrow the U.S.-sponsored regime and reunify the nation. The Geneva convention of 1954 had divided Vietnam at the seventeenth parallel into the communist north and the noncommunist south. The insurgents, by all accounts more popular among the Vietnamese people than the American-sponsored southern regime, used intimidation and assassination of civilian officials but especially excelled in political indoctrination as they fought a "people's war." The U.S. military, trained to fight conventional wars, had vowed to learn counterinsurgency tactics to win the "hearts and minds" of the Vietnamese by providing village security and economic development.

The Americans, however, despite spending over $200 billion in Vietnam, could not master that approach and began to fight as they knew best, with massive firepower and air strikes. U.S. troops and their Vietnamese allies could not compete politically with the NLF and realized that, as one officer explained, "the defeat of insurgencies historically takes years"; instead they set out to destroy the VC and end the war quickly. In 1962 General Paul D. Harkins, head of the Military Assistance Command, Vietnam, believing that technological superiority and especially air support could crush the insurgency, began an aggressive war. The White House ordered deployment of army helicopter companies, fixed-wing aircraft, reconnaissance planes, equipment and chemicals for crop defoliation, and minesweepers and authorized the use of napalm, an incendiary gel that seared human flesh and anything else it touched. Later, Harkins would add cluster bombs, which exploded in midair and released hundreds of "baby" bombs, to the arsenal.

**A South Vietnamese man grieves over his eight-year-old daughter, slain by Viet Cong guerrillas in 1964.** LIBRARY OF CONGRESS

The introduction of such weapons provided short-term benefits, but ultimately the tactics backfired. American military officers repeatedly pointed out that the "lavish" use of artillery, air power, and herbicides was harming and alienating the very people the United States was supposed to help. Instead of "surgically" eliminating the VC, American pilots were indiscriminately bombing peasant hamlets and brutalizing local inhabitants. The allied military force, the Army of the Republic of Vietnam (ARVN) in the south, would likewise capture and shoot anyone left in a burned-out village on grounds of being "suspected VC." Although harsh with senior citizens and children, the ARVN, as U.S. General Edward Rowny observed, "do not really want to tangle with the enemy." Thus violence against civilians grew, and such patterns continued throughout 1963 and 1964. The escalating firepower and growing destruction was not altering the conflict, however, and by early 1965 the NLF was on the verge of victory. President Lyndon B. Johnson that year took decisive steps to further expand the war and ultimately determined the violent nature of the conflict for the remainder of the fighting. These developments are quite clear in several areas especially: the war on the ground, the air war, chemical warfare, and massacres and brutalities directed against civilians.

**Ground War**

Though the country of Vietnam—with its dense jungles and mostly rural population—was particularly well suited for the guerrilla war that the insurgents were fighting, U.S. military commanders tried to wage a conventional war as American forces had in World War II and Korea. Thus, despite lip service to the "hearts and minds" approach, American officers settled on a strategy of attrition, using their huge advantage in weaponry to erode the enemy to the point that southern recruiting and northern replacements could not compensate for their losses. When the "crossover point"—more enemy losses than recruits and replacements—was reached, U.S. success would be imminent.

Attrition, therefore, required massive doses of firepower, often, if not usually, wielded against rural Vietnamese in an indiscriminate manner.

Because it was so difficult to determine which villagers were supporting the Viet Cong and which were neutral or progovernment, American forces often swept through areas and destroyed or burned down entire villages. The U.S. army established "free-fire zones" and conducted "search and destroy" missions in which American firepower might be launched against any Vietnamese or any hamlet in the area. In late 1966–early 1967, for instance, U.S. forces, during Operations Attleboro, Cedar Falls, and Junction City, cleared the "Iron Triangle" area outside Saigon with a "hammer and anvil" tactic, with American units at one end of the war zone driving the enemy toward other U.S. units on the other edge of the battlefield. The resulting destruction, about one thousand enemy killed and a huge complex of tunnels destroyed, had no long-term impact, however. Before the operations, U.S. forces had to clear civilians out of the war zone; then they began attacking any Vietnamese left in the area. By displacing and attacking civilians and soldiers alike, the Americans alienated the very people they were claiming to help, and within six months the enemy returned in full strength, with even more support from the local population. Throughout the war, such patterns—heavy enemy losses but with a corresponding number of strikes against civilians—were always evident and were not only destructive but counterproductive as well.

## Air War

The U.S. Air Force had begun operations in Indochina in 1962, at first spraying defoliants to eliminate the VC's jungle cover, offering air support to the ARVN, and bombing villages to root out suspected enemy strongholds. Those efforts showed few results, however, and in 1965 President Johnson authorized Operation Rolling Thunder, which would become the most sustained air attack in the history of warfare. Johnson's successor, Richard Nixon, would expand that bombing, conducting a massive air campaign against northern Vietnam, Cambodia, and Laos. By 1972 the United States had flown more sorties and dropped more bombs in Vietnam than had all sides combined in World War II.

The air war was waged on both sides of the seventeenth parallel. In the north the U.S. military hoped to destroy the transportation and industrial sectors while also reducing the popular will to fight; in the south U.S. officials sought to thwart infiltration from the north and to attack concentrations of enemy troops. By mid-1965, then, U.S. pilots had flown more than 55,000 sorties against the north and dropped more than 30,000 tons of bombs; a year later those figures rose to 148,000 sorties and 128,000 tons. By late 1966 the United States had also destroyed over 70 percent of northern Vietnam's petroleum-oil-lubricants facilities, and even General Earle Wheeler, chairman of the Joint Chiefs of Staff, conceded that there were no other "major military targets" left. Yet the air war continued and grew. The United States had introduced B-52 bombers into Vietnam in 1965, ushering in a new era in airborne destruction. A single bomber carried more than thirty tons of explosives, and a single mission of six planes could entirely saturate an area of two square miles per sortie.

The destruction was not confined to Vietnam. Between 1964 and 1969, B-52 pilots dropped over 150,000 tons of bombs on the Plain of Jars in Laos alone. In March 1969 Nixon initiated Operation Menu, a full-scale air attack on Cambodia in which tens of thousands of sorties and hundreds of thousands of tons of bombs would not only destroy the countryside but also undermine the Cambodian political landscape and facilitate the rise of the genocidal Khmer Rouge regime.

Vietnam got its share as well. In 1972, in Operation Linebacker, Nixon authorized a nonstop B-52 barrage above the seventeenth parallel, continuing for seven months and tallying 42,000 sorties and more than 150,000 tons of bombs. In December Nixon unleashed Linebacker II, or the so-called Christmas Bombings. Described by one White House aide as "calculated barbarism," U.S. pilots flew about 2,000 sorties and dropped over 40,000 tons of bombs in a ten-day period, hitting virtually every military and communications target in the north, as well as docks, shipyards, neighborhoods, and the biggest hospital in Hanoi. In some places, the B-52s left craters fifty feet in diameter.

All told, the violence of the air war was massive, and one-sided, considering that the north had no effective air force of its own, though the North Vietnamese did damage or destroy thousands of American aircraft via attacks on U.S. bases or the effective use of anti-aircraft weapons. By 1973 the United States had dropped 4.6 million tons of bombs on Vietnam and another 2 million on Cambodia and Laos, destroying about 60 percent of southern Vietnamese hamlets and millions of acres of farmlands and forests, while creating twenty-five million bomb craters and leaving untold

**Children flee accidental napalm bombing by South Vietnamese planes. Tang Bang, South Vietnam, 8 June 1972.** UPI/CORBIS-BETTMANN

amounts of unexploded ordnance that still killed about a thousand Vietnamese per year in the 1990s. A large percentage of the total casualties—about two million Vietnamese (some two-thirds of them above the seventeenth parallel) and three hundred thousand Cambodians and Laotians—died as a result of air strikes.

## Chemical Warfare

President John F. Kennedy, over the objections of military officers, authorized the air force to drop defoliants over southern Vietnam to eliminate the jungle cover used by the VC and destroy crops that might be feeding the enemy. Originally named Operation Hades but renamed Operation Ranch Hand for public relations reasons, the defoliation campaign would bring new forms of "ecocide" to Vietnam. The Air Force, using C-123s outfitted with thousand-gallon tanks and spray nozzles, could saturate a three-hundred-acre area in four minutes, and within weeks all plants, shrubs, grasses, and trees would be dead. In 1967 alone, the Air Force defoliated 1.5 million acres of southern land, and for the entire war dropped about twenty million gallons of chemicals over untold millions of acres of southern Vietnam, contaminating about 1.5 million people in the process.

"Only You Can Prevent Forests" became the motto of those pilots involved in Ranch Hand.

Among the defoliants used, Agent Orange (2,4,5-T), a toxic herbicide containing dioxin, a known carcinogen, was the most infamous. In 1970, however, the U.S. Department of Defense suspended the use of Agent Orange amid numerous reports of birth defects in children whose mothers were exposed to the herbicide. Investigative reporters later discovered that 90 percent of the defoliation program in Vietnam consisted of 2,4,5-T. Accordingly, many American veterans of the war began to report unusual cancers and high rates of birth defects in their own children. In perhaps the most publicized case, the son of Admiral Elmo Zumwalt, Jr., Elmo Zumwalt III, died of cancer, quite possibly from his exposure to dioxins sprayed under his father's command. Thousands of veterans in fact filed a class-action lawsuit against the Veterans Administration and Dow Chemical, maker of Agent Orange; it was settled out of court in 1985.

Another major element in America's chemical war on Vietnam was napalm, a jellied gasoline that both incinerated dwellings and stuck to and burned deeply into human flesh. General Harkins believed in 1962 that the introduction of napalm had made a huge difference; it "really puts the fear of God into the Viet Cong," he boasted, "and that is what counts." Napalm eventually accounted for almost 10 percent of the annual bomb tonnage in Vietnam, with a total of four hundred thousand tons dropped for the entire war. Despite claims by U.S. and southern Vietnamese officials that cases of napalm injuries and deaths were negligible, independent observers touring Vietnamese hospitals found otherwise. They discovered significant numbers of victims and were told that most people struck by napalm died on the spot or before treatment was available. Indeed, one of the more compelling and enduring images of the war was a photo of a young girl running naked on a country road, having torn off her clothes after they were spattered by napalm.

## Civilian Victims

The Vietnam War was marked by atrocities committed against civilians on a vast scale. The NLF, per its concept of "revolutionary morality," used coercion and violence against civilians and officials loyal to the southern regime, referred to as "local tyrants." The southern Vietnamese did the same, on an even larger scale. During the years of the notorious Ngo Dinh Diem regime, perhaps one hundred thousand "suspected" communists or other political dissidents were executed and many more jailed. Once the Americans entered the war in earnest, those levels of violence against noncombatants grew. To be sure, the greatest number of civilian casualties resulted from the extraordinary U.S. air war, while untold others were caused by the often-indiscriminate use of artillery during so-called search-and-destroy operations; but massacre on a more personal level occurred as well.

Atrocities at My Lai, where five hundred unarmed women and children were killed by American soldiers led by William Calley, and at Hue, where hundreds of southern loyalists were killed and buried in mass graves by NLF supporters, were well publicized, but such incidents were not isolated. American officials filled the media with tales of NLF atrocities, but the Vietnamese insurgents, given the nature of a people's war and their political appeal, did not use violence against the local population as a primary weapon. The Americans, however, were poorly trained in guerrilla warfare and trying to engage an elusive enemy on unfamiliar terrain, so frustrated soldiers often lashed out against their putative allies. Indeed, a group of Vietnam veterans, upon returning to the United States, began to expose many of the atrocities committed during the war. In 1971 the "Winter Soldier Investigation" consisted of hundreds of veterans confessing to acts they had seen or com-

**U.S. Marines in Hue after Viet Cong seized two-thirds of the ancient imperial capital during the Tet Offensive.** UPI/CORBIS-BETTMANN

mitted, including torture, rape, and the random killing of noncombatants. Senator Mark Hatfield entered the soldiers' testimonies into the *Congressional Record* while the philosopher Bertrand Russell and Representative Ron Dellums, among others, held public hearings on "war crimes" in Vietnam. The Winter Soldiers, who had a special credibility because of their experience in the war, had to be taken seriously and, despite government attempts to discredit them, attracted a good deal of media attention. As they pointed out, the vast percentage of Vietnamese deaths were civilians. Americans, it seemed, were destroying Vietnam in order to save it.

Vietnam dramatically changed the way the American people thought of violence in wartime. Images of marines burning down a hamlet, a napalm-burned girl running down the road, mass graves, B-52 attacks, and bombed-out villages brought the war home on an immediate and personal level. Untold numbers of Americans joined the antiwar movement because of their revulsion at the violence committed by the U.S. military in Indochina. Vietnam, most agreed, was not "the good war," and in the late 1990s a majority of Americans still believed, according to public opinion polls, that the war was not only a mistake but was "morally wrong."

*BIBLIOGRAPHY*

Buzzanco, Robert. *Masters of War: Military Dissent and Politics in the Vietnam Era.* New York: Cambridge University Press, 1996.

——. *Vietnam and the Transformation of American Life.* Boston: Blackwell, 1999.

Clodfelter, Mark. *The Limits of Air Power.* New York: Free Press, 1989.

Herring, George C. *America's Longest War.* New York: McGraw Hill, 1996.

Hersh, Seymour. *Chemical and Biological Warfare: America's Hidden Arsenal.* Indianapolis: Bobbs-Merrill, 1968.

Karnow, Stanley. *Vietnam: A History.* New York: Viking, 1991.

Kolko, Gabriel. *Anatomy of a War: Vietnam, the United States, and the Modern Historical Experience.* New York: New Press, 1994.

Littauer, Raphael, and Norman Uphoff, eds. *The Air War in Indochina.* Boston: Beacon, 1972.

Vietnam Veterans Against the War. *The Winter Soldier Investigation: An Inquiry into American War Crimes.* Boston: Beacon, 1972.

Weisberg, Barry, ed. *Ecocide in Indochina: The Ecology of War.* San Francisco: Canfield, 1970.

Wilcox, Fred. *Waiting for an Army to Die: The Tragedy of Agent Orange.* New York: Random House, 1983.

Young, Marilyn. *The Vietnam Wars, 1945–1990.* New York: HarperCollins, 1991.

ROBERT BUZZANCO

*See also* **Antiwar Protests; Guerrilla Warfare; Gulf of Tonkin Resolution; My Lai Massacre; War.**

# VIGILANTISM

The American vigilante tradition embodies organized extralegal movements that take the law into their own hands. There were vigilante precedents in Europe, but they did not coalesce to produce a tradition of vigilantism. From its inception in 1767, American vigilantism was a globally unique institution. Mainstream American vigilantism eventually spun off two distinctive versions of the tradition: the mass lynching of African Americans in the South and neovigilantism. Strictly controlled in slavery, southern blacks were seldom lynched before the Civil War. With the end of the war and the abolition of slavery, southern whites soon applied the vigilante technique to the preservation of white supremacy in a slaveless society. Starting with the actions of the Ku Klux Klan in the 1860s and 1870s, which escalated to new heights during the 1880s and 1890s, African Americans in the South were fair game for lynch law, which by 1900 was being carried out on a massive scale. The dynamic of the mass lynching of southern blacks, however, was structured by the state of white-black race relations in the former Confederate states rather than by the issue of law and order that, however skewed and distorted, was central to the mainstream of frontier and western vigilantism.

## The South Carolina Regulators

The first American vigilantes were the South Carolina Regulators, active from 1767 to 1769. In the absence of effective law enforcement in the South Carolina backcountry, the Regulators were formed to battle outlaw gangs. The gangs congregated in their own villages, where they enjoyed whatever they pilfered or plundered, and linked up with an intercolonial network of horse thieves. The gangs abducted young women to serve as paramours in their outlaw villages and raped plantation wives and daughters who were either too old, too young, or too much trouble to be carried off. When they heard of some planter or merchant flush with prosperity, they set upon him, abused his family, and tortured him until he revealed the whereabouts of his valuables.

The law-abiding folk banded together, calling themselves "regulators," to break up the outlaw villages. A two-year vigilante campaign was successful. The gangs were broken up and their leaders pursued all the way to Virginia. The idle, immoral, roguish, and troublesome were captured, received thirty-nine lashes with a whip (or in one case five hundred, accompanied by drum beating and fiddle playing), and those who were thought hopeless were banished from the area. Those deemed "reclaimable" were forced to work—an extralegal system of peonage that kept the lower people out of trouble and helped solve the back-country labor shortage. In the course of their campaign the Regulators executed or killed sixteen outlaws. The now obsolete word *regulator* was the generic term before *vigilante* displaced it in the nineteenth century.

As the South Carolina Regulators became increasingly arbitrary, brutal, and extreme, they were defied by opponents who aptly styled themselves "moderators." A truce between the Regulators and Moderators forestalled a pitched battle. Backing down, the Regulators nonetheless secured from the South Carolina colonial government a guarantee of the creation of district courts and sheriffs. With their movement a resounding success and the Moderators still a potential threat, the Regulators disbanded in 1769. The Regulators and their heirs thrived in the orderly, structured society they created by vigilante action.

**Vigilantes Coast to Coast**

Although there may have been as many as 500 local vigilante bands, one study has documented 326 in operation from 1767 to 1904, about one-third of which operated in the eastern half of the United States; the rest were formed from the 1850s to 1904 in the seventeen contiguous states of the West. Only Utah, which had been settled by the Mormons, who controlled disorder, had no vigilante movement, and Oregon and North Dakota had one each. The three leading vigilante states in the West were California, Texas, and Montana. Twenty-seven of California's forty-three vigilante movements were active during the gold rush decade of the 1850s; the nation's biggest and strongest vigilante movement was active in San Francisco in 1856. Texas had fifty-two vigilante bands, but in no state was the vigilante ethos more deeply rooted than in Montana with two huge episodes

**Seal of the California Vigilance Committee.** CORBIS/
BETTMANN

of vigilantism in the pioneer mining camps of Virginia City and Bannack from 1863–1865 and again in an 1884 sweep of eastern Montana by cattlemen vigilantes out for the blood of horse and cattle thieves.

Although western vigilantism often arose where regular law enforcement was truly weak or almost absent, it is a misconception that such was the only condition under which vigilantes rode. In all too many cases, however, the regular law enforcers did not merely tolerate vigilantes but colluded with them. In fact, vigilante movements often paralleled effective local law enforcement. The view of vigilantes was that a rebuilding of the traditional social structure and values in new frontier communities could be carried out much more effectively by vigilante action than through the routine functioning of the law. A hanging by vigilantes was a graphic warning to all potentially disruptive elements that the values of life and property would be upheld.

**The Ideology and Emotions of Vigilantism**

Headed by the leading men of rural and urban communities, vigilante groups formulated an ideology that they often expressed in a prolific body of exculpatory writings. The ideology of vigilantism had three elements:

1. Under the principle that self-preservation is the first law of nature, vigilantes justified taking the law into their own hands against

the criminal and disorderly who plagued them.

2. Well aware that taking the law into their own hands was, in effect, a revolution against the state, vigilantes pleaded in their behalf for the right of revolution, as exemplified by the War of Independence against Britain.

3. Popular sovereignty was invoked by vigilantes to place themselves above the law. In a classic statement of this belief, vigilantes in northern Indiana declared themselves to be "believers in the *doctrine of popular sovereignty*; that the people of this country are the real sovereigns, and that whenever the laws, made by those to whom they have delegated their authority, are found inadequate to their protection, it is the right of the people to take [that] protection into their own hands, and deal with [the] villains according to their just desserts" (quoted in Brown 1975, p. 117).

These Indiana vigilantes responded to a situation that was typical in the pre–Civil War Midwest and Mississippi Valley. For twenty-five years a bandit-and-blackleg community had flourished in the tamarack thickets and swamps of Noble County. The bandits and their blackleg (cardsharp) allies swore to defend each other as they robbed, murdered, gambled, burned buildings, and dealt in counterfeit money. The culprits, so the vigilantes claimed, seduced many young people of respectable families into lives of crime, debauchery, and prostitution. In 1858 the vigilantes—true to their notion of popular sovereignty—rose up and scattered the blacklegs and bandits.

The northern Indiana movement stood for vigilantes everywhere when it paraded under a banner that read, No EXPENSE TO THE COUNTY—a concise version of the economic rationale for vigilantism. From the Appalachians to the Pacific, the United States was largely underdeveloped frontier territory in which law enforcement and jail costs were often a crucial factor in county budgets. Leading local taxpayers, including vigilante chieftains and their followers, were determined to keep public expenditures low. The view that extralegal action was cheaper, quicker, and more certain than lawful justice was a favorite theme of vigilantes.

There was, however, a lot more to pioneer vigilantism than a concern for local government expenditures. Powerful emotions were expressed, for example, by a prominent spokesman for Montana vigilantes. "We entertain but one sentiment—aversion—deep, strong, and unchangeable for the low, brutal, cruel, lazy, ignorant, sensual and blasphemous miscreants that infest the frontier!" There was also the view that victims of vigilantes were less than human. In 1881 Dr. John E. Osborne, a future governor of Wyoming, attended the lynching of a brutal western outlaw, George ("Big Nose") Parrott. After the hanging Dr. Osborne skinned the corpse and tanned the skin. The preserved skin was made into various mementos, including a pair of shoes that was exhibited for years in a local bank. In like fashion a western vigilante hanging was often admired as a mark of civic virtue and sometimes commemorated by picture postcard photographs of dangling victims.

**Characteristics of Vigilantism**

Vigilante organizations varied greatly in size, from twelve to fifteen members to the six thousand to eight thousand members of the 1856 San Francisco group. Following the precedent of the South Carolina Regulators, vigilantes were typically organized in military-command fashion with constitutions, resolutions, or manifestos to which members subscribed. Like the South Carolinians, vigilantes often tried individuals but almost never found them innocent. Although these trials were mostly pro forma, they were important to the vigilantes, who, as pillars of the community, broke the law with the paradoxical aim of upholding the law. Wary of encouraging anarchy, vigilantes preserved as many of the forms of law as possible while disregarding its substance.

Stemming from the example of Colonel Charles Lynch of Virginia, whose band levied retributive violence against Tory miscreants during the American Revolution, the phrase "to lynch" meant not only the infliction of death but, even more often, corporal punishment, especially whipping. It was not until the middle of the nineteenth century that the definition of lynching was standardized as extralegal execution. From 1767 to 1909, the 326 vigilante movements took 729 lives, the vast majority of whom were white. Not to be forgotten, however, were the 3,220 African Americans lynched in the South from 1880 to 1930, as well as at least 409 southern blacks who were lynched by the Ku Klux Klan from 1868 to 1871. Ballooned by frequent vigilante executions in the West and the mass lynching of southern blacks, the total number of

Americans lynched from 1883 to 1898 easily exceeded the number of legal executions.

Of the very few women lynched in the West, one of the first was the lynching of a Spanish Mexican woman named Josefa (called "Juanita" after her death), who was tried and executed by hungover gold miners in Downieville, California, on 5 July 1851. Josefa's offense was the stabbing to death of a miner who apparently had tried to molest her. "Cattle Kate" (Ella Watson) was hanged in 1889 by a party of Wyoming cattlemen who were convinced, wrongly it appears, that Watson harbored stolen livestock.

**Eminent Americans and Vigilantism**

Local leaders as well as ambitious young men on the way up participated in vigilante movements. Some went into politics and held high office. Five served in the U.S. Senate, one was a congressman, six were state governors, and two were territorial governors. Most of these men were vigilantes in their younger days, but they never regretted or apologized for their actions, including the railroad magnate Leland Stanford, who was also a U.S. senator from and governor of California. Two presidents of the United States explicitly approved of vigilantism: Andrew Jackson and Theodore Roosevelt. President Jackson once advised Iowa settlers to solve a crime problem with vigilantism. As a young rancher in the West, Roosevelt tried mightily to join the Montana vigilante movement that turned out to be the most lethal in American history. Roosevelt was rebuffed, however, by canny vigilante leaders who feared that the loquacious young cattleman would talk too much. Always regretting that he missed the vigilante campaign, Roosevelt in private correspondence after his presidency made a favorable analogy between imperialism (important in his administration) and vigilantism, declaring that both were "very useful to mankind." Although Roosevelt was a vigorous opponent of the lynching of southern blacks, he viewed western vigilantism as a necessity of the frontier era.

Noteworthy, also, are the many distinguished late-nineteenth-century judges, lawyers, and legal scholars who admired vigilantism, including former vigilante Wilbur Fisk Sanders, who was one of the first two U. S. senators from Montana and a founding president of the Montana bar association, and the Supreme Court justice David J. Brewer.

Another ornament of the bar was Charles J. Bonaparte, an aristocratic Baltimore lawyer and patrician reformer of progressive political and economic views. In a speech to the 1890 graduating class of Yale Law School, Bonaparte praised lynch law and announced his belief that "very few innocent men are lynched." In 1906, seven years after he proposed imposing the death sentence in a third conviction for a "serious" offense, Bonaparte became attorney general in the cabinet of President Theodore Roosevelt.

**Pros and Cons**

In 1902 Owen Wister's provigilante novel *The Virginian* (1902) became a runaway best-seller, but the tide of public opinion would within thirty years turn strongly against vigilantism. By the 1930s the staunch control-of-crime doctrine that dominated both mainstream legal thought as well as vigilante attitudes in the nineteenth century was eclipsed by an increasingly strong commitment to strict due process of law. A straw in the wind was Walter Van Tilburg Clark's superb antivigilante novel *The Ox-Bow Incident* (1940), and the equally outstanding 1943 film version of the same title. Contrary to what one might expect, however, neither popular fiction nor movies made much of vigilantism. (A late exception was the series of provigilante *Death Wish* movies of the 1970s and 1980s starring Charles Bronson.)

Although critically praised authors have written much about the lynching of southern blacks, they have, aside from Clark, given only marginal attention to vigilantism. Exceptions include Mark Twain's scathing denunciation of lynch law in one chapter in *The Adventures of Huckleberry Finn* (1884), John Steinbeck's short story "The Vigilante" (1938), and William Saroyan's one-act play *Hello Out There* (1941). The antivigilante pieces by Steinbeck and Saroyan were inspired by a 1933 lynching in San Jose, California. Another notable exception to this slim record is Robert Penn Warren's novel *Night Rider* (1939)—a striking treatment of the treacherous attraction of the vigilante spirit and its insidious impact on individual character.

Even when vigilantism was at its height during the nineteenth century, there were principled opponents who had the courage to speak out. Such a critic was the Reverend William Anderson Scott, who denounced America's biggest and most powerful vigilante movement—that of San Francisco in 1856. Scott delivered a sermon calling for industrial education for the lower classes and for urban charitable institutions as a means of eradicating the root sources of crime. "You may depend upon it," warned Scott, "the stream of blood will never be [stayed] while men take the law into their own hands."

## Neovigilantism

With the waning of traditional frontier vigilantism before 1910, the institution persisted in the form of neovigilantism. The old vigilantism targeted frontier ne'er-do-wells, lower people, and desperadoes, while twentieth-century neovigilantism found its chief targets among Catholics, Jews, immigrants, African Americans, workers and labor leaders, political radicals of the left, and civil libertarians. Although cast in the mold of classic frontier vigilantism, the substance of the potent San Francisco vigilante movement of 1856 was a portent of the neovigilantism that emerged a half century later.

To a considerable extent the San Francisco vigilante episode represented a struggle for power between two opposing religious, class, and ethnic blocs. The vigilante leadership of upper- and middle-class, old American, and Protestant merchants was aligned against a political faction supported by lower-class Irish-Catholic workers. The significance of the San Francisco vigilantes was not the four killers they tried and executed but the expulsions and intimidation of their opponents that they used to seize political control of the city for a decade. The social, economic, and political tensions represented by San Francisco in 1856 were the sort that would later produce the convulsions of neovigilantism. Another indication of the coming wave of neovigilantism was the upper class–led New Orleans movement of 1891, which brazenly lynched eleven Sicilian immigrants with little resistance from the authorities and the governor.

Four decades of neovigilantism were inaugurated on 1 January 1920 by the federal government's nationwide "red raids," which resulted in the arrest of thousands of communists and leftist radicals. Carried out under the color of the law, these raids resembled nothing so much as a giant vigilante roundup. The most remarkable example of the continuity of the vigilante tradition took place in Tampa, Florida, from 1858 to 1936. Tampa ran the gamut of American vigilantism, including the frontier variety as well as a sadistic lynching of an African American in 1903. Most vigorous of all was Tampa's era of neovigilantism from 1887 to 1936, which featured a decades-long antilabor

campaign as well as the sensational 1935 lynching of a political radical—the socialist Joseph Shoemaker. Vigilante-minded members of the Tampa elite were enthusiastic early-twentieth-century sponsors of neovigilante vendettas against the local labor movement, but by the early 1930s mainstream opinion made such attitudes obsolete.

## A Vigilante Road Not Taken

By the late 1960s America was completing ten years of the greatest crime surge in decades. In response, citizen patrol groups sprang up in high-crime urban neighborhoods. Often called "vigilantes" at first, the neighborhood patrol bands aroused the fears of police that they would take the law into their own hands. It seemed that the nation was on the verge of a mass regression to the style of nineteenth-century frontier and western vigilantism. But with few exceptions, thousands of these local patrol groups over the next thirty years eschewed vigilantism and became a welcome and useful supplement to police activity. Thus, grassroots Americans came to a fork in the road that might have led down the path to vigilantism, but they did not take it. Instead, the nation as a whole stuck to the path of middle- and late-twentieth-century respect for rigorous due process of law. At the end of the twentieth century thoughtful Americans were not, however, complacent. They realized that, although historic American vigilantism and lynch law was at its lowest ebb, the vigilante spirit still infused the attitudes of militant groups of various ideologies and at times even tainted the reactions of people of moderate views.

*BIBLIOGRAPHY*

Brown, Richard Maxwell. *The South Carolina Regulators.* Cambridge, Mass.: Harvard University Press, 1963.

——— . *Strain of Violence: Historical Studies of American Violence and Vigilantism.* New York: Oxford University Press, 1975.

Brundage, W. Fitzhugh, ed. *Under Sentence of Death: Lynching in the South.* Chapel Hill: University of North Carolina Press, 1997.

Caughey, John W., ed. *Their Majesties the Mob.* Chicago: University of Chicago Press, 1960.

Culberson, William C. *Vigilantism: Political History of Private Power in America.* New York: Greenwood, 1990.

Hufsmith, George W. *The Wyoming Lynching of Cattle Kate, 1889.* Glendo, Wyo.: High Plains Press, 1993.

Ingalls, Robert P. *Urban Vigilantes in the New South: Tampa, 1882–1936.* Knoxville: University of Tennessee Press, 1988.

Klein, Rachel N. "Ordering the Backcountry: The South Carolina Regulation." *William and Mary Quarterly*, 3d series, 38 (October 1981).

Moses, Norton H. *Lynching and Vigilantism in the United States: An Annotated Bibliography*. Westport, Conn.: Greenwood, 1997.

Mullen, Kevin J. *Let Justice Be Done: Crime and Politics in Early San Francisco*. Reno: University of Nevada Press, 1989.

Rosenbaum, H. Jon, and Peter C. Sederberg, eds., *Vigilante Politics*. Philadelphia: University of Pennsylvania Press, 1976.

Senkewicz, Robert M. *Vigilantes in Gold Rush San Francisco*. Stanford, Calif.: Stanford University Press, 1985.

RICHARD MAXWELL BROWN

*See also* **Civil Disorder; Frontier; Lynching; Militarism; Right to Bear Arms.**

**VIOLENT-CRIME PREVENTION.** *See* Prevention: Violent-Crime Prevention.

# W

## WACO

On the morning of 28 February 1993, seventy-six heavily armed agents of the Bureau of Alcohol, Tobacco, and Firearms (ATF) attempted to serve a search-and-arrest warrant at the Mount Carmel center outside Waco, Texas. The warrant was based on the allegation that the residents of Mount Carmel, a breakaway group from the Seventh-Day Adventist Church that would come to be known as the Branch Davidians, possessed illegal firearms materials and were possibly converting AR-15 semiautomatic rifles into machine guns. Shortly after 9:00 A.M., ATF agents launched a "dynamic entrance" into the communal church to serve their warrant. Overhead, three National Guard helicopters arrived simultaneously.

Within seconds, bursts of gunfire erupted. Four ATF agents were killed and more than twenty were injured. Six Davidians were killed, including one child, along with five pet Alaskan malamute dogs. Five sect members were wounded by ATF gunfire. A cease-fire was reached at noon, but the Davidians refused to surrender. A siege ensued, and 668 Federal Bureau of Investigation agents were eventually called in. The siege lasted for the next fifty-one days. During this period Waco came to dominate the news; the Davidian leader, David Koresh, became a household name.

The siege ended on 19 April when two specially equipped Abrams tanks and four Bradley armored vehicles punched holes into the Mount Carmel structure and fired dozens of CS tear-gas canisters into the building in an attempt to force the Davidians out. Around noon, as high winds swept the area, smoke began pouring from the structure. Within minutes the wood-frame building was engulfed in a fire that killed seventy-four people, including twenty-five children under the age of fifteen. Nine Davidians survived, several of whom were later brought to trial in San Antonio for the killing of federal agents.

Over the next two years thousands of pages of official, journalistic, and academic literature emerged on the Waco affair. One common theme ran through these pages: there was a discrepancy between what the federal government had to say about Waco and what the public believed. This discrepancy led to the creation of two camps of public opinion. The first comprised millions of politically moderate Americans who, despite their distaste for Koresh and his followers, were skeptical of the government's account. The second camp was composed of a more strident group of activists aligned with the American radical right. Spurred on by what would become a cottage industry of books, pamphlets, and videos alleging government conspiracy in the disaster, they became allies of the Mount Carmel cause. From this milieu would come the leaders of the American militia movement.

### Controversies

The bitter controversy over Waco centered on five crucial issues. The first concerned the question

**The Mount Carmel compound afire, 19 April 1993.**
CORBIS/BETTMANN

of who fired the first shot at Mount Carmel. During the siege Koresh claimed that he had gone to the front door of the commune and told the agents to "get back" because there were women and children inside, only to be cut off by a burst of gunfire. The ATF agents claimed that they tried to identify themselves, shouting to Koresh that they had a warrant, but were met with a hail of bullets. Subsequent testimony in the San Antonio trial, as well as testimony from congressional hearings on Waco, offered little to resolve this issue. However, the surviving Davidians were eventually acquitted of murder charges.

The second issue concerned the search-and-arrest warrant. Both the ATF and President Bill Clinton maintained that the Davidians were in possession of "illegally stockpiled weaponry." Koresh and his followers maintained that they owned legal guns; however, they had failed to fill out federal registration forms and pay the fees required for these weapons. With the conflagration came the destruction of nearly all crime scene evidence. Even though the FBI would eventually dig the remains of 396 firearms from the Mount Carmel rubble, including 48 machine guns, the weapons were charred beyond identification, prohibiting a conclusive finding.

The third issue related to the safety of the Mount Carmel children. President Clinton and Attorney General Janet Reno claimed that the children were being "abused significantly" by Koresh. More than any other factor, the charge of child abuse led to Reno's approval of the gassing operation of 19 April. Without it, there likely would have been no fatal assault on the Davidians. In time the government's claim would be seriously undermined. Although one teenage girl would testify before Congress that she had had sexual relations with Koresh, the survivors maintained that the children were never abused by him. In the wake of the final assault, the FBI director, William Sessions, confessed that the bureau had "no contemporaneous evidence" of child abuse, a finding that was further confirmed by the testimony of officials from the Texas Department of Human Services who had interviewed the Mount Carmel children prior to the raid.

The fourth issue related to the military's involvement at Waco. During the 28 February raid, the National Guard helicopters carried more than a dozen armed ATF agents whose role was supposed to be strictly supervisory. Yet during the congressional hearings, ATF agents admitted that they had fired at the Davidians from the helicopters. For the Davidian allies this aerial attack represented a blatant violation of the Posse Comitatus Act, a federal law that forbids the deployment of military forces against civilians unless those civilians are suspected of drug trafficking. The Davidians were not.

The final issue was the fire of 19 April. In his official explanation of the event, Clinton charged that "some religious fanatics murdered themselves." The government would alternatively claim that a Davidian, perhaps Koresh himself, lit a match on the second floor of the compound; a Davidian accidentally kicked over a kerosene lamp on the second floor; a Davidian lit a Molotov cocktail on the second floor. In any event, the spark allegedly ignited the salvaged wood of the Mount Carmel structure, which had been saturated with methylene chloride, a highly combustible petroleum derivative used to suspend the CS gas. A more sinister theory would come to be embraced by the Davidian allies: FBI agents deliberately started the fire with flamethrowers extending from the tank portals, with flash-bang grenades thrown into a second-story window, or with repeated gunfire into the second story. In other words, the U.S. government had committed mass murder, an allegation later confirmed in William Gazecki's award-winning documentary film *Waco: The Rules of Engagement* (1997).

The government's investigation into the Waco incident produced a five-hundred-page Treasury Department report on the ATF raid, known as the *Blue Book*. It recognized "disturbing evidence of flawed decision making, inadequate intelligence gathering, miscommunication, supervisory failures, and deliberately misleading post-raid statements." The *Blue Book* led to the ouster of several top ATF officials and to sweeping reforms in the agency. Public respect for the ATF plummeted. The Justice Department subsequently released a more favorable report on the FBI performance at Waco but failed to provide any evidence for the rationale that Reno had invoked for the FBI's final assault: the need to use CS gas and tanks to prevent Koresh from abusing children.

The searing events of Waco not only animated an unparalleled base of support within the radical right but also fundamentally changed the way many Americans view federal law enforcement. Yet more profoundly, previously isolated voices calling for individual acts of violent resistance to state tyranny began to be heard across the heartland of America. Marking the second anniversary of the Waco disaster, on 19 April 1995 Timothy J. McVeigh bombed the Alfred P. Murrah Federal Building in Oklahoma City, resulting in the death of 168 people and the wounding of hundreds more. The Oklahoma City bombing was the most destructive act of revolutionary terror in American history.

*BIBLIOGRAPHY*

Hamm, Mark S. *Apocalypse in Oklahoma: Waco and Ruby Ridge Revenged*. Boston: Northeastern University Press, 1997.

Kopel, David B., and Paul H. Blackman. *No More Wacos: What's Wrong with Federal Law Enforcement and How to Fix It*. Amherst, N.Y.: Prometheus, 1997.

Reavis, Dick J. *The Ashes of Waco: An Investigation*. Syracuse, N.Y.: Syracuse University Press, 1998.

Tabor, James D., and Eugene V. Gallagher. *Why Waco? Cults and the Battle for Religious Freedom in America*. Berkeley: University of California Press, 1995.

Wright, Stuart A., ed. *Armageddon in Waco: Critical Perspectives on the Branch Davidian Conflict*. Chicago: University of Chicago Press, 1995.

MARK S. HAMM

*See also* **Bureau of Alcohol, Tobacco, and Firearms; Cults; Extremism; Film: Documentary Film; Government Violence Against Citizens; Koresh, David; McVeigh, Timothy; Militias, Unauthorized; Oklahoma City Bombing; Police: Police Violence; Religion; Ruby Ridge.**

# WALKDOWN

In the American West of the nineteenth century, a "walkdown" was an incident in which armed men strode toward each other ready to draw their weapons and fire. The climactic gun duel between hero and villain in Owen Wister's novel *The Virginian* (1902) established the walkdown as a rigid convention in formula fiction about the West and may well have been based on a real walkdown that took place in the summer of 1865 in the courthouse square of Springfield, Missouri. On that occasion James Butler ("Wild Bill") Hickok killed his rival, Dave Tutt, in a confrontation that, as romantically described two years later in *Harper's New Monthly Magazine*, indelibly etched the walkdown in American consciousness. In the fictional print and film versions of the walkdown tradition, the hero is a transitional figure in western life: his gunfighting skill represents the savagery of violence, but it is used, paradoxically, to trump evil in the interest of establishing a peaceable society of civilized values to succeed the sanguinary gunfighting era. Dramatized repeatedly in hundreds of Western films—of which *High Noon* (1952) is a classic example—walkdowns were an authentic if malignant feature of the frontier West. The essence of these gunfights was the showdown that brought to a violent conclusion a festering enmity often based on social, economic, or political factors exacerbated by personal antagonism. Hickok and John Wesley Hardin were among the deadliest western gunfighters. Hardin's most spectacular kill was a showdown shooting of the deputy sheriff Charles Webb in the wild town of Comanche, Texas, on 26 May 1874.

Although the two-man gunfight was at the core of the walkdown, there were battles in which more than one individual to a side blazed away at each other. Such was the noted gunfight near the O. K. Corral in Tombstone, Arizona, in 1881, in which Wyatt Earp and his party bested Billy Clanton and the McLaury brothers. Yet, most western showdown shoot-outs and walkdowns were not famous, such as the obscure incident on 16 October 1867 in Little Lake, Mendocino County, California, that resulted in six deaths. Another little-known but mordant 1867 event was a walkdown near present-day Karnes City, Texas, in which two pairs of range-war shootists fired at each other until three of the four were fatally wounded. The deadliest western showdown took place in 1872, when a jurisdictional dispute turned violent in the Going Snake district of present-day Oklahoma. In this confrontation eight deputy U.S. marshals died at the hands of Cherokees, who were attempting to uphold the authority of their court; in the exchange of gunfire the posse of deputies also killed three Indians. Most but not all such gunfights took place in the West. At Matewan, West Virginia, on 19 May 1920 the pro-union police chief Sid Hatfield shot to death seven men in the course of a bitter labor dispute. Hatfield's seven kills are apparently a one-man record in walkdown history.

*BIBLIOGRAPHY*

Boessenecker, John. *Badge and Buckshot: Lawlessness in Old California*. Norman: University of Oklahoma Press, 1988.

Brown, Richard Maxwell. *No Duty to Retreat: Violence and Values in American History and Society*. New York: Oxford University Press, 1991.

Cawelti, John G. *The Six-Gun Mystique*. Bowling Green, Ohio: Bowling Green University Popular Press, 1975.

Metz, Leon. *John Wesley Hardin: Dark Angel of Texas*. Norman: University of Oklahoma Press, 1996.

Rosa, Joseph G. *Wild Bill Hickok: The Man and His Myth*. Lawrence: University Press of Kansas, 1996.

RICHARD MAXWELL BROWN

*See also* **Gunfighters and Outlaws, Western; Hardin, John Wesley; Hickok, James Butler "Wild Bill"; O. K. Corral Gunfight.**

# WALL STREET, BOMBING OF

"This was the most serious outrage ever perpetrated by the radical in New York," the *Sun and New York Herald* announced on 17 September 1920, the day after a bomb struck Wall Street, killing thirty-three people within twenty-four hours and wounding hundreds more. "In many respects it is the most serious in the history of the country," according to that newspaper account, and it was right in at least one respect: until the bombing of the Alfred P. Murrah Federal Building in Oklahoma City in 1995, the Wall Street explosion of 1920 was the most deadly peacetime bombing on U.S. soil. Within a month, thirty-nine people had died as a result of the blast.

The bomb exploded at 12:01 P.M. on the corner of Wall and Broad Streets, in the heart of New York's financial district. On one corner stood the eminent Morgan bank. Across Broad Street was the New York Stock Exchange. On the other side of Wall Street lay the U.S. Assay Office, just next to the site where George Washington took his first oath as president. At first, detectives from the New York Police Department and representatives of the Morgan bank suggested that the bombing might have been an accident. But the bomb's location soon convinced investigators that the explosion had been a calculated attack on the very foundations of government and society, a violent protest against American capitalism by political radicals.

To commentators at the time, the event seemed of a piece with the tumult of the preceding years: World War I, the Bolshevik Revolution, the Palmer deportation raids, the mass strikes, and the Red Scare. The postwar Red Scare, heaving its last gasps around the country, dragged out well into 1921 in New York, partly in response to the bombing on Wall Street. However, neither investigators at the time nor historians have been able to confirm the widespread suspicion that anarchists or communists planted the bomb. Despite one of the largest criminal investigations in American history and the arrest and interrogation of dozens of politically radical immigrants, the Wall Street bombing was never solved.

A 1920 grand jury in New York did conclude that a bomb wheeled to Wall Street in a horse-drawn cart had caused the explosion. And in 1921 a solution seemed imminent with the arrest in Poland of a German-born American immigrant (and alleged radical) named Wolfe Lindenfeld, who claimed to know who planted the bomb. (He accused the Bolshevik government in Russia of having paid $30,000 for the commission of the crime.) It turned out, however, that Lindenfeld had fabricated his statement, possibly in the hopes of claiming a reward.

In 1991 the historian Paul Avrich identified Mario Buda, an Italian immigrant and self-professed anarchist, as the culprit. According to Avrich, Buda set the bomb in retaliation for the Sacco-Vanzetti arrests. His evidence, however, was far from conclusive.

Ironically, this unsolved crime temporarily boosted the fortunes of the Bureau of Investigation (renamed the Federal Bureau of Investigation in 1933), which had recently come under criticism for its activities during the Palmer raids. For a few crucial months, the Wall Street bombing distracted at-

Aftermath of the Wall Street bombing of 16 September 1920—until 1995 the most deadly bombing in U.S. history. CORBIS/BETTMANN

tention from the bureau's critics and bolstered public support for its claim that a pervasive and violent radical threat necessitated a powerful, secret federal police force capable of combating it.

BIBLIOGRAPHY

Avrich, Paul. *Sacco and Vanzetti: The Anarchist Background.* Princeton, N.J.: Princeton University Press, 1991.

Jaffe, Julian F. *Crusade Against Radicalism: New York During the Red Scare, 1914–1924.* Port Washington, N.Y.: Kennikat, 1972.

Murray, Robert K. *Red Scare: A Study of National Hysteria, 1919–1920.* New York: McGraw-Hill, 1955.

BEVERLY GAGE

*See also* **Anarchism; Bombings and Bomb Scares; Labor and Unions.**

# WAR

*Following the* **Introduction** *are three subentries:* **Causes of; Aftermath of, Physical Aspects;** *and* **Aftermath of, Psychoanalytic Aspects.**

## INTRODUCTION

War is present throughout this *Encyclopedia*, and every aspect of the subject raises its own problems.

The present article merely outlines America's major wars and advances a thesis about them. Individual entries on each war provide further details and analysis.

Not counting battles and skirmishes with Native Americans and pirates, the United States has fought ten wars. Most of them are hard to defend, even the American Revolution (1775–1783), as the differences between Parliament and the colonies could have been worked out peacefully. John Adams said only a third of the colonists wanted independence, which was forced on the rest anyway. Thousands of loyalists who had stayed true to King George III were compelled to emigrate. American slaves suffered also from the outcome of that war, for the British Empire abolished slavery in 1833, thirty years before the United States issued the Emancipation Proclamation. Native Americans suffered a loss as well, for they were no longer under the crown's protection—unlike their brothers in Canada, where Indian "wars" became exceedingly rare.

The War of 1812 (1812–1814) was an accident. The British orders in council that authorized the Royal Navy to interfere with American ships and impress (kidnap) American sailors had been suspended three days before President James Madison declared war. The Treaty of Ghent that ended the war settled little—most of America's disputes with Great Britain having been put aside for discussion later. The war was unpopular at home and resolved nothing.

The Mexican-American War (1846–1848), on the other hand, was no accident. President James K. Polk incited it as a pretext to absorb the Republic of Texas and ended up with a great deal more territory. Mexico was so badly beaten that its hapless government had to cede over five hundred thousand square miles of its territory. It was the greatest hemispheric land grab since the Spanish conquest. Although the Mexican War was unpopular, too, America kept its gains.

The Civil War, America's bloodiest conflict, could not have been avoided except by letting the South secede. Between the Confederate attack on Fort Sumter in April 1861 and May 1865 when the last rebel forces surrendered, 360,000 Union soldiers were killed in battle along with an estimated 135,000 Confederates. The South claimed it was fighting for states' rights, the North to maintain the Union. What Southerners really fought for was the right to own slaves. Few in the North, including President Abraham Lincoln, were abolitionists when the war began. By the time it was over, however, most believed in emancipation. A terrible ordeal for both North and South, the war was nevertheless worth fighting as the Union's cause was just—its meaning captured beautifully by the North's great anthem "The Battle Hymn of the Republic."

The Spanish-American War (1898) began as an effort to free Cuba. Cuba did become independent, although for most Cubans the change made little difference since native rulers proved to be as corrupt and dictatorial as the governors of Spain. But while fighting Spain, the United States also seized Puerto Rico and Guam. It took the Philippine Islands as well, even though many inhabitants wanted complete freedom from American rule. Years of brutal repression followed, after which the United States decided the Filipinos were right after all and laid plans for Philippine independence.

American participation in World War I (1917–1918) made no sense to many observers at the time and to subsequent scholars. The United States had nothing to gain from joining the slaughter. It declared war on Germany in defense of the right of American citizens to travel in a war zone on belligerent ships without getting hurt—a claim never pressed before or since. President Woodrow Wilson came up with a loftier reason by declaring that the conflict was a war to end all wars and that it would make the world safe for democracy. As the Allies were not pledged to this impossible dream, little came of Wilson's "crusade" except German bitterness, another great war in Europe, and much disillusionment at home.

American entry into World War II came late and was pivotal in halting Hitler's plans for unlimited conquest and genocide. Germany threatened American security too. One has only to think of a triumphant Nazi state, armed with atom bombs and intercontinental missiles, which Hitler soon would have possessed had he prevailed in Europe. Imperial Japan was less of a threat to the United States, but it was a menace to Asia and the western Pacific and therefore to vital American interests. Unlike the victory in World War I, winning World War II did make a large part of the world safe for democracy. Not since the Civil War had Americans fought in such a noble cause, or one more important to the nation's future.

The Korean War (1950–1953) probably had to be fought. Once communist North Korea invaded South Korea, the United States was forced to intervene or run the risk of encouraging other such invasions by the communist bloc. The U.S. mistake, after winning the war and driving the enemy out, was to invade North Korea. This brought China into the conflict, turning what might have been a short war into a long, costly stalemate.

America waged war in Vietnam (1964–1973) to prevent the disciplined and heavily armed North from defeating the South's unpopular, corrupt, undemocratic, and incompetent regime. Ironically, American withdrawal and the North's victory enabled America to improve relations with both China and the Soviet Union, which then fell out with each other—and China with Vietnam as well—bringing a stable balance of power to the region. In losing the war America thereby achieved its strategic objectives.

The Persian Gulf War (1991) was designed to restore the regional balance of power, which Iraq had upset by seizing Kuwait the previous year. This was accomplished and Kuwait liberated at very little cost, with U.S. allies paying most of the bill and America losing only 390 men and women—fewer than half to enemy action.

America is, as one historian put it, a country made by war. But it could have been made with fewer wars if the nation had shown greater restraint. Not counting the Revolution, only two were imperative, although a good case can be made for the Korean War—despite the hubris that antagonized China. The Gulf War could have been avoided, but because of smart leadership by President George Bush it became a textbook example of how to conduct a limited war for limited aims. It left loose ends, as all wars do, but remains a model blend of violence and statecraft.

BIBLIOGRAPHY

McPherson, James M. *Battle Cry of Freedom: The Civil War Era.* New York: Oxford University Press, 1988.

Perrot, Geoffrey. *A Country Made by War: From the Revolution to Vietnam, the Story of America's Rise to Power.* New York: Random House, 1989.

Weigley, Russell F. *The American Way of War: A History of United States Military Strategy and Policy.* New York: Macmillan, 1973.

WILLIAM L. O'NEILL

*See also* **American Indian Wars; Antiwar Protests; Cold War; Guerrilla Warfare; Military Culture; Military Interventions;** *and entries on individual wars.*

## CAUSES OF

Ever since Thucydides wrote his *History of the Peloponnesian War* recounting the conflict between Athens and Sparta in the fifth century B.C., philosophers, historians, social scientists, and others have been chronicling war and pondering its causes. Despite this enormous expenditure of intellectual energy, there is little agreement as to the causes of war or the best method for discovering them. Debates within a given discipline are at least as heated as disagreements between scholars in different disciplines.

In his famous book *On War* (1832), Carl von Clausewitz said that war is a "continuation of politics by other means." He meant that war is an instrument of policy, a means of advancing state interests, so that war between states is ultimately a political decision. If we want to understand war—which is often defined as large-scale organized violence between political entities—we must understand why political leaders choose war rather than other means to achieve their desired ends. Although answers to this question are informed by a variety of disciplines, it is political science that tackles the issue most directly, and here we examine some of the leading political theories of the causes of war.

The first step in understanding the causes of war is to classify the enormous number of potential causal factors in a manageable framework. Political scientists often classify the causes of war by the "level of analysis"—individual, nation-state, and international system. The individual level focuses primarily on human nature and on individual political leaders and their belief systems, psychological processes, emotional states, and personalities. The national level includes the type of political system (e.g., democratic or authoritarian), the structure of the economy (capitalist or noncapitalist), the nature of the policy-making process, the role of public opinion and interest groups, ethnicity and nationalism, and political culture and ideology. The international-system level—also called the systemic level—includes the anarchic structure of the international system, the distribution of military and economic power among the leading states, patterns of military alliances and international trade, and so on.

The leading systemic-level approach, and in fact the most influential theory of war in political science, is "realist theory." Realist theory focuses on sovereign states acting rationally to advance their security, power, and wealth in an anarchic international system that lacks a higher authority to mediate disputes between states. Uncertain of their adversaries' intentions, political leaders focus on short-term security needs, assume worst-case scenarios, struggle to increase their power, and use coercive threats to advance their interests, influence their adversaries, and maintain their reputations.

One path to war in realist theory involves the direct conflict of interests between states, at least one of which prefers war to compromise. Another path involves the unintended consequences of actions by those who prefer peace to war and who are driven more by fear than by ambition. Even defensively-motivated efforts by states to provide for their own security through armaments, alliances, and deterrent threats often seem menacing to other states and provoke countermeasures and a spiral of conflict that can gather an irreversible momentum. This is the "security dilemma."

The leading realist theory is balance-of-power theory, which assumes that the primary goal of states is to prevent any single state from achieving a position of dominance. This goal requires that states maintain a balance of power through the internal mobilization of military power and by forming external alliances against potential aggressors.

The theory predicts that this balancing mechanism almost always works to stymie hegemony, either because potential aggressors are deterred by their anticipation of an opposing military coalition or because they are defeated in war after deterrence fails.

Another systemic-level approach, the liberal economic theory of war, downplays the anarchy-bred potential for conflict and stresses rather the potential for international cooperation through free trade. Trade promotes prosperity, which in turn promotes a sense of general satisfaction that is inimical to conflict. An increase of economic interdependence between states discourages war because of its disruptive impact on trade-linked prosperity. Realists, however, question liberals' assumption that trade is always more efficient than military conquest in promoting state wealth. They also argue that because trade and interdependence are usually asymmetrical, they often contribute to conflict rather than deter it. States may be tempted to exploit their trading partner's vulnerabilities and use economic coercion to influence an adversary's policies, thus provoking retaliation, spiraling conflict, and war. This escalatory process is sometimes triggered by domestic economic groups who are especially vulnerable to external developments and who pressure the government for protectionist measures, particularly in bad economic times.

In emphasizing the external forces that shape state decisions for war, systemic-level theories posit that states in similar situations behave in similar ways. The implication is that internal factors have little impact on foreign-policy decisions. There is substantial evidence, however, that the internal makeup of states—particularly their democratic or authoritarian character—has a strong influence on their propensity toward war: democracies rarely if ever go to war with each other.

This "democratic peace" does not mean that democracies are necessarily peaceful. In fact, most analysts have concluded that democracies get involved in wars as frequently as nondemocratic states. We also know that democracies occasionally get involved in crises and use limited amounts of force against other democracies, that they fight imperial wars relatively frequently, and that once involved in war they often adopt a crusading spirit and fight particularly destructive wars. But using standard definitions of democracy (fair, competitive elections and constitutional transfers of executive power) and of war (which is often distin-

guished from lesser conflicts by the threshold of a minimum of one thousand battle-related deaths), there are few if any clear-cut cases of wars between democracies.

It is easier to establish that the democratic peace approximates a law of international behavior than it is to explain why it holds, and in the absence of a good theoretical explanation for this phenomenon, it is difficult to predict how durable it will be. Scholars have proposed several interrelated models to explain why democracies rarely if ever go to war with each other. The "institutional model" argues that checks and balances, the dispersion of power, and the need for public debate in democratic states make it easier for various governmental or societal groups to impede the initiation of war. The "political culture model" suggests that the norms of peaceful conflict resolution that have evolved within democratic societies are extended to relations between democratic states.

Authoritarian leaders, facing fewer constraints on their power, often attempt to exploit the conciliatory tendencies of democracies. This strategy undermines democratic political leaders' expectations that their efforts at peaceful conflict resolution will be reciprocated, reduces their internal constraints on the use of force, and provides additional incentives for democratic regimes to use force against authoritarian regimes to eliminate their violent tendencies. Thus democracies not only respond to attacks by authoritarian states but also initiate wars against them.

One implication of the institutional model of democratic peace is that political leaders are more inclined to war than the public is. This is not always true. Leaders are sometimes precluded by hard-line public opinion from making the concessions that are necessary to prevent war and, in fact, occasionally are forced into wars that they would prefer to avoid. Another lawlike pattern in international politics is that whenever political leaders use force against external adversaries, they benefit, if only temporarily, from a surge in public support. Political leaders, anticipating this "rally 'round the flag" effect, are sometimes tempted to undertake risky foreign ventures in an attempt to distract attention from domestic problems and thereby shore up their political support. This is the "diversionary theory of war."

National-level theories, like systemic-level ones, imply that individuals have little impact, that political leaders' decisions about war and peace are driven by social and economic forces beyond their control. The implication is that substituting one top decision maker for another would not make much difference. Individual-level theories, however, emphasize the impact of individual political leaders, their beliefs about the world and the adversary, and the psychological processes through which they acquire information and make decisions.

One of the most important individual-level causes of war, though one also shaped by political culture and ideology, is misperceptions, especially those pertaining to the capabilities and intentions of adversaries and third states. If leaders exaggerate the hostility of their adversary's intentions, they may overreact to genuinely defensive actions, and thus trigger the spiral toward war. On the other hand, if political leaders underestimate the adversary's hostility or its capabilities, they may fail to build up their own capabilities or fail to demonstrate resolve, either of which undermines deterrence and emboldens the enemy to make war. An underestimation of an adversary's capabilities relative to their own can also engender war by breeding overconfidence in a rapid military victory with minimal costs. This overconfidence is often reinforced by an inflated expectation that one's potential friends will intervene on one's behalf and that one's potential enemies will stay neutral. Military overconfidence can also reinforce hard-line bargaining tactics that often lead to war.

There is no scholarly consensus on which of these causes of war is paramount, whether the causes of war have changed over time, or whether the wars of the future are likely to resemble those of the past. It is clear, however, that war has already changed in important respects. There has been a shift in war from Europe, the primary battleground of the great powers for centuries, to other regions of the world, and from the great powers to other states. This trend is due in part to the stabilizing effects of nuclear weapons on the bipolar rivalry between the superpowers during the Cold War, and perhaps in part to the "security community" that has arisen among the democratic and free-trading European states. This trend has been reinforced by the collapse of the Soviet Union and the end of the Cold War and by the explosion of civil and regional wars outside Europe in the 1990s, although it has been challenged by the waves of conflict in the Balkans in the same period. The intensification of ethnic, national, and religious consciousness in much of the world may change the issues over which wars are fought, and the rise of information-based technologies and the

development of new weapons of mass destruction may affect how wars are fought, but it is unlikely that the ancient plague of war will soon disappear from a world still made up of independent polities engaged in an ongoing struggle for power, wealth, and autonomy.

*BIBLIOGRAPHY*

Clausewitz, Carl von. *On War*. Edited and translated by Michael Howard and Peter Paret. Princeton, N.J.: Princeton University Press, 1976.
Levy, Jack S. "The Causes of War: A Review of Theories and Evidence." In *Behavior, Society, and Nuclear War*. Vol. 1, edited by Philip E. Tetlock et al. New York: Oxford University Press, 1989.
Morgenthau, Hans J. *Politics Among Nations*. New York: Knopf, 1948.
Vasquez, John A. *The War Puzzle*. New York: Cambridge University Press, 1993.
Waltz, Kenneth N. *Man, the State, and War*. New York: Columbia University Press, 1959.

JACK S. LEVY

*See also* **Aggression; Conflict Resolution; War Crimes.**

## AFTERMATH OF, PHYSICAL ASPECTS

The physical effects of war on American veterans have changed with advances in both military medicine and weapons technology. In general, infectious disease, which caused the majority of American casualties prior to World War I, has been replaced by trauma and exposure to toxic chemicals as the primary physical factors affecting war veterans.

Disease was the most common killer of American soldiers in the American Revolution, the War of 1812, the Mexican War, the Civil War, and the Spanish-American War. Disease and malnutrition were especially widespread among soldiers in the Mexican War and the Spanish-American War. Veterans who survived malaria, typhoid, rheumatism, and various camp fevers often suffered painful aftereffects of these diseases. Over the course of the nineteenth century, however, the rate of infectious disease declined among American soldiers.

The experience of Civil War veterans reflected dramatic changes in weapons technology and military medicine, especially the use of rifled muskets, soft lead bullets, and the introduction of anesthetics such as chloroform and ether. Rifled barrels made guns far more accurate than in previous wars, and the capacity of soft lead bullets to expand inside the body after impact made them much more destructive than iron bullets. The absence of aseptic surgical techniques meant that severe wounds usually caused infection and death, unless the limb could be amputated. Amputations, which were rare before the 1860s, became more common in the Civil War because new anesthetics helped overcome both shock and the patient's objections to the procedure.

Two other new inventions, the hypodermic needle and morphine, proved to be a mixed blessing for soldiers. Intravenous morphine and opium pills were both used freely as painkillers in Civil War hospitals. Although reliable addiction rates among veterans are lacking, addiction was often perceived as a particular problem of veterans; in fact, morphine addiction was often known as "soldiers' disease" or "army disease."

Although the introduction of aseptic surgery helped reduce the amputation rate among World War I veterans, survivors of the latter conflict faced problems created by another advance in military technology: poison gas. Mustard agent, a chemical designed to injure and kill humans by destroying soft tissue, especially the eyes, throat, and lungs, was used extensively in trench warfare. Survivors often suffered asthma, chronic bronchitis, emphysema, respiratory cancers, and chronic skin ulcerations. During World War II, more than sixty thousand U.S. soldiers were deliberately exposed to mustard agent for experimental purposes.

Nuclear weapons, the most significant advance in twentieth-century military technology, also had devastating health consequences for some American veterans. Between 1945 and 1963, as many as 250,000 American soldiers were deliberately exposed to nuclear explosions at close range during training exercises. Many of those so-called "atomic soldiers" later developed cancer.

Continuing improvements in military medicine led to falling fatality rates in subsequent wars. But problems associated with exposure to toxic chemicals continued to plague veterans, especially survivors of the Vietnam War and the Gulf War.

Between 1962 and 1971 American forces sprayed over 11 million gallons of a defoliant codenamed Agent Orange on Vietnamese fields and jungles to deprive the North Vietnamese of crops and to create clear lines of sight. Vietnam veterans have ascribed a variety of symptoms to their exposure to Agent Orange, from infertility to precancerous growths, but significant disagreement over the toxic effects of Agent Orange persists among reputable scientists. Estimates of actual exposure to Agent Orange vary due to unreliable records of troop movements in sprayed areas. Surveys show that 25 to 55 percent of all Vietnam veterans believe they were exposed to Agent Orange. In January 1985 seven makers of Agent Orange, including Dow, Monsanto, and Uniroyal, settled a class-action product liability lawsuit that had been

**Vietnam wounded in Walter Reed Army Medical Hospital, 1966.** LIBRARY OF CONGRESS

brought against them for $180 million. The money went to establish a fund for disabled veterans and their survivors, but the companies did not admit that Agent Orange caused any health problems. A 1994 review of the literature by the Institute of Medicine concluded that exposure to Agent Orange was associated with soft tissue sarcoma, chloracne (a severe skin condition), Hodgkin's disease, and non-Hodgkin's lymphoma.

Further advances in weapons technology between the 1960s and the 1990s created new health problems for veterans of the 1990–1991 Persian Gulf conflict. Depleted uranium projectiles threatened not only the enemy but also U.S. soldiers. Used in armor-piercing munitions, depleted uranium is twice as dense as lead, chemically toxic, and about half as radioactive as natural uranium. At least several dozen American soldiers came into contact with depleted uranium dust while salvaging enemy vehicles. In addition, U.S. troops were exposed to smoke from thousands of oil-well fires set by retreating Iraqi troops.

Finally, American soldiers faced Iraq's arsenal of chemical and biological weapons, including mustard agent, nerve agents (chemicals designed to kill humans by causing convulsions and respiratory paralysis), anthrax (an infectious disease characterized by high fever, coughing, vomiting, shock, and death), and botulinum toxin (BT, a naturally occurring poison that causes convulsions and respiratory paralysis). As a precaution, American soldiers in the Gulf were vaccinated against anthrax and BT. They also received self-administered packs of pyridostigmine bromide (PB), a pretreatment against nerve agents to be taken before combat. While the Department of Defense has documented only a few cases of exposure to nerve and mustard agents, most Gulf War veterans got anthrax and BT vaccinations in addition to the PB they took just before going into battle.

American veterans of the Gulf War have complained of a variety of symptoms, including joint pain, fatigue, headache, memory loss, sleep disturbance, and unexplained rashes. Together, these symptoms have come under the unofficial heading of "Gulf War Syndrome," but, as in the case of Vietnam veterans and Agent Orange, poor records of troop movements prohibit decisive scientific conclusions about the causes of these vets' problems. The 1996 final report of the Presidential Advisory Committee on Gulf War Veterans' Illnesses concluded that of all the risk factors noted above, only two warranted further investigation: the long-term effects of low-level exposure to chemical warfare agents and the possible side effects of PB combined with other risk factors.

While advances in military medicine have helped soldiers survive longer on and off the battlefield, simultaneous advances in weapons technology have also created new long-term health problems for veterans.

*BIBLIOGRAPHY*

Dean, Eric T., Jr. *Shook Over Hell: Post-Traumatic Stress, Vietnam, and the Civil War.* Cambridge, Mass.: Harvard University Press, 1997.

Herschbach, Lisa. "Prosthetic Reconstructions: Making the Industry, Re-Making the Body, Modeling the Nation." Paper presented at the seminar of the Interuniversity History of Medicine Consortium, New York Academy of Medicine, 6 January 1999. Available on-line at http://www.nyam.org/library/history/hist99_1.html.

Institute of Medicine. *Veterans and Agent Orange: Health Effects of Herbicides Used in Vietnam.* Washington, D.C.: National Academy, 1994.

Presidential Advisory Committee on Gulf War Veterans' Illnesses. Final Report. Washington, D.C.: U.S. Government Printing Office, 1996.

Rosenberg, Howard L. *Atomic Soldiers.* Boston: Beacon, 1980.

Severo, Richard, and Lewis Milford. *The Wages of War: When America's Soldiers Came Home—From Valley Forge to Vietnam.* New York: Simon and Schuster, 1989.

R. RUDY HIGGENS-EVENSON

*See also* **Environment, Violence Against; Gulf War; Prisoners of War; Vietnam War.**

## AFTERMATH OF, PSYCHOANALYTIC ASPECTS

War by its very nature is violent, and psychoanalysis offers perspectives on the effects of that violence on combatants and civilian victims, their family members and communities, and subsequent generations (descendants) of those exposed to the trauma of war. It has been observed that the psychological aftermath of war trauma is similar in these diverse groups, and that theme—that the human psychological response to the violence of war is similar in all who are involved, directly and indirectly—is the central focus of this essay. From the point of view of the clinical psychoanalyst, in war there are no victors, for everyone suffers comparable psychological damage. A distant and popular American war may have almost no obvious effect on an individual in the United States who does not lose a loved one, while another who directly experiences a loss will be clinically affected in ways more apparently similar to combatants or those living in the countries where combat took

---

### The Story of a Veteran of War

What follows, in vivid detail, is a description of how a veteran of war might manifest the aftereffects of battle.

Sam is a fifty-one-year-old man who fought in Vietnam in 1965 and 1966. He suffers from post-traumatic stress disorder (PTSD), a condition once referred to as shell shock or battle fatigue. The course of Sam's illness has been severe and chronic for over three decades. In the past he has had brief encounters with psychiatrists, but only recently did he decide to pursue treatment again, this time agreeing to weekly psychotherapy in addition to medication. When Sam came to a Veterans Administration hospital six months ago he described enduring and haunting memories, symptomatic of PTSD. He had gone to Vietnam at the age of eighteen, after joining the military at seventeen with his parents' permission. While in Vietnam he repeatedly witnessed death and injury to his fellow soldiers and to the Vietnamese soldiers he was fighting against, but he also sustained serious injury and believed that he would die. He remains particularly horrified about witnessing the death of women and children, and he continues to harbor anger at a fellow soldier, a combat buddy, who attempted suicide by shooting himself after participating in a battle in which civilians were slaughtered.

Sam describes feeling vilified by his community and some of his family upon returning from Vietnam. He felt alternately rejected and misunderstood by his father and his father's friends and associates and smothered by his mother's attention to his physical wounds. Unable to cope with both the rejection and the intense nurturing of his parents, he joined a motorcycle gang and began a chaotic and violent period in his life.

For the next ten years, 1967 to 1977, Sam experienced intense emotional distress, which he tried to self-medicate with alcohol and drug use. He got married, and he and his wife had a child, a son, during these years. He recalls telling his wife that she should leave him because of his turbulent behavior. Later, his condition would be diagnosed as PTSD, but at the time he did not understand what was wrong with him and felt that he was out of control. He experienced diffuse rage and extreme violent behavior, and his wife eventually divorced him after eight years of marriage.

Over the next five years, between the ages of thirty and thirty-five, Sam moved multiple times, starting and either leaving or losing multiple jobs as a low-level manual laborer. He preferred to work outdoors, where he did not feel trapped or crowded, and this kind of work allowed him to avoid almost all social interactions, which made him anxious. A very brief second marriage ended

*(continued)*

---

place. Even so, as a society Americans of current and future generations will be significantly—and similarly—affected by the trauma of that conflict.

It is not well known that the father of psychoanalysis, Sigmund Freud, was under contract with the Carnegie Endowment for International Peace in 1921 to write about the psychoanalytic problem of war, and that just two months after the contract was signed Freud asked to be released from this

obligation because he could make no headway on the topic. Better known is that in his correspondence about war with Albert Einstein in 1932 Freud expressed reservations about the value of what he had to say on the subject.

Since Freud's invention of psychoanalysis, the field has undergone much change, and there is a greater appreciation of the ways in which individual development is determined not just by Freud's

(*continued*)

in divorce. Following the breakup, he did not attempt to form any further relationships, including friendships, feeling strongly that he could not trust anyone enough to risk even a casual relationship.

At age thirty-seven Sam attempted suicide by shooting himself, and while in the hospital for medical care he made a second unsuccessful attempt to kill himself. He was then transferred to a psychiatric unit, but after being discharged he stopped taking his medications and refused further psychiatric treatment of any kind. He did, however, pursue his education, becoming a licensed vocational nurse like his mother, at age forty.

For the next nine years Sam worked at a Veterans Administration hospital as a nurse, with some success. But eventually his PTSD symptoms caught up with him, and he was asked to take early retirement based on medical disability. He then moved to live with his son and grandson.

Sam describes a life in which he is tormented by the trauma of war, a life in which he believes he is guilty of both inflicting violence on others and wrongly surviving retaliatory violence directed at him. (Survivor guilt is central to PTSD, which is also known as the survivor syndrome. Even noncombatant victims of war experience guilt over having done whatever they did to survive. They believe that their survival was achieved at the expense of others.)

Sam is tormented by persistent reexperiences of war trauma in his dreams, in intrusive recollections of Vietnam, and in vivid flashbacks that he finds difficult to separate from real life. He says that he cannot bear to think about Vietnam, that he must put such thoughts out of his mind, and that he cannot associate with other veterans or celebrate Memorial Day. He also describes being emotionally numbed and incapable of intimacy.

Psychoanalysts believe that the trauma of war may create a fundamental psychobiological change in its victims, and Sam shows signs of what may be such change: he has trouble sleeping, is irritable and hypervigilant, is easily startled, and has a bad temper. These symptoms have been hauntingly persistent and have caused significant impairment in every aspect of Sam's life. His struggle has been a long and difficult one, and now, after so many years, he is tentatively willing to begin a treatment that will at best be similarly stressful, but possibly healing.

This description is typical of the severe symptoms that are seen in a traumatized combatant. However, it must be emphasized that noncombatants who were exposed to the trauma of war violence may suffer similarly from PTSD. In others who are traumatized, the clinical picture may be less severe, but nevertheless significant guilt over survival, in addition to other symptoms, may be present.

hypothesized instinctual drives, which he believed created a template for human development and behavior, but by interpersonal and cultural influences. In this new psychoanalytic environment, observations about war are not limited by a conception of violence that holds that aggression is simply in the nature of man. Indeed, the possibilities for understanding the psychological effects of war are enhanced by observations that each individual is influenced by the personalities and experiences of those around him, as well as by the war-related trauma of previous generations. Martin Wangh, a physician and psychoanalyst and a leader in the exploration of intergenerational influences, has written and lectured extensively on how traumatized men returning from war shape the behavior of their societies with respect to violence, and more specifically influence their children to make or avoid war when they become adults.

This essay is based on clinical observations of those who have experienced war trauma, and the study of reports by clinicians who are experienced in making such observations. The sidebar contains a detailed description of a veteran of war, but it should be understood that a noncombatant victim of war, such as a concentration camp survivor or the child of a combatant or survivor, might present a similar clinical picture. Similarly, the specific nature of the conflict does not seem to substantially change the symptoms of psychological trauma observed: violent confrontations in cities in the United States between members of gangs and law-enforcement officials produce clinical pictures similar to those displayed by combatants and victims of conventional battlegrounds.

## The Contagion of War Trauma

The effects of war violence are visited upon family members and upon the communities and descendants of those directly affected by the experience of war. Living family members of concentration camp survivors, for instance, often feel guilty for surviving such violence even if they were thousands of miles away in America when the Nazi Holocaust took place. The children and spouses of war veterans can suffer from the same reactions to war violence as their soldier relative and show similar symptoms of post-traumatic stress disorder. Psychoanalytic understanding of this phenomenon indicates that the actual war survivor subtly imparts the imperative to these family members that they must participate in the central survivor's suffering. Psychological processes such as projection and identification take place, resulting in a psychological contagion of war trauma. All those touched by war—combatants, civilian victims of fighting and efforts at extermination, surviving family members, and descendants—show similar psychological stigmata as a result of the violence of war.

Some of the most interesting psychoanalytic ideas about the nature and causes of war involve hypotheses about how such mechanisms of contagion work within communities, even nations, and operate transgenerationally, causing old conflicts to resurface from generation to generation. Thus, the children of individuals who fought in a war might feel that there are old scores to settle, and would, when they reach maturity, be more likely to promote a similar conflict so that they can take up the cause for which their parents struggled and justify the psychological and physical suffering of their families, their communities, and themselves. Personal psychological traumas, connected to both personal, family, cultural, ethnic, or national myths can in that way be transmitted even to those unborn at the time of a war, perpetuating old hatreds, old sources of guilt, old needs for guilt expiation and self-justification, and in the end leading to new outbreaks of violence.

## Perceptions of Danger in the Aftermath of War

Another area that has been explored by psychoanalysts and psychologists is the nature of perceptions of danger and instability in the aftermath of war. Such perceptions are another effect of war violence and trauma on societies, and can predispose them to future outbreaks of violence. The Cold War between Russia and the United States was an example of this, and the United States practice of nuclear deterrence a central political and military policy through which this could be observed. Nuclear deterrence required the development of a nuclear force of sufficient strength and flexibility that any nuclear attack against the United States would be answered by a successful in-kind attack against the perpetrator.

The policy reflected what for the United States was a fearful experience with the Soviet Union after World War II, as the Soviet military repressed dissent in the block of nations it controlled. The direct threat to the security of the United States during the Cuban Missile Crisis was a particularly galvanizing national experience. But nuclear deterrence also reflected an awareness of the destructive power of the nuclear weapons employed against Japan at the end of World War II, as well as those subsequently developed. The trauma of war violence created national guilt in the United States; the national anticipatory reaction concerning destruction of the world also reflected fears of punishment that were in part related to guilt over using the atomic bomb against civilian populations in Japan. Here, a psychological effect of war violence was significant in its effect on national policy.

From the psychoanalytic perspective, one recognizes that such overwhelming guilt-based traumatic anticipation had to be controlled on a long-term basis, so that people did not live in a constant state of panic. Deterrence policy therefore had to be a self-perpetuating dogma, though it began as a set of potentially useful guidelines after the Soviets had developed their own nuclear capacity. Influenced by unconscious psychological forces, policy makers reasoned that the only way to control devastating weapons of mass destruction was to continue the development of weapons that were even more destructive than those possessed by the other side. A preoccupation with technology developed, and efforts were made to determine and outmatch the numbers of weapons and the delivery systems operated by the Soviets.

Rather than consider other models, especially models that would promote conflict resolution, nuclear-policy makers in the United States assumed that the Soviets would behave rationally only in response to the threat of force, the awareness on their parts of the American capacity to successfully retaliate. Those who disagreed with that perspective were declared naive or accused of operating under false assumptions.

In retrospect, many international relations experts such as Robert Jervis and Patrick Morgan have come to recognize that nuclear deterrence brought the superpowers closer to war, by increasing the level of mutual suspicion and distrust and creating a destabilizing, perpetual arms race. But at the time when deterrence was accepted as the best way to prevent a nuclear war, U.S. experts were sure their ever-vigilant weapons development programs minimized the effect of destabilizing technological advances. Psychoanalysts, on the other hand, would suggest that deterrence was a policy based on a mythology, and in many ways a response to the societal effects of war violence, which operated outside of the conscious awareness of national leaders and the population at large. Contemporary psychoanalysts would further suggest that such thinking and behavior by individuals and groups of individuals at times perpetuates intergroup tensions, and unknowingly contributes to violent or potentially violent interactions between nations.

*BIBLIOGRAPHY*

Egendorf, Arthur, et al. *Legacies of Vietnam: Comparative Adjustment of Veterans and Their Peers.* Washington, D.C.: U.S. Government Printing Office, 1981.

Figley, Charles R., ed. *Stress Disorders Among Vietnam Veterans: Theory, Research, and Treatment.* New York: Brunner/Mazel, 1978.

Jervis, Robert. *Perception and Misperception in International Politics.* Princeton, N.J.: Princeton University Press, 1976.

Josephson, Harold. *James T. Shotwell and the Rise of Internationalism in America.* Cranbury, N.J.: Associated University Presses, 1975.

Morgan, Patrick M. *Deterrence. A Conceptual Analysis.* Beverly Hills, Calif.: Sage, 1977.

Sonnenberg, Stephen M. "Children of Survivors." *Journal of the American Psychoanalytic Association* 22, no. 1 (1974).

Sonnenberg, Stephen M., Arthur S. Blank, Jr., and John A. Talbott, eds. *The Trauma of War: Stress and Recovery in Viet Nam Veterans.* Washington, D.C.: American Psychiatric Press, 1985.

Ursano, Robert J., and Ann E. Norwood, eds. *Emotional Aftermath of the Persian Gulf War: Veterans, Families, Communities, and Nations.* Washington, D.C.: American Psychiatric Press, 1996.

Wangh, Martin. "Some Unconscious Factors in the Psychogenesis of Recent Student Uprisings." *Psychoanalytic Quarterly* 41, no. 2 (1972).

STEPHEN M. SONNENBERG
CATHERINE B. ORSAK

*See also* **Nonviolence; Post-Traumatic Stress Disorder; Prisoners of War; Victims of Violence; Vietnam War.**

# WAR CRIMES

In the most literal sense, war crimes are violations of the customary and codified laws of war. The laws of war are a very specialized subset of international law. Initially, these rules were customary and governed only the conduct of military forces on the battlefield and covered subjects such as the declaration of war, treatment of prisoners and civilians, ransom, quarter, and captured enemy property. Present from the beginning was an effort to draw bold distinction between soldier and civilian.

The emergence of the United States as a global power in the late nineteenth century had a profound effect on the further codification of positive and internationally recognized rules for war. The laws governing Union soldiers in the Civil War were known as General Order No. 100 (also called the Lieber Code). Approved by President Abraham Lincoln on 24 April 1863, the 159 articles covered subjects like guerrilla warfare, retaliation, quarter, and captured enemy property. The Lieber Code was significant because it marked the first time in Western history that the government of a sovereign nation established formal guidelines for the conduct of its army in the field.

General Order No. 100 provided the foundation for a subsequent body of treaty law on the rules of war such as the Hague Conventions. The Hague Conventions of 1899 and 1907 were practical measures designed to prevent excessive suffering in war and related to prisoners, casualties, and spies. Technical issues such as flags of truce, capitulation, armistice, and neutrality were also included. Three of the conventions' declarations addressed technological developments, such as bombs and gas, that fell outside the previously accepted rules of war. The first Hague Conference saw the tentative start of an American-led movement to broaden the laws of war to include acts that had previously been considered beyond the realm of objective judgment.

The expression *war crimes* became familiar during World War I when Prime Minister Lloyd George of Britain called for the extradition and trial of Germany's Kaiser Wilhelm II as a "war criminal." The Versailles Treaty, signed in 1919, reflected the fact that war was no longer a value-free means of dispute resolution. Under Article 227 of the Versailles Treaty, the kaiser was threatened with a trial by an international court. He was not charged with specific war crimes, rather "a supreme offense against international morality and the sanctity of treaties." Unlike the conflict resolutions of old, the victors did not execute a handful of deserving felons and issue an amnesty for acts committed during wartime. Instead, they attempted to broaden the scope of international criminal law to hold individuals personally accountable for acts of nations.

On 3 February 1920, the victors called on the German government to live up to Article 228 of the Versailles Treaty and hand over 854 men accused of war crimes. Germany refused but agreed to try a limited number of men before the German Supreme Court (*Reichsgericht*) in Leipzig. Great Britain, France, and Belgium submitted a revised list of forty-five individuals involved in the most egregious violations of the laws of war. Defendants were charged with mistreating prisoners, shooting civilians, and sinking a hospital ship. In the end, the Leipzig trials were little more than juridical theater and resembled other trials conducted by friendly regimes. As with the trials of American soldiers charged with killing civilians in the Philippines, the stern tone of the judgments was not reflected in the extremely lenient sentences. Ludwig Dithmar and John Boldt—German naval officers who opened fire on Canadian survivors in lifeboats—were sentenced to four years' imprisonment, and both "escaped" after six months.

Reeling from the horrors of trench warfare and other World War I tactics, leaders in the postwar period made great efforts to limit and even outlaw war. The most famous of these efforts was the Kellog-Briand Treaty, or the Pact of Paris, of 1928; however, these rules did little to deter Adolf Hitler's Third Reich. War crimes did not become an issue again until late in World War II, because only victors prosecute war crimes cases. The Moscow Declaration, signed by the United States, the Soviet Union, and the United Kingdom in October 1943, was the first specific commitment to a war crimes trial. After the Axis forces were crushed in 1945, the Allies decided to try Axis leaders in international courts under broadened indictments that forever changed the laws of war. After World War II, there was a sense that the German atrocities were so profound and unprecedented that they required unique judicial action. The London Agreement of 1945 laid the foundations for the trials of the Axis leaders. The first count charged the defendants with planning and waging aggressive war, or "crimes against peace." The second count was a traditional war crimes charge, that is, violations of laws and customs of war; and the third count, "crimes against humanity," broadened the definition of war crimes so that Axis leaders could be charged with injustices committed against German Jews during wartime.

The high-level international war crimes courts (the International Military Tribunal at Nuremberg, the International Military Tribunal for the Far East, and the subsequent Nuremberg trials) were loosely modeled after the London Agreement and Charter. Although the three indictments (London Agreement, Tokyo Charter, and Control Council Law No. 10) differed in small ways, they all contained traditional war crimes charges and the novel aggression, conspiracy, and crimes-against-humanity counts. Nuremberg's International Military Tribunal (IMT), made up of judges from the United States, United Kingdom, France, and the Soviet Union, was the symbolic flagship of Allied war crimes policy. The defendants represented a good cross section of the Third Reich's political and military leadership: Hermann Göring, Albert Speer, Joachim von Ribbentrop, Rudolf Hess, Alfred Jodl, and Karl Dönitz. The trial opened on 6 November 1945. On 21 November Robert Jackson opened the prosecution's case for the Americans. The low point in the IMT came when the Soviet prosecutor charged Nazi Germany with the murders of Polish officers in Katyn. (They had in fact been killed by the Soviets.) When the hotly debated conspiracy and aggression charges were applied, the first court proved conservative, offering

**Hermann Göring standing next to Rudolph Hess at Nuremberg.** LIBRARY OF CONGRESS

no expansive definition of aggression, only vague references to "aggressive acts."

On 1 October 1946 the IMT sentenced twelve men to death, and surprisingly acquitted Hjalmar Schacht, Franz von Papen, and Hans Fritzsche. Acquittals had not been expected by those, especially in Germany, who considered the process to be a show trial. Nuremberg provided an international legal inquiry that was unique in history. Owing to the acrimony surrounding the London Agreement Charter, the courts began and ended divided. The accidental results of this division were carefully considered judgments and dissenting opinions. Although this International Military Tribunal rendered political justice, it was distinct from the Soviet and Nazi versions of the same. The IMT proved that victor trials were not farcical by their nature. The IMT was followed by twelve American trials at Nuremberg under the direction of Brigadier General Telford Taylor. Armed with an indictment modeled after the IMT's, American lawyers tried 187 men at Nuremberg's Palace of Justice between 1947 and 1949. The defendants included the industrialist Alfred Krupp, the diplomat Ernst von Weizsaecker, Einsatzkommando Otto Ohlendorf, the field marshall Wilhelm von List, the judge Rudolf Oeschey, the bureaucrat Hans Lammers, and other high-ranking Third Reich officials. One hundred seventy-seven defendants were judged in

twelve trials between 1947 and 1949. One hundred forty-two were convicted, and twelve were eventually executed.

The IMT stands in stark contrast to the International Military Tribunal for the Far East (IMTFE), or the Tokyo Trials. The trials shared similar indictments in which high government and military leaders were charged with crimes against the peace, war crimes, and crimes against humanity. The IMTFE arraigned twenty-five of Japan's military and civilian leaders on 3 May 1946. Although Emperor Hirohito was not among the defendants, Prime Minister Hideki Tojo and a number of other high-ranking officials were. The tribunal was composed of eleven judges from Australia, Canada, China, France, the Philippines, the Netherlands, New Zealand, the Soviet Union, the United Kingdom, the United States, and India.

The legal historian William Appleman compared the IMTFE to the IMT and found the former "strangely autocratic." Owing to the size of the tribunal and the number of defendants, it took more than two and a half years for the court to reach its verdicts. On 4 November 1948 the IMTFE sentenced seven defendants to death and seventeen were given life terms; three judges issued dissenting opinions.

Only the high-ranking Axis leaders faced the U.S. War Department's aggression, conspiracy, and crimes-against-humanity charges. On the one hand, Axis leaders were given elaborate trials and judged by new standards of international law, while on the other hand, common soldiers and lesser offenders were tried by military commissions with few legal pretenses. The largest number of American war crimes trials were presided over by U.S. military authorities under military law. In Germany, the U.S. Army tried 1,672 individuals in 489 proceedings under military law. The majority of these defendants (more than one thousand) were guards or personnel at Buchenwald, Flossenburg, Mauthausen, Nordhausen, and Mühldorf. The other large group (six hundred) was accused of murdering American pilots. The most famous defendants, however, were the soldiers accused of committing the Malmédy massacre in Belgium, in which eighty-five U.S. prisoners were shot in 1944. On 16 May 1946, seventy-three Waffen SS veterans were charged with various violations of the laws of war. After a five-week trial conducted by the U.S. Army at the Dachau concentration camp in Germany, Joachim Peiper, Sepp Dietrich, and forty-two others were sentenced to death, and twenty-two others were sentenced to life in prison.

*BIBLIOGRAPHY*

Appleman, John Alan. *Military Tribunals and International Crimes.* Westport, Conn.: Greenwood, 1971.

International Military Tribunal. *Trial of the Major War Criminals Before the International Military Tribunal.* Vol. 2. Washington, D.C.: U.S. Government Printing Office, 1949.

Lieber, Francis. *Lieber's Code and the Laws of War,* edited by Richard Shelley Hartigan. Chicago: Precedent, 1983.

Minear, Richard H. *Victor's Justice.* Princeton, N.J.: Princeton University Press, 1971.

Piccigallo, Phillip. *The Japanese on Trial: Allied War Crimes Operations in the East, 1945–1951.* Austin: University of Texas Press, 1979.

Pritchard, R. John, and Sonia Magbanua Zaide, eds. *The Tokyo War Crimes Trial: Index and Guide.* New York: Garland, 1981.

Roberts, Adam, and Richard Guelff, eds. *Documents on the Laws of War.* Oxford, U.K.: Clarendon, 1989.

Smith, Bradley F. *Reaching Judgment at Nuremberg.* New York: Basic, 1977.

———, ed. *The American Road to Nuremberg: The Documentary Record, 1944–1945.* Stanford, Calif.: Hoover Institution Press, 1982.

Taylor, Telford. *The Anatomy of the Nuremberg Trials: A Personal Memoir.* New York: Knopf, 1992.

———. *Nuremberg and Viet Nam.* New York: Bantam, 1971.

Tusa, Ann, and John Tusa. *The Nuremberg Trial.* New York: Atheneum, 1984.

Weingartner, James V. *Crossroads of Death: The Story of the Malmédy Massacre and Trial.* Berkeley: University of California Press, 1979.

Willis, James F. *A Prologue to Nuremberg: The Politics and Diplomacy of Punishing War Criminals of the First World War.* Westport, Conn.: Greenwood, 1982.

Wolfe, Robert, ed. *Americans as Procounsuls: United States Military Government in Germany and Japan, 1944–1952.* Carbondale: Southern Illinois University Press, 1984.

PETER MAGUIRE

*See also* **Holocaust; Human Rights; Mass Murder: Colletive Murder; Military Interventions; My Lai Massacre; World War I; World War II.**

# WAR OF 1812

Sometimes called America's Second War of Independence or Mr. Madison's War, after the president who presided over it, the War of 1812 (18 June 1812–17 February 1815) was a direct outgrowth of the Napoleonic Wars (1803–1815). The United States went to war mainly to force Great Britain to repeal the Orders in Council, which regulated American trade with the European continent, and to give up impressment, the practice of removing seamen from U.S. merchant vessels and forcing them to serve in the Royal Navy.

## Military and Naval Operations

The United States hoped to win this war by conquering Canada and holding it for ransom on the maritime issues, but U.S. invasions of Canada in 1812 and 1813 ended in failure. These failures were partly attributable to government policies over the previous decade that had gutted the defense establishment and left the nation ill-equipped to fight or finance a major war. In addition, there was poor civilian leadership in Washington and weak military leadership in the field, an ill-conceived strategy that focused on peripheral targets, and logistical problems that were nearly insoluble.

Paradoxically, the United States fared much better in 1814–1815, when Napoleon's defeat in Europe freed up British resources and threw the young republic on the defensive. Although a British army burned Washington, D.C., it was repulsed at Baltimore. Another British army was forced to retreat from upstate New York, and a third suffered the most lopsided defeat in British military history at New Orleans.

The United States also fared well in the war on the inland lakes and on the high seas. Naval engagements in this era were usually more deadly than land battles. Round shot, grapeshot, and canister—and the splinters they blasted loose from the wooden ships engaged—often led to casualties of 50 to 75 percent or more. With their enormous fleet, the British had a huge advantage, but U.S. squadrons won major victories on Lake Erie and Lake Champlain, and U.S. warships repeatedly beat British ships on the high seas. Even after the British had bottled up U.S. warships by blockading the Atlantic coast in 1813–1814, U.S. privateers took a heavy toll on British commerce in the English Channel, off the coast of Canada, and in the West Indies.

## Character of the War

The War of 1812 might be considered the last of the North American colonial wars because it so closely resembled the Anglo-French wars that were fought over the fate of the continent between 1689 and 1783. The armies were small (usually no more than five thousand), and the wilderness campaigns were logistical nightmares that made control of the waterways crucial. Indian auxiliaries and militia played a significant role, sometimes ensuring victory but often contributing to defeat, and they were often the perpetrators of atrocities such as killing or injuring prisoners of war or civilians.

The mere threat of an Indian massacre in which no quarter was offered to soldiers or civilians could shape the outcome of a battle. In 1812 British General Isaac Brock played the "Indian card" when he had Detroit under siege, warning his U.S. counterpart, General William Hull, that Britain's Native allies would be beyond his control once the battle was joined. Fearing a massacre, Hull surrendered his entire army. On three other occasions—at Fort Dearborn in 1812 and at the River Raisin and Fort Mims in 1813—Indian massacres took a heavy toll on American soldiers and civilians.

## Domestic Politics and Violence

Politics played an important role in this war as Republicans and Federalists alike tried to exploit the conflict for their own purposes. Republicans (forebearers of the modern Democratic party) hoped to use the war as a vehicle for preserving power, unifying their party, and silencing their domestic foes. For Federalists, the more traditional and conservative party, the war offered the prospect of returning to power by exposing the folly of Republican foreign policy.

The war precipitated domestic violence, most notably in Baltimore, where Republican mobs repeatedly tried to silence the city's outspoken Federalist newspaper, the *Federal Republican.* Three men were killed in these riots, and two others—including Revolutionary War hero Henry "Light-Horse Harry" Lee (the father of Robert E. Lee)—later died from injuries. There was similar violence or threats of violence in other Republican cities in the middle and southern states, but, far from

**Andrew Jackson with the American defenders at New Orleans, 1815.**
CORBIS/BETTMANN

silencing the Federalists, this only added fuel to the antiwar fire.

Federalists everywhere opposed the war, and in Congress they voted as a bloc, opposing the declaration of war and most of the war legislation that ensued. In New England, Federalists went the farthest, writing, speaking, and preaching against the conflict and discouraging enlistments in the army and subscriptions to the war loans. The climax of Federalist opposition was the Hartford Convention (15 December 1814–5 January 1815), a New England conference held to air Federalist grievances, provide for local defense, and propose constitutional amendments to prevent a recurrence of those Republican policies that had proved most injurious to the region.

### Restoration of Peace

The Treaty of Ghent, which brought the War of 1812 to an end, was signed on Christmas Eve of 1814, though slow communications delayed the exchange of ratifications until 17 February 1815. The treaty mentioned none of the maritime causes that had led to the war but simply restored the status quo antebellum. Although militarily the contest ended in a draw, for Republican policy makers the failure to achieve the nation's diplomatic aims meant that the war was actually a failure. But except for diehard Federalists, few Americans remembered it this way. President James Madison proclaimed the war a success, and other Republicans—touting the great victory at New Orleans—echoed him.

### Legacy of War

The war made the reputation of a number of participants, most notably Andrew Jackson and William Henry Harrison, both of whom became president. The war also enhanced the legacy of Anglophobia originally kindled by the American Revolution. Not only were the British blamed for the Indian atrocities in the West, but they were also condemned for their hard campaigning in the Chesapeake Bay region, where they promised freedom to runaway slaves, engaged in the widespread theft and destruction of private property, and, at Hampton, Virginia, committed a host of atrocities against the civilian population. The British were also reviled for mistreating American prisoners of war. In England, in April 1815, American prisoners at Dartmoor rioted to protest a delay in repatriation. British soldiers fired on the prisoners, killing six and wounding sixty others.

This bitter legacy notwithstanding, the level of violence in the conflict was about the same as that of the eighteenth-century colonial wars. Only twenty-three hundred Americans were killed in battle and only forty-five hundred were wounded. Another seventeen thousand Americans, however, probably perished from disease or other causes directly related to the war. British losses were never tabulated but were probably higher because of heavy casualties at New Orleans and the danger of disease during the Atlantic crossing.

*BIBLIOGRAPHY*

Hickey, Donald R. *The War of 1812: A Forgotten Conflict.* Urbana: University of Illinois Press, 1989.

Mahon, John K. *The War of 1812.* Gainesville: University of Florida Press, 1972.

Stagg, J. C. A. *Mr. Madison's War: Politics, Diplomacy, and Warfare in the Early American Republic, 1783–1830.* Princeton, N.J.: Princeton University Press, 1983.

DONALD R. HICKEY

*See also* **War.**

# WASHINGTON, D.C.

In January 1992 a young congressional aide, Tom Barnes, died on a Washington, D.C., street, the victim of a gunshot to the head. Although but one of more than three hundred murder victims in the nation's capital that year, Barnes's death had unusual repercussions. His boss, the U.S. senator Richard Shelby of Alabama, utilizing the power bestowed on Congress of exclusive jurisdiction over the federal district, reacted forcefully by introducing legislation requiring Washington residents to vote on a referendum reinstating the death penalty. Rejected by a two-to-one margin, the referendum nonetheless heightened national attention to the rising level of violence in Washington. Also, typical for a city situated at the South's border, it affirmed the close association between violence and race.

Created out of the two largest slaveholding states in the nation, Maryland and Virginia, the District of Columbia retained slavery well into the Civil War. Abolitionists, however, made the district an early target of their attention. Establishment of an abolitionist society in Washington in 1831 and Nat Turner's rebellion in nearby Virginia the same year intensified racial unrest in the area. Four years later, protracted violence shook Wash-

**Racial clash over the integration of a public swimming pool in Anacostia, 1949.**
COPYRIGHT WASHINGTON POST; REPRINTED BY PERMISSION OF THE D.C. PUBLIC LIBRARY.

ington after reports that a black house servant in possession of abolitionist literature had attempted to murder his white owner. Over the next three days, whites destroyed a number of properties owned or operated by African Americans. Although blacks were the object of the violence, the chief public response to the disturbance was the tightening of existing codes restricting African Americans' free association and employment. Further conflict followed the Compromise of 1850. Although this legislation abolished the slave trade in Washington, by granting slave owners the authority to retrieve runaways, it generated clashes between owners or their agents and those who sympathized with the escaped slaves.

Washington avoided further civil disorders in the nineteenth century, but the relative peace lasted only until shortly after World War I. In July 1919 a relatively minor incident unleashed four days of violence in which white mobs stormed black neighborhoods, where they in turn were met with gunfire. Prompted in part by a national Red Scare in which African Americans were accused of being sympathizers with the new Communist regime in Russia, the Washington incident claimed as many as forty lives.

Such clashes were the exception in D.C. during the early twentieth century, however. Rigid enforcement of the color line into the 1950s did not eliminate racial hostility, but discouraged its open

expression. Following a 1948 Supreme Court decision striking down restrictive housing covenants, whites organized to keep African Americans from moving into some of Washington's older neighborhoods. Ultimately, whites chose relocation over violence and physical intimidation of the kind that characterized similar transitions in industrial neighborhoods in Chicago and Detroit. Racial conflict did erupt in the predominantly white Anacostia section of Washington, D.C., following desegregation of swimming facilities there in 1949. Resistance to court-ordered desegregation of Washington's schools in 1954 was vocal but generally without serious incident.

Racial tensions increased as the Civil Rights movement moved north from the Deep South. A growing militancy put Washington's black residential majority increasingly at odds with federal authorities. Even as black activists challenged a massive highway plan for Washington in congressional hearings in April 1968, news of Martin Luther King's assassination provoked Washington's worst incidence of civil disorder. By the time peace was restored, twelve persons were dead and seventy-six hundred arrested. More than twelve hundred buildings had burned, generating property damage of $24.7 million.

Among those propelled to prominence in the turbulent 1960s was the civil rights activist Marion Barry, who proclaimed in the aftermath of the 1968

409

**National Guardsmen patrol during race riots in Washington, D.C., April 1968.** Hulton Getty/Liaison Agency

disturbances that Washington would burn again if African Americans were not given the chance to rebuild the city themselves. Such tactics, Fred Siegel charged in a 1997 book, *The Future Once Happened Here*, characterized a new style of politics that put public treasuries at the mercy of threats of civil unrest. Barry was not long in joining the mainstream as an elected politician, but as Siegel reports, he did not hesitate to invoke the specter of racial turmoil as leverage when it came to dealing with the white establishment.

Having clashed repeatedly with the police as a young activist, Barry maintained an adversarial relationship with law enforcement once in office as mayor, reducing the number of men on the Washington force from a high of fifty-one hundred in the late 1960s to thirty-six hundred in 1981. Congress insisted on putting more officers on the street, but as a crack epidemic and a deep recession

took hold in the mid-1980s, violent crime rose precipitously, leading to Washington's reputation as "the murder capital" of the country. By 1988 drug arrests in the city were made at the rate of one every twenty minutes; burglaries at the rate of one an hour. The city's murder rate of sixty per ten thousand residents far exceeded that of New York City, where the rate was twenty-five per ten thousand. In 1989 the brother of Washington's police chief, Maurice Turner, died in a drug-related incident.

In May 1991 the city suffered further turbulence, this time when a black policewoman fired on a Latino man who was resisting arrest for intoxication. Scores of Latinos poured into nearby streets, burning cars and looting stores. While no deaths followed three nights of disorder, the clashes were responsible for the fifty injuries (mostly police) and severe damage or destruction of thirty-one buildings and sixty-six police cruisers. Like African Americans before them, Latino leaders claimed that the violent nature of the incident stemmed from frustrations built up over many years of discrimination.

Following the national trend, Washington saw a significant drop in its murder rate at the end of the 1990s, down 24 percent in 1997 despite continuing turmoil in the police department. Such progress did not eliminate either the tensions between local residents and their federal overseers or the perception around the country that, for all its monumental splendor, Washington, D.C., remains a dangerous place to live. Such views are likely to persist as long as Washington remains so starkly divided between those with money and power and those who have neither.

BIBLIOGRAPHY

Gillette, Howard. *Between Justice and Beauty: Race, Planning, and the Failure of Urban Policy in Washington, D.C.* Baltimore: Johns Hopkins University Press, 1995.

Jaffe, Harry S., and Tom Sherwood. *Dream City: Race, Power, and the Decline of Washington, D.C.* New York: Simon and Schuster, 1994.

Melder, Keith, comp. *City of Magnificent Intentions*. 2d ed. Washington: Intac, 1998.

Siegel, Fred. *The Future Once Happened Here: New York, D.C., L.A., and the Fate of America's Big Cities.* New York: Free Press, 1997.

HOWARD GILLETTE, JR.

*See also* **Urban Violence.**

# WATTS RIOT

On 11 August 1965 dusk was settling on Los Angeles, then the third largest city in the United States, when Marquette Frye, a young African American, and his brother were stopped by the California Highway Patrol just outside of the neighborhood known as Watts. Frye was detained not far from his home, and his irate mother quickly appeared on the scene and began to berate her son. Matters quickly spun out of control, and soon the officers were in the process of hauling Frye, his brother, and his mother to jail. There was resistance, particularly from Frye's mother, and soon a crowd began to gather and question the authorities sharply. Then Los Angeles Police Department (LAPD) officers, whose reputation for brutality against African Americans was well established, appeared on the scene. Their presence inflamed the large crowd further, especially when the rumor arose that a young, pregnant black woman had been handled roughly by the officers. This rumor proved to be false, but it provided the spark that converted a routine traffic stop into one of the largest and most devastating episodes of civil unrest in U.S. history.

By 18 August 1965 at least thirty-four people had been killed, almost all of whom were black, in an event that was dubbed by many as the Watts Riot and by others as the Watts Uprising. Only a few apartment buildings and churches were burned to the ground; particularly hard hit, however, were retail stores that were perceived as being exploitative. Property damage was estimated at $200 million, with outposts of major retail chains and supermarkets hit particularly hard.

In retrospect, it is not surprising that the black population of Los Angeles exploded in 1965. As black migrants began pouring into Los Angeles, particularly during World War II, they found that housing opportunities were limited and that there were certain neighborhoods that they could enter only at the risk of a confrontation with police or angry whites. Many stores in the areas of South Los Angeles that served blacks were notorious for selling inferior goods at exorbitant prices. Mass transit was limited in a city and county that already were prime examples of a sprawling megalopolis; since most jobs in the area were distant from the areas where African Americans resided, the absence of transportation often left blacks stranded—and unemployed—in a metropolis crisscrossed by freeways.

The consequences of this unrest were widespread. Ironically, the turbulence beset Los Angeles shortly after President Lyndon Baines Johnson had signed the Voting Rights Act of 1965. The president and his Democratic Party fully expected that adding millions of blacks to the voting rolls would seal their domination of national politics for the next generation. Instead, the civil unrest in Los Angeles helped to spark what was termed a "white backlash" against the Civil Rights movement, which—along with other factors—caused a number of white voters to desert the Democrats and join the Republicans. The immediate beneficiary was the former actor Ronald Reagan, who defeated the once-popular Democratic incumbent Edmund G. "Pat" Brown for governor in 1966. A key factor in Reagan's successful campaign was his pledge that the kind of turmoil and violence that had hit South Los Angeles would not occur during his tenure, in part because of his promise of tough "law and order" policies.

Blacks were also affected by the aftermath of the events of August 1965. The Nation of Islam, whose mosque was a major target of assault by the LAPD during the height of the unrest, gained in popularity; the group was perceived as a militant alternative to the moderation of the National Association for the Advancement of Colored People and was viewed as unafraid to confront police misconduct. Ironically, a few months earlier Malcolm X, a former member of the Nation of Islam who had broken away to form his own group, had been slain in New York City—reportedly by former comrades in the Nation of Islam—in part because he wanted the group to follow a secular path, highlighting the issue of police misconduct. In Los Angeles, the Nation of Islam had followed precisely this path, which led to a murderous police assault on their place of worship.

A Community Alert Patrol was initiated to monitor the LAPD; this proved to be a precursor of the Black Panther Party, which was founded in Oakland, California, in 1966. The Black Panthers, whose chapter in Los Angeles proved to be one of its most influential, was deeply influenced by gangs, many of which were heavily involved in the civil unrest.

Gangs were among the few organized groups among blacks that appeared to be militant in Los Angeles in August 1965, and they certainly were the only organized groups poised to take advantage of the turmoil. The merchandise they seized and the weapons they obtained ensured that they

411

would enjoy an even higher profile in the coming years.

The Civil Rights movement, symbolized by Martin Luther King, Jr., an apostle of nonviolence, was placed on the defensive by the events of August 1965. King traveled to Los Angeles as the embers were still smoldering; there he found a great deal of skepticism. Nonviolence, which had been embraced in the Deep South, was not viewed as positively in black Los Angeles. The events in Watts compelled King to expand his crusade, as he sought to move beyond the de jure segregation of the South to the de facto segregation of the North and West.

President Johnson appointed a commission headed by former Central Intelligence Agency director John McCone that extensively investigated the events of August 1965; when Los Angeles exploded again in 1992, however, it seemed clear that the underlying causes of the uprising in Watts had not been addressed.

BIBLIOGRAPHY

Bullock, Paul. *Watts, the Aftermath: The Inside View of the Ghetto.* New York: Grove, 1969.

Horne, Gerald. *Fire This Time: The Watts Uprising and the 1960s.* Charlottesville: University Press of Virginia, 1995.

O'Toole, James. *Watts and Woodstock: Identity and Culture in the United States and South Africa.* New York: Holt, Rinehart and Winston, 1973.

GERALD HORNE

*See also* **Los Angeles; Los Angeles Riots of 1992; Riots.**

# WEAPONS

*This entry has five parts:* **Biological and Chemical, Conventional, Handguns, Nuclear,** *and* **Stun and Shock Devices**

## BIOLOGICAL AND CHEMICAL WEAPONS

Biological and chemical weapons have been viewed in most societies as particularly abhorrent. As a result, even though their means of production and devastating effects have long been understood, they have rarely been used. In the twentieth century, poison gas was used in World War I by all the warring parties, including the United States. Such weapons were not used extensively again until Iraq's chemical weapon attacks against Iran during the 1980s.

Since then, these weapons have become a subject of increasing concern. By the mid-1990s, United States authorities estimated that more countries than ever were developing these weapons. Some two dozen countries were suspected of having chemical weapons programs, and as many as seventeen of having biological weapons programs.

Chemical and biological weapons are often considered as similar threats because they share several characteristics. Both are relatively inexpensive and easy to produce. Small amounts of either type can debilitate or kill many people; both types are therefore considered weapons of mass destruction. Also, since the usual means of delivery involves releasing them into the air, these weapons may kill indiscriminately. While chemical and biological weapons have features in common, they also bear important and distinctive characteristics.

### Chemical Weapons

Chemical warfare agents are inanimate materials that can cause injury or death upon exposure. One type of chemical weapon primarily affects the surfaces with which it comes in contact. Another type damages the general nervous system after being introduced into the body. Examples of the first category include phosgene gas, chlorine gas, hydrogen cyanide, and mustard gas. (Mustard is actually composed of tiny droplets that are dispersed in the air as if a gas.)

The principal action of phosgene, chlorine, and hydrogen cyanide occurs through inhalation. Phosgene is a choking agent that causes the lungs to fill with water, while chlorine destroys the cells that line the respiratory system. Hydrogen cyanide, which is sometimes described as a blood agent, blocks oxygen from reaching the blood. Mustard is a blistering agent that damages any surface it contacts, including the skin, eyes, and lungs. It may cause death by respiratory failure.

The second category, nerve agents, blocks the transmission of nerve messages throughout the body. These substances include sarin, soman, tabun, and VX. All act by disrupting the normal action of a neurotransmitter called acetylcholine. Whether exposure is through inhalation or absorption by the skin, a single drop of nerve agent can shut down the body's nervous system. The most powerful of this group is VX, but all can cause death within minutes after exposure.

Herbicides are chemicals that kill vegetation. Agent Orange, for example, was used extensively as a defoliant by U.S. forces during the Vietnam

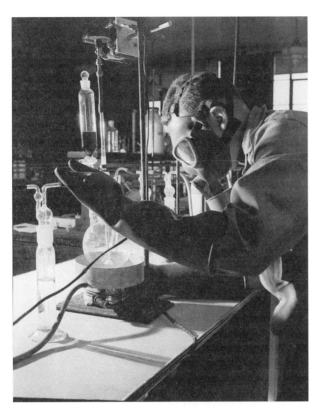

**Preparing mustard gas for smell-identification training for air raid wardens, 1942.** CORBIS/BETTMANN

War. In high concentrations it is considered a possible cause of cancer and other illnesses. Though the scientific evidence is inconclusive, many veterans of the Vietnam War have linked their subsequent ailments to exposure to Agent Orange. Some people regard herbicides as chemical weapons if used for hostile purposes. But there is no universal agreement about this, since herbicides are not intended to cause direct injury to humans or animals.

### Biological Weapons

Biological warfare agents include bacteria, viruses, fungi, and other microorganisms that can kill or incapacitate. Since they can reproduce, biological agents have the unique potential to make an environment more dangerous over time. If used for hostile purposes, any disease-causing microorganism could be considered a weapon. But specific characteristics of certain agents make them more likely to be used than others.

Some potential warfare agents can make their victims very sick but not necessarily kill them. Examples include the microorganisms that cause tu-

laremia, Q fever, and yellow fever. After suffering debilitating illness, victims of these diseases often recover, although not always. Other agents are more likely to be lethal. The bacteria that cause bubonic plague and the virus that causes smallpox can kill large numbers of people if untreated. Early antibiotic treatment usually cures plague victims, and smallpox vaccinations, when given before exposure to the virus, can prevent the disease.

Anthrax bacteria are considered likely weapons because of their particular features. They can exist as hardy, shell-like forms called spores. If inhaled, the spores pass through the respiratory tract into the body where they can become active and highly lethal. Anthrax bacteria are usually found under the soil surface and primarily cause disease in cattle and other grazing livestock. But if released into the air and inhaled, a few thousand spores can be fatal.

Botulinum toxin is also lethal in tiny doses. Although often categorized as a biological weapon, the toxin is not itself a living agent, but a product of the bacterium *Clostridium botulinum*. The toxin is dangerous whether inhaled or ingested in food or drink. Botulinum toxin is so potent that a gallon is enough to poison a small city's water supply. But because water purification systems would neutralize the toxin, the risk to users would be minimal.

### History

Poisons have been used for hostile purposes periodically throughout human history. Although poisons could be developed from mineral, plant, or animal sources, historically there was little distinction drawn between poison and disease. Whatever their source, poisons were used to assassinate people, to contaminate wells, and to cause other kinds of harm or injury.

Only after the nineteenth-century discovery that microorganisms were the cause of disease did the understanding of the difference between biological and chemical agents as weapons become clear. Because it was discovered that contagion from certain diseases could become widespread, attacks with contagious agents became especially notorious. One famous instance of biological warfare occurred in the fourteenth century when the Tartars reportedly hurled plague-infected cadavers into the walled city of Caffa, a seaport in southern Russia. Another incident took place in 1763 in colonial America, when the British gave blankets from their smallpox infirmary to Indian chiefs in the area around Fort Pitt (later Pittsburgh) in hopes of transmitting the disease. Both cases presumably resulted in epidemics in the targeted populations.

## Use of Chemical and Biological Weapons

The first large-scale attacks with chemical weapons occurred during World War I. Usage began in 1915 when German troops released chlorine gas from cylinders as the wind blew toward French lines a few hundred yards away. The yellow-green cloud enveloped the French soldiers, who choked and panicked. As the war continued, phosgene and other chemical weapons were introduced in battle, culminating with Germany's introduction of mustard gas in 1917. By the end of the war in 1918, all the major powers had used chemical weapons.

For a short period after the war, military analysts debated the utility and ethics of using poisonous weapons. The suffering caused by the gas attacks led to the 1925 Geneva Protocol, which bans the use of chemical or bacteriological agents in war. The protocol encouraged an international norm that subsequently helped deter the use of these weapons.

In the hundreds of wars and skirmishes after World War I, few involved poisonous weapons. Exceptions included Italy's limited use of chemical arms against Ethiopia in the 1930s and Egypt's against Yemen in the 1960s. Some considered the U.S. use of herbicides during the Vietnam War as chemical warfare, although this interpretation was disputed. Not until the 1980s, when Iraq attacked Iran with gas during their eight-year war, were chemical weapons again used extensively for a prolonged period of time.

Although Iraq denied using chemical weapons, UN inspectors repeatedly discovered that they were doing so. Still, no international agency or country tried to stop Iraq's actions. As a result, in the 1991 Persian Gulf War, many nations that had been silent about Iraq's actions against Iran faced a chemically and biologically equipped Iraq on the battlefield.

Ground fighting in the Gulf War lasted only a few days, and Iraq apparently did not fire any chemical or biological agents. But the experience prompted renewed attention to the problem of such weapons. In 1995 a Japanese cult called Aum Shinrikyo released sarin nerve agent in the Tokyo subway, killing twelve people and injuring 5,500. Cult leaders reportedly told authorities that their choice of weapon was inspired by the publicity about Iraq's chemical arms.

The only extensive biological attacks in the twentieth century were by Japan against China in the late 1930s and 1940s. The Japanese dropped plague and other bacteria from airplanes over several towns, causing outbreaks of disease. The only large-scale terrorist attack with a biological

**German troops releasing gas during World War I. A change of wind could be disastrous.** HULTON GETTY/LIAISON AGENCY

weapon occurred in 1984. Members of the Rajneesh cult in Wasco County, a rural area of Oregon, placed salmonella bacteria in the salad bars of several restaurants. It was discovered that this act was a rehearsal for a later effort to make potential voters sick on election day, so that the cult's candidate would win. Although 750 people became ill, none died. Evidently, the cult did not carry out its election-day plan.

### The United States and Chemical and Biological Warfare

U.S. military forces engaged in chemical warfare during World War I. Like the other major powers in the war, the United States produced and used mustard and other agents. The agony suffered by the wartime victims of poison gas prompted the United States to take a lead in negotiating the establishment of the 1925 Geneva Protocol. Paradoxically, the Senate did not hold a vote to ratify, and the United States remained one of the few major powers not a party to the agreement. Nevertheless, the United States stopped producing poison gas and effectively abided by the terms of the protocol. (The Senate ultimately ratified the protocol in 1975.)

In the early 1940s, after the United States entered World War II, the army revived the chemical corps and embarked on a biological weapons program as well. Except for Japan, the warring parties refrained from using chemical or biological weapons. Although the Germans did not use gas as a battlefield weapon, they gassed to death millions of Jews and other nonmilitary victims.

With the beginning of the Cold War in the late 1940s, the United States embarked on ambitious chemical and biological weapons programs. Besides maintaining large stocks of these weapons, the U.S. Army conducted mock biological warfare tests over cities in the United States. As the public later learned, between 1949 and 1969 the army had released bacteria and chemicals in hundreds of populated areas throughout the country. The purpose was to see how the agents would spread and survive. The targeted areas included San Francisco, Minneapolis, St. Louis, Washington National Airport, and the New York City subway. Millions of people were exposed to the bacteria and chemicals that were released during these tests.

The army's test agents included the bacteria *Serratia marcescens* and *Bacillus subtilis* and the chemical zinc cadmium sulfide. The test agents, which the army called simulants, were not as dangerous as actual warfare agents, such as the bacteria that cause anthrax or plague. Nonetheless, scientific studies available at the time of the tests suggested that the simulant agents posed risks to members of the public.

The tests over populated areas ended in 1969. That year the United States also declared that it was destroying its biological weapons and eliminating its offensive program. The initiative was soon joined by the Soviet Union and others who established the 1972 Biological Weapons Convention (BWC). The convention bans the development, production, or stockpiling of biological and toxin weapons. The treaty allows for protective biological programs, and the United States continues a biological defense research program. Suspicions that the Soviets continued an illegal offensive program were confirmed in 1992, after the breakup of the communist regime.

Even after destroying its biological weapons stocks, the United States maintained an offensive chemical program. But in a 1990 agreement with the Soviet Union one year before its demise, both countries pledged to destroy their chemical arsenals. The decision was reaffirmed by Russia and the other former Soviet republics, who became parties to the 1993 Chemical Weapons Convention (CWC). The CWC prohibits the development, production, or stockpiling of chemical weapons.

The United States became a party to the chemical treaty in 1997, and by the end of the year, 160 countries had signed the agreement. Unlike the BWC, which has no provisions for verification or enforcement, the CWC provides for onsite inspections and penalties for noncompliance. Negotiations were under way during the late 1990s to strengthen the biological treaty with similar provisions.

At the close of the twentieth century, two conflicting trends became evident. Although some countries were suspected of developing poison weapons, many more had accepted the international agreements that banned these weapons.

*BIBLIOGRAPHY*

Cole, Leonard A. *Clouds of Secrecy: The Army's Germ Warfare Tests over Populated Areas.* Lanham, Md.: Rowman and Littlefield, 1988, 1990.

———. *The Eleventh Plague: The Politics of Biological and Chemical Warfare.* New York: W. H. Freeman, 1997.

Morel, Benoit, and Kyle Olson, eds. *Shadows and Substance: The Chemical Weapons Convention.* Boulder, Colo.: Westview, 1993.

SIPRI (Stockholm International Peace Research Institute). *The Problem of Chemical and Biological Warfare.* 4 vols. New York: Humanities Press, 1971–1975.

Wright, Susan, ed. *Preventing a Biological Arms Race.* Cambridge, Mass.: Massachussetts Institute of Technology Press, 1990.

LEONARD A. COLE

*See also* **Disarmament and Arms Control; War, Aftermath of.**

### CONVENTIONAL

### The Gunpowder Era: Colonial Years to the Civil War

*Land Warfare.* Armed conflict in the new English colonies of the Atlantic seaboard was an accepted fact. The war between the colonizing powers (England, France, Spain, and Holland) could erupt at any time; consequently, the initial settlers were well armed with the newest military technology. Initially, the colonials were armed with matchlock (burning fuse) muskets; these were replaced in the early 1700s by the more effective flintlock (using a stone flint). The latter became the mainstay of U.S. infantry weapons until the mid-1800s. The inherent inaccuracy of the weapon system could be overcome only by massing units in long, linear formations. Popular images of soldiers standing shoulder-to-shoulder are based in fact, as commanders attempted to fire thousands of lead balls at relatively short ranges in order to increase their chances of killing an enemy; they then charged the enemy with bayonets, daggerlike attachments placed on the end of the musket.

American artillery pieces from 1605 to the mid-nineteenth century were bronze, smoothbore, muzzle-loading cannons that had a variety of uses, from large, ship-carried naval guns to small, mobile field artillery. Three types of artillery came into existence in the gunpowder era: guns, flat-trajectory, long-range weapons generally used by ships; mortars, stubby, high-trajectory, short-range cannons meant for siege warfare and capable of massive damage to enemy fortifications; and howitzers, the term encompassing the wide range of artillery pieces that were neither guns nor mortars. These are the classic "cannons" of the American Revolution and Civil War. The most famous howitzer was the twelve-pounder Napoleon of the Civil War era. The artillery of the period employed explosive shell, canisters (antipersonnel rounds that resembled coffee cans filled with lead shot), and solid cannonballs.

*Naval Warfare.* Wooden-hulled warships, ranging from small one- or two-gun sloops to massive ships with one hundred or more guns, plied the American seaways throughout the era. Naval artillery varied in size; in general, the larger the ship the larger and more numerous the guns. Tactics of the time were based on the broadside: mass, successive firing of cannons at an opposing ship. Like land-based warfare, war at sea attempted to overcome the inherent inaccuracy of the smoothbore cannon with firepower; in effect, a naval commander would shoot large numbers of cannonballs at an opponent in hopes of getting a few hits.

Given the toughness of wooden ships and the simple fact that wood naturally floats, war at sea in this period was often decided not by long-range artillery duels but by boarding. The attacking ship would grapple an enemy ship with ropes and hooks, pulling the vessels together. The attacker would then send armed troops across and either eliminate the enemy's crew or force their surrender. With grappling and boarding, naval warfare became as bloody as its land counterpart.

### Industrialized War: The Civil War to World War I

*Land Warfare.* The Civil War exemplifies mid-nineteenth-century changes in warfare. Early rifles were slow to load, making them useless in large numbers. The French army officer Claude-Étienne Minié overcame this difficulty by developing a conical bullet that was smaller than the barrel, and thus loaded as fast as a smoothbore musket. The bullet would then "swell" into the barrel's rifling. The effective range of muskets jumped to over 250 meters while still maintaining a rate of fire of three rounds per minute. The percussion cap, a copper cap filled with a small amount of mercury fulminate, replaced the flintlock mechanism. The combination of the percussion cap, the "Minié ball," and the use of obsolete mass tactics was in large part responsible for the Civil War's total of some 620,000 casualties—more than any other war in U.S. history.

The Civil War also served as an impetus for the invention of the working repeating rifle. But it was the inventor Richard Gatling who would change the nature of warfare in the modern era: Gatling's gun was a hand-cranked .58-caliber machine gun with a rate of fire of nearly nine hundred rounds per minute. It saw only limited use in the final year of the Civil War but was the forerunner of modern machine guns and the first machine gun of the U.S. Army, replaced by more advanced models after the Spanish-American War of 1898.

*Naval Warfare.* Naval warfare went through massive changes in the era between the 1860s and World War I, as wooden warships were replaced by ironclad and all-steel ships. Broadside tactics were discarded as pivot-mounted cannons with eight- to twelve-inch bores became the standard armament of warships. Later, a rotating turret—first seen on the USS *Monitor,* the Union ironclad that fought its famous battle against the Confederate ironclad CSS *Virginia* in 1862—replaced the pivot-gun. Among the warship's many roles were that of battleship, a warship capable of withstanding the heaviest damage in a battle line, and cruiser, serving as commerce-raider and commerce-protector. As naval guns became capable of firing longer ranges and ships became tougher, new weapons were developed to counter the changes. Torpedoes, long metal tubes filled with explosives and containing a small motor for propulsion, came into use in the early 1900s, and explosive mines, first used in the Civil War, became important weapons of the U.S. Navy before World War I.

## Era of the World Wars: World War I and World War II

*Land Warfare.* When the armies of Europe clashed in 1914, few could say what the outcome would be. The U.S. military, while experimenting with new technology before the war, was completely unprepared for the mobilization of nearly five million men in the army and navy. The U.S. Army's basic weapons of World War I can be broken down into two categories: small arms (including machine guns) and artillery. The basic weapon of the doughboy (infantryman) was the Springfield M1903 rifle, capable of firing six shots without reloading and hitting targets six hundred meters away. American-made machine guns included the M1917 .30-caliber Browning machine gun, a water-cooled monster capable of firing over six hundred rounds per minute; and the .30–06 Browning automatic rifle, a light machine gun that is considered the grandfather of modern assault rifles. During World War II, the infantryman was armed with many of the same weapons as his 1917 predecessor, with the notable exception of the M1 Garand semiautomatic rifle. As a monument to its industrial power, the United States became the

only nation in World War II to have a semiautomatic rifle as its mass-issued, primary infantry weapon.

American artillery was lacking in numbers, but not capability, in 1917. Like many of the European powers, the United States had adopted a breech-loading, pneumatic-recoil artillery piece, but lacked sufficient numbers to arm troops going to France. The French M1898, the famous "French 75," became the main artillery piece of the U.S. Army in World War I. It also used a pneumatic-recoil system, allowing for accurate and rapid fire due to absorption of the recoil of the piece without pushing the gun backward. This set the stage for indirect artillery fire (versus direct or line-of-sight fire) used by all modern armies. By 1945, American artillery had increased in size and capability, from 75-millimeter howitzers that could be carried by a mule train, to 155-millimeter "Long Toms" capable of hitting targets at ranges of eight to ten miles.

With the invention by Britain of the tank in 1915, warfare took another major turn. The United States used British and French tank designs to limited effect in 1917–1918 and relegated the tank to an infantry-support role. Following World War I, the U.S. Army's tank corps was disbanded, and the few tanks produced by the United States prior to 1939 were parceled out in small numbers to infantry units. The U.S. Army faced the main question of pre-1939 tank designers—are tanks meant to replace horse cavalry in the mobile role, or are they meant to be slow-moving fortresses to support walking infantrymen? When World War II began, the U.S. Army was still divided on the subject, finally compromising by designating three categories for tanks (light, medium, and heavy) and organizing them in specialized units, such as cavalry groups (regimental-sized elements supporting corps-sized units), tank battalions, and tank destroyer battalions (specially designed antitank artillery pieces mounted on a tank chassis). By 1945, American military leaders realized that the medium tank, especially the M4A3 Sherman and its later models, formed the backbone of armored warfare, combining infantry-support capabilities with speed. Additionally, the Sherman could be built in huge numbers. Over forty-one thousand Sherman tanks were built by U.S. factories from 1940 to 1945 and saw action in the armies of all the Allied powers. Despite its inferiority to the German tank models, such as the Tiger and Panther, the Sherman tank continued to serve as the front-line U.S. tank of World War II.

**Dismantling a 75-mm howitzer, 1942. Photo by Jack Delano.** LIBRARY OF CONGRESS

*Air Warfare.* World War I saw the birth of mechanized aerial warfare, beginning with reconnaissance missions and ending with the first strategic bombing raids of enemy cities. By 1919, the United States, along with all other industrialized nations, realized that the airplane was a crucial part of a nation's war machine. American airpower from 1919 to 1945 can be divided into three categories. First, the fighter plane (or the pursuit, or interceptor, plane) was the most-produced aircraft type of the period. Fighter aircraft could serve as defenders over beachheads or cities, were relatively cheap to produce, and in general required only one pilot. Beginning with biplanes, such as the French Spad XIII in 1918 and ending with high-performance piston-driven planes of 1945 like the P-51 Mustang, the fighter plane formed the basis of American airpower.

Second, the medium, or tactical, bomber attempted to fill both the role of ground-support aircraft and light bomber. However, ground-to-air communication between bombers and the troops they supported was in its infancy, and most medium bombers tended to be used for interdiction missions. Interdiction consisted of air raids aimed at stopping enemy forces from reaching the battlefield; for example, an air attack might be aimed at destroying a key bridge. The main U.S. medium

bomber of World War II was the B-25 Mitchell, with nearly ten thousand produced. In general, most ground-support missions were flown not by specific bomber-class airplanes, but by multirole fighters such as the P-47 Thunderbolt and F6F Hellcat, effectively creating their own typology, that of the fighter-bomber.

Third, strategic bombing appealed greatly to American policy makers. Isolationism, fear of invasion, and budgetary constraints of the 1920s and 1930s all played a role in encouraging the growth of U.S. heavy bombers, the epitome of which in World War II was the B-17 Flying Fortress. Bristling with thirteen .50-caliber machine guns, and carrying an average bomb load of six thousand pounds, the B-17 was considered a superweapon of its day. Other heavy-bomber models followed in the war years, such as the B-24 Liberator and the B-29 Superfortress, the latter capable of carrying more than three times the B-17's bomb load. It was a B-29 that inaugurated the nuclear age in August 1945 by dropping the atomic bomb on Hiroshima, Japan.

The U.S. bombing campaigns against Germany and Japan, while debatable in their effectiveness, demonstrated the devastation that could be wrought by fleets of thousands of heavy bombers. The heavy bomber served in a variety of other roles, from antisubmarine patrols in the North Atlantic to ground-support during the massive carpet-bombing raids on enemy ground units. These aircraft serve as the pattern of U.S. heavy-bomber design to the present, relying on toughness, speed, and technological innovation to defeat opponents.

*Naval Warfare.* The invention of the airplane and the continued development of the submarine determined U.S. naval strategy and operations from 1919 to 1945. The early experiments with ship-launched aircraft soon led to the use of seaplanes carried on large surface ships, such as battleships and heavy cruisers. The launching of the first U.S. aircraft carrier in 1922, the USS *Langley,* was followed in the early 1930s by the first large, or fleet, carriers. Capable of carrying up to seventy airplanes, the aircraft carrier was initially designed as a support vessel that would spot enemy ships for the big-gun battleships to engage. The airplanes on an aircraft carrier included dive bombers (which attacked by diving on a ship in an almost vertical dive and then releasing its bomb), torpedo bombers (carrying a single torpedo capable of sinking most ships and badly damaging even the largest), and fighters (used to escort bombers to their targets and to defend the friendly ships). The aircraft carrier became the primary determination of a fleet's strength, especially after the devastating Japanese raid on Pearl Harbor, Hawaii, in December 1941. By 1945, battleships had been diverted to supporting amphibious invasions or providing antiaircraft protection to the aircraft carriers, while the carriers became the big ships of the U.S. Navy, capable of a multitude of roles, from antishipping to ground support.

As much as the aircraft carrier, the submarine determined U.S. victory over Japan by 1945. U.S. naval designers in the 1920s and 1930s determined that Japan was the most probable near-term enemy and designed long-range submarines toward the threat. Their planning had paid off by 1945, since U.S. submarines literally destroyed the Japanese merchant fleet to an extent only dreamed of by other submarine-using nations. Some 1,286 Japanese merchant vessels were sunk by U.S. and Allied submarines in the war, accounting for well over half of the total lost. The resulting effect was the economic and industrial collapse of the Japanese home islands and the isolation of Japanese troops from resupply and reinforcement. By the end of the war, the United States had produced the largest navy in history, including 141 aircraft carriers (including small escort carriers intended for antisubmarine work), 203 submarines, and over 750 cruisers and destroyers. The aircraft carrier and submarine had become the main weapons of the U.S. Navy, and continued their dominance in U.S. naval policy for the rest of the twentieth century.

## The Cold War and After

*Land Warfare.* The coming of the nuclear age at the end of World War II was believed by many to end the role of the foot soldier in war. However, the realities of the Cold War soon demonstrated the need for a graduated scale of war, from counterguerrilla operations to planning for a World War II–style conflict in Central Europe against the Warsaw Pact. The Korean War (1950–1953) and commitment to the North Atlantic Treaty Organization (NATO) led to rearmament and expansion of the U.S. Army beginning in the 1950s and continuing until 1989. The perceived Soviet threat in Europe pushed further technological refinements during the Cold War, and Congress provided ample funding for new weapons systems. The U.S. Army received a new main battle tank (or MBT) every decade or so, added larger and more mobile field artillery (including nuclear-capable 8-inch and 155-millimeter guns), developed advanced missile artillery such as Pershing and MLRS (multiple launch rocket system) surface-to-surface missiles, and introduced new small arms such as the M60 machine gun and the M16 rifle.

In the early 1960s, development of effective counterinsurgency forces resulted in the organization of the Special Forces (or Green Berets) and the growth of airmobile operations based on helicopters. The Vietnam War (1965–1973) became the testing ground for both Special Forces and the helicopter in combat. The use of Special Operations Forces (SOF) continues today in counterinsurgency, foreign military training, and counterterrorism programs of the U.S. military. The helicopter matured in the late 1960s from a mode of transportation to a direct-combat weapon. Attack helicopters, such as the heavily armed and capable AH-1 Cobra, entered the army inventory as tank busters and ground-support aircraft, fulfilling the role held earlier by the fighter-bombers of World War II. Again, the Cold War spurred further development, and later models of the Cobra, and the newer AH-64 Apache, formed the mainstay of U.S.

Army and Marine Corps aviation well into the 1990s. During the 1991 Persian Gulf War, attack helicopters and modern MBTs, such as the M1A2 Abrams, demonstrated the destructive power of conventional weapons on the land battlefield.

As antitank artillery had been developed before and during World War II, military planners looked for a new method of stopping modern armor. The 1973 Yom Kippur War, in which Egypt and Syria attacked Israel, saw the rise of the antitank missile and brought infantrymen back on par with the tank. The United States responded to the demonstration of the Arab states' Soviet-produced weaponry by developing the TOW (*t*ube-launched, *o*ptically tracked, *w*ire-guided) antitank missile in the late 1960s and early 1970s and thereafter continued to develop a variety of antitank missiles. The increased speed of aircraft demanded the development of effective air-defense missiles for the U.S. ground forces. Beginning in the 1950s, numerous systems entered the inventory, from the Nike high-altitude and Hawk low-altitude air-defense missiles to shoulder-fired missiles such as the Stinger (which Afghani guerrillas effectively used during the 1979–1989 Soviet invasion of Afghanistan). The United States also continued to develop longer-range antiair missiles and by the late 1980s the U.S. inventory included the Patriot missile (used in the Gulf War) and the vehicle-mounted Avenger system.

*Air Warfare.* The Cold War also encouraged the development of nuclear-capable heavy bombers. The U.S. Air Force's Strategic Air Command (SAC) grew in size and capability throughout the Cold War, while its tactical (ground-support) mission diminished in importance. However, the Korean War and the Vietnam War demonstrated that airpower still had a major role to play in a nonnuclear war. In Korea, World War II–vintage aircraft continued to provide the traditional ground-support role, from direct support to U.S. and United Nations ground forces to interdiction missions along vulnerable enemy supply lines. In Vietnam, U.S. and South Vietnamese aircraft interdicted the Ho Chi Minh Trail, attacked enemy troop concentrations, and performed critical surveillance missions. Additionally, the F-111 strike bomber, a supersonic jet bomber that continued the tradition of the medium bombers of World War II, was widely used against key targets in North Vietnam. Even the B-52s, the mainstay of the air force's nuclear-bomber force, saw heavy action in the Vietnam War. B-52s provided carpet-bombing strikes against large North

Vietnam Army troop formations around Khe Sanh in 1968 and the 1972 air raids on Hanoi. Even as late as the 1991 Gulf War, B-52s were used in carpet-bombing roles in support of U.S. ground forces.

The Arab-Israeli wars of 1967 and 1973, and the U.S. experience over the skies of North Vietnam, demonstrated to both East and West the vulnerability of aircraft to surface-to-air missiles (commonly called SAMs) and advanced radar defenses. In response to the growing threat of surface-based air defense, the United States poured large amounts of funding into developing radar-defeating technology, and by the late 1980s the research had paid off with the introduction of the F-117 Stealth fighter and, by the early 1990s, of the B-2 Stealth bomber. Stealth technology uses advanced alloys, radar-deflecting and -absorbing materials, and computer-designed aircraft in an attempt to make an airplane "invisible" to radar. Intended to be a deep-strike aircraft in a U.S.-Soviet war, the Stealth fighter and bomber have become key parts of selective employment of combat strength in areas critical to U.S. interests.

The U.S. Air Force's heavy-bomber fleet, by the late 1970s, had also adopted the cruise missile for "standoff" missions, enabling aircraft to fire missiles well out of range of enemy air defenses. The cruise missile is a subsonic missile that uses state-of-the-art computers and satellite navigation to guide it to its target, and it has a range of nine hundred to twelve hundred miles. Some strategists see the cruise missile as the perfect weapon, combining accuracy and explosive power with little to no danger to the launching aircrew. Other "smart" weapons, such as laser- and television-guided bombs, were developed from the mid-1960s onward, and have been widely used since 1990.

*Naval Warfare.* Naval warfare after 1945 continued to focus on the aircraft carrier as the main tool of force projection. Aircraft carriers grew in size and capability and could fill a multitude of roles. U.S. Navy carriers saw action in every conflict from Korea to the Gulf War.

Improvements in communications and navigation, using space-based satellites and high-altitude reconnaissance aircraft, and the development of a nuclear-powered fleet revolutionized naval warfare. Surface vessels, with the exception of the carriers, became smaller, faster, and deadlier than ever before. To counter the threat of air attack, new antiaircraft missiles were developed; to replace the big guns of the battleships, antiship missiles were used (such as the Harpoon); and to fight the submarine threat, a new generation of antisub weapons, including antisubmarine torpedoes and missiles, came into use. By the late 1980s, cruise missiles became one of the main weapons on larger surface ships. Because of political considerations, such as the ability of the navy to operate for long periods of time from international waters without the need for land-based facilities, the U.S. Navy has become the first-response force to areas in which the United States deploys military forces. Nuclear-powered supercarriers, with crews of over five thousand sailors and a host of smaller escort and support vessels, are routinely dispatched to deal with military crises, well before either land or air forces become involved.

*Information and Space Warfare.* The invention of the computer in the 1940s, and its applicability to military uses, has led to a new frontier of conflict, information warfare. The U.S. military's large and complex command, control, communications, and information (C3I) systems are largely dependent on computers for operation. Consequently, the armed services have devoted large resources to the development of counterintrusion and intrusion assets. The future of warfare may well depend on the proper operation of computers and their defense.

The military use of space grew throughout the Cold War, beginning with the reaction to the Soviet launching of Sputnik in 1957. U.S. military planners developed a variety of navigational satellites that could assist in air, sea, and ground movement, and sponsored the use of intelligence-gathering "spy" satellites. By the 1980s the U.S. military had become dependent on satellites for everything from television for troops stationed overseas to highly classified reconnaissance on Warsaw Pact military operations and nuclear-weapons testing. Every weapons system gives rise to a counter-weapon, and use of satellites led to development of the ASAT (antisatellite) system. An ASAT missile could be fired from a high-altitude warplane to destroy or damage low-flying satellites, the very satellites most valuable to military commanders. Military use of space for a variety of functions keeps expanding and the digitalization and computerization of the U.S. Armed Forces continues.

## The Future of Conventional Warfare

*Lethal Warfare.* As the history of the post-1945 era has demonstrated, the likelihood of a nonaccidental nuclear war is remote. In stark contrast, conventional warfare, from infantry-based battles in the hills of Korea to tank duels in the Iraqi desert, has continued to be the primary way in which nations conduct war. The development of aircraft, ships, and ground weapons, especially those that involve cutting-edge computer technology, was proceeding at an exponential rate at the end of the twentieth century, but the era of the "push-button war" (as stated by some strategists in the late 1940s) had yet to arrive. Conventional forces continued to be dependent upon men and women to operate the machinery of conflict, despite rapidly developing technology.

*Nonlethal Warfare.* Beginning with tear gases, rubber bullets, and other equipment used by riot control forces, the U.S. military has done extensive testing and development of nonlethal weapons. In the post–Cold War world, the applicability of weapons that do not kill opponents but instead temporarily paralyze or immobilize them is of great use. U.S. forces on humanitarian or peace-keeping missions, for example, require weapons that do not kill their targets. In the future, nonlethal weapons, from "sticky foam," which literally glues a target into place, to lasers, sonic beams, and other such devices once placed in the realm of science fiction, will likely have a bigger role in conjunction with conventional lethal weapons.

BIBLIOGRAPHY

Boyne, Walter J. *Beyond the Wild Blue: A History of the United States Air Force, 1947–1997.* New York: St. Martin's, 1997.

Coggins, Jack. *Arms and Equipment of the Civil War.* Garden City, N.Y.: Doubleday, 1962.

Doughty, Robert A., Ira D. Gruber, et al. *Warfare in the Western World.* Vols. 1 and 2. Lexington, Mass.: Heath, 1996.

Ellis, John. *The World War II Databook: The Essential Facts and Figures for All Combatants.* London: Aurum, 1993.

Hogg, Ian. *Weapons That Changed the World.* New York: Arbor House, 1986.

Howarth, Stephen. *To Shining Sea: A History of the U.S. Navy, 1775–1991.* New York: Random House, 1991.

Kirk, John, and Robert Young. *Great Weapons of World War II.* New York: Walker, 1967.

Leach, Douglas E. *Arms for Empire: A Military History of the British Colonies in North America, 1607–1763.* New York: Macmillan, 1973.

Mason, Tony. *Airpower: A Centennial Appraisal.* Washington: Brassey's, 1994.

Pemsel, Helmut. *A History of War at Sea: An Atlas and Chronology of Conflict at Sea from Earliest Times to the Present.* Annapolis, Md.: Naval Institute Press, 1979.

Weigley, Russell F. *The American Way of War.* New York: Macmillan, 1973.

ROBERT R. MACKEY

*See also* **War** *and entries on individual conflicts.*

## HANDGUNS

The term *handgun* originated in or before the sixteenth century. Originally the term referred to a rifle that was small and light enough that it could be supported by one's arm, as opposed to one that could be fired only when settled on a rest. By the eighteenth century, however, the term had its present meaning of a firearm designed to be fired with one hand.

### Handguns Versus Long Guns (Rifles and Shotguns)

Handguns originally had one or more barrels, which had to be loaded individually through the muzzle, which was held pointing up so loose (black) gunpowder could be poured down into it. The powder was then compacted by having a patch of cloth pushed against it with a ramrod, and then a bullet was dropped on top and compacted again with the ramrod. Firing involved pulling back an external hammer, which would fall when the trigger was pulled, igniting some powder that had been placed in a pan under the hammer, which, in turn, ignited the powder in the barrel. Misfires would commonly occur because the powder in either place had become wet or otherwise inoperative.

Until late in the eighteenth century, a variety of ways were used to get the powder in the pan to ignite. The most important was the flintlock, which, as the name implies, used a flint to generate a flame when the hammer fell. The early nineteenth century saw the appearance of guns with a metal cap (percussion cap) filled with fulminate of mercury, which would ignite when the hammer fell on it. In the pre-revolver era long guns operated in the same general fashion.

Modern handguns (and long guns) fire a fixed cartridge that contains smokeless powder and a bullet seated in the cartridge's open end. At the opposite end is a primer. Igniting when hit by the firing pin, the primer fires the smokeless powder. The powder does not explode, rather, it burns, creating expanding gases that have no way of escaping except by pushing the bullet down the gun's barrel.

The longer the barrel, the more velocity can be imparted to the bullet before it reaches the open air, one of several reasons rifles are much deadlier than handguns. Many rifle bullets can penetrate through fifty or more inches of wood; thus they are capable of penetrating one body and wounding others beyond. Furthermore, rifle bullets tend to tumble end over end when they encounter the naturally destabilizing medium of a body. Tumbling is largely irrelevant to the use of handguns because their bullets are only slightly longer than they are wide, but a tumbling rifle bullet greatly increases the severity of any wound. Depending on the caliber of the gun, only 15 percent of those shot with handguns die, while 50 percent or more of those shot with high-caliber rifles die.

Shotguns are even deadlier. A shotgun is a weapon with a long barrel (minimum eighteen inches and generally of large diameter) designed to be fired from the shoulder. It fires either a huge slug or multiple large pellets (used for deer hunting) or many small pellets (called birdshot). With one pull of the trigger a single-shot 12-gauge hunting shotgun (costing as little as $69) loaded with 00 buckshot discharges as many missiles of comparable size at comparable velocity as the fifteen-shot U.S. Armed Forces Beretta M-9 semiautomatic pistol, which sells for over $600. Among victims intentionally shot with a 12-gauge shotgun, two-thirds or more die.

A further technical characteristic of modern handguns is that, unlike long guns, they are generally designed so that they do not fire if dropped. Also, unlike most long guns, handgun firing mechanisms require too much strength to be actuated by very small children. This, along with their lower lethality and penetration, is reflected in accidental-death trends. In the twenty-year period from 1967 to 1986, the rate of fatal gun accidents fell almost two-thirds, a reduction of roughly 1,500 deaths annually. Not coincidentally, during that same period the number of civilian-owned handguns in America increased by 173 percent, and the handgun replaced the long gun as the weapon most often used for defense in American homes. At the end of the twentieth century long guns accounted for less than 10 percent of the firearms kept loaded at any one time in American homes. Long guns are so disproportionately accident-prone and deadly that they are involved in 59 percent of fatal gun accidents.

### Types of Handguns

With the exception of rarely encountered aberrant types of pistols such as high-bolt-action pistols, modern handguns are divided into two types: the semiautomatic pistol, which first appeared about 1892, and the revolver, which was perfected by the American inventor Samuel Colt from the

1830s on. Revolvers have a cylinder that holds five to nine shots, depending on the cartridge caliber. Because most nineteenth-century revolvers could go off if dropped, a prudent owner would leave the chamber directly beneath the hammer, or firing pin, empty. Until late in that century revolvers were "single-action," that is, the hammer had to be manually cocked. This rotated the cylinder, bringing a loaded chamber under the hammer; by pulling the trigger, the cocked hammer would descend, firing the round. To continue firing required recocking the hammer, thereby rotating another loaded chamber into play, and pulling the trigger again. (Unlike semiautomatic pistols, revolvers have no safety mechanism to prevent their being fired after being cocked. Revolvers were never intended to be carried in the cocked mode, for any slight pressure on the trigger will discharge a cocked revolver.)

The cartridge had not yet been invented, and early revolvers were "cap and ball" weapons: The black powder was secured in the cylinder chambers on one end by a metal cap containing fulminate of mercury, while the bullet capped the other end. When the hammer struck the cap, it fired the powder, thereby propelling the bullet down the barrel. Early Colt revolvers resembled semiautomatic pistols (but not modern revolvers) in having interchangeable cylinders; one could carry multiple loaded spare cylinders so that, having fired the revolver dry, the empty cylinder could be dropped out and replaced with another loaded cylinder.

By the end of the nineteenth century three major improvements had occurred:

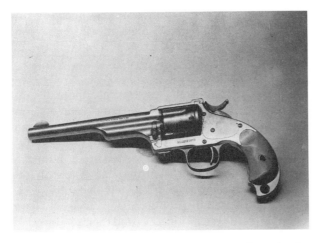

**An 1873 model .44-caliber Hopkins and Allen pistol used by Jesse James.** LIBRARY OF CONGRESS

1. The "double-action" revolver, which can be fired by simply pulling the trigger without first cocking the hammer, was introduced. (Double-action revolvers can generally fire single action as well, by first manually cocking the hammer and then pulling the trigger. Single action is generally used for target accuracy since the single-action trigger pull is much lighter and smoother than the double action.) Today virtually all revolvers manufactured are double action; indeed, there is a trend toward producing double-action-only revolvers because they are safer than those that allow firing in the single-action mode.
2. The fixed cartridge rendered "cap and ball" weapons obsolete.
3. Black powder (so-called because discharging the firearm resulted in a cloud of black smoke) was replaced with smokeless powder, which is more powerful, reliable, and safe. Smokeless powder and the invention of the fixed cartridge made the semiautomatic pistol practicable.

Unlike the revolver, which uses a round cylinder in which holes are placed to accommodate the cartridges, the semiautomatic handgun has a long, straight magazine with a spring in the bottom. The cartridges are loaded into the magazine, which is normally seated in the grip and detachable for loading. There is a slide at the top over the magazine. Manually pulling the slide to the rear takes the top cartridge from the magazine, placing it in the firing chamber, and simultaneously cocks the firing mechanism. Firing produces recoil, which in the semiautomatic is directed so that it automatically recycles the slide, putting the next cartridge in the chamber. The trigger may then be pulled again and again until the magazine is empty. (By contrast, a fully automatic firearm fires multiple rounds from one trigger pull and continues to fire as long as the trigger is held back. Generally, fully automatic guns are available only as long guns because recoil makes fully automatic pistols uncontrollable.)

Unlike revolvers, many semiautomatics have a safety so that they may be carried safely with a shell in the firing chamber and the hammer cocked ("cocked and locked"). On earlier semiautomatics, however, the safety only locks the trigger. It does not prevent accidental discharge if the pistol is dropped. Designs developed from the mid–

## Firearm Availability and Homicide Rates

Firearm availability is not invariably or even usually associated with high homicide rates. The criminologist Gary Kleck's 1997 survey of homicide rates and firearm ownership in thirty-six developed nations found no significant correlation between these two factors. Likewise, murder rates appear to have substantially decreased since firearms became available in the mid-fifteenth century. As indicated in the table, over a twenty-year period a 68.3 percent increase in total U.S. firearms and a 105.8 percent increase in handguns corresponded with a slight decline—not an increase—in the homicide rate. Increases in handgun and total gun ownership since 1994 have coincided with a 14.6 percent decline from the 1975 homicide rate. Two caveats are necessary, however. First, these figures refer only to nongovernment homicide. In the twentieth century more people were killed by governments than by criminals. Second, the long-term decline in civilian homicide has been subject to occasional upswings. For instance, after World War II, homicide rates remained stable in the United States and then doubled between 1960 and 1973; the rate then stabilized again at eight to ten per hundred thousand until the mid-1990s, when it began to dip a little below eight. European murder rates rose steadily at a much faster rate than the American rate but still remained lower because Europe started out with a much lower rate in the early twentieth century. Again, however, there is no consistent relation to firearm ownership.

ally all the world's other armies and police agencies. First, its recoil is partially absorbed in cycling the slide, producing less felt recoil. Second, its magazine holds more rounds (commonly eight to sixteen) than a comparable caliber revolver (usually six). Finally, it can be reloaded much more rapidly.

How strongly European police preferred the semiautomatic pistol over the revolver was illustrated by the reaction of German police when the U.S. occupation forces equipped them with fine Smith and Wesson revolvers after World War II. As soon as Germany attained independence, German police disposed of the revolvers, replacing them with cheap Spanish pistols, which was all they could then afford. An incident in 1972 dramatized for European police the major advantage of the revolver (though well-maintained semiautomatics are highly reliable, the inherently simpler revolver is even more reliable with less care). While trapped in a procession, British Princess Anne's limousine was attacked by a man armed with two .22-caliber revolvers. Her bodyguard jumped out with the highly-thought-of Walther PPK semiautomatic, which jammed. (He threw it at the attacker and then subdued him barehanded, despite receiving multiple bullet wounds.) In the wake of this incident, some European police forces, particularly the French, returned to the revolver.

Semiautomatic pistols are the subjects of multiple mythologies. It is, for instance, not true that they fire faster than revolvers. In fact, they are slightly slower, though the difference is so small as to be immaterial. Neither are semiautomatics more lethal shot-for-shot. The most common revolvers (.38 special and .357 magnum) and semiautomatics (.380 and 9mm parabellum) fire virtually identical-diameter bullets, albeit at different velocities.

### Handguns and Crime

Semiautomatics are theoretically more deadly because of their greater magazine capacity and more rapid reloading capability. In incidents where criminals discharge a handgun, however, on average less than three rounds are fired, so the difference between a six-shot revolver and a fifteen-shot semiautomatic is irrelevant. Nor are semiautomatics used disproportionately in crime. True, both sales of semiautomatics and their use by criminals have slowly risen. But the proportion of gun crimes that involve semiautomatic pistols does not exceed the proportion of handguns that are semi-

twentieth century on (including firing-pin-locking devices, since the 1950s), particularly on the so-called double-action semiautomatic, do preclude such accidental discharge. In the double action, after cycling the slide to bring a cartridge into the chamber, the hammer can be deactivated—from which position it can nevertheless be fired by a single long, heavy trigger pull. Thereafter, of course, the recoil cycles the slide automatically for every successive shot.

While the British army clung to the revolver until well after World War II and American police did so into the 1970s, three major advantages of the semiautomatic dictated its adoption by virtu-

U.S. Murder Rates and Increases in Gun Ownership, 1974–1998.

| | Total Gun Ownership | | Guns per 1,000 Population | | Homicide Rate per 100,000 Population |
|---|---|---|---|---|---|
| | Handguns | All Guns | Handguns | All Guns | |
| 1974 | 39,086,637 | 134,587,281 | 192.8 | 657.1 | 9.8 |
| 1998 | 94,890,222 | 254,512,056 | 372.8 | 942.6 | 6.2 |

SOURCE: Figures for 1998 based on the FBI's preliminary annual release estimate for the 1998 homicide rate; the Bureau of the Census mid-range estimate for the 1998 U.S. population; and an estimate for gun sales for the years 1995–1997 based on averaging gun sales for the years 1992–1994 as given in Kleck, Gary, *Targeting Guns: Firearms and Violence in America* (New York: de Gruyter, 1997).

automatic. Indeed, the proportion of gun crimes that involve semiautomatic pistols is slightly less than the proportion of semiautomatics in the entire stock of handguns. It has been suggested that changes in criminal firearm preferences follow patterns set by the group criminals most respect, the police. In the 1960s, when police switched from .38 specials to the much more powerful magnum revolvers, some criminals followed suit, as they did beginning in the 1970s when police moved to the less deadly (but with a greater magazine capacity) 9 mm semiautomatic. Nonetheless, for many decades the primary murder weapons have been .38 specials and .357 magnum revolvers.

Four to seven million new firearms are sold annually to civilians in the United States; two to four million of them are handguns. But the total stock of firearms is more difficult to estimate than the total stock of any comparably priced consumer items, such as television sets. Handguns possessed by avid target shooters, like televisions possessed by avid watchers, might have a life expectancy of three to five years, although, as with televisions, replacement of crucial parts could extend life for a further three to five years. A handgun that is shot only five hundred times a year would have a life expectancy of two hundred to six hundred years; and a handgun that is simply kept for self-defense without ever being shot has an unlimited life expectancy if kept minimally well maintained.

On the basis of available figures for firearms sales since 1898, it is estimated that as of 1994 American civilians owned over 235.5 million firearms, which is equivalent to 904 firearms for every 1,000 Americans, with handguns exceeding 84.5 million (see table). This does not mean, however, that firearms are more available in the United States than anywhere else. Availability is greatest in Israel, where every law-abiding, responsible adult Jewish applicant is licensed to own and carry a handgun, while the government loans out millions of arms for use by those who do not own a gun.

*BIBLIOGRAPHY*

DiMaio, Vincent. *Gunshot Wounds: Practical Aspects of Firearms, Ballistics, and Forensic Techniques.* New York: Elsevier, 1985.

Ezell, Edward C. *Small Arms of the Western World.* 11th ed. Harrisburg, Penn.: Stackpole, 1977.

Fackler, Martin L. "Gunshot Wound Review." *Annals of Emergency Medicine* 28 (1996).

Hogg, Ian, and John Weeks. *Pistols of the World.* 3d ed. Northridge, Ill.: DBI, 1992.

Kleck, Gary. *Targeting Guns: Firearms and Violence in America.* New York: de Gruyter, 1997.

Polsby, Daniel D., and Don B. Kates. "American Homicide Exceptionalism." *University of Colorado Law Review* 69, no. 4 (fall 1998).

———. "Of Holocausts and Gun Control." *Washington University Law Quarterly* 75, no. 4 (1997).

DON B. KATES

*See also* **Gun Control; Gun Violence: Overview** *and* **Gun Culture; Saturday Night Specials.**

## NUCLEAR

On 6 August 1945 air raid sirens wailed above the ancient city of Hiroshima, Japan, as three B-29 Superfortress bombers flew overhead. Many Japanese ignored the alarms for such a small flight of American planes. Moments later, a brilliant flash, followed by a wave of searing fire, destroyed the city and killed ninety thousand people. The nuclear age had begun.

### History of U.S. Nuclear Weapons Development

American nuclear weapons development can be directly traced to a 1939 letter from physicist

Albert Einstein to President Franklin D. Roosevelt. Einstein, a refugee from Nazi Germany, alerted Roosevelt to the possibility of German development of a fission bomb of unimaginable destructive power. Roosevelt responded by beginning one of the most expensive and secretive government programs ever devised: the Manhattan Project. Under the leadership of physicist Robert J. Oppenheimer, the Manhattan Project tested the first nuclear weapon at Alamogordo, New Mexico, in July 1945. Two additional bombs were immediately produced, code-named Fat Man and Little Boy after their distinctive design differences (one was stubby and round, the other long and cigar-shaped). Little Boy was dropped on Hiroshima, while Fat Man demolished the city of Nagasaki, Japan, on 8 August 1945, leading to Japanese surrender later that month.

From 1945 to 1949 the atomic bomb program was an American monopoly. Serious consideration was given to nuclear disarmament as envisioned in the United Nations Charter; however, the rise of the U.S.-Soviet Cold War prevented the implementation of an international nuclear weapons control agency. When the Soviets tested their first atomic bomb in 1949, the United States responded by developing the fusion bomb (also known as the hydrogen bomb, the thermonuclear bomb, or simply the H-bomb). In simple terms, the H-bomb combined two atomic nuclei into a single nucleus, and the resultant energy constituted the explosive

power of the bomb; the fission bomb relied on the opposite principle of splitting a nucleus into two or more separate atomic nuclei, with the explosion being generated by the released energy.

Throughout the twentieth century nuclear weapons varied only in terms of their explosive power. In contrast, the delivery systems that carried the bombs, from manned bombers to submarines to land-based missiles and artillery, changed dramatically. It was these delivery systems that shaped the employment and politics of nuclear war.

## Nuclear Delivery Systems: Bombers and Missiles

For the United States and the USSR, the atomic bomb presented a dilemma. Was it a political-strategic weapon, a "doomsday device" reserved as a last resort, if even then, or was it just another weapon, albeit much more destructive? This dichotomy affected the development of a wide variety of delivery systems for nuclear weapons.

Initially, the manned bomber was the primary means of delivering nuclear weapons. The bomber, whether the propeller-driven B-29 or the later B-2 Stealth, possessed several advantages and one major disadvantage. First, the manned bomber was a perfect "political" weapon. During the Cold War, the United States or the Soviet Union could indicate their level of military readiness by placing their respective nuclear bomber fleets on alert. This

**Atomic bomb of the "Fat Man" variety, the kind dropped on Nagasaki on 9 August 1945.** CORBIS

would send a strong signal to the opposing side about their resolve and military preparedness. Second, bombers could be recalled if a crisis situation receded. For example, a diplomat could show his nation's peaceful intentions by canceling a bombing mission already in the air. Additionally, flight times from the United States to the Soviet Union, and vice versa, were numbered in hours, giving ample time for high-level diplomacy to bring about an end to the crisis. Lastly, the bomber had a variety of nonnuclear roles, such as conventional bombing missions. However, the bomber also had a glaring weakness: it was an airplane. Aircraft are vulnerable to enemy air defenses such as interceptor aircraft or missiles, weather, and mechanical breakdown. It was these weaknesses that led both superpowers to develop the second major delivery system for nuclear weapons—the ballistic missile.

Ballistic missiles descended directly from the German V-2 rockets of World War II. In their simplest version ballistic missiles are fired from one location and projected to extremely high altitudes to descend upon their targets, somewhat like very-long-range artillery shells. In their most advanced incarnation, ballistic missiles equipped with advanced guidance systems can strike targets from ten thousand miles away with an estimated fifty-foot margin of error. American nuclear-capable missiles emerged in the mid-1950s with the Titan I and Atlas rockets, able to deliver a one-megaton (equal to the explosive power of one million tons of TNT) nuclear warhead at a range of 5,500 and 6,250 miles, respectively. Under U.S. Air Force control, these first intercontinental ballistic missiles (ICBMs) were deployed beginning in 1959 at locations that could hit Soviet cities.

The U.S. Army and Navy also developed their own nuclear weapons programs. For the army, a series of tactical nuclear weapons, limited in yield to as little as .02 kilotons, emerged as part of the Pentomic Division program, which attempted to redesign ground forces around the new weapons. Although the Pentomic Division program was eventually deemed a failure due to poor planning, tactical nuclear weapons remained a central facet of army defense planning, especially in Western Europe. The navy, in contrast, developed a strategic nuclear program that competed with the air force program in many respects. Although the navy kept nuclear-capable aircraft on its carriers from the early 1950s onward, it did not begin development of sea-launched ballistic missiles (SLBMs) until the end of the decade. The USS

*George Washington*, the first SSBN (in naval terminology, *SS* stands for "submarine," while *BN* stands for "ballistic, nuclear"), carried the new Polaris missile, a solid-fuel rocket with a range of nearly 2,850 miles.

The nuclear-missile-carrying submarine presented an interesting dilemma to diplomats and policy makers. It was either a revenge weapon, meant to hit an enemy that had already attacked, or a "first strike" weapon, meant to launch a surprise attack on an unprepared foe. Unlike nuclear bombers, the SSBNs were designed and employed in secrecy and were useless in brinkmanship politics. Since they could stealthily approach an enemy's coastline before launching, they could cut the missile warning time down from between twenty and thirty minutes to between five and ten minutes, depending on the target's location. The Soviet Union responded by building its own SLBM force, as did France and the United Kingdom. By the mid-1960s a new naval arms race, focused on the SLBM, had begun, as both superpowers developed newer submarines and antisubmarine forces.

In the 1970s newer and more accurate intermediate-range ballistic missiles (IRBMs) and cruise missiles were introduced in Europe and Japan as part of a U.S. strategy to spread a "nuclear umbrella" over its allies. It was these deployments that inaugurated the first widespread antinuclear protests against U.S. policy in Europe and in America, beginning a process of policy change that would shape both the doctrine and development of American nuclear weapons.

**American Nuclear Strategy: 1945–1999**

Initially, the United States had no stated nuclear weapons policy. The president controlled the weapons themselves, authorizing use only on his personal order. For military commanders, nuclear weapons were seen as a newer and more devastating bomb, but a bomb nonetheless. When Dwight D. Eisenhower assumed office in 1953, a new policy, called the "New Look," was established, which became popularly known as "massive retaliation." The policy did not advocate responding to any Soviet aggression with nuclear war, but established that nuclear weapons would be considered one of the primary means of U.S. response in such a case. This program allowed Eisenhower to cut back on expensive conventional land forces (tanks, artillery, etc.) and depend more on less costly nuclear programs. During the

Eisenhower administration the concept of limited nuclear war was also developed. Limited nuclear war was, in effect, the use of small (tactical) nuclear weapons aimed at military targets. This contrasted with strategic, or total, nuclear war, which aimed at the destruction of a nation's infrastructure and population.

With the election of John F. Kennedy in 1960, American nuclear strategy changed again. Kennedy's "flexible response" strategy reversed Eisenhower's nuclear weapons focus by stating that the United States would use a graduated response to Soviet challenges. This called for an expansion of the conventional armed forces and gave the president a viable nonnuclear option for war. Kennedy's secretary of defense, Robert S. McNamara, further refined the American nuclear weapons program, developing the concept of the nuclear triad of land-based missiles, SLBMs, and the bomber force. By the mid-1960s the United States possessed enough nuclear weapons and delivery systems not only to launch a nuclear war but also to absorb a Soviet strike and respond effectively.

The Cuban missile crisis of October 1962 presented the first test of the American system. When it was discovered that the Soviets had transported IRBMs to Cuba, only ninety miles from the continental United States, American policy makers responded by demanding that the weapons be withdrawn. U.S. forces were placed on DEFCON (defense condition) 2, the highest state of alert short of all-out war, and plans were made for an invasion of Cuba. Unknown to U.S. leaders, the Soviets had authorized the use of tactical nuclear weapons if the Americans invaded Cuba; such a policy would have probably led to an all-out nuclear exchange. Luckily, Soviet leader Nikita Khrushchev and Kennedy reached an agreement for a mutual withdrawal of missiles (the Soviet Union from Cuba, the United States from Turkey) and the crisis passed. However, the Cuban missile crisis had two main results. For people in the United States and other free-world nations, the specter of nuclear war became a growing concern and spawned the birth of the first organized antinuclear movements. In contrast, the USSR saw the withdrawal of missiles from Cuba as a policy defeat due to military weakness. Consequently the Soviet nuclear program went into high gear, with production surpassing the total number of American nuclear warheads by 1970 (1,299 Soviet ICBMs versus 1,054 U.S. missiles). However, like many issues surrounding the Cold War, the number of delivery systems often masked the total destructive power available to both sides. Despite the best Soviet efforts to achieve parity with the U.S. by 1970, it was not until the mid-1980s that the USSR actually surpassed the total number of nuclear warheads available for deployment. The table below outlines the rapid growth and decline of the total nuclear warheads (including artillery shells) available to the superpowers from 1960 to 1990:

| Year | U.S. | USSR |
|------|------|------|
| 1960 | 31,200 | 6,100 |
| 1970 | 27,000 | 20,000 |
| 1980 | 22,000 | 40,000 |
| 1990 | 15,000 | 27,000 |

In response to the growing Soviet nuclear capability, the American strategy changed once again. Mutual assured destruction, known by its unfortunate acronym MAD, became the stated U.S. policy by the late 1960s, a recognition of mutual U.S. and Soviet vulnerability to nuclear destruction. By the 1970s a relatively stable "balance of terror" existed between the superpowers. Since neither side possessed a marked advantage in weaponry, two options for further developments existed. First, either could push for more destructive, accurate, advanced weapons. Both did. The United States and the Soviet Union developed newer missiles throughout the 1970s and 1980s, introducing such innovations as multiple-warhead missiles (MIRVs, or multiple independent reentry vehicles, literally self-guiding warheads that broke apart in orbit and traveled to separate targets), mobile missile launchers, and the neutron bomb (which limited collateral damage to infrastructure, effectively leaving buildings intact while killing people). Also, the United States began the Strategic Defense Initiative (SDI) in the 1980s, a project of the Reagan administration that became known as Star Wars due to its emphasis on futuristic weaponry intended to deflect or destroy incoming missiles. Extremely expensive, SDI existed as long as the Soviet threat did; with the 1989 collapse of the Soviet Union, SDI (as a national "nuclear defense shield") was doomed, as were many of the expensive nuclear weapons development programs of the Cold War.

The second option, disarmament, was also pursued by both powers. The impact of antinuclear movements in the Western democracies in driving

President Ronald Reagan addresses the nation about the Strategic Defense Initiative, 23 March 1983. CORBIS/BETTMANN

this program forward should not be underestimated. The goal of both sides was a program of limitation/reduction that guaranteed MAD, but also limited proliferation to nonnuclear countries and eliminated extremely costly, but redundant, nuclear programs. The first such conference, the Strategic Arms Limitations Treaty (SALT I) talks, began in late 1969. A limited success, it set the pattern for later conferences such as SALT II in 1979, and the Strategic Arms Reduction Treaty, or START, talks in 1991 and 1993. START I was signed by President George Bush and Premier Mikhail S. Gorbachev in July 1991 and reduced the strategic (but not tactical) nuclear arsenals of both nations; the former Soviet Union reduced its warheads from 11,012 to 6,163, the U.S. from 12,646 to 8,556. START II, signed in January 1993 by the new Russian leader Boris Yeltsin and President Bush, who was then leaving office, further reduced the numbers; the former Soviet Union reduced to 3,000 and the U.S. to 3,500 warheads.

### Environmental Effects of Nuclear Weapons

From the production to the use of nuclear weapons, significant dangers exist to the environment. Production of the weapons, especially in nations without adequate environmental laws and controls, often results in large amounts of highly toxic radioactive waste materials. Above-ground tests of nuclear weapons by all the nuclear-capable nations (especially the U.S., the Soviet Union, France, and China) spread low-level radioactive fallout for hundreds of miles from the test sites. Consequently, the United States and the USSR turned to underground testing in the 1960s, while France focused its nuclear testing on uninhabited islands in the South Pacific.

The use of a nuclear device is devastating to the environment; the all-out nuclear war envisioned by many during the height of the Cold War could well have been apocalyptic. Beginning in the early 1980s, and gaining popularity in the United States in movies and numerous books, the concept of "nuclear winter" came to be understood as the likely result of a massive nuclear war between the superpowers. The concept is based on the fallout produced by above-ground testing in the 1950s and several natural disasters (including the explosions of Krakatoa in the nineteenth century and Mount St. Helens in the twentieth century). In effect, some scientists believed that the large amounts of dust, ash, and debris scattered in a chain of nuclear explosions would fill the upper atmosphere for months, possibly even years. Consequently, the majority, if not all, of sunlight would be blocked, killing most crops and plunging temperatures below freezing in much of the world. Fortunately, the theory was never proven, and remained under debate in the late 1990s.

### The Future of Nuclear War

For the United States, nuclear weapons remain a fixed part of national defense. American missile submarines, nuclear-capable surface ships, bomb-carrying aircraft, and even conventional field artillery maintain the ability to use nuclear weapons. Although technical developments may shape the delivery or yield of nuclear weapons, their employment remains under the firm control of the president.

Threats to the United States from new nuclear powers and from terrorist organizations, however, can be expected to increase in the future. With the explosion of information, and the lowering of borders and security in the post–Cold War world, the spread of nuclear weapons information and materials to nations and nonstate organizations has greatly expanded. Although the Cold War has ended, the threat of nuclear war has not. When the first bomb was tested in 1945, the nuclear genie was released from the bottle. It is still with us today.

*BIBLIOGRAPHY*

Addington, Larry H. *The Patterns of War Since the Eighteenth Century.* Bloomington: Indiana University Press, 1994.

Brodie, Bernard. *Strategy in the Missile Age.* Princeton, N.J.: Princeton University Press, 1959.

Brodie, Bernard, ed. *The Absolute Weapon: Atomic Power and World Order.* New York: Harcourt, Brace, 1946.

Doughty, Robert A., et al. *Warfare in the Western World.* Vol. 2. Lexington, Mass.: Heath, 1996.

Freedman, Lawrence. *The Evolution of Nuclear Strategy.* New York: St. Martin's, 1981.

Mandelbaum, Michael. *The Nuclear Question: The United States and Nuclear Weapons, 1946–1976.* Cambridge, U.K.: Cambridge University Press, 1976.

Midgley, John J. *Deadly Illusions: Army Policy for the Nuclear Battlefield.* Boulder, Colo.: Westview, 1986.

Osgood, Robert E. *Limited War: The Challenge to American Strategy.* Chicago: University of Chicago Press, 1957.

ROBERT R. MACKEY

*See also* **Disarmament and Arms Control; Environment, Violence Against; Hiroshima and Nagasaki; Literature: Nuclear War Fiction; Strategic Defense Initiative (SDI).**

## STUN OR SHOCK DEVICES

The 1980s and 1990s witnessed increasing use of electroshock devices both in the United States and in foreign countries. Such devices, which deliver up to 300,000 volts of electricity at low amperage on contact with their targets, are employed widely by U.S. police departments and corrections systems. Some types of the devices, especially stun guns, were becoming more readily available to the general public in the late 1990s. Electroshock weapons are frequently used for torture in some foreign countries, and the export of such equipment from the United States appeared to be growing at the end of the twentieth century.

Electroshock devices fall into four major categories: stun guns (or batons), which are handheld devices that deliver shocks on contact; taser guns, which fire darts that are attached to the weapons by wires and deliver a shock when the dart, which can travel as far as thirty feet, catches in the target's skin or clothing; electric shields, which are handheld electrified shells often used in riot control; and stun belts, which are strapped around a subject's waist and activated at the push of a button from distances up to three hundred feet, delivering a shock that invariably causes the victim to fall to the floor and occasionally to urinate, defecate, or become unconscious.

Manufacturers, of which there were close to fifty in the United States as of 1999, argue that these weapons give authorities nonlethal alternatives to guns and truncheons and that the threat of a shock is often sufficient to control a subject's behavior. Police and prison officials who have endorsed the products, particularly the taser gun and the stun belt, appreciate that control can be effected without direct physical contact with a target. Though the taser gun may leave two burns that look like a vampire bite on the skin, most devices can be applied without leaving marks, which critics contend may encourage their inappropriate application.

Many U.S. police departments use stun and taser guns to control allegedly unruly suspects or prisoners. Police used a taser gun on Rodney King in a notorious videotaped incident in Los Angeles in 1991. Stun belts are used during the transport of prisoners, occasionally on defendants in criminal trials, and increasingly on chain gangs, as for instance in Wisconsin, which adopted the practice in 1997. One manufacturer recommends the use of such belts to transport the mentally ill as well.

Human rights officials and some doctors have raised questions about the use of stun or shock devices, which, in their view, have not been adequately tested on human subjects to determine medical implications and may violate international human rights strictures against cruel, inhumane, and degrading punishment. The medical concerns relate to the fact that electric shocks can depolarize skeletal muscles and therefore, at least theoretically, depolarize heart muscles and cause defibrillation or arrhythmia. The policy of the U.S. Bureau of Prisons as of 1999 was not to use stun belts on prisoners with heart disease, though whether all prisoners were being adequately tested for such disease was uncertain. Certainly it is not possible to screen subjects for prior physical problems when a stun gun or electric shield is used in the course of police work, and several deaths have been attributed to the use of taser guns, particularly on people under the influence of drugs. At least one death was directly attributed to the use of an electric riot shield.

As of 1999, the human rights group Amnesty International had identified forty-nine countries in which electric-shock equipment was commonly used, including China, Mexico, Saudi Arabia, and Turkey, where such equipment was being used to torture and maltreat prisoners. In Tibet, for example, Chinese prison guards regularly apply shock batons to the teeth, ears, and genitalia of teenage Tibetan nuns and monks imprisoned for advocating Tibetan freedom.

Human rights groups suspect that U.S. manufacturers are exporting shock devices to countries that use them for torture, but because the U.S. Commerce Department classifies such devices not as torture equipment (the export of which it restricts) but as police equipment, it is difficult to know for certain. As of 1999, the Commerce Department had yet to make public the details of such exports, nor did it restrict the resale of such equipment to third-party countries.

Furthermore, the sale of such devices, specifically stun guns, to the general public was increasing at the end of the twentieth century. One U.S. manufacturer acknowledged that its devices, marketed as weapons of self-defense, were available through variety stores, gun shops, uniform stores, and flea markets. Some observers were predicting that eventually it would be as common to carry a stun gun as it is to carry a whistle or a can of mace and that electric-shock devices, including the stun belt, would someday be used as instruments of punishment or restraint in schools and hospitals.

BIBLIOGRAPHY

Amnesty International. *Arming the Torturers: Electro-Shock Torture and the Spread of Stun Technology.* New York: Amnesty International, March 1997.

Cusac, Anne-Marie. "Stunning Technology." *Progressive*, July 1996.

Robinson, M. N., et al. "Electric Shock Devices and Their

Effects on the Human Body." *Medical Science and Law* 30, no. 4 (1990).

WILLIAM F. SCHULZ

*See also* **Police: Police Brutality; Prisons; Torture.**

## WEATHERMAN AND WEATHER UNDERGROUND

Weatherman, an offshoot of the Students for a Democratic Society (SDS), and the Weather Underground, a clandestine organization of radical bombers, were the two most violent political groups to emerge from the white student left of the 1960s. Consciously adapting third-world guerrilla strategies to conditions in the United States, they destroyed government and private property and generated a myth about themselves as armed and dangerous revolutionaries. Though small in numbers (never more than several hundred dedicated members), both groups played a pivotal role in the American movement to end the war in Vietnam. They attracted widespread media attention, and they propelled other groups, including the Yippies, to take decisive steps to end the war.

Weatherman—the name was borrowed from Bob Dylan's 1965 song "Subterranean Homesick Blues"—emerged at the fractious 1969 SDS national convention. The leaders of the group—Mark Rudd, a spokesman for the students during the campus uprisings at Columbia University in 1968; Bernardine Dohrn, a University of Chicago law school graduate; and Billy Ayers, the scion of an elite Chicago family—expelled the Progressive Labor (PL) faction of SDS, which was urging students to unite with workers. Weathermen seized control of the SDS national office in Chicago and took over the SDS newspaper, *New Left Notes*, renamed *Fire!*, which they used to encourage white youth to reject their social privilege and join black revolutionaries and dismantle the American empire.

Insisting that blue-collar workers had been corrupted by capitalism and that proletarian revolution was impossible in the United States, Weatherman created its own version of the Red Guards, the roving bands of students that disrupted China during Mao Zedong's Cultural Revolution of the 1960s. Members of Weatherman invaded public high schools in New York, and in Detroit they held teachers captive and incited students to rebel.

In October 1969 Weatherman staged what became known as the Days of Rage, a series of violent protests in Chicago that began with the bombing of the statue of a policeman in Haymarket Square and included a rally in Lincoln Park to commemorate Che Guevara's death in Bolivia in 1967. Wearing boots and helmets and carrying rocks and clubs, nearly three hundred demonstrators smashed windows in cars and banks. After five days of bloody street battles and fierce confrontations with the police, most of the protesters were arrested, charged with rioting, and incarcerated in the Cook County jail.

Then, in the winter of 1969–1970 Weatherman evolved into the Weather Underground, whose anonymous members acting in underground collectives committed acts of sabotage and terrorism. A New York City collective firebombed the house of John Murtagh, the presiding judge in the trial of twenty-one Black Panthers who were charged with conspiring to bomb police stations, department stores, and New York City landmarks, including the Bronx Botanical Gardens. The Weathermen then began to make antipersonnel weapons that were to be detonated at Fort Dix in New Jersey. On 6 March 1970, one of the bombs accidentally exploded, killing three Weather Underground members and precipitating an investigation by the Federal Bureau of Investigation.

Soon thereafter, Bernardine Dohrn, the leader of the group, criticized the Weather Underground's extremism in a document entitled "New Morning—Changing Weather." During the 1970s, however, the organization set off nearly twenty bombs in government buildings, including the New York City Police Headquarters, the U.S. Capitol, and the Pentagon, and issued a series of communiqués to the media stating that revolutionary violence was the only way to change the society.

The Weather Underground's bombs caused minor structural damage to buildings and minor disruption of government operations, but as warnings were phoned in ahead of time, there were no injuries to persons. Although the FBI conducted an intensive hunt for Dohrn, Ayers, and Rudd, all three eluded capture during the decade in which they were fugitives.

When the Vietnam war ended, the group lost much of its raison d'être. The number of bombings declined from six in 1970 to one in 1974. However, there were as many as four bombs in 1975—at the Department of Defense in Oakland, California, the Banco de Ponce in New York City, the Agency for International Development in Washington, D.C., and the Kennecott Corporation in Salt Lake City.

Charting a new direction, the organization published and distributed a manifesto, entitled *Prairie Fire,* that called for the creation of a communist party that would wage class warfare and establish a dictatorship of the proletariat. Ideological debate ensued and intensified, factionalism increased, and the group was torn apart in the late 1970s, with some former members rejecting politics completely and with others trying to redefine revolution in splinter groups like the Prairie Fire Organizing Committee and the May 19th Communist Organization. Bernardine Dohrn and Bill Ayers were accused of counterrevolutionary politics and expelled from the organization, and although they had sworn never to surrender to the authorities, they turned themselves in and never faced time in prison for their role in the Weather Underground. "Guilty as hell, free as a bird—America is a great country," Ayers observed. Others followed their example. Most Weather Underground members soon found a place for themselves in the society they had rejected. Others joined with the Black Liberation Army (BLA), a violent urban guerrilla organization. In 1981 BLA took part in an armed robbery in which two police officers and a security guard were murdered, and after arrests and a trial under the tightest security, the Weather Underground defendants Kathy Boudin, Judy Clark, and David Gilbert were sentenced to long prison terms. Boudin received twenty years to life, the others three consecutive terms of twenty-five years to life. A decade earlier, they might have become symbols of rebellion, but in the 1980s and 1990s they were largely forgotten, much as the Weather Underground passed into historical obscurity. Still, the organization has taken on a mythic identity in Hollywood films, including Jeremy Kagan's *Katherine* (1975) and Sidney Lumet's *Running on Empty* (1988), and in popular literature, including Marge Piercy's *Vida* (1979) and Philip Roth's *American Pastoral* (1997).

*BIBLIOGRAPHY*

Jacobs, Harold, ed. *Weatherman.* Berkeley, Calif.: Ramparts, 1970.

Raskin, Jonah, ed. *The Weather Eye: Communiqués from the Weather Underground, May 1970–May 1974.* San Francisco: Union Square, 1974.

Weather Underground Organization. *Prairie Fire: The Politics of Revolutionary Anti-Imperialism.* San Francisco: Communications Company, 1974.

JONAH RASKIN

*See also* **Bombings and Bomb Scares; Extremism; New Left; Yippie!**

# WEEGEE (ARTHUR FELIG)
## (1899–1968)

Arthur Felig, born Usher Fellig in Austria, came to the United States in 1910 with his family. He boasted that he earned his professional name Weegee—his own rendition of Ouija, a board system used by clairvoyants—for his uncanny ability to be the first photographer on the scene of a calamity. His American childhood was shaped by the experiences of a large, Jewish immigrant family living in the tenement district of New York City's Lower East Side. For a while Weegee worked to help support his family, but at the age of fifteen he quit school and left home. He led a transient existence in Manhattan's downtown areas, taking what employment he could find and sleeping in charity missions and parks when he could not afford lodging. At this time Weegee was introduced to commercial photography through jobs as an assistant and as a street tintype portraitist.

In the mid-1920s, Weegee obtained a regular position with Acme Newspictures as a darkroom technician and printer, and in handling images for the popular press his sensibility was formed: "At Acme history passed through my hands. Fires, explosions, railroad wrecks, ship collisions, prohibition gang wars, murders, kings, presidents, everybody famous and everything exciting" (Weegee 1961, p. 28). Within the agency Weegee advanced to a position as a news photographer known for his human-interest assignments on the city beat. In 1935 he left Acme to begin freelance work, and by 1938 he had established his identity in the media as Weegee. Many of his news leads came through listening in on calls to the central Manhattan police station, which he followed on a shortwave radio installed in his automobile. Over the next ten years he produced his signature photography, and several of his images of crime, accidents, and disaster were exhibited at the Photo League and the Museum of Modern Art, beginning in 1941 with the one-man show "Murder Is My Business."

Weegee covered local New York stories in the night hours equipped with a high-watt flashgun. His camera lens roamed from Bowery drunks to socialites uptown and from three-alarm fires to vice arrests, but the best-known photographs feature crime and accident victims. In these photographs a stark, momentary radiance from the flash penetrates the city's impersonal, almost funereal blackness to reveal a few fateful truths about modern urban existence. The injured or dead body of the victim is captured in an awkward or absurd posture, typically in the picture's foreground space. In many instances the body is brightly illuminated as if on display for the policemen and bystanders gathered around, some of whom watch impassively while others are animated by the diversion. Through the asymmetries in Weegee's composition and lighting and an imbalance in the mood of the scene, these images offer a deadpan perspective on human mayhem. In his choice of subject matter and form, Weegee crafted the sensational yet detached style of a daily tabloid press, a style that has maintained currency in the news, fashion, and art worlds.

This photography, accompanied by a version of hard-boiled prose, was published in his book *Naked City* (1945). In this period Weegee began to experiment with distortion lenses and other mechanical devices to manipulate the photograph, and he made some short motion-picture films with a 16 mm handheld camera. He left for Hollywood in late 1947 with high ambitions but found work only as a movie consultant and as a bit player. His grotesque visual account of life in the dream factory was published in *Naked Hollywood* (1953), which

**Weegee, 1945.** CORBIS/BETTMANN

contains some distorted and manipulated images. After returning to New York in 1952, he continued to apply these optical devices in making celebrity portraits, several of which were published in major magazines. From this time until his death in 1968, Weegee contracted to photograph advertising campaigns, official functions, and public figures; he no longer covered crime or disaster. He also lectured, traveled in Europe on assignment, and wrote a brashly self-promoting autobiography.

*BIBLIOGRAPHY*

Barth, Miles, ed. *Weegee's World*. Boston: Little, Brown, 1997.
Weegee. *Naked City*. New York: Essential Books, 1945.
———. *Weegee by Weegee: An Autobiography*. New York: Ziff-Davis, 1961.
———. *Weegee's People*. New York: Essential Books, 1946.
Weegee, and Mel Harris. *Naked Hollywood*. New York: Pellegrini and Cudahy, 1953.

JAMES GOODWIN

*See also* **Journalism; Photography.**

# WEST

In the geographic West—the area west of the Mississippi River—violence has taken on an astonishing and convoluted array of forms, shapes, and contexts. In and of itself, violence in the West is like that in any other area of the nation: it has been perpetrated by people on their own kind and on other peoples as well as on animals and the physical world. It has been driven by politics, greed, and spite; it has occurred arbitrarily, accidentally, and by design; and it has been committed by groups and individuals for personal reasons and for community purposes.

Nothing distinguishes actual violence in the American West from any other region of the country or part of the world except the singular American notion that one has no duty to retreat from conflict. This idea, which allows people to legally stand their ground and fight rather than give way until threatened with severe bodily harm, flouted English common law, which required that people give way when faced with threats, resorting to violence only when there are no other options. "A man is not born to run away," wrote the Supreme Court justice Oliver Wendell Holmes in 1921, codifying into law the practices of American experience. The stand-your-ground-and-fight ethic of the West helped make American violence endemic; it

symbolized the virtue of a doctrine that promoted rather than discouraged physical confrontation.

## Westward Expansion

In 1803, as Thomas Jefferson charged the explorers Meriwether Lewis and William Clark to travel over the nation's new acquisition, the Louisiana Purchase, intragroup violence characterized life among the various Native American groups in the West. Rivalries among native peoples—sometimes for economic reasons and other times for social ones—were encoded into their relationships; they lived in close proximity and fought continually over resources—game, water, trade goods, and other necessities of life. Although the immi-

### The West and the National Creation Myth

The acceptance of violence as part of the myth of national creation has cast ordinary violence in the West in high relief for Americans past and present. The West is the location of the Pueblo Indian creation myth, which centers on *sipapu*, the figurative hole in the earth from which their people emerged in the beginning of the world. The image of the West, especially in the conquest of the region by settlers between 1848 and 1890, also serves a mythic purpose for Americans. In the post–Civil War West, the United States emerged and reinvented itself, shedding slavery, sectionalism, and states' rights, and became an American nation that persisted until its post-Watergate fragmentation. The new nation embodied in the West transcended the inherent flaws of the first republic, impaled on its own inconsistencies by the shelling of Fort Sumter, South Carolina; the West healed the hole in the heart of the nation born anew after its epic and cataclysmic tragedy of the Civil War. The revised national creation myth gave the West a primacy in American life and thinking that grew from innocence and the potential for reinvention. When Americans paid homage to their national and nationalistic roots, they did not look to Independence Hall in Philadelphia; they went West as their forefathers did, to find self and create society, to build fresh in the detritus of the old. In doing so they gave every event, but especially violence in the West, a kind of standing and significance enjoyed by no other part of the nation.

grants to the American republic saw all such people as "Indians," Native Americans were members of a thousand or more different nations with long histories of conflict among themselves.

At least some of the conflict among Native Americans could be attributed to the acquisition of the horse, which was brought to the New World by the Spanish in the sixteenth century. Horses transformed the lives of some western Native American peoples, Apache, Cheyenne, Comanche, and Lakota, or Sioux, prominent among them, giving them range and power that they had never before experienced. The designation of the plains of west Texas and southeastern New Mexico as first the *Apachería,* when this land was dominated by the eastern Apache peoples, and later the *Comanchería,* territory of the vaunted horsemen of the southern plains, testified to the power of the horse. The expansion of Lakota people west from Minnesota onto the plains, a process that began in about 1700 and reached its apex in the first half of the nineteenth century with the virtual enslavement of the Mandan, Hidatsa, and other sedentary peoples of the Missouri River basin, revealed the power of the horse to transform the relationships between Native American peoples. As a result of that Lakota expansion, Pawnee gave assistance to the Americans against the Lakota (as portrayed in Kevin Costner's 1990 film, *Dances with Wolves*) and General George Armstrong Custer was assisted by Crow Indian scouts at the Battle of Little Bighorn, in the heart of the Crow homeland.

When Lewis and Clark ventured up the Missouri River in search of the Pacific Ocean, they were not above using violence to achieve their ends. Outnumbered and among the few whites and almost certainly the first Americans most Native Americans had ever encountered, the party killed only two Native Americans during their three-year journey. That number did not mean the trip was free of violence. When necessary, the entourage made a show of force and even grappled with the Indians on occasion, using the threat of violence to coerce cooperation and not hesitating to fight when the leaders deemed it necessary. This specter of violence to compel cooperation was among the most effective tools of persuasion enjoyed by this small group of voyagers among many who might become their enemies.

Beginning with Lewis and Clark, the threat of violence in place of violence itself became part of the cultural baggage of Indian-white relations in the West. The pattern started with the settlement of the continent by the Spanish and the English and had been transmitted across the Cumberland Gap, through the Ohio Valley, and on to the trans-Mississippi West. When the threat failed to achieve the desired results, real violence often followed. It showed both the determination of the Americans and their willingness to resort to whatever means they had available to achieve their ends.

Another factor in the early nineteenth century was the presence of the outposts of New Spain in Texas, New Mexico, and California (and a few small ones in Arizona). In 1821 these outliers became part of the new Mexican nation, loosely tied to the core of their culture in the central highlands of Mexico. Violence between the Spanish and Native Americans began with the arrival of the Vázquez de Coronado expedition on the Rio Grande in 1540 and continued throughout the Spanish era. Sixteenth-, seventeenth-, and eighteenth-century Spaniards moved north for one of two reasons: to save souls for their God or to acquire wealth from what they thought were the cities of Cíbola, where they believed great quantities of gold were hidden. In the process of chasing either dream, they resorted to violence to compel the cooperation of the sedentary Pueblo peoples of New Mexico and the neophytes they drew to their California missions. By 1800 a history of resentment and violence that culminated in a pattern of raiding by the most mobile Indian groups, the Comanche and Kiowa in Texas and eastern New Mexico and the Navajo and Utes in northern New Mexico and Colorado, coupled with weak Spanish and Mexican institutions in the north, led to parity in power that was based on the ability to wage war. For the Republic of Mexico, the situation dictated that the new nation's hold on its north was tenuous indeed.

The Texas revolution of the 1830s illustrated the weakness of Mexico's hold and foreshadowed the American takeover of what is now the Southwest. In search of economic development, the Mexican government gave impresario grants to Americans who wanted to settle in central Texas; chief among them were Moses Austin and his son, Stephen F. Austin. The only stipulations were that impresarios had to convert to Catholicism, become Mexican citizens, and agree to abide by Mexican laws, which meant engaging in commercial trade with the distant city of Chihuahua but not with nearby New Orleans. The Austins and other impresarios nominally agreed, but, far from the institutions of Mexican society and tempted by the quick profits that could be earned in direct trade with the

United States, they often ignored the law. By 1830 Anglo-Americans outnumbered Mexicans by almost ten to one in central Texas, and many Mexican merchants recognized the desirability of shedding their largely useless economic relationships with Mexico for the far more fruitful ones with New Orleans and St. Louis. The result was a cross-cultural Anglo and Hispanic revolution against Mexico that freed Texas and made it an independent nation.

The Texas revolution gave the United States one of its abiding mythologized episodes of violence—the massacre of the defenders of the Alamo in San Antonio—as well as a massacre at Goliad and the eventual triumph of the "Texican" (as they were known) forces at the battle of San Jacinto along what is now the Houston ship channel. The little mission in San Antonio provided the high drama of self-sacrifice in a hopeless cause. Americans who had gone to Texas, usually as a result of their own misdeeds in the United States, died there in high style along with Anglo- and Spanish-speaking Texicans. Although national mythology suggested that they died fighting, many were massacred after the fact like earlier Texican fighters at Goliad. The Mexican president General Antonio López de Santa Anna became a villain first in Texican lore and then in American lore, ultimately becoming the prototypical despot against whom to fight for democracy. Valor became attached to the sacrifice at the Alamo in a fashion unparalleled in the United States except, in later years, by the battles of Gettysburg (1863) and perhaps Shiloh (1862) in the Civil War and by the Battle of the Bulge (1944) and the assault on Iwo Jima (1944–1945) in World War II. The defense and ultimate surrender of the Alamo set a mythic heroic standard for the nation that continues to be the basis for measuring the national will to sacrifice.

The Texas revolution also foreshadowed the Mexican War. In 1846 the United States invaded Mexico with the goal of annexing the area north of the Rio Grande and extending the American nation to the Pacific Ocean in the south as well as in Oregon. Historians generally agree that this was a war of unbridled aggression, a case of a new and powerful nation flexing its muscles against a weaker and disorganized neighbor. The Treaty of Guadalupe Hidalgo ended the war and gave the United States much of what had been northern Mexico—including present-day California, New Mexico, and much of Arizona. Cloaked in the rhetoric of Manifest Destiny, which made the United States the sole nation with a legitimate claim to North America, the Mexican War exemplified the use of violence as a tool of national policy.

Expansionism had already become an American watchword. As those who thought a democracy would lose its virtue if it covered an entire continent were swept aside, westward expansion developed momentum. The Oregon Trail, a nearly two-thousand-mile journey from Missouri to the Willamette Valley of Oregon, became the leading path to the West. Throughout the 1840s—before and after the Mexican War—thousands streamed along the trail to reinvent themselves in the lush valleys of Oregon. Occasional violence permeated the trail, although much of it was inadvertent—accidental death and injury from firearms reached peculiarly high proportions along the trail—but the ongoing stream of travelers provoked diplomatic, social, and violent response from the Native Americans whose lands they traversed.

Throughout the first half of the nineteenth century, Native Americans crowded onto the plains, increasing competition among themselves and with overland travelers for the scarce resources of the waterways of the plains. The growing number of horses that Native Americans possessed, a measure of wealth and status for many tribes, began to crowd out the buffalo, inaugurating fierce competition for grasses that led to renewed rivalries among some groups and new contests of power between others. Especially in the narrow river plains, where many necessary resources existed, the competition among native peoples and traveling settlers became heated. Direct violence and indirect violence (i.e., destruction of the staples of Indian life) often resulted.

The same era, the period just before the Civil War, also revealed the way in which the geographic West became a location for violence as a result of the politics of the rest of the nation. The battle for Bleeding Kansas, the often violent contest between free- and slave-staters for the control of the Kansas territory, showed that geography was no barrier to the spread of violence based in politics. Advocates of the expansion of slavery, called Missouri Ruffians by their Kansas free-state neighbors, crossed the border to wreak havoc. Their most violent attack was a raid on Lawrence, Kansas, in 1856 that killed one man and destroyed the town. In retaliation, the zealous abolitionist

**Armed 19th-century settlers, prepared for clashes with Native Americans.** LIBRARY OF CONGRESS

John Brown, who later led a raid on the federal arsenal at Harpers Ferry, Virginia, and his followers killed five proslavery men and mangled their bodies. A civil war in the Kansas territory in which more than two hundred people died followed. The sectionalism of the nation had caused an episode of violence in the West that foreshadowed the future disruption of the nation.

After the Civil War, in which battles were fought as far west as Glorieta Pass in New Mexico, the real westward expansion began and with it the violence associated with conquering the region. Beginning in the 1850s, the U.S. Army began to clear the way for settlement, chasing Native Americans from their homelands and pursuing them until they surrendered and acceded to life on reservations. In the Southwest in the early 1860s, Christopher "Kit" Carson led troops commanded by Brevet General James H. Carleton in pursuit of the Mescalero Apache and Navajo, who were subdued and brought back to the miserable living conditions of a reservation called the Bosque Redondo in eastern New Mexico. Carson's strategy was to attack in the winter, when hunter-gatherer peoples were least mobile and dependent on the food stores they collected during the rest of the year. By destroying Native American stores, Carson was able to bring Indian people to their knees. His strategy became standard practice throughout the West and provided the American military with many of its successes.

Native American responses took many forms. Uprisings, such as the Lakota revolt in Minnesota in August 1862, provided one kind. Although the Lakota (Dakota Sioux) killed a number of whites, the uprising was brutally put down and its leaders "weighed," or hung. Another response was to flee, as did some Navajo who went to the far western parts of the reservation and remained there, apart from their kinsmen, who were forced into New Mexico. Other Native Americans broke out from the reservations. In 1869 Dull Knife and his Cheyenne were sent to a reservation in Indian Territory instead of the one they expected to be sent to near Fort Robinson, Nebraska. Starving on their new reservation, they sought to return home to the lands from which they originated. On the way, they tangled with settlers and the military, destroying some farmsteads and killing people, as national reporters tracked their progress.

Dull Knife's breakout signaled an end of one kind of Indian war and the beginning of another. Before 1870 the contests between Native Americans and the United States determined who would

437

control the land. The tactics of the Americans, from the indiscriminate killing of the buffalo to eliminate (in the words of one general) "the Indians' commissary," to the kinds of military techniques used, were aimed at subduing free peoples in control of their destinies. After 1870, even in dramatic cases such as George Armstrong Custer's debacle at the Battle of Little Bighorn or Chief Joseph's aborted trek to Canada, the military generally engaged in pursuing people who had already been defeated and were trying to reconstitute their old lifeways in a hostile political, economic, and social environment. The great exceptions to this rule, the Mescalero Apache leader Victorio in 1878–1880 and the Chiracahua leader Geronimo later in the 1880s, both had the benefit of crossing the Mexican border, beyond which they could find shelter from the American military. Unlike the Lakota, Cheyenne, or Navajo, they could maintain an intact free world beyond the reach of the U.S. Army and could cross the border for the purpose of raiding and disruption as much as to recover territory. Their resistance was longer-lived and more difficult for the army to defeat than even that of the famed Sitting Bull, who in the end sought refuge north of the Canadian border. Like another famous Lakota leader, Crazy Horse, who was murdered on a reservation in the custody of the military, Sitting Bull was also murdered, by Indian police sent by the reservation superintendent to arrest him. When Indian response became spiritual rather than physical, as in the Ghost Dance religion of the early 1890s, the response of the American military remained violent. The massacre of more than 150 Ghost Dancers at Wounded Knee in December 1890 revealed the limitations of even spiritual resistance. Despite the dramatic fall of Custer and the 250 or more men who died with him almost fifteen years before the Ghost Dance, in a larger geopolitical sense Custer's military action was a minor episode in a story forcefully unfolding toward its conclusion.

The economic activities that cleared the way for Anglo-American settlement brought their own forms of violence in their wake. The cattle trade was rife with violence, for the trails covered more than six hundred miles from Texas to the various railheads in Kansas and, even farther along the western route, in Wyoming. Battles with outlaws and rustlers were common along the trails, and Indian resentment of the cattle that passed through Indian Territory, eating the grasses and drinking the water supply with the cattle drivers rarely pay-

ing for the privilege, spurred confrontations that sometimes led to conflict. Making a living in the West often meant encroaching on others.

The cow towns at the end of the trail were also marked by their share of violence. Although many towns, such as Wichita, Kansas, required cowboys to exchange their sidearm for a token before entering town, each town was adjacent to an area where nearly anything went. Called Devil's Addition outside Abilene, Kansas, and Delano outside Wichita, such places did not officially sanction violence but did little to prevent it. In this part of the country where legal institutions were not firm, individuals often resorted to whatever means necessary to redress any real or imagined wrong.

This meant that social banditry—violence that had as its purpose not only individual gain but also attacks on the power structure—played important roles as the institutions of American society took shape in the West. The first social bandits to attain heroic stature in the West were Hispanics who challenged the status quo in mid-nineteenth-century California: the neomythical Joaquin Murietta, a Spanish-era legendary Robin Hood–like bandit, typified such figures. In an Anglo-American context, the notorious outlaw Jesse James and his gang were also folk heroes, exemplifying not only southern states' rights resistance to the consolidation of the Union after the Civil War but also an agrarian ethic and culture that was being diminished by the spread of industrialization. James's two primary targets were banks and railroads, both exemplifying the consolidation of capital and power that industrialization brought. Later social banditry was more futile, but equally romantic. Gregorio Cortez, a *tejano* (Hispanic Texan) who shot and killed a sheriff over a misunderstanding and fled for the Mexican border, became the subject of a widely sung *corrido*, a popular ballad that lamented his fate as an example of the plight of Spanish speakers in turn-of-the-century Texas. Cortez's act, his desperate flight for freedom and safety, spoke volumes to Hispanics in a harsh, Anglo-dominated society.

Based in the mythology of the West, the social bandit became an important figure in American popular culture. From Gregorio Cortez onward, social bandits resisted the system or lived apart from it. Many nineteenth-century outlaws were regarded as social bandits. Tom Horn, Butch Cassidy, and others became legendary figures. The social bandit also had resonance in the twentieth century. Captain America, played by Peter Fonda in *Easy*

*Rider* (1969), offers one example, as do the heroines of *Thelma and Louise* (1991).

## Industrialization

The introduction of industrial labor in the West also led to violence, especially in the mining industry. Violence had been closely associated with mining since the gold rush, when Anglo-American miners banded together to force out foreign, sometimes more experienced, miners who were more successful than they were. The transition of mining from individuals to corporations demanded countless workers, and the mining companies had an investment in keeping wages down and conditions difficult. Mining was paid as piecework, with miners weighing their individual bags of ore on sometimes crooked scales. When labor began to organize in the 1870s, violence against workers and, in response, violence by workers against corporate America was rife. From the Haymarket Square riot in Chicago in 1886 to the murder of former governor Frank Steunenberg of Idaho in 1905, the execution by firing squad of the organizer Joe Hill in 1914, and the Ludlow Massacre in 1914 to the murder of Wesley Everest of the Industrial Workers of the World (IWW, also known as the Wobblies) outside of Centralia, Washington, in 1919, violence permeated the conflict between corporate America and workers who sought to organize.

Farmers, who felt the same pressure as workers in an industrializing society, also organized, and although the violence associated with the agrarian revolt was largely symbolic, it played a large role in shaping the perception of grass-roots politics in the nation. One of the farmers' organizations, the Farmer's Alliance, was founded in Lampasas, Texas, in 1875 to combat rustling. The movement grew, developing a political platform and considerable political clout by the early 1890s in southern, western, and silver-producing states. Populism, as this agrarian movement was labeled, made the most gains in states where the two-party system functioned poorly—in the West typically where Republicans dominated and Democrats were scarce. The response to Populist success often included symbolic violence. In 1894 the Republican members of the Kansas legislature refused to seat Populists who won election; they even had a picture taken of the Republican delegation on the steps of the state capitol, showing all members armed to the teeth, and circulated it widely in a vain attempt to further discourage Populist delegates.

## The Twentieth Century

Racial violence also took on new, more organized forms in the twentieth century. The history of African Americans, Hispanics, Chinese, and other nonwhite minorities in the West has been as rife with violence as that of Native Americans. In the twentieth century, violence as a form of social control became common. One powerful example was the race riot in Tulsa, Oklahoma, in 1921 that decimated the prosperous African American community there. Oklahoma, formerly Indian Territory, had been the first multicultural state in America; it was not only a place to send displaced Native Americans but also a haven for runaway slaves from the South before the Civil War and for freedmen afterward. During enforced segregation, African American business grew, for only occasionally did white business seek African American markets. By the 1920s in Tulsa, African American companies handled much of the insurance in African American communities across the nation. As a result of a pretext, whites attacked the black community on 31 May 1921, and instead of seeking to stop the violence, the Oklahoma National Guard assisted the attackers; in fact, a National Guard airplane reportedly bombed part of the African American section of town. The community was destroyed and took years to recover. Thus, the power of the state had supported mob violence against African Americans.

Up the road from Tulsa, on the Osage Trust Lands, a similar saga took shape. Osage land was rich with oil, and members of the tribe became wealthy from leasing their land. A number of local Anglo-Americans conspired with outside interests to divest the Osage of their oil-bearing land. When such tactics did not work, the group resorted to murder, killing a number of the important landowners and swindling their heirs. A concerted effort by federal Justice Department officials put an end to the crimes, but the situation clearly illustrated the susceptibility of nonwhites to locally sanctioned violence anywhere in the West.

Hispanics felt the same pressures, especially in Texas, where a caste system developed that kept Spanish-speaking people in their so-called place. As elsewhere in the country, a system that used law and, when necessary, the threat or actuality of extralegal violence to limit Hispanic opportunities and contain Hispanic aspirations became a common device of social control. This system mirrored the situation of African Americans in the South and inspired a collective hopelessness that only great social upheaval could change.

The Great Depression of the 1930s and World War II provided the context for a change not only in the old social system but also in the nature and location of violence. The poverty of the depression drew thousands to California, many from the decimated Dust Bowl region of the Great Plains. These poverty-stricken Anglo-Americans, called Okies, suffered many of the same indignities as did non-whites of similar economic circumstances: signs that read "No Okies Allowed" became as common in 1930s California as those that evoked the same sentiment about African Americans. In some cases Okie migrant camps were attacked by people who felt threatened either by the mere presence of Okies, who were regarded as bringing the level of a community down, or by the aspirations Okies had to permanence, decent wages, and other tenets of middle-class life.

World War II transformed the demography of the American West, bringing millions to cities, especially on the coast, and providing new urban venues to continue the history of violence. Towns such as Albuquerque and Wichita became cities, Los Angeles and San Francisco grew dramatically, and the populations of all became diverse. Hundreds of thousands of soldiers and sailors passed through the Presidio at San Francisco and the port at San Diego and countless other places on their way to the war in the Pacific. Xenophobic servicemen and recalcitrant local youth often clashed, especially over cultural differences such as types of clothing. In Los Angeles especially, a view of Mexican American youth as threatening permeated the region. The famous Sleepy Lagoon case of 1942, in which nineteen Mexican American gang members were tried for the death of one of their peers at an East Los Angeles swimming hole, illustrated the prevailing sentiments. The Zoot-Suit Riot of 1943 involved rioting servicemen who captured Hispanic, African American, and Filipino youths dressed in zoot-suits, long-coated suits with pegged trousers, which the servicemen felt symbolized disrespect for the conventions of American society. The soldiers beat the young men, stripped them of their clothes, and left them bleeding in the streets. Later allegations that simply being black, Hispanic, and Asian had led to the attack were largely substantiated. Urban violence mirrored the social-control functions of rural violence and could viciously uphold the class and racial status quo of the war.

As elsewhere in the nation, the decades following World War II offered prosperity in the West, an increase in expectations, and, after 1960, a statistically enormous increase in violent crime. Social theorists tied this increase in crime to the rise of youth culture, the growing number of young people, and the liberalization of American culture, which after 1960 began the long and uneven process of becoming inclusive. In this liberalization the rigid standards that had governed much of American life in the twentieth century loosened and a wider range of behaviors became acceptable. By the middle of the 1960s, the nation was engaged in an enormous cultural revolution that eventually altered nearly everything about American life. That movement found its initial manifestation in the San Francisco Bay Area at the University of California at Berkeley. Borrowing the techniques of the Civil Rights movement, the nonviolent direct action advocated by Mohandas K. Gandhi and Martin Luther King, Jr., students at Berkeley first protested for the right to organize political activity on campus and later against the Vietnam War. Although most student protest remained nonviolent, a certain amount of property damage and occasional personal violence occurred, sometimes resulting from the efforts of the California state police. Pitched battles between police and students became a feature first on the Berkeley campus and later on college campuses all across the West.

At about this same time, a group of social outcasts and misfits called the Hell's Angels burst on the national scene. Headquartered in California, this group of outlaw motorcyclists, colloquially called bikers, became a symbol not only of the postwar changes in American society but also of its violence and growing incivility. The Hell's Angels settled their scores with violence; it was a form of sport and ritual with the club. They also stood up for what they believed was Americanism, in more than one instance attacking student antiwar protesters. In a bizarre development in 1969, the touring rock group the Rolling Stones selected the Hell's Angels to police the Stones' free concert at Altamont Speedway outside of San Francisco. Poorly suited for the responsibility, the Hell's Angels ended up stabbing to death a young African American man who arrived at the concert with a white woman—anathema to the Angels—and who in the course of the fracas brandished a gun. It was a sad ending to the decade of the counterculture, the movement to culturally reinvent the United States that professed peace, love, and an end to war; the incident was an example of the endemic nature of violence in American and western life.

Also in the 1960s, in Los Angeles, racial violence found a new manifestation. In the Watts area of Los Angeles in 1965, an African American man named Marquette Frye was stopped by police on a hot summer night. The relationship between the police and the African American community was strained at best; headed by Chief Edwin Parker, the Los Angeles police force seemed like an occupying army to African Americans, and tensions ran high. A crowd gathered around Frye, and a violent uprising that destroyed Watts and South Central Los Angeles ensued, leaving more than thirty people dead and destroying millions of dollars' worth of property. The National Guard and federal troops were required to restore order, but the wounds did not heal.

Relations improved only minimally between the police and African Americans in Los Angeles during the following two decades; a similar lack of communication and respect typified relations throughout the nation. Tensions erupted in 1991, when five Los Angeles police officers savagely beat Rodney King, an African American, prompting outrage in the African American community. This anger turned to violence in 1992, when an all-white jury acquitted the officers. Again South Central erupted in violence, including a savage attack by African Americans on a white truck driver, Reginald Denny, and looting by blacks of Korean-owned stores. More than forty people died before the riot was quelled days later.

By the 1990s, in urban areas the threat of an uprising and street crime forced people to consider their activities in light of their safety. Polarized race and class relations contributed to a widespread fear of violence, and the spread of Los Angeles gangs such as the Crips and the Bloods to smaller cities spelled a more violent future. In rural areas the prevalence of gun ownership contributed to a disproportionate rate of violent death, both accidental and intentional. Although national crime figures showed a decrease in violent crime beginning in the mid-1990s, the impression of vulnerability to violence remained. As the twentieth century ended, in the West as elsewhere in the nation Americans feared the encroachment of violence on their lives.

BIBLIOGRAPHY

Baldassare, Mark, ed. *The Los Angeles Riots: Lessons for the Urban Future.* Boulder, Colo.: Westview, 1994.

Brown, Richard Maxwell. *No Duty to Retreat: Violence and Values in American History and Society.* Oxford: Oxford University Press, 1991.

Davis, Mike. *City of Quartz: Excavating the Future in Los Angeles.* New York: Verso, 1991.

Halliburton, R., Jr. *The Tulsa Race War of 1921.* San Francisco: R and E Research Associates, 1975.

Hogan, Linda. *Mean Spirit.* New York: Atheneum, 1990.

Lukacs, J. Anthony. *Big Trouble: A Murder in a Small Western Town Sets Off a Struggle for the Soul of America.* New York: Simon and Schuster, 1997.

Marks, Paula Mitchell. *"And Die in the West": The Story of the OK Corral Gunfight.* New York: William Morrow, 1989.

Paredes, Américo. *"With His Pistol in His Hand": A Border Ballad and Its Hero.* Austin: University of Texas Press, 1958.

Slotkin, Richard. *The Fatal Environment: The Myth of the Frontier in the Age of Industrialization, 1800–1890.* New York: Atheneum, 1985.

———. *Gunfighter Nation: The Myth of the Frontier in Twentieth-Century America.* New York: Atheneum, 1992.

———. *Regeneration Through Violence: The Mythology of the American Frontier, 1600–1860.* Middletown, Conn.: Wesleyan University Press, 1973.

Utley, Robert. *The Lance and the Shield: The Life and Times of Sitting Bull.* New York: Henry Holt, 1993.

HAL ROTHMAN

*See also* **Agrarian Violence; American Indians; Crazy Horse; Custer, George Armstrong; Frontier; Gunfighters and Outlaws, Western; Industrial Workers of the World; Labor and Unions; Los Angeles Riots of 1992; No Duty to Retreat; Race and Ethnicity; Sitting Bull; Vigilantism; Wounded Knee, 1890; Zoot-Suit Riot;** *and individual places and wars.*

# WESTERN CIVIL WAR OF INCORPORATION

The Western Civil War of Incorporation (WCWI) was the aggregate of more than forty violent local conflicts that pervaded the American West from the 1850s to 1919. At the core of the WCWI was the conservative, consolidating authority of capital that was, according to the scholar Alan Trachtenberg, "incorporating" America into a tightly controlled social and economic order during the late nineteenth century. Central to the WCWI were ten episodes (1857–1901) in which small ranchers and farmers resisted the incorporating efforts of land-monopolizing forces. In line with the industrializing and urbanizing trend in the West, the main thrust of incorporation then moved from the farm-and-ranch country to the mills and mines of the vast region. Pacing the industrial and urban phase of incorporation was Colorado's Thirty Years' War (1884–1914), in which unionized hard-rock and soft-coal miners fought the incorporating drive of leading companies. Another very violent struggle was the 1890s Coeur d'Alene War in northern Idaho between the mine and mill companies and the miners and mill workers. As the early twentieth century unfolded, a dynamic new anti-incorporating force burst on the scene in the form of a radical, anticapitalist labor union, the Industrial Workers of the World (IWW), whose members were often called "Wobblies." From Puget Sound to Bisbee, Arizona, and from California to Montana, the Wobblies carried the fight against the incorporating element, whose response was to redouble its effort to master the situation. The IWW organized timber workers, miners, mill hands, and itinerant harvesters in western fields.

The boomtown phase of the WCWI was centered in the Kansas cattle towns, but boomtown disorder also exacerbated incorporating conflict in such communities as Tombstone, Arizona (1878–1881), and Goldfield, Nevada (1907).

It was, however, the combat of homesteaders against the incorporating forces of landed wealth and power that intrigued Americans. In states and territories such as New Mexico, Nebraska, California, Texas, Arizona, Wyoming, and Oregon there were outbreaks of outlaw and vigilante activity. The point men on the opposing sides of this phase of the WCWI were incorporation gunfighters versus resister gunfighters. Frank Canton, Tom Horn, "Wild Bill" Hickok, and Wyatt Earp were just a few of the incorporation gunfighters. Resister gunfighters were common, and many became famous, including Billy the Kid, Jesse James, John Wesley Hardin, Nate Champion, and Nick Ray. Heroic resister gunfighters were often idolized by law-abiding people of small means who feared and detested wealthy, powerful incorporators.

### Johnson County War

A high point in this regional civil war was the 1892 Johnson County War, part of some fifteen years of Wyoming cattle-range conflict from the late 1880s to 1901. Trouble began when wealthy and arrogant aristocrats from Britain and the eastern United States invested heavily in the Wyoming cattle industry and then went west to look after their extensive herds. These "cattle kings" alienated small ranchers, cowboys, and farmers, and insults and injured feelings escalated to actual conflict when a rustler element—sometimes joined by

basically honest folk building up their own small ranches—began to run off maverick cattle claimed by the ranching nabobs. The big ranchers formed the Wyoming Stock Growers' Association in 1873 to subdue the insurgent rustler and small landholder element and to incorporate it into a social and economic order dominated by the elite. As with many other struggles in the WCWI, the Wyoming range conflict was heavily politicized. Republicans supported the big cattlemen while Democrats and Populists opposed them. The Republicans, from its state party chairman and Wyoming's two U.S. senators to President Benjamin Harrison, aided and abetted the beef barons.

By 1892 Johnson County had become the center of Wyoming resistance to rangeland incorporation. Borrowing a leaf from the book of the highly successful vigilante movement in Montana that eight years earlier, in 1884, devastatingly squelched range-country banditry, the cattle kings of Wyoming organized their own vigilante band, which was led by the big rancher Frank Wolcott, included gunfighter and range-detective Frank Canton in a key role, and recruited gunslinging mercenaries all the way from Texas. The vigilantes scored big when, in early April 1892, they invaded Johnson County and surrounded and killed two of their prime targets—the resister gunfighters Nate Champion and Nick Ray. But before the invaders could capture the Johnson County seat, Buffalo, outraged citizens rallied and put them under siege. It was only through the intervention of President Harrison and a detachment of U.S. Army troops that a massacre of the invaders was forestalled. The surprising upshot of the Johnson County War was a stunning setback for the incorporators. The Johnson County War was reported in newspapers nationwide and caught the attention of both friends and foes of incorporation. One of the former was the eastern writer Owen Wister, whom the Johnson County War inspired to write the proincorporation novel *The Virginian* (1902), a national best-seller that initiated the linkage of the very real Johnson County War to the myth and legend of the West as purveyed by fiction and in film. Jack Schaefer's novel *Shane* (1949) was loosely based on the Johnson County War, as was the classic Western movie *Shane* (1953), directed by George Stevens. In its depiction of an oppressive local cattleman bent on destroying a neighboring faction of small farmers, the film captures the tension and tragedy of many episodes in the WCWI, not just the Johnson County War. A perceptive treatment of the Johnson County War is the anti-incorporation novel *Riders of Judgment* (1957) by Frederick Manfred and based on the lives of Champion and Ray. The first scholarly treatment of the Johnson County War was Helena Huntington Smith's *The War on Powder River* (1966).

A flawed but powerful film about the Johnson County War is *Heaven's Gate* (1980), directed by Michael Cimino. Lacking the brilliant simplicity of *Shane*, *Heaven's Gate* departs from the reality of the Johnson County War in its portrait of the anti-incorporating small landholders as "ethnics" (white immigrants) from Europe. In fact, the Johnson County resisters to the big cattlemen were mainly "Anglos" and nonimmigrants, as was usually the case with rural opponents of the incorporation of the American West. The Johnson County War was only a temporary setback for the cattle magnates of Wyoming. They altered their tactics, turning from vigilantism to the services of a lethal bounty hunter, Tom Horn, who picked off rustlers from ambush. By 1910 the rangeland of Wyoming was a part of the fully incorporated West. Horn's murder-for-money career had ended in 1903 with his legal execution for a bungled ambush that found him mistakenly killing a young boy rather than his intended rustler victim. The last stand for the resister side in the WCWI was mounted by the IWW in four violent outbreaks during World War I. In all of these events (Everett, Washington, 1916; Bisbee, Arizona, 1917; Butte, Montana, 1917; and Centralia, Washington, 1919), the Wobblies were losers. By 1920 the West was fully incorporated and stayed that way until the turbulence and insurgency of the 1960s resulted in the disincorporation of the West as well as the entire nation.

*BIBLIOGRAPHY*

Brown, Richard Maxwell. *No Duty to Retreat: Violence and Values in American History and Society.* New York: Oxford University Press, 1991. Chapters 2 and 3 formulate the concept of the WCWI and enlarge upon it.

———. "Violence." In Clyde A. Milner II, Carol A. O'Connor, and Martha A. Sandweiss, eds. *The Oxford History of the American West.* New York: Oxford University Press, 1994. This essay lists and maps forty-two episodes in the WCWI.

Lukas, J. Anthony. *Big Trouble.* New York: Simon and Schuster, 1997. A monumental contribution to the history of the Western Civil War of Incorporation.

Papanikolas, Zeese. *Buried Unsung: Louis Tikas and the Ludlow Massacre.* Salt Lake City: University of Utah Press, 1982.

Slotkin, Richard. *Gunfighter Nation: The Myth of the Frontier in Twentieth-Century America.* New York: Atheneum, 1992.

Trachtenberg, Alan. *The Incorporation of America: Culture and Society in the Gilded Age.* New York: Hill and Wang, 1982.

RICHARD MAXWELL BROWN

*See also* **Agrarian Violence; Gunfighters and Outlaws, Western; Industrial Workers of the World; Mussel Slough Conflict; West.**

## WHISKEY REBELLION

The so-called Whiskey Rebellion, centered in western Pennsylvania, began with resistance to the national excise act that was passed in early 1791; it climaxed in July 1794 in an explosion of violence that led to the greatest use of force by the national government against internal dissent prior to the Civil War. The episode then ended anticlimactically with the trials of several supposed rebels in Philadelphia during the spring and summer of 1795. These incidents fit the pattern of a traditional "regulation," in which the economically pressed use violence not to overthrow a government, as in a true rebellion, but to prevent the implementation of legislation (also opposed by better-off moderates) that would cause additional hardship.

In western Pennsylvania commercialization and population growth led to the development of thriving towns whose shopkeepers, attorneys, and artisans served the more market-oriented farmers. But poorer folk, landless tenants, and landowners who lacked the means to enter the growing market depended on neighbors who owned a small still to produce whiskey, a product used for both local consumption and wider commerce. Both richer and poorer residents of the area became suspicious of those in the eastern part of the state, who they believed remained indifferent to western interests; they were also suspicious of the new national government, which seemed unwilling or unable to remove threats to their safety posed by the Native Americans north and west of the Ohio River.

In order to implement the Excise Act of 1791, the national government appointed large numbers of collectors to register stills and to receive the payment of taxes on the production of whiskey and other spirits. Westerners accused of violating the law discovered that they would be summoned to the Federal District Court in distant Philadelphia. The political and economic leaders within the region opposed the law, but some eventually accepted positions as collectors, and a few of the more commercial distillers began to register their stills and pay the tax. Many poorer westerners became "regulators" and took effective, sometimes painful but not lethal, action—tarring and feathering and burning barns and occasionally houses—against collectors and registered still owners. Those led by "Tom the Tinker," an anonymous pamphleteer, shot holes in registered stills. These local, sporadic acts created a climate of fear that prevented the effective collection of the excise.

By 1792 national leaders, notably Secretary of the Treasury Alexander Hamilton and President George Washington, came to believe that local politicians had mobilized this resistance to discredit their administration and to provoke separation from the nation. In the summer of 1794 their decision to punish unregistered still owners precipitated an outbreak of violence that gave them the opportunity to crush the regulators. At first the federal marshal from Philadelphia had little difficulty in serving his writs in several of the western counties; but when he joined General John Neville, the officer responsible for collections throughout all of western Pennsylvania, they ran into difficulties along the Washington-Allegheny county line. Angered by Neville's attempt to enforce the act, several locals attacked the general's house but were beaten off with one man killed. A local militia unit then joined the regulators. Meanwhile Neville had requested and received a small number of national troops from the garrison in nearby Pitts-

burgh. The ensuing confrontation resulted in the death of the leader of the militia and the burning and destruction of Neville's house. A few days later other regulators stopped the United States mail near Greensburg and seized several letters written by Pittsburgh notables that revealed their opposition to the regulation. In the eyes of Washington and Hamilton, attacking an important collector, battling with national troops, and interfering with the United States mail had escalated regulation into rebellion; but before ordering their forces into western Pennsylvania, in conjunction with the state of Pennsylvania they sent commissioners to the region to negotiate with the westerners.

The westerners, both moderates and regulators, decided to hold a special convention at Parkinson's Ferry (now Monongahela). Meanwhile five to seven thousand militiamen who were assembled at Braddock's Field, a few miles from Pittsburgh, decided to accept the exile (from Pittsburgh) of several writers of the intercepted letters and to march through the city. Although nonviolent, these actions exacerbated the fear of the moderates. At the same time the regulation, with its barn burnings, symbolic liberty poles, and resigning collectors, spread to central and eastern Pennsylvania and western Virginia and Maryland.

The western moderates took control at the Parkinson's Ferry assembly and convinced the delegates to appoint a committee to negotiate with the national and state commissioners. They also converted a majority of the representatives at a later

**Tarring-and-feathering a government inspector during the Whiskey Rebellion, 1794.** CORBIS/BETTMANN

assembly at Brownsville to accept the terms demanded by the commissioners, worked diligently to have as many westerners as possible sign oaths to support the government, and won the state and national elections held in the region during October. But all this failed to convince either the commissioners or the two governments that the moderates could control the rioters.

Thus, a massive militia army of almost thirteen thousand men, mobilized from eastern Pennsylvania, Maryland, Virginia, and New Jersey, marched against the region in November 1794 and met no resistance. Alexander Hamilton and other important national figures who accompanied the army could uncover no evidence that linked any of the local political leaders to the regulators, except for David Bradford, a prominent Washington County attorney who fled to Spanish territory at Natchez. They seized some smaller fry, but eventually released most of them at Philadelphia. Only two individuals, one retarded and the other perhaps insane, faced execution for all this action. President Washington pardoned both, thus ending the "rebellion."

Although it occasioned an effective early use of national power, the Whiskey Rebellion did make politicians leery of levying heavy direct taxes. Indeed, the Jeffersonians repealed the excise in the early 1800s, and except for a few years during the War of 1812, the nation imposed no further excise tax until the Civil War.

*BIBLIOGRAPHY*

Baldwin, Leland D. *Whiskey Rebels*. Pittsburgh: University of Pittsburgh Press, 1939.
Boyd, Steven R., ed. *The Whiskey Rebellion: Past and Present Perspectives*. Westport, Conn.: Greenwood, 1985.
Elkins, Stanley, and Eric McKitrick. *The Age of Federalism*. New York: Oxford University Press, 1993.
Slaughter, Thomas P. *The Whiskey Rebellion: Frontier Epilogue to the American Revolution*. New York: Oxford University Press, 1986.

VAN BECK HALL

*See also* **Civil Disorder; Riots.**

# WHITE SLAVERY

The "white slave" scare of the Progressive Era provides an example of social anxiety about women's changing status in American culture and a study of legislative and judicial response to a social problem. In the long run, white slavery proved more smoke than fire, but the statutory and cultural heritage of the white slave fear of 1907 to 1914 spanned the twentieth century.

In the early twentieth century, antiprostitution became a major urban reform effort and reflected the cultural concerns about immigration, urbanization, and women's status. As young people, especially young unmarried women, moved to the city from American rural areas and from overseas, urban centers became a threatening forum of social interaction. Most American cities and towns contained vice districts. The most famous was New Orleans's "Storyville," but numerous others existed, such as Chicago's "Levee" and Houston's "Reservation." What confounded middle-class social reformers was how urban brothels in these districts found the women to staff their businesses.

Antiprostitution activists believed that low wages explained some of the labor supply, but they also fixed on syndicates of foreign men, especially Jews, who either imported women into the country to staff brothels or captured American girls and women and forced them into brothel work. This form of coerced prostitution, popularly called white slavery, captured the nation's imagination, and the media poured out books, articles, and movies depicting the evil city and white slavery. In response, numerous local antiprostitution organizations formed. They raised funds; investigated vice conditions in their localities; published a vice report; and lobbied city, county, and state government to enact stricter penalties and policies against prostitution and bawdy houses. The best known of these reports are *The Social Evil* (1902) from New York City and *The Social Evil in Chicago* (1911).

Although newspapers and reformers had occasionally used the term *white slaves* to refer to prostitutes or to Mormon wives, the white slave scare started in Chicago, a booming metropolis with multiethnic communities. In 1907 the muckraking journalist George Kibbe Turner published an article in *McClure's Magazine* charging that a "loosely organized association . . . largely composed of Russian Jews" supplied women to Chicago's brothels and did so with the knowledge of city officials. A local prosecutor, Clifford G. Roe, then undertook a series of prosecutions of keepers of bawdy houses after he claimed to have discovered a note thrown from a brothel by a young woman who alleged she was being kept as a white slave. Other newspapers, magazines, and prosecutors picked up the theme. By 1913 the *San Francisco Examiner* ran a story claiming that sixty thousand women a year were kidnapped and forced into brothel prostitution.

Edwin W. Sims, a U.S. attorney in Chicago, did more than publicize the problem. He convinced his friend and U.S. congressman James R. Mann that federal legislation was needed to deal with the interstate and international trade in women. Mann introduced a bill in Congress on 6 December 1909 to punish the interstate transportation of women for "prostitution, or debauchery, or for any other immoral purpose." His bill, built on Congress's power under the interstate commerce clause of the Constitution, encountered little opposition, and almost no discussion occurred of what the phrase "immoral purpose" meant. President William Howard Taft signed the White-Slave Traffic (Mann) Act into law on 25 June 1910.

While the statute caught its share of persons running brothels and even those involved in consensual sex and trysts, the Mann Act did not destroy white slavery since no such institution existed. Most Mann Act prosecutions did not involve syndicates of foreign men "enslaving" women to work in brothels but, rather, implicated the voluntary interstate transportation of adult women willing to work as prostitutes in low bars and theaters. From the 1920s through the 1940s the Justice Department and the Federal Bureau of Investigation uncovered and prosecuted such behaviors as it sought to uphold a federal standard of morality. Occasionally the Mann Act proved useful in prosecuting political radicals, such as the 1944 trial of communist sympathizer Charlie Chaplin (the jury acquitted him of the charge). But by the 1950s Mann Act prosecutions drastically declined as social and cultural values changed. Revised in 1978 and 1986, the Mann Act endures in federal statutes, and interstate or foreign transportation of a person for prostitution "or any sexual activity for which any person can be charged with a criminal offense" is a federal crime.

White slavery and the Mann Act demonstrate the power of popular perception and hysteria, the impact of tensions within the culture, and the longevity of statutes past their initial purpose.

BIBLIOGRAPHY

Connelly, Mark Thomas. *The Response to Prostitution in the Progressive Era*. Chapel Hill: University of North Carolina Press, 1980.

Grittner, Frederick K. *White Slavery: Myth, Ideology, and American Law*. New York: Garland, 1990.

Langum, David J. *Crossing over the Line: Legislating Morality and the Mann Act*. Chicago: University of Chicago Press, 1994.

Young, Mary de. "Help, I'm Being Held Captive! The White Slave Fairy Tale of the Progressive Era." *Journal of American Culture* 6 (spring 1983).

THOMAS C. MACKEY

*See also* **Prostitution.**

# WHITMAN, CHARLES
(1941–1966)

From the observation deck of the twenty-seven-story tower of the University of Texas at Austin, Charles Joseph Whitman looked out over the city of Austin on 1 August 1966 and rained down a shower of bullets on the passersby below.

Whitman, born in Lake Worth, Florida, was a twenty-five-year-old junior at the university. He was married and was taking an intense summer course load of fourteen hours as a student in archi-

**Charles Whitman.** CORBIS/BETTMANN

tectural engineering. Whitman had been an Eagle Scout and served in the U.S. Marine Corps. A few months before the shooting, Whitman's mother left his father after years of abuse. This abusive nature had been passed on to Whitman, who admitted to a psychiatrist that he had twice beaten his wife.

Around midnight on 1 August 1966 Whitman stabbed his mother and then shot her in the back of the head. In unaddressed notes, Whitman indicated that he killed his mother in order to end her misery. He picked up his wife at her job and brought her home, where he stabbed her three times, apparently to save her the embarrassment of his later actions. He also expressed his deep hatred for his father in his notes.

Whitman then prepared for his upcoming attack. He gathered several types of guns, as well as food and water. After entering the tower building he paused and took the time to kill Edna Townsely, the receptionist at the entrance to the observation deck. It is probable that this delay saved the lives of dozens of others, as Whitman just missed the 11:30 changing of classes, when more than a thousand students would have been within shooting range from the tower. As it was, many were safely in their classrooms when Whitman started shooting at 11:48.

Whitman's vantage from the tower allowed him to shoot out in all directions and at great distances. Among Whitman's victims was a pregnant woman, whose child died though she did not; a young newspaper boy; an Englishman with a pregnant wife and two children in England; and a Peace Corps trainee. Billy Speed, an Austin policeman, was shot down when he returned fire on Whitman. The police sent out a low-flying airplane, which Whitman fired upon, driving the plane back, with the tower serving as an effective shield. Finally, a group of police officers was able to reach the observation deck and overtake Whitman. After ninety-six minutes of firing upon Austin, Whitman was shot and killed. He had taken sixteen people with him. His motives remain unknown, but an autopsy, which Whitman specifically requested be done in one of his notes, revealed that he had a brain tumor.

The observation deck was closed in 1975 because several people had committed suicide by jumping from the tower. In November 1998 the university announced that the observation deck would be opened to the public, after safety barriers had been installed.

BIBLIOGRAPHY

Kelleher, Michael D. *Flash Point: The American Mass Murderer*. Westport, Conn.: Praeger, 1997.
Lavergne, Gary M. *A Sniper in the Tower: The Charles Whitman Murders*. Denton: University of North Texas Press, 1997.

TRACY W. PETERS

*See also* **Mass Murder: Individual Perpetrators.**

## WIFE BEATING. *See* Spousal Abuse.

## WILD BILL HICKOK. *See* Hickok, James Butler "Wild Bill."

## WILDING AND BERSERKING

*Wilding* and *berserking* refer to criminal assaults with particular sets of characteristics. Although the terms are not synonymous and do not have the same origins, both have been used in the 1980s and 1990s to label extremely violent crimes. Both terms are the subject of debate, and both are open to interpretation—*berserking* being more indeterminate because it is rarely used. *Wilding* is the more common, and thus more meaningful, label.

### Wilding

The definition of *wilding* has been the subject of extensive debate, with some claiming that crimes with a racial component, especially crimes by black assailants against white victims, are more likely to attract the label. In general, the term has been used to refer to crimes committed by an informal group of people (rather than members of a recognized gang, club, or organization), almost always teenage or young adult males. The crimes are motivated solely by the desire to have fun or to experience a thrill, and those who commit them show little or no remorse. Thus, this type of attack is sometimes labeled a "thrill crime." Such attacks usually involve several victims and take place over a substantial time period, perhaps several hours. A rampaging group will attack anyone in its path, making wilding an opportunistic crime. Crimes described as wildings usually involve weapons such as bats, clubs, rocks, and sticks, but seldom guns; they often result in the serious injury, but not the death, of their victims. Activities similar to those now labeled as wildings have taken place in urban environments for hundreds of years and are thus nothing new. However, most discussions of wilding include lamentations about the increasing callousness of youth, the moral decay of the contemporary urban environment, and the desperation and hopelessness increasingly felt by urban teenagers. Thus, these elements have become part of what wilding means.

The term *wilding* was first used in connection with the New York City case of 1989 in which a group of African American and Hispanic boys ran through Central Park attacking a number of people and damaging property. The case became especially prominent in the media in part because of one victim, the "Central Park Jogger," who was raped, beaten, and left for dead. The victim, a young Caucasian investment banker, survived and eventually emerged from her coma. The case resulted in convictions for crimes ranging from robbery to rape. The term *wilding* was reportedly taken from a statement made by one of the boys and was initially treated in the news as a term routinely used by young males to describe this type of activity. However, others have claimed that the boy may actually have been saying "wild thing" and was misunderstood. Whatever the case, wilding is not a term with an official or legal origin and is not used as a category for government crime statistics; rather, the term originated from personal comments and news reporters' interpretation and use of them.

Only a few cases have been labeled wildings since 1989. They include a 1990 case in Louisville, Kentucky, similar to the 1989 crime, in which six African American youths attacked and beat two dozen Caucasian victims, three of whom were rendered comatose. Other cases involved murder: in 1990 eight teenagers and young adults raped, beat, and killed a prostitute in Boston; in 1997, two bored youths in Franklin, New Jersey, deliberately lured pizza deliverers and killed them. In 1996 a second Central Park case, which again involved a savage group attack on a woman jogger, gained national attention as a wilding. In every case subsequent to the Central Park case of 1989, there has been public debate as to whether wilding was an appropriate label, especially where the crimes diverged from the pattern of opportunistic, random attacks short of murder. Local journalists and commentators are continually debating the definition

of the term and using it to label other, less visible cases.

Various explanations have been given for wilding behavior. These include poor living conditions or extreme poverty, substandard education, the lack of strong family bonds, the absence of positive role models, boredom, the lack of adequate social and recreational outlets, the need to feel power and to belong to a group, and a decline in morality and accountability in society in general. This final cause is explored by Charles Derber, whose book defines wilding broadly to mean crimes, including white-collar crimes, characterized by a "degenerate form of individualism."

## Berserking

*Berserking,* connoting horrific, purposeless, and out-of-control crime, is not often used. The word *berserker,* which refers to the perpetrator of such crimes, is somewhat more common. Criminals labeled as such are usually individuals (not members of violent groups) who cause the deaths of multiple victims, but the term has been applied to the actions of groups as well. *Berserker* is borrowed from Scandinavian mythology, where it referred to fearless warriors (literally "bear shirts") who howled like beasts in battle, used no protective armor, and focused intensely on the fight.

Several criminals at the end of the twentieth century have been called berserkers. Craig ("Berserker") Bjork was convicted of murdering his infant sons, his girlfriend, her friend, and a fellow prison inmate. A group of Hell's Angels bikers in Canada who committed multiple atrocities, including murders, were called berserkers. The term was used as a forehead tattoo by the Freeman brothers, Bryan and David, who, along with their cousin, murdered their parents and younger brother in 1990. *Berserking* (like *berserker*) has been used too infrequently in reports of criminal cases to warrant sustained debate over crimes to which it can legitimately be applied.

*BIBLIOGRAPHY*

Benedict, Helen. "The Jogger and the Wolfpack: The 1989–1990 Central Park Jogger Case." In *Virgin or Vamp: How the Press Covers Sex Crimes,* edited by Benedict. New York: Oxford University Press, 1992.

Derber, Charles. *The Wilding of America: How Greed and Violence Are Eroding Our Nation's Character.* New York: St. Martin's, 1996.

Sullivan, Timothy. *Unequal Verdicts: The Central Park Jogger Trials.* New York: Simon and Schuster, 1992.

LISA M. CUKLANZ

*See also* **Teenagers; Thrill Crime.**

## WILD WEST SHOWS. *See* Cody, William "Buffalo Bill."

## WINCHESTER, OLIVER FISHER (1810–1880)

Oliver Winchester is less aptly characterized as a gunsmith or craftsman than as an industrialist and entrepreneur. He became famous for his development and manufacture of the Winchester rifle, a shoulder gun that profited greatly from the inventions and improvements of such men as Horace Smith, D. B. Wesson, Tyler Henry, Nelson King, Christopher Spencer, B. B. Hotchkiss, and John M. Browning.

Born in Boston on 30 November 1810, Winchester spent his youth and early manhood casting about for a suitable career. He held jobs as a farmhand, carpenter's apprentice, clerk, construction worker, manager of a Baltimore men's clothing store, and operator of an import business in New York. In 1850, having gravitated to New Haven, Connecticut, he and a partner, John Davies, ran a thriving shirt-manufacturing company. His success in this undertaking enabled him to indulge his growing interest in firearms, and in the mid-1850s he became principal stockholder and owner of the Volcanic Repeating Arms Company, reorganized in 1857 as the New Haven Arms Company and later, in 1866, as the Winchester Repeating Arms Company. By shrewdly utilizing the skills and patents of men of inventive genius, Winchester launched a company that would eventually become the world's largest manufacturer of guns and ammunition. Well before his death on 11 December 1880, he had become one of New Haven's leading citizens, donating property and money to Yale University and serving in 1866–1867 as Connecticut's lieutenant governor.

The products of the Winchester company have played a part during various wars: the Civil War, World War I, World War II, the Vietnam War, and even the Persian Gulf War. The company's contributions to World War II are especially noteworthy and "included 15 billion rifle and machine gun cartridges, 1.5 billion pounds of cartridge metals, and one hundred million pounds of aluminum, in addition to hundreds of thousands of M1 Garand rifles and M1 carbines" (Wilson 1991, p. 179). Despite such facts, the Winchester name is associated less with military conflict than with the rugged adventures and garish colors of American social and cultural history. Often described as "the gun that won the West," the Winchester rifle was popular with frontier settlers, lawmen, and hunters. It was prized as well by Native Americans, and Sioux warriors used it in the battle against General George Armstrong Custer at Little Bighorn. A model 1873 Winchester was owned by the outlaw Billy the Kid, as well as by Pat Garrett, the sheriff who shot the Kid. In his Wild West Show, William F. "Buffalo Bill" Cody fired Winchester rifles, as did other members of his troupe, including Annie Oakley. President Theodore Roosevelt owned various Winchester longarms, including big-game guns that he and his son Kermit used on their 1909–1910 safari in Kenya. Legend has it that they practiced for their East African adventure on the White House lawn. Many Texas Rangers relied on Winchesters, including Frank Hamer, the man who pursued and killed Bonnie Parker and Clyde Barrow. From 1860 to 1895 Winchesters were often glamorized in dime novels. In the twentieth century, they were conspicuous props in such television shows as *The Rifleman* (1958–1963), starring Chuck Connors, and in countless Western movies, including *Winchester '73* (1950) and *Carbine Williams* (1952), both starring James Stewart, *Vera Cruz* (1953), starring Gary Cooper and Burt Lancaster, and *True Grit* (1969), starring John Wayne.

BIBLIOGRAPHY

Williamson, Harold Francis. *Winchester, the Gun That Won the West.* New York: A. S. Barnes, 1952.
Wilson, R. L. *Winchester, an American Legend: The Official History of Winchester Firearms and Ammunition from 1849 to the Present.* New York: Random House, 1991.

DONALD D. KUMMINGS

*See also* **Weapons.**

## WITCHCRAFT

Witchcraft has often been defined by those seeking to eradicate it, that is, by witch-hunters, and

Nineteenth-century depiction of a Puritan woman accused of witchcraft. Woodcut by Douglas Volk, 1885. CORBIS/BETTMANN

violence has characterized witch-hunting to a far greater extent than it has the practice of witchcraft itself. Witchcraft accusations have centered on perceived diabolical wrongdoing, or *maleficium*. In colonial America it was presumed that the accused had done harm to the accusers or their families; "witches" were suspected of a range of malefic acts, from relatively minor and annoying deeds, like turning butter rancid, to more egregious acts, such as making cows ill, brutally beating victims, or even causing childhood disease and death. The accused usually denied such *maleficium*, along with more general accusations of witchcraft. But early American witch-hunts continued despite such protestations, ultimately resulting in the jailing of over three hundred suspects and the hanging deaths of thirty-five people from 1620 to 1725. The most notorious episode of witch-hunting occurred in Salem, Massachusetts, in 1692–1693.

In seventeenth-century New England, Puritans understood witchcraft as a pact forged between a witch (usually a woman) and the devil. Ministers, magistrates, and laity sought to eliminate witchcraft, thus defined, from their godly commonwealth. Evidence brought to court during the trials sought to associate an accused witch with the devil's deeds. The most desirable piece of evidence would have been an eyewitness account of the accused signing the devil's book; if this was not available, then evidence of wrongdoing inspired by the devil could also serve. Because women tended to see themselves as weak and sinful, under pressure they sometimes conflated ordinary

sin (in Puritan theology, an implicit covenant with the devil) with an actual pact with the devil (signing one's name in the devil's book); hence some fifty women confessed to witchcraft.

Throughout U.S. history, the concept of "witch" and charges of witchcraft have helped to set and police the boundaries of female normality and acceptable behavior. Arguing against Iowa's proposed Equal Rights Amendment in 1992, for example, Pat Robertson expounded to members of the Christian Coalition that the feminist movement was "a socialist, anti-family political movement that encourages women to leave their husbands, kill their children, practice witchcraft, destroy capitalism, and become lesbians." Women who have challenged cultural notions of appropriate conduct, whether intentionally or unintentionally —even women who have wholeheartedly embraced social norms—have been (and still are) vulnerable to masculine apprehension and mistrust, and in extreme cases to accusations of witchcraft. Although "witches" in early America could be either male or female, witchcraft, witch-hunting, and womanhood are inextricably linked in American history and indeed in the history of the Western world.

If we leave behind the Puritan definition of witchcraft, requiring signature in the devil's book, and consider more broadly forms of magical practice designed to harness spiritual power, then perhaps it could be argued that witchcraft has taken place. Even Puritans were known to practice magic; for example, they placed horseshoes above their doorways to ward off sickness. Magic, healing, and religion coexisted uneasily in this early modern world, a world in which medical science, as it is known today, did not exist.

European Americans were not alone in their attempts to manipulate the supernatural world. Native Americans and African Americans have also practiced divination, spirit possession, and other forms of magic throughout U.S. history. Women in particular have often found their voices through religion, which in various ways has authorized their speech, even leadership, at times when women have otherwise lacked a legitimate public place and status. Members of African American Spiritualist churches, for example, have confronted a striking irony: though empowered by their faith and their practice of spirit possession, women have simultaneously incurred a liability. Practices tainted by their association with "witchcraft"—conjuring spirits or the use of charms—have been broadly stigmatized as dangerously superstitious, if not savage.

### Modern Practice

If most people assume that witchcraft is a violent manipulation of spiritual power, then contemporary practitioners of Wicca bear the brunt of these misunderstandings about witchcraft and magical practice. Old tensions involving the terms *witchcraft* and *witch* persist. Many eagerly adopt the terms in solidarity with the thousands persecuted for witchcraft in earlier centuries (especially in Europe); yet just as many search for other terms that will not tie them to the traditional image of the malicious hag.

Modern practitioners of Wicca insist their craft is nonviolent. These self-described witches are predominantly women, and they frequently see their witchcraft as a political as well as a religious calling, serving to redefine female identity and give women an important source of power in their fight to liberate women from second-class status. For many witches, witchcraft is not an isolated practice but the name given to a full religious worldview involving pantheism, goddess worship, environmentalism, and personal meditative and therapeutic practices. Issues of magical practice are controversial among spiritual feminists, whether they call themselves witches or not. They recognize magic's efficacy but realize that its use entails responsibility. The majority insist that the magic they practice is "positive"; in fact, they espouse the "threefold law" as a self-monitoring guideline: what you send re-

turns three times over. Negative energy will revisit those who knowingly dispatch it.

Despite Wicca's positive emphasis on rituals and practices that glorify women's power and affirm their bodies, there are critics of contemporary witchcraft. Opponents generally associate the craft with Satanism, a completely different sort of religious ideology. Witchcraft, in fact, has nothing to do with Satanism: because witches do not consider themselves Christian, they neither believe in nor worship God or Satan. Nevertheless, by assuming the label of "witch," those practicing "witchcraft" become weighted by all of the baggage associated with the term, including a history in this country of association with the devil derived from the colonial witch trials.

Witchcraft has been assumed to be violent, but in fact the vigorous witch-hunting efforts in America have proven to be far more so. As a means of legitimating violence against vulnerable members of society, scapegoating and witch-hunting have persisted far beyond the colonial period and beyond the bounds of alleged sorcery itself.

*BIBLIOGRAPHY*

Demos, John Putnam. *Entertaining Satan: Witchcraft and the Culture of Early New England.* New York: Oxford University Press, 1982.

Eller, Cynthia. *Living in the Lap of the Goddess: The Feminist Spirituality Movement in America.* New York: Crossroad Publishing, 1993.

Hall, David D., ed. *Witch-Hunting in Seventeenth-Century New England: A Documentary History, 1638–1692.* Boston: Northeastern University Press, 1991.

Reis, Elizabeth, ed. *Spellbound: Women and Witchcraft in America.* Wilmington, Del.: Scholarly Resources, 1998.

ELIZABETH REIS

See also **Folk Culture; Religion; Salem Witch Trials; Satanism, Modern.**

**WOBBLIES.** *See* Industrial Workers of the World.

# WOMEN

*Following the Overview are two subentries: Outlaws and Women Who Kill.*

## OVERVIEW

Violence against women, in varying forms and degrees, is a near universal phenomenon that has roots reaching back to the earliest periods of recorded history. Throughout the history of the United States, beginning in the colonial period, violence against women has been at various times both condoned and ignored. While theories on the roots of such violence have become more elaborated over the years, the subordination of women, in differing degrees, to male control and authority has remained a constant underlying theme. At the beginning of the twenty-first century as in the past, such subordination and oppression exist simultaneously within interpersonal and familial relationships as well as in institutional and societal spheres, being reinforced through economic, religious, political, medical, educational, and cultural structures.

**Colonial Period**

In the early colonial period, beginning in the seventeenth century, the Puritans incorporated English common law into their newly founded society as the basis for justice and order. This set of laws was heavily influenced by biblical (and specifically, Mosaic) codes. Hence, the criminal law system was seen as the law of God and was used to judge and enforce the community's religious morality. Within this set of laws married women were considered legal nonentities, without political rights, who were essentially incorporated under the authority of their husbands. Moreover, all money earned or inherited by the wife was under the control of the husband.

Spousal abuse then, as over the centuries that followed, could take numerous forms, including physical violence, emotional and sexual abuse, threats of violence or abuse, and, more critical in the colonial context, abandonment. Women in this period had few economic or political options, and it was generally necessary for families and the community to work together as a whole for survival. If a husband deserted his family, it often became difficult or impossible for women and children to subsist. In such cases colonial courts either required the husband to provide financially for his family or the family became a ward of the local parish.

At this time, to beat one's wife was an accepted male prerogative although it was not an unlimited legal privilege. The key differentiation was whether the chastisement was considered "within moderation." One example of such moderation was the "rule of thumb," which stipulated that the size of weapon a husband could use to beat his wife could be no larger around than the circumference of his thumb. Previous to this guideline, English common law stated that a husband could chastise his wife with any "reasonable instrument." Numerous legal and judicial accounts exist of threatened or enacted spousal violence that surpassed "moderation" and for which fines and punishments were levied.

Rape under English common law was defined simply as "carnal knowledge," meaning the forced entrance of the penis into the vagina. By 1648, in the Old Testament–based legal code of the Massachusetts Bay Colony known as the Body of Liberties, rape was declared an offense that carried the penalty of death, even though there was no direct biblical tenet that required capital punishment for this crime. This penalty was extreme compared to other colonies, which used lesser corporal and financial punishment in cases of rape. Of the rape cases that went to trial in the colonies, however, the perpetrator was often from a lower social class than the victim, or the victim was a married woman who could prove resistance. It was the responsibility of the victim to show physical proof that the sexual contact was nonconsensual, making it difficult to achieve a guilty verdict against rapists in many cases.

Another section of English common law included the Common Scold Law, for women only, which called for use of the brank (or "scold's bridle") or a public dunking stool as punishment for those who were declared to be troublesome and angry, "wrangled" with their neighbors, too often rebuked their husbands, or in other ways broke the peace. The brank was made of an iron frame and was designed to form a cage around the woman's head; it included a sharpened or spiked piece of metal that was then forced into her mouth to curb her tongue. Thus "bridled," the convicted "scold" was paraded through the streets on a chain and might be tied to a pillory, whipping post, or market cross. Dunking stools were also widely used against women convicted of scolding. In this case women were strapped onto a chair or stool that was extended over water and could be raised and lowered, to plunge them up and down.

One particularly cruel and gruesome example of violence against women in the United States was the witch-hunts and trials of the late seventeenth and early eighteenth centuries. Witch trials began first during the Spanish Inquisition in the late fifteenth century; however, this phenomenon spread throughout much of Europe and to the American colonies. Suspected witches were searched for a "devil's teat," moles, other skin blemishes, or places that did not bleed when pricked with a needle. Research has revealed that most accused and convicted witches were middle-aged women with few or no children, often widowed, generally in low social positions, sometimes involved in conflict with another community member, and often considered abrasive by neighbors. Evidently, many of these women were neither safely enough lodged within an immediate patriarchal-headed family to avoid scrutiny nor passive and submissive enough to fit within Puritan gender norms for women.

There are limited written records detailing the existence or forms of violence against women within native North American cultures of the colonial period. Early-eighteenth-century accounts left by women such as Mary Jemison (who lived among the Seneca Indians) and by the priest Chrestien Le Clercq (whose accounts of travel on the Gaspé Peninsula of Quebec includes critical interpretations of Micmac Indian women's "ambition to act the patriarch") often reveal a more equitable distribution of power in the gender roles of Native men and women. Previous to these accounts is a detailed record kept by a Jesuit in the sixteenth century who visited the Iroquois in what is now New York State and documented their way of life before European colonial impact. Their social structure was matrilinear and matrilocal, with the inheritance of the fruits of the land being passed from mother to daughter. Further, Iroquois women had control of the distribution of resources in the longhouses and seemed, generally, to have roles of leadership. Overall, his account gives no hints of gender-based violence, but instead depicts peaceable social interaction among the tribe's members.

## Independence and Nationhood

The new nation of the United States of America was born in 1776. Intertwined in the process of colonial independence were the motivational ideals of democracy, freedom, and equality; however, these were not legally extended beyond white, land-owning men. Early in the formation of the new nation's laws, Abigail Adams in letters to her husband, John Adams, advocated for the rights of white women to increased freedom within marriage. Unfortunately, neither of these aims were achieved in her lifetime. Instead women were encouraged to be patriotic and republican within

their roles as wives and mothers, instilling moral fortitude in the nation's future male citizens. Women's roles thus continued to be largely relegated to domestic and private affairs, with little political or legislative influence over their own lives or personal safety from violence.

As the nation grew, increasing numbers of African slaves were bought by Americans and forced to labor mainly in the burgeoning agricultural industries. The treatment of slaves varied from owner to owner. Generally, the lives of these women, men, and children were harsh and often conditions were brutally oppressive. Women under slavery were vulnerable to sexual assault by their owners as well as to severe physical and psychological violence. No recourse or refuge from such violence existed and, from the master's perspective, the children that often resulted from these rapes simply served to enlarge his resources. Further, women were frequently separated from their children and other family members, any of whom could be sold at any time to another master. This horrific treatment of enslaved African women as sexual chattels and inhuman objects produced a profoundly detrimental legacy of continued racism and sexual violence against African American women in American society into the twenty-first century.

## Industrial Age

With the advent of the Industrial Revolution in the later part of the eighteenth century, social roles within families began to change. Patriarchal control over the time, resources, activities, and sexuality of women began slowly to weaken. Women of all classes were eventually seen not as morally inferior to men, but as responsible by virtue of their natural purity to control men's innate lust. As a result, women who were raped or in other ways sexually assaulted were considered "fallen." Often a woman was both blamed for the man's crime and socially stigmatized by the attack. Further, as young women of lower classes from rural and immigrant backgrounds began to work and live in city settings, less traditional protection was available through one's family. Coupled with insufficient legal protection, women became, in the views of perpetrators, seemingly more accessible to rape. Other influences in this period were social theorists' views on the "natural" patriarchal family structure and causes of violence against women. This perspective was felt justified by the superior strength and reason of men as juxtaposed against the "natural" passivity and compliance of women. A slightly later addition to this argument was the human male's dominant urge to reproduce, which was seen as leading to behavior that in the twentieth century was defined as rape.

In the field of medicine during this period particularly brutal experimental surgeries were carried out on a number of slaves. In late 1850s a surgeon named Marion Sims began his work on enslaved African American women whom he had purchased for this purpose. Anarcha, one of these women, was operated on twenty-nine times without anesthesia by Sims, to practice and perfect his surgical techniques. Sims and many other physicians of the day firmly held the racist misconception that "savage" women of African descent were capable of withstanding extreme pain.

With the American expansion westward came numerous clashes with Native American and Mexican resistors. As U.S. forces seized and then attempted to control what is currently the American Southwest, the women of the conquered populations were widely victimized with rape and other acts of sexual violence as additional demoralizing tactics of warfare. Further, in California between 1850 and 1860 apprenticeship laws allowed for the abduction and sale of Native Americans, especially young women and children, into "indentured servitude." This terminology was essentially a euphemism for enslavement carried out as a business enterprise.

### Reform Era and First-Wave Feminism

By the second half of the nineteenth century, as the Industrial Revolution gained ever increasing momentum, its negative social, economic, and cultural effects were becoming obvious. The population was shifting significantly from rural to urban areas in search of employment and prosperity, however, by the 1850s numerous inner cities became increasingly overcrowded, developing serious social and health problems. Discontent among workers grew steadily and focused largely on poor wages, unlimited working hours, discrimination based on ethnicity or gender, and the seemingly unchecked power of large trusts and businesses. A reform movement began in the 1850s in the churches of the northeast. Growing out of a recognized acute need for social, economic, and legislative change, it worked toward such goals as abolition, temperance, and education.

Numerous middle- and upper-class women took part in these activities, and the experience of the movement became a catalyst for women to unify in the pursuit of political and legal rights. In July 1848 a group of pioneering feminist activists met at Seneca Falls, New York, for the first official discussions of women's rights. The women who orchestrated the meeting, including Elizabeth Cady Stanton, Lucretia Mott, Martha C. Wright, Jane Hunt, and Mary Ann Clintock, planned to focus on the social, civil, and religious rights of women. Out of this landmark meeting was born the suffrage movement, which sought the right for women to vote. Although this goal was not realized until 1920, a tremendous amount of time and resources were dedicated to its fulfillment over a seventy-two-year struggle. Despite this enormous achievement for the rights of women and the close work of some suffragettes within the abolitionists, there still existed within the suffrage movement, as within American society at large, varying degrees of discrimination based on ethnicity, class, and immigration status. These at times caused significant divisions among suffrage.

Among the most influential texts initiating the reform movement was *The Vindication of the Rights of Women*, written by the British feminist Mary Wollstonecraft in 1792. By the mid-1800s, Wollstonecraft's treatise—which refuted the assumption that male nature and virtues are superior to (or even different from) those of women, and further argued that all of humanity has been equally endowed with reason and rationality—had become virtually a Bible for activists in the first wave of the feminist movement in the United States. Later, *The Subjection of Women* (1869), written by John Stuart Mill and published in England, argued in support of equal rights for women. According to Mill, "the vilest malefactor has some wretched women tied to him, against whom he can commit any atrocity except killing her, and, if tolerably cautious, can do that without much danger of the legal penalty" (Wilson 1997).

Also of importance was the social theory proposed by Karl Marx in *The Communist Manifesto* (1848), and then applied more specifically to women by Friedrich Engels in *The Origin of the Family, Private Property, and the State* (1884), which offered feminists a framework to analyze domestic and other violence against women in terms of capitalism and private property. These German-born theorists viewed women as economic dependents first of their fathers and then of their husbands. They argued that women exchanged their domestic and sexual services for economic security in the legal, monogamous family, a set of circumstances that had parallels, in some ways, to slave ownership. Engels held that the emergence of private property and its control by men were the primary historical events from which modern social order and systematic gender violence originated.

Over the course of the nineteenth century, and as a result of women's social and political activity, legislation and sanctions involving domestic violence slowly changed. By the 1870s states began rejecting the codified prerogative of husbands to batter their wives. In 1874 the North Carolina Supreme Court made a ruling against spousal battery; however, the court went on to state that "if no permanent injury has been inflicted, nor malice, cruelty nor dangerous violence shown by the husband, it is better to draw the curtain, shut out the public gaze and leave the parties to forget and forgive" (Wilson 1997). As this account exemplifies, the laws surrounding domestic violence were changing, yet it was still perceived as a socially tolerated and private matter.

In the decade following the end of the Civil War, societies for the prevention of cruelty to children began to address family violence. Between 1875 and 1900, such organizations were part of the general reform movement and were heavily influenced by feminist views. Nonetheless, the participants in these societies at first tried to avoid intervening in cases of spousal abuse. Only after

increasing numbers of battered women requested aid that they were unable to attain through their family and friends did societies for the prevention of cruelty to children begin to offer monetary help and sometimes housing. Police protection at this time was limited, and many officers sympathized with the husband's frustrations and downplayed the seriousness of assaults against wives.

During the nineteenth and early twentieth centuries, violence against women continued in the field of medicine. Sigmund Freud, the founder of psychoanalysis, heard disclosures of sexual abuse by numerous women he treated. Although he initially believed the accounts and published his findings, under pressure from his peers he recanted, and ultimately he recast his diagnosis of these experiences as mere fantasies. Moreover, with Freud's creation of "hysteria" as a neurosis, American physicians such as Isaac Ray and Robert Battery accepted the purported idea that women's susceptibility to this disease, as well as to insanity and criminal impulses, was caused by their sexual organs. As a result, clitoridectomies were performed to cure masturbation and hysteria and to make women less rebellious, and hysterectomies were undertaken to cure insanity.

### Early Twentieth Century

Shortly after the achievement of women's suffrage in 1920 and until the early 1960s, the feminist

**Suffragettes from nearly every state in the Union converge on the U.S. Senate to petition for equal voting rights, early twentieth century.**
CORBIS/HULTON-DEUTSCH COLLECTION

455

movement experienced a distinct recession. During the Progressive Era, roughly between 1900 and the 1930s, there was a shift in social and political activity that called for a more equal distribution of economic wealth and authority, the creation of widespread social support and welfare systems, and the understanding that progress as a nation must be organized and guided. In this period, relationship violence was incorporated under the umbrella of the new profession of social work. At this time marital violence was largely portrayed as mutual, and its causes were often attributed to environmental stressors, lack of education, or lack of mental integrity. Further, women were generally held responsible for the tone and setting of the family environment. Of critical importance in this era was the maintenance of the modern nuclear family, a value that superseded dealing with the violence that continued to be experienced by women.

In the 1940s and 1950s the focus shifted toward psychiatric understanding of relationship violence. Victims of abuse were often diagnosed as having complex mental disorders resulting from sexual repression, a failure to accept their femininity, frigidity, or masochism, among other causes. Victims were treated for these "neuroses," with little regard for targeting the abusers who perpetrated the assaults. As in previous decades, the preservation of the ideal of the conventional family was the overarching theme.

### Second-Wave Feminism

The women's liberation movement that emerged in the 1960s and 1970s sought generally to achieve equality of power for women by eliminating the enforcement or restriction of gender roles. This revival of feminism also raised a broader awareness of issues that coalesced into specific struggles to oppose relationship violence, rape, and other forms of sexual assault against women. The anti-rape movement, for example, stimulated the emergence of grassroots community rape-crisis centers, whose advocacy efforts led to widespread social awareness of what constitutes rape, its magnitude, and the community responses needed to end violence and support survivors. The battered women's movement focused on aiding victims of domestic violence as well as raising social consciousness and working toward legislative reform.

These movements and the groups that formed within them were grounded in a feminist social

**Women's liberation demonstration, 1970.** CORBIS/ BETTMANN

analysis that argued that profound power differentials in patriarchal society nurtured oppression and inequity. Theorists such as Gayle Rubin, Dorothy Dinnerstein, and Nancy Chodorow held that numerous forms of oppression and violence were linked to the enforcement of gender roles, with women being seen as "naturally" passive, submissive, weak, and in need of male protection, and men being seen as "naturally" independent, strong, unemotional, and programmed to protect and control women. The institutionalization of this perspective has supported economic, educational, political, legal, and social privileges advantaging men—and yielded a social framework in which the use of violence against women is allowed and even openly condoned, especially if the abuser were a father or husband.

Even as great strides were made in public awareness about rape and domestic violence, however, profoundly damaging and criminal medical violence was carried out against women in the form of forced sterilization, with the vast majority of the victims being women of color. The roots of this phenomenon date to the emergence of eugenics during the Progressive Era. Some theorists argued that racial differences were biologically based and that therefore steps should be taken to limit the number of immigrants allowed into the United States and to curb reproduction among minority populations who were seen as racially inferior. Most widely affected were African American, Latina, Puerto Rican, and Native American women who were targeted for sterilization regardless of their consent and, in some cases, without their prior knowledge. It has been estimated that during 1972 alone as many as two hundred thousand women, and a small number of men, were sterilized through federal funding (Marilyn French, *The War Against Women,* London: Hamish Hamilton Ltd., 1992, p. 102). By the end of the 1970s, more than 35 percent of women of childbearing age in Puerto Rico and 24 percent of Native American women in the United States had been forced into sterilization.

### Rape and the Anti-Rape Movement

Throughout most of U.S. history women who have been victims of rape or other forms of sexual assault have generally been judged with suspicion, viewed either as liars or as temptresses who invited the assault. Further, the burden of proof rested predominantly on the victim, making sexual crimes extremely difficult to convict. When reported, rapes were often treated by police and prosecuting attorneys with skepticism or disinterest.

During the 1970s, however, women organized grassroots rape-crisis centers that offered legal and medical advocacy, engaged in political lobbying, and devoted themselves to community-awareness efforts to change the ways that rape was often condoned. The first rape-crisis centers were developed under the auspices of the National Organization for Women (NOW), established in 1966 to work toward legal equity and access for women to the opportunities held by men. Anti-rape activism was a catalyst for the emergence of significant scholarship concerning violence against women that confronted long-standing myths.

Intrinsic to the change process was the development of language, concepts, and definitions to describe the manifestations and causes of relationship violence, rape, and other forms of sexual assault. In September 1971 Susan Griffin published

a groundbreaking article in *Ramparts* titled "Rape: An All-American Crime," in which she reported that forcible rape was the most frequently committed violent crime in America and powerfully described how rape, or the fear of it, was a part of women's everyday lives. In 1975 Susan Brownmiller published *Against Our Will: Men, Women and Rape,* in which she defined rape as "a conscious process of intimidation by which all men keep all women in a state of fear"(p. 5). That same year Diana Russell argued, in *The Politics of Rape,* that if men were socialized not to separate sexual feelings from those of care and warmth, rape would be rare and significantly fewer men would be sexually coercive to women in less extreme ways.

Anti-rape activism ultimately elicited widespread changes in federal and state laws regarding rape. Legislation was enacted to broaden the definition of rape and alter the procedures followed in rape trials. For example, rape was changed to a gender-neutral crime, permitting the offense of male-on-male rape to be prosecuted, and criminal penetration was expanded from vaginal to include oral and anal sodomy. Finally, evidence rules requiring corroboration witnesses were dropped and limits were placed on the admission of the victim's sexual history. In 1978 a landmark case occurred in a local-level Oregon criminal court, when for the first time in U.S. court history a husband currently living with his wife was tried for marital rape (although he was not convicted). Under pressure from the anti-rape movement, the National Center for the Prevention and Control of Rape (NCPCR) was created within the National Institute of Mental Health (NIMH) in 1976 through federal legislation to sponsor research, education, and training programs that would investigate the causes of sexual assault, its impact on the mental health of victims, and effective strategies for its treatment and prevention. A survey conducted by the NCPCR indicated that by 1979 community-based rape-crisis centers had been established in at least one community in every state as well as in the District of Columbia and Puerto Rico. In the years after its formation the NCPCR was reorganized several times. In 1990, sexual-assault research was incorporated under the broader research scope of the violence and traumatic stress studies at NIMH, with rape studies losing visibility and autonomy in the process. In 1998 NIMH ceased to do research specifically on sexual assault. Federal initiatives against rape and sexual assault were subsumed under the aegis of domestic violence, where they tended to recede from awareness.

## Initiatives Against Partner Violence

The 1970s saw the first widespread opening of shelters and telephone hotlines officially committed to victims of domestic violence. Women had long resisted battery on the individual level and more rarely at the community level, but now they began to achieve considerable gains politically, ideologically, and socially. The National Coalition Against Domestic Violence was formed in 1978 during a meeting of the U.S. Commission on Civil Rights that was specifically focused on battered women. In the short span between 1975 and 1995 the number of shelters in the United States sprang from fewer than twenty to more than twelve hundred.

Activists also organized educational and media campaigns and lobbied for legislative reforms of criminal and civil statutes. In 1979 both the Interdepartmental Committee on Domestic Violence, with representatives from twelve federal agencies, and the Office of Domestic Violence (ODV) were created by President Jimmy Carter. The ODV was later dismantled by President Ronald Reagan. In the 1990s, services and research on violence against women were addressed primarily by the Department of Justice and the Centers for Disease Control and Prevention, making criminal justice and public health vocabulary the dominant languages in which the issues are articulated. The concept models that predominate in public health and criminology do not address socially constructed gender roles of the privileges male domination created. Thus, they decontextualize the consideration of male violence against women.

## Landmarks in Social Science Research

*Date Rape.* The sociologist Eugene Kanin first studied sexual aggression among college students in 1957. His work is historic because he was the first to think of sexual aggression outside of the "criminal element," suggesting that it could even be found in ordinary college students. In 1974 Ann Burgess and Lynda Holmstrom wrote "The Rape Trauma Syndrome," a research study that described a specific set of widely experienced effects of rape on victims. Although these investigators were learning that many survivors of rape knew their attacker, the term *date rape* was not coined until 1982, when an article published in *Ms.* magazine discussed the research findings of Mary Koss

concerning rates of sexual aggression and victimization on the college campus. The phenomenon of marital rape was identified both by Lenore Walker, in *The Battered Woman* (1979), and Diana Russell, in *Rape in Marriage* (1982), who estimated that between 30 percent and 40 percent of battered women were also sexually assaulted. These studies were critical in providing a language with which to discuss acts that had heretofore gone largely unnamed and unexamined. The first nationally representative survey of rape prevalence independent of federal crime statistics was released in April 1992 by the National Victims Center. The finding that 13 percent of American women had been raped was front-page news across the nation. The most recent nationally representative data are from the National Violence Against Women Survey, funded by the U.S. Department of Justice and the Centers for Disease Control and Prevention. The reported rape prevalence was 17.6 percent among women when completed and attempted rape were added together, as is typically done with crime statistics. The rate for completed rape alone was 14.8 percent (Tjaden and Thoennes 1998, pp. 1–16).

*Domestic Violence.* Research in the area of intimate violence also began to be undertaken in the mid-1970s. In 1975 the first nationally representative survey of violence in families indicated that 28 percent of married couples reported the occurrence of at least one physical assault between them (Straus, Gelles, and Steinmetz 1980). A decade later, a second nationwide family violence survey reported that one out of eight men surveyed admitted to physically assaulting their wives in the past twelve months (Straus and Gelles 1990). Although women admit to a similar level of violent acts, Angela Browne argues in "Violence Against Women by Male Partners" (*American Psychologist* 48, 1993, pp. 1077–1087) that men primarily perpetrate the most serious acts, those characterized by physical harm, sexual aggression, forcible restraint, and threats to injure or kill. Although men are more likely to be injured by strangers than by people they know, crime and emergency-room statistics show that women are more likely to be attacked, raped, injured, or killed by former or current male partners than by any other type of perpetrator. In 1992 the American Medical Association formally acknowledged the problem of domestic violence, which was defined as "a pattern of coercive behaviors that may include repeated battering and injury, psychological abuse, sexual assault, progressive social isolation, deprivation, and intimidation." In 1996 the American Psychological Association convened the Presidential Task Force on Violence and the Family that formally defined intimate violence as "abuse, battering and sexual assault whether individuals are married, dating, living together, separated, or divorced."

*Lesbians and Violence.* Only since the late 1980s has relationship violence been studied in same-sex couples. Claire Renzetti reported in 1992 that heterosexual and homosexual intimate violence occurred at about the same rate and attributed the delay in investigating abuse between lesbian partners to pervasive heterosexism in the social sciences and to stereotypes of women as nonaggressive. Studies by Kerry Lobel in 1986 and Valli Kanuha in 1990, among others, indicated that from 17 percent to 46 percent of lesbians reported being abused by a female partner. Lesbians are also subject to attacks by antigay perpetrators in which they are victimized through verbal, physical, or sexual attacks, including rape, according to research done by Linda Garnets, Gregory M. Herek, and Barrie Levy in 1990.

*Elder Abuse.* Another understudied area is abuse of elderly women. Because of mandatory reporting laws for abuse of vulnerable elderly persons, the problem is known to exist, but many existing studies are marred by poor individual and institution response levels, and reliable estimates of incidence and prevalence rates are unavailable. Factors such as poverty, chronic ill health, and long-term dependency on others for daily care are experienced disproportionately by women as they age and may contribute to higher risks for elder abuse among them.

*Risk Factors for Sexual Assault Victimization.* Existing research involving vulnerability factors for intimate violence, sexual assault, or both indicates that the most powerful predictor across this crime category is female gender, particularly when the research focus is limited to cases where physical injury was sustained. Age is also an effective predictor, as levels of vulnerability vary greatly across the life span. Data from the National Violence Against Women Survey showed that slightly more than half of rape victims were younger than eighteen years old when first assaulted (Tjaden and Thoennes 1998). The family plays a vital role in the perpetuation and reinforcement of behaviors and attitudes that foster violence against girls and women. In her article "Does Violence Beget Violence? A Critical Examination of the Literature"

(1989), Cathy Widom estimates that one third of children who are abused or exposed to violence in childhood subsequently become violent as adults. Further, women who are sexually abused in childhood are more likely to be physically abused by male partners in adulthood.

## Contemporary Public Policy

Public policy changes are among the most important tools to achieve significant and lasting reductions in violence against women. In 1994 the landmark Violence Against Women Act (VAWA) was passed into law as the first U.S. federal legislation directly addressing gender-based crimes. Through VAWA the government allotted $1.6 billion to support increased police personnel, higher levels of prosecution, more severe penalties for perpetrators, and extended victim services. Five years later, follow-up legislation known as VAWA II was being drafted to extend those initiatives. Proposed amendments aimed for a better understanding of the extent and causes of violence against women and called for systematic examination of the effectiveness of specific education, prevention, and intervention approaches. To this end, interdisciplinary research efforts would be encouraged through federal support mechanisms and maintained with long-term funding allocations. Additional proposed initiatives included (1) an analysis of the uniformity and consistency of rape and sexual-assault laws at the state level, especially as they applied to acquaintances or intimates; (2) identification of criminal justice reforms that would increase case prosecution; (3) mandated educational and training programs for judges, prosecutors, police, and victim advocates; (4) significantly increased levels of punishment for sexual and violent assaults; (5) state-funded forensic rape exams; and (6) federal provision of grants to states to implement innovative programs aimed at increasing arrests, prosecution, and conviction rates in relationship violence, rape, or other sexual assault cases.

## Research Initiatives

A review of research agendas developed by federal advisory organizations, including the National Research Council, point to areas of agreement on fruitful directions for future research on violence against women. Work should continue to improve the reliability and validity of estimates of incidence and prevalence rates, and these studies should be extended to groups that might be at high risk for violence by virtue of race, ethnicity, age, disability, language, sexual orientation, socioeconomic status, and migrant, immigrant, or refuge status. Suggested quantitative and qualitative studies include (1) continued examination of risk factors for diverse perpetrators and victims, (2) evaluation of short- and long-term effects of programs used to prevent sexual and intimate partner violence, (3) appraisal of interventions designed for children and adolescents, (4) analysis of the informal strategies and processes employed by women to end violence in their lives, and (5) assessment of the current availability of and need for legal assistance. Research should be broadened to include examination of emotional or psychological abuse, correlations of violence and abuse to various diseases, and the long-term effects of chronic violence over the life span.

Contemporary scholarship on the causes of violence identifies multiple causes, operating across the life span, from the level of the individual to the broader society. It is generally agreed that the expression of aggression toward women is socially shaped. Because violence against women occurs within the larger context of a sociocultural environment, it is vital scholarly work to aim for greater understanding of those factors that socially and institutionally condone and maintain violence against women, including features that contribute to continuation of an oppressive imbalance of power between men and women. Advances in knowledge must be accompanied by social policies that address the factors rendering women economically and socially unequal and too often dependent on potentially abusive male partners. These initiatives include (1) enforcing pay equity, (2) eliminating discrimination in wage and hiring practices, (3) developing economic strategies for addressing women's traditional roles in dependent care, including care of children and the elderly, (4) support of reproductive freedom, and (5) fostering increasing representation of women in leadership roles.

## BIBLIOGRAPHY

Bart, Pauline B., and Eileen Geel Moral, eds. *Violence Against Women: The Bloody Footprints*. Newbury Park, Calif.: Sage, 1993.

Brownmiller, Susan. *Against Our Will: Men, Women, and Rape*. New York: Simon and Schuster, 1975.

Cardarelli, Albert P., ed. *Violence Between Intimate Partners: Patterns, Causes, and Effects*. Needham Heights, Mass.: Allyn and Bacon, 1997.

Council on Scientific Affairs, American Medical Association. "Violence Against Women: Relevance for Medical Practitioners." *Journal of the American Medical Association* 267, no. 23 (1992).

Crowell, Nancy A., and Ann W. Burgess, eds. *Understanding Violence Against Women*. Washington, D.C.: National Academy Press, 1996.

Garnets, Linda, Gregory M. Herek, and Barrie Levy. "Violence and Victimization of Lesbians and Gay Men: Mental Health Consequences." *Journal of Interpersonal Violence* 5, pp. 366–383.

Gelles, Richard J., and Donileen R. Loseke, eds. *Current Controversies on Family Violence*. Newbury Park, Calif.: Sage, 1993.

Kanuha, Valli. "Compounding the Triple Jeopardy: Battering in Lesbian-of-Color Relationships." *Women and Therapy* 9, pp. 169–184.

Koss, Mary P., Lisa Goodman, Angelo Browne, Louise F. Fitzgerald, Gwen Keita, and Nancy Russo. *No Safe Haven: Male Violence Against Women at Home, at Work, and in the Community*. Washington, D.C.: American Psychological Association, 1994.

Lobel, Kerry, ed. *Naming the Violence: Speaking About Lesbian Battering*. Seattle: Seal Press, 1986.

O'Toole, Laura L., and Jessica R. Schiffman, eds. *Gender Violence: Interdisciplinary Perspectives*. New York: New York University Press, 1997.

Renzetti, Claire. *Violent Betrayal: Partner Abuse in Lesbian Relationships*. Newbury Park, Calif.: Sage, 1992.

Russell, Diana E. H. *The Politics of Rape: The Victim's Perspective*. New York: Stein and Day, 1975.

Skinner, Ellen, ed. *Women and the National Experience: Primary Sources in American History*. Reading, Mass.: Addison-Wesley, 1996.

Straus, Murray A., Richard J. Gelles, and Suzanne K. Steinmetz. *Behind Closed Doors: Violence in the American Family*. Garden City, N.Y.: Anchor Press/Doubleday, 1980.

Straus, Murray A., and Richard J. Gelles, eds. *Physical Violence in American Families: Risk Factors and Adaptation to Violence in 8,145 Families*. New Brunswick, N.J.: Transaction, 1990.

Tjaden, Patricia G., and Nancy Thoennes. "Prevalence, Incidence, and Consequences of Violence Against Women Survey." *National Institute of Justice Centers for Disease Control and Prevention Research in Brief*. November 1998.

Walker, Lenore E. *The Battered Woman*. New York: Harper and Row, 1979.

Warshaw, Robin. *I Never Called It Rape: The* Ms. *Report on Recognizing, Fighting, and Surviving Date and Acquaintance Rape*. New York: HarperPerennial, 1994.

Widom, Cathy S. "Does Violence Beget Violence? A Critical Examination of the Literature." *Psychological Bulletin* 106 (1989).

Wilson, Karen J., ed. *When Violence Begins at Home: A Comprehensive Guide to Understanding and Ending Domestic Abuse*. Alameda, Calif.: Hunter House, 1997.

MARY P. KOSS
CAROLYN HOUSE-HIGGINS

See also **Abortion; Domestic Violence; Endocrinology: PMS and Female Violence; Gender; Pornography; Rape; Sex Differences; Sex Offenders; Sexual Harassment; Spousal and Partner Abuse; Suffrage.**

## OUTLAWS

Romantic notions about crime and violence energize much of the thinking about the nineteenth century's Old West, a place associated with the unique geographical region between the Mississippi River and the Pacific Coast. The western outlaw, a character who ranged across the West for four decades after the Civil War, remains central to a rhetoric that endorses the philosophy of taking the law into one's own hands. Whether a single gunfighter dressed in black or one of a gang of stage, bank, or train robbers, these western outlaws emerge as a distinctly masculine group, making a living by the pursuit of crime, often defined as "noble" or "heroic" in popular conventions. While there are many flaws inherent in this portrayal of western banditry, no assumption is more flawed than the idea that only men broke the law in the post–Civil War West.

Women from a variety of ethnic and cultural backgrounds lived among lawbreakers and had knowledge of and contributed to illegal activity in the West. Among these women were female felons who committed a single, often spontaneous, crime, such as arson or homicide. Some were repeat offenders, charged with forgery or grand larceny as well as other petty crimes. Generally, none of these women criminals would have been termed *outlaws* by law-enforcement personnel or the public. Their criminal lives lacked the dramatic clashes with the law and subsequent sensational publicity essential to the outlaw label.

Outlaw women, like their male counterparts, lived from time to time on both sides of the law, pursuing crime as a part-time occupation. On occasion, the illegal aspects of their lives overtook them and they engaged in criminal activity, especially with guerrilla characteristics (hit-and-run tactics), on a regular basis.

Outlaw women can be divided into three categories. The first includes those women who aided and abetted the criminal pursuits of their husbands, brothers, sons, and companions. The second encompasses women recognized as outlaws in their own right. A third category remains underresearched—that of female cross-dressers who made their way through western history undetected in their male garb. How many such women—like the prostitute Nina Patchen, who on occasion wore men's clothing, or Josephine Monaghan, who dressed and worked as a cowboy—rode with outlaw gangs cannot be ascertained.

### Outlaw Accomplices

Women who assisted the criminal activities of the men around them have sketchy identities in historical records. Law-enforcement officials, intent on arresting or killing male offenders, often overlooked these women, who slipped into historical obscurity as their felonious male companions died violently or entered a penitentiary. The women themselves made good use of the invisibility afforded them by prevailing notions of female passivity and by the conviction of nineteenth-century criminologists that habitual criminal behavior was almost exclusively the province of men.

Male criminals were unlikely to draw attention to the lawbreaking wife, companion, mother, or sister, who might be the only remaining provider for the children and elderly of the outlaw family. For example, Molly Evans and her daughter Eva kept the family together when Christopher Evans abandoned farming and—along with his hired hand John Sontag—turned to train robbery in the 1890s. After a series of holdups and gun battles in which California law officers died, Evans served seventeen years of a life sentence in Folsom prison. During her husband's imprisonment, Molly Evans supported the family by taking in wash and working in local factories. Eva Evans always skirted the edges of her father's criminal escapades, was engaged to John Sontag before his death from infected gunshot wounds, participated in plans for at least one prison break, and worked to secure a pardon for her aging parent. In 1911, Eva greeted her father after his discharge from the penitentiary and took him to Portland, Oregon, where the family was reunited.

Family loyalty intensified when outlaws came from ethnic or racial groups that in the best of circumstances struggled with the Anglo institutions of the West. African Americans, Asian Americans, Native Americans, and Spanish-speaking people learned from a range of experiences in the West that self-protection demanded group loyalty in the face of law-enforcement procedures determined primarily by Anglo Americans. Few were willing to incriminate others—male or female—from their own ethnic communities.

Accordingly, the exact nature and extent of the involvement of western women who assisted in the criminal activities of men will never be completely understood. Nonetheless, some achieved sufficient fame to serve as examples of women outlaws who lived within the vice community of the West and participated to some degree in its activities.

For example, Zerelda James Samuel, the mother of Jesse and Frank James, was connected closely to the criminal activities of her children and their associates. Long suspected of harboring her sons and their gang, Zerelda Samuel lost a hand in a fire-bomb attack on the family home in Kearney, Missouri, in 1875. She responded with vigor, proclaiming her innocence and soliciting public sympathy for herself and a young son lost in the assault. After the collapse of the James gang and the death of Jesse James in 1882, Zerelda exploited the family homestead for its tourist potential until her own demise in 1911. Her part in encouraging and supporting the crimes of the James brothers and their gang remains ambiguous. She—as well as Zee Mimms and Jane Bliven, the wives of Jesse James and outlaw Bill Dalton—remains a symbol of the many women who, well informed about the outlaw lives of their western men, could be described, at the least, as outlaw accomplices.

**Known Outlaws**

Women who embraced criminality more openly represent another category of women outlaws—those who, in their own lifetimes, earned public names as lawbreakers. For these women retribution and punishment was often swift and violent. For example, in 1889 Wyoming vigilantes hanged Ella "Cattle Kate" Watson. Watson, a known prostitute, had acquired both land and cattle by suspect means, according to local lore. Although reasons for her lynching were only slightly investigated, jealousy about Watson's property and the possible illegal way she amassed it may have contributed to her murder, for which no one was ever convicted.

The most famous woman outlaw was Belle Starr, the "Bandit Queen of the West," born Myra Maybelle Shirley in Missouri in 1848. Most accounts of Belle Starr obscured the violent realities of her short life because they employed the language of sensational journalism and exaggerated the importance of a single photograph of Starr dressed in black velvet and holding a gun.

At a young age, Starr found herself surrounded by larceny, horse stealing, and murder through the actions of her male relatives and associates. Her direct involvement in criminal activity often seemed circumstantial or conflated by so-called eyewitnesses, but each suspicious rumor, criminal charge, and court appearance gave her greater appeal to journalists and legend-builders. A conviction in 1883 for horse stealing solidified her outlaw identity. Her association with Native Americans, and especially her marriage in 1880 to Cherokee Sam Starr, irrevocably set her apart from the Anglo community as a woman of questionable character.

Disorder and difficulty marked her relationships with her neighbors, husbands, lovers, and children. As an adult, she lived close to poverty, scratching out a farming life between bouts with the law. Despite numerous, flamboyant tales of Starr riding with the Younger gang, robbing banks, and shooting up saloons, there is no reliable evidence to substantiate these rumors. Ambushed and shot in the back at age forty, Belle Starr left a murky legacy concerning the woman outlaw in the West.

Few western women achieved the tabloid recognition of Belle Starr, but some did become local figures of notoriety. In 1899 Arizona inmate Pearl Hart, advertised in the local press as a highway bandit, was photographed in several different poses and clothing styles, including men's apparel, a sidearm, and a shotgun. It may be that someone at the penitentiary hoped to capitalize on Hart's sensational name by selling the images. In 1902, Hart claimed to be pregnant, secured an early release from her sentence, and disappeared, but her name remains linked to the popular tales of the old territorial prison at Yuma, Arizona.

The western woman who perhaps most closely fit the definition of an outlaw made her mark not in the Old West, but during the Great Depression. Bonnie Parker, born in 1910, earned her infamous reputation through a string of violent crimes committed with fellow Texas native Clyde Champion Barrow. When the teenaged waitress met Barrow, her husband of three years was serving a ninety-nine-year sentence in a Texas penitentiary. Her relationship with Barrow quickly centered on his small-time criminal career. In 1932 Parker achieved national fame when she and Barrow, with their ever-changing gang, embarked on a series of highly publicized gas station and grocery store robberies across the Southwest, leaving twelve people murdered.

**Pearl Heart, 1899.** COURTESY OF THE ARIZONA HISTORICAL SOCIETY/TUCSON, AHS# 28916

Bonnie and Clyde survived impossible odds in deadly gun battles with law-enforcement officers and escaped time and again in one stolen vehicle after another. These outlandish, bloody episodes, combined with the well-publicized support of their large families, created sympathy for Bonnie and Clyde among some Depression-weary Americans. On 23 May 1934, the saga of Bonnie and Clyde ended when the pair died on a rural Louisiana road in a torrent of rifle and machine-gun fire from police weapons. Their deaths were as violent as those inflicted on their victims. Like Belle Starr before her, Bonnie Parker, a poor woman with limited educational and cultural resources, assumed a folk-legend status that had little connection to her life and character. Photographs that showed Parker as a cigar-smoking, shotgun-toting outlaw played well for the public audience, for they highlighted the romance of her story, ignored the economic deprivation of her life, and belied the

brutality of the murderous events with which she was involved. Parker's life refutes the notion that women outlaws were incapable of aggressive, criminal behavior, even as it underscores the economic and cultural aspects that fueled female lawbreaking.

Even with a life as well documented as Parker's, knowledge about women outlaws in the West remains superficial and myth-laden. Accounts of such women depend on slim documentation and tend to highlight glamour in criminality. Language like "wild cat," "sexy sinner," and "gun-toting honey" ridicules the social forces shaping these women and portrays them as subjects of adventure and merriment. Seldom have significant questions been asked about the lives of women outlaws and the nature of their criminality.

Disruptive social conditions and economic uncertainty in the West contributed to the behavior of women outlaws. Women turned to crime because of their close relationships with male criminals, but also because they believed that through crime they could secure money. Classification as an outlaw appeared to depend on the public responses to a woman's crime and subsequent legal troubles, especially if the offender came from the poorer classes of westerners.

As the characters of the West—cowboys, gunfighters, marshals—were being delineated for American audiences, the presence of a few atypical, female criminals added exactly the spice that was needed to complete the public's picture of western outlaws. A handful of female outlaws served to add color to the western story; a substantial number would have made a very different statement about violence, class, and race in the American West. In fact, it is unlikely that society wanted to examine too closely the realities of violence and the criminal lives of western women. To have done so might have revealed that such lives among women were more usual than anyone generally thought, a realization that would have demanded a more thorough social and political response to the complexities of western crime and cultural interactions. History is left with the lives of Belle Starr and Bonnie Parker, told in a fragmented and fanciful style. These women represented only part of a multifaceted and shrouded story about western women and crime.

*BIBLIOGRAPHY*

Croy, Homer. *Jesse James Was My Neighbor.* New York: Duell, Sloan, and Pearce, 1949.

Fisher, Vardis, and Opal Laurel Holmes. *Gold Rushes and Mining Camps of the Early American West.* Caldwell, Idaho: Caxton, 1968.

Jeffrey, John Mason. *Adobe and Iron: The Story of the Arizona Territorial Prison.* La Jolla, Calif.: Prospect Avenue, 1969.

Lombroso, Cesare, and William Ferreo. *The Female Offender.* New York: D. Appleton, 1900.

Phillips, John Neal. *Running with Bonnie and Clyde: The Ten Fast Years of Ralph Fults.* Norman: University of Oklahoma Press, 1996.

Secrest, William B. *Lawmen and Desperadoes: A Compendium of Noted, Early California Peace Officers, Badmen, and Outlaws, 1850–1900.* Spokane, Wash.: Arthur H. Clarke, 1994.

Settle, William A., Jr. *Jesse James Was His Name; or, Fact and Fiction Concerning the Careers of the Notorious James Brothers of Missouri.* Columbia: University of Missouri Press, 1966.

Shirley, Glenn. *Belle Starr and Her Times: The Literature, the Facts, and the Legends.* Norman: University of Oklahoma Press, 1982.

ANNE M. BUTLER

*See also* **Barker, Ma "Arizona Kate"; Bonnie and Clyde; Frontier; Gunfighters and Outlaws, Western; Prisons: Women Prisoners; West.**

## WOMEN WHO KILL

The general public has long viewed women who kill with both fascination and derision. Cultural norms prescribe nonviolent behavior for women; women are socialized to suppress anger and not express it through aggressive, much less violent, behavior. Not surprisingly, women who kill have historically received a great deal of public attention and notoriety. Lucretia Borgia, Lizzie Borden (although she was found not guilty by the jury), and Bonnie Parker are just three examples of "celebrity" female killers. Until the late twentieth century, however, homicide researchers neglected women who kill—ironically for the same reason that these women captured public allure: there were so few of them.

Table 1 shows that between 1980 and 1996, women committed only 11–15 percent of homicides. While there were periodic rises and dips in these figures, changes over the last four decades of the twentieth century were not dramatic. During the 1970s some criminologists sounded the alarm that women were becoming more violent and that their rate of increase for violent crime was greater than that of men. Other criminologists, however, argued that the statistics showed a decrease in violence by women. Although the statistics appeared to favor the latter view, the debate was significant in that it generated considerable interest in

TABLE 1. Homicides by Sex of Offender, 1980–1996

| Year | Male | Female | Unknown | Offenders Who Are Female (%) |
|---|---|---|---|---|
| 1980 | 10,722 | 2,000 | 306 | 15.35 |
| 1985 | 8,887 | 1,548 | 64 | 14.74 |
| 1990 | 9,231 | 1,357 | 134 | 12.66 |
| 1996 | 7,227 | 914 | 98 | 11.09 |

Figures are for homicides involving single offenders who murdered single victims only. Homicides involving multiple offenders with single victims, single offenders with multiple victims, and multiple offenders with multiple victims have been excluded.

female offenders. Researchers began paying closer attention to gender as a variable in homicide studies, and their work from the 1970s onward reveals important patterns in female homicide offending.

### Who Are Women Who Kill?

Research profiling female killers shows them to be typically in their twenties and thirties, currently or previously married, and unemployed. Although being unemployed may indicate at least middle-class socioeconomic status (i.e., the women do not need to work because they have a partner who supports them), most female homicide offenders have limited education (less than twelve years), which constrains their job opportunities and suggests low socioeconomic status. Because most of these women also have children, lack of affordable, quality childcare also restricts employment options. Researchers report that female homicide offenders who are employed at the time of the offense usually hold low-paying, low-status occupations. Women of color are overrepresented among women arrested for homicide.

Although the general profiling of female homicide offenders is useful, there is important variation across both offender and victim characteristics when the circumstances under which women kill are taken into account.

### When and Why Women Kill

*Intimate Relationships.* When women kill, their likely victims are people with whom they have had an intimate relationship. Husbands and boyfriends make up the largest victim category of female killers.

When women kill husbands or boyfriends, it is often while defending themselves from a partner's abuse or because they are in danger of being critically injured or killed by their partner. According to the law professor Holly Maguigan, 75 percent of women who kill husbands or boyfriends do so during a confrontation.

When battered women kill their partners in nonconfrontational situations, observers sometimes question whether the killing was necessary. Research shows that most battered women do call the police on numerous occasions and repeatedly leave or try to leave their abusive partners. Some battered women obtain protection orders from the courts. These steps, however, do not guarantee the abuse will stop. Research indicates that about 50 percent of female homicide victims each year are killed in a separation attack, that is, when they tried to leave their batterer. A large number of women are killed when they attempt to get help by taking actions such as calling the police or having a protection order issued.

One widely cited explanation of these types of cases is known as battered woman's syndrome. Battered woman's syndrome is a form of post-traumatic stress disorder (PTSD), in which a traumatic experience—in this case repeated abuse by one's partner—produces intense fear and feelings of helplessness in the victim. Learned helplessness is a central feature of battered woman's syndrome and refers to the battered woman's perception that she has no viable option for escaping or avoiding the violence. She may also experience a variety of physical and psychological symptoms of PTSD, including numbness, sweating, heart palpitations, an inability to concentrate, sleep disturbances, intense shame, and hypervigilance regarding her partner's words and behavior. Given the pattern of abuse she has experienced and her undiluted fear of the batterer, a battered woman may reasonably perceive herself to be in imminent danger even when not engaged in a confrontation with her partner at the time of the homicide.

But the theory of battered woman's syndrome has been criticized for several reasons, especially as a defense for battered women who kill. For example, battered woman's syndrome implies psychological pathology in the woman killer, which raises doubts about her ability to make reasonable decisions. A second problem with the theory is it appears unable to explain how a woman who has learned helplessness suddenly decides to defend herself proactively against an abuser. Third, there is considerable variation in battered women's reactions to abuse; not all battered women who kill

exhibit clinical symptoms of battered woman's syndrome.

Another theory, developed by the criminologist Robin S. Ogle, is intended to explain killing by women in any context, not just when they are involved in abusive relationships, but it clearly applies to battered women who kill. Ogle points out that women experience a higher level of stress in their everyday lives than do men. This stress derives from such sources as role conflict (e.g., balancing employment and family responsibilities), institutional discrimination (e.g., unequal pay, glass ceilings), and internalization of a devalued status (e.g., beliefs that women are emotional, less intelligent than men, and submissive). Women with other devalued social statuses (e.g., poor women, women of color) experience an even greater level of everyday stress. But because of gender socialization, women, unlike men, do not cope with life stress through anger and aggression. Instead, women typically internalize the anger as hurt and guilt, and they repress aggression. Some women do this so strongly that they develop an overcontrolled personality: an extreme inhibition of the ability to express anger and aggression. However, psychologists have found that individuals with overcontrolled personalities may end up exploding in anger and aggression, particularly when chronic, high-level, situational stress (e.g., social isolation, fear, or significantly reduced resources) becomes overwhelming, breaking down inhibitions.

Ogle maintains that battering worsens the effects of all these factors on women. Battering certainly increases everyday stress in the lives of victims, creating fear and lowering self-esteem. Batterers also typically restrict victims' resources and isolate victims from relatives, friends, and others. The battered woman who kills is an overstressed, overcontrolled personality who lashes out violently against her abuser when situational pressures finally become unbearable. However, while Ogle's theory has some appeal, it does not adequately account for the many—perhaps even the majority of—severely battered women who do not kill their abusers.

Children are a second category of intimates who may be killed by women. Most child homicide victims are killed by their mothers. Many people have difficulty understanding how a mother could kill her child; they assume that such a woman must be mentally ill. Research indicates, however, that women who kill their children rarely exhibit symptoms of psychopathology. Rather, some researchers argue that women's higher rate of child homicide is related to the greater amount of time they spend with children. Because mothers are their children's primary caregivers, they experience the lion's share of the stress and frustration that child rearing often entails. Children's small size and inability to defend themselves increase their vulnerability. Infants less than a year old are significantly more likely to be killed than older children.

Some theorists, though, explain neonaticide (the killing of newborns) in sociobiological terms. They argue that parental investment in offspring is a limited resource. Sometimes—for example, when the child's prospects for survival to adulthood are poor—a mother must choose between investing in a newborn or in other current or future children. According to these theorists, mothers who are most likely to kill their babies are young, unmarried, poor, and socially isolated—in other words, women who would be rearing children under less than ideal conditions. While provocative, this theory cannot explain why mothers kill their older children.

Other intimates who may be murdered by women are elderly parents, although these make up only a small percentage of all homicides, including homicides committed by women. The murder of an elderly parent by an adult daughter may be explained by the fact that daughters are more likely than sons to assume responsibility for caregiving to the infirm and elderly. The majority of these women work outside the home but also have children of their own still living at home. The stress arising from these conflicting demands may become so overwhelming that the women resort to violence that can, intentionally or unintentionally, result in homicide.

*Friends, Acquaintances, and Strangers.* Although many researchers have noted the difficulties inherent in trying to distinguish friends from acquaintances, it is generally accepted that friends are more intimate than acquaintances and have longer, more mutually reinforcing interactions. Acquaintances include neighbors, classmates, coworkers, employers, and employees.

Researchers have found that women are approximately twice as likely to kill acquaintances as they are to kill friends, although both groups combined represent only about a quarter of the total victims of female homicide offenders. Most of these victims, whether friends or acquaintances, are men.

What motives do female homicide offenders offer to explain the killing of a friend or acquaintance? Among the most common motives for the killing of friends are romantic triangles or arguments as well as contentions over money or property. These factors frequently lead to the killing of acquaintances as well, but acquaintances are also more likely than friends to be killed during the commission of another crime, such as a robbery. Women rarely kill friends while committing other crimes, but female homicide offenders often claim self-defense when the victim was a friend or acquaintance.

Stranger homicide is rare, especially stranger homicide committed by women. In her analysis of female homicide offenders, criminologist Coramae Richey Mann reports that the proportion of women who kill strangers showed little variation during the second half of the twentieth century. Compared with women who kill intimates, friends, and acquaintances, women who kill strangers are more likely to act with accomplices, usually men, and are more likely to kill strangers during the commission of another felony offense. But as Mann points out, despite their rarity, women who kill strangers are typically considered by the public to be more dangerous than women who kill intimates, friends, or acquaintances. This perception stems from the belief that the woman who kills a stranger, rather than acting in self-defense or a spontaneous emotional outburst, is motivated by money and greed or the thrill of killing in its own right. According to Mann, stranger victims are less likely than other murder victims to have done anything to precipitate their death, and strangers are five times more likely than friends or acquaintances to be killed for economic gain.

**Future Directions**

Despite the growth in empirical research during the last two decades of the twentieth century on women who kill, there remained significant gaps in the literature. Of particular concern is the view promoted in the popular media during the 1990s that women are as violent as men. Proponents of this view claimed that the official statistics mask women's true participation in violent crime because "chivalrous" criminal justice professionals accept gender stereotypes of women as passive and nonviolent (Kelleher and Kelleher 1998; Pearson 1998). Criminologists, however, have found little evidence to support the notion of chivalry in the criminal justice system. What is needed is more careful analysis and theorizing of the gendered nature of killing and victimization. Such analysis and theorizing must contextualize violent behavior by women and men and examine how it is culturally mediated, that is, how it is influenced not only by gender, but also by the intersection of gender with other social locating variables, including race and ethnicity, class, age, and sexual orientation. Clearly, women sometimes kill, but when they do they are not necessarily "acting like men." The available data indicate that killing by women and killing by men are quantitatively different. Researchers must now address how they are qualitatively different.

*BIBLIOGRAPHY*

Browne, Angela, and Kirk R. Williams. "Gender, Intimacy, and Lethal Violence: Trends from 1976 through 1987." *Gender and Society* 7, no. 1 (1993).

Bureau of Justice Statistics. *Criminal Victimization in the United States.* Washington, D.C.: U.S. Department of Justice, 1997.

Dutton, Mary Ann. "Understanding Women's Responses to Domestic Violence: A Redefinition of Battered Women Syndrome." *Hofstra Law Review* 21, no. 4 (1993).

Kelleher, Michael D., and C. L. Kelleher. *Murder Most Rare: The Female Serial Killer.* New York: Praeger, 1998.

Maguigan, Holly. "Battered Women and Self-Defense: Myths and Misconceptions in Current Reform Proposals." *University of Pennsylvania Law Review* 140, no. 2 (1991).

Mann, Coramae Richey. *When Women Kill.* Albany: State University of New York Press, 1996.

Ogle, Robin S., Daniel Maier-Katkin, and Thomas J. Bernard. "A Theory of Homicidal Behavior Among Women." *Criminology* 33, no. 2 (1995).

Pearson, Patricia. *When She Was Bad: Violent Women and the Myth of Innocence.* New York: Viking, 1998.

Seagrave, Kerry. *Women Serial and Mass Murderers: A Worldwide Reference, 1580 Through 1990.* Jefferson, N.C.: McFarland, 1992.

Sommers, Ira, and Deborah Baskins. "Sex, Race, Age, and Violent Offending." *Violence and Victims* 7, no. 3 (1992).

CLAIRE M. RENZETTI

*See also* **Barker, Ma "Arizona Kate"; Bonnie and Clyde; Borden, Lizzie; Infanticide and Neonaticide; Post-Traumatic Stress Disorder; Smith, Susan; Spousal and Partner Abuse; Wuornos, Aileen.**

# WORKPLACE

Workplace violence is among the fastest-growing causes of injury suffered by the workforce in the United States. Assaults and violent acts cause 20 percent of all occupational deaths, second only to transportation deaths. Homicide in the workplace, once limited to sporadic events in a few industries, now threatens workers in all industries and occupations. In many states, especially those with large metropolitan areas, homicide in the workplace has surpassed transportation-related incidents as the leading cause of death in at least one of the past three years.

The first research to identify the extent of violence in the workplace began in the early 1980s, although programs designed to reduce incidents of robbery and related incidents of homicide date to the early 1970s. Since the recognition of violence as a serious and common workplace threat, many agencies have begun to examine issues of causation and effect. The Centers for Disease Control and Prevention declared workplace homicide an epidemic in 1992, and agencies such as the Bureau of Labor Statistics and the National Institute for Occupational Safety and Health have begun focusing more attention on the area. Although much has been learned, this knowledge is still outweighed by what is not known. Workplace violence was brought to public attention through media coverage of events that led to multiple homicides and involved coworkers or disgruntled former employees. However, media coverage rarely depicts the types, frequency, and common characteristics of workplace violence. The typology presented here provides a framework for understanding the etiology of workplace violence, and an examination of the research on incidence and prevention suggests measures for addressing the problem.

## Typology

Workplace violence involves a diverse array of industries, occupations, events, and outcomes. Several agencies and researchers have developed a typology to characterize the etiologic factors that identifies four categories of violent events in the workplace. These categories are based on the perpetrator's relationship to the business in which the event occurred:

Type I: The perpetrator has no legitimate relationship to the business or its employees and is usually committing a criminal act prior to the violence. Criminal acts include robbery, shoplifting, and loitering.

Type II: The perpetrator has a legitimate relationship with the business and becomes violent during a business transaction. This category includes customers, clients, patients, students, inmates, and any other group for which the business provides services.

Type III: The perpetrator is an employee or past employee of the business who attacks or threatens another employee(s) or past employee(s).

Type IV: The perpetrator does not have a relationship with the business but has a personal relationship with the intended victim. This category includes victims of domestic violence assaulted while at work.

Different businesses have different risks for each type of violence, and recognizing the types of violence that occur in business settings is crucial for identifying appropriate intervention strategies. The following sections discuss the incidence and characteristics of workplace violence, the risk factors that place certain businesses at higher risk for violence, and approaches to preventing violence in different workplace settings.

### Incidence

*Homicide.* The Census of Fatal Occupational Injuries (CFOI), conducted annually by the U.S. Department of Labor, Bureau of Labor Statistics, is the most comprehensive data-collection system for occupation-related deaths. Reports are collected by each state from death certificates, autopsy reports, and other sources. In 1997, CFOI reported 856 workplace homicides, corresponding to 0.65 homicides per 100,000 U.S. workers. The number of workplace homicides reported through CFOI since its inception in 1992 showed an increase from 1992

through 1994 followed by a decrease from 1995 to 1997.

Although the CFOI is the most comprehensive national source for statistics on occupational deaths, it may undercount the number of violence-related deaths because of misclassification and inconsistent coding between states. Researchers conducting detailed studies have reported the rate of workplace homicide to range between 0.71 and 1.53 per 100,000 workers per year.

*Nonfatal Violence.* The number of workplace assaults leading to injury but not death is unknown, but it probably greatly exceeds the number of fatalities. The number of stress-related problems resulting from violent events may exceed that of both injury and homicide. Estimates from published studies of nonfatal violent victimization at work show a wide range, from 43 to 220 assaults per 100,000 employees per year. Other findings estimate that nonfatal events are from fifty to one hundred times more frequent than fatal events. According to the National Crime Victimization Survey, an average of 1.5 million workers were assaulted while on duty each year from 1992 to 1996.

Research enumerating the number of violent nonfatal workplace injuries is complicated because no single reporting mechanism exists and many events go unreported. Furthermore, many results are difficult to compare because the outcomes studied vary widely, ranging from serious injuries leading to time away from work to noninjury stress-related events.

*Workers at Risk.* Risks for workplace homicides are not evenly distributed among the workforce. Blacks, Asians and Pacific Islanders, Hispanics,

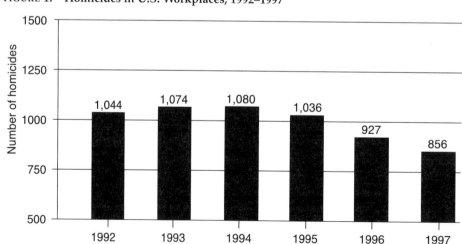

FIGURE 1. Homicides in U.S. Workplaces, 1992–1997

## Scenarios of Types of Workplace Violence

Type I: Perpetrator has no legitimate business relationship and enters business with criminal intentions.

Scenario: Two men in their mid-twenties entered a liquor store at approximately 8 P.M. They drew guns and demanded that the clerk, the only other person at the store at the time, hand over all the money. The clerk opened the cash drawer, which had a significant amount of cash, took out about $100 to hand to one of the robbers, and then quickly shut the cash drawer. The other robber said that he saw more money in the drawer and that the employee had better hand it over. The clerk insisted there was no more money, although there was. The second perpetrator then shot the clerk, opened the drawer to remove the remaining money, and the robbers fled. The employee was fatally wounded, and the robbers were never apprehended.

Type II: The perpetrator is a client, patient, or inmate of the business.

Scenario: The nursing staff in an assisted-living home in the Midwest was recently reduced because of budget cuts. The activity of transferring patients between bed and chair, once supervised by nurses, was taken over by orderlies. An elderly man suffering from dementia had developed a very strong attachment to the nursing staff and had an extreme distrust of strangers. When a new orderly tried to put him in his chair for dinner, he became very distraught, biting and kicking the orderly. Although the elderly man was not injured in the encounter, the orderly had three open bite marks on his arm and hand.

Type III: The perpetrator is a current or past employee of the business.

Scenario: An office supply company, under new management, redrew boundaries for its sales team and changed the commission structure. One employee, who felt that his new area was drawn specifically to reduce his number of clients and that the revamped commission structure was unfair, complained to his manager. The manager, who was new and intimidated by the employee, had him transferred to another store without informing the manager of the second store of the complaints. The employee, who felt the transfer had been made just to get rid of him, complained to the manager at his second store. This manager told him that he would have to adjust to the new environment. The employee grew more upset at work and started making unflattering comments about the business and talked to other employees of retaliation against the management. It is unknown if the employees reported this threat to the management. The employee, as he became more upset with the work environment, starting losing clients and made lower commissions, which resulted in his being put on probation. The next week, the employee entered a managers' meeting with a handgun and opened fire, injuring three managers.

Type IV: The perpetrator is a personal acquaintance of the intended victim and does not have an independent relationship with the business.

Scenario: A woman left her abusive husband and moved in with her sister without telling her husband where she was staying. He started coming by her workplace and vandalizing her car while she was at work. She did not report this vandalism to anyone at the time. After a week in which her car window was broken, obscenities were scrawled on her windshield, and her tires were slashed, the estranged husband then started entering the workplace shouting threats at the employee. She hid in the bathroom when the other employees saw him coming, but no other action was taken. After several days of persistent threats, he came in with a gun and opened fire on the office. One employee was fatally wounded and another nonfatally wounded before the perpetrator could be restrained by security guards. The wife was not injured.

Work-Related Homicides, United States, 1997

| | Number | Percentage | Rate per 100,000 Workers |
|---|---|---|---|
| Total | 856 | 100 | 0.654 |
| *Gender* | | | |
| Male | 711 | 83.1 | 1.00 |
| Female | 145 | 16.9 | 0.24 |
| *Age* | | | |
| ≤ 24 | 87 | 10.2 | 0.45 |
| 25–34 | 214 | 25.0 | 0.66 |
| 35–44 | 215 | 25.1 | 0.59 |
| 45–54 | 170 | 19.9 | 0.63 |
| 55–64 | 119 | 13.9 | 0.98 |
| ≥ 65 | 51 | 6.0 | 1.36 |
| *Type of Event* | | | |
| Type I: Crime | 731 | 85.4 | N/A |
| Type II: Client | 25 | 2.9 | |
| Type III: Employee | 56 | 6.5 | |
| Type IV: Personal Acquaintance | 44 | 5.1 | |
| *Cause* | | | |
| Shooting | 705 | 82.4 | N/A |
| Stabbing | 73 | 8.5 | |
| Other | 78 | 9.1 | |

SOURCE: Number of homicides from the Census of Fatal Occupational Injuries, U.S. Department of Labor, Bureau of Labor Statistics; workforce population from the Current Population Survey, U.S. Bureau of the Census.

and new immigrants of any ethnicity have an elevated risk compared with their proportion in the workforce. Work-related homicide rates are three to five times higher for males than for females, although the proportion of homicides among all occupational deaths is higher for females. In 1997, CFOI reported 711 work-related homicides for males and 145 for females, with corresponding rates of 1.00 per 100,000 male and 0.24 per 100,000 female workers. Although rates for males are higher, homicides made up only 12 percent of all male occupational deaths but 31 percent of female occupational deaths. Until 1997, workplace homicide was consistently the leading cause of death for females at work in all years since national statistics have been collected.

Over half of the workplace homicide victims are workers between the ages of twenty-five and forty-four. However, rates are highest for very young and very old workers. The 1995 CFOI report, as well as many independent studies, shows steady increases in homicide rates with increasing age, especially among workers over age sixty-five. The few statistics available on adolescent employees show them to be at very great risk.

*Workplace Violence by Type.* Although the focus of media attention and many prevention programs is on Type III violence, Type I violence is the most frequent cause of homicide. In 1997, 85.4 percent of all workplace homicides were Type I, with other types each accounting for less than 10 percent.

Although homicides are predominantly Type I events, nonfatal assaults have a very different distribution. In California, during a four-month study period in 1994, 29.7 percent of workplace assaults were Type I, 62.5 percent were Type II, 5.6 percent were Type III, and 0.2 percent were Type IV. Type I and Type IV events are often considered the most lethal, although when Type III events do lead to fatality, they often cause multiple fatalities.

*Industry and Occupation.* Type I events are concentrated in the retail, service, and transportation industries, where employees have contact with the public and with cash transactions. Over 80 percent of both fatal and nonfatal events in grocery stores, drugstores, liquor stores, taxicabs, and law enforcement and private security agencies are Type I events. Hospitals, institutions, schools, and correctional facilities experience predominantly Type II events, and these are largely nonfatal. Type III events are distributed throughout many types of industries but are the most common type found in professional and private corporations, which overall have very few violent events in the workplace. Type IV events, which have been the subject of fewer studies than the other types, have not been identified as specifically concentrated in particular industries.

*Cause of Injury.* Shootings account for over 80 percent of all workplace homicides but are less frequent among nonfatal events. In nonfatal events, hitting, kicking, punching, and biting account for approximately 75 percent of all injuries. Excluding homicides, firearms are responsible for injury in 4 to 17 percent of events depending on the source of the report.

**Risk Factors**

Factors that place individual businesses at high risk for workplace homicide, assault, and

470

threats vary according to the type of event under consideration.

*Type I.* Risk factors for Type I violence are the broadest and most complex of the four types of events. Businesses at high risk of Type I violence are generally characterized as having high contact with the public; involving exchange of money; delivering services, goods, or passengers; isolated; open late at night or during early morning hours; and located in high-crime areas.

Research studies conducted after the early 1970s examining convenience stores have helped identify specific characteristics of businesses that can place them at high risk of Type I violence. These include the following:

1. poor cash-handling procedures
2. poor visibility into and within the business
3. poor lighting in and around the store
4. easy access or escape routes
5. location in heavy traffic, near single-family homes, or in high-crime neighborhoods
6. lack of adequate employee training
7. lack of adequate safety procedures and equipment

Other proposed risk factors that do not have consistent support include having only one clerk on duty (especially a female clerk), keeping late store hours, having few customers, few cars parked in front, no back room, the presence of gas pumps, and the presence of pay phones and automatic teller machines. Different studies have found different relationships between robberies and robbery-related injury, suggesting that risk factors may vary within business types, regions, and communities.

Preliminary studies of robbery-related injuries have found that employee behavior during a robbery can drastically affect the potential for injury. Many injuries during robberies occur when the employee resists, tricks, argues, or pursues the robber.

Although research has not been conducted to identify specific risk factors for other industries at high risk of Type I workplace violence, many of the risk factors associated with convenience store robberies can be generalized to other public establishments. Security guards, who by the nature of their job protect individuals or valuables, are at high risk of assault, often in settings at high risk of robbery. Taxicab drivers and employees of motels, drinking establishments, restaurants, and liquor stores share many of the same risk factors as convenience store workers. Taxicab drivers, who have the highest rates of workplace homicide, are at risk because assailants have easy access to the driver, a quick and easy getaway with anonymity, and a low likelihood of interference. No comprehensive studies identifying risk factors in these settings have been completed.

Research from the perspective of the robber has also contributed to understanding Type I workplace violence. According to a 1995 survey of 310 incarcerated robbers, the things that most attracted them to a location were, in order of importance, an easy escape route, a high take (large amount of accessible money), anonymity during the robbery, lack of active police patrol, lack of armed clerks, and a low potential for interference. The presence of cameras and alarms were also considerations but were lower in priority as defined by the robbers.

*Type II.* Although Type II events are not the primary cause of homicides, they may be the most prevalent type of nonfatal injuries. Risk factors for Type II violence include working with unstable or volatile persons, working in unsecured locations, and working in community-based settings. These characteristics are found in many occupations, including law enforcement, health and mental health care, social service, education, and transportation. Service providers in institutional settings, such as correctional facilities and mental health wards, have very high rates of Type II events. Workers in bars and restaurants and taxicab drivers also deal frequently with volatile customers, and Type II events occur in these settings.

Although many risk factors for Type II workplace assault have been identified, the very necessity of working with high-risk clients is the major predictor. Health-care providers are among those at highest risk of Type II workplace violence. There are many scenarios that lead to assault, but perhaps the most common is the health-care provider who cares for mentally disabled, unstable, or disoriented patients, including those under the influence of drugs or elderly persons suffering from dementia. Thus, workers in mental institutions, skilled nursing, and emergency departments have very high rates.

In these settings environmental control, training and staffing procedures, and an understanding of the characteristics of the potential perpetrator are important issues. Workplaces that have poor lighting, isolated areas, and floor plans that hinder communication and visualization between offices have all been identified as high-risk settings. These risk factors are evident in many hospitals, schools, and similar institutions, which are often in older buildings and lack the resources for extensive maintenance or renovation. For example, treatment areas that are not visible to a main nursing station are more likely places for assault than areas in which the behavior of the perpetrator is visible. School rooms, such as those in isolated barracks, that have small windows or no windows at all, and that do not open into public areas, may place teachers at higher risk.

Controlling the environment is especially difficult in occupations in which the employee provides services at the client's home. In home-care situations the worker is isolated from other employees, is unfamiliar with the environment, and often has no ability to communicate the need for help.

Research in the health-care setting has found that staff shortages and a lack of trained, regular staff increased the incidence of violence. Inadequate staffing pressures the available staff to work quickly and possibly miss potential signs of danger. Furthermore, as clients wait long periods for what they may see as inadequate attention, hostility and the potential for violence increase.

*Type III.* Type III events, although not a common cause of homicide or injury, may be the most common cause of harassment. The most common victim of a Type III event is a co-employee, supervisor, or manager of the perpetrator. A scenario that garners much media attention is the recently fired worker who returns to assault the persons seen by that worker as responsible for the termination; but these events are not common.

Characterizing the perpetrator of Type III violence is difficult because there are many variations; but one uniting characteristic is the perpetrator's notion of unfair or disrespectful treatment. This notion could be a reality or a consequence of psychosocial and mental factors. The focus of the perpetrator's hostility can be an individual, a group of individuals, or the workplace itself. In most scenarios of Type III violence, the perpetrator's sense of having been unfairly treated grows over time, and there are usually early signs of trouble.

Several researchers have identified historical characteristics for Type III perpetrators, but no list has high sensitivity or specificity in predicting violent behavior. Though recognition of these characteristics can help workplaces take early action to prevent growing hostility and potential violence, these characteristics are not meant to be screening tools for hiring, and in many instances doing so would be illegal. S. Anthony Baron (1996) identified common characteristics of Type III perpetrators:

1. drug or alcohol abuse
2. serious stress or multiple life stressors
3. unshakable depression
4. continual excuses or blaming others; failure to take responsibility for actions
5. high levels of aggression and aggressive behavior
6. low job satisfaction, with feelings of mistreatment or inappropriate rewards
7. poor interpersonal relationships
8. socially inappropriate or unacceptable behavior
9. unusual or changed behavior, evident in work or with coworking interactions
10. psychotic or paranoid behavior

One of the most prevalent risk factors for Type III violence is a management or personnel system that does not recognize potential perpetrators or does not have policies in place to handle problems that have been identified. Baron has also identified characteristics of the work environment that do not recognize and may even promote the potential for violence:

1. organizational problems regarding personnel that go largely ignored
2. chronic labor-management conflict
3. preferential treatment of some employee groups
4. a dehumanizing work environment
5. ineffective and poorly defined grievance procedures
6. lack of mutual respect among employees and departments
7. ineffective horizontal and vertical communication
8. lack of consistency in management practices
9. increased workload with few rewards or resources
10. insufficient attention to physical environment and security measures

Environmental design is also influential in predicting Type III assault. Workplaces that lack adequate facilities to perform the work required and that have isolated work areas increase the potential for violence. Failure to control entrances and exits can also be a risk factor when a perpetrator has decided to initiate a violent event.

*Type IV.* Type IV workplace violence is the least studied and probably the most underreported. The violence occurs at the victim's workplace, but it is the personal relationship, not the workplace itself, that precipitates the event. Factors external to the business make these events the most difficult to characterize and prevent.

The most common scenario for Type IV violence involves a domestic dispute between a couple who have recently separated. The perpetrator, who knows that the victim must go to work, may stalk, threaten, or assault the victim in this known location. Other employees may get caught in the violence either by trying to protect the victim or simply by being in the vicinity.

The risk factors for these types of events are largely associated with an unresponsive workplace. Lack of communication and policies to help protect a threatened worker, lack of adequate management personnel to listen to and take action about a complaint, and a working environment that lacks adequate security can all exacerbate this type of violence.

**Prevention**

Just as risk factors vary by the type of violence, so do prevention measures. Although the specific steps for effective prevention programs are diverse, for most business settings the considerations must include the environmental design of the business, management practices, employee training, maintenance of the program, and surveillance and reporting procedures.

*Type I.* The first research in preventing Type I violence focused on environmental control, when in 1971 C. Ray Jeffery coined the motto Crime Prevention Through Environmental Design (CPTED). The goal of CPTED was to modify work environments to reduce vulnerability to crime, allowing store managers direct control of the environment rather than having them rely on indirect control of criminal behavior.

Evaluations of programs incorporating these types of measures, most of which have been in the convenience store setting, have found great success, with reported reductions of robberies between 13 and 24 percent. On the basis of some of this research, the Gainesville, Florida, police department analyzed convenience store robbery data and implemented a city ordinance that required the following components: an unobstructed view of the cash register and sales area, conspicuous signs indicating little available cash, a drop-time release safe, brightly lit parking lots, security cameras, and mandatory robbery-prevention training. One year later the combined factors led to a 64 percent reduction in convenience store robberies in Gainesville and a 75 percent reduction in the number of robberies between 8 P.M. and 4 A.M. These results, however, did not control for stores that closed for business during the study period. This research led to the Florida Convenience Store Security Act of 1990, which was amended in 1992.

Most of these prevention strategies have yet to be tested in other business settings, and many approaches to prevention, including employee training, have yet to be scientifically evaluated at all. Effective environmental design changes differ depending on the community and the individual store; modifications need to be studied at the local level before standards can be adopted for large areas.

*Type II.* The main focus of prevention for Type II events is on employee training and implementation of safety procedures. Training should focus on communication skills, such as how to recognize and defuse a hostile client, how to work effectively with clients with known violent tendencies, and how to evaluate and respond to new clients in new settings, and on enacting policies to report events when they occur. Other safety procedures can include maintaining adequate staffing, use of safety teams and security guards, and developing clear lines of communication about violent events.

Environmental designs can also prevent Type II violence. Increasing visibility so that workers are not isolated with potentially dangerous clients can be accomplished through open floor plans, the use of central workstations, use of closed-circuit monitors, and maintaining adequate lighting. Personal alarms are useful when isolated working areas are unavoidable. Seclusion or security rooms can be helpful to isolate violent individuals, and barriers can be used in some settings to separate employees from clients.

The types of successful prevention measures depend on the individual characteristics of the business. Few of these measures have been scientifically evaluated.

*Type III.* The prevention of Type III events focuses on employer-employee and employee-employee relationships and is based in management style and communication procedures. Although many of the early prevention measures focused on hiring and screening procedures, these have not proven to be effective and often violate employment laws. Because most Type III events build over a period of time, the most effective prevention is the implementation of systems that can recognize trouble and intervene in the early stages. These can include giving employees access to personnel, such as a mediator or ombudsman, with whom they can speak freely and confidentially; procedures by which potentially dangerous events are communicated between employees, managers, and supervisors; and the availability of counseling services for employees.

The general tenor and environment of the workplace can also play a role in increasing or decreasing violence. Training managers in good communication and listening skills, encouraging staff to share ideas and credit for good work, and maintaining a positive environment can all prevent the buildup of tensions.

Because many violent events occur after an employee has been released from service, prevention programs should include strategies to deal effectively with employment termination. Although many approaches have been suggested, few have been evaluated. Some methods include using a team rather than an individual to give notice, giving notice late on Friday so the employee has the weekend to cool down, and providing exit counseling and job training. If there is any indication that violence might erupt, employers should ensure that the employee cannot gain access to the workplace by collecting all keys held by the employee, keeping doors locked and secured, hiring security if needed, and instructing all workers to contact authorities if the employee is seen on the premises.

*Type IV.* Since Type IV events are the most difficult to characterize and to predict, they are the most difficult to prevent. The most effective approach is to have an open line of communication between employees and management, so that an individual who should not be at the work site can be identified, and to have procedures in place to alert authorities if the undesirable individual is seen. Further measures include escorting employees to parking lots, keeping entrances and exits locked and monitored, and maintaining clear visibility to the employee's work area. Few comprehensive plans for the prevention of Type IV events are available, and no scientific evaluations have been published.

The causes of workplace violence are complex, and the appropriate prevention strategies will vary in each individual workplace. Although there is much to be learned about which strategies are successful, it is imperative that employers seek to understand the risk in their workplaces and to take steps to prevent violent events.

*BIBLIOGRAPHY*

Bachman, Ronet. "Violence and Theft in the Workplace." Washington, D.C.: U.S. Department of Justice, Bureau of Justice Statistics NCJ-148199, 1994.

Baron, S. Anthony. "Organizational Factors in Workplace Violence: Developing Effective Programs to Reduce Workplace Violence." In *Violence in the Workplace: Occupational Medicine: State of the Art Reviews.* Vol. 11, no. 2, edited by Robert Harrison. Philadelphia: Hanley and Belfus, 1996.

Castillo, Dawn N., and E. Lynn Jenkins. "Industries and Occupations at High Risk for Work-Related Homicide." *Journal of Occupational Medicine* 36, no. 2 (1994).

Clifton, Wayland, Jr., and P. T. Callahan. *Convenience Store Robberies: An Intervention Strategy by the City of Gainesville, Florida*. Gainesville, Fla.: Gainesville Police Department, 1987.

Davis, Harold. "Workplace Homicides of Texas Males." *American Journal of Public Health* 77 (1987).

Erickson, Rosemary J. *Armed Robbers and Their Crimes*. Seattle: Athena Research Corporation, 1996.

Hales, Thomas, et al. "Occupational Injuries Due to Violence." *Journal of Occupational Medicine* 30, no. 6 (1988).

Howard, John. "State and Local Regulatory Approaches to Preventing Workplace Violence." In *Violence in the Workplace: Occupational Medicine: State of the Art Reviews*. Vol. 11, no. 2, edited by Robert Harrison. Philadelphia: Hanley and Belfus, 1996.

Hunter, R. D. "Convenience Store Robbery in Tallahassee: A Reassessment." *Journal of Security Administration* 13, no. 1 (1990).

Jeffery, C. Ray. *Crime Prevention Through Environmental Design*. Beverly Hills, Calif.: Sage, 1971.

Jeffery, C. Ray, et al. "Crime Prevention and Computer Analysis of Convenience Store Robberies in Tallahasee, Florida." *Florida Police Journal* 34 (1987).

Kraus, Jess F., Bonnie Blander, and David L. McArthur. "Incidence, Risk Factors, and Prevention Strategies for Work-Related Assault Injuries: A Review of What Is Known, What Needs to Be Known, and Countermeasures for Intervention." *Annual Review of Public Health* 16 (1995).

National Institute for Occupational Safety and Health. "Prevention of Homicide in the Workplace Alert." Washington, D.C.: DHHS (NIOSH), September 1993.

———. "Violence in the Workplace: Risk Factors and Prevention Strategies." *Current Intelligence Bulletin* 57. Washington, D.C.: DHHS (NIOSH), June 1996.

Northwestern National Life Insurance Company. "Fear and Violence in the Workplace: A Survey Documenting the Experience of American Workers." Minneapolis, 1993.

Peek-Asa, Corinne, et al. "Incidence of Nonfatal Workplace Assault Injuries Determined from Employee Reports in California." *Journal of Occupational and Environmental Medicine* 39, no. 1 (1997).

Simonowitz, Joyce A. "Health Care Workers and Workplace Violence." In *Violence in the Workplace: Occupational Medicine: State of the Art Reviews*. Vol. 11, no. 2, edited by Robert Harrison. Philadelphia: Hanley and Belfus, 1996.

Toscano, G. *National Census of Fatal Occupational Injuries, 1996*. Washington, D.C.: U.S. Department of Labor, Bureau of Labor Statistics, 1997.

Warchol, Greg. *Workplace Violence, 1992–1996*. Report NCJ 168634. Washington, D.C.: U.S. Department of Justice, Office of Justice Programs, Bureau of Justice Statistics, 1998.

Windau, J., and G. Toscano. "Workplace Homicides in 1992." In *Fatal Workplace Injuries in 1992: A Collection of Data and Analysis*. Report 870. Washington, D.C.: U.S. Department of Labor, Bureau of Labor Statistics, April 1994.

CORINNE PEEK-ASA

*See also* **Child Labor; Corporations; Sexual Harassment; Sweatshops.**

# WORLD TRADE CENTER BOMBING

At 12:18 P.M. on Friday, 26 February 1993, a bomb containing approximately twelve hundred pounds of explosives detonated in an underground garage at the World Trade Center complex in New York City. The explosion killed six people, injured more than one thousand, and caused $500 million in damage. Not since the Civil War had the United States seen so many people injured in a single event. As of late 1999, the bombing remained the worst act of international terrorism committed on U.S. soil.

A few days after the blast, investigators recovered the vehicle identification number (VIN) from the yellow Ford Econoline van that was used to transport the bomb. The VIN belonged to a vehicle owned by a truck rental agency in Jersey City, New Jersey, that had been rented to Mohammed A. Salameh three days before the bombing. After reporting the van stolen, Salameh returned to the rental agency to retrieve his $400 deposit, where federal agents arrested him on 4 March 1993. Salameh handled the money transactions involved in purchasing the chemicals for the bomb and in renting the storage unit to store materials, and mixed the chemicals to make the bomb. He also rented the yellow van and drove it to a service station in New Jersey for gas, but he did not drive the van to the World Trade Center.

On 9 March 1993 police questioned Ahmad M. Ajaj about the bombing and arrested him later that day. Nidal A. Ayyad was arrested on 10 March 1993. Mahmoud Abouhalima was arrested in Egypt on 24 March 1993 and returned to the United States.

Almost one year after the incident, four of six defendants indicted for the bombing were convicted. On 24 May 1994 U.S. District Judge Kevin Thomas Duffy sentenced Salameh, Ayyad, Abouhalima, and Ajaj each to 240 years in prison and fined them each $250,000. Judge Duffy determined the sentence by calculating the life expectancy of the six killed in the blast—180 years—and then adding 60 years for each of the two other counts. The two remaining defendants—Ramzi Ahmed Yousef, who was the mastermind behind the bombing, and Abdul Rahman Yasin—were indicted in

**Beneath the World Trade Center, February 1993.** CORBIS/REUTERS

absentia. (Yousef was arrested on 7 February 1995 in Islamabad and returned to United States; as of late 1999 Yasin was still at large.)

In January 1995 jury selection began for the trial of the blind Egyptian sheik Omar Abdel Rahman, spiritual adviser to the four men convicted of the bombing. Rahman was accused of "plotting a war of urban terrorism" in response to U.S. support of Israel and Egypt. On 1 October 1995, bringing the biggest trial involving international terrorism in U.S. history to a close, a federal jury found the sheik and nine other defendants guilty on forty-eight of fifty charges. These defendants were not accused of the World Trade Center bombing but of seditious conspiracy in plotting to bomb the landmark towers and other landmarks as part of a jihad, or holy war, to undermine U.S. support for Egypt and Israel. Sheik Rahman was sentenced to life in prison.

Yousef, the mastermind behind the bombing, was apprehended in Islamabad on 7 February 1995 by Pakistani and U.S. agents acting on a tip, turned over to U.S. agents, and taken back to the United States. During his flight back to the United States, Yousef told federal agents how he planned to topple one of the 110-story towers into the other so that many people would be killed. Yousef and another accomplice, Eyad Ismoil, were later found guilty of a plot to bomb the World Trade Center.

Prosecutors charged Ismoil with driving the bomb-laden truck into the center's subterranean garage. Ismoil insisted that he thought he was delivering shampoo. Before receiving his sentence of life plus 240 years in prison on 8 January 1998 before Judge Duffy, Yousef proclaimed, "I am a terrorist, and I am proud of it." As of late 1999 Abdul Yasin remained the only conspirator in the bombing still at large.

*BIBLIOGRAPHY*

Dwyer, Jim, et al. *Two Seconds Under the World: Terror Comes to America—The Conspiracy Behind the World Trade Center Bombing.* New York: Crown, 1994.

Kushner, Harvey W. *Terrorism in America: A Structured Approach to Understanding the Terrorist Threat.* Springfield, Ill.: Thomas, 1998.

U.S. Congress. House of Representatives. Committee of the Judiciary. Subcommittee on Crime and Criminal Justice. *World Trade Center Bombing: Terror Hits Home.* 103d Cong., 1st sess., 1993.

HARVEY W. KUSHNER

*See also* **Bombings and Bomb Scares; Terrorism.**

# WORLD WAR I

There were three aspects of World War I (1914–1918) that intersected with long-term trends of collective violence in American history. The first was the mobilization of a mass army, the transport of the vanguard to France, and the deployment of over one million men on the field of battle. There was a second facet of organized violence that never left the continental United States. It grew out of military mobilization, though its roots were deep: Racial violence erupted in areas where black soldiers were quartered in segregated urban areas of the South. This series of episodes intersected with a collective intolerance related to the presence within American society of millions of people of German and Austrian descent.

A third facet of the history of violence is both private and public. The road back for many men who had served was a difficult one. It must be noted that the horror of World War I was not duly represented through works of fiction, poetry, or, especially, film in the United States. The history of violence is incomplete unless it recognizes the sanitization and representation of warfare in postwar America, in particular through the medium of film. Though there were many representations of World War I that raised doubts as to the heroic nature of conflict, most cinematic treatments of the war were melodramas that usually linked war to a heroic adventure or a love story. The war became domesticated in this way, helping to smooth the path for U.S. involvement in an even more violent and brutal conflict.

## In Europe

*Military Participation.* In global terms, the American commitment to war between April 1917 and November 1918 was limited. Of a total of about 25 million men of military age, about 4.3 million served in uniform. In other words, men of military age had about a one-in-five chance of seeing military service; meanwhile, French and German men of the same age group had a four-in-five chance of serving.

American casualties were also relatively light. Approximately 114,000 Americans died while on active service. As in all other combatant countries, this number reflected not only the heavy toll of industrialized warfare but also the coincidence of mobilization with the appearance of the worst influenza epidemic in history. Estimates vary, but it would be safe to estimate that American combat losses totaled about 50,000 men. Considering all deaths during active service, the number of American losses in proportion to the total who served in the war is relatively slight. American forces lost

2.7 percent of the total mobilized, Britain and Russia about 12 percent, France and Germany about 16 percent, and Serbia a staggering 37 percent. In the context of American history such losses were substantial although they were not on the scale of the losses during the Civil War. They were, however, greater than those registered during the Vietnam conflict

*Defeating Germany.* What did this investment in men and material achieve? The historical consensus is that American firepower did not win the war. It was not what the American expeditionary force achieved in the field that helped shift the balance of military power, but what it offered the Allies for the future that made the difference. The proven ability of American forces to organize a vast logistical operation to move armies across the Atlantic convinced the German high command that Germany could not carry on the war after its last major offensive had ground to a halt outside Paris in June and July 1918.

By then there were over 500,000 trained U.S. troops in France, and each month brought another 250,000, swelling available manpower in late 1918 to 2,000,000 men. This reservoir had to be tapped, despite commanding general John J. Pershing's caution about throwing his men into action and despite his commitment to keeping American forces separate from the Allies.

At Cantigny on the Somme in May, American troops had helped fill the gaps between French and British lines created by the German offensive. The Second Division helped stem the German offensive farther south at Belleau Woods and Château-Thierry. Farther to the east, at St. Mihiel on 12 September 1918, five hundred thousand American troops went into action to eliminate a German salient established four years earlier. The Germans retreated, leaving over fifteen thousand prisoners behind.

American troops were at the heart of the Meuse-Argonne offensives that followed. On 26 September 1918, nine U.S. divisions went into action, supported by 189 tanks and 800 airplanes. Over the following seven weeks, more than one million U.S. soldiers were in action. There were approximately 120,000 casualties before the armistice was declared on 11 November 1918.

The significance of this set of military operations was not limited to these eighteen months of conflict. World War I was a moment of initiation into the nature of industrialized warfare for many men who went on to play significant parts in

**Wounded British and German troops in the streets of Quentin, France, after the second battle of the Somme, 1918.** HULTON GETTY/LIAISON AGENCY

World War II. Harry Truman saw service with the Artillery Corps. Captain George C. Marshall was entrusted with the job of opening two officer-training camps in Plattsburg, New York. He was one of the first Americans to step ashore in France and served with distinction as a staff officer. George S. Patton also served in France in 1917–1918. He set up the first American Tank Corps. Commanding the Forty-second Infantry Rainbow Division—with men from twenty-six states—was Colonel Douglas MacArthur. These men were among the millions who came into contact with a new kind of war, one which would return in an even more violent form just two decades later.

**In the United States**

The scale of mobilization in World War I and, later, the number of casualties brought several waves of a violent form of "Americanism." The first victims of this aggressive nationalism were people of German origin. One man, Robert Prager, was lynched in April 1918 near St. Louis, Missouri; his sole offense was that he had been born in Germany. He was stripped, bound with an American flag, and hanged, while some five hundred witnesses cheered. His murderers were quickly apprehended, and in the ensuing trial the perpetrators claimed the lynching had been a "patriotic

murder." They were acquitted after just twenty-five minutes of deliberation.

Some symbolic violence had menacing overtones. German street names were changed: Hamburg Street in Brooklyn became Madison Street. When schoolchildren were filmed taking turns throwing German books onto a fire, the concept of national war as war against an entire culture and an entire people took a step forward.

In the United States, there was another dimension of wartime violence that was peculiarly American. World War I unleashed a wave of racial violence, partly related to military mobilization and partly related to the recruitment of southern black labor in northern cities. Although there were similar echoes of racial intolerance in Europe, none of it exploded in the same way it did in the United States.

In 1917 the Third Battalion of the Twenty-fourth Infantry, made up of African American soldiers, was stationed at a new compound at Camp Logan near Houston, and a racial incident occurred. On 23 August a black soldier tried to stop two white policemen from abusing a black woman. He was beaten and arrested. A second soldier was arrested after asking what had happened to the first man in custody. About one hundred black soldiers seized weapons and marched toward the city. In the ensuing shoot-out, twenty people were killed: four white policemen, four black soldiers, and twelve white bystanders.

More than one hundred soldiers were arrested and sent to the prison stockade at Fort Bliss, near El Paso, Texas. In November of the same year, the men were tried at Fort Sam Houston. Thirteen men were sentenced to death. Forty-one received life sentences, four received shorter sentences, and the rest were acquitted. The thirteen condemned men were hanged on 11 December 1917. There had been no review of the sentences by either the War Department or by President Woodrow Wilson—despite appeals made to them.

Two additional trials followed. At one trial, sixteen more men were sentenced to death. This time the president reviewed the trial record personally, on the advice of Newton Baker, secretary of war. Wilson and Baker agreed to commute ten of the sentences, but six more condemned men were hanged.

The Houston incident was only one of many. Endemic racial tensions intensified in wartime and not only in the army. Black workers migrated to northern cities to staff booming factories during the war. Their presence in the north after the war, and the violence that broke out in a number of northern cities, may be traced back to the demands of the war economy of 1917–1918.

## The Aftermath

*Violence Endured.* The most visible legacy of the war were the disabled who returned home after the conflict. Over two hundred thousand U.S. soldiers were wounded in active service. They suffered from every kind of disability. The amputees and physically injured men were aided by the Veterans Administration. More problematic was the fate of those with psychological wounds. Of the roughly ninety-seven thousand American soldiers admitted to army hospitals for psychological disabilities, approximately forty-two thousand received disability discharges. American psychiatrists were as much in the dark as their colleagues in Europe as to how to help these traumatized men. Through the work of these psychiatrists, however, army physicians were better able to diagnose and treat soldiers in World War II who suffered from the condition called "combat fatigue."

*Violence Contained.* One of the legacies of the war was the conviction that something had to be done to prevent this paroxysm of violence from

returning. That was the impetus behind Woodrow Wilson's effort to convince the U.S. Senate to ratify the peace treaty ending the war. But opponents of the treaty were wary of its central plank—the creation of a League of Nations. This institution was intended by Wilson to serve as a forum for discussion, a way of regulating violence. But the opponents of the league feared that it would compromise U.S. sovereignty. They won, but the story was repeated again after World War II. This time, a different kind of league—the United Nations—emerged as a barrier against future wars.

*Violence Reconfigured.* The impact of World War I had an important cultural dimension; it is relevant to note how contemporaries understood and misunderstood the experience of organized violence on a mass scale. Representations of violence took many forms during and after the war. There were many memoirs and some enduring poetry and fiction. Among the literary works that have endured are *The Enormous Room* (1920) by E. E. Cummings, *Three Soldiers* (1921) by John Dos Passos, and *A Farewell to Arms* (1929) by Ernest Hemingway.

The most important source for the dissemination of images of war is the medium of film. Just at the time of World War I, the film industry and

*All Quiet on the Western Front* (1930). CORBIS/BETTMANN

479

filmmakers like Charlie Chaplin had come into their own as the creators of mass entertainment. The war was a box-office bonanza, both for the domestic market and for the export market. American moviemakers usually placed the conflict of war within a story of romance, adventure, or comedy, and thereby re-created it in a mythical form that was more palatable than the event itself. One exception is *All Quiet on the Western Front* (1930), based on the novel of the same title by Erich Maria Remarque, a successful antiwar film in which American actors convincingly play the sacrificed generation of Germans. Most other films, however, helped bury the past by re-creating it in a sanitized form that moviegoers would accept. Gary Cooper in the title role of *Sergeant York* (1941) portrayed a pacifist hillbilly-turned-sharpshooter and Congressional Medal of Honor winner—a hero suited to the buildup to American entry into World War II.

*BIBLIOGRAPHY*

Grimshaw, Allen D., ed. *Racial Violence in the United States.* Chicago: Aldine, 1969.

Marshal, Samuel Lyman Atwood. *World War I.* New York: American Heritage, 1971.

Nagler, Jörg. "Enemy Aliens in the USA, 1914–1918." In *Minorities in Wartime,* edited by Panikos Panayi. Providence, R.I.: Berg, 1993.

Peterson, H. C., and Gilbert C. File. *Opponents of War.* Madison: University of Wisconsin Press, 1957.

Rollins, Peter C., and John E. O'Connor, eds. *Hollywood's World War I: Motion Picture Images.* Bowling Green, Ohio: Bowling Green State University Popular Press, 1997.

Schaffer, Ronald. *America in the Great War: The Rise of the Welfare State.* New York: Oxford University Press, 1991.

Schuler, Edgar A. "The Houston Race Riot, 1917." *Journal of Negro History* 29 (1944): 300–338.

JAY WINTER

*See also* **Weapons: Biological and Chemical.**

# WORLD WAR II

## Overview

*The Chronology of War.* The war began on 1 September 1939, when Germany attacked Poland. Great Britain and France declared war on Germany on 3 September. In April 1940 Adolf Hitler's forces invaded Denmark and Norway. Germany then attacked Belgium, Holland, and France. The British army was evacuated from Dunkirk, and

France surrendered on 16 June. Italy joined Germany, forming the Axis. The British won the aerial Battle of Britain in summer 1940, preventing an invasion.

President Franklin D. Roosevelt determined that the United States could not be idle in a world threatened by militant aggression. September 1940 saw a peacetime draft, and in late autumn, lend-lease was introduced; the Lend-Lease Act, passed in March 1941, gave Britain war tools in return for military bases and trade concessions. America provided naval protection for British Atlantic convoys.

In April and May 1941, Germany took Greece and Crete. Axis forces advanced east in North Africa, threatening the Suez Canal. On 22 June 1941 Hitler invaded Russia. Then, after huge territorial gains, Germany's assault faltered and, in February 1942, the Russians assumed the offensive. The Germans had already lost 1,164,000 men on the eastern front.

On 7 December 1941 the Japanese attacked the American naval base at Pearl Harbor as part of a broad offensive in the Far East. This brought the United States into the war. In Europe, U.S. and British forces won North Africa in fighting from October 1942 to May 1943. The Allies then attacked Sicily in July and Italy in September. The Italians quickly surrendered but the Germans fought on in difficult mountainous terrain until May 1945.

Naval control of the Atlantic was won by mid-1943 and Germany's air power was destroyed by early 1944 at huge cost. In July 1943 alone, the United States lost one hundred planes and one thousand crewmen. On D-Day, 6 June 1944, the Allies invaded Normandy. Vicious hedgerow fighting ended in an Allied breakout on 25 July and a swift armored advance. Paris was liberated on 25 August. Attempts to enter Germany before winter failed, but Hitler's December counterattack in the Battle of the Bulge was unsuccessful and the German offensive was stopped. Defeated in east and west, Germany capitulated on 7 May 1945.

In the Pacific, Japan made huge initial gains, including the Philippines, Thailand, Indochina, Burma, and Malaya. But the advance was blunted in the naval-air Battle of Midway in June 1942, and by midyear, eventual Allied victory was assured. Allied forces under General Douglas MacArthur advanced north from New Guinea to recapture the Philippines, while Admiral Chester Nimitz struck west across the central Pacific from Hawaii. Vicious fighting on islands like Guadalcanal, Okinawa, and Iwo Jima was intensified latterly by

**American wounded at Omaha Beach, June 1944.** NATIONAL ARCHIVES

Japanese suicide attacks. An Allied naval blockade of Japan and airborne bombing of major cities presaged an invasion, but after atomic bombs were dropped on Hiroshima and Nagasaki on 6 and 9 August, Japan surrendered on 2 September 1945.

*America's Accomplishment.* U.S. mobilization was highly effective: by 1945, sixteen million Americans had worn uniform. American forces finally dominated in Western Europe and Asia. Democracy and industrial capitalism, questioned during the Great Depression of the 1930s, had been vindicated. A relatively united America became the "arsenal of democracy," equipping its own and other Allied forces with 86,000 tanks, 296,000 planes, 71,000 warships, and other armaments. Militaristic, authoritarian systems were vanquished and Nazi racist evil was eradicated. The United States emerged a prosperous superpower at relatively low cost: three hundred thousand dead versus some twenty million for the Soviet Union.

*The "Good War" Myth.* So great was the Allied victory in World War II that the conflict came to be dubbed the "Good War." As Studs Terkel has written, in retrospect the war was a time when everything seemed to work to the advantage of the United States and all problems found solutions. The power of this mythic view has obscured other, problematic features of the conflict. These are considered below in thematic categories linked to questions of violence.

### Fighting the War

*Brute Force.* The war is popularly imagined as an antiseptic contest of sleek fighting machines streaking across open landscapes. This has fed a fascination with high-tech weapons, illustrated in computer games and movies from *Star Wars* (1977) to *Top Gun* (1986). The image is most accurate for early phases of the war when Axis forces, notably Germany—waging blitzkrieg, or "lightning," war—eviscerated opponents who had obsolete equipment and antiquated organization. The Axis needed to win swift victories in breadth to avoid a war of depth or attrition, for which they lacked the human and economic resources. As the tide turned for the Allies, retaking ground against veteran opponents was often brutally grinding, resembling the static fighting of World War I. In

481

**Douglas "Dauntless" dive-bombers sank four Japanese carriers at Midway in June 1942.**
THE GRANGER COLLECTION, NEW YORK

Russia, Italy, Normandy, and the Pacific, advances exacted a huge cost. John Ellis has described this as "brute force" combat.

*Maximum Firepower.* Since 1865 Americans have fought overseas, and they have been understandably chary about their young dying on foreign fields. The United States in World War II also produced vast quantities of munitions. This equation led to the use of overwhelming firepower to save friendly lives. But it also meant massive destruction to the environment. The trend was exacerbated by a phenomenon noted by S. L. A. Marshall in 1947: only about 18 percent of infantry fired their weapons in action; hence, heavy weapons and artillery had to kill through the laying down of massive firepower intended to destroy everything in the path of the advancing forces. The legacy of this blanket fire was exemplified in Vietnam, where the terrain and ecology were devastated by American force.

*Airborne Destruction.* Before World War II, America opposed aerial bombing against civilians and condemned carpet bombing by fascists in Spain and Japan in China. The war eroded this stance. In Europe, U.S. bombers originally tried to avoid civilian targets but by 1944 they accompanied the British in area bombing of cities like Munster, Berlin, and Dresden. Japanese civilians were targeted from the start, and firebombing, tested first at Hamburg, devastated cities like Nagoya, Osaka, and Tokyo.

The U.S. government has not been candid about the crudity of aerial warfare, creating the illusion that hostile governments can be punished through "surgical strikes" that minimize civilian losses. In fact, in every war up through the 1990s, 90 percent of bombs (dropped by the United States or any other air force) missed their immediate targets.

*War Psychosis.* Prolonged fighting, especially between hostile ethnic groups, intensifies rage, called war psychosis. This widens the circle of accepted violent acts. Psychosis was highest on the Russian and Pacific fronts. The surprise attack on Pearl Harbor and Japanese atrocities against captives fed a preexisting mistrust of Asians. Ferocious fighting engendered what John Dower called a mutual "war without mercy." Some Allied soldiers killed or tortured Japanese prisoners. Genocide was publicly advocated and the firebombing program cost at least 670,000 civilian deaths. Although there were strong military reasons for using atom bombs, their deployment was made morally acceptable by previous mutual ferocity.

The war in the West was more restrained but evidenced some abuse of noncombatants and questionable destruction of civilian infrastructure. Hatred of Nazism intensified in the wake of concentration camp openings: James Bacque has charged that up to one million German prisoners in American and French hands died of neglect.

Hollywood failed to deal candidly with war psychosis; in wartime movies like *Bataan* (1943), only the enemy committed atrocities. This misled

482

## The Bombing of Dresden

The ancient city of Dresden was subjected to a huge bombing mission by the Western Allies, on 13–14 February 1945, which targeted the central city. The assault was in three waves, two by the British, employing a technique perfected in the bombing of Hamburg in 1943. Around 10 P.M. on 13 February, bombers dropped high explosives to blow open windows and roofs, followed by incendiaries to start fires. About 1:30 A.M. the next morning, bombers dropped more high explosives to spread the flames and hit neighboring fire brigades entering Dresden. An inferno covered about eight square miles of the city center, with temperatures reaching nine hundred degrees. Convection currents feeding the blaze sucked in victims from blocks away, and many people were asphyxiated or roasted in bomb shelters. Just after noon on 14 February, American planes re-bombed Dresden and strafed refugees. Estimates of the final death toll vary widely; a reasonable number would be at least eighty thousand.

British and American authorities have never adequately explained the purpose of destroying this medieval city. Neither the railway network nor the light industrial sectors were major targets. Perhaps this was a demonstration to the Soviets (in whose path Dresden lay) of Western military potential in the postwar world. It was also an example of prolonged conflict producing war psychosis.

The attack is the subject of the 1969 novel *Slaughterhouse Five* by Kurt Vonnegut, who survived the Dresden bombing.

young men who later fought in Vietnam about the inevitable mutual rage of ethnic warfare.

## Society Under Strain

*Ethnic and Sexual Stresses.* A war against Nazism abroad inevitably brought challenges to discrimination at home, exemplified in the "Double V" campaign to defeat fascism abroad and racism at home. African Americans endured segregation in civilian and military life. Black soldiers faced danger as frontline service troops but were denied combat status. President Roosevelt narrowly averted a civil rights march on Washington in mid-1941 by banning discrimination in government and defense industries.

Japanese residents—including citizens—living on the Pacific coast were interned. Hispanics in the west also suffered discrimination even though, like other ethnic minorities, they were subject to drafting. In 1943 alone, ethnic tensions fueled rioting in Detroit, Philadelphia, San Diego, and Chicago.

Wartime gave women greater employment opportunities but they were criticized for abandoning family. Female service personnel were stereotyped as nymphomaniacs, sometimes harassed and even raped. Homosexuals who survived induction screening suffered bullying and harsh prison sentences if their sexual orientation was detected later. Aggression against women and homosexuals reflected a wider social tolerance of abuse. Both were denied GI benefits, arguably a form of psychological violence.

*Juvenile Delinquency.* Although home-front life was keynoted by prosperity and opportunity, social instability was engendered by massive population shifts to urban industrial concentrations, by troop movements, and by the dislocations of normal life inevitable in war. Fathers or elder brothers might be drafted, both parents could be fully employed, often on night shift, along with older children, leaving younger siblings unsupervised and resentful of neglect. Uncontrolled teenage freedom sparked fears of delinquency. The Federal Bureau of Investigation claimed juvenile crime rose each war year—by over 40 percent in 1943 alone. Although social workers disputed the figures, undoubtedly adolescent sexual promiscuity and antisocial behavior, including theft, vandalism, and gang violence, did increase. Adult fears of rising delinquency continued into the mid-1950s.

## Long-Range Implications

*The Cold War.* The incompatibility of the Allied nations' political systems was obscured by mutual need during the conflict. But peacetime differences revealed the latent antagonism between Western democratic capitalism and Soviet communism. The failure of the wartime alliance to reach lasting cooperation meant that the postwar period was characterized by international insecurity, with threatening diplomatic crises, a superpower arms race, covert military operations, and limited but

## Combat Trauma and Readjustment

It is popularly believed that "Good War" veterans did not suffer post-traumatic stress disorder, previously known as battle trauma or combat fatigue. This is a misconception. Because twelve of thirteen soldiers saw no combat, they experienced little trauma. However, for the minority in combat, psychological costs were high. Of eight hundred thousand combat veterans, 37.5 percent had psychiatric discharges. Studies over fifteen years suggested that many continued to suffer anxiety and depression. Combat trauma caused numerous readjustment problems for veterans, including alcoholism, employment instability, violence and family abuse, and divorce.

Adjustment was most difficult for the immature or least educated. Of veterans discharged for inability to function, 66.6 percent of those with a high school diploma or above could aspire to a full recovery, versus only 37.6 percent for those with an elementary education. Tragically, the least educated were usually privates in combat units if white, or in the often equally dangerous quartermaster battalions if black. The better educated typically became officers or entered special branches such as intelligence. For the undereducated, symptoms of trauma such as chronic jitters (40 percent of combat soldiers reported this complaint) and failure to obtain a job or to pursue further education—a lack of motivation accompanied by heavy drinking and the seeking of solace in bars—tended to be prolonged. Many failed to use the GI Bill. Probably 80 percent of those who graduated from college under the Bill were middle-class veterans who would have attended anyway.

costly wars in client countries of the great powers, notably Korea and Vietnam.

*The Military Industrial Complex.*   Many GIs came home horrified by the devastation they saw overseas and determined that such havoc would never be wreaked on American soil. Americans' perception that they were living in a seemingly hostile, unreasonable world was increased when in 1949 Russia successfully exploded an atom bomb and China fell to communism. The government had failed to prepare the public adequately as to the likelihood of these events. Altogether, these events fueled a view of America as a fortress protected by bombs and then missiles manufactured by increasingly powerful defense industries, whose alliance with government had begun in World War II. After the Korean War, and a huge expansion in ground forces, there was a corresponding increase in the production of arms and equipment. Arguably, this development of immense force was out of balance with other national needs and undercut the competitiveness of much American business, which became dependent on guaranteed government contracts, with toleration of overruns and inefficiency. The arms race may also have precluded exploration of other avenues to world security.

*The Munich Analogy.*   In September 1938 Britain and France agreed to German demands for the cession of Czechoslovakian territory. This was partly to buy time for rearmament. But, since the war, Americans have used Munich to discredit diplomatic solutions to international disputes as "appeasement." The Munich analogy was cited to justify the war in Vietnam and to prevent a nonviolent response (the imposition of sanctions) to the 1990 Iraqi invasion of Kuwait.

*Officially Sanctioned Covert Violence.*   The combat veteran and professor Paul Fussell has noted that our perception of the Nazi enemy as purely evil allowed us to perceive ourselves as entirely good. Therefore, all of our actions during the war could be justified. Actually, according to Fussell, we were not entirely good, only less evil than our opponents. Americans tortured prisoners, targeted civilians, talked of genocide, ignored many of Hitler's victims, and sanctioned covert operations by the Office of Strategic Services (OSS), which may have been justified in the circumstances but left a dubious legacy of official violence. Assassination is an example. The wartime Allies targeted Nazis such as Obergruppenfuhrer Reinhard Heydrich, a ruthless killer. But the Central Intelligence Agency, the successor to the OSS, is also tied to political assassinations, as well as training and support of terrorists, destabilization of sovereign governments, covert attacks on peaceful states, arms dealing, even possible complicity in drug trafficking. Such acts, although highly questionable, have been seen by the United States as acceptable because of its assumption of moral superiority acquired in World War II.

**U.S. Army troops uncover some of the horrors of the concentration camp at Dachau, May 1945.** HULTON GETTY/LIAISON AGENCY

*The Shadow of Annihilation.* At the heart of the Cold War arsenal are nuclear weapons, descendants of those used in 1945. Many people believe that these are necessary to American security. But they also mean that humankind lives with the constant possibility of annihilation. Some children growing up under this shadow suffered diffuse emotional stresses from the suppressed nightmare of violent death. Because of the positive-thinking philosophy in place during the Cold War, adults largely failed to address children's fears. It has been suggested by scholars like Robert Jay Lifton that the fear of premature annihilation may have helped to produce a sense of futility regarding large public questions, a felt loss of personal control and pointlessness, cynicism about human motivation, a culture of present-centered materialism with little future planning, and a morbid fascination with random violence and unexpected death, which has affected both entertainment and daily life.

**The Balance Sheet**

In one sense, World War II saw a triumph of light over dark. The organized forces of aggressive militarism, racism, and terror as a guiding principle were defeated. The Western Allies fought for four principles: freedom of speech, freedom of religion, freedom from fear, and freedom from want.

In another sense, this most costly war in history continued the undermining of humankind's sense of common virtue and belief in moral progress that began with World War I. From 1945 on, the continuance of life has been uncertain. When the Nazi death camps were opened, we saw the depths to which our species can descend when technology and organizational method are harnessed for destructive purposes. Although Nazism appalls most, it openly fascinates some white supremacist groups and its evil is belittled by organizations such as the Institute for Historical Review and the Liberty Lobby. The war saw an orgy of killing, not only in camps but in war zones like Russia, where no mercy was given. Americans shared in this butchery, notably in the Pacific, but also in Europe, where hitherto unimagined destruction was rained from the air. War psychosis affected all the belligerents. A long-term legacy of total war appears to have been a lowered sense of the sacredness of life and an increasing acceptance of random violence and death in both entertainment and actuality.

*BIBLIOGRAPHY*

Adams, Michael C. C. *The Best War Ever: America and World War II.* Baltimore: Johns Hopkins University Press, 1994.
Bacque, James. *Other Losses: An Investigation into the Mass Deaths of German Prisoners at the Hands of the French and Americans After World War II.* Toronto: Stoddart, 1989.

Bérubé, Allan. *Coming Out Under Fire: The History of Gay Men and Women in World War Two.* New York: Free Press, 1990.

Dalfiume, Richard M. *Desegregation of the U.S. Armed Forces: Fighting on Two Fronts, 1939–1953.* Columbia: University of Missouri Press, 1969.

Dower, John W. *War Without Mercy: Race and Power in the Pacific War.* New York: Pantheon, 1986.

Ellis, John. *Brute Force: Allied Strategy and Tactics in the Second World War.* New York: Viking, 1990.

Fussell, Paul. *Thank God for the Atom Bomb and Other Essays.* New York: Summit, 1988.

Gilbert, James B. *A Cycle of Outrage: America's Reaction to the Juvenile Delinquent in the 1950s.* New York: Oxford University Press, 1986.

Ginzberg, Eli, with James K. Anderson, Sol W. Ginsburg, and John L. Herma. *The Ineffective Soldier.* New York: Columbia University Press, 1959.

Gray, J. Glenn. *The Warriors: Reflections on Men in Battle.* New York: Harper and Row, 1970.

Grossman, Dave. *On Killing: The Psychological Cost of Learning to Kill in War and Society.* Boston: Little, Brown, 1995.

Havinghurst, Robert J., with John W. Baughman, Ernest W. Burgess, and Walter H. Eaton. *The American Veteran Back Home: A Study of Veteran Readjustment.* New York: Longmans, Green, 1951.

Irving, David. *The Destruction of Dresden.* London: Kimber, 1963.

Lifton, Robert Jay, and Richard Falk. *Indefensible Weapons: The Political and Psychological Case Against Nuclearism.* New York: Basic, 1982.

Lipstadt, Deborah E. *Denying the Holocaust: The Growing Assault on Truth and Memory.* New York: Plume, 1994.

Manchester, William. *Goodbye Darkness: A Memoir of the Pacific War.* Boston: Little, Brown, 1980.

Marshall, S. L. A. *Men Against Fire: The Problem of Battle Command in Future War.* New York: William Morrow, 1947.

Rubenstein, Richard L. *The Cunning of History: The Holocaust and the American Future.* New York: Harper and Row, 1975.

Schaffer, Ronald. *Wings of Judgement: American Bombing in World War II.* New York: Oxford University Press, 1985.

Schrijvers, Peter. *The Crash of Ruin: American Combat Soldiers in Europe During World War II.* New York: New York University Press, 1998.

Sledge, E. B. *With the Old Breed, at Peleliu and Okinawa.* New York: Oxford University Press, 1990.

Taylor, Telford. *Nuremberg and Vietnam: An American Tragedy.* Chicago: Quadrangle, 1974.

Terkel, Studs. *"The Good War": An Oral History of World War Two.* New York: Pantheon, 1984.

Winkler, Allan M. *Home Front U.S.A.: America During World War II.* Arlington Heights, Ill.: Harlan Davidson, 1986.

MICHAEL C. C. ADAMS

*See also* **D-Day; Hiroshima and Nagasaki; Holocaust; Pearl Harbor; War; War Crimes; Weapons: Nuclear.**

# WOUNDED KNEE, 1890

The Wounded Knee massacre of 1890 occurred as a result of the U.S. army's campaign to suppress the Ghost Dance, an anticolonial religious movement, on Lakota Indian reservations in South Dakota.

## Background, 1850–1889

Conflict between Lakotas (one of seven divisions of the Sioux) and the United States first emerged along the Oregon Trail in the 1850s. Under the Treaty of 1868, many Lakotas agreed to peace in exchange for a permanent reservation and the abandonment of U.S. forts along the Bozeman Trail. After the 1874 discovery of gold in the Black Hills, miners illegally entered the Great Sioux reservation. Two years later, the government forced Lakotas to cede the Black Hills without obtaining the required number of signatures under the 1868 treaty. The government further demanded that Lakotas abandon unceded hunting grounds in present-day Wyoming and Montana. When Lakotas refused, a military expedition was launched to subdue them. Although Lakotas and their Cheyenne and Arapaho allies were victorious at the Battle of Little Bighorn on 25 June 1876, the army completed its conquest of the Lakotas in 1877.

With Lakotas subsequently living on the reservation, government officials began a program of assimilation. Government agents, assisted by Christian missionaries, encouraged Lakotas to farm, forced Lakota children to attend school, and attempted to destroy Lakota religion, culture, and political organization. Assimilationists also advocated a policy of allotment whereby Indian families would reside on separate tracts of land, become market-oriented farmers, and lose their tribal identity. This policy was adopted under the 1887 Dawes Act. At the same time, railroads, speculators, politicians, and settlers with interests in Dakota Territory calculated that after allotment Lakotas would require only half their remaining land.

In 1882 and 1888, Lakotas successfully resisted efforts to force them to make land cessions. But an 1889 commission, headed by General George Crook, used a combination of threats and promises to obtain enough Lakota signatures to break the Great Sioux reservation into four smaller reserves. Although Crook promised Lakotas that the government would not reduce their rations, Congress cut Indian appropriations, resulting in diminished rations in the winter of 1889–1890. By this time,

Lakotas had endured a long string of broken promises, the theft of their land, an assault on their culture, and deterioration of economic and social conditions. Many were ready to embrace a new religion that promised an end to colonialism.

**The Ghost Dance**

The Ghost Dance originated with the teachings of a Paiute prophet, Wovoka (also known as Jack Wilson). In the late 1880s, Wovoka foretold a cataclysmic event that would result in the destruction or removal of whites and the creation of a new world for Indians in which game would be restored and dead ancestors would return. Wovoka instructed his followers to perform a dance that became known as the Ghost Dance. Although many non-Indians thought that Wovoka claimed to be the Son of God, it is doubtful he made this claim.

In 1889 a Lakota delegation journeyed to Wovoka's home in Nevada. There, along with representatives of several other tribes, they learned of the Ghost Dance. After the delegation returned in early 1890, many Lakotas formed encampments where they performed the new dance and saw visions of the world to come. Although the Ghost Dance threatened the authority of the government and its project of assimilation, most agents believed that the dance would eventually die out. Some, however, attempted to use the reservation police to stop the dances. When confronted, the dancers, wearing "ghost shirts" that they believed made them invulnerable to bullets, brandished weapons. Although some historians have maintained that the Lakotas altered Wovoka's originally peaceful teaching into one of militant hostility toward whites, Lakotas continued to rely on supernatural means to achieve the new world. Their only displays of militance were defensive responses to attempts to suppress the dance.

**Military Intervention**

In early October 1890, a new agent, Daniel F. Royer, assumed charge at the Pine Ridge reservation. Ill-equipped to understand or respond to the Ghost Dance, Royer began to demand military intervention. On 17 November, troops were authorized. Some historians have argued that the

The burial of Sioux Indians massacred by white settlers during the battle of Wounded Knee, 1890. HULTON GETTY/LIAISON AGENCY

government sent troops in response to fears of nearby settlers, but scholarship in the 1990s shows that settlers did not begin to manifest alarm about the Ghost Dance until after military mobilization was under way.

The army's strategy, developed by General Nelson A. Miles, was to use an overwhelming display of force to cow Lakotas into surrendering. At first, this plan was effective. But on 15 December the Standing Rock reservation Indian police killed Sitting Bull during an attempt to arrest him. Fearing for their lives, many of Sitting Bull's followers fled south to the camp of Big Foot on the Cheyenne River. On 23 December, Big Foot and his people eluded military surveillance and moved farther south toward the Pine Ridge reservation. Although army officers believed Big Foot intended to join the remaining Lakotas in the Badlands, when the army finally intercepted Big Foot at Wounded Knee Creek on 28 December, he was only twenty miles from the headquarters of the Pine Ridge reservation and obviously headed to that destination.

**Wounded Knee**

On 29 December, as the Seventh Cavalry, under the command of Colonel James W. Forsyth, attempted to disarm Big Foot's people, a shot was fired. Although it is uncertain who fired this shot, the most likely scenario is that a gun belonging to Black Coyote went off as he struggled with soldiers to prevent its confiscation. In any event, troops immediately opened fire. While some Lakota men returned fire, most fled along with women and children. Over the next several hours, soldiers pursued Lakotas, firing indiscriminately at men, women, and children. Four Hotchkiss guns on a nearby hill fired into a ravine where some Lakotas sought refuge. According to contemporary government sources, 153 Lakotas and 25 soldiers died. Modern (post-1980) investigations, however, indicate that the army killed at least 300 Lakotas, including many women and children, in the 1890 massacre at Wounded Knee.

Wounded Knee has often been described as the last episode in the period of warfare between Indian nations and the United States. It is more accurate, however, to see this episode in relation to the government's policy of forcing already conquered peoples to become assimilated to American cultural norms and of liquidating their lands. A few Lakotas continued to dance the Ghost Dance

over the next few years, but the slaughter at Wounded Knee was a terrible demonstration of the costs of openly defying the reservation system.

*BIBLIOGRAPHY*

DeMallie, Raymond J. "The Lakota Ghost Dance: An Ethnohistorical Account." *Pacific Historical Review* 51 (November 1982).

Mooney, James. *The Ghost-Dance Religion and the Sioux Outbreak of 1890.* 1896. Reprint. Lincoln: University of Nebraska Press, 1991.

Ostler, Jeffrey. "Conquest and the State: Why the United States Employed Massive Military Force to Suppress the Lakota Ghost Dance." *Pacific Historical Review* 65 (May 1996).

Utley, Robert M. *The Last Days of the Sioux Nation.* New Haven, Conn.: Yale University Press, 1963.

JEFFREY OSTLER

*See also* **American Indians: American Indian Wars; Sitting Bull; Wovoka.**

# WOUNDED KNEE, 1973

The 1973 siege at Wounded Knee, South Dakota, took place in a period of unprecedented Indian activism that began four years earlier with the occupation of Alcatraz in San Francisco Bay, California. The siege was part of a national struggle between the American Indian Movement (AIM) and the federal government. It also involved a local battle in South Dakota between Oglala Sioux supporters and opponents of the Pine Ridge reservation's tribal government.

The Pine Ridge reservation and nearby white communities became a focal point of Indian activism in 1972. In February 1972 AIM activists converged on Gordon, Nebraska, to protest the murder of Raymond Yellow Thunder, an Oglala Sioux, by four white youths. Following the Trail of Broken Treaties (a protest group that went to Washington to protest broken treaties and to publicize current grievances) and AIM's occupation of the Bureau of Indian Affairs (BIA) building in Washington, D.C., in November, AIM members, including Russell Means, an Oglala Sioux, prepared to support ongoing efforts by the Oglala Sioux Civil Rights Organization (OSCRO) to impeach the tribal chairman Richard Wilson on charges of malfeasance, corruption, and use of his "goon squad" to intimidate opponents. Tensions increased on 6 February 1973, when AIM members set the county

**American Indians stand guard outside Sacred Heart Catholic Church at Wounded Knee after members of the American Indian Movement took control of the town, 3 March 1973.** UPI/CORBIS-BETTMANN

courthouse on fire in Custer, South Dakota, as part of a protest against the killing of another Oglala Sioux, Wesley Bad Heart Bull. On 27 February, following the failure of a final attempt to impeach Wilson, OSCRO and AIM occupied a trading post at Wounded Knee, the site of the 1890 massacre. Federal law-enforcement officials, including Federal Bureau of Investigation agents, and BIA police surrounded Wounded Knee. Within a few days, journalists from the around the world arrived.

After an intense firefight on 8 March, a cease-fire was declared. An agreement to end the occupation was almost reached, but it broke down in the face of the Federal Bureau of Investigation's insistence on prosecuting perpetrators of alleged crimes at Wounded Knee. On 11 March 1973, Indians invoked the Treaty of 1868 and declared the Independent Oglala Nation. After a heavy firefight on 27 March, a new round of negotiations began. On 5 April, an accord was reached that called for Indian leaders to meet government officials in Washington, D.C., to discuss treaty rights and the dismal conditions on reservations. This accord also failed in disputes over the timing of disarmament. On 25 April inside Wounded Knee, Frank Clear-

water died of wounds suffered eight days earlier during a skirmish. The next day, in the most intense firefight yet, federal agents killed Buddy Lamonte. Fearing that the government was about to launch an all-out assault, Indian leaders entered a third round of negotiations. On 5 May, an agreement was reached calling for a meeting on treaty rights between Indian leaders and government officials that would set the stage for further talks in Washington, D.C. The siege ended on 7 May. A preliminary meeting was held on 30 May, but officials of President Richard M. Nixon's administration declined to hold further discussions.

Wounded Knee marked the high point of the Indian activism of the late 1960s and early 1970s. Over subsequent years, AIM was crippled by internal divisions and government repression. Among Indian people decades after the siege, its legacy remains controversial.

*BIBLIOGRAPHY*

Burnette, Robert, and John Koster. *The Road to Wounded Knee.* New York: Bantam, 1974.
Dewing, Rolland. *Wounded Knee II.* Chadron, Neb.: Great Plains Network, 1995.

Smith, Paul Chaat, and Robert Allen Warrior. *Like a Hurricane: The Indian Movement from Alcatraz to Wounded Knee.* New York: New Press, 1996.

JEFFREY OSTLER

*See also* **American Indian Movement.**

# WOVOKA

Wovoka, also known as Jack Wilson, was a Numu, or Northern Paiute Indian, born around 1856 in Nevada. He was the prophet of the 1890 Ghost Dance religion, which was pan-tribal, otherworldly, and apocalyptic and had pacifist and accommodationist ideals, that is, a belief that the Indians should attempt to live peacefully with white people and be willing to make whatever accommodations were necessary to achieve this. Although these tenets would seem conducive to inspiring harmony between whites and Indians, the messianic fervor surrounding Wovoka and the Ghost Dance was one of the factors that precipitated the massacre at Wounded Knee in South Dakota on 29 December 1890.

Wovoka's father, Buckskin or Numuraivo, was a powerful shaman hostile to white settlers; his mother, Tiya, by contrast, was willing to labor for them. Tiya may well have worked for the Wilsons, the pioneer Missouri couple who employed Wovoka, exposed him to Presbyterianism, and allowed him to live on their land in Mason Valley and share meals with them. One day, while cutting trees in the Sierra Nevada Mountains for the couple, Wovoka, whose name means woodcutter, became ill. Through some combination of high fever, a solar eclipse, and what he later described as a "loud noise" on 1 January 1889, Wovoka had a vision in which he received a message from God.

Three years later, on 1 January 1892, Wovoka explained this vision, with the aid of interpreters, to James Mooney, an Irish American from the Bureau of American Ethnology. According to his own account, Wovoka was told by God to spread the following message among the Indians: "be good and love one another, have no quarreling, and live in peace with whites," and "put away all the old practices that savored of war." Wovoka's vision was clearly bicultural: his people would carry on with their traditional circle or round dance, even as they embraced central tenets of the conquering white Christians—the Protestant work ethic and

the commandments against lying, stealing, and homicide. According to his vision, Ghost Dance religion elevated Wovoka to the status of "President of the West," in which capacity he would share political power with President Benjamin Harrison.

While logically one might contend that it was his fear of arrest following the Wounded Knee massacre that caused Wovoka to alter an originally hostile antiwhite ideology, an earlier interview, given nearly one month prior to Wounded Knee, dispels these suspicions: through an interpreter, Wovoka told the army scout Arthur Chapman that "people . . . must not fight, there must be peace all over the world." He also explained, "I told all the headmen who came to see me . . . that when they went home to say to their people . . . they must keep the peace"; if they did not, Wovoka would "help the soldiers to make them stop."

In western Nevada, where Wovoka lived, Indians participated in the regional economy, making Indian wars a thing of the past. However, in South Dakota life for the seven tribes of Western Sioux (also known as the Lakota) was reminiscent of conditions—conquest, starvation, disease, cultural interference, and widespread deprivation—that gave rise to the 1870 Ghost Dance, an earlier religious movement in Nevada that Wovoka no doubt was aware of. Compounding these deplorable conditions, the discovery of gold in the Black Hills of South Dakota between 1876 and 1877 led whites to appropriate the Lakota's land for themselves and to reduce the size of the Great Sioux Reservation by one-half. The Indians of South Dakota heard that a savior had appeared on Earth to punish the white man. Red Cloud, accordingly, dispatched a delegation to visit Wovoka in Nevada in the fall of 1889 and investigate. Since none of the delegation's leaders spoke Paiute, the interpretation of Wovoka's message must have been faulty. In fact, it remains a mystery how or if his words were understood at all. When the delegation returned home the following spring, instead of conveying the original 1890 Ghost Dance promise to Indians of reward for adherence to Wovoka's teachings and admonishments against fighting, they persuaded the Lakota that their dead would be resurrected, along with all sixty million buffalo exterminated from 1882 to 1884. They also predicted that a natural disaster or apocalypse would result in the elimination of all whites and the restoration of the Lakota culture of pastoral nomadism. One member of the Lakota delegation gave the date of the coming apocalypse as November

1890. This predicted date was not far off the mark; however, the anticipated results of this apocalypse were horribly inaccurate: in the early morning hours of 29 December, in revenge for Lieutenant Colonel George Armstrong Custer's defeat at Little Bighorn on 25 and 26 June 1876, 370 Lakota, mostly women and children, were forced from their tepees and massacred at Wounded Knee. Conditions among the Lakota had so deteriorated by this time that the commissioner of Indian affairs, in his list of the twelve causes of the "outbreak" that the massacre put down, stressed economic privations as the most significant, listing the "Messiah craze"—a term used to describe the intense fervor surrounding Wovoka's exalted status among his people—at number eleven.

Wovoka refused to discuss his vision after the massacre. He told Mooney that "whites lied" and "Indians disobeyed," referring to his belief that whites had described his religion as hostile and that Indian delegates had not relayed his message correctly. Thereafter, he settled into a life of modest celebrity. Delegations continued to visit him. He supported his wife, Mary (Tuma), and three surviving children, Lucy, Ida, and Alice, with money he made as a shaman as well as from selling his likeness and Ghost Dance relics (sacred paints, magpie and eagle feathers, hats and clothing he had worn) to Indians across the nation, who sent money through the mail. He twice traveled to Oklahoma, where he was feted. At home he worked on behalf of temperance and Warren Harding's presidential campaign in 1920.

Wovoka never lost faith in his vision. On learning of World War I, he expressed a desire to end the "German war" by sending "ice bombs." Local whites who knew him well reported Wovoka's final prophecy, that if he reached heaven he would "shake the earth." In a cabin at the Yerington Indian Colony in Mason Valley, he died of kidney failure on 28 September 1932, his age listed on the Nevada death certificate as seventy-four, although it was probably seventy-six.

BIBLIOGRAPHY

Bailey, Paul. *Wovoka: The Indian Messiah.* Los Angeles, Calif.: Westernlore, 1957.

DeMaillie, Raymond J. "The Lakota Ghost Dance: An Ethnohistorical Account." *Pacific Historical Review* 51 (1982): 385–405.

Hittman, Michael. *Wovoka and the Ghost Dance.* 2d ed. Lincoln: University of Nebraska Press, 1997.

Miller, David. *Ghost Dance.* Lincoln: University of Nebraska Press, 1959.

Mooney, James. *The Ghost-Dance Religion and the Sioux Outbreak of 1890.* Lincoln: University of Nebraska Press, 1991.

MICHAEL HITTMAN

*See also* **American Indians; Cults; Religion; Wounded Knee, 1890.**

# WRESTLING, PROFESSIONAL

Wrestling is one of the oldest sporting activities known to the human race, and it has a long history in the United States. American Indians held wrestling matches before the arrival of Europeans. In colonial America and thereafter, wrestling became commonplace, especially at social gatherings. Presidents George Washington and Abraham Lincoln, to cite two famous examples, were well known for their wrestling prowess. Until the Civil War, wrestling was done on an amateur basis; but by the late 1800s the social nature of wrestling began to change. At this time some wrestlers became so celebrated that spectators paid to watch wrestling matches, often at county fairs. This was the beginning of professional wrestling in the United States.

### Evolution of Professional Wrestling

At the turn of the twentieth century, professional wrestling was a popular American spectator sport. Baseball was still developing, basketball and football had not yet captured national attention, and boxing was considered somewhat vulgar. George Hackenschmidt and Frank Gotch, the two most publicized professional wrestlers of this era, fought a series of popular matches between 1904 and 1911. In 1911 at Chicago's Comiskey Park, Gotch defeated Hackenschmidt in front of thirty-three thousand paying spectators, at the time the largest attendance ever for a sporting event in the United States (except horse racing). Soon after this event, professional wrestling began a downward turn. Matches were increasingly fixed, and when this became public knowledge, sports reporters and fans eventually lost interest. By the 1940s professional wrestling was nearly dead.

By showcasing large, colorful athletes such as Gorgeous George and Nature Boy Buddy Rogers, network television revived popular interest in professional wrestling during the 1950s. Wrestling fans were treated to physical contests between good and evil—a passion play with doses of man-to-man violence. But by the 1960s, with wrestling programs' ratings sagging, the national networks dropped them. Regional wrestling alliances emerged, each with its own "national" champion. Professional wrestling had not disappeared, but it was relegated to a background position in the world of sports entertainment.

In the early 1980s Vince McMahon used cable television to transform his World Wrestling Federation (WWF) into a national phenomena. In the late 1990s, the WWF and the media mogul Ted Turner's World Championship Wrestling (WCW) were the two preeminent professional wrestling alliances. Both were economically powerful organizations with tremendous fan followings.

Professional wrestling in the United States has taken many turns, but its constant feature is an association with physical violence. The earliest professional wrestlers, like their amateur counterparts, engaged in wrestling as sport. The violence of early wrestling was found in the basic confrontation of two individuals trying to subdue each other physically. By definition, legitimate wrestling entails a certain amount of violence. As professional wrestling came to be identified more as entertainment than sport, most of the violence of professional wrestling became staged rather then genuine.

## Forms of Staged Violence

In the WWF and WCW, violence is frequent and spectacular, taking three main forms. First, there is the violence of intimidation. Professional wrestlers commonly threaten their opponents and others (e.g., family, friends, business associates) with vows to humiliate, injure, or even kill them. The WWF's Stone Cold Steve Austin perpetrated one of the most elaborately staged threats of 1998. Dressed in military battle gear, Austin held Vince McMahon hostage at gunpoint, tied him up in the center of the ring, and threatened to kill him (so afraid was McMahon that viewers saw "evidence" of his wetting his pants). Of course, Austin did not shoot McMahon, even though many in the crowd were yelling, "Kill him!" Not only individual wrestlers issue threats. There has been a proliferation of factions in both the WWF and the WCW, with the "Wolfpack" being one of the most popular groups in the WCW. The lyrics to the Wolfpack theme song contain this threat: "Don't turn your back on the Wolfpack, you might end up in a body bag."

A second form of violence is the destruction of property. Occasionally, professional wrestlers will

**A professional wrestling match between the Crusher and Bobby Duncan.** CORBIS/
BETTMANN

ransack a residence or office; most commonly they damage arena property, both backstage and at ringside—typically including chairs, tables, doors, lights, computers, and even bathroom facilities.

The final and most significant form of violence is bodily harm, which can take place in or out of the ring. Wrestlers are hit with chairs, hammers, bats, canes, chains, and barbed wire. In February 1999 WCW wrestler Hardcore Hak boasted to a Minneapolis audience that he was the first man to wrap barbed wire around a bat and use it to smash a man's head. Wrestlers can be even more imaginative in their choice of weapons. For example, on Super Bowl Sunday of 1999, Mankind, a WWF wrestler, used a forklift to drop a wooden platform holding kegs of beer on top of former WWF champion The Rock. Such violent attacks can feature a considerable amount of blood (or an artificial red substance that looks like blood). Moreover, on occasion, beaten wrestlers are shown being taken away in an ambulance, presumably headed for a hospital. Although not all wrestling fans agree, it is generally understood that virtually all physical attacks are choreographed. However, even staged violence can harm the wrestling participants.

### Concerns of Critics

With violence increasingly prominent in professional wrestling, critics have voiced several concerns. Many believe that the violence in professional wrestling is more sensationalist than ever, perhaps owing to the fact that violence has become a common, and accepted, part of social life. To attract audience attention, wrestling promoters have pushed the limits. Rather than use a two-by-four to chase after opponents, as was done by wrestler Jim Duggan in the 1980s, Scott Hall, a popular wrestler of the 1990s, uses a taser (a shock weapon used in police work) for the same purpose. Advances in technology have provided even greater opportunities for violence. For example, Kane, a famous wrestler in the WWF, is portrayed as capable of sending lightning bolts in the direction of opponents. Kane used this method to set a man (a stuntman in a special suit) on fire.

Professional wrestling has also tended to cartoonishly trivialize violence. In early 1998 two WWF wrestlers were thrown into a dumpster, which was then rolled off an eight-foot embankment. An ambulance arrived, and the television audience was told that the wrestlers were taken to the emergency room of the nearest hospital. Word was passed along that the victims were seriously

injured, yet these wrestlers, dressed in hospital gowns, reappeared toward the end of the program to chase down their rivals. The cartoon nature of wrestling violence has been taken to its literal extreme in MTV's popular *Celebrity Death Match* series, a program featuring animated clay characters. Some of the matches highlighted on this program include Michael Jordan versus Dennis Rodman; David Letterman versus Jay Leno; Prince (the rock star) versus Prince (Charles of England); and Hillary Clinton versus Monica Lewinsky. These matches invariably depict heads severed, limbs pulled completely out, and bodies disemboweled.

In the 1980s and earlier, violence in professional wrestling was played out with a good-versus-evil script. Typically, "good" wrestlers used legitimate violence to overcome the illegitimate violence of "bad" wrestlers. Today the good-versus-evil story line in professional wrestling is far less pronounced. Professional wrestlers, perhaps mimicking society, are neither good guys nor bad guys but a combination. Many "bad" wrestlers have become fan favorites, such that the use of violence is applauded regardless of who uses it or for what purpose it is used.

Staged violence in professional wrestling is a regular occurrence, spectacular in form and frequently trivialized, that is often pitched to an audience of children. Another one of professional wrestling's features is violence against women. Over the years, women have played a role in professional wrestling, but it has almost always been subservient. At times women are victims of violence: in February 1999 the wife of Diamond Dallas Page of the WCW was shown on television being kidnapped by another wrestler and then thrown out of a car. More generally, women in professional wrestling are the victims of threats, especially sexual threats.

Professional wrestling has become big-time entertainment, selling out large stadiums and garnering high television ratings. Making use of the latest technology in stage design and performance production, professional wrestling is a spectacular display of graphic interpersonal violence. Many observers say that the violence in professional wrestling is just entertainment and that it causes no real harm. Some even suggest that staged violence experienced vicariously lessens the frequency of actual violence. However, many others argue quite the opposite, that media violence contributes to a desensitization to violence and increased aggression.

*BIBLIOGRAPHY*

Johnson, Kirk. "Professional Wrestling Cuts Good Guys from the Script." *New York Times,* 30 March 1998.

Maguire, Brendan, and John F. Wozniak. "Racial and Ethnic Stereotypes in Professional Wrestling." *Social Science Journal* 24, no. 3 (1987).

Morton, Gerald, and George O'Brien. *Wrestling to Rasslin: Ancient Sport to American Spectacle.* Bowling Green, Ohio: Bowling Green State University Press, 1985.

*The Unreal Story of Professional Wrestling.* Video produced by Actuality Productions, Inc., for the Arts and Entertainment Network, 1998.

BRENDAN MAGUIRE
JOHN F. WOZNIAK

*See also* **Spectacle, Violence as; Sports.**

## WRONGFUL DEATH

U.S. law stipulates that a person is liable under the civil law when his or her negligent actions cause the death of another, defined by the law as *wrongful death.* This has not always been the case.

Under Anglo-Saxon law in the medieval era, homicide in all forms was regarded as a civil offense, and damages for killing a person were payable to the deceased's relatives. Initially, the amount paid was set by arbitration; later, a scale of payments was established based on the decedent's social rank. Over time killing came to be viewed as an offense against the state, and by the late thirteenth century every homicide was a criminal offense. Accidental homicides were not punished by death, but the property of the defendant was forfeited to the state, making any civil action useless.

In 1808 the British lord chief justice Lord Ellenborough, in *Baker v. Bolton,* set the English common-law precedent denying recovery for the death of a human killed by the negligence of another. In that case the plaintiff sued the owners of a stagecoach that had overturned, causing the death of his wife. The jury was instructed that "in a civil court, the death of a human being could not be complained of as an injury." Ellenborough may have mistakenly believed that the death was a crime, making a civil action useless. Despite its lack of precedent or reasoning, *Baker* was parroted and followed by other judges, becoming a tenet of English common law. U.S. courts adopted *Baker,* and thus American common law also bars recovery for wrongful death.

In effect, *Baker* made it cheaper for the defendant to kill the plaintiff than to injure her, and thus

---

### Examples of Wrongful Death Due to Medical Malpractice

1. Giving a patient excessive Demoral to relieve pain, causing respiratory distress leading to death.

2. Failure to recognize congestive heart failure over several days; instead diagnosing the condition as flu during repeated visits to the clinic, with the patient dying while being driven in (again) to the hospital.

3. Admitting a patient for a couple of days because of a suspected heart attack, but concluding that symptoms were gastrointestinal without performing further diagnostic testing that would have revealed coronary artery disease needing treatment (such as bypass surgery or angioplasty), with the result that the patient is discharged and dies from a massive heart attack on the ride home.

4. Negligent dissection of the coronary artery during cardiac catherization, causing the patient's death.

---

the rule was greatly criticized. The injustice of the common-law rule was remedied in England in 1846 by the passage of Lord Campbell's Act, which allowed a suit by family members for the damage caused by the loss due to wrongful death—that is, where the death was caused by the neglect of another. In the United States, statutes based on the act were passed by the various states, the first being New York in 1847. By the end of the twentieth century, there were statutes in all states that provide a right to recover for wrongful death.

Although state statutes vary, generally heirs may bring an action for economic and noneconomic loss resulting from the death. Economic loss generally includes loss of earnings, employment benefits, social security or private pension payments, and burial or cremation costs. Noneconomic loss generally includes the loss of love, society, companionship, and support. The law does not allow recovery for grief, nor does it generally allow the recovery of punitive damages in these cases (as with the California case of *Krouse v. Graham,* 1977).

A survival action may also be brought by the estate of the deceased to recover damages suffered by the decedent before his or her death. Damages such as medical bills and wage loss, and in appropriate cases, punitive damages, may be recovered.

*BIBLIOGRAPHY*

Flahavan, William F., et al. *California Practice Guide: Personal Injury.* Encino, Calif.: Rutter Group, 1998.
Speiser, Stuart M., Charles F. Krause, and Juanita M. Madole. *Recovery for Wrongful Death and Injury.* New York: Clark Boardman Callaghan, 1992.

MONTY A. MCINTYRE

*See also* **Crime, Legal Definitions of; Homicide.**

## WUORNOS, AILEEN
### (1956– )

Aileen Wuornos was arrested in 1991 and subsequently convicted of killing seven men along Florida highways during acts of prostitution. Wuornos was given the death penalty for her crimes. The nature of Wuornos's motivations remains debated, however. Wuornos claimed she carried a gun for protection and killed in self-defense, only when men were trying to rape or physically harm her. She asserted that she needed to use self-defense all seven times and that the issue the court should have considered was the principle of self-defense, not the number of times she had to resort to it. Others maintain that Wuornos is the first female serial murderer—that she premeditatedly intended to kill her victims and lured them to their demise.

Some attribute Wuornos's violence to an abusive childhood. Abandoned by her mother, abused by her father (who eventually committed suicide in prison after being convicted for kidnapping and sodomizing a child), and raised primarily by her grandparents, Wuornos became a prostitute at age fourteen and was familiar with drug and alcohol use early on. Nick Broomfield, in his documentary *Aileen Wuornos: The Selling of a Serial Killer* (1992), claims that Wuornos has been viewed as "anything from a neglected and abused child who hates her father and is murdering him over and over again to a sadist who takes pleasure in the agony of her victims." In an interview from the documentary, Wuornos says that she is being made "to look like a monster and deranged like a Jeffrey Dahmer, which I'm not."

**Aileen Wuornos, 1991.** CORBIS/REUTERS

The curious circumstances and individuals surrounding Wuornos's convictions and trials have sparked some controversy over whether Wuornos received justice in the court system. The first man Wuornos killed, Richard Mallory, had been incarcerated for ten years for violent sexual assault prior to meeting Wuornos. Yet, despite Wuornos's claims of self-defense and a vivid description in court of how Mallory severely physically abused Wuornos and threatened her life, this evidence was not presented by the defense or prosecution at Wuornos's trial. Also, shortly after being imprisoned, Wuornos was adopted by Arlene Pralle, a born-again Christian. Under the influence of Pralle and Pralle's lawyer, Steve Glazer, Wuornos changed her plea from "not guilty" to "no contest," a change which effectively became the legal equivalent of a guilty plea, with a death sentence attached. Pralle believed, and Wuornos concurred for a short time, that pleading "no contest" would make peace with God and save Wuornos in the next world. Wuornos later lamented her trust of

Pralle and Glazer and her change of plea, questioning their economic motivations. Whether Pralle and Glazer were involved in potential movie or book deals about Wuornos remains uncertain.

Wuornos's lover at the time of the murders, Tyria Moore, was seen driving in one of the murdered men's cars with Wuornos, but Moore was given immunity from charges in the case, in exchange for lying to Wuornos to make her confess to the murders. As of 1999, Wuornos was on death row awaiting execution.

BIBLIOGRAPHY

Griggers, Camilla. *Becoming Woman*. Minneapolis: University of Minneapolis Press, 1997.

Hart, Lynda. *Fatal Women*. Princeton, N.J.: Princeton University Press, 1994.

Levin, Jack, and James Alan Fox. "Female Serial Killers." In *Female Criminality: The State of the Art*, edited by Concetta C. Culliver. New York: Garland, 1993.

Myers, Alice, and Sarah Wight. "Introduction." In *No Angels: Women Who Commit Violence*, edited by Myers and Wight. San Francisco: HarperCollins, 1996.

Skrapec, Candice. "The Female Serial Killer." In *Moving Targets*, edited by Helen Birch. Berkeley: University of California Press, 1994.

VALERIE KARNO

*See also* **Film: Documentary Film; Serial Killers; Women: Women Who Kill.**

# X-Z

**XENOPHOBIA.** *See* Foreign Intervention, Fear of; Nativism.

## YIPPIE!

For a brief moment in the late 1960s and early 1970s, Yippie! exerted an influence on the American cultural and political scene far exceeding its intangible structure and minuscule numbers. A mythic group far more than a clearly defined organization, Yippie! derived its power from the creativity of its charismatic figureheads Abbie Hoffman and Jerry Rubin, its ability to channel the rebellion of youth, and its knack for attracting television coverage.

Based in New York and made up mostly of men over the age of thirty, Yippie! appealed to high school students, college dropouts, and hippies who flocked to Manhattan's East Village and San Francisco's Haight-Ashbury. The name Yippie! itself was intended to convey a sense of utopian freedom that Rubin, Hoffman, and their friends felt was missing from puritanical American society and from both the stodgy Old Left and the rigid New Left. Insisting that the American empire would be undermined by sexual liberation, the recreational use of marijuana, and raucous rock and roll, Yippie! advocated grassroots cultural revolution. Hoffman, Rubin, and company hoped to generate a new political animal—part long-haired hippie, part urban guerrilla—that would dominate the landscape of rebellion. In the winter of 1968, Yippie! announced plans for a Festival of Life in Chicago that would protest the Vietnam War as well as the Democratic National Convention.

The first major Yippie! event took place in Manhattan's Grand Central Station. Firecrackers and cherry bombs exploded, the terminal's clocks were vandalized, the walls spray-painted with graffiti. The police waded into the crowd and clubbed demonstrators. At a press conference, a New York Civil Liberties Union speaker described it as the "worst display of police brutality I've ever seen outside of Mississippi."

In March 1968, when President Lyndon Johnson announced he would not run for reelection, Yippie! plans for the Festival of Life fizzled. Then, in June, when Robert Kennedy, the front-running Democratic candidate, was assassinated in Los Angeles, Yippie! revived its plans. Hoffman and Rubin escalated their verbal high jinks, threatening to dump the hallucinogenic drug LSD into the reservoirs of Chicago, kidnap delegates, and sabotage the telephone system. The authorities took these provocative statements at face value. Mayor Richard Daley refused to grant the Yippies a permit to hold the Festival of Life and announced that anyone coming to Chicago with the aim of promoting violence would be treated as a common criminal. On the eve of the convention, as though to prove they meant business, the police shot and killed a seventeen-year-old Native American named Dean Johnson allegedly because he reached for a pistol when stopped for routine questioning, but by

Yippie! accounts simply because he was a young, Native American protester. The Yippies prepared for battle. In Lincoln Park—on the shore of Lake Michigan, and miles from the Amphitheater where the nominating convention was taking place— demonstrators received training in "mobile street tactics," and at the Federal Building, Hoffman held a press conference to announce the eighteen-point Yippie! program, which called for an immediate end to the war in Vietnam, the abolition of money, and the disarming of all police. Moreover, the Yippies announced they were running a pig for President. But Pigasus, their corn-fed candidate, was taken into custody and the Yippies were arrested and charged with disorderly conduct.

Confrontations intensified between the authorities and the insurgents. In Grant Park, across the street from the hotel where many delegates were staying, the police attacked the protesters with tear gas and clubs, and the protesters retaliated with rocks and bottles. On 27 August the battle came to a climax outside the Hilton Hotel. Yippies, members of Students for a Democratic Society (SDS), and supporters of the antiwar candidate Eugene McCarthy linked arms and chanted "the whole world is watching." The police attacked, and as the media observed, "all hell broke loose." More than a thousand people, including reporters and innocent bystanders as well as militant demonstrators were injured and nearly two hundred people were arrested. Network television broadcast the violence to a shocked nation.

Abbie Hoffman called Chicago the place "where the facade of a democratically run convention was washed down the streets with the blood of young people." The *New York Times* reporter Tom Wicker wrote that "everything since Chicago has had a new intensity—that of polarization, of confrontation, of antagonism, and fear."

In the wake of the "police riot" (so described by the National Commission on the Causes and Prevention of Violence), Yippie! became a household word, and Hoffman and Rubin were catapulted into the national spotlight. Indicted on federal charges of conspiracy and crossing state lines with the intent of rioting, they traveled across the country promoting rebellion and spreading the myth of Yippie! In late September 1969, they went on trial with Tom Hayden, David Dellinger, Rennie Davis, John Froines, Lee Weiner, and Bobby Seale, the chairman of the Black Panther Party.

Hoffman and Rubin defined the issues in the five-month courtroom drama, upstaging Judge Julius Hoffman, who had a reputation as a liberal and who belonged to Chicago's elite Jewish community. On one occasion, Hoffman and Rubin came to court wearing judicial robes over police uniforms. On another occasion late in the trial, Abbie Hoffman launched into a verbal assault, in Yiddish, on Judge Hoffman, accusing him of betraying his fellow Jews and collaborating with the gentile establishment.

At every step, Hoffman and Rubin insisted that the government had engaged in a conspiracy to deprive the protesters of their constitutional rights, and argued that the police rather than the demonstrators had precipitated the violence at the convention. Moreover, they argued that the trial of the "Chicago Eight," as the defendants were dubbed, was a government attempt to repress the counterculture of the 1960s. Pete Seeger, Arlo Guthrie, and Allen Ginsberg appeared in court to lend credence to the Yippie! case. Most observers agreed that Hoffman's testimony was the high point of the trial. On the witness stand he insisted that he was an "orphan of America" and that the Yippie! protests in Chicago were meant to create a culture of liberation, not to destroy society.

Four of the defendants, including Hoffman and Rubin, were found not guilty of conspiracy but guilty of crossing state lines with the intention of creating a riot. Yippie! supporters rallied against the verdict across the country, battling the police and destroying property, including a branch of the Bank of America in Isla Vista, California. After a long appeals process, the convictions were finally overturned in 1972 when the U.S. Court of Appeals upbraided Judge Hoffman and the federal prosecutors for denying the defendants their constitutional right to a fair trial.

In the 1970s the Yippies tried to reinvent themselves as the Youth International Party, but their freewheeling, anarchistic style was anathema to the demands of a formal political organization and the effort failed, though there was one last flicker in Miami at the 1972 Democratic and Republican National Conventions. In the mid-1980s Hoffman and Rubin debated one another on college campuses: Hoffman defended Yippie! and encouraged students to protest; Rubin went to work on Wall Street and celebrated the values of self-advancement, commercial success, and consumerism that were associated with "Yuppies," the young, upwardly mobile urban professionals who became an integral part of the social landscape of the 1980s. Black Panther survivors and SDS veterans held reunions in the 1990s that rallied the faithful, but without Hoffman, who had committed suicide in 1989, the scattered former Yippies lacked a compelling figure who might have carried on the spirit of irreverence that had energized the group and propelled it into the forefront of the generational conflict that polarized America in the 1960s.

BIBLIOGRAPHY

Krassner, Paul. *Confessions of a Raving Unconfined Nut.* New York: Simon and Schuster, 1993.
McNeill, Don. *Moving Through Here.* New York: Knopf, 1970.
Raskin, Jonah. *For the Hell of It: The Life and Times of Abbie Hoffman.* Berkeley: University of California Press, 1996.

JONAH RASKIN

*See also* **Antiwar Protests; Hoffman, Abbie; Weatherman and Weather Underground.**

## ZODIAC KILLER

In July 1969 editors at three northern California newspapers received letters from an anonymous author claiming responsibility for three murders and an attempted homicide that had until then remained unsolved. The first two murders had occurred on 20 December 1968, and the third murder and attempted homicide occurred on 5 July 1969. What distinguished these letters from others also claiming responsibility was that the author, who, for reasons that are still unknown, called himself Zodiac, listed information about the cases that had never been publicized. Each correspondence also included one-third of a cipher that the writer claimed encoded his real name. After the newspapers published the cipher, readers solved it. Although the code did not contain the killer's name, this event marked the beginning of the media's involvement in the Zodiac case—an involvement that provoked questions about the public's right to know and the press's responsibility in dangerous cases.

Zodiac continued actively to seek publicity; by 1978 the correspondences positively attributed to him numbered twenty-one. In those that followed the original letters, he claimed responsibility for attacking nine people across California: three of these victims escaped, the other six died. Unlike the crimes of many serial killers, Zodiac's murders did not evidence a particular style that identified a single perpetrator. He fired on some of his victims from a distance; others he bound with clothesline and stabbed. He shot his last known victim in the head at close range. In the absence of an identifying style, Zodiac's letters were the only clue linking these crimes together, and he made certain to include specific information—unpublicized facts about the murders, scraps of a victim's bloodstained clothing—so that investigators could verify the letters' authenticity.

In most of his correspondence Zodiac taunted the police for failing to catch him. He also demanded that his letters be published and threatened violence if they were not. In October 1969 the *San Francisco Chronicle* published a threat in which Zodiac expressed a desire to kill an entire school bus full of children. The public panicked, and police forces, school districts, and terrified parents throughout northern California implemented preventive measures to ensure children's safety. The publicity delighted Zodiac, who requested that his next letter be printed on the front page and threatened that he would kill again if it was not. The press complied.

The Zodiac killer's attention-seeking behavior defines a specific kind of criminal: one who commits crime to achieve glory. His ability both to commit crimes and to escape detection signified to Zodiac his own superiority and uniqueness; this sense of himself was reinforced positively when the media capitulated to his demands for publicity. He then used each attack to taunt the police publicly. Over time people began to wonder if the press's publicizing the correspondence had become the killer's incentive to commit further crimes. The extreme panic resulting from the publication of the school-bus threat caused the press to question its role in creating sensationalism and fear. This role was not limited to newspapers: in the late 1960s and early 1970s fictional accounts of serial homicides drew great public interest. The 1971 film *Dirty Harry* was, in fact, closely based on the Zodiac case.

In the early 1990s a strikingly similar case emerged. A murderer calling himself the Zodiac Killer shot seven people and stabbed one person one hundred times in New York City. He wrote letters to the press in which he claimed to choose victims on the basis of their astrological signs. Investigators at first speculated that this might be the same killer as the California Zodiac. The New York City Zodiac was, however, apprehended: in 1996 police arrested and later convicted Heriberto Seda for the killings. Evidence definitively proved that

Seda was not the Zodiac killer from northern California, who was never caught.

BIBLIOGRAPHY

Egger, Steven A. *The Killers Among Us: An Examination of Serial Murder and Its Investigation.* Upper Saddle River, N.J.: Prentice Hall, 1998.

Graysmith, Robert. *Zodiac.* New York: Berkley, 1987.

Holmes, Ronald M., and Stephen T. Holmes. *Serial Murder.* 2d ed. Thousand Oaks, Calif.: Sage, 1998.

Jenkins, Philip. *Using Murder: The Social Construction of Serial Homicide.* New York: Aldine de Gruyter, 1994.

Sears, Donald J. *To Kill Again: The Motivation and Development of Serial Murder.* Wilmington, Del.: Scholarly Resources, 1991.

"Signs Point to a Zodiac Suspect." *U.S. News & World Report,* 1 July 1996.

D. LEFLER

*See also* **Serial Killers.**

## ZOOT-SUIT RIOT

The Zoot-Suit Riot in Los Angeles was the first in a wave of race riots that swept through the United States in 1943. In the early evening of 3 June, about fifty sailors from the Naval Reserve Armory near Chavez Ravine in Los Angeles stormed through the mostly Mexican American neighborhoods that lay between their post and downtown Los Angeles. The sailors stripped zoot-suits off young civilian men and beat those who resisted. The next day, as news of the fighting spread, military men stationed throughout southern California poured into Los Angeles by the hundreds and attacked anyone they could find who was wearing a zoot-suit. For several nights, military men and some civilians gathered in downtown Los Angeles to organize their assaults on the predominantly Mexican American neighborhoods of East Los Angeles and the black neighborhoods of Watts. In both areas, they met stiff resistance from the local youth, who organized to protect their homes and neighborhoods. The Los Angeles Police Department responded to the riot by jailing hundreds of young Mexican American, black, and working-class white men "for their own protection." The weeklong riot effectively stopped when the army and navy commanders in southern California took the crisis seriously and confined military men to their bases.

The origins of the zoot-suit are unclear, although its stylistic antecedents can be traced back to gentlemanly fashion standards of earlier decades. By the late 1930s, the zoot-suit—also known as the "killer-diller" in the South and the "drape-shape" or "tacuche" on the West Coast—was a broad-shouldered fashion worn exclusively by African American jazz artists, hipsters, and young aficionados of jazz music and culture. Most Americans across the color line considered the zoot-suit garish and inappropriate at best; at worst, they saw the fashion as an affront to the unwritten code of segregation that demanded racial minorities to act discreet, decorous, and deferential in public. For working-class Mexican American, Jewish, Italian American, and black youth, however, the zoot-suit was only one of the ways in which they fashioned their own cultural identities—often in defiance of social expectations—through jazz culture. For the military and civilian men who rioted, destroying the zoot-suit was as much a focused show of power designed to reassert the abrogated norms of segregation and white privilege as it was an expression of wartime anxieties.

White and minority activists blamed the riot on the Los Angeles newspapers, and most scholars since then have attributed negative reporting, anti-Mexican sentiments, or wartime anxiety as the cause of the riot. Sailors rioted the first night, however, in response to a series of escalating local confrontations over social space, and the Zoot-Suit Riot unfolded during the following week along numerous social fault lines. The riot was as much about race as it was about the use of social space, about the changing social boundaries brought on by World War II, and about the social conflicts between military men and civilians. Unlike the riots that followed in other cities that year, from San Diego to Detroit to Harlem in New York City, there were no reported murders, rapes, or serious damage to property in connection with the Zoot-Suit Riot, and in only a few cases was there serious injury. Instead, much of the mob violence revolved around the curious practice of destroying zoot-suits, which started almost from the moment the expensive fashion first appeared on the streets of the city around 1940.

The Zoot-Suit Riot in Los Angeles created an international embarrassment for the United States. The Axis radio quickly pointed out that, contrary to Allied propaganda, American society was

**The aftermath of the Zoot-Suit Riot.** AP/WIDE WORLD PHOTOS

deeply racist. At home, Mexican Americans and blacks continued to undermine segregation practices throughout the war, after having successfully resisted direct attacks on their communities. Los Angeles politicians made new efforts after the riot to work with the Mexican American communities of Los Angeles by appointing prominent Mexican Americans to civic advisory boards and wartime committees in an attempt to foster greater unity. Political activists on the left found new cause to level heavy critiques against the hypocrisy of segregation, and they renewed their efforts to organize within black and Mexican American communities for social justice.

BIBLIOGRAPHY

Chibnall, Steve. "Whistle and Zoot: The Changing Meaning of a Suit of Clothes." *History Workshop: A Journal of Socialist and Feminist Historians* 20 (fall 1985).

Cosgrove, Stuart. "The Zoot-Suit and Style Warfare." *History Workshop: A Journal of Socialist and Feminist Historians* 18 (fall 1984).

Mazón, Mauricio. *The Zoot-Suit Riots: The Psychology of Symbolic Annihilation.* Austin: University of Texas Press, 1984.

Pagán, Eduardo Obregón. "Sleepy Lagoon: The Politics of Youth and Race in Wartime Los Angeles, 1940–1945." Ph.D. diss. Princeton University, 1996.

EDUARDO OBREGÓN PAGÁN

*See also* **Fashion; Los Angeles; Mexican Americans; Nativism; Riots.**

# Appendix

The following lists of (1) organizations, (2) publications, and (3) Web resources more or less centrally concerned with violence in America are highly selective. Indeed, an exhaustive directory of government, public, and private agencies; associations, foundations, and institutes; and their newsletters, reports, bulletins, journals, and other periodicals would require a separate volume, especially if the large and growing number of college and university violence research centers and municipal and state offices were included. These lists then are designed only to identify some major and representative groups and publications that seek to understand and address American violence in its various past and present manifestations. Users of this encyclopedia will not be surprised to find that electronic resources for information on violence in America are multiplying faster than print media can record.

Two important government publications for researchers to consider are the Uniform Crime Reports (UCR) and the National Crime Victimization Survey (NCVS). The UCR, published by the Federal Bureau of Investigation and available on its Web site (see below as well as the titled entry in the encyclopedia), is a view of crime based on the submission of statistics by city, county, and state law-enforcement offices. This report includes only known offenses and persons arrested. The offenses include murder, nonnegligent manslaughter, forcible rape, robbery, aggravated assault, burglary, larceny-theft, motor vehicle theft, and arson. In contrast, the NCVS, compiled by the U.S. Department of Justice (see below and entry in the encyclopedia), is an ongoing survey of households about their victimization from the following crimes: rape, sexual assault, robbery, assault, aggravated assault, theft, burglary, and motor vehicle theft *including those crimes not reported to the police*. This report does not include homicide because homicide victims cannot be interviewed. Another document useful to researchers is the *Statistical Handbook on Violence in America*, edited by the Violence Research Group and published by Oryx Press.

A subject index (beginning on p. 530) identifies the principal organizations dealing with particular aspects of violence and prevention.

Ronald Gottesman
Nikki Senecal

# ORGANIZATIONS

**Abusive Men Explore New Directions**
*Provides training programs, conventions, and publications.*
789 Sherman Street
Suite 580
Denver, CO 80203
Tel.: (303) 832-6363

**Albert Einstein Institution**
*Supports and conducts research, political studies, and education on the potential of nonviolent action.*
427 Newbury Street
Boston, MA 02115
Tel.: (617) 247-4882
Fax: (617) 247-4035
E-mail: einstein@igc.org

**American Association of Suicidology**
*Brings together people in various disciplines and fields who share a common interest in the prevention of suicide and self-destructive behavior.*
4201 Connecticut Avenue, NW
Suite 408
Washington, DC 20008
Tel.: (202) 237-2280
Fax: (202) 237-2282

**American Bar Association**
*National group representing the legal profession, has several commissions that deal with violence, such as the Commission on Domestic Violence and the Commission on Gun Violence.*
750 North Lake Shore Drive
Chicago, IL 60611
Tel.: (312) 988-5000
E-mail: info@abanet.org
URL: http://www.abanet.org

**American Civil Liberties Union**
*Advocates for individual rights—litigating, legislating, and educating the public on a broad array of issues affecting individual freedom in the United States.*
125 Broad Street
18th Floor
New York, NY 10004-2400
Tel.: (212) 549-2500 or (212) 344-3005
URL: http://www.aclu.org

**American Correctional Association**
*Seeks to create effective correctional solutions; publishes a professional journal and many other works for corrections administrators and specialists.*
4380 Forbes Boulevard
Lanham, MD 20706-4322
Tel.: (301) 918-1874 or (800) 222-5646
E-mail: problems@corrections.com
URL: http://www.corrections.com/aca

**American Foundation for Suicide Prevention**
*Seeks to prevent suicide through research, education, and treatment.*
120 Wall Street
New York, NY 10005
Tel.: (212) 363-3500
Fax: (212) 363-6237
E-mail: hhendin@afsp.org
URL: http://www.afsp.org

**American Medical Association**
*Promotes the art and science of medicine and the betterment of public health.*
515 North State Street
Chicago, IL 60610
Tel.: (312) 464-5000
URL: http://www.ama-assn.org

**American Peace Network**
*Educational organization dedicated to promoting human progress and survival by correcting worldwide political mismanagement and downsizing excessive military institutions.*
610 Ethan Allen Avenue
Takoma Park, MD 20912
E-mail: admin@apn.org
URL: http://www.apn.org

**American Peace Society**
*Advances peaceful means of "avoiding and adjusting difference among nations." Publishes* World Affairs.
1319 Eighteenth Street, NW
Washington, DC 20036-1802
Tel.: (202) 296-6267

**American Psychological Association**
*Largest organization of psychologists in the United States; includes special divisions for those with interest in youth violence.*
750 First Street, NE
Washington, DC 20002
Tel.: (202) 336-5500
URL: http://www.apa.org

**American Society for the Prevention of Cruelty to Animals**
*Promotes humane principles, prevents cruelty, and alleviates pain, fear, and suffering of animals through nationwide information, awareness, and advocacy programs. Publications include* Animal Watch.
424 East Ninety-second Street
New York, NY 10128-6804
Tel.: (212) 876-7700
Fax: (212) 876-9571
URL: http://www.aspca.org

## American Society of Criminology
*International organization committed to bringing together a multidisciplinary forum fostering criminology study, research, and education.*
1314 Kinnear Road
Suite 212
Columbus, OH 43212-1156
Tel.: (614) 292-9207
Fax: (614) 292-6767
E-mail: asc41@compuserve.com
URL: http://www.asc41.com

## American Women's Self-Defense Association
*Promotes rape prevention awareness and self-defense. "You have an absolute right to defend yourself."*
713 North Wellwood Avenue
Lindenhurst, NY 11757
Tel.: (888) STOP-RAPE or (516) 226-8383
Fax: (516) 226-5454

## Amnesty International
*Worldwide movement that works to promote all human rights enshrined in the Universal Declaration of Human Rights and other international standards. Campaigns to free all prisoners of conscience; ensure fair and prompt trials for political prisoners; abolish the death penalty, torture, and other cruel treatment of prisoners; end political killings and "disappearances"; and oppose human rights abuses.*
322 Eighth Avenue
New York, NY 10001
Tel.: (212) 463-9193
Fax: (212) 463-9193 or (212) 627-1451
URL: http://www.amnesty.org

## Animal Protection Institute of America
*National advocacy group to protect animals from abuse.*
2831 Fruitridge Road
Sacramento, CA 95820
Tel.: (916) 731-5521 or (800) 348-7387
Fax: (916) 731-4467
E-mail: onlineAPI@aol.com
URL: http://www.api4animals.org

## Anti-Defamation League
*Fights anti-Semitism and bigotry here and abroad; serves as a public resource for government, media, law-enforcement agencies, and the public at large.*
823 UN Plaza
New York, NY 10017
URL: http://www.adl.org

## Barrios Unidos
*Multicultural nonprofit organization that seeks to prevent and curtail violence among young people.*
1817 Soquel Avenue
Santa Cruz, CA 95062
Tel.: (831) 457-8208

Fax: (831) 457-0389
E-mail: barriosunidos@cruzio.com

## Bureau of Alcohol, Tobacco, and Firearms
*Law-enforcement organization within the U.S. Department of Treasury dedicated to reducing violent crime and protecting the public. Enforces federal laws regarding alcohol, tobacco, firearms, explosives, and arson.*
650 Massachusetts Avenue, NW
Washington, DC 20226
Tel.: (202) 927-7777
Fax: (202) 927-7862
URL: http://www.atf.treas.gov/welcome.htm (Field offices and hotline phone numbers are available on Web site.)

## Bureau of Justice Statistics
*A component of the Office of Justice Programs in the U.S. Department of Justice that provides the United States' primary source for criminal justice statistics. Collects, analyzes, publishes, and disseminates information on crime, criminal offenders, victims of crime, and the operation of justice systems at all levels of government.*
Office of Justice Programs
U.S. Department of Justice
810 Seventh Street, NW
Washington, DC 20531
Tel.: (202) 307-0765
E-mail: askbjs@ojp.usdoj.gov
URL: http://www.ojp.usdoj.gov/bjs/welcome.html

## Carter Center
*Group of organizations focused on international cooperation, conflict resolution, and the alleviation of poverty in the United States.*
1 Copenhill
Suite 453
Freedom Parkway
Atlanta, GA 30307
Tel.: (404) 331-3900
URL: http://www.CarterCenter.org

## Cease Fire, Inc.
*Dedicated to saving lives by reducing the number of handgun-related deaths and injuries in the United States.*
P.O. Box 33424
Washington, DC 20033-0424
E-mail: info@ceasefire.org
URL: http://www.ceasefire.org

## Center for Communication and Social Policy
*Conducts research of communication policy issues and seeks to improve methods of conflict resolution. Home to the Violence Prevention Evaluation Project, which conducts the largest ongoing scientific study of television violence.*
Institute for Social, Behavioral, and Economic Research
University of California, Santa Barbara
Santa Barbara, CA 93016

Tel.: (805) 893-7879
Fax: (805) 893-7390
E-mail: ccsp@omni.ucsb.edu
URL: http://www.ccsp.ucsb.edu

**Center for Defense Information**
*Independent nonprofit research organization that monitors military affairs throughout the world.*
1779 Massachusetts Avenue, NW
Washington, DC 20036
Tel.: (202) 332-0600
Fax: (202) 462-4559
E-mail: info@cdi.org
URL: http://www.cdi.org

**Center for Democratic Renewal**
*Multiracial, multiethnic, interfaith nonprofit organization that seeks a nonviolent response to hate groups and white supremacists.*
P.O. Box 50469
Atlanta, GA 30302-0469
Tel.: (404) 221-0025

**Center for Nonviolent Communication**
*Attempts to strengthen our ability to inspire compassion from others and to respond compassionately to others and to ourselves.*
P.O. Box 2662
Sherman, TX 75091-2662
Tel.: (903) 893-3886
Fax: (903) 893-2935
E-mail: cnvc@compuserve.com
URL: http://www.cnvc.org

**Center for Research on the Influences of Television on Children**
*Conducts basic and applied research related to electronic media and children. Publishes reports in scientific journals and book chapters.*
Division of Child Development and Family
  Relationships
Department of Human Ecology
115 GEA / A2700
University of Texas at Austin
Austin, TX 78712-1097
Tel.: (512) 471-3141
URL: http://www.critc.he.utexas.edu

**Center for the Applied Study of Prejudice and Ethnoviolence**
*Studies and responds to prejudice, discrimination, conflict, and violence. Collects, analyzes, produces, and disseminates information on prevention and response to violence. Publishes the bimonthly newsletter* Perspectives.
2743 Maryland Avenue
Baltimore, MD 21218
Tel.: (410) 366-9654

Fax: (410) 366-9656
E-mail: prejinst@aol.com
URL: http://www.prejudiceinstitute.org

**Center for the Prevention of School Violence**
*Serves as a primary point of contact for dealing with school violence. Resource for information, program assistance, and research about school violence.*
20 Enterprise Street
Suite 2
Raleigh, NC 27607-7375
Tel.: (919) 515-9397 or (800) 299-6054
Fax: (919) 515-9561
URL: http://www.ncsu.edu/cpsv

**Center for the Prevention of Sexual and Domestic Violence**
*An interreligious educational resource center that addresses issues of sexual and domestic abuse. Seeks to engage religious leaders in ending abuse.*
936 North Thirty-fourth Street
No. 200
Seattle, WA 98103
Tel.: (206) 634-1903
Fax: (206) 634-0115
E-mail: cpsdv@cpsvd.org
URL: http://www.cpsdv.org

**Center on Human Policy**
*Seeks to ensure the rights of people with disabilities.*
Syracuse University
805 Crouse Avenue
Syracuse, NY 13244-2280
Tel.: (315) 443-3851 or (800) 849-0826
E-mail: thechp@sued.syr.edu

**Center on War and the Child**
*Serves to inform and educate the public about the militarization of children and their victimization by war.*
P.O. Box 487
35 Benton Street
Eureka Springs, AR 72632
Tel.: (501) 253-8900

**Centers for Disease Control and Prevention**
*Promotes health and quality of life by preventing and controlling disease, injury, and disability. Underwrites research on violence.*
1600 Clifton Road, NE
Atlanta, GA 30333
Tel.: (800) 311-3435
URL: http://www.cdc.gov

**Center to Prevent Handgun Violence**
*Educational and research affiliate of Handgun Control, Inc.*
1225 I Street, NW
Suite 1100
Washington, DC 20005

Tel.: (202) 289-7319
Fax: (202) 408-1851
URL: http://www.handguncontrol.org/research.htm

**Central Intelligence Agency**
*Collects, evaluates, and disseminates foreign intelligence reports to assist the president, the National Security Council, and all who make and execute U.S. national security policy. Conducts counterintelligence and special activities related to national security as directed by the president.*
Washington, DC 20505
Tel.: (703) 482-1100 (switchboard), (703) 482-7677 (public affairs), or (703) 613-1287 (freedom of information)
URL: http://www.cia.gov/index.html

**Centre for Comparative Criminology and Criminal Justice**
*Established within the School of Sociology and Social Policy to promote research, teaching, advice, and consultation on matters related to crime and deviant behavior.*
University of Wales
Bangor
Gwynedd LL57 2DG
United Kingdom
Tel.: (02148) 351-151
URL: http://www.bangor.ac.uk

**Child Abuse Prevention Association**
*Seeks to prevent and treat all forms of child abuse by creating changes in individuals, families, and society that strengthen relationships and promote healing.*
503 East Twenty-third Street
Independence, MO 64055
Tel.: (816) 252-8388
Fax: (816) 252-1337
E-mail: capa@childabuseprevention
URL: http://www.childabuseprevention.org

**Childhelp U.S.A.**
*Dedicated to meeting the physical, emotional, educational, and spiritual needs of abused and neglected children. Focuses on treatment, prevention, and research. Operates the Childhelp National Child Abuse Hotline.*
National Headquarters
15757 North Seventy-eighth Street
Scottsdale, AZ 85260
Tel.: (800) 422-4453 (hotline), (800) 2 A-CHILD (TDD), or (480) 922-8212
Fax: (480) 922-7061
URL: http://www.childhelpusa.org

**Children's Bureau**
*Responsible for assisting states in the delivery of child welfare services including those that protect children from child abuse and neglect. Invests in staff training and technological and innovative programs.*
Department of Health and Human Services
Administration for Children and Families

200 Independence Avenue, SW
Washington, DC 20201
Tel.: (202) 260-5140 (director)
Fax: (202) 260-9345
URL: http://www.acf.dhhs.gov/programs/cb/

**Children's Defense Fund**
*Works "to ensure every child a healthy start, a head start, a fair start, a safe start, and a moral start in life, and successful passage to adulthood with the help of caring families and communities."*
National Headquarters
25 E Street, NW
Washington, DC 20001
Tel.: (202) 628-8787
E-mail: cdinfo@childrensdefense.org
URL: http://www.childrensdefense.org

**Children's Rights of America, Inc.**
*Works to rescue troubled children when all other avenues have failed.*
500 Sugar Mill Road
Building B
Suite 220
Atlanta, GA 30350
Tel.: (770) 998-6698 or (800) 442-HOPE

**Child Welfare League of America, Inc.**
*The nation's oldest and largest membership-based child welfare organization, committed to promoting the well-being of children, youths, and their families, and protecting every child from harm. Assists over 2.5 million abused and neglected children and their families each year with a wide range of services.*
440 First Street, NW
3d Floor
Washington, DC 20001-2085
Tel.: (202) 638-2952
Fax: (202) 638-4004
URL: http://www.cwla.org

**Coalition Against Trafficking in Women**
*Works internationally to combat all forms of sexual exploitation, especially prostitution and trafficking of women and children.*
316 Roosevelt Hall
University of Rhode Island
Kingston, RI 02881
Tel.: (401) 874-2757
Fax: (401) 874-4527
E-mail: dhughes@uriacc.uri.edu
URL: http://www.uri.edu/artsci/wms/hughes/catw

**Coalition to Stop Gun Violence**
*National coalition of educational, professional, and religious organizations that seeks to ban sales and private possession of handguns.*

1000 Sixteenth Street, NW
Suite 603
Washington, DC 20036
Tel.: (202) 530-0340
Fax: (202) 530-0331
E-mail: noguns@aol.com
URL: http://www.csgv.org

### Colloquium on Violence and Religion

*Scholarly group that aims to "explore, criticize, and develop the mimetic model of the relationship between violence and religion in the genesis and maintenance of culture." Sponsors conferences, a bulletin available to members, and the journal* Contagion: Journal of Violence, Mimesis, and Culture.
Professor Sandor Goodhart
Executive Secretary, COV&R
Department of English
1356 Heavilon Hall
Purdue University
West Lafayette, IN 47907-1356
Tel.: (765) 494-3720 or (765) 494-3740 (department)
Fax: (765) 494-3780
E-mail: Goodhart@purdue.edu, dculbert@kent.edu
  (Diana Culbertson, COV&R president), or
  jshinnic@io.com (Julie Shinnick, COV&R treasurer)

### Commission for Racial Justice

*Has a wide focus; works against injustices ranging from capital punishment to racially motivated violence. Also works with women victims of spousal battery and advocates penal reform.*
700 Prospect Avenue
Cleveland, OH 44115-1110
Tel.: (216) 736-2100

### Commission for Social Justice

*An Italian antidefamation league.*
Order of the Sons of Italy in America
Anti-defamation Branch
219 East Street, NE
Washington, DC 20002
Tel.: (202) 547-2900

### Committee Against Anti-Asian Violence

*Works with the Asian community on issues of racially motivated violence and police brutality. Brings together Asians of different nationalities, ethnicities, and generations to address issues of racism, anti-immigration discrimination, and economic injustice; assists victims of violence.*
191 East Third Street
New York, NY 10009
Tel.: (212) 473-6485
Fax: (212) 473-5569
E-mail: CAAV@dti.net

### Community United Against Violence

*Nonprofit agency that addresses and prevents hate violence against lesbians, gay men, bisexuals, and transgendered persons. Also seeks to prevent same-sex domestic violence.*

973 Market Street
No. 500
San Francisco, CA 94103
Tel.: (415) 333-HELP (24-hour crisis line) or
  (415) 777-5500 (business)
Fax: (415) 777-5565

### Conflict Resolution Center International

*Multinational organization that supports mediators of interracial, tribal, religious, ethnic, or intercommunal disputes. Publishes* Conflict Resolution Notes *and an annual* Conflict Resolution Resource Directory.
204 Thirty-seventh Street
No. 203
Pittsburgh, PA 15201-1859
Tel.: (412) 687-6210
Fax: (412) 687-6232
E-mail: crcii@igc.apc.org
URL: http://www.conflictres.org

### Congress of Racial Equality

*Seeks to establish equality for all people regardless of race, creed, sex, age, disability, religion, or ethnic background. CORE works to identify and expose acts of discrimination.*
817 Broadway
3d Floor
New York, NY 10003
Tel.: (212) 598-4000
E-mail: corenyc@aol.com
URL: http://www.core-online.org

### Creative Response to Conflict, Inc.

*Conducts workshops in conflict resolution, peer mediation, bias awareness, and group problem solving with children, administrators, teachers, and community groups.*
Children's Response to Conflict
521 North Broadway
Nyack, NY 10960
Tel.: (914) 353-1796
Fax: (914) 358-4924
E-mail: ccrcnyack@aol.com

### Crime Stoppers International

*Develops local organizations to provide crime-solving assistance to law enforcement. Publishes* The Caller.
P.O. Box 30413
Albuquerque, NM 87190-0413
Tel.: (808) 322-9969 (Dr. Alan Pratt, president) or (800)
  245-0009 (Judge Richard Carter, general counsel)
URL: http://www.c-s-i.org

### Death Penalty Information Center

*Offers analysis and information on issues regarding capital punishment to the public and the media.*
1320 Eighteenth Street, NW
5th Floor
Washington, DC 20036
Tel.: (202) 293-6970

Fax: (202) 822-4784
E-mail: dpic@essential.org
URL: http://www.essential.org/dpic

**Domestic Violence Project of the American Academy of Facial, Plastic, and Reconstructive Surgery**
*Surgical group involved in helping victims of domestic violence. Offers complimentary consultation and surgery.*
Facial Plastic Surgery
American Academy of Facial Plastic and Reconstructive Surgery
310 South Henry Street
Alexandria, VA 22314
Tel.: (703) 299-09291 or (800) 332-FACE
http://www.aafprs.org/about/dvproject.html

**Drug Enforcement Administration**
*Enforces the controlled substance laws and requirements of the United States and investigates and prepares prosecution of those involved in growth, manufacture, or distribution of controlled substances.*
U.S. Department of Justice
Information Services Section (CPI)
700 Army-Navy Drive
Arlington, VA 22202
URL: http://www.usdoj.gov/dea

**Duluth Domestic Abuse Intervention Project**
National Training Project
*Publishes and distributes training materials (books, curricula, reports, manuals, and videotapes). Conducts training seminars for people who assist victims of domestic violence and those in the criminal justice system.*
202 East Superior Street
Duluth, MN 55802
Tel.: (218) 722-2781
Fax: (218) 722-0779

**Educational Fund to End Handgun Violence**
*Maintains a firearms litigation clearinghouse. Committed to public education on handgun violence.*
1000 Sixteenth Street, NW
Suite 603
Washington, DC 20036
Tel.: (202) 530-5888
Fax: (202) 530-0331
E-mail: EdFund@aol.com
URL: http://www.endhandgunviolence.org

**Educational Information and Resource Center**
*A public agency that specializes in education-related programs and services for parents, schools, communities, and nonprofit organizations throughout New Jersey.*
606 Delsea Drive
Sewell, NJ 08080
Tel.: (609) 582-7000
URL: http://www.eirc.org

**EMERGE: Counseling and Education to Stop Male Violence**
*Provides technical assistance and training for human services and law-enforcement professionals and distributes publications and information.*
2380 Massachusetts Avenue
Suite 101
Cambridge, MA 02141
Tel.: (617) 547-9870
Fax: (617) 547-0904

**End Violence Against the Next Generation, Inc.**
*Researches, collects, and disseminates information on and promotes alternatives to corporal punishment.*
977 Keeler
Berkeley, CA 94708

**Equality Now**
*Multinational organization that protects and defends the civil, political, economic, and social rights of girls and women worldwide. Concerned with rape, domestic violence, female infanticide, female genital mutilation, sexual harassment, pornography, gender discrimination, and political representation.*
P.O. Box 20646
Columbus Circle Station
New York, NY 10023
E-mail: info@equalitynow.org
URL: http://www.equalitynow.org

**Family Violence Prevention Fund**
*National nonprofit organization that focuses on domestic-violence education, prevention, and public-policy reform.*
383 Rhode Island Street
Suite 304
San Francisco, CA 94103-5133
Tel.: (415) 252-8900
Fax: (415) 252-8991
E-mail: fund@fvpf.org
URL: http://www.fvpf.org

**Family Violence Research Program**
*Studies all aspects of family violence and abuse including the physical and sexual abuse of children, corporal punishment of children, physical abuse of spouses, dating violence, elder abuse, intrafamily homicide, rape and marital rape, violence between siblings, pornography, and abduction.*
Family Research Laboratory
126 Horton Social Science Center
University of New Hampshire
Durham, NH 03824-3586
Tel.: (603) 862-1888
Fax: (603) 862-1122
E-mail: mas2@christa.unh.edu
URL: http://www.unh.edu/frl

**Federal Bureau of Investigation**
*Investigates violations of federal criminal law.*
Office of Public and Congressional Affairs

509

J. Edgar Hoover Building
935 Pennsylvania Avenue, NW
Washington, DC 20535-0001
Tel.: (202) 324-3000 (Consult local phone book for local field offices.)
URL: http://www.fbi.gov

**Federal Communications Commission**
*Regulates U.S. communications, including the v-chip, which blocks the viewing of violent, sexual, and indecent material broadcast on television.*
445 Twelfth Street, SW
Washington, DC 20554
Tel.: (202) 418-0190
E-mail: fccinfo@fcc.gov
URL: http://www.fcc.gov (FCC homepage) or http://www.fcc.gov/vchip (v-chip homepage)

**Federal Law Enforcement Training Center**
*Provides training for law-enforcement professionals. Also conducts law-enforcement research and development, and seeks to share technology.*
Glynco, GA 31524
Tel.: (912) 267-2100
URL: http://www.ustreas.gov/fletc

**Fortune Society**
*Sponsors educational programs and publishes about prisons and criminal justice.*
39 West Nineteenth Street
New York, NY 10011
Tel.: (212) 206-7070

**Gay and Lesbian Alliance Against Defamation**
*National organization to oppose media and public defamation of gay and lesbian individuals.*
150 West Twenty-sixth Street
Suite 503
New York, NY 10001
Tel.: (212) 807-1700
Fax: (212) 807-1806

**Guardian Angels**
*Unarmed volunteers organized to deter crime.*
982 East Eighty-ninth Street
Brooklyn, NY 11236
Tel.: (718) 649-2607 or (212) 967-0808 (Manhattan)
Fax: (718) 649-5705 or (212) 967-6030 (Manhattan)

**Henry F. Guggenheim Foundation**
*Sponsors scholarly research on problems of violence, aggression, and dominance; provides research grants and dissertations fellowships. Publishes the* Henry F. Guggenheim Review *and sponsors conferences.*
527 Madison Avenue
New York, NY 10022
Tel.: (212) 644-4907

Fax: (212) 644-5110
URL: http://www.hfg.org

**Holocaust Memorial Museum, United States**
*National institute for the documentation, study, and interpretation of Holocaust history. Serves as a memorial to the victims of the Holocaust.*
100 Raoul Wallenberg Place
Washington, DC 20024-2150
Tel.: (202) 488-0400
URL: http://www.ushmm.org

**Human Rights Advocates**
*International human rights lawyers' and professionals' organization. Provides education about human rights law.*
P.O. Box 5675
Berkeley, CA 94705
Tel.: (510) 540-8017
Fax: (510) 540-1947

**Human Rights Campaign Fund**
*Advances lesbian and gay civil rights by lobbying Congress and advancing candidates who support lesbian and gay civil rights and increased funding for women's health and AIDS research and treatment.*
919 Eighteenth Street, NW
Suite 800
Washington, DC 20006
Tel.: (202) 628-4160

**Human Rights Workshop**
*A biweekly interdisciplinary human rights workshop that considers conceptual questions relating to human rights and duties, clashes between competing legal and normative systems, and problems that arise in particular historical or contemporary situations as they affect human rights.*
Neal Enssle, Student Coordinator
E-mail: n-enssle@uchicago.edu
Tel.: (773) 752-1927
URL: http://www.uchicago.edu/cis/human-rights

**Incest Survivors Resource Network International**
*An educational resource network for survivors and professionals who work with survivors. Operates an international help line.*
P.O. Box 7375
Las Cruces, NM 88006-7375
E-mail: ISRNI@zianet.com
URL: http://www.zianet.com/ISRNI

**Indian Health Service**
*Agency within the U.S. Department of Health and Human Services responsible for providing federal health services to American Indians and Alaska Natives.*
Communications Staff
Room 6-35

Parklawn Building
5600 Fishers Lane
Rockville, MD 20857
Tel.: (301) 443-3593
Fax: (301) 443-0507
URL: http://www.ihs.gov

## Institute for Defense Analyses
*Nonprofit corporation that promotes national security and public interests by assisting the Office of Defense. Does not work directly for military departments, private industry, or foreign governments.*
1801 North Beauregard Street
Alexandria, VA 22311
Tel.: (703) 845-2300
Fax: (703) 845-2588
URL: http://www.ida.org

## Institute for Defense and Disarmament Studies
*Seeks to demilitarize world affairs, end reliance on nuclear weapons, and bring about world peace.*
675 Massachusetts Avenue
Cambridge, MA 02139
Tel.: (617) 354-4337
Fax: (617) 354-1450

## Institute for Mediation and Conflict Resolution
*Promotes voluntary community conflict resolution.*
384 East 149th Street
Room 330
Bronx, NY 10455
Tel.: (718) 585-1190
Fax: (718) 585-1962
E-mail: imcrmed@nyct.net

## Institute for Peace and Justice
*Committed to working for peace by seeking justice. Attempts to find alternatives to violent conflict resolution.*
4144 Lindell Boulevard
Suite 408
St. Louis, MO 63108
Tel.: (314) 553-4445
Fax: (314) 553-1017
E-mail: ppjn@aol.com
URL: http://members.aol.com/ppjn

## Institute for the Study of Genocide
*Furthers discussion and scholarship on the causes and prevention of genocide with reference to the role of law and justice agencies. Publishes a semiannual newsletter and runs conferences.*
Professor Orlanda Brugnola
John Jay College of Criminal Justice
Tenth Avenue Building
Room 325
New York, NY 10019
Tel.: (212) 237-8334

URL: http://www.jjay.cuny.edu/academic/center_res/ins_genocide.html

## Institute for Victims of Trauma
*Organization for professionals specializing in crisis intervention, the treatment of post-traumatic stress, and the study of terrorism. Assists victims of political violence, accidents, and man-made and natural disasters; also provides help for friends and families of direct victims.*
6801 Market Square Drive
McLean, VA 22101
Tel.: (703) 847-8456
Fax: (703) 847-0470
E-mail: ivt@microneil.com
URL: http://www.microneil.com/ivt

## Institute of Medicine
*Provides information and advice concerning health and science policy to government, the corporate sector, the professions, and the public.*
National Academy of Sciences
2101 Constitution Avenue, NW
Washington, DC 20418
Tel.: (202) 334-2000
E-mail: wwwfdk@nas.edu
URL: http://www2.nas.edu/iom

## International Association for the Study of Organized Crime
*Encourages and supports research on organized crime. Publishes* Criminal Organizations *newsletter.*
Office of International Criminal Justice
University of Illinois, Chicago
1033 West Van Buren Street
MC 777
Chicago, IL 60607-2919

## International Association of Chiefs of Police
*Recognizes excellence in law enforcement through award programs and provides educational opportunities to enhance work, find solutions, and make informed decisions. Offers a myriad of information to professional law enforcers; exchanges information throughout the world. Publishes* Police Chief *magazine.*
515 North Washington Street
Alexandria, VA 22314
Tel.: (703) 836-6767 or (800) THE-IACP
Fax: (703) 836-4543
URL: http://www.theiacp.org

## International Association of Official Human Rights Agencies
*Multinational organization of government human rights agencies with enforcement powers to foster relations and enhance human rights procedures.*
444 North Capitol Street
Suite 408
Washington, DC 20001

Tel.: (202) 624-5410
Fax: (202) 624-8185

**International Centre for Comparative Criminology**
*Promotes exchanges between North American and European criminologists.*
University of Montreal
CP 6128, Succursale Centre-ville
Montreal PQ H3C 3J7
Canada
Tel. (514) 343-7065
URL: http://www.cicc.umontreal.ca

**International Centre for the Prevention of Crime**
*Assists cities and countries to reduce delinquency and violence around the world.*
507 Place d'Armes
Bureau 2100
Montreal APH2Y 2W8
Canada
Tel.: (514) 288-6731
Fax: (514) 288-8763
E-mail: icpc@crime-prevention-intl.org
URL: http://www.crime-prevention-intl.org

**International Communication Association**
*The major international organization for communication research. Publishes* Human Communications, Communication Theory, *and* Journal of Communications.
P.O. Box 9589
Austin, TX 78766
Tel.: (512) 454-8299
Fax: (512) 451-6270
E-mail: icahdq@uts.cc.utexas.edu
URL: http://www.icahdq.org

**International Criminal Police Organization**
*Seeks to involve all nations in voluntary exchange of information about crimes and criminals. Examines the international behavior of criminals including crimes planned in one country and committed in another, similar offenses committed in more than one country, escapes across borders, transfer of illicit gains, and concealing of objects used to commit crimes in another country. Some offenses, such as currency counterfeiting, trafficking in humans, and drug trafficking, are covered by international conventions.*
INTERPOL
200 Quai Charles de Gaulle
69006 Lyons
France
Tel.: (33) 4 72 44 70 00
Fax: (33) 4 72 44 71 63

**International Gay and Lesbian Human Rights Commission**
*Monitors, documents, exposes, and responds to human rights violations against lesbians, gay men, bisexuals, and people with AIDS/HIV.*

1360 Mission Street
Suite 200
San Francisco, CA 94103
Tel.: (415) 255-8680
Fax: (415) 255-8662
URL: http://www.iglhrc.org

**International League for Human Rights**
*Supports adherence to international human rights regulations.*
432 Park Avenue South
Suite 1103
New York, NY 10016
Tel.: (212) 684-1221
Fax: (212) 684-1696
URL: http://www.ilhr.org

**International Society for Research on Aggression**
*International and interdisciplinary society of scholars and scientists interested in the scientific study of aggression and violence. Publishes* Aggressive Behavior.
Gordon Russell
Executive Secretary
1 Mckenzie Crescent
Sidney, BC V8L 5Y7
Canada
E-mail: donnerst@sscf.ucsb.edu (Ed Donnerstein, president-elect)
URL: http://www.israsociety.com

**International Women's Rights Action Watch**
*Calls attention to the violation of women's rights. In accordance with the Convention on the Elimination of All Forms of Discrimination.*
Hubert Humphrey Institute of Public Affairs
University of Minnesota
301 Nineteenth Avenue South
Minneapolis, MN 55455
Tel.: (612) 625-5093
Fax: (612) 624-0068
E-mail: iwraw@hhh.umn.edu

**Jewish Defense League**
*Controversial activist group that provides education, helps build pride in Jewish tradition, aids Jews everywhere, and seeks to change the Jewish image by all means, "including strength and violence."*
P.O. Box 480370
Los Angeles, CA 90048
Tel.: (818) 980-8535
Fax: (781) 634-0338
E-mail: jdljdl@aol.com
URL: http://www.jdl.org

**Jewish Defense Organization**
*"Training Jews to defend themselves against Nazi terror."*
P.O. Box 159
New York, NY 10150

Tel.: (212) 252-3383
E-mail: JudeaM@jdo.org
URL: http://www.jdo.org

**John M. Olin Foundation, Inc.**
*Sponsors projects that strengthen economic, political, and cultural institutions and promotes study of the connections between economic and political freedoms.*
330 Madison Avenue
22d Floor
New York, NY 10017
Tel.: (212) 661-2670
Fax: (212) 661-5917
URL: http://www.jmof.org

**Johns Hopkins Center for Gun Policy and Research**
*Dedicated to preventing gun-related deaths and injuries.*
School of Public Health
624 North Broadway
Baltimore, MD 21205
Tel.: (410) 955-3995
Fax: (410) 614-9055
E-mail: jhcgpr@jhsph.edu
URL: http://www.jhsph.edu/gunpolicy

**Kids Count**
*National state-by-state effort to track the status of children in the United States. Provides for the educational, social, economic, and physical well-being of children.*
Annie East Casey Foundation
701 Street Paul's Street
Baltimore, MD 21202
Tel.: (410) 547-6600
Fax: (410) 547-6624
E-mail: webmail@aecf.org
URL: http://www.kidscount.org

**Klanwatch**
*Established by the Southern Poverty Law Center to track Ku Klux Klan activity; also covers other hate groups. (See the Southern Poverty Law Center, below.)*
Intelligence Center
Southern Poverty Law Center
400 Washington Avenue
Montgomery, AL 36104
URL: http://www.splcenter.org/intelligenceproject/ip-index.html

**LAMBDA GLBT Community Services**
*A nonprofit gay and lesbian agency that provides services to help gay teens in trouble, prevent homophobic attacks, and assist survivors of hate crimes and same-gender violence.*
Gay and Lesbian Anti-Violence Project
P.O. Box 31321
El Paso, TX 79931-0321
Tel.: (915) 562-GAYS (administration), (800) 616-HATE (National GLBT Hate Crimes Hotline)

E-mail: AVP@lambda.org
URL: http://www.lambda.org

**Law and Society Association**
*International, interdisciplinary group of scholars who study the intersection of law and politics, society, economics, and culture. Publishes* Law and Society Review *as well as a newsletter.*
University of Massachusetts
P.O. Box 33615
Amherst, MA 01003-3615
Tel.: (413) 545-4617
Fax: (413) 545-1640
E-mail: lsa@legal.umass.edu
URL: http://www.lawandsociety.org

**MacArthur Foundation**
*Private grant-making institution dedicated to helping groups and individuals foster lasting improvement in the human condition. Funds research, policy development, dissemination of information, education, and training programs.*
Office of Grants Management
140 South Dearborn Street
Chicago, IL 60603
Tel.: (312) 726-8000 or (312) 920-6285 (TDD)
Fax: (312) 920-6258
URL: http://www.macfdn.org

**Martin Luther King, Jr., Center for Nonviolent Social Change**
*Dedicated to carrying forward the legacy and work of Martin Luther King, Jr., through research, education, and training in the principles, philosophy, and methods of nonviolence.*
The King Center
449 Auburn Avenue, NE
Atlanta, GA 30312
Tel.: (404) 524-1956
Fax: (404) 526-8969
E-mail: MLKctr@aol.com

**Meiklejohn Civil Liberties Institute**
*Advocates for human rights and peace law through U.S. and UN laws and processes. Publishes and distributes anthologies on human rights and peace law and a directory of human rights organizations and periodicals.*
P.O. Box 673
Berkeley, CA 94701-0673
Tel.: (510) 848-0599
Fax: (510) 848-6008
E-mail: mcli@igc.org
URL: http://www.sfsu.edu/~mclicfc

**Men Overcoming Violence**
*Committed to ending men's violence. Provides counseling to batterers and prevention groups for gay men; also runs a youth program.*
1385 Mission Street
Suite 300

San Francisco, CA 94103
Tel.: (415) 626-6683
Fax: (415) 626-6704
E-mail: move@slip.net
URL: http://www.menovercomingviolence.org

**Mexican American Legal Defense
and Educational Fund**
*National nonprofit organization protects and promotes the
civil rights of the more than twenty-nine million Latinos
living in the United States.*
National Headquarters
Los Angeles Regional Office
634 South Spring Street
11th Floor
Los Angeles, CA 90014
Tel.: (213) 629-2512
Fax: (213) 629-0266
URL: http://www.maldef.org

**Milton S. Eisenhower Foundation**
*Invests in and supports economic development of urban areas
to reduce crime, welfare dependency, drug abuse, and school
dropout rate.*
1660 L Street, NW
Suite 200
Washington, DC 20036
Tel.: (202) 429-0440
Fax: (202) 452-0169

**M. K. Gandhi Institute for Nonviolence**
*Seeks to prevent violence and resolve conflicts through
research, education, and programming. Promotes the
principles of nonviolence.*
Christian Brothers University
650 East Parkway South
Memphis, TN 38104
Tel.: (901) 452-2824
Fax: (901) 452-2775
E-mail: questions@gandhiinstitute.org
URL: http://www.gandhiinstitute.org

**Mothers Against Drunk Driving**
*Aims to stop drunk driving and supports victims; seeks to
prevent underage drinking.*
511 East John Carpenter Freeway 700
Irving, TX 75062
Tel.: (214) 744-6233 or (800) GET-MADD
E-mail: info@madd.org
URL: http://www.madd.org or http://www.madd.org/
  chapters/default.shtml (local chapter directory)

**National Alliance for Safe Schools**
*Nonprofit research, training, and technical assistance
organization. Dedicated to promotion of an orderly
educational environment.*

P.O. Box 1068
College Park, MD 20741
Tel.: (301) 935-6063
Fax: (301) 935-6069
E-mail: nass@erols.com
URL: http://www.safeschools.org

**National Alliance of Sexual Assault Coalitions**
*A national organization that focuses on public policy and
public education to end sexual violence. Represents public-
policy interests of sexual-assault victims on the federal level.*
Gail Burns Smith
c/o Connecticut Sexual Assault Crisis Services, Inc.
110 Connecticut Boulevard
East Hartford, CT 06108
Tel.: (860) 282-9881
E-mail: coalition@connsacs.org
URL: http://www.connsacs.org/alliance.htm

**National Association for the Advancement
of Colored People**
*Promotes political, educational, social, and economic equality
of minority group citizens in the United States. Publishes
Crisis.*
Washington Bureau
1025 Vermont Avenue, NW
Suite 1120
Washington, DC 20005
Tel.: (202) 638-2269 or (410) 358-8900 (national office)
URL: http://www.naacp.org

**National Association of Child Advocates**
*Committed to strengthening state and local child-advocacy
organizations.*
1522 K Street, NW
Suite 600
Washington, DC 20005-1202
Tel.: (202) 289-0777
Fax: (202) 289-0776
E-mail: naca@childadvocacy.org
URL: http://www.childadvocacy.org

**National Association for Children of Alcoholics**
*Provides education for the children of alcoholics, and their
doctors, nurses, teachers, parents, clergy, and clinicians.*
11426 Rockville Pike
Suite 100
Rockville, MD 20852
Tel.: (888) 554-COAS
Fax: (301) 468-0987
E-mail: nacoa@erols.com
URL: http://www.health.org/nacoa

**National Association of Counsel for Children**
*Professional membership association that works to improve
the legal protection and representation of children by training
and educating child advocates and by effecting policy and
legal systems improvement.*

1825 Marion Street
Suite 340
Denver, CO 80218
Tel.: (888) 828-NACC or (303) 864-5320
Fax: (303) 864-5351
E-mail: advocate@NACCchildlaw.org
URL: http://NACCchildlaw.org

### National Association of Criminal Defense Lawyers

*Seeks to ensure justice and due process for persons accused of crimes of misconduct. Committed to preserving fairness within the American criminal justice system.*
1025 Connecticut Avenue, NW
Suite 901
Washington, DC 20036
Tel.: (202) 872-8600
Fax: (202) 872-8690
E-mail: assist@nacdl.com
URL: http://www.criminaljustice.org

### National Association of Juvenile Correctional Agencies

*Organization for heads of juvenile correctional agencies and others responsible for juvenile delinquency programs.*
3401 West End Avenue
Suite 400
Nashville, TN 37203
Tel.: (615) 250-0000
Fax: (615) 896-5968

### National Center for Assault Prevention

*Multinational organization that seeks to prevent interpersonal violence against vulnerable populations, including children and adolescents, older people, and mentally retarded or developmentally disabled adults and children.*
606 Delsea Drive
Sewell, NJ 08080
Tel.: (609) 582-7000 or (800) 258-3189
Fax: (609) 582-3588

### National Center for Health Statistics

*The primary federal organization responsible for collecting, analyzing, and disseminating health statistics. Provides relevant, timely, and statistical information on accidental injury, firearm mortality, and homicide.*
U.S. Department of Health and Human Services
Centers for Disease Control and Prevention
6525 Belcrest Road
Hyattsville, MD 20782-2003
Tel.: (301) 436-8500
E-mail: nchsquery@cdc.gov
URL: http://www.cdc.gov/nchswww

### National Center for Injury Prevention and Control

*Program that seeks to reduce injury, disability, and death associated with home and recreational injuries.*
Mailstop K65
4770 Buford Highway NE
Atlanta, GA 30341-3724

Tel.: (770) 488-1506
Fax: (770) 488-1667
E-mail: ohcinfo@cdc.gov
URL: http://www.cdc.gov/ncipc

### National Center for Missing and Exploited Children

*Serves as the nation's resource center for child protection and spearheads national efforts to locate and recover missing children and to raise public awareness about ways to prevent child abduction, molestation, and sexual exploitation.*
Charles B. Wang International Children's Building
699 Prince Street
Alexandria, VA 22314-3175
Tel.: (703) 274-3900 or (800) THE-LOST
  / 800-843-5678 (24-hour hotline)
Fax: (703) 274-2220
URL: http://www.missingkids.com

### National Center for Prosecution of Child Abuse

*To help educate prosecutors on social violence and related medical and scientific advances.*
American Prosecutors Research Institute
99 Canal Center Plaza
Suite 510
Alexandria, VA 22314
Tel.: (703) 739-0321
Fax: (703) 549-6259
URL: http://www.Ndaa-apri.org

### National Center for the Study of Corporal Punishment and Alternatives

*Studies the psychological and educational aspects of school and home discipline and their relationship to aggression and violence.*
Temple University
253 Ritter Annex
Philadelphia, PA 19122
Tel.: (215) 204-6091
Fax: (215) 204-6013

### National Center for Victims of Crime

*A resource and advocacy center for victims of crime. Delivers training and technical assistance to victim service providers and allied professionals concerned with the impact of crime and the ways in which victims can regain control of their lives.*
2111 Wilson Boulevard
Suite 300
Arlington, VA 22201
Tel.: (703) 276-2880 or (800) FYI-CALL
Fax: (703) 276-2889
URL: http://www.ncvc.org

### National Center for Youth Law

*Uses the law to improve the lives of poor children and to protect them from the harms of poverty. Involved in issues of child support, child welfare, adolescent housing, and public benefits.*

114 Sansome Street
Suite 900
San Francisco, CA 94104-3820
Tel.: (415) 543-3307
E-mail: info@youthlaw.org
URL: http://www.youthlaw.org

### National Center on Institutions and Alternatives
*Provides training, technical assistance, research, and direct services to criminal justice, social services, and mental health organizations. Explores alternative sentences and treatments for offenders.*
3125 Mt. Vernon Avenue
Alexandria, VA 22305
Tel.: (703) 684-0373
Fax: (703) 684-6073
E-mail: info@ncianet.org
URL: http://www.ncianet.org/ncia

### National Children's Coalition
*Central resource and reference center for child abuse, teen suicide, and violence against and by children and teens.*
267 Lester Avenue
Suite 104
Oakland, CA 94606
Tel.: (500) 675-KIDS or (510) 286-7916
E-mail: YouthKids@aol.com

### National Clearinghouse for Alcohol and Drug Information
*World's largest resource for information on substance abuse.*
Center for Substance Abuse
Prevention of Substance Abuse and Mental Health
Services Administration
U.S. Department of Health and Human Services.
P.O. Box 2345
Rockville, MD 20847-2345
Tel.: (800) 729-6686 or (800) 487-4889 (TDD)
Fax: (301) 468-6433
URL: http://www.health.org/about.htm

### National Clearinghouse for the Defense of Battered Women
*Provides resources and information to the defense teams of battered women charged with crimes.*
125 South Ninth Street
Suite 302
Philadelphia, PA 19107
Tel.: (215) 351-0010
Fax: (215) 351-0779

### National Clearinghouse on Child Abuse and Neglect
*Provides information on prevention, identification, and treatment of child abuse and neglect and related child welfare issues.*
Department of Health and Human Services
330 C Street, SW
Washington, DC 20447

Tel.: (703) 385-7565
Fax: (703) 385-3206
E-mail: Nccanch@calib.com
URL: http://www.calib.com/nccanch

### National Clearinghouse on Marital and Date Rape/ Women's History Library
*Provides education on rape prevention through speakers, publications, and consultations by phone or in person.*
2325 Oak Street
Berkeley, CA 94708
Tel.: (510) 524-1582
E-mail: ncmdr@aol.com
URL: http://members.aol.com/ncmdr/index

### National Coalition Against Domestic Violence
*Serves as an information and referral center for victims and survivors of abuse. Builds coalitions, provides training and technical assistance, contributes to public education and awareness and to public-policy development and monitoring.*
National Office
P.O. Box 18749
Denver, CO 80218-0749
Tel.: (303) 839-1852 or (800) 799-7233 (National Domestic
  Violence hotline)
Fax: (303) 831-9251
URL: http://www.ncadv.org

### National Coalition Against Sexual Assault
*A feminist organization that provides leadership to end sexual violence and all forms of oppression through advocacy, education, and public policy.*
125 North Enola Drive
Enola, PA 17025
Tel.: (717) 728-9764
Fax: (717) 728-9781
E-mail: ncasa@redrose.net
URL: http://www.ncasa.org

### National Coalition on Television Violence
*Nonprofit organization that aims to reduce the amount of gratuitous violence on television.*
5132 Newport Avenue
Bethesda, MD 20816
Tel.: (301) 986-0362
E-mail: kmcr@mediaone.net
URL: http://www.nctvv.org

### National Coalition to Abolish Corporal Punishment in Schools
*Coalition of state and national organizations to abolish corporal punishment as a form of discipline in schools.*
Center for Effective Discipline
155 West Main Street
No. 1603
Columbus, OH 43215
Tel.: (614) 221-8829
Fax: (614) 221-2110

E-mail: nblock@infinet.com
URL: http://www.stophitting.com

## National Committee for the Prevention of Child Abuse
*Dedicated to improving health and well-being of children. Sponsors programs, research, and media campaigns at state and local level to provide leadership to child abuse prevention organizations nationwide.*
200 South Michigan Avenue
17th Floor
Chicago, IL 60604-4357
Tel.: (312) 663-3520
Fax: (312) 939-8962
URL: www.childabuse.org

## National Committee for the Prevention of Elder Abuse
*Seeks to promote an understanding of the problem of elder abuse and to develop services to protect the elderly and reduce abuse and neglect.*
Institute on Aging
119 Belmont Street
Worcester, MA 01605
Tel.: (508) 793-6166

## National Communication Association
*The largest national organization for promoting communication scholarship and education.*
5105 Backlick Road
Building E
Annandale, VA 22003
Tel.: (703) 750-0533
Fax: (703) 914-9471
URL: http://www.natcom.org

## National Conference on Peacemaking and Conflict Resolution
*Nonmembership organization that biennially hosts the largest conference in the field of conflict resolution.*
Institute for Conflict Analysis
4400 University Drive
Fairfax, VA 22030-4444
E-mail: ncper@gmu.edu
URL: http://www.gmu.edu/departments/ncpcr

## National Consortium on Violence Research
*A multidisciplinary research and training center specializing in violence research with the aim of advancing basic scientific knowledge about the causes of or contributing factors to interpersonal violence.*
H. John Heinz III
School of Public Policy and Management
Carnegie Mellon University
5000 Forbes Avenue
Pittsburgh, PA 15213
Tel.: (412) 268-8269
Fax: (412) 268-7036
URL: http://www.ncovr.heinz.cmu.edu

## National Council on Child Abuse and Family Violence
*Provides information and referrals on spouse, child, and elder abuse through a toll-free hotline. Offers assistance and information for community-based programs and publishes brochures, periodicals, and a newsletter.*
1155 Connecticut Avenue, NW
Suite 400
Washington DC 20036
Tel.: (202) 429-6695 or (800) 222-2000
E-mail: nccafv@aol.com

## National Council on Crime and Delinquency
*Conducts research and initiates programs and policies to reduce crime and delinquency. Seeks to influence public policies that affect the nature of crime and delinquency and the future of the justice system. Encourages citizen involvement in effective, humane, fair, and economically sound solutions to criminal justice problems.*
685 Market Street
No. 620
San Francisco, CA 94105
Tel.: (415) 896-6223
Fax: (415) 896-5109
URL: http://nccd-crc.org

## National Crime Prevention Council
*Private nonprofit organization that seeks to prevent crime through community involvement.*
1700 K Street, NW
2d Floor
Washington, DC 20006-3817
Tel.: (202) 466-6272
Fax: (202) 296-1356
URL: http://www.ncpc.org

## National Crime Prevention Institute
*Provides information, technical assistance, and training to police, criminal justice planners, security personnel, and community representatives in crime prevention.*
Justice Administration
University of Louisville
Louisville, KY 40292
Tel.: (502) 852-6987
Fax: (502) 852-6990
E-mail: jcfryrol@gwise.louisville.edu
URL: http://www.louisville.edu/a-s/ja/prog.html

## National Data Archive on Child Abuse and Neglect
*Facilitates research relevant to child maltreatment field. Operates listserves and sponsors training institutes and workshops.*
Family Life Development Center
College of Human Ecology
Cornell University
MUR Hall
Ithaca, NY 148853
Tel.: (607) 255-7794

E-mail: datacan@cornell.edu
URL: http://www.ndacan.cornell.edu

## National Domestic Violence Hotline
*Answers about ten thousand calls per month from those experiencing domestic violence, and their family and friends. A project of the Texas Council on Family Violence in conjunction with the U.S. Department of Health and Human Services.*
P.O. Box 161810
Austin, TX 78731-3074
Tel. (800) 799-SAFE or (800) 787-3224 (TDD)

## National Gay and Lesbian Task Force
*Lobbies Congress, organizes grassroots action for gay freedom and full civil rights. Seeks to eliminate prejudice based on sexual orientation.*
1700 Kalorama Road, NW
Washington, DC 20009
Tel.: (202) 332-6483
Fax: (202) 332-0207
URL: http://www.ngltf.org

## National Institute for Occupational Safety and Health
*The only federal institute responsible for conducting research and making recommendations for the prevention of work-related illnesses and injuries. Investigates hazardous working conditions; evaluates hazards in the workplace; creates and disseminates methods for preventing disease, injury, and disability; researches and provides recommendations for worker protection; provides education and training for occupational-safety-and-health workers.*
Hubert H. Humphrey Building
200 Independence Avenue, SW
Room 715H
Washington, DC 20202
Tel.: (800) 35-NIOSH (technical inquiries)
URL: http://www.cdc.gov/niosh

## National Institute of Justice
*The research and development branch of the Department of Justice.*
Office of Justice Programs
810 Seventh Street, NW
Washington, DC 20531
Tel.: (202) 616-2318
Fax: (202) 307-6394
URL: http://www.ojp.usdoj.gov/nij

## National Institute of Mental Health
*Conducts and supports research nationwide on mental illness.*
NIMH Public Inquiries
6001 Executive Boulevard
Room 8184 MSC 9663
Bethesda, MD 20892-9663
Tel.: (301) 443-4513
Fax: (301) 443-4279

E-mail: nimhinfo@nih.gov
URL: http://www.nimh.nih.gov

## National Institute on Drug Abuse
*Established in 1974, NIDA supports over 85 percent of the world's research on health aspects of drug abuse and addiction. Designs and develops new medicines for addiction; studies the impact of drug exposure on children; seeks effective drug-abuse prevention and treatment; does research and disseminates this knowledge to policy makers and practitioners.*
National Institute of Health
6001 Executive Building
Bethesda, MD 20892-9561
Tel.: (301) 443-6245
E-mail: information@lists.nida.nih.gov.
URL: http://www.nida.nih.gov

## National Institutes of Health
*Federal biomedical research institute that conducts and supports research throughout the United States and abroad; trains research investigators; and generates new knowledge to help prevent, detect, diagnose, and treat disease and disability.*
NIH Office of Communications and Public Liaison
Bethesda, MD 20892
Fax: (301) 402-4541
E-mail: NIHinfo@od.nih.gov
URL: http://www.nih.gov

## National Organization for Victim Assistance
*Private, nonprofit organization committed to the recognition and implementation of victim rights through public-policy work, victim services, and professional development for people who work with crime victims. Sponsors a hotline for victims of crime.*
1757 Park Road, NW
Washington, DC 20010
Tel.: (202) 232-6682 or (800) TRY-NOVA (hotline)
Fax: (202) 462-2255
E-mail: nova@try-nova.org
URL: http://www.try-nova.org

## National Organization for Women
*Seeks political, social, legal, and economic equality between men and women through grassroots organizing, lobbying, litigation, protests, and demonstrations.*
1000 Sixteenth Street, NW
Suite 700
Washington, DC 20036
Tel.: (202) 331-0066
Fax: (202) 785-8576
E-mail: now@now.org
URL: http: //www.now.org

## National Organization on Male Sexual Victimization
*Committed to the prevention, treatment, and elimination of the sexual victimization of boys and men through research, education, advocacy, and activism.*

P.O. Box 20782
West Palm Beach, FL 33416
Tel.: (800) 738-4181
E-mail: mail@malesurvivor.com
URL: http://www.malesurvivor.com

**National Resource Center on Domestic Violence**
*Furnishes information and resources to advocates, policy makers, and the media.*
6400 Flank Drive
Suite 1300
Harrisburg, PA 17112
Tel.: (800) 537-2238
Fax: (717) 545-9456

**National Rifle Association**
*Dedicated to lawful, effective, responsible, and safe use of firearms. Maintains institute for legal action.*
11250 Waples Mill Road
Fairfax, VA 22030
Tel.: (800) NRA-3888
URL: http://www.nra.org

**National Urban League**
*Assists African Americans in achieving social and economic equality; provides advocacy, program services, and research. Branches in major cities.*
120 Wall Street
New York, NY 10005
Tel.: (212) 558-5300
Fax: (212) 344-5332
E-mail: info@nul.org
URL: http://www.nul.org

**Nonviolence International**
*Interested in bringing about social and political change through nonviolent means. Serves as an educational and resource center for active nonviolence. Publishes* Frontline.
P.O. Box 39127
Friendship Station, NW
Washington, DC 20016
Tel.: (202) 244-0951
Fax: (202) 244-6396
E-mail: nonviolence@igc.apc.org
URL: http://www.igc.org/nonviolence

**North American Association of Wardens and Superintendents**
*National organization for the heads of male and female detention, penal, and correctional institutes. Focuses on the problems and programs of correctional institutes; promotes the care, custody, and treatment of offenders and the management of institutions.*
Pat Keohane, President
714 Meramac Lane
Nixa, MO 65714
Tel.: (417) 725-8328 (home) or (417) 862-7543 (work)
Fax: (417) 837-1717

**Office for Civil Rights**
*Ensures equal access to education by enforcing civil rights. Publishes guidance on issues related to Title VI, Title IX, and affirmative action, including the protection of children from sexual harassment and hate crimes.*
U.S. Department of Education
Customer Service Team
Mary East Switzer Building
330 C Street, SW
Washington, DC 20202
Tel.: (800) 421-3481, (202) 205-5166, or (202) 205-5166
Fax: (202) 205-9862
E-mail: OCR@ED.gov
URL: http://www.ed.gov/offices/OCR

**Office of Juvenile Justice and Delinquency Prevention**
*Furnishes facts, figures, grant funding, and conference publications regarding juvenile justice, delinquency prevention, violence, and victimization.*
U.S. Department of Justice
Office of Justice Programs
810 Seventh Street, NW
Washington, DC 20531
Tel.: (202) 307-0751
Fax: (202) 307-2093
URL: http://www.ojjdp.ncjrs.org

**Parents Anonymous**
*A child-abuse-prevention organization dedicated to strengthening families through strategies that promote mutual support and parent leadership.*
675 West Foothill Boulevard
Suite 220
Claremont, CA 91711-3416
Tel.: (909) 621-6184
Fax: (909) 625-6304
URL: http://www.parentsanonymous-natl.org

**Parents of Murdered Children**
*Dedicated to murder prevention and survivor support.*
100 East Eighth Street, B-41
Cincinnati, OH 45202
Tel.: (888) 818-POMC
Fax: (513) 345-4489
E-mail: NatlPOMC@aol.com
URL: http://www.pomc.org

**Parents and Teachers Against Violence in Education**
*Opposes corporal punishment and other types of violent punitive techniques in schools. Seeks a violence-free environment for children.*
P.O. Box 1033
Alamo, CA 94507-7033
Tel.: (925) 831-1661
Fax: (925) 838-8914
E-mail: ptave@silcon.com

**Partnership Against Domestic Violence**
*Offers help to battered women.*
P.O. Box 54383
Atlanta, GA 30308
Tel.: (404) 873-1766

**Peace Links**
*Educates on peace issues and assists in developing grass roots organizing to develop alternatives to violence and ending the threat of nuclear weapons.*
666 Eleventh Street, NW
Suite 200
Washington, DC 20001
Tel.: (202) 783-7030
Fax: (202) 783-7040
E-mail: peacelinks@igc.apc.org

**People for the American Way**
*Committed to the American values of pluralism, diversity, freedom of expression, and freedom of religion. Aims to counter bigotry and intolerance. Publishes issue papers, reports, and books.*
2000 M Street, NW
Suite 400
Washington DC 20036
Tel.: (202) 467-4999
URL: http://www.pfaw.org

**Physicians for a Violence-free Society**
*National nonprofit organization of physicians, other members of the healthcare community, and concerned citizens committed to reducing violence in the United States. Publishes* Action Notes, *a bimonthly educational newsletter.*
San Francisco General Hospital
1001 Potrero Building 1
Room 300
San Francisco, CA 94110
Tel.: (415) 821-8209
Fax: (415) 282-2563
E-mail: pvs@pvs.org
URL: http://www.pvs.org

**Physicians for Human Rights**
*An organization of health professionals, scientists, and concerned citizens that uses knowledge and skills of the medical and forensic sciences to investigate and prevent violations of international human rights and humanitarian law.*
100 Boylston Street
Suite 702
Boston, MA 02116
Tel.: (617) 695-0041
Fax (617) 695-0307
URL: http://www.phrusa.org

**Resource Center on Domestic Violence, Child Custody, and Protection**
*Operated by the National Council of Juvenile and Family Court Judges. Provides general information, consultation, and training related to protection and custody issues in domestic-violence cases.*
National Council of Juvenile and Family Court Judges
Family Violence Department
P.O. Box 8970
Reno, NV 89507
Tel.: (800) 527-3223 or (775) 784-6012

**SEASON for Nonviolence**
*Annual event to create awareness of the principles of nonviolence.*
1565 Maple Avenue
Suite 204-205
Evanston, IL 60201
Tel.: (847) 866-9525
Fax: (847) 866-9526
E-mail: seasonnv@aol.com
URL: http://www.gandhiking.com

**Second Amendment Foundation**
*Promotes right to bear arms.*
12500 NE Tenth Place
Bellevue, WA 98805
Tel.: (800) 486-6963
Fax: (425) 451-3959
URL: http://www.saf.org

**Sentencing Project**
*Explores alternative sentencing options and examines social effects of imprisonment.*
918 F Street, NW
Suite 501
Washington, DC 20004
Tel.: (202) 628-0871
Fax: (202) 628-1091
E-mail: staff@sentencingproject.com
URL: http://www.sentencingproject.org

**Sex Addicts Anonymous**
*Support group helps members recover from sex addiction or dependency.*
International Service Organization of Sex Addicts Anonymous
P.O. Box 70949
Houston, TX 77270
Tel.: (713) 869-4902 or (800) 477-8191
E-mail: info@saa-recovery.org
URL: http://www.sexaa.org

**Simon Wiesenthal Center**
*International center for information on the Holocaust, the defense of human rights, and the Jewish people. Fights bigotry and anti-Semitism. Maintains a library, archives on the Holocaust, twentieth-century genocides, anti-Semitism, racism, and related issues. Also maintains the Museum of Tolerance.*
9750 West Pico Boulevard
Los Angeles, CA 90035

Tel.: (310) 553-9036
URL: http://www.wiesenthal.com

**Southern Poverty Law Center**
*Nonprofit organization that combats hate, intolerance, and discrimination through education and litigation. The Intelligence Project monitors hate and extremist activity throughout the United States and oversees, with the investigative and publishing activities of Klanwatch and the Militia Task Force.*
Requests for assistance:
Request
Legal Department
SPLC
P.O. Box 2087
Montgomery, AL 36104
Other requests:
400 Washington Avenue
Montgomery, AL 36104
URL: http://www.splcenter.org

**Stop Prisoner Rape, Inc.**
*Committed to preventing the rape, sexual slavery, forced prostitution, and sexual harassment of male and female prisoners, to bringing these matters to the public's attention, and to helping survivors of jailhouse rape.*
P.O. Box 632
Fort Bragg, CA 55473
Tel.: (707) 964-0820
E-mail: roanne@mcn.org
URL: http://www.spr.org

**Survivors of Incest Anonymous**
*International network of self-help meetings, offering a twelve-step recovery program. Publishes self-help materials.*
P.O. Box 21817
Baltimore, MD 21222-6817
Tel.: (410) 282-3400

**Trauma Foundation**
*Seeks to reduce injuries and deaths by focusing on policy development and advocacy. Sponsors programs to prevent violence.*
San Francisco General Hospital
Building 1, Room 300
San Francisco, CA 94110
E-mail: tf@tf.org
URL: http://www.traumafdn.org

**U.S. Department of Defense**
*To provide military forces, to deter war, and to protect national security.*
Office of the Assistant Secretary of Defense for Public Affairs
1400 Defense Pentagon
Room 1E757
Washington, DC 20301-1400
Tel.: (703) 697-5737

E-mail: dpcintrn@osd.pentagon.mil
URL: http://www.defenselink.mil

**U.S. Department of Health and Human Services**
*Principal government agency to protect the health of Americans, providing essential human services through over three hundred programs.*
200 Independence Avenue, SW
Washington, DC 20201
Tel.: (202) 619-0257 or (877) 696-6775
E-mail: hhsmail@os.dhhs.gov
URL: http://www.hhs.gov

**U.S. Department of Justice**
*Administers government agencies concerned with investigation and prosecution of federal crimes, representing the United States in court, managing federal prisons, and enforcing immigration laws. Provides federal leadership in preventing and controlling crime.*
950 Pennsylvania Avenue, NW
Washington, DC 20530-0001
E-mail: web@usdoj.gov
URL: http://www.usdoj.gov or http://www. ojp.usdoj.gov/ovc (Office for Victims of Crime)

**Victim Services**
*Serving victims of domestic violence, incest, rape, sexual assault, elder abuse, and other crimes.*
2 Lafayette Street
New York, NY 10007
Tel.: (212) 577-7700, (212) 577-7777 (24-hour crime victims hotline), (800) 621-HOPE (24-hour domestic violence hotline), (718) 899-4000 (New York immigration hotline), or (212) 227-1227 (elder abuse hotline)
URL: http://www.victimservices.org

**Violence Against Women Grants Office**
*Administers the Department of Justice discretionary grant programs under the Violence Against Women Act of 1994.*
Office of Justice Programs
U.S. Department of Justice
810 Seventh Street, NW
Washington, DC 20531
Tel.: (202) 307-6026
Fax: (202) 305-2589
URL: http://www.ojp.usdoj.gov/vawgo

**Violence Policy Center**
*Works to reduce gun death and injury in the United States through advocacy, research, and public-education activities.*
1140 Nineteenth Street, NW
Suite 600
Washington, DC 20036
Tel.: (202) 822-8200
Fax: (202) 822-8205
E-mail: comment@vpc.org
URL: http://www.vpc.org

**VOICES in Action, Inc./Victims of Incest Can Emerge Survivors**
*International organization that provides assistance to victims of incest and child sexual abuse and generates public awareness of the prevalence of incest. Publishes the newsletter* Chorus.
P.O. Box 148309
Chicago, IL 60614
Tel.: (773) 327-1500 or (800) 7-VOICE-8
E-mail: voices@voices-action.org
URL: http://www.voices-action.org

**Women Against Military Madness**
*Fights injustice and attempts to end militarism. Seeks higher priority in U.S. budget for fighting poverty and ending hunger.*
310 East Thirty-eighth Street
No. 225
Minneapolis, MN 55409-1300
Tel.: (612) 827-5364
Fax: (612) 827-6433

**Women's International League for Peace and Freedom—U.S. Section**
*Works nonviolently to achieve world disarmament, full rights for women, racial and economic justice, and an end to all forms of violence. Works to establish conditions that can assure peace, freedom, and justice. Publishes* Building Peace, Peace and Freedom, *and newsletters.*

1213 Race Street
Philadelphia, PA 19107-1691
Tel.: (215) 563-7110
Fax: (215) 563-5527
E-mail: wilpf@wilpf.org
URL: http://www.wilpf.org

**Women Strike for Peace**
*Organization focusing on peace activism, disarmament, and anti-intervention. Publishes monthly legislative alert.*
110 Maryland Avenue, NE
Suite 102
Washington, DC 20002
Tel.: (202) 593-6948 or (202) 543-2660
Fax: (202) 544-9613

**World Health Organization**
*International UN agency that works toward the highest level of health—"complete, physical, mental, and social well-being" for all people. Publishes several journals in a variety of languages.*

Headquarters:
Ave Appia 20
1211 Geneva 27
Switzerland
Tel.: 00-41-22-791-2111
Fax: 00-41-22-791-0746
E-mail: info@who.int
URL: http://www.who.org

Regional Office:
525 Twenty-third Street, NW
Washington, DC 20037
Tel.: (202) 974-3000
Fax: (202) 974-3663
E-mail: info@who.ch
URL: http://www.paho.org

# JOURNALS

*Aggressive Behavior*
*Publishes articles and research on overt or implied conflict behaviors.*
ISSN: 0096-140X
Editor: Ronald Baenninger
Published bimonthly by:
John Wiley & Sons
Customer Service
605 Third Avenue
New York, NY 10158-0012
Tel.: (212) 850-6645
Fax: (212) 850-6021
E-mail: subinfo@wiley.com
URL: http://www.interscience.wiley.com

*American Journal of Sociology*
*Publishes analysis and research in the social sciences.*
ISSN: 0002-9602
Editor: Roger V. Gould
Published bimonthly by:
University of Chicago Press
Journals Division

P.O. Box 37005
Chicago, IL 60637
Tel.: (773) 753-3347
Fax: (773) 753-0811
E-mail: orders@journals.uchicago.edu

*American Sociological Review*
*Publishes original work of interest to sociologists in general, especially that which advances the understanding of fundamental social processes and important methodological innovations.*
ISSN: 0003-1224
Editor: Glenn Firebaugh
Published bimonthly by:
American Sociological Association
1307 New York Avenue, NW
Suite 700
Washington, DC 20005
Tel.: (202) 383-9005 or (202) 872-0486 (TDD)
Fax: (202) 683-0882
E-mail: subscriptions@asanet.org

*Child Abuse and Neglect: The International Journal*
*International, multidisciplinary forum on all aspects of child abuse and neglect, with an emphasis on prevention and treatment.*
ISSN: 0145-2134
Editor: Richard D. Krugman
Published monthly by:
Elsevier Science
Regional Sales Office
P.O. Box 945
New York, NY 10159-0945
Tel.: (212) 633-3730/3731 or (888) 4ES-INFO
Fax: (212) 633-3680
E-mail: sm.wilkinson@elsevier.co.uk
URL: http://www.elsevier.com

*Child and Youth Care Forum*
*Designed to provide a medium for communication and debate on practice, training, theory, research, and professional issues for personnel in child and youth care settings.*
ISSN: 1053-1890
Editor: Jerome Beker
Published bimonthly by:
Kluwer Academic/Plenum Publishers
233 Spring Street
New York, NY 10013-1578
Tel.: (212) 620-8085
Fax: (212) 463-0742
E-mail: bischoff@plenum.com

*Child Development*
*Publishes original articles exploring all aspects of child development from prenatal stages through adolescence. A publication of the Society for Research in Child Development.*
ISSN: 0009-3920
Editor: Marc H. Bornstein
Published bimonthly by:
Blackwell Publishing
Subscription Department
350 Main Street
Malden, MA 02148
Tel.: (800) 835-6770
Fax: (781) 388-8232
E-mail: subscrip@blackwellpub.com

*Child Maltreatment*
*Publishes on theory, practice, and policy issues in the field of child abuse and neglect. Journal of the American Professional Society on the Abuse of Children.*
ISSN: 1077-5595
Editor: Mark Chaffin
Published quarterly by:
Sage Publications, Inc.
2455 Teller Road
Thousand Oaks, CA 91220
Tel.: (805) 499-0721
Fax: (805) 499-0871

E-mail: info@sagepub.com
URL: http://www.sagepub.com

*Children and Youth Services Review*
*An international, multidisciplinary review of the welfare of young people. Publishes critical scholarship regarding service programs for youths and children.*
ISSN: 0190-7409
Editor: Duncan Lindsey
Published monthly by:
Elsevier Science
Customer Support Department
P.O. Box 945
New York, NY 10010
Tel.: (212) 633-3730/3731 or (888) 4ES-INFO
Fax: (212) 633-3680
E-mail: usinfo@elsevier.com

*Children's Legal Rights Journal*
*Focuses on the relationship between the legal profession and children.*
ISSN: 0278-7210
Editor: Robyn Kaufman
Published quarterly by:
William S. Hein and Co, Inc.
1285 Main Street
Buffalo, NY 14209
Tel.: (800) 828-7571

*Child Welfare*
*Publishes work that helps to extend existing knowledge in any child or family welfare or related service.*
Published bimonthly by:
Child Welfare League of America, Inc.
c/o PMDS
P.O. Box 2019
Annapolis Junction, MD 20701
Tel.: (800) 407-6273
Fax: (301) 206-9789

*Crime and Delinquency*
*Addresses specific economic, social, or political policy or programs or interest to criminal justice professionals. Published in cooperation with the National Council on Crime and Delinquency.*
Editor: Don Gibbons
Published quarterly by:
Sage Publications, Inc.
2455 Teller Road
Thousand Oaks, CA 91320
Tel.: (805) 499-0721
Fax: (805) 499-0871
E-mail: info@sagepub.com
URL: http://www.sagepub.com

*Crime, Law, and Social Change:*
*An International Journal*
*Publishes articles related on the political economy of organized crime at the transnational, national, regional, and local levels anywhere in the world.*

ISSN: 0925-4994
Editor: Alan Block
Published eight times yearly by:
Kluwer Academic Publishers
U.S. subscriptions:
101 Philip Drive
Assinippi Park
Norwell, MA 02061
Tel.: (781) 871-6600
Fax: (781) 871-6528
URL: http://www.wkap.nl

### Criminal Justice and Behavior
*Official publication of the American Association of Correctional Psychology. Publishes timely, well conceived, lively scholarship that advances knowledge and expertise of professionals and academics in forensic psychology.*
ISSN: 0093-8548
Editor: Curt R. Bartol
Published quarterly by:
Sage Publications, Inc.
2455 Teller Road
Thousand Oaks, CA 91320
Tel.: (805) 499-0721
Fax: (805) 499-0871
E-mail: info@sagepub.com
URL: http://www.sagepub.com

### Criminal Justice Ethics
*Publishes articles focusing on ethical issues in criminal justice relating to police, courts, corrections, and legal philosophy.*
ISSN: 0073-129X
Editors: William C. Heffernan, John Kleinig,
     Timothy Stevens
Published semiannually by:
Institute of Criminal Justice Ethics
John Jay College
555 West Fifth-seventh Street
Suite 601
New York, NY 10019-1029
Tel.: (212) 237-8033
Fax: (212) 237-8030
E-mail: cjejj@cunyvm.cuny.edu
URL: http://wwwlib.jjay.cuny.edu/cje

### Criminal Justice Policy Review
*Multidisciplinary journal publishes quantitative and qualitative analysis of justice policy.*
ISSN: 0887-4034
Editor: Robert Mutchnick
Published quarterly by:
Indiana University Press
601 North Morton Street
Bloomington, IN 47404-3797

### Criminal Justice Review
*Focuses on regional and national trends and problems and on research on criminal justice issues, institutions, and processes.*

ISSN: 0734-0168
Editor: Richard J. Terrill
Published semiannually by:
College of Public and Urban Affairs
Georgia State University
Box 4018
Atlanta, GA 30302-4018

### Criminology
*Publishes theoretical, empirical, methodological research on crime and deviant behavior.*
ISSN: 0011-1384
Editor: Robert J. Bursik, Jr.
Published quarterly by:
American Society of Criminology
1314 Kinnear Road
Suite 212
Columbus, OH 43212-1156
Tel.: (614) 292-9207
Fax: (614) 292-6767
E-mail: asc41@compuserve.com
URL: http://www.asc41.com

### Criminology, Penology, and Police Science Abstracts
*International abstracts covering etiology of crime and juvenile delinquency, control and treatment of offenders, criminal procedure, administering justice, and forensic and police sciences.*
ISSN: 0928-8759
Editors: J. J. M Van Dijk, K. Van Leeuwen
Published bimonthly by:
Kugler Publications
P.O. Box 11188
1001 GD Amsterdam
The Netherlands

### Defence and Peace Economics
*Considers all aspects of economics of defense, disarmament, conversion, and peace.*
ISSN: 1043-0717
North American Editor: Professor William Rogerson
Published quarterly at:
P.O. Box 32160
Newark, NJ 07102
Tel.: (800) 545-8398
Fax: (973) 643-7676

### Family Violence and Sexual Assault Bulletin
*Publishes original papers concerning family violence and sexual assault issues, treatment, research, and programs. Subscription requires membership in the Family Violence and Sexual Assault Institute.*
Editor: Robert Geffner
Published quarterly by:
Family Violence and Sexual Assault Institute
7120 Herman Jared Drive
Fort Worth, TX 76180
Tel.: (817) 485-2244
Fax: (817) 485-0660

524

E-mail: fvsai@iamerican.net
URL: http://www.fvsai.org

## Homicide Studies
*Disseminates information concerning research, public policy, and applied knowledge pertinent to the study of homicide.*
Editor: M. Dwayne Smith
Published quarterly by:
Sage Publications, Inc.
2455 Teller Road
Thousand Oaks, CA 91220
Tel.: (805) 499-0721
Fax: (805) 499-0871
E-mail: info@sagepub.com
URL: http://www.sagepub.com

## Human Rights
*Publishes news articles, features, and commentary on human rights and responsibilities.*
ISSN: 0046-8185
Editor: Jessica Washington
Published quarterly by:
ABA Publishing
Individual Rights and Responsibilities Section
750 North Lake Shore Drive
Chicago, IL 60611
Tel.: (312) 988-5990
Fax: (312) 988-6081

## Human Rights Law Journal
*Publishes articles, reports, and documentation on constitutional law and decisions of the Supreme Court regarding human rights.*
ISSN: 0174-4704
Editor: Erika Engel
Published monthly by:
International Institute of Human Rights
3608 512th Street
Arlington, VA 22204

## International Journal of Comparative and Applied Criminal Justice
*Publishes articles concerning international criminal justice, especially those that compare the response to an issue in several countries.*
ISSN: 0192-4036
Editor: Dae H. Chang
Published by:
Department of the Administration of Justice
Box 135
Wichita State University
Wichita, KS 67260-0135
Tel.: (316) 978-6517
Fax: (316) 978-3626

## International Journal of Group Tensions
*Official publication of the International Organization of the Study of Group Tensions. Publishes philosophy, theory, and empirical and methodological studies of conflict in human group relations.*
ISSN: 0047-0732
Editors: Benjamin B. Wolman, Herbert H. Kraus
Published quarterly by:
Kluwer Academic/Plenum Publishers
233 Spring Street
New York, NY 10013-1578
Tel.: (212) 620-8085
Fax: (212) 463-0742
E-Mail: bischoff@plenum.com

## International Journal of Offender Therapy and Comparative Criminology
*Provides a forum for research, discussion, and treatment of variables associated with crime and delinquency with an emphasis on theoretical and clinical treatment of offenders.*
ISSN: 0306-624X
Managing Editor: George Palermo
Published quarterly by:
Sage Publications, Inc.
2455 Teller Road
Thousand Oaks, CA 91220
Tel.: (805) 499-0721
Fax: (805) 499-0871
E-mail: info@sagepub.com
URL: http://www.sagepub.com

## International Journal of the Sociology of Law
*Publishes theoretical and empirical studies of law as a social process, with an international perspective.*
ISSN: 0194-6595
Editors: John Carrier, Stephen Savage
Published quarterly by:
Harcourt Brace and Co, Ltd.
Journals Subscription Department
Foots Cray
High Street
Sidcup
Kent DA1 5HP
United Kingdom
Tel.: (01 81) 308-5700

## Journal of Abnormal Child Psychology
*Publishes theoretical and empirical research to aid scientists and practicing professionals concerned with child and adolescent psychopathology.*
ISSN: 0091-0627
Editor: Susan B. Campbell
Published bimonthly by:
Kluwer Academic/Plenum Publishers
233 Spring Street
New York, NY 10013-1578
Tel.: (212) 620-8013
Fax: (212) 807-1047

## Journal of Child and Family Studies
*An international forum on applied research, program evaluation, and service and policy issues dealing with the*

*early identification, prevention, diagnosis, treatment, and rehabilitation of emotional disorders in children, youth, and family focusing on mental health, including broad themes of child abuse and neglect, family stress, and substance abuse.*
ISSN: 1062-1024
Editor: Nirbhay North Singh
Published quarterly by:
Kluwer Academic/Plenum Publishers
233 Spring Street
New York, NY 10013-1578
Tel.: (212) 620-8085
Fax: (212) 463-0742
E-Mail: bischoff@plenum.com

### Journal of Child Sexual Abuse
*Publishes work on research, treatment, and program innovations for victims, survivors, and offenders.*
ISSN: 1053-8712
Editor: Robert A. Geffner
Published quarterly by:
Haworth Press
10 Alice Street
Binghamton, NY 13904-1580
Tel.: (800) 426-6784
Fax: (800) 895-0582
E-mail: getinfo@haworth.com

### Journal of Criminal Justice
*International journal disseminates new information, ideas, and methods to practitioners and academics in criminal justice. Discusses different aspects of criminal justice in relation to each other.*
ISSN: 0047-2352
Editor: Kent B. Joscelyn
Published bimonthly by:
Elsevier Science
Regional Sales Office
P.O. Box 945
New York, NY 10159-0945
Tel.: (212) 633-3730/3731 or (888) 4ES-INFO
Fax: (212) 633-3680
URL: http://www.elsevier.com

### Journal of Criminal Law and Criminology
*Publishes scholarly articles focusing on criminal law.*
ISSN: 0091-4196
Editor: Mark Josephson
Published quarterly by:
Northwestern School of Law
Office of Legal Publications
357 East Chicago Avenue
Chicago, IL 60611

### Journal of Elder Abuse and Neglect
*Devoted to the study of causes, treatment, effects, and prevention of mistreatment of the elderly. Free to members of the National Committee for the Prevention of Elder Abuse, Inc.*

Editors: Rosalie S. Wolf, Susan McMurray Anderson
Published by:
The Institute on Aging
The Medical Center of Central Massachusetts
119 Belmont Street
Worcester, MA 01605

### Journal of Emotional Abuse
*First journal to focus exclusively on nonphysical aggression, intimidation, and harassment.*
ISSN: 1092-6798
Coeditors: Robert A. Geffner, B. B. Robbie Rossman
Published quarterly by:
Haworth Press
10 Alice Street
Binghamton, NY 13904-1580
Tel.: (800) 426-6784
Fax: (800) 895-0582
E-mail: getinfo@haworth.com

### Journal of Family Violence
*Publishes information on clinical and investigative efforts regarding all forms of family violence and its precursors.*
ISSN: 0885-7482
Editors: Vincent B. Van Hasselt, Michel Hersen
Published quarterly by:
Kluwer Academic/Plenum Publishers
233 Spring Street
New York, NY 10013-1578
Tel.: (212) 620-8013
Fax: (212) 463-0742
E-Mail: cloutier@plenum.com

### Journal of Interpersonal Violence
*Covers domestic violence, child sexual abuse, rape and sexual assault, and other violent crimes.*
ISSN: 0886-2605
Editor: Jon R. Conte
Published monthly by:
Sage Publications, Inc.
2455 Teller Road
Thousand Oaks, CA 91220
Tel.: (805) 499-0721
Fax: (805) 499-0871
E-mail: info@sagepub.com
URL: http://www.sagepub.com

### Journal of Offender Rehabilitation
*Publishes research and concepts on rehabilitation in custodial and community settings.*
ISSN: 1050-9674
Editor: Nathaniel J. Pallone
Published quarterly by:
Haworth Press
10 Alice Street
Binghamton, NY 13904-1580
Tel.: (800) 426-6784

Fax: (800) 895-0582
E-mail: getinfo@haworth.com

### Journal of Quantitative Criminology
*Publishes material that applies quantitative techniques to substantive, methodological, evaluative concerns of interest to the criminology community.*
ISSN: 0748-4518
Editor: Michael D. Maltz
Published quarterly by:
Kluwer Academic/Plenum Publishers
233 Spring Street
New York, NY 10013-1578
Tel.: (212) 620-8027
Fax: (212) 463-0742
E-mail: ewerner@plenum.com

### Journal of Research in Crime and Delinquency
*Published in cooperation with the National Council on Crime and Delinquency. Reports on original research, new theory, and critical analysis especially pertinent to the field of crime and delinquency.*
ISSN: 0022-4278
Editor: Mercer L. Sullivan
Published quarterly by:
Sage Publications, Inc.
2455 Teller Road
Thousand Oaks, CA 91220
Tel.: (805) 499-0721
Fax: (805) 499-0871
E-mail: info@sagepub.com
URL: http://www.sagepub.com

### Journal of Social Distress and the Homeless
*International, interdisciplinary forum on psychosocial distress and disorganization and their relationship to wider issues in the fields of criminal justice, education, economics, homelessness, violence, and racial tensions.*
ISSN: 1053-0789
Editor: Robert West Rieber
Published quarterly by:
Kluwer Academic/Plenum Publishers
233 Spring Street
New York, NY 10013-1578
Tel.: (212) 620-8085
Fax: (212) 463-0742
E-Mail: bischoff@plenum.com

### Journal of Traumatic Stress
*Publishes information on biopsychosocial aspects of traumatic events such as war, disaster, accident, violence, abuse, hostage taking, or life-threatening illness.*
ISSN: 0894-9867
Editor: Dean G. Kilpatrick
Published quarterly by:
Kluwer Academic/Plenum Publishers
233 Spring Street
New York, NY 10013-1578

Tel.: (212) 620-8085
Fax: (212) 463-0742
E-Mail: bischoff@plenum.com

### Justice Quarterly
*Publishes scholarly articles on criminal justice and on criminal and justice studies.*
ISSN: 0741-8825
Editor: Finn Esbensen
Published quarterly by:
Academy of Criminal Justice Sciences
1500 North Beauregard Street
Suite 101
Alexandria, VA 22311
Tel.: (800) 757-ACJS

### Law and Human Behavior
*Provides a multidisciplinary forum to study the relationship between human behavior and the law, the legal system, and the legal process. Official journal of the American Psychology-Law Society, a division of the American Psychological Association.*
ISSN: 0147-7307
Editor: Richard L. Wiener
Published bimonthly by:
Kluwer Academic/Plenum Publishers
233 Spring Street
New York, NY 10013-1578
Tel.: (212) 620-8027
Fax: (212) 463-0742
E-mail: ewerner@plenum.com

### MHQ: The Quarterly Journal of Military History
*Publishes articles on all aspects of military history.*
ISSN: 1040-5992
Editor: Robert Cowley
Published quarterly by:
MHQ Subscriptions Office
P.O. Box 597
Mount Morris, IL 61054
Tel.: (800) 827-1218

### Negotiation Journal: On the Process of Dispute Settlement
*Committed to the development of better techniques for negotiating differences.*
ISSN: 0748-4526
Editor: J. William Breslin
Published quarterly by:
Kluwer Academic/Plenum Publishers
233 Spring Street
New York, NY 10013-1578
Tel.: (212) 620-8027
Fax: (212) 463-0742
E-mail: ewerner@plenum.com

### Omega: The Journal of Death and Dying
*Guide for clinicians, social workers, and health care professionals dealing with patients with problems such as terminal illness, fatal accidents, suicide, and bereavement.*

ISSN: 0030-2228
Editor: Robert J. Kastenbaum
Published eight times a year by:
Baywood Publishing Company, Inc.
26 Austin Avenue
Box 337
Amityville, NY 11701
Tel.: (516) 691-1270
Fax: (516) 691-1770

## Patterns of Prejudice

*Publishes scholarly articles on the national and international conditions, causes, and manifestations of racial, religious, and ethnic discrimination and prejudice, with particular reference to anti-Semitism. Published in connection with the Institute of Jewish Affairs.*
ISSN: 0031-322X
Editors: David Cesarani, Anthony R. Kushner
Published quarterly by:
Sage Publications, Inc.
2455 Teller Road
Thousand Oaks, CA 91220
Tel.: (805) 499-0721
Fax: (805) 499-0871
E-mail: info@sagepub.com
URL: http://www.sagepub.com

## Protecting Children

*Publishes work essential for human services professionals, focusing on research, treatment, and advocacy on child abuse and neglect.*
ISSN: 0893-4231
Editor: Robyn Alsop
Published quarterly by:
The American Humane Association, Children's Division
Department No. 0828
Denver, CO 80263-0828
Tel.: (303) 792-9900
Fax: (303) 792-5333
E-mail: children@americanhumane.org

## Social Forces

*Publishes sociological inquiry. Also explores issues related to social psychiatry, anthropology, political science, history, and economics.*
ISSN: 0037-7732
Editor: Richard L. Simpson
Published quarterly by:
Journals Department
UNC Press
P.O. Box 2288
Chapel Hill, NC 27515-2288
Tel.: (919) 966-3561 ext. 256 or (800) 272-6817
Fax: (919) 966-3829
E-mail: uncpress_journals@unc.edu
URL: http://www.irss.unc.edu/sf

## Social Justice

*Publishes on social justice issues, including crime and justice, justice and the world system, and women and welfare reform.*
ISSN: 0094-7571
Managing Editor: Gregory Shank
Published quarterly by:
Global Options
P.O. Box 40601
San Francisco, CA 94140
Tel.: (415) 550-1703
E-mail: socialjust@aol.com

## Social Problems

*Publishes critical perspectives on contemporary social issues, including conflict, social action, and change; crime and juvenile delinquency; substance use, law, and society. A publication of the Society for the Study of Social Problems.*
ISSN: 0037-7791
Editor: David Smith
Published quarterly by:
University of California Press
Journals Division
200 Center Street
Suite 303
Berkeley, CA 94704-1223
Tel.: (510) 642-4191
Fax: (510) 642-9917
E-mail: journals@ucop.edu

## Studies in Conflict and Terrorism

*Focuses on physical conflict short of formal war and on nonphysical conflict of an economic, political, or social nature.*
ISSN: 1057-610X
Editors: George K. Tan, Bruce Hoffman
Published quarterly by:
Taylor & Francis, Inc.
47 Runway Road
Suite G
Levittown, PA 19057
Tel.: (215) 785-5800 or (800) 821-8312
Fax: (215) 269-8368

## Suicide and Life Threatening Behavior

*Official publication of the American Association of Suicidology. Addresses emergent theoretical, clinical, and public health approaches to violent, self-destructive, and life-threatening behaviors.*
ISSN: 0363-0234
Editor: Morton M. Silverman
Published quarterly by:
Guilford Press
72 Spring Street
New York, NY 10012
Tel.: (800) 365-7006
Fax: (212) 966-6708

## Terrorism and Political Violence

Publishes articles that study all aspects of terrorism and political violence.

ISSN: 0954-6553
Editors: David C. Rapoport, Paul Wilkinson
Published quarterly by:
ISBS
5804 NE Hassalo Street
Portland, OR 97213-3644
Tel.: (800) 944-6190
Fax: (503) 280-8832

## Trends in Organized Crime

*Publishes information and analyses of international efforts to anticipate and counter organized-crime activities.*
ISSN: 1084-4791-11-1
Editor: Roy Godson
Published quarterly by:
Transaction Publishers
390 Campus Drive
Somerset, NJ 07830
Tel.: (888) 999-6778
Fax: (732) 748-9801
E-mail: orders@transactionpub.com
URL: http://www.transactionpub.com

## Victimology: An International Journal

*Covers issues related to victims of crime, rape, child abuse, or spouse abuse, and victim or witness services.*
Editor: Emilio C. Viano
Published quarterly by:
Victimology, Inc.
2333 North Vernon Street
Arlington, VA 22207
Tel.: (703) 528-3387

## Violence Against Women

*Publishes empirical research as well as historical and cultural analysis on all aspects of violence against women.*
ISSN: 1077-8012
Editor: Claire M. Renzetti
Published monthly by:
Sage Publications, Inc.
2455 Teller Road
Thousand Oaks, CA 91220
Tel.: (805) 499-0721

Fax: (805) 499-0871
E-mail: info@sagepub.com
URL: http://www.sagepub.com

## Violence and Abuse Abstracts: Current Literature in Interpersonal Violence

*Publishes abstracts and bibliographical data on all aspects of violence and abuse: medical, legal, psychological, and social.*
ISSN: 1077-2197
Published quarterly by:
Sage Publications, Inc.
2455 Teller Road
Thousand Oaks, CA 91220
Tel.: (805) 499-0721
Fax: (805) 499-0871
E-mail: info@sagepub.com
URL: http://www.sagepub.com

## Violence and Victims

*Publishes cross-disciplinary theory and research regarding policy and practice in all areas relating to interpersonal violence and victimization.*
ISSN: 0886-6708
Editor: Roland D. Maiuro
Published quarterly by:
Springer Publishing Company
536 Broadway
New York, NY 10012-3955
Tel.: (212) 431-4370
Fax: (212) 941-7842
E-mail: contactus@springerjournals.com

## Women and Criminal Justice

*Devoted specifically to international and interdisciplinary scholarly research dealing with women and criminal justice.*
ISSN: 0897-4454
Editor: Donna C. Hale
Published quarterly by:
Haworth Press
10 Alice Street
Binghamton, NY 13904-1580
Tel.: (800) 426-6784
Fax: (800) 895-0582
E-mail: getinfo@haworth.com

# WEB RESOURCES

## Antistalking Web Site

*Provides information about stalkers and stalking, prevention and response for victims, law enforcement, mental health professionals, researchers, educators, and legislators.*
E-mail: comments@antistalking.com
URL: http://www.antistalking.com

## Campus Safety

*Provided by Security on Campus, Inc., "the only national, nonprofit organization geared specifically and exclusively to the prevention of college and university campus violence and other crimes," this site supplies information on campus crime and prevention for current and prospective students, parents,*

and community members. Visitors to the site will find campus crime statistics (in pdf format), detailed summaries, and the full text of campus security laws, victim-assistance and binge-drinking-prevention resources, and links to recent campus crime news. Users can also subscribe for e-mail notification of site updates.
URL: http://www.campussafety.org

**Corrections Connection**
*An on-line resource for news and information on corrections.*
URL: http://www.corrections.com

**Federal Statistics Web Resource**
*Maintains links to statistics from more than seventy U.S. government agencies.*
URL: http://www.fedstats.gov

**Human Rights Internet**
*Provides access to information and documents from and to international human rights workers.*
E-mail: hri@hri.ca
URL: http://www.hri.ca

**Institute for Global Communications (Justice Web)**
*Complete on-line service for those working on peace, economic and social justice, human rights, environmental protection, labor issues, and conflict resolution.*
URL: http://www.igc.org

**Justice Information Center**
*Searchable service of the national criminal justice reference service covering such topics as corrections, courts, criminal justice statistics, drugs and crime, juvenile justice, law enforcement, and crime prevention. Has an abstracts database.*
URL: http://www.ncjrs.org

**Juvenile Justice Clearinghouse**
*Contains information on juvenile justice.*
URL: http://www.fsu.edu/~crimdo/jjclearinghouse

**Minnesota Center Against Violence and Abuse**
*Electronic clearinghouse of international information about violence and abuse. Extensive resources on everything from domestic violence to terrorism, from child abuse to elder abuse.*
URL: http://www.mincava.umn.edu

**National Coalition of Anti-Violence Programs**
*National coalition of lesbian, gay, bisexual, transgender, and HIV-positive people; provides victim assistance, advocacy, and documentation programs to educate the public about the extent and severity of hate crimes. Gives addresses of local services.*
URL: http://www.avp.org

**Nonviolence Web**
*Home to various peace groups on the Web*
E-mail: nvweb@nonviolence.org
URL: http://www.nonviolence.org

**Pacific Center for Violence Prevention**
*Supports community-based violence prevention in California and works to reduce youth access to drugs, alcohol, and firearms. Despite the center's focus on California, a large number of violence-prevention resources are available to all users.*
URL: http://www.pcvp.org

**Resources for Youth**
*Public education campaign to increase public and private investment in organizations seeking to reduce violence against youth.*
E-mail: info@preventviolence.org
URL: http://www.preventviolence.org

**United Nations Crime and Justice Information Network**
*Provides global crime prevention and criminal justice information.*
URL: http://www.uncjin.org

**Violence Against Women Online Resources**
*Provides up-to-date information on intervention to prevent violence against women to law, criminal justice, advocacy, and social services personnel.*
URL: http://www.vaw.umn.edu

**Web of Justice**
*Developed by the Pinellas County (Florida) Department of Justice Coordination for those researching criminal justice issues.*
URL: http://www.co.pinellas.fl.us/bcc/juscoord/exploremain.htm

# SUBJECT INDEX

A selective list of organizations, journals, and web resources that deal with the following aspects of violence, its victims, and its perpetrators.

**Publications:** *Family Violence and Sexual Assault Bulletin; Journal of Family Violence; Journal of Interpersonal Violence; Violence Against Women.*

**Web Resources:** Minnesota Center Against Violence and Abuse; Violence Against Women Online Resources.

## Elder Abuse

**Organizations:** National Committee for the Prevention of Elder Abuse; National Council on Child Abuse and Family Violence; Victim Services.

**Publications:** *Journal of Elder Abuse and Neglect; Journal of Family Violence.*

**Web Resources:** Minnesota Center Against Violence and Abuse.

## Gay and Lesbian

**Organizations:** Community United Against Violence; Gay and Lesbian Alliance Against Defamation; Human Rights Campaign Fund; International Gay and Lesbian Human Rights Commission; LAMBDA GLBT Community Services; Men Overcoming Violence; National Gay and Lesbian Task Force.

## Government Agencies

**Organizations:** Bureau of Alcohol, Tobacco and Firearms; Bureau of Justice Statistics; Centers for Disease Control and Prevention; Central Intelligence Agency; Drug Enforcement Administration; Federal Bureau of Investigation; Federal Communications Commission; Federal Law Enforcement Training Center; Indian Health Service; National Institute for Occupational Safety and Health; National Institute of Justice; National Institute of Mental Health; National Institute on Drug Abuse; National Institutes of Health; Office for Civil Rights; Office of Juvenile Justice and Delinquency Prevention; U.S. Department of Defense; U.S. Department of Health and Human Services; U.S. Department of Justice.

**Web Resources:** Federal Statistics Web Resource.

## Grantmaking

**Organizations:** Henry F. Guggenheim Foundation; MacArthur Foundation; Milton S. Eisenhower Fund; Violence Against Women Grants Office.

## Guns and Gun Control

**Organizations:** Bureau of Alcohol, Tobacco, and Firearms; Ceasefire; Center to Prevent Handgun Violence; Coalition to Stop Gun Violence; Educational Fund to End Handgun Violence; Johns Hopkins Center for Gun Policy and Research; National Rifle Association; Second Amendment Foundation; Violence Policy Center.

**Web Resources:** Pacific Center for Violence Prevention.

## Hate Crime

**Organizations:** Center for Democratic Renewal; Community United Against Violence; Klanwatch; LAMBDA GLBT Community Services; Office for Civil Rights; People for the American Way; Simon Wiesenthal Center; Southern Poverty Law Center.

**Publications:** *Patterns of Prejudice.*

**Web Resources:** National Coalition of Anti-Violence Programs.

## Health and Physicians

**Organizations:** American Medical Association; American Psychological Association; Centers for Disease Control and Prevention; Domestic Violence Project of the American Academy of Facial, Plastic, and Reconstructive Surgery; Indian Health Service; International Centre for Comparative Criminology; Institute of Medicine; National Center for Health Statistics; National Center for Injury Prevention and Control; National Institute for Occupational Safety and Health; National Institute of Mental Health; National Institute on Drug Abuse; National Institutes of Health; Physicians for a Violence-free Society; Physicians for Human Rights; Sex Addicts Anonymous; U.S. Department of Health and Human Services; World Health Organization.

**Publications:** *International Journal of Offender Therapy and Comparative Criminology; Journal of Abnormal Child Psychology; Journal of Traumatic Stress; Omega: Journal of Death and Dying.*

## Homelessness

**Publications:** *Journal of Social Distress and the Homeless.*

## Incest

**Organizations:** Incest Survivors Resource Network International; Survivors of Incest Anonymous; Victim Services; VOICES in Action, Inc.

## International Organizations

**Organizations:** Amnesty International; Center for the Prevention of Sexual and Domestic Violence; Conflict Resolution Center International; Crime Stoppers International; Human Rights Advocates; Incest Survivors Resource Network International; International Association for the Study of Organized Crime; International Association of Chiefs of Police; International Association of Official Human Rights Agencies; International Centre for Comparative Criminology; International Centre for the Prevention of Crime; International Communication Association; International Criminal Police Organization (INTERPOL); International Gay and Lesbian Human Rights Commission; International League for Human Rights; International Society for Research on Aggression; International Women's Rights Action Watch; Law and Society Association; Nonviolence International; Sex Addicts Anonymous, Inc.; Survivors of Incest Anonymous; VOICES in Action, Inc.; Women's International League for Peace and Freedom; World Health Organization.

**Publications:** *Child Abuse and Neglect: The International Journal; Children and Youth Services Review; Crime Law and Social Change: An International Journal; Criminology, Penology, and Police Science Abstracts; International Journal of Group Tensions; International Journal of Offender Therapy and Comparative Criminology; International Journal of the Sociology of Law; Journal of Child and Family Studies; Journal of Criminal Justice; Journal of Social Distress and the Homeless; Patterns of Prejudice; Trends in Organized Crime; Victimology: An International Journal; Women and Criminal Justice.*

**Web Resources:** Human Rights Internet; United Nations Crime and Justice Information Network.

## Law and Legal Services

**Organizations:** American Bar Association; American Civil Liberties Union; Amnesty International; Death Penalty Information Center; Drug Enforcement Administration; Human Rights Advocates; Law and Society Association; Mexican American Legal Defense and Education Fund; National Association of Child Advocates; National Association of Council for Children; National Association of Criminal Defense Lawyers; National Center for the Prosecution of Child Abuse; National Center for Youth Law; National Clearinghouse for the Defense of Battered Women; Southern Poverty Law Center.

**Publications:** *Children's Legal Rights Journal; Crime Law and Social Change; Human Rights Law Journal; International Journal of the Sociology of Law; Journal of Criminal Law and Criminology; Law and Human Behavior.*

## Law Enforcement

**Organizations:** Bureau of Alcohol, Tobacco, and Firearms; Crime Stoppers International; Federal Bureau of Investigation; Federal Law Enforcement Training Center; Guardian Angels; International Association of Chiefs of Police; International Criminal Police Organization (INTERPOL); National Council on Crime and Delinquency; National Crime Prevention Institute; U.S. Department of Justice.

**Publications:** *Crime, Law, and Social Change; Criminology, Penology, and Police Science Abstracts.*

**Web Resources:** Justice Information Center

## Military

**Organizations:** Center for Defense Information; Institute for Defense Analysis; U.S. Department of Defense.

**Publications:** *MHQ: The Quarterly Journal of Military History.*

## Minorities

**Organizations:** Anti-Defamation League; Barrios Unidos; Center for Democratic Renewal; Commission for Racial Justice; Committee Against Anti-Asian Violence; Holocaust Memorial Museum; Indian Health Service; Jewish Defense League; Jewish Defense Organization; Mexican American Legal Defense and Education Fund; National Association for the Advancement of Colored People.

**Publications:** *Patterns of Prejudice.*

## Organized Crime

**Organizations:** International Association for the Study of Organized Crime.

**Publications:** *Crime, Law, and Social Change; Trends in Organized Crime.*

## Peace and Nonviolence

**Organizations:** Albert Einstein Institution; American Peace Network; American Peace Society; Carter Center; Institute for Defense and Disarmament Studies; Institute for Peace and Justice; M. K. Gandhi Institute for Nonviolence; Peace Links; SEASON for Nonviolence; Women's International League for Peace and Freedom; Women Strike for Peace.

**Publications:** *Defence and Peace Economics.*

**Web Resources:** Institute for Global Communications (Justice Web); Nonviolence Web.

## Prevention

**Organizations:** American Foundation for Suicide Prevention; Barrios Unidos; Center for Communication and Social Policy; Center for the Prevention of School Violence; Center for the Prevention of Sexual and Domestic Violence; Centers for Disease Control and Prevention; Child Abuse Prevention Association; Coalition Against Trafficking in Women; Community United Against Violence; Family Violence Prevention Fund; Family Violence Research Program; Guardian Angels; International Centre for the Prevention of Crime; Men Overcoming Violence; Mothers Against Drunk Driving; National Center for Assault Prevention; National Center for Injury Prevention and Control; National Council on Crime and Delinquency; National Crime Prevention Council; National Crime Prevention Institute; Office of Juvenile Justice and Delinquency Prevention; Parents of Murdered Children; Physicians for a Violence-free Society; Society for the Prevention of Cruelty to Animals; Trauma Foundation.

**Web Resources:** Antistalking Website; Justice Information Center; Pacific Center for Violence Prevention; United Nations Crime and Justice Information Network.

## Prisons and Prisoners

**Organizations:** American Correctional Association; Commission for Racial Justice; Death Penalty Information Center; Fortune Society; National Association of Juvenile Correctional Agencies; National Center on Institutions and Alternatives; National Center for Youth Law; North American Association of Wardens and Superintendents; Office of Juvenile Justice and Delinquency Prevention; Sentencing Project; Stop Prisoner Rape.

**Publications:** *Criminology, Penology, and Police Science Abstracts; International Journal of Offender Therapy and Comparative Criminology; Journal of Offender Rehabilitation.*

**Web Resources:** Corrections Connection; Institute for Global Communications; Justice Information Center.

## Professional Organizations

**Organizations:** American Bar Association; American Medical Association; American Psychological Association; American Society of Criminology; Domestic Violence Project of the American Academy of Facial, Plastic, and Reconstructive Surgery; Human Rights Advocates; Institute for Victims of Trauma; International Association of Chiefs of Police; International Association of Official Human Rights Agencies; International Communication Association.

**Publications:** *American Journal of Sociology; American Sociological Review.*

## Rape and Sexual Assault

**Organizations:** American Women's Self-Defense Association; Equality Now; Family Violence Research Program; National Alliance of Sexual Assault Coalitions; National Clearinghouse on Marital and Date Rape/Women's History Library; National Coalition Against Sexual Assault; National Organization on Male Sexual Victimization; Victim Services.

**Publications:** *Family Violence and Sexual Assault Bulletin; Journal of Interpersonal Violence.*

## Research

**Organizations:** Center for Communication and Social Policy; Center for Defense Information; Center to Prevent Handgun Violence; Center for Research on the Influence of Television on Children; Educational Information and Resource Center; Family Violence Research Program; Holocaust Memorial Museum; Human Rights Workshop; Institute for the Study of Genocide; International Association for the Study of Organized Crime; International Society for Research on Aggression; John M. Olin Institute for Strategic Studies; Johns Hopkins Center for Gun Policy and Research; Kids Count; National Alliance for Safe Schools; National Center for Health Statistics; National Center for the Study of Corporal Punishments and Alternatives; National Children's Coalition; National Clearinghouse for Alcohol and Drug Information; National Clearinghouse on Child Abuse and Neglect; National Clearinghouse on Marital and Date Rape; National Clearinghouse for the Defense of Battered Women; National Consortium on Violence Research; National Data Archive on Child Abuse and Neglect; National Institute of Justice; National Resource Center on Domestic Violence; Resource Center on Domestic Violence, Child Custody, and Protection; Second Amendment Foun-

dation; Simon Wiesenthal Center; Violence Policy Center.

**Publications:** *Violence and Abuse Abstracts.*

**Web Resources:** Minnesota Center Against Violence and Abuse; Pacific Center for Violence Prevention.

## Religion

**Organizations:** Anti-Defamation League; Center for the Prevention of Sexual and Domestic Violence; Colloquium on Violence and Religion.

## School Violence

**Organizations:** Center for the Prevention of School Violence; Children's Defense Fund; Educational Information and Resource Center; End the Violence Against the Next Generation; National Alliance for Safe Schools; National Center for the Study of Corporal Punishment and Alternatives; National Children's Coalition; National Coalition to Abolish Corporal Punishment in Schools; Parents and Teachers Against Violence in Education.

**Web Resource:** Campus Safety.

## Suicide and Life-Threatening Behavior

**Organizations:** American Foundation for Suicide Prevention; American Association of Suicidology; National Center for Injury Prevention and Control; National Children's Coalition.

**Publications:** *Suicide and Life Threatening Behavior.*

## Television and the Media

**Organizations:** Center for Communication and Social Policy; Center for Research on the Influences of Television on Children; National Coalition on Television Violence.

## Terrorism

**Organizations:** Institute for Victims of Trauma.

**Publications:** *Studies in Conflict and Terrorism; Terrorism and Political Violence.*

**Web Resources:** Minnesota Center Against Violence and Abuse.

## Victims Rights and Services

**Organizations:** Amnesty International; Child Abuse Prevention Association; Childhelp U.S.A.; Child Welfare League of America, Inc.; Committee Against Anti-Asian Violence; Community United Against Violence; Domestic Violence Project of the American Academy of Facial, Plastic, and Reconstructive Surgery; Incest Survivors Resource Network International; Institute for Victims of Trauma; LAMBDA GLBT Community Services Anti-Violence Project; Mothers Against Drunk Driving; National Center for Victims of Crime; National Domestic Violence Hotline; National Organization for Victim Assistance; Parents of Murdered Children; Southern Poverty Law Center; Stop Prisoner

Rape; Survivors of Incest Anonymous; Victim Services; VOICES in Action, Inc.

**Publications:** *Victimology: An International Journal; Violence and Victims.*

## War

**Organizations:** Center for Defense Information; Center on War and the Child; Holocaust Memorial Museum; Institute of Defense Analyses; Women Against Military Madness.

**Publications:** *International Journal of Group Tensions; Journal of Traumatic Stress.*

## Women

**Organizations:** American Women's Self-Defense Association; Battered Women's Movement; Center for the Prevention of Sexual and Domestic Violence; Coalition Against Trafficking in Women; Domestic Violence Project of the American Academy of Facial, Plastic, and Reconstructive Surgery; Equality Now; International Women's Rights Action Watch; National Clearinghouse for the Defense of Battered Women; National Organization for Women; Violence Against Women Grants Office; Women Against Military Madness; Women's International League for Peace and Freedom; Women Strike for Peace.

**Publications:** *Violence Against Women; Women and Criminal Justice.*

**Web Resources:** Violence Against Women Online Resources.

## Youth

**Organizations:** Barrios Unidos; Center for the Prevention of School Violence; Center for Research on the Influences of Television on Children; Center on War and the Child; Child Abuse Prevention Association; Childhelp U.S.A.; Children's Defense Fund; Children's Rights of America, Inc.; Child Welfare League of America, Inc.; Educational Information and Resource Center; End the Violence Against the Next Generation; Kids Count; National Alliance for Safe Schools; National Association of Child Advocates; National Association of Council for Children; National Association of Juvenile Correctional Agencies; National Center for Missing and Exploited Children; National Center for the Study of Corporal Punishment and Alternatives; National Center for Youth Law; National Children's Coalition; Office of Juvenile Justice and Delinquency Prevention; Parents and Teachers Against Violence in Education.

**Publications:** *Child and Youth Care Forum; Child Development; Children and Youth Services Review; Children's Legal Rights Journal; Child Welfare; Journal of Abnormal Child Psychology.*

**Web Resources:** Juvenile Justice Clearinghouse; Pacific Center for Violence Prevention; Resources for Youth.

# About the Editors

**RONALD GOTTESMAN, EDITOR IN CHIEF**
Ronald Gottesman, professor of English at the University of Southern California, was organizing editor for the first edition of the *Norton Anthology of American Literature*, now in its fifth edition. Gottesman established and directed the Center for Humanities at the University of Southern California, was the founding editor of two journals, and editor in chief or coeditor of five major book series in literature and film. *Perspectives on Citizen Kane*, edited and with an introduction by Gottesman, was published in 1996, and his coedited volume *Playing to the Camera: Film Actors Discuss Their Craft* was published in 1998. Gottesman has served as a consultant for many nonprofit organizations, such as the Aspen Institute.

**RICHARD MAXWELL BROWN, CONSULTING EDITOR**
Richard Maxwell Brown is the author of *Strain of Violence: Historical Studies of American Violence and Vigilantism* (1975), *No Duty to Retreat: Violence and Values in American History and Society* (1991), and many other works on American violence and vigilantism. He has served as a consultant to the National Commission on the Causes and Prevention of Violence (1968–1969) and is Beekman Professor Emeritus of Northwest and Pacific History at the University of Oregon.

## THE ADVISORY BOARD

**LAURA A. BAKER**
University of Southern California
Department of Psychology

**HOWARD BECKER**
University of California, Santa Barbara
Department of Sociology

**ERIC FONER**
Columbia University
Department of History

**JAMES GILLIGAN**
Cambridge Hospital
Cambridge, Massachusetts

**SANDER L. GILMAN**
University of Chicago
Departments of Germanic Studies and
Psychiatry

**JAMES A. INCIARDI**
University of Delaware
Center for Drug and Alcohol Studies

**W. J. T. MITCHELL**
University of Chicago
Departments of English and Art History

**ALEX PIQUERO**
Temple University
Department of Criminal Justice

# List of Contributors

**ABRAHAMSON, AMY C.**
University of Southern California
Department of Psychology
*Health and Medical Factors: Diet and Nutrition*

**ABZUG, ROBERT H.**
University of Texas at Austin
Departments of History and American Studies
*Holocaust*

**ADAMS, MICHAEL C. C.**
Northern Kentucky University
Department of History
*World War II*

**ALBINI, JOSEPH L.**
University of Nevada, Las Vegas
Department of Criminal Justice
*Black Hand*
*Mafia*

**ALPERT, GEOFFREY P.**
University of South Carolina
College of Criminal Justice
*Police: Overview*

**ALVAREZ, ALEXANDER**
Northern Arizona University
Department of Criminal Justice
*Statistics and Epidemiology*

**ANBINDER, TYLER**
George Washington University
Department of History
*Catholics*
*Nativism*

**ANDERSON, ELIJAH**
University of Pennsylvania
Department of Sociology
*Urban Violence*

**ANDERSON, FRED**
University of Colorado at Boulder
Department of History
*American Revolution: Military Campaigns*
*French and Indian War*

**ARCHER, JOHN**
University of Central Lancashire
Department of Psychology
*Sex Differences*

**ARCHIBALD, MATTHEW E.**
University of Washington, Seattle
Department of Sociology
*Draft Riots*
*Drunk Driving*

**ARTHUR, PAUL**
Montclair State University
Department of English
*Film: Documentary Film*

**BACHIN, ROBIN F.**
University of Miami
Department of History
*Sports*

**BACHMAN, RONET**
University of Delaware
Department of Sociology and Criminal Justice
*Rape: Incidence and Legal and Historical Aspects*

**BAILIE, GIL**
Florilegia Institute
Sonoma, California
*Theories of Violence: Religion*

**BAKER, LAURA A.**
University of Southern California
Department of Psychology
*Aggression*

BAKER, LAURA A. (*continued*)
*Psychophysiology: Vagal Tone*
*Smoking*
*Theories of Violence: Biology*
*Theories of Violence: Psychology*

BALBONI, ALAN
Community College of Southern Nevada, North Las Vegas
Department of Philosophical and Regional Studies
*Giancana, Sam*
*Las Vegas*

BALCH, ROBERT W.
University of Montana, Missoula
Department of Sociology
*Heaven's Gate*

BALMER, RANDALL
Barnard College
Columbia University
*Snake Handlers*

BANKS, NANCY A.
Columbia University
Department of History
*Luciano, "Lucky"*
*Pearl Harbor*
*Schools: Integration*
*Valachi, Joseph*

BANKS, ROSIE L.
University of Chicago
Department of English
*Chicano Moratorium*

BARLOW, MELISSA HICKMAN
University of Wisconsin–Milwaukee
School of Social Welfare
*Journalism*

BATEMAN, ROBERT L., III
United States Military Academy
Department of History
*Radio: Military and Police Uses*
*Private Security: Private Police*

BEASLEY, JERRY L.
Radford University
Department of Physical and Health Education
*Martial Arts*

BELT, TODD
University of Southern California
Department of Political Science
*Muslims*

BENGE, G. JACK, JR.
Bowling Green State University
Department of History
*Dred Scott Decision*

BLAKELY, EDWARD J.
New School University
Robert J. Milano School of Policy and Management
*Private Security: Gated Communities*

BLANCHARD, DALLAS A.
University of West Florida
Department of Sociology and Anthropology
*Abortion*

BLOCK, ALAN A.
Pennsylvania State University
Jewish Studies Program
*Costello, Frank*
*Diamond, Jack "Legs"*
*Organized Crime*

BLOCK, CAROLYN REBECCA
Illinois Criminal Justice Information Authority
*Homicide*

BOGGS, COLLEEN GLENNEY
University of Chicago
Department of English
*Pullman Strike*

BOLSTER, W. JEFFREY
University of New Hampshire
Department of History
*Privateers*

BORINSKY, ALICIA
Boston University
Department of Latin American Studies
*Machismo*

BOSKIN, JOSEPH
Boston University
Department of History
*Humor*

BOWEN, DEIRDRE M.
University of Washington, Seattle
Department of Sociology
*Gilmore, Gary*
*Kidnapping*

BOWKER, LEE H.
Humboldt University
Department of Sociology
*Prisons: Prison Violence*

BOYERS, ROBERT
Skidmore College
School of Arts and Letters
*Literature: Poetry*

BRADAC, JAMES J.
University of California, Santa Barbara
Department of Communication
*Language and Verbal Violence: Overview*

BRADDOCK, JOMILLS HENRY
University of Miami
Department of Sociology and Center for
  Research on Sport in Society
*Sports*

BRANDS, H. W.
Texas A&M University at College Station
Department of History
*Cold War*

BRAVIN, JESS
*The Wall Street Journal*
California Edition
*Manson, Charles*

BRENNAN, PATRICIA A.
Emory University
Department of Psychology
*Developmental Factors: Perinatal*

BRINEGAR, JERRY L.
New Beginnings Marriage and Family Therapy
Athens, Georgia
*Sibling Abuse*

BRODY, DAVID
University of California, Davis
Department of History, Emeritus
*Labor and Unions*

BRODY, DAVID
University of Delaware
Department of Art History
*Painting*

BROIDY, LISA MARIE
University New Mexico
Department of Sociology
*Developmental Factors: Childhood*

BROWN, BILL
University of Chicago
Department of History
*Posters*

BROWN, RICHARD MAXWELL
University of Oregon
Department of History
*Overview of Violence in the United States*
*"Fifty-four Forty or Fight"*
*Mussel Slough Conflict*
*No Duty to Retreat*
*Vigilantism*
*Walkdown*
*Western Civil War of Incorporation*

BROWNE, NICK
University of California, Los Angeles
Department of Film and Television
*Film: Aesthetics of Violence*

BRUNDAGE, W. FITZHUGH
University of Florida
Department of History
*Lynching*

BUENKER, JOHN D.
University of Wisconsin–Parkside
Department of History
*Theories of Violence: Overview I*
*Theories of Violence: History*

BURG, B. R.
Arizona State University
Department of History
*Piracy*

BURKE, TOD W.
Radford University
Department of Criminal Justice
*Carjacking*

BURNS, RICHARD DEAN
California State University, Los Angeles
Department of History, Emeritus
*Disarmament and Arms Control*

BURTON, ORVILLE VERNON
University of Illinois at Urbana
*Bosket Family*

BUSHWAY, SHAWN
University of Maryland College Park
Department of Criminology and Criminal
  Justice
*Recidivism of Violent Offenders: Overview*

BUTLER, ANNE M.
Utah State University
Department of History
*Prisons: Women Prisoners*
*Women: Outlaws*

BUZZANCO, ROBERT
University of Houston
Department of History
*Vietnam War*

CAMPBELL, PATRICIA J.
Editor and Author
Fallbrook, California
*Literature: Children's and Young Adult
Literature*

CANNON, LOU
The Washington Post
*Los Angeles Riots of 1992*

CAPECI, DOMINIC J., JR.
Southwest Missouri State University
Department of History
*Detroit*

CAPRIO, TEMBY
University of Chicago
Department of Germanic Studies
*Loeb, Richard, and Nathan Leopold*

CAREY, GREGORY
University of Colorado at Boulder
Institute for Behavioral Genetics
*Genetics: Twins, Families, and Adoptions*

CARMODY, DIANNE CYR
Old Dominion University
Department of Sociology and Criminal Justice
*Rape: Incidence and Legal and Historical Aspects*

CASEY, KAREN A.
Lynn University
School of Graduate Studies
*Sexual Harassment*

CASSIDY, KEITH
University of Guelph
Department of History
*Roe v. Wade* (sidebar in *Abortion*)

CHAFFIN, TOM
Emory University
Department of History
*Filibustering Expeditions*

CHANG, EDWARD TAEHAN
University of California, Riverside
Department of Ethnic Studies
*Korean Americans*

CHEMERINSKY, ERWIN
University of Southern California
School of Law
*Hate Crime*

CHRISTOPHER, RUSSELL L.
Columbia University
Faculty of Law
*Self-Defense and Security*

CHURCHILL, WARD
University of Colorado at Boulder
Department of Ethnic Studies
*American Indian Movement*

CLARKE, JAMES W.
University of Arizona
Department of Political Science
*Assassinations
Hinckley, John W., Jr.
Ray, James Earl
Sirhan Sirhan*

CLEAR, TODD R.
Florida State University
School of Criminology and Criminal Justice
*Prisons: Riots*

COATE, CHARLES
Eastern Oregon University
Department of History
*Dallas, Claude*

COCCARO, EMIL F.
University of Chicago
Pritzker School of Medicine
*Neurotransmitters: Serotonin*

COFFEY, COLLEEN M.
University of Colorado at Boulder
Department of Psychology
*Genetics: Twins, Families, and Adoptions*

COGAN, FRANCES B.
University of Oregon
Honors College
*Prisoners of War*

COHEN, ADAM MAX
University of Virginia
Department of English
*Black Panthers
Cleaver, Eldridge
Freedom Rides
Newton, Huey*

COLE, LEONARD A.
Rutgers, the State University of New Jersey,
Newark
Department of Political Science
*Weapons: Biological and Chemical*

COMINGS, DAVID E.
City of Hope Medical Center
Duarte, California
*Genetics: Molecular—Humans*

CONE, JAMES H.
Union Theological Seminary
New York, New York
*King, Martin Luther, Jr.*
*Malcolm X*

COODLEY, LAUREN HELENE
Napa Valley College
Department of History
*Industrial Workers of the World*

COOK, BERNIE
Georgetown University
Department of English
*Film: Censorship*
*Television: Violent Genres*

COOPER, CYNTHIA A.
Southern Illinois University at Edwardsville
Department of Mass Communication
*Television: Historical Overview*

COSTANZO, MARK
Claremont McKenna College and Claremont
Graduate University
*Execution, Methods of*

COUNTRYMAN, EDWARD
Southern Methodist University
Department of History
*American Revolution: Overview*
*Boston Massacre*

COURTOIS, CHRISTINE A.
Psychiatric Institute of Washington, D.C.
Posttraumatic Disorders Program
*Incest*

COURTWRIGHT, DAVID T.
University of North Florida
Department of History
*Frontier*
*Gender*

CRAIN, CALEB
Author
New York, New York
*Cannibalism*

CUKLANZ, LISA M.
Boston College
*Wilding and Berserking*

CURRY, G. DAVID
University of Missouri–St. Louis
Department of Criminology and Criminal
Justice
*Gangs*
*Robbery*

DANIELS, ROGER
University of Cincinnati
Department of History
*Asians*
*Chinese Exclusion Act*
*Japanese Americans*
*Japanese Americans, Incarceration of*

DAS, VEENA
Delhi School of Economics and
New School for Social Research
*Victims of Violence: Social Suffering*

DAVIS, CHAYNA J.
University of Colorado at Boulder
Institute for Behavioral Genetics
*Genetics: Twins, Families, and Adoptions*

DEARMENT, ROBERT K.
Author and Historian
Sylvania, Ohio
*Calamity Jane*
*Hickok, James Butler "Wild Bill"*
*Holliday, John Henry "Doc"*
*Huddleston, Ned*
*Scarborough, George Adolphus*

DECKER, SCOTT H.
University of Missouri–St. Louis
Department of Criminology and Criminal
Justice
*Gangs*
*Robbery*

DÉGH, LINDA
Indiana University
Folklore Institute
*Folk Narratives: Overview*

**DENNO, DEBORAH W.**
Fordham University Law School
*Health and Medical Factors: Lead*

**DEVERELL, WILLIAM**
California Institute of Technology
Division of the Humanities and Social Sciences
*Los Angeles Times Building, Bombing of*

**DEVINE, JOHN**
Author and Consultant
New York City
*Schools: Overview*

**DIETZ, ERIK**
University of Massachusetts at Lowell
Department of Criminal Justice
*Assault*
*Sentencing*

**DINAN, JOHN J.**
Wake Forest University
Department of Politics
*Civil Liberties*

**DINNERSTEIN, LEONARD**
University of Arizona
Department of History
*Frank, Leo*
*Immigration*
*Jews*

**DOTSON, BILL**
University of Chicago
Department of English
*Road Rage*
*Strategic Defense Initiative*

**DUBOFSKY, MELVYN**
Binghamton University, State University of
    New York
Department of History
*Haywood, William*
*Strikes*

**DUSENBURY, LINDA**
Cornell Medical University
Weill Medical College
*Schools: Antiviolence Curricula*

**DYKSTRA, ROBERT R.**
University at Albany, State University of
    New York
School of Public Policy
*Dodge City*

**EARLE, JONATHAN**
University of Kansas
Department of History
*Abolition*

**EASTMAN, CAROLYN**
Johns Hopkins University
Department of History
*Long Walk of the Navajo*

**EDWARDS, JEROME E.**
University of Nevada, Reno
Department of History
*Gambling*

**EISENSTEIN, ZILLAH**
Ithaca College
Department of Political Science
*Hate, Politics of*

**ETHINGTON, PHILIP J.**
University of Southern California
Department of History
*Los Angeles*

**EVERITT, DAVID**
Freelance Writer and Author
Huntington, New York
*Berkowitz, David "Son of Sam"*
*Bundy, Ted*
*Dahmer, Jeffrey*
*DeSalvo, Albert*
*Fish, Albert*
*Gacy, John Wayne*
*Gein, Ed*
*Holmes, H. H.*
*Lucas, Henry Lee*
*Panzram, Carl*
*Unruh, Howard*

**EWING, CHARLES PATRICK**
University at Buffalo, State University of
    New York
School of Law
*Teenagers*

**FABIANIC, DAVID**
University of Central Florida
Department of Criminal Justice and Legal
    Studies
*Hoffa, Jimmy*
*Hoover, J. Edgar*

**FARMER, MARY J.**
Bowling Green State University
Department of History
*Black Codes*

FARRINGTON, DAVID P.
   Cambridge University
   Institute of Criminology
      *Psychophysiology: Heart Rate*

FAVAZZA, ARMANDO R.
   University of Missouri–Columbia
   Department of Psychiatry and Neurology
      *Mutilation of the Body*

FEARNOW, MARK
   Pennsylvania State University
   School of Theatre
      *Theater*

FEELEY, MALCOLM
   University of California, Berkeley
   School of Law
      *Deadly Force*

FELLMAN, MICHAEL
   Simon Fraser University
   Department of History
      *Guerrilla Warfare*
      *James, Jesse*

FERRELL, JEFF
   Northern Arizona University
   Department of Criminal Justice
      *Graffiti*

FESSLER, PAUL R.
   Culver-Stockton College
   Department of History
      *German Americans*

FISHBEIN, DIANA H.
   Research Triangle Institute
   Transdisciplinary Behavioral Science Program
      *Neurotransmitters: Dopamine, Norepinephrine,*
         *and Their Metabolic Enzyme, Monoamine*
         *Oxidase*

FLEMING, DAN
   University of Ulster at Coleraine
   School of Media and the Performing Arts
      *Toys and Games*

FLOR-HENRY, PIERRE
   University of Alberta
   Clinical Diagnostics and Research Center
      *Neuropsychology: Hemispheric Laterality*

FOOTE, KENNETH E.
   University of Texas at Austin
   Department of Geography
      *Memorials*

FRANCIONE, GARY L.
   Rutgers, the State University of New Jersey,
      Newark
   School of Law
      *Animals, Violence Against*

FRANK, ANDREW KEVIN
   California State University, Los Angeles
   Department of History
      *South*

FRANKLIN, H. BRUCE
   Rutgers, the State University of New Jersey,
      Newark
   Department of English
      *Literature: Nuclear War Fiction*

FRIEDMAN, LAWRENCE M.
   Stanford University
   School of Law
      *Crime and Punishment in American History*

FRIMAN, H. RICHARD
   Marquette University
   Department of Political Science
      *Drugs: Drug Trade*

FURNISS, MAUREEN RUTH
   Chapman University
   Department of Film Studies
      *Film: Animation*

FYFE, JAMES J.
   Department of Criminal Justice
   Temple University
      *Police: Police Brutality*
      *Police: Police Use of Force*

GAGE, BEVERLY
   Columbia University
   Department of History
      *Wall Street, Bombing of*

GALLAGHER, EUGENE V.
   Connecticut College
   Department of Religious Studies
      *Cults*
      *Koresh, David*

GARBARINO, JAMES
   Cornell University
   Department of Human Development
      *Poverty*

GARVER, NEWTON
   University at Buffalo, State University of
      New York
   Department of Philosophy
      *Nonviolence*

GATZKE, LISA M.
University of Southern California
Department of Psychology
*Psychophysiology: EEG*

GIBBONS, PATRICK
University of California, Los Angeles
Emergency Medicine Center
*Medicine and Violence: Emergency*
*Medicine*

GIGLIO, JAMES N.
Southwest Missouri State University
Department of History
*Kennedy, John F.*
*Kennedy, Robert F.*

GILJE, PAUL A.
University of Oklahoma
Department of History
*Irish Americans*

GILLETTE, HOWARD, JR.
Rutgers, the State University of New Jersey,
Camden
Department of History
*Washington, D.C.*

GILLIGAN, JAMES
Cambridge Hospital
Cambridge, Massachusetts
*Psychological Violence*
*Structural Violence*

GINDHART, MARIA P.
University of Pennsylvania
Department of History of Art
*Sculpture*

GLADMAN, KIMBERLY R.
New York University
Department of Comparative Literature
*Literature: Pulp Fiction*
*Spillane, Mickey*

GOLDMAN, MARTIN S.
Merrimack College
Center for the Study of Jewish-Christian
Relations
*Crazy Horse*

GOLOMB, BEATRICE A.
University of California, San Diego
Department of Medicine
*Health and Medical Factors:*
*Cholesterol*

GONZÁLEZ, GASPAR
Yale University
American Studies Program
*Film: Representing Gender, Race, and Ethnicity*

GOODMAN, JAMES
Rutgers, the State University of New Jersey,
Newark
Department of History
*Scottsboro Case*

GOODWIN, JAMES
University of California, Los Angeles
Department of English
*Photography*
*Weegee (Arthur Felig)*

GOULART, RON
Author
Weston, Connecticut
*Comics*

GRANT, BARRY KEITH
Brock University
Department of Communication, Popular
Culture, and Film
*Film: Landmark Films*

GRAY, CHRIS HABLES
University of Great Falls
Department of Cultural Studies and Technology
*Politics: Government*
*Politics: Political Campaigns*

GREENE, JACK R.
Temple University
Department of Criminal Justice and Center for
Public Policy
*Police: Overview*

GRIMSHAW, ALLEN D.
Indiana University
Department of Sociology
*Riots*

GRISWOLD DEL CASTILLO, RICHARD
San Diego State University
Department of Chicana and Chicano Studies
*Mexican Americans*

GROSS, BRUCE H.
University of Southern California
School of Medicine
Department of Psychiatry and the Behavioral
Sciences
*Forensic Psychiatry*

HAAS, KENNETH C.
University of Delaware
Department of Sociology and Criminal Justice
*Confessions, Coerced*
*Corporal Punishment*
*Cruel and Unusual Punishment*

HACSI, TIMOTHY A.
Harvard University
Harvard Children's Initiative
*Child Labor*

HADDEN, SALLY E.
Florida State University
Department of History and College of Law
*Fugitive Slave Acts*

HAGERMAN, EDWARD
York University
Department of History
*Militarism*

HAINES, DVIDA W.
George Mason University
Department of Sociology and Anthropology
*Vietnamese Americans*

HALBROOK, STEPHEN P.
Attorney
Fairfax, Virginia
*National Rifle Association*
*Right to Bear Arms*

HALL, VAN BECK
University of Pittsburgh
Department of History
*Whiskey Rebellion*

HAMM, MARK S.
Indiana State University
Department of Criminology
*McVeigh, Timothy*
*Ruby Ridge*
*Waco*

HAMM, RICHARD F.
University at Albany, State University of
New York
Department of History
*Prohibition and Temperance*

HAMPSON, RICK
*USA Today*
*Gambino, Carlo*
*Genovese, Vito*
*Gotti, John*

HANAGAN, MICHAEL P.
New School University
Center for Studies of Social Change
*American Violence in Comparative Perspective*

HANSOM, PAUL
University of Southern California
Writing Program
*Black Dahlia Case*
*G-men*
*My Lai Massacre*

HARRIES, KEITH
University of Maryland Baltimore County
Department of Geography and Environmental
Systems
*Geography of Violence*

HARRIS, ROBERT L., JR.
Cornell University
Africana Studies and Research Center
*African Americans*

HAWKINS, DARNELL F.
University of Illinois at Chicago
Departments of African-American Studies,
Sociology, and Criminal Justice
*Race and Ethnicity*

HAWLEY, F. FREDERICK
Western Carolina University
Department of Criminal Justice
*Gun Violence: Gun Culture*

HEARN, CHESTER G.
Author
Potts Grove, Pennsylvania
*Harpers Ferry, Raid on*

HEIDE, KATHLEEN M.
University of South Florida, Tampa
Department of Criminology
*Parricide*

HEINEMAN, KEN
Ohio University
Department of History
*Antiwar Protests*

HENDIN, HERBERT
New York Medical College
Department of Psychiatry
*Assisted Suicide and Euthanasia*
*Suicide*

HENNESSY, JAMES J.
Fordham University School of Education
Division of Educational and Psychological
  Services
*Thrill Crime*

HENRY, BILL C.
Colby College
Department of Psychology
*Neuropsychology: Brain Function*

HERZOG, TODD
University of Chicago
Department of Germanic Studies
*Copycat Violence*
*Scapegoat*
*Spectacle, Violence as*

HICKEY, DONALD R.
Wayne State College, Nebraska
Department of History
*War of 1812*

HIETTER, PAUL T.
Mesa Community College, Phoenix, Arizona
Department of Social Sciences
*Phoenix*

HIGGENS-EVENSON, R. RUDY
San Francisco State University
Department of History
*Booth, John Wilkes*
*Brown, John*
*Depressions, Economic*
*War: Aftermath of, Physical Aspects*

HIRSCH, ARNOLD R.
University of New Orleans
Department of History
*New Orleans*

HITTMAN, MICHAEL
Long Island University, Brooklyn
Department of Anthropology, Sociology, and
  Social Work
*Wovoka*

HO, HSIU-ZU
University of California, Santa Barbara
Department of Education and Psychology
*Endocrinology: PMS and Female Violence*

HODOS, JEROME
University of Pennsylvania
Department of Sociology
*Urban Violence*

HOFER, MATTHEW R.
University of Chicago
Department of English Language and Literature
*Language and Verbal Violence: Legal Status*

HOGAN, NANCY GRIER
University of Chicago
Pritzker School of Medicine
*Jehovah's Witnesses*
*Medicine and Violence: Medical Experimentation
  on the Mentally Ill*
*Neurotransmitters: GABA*

HONG, FORREST
LivHOME, Inc., Los Angeles, California
Community Outreach and Education
*Domestic Violence*

HORNE, GERALD
University of North Carolina, Chapel Hill
Institute of African American Research
*MOVE Bombing*
*Watts Riot*

HOUSE-HIGGINS, CAROLYN
University of Exeter
Department of Women's Studies
*Women: Overview*

HUGGINS, MARTHA K.
Union College, Schenectady, New York
Department of Sociology
*Foreign Police, U.S. Training of*

HUMMEL, RICHARD L.
Eastern Illinois University, Charleston
Department of Sociology and Anthropology
*Hunting*

HUNT, ALFRED
Purchase College, State University of New York
Department of History
*Slave Rebellions*

HUNT, DARNELL M.
University of Southern California
Department of Sociology
*Simpson, O. J., Murder Trials*

INCIARDI, CRAIG J.
Rock and Roll Hall of Fame
*Music: Popular*

INCIARDI, JAMES A.
University of Delaware
Center for Drug and Alcohol Studies
*Bounty Hunters*
*Criminal Justice System*

**INCIARDI, JAMES A.** (*continued*)
*Drugs: Drugs and Crime*
*Genovese, Kitty, Murder of*
*Goetz, Bernhard H.*
*Hijacking*
*Plea Bargaining*
*Starkweather, Charles, and Caril Ann Fugate*

**INGALLS, ROBERT P.**
University of South Florida
Department of History
*Cuban Americans*

**ISHIKAWA, SHARON S.**
University of California, Los Angeles
Department of Psychology
*Temperament*

**ISSEL, WILLIAM**
San Francisco State University
Department of History
*San Francisco*

**JENNINGS, FRANCIS**
The Newberry Library
D'Arcy McNickle Center for the History of the
    American Indian, Emeritus
*American Indians: Overview*

**JENSEN, ROBERT**
University of Texas at Austin
Department of Journalism
*Pornography*

**JOHNSON, IDA M.**
University of Alabama
Department of Criminal Justice
*Incidence of Violence*

**JOHNSON, LOCH K.**
University of Georgia
Department of Political Science
*Central Intelligence Agency*

**JOHNSON, ROBERT**
American University, Washington, D.C.
Department of Justice, Law, and Society
*Death Row*

**JONES, HOWARD**
University of Alabama
Department of History
*Amistad Case*

**JONES, JACK**
Journalist
Naples, New York
*Lennon, John, Murder of*

**JONES, JACQUELINE**
Brandeis University
Department of American History
*Class*

**JOSELIT, JENNA WEISSMAN**
Princeton University
Department of American Studies
*Lansky, Meyer*
*Lepke, Louis*
*Murder, Inc.*
*Schultz, "Dutch" (Arthur Flegenheimer)*
*Siegel, Benjamin "Bugsy"*

**KANE, ROBERT**
Portland State University
Division of Administration of Justice
*Police: Police Brutality*
*Police: Police Use of Force*

**KANER, ANGELICA**
Yale University School of Medicine
Department of Psychiatry
*Anorexia and Bulimia*

**KANN, MARK E.**
University of Southern California
Department of Political Science
*Government Commissions*
*Jackson State*
*Kent State*
*New Left*

**KAPLAN, JEFFREY**
Helsinki University
Renvall Institute
*Religion*
*Satanism, Modern*

**KARNO, VALERIE**
University of Southern California
Department of English
*Wuornos, Aileen*

**KASTENBAUM, ROBERT**
Arizona State University
Department of Communication, Emeritus
*Thanatology*

**KATES, DON B.**
Pacific Research Institute for Public Policy
*Saturday Night Specials*
*Weapons: Handguns*

**KAWIN, BRUCE F.**
University of Colorado at Boulder
Department of English and Film Studies
*Film: Violent Genres*

**KENNY, KEVIN**
Boston College
Department of History and Irish Studies
Program
*Molly Maguires*

**KERSTEN, ANDREW E.**
University of Wisconsin–Green Bay
Department of History
*Suffrage*

**KETZ, LOUISE B.**
Louise B. Ketz Agency
New York, New York
*Alamo*
*Blackbeard*
*Cody, William "Buffalo Bill"*
*Garrett, Pat*
*Kidd, Captain William*
*Mexican War*
*Quantrill's Raid*
*Spanish-American War*

**KIMMEL, MICHAEL S.**
State University of New York at Stony Brook
Department of Sociology
*Masculinity*

**KINLOCK, TIMOTHY**
University of Baltimore and Friends Research
Institute
Division of Criminal Justice, Criminology, and
Social Policy
*Drugs: Drug Prevention and Treatment*

**KIPNIS, LAURA**
Northwestern University
Department of Radio-Television-Film
*Serial Killers, Representations of*

**KLOCKARS, CARL B.**
University of Delaware
Department of Sociology and Criminal Justice
*Police: Community Policing*

**KNOX, SARA LOUISE**
University of Western Sydney
Faculty of Social Inquiry
*Literature: Popular Fiction*

**KOPEL, DAVID B.**
Independence Institute
Golden, Colorado
*Police: Police Violence*

**KOSS, MARY P.**
University of Arizona, Tucson
Department of Public Health, Family and
Community Medicine, Psychiatry, and
Psychology
*Women: Overview*

**KRASE, JERRY**
Brooklyn College, City University of New York
Department of Sociology
*Crown Heights Riot*

**KRAUS, JOE**
Oakton Community College, Des Plaines,
Illinois
Department of English
*Dillinger, John*
*St. Valentine's Day Massacre*

**KREBS, CHRISTOPHER R.**
Florida State University
School of Criminology and Criminal Justice
*Prisons: Riots*

**KRIESBERG, LOUIS**
Syracuse University
Department of Social Conflict Studies, Emeritus
*Conflict Resolution: International and
Institutional*

**KRSTULJA, WALTER F.**
Attorney and Forensic Consultant
Orange, California
*Forensic Science*

**KRUESI, MARCUS J. P.**
University of Illinois at Chicago
Department of Psychiatry
Institute for Juvenile Research
*Neurotransmitters: Overview*

**KUMMINGS, DONALD D.**
University of Wisconsin–Parkside
Department of English
*Deringer, Henry, Jr.*
*Remington, Eliphalet*
*Winchester, Oliver Fisher*

**KURTZ, LESTER R.**
University of Texas at Austin
Departments of Sociology and Asian Studies
*Methodologies of Violence Research*

**KUSHNER, HARVEY W.**
Long Island University
Department of Criminal Justice
*Atlanta Centennial Olympic Park, Bombing of*

KUSHNER, HARVEY W. (*continued*)
*Bombings and Bomb Scares*
*Letter Bombs*
*Unabomber*
*World Trade Center Bombing*

KWONG, PETER
Hunter College, City University of New York
Department of Urban Affairs and Planning
*Chinese Americans*

LAGASSÉ, MAUREEN A.
University of Virginia
Department of English
*Howard Beach Incident*

LAMAY, CRAIG L.
Northwestern University
Medill School of Journalism
*Television: Children's Television*

LANE, ROGER
Haverford College
Department of History
*Capital Punishment*

LANGLEY, LESTER D.
University of Georgia
Research Department of History
*Military Interventions: Overview*

LAPSANSKY, EMMA J.
Haverford College
Department of History
*Quakers*

LARSEN, LAWRENCE H.
University of Missouri–Kansas City
Department of History
*Kansas City*

LEDERER, SUSAN E.
Yale University School of Medicine
Section of the History of Medicine
*Medicine and Violence: Overview*
*Sterilization, Involuntary*
*Tuskegee Syphilis Study*

LEE, MATTHEW T.
University of Delaware
Department of Sociology and Criminal Justice
*Symbolic Violence*

LEFLER, D.
University of Chicago
Department of English
*Zodiac Killer*

LEONARD, STEPHEN J.
Metropolitan State College of Denver
Department of History
*Denver*

LEONARD, THOMAS C.
University of California, Berkeley
Graduate School of Journalism
*Muckrakers*

LEVAO, RONALD
Rutgers, the State University of New Jersey,
New Brunswick
Department of English
*Boxing*

LEVINE, MARTIN LYON
University of Southern California
Department of Law, Gerontology, Psychiatry
and the Behavioral Sciences
*Torture*

LEVY, JACK S.
Rutgers, the State University of New Jersey,
New Brunswick
Department of Political Science
*War: Causes of*

LEWIS, BARBARA WILLIAMS
University of Texas at Austin
Department of English
*Bowie, James*

LEWIS, CATHERINE F.
University of Connecticut Health Center
Department of Psychiatry
*Infanticide and Neonaticide*

LEWIS, DAN A.
Northwestern University
Department of Education and Social Policy
*Costs of Violent Crime*

LEWIS, DAVID LEVERING
Rutgers, the State University of New Jersey,
New Brunswick
Department of History
*National Association for the Advancement of
Colored People*

LEWIS, PATRICIA SCHEIERN
University of Chicago
Department of English
*Fine Arts*

551

**LI, W. CHERRY**
Santa Monica College, California
Department of Academic Computing
*Internet*

**LILIENFELD, SCOTT O.**
Emory University
Department of Psychology
*Health and Medical Factors: Body Types*

**LILLY, J. ROBERT**
Northern Kentucky University, Highland
Heights
Department of Sociology
*Stalking*

**LIPINSKI, DANIEL**
Duke University
Department of Political Science
*Terrorism*

**LIPPARD, CHRIS**
University of Utah
Film Studies Program
*Film: Directors*

**LIPSTADT, DEBORAH E.**
Emory University
The Institute for Jewish Studies
*Neo-Nazis*

**LIU, JIANG-HONG**
University of California, Los Angeles
School of Nursing
*Prevention: Early Health Preventions*

**LONSDALE, KATHLEEN**
University of Southern California
Department of English
*Atlanta Child Murders*

**LOUGHRAN, TRISH**
University of Chicago
Department of English
*Alien and Sedition Acts*

**LYKKEN, DAVID**
University of Minnesota
Department of Psychology, Emeritus
*Eugenics*

**LYNAM, DONALD**
University of Kentucky
Department of Psychology
*Developmental Factors: Puberty and Adolescence*

**McBRIDE, DUANE C.**
Andrews University
Department of Behavioral Sciences
*Drugs: Drugs and Violence*

**McBROOME, DELORES NASON**
Humboldt State University
Department of History
*Southern Christian Leadership Conference*

**McCORD, JOAN**
Temple University
Department of Criminal Justice
*Intergenerational Transmission of Violence*

**McELRATH, KAREN**
Queens University, Belfast
Department of Sociology and Social Policy
*Vandalism and Violence Against Property*

**McGARY, HOWARD**
Rutgers, the State University of New Jersey,
New Brunswick
Department of Philosophy
*Theories of Violence: Philosophy*

**McINTYRE, LANN G.**
McIntyre & McIntyre
San Diego, California
*Crime, Legal Definitions of*

**McINTYRE, MONTY A.**
McIntyre & McIntyre
San Diego, California
*Wrongful Death*

**MACKEY, ROBERT R.**
United States Military Academy
Department of History
*Foreign Intervention, Fear of*
*Military Interventions: Peacekeeping Missions*
*Mormons*
*Weapons: Conventional*
*Weapons: Nuclear*

**MACKEY, THOMAS C.**
University of Louisville
Department of History
*Enforcement Acts*
*White Slavery*

**MacNEIL, GORDON**
University of Alabama
School of Social Work
*Gun Violence: Overview*

**MADRIZ, ESTHER**
University of San Francisco
Department of Sociology
*Theories of Violence: Overview II*

**MAGUIRE, BRENDAN**
Western Illinois University
Department of Sociology and Anthropology
*Wrestling, Professional*

**MAGUIRE, PETER**
Independent Scholar
New York, New York
*Ultimate Fighting*
*War Crimes*

**MALES, MIKE A.**
University of California, Irvine
School of Social Ecology
*Children*

**MARC, DAVID**
Syracuse University
S. I. Newhouse School of Public
Communications
*Popular Culture*

**MARTINEZ, RAMIRO, JR.**
University of Delaware
Department of Sociology and Criminal Justice
*Symbolic Violence*

**MARX, GARY T.**
Massachusetts Institute of Technology, Emeritus
*Social Control*

**MAXSON, STEPHEN C.**
University of Connecticut
Department of Psychology
*Animal Studies of Aggression and Violence*

**MEDNICK, SARNOFF A.**
University of Southern California
Social Science Research Institute
*Developmental Factors: Prenatal*
*Genetics: Chromosomal Abnormalities*
*Recidivism of Violent Offenders: Genetic Factors*

**MERANZE, MICHAEL**
University of California, San Diego
Department of History
*Prisons: Overview*

**MERCILLIOTT, FREDERICK**
Chowan College
Department of Criminal Justice
*Arson and Fire*

**MERCY, JAMES A.**
Centers for Disease Prevention and Control
National Center for Injury Prevention and
Control
*Gun Violence: Epidemiology of Injuries*

**MILLER, RANDALL M.**
Saint Joseph's University
Department of History
*Philadelphia*

**MITCHELL, W. J. T.**
University of Chicago
Departments of English and Art History
*Representation of Violence*

**MOON, MICHAEL**
John Hopkins University
Department of English
*Gay Bashing*

**MOORE, JACK B.**
University of South Florida
Department of English
*Du Bois, W. E. B.*
*Skinheads*

**MOORE, LEONARD J.**
McGill University
Department of History
*Ku Klux Klan*

**MORGAN, ALEX B.**
Emory University
Department of Psychology
*Health and Medical Factors: Body Types*

**MORIARTY, LAURA J.**
Virginia Commonwealth University
Department of Criminal Justice
*Campus Violence*

**MORRISON, EMORY**
University of Washington, Seattle
Department of Sociology
*Birth Order and Birth Spacing*
*Capitalism*

**MOURE-ERASO, RAFAEL**
University of Massachusetts at Lowell
Department of Work Environment
*Sweatshops*

**MUHAMMAD, KHALIL GIBRAN**
Rutgers, the State University of New Jersey,
New Brunswick
Department of History
*National Association for the Advancement of
Colored People*

553

NATHANSON, DONALD L.
Jefferson Medical College
The Sylvan S. Tomkins Institute
*Emotion*
*Shame*

NEWTON, MICHAEL
Freelance Author
Nashville, Indiana
*Mass Murder: Individual Perpetrators*

NOCK, MATTHEW K.
Yale University
Department of Psychology
*Suicide*

NORWOOD, ANN E.
Uniformed Services University
F. Edward Herbert School of Medicine
Department of Psychiatry
*Post-Traumatic Stress Disorder*

NOYES, JOHN K.
University of Cape Town
Department of Classical Languages and
Literatures
*Sadism and Masochism*

O'BRIEN, ROBERT M.
University of Oregon
Department of Sociology
*National Crime Victimization Survey*

OKRENT, NICHOLAS E.
Columbia University
Department of Philosophy
*Miami*

O'NEILL, WILLIAM L.
Rutgers, the State University of New Jersey,
New Brunswick
Department of History
*War: Introduction*

ORSAK, CATHERINE B.
University of Texas
Southwestern Medical Center at Dallas
Department of Psychiatry
*War: Aftermath of, Psychoanalytic Aspects*

OSTLER, JEFFREY
University of Oregon
Department of History
*Sitting Bull*
*Wounded Knee, 1890*
*Wounded Knee, 1973*

OTTERBEIN, KEITH F.
University at Buffalo, State University of
New York
Department of Anthropology
*Theories of Violence: Anthropology*

PAGÁN, EDUARDO OBREGÓN
Williams College
Department of History
*Zoot-Suit Riot*

PAINTER, NELL IRVIN
Princeton University
Department of History
*Slavery*

PALETZ, DAVID L.
Duke University
Department of Political Science
*Terrorism*

PALLONE, NATHANIEL J.
Rutgers, the State University of New Jersey,
New Brunswick
Center of Alcohol Studies
*Thrill Crime*

PARKER, GREGORY L.
Columbia University
Department of History
*Gatling, Richard Jordan*
*Gulf of Tonkin Resolution*
*Suburban Violence*
*Tampering, Product*

PASCHEL, JARRETT
University of Washington
Department of Sociology
*Barker, Ma "Arizona Kate"*
*Kelly, George "Machine Gun"*
*McCarthy, Joseph R.*
*Tarring and Feathering*

PATERSON, THOMAS G.
University of Connecticut
Department of History
*Contras*
*Cuban Missile Crisis*

PATRICK, CHRISTOPHER J.
University of Minnesota
Department of Psychology
*Psychopathy, Biology of*

**PEAK, JASON W.**
Attorney
Reno, Nevada
*Sex Offenders*

**PEAK, KENNETH J.**
University of Nevada, Reno
Department of Criminal Justice
*Sex Offenders*

**PEBWORTH, MICHAEL JONATHAN**
University of Oregon
Department of History
*Atlanta*
*Haiti, Rebellion in*
*Red Scare*
*St. Louis*
*Seattle*

**PEEK-ASA, CORINNE**
University of California, Los Angeles
Southern California Injury Prevention Research
    Center
*Workplace*

**PERSELLIN, KETURA**
Freelance Writer
Philadelphia, Pennsylvania
*Fashion*

**PETERS, TRACY W.**
University of Washington, Seattle
Department of Sociology
*Cassidy, Butch, and the Sundance Kid*
*Corona, Juan*
*Floyd, Charles Arthur "Pretty Boy"*
*Hunt, Joe*
*Lindbergh Kidnapping Case*
*Nelson, George "Baby Face"*
*Speck, Richard*
*Whitman, Charles*

**PHILLIPS, MICHAEL**
University of Texas at Austin
Department of History
*Dallas*
*Houston*

**PINSKER, MATTHEW**
Millersville University
Department of History
*Civil War*

**PIQUERO, ALEX**
Temple University
Department of Criminal Justice
*Age and the Life Cycle*

**POK, BINH H.**
City University of New York
Graduate School and University Center
*Borden, Lizzie*

**POPE, CARL E.**
University of Wisconsin–Milwaukee
Department of Criminal Justice
*Crime and Violence, Popular Misconceptions of*

**POPE, DANIEL**
University of Oregon
Department of History
*Advertising*

**POWELL, LAWRENCE N.**
Tulane University
Department of History
*Long, Huey*

**PROCTER, BEN**
Texas Christian University
Department of History
*Hearst, William Randolph*

**PULA, JAMES S.**
Utica College of Syracuse University
School of Graduate and Continuing Education
*Polish Americans*

**QUIRK, JEFFREY T.**
Pennsylvania State University
Department of Biobehavioral Health
*Endocrinology: Overview*

**RABLE, GEORGE C.**
University of Alabama
Department of History
*Reconstruction*

**RAFFETY, MATTHEW TAYLOR**
Columbia University
Department of History
*Boston*
*Chicago*
*Symbionese Liberation Army*

**RAINE, ADRIAN**
University of Southern California
Department of Psychology
*Neuropsychology: Brain Imaging*
*Prevention: Early Health Preventions*
*Psychophysiology: Autonomic Activity*
*Temperament*

555

RASKIN, JONAH
University of California, Berkeley
Department of Communication Studies
*Hoffman, Abbie*
*Weatherman and Weather Underground*
*Yippie!*

REED, JOHN SCOTT
San Diego State University
Department of History
*Gun Control*

REIS, ELIZABETH
University of Oregon
Department of History
*Salem Witch Trials*
*Witchcraft*

RENSHON, STANLEY A.
City University of New York
Department of Political Science
*Gulf War*

RENZETTI, CLAIRE M.
St. Joseph's University
Department of Sociology
*Women: Women Who Kill*

RESNICK, PHILLIP J.
Case Western Reserve University
Department of Psychiatry
*Infanticide and Neonaticide*

REYNOLDS, MIKE
University of Southern California
Department of English
*Oswald, Lee Harvey*
*Ruby, Jack*

ROBERTS, ALBERT R.
Rutgers, the State University of New Jersey,
Piscataway
Department of Administration of Justice
*Gun Violence: Overview*
*Rehabilitation of Violent Offenders*
*Spousal and Partner Abuse*
*Victims of Violence: Overview*

ROBERTS, BEVERLY J.
American Red Cross of New Jersey
*Prostitution*
*Rehabilitation of Violent Offenders*

ROBERTS, GARY L.
Abraham Baldwin College
Department of History
*Billy the Kid*
*Canton, Frank*
*Clanton Gang*
*Colt, Samuel*

ROBERTS, GARY L. (*continued*)
*Dalton Gang*
*Earp Brothers*
*Gunfighters and Outlaws, Western*
*Hardin, John Wesley*
*Masterson, William "Bat"*
*O. K. Corral Gunfight*
*Sand Creek Massacre*

ROLLE, ANDREW
Occidental College
Department of History
*Bridger, Jim*
*Frémont, John Charles*

RORABAUGH, W. J.
University of Washington, Seattle
Department of History
*Free Speech Movement*

ROSENBAUM, ALAN
University of Massachusetts Medical School
*Neuropsychology: Head Injury*

ROSENFELD, RICHARD
University of Missouri–St. Louis
Department of Criminology and Criminal
Justice
*Theories of Violence: Behavioral Sciences*

ROTH, MITCHEL
Sam Houston State University
Department of History
*Bonnie and Clyde*

ROTHMAN, HAL
University of Nevada, Las Vegas
Department of History
*West*

ROWE, DAVID C.
University of Arizona
Department of Family Studies
*Nature vs. Nurture*

RUBENSTEIN, RICHARD E.
George Mason University
School of Public Affairs
*Militias, Authorized*

RUSSO, ALEXANDER
Brown University
Department of American Civilization
*Radio: Popular*

RYAN, PATRICK J.
Long Island University, Emeritus
*Capone, Al*
*Ness, Eliot*

**SANTIAGO-IRIZARRY, VILMA**
Cornell University
Department of Anthropology and Latino
    Studies Program
*Puerto Ricans*

**SAUM, CHRISTINE A.**
University of Delaware
Center for Drug and Alcohol Studies
*Uniform Crime Reports*

**SAYRE, HENRY M.**
Oregon State University
Department of Art
*Performance Art*

**SCARPA, ANGELA**
Virginia Polytechnic Institute and State
    University
Department of Psychology
*Child Abuse: Physical*
*Endocrinology: Hormones in Child Abuse*

**SCARPACI, VINCENZA**
University of Oregon
Department of History
*Sacco-Vanzetti Case*

**SCHAAL, BENOIST**
Centre National de la Recherche Scientifique
Nouzilly, France
*Endocrinology: Testosterone*

**SCHECHTER, HAROLD**
Queens College, State University of New York
Department of English
*Cunanan, Andrew*
*Serial Killers*

**SCHEESE, DON**
Gustavus Adolphus College
Department of English
*Environment, Violence Against*

**SCHILDGEN, ROBERT**
*Sierra* magazine and University of California
    Publishing Program
*Menendez, Erik and Lyle*

**SCHNEIROV, RICHARD**
Indiana State University
Department of History
*Haymarket Square Riot*

**SCHRIGER, DAVID**
University of California, Los Angeles
Emergency Medicine Center
*Medicine and Violence: Emergency Medicine*

**SCHULZ, WILLIAM F.**
Amnesty International USA
*Amnesty International*
*Human Rights*
*Weapons: Stun or Shock Devices*

**SENECAL, NIKKI**
University of Southern California
Department of English
*Smith, Susan*
*Theories of Violence: Feminism*

**SHAPIRO, HERBERT**
University of Cincinnati
Department of History
*Civil Rights Movements*

**SHINNICK, JULIA**
National Coalition of Independent Scholars
*Music: Musicals*

**SHUCARD, ALAN**
University of Wisconsin–Parkside
Department of English
*Bureau of Alcohol, Tobacco, and Firearms*
*Moran, George "Bugs"*

**SHULMAN, ROBERT**
University of Washington, Seattle
Department of English
*Literature: Fiction*

**SIEGEL, LARRY**
University of Massachusetts at Lowell
Department of Criminal Justice
*Assault*
*Sentencing*

**SIEGEL, MARCIA B.**
Independent Scholar
Rockport, Massachusetts
*Dance*

**SIKORA, FRANK**
Journalist
Birmingham, Alabama
*Church Bombings*

**SILLITOE, LINDA**
Journalist and Author
Mesa, Arizona
*Hofmann, Mark*

**SILVERMAN, MORTON M.**
University of Chicago
Department of Psychiatry
*Self-Destructiveness*

SIMON, RON
Columbia University and Museum of Television and Radio
*Television: Censorship*

SIMPSON, CHRISTOPHER
American University, Washington, D.C.
School of Communication
*Government Violence Against Citizens*

SINGER, MARGARET THALER
University of California, Berkeley
Department of Psychology
*Jonestown*

SLUTSKE, WENDY S.
University of Missouri–Columbia
Department of Psychology
*Alcohol and Alcoholism*

SMEAD, HOWARD
University of Maryland College Park
Department of History
*Civil Disobedience*
*Civil Disorder*

SMITH, CATHERINE PARSONS
University of Nevada, Reno
Department of Music
*Music: Classical*

SOKOL-KATZ, JAN
University of Miami
Department of Sociology and Center for Research on Sport in Society
*Sports*

SONN, RICHARD D.
University of Arkansas, Fayetteville
Department of History
*Anarchism*

SONNENBERG, STEPHEN M.
Baylor College of Medicine
Department of Psychiatry and Behavioral Sciences
*War: Aftermath of, Psychoanalytic Aspects*

STANNARD, DAVID E.
University of Hawaii
Department of American Studies
*American Indians: American Indian Holocaust*

STARR, RAYMOND G.
San Diego State University
Department of History, Emeritus
*San Diego*

STAUB, ERVIN
University of Massachusetts at Amherst
Department of Psychology
*Bystanders*
*Mass Murder: Collective Murder*
*Peacemaking*

STERN, KENNETH S.
American Jewish Committee
*Militias, Unauthorized*

STINE, HOWARD E.
University of Washington, Seattle
Department of Sociology
*Hiroshima and Nagasaki*

STOCK, CATHERINE McNICOL
Connecticut College
Department of History and American Studies
*Agrarian Violence*

STONER, MADELEINE R.
University of Southern California
School of Social Work
*Homelessness*

STRICKLAND, RENNARD
University of Oregon
School of Law
*Trail of Tears*

STURTEVANT, WILLIAM C.
Smithsonian Institution
Department of Anthropology
*Scalping*

SURRATT, HILARY L.
University of Delaware
*Maternal Prenatal Violence*

SUSMAN, ELIZABETH J.
Pennsylvania State University
Department of Biobehavioral Health
*Endocrinology: Overview*

SUSSMAN, STEVE
University of Southern California
Institute for Health Promotion and Disease Prevention Research
*Tobacco Industry*

SWAGERTY, WILLIAM R.
University of Idaho
Department of History
*Chief Joseph*

TAL, KALÍ
University of Arizona, Tucson
Arizona International College
*Literature: Nonfiction Prose*

TEHRANI, JASMINE A.
University of Southern California
Social Science Research Institute
*Developmental Factors: Prenatal*
*Genetics: Chromosomal Abnormalities*
*Recidivism of Violent Offenders: Genetic Factors*

TERRY, YVONNE M.
Andrews University
Department of Behavior Sciences
*Drugs: Drugs and Violence*

THEOHARIS, ATHAN G.
Marquette University
Department of History
*Federal Bureau of Investigation*

THORNTON, J. MILLS, III
University of Michigan
Department of History
*Montgomery Bus Boycott*

TOCH, HANS
University at Albany, State University of
New York
School of Criminal Justice
*Prisons: Prison Conditions*

TORRES, ADRIANA N.
New York University
Shirley M. Ehrenkranz School of Social Work
*Drive-by Shooting*

TREMBLAY, RICHARD E.
University of Montreal
Department of Psychiatry and Psychology
*Endocrinology: Testosterone*

TRICKETT, PENELOPE K.
University of Southern California
School of Social Work
*Child Abuse: Sexual*

TURK, AUSTIN T.
University of California, Riverside
Department of Sociology
*Oklahoma City Bombing*

TURNER, THOMAS R.
Bridgewater State College
Department of History
*Lincoln, Abraham*

TURPIN, JENNIFER
University of San Francisco
Department of Sociology
*Methodologies of Violence Research*
*Prevention: Violent-Crime Prevention*
*Theories of Violence: Political and Social Sciences*

URSANO, ROBERT J.
Uniformed Services University
F. Edward Herbert School of Medicine
Department of Psychiatry
*Post-Traumatic Stress Disorder*

VALENTE, SHARON M.
University of Southern California
Department of Nursing
*Child Abuse: Ritual*

VALENTINE, PAMELA VEST
University of Alabama at Birmingham
Department of Government and Public Service
*Fight-or-Flight Syndrome*

VAN HULLE, CAROL A.
University of Colorado at Boulder
Institute for Behavioral Genetics
*Genetics: Twins, Families, and Adoptions*

VECOLI, RUDOLPH J.
University of Minnesota
Department of History
*Italian Americans*

VITALE, ALEX S.
Brooklyn College
Department of Sociology
*New York*

VORRASI, JOSEPH A.
Cornell University
Department of Human Development
*Poverty*

WACHS, ELEANOR
Harvard University
Radcliffe Seminars
*Folk Culture*
*Folk Narratives: New York City Crime-Victim*
*Stories*

WALLER, ALTINA L.
University of Connecticut, Storrs
Department of History
*Feuds*

WALSH, ANTHONY
Boise State University
Department of Criminal Justice
*Rape: Biosocial Aspects*
*Sociobiology*

559

WARD, MICHELLE
University of Southern California
Department of Psychology
*Smoking*

WARTERS, WILLIAM C.
Wayne State University
College of Urban, Labor, and Metropolitan
Affairs
*Conflict Resolution: Interpersonal*

WEBBER, MICHAEL J.
University of San Francisco
Department of Sociology
*Theories of Violence: Political and Social Sciences*

WEINBERG, LEONARD
University of Nevada, Reno
Department of Political Science
*Extremism*

WEISHEIT, RALPH A.
Illinois State University
Department of Criminal Justice
*Rural Violence*

WEISS, HAROLD J., JR.
Jamestown Community College, Jamestown,
New York
Department of History
*Texas Rangers*

WEISSBERG, ROGER
University of Illinois at Chicago
Department of Psychology and Education
*Schools: Antiviolence Curricula*

WELLS, ANNE SHARP
George C. Marshall Foundation
*Korean War*

WERTH, JR., JAMES L.
American Psychological Association
*Euthanasia*

WEST, ELLIOTT
University of Arkansas, Fayetteville
Department of History
*American Indians: American Indian Wars*

WILBANKS, WILLIAM
Florida International University
Department of Criminal Justice, Emeritus
*Miami*

WILBER, KATHLEEN H.
University of Southern California
School of Gerontology and School of Policy,
Planning, and Development
*Elder Abuse*

WINTER, JAY
Cambridge University
Pembroke College
*World War I*

WOLFE, CHARLES
University of California, Santa Barbara
Department of Film Studies
*Film: Overview*

WOOSTER, ROBERT
Texas A&M Universities at Corpus Christi
Department of Humanities
*Custer, George Armstrong*
*D-Day*
*Military Culture*

WOZNIAK, JOHN F.
Western Illinois University
Department of Sociology and Anthropology
*Wrestling, Professional*

WRIGHT, JOHN PAUL
East Tennessee State University
Department of Criminal Justice and
Criminology
*Corporations*

WYATT-BROWN, BERTRAM
University of Florida
Department of History
*Dueling*
*Honor*

YARALIAN, PAULINE S.
University of Southern California
Department of Psychology
*Neuropsychology: Brain Imaging*
*Psychophysiology: Autonomic Activity*

ZIMMERMAN, BRIAN
University of Chicago
Department of English
*Tet Offensive*
*Video Games*

# Index

Note: Volume numbers precede page numbers in **boldface.** Page numbers in **bold-face** refer to the main entry or subentry on the subject. Pages with illustrations, tables, or graphs are cited in *italics*.

and control of aggression, **3:**329a

fearlessness and fearfulness and, **3:**278a

Anarchism, **1:105b–107b**

and Haymarket Square bombing (1886), **1:**157a–158a, 213b–214a; **2:**97a–99a; **3:**225a–b

Italian Americans and, **2:**183b–184a; **3:**75a–78a

and labor movement, **2:**239b

and Wall Street bombing (1920), **3:**392b

*Anarchist Cookbook, The* (Powell), **1:**107a, 157a

Anastasia, Albert, **2:**2b, 30b, 297a, 415a

Ancient Order of Hibernians (AOH), **2:**403b

Ancient world

infanticide in, **2:**171b

sports violence in, **3:**198b–199a

Andelman, Bob, **3:**198a

Anderson, Bloody Bill, **2:**189b

Anderson, Jack, **2:**413b

Andersonville prison camp (Georgia), **2:**357a, 589a–b, 593a

Andrews, Dana, **2:**43b

Andrews, Joan, **3:**34a

Androcur (cyproterone acetate), **3:**12a–b

Androgens

rape and, **3:**11b–12a

*See also* Testosterone

Andromorphy, **2:**101a

Andros, Edmund, **1:**75b, **168b**

Anger

Darwin on, **2:**443b

and memory, **1:**35a

and violence, **1:**456a

Anger, Kenneth, *Fireworks,* **1:**517a

Anger-rage, affect of, **1:**457b

Angiolillo, Michelle, **2:**183b

Anglo-French colonial wars, **1:**591a

French and Indian War, **1:**75b–76a, **590b–594a**

Angry Arts Festival, **2:**512b

Animal ethics, modern, **1:**115a–b

Animals

aggression in, **1:**54b

ethological theory of, **2:**443b–444a

evolutionary theory of, **2:**444a–b

human aggression compared with, **1:**116b

proximate versus ultimate explanations of, **2:**444b–445a

sex differences in, **1:**117a; **2:**445a–b

in children's literature, **2:**277b

Descartes on, **1:**107b–108b

as executioners, **1:**491b

humane-treatment principle, **1:**108b–109b

human uses of, **1:**109b–113a

as property, **1:**113a–114a

snake handling, **3:173a–174b**

violence against, **1:107b–116a,** 108a, 112a. *See also* Hunting

Animal sacrifice, satanist, **3:**92b

Animal studies

of aggression and violence, **1:**54b, **116a–120b**

of fearlessness and fearfulness, **3:**279a

Animal waste, pollution from, **1:**474a

Animal welfare laws, **1:**109a–b, 113b–114a

Animation, **1:537a–540b; 3:**272a

early, **1:**537a–538b

monitoring content of, **1:**539a–540b

violence for humorous effect in, **1:**538b–539a

Annan, Kofi, **1:**180a

Anomic suicide, **3:**237b

Anomie-strain theory, **3:**306a

Anonymous bomb threats, **1:**156a

Anorexia, **1:120b–122a; 3:**128b

Antarctic Treaty, **1:**414a–b

Antebellum era

labor violence in, **3:**224a–b

melodrama in, **3:**292b–293a

southern violence in, **3:**184a–186a

urban violence in, **3:**354a–355a

Antheil, George, **2:**417b

Anthony, Susan B., **2:**486a

Anthrax, **3:**399a, 413b

Anthropology, theories of violence, **3:302b–305a**

Antiabolitionist riots, **1:**261b; **3:**53a–54a

Antiabortion movement, **1:**25a

and civil disobedience, **1:**243b

demonstrations, **1:***26a–b*

participants in, **1:**28a–b, *255a–b*

violence espoused by, **1:**25b–28b; **2:**621a; **3:**34a–b

Web site, **2:**178a

Anti-androgens, chemical castration of rapists using, **3:**12a–b

Anti-Arson Act (1982), **1:**185b

Anti-Car Theft Act (1992), **1:**208a–b

Anti-Chinese movement, **1:**233a, 234b, 235a–b

cartoon satirizing, **1:***235a–b*

Anti-Defamation League (ADL), **2:**94b

Antietam, Battle of, **1:**270a–b, 272b

Antigovernment sentiment

in Christian Identity movement, **3:**33b

extremism and, **1:**496b–497a

riots, **3:**53b, 54a–b

Ruby Ridge and, **3:**71a

in rural areas, **3:**73b–74a

in western states, **3:**73b

Anti-Imperialist League, **1:**124a

Anti-Japanese movement, **2:**190b

Antinomian violence, **3:**34b–36a

Heaven's Gate cult suicide as, **3:**36a

Jonestown massacre as, **3:**35a–36a

Waco as, **3:**36a

Anti-rape movement, **3:**312a, 456a, 457a–b

Anti-Saloon League, **2:**622a

Anti-segregation movement, **1:**236b–237a

Anti-Semitism, **2:**94b–95a

in Atlanta (Georgia), **1:**139a

in Christian Identity movement, **3:**33a–b

Crown Heights Riot, **1:355b–357a**

demonstration supporting, **2:***197b*

in Ford (Henry) newspaper series, **3:**33a–b, 38a

Frank's (Leo) trial and, **1:**585a–b

and hate crimes, **2:**96a

Holocaust revelations and, **2:**125b

on Internet, **2:**179b–180a

Jewish immigration in 1920s and, **3:**38a

linguistic aspects of, **2:**246b

neo-Nazis and, **2:**451a–b

as violence to Jewish identities, **3:**249b

Antislavery riots, **3:**54a

Anti-Slavery Society, meeting of, **1:***262a–b*

Antisocial behavior

autonomic activity and, **2:**635a–637b, 639a–641a; **3:**309a

childhood factors for, **1:**402a–403b

genetic factors for, **2:**24a–25b

heritability of, **2:**26a, 27a, 28a

perinatal factors for, **1:**400a–402a

prenatal factors for, **1:**398a–400a

Antisocial personality disorder, **1:**64a; **2:**507a

and alcohol dependence, **1:**64a–b, 65a–b

versus psychopathy, **2:**631b–632a

Antiterrorism and Effective Death Penalty Act (1996), **1:**185b, 258b

Anti-Terrorism Assistance Program, and foreign-police training, **1:**572b

Antiterrorism measures, **3:**283a–b, 283b–284a

civil liberties and, **3:**283b–284a

media as, **3:**282b

Antiviolence curricula, **3:**108b, **112a–114b**

recommended elements, **3:**112b–114a

Antiwar protests, **1:122b–127a,** *242a–b*

in 1960s, **1:**288b–289a

allusions to Holocaust in, **2:**126a–b

assaults on protesters, **3:**56a

Chicano Moratorium, **1:216a–217a; 2:**365a

as civil disobedience, **1:**242a–b

Civil War and, **1:**123b

Hoffman (Abbie) and, **2:**120b

Jackson State demonstrations, **1:**191a, 289a; **2:187a–188b,** 217b

Kent State demonstrations, **1:**126b, 191a, 289a; **2:216a–218a,** 392b

military intervention in, **2:**392b

posters used for, **2:**574a–b

Revolutionary War and, **1:**123a

riots caused by, **3:**54b

student, **1:**190b–191a, *191a–b*

Vietnam War and, **1:**125b–126b, *126a–b,* 242a, 245b–246a; **3:**383a

women and, **3:**313a

World War I and, **1:**124a–125a

World War II and, **1:**125a–b

Antonowicz, D. H., **3:**28b–29a

Antonucci, Danny, **1:**540a

Antrim, William, **1:**146a. *See also* Billy the Kid

Anxiety, child abuse and, **1:**221b

AOG. *See* Army of God

AOH. *See* Ancient Order of Hibernians

Apaches

in American Indian wars, **1:**2b, 89a–b

atrocities committed by, **1:**598b

Mescalero, **1:**88b; **3:**437a

O. K. Corral gunfight, **1:**277a, 277b, 450b; **2:**73b, 124a, **489a–490b;** **3:**391b
rough-and-tumble fighting, **1:**244b
in St. Louis (Missouri), **3:**80b–82a
in San Diego (California), **3:**87a–b
Texas Rangers, **3:288b–290b**
twentieth-century, **1:**599b–601a
vigilantism, **1:**7b–8a, 599a–b; **2:**518b; **3:**384a–386a, 387a
*See also* Gunfighters and outlaws, Western
Frost, J. William, **2:**645a
Frost, Robert, **2:**282b
Frustration-aggression hypothesis, **3:**198a, 322b, 323a
Frye, Marquette, **3:**411a, 441a
*Frye v. United States*, **1:**582a
FSM. *See* Free Speech Movement
Fuerzas Armadas Revolucionarias de Colombia (FARC), **1:**439a–b
Fugate, Caril Ann, **3:215b–216b,** *216a*
Fugitive-recovery agents, **1:**172a, 173a–b
Fugitive Slave Acts, **1:601b–603b**
of 1793, **1:**263a, 602b
of 1850, **1:**263a, 603a
cartoon on, **1:***602a–b*
Fuhrman, Mark, **3:**156b
Fujisaki, Hiroshi, **3:**157b
Fulbright, J. William, **2:**63b
Fuller, Wes, **2:**490a
*Full Metal Jacket* (film), **1:**526b
Fulminante, Oreste, **1:**296a
*Furman v. Georgia*, **1:**202a, 340b, 346a–b, 359a
Fusion bomb, **3:**426a–b
Fussell, Paul, **3:**484b
Fyfe, James J., **2:**543a

# G

GABA (gamma-aminobutyric acid), **2:470a–b**
Gabrielli, William, **2:**462b; **3:**21a–b
Gacy, John Wayne, **2:1a–2a,** *2a*
Gaddis, Thomas, **2:**504a
Gadsby, Jane, **3:**364b
Gag animation, **1:**537b
Gage, Lyman, **2:**98b–99a
Gage, Thomas, **3:**49a
Gagliano, Joseph, **2:**496a
Gaines, William, **1:**292a
Gaither, Billy Jack, **2:**19b
Galás, Diamanda, **2:**417a
Galen of Pergamon, **3:**278b
Gall, Franz Joseph, **3:**307a
Galleani, Luigi, **2:**183b; **3:**77a
Galleanisti, **2:**183b–184a
Galski, Thomas, **2:**463b
Galton, Francis, **1:**484a, 484b; **2:**447a
eumemic suggestion of, **1:**486b
Galtung, Johan, **2:**362b; **3:**229b
Gambino, Carlo, **2:2a–3b,** *3a,* 31a
and Gotti (John), **2:**45b
Gamble, J. W., **1:**359b
Gambling, **2:3b–6a**
Costello (Frank) and, **1:**318a

Holliday (John Henry "Doc") and, **2:**123b
Kefauver Committee on, **2:**4a–b
Lansky (Meyer) and, **2:**253a
organized crime and, **2:**493b
as popular recreation, **2:**4b–5a
Schultz (Dutch) and, **2:**493b
Siegel (Benjamin "Bugsy") and, **3:**154a–b
in South, historical, **3:**199b
Games. *See* Role-playing games; Toys; Video games
Game theory
aggression according to, **1:**117b–118a
conflict resolution according to, **1:**298a
Gamma-aminobutyric acid (GABA), **2:**470a–b
Gandhi, Mohandas K.
and civil disobedience, **1:**239a–240a, 242b; **2:**486a
and Civil Rights movement, **1:**241a
influence on King (Martin Luther, Jr.), **1:**241b–242a; **2:**224b
nonviolence of, **2:**486b
on poverty, **2:**577b; **3:**230a
Gangbang (rumble), **1:**424a
*Gangbusters* (radio program), **3:**9a
Gang rape
of Central Park jogger (1989), **3:**261a
women's march in defense of rapists (1983), **3:**250a
Gangs, **2:6a–13b**
and crime, **2:**7a, 8b–11b
and drive-by shooting, **1:423b–425b**
and drugs, **2:**11b–12a
elements of, **2:**6b–7a
and fashion, **1:**500b
and graffiti, **2:**7a, 58b–60a
and gun culture, **2:**83b
honor codes and, **2:**137a
in Los Angeles (California), **2:**9a–b, 12a, 290b–291a
machismo and, **2:**306b
membership in, determining, **2:**7a–b
origins and evolution of, **2:**8b–9a
outlaw, vigilantism against, **3:**383b–384a, 385a
police search of members, **2:***8a–b*
police toleration of, **3:**177a
in prison, **2:**604b, 606b
responding to, **2:**12b–13a
skinhead, **3:**161a–162b
and social institutions, **2:**12a–b
teenage, **3:***256a–b*
urban violence by
in antebellum period, **3:**355b
in mid-twentieth century, **3:**357a
Vietnamese American, **3:**377a–b
Watts riot and, **3:**411b–412a
women in, **2:**12a, 306b–307a
Gangster films, **1:**519b–520a, 528b–529a, 533a; **2:**42b, 565b–566a
Gangster rap, **2:**422b–423a, 566a
Gans, Harper, **2:**104b
Gans, Joe, **1:**175a
Gantz, John, **1:**389a
GAO. *See* General Accounting Office

Gara, Larry, **2:**483b
Garbarino, James, **2:**580a, 630a
Garcia, Allesandro, **2:**333a–b
Gardner, Alexander, **1:**558a; **2:**520b, 522b
Gardner, John, **2:**420a
Garfield, James, **1:**275b
memorial statue of, **2:**357a
Garfinkel, Harold, **3:**246b–247a
Gargullo, Merlita, **3:**193b–194a
Garment industry
labor law violations in California (1990s), **3:**244a–245a, *245a*
sweatshops, **3:243a–245a,** *244a–b*
Garnet, Henry Highland, **1:**22a, 263a
sources of inspiration for, **2:**90b
Garnets, Linda, **3:**459a
Garnier, Gilles, **3:**133b
Garrett, H. Lawrence, III, **2:**380a
Garrett, Pat, **1:**146b–147a; **2:13b–15a,** 73b
slaying Billy the Kid, **2:***14a–b*
Garrison, William Lloyd, **1:**21b, 123a–b, 263a, 444b; **2:**433a
Gartner, Rosemary, **3:**323a
Garvey, Marcus, **1:**496b; **2:**311b, 312a
Gary, Joseph E., **1:**157b; **2:**98b
Gas
lethal, execution by, **1:**494a
poison, **3:**398a, 415a
Gasoline bomb, **1:**127b
Gastil, Raymond D., **2:**35a
Gated communities, **2:**614a–616b
Gates, Daryl, **2:**292b, 293a, 553b, 554b
Gates, Henry Louis, Jr., **1:**286a
Gatling, Richard Jordan, **2:15a–16a,** *15a;* **3:**416b
Gatling gun, **2:**15a–16a; **3:**416b–417a
Gault, Gerald, **1:**335b
Gault, Tip, **2:**143b, 144a
Gay bashing, **2:16a–20b**
definition of, **3:**209a
hate crimes, **2:**95a–b
literature on, **2:**278b
in military, **2:**380b–381a
in rap music, **2:**422b
by Satanists, **3:**93a
by skinheads, **3:**162a
Stonewall riots (1969), **2:**17b, 18a; **3:**56b, 302a
television censorship and, **3:**265a, 269a
White Night Riot (1979), **3:**91a
Gaynor, William, **2:**523b
Gay rights activism, **3:**302a
and civil disobedience, **1:**243b
origins of, **2:**17b
Gazecki, William, **3:**391a
*Waco: The Rules of Engagement,* **1:**542b–543a
Gedney, Thomas, **1:**102a
Geertz, Clifford, **3:**194b
Gein, Ed, **2:20b–21b,** *21a;* **3:**134b
films based on life of, **1:**520a; **2:**20b
home of, **3:**135a–b
Geller, William A., **2:**549b
Gelles, Richard J., **1:**147b; **2:**169a
Gender, **2:21b–22b**
and alcohol-related violence, **1:**61a–b
and alcohol use, **1:**59b, 60a

torture of, by Immigration and
Naturalization Service, **3**:334b
violence against, in St. Louis
(Missouri), **3**:82a
violent behavior of, **3**:3b, 4b
*See also specific groups*
Immigration, **2:155a–163b**
Alien and Sedition Acts, **1:66a–67a,**
254b
and anti-Catholic sentiment, **1**:210a;
**3**:38a
anti-Semitism and, **3**:38a
Chinese, **1**:232b; **2**:440b
Chinese Exclusion Act (1882), **1**:233a,
**234b–236a; 2**:441b
in colonial era, **2**:155b–156b
and ethnic tensions
in Boston (Massachusetts),
**1**:169b–170a
in Detroit (Michigan), **1**:394b
in Los Angeles (California), **2**:290b
and extremism, **1**:496a
German, **2**:37b
Irish, **1**:169b, 211a; **2**:155b, 156b–157a,
439a
Korean, **2**:226b
in nineteenth century, **2**:156b–159b,
440a; **3**:355a–b
Polish, **2**:555b–556a
post–Civil War, **1**:14a–b
postindependence, **2**:438b–439a
Puerto Rican, **2**:641b
Sacco-Vanzetti case and, **3**:75b
in twentieth century, **2**:160a–163a, 442b
vigilante religious violence and, **3**:38a
to Western Europe, **3**:1a
Immigration and Naturalization Service,
torture by, **3**:334b
Imperial Food Products sweatshop fire
(1991), **3**:244a–b
Imperialism, **2**:372b–373a, 389a–391a,
392a
Imprecatory prayer, in pro-life rescue
movement, **3**:34b
Impulsivity
and juvenile substance abuse and
violence, **3**:256b
and suicide, **3**:240a
and thrill-seeking behavior, **3**:328b
Incapacitation, as sentencing goal, **3**:131a
Incarceration
of conscientious objectors, **2**:482b–483b
effect of, misconceptions regarding,
**1**:345b–346a
history of, **3**:130b
as incapacitation, **3**:131a
reformative, **2**:594a–595a
shock (boot camp), **3**:132b
*See also* Prisons
Ince, Thomas, **1**:514b
Incest, **2:163a–166a**
bystanders to, **1**:187b–188a
consequences of, **2**:164b–165b
definition of, **2**:163b
prevalence of, **2**:163b, 164a
in slave-owning families, **3**:170a
treatment protocols for, **2**:165b

Inciardi, James A., **2**:625b
Incidence of violence, **2:166a–170a**
domestic violence, **2**:168b–169a
elder abuse, **1**:453b–454a
homicide, **2**:166b–167b
physical assault, **2**:168b
rape, **2**:167b–168a; **3**:13b–14b
workplace, **3**:468a–470b, *468a–b, 470a*
*See also* Statistics
*Incidents in the Life of a Slave Girl* (Jacobs),
**2**:264a
Inclusive fitness, and child abuse and
neglect, **3**:181a
*In Cold Blood* (Capote), **2**:274a, 333a–b
Income
victimization by, **3**:367a, 367b
*See also* Socioeconomic status
Incompetency, issue of, in criminal-court
proceedings, **1**:574a–575b
Incorporation, **1**:14a–15b; **2**:71a
Western Civil War of, **3:441b–443b**
Indentured servants, **3**:184a
abuse of, **1**:279a–b
American Indians as, **3**:454a
in Bacon's Rebellion, **1**:57a
children as, **1**:227a
immigrants as, **2**:156a
Indeterminate sentence, **1**:334b; **3**:131a–b
Index crimes, **2**:250b–251a; **3**:219a,
351b–352a
in rural versus urban areas, **3**:72a
*See also* Legal definitions; Uniform
Crime Reports
India
anticolonial campaign in, **1**:239b–240a
execution methods in, **1**:491b
murder rate in, **2**:31b–32a
poverty rate in, **2**:579b
violence levels in, **2**:32a–b
Indiana, vigilantism in, **3**:385a
*Indian Ghost Dancer, The* (Bartlett), **3**:121b
Indian removal. *See* Trail of Tears
Indian Removal Act (1830), **3**:344a
Indians
in Africa, mistreatment of, **1**:129b
American. *See* American Indians
in U.S., mistreatment of, **1**:130a
Indian War of 1864, **3**:86a
*Indicators of School Crime and Safety* report,
**3**:103b, 104b–105b
Indictment, **1**:353a
Individual violence, and collective
violence, **2**:359b–360a
Indonesia, Chinese in, **1**:129b
Industrial conflict, **1**:9a–b
*See also* Labor unrest
Industrial Revolution
American, **1**:312b–313a
and immigration, **2**:156b
Industrial society
and popular culture, **2**:563a–564a
structured order in, **1**:16b
transition to information society,
violence associated with,
**1**:16a–17a
violent climate of, **2**:73a
Industrial violence. *See* Labor unrest

Industrial Workers of the World (IWW),
**2:170a–171a,** 241a
campaign against incorporation, **1**:15b
and civil disobedience, **1**:240b
disturbances involving
in San Diego (California), **3**:87b–88b
in Seattle (Washington), **3**:124a–b
and extremism, **1**:497b
founding of, **1**:106a
Haywood (William "Big Bill") and,
**2**:99b–100a
headquarters in Seattle (Washington),
**1**:*15a–b*
Red Scare of 1919–1920 and, **3**:26b
violence against, **1**:125a, 283b; **2**:558a
and Western Civil War of
Incorporation, **3**:442a
Inequality
as cause of riots, **3**:62b–63a
as cause of violence, **3**:230a, 232b–233a
and racial differences in criminal
violence rates, **3**:4b–5a
and racial violence, **3**:5a, 61b
in school spending, **3**:116b
as structural violence, **3:229b–233b**
Infancy
manifestations of aggression in, **1**:51a
tendencies toward violence in, **1**:402b
Infanticide, **2:171a–174a; 3**:465b–466a
in animals, **1**:118a–b
crime characteristics of, **2**:172b–173a
definition of, **2**:171b
evolutionary/sociobiological
explanation for, **3**:181a–b
legal issues regarding, **2**:173a–b
rate of, **2**:171b
*Infantry Journal*, articles on radio
published in, **3**:7a–b
Infibulation, **2**:427a
Influenza, prenatal exposure to, effects of,
**1**:398a–b, *399a*
Informants, police, nonenforcement
policies toward, **3**:176a–177a
Information (document), **1**:353a–b
Information society, **1**:17b–18a
transition to, violence associated with,
**1**:16a–17a
Information warfare, **3**:421a
Informed consent
of mentally ill, **2**:349b, 351a–b
Nuremberg Code and, **2**:350a
patient, **2**:338a–b
principle of, **1**:135b
*In Front of the Children: Screen
Entertainment and Young Audiences*
(Bazalgette and Buckingham), **1**:539a
INF Treaty, **1**:414a–b
Ingenito, Ernest, **2**:330a
*Ingraham v. Wright*, **1**:308a–b, 311b
In-group bias, **2**:247b
Initial appearance, in criminal justice
process, **1**:352a–b
Injection, lethal, execution by, **1**:494a;
**2**:145b
Injuries
blunt, **2**:343b–344a, 459a
carjackings and, **1**:206b

representations of, **2:**184a, 184b–185a, 565b

reputation for violence, **2:**182b

Sacco-Vanzetti case, **1:**107a; **2:**160b–161a, 184a; **3:75a–78a**

secret societies of, **1:**100a

violence against, **2:**442a, 474b

zoot-suits and, **3:**500b

Italy, Mafia in, **2:**310b–311a

*I, the Jury* (Spillane), **3:**196b, 197a

Ito, Lance A., **3:**156b

Iverson, Sherrice, **2:**29b

Ives, Charles, songs of, **2:**416b–417a, 417b

Ives "Destroyers" (toys), **3:**338b, 339b

IWW. *See* Industrial Workers of the World

# J

Jack Broughton's Rules of 1743 (boxing), **1:**174b, 175a

Jacklin, Carol, **2:**446a–b

Jackson, Andrew

and American Indian holocaust, **1:**79b; **2:**322b

in American Indian wars, **1:**84b, 85a

and dueling, **1:**446a

and Indian removal, **3:**344a–b

and invasion of Florida, **2:**385b

maternal legacy of, **2:**319a

and vigilantism, **1:**8a; **3:**386a

in War of 1812, **3:**407a–b, 408a

Jackson, Jimmie Lee, **1:**268b

Jackson, John J., **3:**197b

Jackson, Kenneth, **3:**234a

Jackson, Pamela Irving, **2:**9b

Jackson, Thomas J. "Stonewall," **2:**92b, 372a

death of, **2:**382a

Jacksonian era

class-related violence in, **1:**280b

riots in, **1:**247b–248a

Jackson State College/University riots (1970), **1:**191a, 289a; **2:187a–188b,** 217b

*Jackson v. Bishop,* **1:**311a–b, 360a

Jack the Ripper, **3:**133b

and copycat violence, **1:**305a

JACL. *See* Japanese American Citizens' League

Jacob, story of, **3:**153b

Jacobs, Harriet, *Incidents in the Life of a Slave Girl,* **2:**264a

Jacobs, Mike, **1:**179b

"Jacob Wetterling Act" (1994), **3:**145a

Jagger, Mick, **1:**542b; **2:**422a

Jails. *See* Prisons

Jamaica, pirates in, **2:**528a–b

James, Frank, **1:**13a, 375a; **2:**72a, 188b–189a, 190a, 647a

James, Jesse, **1:**13a, 563b; **2:**72a, 72b, **188b–190b,** *189b;* **3:**438b

pistol used by, **3:***423a*

as resister to incorporation, **3:**442a

James Bond series, **1:**517a, 530b

James gang, **1:**377b; **2:**189a–190a, 647a; **3:**462a

Jameson, Fredric, **3:**46b

Jamestown (Virginia)

burning of (1676), **3:**183b, *184a–b*

Indian attacks on, **1:**73b, 80b–81a; **3:**31a

Janis, Irving, **3:**320a–b

Janney, Samuel, **2:**646a

Janowitz, Morris, **3:**61a

*Janus Report,* on sadomasochism, **3:**79a

Japan

Hiroshima and Nagasaki, **2:116b–119a,** *117a–b,* 275a, 323b–324a; **3:**425b

homicide rate in, **1:**17a

and human medical experimentation, **2:**349b

infanticide in, **2:**171b

Koreans in, mistreatment of, **1:**129b

nerve agent used in, **3:**414b

Pearl Harbor attack, **2:510a–511a,** *511a–b*

use of biological weapons against China, **3:**414b

Japanese American Citizens' League (JACL), **2:**194b

Japanese Americans, **2:190b–192b**

discrimination of, **2:**192b–193a

evacuation of, **2:***194a*

incarceration of, **1:**258a, 266b, 570b; **2:**162a, 191b–192a, **192b–195b**

violence against, **1:**130a; **2:**191a, 193b, 519a

Japanese prisoners of war, in World War II, **2:**591b–592a

Jarrell, Randall, **2:**283b–284a, 285b

Javogues, Claude, **1:**97b

*Jaws* (film), **1:**533a

Jealousy

and dating violence, **1:**193a

evolutionary underpinnings of, **3:**179b–180a

Jeffers, Robinson, **2:**283a–b

Jefferson, Thomas, **1:**261a

and Alien Acts, **1:**67a

and American Indian holocaust, **1:**79a–b

on continuous revolution, **3:**44b, 73b

and Declaration of Independence, **2:**438b

and filibusters, **1:**511a

and military interventions, **2:**385b

on slavery's impact on owners, **3:**169b

on violence, **3:**318a

and westward expansion, **3:**434b

on white southern violence, **3:**183a

Jeffries, Jim, **1:**175b; **3:**202a–b, *203a–b*

Jehovah's Witnesses, **2:195b–196b**

and freedom of speech issue, **1:**255a

Jemison, Mary, **3:**453a

Jenkins, Josh, **2:**332a

Jenkins, Will, **2:**275a

Jennings, Henry, **2:**114a

Jenny Craig Weight Loss Center, symbolic violence against women, **3:**250b–251a

Jerome, "Black Jack," **1:**390a

*Jerry Springer Show,* **3:**263a–b, 264b

Jervis, Robert, **3:**403a

Jewell, Richard, **1:**140b

Jewish Chronic Disease Hospital experiments (1963), **2:**349b

Jews, **2:197a–198b**

versus African Americans, **1:**252b

and anarchism, **1:**105b

attacks on, **2:**157b, 159a–b, 161b. *See also* Anti-Semitism

conspiracy theories regarding, **2:**451a

derogatory terms for, **2:**156b

discrimination of, **2:**197a

end to, **1:**300b

Eastern European, attacks on, **2:**159a, 161b

hate crimes against, **2:**94b–95a, 96a

lynching of, **1:**585b

mass suicide at Masada (A.D. 73), **3:**241a–b

in Nazi Germany, **1:**186a. *See also* Holocaust

and organized crime, **1:**395b; **2:**494a–b

stereotypes regarding, **2:**149a

symbolic violence to identities of, **3:**249b

vandalism targeting, **3:**363b

victimization of, **2:**197b–198b

voting rights of, **2:**156a

and white slavery, **3:**445b

zoot-suits and, **3:**500b

Jim Crow laws

and southern violence, **3:**186b–187a

*See also* Segregation

*Job, the Victim of His People* (Girard), **3:**96a

Jodl, Alfred, **3:**404b

John, Richard, **3:**20a

John Birch Society, **1:**496a, 571a

*John Gabriel Borkman* (Ibsen), **2:**629a, *629b*

*Johnny Johnson* (musical), **2:**419b–420a

Johnson, Andrew

attempted assassination of, **1:**164a

Reconstruction policies and violence, **3:**23a–b

Johnson, Captain Charles, **2:**529a

Johnson, Dean, **3:**497b

Johnson, Diane, *The Shadow Knows,* **2:**264a

Johnson, Frank M., Jr., **1:**237a

Johnson, George, **1:**70b

Johnson, Hinton, **2:**424a

Johnson, Jack, **1:**175b; **3:**202a–b

Johnson, James Weldon, **1:**240a, **442b; 2:434a**

Johnson, Lyndon B., **1:**275b

assault on, in Dallas (Texas), **1:**375b

and civil rights, **1:**268b

community-based corrections and, **3:**28a

and Gulf of Tonkin Resolution, **2:**63b–64a

investigation on causes of violence under, **3:**260a–b

and King (Martin Luther, Jr.), **2:**225b

and Vietnam War, **2:**134b; **3:**286b, 379a–b, 380a

Khe Sanh, **3:**287a–b

Tet Offensive, **3:**288a

and violence commissions, **2:**47a, 49b–50a, 51a, 53a, 54a, 54b

and Watts riot, **3:**412a

# O

See also Child abuse, sexual; Rape;
Sexual assault
*Sex Crimes in History* (Masters and Lea),
3:133a
Sex differences, **3:140b–144a**
in aggression, **1:**117a; **2:**176a, 445a–b,
446a–b
cross-cultural studies of, **2:***448b,*
448b–449a
in brain structure, **1:**461b; **2:**461b
evolutionary psychology explanation
of, **3:**140b–141a
gender socialization theories of, **3:**181b
opposite-sex violence, **3:**142a–143b
same-sex violence, **3:**141a–142a,
*142a–b, 143a*
sociobiological explanation of,
**3:**181b–182a
and symbolic meanings of violence,
**3:**247a
in testosterone levels, **1:**466a–b
*See also* Gender; Men; Women
Sex drive, male, and rape, **3:**11b–12a
Sex-killers. *See* Serial killers
Sex offenders, **3:144a–147a**
characteristics of, **3:144b**
definition of, 3:144a
legal and legislative trends concerning,
**3:144b–146a**
chemical castration, 3:146a
civil commitment laws, 3:145b–146a
registration and community
notification of, 3:145a–b
treatment of, effectiveness of, **3:146a–b**
*See also* Rapists
*Sex Pistols* (punk band), **2:**421a
Sex-role attitudes, and dating violence,
**1:**193a
Sexual abuse
of children, **1:223b–226b**
chemical castration of molesters,
3:146a
civil commitment laws, 3:145b–146a
and cortisol levels, 1:223a–b, 228a,
463b–464a
definition of, 1:224a
diagnosis of, 2:345b
effects of, 1:224b–226a
incest as, 2:163b–165b
Internet and, 2:178b–179b
legal trends, 3:144b–146a
offender registration and notification
laws and, 3:145a–b
prevalence of, 1:223b
ritual, 1:222b
in slave-owning families, 3:170a
statistics on, 3:144b
and eating disorders, **1:**121a
emergency care for, **2:**346a
literature on, **2:**278a
Sexual assault, **1:**132b
by athletes, **3:**205b–206a
by partners, **3:**209a–b
statistics on, 3:144b
problems in collection of,
3:220b–221a
*See also* Rape

Sexual behavior
criminal
changing definitions of, **3:**144a–b
*See also* Sex crimes
laws controlling, **1:**336b–337a, 338a
polygamy, and Mormon Wars,
**3:**36b–37b
in prisons, **1:**346b–347a; **2:**606b–607a,
612b
problems with, child sexual abuse and,
**1:**225a
religious violence based on, **3:**36a–b
sadism and masochism, **3:78a–80b**
Sexual harassment, **3:147a–151a**
in armed forces, **2:**380a–b
definitions of, **3:**148b, 149a–b
impact of, **3:**150a–b
laws on, **3:**147b–149a
levels of, **3:**149b
perpetrators of, **3:**150a
prevalence of, **3:**149b–150a
in schools, Supreme Court definition
of, **3:**100b
Sexuality, and violence, **1:**192b
in advertising, **1:**33b
in film, **1:**528a, 534b
gay bashing, **2:16a–20b**
Sexually Violent Predator (SVP) Act
(1997), **1:**577b–578a
Sexual maturation, and crime, **1:**405a
*Sexual Personae* (Paglia), **3:**136a
Sexual psychopathology, of serial killers,
**3:**136a
Sexual selection theory of violence,
**2:**445a–b
confirmation of, **2:**449a
Sexual violence
as class-related violence, **1:**280b
on college campuses, **1:**192b–193a
feminist theories of, **3:**312a–b
feminist view of, **2:**569b
interventions for, **2:**586b–587a
popular misconceptions of,
**1:**346b–347a
on television, **3:**273b–274a
Seymor, Horatio, **1:**420b
*Shadow, The* (radio program), **3:**9a
*Shadow Knows, The* (Johnson), **2:**264a
Shaeffer, Rebecca, **2:**256b
Shahn, Ben, **2:**525a
Sacco-Vanzetti case and, **3:**77a
Shakers, **2:**484a
Shakespeare, William, **3:**292a–b
Shakur, Tupac, **2:**423a
Shamans, **2:**427b
Shame, **3:151a–152b**
behavioral reactions to, **3:**151b–152b
compass of, **3:**151b–152a, *151b*
and death of self, **2:**628a–b
emotions related to, **3:**151a
and poverty, **3:**232a–233a
poverty and, **2:**580a–b
in public life, **3:**152a–b
and violence, **2:**580a
Shame-humiliation, affect of, **1:**459a
Shan, Ben, **2:**499b
*Shane* (Schaefer), **3:**442b

Shannon, Duncan, **2:**368a
Shannon, Lyle W., **2:**35a
Shannon, Rachelle, **1:**27a
Shannon, Shelly, **3:**34b
Shapiro, Herbert, **1:**248b
Shapiro, Jacob "Gurrah," **1:**406b–407a;
**2:**493b
Shapiro, J. Irwin, **2:**29a
Shapiro, Miriam, **2:**512b
Sharecroppers Union, **1:**266b, 283b
Sharieff, Raymond, **2:**424a
Sharp, Hary, **2:**338b
Sharpe, Violet, **2:**262a
Sharpsteen, Ben, **1:**537b
Shaw, Clifford R., **3:**300a
Shaw, Herman, **3:**346b
Shawn, Wallace, *Aunt Dan and Lemon,*
**3:**294b
Shawnees
conflicts with colonists, **1:**2b
image of, **1:**76a
in Revolutionary War, **1:**82b
Shays, Daniel, **1:**94a, 280a; **2:**397b
Shays's Rebellion, **1:**57a, *94a,* 94a–b, 280a,
390b–391a, 496b; **3:**54a
suppression of, **2:**397b
Sheets, J. Gary, **2:**121b
Sheets, Kathleen, **2:**121b
Shelby, Richard, **3:**408b
Sheldon, William, **2:**101a
Sheley, Joseph, **2:**76b
Shelters, domestic violence, **3:**209b–210b
Shelton, Robert, **2:**235a
Shengold, Leonard, **2:**629a
Shepard, Matthew, **2:**19b, 94a; **3:**302a
candlelight vigil for, **2:***19a–b*
Shepard, William, **1:**57a
*Sheppard v. Maxwell*, **1:**334b
Sheridan, Philip, **1:**275a
in American Indian wars, **1:**88a; **2:**372a
and Custer (George Armstrong),
**1:**370a, 371a
on frontier violence, **1:**599a; **2:**474a
*Sheriff Jay Printz v. United States*, **2:**437b;
**3:**51b
Sherman, William Tecumseh, **1:**273b,
274b–275a, *275a–b*
and American Indians, **2:**288b–289a
march to the sea, **1:**127b–128a, 138b;
**2:**56a, 559a
in post–Civil War era, **2:**372a
Sherman Anti-Trust Act (1890), applied
to labor, **1:**214a; **2:**643b
Sherrill, Patrick, **2:***330a–b,* 332a
Sherrill, Robert, **2:**437b; **3:**94a–b
Sherry, Michael, **2:**559b
Sherwin, I., **2:**463a
Sherwood, Harry, **2:**4a
Sherwood, Robert E., **3:**294a–b
Sherwood, Sam, **2:**401b–402a
Shields, Henry, **1:**294b
Shields, James, **2:**259b
Shillady, John R., **2:**434b
Shining Path, and drug trade, **1:**439b
Shirley, Myra Maybelle. *See* Starr, Belle
Shivaree, **3:**254b
*Shivers* (film), **1:**528a

# W

Waco (Texas) incident, **1:**366b–367a, 503b; **2:**554a–b; **3:389a–391b,** *390a*
  and BATF, **1:**185b
  as government violence against citizens, **2:**57a
  legacy of, **3:**36a, 71a
  McVeigh (Timothy) response to, **2:**308b
  and militia ideology, **2:**401a
  as religious violence, **3:**36a
  sexual abuse revelations and, **3:**36b, 390b
  site of, **2:**356b
*Waco: The Rules of Engagement* (film), **1:**542b–543a
Wacquant, Loic J. D., **3:**247a
Wadsworth, Michael E. J., **2:**639a
Wages, decline in, and cost of crime, **1:**320a–b
Wagner Act (1935), **2:**242b
  impact of, **2:**242b–243a
*Wag the Dog* (film), **3:**47b
Wakasa, James Hatsuki, **2:**194b
Walcott, Jersey Joe, **1:***176a–b*
Wald, Lilian, **2:**160a
Wales, guerrilla warfare in, **2:**61a
Walkdown, **2:**73b; **3:391b–392a**
Walker Colt (pistol), **1:**290a
Walker, David, **1:**22a, 262a
  *Appeal,* **3:**164b, 185a
  sources of inspiration for, **2:**90b
Walker, Edwin, **2:**498b
Walker, Lenore, **3:**458b
Walker, Mickey, **1:**175b
Walker, Samuel, **1:**290a, 345b; **3:**28b
Walker, William, **1:**511b–512a; **2:**386b, 387a–b, *387b*
Walker, Zachariah, **2:**433b–434a
Walker's War, **1:**181a
Wallace, Bill "Superfoot," **2:**317a
Wallace, George, **2:**369a, 562a
  opposition to desegregation, **3:**115a, 187b
Wallace, J. F., **2:**456a
Wallace, Lew, **1:**146b
Wallace, Michael, **1:**244a
Wallace, William, **1:**271a
Wallace-Burke Gun Club, **1:***600a–b*
Walley, Merritt, **1:**390a
Walling, William English, **2:**433b
Wall Street bombing (1920), **1:**106b–107a; **2:**183b–184a; **3:**76b, **392a–393a**
  aftermath of, **3:***393a–b*
Walnut Street Jail, **1:**310a–b; **2:**594b–595a
Walpurgisnacht, **3:**91b
Walters, Bronco Bill, **3:**97b
Walter, Virginia, *Making Up Mega-boy,* **2:**277a
Wampanoags
  in King Philip's War, **1:**74b–75b
  relations with colonists, **1:**81a
Wangh, Martin, **3:**401b
War, **3:393a–403b**
  advertising in, **1:**30a–32a
  aftermath of
    physical aspects of, **3:397b–399b**

psychoanalytic aspects of, **3:399b–403b**
  American way of, **2:**559a–b
  causes of, **3:395a–397b**
  class dimension in, **1:**278b
  commemoration of victims of, **2:**354b–355a
  definition of, **3:**395a
  films on, **1:**386a, 513b, 525a–b, 533a–b
  friendly fire in, **2:***381a–b,* 381b–383b
  and genocide, **2:**320b
  hate crimes during, **2:**96a
  honor and, **2:**133b–135a
  horrors of, **1:**270a–b, 271a
    photographic images of, **2:**431b, *432a–b,* 521b, 522a
  Lieber Code of, **1:**411b
  literature on, **2:**263b–264a
    poems, **2:**283b–284a
    young adult, **2:**279a–b
  movement to outlaw, **1:**412b
  music about, **2:**416b–417a, 419b–420a
  nonviolence in, **2:**482b–483b
  prisoners of. *See* Prisoners of war
  propaganda, **2:**572b–574a
  race-based grounds for, **3:**2b
  racial differences in aggression as pretexts for, **3:**2a–b
  reporting on, **2:**108b–109b, 201b, 371a, 520b, 521a–522b
  in sculpture, **3:**122a
  soldiers returning from, rehabilitation of, **2:**309a
  southern attitude toward, **3:**186a–b
  U.S. involvement in, **3:393b–395a**
  victory in, racial superiority as reason for, **3:**2b
  violence against civilians in, **2:**323a–b
  *See also specific wars*
War crimes, **3:403b–406b**
  My Lai massacre, **2:430b–432b,** *432a–b*
Ward, Jim, **2:**428a–b
Ward, Lynn, **1:**216b
Ward, Michael, **2:**411b
Ward, Nathaniel, **1:**357b
Wardell, D., **2:**462b
Warhol, Andy, **1:**558a–b
  *Electric Chair,* **1:***558b*
Warmoth, Henry Clay, **2:**287b
Warner, Matt, **1:**208b
Warner, Volney, **1:**68a
Warner Bros., **1:**538a
War of 1812, **3:**393b–394a, **406b–408b**
  character of, **3:**407a–b
  domestic politics and, **3:**407b–408a
  legacy of, **3:**408a–b
  military operations in, **3:**406b–407a
  Native Americans in, **1:**84a–b
  New Orleans (Louisiana) during, **2:**473b–474a
  prisoners of war in, **2:***589b;* **3:**408a
  privateers in, **2:**613b–614a
War of Independence. *See* American Revolution
War of Indian Independence. *See* Pontiac's War

*War of the Worlds* (radio broadcast), **3:**9b–10a
Warrant, arrest, **1:**351b
War Relocation Authority (WRA), **2:**192a, 193b
Warren, Earl, **1:**339b
  on cruel and unusual punishment, **1:**358b
Warren, Joseph, **1:**171a
Warren, Robert Penn, *Night Rider,* **3:**386b
War Resisters' International, **1:**412b
War Resisters League, **1:**125a
Warshow, Robert, **2:**565b
Wartella, Ellen, **3:**263a
War toys
  campaigns against, **3:**341a–b
  historical contexts of, **3:**339a–340b, *339b*
  *Star Wars,* **3:**342a
Washington, Booker T., Du Bois on, **1:**443a
Washington (D.C.), **3:408b–410**
  homicide rate for, **2:***35b;* **3:**410b
  racial violence in, **3:**408b–409b
  road rage programs in, **3:**65a
  violent crime rates in, **2:***33a–b*
Washington, George, **1:**184b
  American Indian wars and, **1:**82b, 83a
  farewell address (1796) of, **1:**410b
  and military interventions, **2:**385b
  and pacifist movement, **1:**123a
  in Revolutionary War, **1:**95a–96b
  and Whiskey Rebellion, **2:**398a; **3:**444a, 445a
Washington, Madison, **1:**37a
Washington, Treaty of (1871), **1:**411b
Washington Naval System, **1:**412a–b
*Washington Post,* Unabomber manifesto published in, **3:**350b
Washington State
  law against assisted suicide in, **1:**137b
  Moses Lake school shooting, **3:***104a–b*
  Red Scare mob violence in, **3:**26b
  timber strike of 1916, **3:**124a–b
  Tylenol tampering deaths in, **3:**253a
  *See also* Seattle
Washita River (Oklahoma) massacre (1868), Indian casualties in, **1:**3b
Water pollution, **1:**478b–479a
  animal agriculture and, **1:**111a
Watie, Stand, **1:**85b
Watson, Brook, **2:**500b
Watson, Charles "Tex," **2:**315a
Watson, Ella "Cattle Kate," **1:**336b; **3:**386a, **462a**
Watson, John, **3:**320a
Watson, Tom, **1:**14b
*Watson and the Shark* (Copley), **2:**500a–501a, *500a–b*
*Watson v. State,* **3:**94a
Watts riot, **1:**5b, 284b; **2:**547b; **3:411a–412a,** 441a
  consequences of, **3:**411b–412a
  government commission on, **2:**48b
  predisposing factors for, **3:**411a
Waugh, Evelyn, *Loved One, The,* **3:**291a
Wayne, Anthony, **1:**83a
Wayne, John, **1:**552b, 554a, *554a–b*

"good war" myth of, **3**:481a–b
graffiti during, **2**:58b
hate crimes during, **2**:96a
interservice rivalries in, **2**:384a
Kennedy (John F.) in, **2**:211a
long-range implications of, **3**:483b–485a
mass killing of civilians during, **2**:323b–324a
medical care during, **2**:342b
Mexican Americans in, **2**:364b
mobile warfare in, **1**:424a
National Rifle Association during, **2**:437a
nonviolence during, **2**:483a
Pearl Harbor attack, **2**:510a–511a, *511a–b*
  and U.S. espionage, **1**:211b–212a
photographic images of, **2**:521b
prisoners of war in, **2**:589b, *589b, 591a–592a*
private firearms in, **3**:51a
propaganda during, **2**:573a–574a
radio in, **3**:7b–8a
right to bear arms and, **3**:51a
social strain during, **3**:483a–b
U.S. accomplishment in, **3**:481a
use of atomic bomb in, Hiroshima and Nagasaki, **2**:116b–119a
U.S. participation in, **3**:394b
war-crime trials, **3**:404b–406a
war toys of, **3**:339a, *339b*
weapons of, **3**:417a–419b
World Wide Web. *See* Internet
World Wrestling Federation (WWF), **3**:492a
  television advertisement of, **1**:33b
Worster, Donald, **1**:473b
Wounded Knee (1890), **1**:90b; **3**:33a, 438a, **486b–488b**, 491a
  Indian casualties in, **1**:3b
  memorial at, **2**:*357a–b*
Wounded Knee (1973), **1**:67b–68a; **3**:488b–490a
Wovoka (Paiute prophet), **1**:90a; **3**:32b, **487a**, 490a–491a
WPC. *See* Workingmen's Party of California
WRA. *See* War Relocation Authority
Wrestling, **2**:567a
  Dempsey-Montana match, **3**:*202a–b*
  professional, **3**:491b–494a
    evolution of, **3**:491b–492a
    forms of staged violence in, **3**:492b–493a
    television and, **3**:202b–203a
Wright, Andy, **3**:118a, *119a–b*
Wright, James, **2**:76b, **78b**
Wright, Martha C., **3**:454b
Wright, Norris, **1**:173b
Wright, Richard, *Native Son,* **2**:264b–265a
Wright, Roy, **3**:118a
Wright, Susan Webber, **3**:148a

Wrongful death, **3**:494a–495a
WSGA. *See* Wyoming Stock Growers Association
WSP. *See* Women Strike for Peace
WU. *See* Weather Underground
Wuornos, Aileen, **3**:495a–496b, *495b*
  documentary film about, **1**:543a–b
Wurmser, Leon, **3**:151a
WWF. *See* World Wrestling Federation
Wyatt, Gail, **1**:225b
Wyatt, Zip, **2**:71b
Wyman, David, **2**:126b
Wyoming
  Johnson County War, **2**:71b; **3**:442a–443a
  Massacre (1778), **1**:*72a–b*
Wyoming Stock Growers Association (WSGA), **1**:195a–b

# X

*X-Files, The* (television show), **3**:276b
X films, **1**:547a
XYZ affair, **1**:66a

# Y

Yablonski, Jock, **2**:557b
Yachtjacking, **2**:114b
Yakima War, **1**:89a–b, **217b**
Yale, Frankie, **1**:204b
Yamamoto, Isoroku, **2**:510b
Yamassees, **1**:2b, 81b
Yancey, William L., **1**:445b
Yasin, Abdul Rahman, **1**:160b; **3**:475b, 476b
Y chromosome, extra copy of, **2**:22b–24a, 447b
Yeager, Robert C., *Seasons of Shame,* **3**:197b
Yellow journalism, **2**:201a–b
Yellowstone Expedition, **1**:370b
Yellow Thunder, Raymond, **1**:67b; **3**:488b
Yeudall, Lorne T., **2**:462a
Yippie!, **2**:120b; **3**:497a–499a
Y2K, **1**:17b
Yoko, Ota, **2**:117b
York, Alvin, **2**:83b
Yorktown, Battle of, **1**:96b
Young, Brigham, **2**:408a, 408b, 409a–b; **3**:37a–b
Young, Coleman, **1**:397a; **2**:72b, 647a
Young, Kevin, **3**:201a
Young, Mahonri, **3**:121b–122a
Younger brothers, **1**:377b; **2**:647a
Younger, Cole, **2**:190a
Young males
  African American, victimization of, **3**:367a
  homicide rates for, **2**:318b
  rape by, evolutionary/sociobiological explanation for, **3**:180a

skinhead subcultures, **3**:160b–162a
suicide rate of, **3**:238a
violence against men, **3**:141a–142a
  assault, **3**:141b, *143a*
  homicide, **3**:141a–b, *142a–b*
  as honor contests, **3**:248b
  *See also* Men; Teenagers
Yousef, Ramzi Ahmed, **1**:160a, 160b; **2**:425a; **3**:475b–476b
Youth International Party (Yippies), **1**:157a
Youth violence
  and criminal justice system, **2**:12b
  guns and, **2**:76a–77a
  poverty and, **2**:577a, 578a
  statistics on, **2**:577a–b
  *See also* Juvenile delinquency
Yucca Mountain, **1**:481a
Yugoslavia
  ethnic cleansing in, international response to, **2**:396b
  NATO bombing campaign in, **2**:374a
  peacekeeping mission in, **2**:395a
  *See also* Bosnia; Kosovo

# Z

Zahn, Gordon, **2**:486b
Zale, Tony, **1**:176a
Zamora, Ronnie, **3**:260b
Zane, Arnie, **1**:381a–b
Zangara, Giuseppe, **1**:131b, 341a; **2**:368a–b
Zapruder, Abraham, **1**:540b–541a, 548b
Zebra case, **2**:424b; **3**:90b
Zeehanderlaar, Felix, **2**:294a
Zeichner, A., **2**:455b
Zero-tolerance policy, **2**:537b–538a
  for school violence, **3**:102b
Zimbardo, Philip, **3**:320a
Zimmer, Andrew, **2**:*330a–b*, 332b
Zimmerman telegram, **1**:570a
Zimring, Franklin, **2**:74b, 250b; **3**:93b
Zionist Occupation Government (ZOG), **1**:367b
Zipes, Jack, **1**:539b
Zodiac killer, **3**:499a–500a
ZOG. *See* Zionist Occupation Government
Zombie movies, **1**:522b–523a
*Zoo Story, The* (Albee), **3**:294b
Zoot-Suit Riot, **1**:249a; **2**:161b–162a, 290a; **3**:440a, **500a–501b**, *501a–b*
  fashion and, **1**:500b
Zumwalt, Elmo, III, **3**:381b
Zumwalt, Elmo, Jr., **3**:381b
Zwerg, Jim, **1**:586b
Zwerin, Charlotte, *Gimme Shelter,* **1**:542b
Zwick, Edward, *Glory,* **1**:516b
Zwillman, Abner "Longy," **2**:493b
Zylicz, Zbigniew, **1**:137a